| 1946 | 1947 | 1948 | 1949 | 1950 | 1951 | 1952 | 1953 | 1954 | 1955 | 1956 | 1957 | 1958 | |
|---|---|---|---|---|---|---|---|---|---|---|---|---|---|
| $143.8 | $161.7 | $174.8 | $178.1 | $192.0 | $207.1 | $217.1 | $229.7 | $235.8 | $253.7 | $266 | | | |
| 30.7 | 34.0 | 45.9 | 35.3 | 53.8 | 59.2 | 52.1 | 53.3 | 52.7 | 68.4 | 71 | | | |
| 27.5 | 25.5 | 32.0 | 38.4 | 38.5 | 60.1 | 75.6 | 82.5 | 75.8 | 75.0 | 79 | | | |
| 7.6 | 11.6 | 6.5 | 6.2 | 1.9 | 3.8 | 2.4 | .6 | 2.0 | 2.2 | 4 | | | |
| 209.6 | 232.8 | 259.1 | 258.0 | 286.2 | 330.2 | 347.2 | 366.1 | 366.3 | 399.3 | 420 | | | |
| 13.9 | 17.2 | 20.3 | 21.9 | 23.9 | 27.6 | 29.6 | 31.6 | 33.1 | 35.3 | 38 | | | |
| 195.7 | 215.6 | 238.8 | 236.1 | 262.3 | 302.6 | 317.6 | 334.5 | 333.2 | 364.0 | 381 | | | |
| 17.4 | 21.0 | 19.8 | 23.4 | 26.1 | 30.3 | 31.8 | 34.8 | 34.1 | 36.0 | 34 | | | |
| 178.3 | 194.6 | 219.0 | 212.7 | 236.2 | 272.3 | 285.8 | 299.7 | 299.1 | 328.0 | 346 | | | |
| 6.1 | 5.8 | 5.4 | 5.9 | 7.1 | 8.5 | 9.0 | 9.1 | 10.1 | 11.5 | 12.9 | 14.9 | 15.2 | 10 |
| 9.1 | 11.3 | 12.4 | 10.2 | 17.9 | 22.6 | 19.4 | 20.3 | 17.6 | 22.0 | 22.0 | 21.4 | 19.0 | 11 |
| 1.9 | 4.6 | 9.6 | 9.6 | 6.9 | 7.0 | 7.5 | 6.4 | 7.9 | 12.3 | 9.9 | 9.2 | 7.1 | 12 |
| 16.1 | 17.0 | 16.9 | 18.5 | 21.8 | 19.4 | 20.5 | 22.1 | 24.6 | 26.4 | 28.8 | 32.5 | 36.7 | 13 |
| 177.3 | 189.8 | 208.5 | 205.6 | 226.1 | 253.7 | 270.4 | 286.1 | 288.2 | 308.8 | 330.9 | 349.3 | 359.3 | 14 |
| 18.7 | 21.4 | 21.1 | 18.5 | 20.6 | 28.9 | 34.0 | 35.4 | 32.5 | 35.4 | 39.6 | 42.4 | 42.2 | 15 |
| 158.6 | 168.4 | 187.4 | 187.1 | 205.5 | 224.8 | 236.4 | 250.7 | 255.7 | 273.4 | 291.3 | 306.9 | 317.1 | 16 |
| 477.0 | 468.3 | 487.7 | 490.7 | 533.5 | 576.5 | 598.5 | 621.8 | 613.7 | 654.8 | 668.8 | 680.9 | 679.5 | 17 |
| −14.7 | −1.8 | 4.1 | .6 | 8.7 | 8.1 | 3.8 | 3.9 | −1.3 | 6.7 | 2.1 | 1.8 | −.2 | 18 |
| 3374 | 3249 | 3326 | 3289 | 3504 | 3722 | 3799 | 3882 | 3764 | 3946 | 3960 | 4031 | 3885 | 19 |

| 1946 | 1947 | 1948 | 1949 | 1950 | 1951 | 1952 | 1953 | 1954 | 1955 | 1956 | 1957 | 1958 | |
|---|---|---|---|---|---|---|---|---|---|---|---|---|---|
| 58.5 | 66.9 | 72.1 | 71.4 | 72.1 | 77.8 | 79.5 | 80.1 | 80.5 | 80.2 | 81.4 | 84.3 | 86.6 | 20 |
| 35.0 | 39.4 | 41.1 | 38.8 | 44.9 | 48.7 | 50.6 | 54.8 | 51.9 | 58.5 | 61.1 | 61.9 | 57.9 | 21 |
| 110.0 | 113.1 | 111.5 | 111.2 | 116.2 | 122.7 | 127.4 | 128.8 | 132.3 | 135.2 | 136.9 | 135.9 | 141.1 | 22 |
| 141.4 | 144.1 | 146.6 | 149.2 | 152.3 | 154.9 | 157.5 | 160.2 | 163.0 | 165.9 | 168.9 | 172.0 | 174.9 | 23 |
| 57.5 | 59.3 | 60.6 | 61.3 | 62.2 | 62.0 | 62.1 | 63.0 | 63.6 | 65.0 | 65.5 | 66.9 | 67.6 | 24 |
| 2.3 | 2.3 | 2.3 | 3.6 | 3.3 | 2.1 | 1.9 | 1.8 | 3.5 | 2.9 | 2.8 | 2.9 | 4.6 | 25 |
| 3.9 | 3.9 | 3.8 | 5.9 | 5.3 | 3.3 | 3.0 | 2.9 | 5.5 | 4.4 | 4.1 | 4.3 | 6.8 | 26 |
| 8.4 | 11.6 | 14.4 | 17.4 | 25.6 | 27.3 | 32.6 | 36.7 | 38.2 | 45.3 | 49.3 | 52.2 | 52.7 | 27 |

(Continued on back cover)

# ECONOMICS
Principles, Problems, and Policies

# ECONOMICS
## Principles, Problems, and Policies

**Campbell R. McConnell**

**Professor of Economics**
**University of Nebraska—Lincoln**

**Eighth Edition**

**McGraw-Hill Book Company**

New York   St. Louis   San Francisco   Auckland
Bogotá   Hamburg   Johannesburg   London
Madrid   Mexico   Montreal   New Delhi
Panama   Paris   São Paulo   Singapore
Sydney   Tokyo   Toronto

# ECONOMICS
## Principles, Problems, and Policies

567890 DODO 898765432

This book was set in Century Schoolbook by York
Graphic Services, Inc. The editors were Bonnie E.
Lieberman, Marjorie Singer, and Edwin Hanson; the
designer was Merrill Haber; the production supervisor
was Phil Galea. New drawings were done by J & R
Services, Inc.
R. R. Donnelley & Sons Company was printer and
binder.

**Library of Congress Cataloging in Publication Data**

McConnell, Campbell R
    Economics: principles, problems, and policies.

    Includes index.
    1. Economics. I. Title.
HB171.5.M139  1981      330      80-22408
ISBN 0-07-044930-9

TO MEM

# CONTENTS

# PART FOUR    ECONOMIC GROWTH: ANALYSIS AND POLICY

# PART FIVE  THE ECONOMICS OF THE FIRM AND RESOURCE ALLOCATION

# PREFACE

As is true of any other activity, the authoring of a textbook entails both costs and benefits. The primary cost is the investment of an inordinate amount of time. One of the less obvious benefits is the opportunity for revision. Although it is a highly demanding and sometimes dreary undertaking, revision affords the chance for improvement—to delete the archaic and install the novel, to rectify errors of omission or commission, to rephrase potentially misleading statements, to introduce more relevant illustrations, to bring more pertinent data to bear, to upgrade organizational logic—in short, to build constructively upon a tested framework of ideas. Much of my time these past two years has been devoted to the preparation of this eighth edition of *Economics*. I hope and trust that those who examine this new edition will agree that I have exploited fully the opportunity afforded me. In my judgment this is the most extensive revision of *Economics* undertaken in the twenty years of its existence.

Although the eighth edition bears only a modest resemblance to the first, the basic purpose remains the same: to introduce the beginning economics student to those principles essential to an understanding of fundamental economic problems and the policy alternatives society may utilize to contend with these problems. It is hoped that the ability to reason accurately and objectively about economic matters and the development of a lasting interest in economics will be two valuable byproducts of this basic objective. Furthermore, my intention remains that of presenting the principles and problems of economics in a straightforward, logical fashion. To this end great stress has been put upon clarity of presentation and organization.

## ☐ THE EIGHTH EDITION

Each chapter in the eighth edition has been subjected to a topic-by-topic, line-by-line evaluation; none has escaped content revision, rewriting for greater clarity, organizational improvement, and updating. The extensiveness of this revision reflects a variety of considerations: the insightful suggestions of some twenty-six scholars who reviewed the seventh edition; new developments in the domestic and world economies *and* concomitant changes in economic theory and policy; and, in no small measure, continued growth in the number of excellent competing tests on the market.

Let me first single out some of the more salient changes and then summarize the revisions on a part-by-part basis. It is to be emphasized that this presentation is selective. The *Instructor's Manual* incorporates a more detailed statement of the revisions on a chapter-by-chapter basis.

△ **Salient Changes**

The most visible change in the eighth edition is the replacement of the old Chapter 39 on the economics of war and defense with a new chapter on the economics of the energy crisis. Three other chapters have been thoroughly overhauled and, with only slight exaggeration, might be regarded as new. Specifically, Chapter 10 on cyclical fluctuations has been made more analytical and less descriptive. In addition to extensive reorganization, new emphasis is placed upon such matters as the various causes of inflation, the possible relationships between the price level and aggregate output, the measuring of unemployment, and the like. Chapter 29 on oligopoly now centers upon four models—kinked demand, collusion, price leadership, and cost-plus pricing—and concludes with a case study of how oligopoly has functioned in the automobile industry. The extensive treatment of game theory found in the seventh edition has been omitted and real-world illustrations now abound. The net result, I believe, is a tighter and more relevant introduction to oligopoly behavior. Chapter 34 on antitrust and regulation has also been recast. The structure-versus-behavior controversy is highlighted in discussing antitrust policy. Material on industrial regulation has been reworked to stress regulatory problems and the recent supply-and-demand theory of regulation is introduced. Finally, the new social regulation—its purposes and the furor surrounding it—is discussed.

At least two other chapters fall into the "extensively revised" category. Chapter 18 on stagflation contains important new material on supply-side economics and its policy prescriptions. Chapter 37 on income inequality now embodies a discussion of the Lorenz Curve, focuses more clearly upon the equality-efficiency trade-off as the core of the income distribution debate, and features an improved presentation of the negative income tax proposal.

△ **Part-by-Part Revisions**

Consider now the highlights of the eighth edition on a part-by-part basis.

**1  Introductory**  The introductory material of Part 1 has been trimmed extensively. For example, in Chapter 3 the technical discussion of comparative advantage has been deferred to Chapter 41 and the presentation of the circular flow model has been truncated. Chapter 7 has been tightened by eliminating less relevant topics and those concepts which will be explored more fully in later chapters. Each of the eight chapters in Part 1 has been condensed through a prudent pruning of excess verbiage. This is not to say there is no new material. For example, in Chapter 1 a new short section integrates its facts-theory-policy discussion through a simple application. In Chapter 2 a number of applications of the production possibilities curve are summarized. And Chapter 8 now features a discussion of the tax revolt. But overall instructors will find it possible to move through the introductory chapters more rapidly than in earlier editions.

**2  Macroeconomics**  Major changes in Part 2 include the following. The organization of Chapter 9 has been improved by deferring the discussion of how money GNP is deflated until after the two approaches to calculating GNP have been discussed. A brief section on the subterranean economy has also been added. The extensive revision of Chapter 10 has already been noted. In Chapter 12 the section on planned and actual investment has been recast for greater clarity; the definition and algebraic derivation of the multiplier have been made explicit; and the recessionary and inflationary gaps are now presented on separate diagrams. Chapter 13 has undergone important organizational and pedagogical improvements. The most important content changes involve new material on the political business cycle and the use of government purchases and taxes as policy options.

**3 Money** The analytics of the money market have been shifted from Chapter 32 to Part 3. Hence, Chapter 14 begins with a careful treatment of the demand for money. This analysis is carried over into Chapter 16 to permit a more comprehensive model of the money market and monetary policy within the Keynesian system. Chapter 15 has been tightened somewhat to allow for a new introductory section on the historical evolution of fractional reserve banking. The section on the monetary multiplier has been reworked for greater clarity. The revised Chapter 17 on monetarism embodies improved organization, a simplified discussion of the velocity of money, and an extension of the rules-versus-discretionary policy debate to include important new material on the rational expectations theory. The reworking of Chapter 18 to include supply-side economics and policy has already been documented.

**4 Growth** In Chapters 19 and 20 I have tried to make amends for the relative neglect of the productivity concept in earlier editions. Thus in Chapter 19 the discussion of diminishing returns is more intuitive and emphasizes output per worker, that is, labor productivity. The determinants of labor productivity are made explicit and a new section applies these determinants to the slowdown in productivity growth which has plagued the United States since the mid-1960s. Chapter 20's discussion of growth in the United States is also recast to emphasize that increases in real output stem either from improvements in labor productivity or increases in labor inputs.

**5 Microeconomics** A number of significant organizational changes have been made in the microeconomics chapters. The material on consumer demand as viewed from the vantage point of the individual firm has been shifted from Chapter 23 to Chapters 26 and 27. This makes Chapter 23 more manageable as to length *and* sensibly locates the discussions of demand and marginal revenue curves. Similarly the technical statement of the law of diminishing returns, which formerly appeared in Chapter 19 on growth theory, is now located at the beginning of Chapter 25 on production costs. This will permit students to better understand how diminishing returns affects the shapes of the short-run cost curves. Some of the more significant content changes in Part 5 include (1) more applications and illustrations of elasticity of demand in Chapter 23; (2) a new appendix on indifference curve analysis in Chapter 24; (3) a revision of the discussion of price discrimination in Chapter 27; (4) a tightening and empirical updating of Chapter 28's section on advertising; and (5) the reorganization and rewriting of Chapter 30's section on the least-cost and profit-maximizing combinations of resources to improve the logic and clarity. The extensive revision to which Chapter 29 on oligopoly was subjected has already been detailed.

**6 Problems** Many of Part 6's revisions have already been mentioned: (1) the thorough rewrite of Chapter 34 on antitrust and regulation; (2) the organizational and content changes in Chapter 37 on income distribution; and (3) the entirely new Chapter 39 on energy. In addition, Chapter 35 on agriculture now includes a bit more material on the parity concept and the related fact that public policy has backed off somewhat from the freer-market policies of the mid-1970's. Chapter 38 on labor problems has been shortened somewhat. In addition, the section on public-sector unionism has been reworked and the crowding hypothesis has been stressed in the section on sex discrimination.

**7 International** Chapter 41 on comparative advantage and the macroeconomic effects of international trade reflects some tightening of the presentation and an improved explanation of how net exports affect aggregate demand. Chapter 42 is also leaner and includes an improved discussion of the economic effects of tariffs. The discussions of fixed and floating exchange rates—and the prerequisites to the effective functioning of both systems—are brought into better focus in Chapter 43. The determinants of exchange rates under a floating system are stressed and a discussion of the 1977–1978 dollar crisis is included. The historical-descriptive material of Chapter 44 has been greatly condensed. Finally, Chapter 45 on the Soviet economy has been reworked for the new 1977 Constitution, some new perspectives on the Liberman reforms, and more current information on Soviet growth.

△   "Last Word" Minireadings

The built-in minireadings introduced in the sixth edition were enthusiastically received by most users. These "Last Word" selections serve several purposes: some provide meaningful real-world applications of economic concepts; others reveal "human interest" aspects of economic problems; and still others challenge the concepts and interpretations of mainstream economics. The minireadings are purposely placed at the end of each chapter so as not to interrupt the continuity of the text material. One-third of the "Last Words" are new in the eighth edition.

☐   PRODUCT DIFFERENTIATION

In terms of content I feel this text embraces a number of departures in content and organization which perhaps distinguish it from other books in the field.

1   The principles course frequently fails to provide students with a comprehensive and meaningful definition of economics. To remedy this shortcoming, one complete chapter (Chapter 2) is devoted to a careful statement and development of the economizing problem

and an exploration of its implications. The foundation thereby provided should be helpful in putting the many particular subject areas of economics into proper perspective.

2   For better or worse, government is obviously an integral and increasingly important component of modern capitalism. Its economic role, therefore, should not be treated piecemeal or as an afterthought. This text introduces the economic functions of government early and accords them systematic treatment (Chapters 6 and 8).

3   This volume puts considerable emphasis upon the crucial topic of economic growth. Chapter 19 summarizes growth theory. Chapter 20 discusses American growth, the growth controversy, and the Doomsday models. Chapter 21 draws upon the conceptual framework of Chapter 19 in treating the obstacles to growth which plague the underdeveloped countries. An important segment of Chapter 45 concerns the growth record and prospects of Soviet Russia's command economy. Beyond this it will be found that the chapters on price theory pay special attention to the implications that the various market structures have for technological progress.

4   It is understandable that the elusiveness of general equilibrium analysis eminently qualifies this topic for omission at the principles level. The result, however, is a grievous shortcoming of most introductory courses. A sincere effort is made in this book to remedy this deficiency. Specifically, an entire chapter (Chapter 5) is devoted to the notion of the price system, and another chapter (Chapter 33) explicitly outlines in more sophisticated terms the nature and significance of general equilibrium analysis.

5   I have purposely given considerable attention to microeconomics in general and to the theory of the firm in particular. There are two reasons for this emphasis. In the first place, the concepts of microeconomics are difficult for most beginning students. Short expositions usually compound these difficulties by raising more questions than they answer. Secondly, I have coupled analysis of the various

market structures with a discussion of the social implications of each. The impact of each market arrangement upon price and output levels, resource allocation, and the rate of technological advance is carefully assessed.

6 Part 6 provides a broad spectrum of chapters on current socioeconomic problems. As most students see it, this is where the action is. I have sought to guide the action along logical lines through the application of appropriate analytical tools. My bias in Part 6 is in favor of inclusiveness; each instructor can effectively counter this bias by omitting those chapters felt to be less relevant for a particular group of students.

## ☐ ORGANIZATION AND CONTENT

In terms of organization, this book has been written with the conviction that the basic prerequisite of an understandable economics text is the logical arrangement and clear exposition of subject matter. This concern with organization is perhaps most evident in Part 1, which centers upon the step-by-step development of a comprehensive and realistic picture of American capitalism. This coherent group of introductory chapters is substituted for the traditional smattering of more or less unrelated background topics that ordinarily introduce the student to the study of economics.

Throughout this volume the exposition of each particular topic and concept is directly related to the level of difficulty which in my experience the average student is likely to encounter. It is for this reason that national income accounting, microeconomics, and to a lesser degree, employment theory are purposely accorded comprehensive and careful treatments. Simplicity in these instances is correlated with comprehensiveness, not brevity. Furthermore, my experience suggests that in the treatment of each basic topic—employment theory, money and banking, international economics, and so forth—it is highly desirable to couple analysis and policy. A three-step development of basic analytical tools is employed: (1) verbal description and

illustration, (2) numerical examples, and (3) graphic presentation based upon these numerical illustrations.

As noted in the summary of major eighth edition changes, the material is organized around seven basic topics: (1) an introduction to American capitalism; (2) national income, employment, and fiscal policy; (3) money and monetary policy; (4) economic growth; (5) economics of the firm and resource allocation; (6) current economic problems; and (7) international economics and the Soviet economy.

Part 1 is designed to introduce the method and subject matter of economics and to develop the ideological framework and the factual characteristics of American capitalism. This group of chapters develops in an orderly fashion the overall picture of how our economy operates. After an introduction to the methodology of economics in Chapter 1, an entire chapter is devoted to defining and explaining the economizing problem. Chapters 3 to 5 develop the capitalistic ideology and the notion of the most fundamental institution of capitalism—the price system. Early emphasis upon the price system is designed to provide the necessary orientation for the detailed treatment of pricing found in Part 5 and to contribute to an understanding of the national income analysis in Part 2 and, more specifically, the topics of inflation and deflation. Chapter 6 introduces government as a basic economic component of modern capitalism; government's economic functions are systematically explained and evaluated. Upon this superstructure of a mixed public-private economy, Chapters 7 and 8 add the factual information concerning the private and public sectors of the economy, thereby making our mixed capitalism model much more realistic. However, instructors who wish to minimize institutional material may choose to omit Chapters 7 and 8.

Part 2 treats national income analysis and fiscal policy. Chapter 9 on national income accounting reflects my conviction that this difficult topic merits detailed treatment. Some instructors may choose to truncate this discussion by omitting or deemphasizing the income approach to GNP. Chapter 10 treats the characteristics, causes, and consequences of cyclical fluctuations. The next three chapters are devoted to neo-Keynesian employment theory, fiscal policy, and the public debt.

Part 3 emphasizes the balance sheet approach to money and banking. This approach seems most in accord with the goal of providing the student with an analytical tool needed in reasoning through, as opposed to memorizing, the economic impact of the various basic banking transactions. Just as fiscal policy is linked directly to income theory in Part 2, monetary policy immediately follows the discussion of money and banking. Monetarism is portrayed as an alternative to Keynesianism and this is followed by a rather detailed look at the distressing macroeconomic events of the past decade. The first half of the book is completed with Part 4 on economic growth in both the United States and the underdeveloped nations and problems related thereto.

For reasons already noted, the treatment of pricing and resource allocation in Part 5 is purposely detailed. Throughout Chapters 26 to 29 emphasis is placed upon the social implications of the various market structures. What is the significance of each market structure for price and output levels, resource allocation, and technological progress? Emphasis in the discussion of distribution—Chapters 30 to 32—is generally in accord with the relative quantitative importance of the various market shares in our economy. I have not belabored the analysis of interest, rent, and profits where, it seems to me, economic analysis is rather tentative. Chapter 33 provides a capstone discussion of general equilibrium, including an introduction to input-output analysis.

Part 6 deals largely with domestic issues: the monopoly problem, the farm problem, the problems of the cities, the economics of inequality and poverty, labor relations and collective bargaining, the energy problem, and the radical critique. Excepting Chapter 40, in each of these chapters an attempt has been made to (1) describe the historical and factual background of the problem, (2) analyze its causes and effects, (3) explore government policy, and (4) offer a thought-provoking discussion of public policy alternatives. As noted, instructors may choose to use the chapters of Part 6 selectively.

The first four chapters of Part 7 survey international trade and finance with some rigor. Finally, Chapter 45 offers a relatively comprehensive discussion of the Soviet economy, emphasizing its planning processes and its growth prospects.

End-of-chapter summaries provide a concise, pointed recapitulation of each chapter. Much thought has gone into the end-of-chapter questions. The first question at the end of each chapter is a list of important terms and concepts encountered in that particular chapter. Because the introductory course is heavily imbued with terminology, this listing should prove helpful. Though purposely intermixed, all other questions are of three general types. Some are designed to highlight the main points of each chapter. Others are "open-end" discussion or thought questions. Wherever pertinent, numerical problems which require the student to derive and manipulate key concepts and relationships are employed. Numerical problems are stressed in those chapters dealing with national income accounting and analysis, money and banking, and price theory. Some optional "advanced analysis" questions accompany certain theory chapters. These problems usually involve the stating and manipulation of certain basic concepts in equation form. Answers to all quantitative questions are found in the *Instructor's Manual*. The bibliographical references at the end of each chapter are designed to provide both breadth and depth for the ambitious student. Yet care has been taken to see that these references are not beyond the grasp of the average college sophomore.

## ☐ ORGANIZATIONAL ALTERNATIVES

Though economics instructors are in general agreement as to the basic content of a principles of economics course, there are considerable differences of opinion as to what particular arrangement of material is best. The structure of this book is designed to provide considerable organizational flexibility. And I am happy to report that users of prior editions have informed me that they accomplished substantial rearrangements of chapters with little sacrifice of continuity. Though I have chosen to move from macro- to microeconomics, there is no reason why the introductory material of Part 1 cannot be followed immediately by the micro-analysis of Part 5. Similarly, in my judgment money and banking can best be taught after, rather than before, national income analysis. Those who disagree will encounter no special problems by preceding Chapter 9 with Chapters 14, 15, and 16. Furthermore, some instructors will prefer to intersperse the microeconomics of Part 5 with the problems chapters of Part 6. This is easily accomplished. Chapter 35 on the farm problem may follow Chapter 26 on pure competition; Chapter 34 on antitrust and regulation may follow Chapters 27 to 29 on imperfect competition. Chapter 38 on labor unions and collective bargaining may either precede or follow Chapter 31 on wages, and Chapter 37 on income inequality may follow Chapters 31 and 32 on the distributive shares of national income.

Other rearrangements to consider include the placement of Chapter 10 on the business cycle after either Chapter 12 or 13 and the shifting of Chapter 22 on market structures so that it is considered after Chapter 25. Finally, because the energy problem and its consequences are international in scope, one can see advantages in considering Chapter 39 after either Chapter 43 or 44.

Those who teach the typical two-semester course and who feel comfortable with the book's organization will find that, by putting the first four parts in the first semester and Parts 5 through 7 in the second, the material is divided both logically in terms of content and quite satisfactorily in terms of quantity and level of difficulty between the two semesters. For those instructors who choose to put more emphasis upon international economics, it is

suggested that Parts 1, 2, 3, and 7 be treated the first semester and Parts 4, 5, and 6 the second. For a course based on three quarters of work I would suggest Chapters 1 through 13 for the first quarter, 14 through 33 for the second, and 34 through 45 for the third. Finally, those interested in the one-semester course will be able to discern several possible groups of chapters that will be appropriate to such a course. Tentative outlines for three one-semester courses, emphasizing macroeconomics, microeconomics, or a survey of micro and macro theory, follow this preface on page xxxi.

☐  SUPPLEMENTS

The seventh edition of *Economics* is accompanied by a wide range of useful supplements, making it one of the most complete instructional packages available for the principles course.

The fifth edition of *Economic Issues: A Book of Readings* remains available as a supplement for this or any other mainstream textbook.

Professor Robert C. Bingham of Kent State University has prepared two valuable supplements. First, students have found his *Study Guide* to be an indispensable aid. It contains for each chapter an introductory statement, a checklist of behavioral objectives, an outline, a list of important terms, fill-in questions, problems and projects, objective questions, and discussion questions. An extensive glossary is found at the conclusion of the volume. The *Guide* comprises, in my opinion, a superb "portable tutor" for the principles student. Second, Professor Bingham's *Economic Concepts* provides carefully designed programmed materials for all the key analytical areas of the principles course.

My *Instructor's Manual* includes some comments of a pedagogical character and, more important, is a reservoir of objective and essay questions. In addition to a more attractive format, the eighth edition of the *Manual* has been substantially expanded with the addition of some 500 new multiple-choice questions. As noted earlier, answers to all the test's quantitative end-of-chapter questions are provided for the convenience of instructors.

The old tear-and-paste *Test File* associated with earlier editions of *Economics* has fallen prey to technological progress. The eighth edition *Instructor's Manual* is keyed to a computerized test service, the EXAMINER system. All the true-false and multiple-choice questions in the *Instructor's Manual* are coded with computer numbers so that instructors desiring to prepare and grade quizzes and examinations can do so by using this system. Detailed information needed to implement this system can be found in the *Instructor's Manual.*

Color transparencies and black-and-white enlarged transparency masters for overhead projectors are available to those desiring these classroom aids.

## ☐ DEBTS

The publication of this eighth edition extends the life of *Economics* into its third decade. The acceptance of *Economics,* which was generous from the outset, has expanded with each edition. This kind reception has no doubt been fostered by the many teachers and students who have been kind enough to give me the benefit of their suggestions and criticisms.

The eighth edition has benefited from many perceptive reviews. The contributors of these reviews, to whom I am especially grateful, are Fred J. Abraham, University of Northern Iowa; Joseph E. Barr, Framingham State University; Bruce L. Beatty, El Camino College; Deepak Bhattasali, Boston University; Norman Caldwell, Iowa Central Community College; E. D. Chastain, Auburn University; Betty Chu, San Jose State University; Edwin M. Cobb, Elgin Community College; Norman V. Cure, Macomb County Community College; Pritam S. Dhillon, Cook College; Theodore Frickel, Utah State University; David G. Garraty, Thomas Nelson Community College; Frank W. Gery, St. Olaf College; Jack B. God-dard, Northeastern Oklahoma State University; Nicholas D. Grunt, Tarrant County Junior College, South Campus; Thomas W. Hiestand, Concordia College; James B. McCollum, Columbus College; Vincent R. McDonald, Howard University; Douglas G. Madigan, Robert Morris College; H. C. Milikien, American River College; Duane B. Oyen, University of Wisconsin, Eau Claire; Sam F. Parigi, Lamar University; Manuel Rios, Laredo Junior College; William Tabel, Thornton Community College; Percy O. Vera, Sinclair Community College; and Kenneth Weiher, University of Texas.

My colleagues at the University of Nebraska-Lincoln continue to generously share knowledge of their specialties with me and to provide encouragement. Professor W. H. Pope of Ryerson Polytechnical Institute has made many invaluable suggestions in his preparation of the second Canadian edition of *Economics.* My three children—Lauren, Curt, and Beth—have been active participants in the preparation of this edition. By some twist of fate, all are economics majors and, therefore, have been able to assist, not only in such routine tasks as index preparation, but also in proofreading and the evaluation of new material. I am pleased to acknowledge publicly their help.

Lastly, I am greatly indebted to the many professionals at McGraw-Hill—and in particular Peter Nalle, Bonnie Lieberman, Mel Haber, Lee Catalano, Kathi Benson, Phil Galea, and Ed Hanson—for their expertise in the production and distribution of this book. My greatest debt is to Marjorie Singer for direct supervision of this revision.

Given this myriad of assistance, I see no compelling reason why the author should assume full responsibility for errors of omission or commission. But I bow to tradition.

*Campbell R. McConnell*

# Three Suggested Outlines for One-Semester Courses

# AN INTRODUCTION TO AMERICAN CAPITALISM

## PART ONE

# The Nature and Method of Economics

# chapter 1

Man, unfortunate creature, is plagued with wants. He wants, among other things, love, social recognition, and the material necessities and comforts of life. Man's striving to improve his material well-being, to "make a living," is the concern of economics. More specifically, economics is the study of man's behavior in producing, exchanging, and consuming the material goods and services he wants.

But a more sophisticated definition of our subject matter is in order. We are, indeed, characterized by both biologically and socially determined wants. We seek food, clothing, shelter, and a myriad of goods and services which we associate with a comfortable or affluent standard of living. We are also blessed with certain aptitudes and are surrounded by quantities of property resources—both natural and manufactured. The obvious action is to use the available human and property resources—labor and managerial talents, tools

and machinery, land and mineral deposits—to produce goods and services which satisfy these wants. And this, of course, is precisely what is done through the organizational mechanism we call the economic system.

Quantitative considerations, however, rule out an ideal solution. The blunt fact is that the totality of our material wants is beyond the productive capacity of available resources. Hence, absolute material abundance is not a possible outcome. This unyielding fact is the basis for our definition of economics: *Economics is concerned with the efficient utilization or management of limited productive resources for the purpose of attaining the maximum satisfaction of human material wants.* Though it may not be self-evident, all the headline-grabbing issues of the day—inflation, unemployment, the energy problem, poverty and inequality, pollution, government regulation of business, and the rest—have their roots in the issue of using scarce resources efficiently.

In the present chapter, however, we must resist the temptation to plunge into the problems and issues of the day. Our immediate concern is with some basic preliminary matters. In particular, we seek answers to the following questions:

**1** Of what importance or consequence is the study of economics?

**2** How should we study economics—what are the proper procedures? What is the character of the methodology of economics?

**3** What specific problems, limitations, and pitfalls might we encounter in studying economics?

## ☐ THE AGE OF THE ECONOMIST

Is economics a discipline of consequence? Is the study of economics an endeavor worthy of one's time and effort? Some four decades ago John Maynard Keynes (1883–1946)—clearly the most influential economist of this century—offered a telling response:

> The ideas of economists and political philosophers, both when they are right and when they are wrong, are more powerful than is commonly understood. Indeed the world is ruled by little else. Practical men, who believe themselves to be quite exempt from any intellectual influences, are usually the slaves of some defunct economist.

The ideologies of the modern world which compete for our minds have been shaped in substantial measure by the great economists of the past—Adam Smith, John Stuart Mill, David Ricardo, Karl Marx, and John Maynard Keynes.[1] And it is currently commonplace for world leaders to receive and invoke the advice and policy prescriptions of economists; "the

political economist is now a fixture in the high councils of government."[2] To illustrate: The President of the United States benefits from the ongoing counsel of his Council of Economic Advisers. The broad spectrum of economic issues with which political leaders must contend, and on which they must assume some tenable posture, is suggested by the contents of the annual *Economic Report of the President:* unemployment and inflation, economic growth and productivity, taxation and public expenditures, poverty and income maintenance, the balance of payments and the international monetary system, labor-management relations, manpower development and training, pollution, discrimination on the basis of race and sex, competition and antitrust, to enumerate only a few of the areas covered.

### △  Economics for Citizenship

These comments correctly imply that a basic understanding of economics is essential if we are to be well-informed citizens. Most of the specific problems of the day have important economic aspects, and as voters we can influence the decisions of our political leaders in coping with these problems. Should America adopt mandatory price and wage controls to restrain inflation? Should we make a national commitment to the development of new sources of energy? Should we attempt to break up the huge corporations which seem to dominate certain segments of our economy? What can be done to reduce unemployment? Are existing welfare programs effective and justifiable? Should we continue to subsidize farmers? Is there any justification for protecting certain industries from foreign competition? Should income be distributed more equally? Since the answers to such questions are determined by our elected officials, intelligence at the polls requires that we have a basic working knowledge of economics.

---

[1] Either of the following two volumes—Robert Heilbroner, *The Worldly Philosophers,* 4th ed. (New York: Simon and Schuster, Inc., 1972), or Daniel R. Fusfeld, 3d ed., *The Age of the Economist* (Chicago: Scott, Foresman and Company, 1977)—will provide the reader with a fascinating introduction to the historical development of economic ideas.

[2] Walter W. Heller, *New Dimensions of Political Economy* (New York: W. W. Norton & Company, Inc., 1967), p. 14.

△ **Personal Applications**

Economics is also a vital discipline for somewhat more mundane and immediate reasons. Economics is of practical value in business. An understanding of the overall operation of the economic system puts the business executive in a better position to formulate policies. The executive who understands the causes and consequences of inflation is better equipped during inflationary periods to make more intelligent decisions than otherwise. Indeed, more and more economists are appearing on the payrolls of large corporations. Their job? To gather and interpret economic information upon which rational business decisions can be made. Also, economics gives the individual as a worker and income receiver some insights as to how to become more secure in facing the effects of inflation and unemployment. How can one "hedge" against the reduction in the purchasing power of the dollar which accompanies inflation? What occupations are most immune to unemployment?

In spite of its practical benefits, however, the reader must be forewarned that economics is an academic, not a vocational, subject. Unlike accounting, advertising, corporation finance, and marketing, economics is not primarily a how-to-make-money area of study.[3] A knowledge of economics may be helpful in running a business or in managing one's personal finances, but this is not its primary objective. In economics, problems are usually examined from the social, not from the individual, point of view. The production, exchange, and consumption of goods and services are discussed from the viewpoint of society as a whole, not from the standpoint of one's own bankbook.

□ **METHODOLOGY**

What do economists do? What are their goals? What procedures do they employ? The

[3] An economist has been defined as an individual with a Phi Beta Kappa key on one end of a watch chain and with no watch on the other.

title of this volume—*Economics: Principles, Problems, and Policies*—contains a thumbnail answer to the first two questions. Economists derive economic *principles* which are useful in the formulation of *policies* designed to solve economic *problems*. The procedure employed by the economist is summarized in Figure 1-1. The economist must first ascertain and gather the facts which are relevant to consideration of a specific economic problem. This task is sometimes called "descriptive economics." The economist then puts this collection of facts in order and summarizes them by "distilling out" a principle, that is, by generalizing about the way individuals and institutions actually behave. Deriving principles from facts

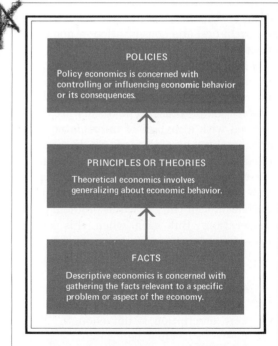

FIGURE 1-1  THE RELATIONSHIP BETWEEN FACTS, PRINCIPLES, AND POLICIES IN ECONOMICS

In studying any problem or segment of the economy, the economist must first gather the relevant facts. These facts must then be systematically arranged, interpreted, and generalized upon. These generalizations are useful not only in explaining economic behavior, but also in predicting and therefore controlling future events.

is called "economic theory" or "economic analysis." Finally, the general knowledge of economic behavior which economic principles provide can then be used in formulating policies, that is, remedies or solutions, for correcting or avoiding the problem under scrutiny. This final aspect of the field is sometimes called "applied economics" or "policy economics."

Continuing to use Figure 1-1 as a point of reference, let us now examine this three-step procedure in more detail.

## △ Descriptive Economics

All sciences are empirical. All sciences are based upon facts, that is, upon observable and verifiable behavior of certain data or subject matter. In the physical sciences the factual data are inorganic. As a social science, economics is concerned with the behavior of individuals and institutions engaged in the production, exchange, and consumption of goods and services.

The first major step, then, in investigating a given problem or a specific segment of the economy is to gather the facts. This can be an infinitely complex task. The world of reality is cluttered with a myriad of interrelated facts. The economist therefore must use discretion in fact gathering. One must distinguish economic from noneconomic facts and then determine which economic facts are relevant and which are irrelevant for the particular problem under consideration. But even when this sorting process has been completed, the relevant economic facts may appear diverse and unrelated.

## △ Economic Theory

A conglomeration of facts is relatively useless; mere description is not enough. To be meaningful, facts must be systematically arranged, interpreted, and generalized upon. This is the task of economic theory or analysis. Principles and theories—the end result of economic analysis—bring order and meaning to a number of facts by tying these facts together, putting them in correct relationship to one another, and generalizing upon them.

"Theories without facts may be barren, but facts without theories are meaningless."[4]

The interplay between the levels of fact and theory is more complex than Figure 1-1 indicates. Principles and theories are meaningful statements drawn from facts, but facts, in turn, serve as a constant check on the validity of principles already established. Facts—how individuals and institutions actually behave in producing, exchanging, and consuming goods and services—change with time. This makes it essential that economists continuously check existing principles and theories against the changing economic environment. The history of economic ideas is strewn with once-valid generalizations about economic behavior which were rendered obsolete by the changing course of events.

**Terminology**  A word on terminology is essential at this juncture. Economists talk about "laws," "principles," "theories," and "models." These terms all mean essentially the same thing: generalizations, or statements of regularity, concerning the economic behavior of individuals and institutions. The term "economic law" is a bit misleading because it implies a high degree of exactness, universal application, and even moral rightness. So, to a lesser degree, does the term "principle." And some people incorrectly associate the term "theory" with idle pipe dreams and ivory-tower hallucinations, divorced from the facts and realities of the world. The term "model" has much to commend it. A model is a simplified picture of reality, an abstract generalization of how the relevant data actually behave. In this book these four terms will be used synonymously. The choice of terms in labeling any particular generalization will be governed by custom or convenience here. Hence, the relationship between the price of a product and the quantity consumers purchase will be called

[4]Kenneth E. Boulding, *Economic Analysis: Microeconomics,* 4th ed. (New York: Harper & Row, Publishers, Incorporated, 1966), p. 5.

the "law" of demand, rather than the theory or principle of demand, because it is customary so to designate it.

Several other points regarding the character and derivation of economic principles are in order.

**Generalizations**  Economic principles are *generalizations* and, as the term implies, characterized by somewhat imprecise quantitative statement. Economic facts are usually diverse; some individuals and institutions act one way and some another way. Hence, economic principles are frequently stated in terms of averages or statistical probabilities. For example, when economists say that the average household earned an income of about $15,060 in 1978, they are making a generalization. It is recognized that some households earned much more and a good many others much less. Yet this generalization, properly handled and interpreted, can be very meaningful and useful. Similarly, economic generalizations are often stated in terms of probabilities. For example, a researcher may tell us that there is a 95 percent probability that every $1.00 reduction in personal income taxes will result in a $.92 increase in consumer spending.

**"Other Things Equal" Assumption**  Like other scientists, economists make use of the *ceteris paribus,* or "other things being equal," assumption in constructing their generalizations. That is, they assume all other variables except the one under consideration are held constant. This technique simplifies the reasoning process by isolating the relationship under consideration. To illustrate: In considering the relationship between the price of product X and the amount of X purchased, it is most helpful to assume that, of all the factors which might influence the amount of X purchased (for example, the price of X, the prices of other goods, consumer incomes and tastes), only the price of X varies. The economist is then able to focus upon the "price of X-purchases of X" relationship without reasoning being blurred or confused by the intrusion of other variables.

In the physical and biological sciences controlled experiments usually can be performed where "all other things" are in fact held constant. Thus, the assumed relationship between two variables can be empirically tested with great precision. But economics is not a laboratory science. The economist's process of empirical verification is based upon "real world" data generated by the actual operation of the economy. In this rather bewildering environment "other things" do change. Despite the development of rather sophisticated statistical techniques designed to hold other things equal, such controls are less than perfect. As a result, economic principles are less certain and less precise than those of the laboratory sciences.

**Abstractions**  Economic principles, or theories, are necessarily abstractions. They do not embody the full bloom of reality. The very process of sorting out noneconomic and irrelevant facts in the fact-gathering process involves abstracting from reality. Unfortunately, the abstractness of economic theory prompts the uninformed to identify theory as something which is impractical and unrealistic. This is nonsense! As a matter of fact, economic theories are practical for the simple reason that they are abstractions. The level of reality is too complex to be very meaningful. Economists theorize in order to give meaning to a maze of facts which would otherwise be confusing and useless and to put facts into a more usable, practical form. Thus, to generalize is to abstract; generalization for this purpose is practical, and therefore so is abstraction. An economic theory is a model—a simplified picture or map—of some segment of the economy. This model enables us to understand reality better *because* it avoids the details of reality. Finally, theories—*good* theories—are grounded on facts and therefore are realistic. Theories which do not fit the facts are simply not good theories.

**Induction and Deduction**   In saying that economists distill principles from facts we are describing the *inductive* or empirical method. Here we begin with an accumulation of facts which are then arranged systematically and analyzed so as to permit the derivation of a generalization or principle. Induction moves from facts to theory, from the particular to the general. We must now note that, in terms of Figure 1-1, economists frequently set about their task by beginning at the level of theory and proceed to the verification or rejection of this theory by an appeal to the facts. This is the *deductive* or hypothetical method. Thus, economists may draw upon casual observation, insight, logic, or intuition to frame a tentative, untested principle called an *hypothesis*. For example, they may conjecture, on the basis of "armchair logic," that it is rational for consumers to buy more of a product when its price

is low than when its price is high. The validity of this hypothesis must then be tested by the systematic and repeated examination of relevant facts. The deductive method goes from the general to the particular, from theory to facts. Most economists view deduction and induction as complementary, rather than opposing, techniques of investigation. Hypotheses formulated by deduction provide guidelines for the economist in gathering and systematizing empirical data. Conversely, some understanding of factual evidence—of the "real world"—is prerequisite to the formulation of meaningful hypotheses.

**Graphic Expression**   Theories, or models, can be expressed in many ways. For example, the physicist and the chemist illustrate their theories by building Tinker-Toy arrangements of multicolored wooden balls that represent protons, neutrons, and so forth, held in proper relationship to one another by wires or sticks. Economists are not so lucky as to have theories that lend themselves to such tangible demonstrations. *Economic models may take the form of verbal statements, numerical tables, mathematical equations, or graphs.* The last are particularly helpful and will be used throughout this book. Most of the principles we shall encounter will explain the relationship between just two sets of economic facts, for example, the relationship between the price of a specific product and the quantity of it which consumers buy. Simple two-dimensional graphs are a convenient and clear way of visualizing and manipulating these relationships.

As shown in Figure 1-2, graphs are drawn on squared paper divided into four quarters, or quadrants, by a horizontal axis and a vertical axis, which intersect at right angles. The point of intersection is called the *origin*. Each axis has a scale of numerical values. On the vertical axis, all values above the origin are positive, and all values below are negative. On the horizontal axis, values to the right of the origin are positive; those to the left are negative. The

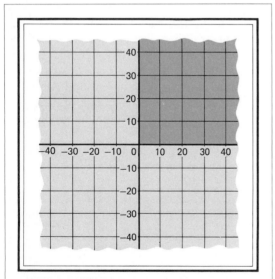

**FIGURE 1-2   ECONOMIC PRINCIPLES CAN BE EXPRESSED GRAPHICALLY**

Two-dimensional graphs are a convenient way of presenting and manipulating relationships between data. The relationship between two sets of economic data with positive numerical values is shown in the northeast quadrant of the chart.

point of intersection, that is, the origin, designates zero. Though the vertical and horizontal
scales in Figure 1-2 measure the same numerical values, this need not be the case. Each unit
on the vertical axis may measure $1, while the
same distance on the horizontal axis may denote 1000 bushels of corn.

In elementary economics we are virtually
always concerned with the relationship between two sets of economic facts, the values of
which are positive. Hence, we are concerned
with the upper right-hand (northeast) quadrant where both scales measure positive
values.

Now let us explore an example or two to
illustrate the construction and interpretation
of graphs. Suppose detailed factual investigation reveals that, other things being equal, the
relationship between the price of corn per
bushel and the amount farmers are willing to
produce and offer for sale per year is as shown
in Table 1-1.

How can this be shown graphically? Simply by putting the two sets of facts—product
price and quantity supplied—on the two axes
of the chart and locating the five combinations

**TABLE 1-1**
**The Quantities of Corn Farmers will Supply
at Various Prices (*hypothetical data*)**

| Price per bushel | Bushels supplied per year |
|---|---|
| $5 | 12,000 |
| 4 | 10,000 |
| 3 | 7,000 |
| 2 | 4,000 |
| 1 | 1,000 |

of price-quantity supplied as shown in Table
1-1. Convention or convenience dictates which
set of facts goes on the vertical axis and which
on the horizontal axis. By convention, economists put "price" on the vertical and "quantity" on the horizontal axis, as indicated in Figure 1-3. The five price-quantity combinations
are plotted on the chart by drawing perpendiculars from the appropriate points on the two
axes. For example, in plotting the $5–12,000-
bushel combination, perpendiculars must be
drawn across from the vertical (price) axis at
$5 and up from the horizontal (quantity-
supplied) axis at 12,000 bushels. Their point of
intersection locates the $5–12,000-bushel com-

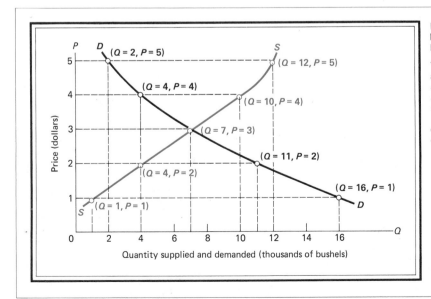

**FIGURE 1-3 GRAPHING
DIRECT AND INVERSE
RELATIONSHIPS**

Two sets of economic data which
are directly related, such as price
and quantity supplied, graph as
an upsloping curve (*SS*). Two
sets of data which are inversely
related, such as price and
quantity demanded, graph as a
downsloping curve (*DD*).

bination on the graph. The same procedure locates the other four price-quantity combinations. If it is assumed that the same general relationship between price and quantity supplied will prevail at all points between the five graphed, a line or curve can be drawn to connect these points. In this instance the two sets of data are *directly related;* that is, price and quantity supplied change in the same direction. As price increases, the quantity supplied increases. As price declines, so does the quantity supplied. When two sets of data are directly related, they will always graph as an *upsloping* line or curve, such as *SS* in Figure 1-3.

Now suppose fact gathering reveals that the price of corn and the quantity which consumers will buy per year are related in the manner shown in Table 1-2. These data indicate that consumers will demand more corn when its price is low than they will when the price is high; that is, price and quantity are *inversely related*. If price increases, the amount purchased will decline. If price declines, the quantity purchased will increase. An inverse relationship will always graph as a *downsloping* line or curve, such as *DD* in Figure 1-3.

Anticipating Chapter 4, we note in passing that Figure 1-3 constitutes a basic economic model of a market. That is, by combining the direct relationship between price and quantity supplied—called the *law of supply*—and the inverse relationship between price and quantity demanded—labeled the *law of demand*—

we have constructed a simple economic model. Hence, we will find in Chapter 4 that the intersection of these two curves identifies the market price ($3 in this case) and the quantity of the product (7000 bushels) which will be bought and sold. Although this model is very simple, we shall discover in later chapters that it has wide applicability and great explanatory power.

**Dangers of Models**   When properly constructed and interpreted, economic models are invaluable tools. But we must be aware of certain potential dangers in deriving and applying these models.

**1**   The fundamental danger in constructing an economic model or principle is that the economist might fail to distinguish correctly between relevant and irrelevant facts. If the economist "boils out" some relevant facts, the resulting principle may be a disjointed, misleading, and, at best, incomplete analytical tool. A related difficulty stems from the possibility that an economist might abstract from too many facts and construct a model which is hyperabstract and truly out of touch with reality.

**2**   In applying economic models, we must always recognize them for what they are—useful first approximations. It is easy, but dangerous, to slip into the practice of becoming so enamored of the logical clarity of a model that we forget it is only a rough outline of reality. There may be many omissions between a simplified economic model and reality.

**3**   We must be on guard in applying economic models so as not to impute any ethical or moral qualities to them. Economic models are the analytical tools of the economist and, as such, they are ethically neutral. Because they are constructed of facts, economic models afford general statements about "what is," not indications of "what ought to be." Figure 1-3 does not tell us that farmers *should* supply more corn at higher prices than at lower prices, but, rather, that they *actually do*.

**TABLE 1-2**
**The Quantities of Corn Consumers will Purchase at Various Prices (*hypothetical data*)**

| Price per bushel | Bushels demanded per year |
|---|---|
| $5 | 2,000 |
| 4 | 4,000 |
| 3 | 7,000 |
| 2 | 11,000 |
| 1 | 16,000 |

△ **Policy Economics**

We value economic principles for the knowledge they contain. Economic models can help us understand why prices rise or fall, what causes unemployment, why shortages or surpluses of products occur, and so on. But more importantly, economic theory is the basis for *economic policy*; that is, our understanding of economic principles can be applied in resolving specific problems and in furthering the realization of society's overall goals. Economic principles are extremely valuable as predictive devices. And accurate prediction is obviously required if we want to alter some event or outcome. More specifically, if some undesirable event (such as unemployment or inflation) can be predicted or understood through economic theory, we may then be able to influence or control that event. Or, if we cannot control an outcome, at least we gain from prediction invaluable time to prepare for adjusting to its consequences. Ability to predict a rainstorm does not give us control over the weather, but it does permit us to prepare for it by carrying a raincoat and an umbrella.

**Values**  It is evident that value judgments—opinions as to what is desirable or undesirable—come into the picture at this juncture. Descriptive economics and economic theory are both concerned with facts—the former immediately and the latter once removed. Policy economics necessarily entails value judgments as to the desirability of certain events. When operating at this level, economists are no longer functioning as scientists per se, but, rather, as policy makers. They are dealing not only with facts, but also with values.

An example or two will help at this point. Our previously noted law of demand is the basis for one illustration: "Consumers generally buy more of a product at a low price than they do at a high price." Suppose a clothing merchant has a large overstock of summer clothing at a time when shipments of fall and winter clothing are due. The merchant must somehow get rid of this undesired surplus stock of summer wear. Our law of demand helps the merchant solve this problem by predicting how consumers will react to price changes. In particular, the principle predicts that the merchant will be able to increase sales and "move" the surplus by lowering prices. He will formulate price policies accordingly, and "run a sale." The surplus disappears.

A second example, of greater consequence to the economy as a whole, involves the fundamental principle that, within certain limits, there is a direct relationship between total spending and the level of employment in the economy. "If total spending increases (decreases), the volume of employment will rise (fall)." This principle can be invaluable to government in determining its economic policies. For example, if government economists note that available statistics indicate an actual slackening of total expenditures, the principle will permit them to predict the undesirable consequence of unemployment. Aware of this anticipated result, public officials are now in a position to set in motion certain government policies designed to bolster total spending and head off expected unemployment. In short, we must be able to predict in order to effectively control. Economic principles help make prediction possible.

**Economic Goals**  It is important at this point that we note, and reflect upon, a number of economic goals or values which are widely, though not universally, accepted in our society and, indeed, in many other societies. These goals may be briefly listed as follows:

*1  Economic growth*  The production of more and better goods and services, or, more simply stated, a higher standard of living, is desired.

*2  Full employment*  Suitable jobs should be available for all who are willing and able to work.

*3  Price stability*  Sizable upswings or downswings in the general price level, that is, inflation and deflation, should be avoided.

**4  *Economic freedom***  Business executives, workers, and consumers should enjoy a high degree of freedom in their economic activities.

**5  *An equitable distribution of income***  No group of citizens should face stark poverty while other citizens enjoy extreme luxury.

**6  *Economic security***  Provision should be made for those who are chronically ill, disabled, handicapped, aged, or otherwise dependent.

Now this list of widely accepted goals[5] provides the basis for several significant points. First, note that this or any other statement of basic economic goals inevitably entails problems of interpretation. What are "sizable" changes in the price level? What is a "high degree" of economic freedom? What is an "equitable" distribution of income? Although most of us might accept the above goals as generally stated, we might also disagree very substantially as to their specific meanings and hence as to the types of policies needed to attain these goals. It is noteworthy that, although goals 1 to 3 are subject to reasonably accurate measurements, the inability to quantify goals 4 to 6 undoubtedly contributes to controversy over their precise meaning.

Second, certain of these goals are complementary in that to the extent one goal is achieved, some other goal or goals will also tend to be realized. For example, the achieving of full employment (goal 2) obviously means the elimination of unemployment, a basic cause of low incomes (goal 5) and economic insecurity (goal 6). Furthermore, considering goals 1 and 5, it is generally agreed that the sociopolitical tensions which may accompany a highly unequal distribution of income are tempered to the extent that most incomes rise absolutely as a result of economic growth.

[5]There are other goals which might be added. For example, the realization of balance in our international trade and finance is an important national goal, as is improvement of the physical environment.

Third, some goals may be conflicting or mutually exclusive. Some economists argue that those forces which further the attainment of economic growth and full employment may be the very same forces which cause inflation. In fact, the apparent conflict between goals 2 and 3 has been at the forefront of economic research and debate in recent years. Goals 1 and 5 may also be in conflict. Many economists point out that efforts to achieve greater equality in the distribution of income may weaken incentives to work, invest, innovate, and take business risks, that is, to do the things that promote rapid economic growth. They argue that government tends to equalize the distribution of income by taxing high-income people quite heavily and transferring those tax revenues to low-income people. The incentives of a high-income individual will be diminished because taxation reduces one's income rewards. Similarly, a low-income person will be less motivated to work and engage in other productive activities when government stands ready to subsidize that individual. In Chapter 37 we will encounter a more sophisticated statement of this conflict.

This leads us to a fourth point: When basic goals do conflict, society is forced to develop a system of priorities for the objectives it seeks. To illustrate: If full employment and price stability are to some extent mutually exclusive, that is, if full employment is accompanied by some inflation *and* price stability entails some unemployment, society must decide upon the relative importance of these two goals. Suppose the relevant choice is between, say, a 7 percent annual increase in the price level accompanied by full employment on the one hand, and a perfectly stable price level with 8 percent of the labor force unemployed on the other. Which is the better choice? Or how about a compromise goal in the form of, say, a 4 percent increase in the price level each year with 6 percent of the labor force out of work? There is obviously ample room for disagreement here.

**Formulating Economic Policy**  The creation of specific policies designed to achieve the broad economic goals of our society is no simple matter. A brief examination of the basic steps in policy formulation is in order.

**1**  The first step is to make a clear statement of goals. If we say that we have "full employment," do we mean that everyone between, say, 16 and 65 years of age has a job? Or do we mean that everyone who wants to work has a job? Should we allow for some "normal" unemployment caused by workers' voluntarily changing jobs?

**2**  Next we must state and recognize the possible effects of alternative policies designed to achieve the goal. This entails a clear-cut understanding of the economic impact, benefits, costs, and political feasibility of alternative programs. Thus, for example, economists currently debate the relative merits and demerits of fiscal policy (changing government spending and taxes) and monetary policy (altering the supply of money) as alternative means of achieving and maintaining full employment (Chapter 17).

**3**  We are obligated to both ourselves and future generations to look back upon our experiences with chosen policies and evaluate their effectiveness; it is only through this type of evaluation that we can hope to improve policy applications. Did a given change in taxes or the supply of money alter the level of employment to the extent originally predicted? If not, why not?

△  **Recapitulation**
It might be useful at this juncture to bring the salient points of our discussion together in a brief illustration. Suppose we decide to investigate the relationship between income and consumption for the economy as a whole. To gather the relevant *facts* in this instance we simply turn to published government documents and record the relevant data, a sampling of which is shown in Table 1-3. Do these data suggest a *principle?* They clearly do: Examin-

**TABLE 1-3**
The Relationship between Disposable Income and Consumption (columns 2 and 3 in billions of dollars)

| (1) Year | (2) Disposable income | (3) Consumption | (4) = (3) ÷ (2) Consumption/ Disposable income |
|---|---|---|---|
| 1960 | $  349 | $  325 | 93% |
| 1963 | 403 | 375 | 93 |
| 1966 | 510 | 465 | 91 |
| 1969 | 630 | 580 | 92 |
| 1972 | 801 | 733 | 92 |
| 1975 | 1,087 | 979 | 90 |
| 1978 | 1,451 | 1,340 | 92 |

*Source: Economic Report of the President, 1979.*

ing columns 2 and 3, we observe that *consumption varies directly with disposable (after-tax) income.* But our generalization will be more useful if it can be quantified. This is achieved through column 4 wherein consumption is expressed as a percentage of disposable income. Our generalization can now be stated with greater precision: *Households consume approximately 92 percent of their disposable incomes.* Is this knowledge useful for public *policy?* Yes, indeed! Suppose that the total level of spending is so low that the national output is far below the economy's productive potential and we are faced with the problem of substantial unemployment. Our generalization will permit economists to predict the size of the tax cut which will be required to increase disposable incomes and stimulate consumer spending sufficiently so as to restore production to the full-employment level.

☐  **TWO CHEERS FOR ECONOMISTS**
How successful have economists been in formulating economic principles and applying them to economic problems? What is the current "state of the art"? This is a broad and complex question to which there are no simple, unqualified answers.

There is, on the one hand, substantial evidence that economics has achieved rapid and significant progress in recent decades. The flow of scholarly articles, monographs, and treatises on a vast spectrum of economic questions has been "swelling like a tidal wave," reflecting a knowledge explosion in the discipline. Furthermore, economists take considerable pride in the fact that their discipline is the only social science for which the Swedish Academy of Science awards a Nobel Prize. And, as noted at the outset of this chapter, the counsel and advice of economists are systematically sought and applied by governments at all levels and of all ideologies.

Yet, there is an undercurrent of dissatisfaction with the accomplishments of economics. As one critic has put it, the light of economic understanding "is curiously uneven. Some parts of the social machinery are brilliantly lit. Other parts are left shadowy or totally dark."[6] Although interrelated and somewhat overlapping, the criticisms of economics run along the following lines.

**1   Hyperabstraction**   One frequently voiced criticism is that the ability of economists to "theorize" in the sense of reasoning abstractly has outrun the base of factual data. Because of the application of mathematics to economics and the availability of computers, economists can construct and manipulate highly complex models involving in some instances hundreds of equations. But, it is argued, the economic relationships shown in these equations are often *assumed* or based upon sketchy and questionable empirical evidence. To a degree, economics has lost touch with reality in that it is often difficult, if not impossible, to verify or reject economic theories in the light of reliable empirical facts.

**2   Dodging Values**   In their desire to maintain scientific objectivity, economists

have generally tended either to avoid, or to approach timidly, those problems or issues which are immersed in subjective value judgments. Stated differently, economics has increasingly limited itself to quantifiable aspects of human behavior and has skirted qualitative questions in the name of scientific purity. Notable example: Economists have had relatively little to say concerning the highly relevant question of how income ought to be distributed. The reason: There is no scientific way of calculating the gain to person B and the loss to person A as dollars are shifted from A to B. These gains and losses are subjective and nonmeasureable. Consequently, economists have largely dodged the question of income redistribution. Incidentally, some observers hold that the entire field of economics is based upon the value judgment that "more is better," that is, it is desirable to have more output rather than less, and therefore find it ironic that economists shun certain issues wherein values are inherently involved.

**3   Disciplinary Myopia**   Economists have been criticized for an unwillingness to look across disciplinary boundaries and acknowledge the importance of other disciplines in explaining real-world events. Real-world problems *are* multidisciplinary in character; that is, in addition to economics these problems entail social, political, cultural, historical, and psychological aspects. As a result, the purely economic analysis of these problems entails a limited and unrealistic understanding of them and, consequently, ineffective and misguided policy recommendations. First example: Many studies of the problems of the less developed countries have resulted in ineffective growth policies for these nations, not because of faulty economic analyses, but because of a failure to grasp the sociocultural milieu, the historical background, the political institutions, and the attitudinal characteristics of the country. Second example: It is contended that the insistent inflation of the 1970s is *not* explainable in terms of accepted economic theory

[6]Robert L. Heilbroner, "On the Limited 'Relevance' of Economics," *The Public Interest,* Fall 1970, p. 81.

(as presented in Part 2), but, rather, in terms of political decisions and the exertion of *power*. In particular, the formation of the oil cartel by the Organization of Petroleum Exporting Countries (OPEC) caused a dramatic power shift internationally, the major consequence of which has been dramatic increases in petroleum prices and worldwide inflation.[7]

**4   Real-World Dynamics**   Changes in the "facts" of the real world have a persistent tendency to render the existing body of economic knowledge obsolete and irrelevant. The composition of output and the structure of industry are constantly changing; the legislative and institutional framework of the economy vary through time; the relative significance and goals of the governmental sector are continuously shifting; the scope and character of our economic relationships with the rest of the world have altered considerably; and so on. Hence, a growing number of economists feel that widely accepted theories which provided an understanding of the Depression economy of the 1930s and the war-induced prosperity of the 1940s are less applicable to the economy of the 1970s and 1980s wherein inflation and unemployment have tended to persist simultaneously.

□   **PITFALLS TO STRAIGHT THINKING**
Our discussion of the economist's procedure has, up to this point, skirted some of the specific problems and pitfalls frequently encountered in attempting to think straight about economic problems. Consider the following impediments to valid economic reasoning.

[7]See Robert Lekachman, *Economists at Bay* (New York: McGraw-Hill Book Company, 1976), particularly chap. 1, and John Kenneth Galbraith, "Power and the Useful Economist," *American Economic Review,* March 1973, pp. 1–11. The ideas expressed in these first three criticisms of orthodox economics are associated with an alternative conception of the economy known as "institutional economics" or "evolutionary economics." The interested reader should consult Allan G. Gruchy, *Contemporary Economic Thought* (Clifton, N.J.: Augustus M. Kelley, Publishers, 1972).

△   **Bias**
In contrast to a neophyte physicist or chemist, the budding economist ordinarily brings into economics a bundle of biases and preconceptions about the field. For example, one might be suspicious of business profits or feel that deficit spending is evil. Needless to say, biases may cloud our thinking and interfere with objective analysis. The beginning economics student must be willing to shed biases and preconceptions which are simply not warranted by facts.

△   **Loaded Terminology**
The economic terminology to which we are exposed in newspapers and popular magazines is sometimes emotionally loaded. The writer—or more frequently the particular interest group he or she represents—may have a cause to further or an ax to grind, and terms will be slanted to solicit the support of the reader. Hence, we may find a governmental flood-control project in the Great Plains region called "creeping socialism" by its opponents and "intelligent democratic planning" by its proponents. We must be prepared, therefore, to discount such terminology in achieving objectivity in the understanding of important economic issues.

△   **Definitions**
No scientist is obligated to use common-sense or immediately understandable definitions of his or her terms. The economist may find it convenient and essential to define terms in such a way that they are clearly at odds with the definitions held by most people in everyday speech. So long as the economist is explicit and consistent in these definitions, he or she is on safe ground. A typical example: The term "investment" to John Q. Citizen is associated with the buying of bonds and stocks in the securities market. How often have we heard someone talking of "investing" in General Motors stock or government bonds? But to the economist, "investment" means the purchase of real capital assets such as machinery

and equipment, or the construction of a new wing on a factory building, not the purely financial transaction of swapping cash or part of a bank balance for a neatly engraved piece of paper.

△ **Fallacy of Composition:**
  **Macro and Micro**

Another pitfall in economic thinking is to assume that "what is true for the individual or part is necessarily also true for the group or whole." This is a logical fallacy; it is *not* correct. The validity of a particular generalization for an individual or part does not necessarily ensure its accuracy for the group or whole.

A noneconomic example may help: You are watching a football game on a sunny autumn afternoon. The home team executes an outstanding play. In the general excitement, you leap to your feet to get a better view. *Generalization:* "If you, *an individual,* stand, then your view of the game is improved." But does this also hold true for the group—for everyone watching the game? Certainly not! If everyone stands to watch the play, everyone—including you—will probably have the same or even a worse view than when seated!

Consider an example or two from economics: A wage increase for Smith is desirable because, given product prices, it increases Smith's purchasing power and standard of living. But if everyone realizes a wage increase, product prices will rise, that is, inflation will occur. Therefore, Smith's standard of living may be unchanged as higher prices offset this larger salary. Second illustration: An *individual* farmer who is fortunate enough to reap a bumper crop is likely to realize a resulting income that is larger than usual. This is a correct generalization. Does it apply to farmers as a *group?* Possibly not, for the simple reason that to the individual farmer, crop prices will not be influenced (reduced) by this bumper crop, because each farmer is producing a negligible fraction of the total farm output. But to farmers as a group, prices vary inversely with

total output.[8] Thus, as all farmers realize bumper crops, the total output of farm products rises, thereby depressing prices. If price declines overbalance the unusually large output, farm incomes *fall.*

In a sense, these comments on the fallacy of composition boil down to this: There are two essentially different levels of analysis at which the economist may derive laws concerning economic behavior. The level of *macroeconomics* is concerned either with the economy as a whole or with the basic subdivisions or aggregates—such as the government, household, and business sectors—which make up the economy. An aggregate is a collection of specific economic units which are treated *as if* they were one unit. Thus, we might find it convenient to lump together the 15 million businesses in our economy and treat them as if they were one huge unit. In dealing with aggregates, macroeconomics is concerned with obtaining an overview, or general outline, of the structure of the economy and the relationships among the major aggregates which constitute the economy. No attention is given to the specific units which make up the various aggregates. It is not surprising, then, to find that macroeconomics entails discussions of such magnitudes as *total* output, the *total* level of employment, *total* income, *total* expenditures, the *general* level of prices, and so forth, in analyzing various economic problems. In short, macroeconomics examines the forest, not the trees. It gives us a bird's-eye view of the economy.

On the other hand, *microeconomics* is concerned with *specific* economic units and a *detailed* consideration of the behavior of these individual units. When operating at this level of analysis, the economist figuratively puts an economic unit, or very small segment of the economy, under the microscope to observe the details of its operation. Here we talk in terms of an individual industry, firm, or household and concentrate upon such magnitudes as the

---

[8]This assumes there are no government programs which fix farm prices.

output or price of a *specific* product, the number of workers employed by a single firm, the revenue or income of a particular firm or household, the expenditures of a given firm or family, and so forth. In microeconomics we examine the trees, not the forest. Microeconomics is useful in achieving a worm's-eye view of some very specific component of our economic system.

The basic point is this: The fallacy of composition reminds us that *generalizations which are valid at one of these levels of analysis may or may not be valid at the other.*

△  **Prosperity and Depression**

Closely related to the fallacy of composition is the fact that notions or ideas which are valid during prosperity may be invalid during depression, or vice versa. Some economic principles rest upon a specific presupposition concerning the phase of the business cycle; the validity of a given principle may depend upon the existence of good times or bad times. For example, the economist deems thrift or saving as economically beneficial and therefore desirable during periods of prosperity involving sharp inflation. Why? Because, as we shall discover, a high level of saving will tend to reduce inflationary pressure. Yet, during periods of depression, the economist is equally correct in generalizing to the effect that saving is an economic vice, the reason being that too much saving is the immediate cause of unemployment or depression.

△  **Cause and Effect: Post Hoc Fallacy**

Still another hazard in economic thinking is to assume that simply because one event precedes another, the first is necessarily the cause of the second. This kind of faulty reasoning is known as the *post hoc, ergo propter hoc,* or "after this, therefore because of this" fallacy.

A classic example clearly indicates the fallacy inherent in such reasoning. Suppose that early each spring the medicine man of a native tribe performs his ritual by cavorting around the village in a green costume. A week or so later the trees and grass turn green. Can we safely conclude that event A, the medicine man's gyrations, has caused event B, the landscape's turning green? The rooster crows before dawn, but this doesn't mean the rooster is responsible for the sunrise!

It is especially important in analyzing various sets of empirical data *not* to confuse correlation with causation. *Correlation* is a technical term which indicates that two sets of data are associated in some systematic and dependable way; for example, we may find that when X increases, Y also increases. But this does not necessarily mean that X is the cause of Y. The relationship could be purely coincidental or determined by some other factor, Z, not included in the analysis. Example: Economists have found a positive correlation between education and income. In general, people with more education earn higher incomes than do people with less education. Common sense prompts us to label education as the cause and higher incomes as the effect; more education suggests a more productive worker and such workers receive larger monetary rewards. But, on second thought, might not causation run the other way? That is, do people with higher incomes buy more education, just as they buy more automobiles and more steaks? Or is the relationship explainable in terms of still other factors? Are education and income positively correlated because the bundle of characteristics—ability, motivation, personal habits—required to succeed in education are the same characteristics required to be a productive and highly paid worker? Upon reflection, seemingly simple cause-effect relationships—"more education results in more income"—may prove to be suspect or perhaps flatly incorrect.

In short, cause-and-effect relationships are typically not self-evident in economics; the economist must look carefully before leaping to the conclusion that event A caused event B. Certainly the simple fact that A preceded B is not sufficient to warrant any such conclusion.

## Summary

**1**  Economics is concerned with the efficient use of scarce resources in the production of goods and services to satisfy material wants.

**2**  Economics is studied for several reasons: ***a.*** It provides valuable knowledge concerning our social environment and behavior; ***b.*** it equips a democratic citizenry to render fundamental decisions intelligently; ***c.*** although not a vocational discipline, economics may provide the business executive with valuable information.

**3**  Economics is based upon facts concerning the activities of individuals and institutions in producing, exchanging, and consuming goods and services.  The task of descriptive economics is the gathering of those economic facts which are relevant to a particular problem or specific segment of the economy.

**4**  These facts are then studied, arranged, and generalized upon.  The resulting generalizations are called "principles," "theories," or "models."  The derivation of these principles is the task of economic theory.

**5**  Economic principles have several noteworthy characteristics.  First, they are generalizations and, as such, are subject to exceptions and elude quantitatively precise statement.  Further, economic principles are models of reality and hence are abstract; their usefulness depends upon this abstraction.  Finally, economic principles often can be conveniently expressed on two-dimensional graphs.

**6**  Economic principles are particularly valuable as predictive devices; they are the bases for the formulation of economic policy designed to solve problems and control undesirable events.

**7**  Economic growth, full employment, price stability, economic freedom, equity in the distribution of income, and economic security are all widely accepted economic goals in our society.  Some of these goals are complementary; others are mutually exclusive.

**8**  There are numerous pitfalls in studying economics which the beginner may encounter.  Some of the more important chuckholes strewn along the road to economic understanding are ***a.*** biases and preconceptions, ***b.*** terminological difficulties, ***c.*** the fallacy of composition, ***d.*** the fact that the validity of some economic ideas may depend upon the stage of the business cycle, and ***e.*** the difficulty of establishing clear cause-effect relationships.

## Questions and Study Suggestions

**1**  Key terms and concepts to remember: descriptive economics; economic theory; policy economics; generalizations or principles; "other things equal" assumption; direct and inverse relationships; induction and deduction; value judgments; economic goals; fallacy of composition; macroeconomics and microeconomics; *post hoc, ergo propter hoc* fallacy; correlation and causation.

**2**  Explain in detail the interrelationships between economic facts, theory, and policy.  Critically evaluate: "The trouble with economics is that it is not practical.  It has too much to say about theory and not enough to say about facts."

**3**  Analyze and explain the following quotation:[9]

---

[9] Henry Clay, *Economics for the General Reader* (New York: The Macmillan Company, 1925), pp. 10–11.

Facts are seldom simple and usually complicated; theoretical analysis is needed to unravel the complications and interpret the facts before we can understand them . . . the opposition of facts and theory is a false one; the true relationship is complementary. We cannot in practice consider a fact without relating it to other facts, and the relation is a theory. Facts by themselves are dumb; before they will tell us anything we have to arrange them, and the arrangement is a theory. Theory is simply the unavoidable arrangement and interpretation of facts, which gives us generalizations on which we can argue and act, in the place of a mass of disjointed particulars.

4   Of what significance is the fact that economics is not a laboratory science? What problems may be involved in deriving and applying economic principles?

5   "Like all scientific laws, economic laws are established in order to make successful prediction of the outcome of human actions."[10]   Explain.

6   "Abstraction . . . is the inevitable price of generality . . . indeed abstraction and generality are virtually synonyms."[11]   Explain.

7   Briefly explain the use of graphs as a means of presenting economic principles. What is an inverse relationship? How does it graph? What is a direct relationship? How does it graph? Graph and explain the relationships one would expect to find between *a.* the number of inches of rainfall per month and the sale of umbrellas, *b.* the amount of tuition and the level of enrollment at a university, and *c.* the size of a university's athletic scholarships and the number of games won by its football team. In each case cite and explain how considerations other than those specifically mentioned might upset the expected relationship. Is your second generalization consistent with the fact that, historically, enrollments and tuition have both increased? If not, explain any difference.

8   To what extent would you accept the six economic goals stated and described in this chapter? What priorities would you assign to them? It has been said that we seek simply four goals: progress, stability, justice, and freedom. Is this list of goals compatible with that given in the chapter?

9   Analyze each of the following specific goals in terms of the six general goals stated on pages 11–12, and note points of conflict and compatibility: *a.* The lessening of environmental pollution; *b.* increasing leisure; and *c.* protection of American producers from foreign competition. Indicate which of these specific goals you favor and justify your position.

10   Interpret the curve in Figure 18-2 on page 352, indicating the nature of the public policy dilemma it illustrates. Which of the choices posed by the curve do you prefer? Why?

11   Explain and give an illustration of *a.* the fallacy of composition, and *b.* the "after this, therefore, because of this" fallacy. Why are cause-and-effect relationships difficult to isolate in the social sciences?

12   "Economists should never be popular; men who afflict the comfortable serve equally those who comfort the afflicted and one cannot suppose that American capitalism would long prosper without the critics its leaders find such a profound source of annoyance."[12]   Interpret and evaluate.

[10]Oskar Lange, "The Scope and Method of Economics," *Review of Economic Studies,* vol. 13, 1945-1946, p. 20.

[11]George J. Stigler, *The Theory of Price* (New York: The Macmillan Company, 1947), p. 10.

[12]John Kenneth Galbraith, *American Capitalism,* rev. ed. (Boston: Houghton Mifflin Company, 1956), p. 49.

## Selected References

Boulding, Kenneth E.: *Economics as a Science* (New York: McGraw-Hill Book Company, 1970).

Helppie, Charles, James Gibbons, and Donald Pearson: *Research Guide in Economics* (Morristown, N.J.: General Learning Press, 1974).

Hough, Robbin R.: *What Economists Do* (New York: Harper & Row, Publishers, Incorporated, 1972).

Keynes, J.N.: *The Scope and Method of Political Economy,* 4th ed. (New York: The Macmillan Company, 1930).

Lange, Oskar: "The Scope and Method of Economics," *Review of Economic Studies,* vol. 13, 1945–1946, pp. 19–32.

Lekachman, Robert: *Economists at Bay* (New York: McGraw-Hill Book Company, 1976).

Papps, Ivy, and Willie Henderson: *Models and Economic Theory* (Philadelphia: W. B. Saunders Company, 1977).

Stigler, George J.: *The Theory of Price* (New York: The Macmillan Company, 1947), chap. 1.

Ward, Benjamin: *What's Wrong with Economics?* (New York: Basic Books, Inc., Publishers, 1972).

# LAST WORD
## Economics and Gasoline Conservation

An interesting application of economic analysis to the problem of gasoline conservation follows. Using data for 21 nations, a rather pronounced inverse relationship is found between the amount of gas consumed and its price. The policy implication is that a special tax upon gasoline in the United States would be an effective means of restricting consumption.

There is now a large body of econometric and engineering evidence indicating very substantial responses of energy demand to changes in price over time. An oversimplified but revealing way of demonstrating the long-run response is to show for a single year consumption differences across countries that have had wide and long-standing differences in the levels of energy prices. If differences in the energy price levels have persisted for some time, the consumption variations (controlling for variations in incomes) should reveal long-run responses.

Availability of data allowed such an experiment for petroleum use in transportation in 1975 (see figure).

Countries that charged their consumers the highest prices for motor gasoline showed the lowest transportation petroleum use relative to their national income. In the United States and Canada, on the other hand, where gasoline prices were less than 50 percent of levels elsewhere, the intensity of oil consumption was approximately double that of the other countries. These results are particularly significant because the variation in prices between these countries is largely due to differences in gasoline tax levels.

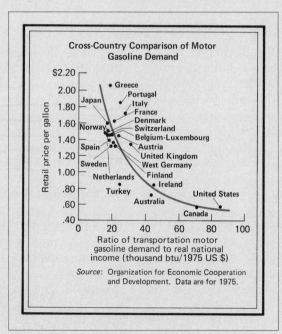

Cross-Country Comparison of Motor Gasoline Demand

*Source*: Organization for Economic Cooperation and Development. Data are for 1975.

*Economic Report of the President, 1978* (Washington, D. C.), pp. 189–190, abridged.

# An Introduction to the Economizing Problem

chapter 2

The primary objective of this chapter is to introduce and explore certain fundamental considerations which constitute the foundation of economic science. Basically, we want to expand upon the definition of economics introduced in Chapter 1 and explore the essence of the economizing problem. To this end, we shall illustrate, extend, and modify our definition of economics by the use of so-called production possibilities tables. We shall then restate and discuss the economizing problem in terms of certain practical questions. Finally, we shall survey briefly the different ways in which institutionally and ideologically diverse economies go about "solving" or responding to the economizing problem.

## □ THE FOUNDATION OF ECONOMICS

Two fundamental facts provide a foundation for the field of economics. It is imperative that we carefully state and fully understand these two facts, since everything that follows in our study of economics depends directly or indirectly upon them. The first fact is this: *Society's material wants, that is, the material wants of its citizens and institutions, are virtually unlimited or insatiable.* Second: *Economic resources—the means for producing goods and services—are limited or scarce.*

## △ Unlimited Wants

Let us systematically examine and explain these two facts in the order stated. In the first statement, precisely what do we mean by "material wants"? We mean, first, the desires of consumers to obtain and use various *goods* and *services* which give pleasure or satisfaction.[1] An amazingly wide range of products fills the bill in this respect: houses, automobiles, toothpaste, pencils, onions, sweaters, and the like.

[1]This definition leaves a variety of wants—recognition, status, love, and so forth—for the other social sciences to worry about.

In short, innumerable products which we sometimes classify as *necessities* (food, shelter, clothing) and *luxuries* (perfumes, yachts, mink coats) are all capable of satisfying human wants. Needless to say, what is a luxury to Smith may be a necessity to Jones, and what is a commonplace necessity today may have been a luxury a few short years ago.

But services may satisfy our wants as much as tangible products. A repair job on our car, the removal of our appendix, a haircut, and legal advice have in common with goods the fact that they satisfy human wants. On reflecting, we realize that we indeed buy many goods, for example, automobiles and washing machines, for the services they render. The differences between goods and services are often less than they seem to be at first.

Material wants also include those which businesses and units of government seek to satisfy. Businesses want factory buildings, machinery, trucks, warehouses, and other things that assist them in realizing their production goals. Government, reflecting the collective wants of its citizenry or goals of its own, seeks highways, schools, hospitals, and military hardware.

As a group, these material wants are, for practical purposes, *insatiable,* or *unlimited.*[2] This means that material wants for goods and services are incapable of being completely satisfied. A simple experiment will help to verify this point: Suppose we are asked to list those goods and services we want but do not now possess. If we take time to ponder our unfilled material wants, chances are our list will be impressive. And over a period of time, our wants multiply so that, as we fill some of the wants on the list, at the same time we add new

ones. Material wants, like rabbits, have a high reproduction rate. The rapid introduction of new products whets our appetites, and extensive advertising tries to persuade us that we need countless items we might not otherwise consider buying. Not too many years ago, the desire for color television, air conditioners, video recorders, digital watches, and tubeless tires was nonexistent. Furthermore, we often cannot stop with simple satisfaction: the acquisition of a Pinto or Chevette has been known to whet the appetite for a Porsche or Jaguar.

In summary, we may say that at any given time the individuals and institutions which constitute society have innumerable unfulfilled material wants. Some of these wants—food, clothing, shelter—have biological roots. But some are also influenced by the conventions and customs of society: the specific kinds of food, clothing, and shelter we seek are frequently determined by the general social and cultural environment in which we live. Over time, wants change and multiply, abetted by the development of new products and by extensive advertising and sales promotion.

Finally, let us emphatically add that the overall end or objective of all economic activity is the attempt to satisfy these diverse material wants.

### △  Scarce Resources

Consider now the second fundamental fact: *Economic resources are limited or scarce.* What do we mean by "economic resources"? In general, we are referring to all the natural, human, and manufactured resources that go into the production of goods and services. This obviously covers a lot of ground: factory and farm buildings and all sorts of equipment, tools, and machinery used in the production of manufactured goods and agricultural products; a variety of transportation and communication facilities; innumerable types of labor; and, last but not least, land and mineral resources of all kinds. There is an apparent need for a simplified classification of

---

[2]It should be mentioned in passing that the fallacy of composition is relevant here. Our wants for a *particular* good or service can obviously be satisfied; that is, over a short period of time we can get sufficient amounts of toothpaste or beer. Certainly one appendicitis operation is par for the course. But goods *in general* are another story. Here we do not, and presumably cannot, get enough. We shall say more about the satisfying of wants for specific goods in Chapter 24.

such resources, which we shall meet with the following categories: (1) *property* resources—land or raw materials and capital; (2) *human* resources—labor and entrepreneurial ability.

**Resource Categories**   What does the economist mean by *land?* Much more than do most people. Land refers to all natural resources—all "free gifts of nature"—which are usable in the productive process. Such resources as arable land, forests, mineral and oil deposits, and water resources come under this general classification. What about *capital?* Capital, or investment goods, refers to all manufactured aids to production, that is, all tools, machinery, equipment, and factory, storage, transportation, and distribution facilities used in producing goods and services and getting them to the ultimate consumer. *Capital goods* ("tools") differ from *consumer goods* in that the latter satisfy wants directly, whereas the former do so indirectly by facilitating the production of consumable goods. We should note especially that the term "capital" as here defined does *not* refer to money. True, business executives and economists often talk of "money capital," meaning money which is available for use in the purchase of machinery, equipment, and other productive facilities. But money, as such, produces nothing; hence, it is not to be considered as an economic resource. *Real capital*—tools, machinery, and other productive equipment—is an economic resource; *money* or *financial capital* is not. *Labor* is a broad term which the economist uses in referring to all man's physical and mental talents usable in producing goods and services (with the exception of a special set of human talents—entrepreneurial ability—which, because of their special significance in a capitalistic economy, we choose to consider separately). Thus the services of a ditch-digger, retail clerk, machinist, teacher, professional football player, and nuclear physicist all fall under the general heading of labor.

Finally, what can be said about this special human resource which we label *entrepreneurial ability,* or, more simply, *enterprise?* We shall give the term a specific meaning by assigning four related functions to the entrepreneur.

**1**   The entrepreneur takes the initiative in combining the resources of land, capital, and labor in the production of a good or service. Both a sparkplug and a catalyst, the entrepreneur is at once the driving force behind production and the agent who combines the other resources in what is hoped will be a profitable venture.

**2**   The entrepreneur has the chore of making basic business-policy decisions, that is, those nonroutine decisions which set the course of a business enterprise.

**3**   The entrepreneur is an innovator—the person who attempts to introduce on a commercial basis new products, new productive techniques, or even new forms of business organization.

**4**   The entrepreneur is obviously a risk bearer. This is apparent from a close examination of the other three entrepreneurial functions. The entrepreneur in a capitalistic system has no guarantee of profit. The reward for his or her time, efforts, and abilities may be attractive profits *or* losses and eventual bankruptcy. In short, the entrepreneur risks not only time, effort, and business reputation, but his invested funds and those of his associates or stockholders.

**Resource Payments**   We shall see shortly how these resources are provided for business institutions in exchange for money income. The income received from supplying property resources—raw materials and capital equipment—is called *rental* and *interest income.* The income accruing to those who supply labor is called *wages* and includes salaries and various wage and salary supplements in the form of bonuses, commissions, royalties, and so forth. Entrepreneurial income is called *profits,* which, of course, may be a negative figure—that is, losses.

These four broad categories of economic

resources, or _factors of production_ as they are often called, leave room for debate when it comes to classifying specific resources. For example, suppose you receive a dividend on some General Motors stock which you may own. Is this an interest return for the capital equipment which the company was able to buy with the money you provided in buying GM stock? Or is this return a profit which compensates you for the risks involved in purchasing corporate stock? What about the earnings of a one-person general store where the owner is both the entrepreneur and the labor force? Are the owner's earnings to be considered as wages or profit income? The answer to both queries is "some of each." The important point is this: Although we might quibble about classifying a given flow of income as wages, rent, interest, or profits, all income can be listed without too much arbitrariness under one of these general headings.

**Relative Scarcity**  All economic resources, or factors of production, have one fundamental characteristic in common: _Economic resources are scarce or limited in supply._ Our "spaceship earth" contains only limited amounts of resources which can be put to use in the production of goods and services. Quantities of arable land, mineral deposits, capital equipment, and labor (time) are all limited; that is, they are available only in finite amounts. Because of the scarcity of productive resources and the constraint this scarcity puts upon productive activity, output will necessarily be limited. Society will _not_ be able to consume all the goods and services it might want. Thus, in the United States—one of the most affluent nations on earth—output per person was limited to $10,737 in 1979.

☐  **ECONOMICS DEFINED**

Given that wants are unlimited and resources are scarce, economics can be defined as _the social science concerned with the problem of using or administering scarce resources (the_

_means of producing) so as to attain the greatest or maximum fulfillment of society's unlimited wants (the goal of producing)._ Economics is concerned with "doing the best with what we have." If our wants are virtually unlimited and our resources are scarce, we cannot conceivably satisfy all society's material wants. The next best thing is to achieve the greatest possible satisfaction of these wants. Economics is a science of efficiency—efficiency in the use of scarce resources.

Precisely what is meant by _efficiency_ as economists use the term? It means something akin to, but not identical with, the term "efficiency" as used in engineering. The mechanical engineer tells us that a steam locomotive is only "10 percent efficient" because a large part—some 90 percent—of the energy in its fuel is not transformed into useful power but is wasted through friction and heat loss. The maximum output of usable power is not derived from the inputs of fuel.

Economic efficiency is also concerned with _inputs_ and _outputs._ Specifically, it is concerned with the relationship between the units of scarce resources which are put into the process of production and the resulting output of some wanted product; economic efficiency deals with inputs of scarce resources and outputs of useful products.

△  **Full Employment and**
  **Full Production**

Society wants to use its scarce resources efficiently; that is, it wants to get the maximum amount of goods and services produced with its limited resources. To achieve this it must realize both full employment and full production.

By _full employment_ we mean that all available resources should be employed. No workers should be involuntarily out of work; the economy should provide employment for all who are willing and able to work. Nor should capital equipment or arable land sit idle. Note we say _available_ resources should be employed. Each society has certain customs and practices which determine what particular resources are available for employment. For example, legislation and custom provide that children and the very aged should not be employed. Similarly, it is desirable for productivity to allow farmland to lie fallow periodically.

By *full production* we simply mean that resources should be allocated efficiently; that is, employed resources should be utilized so as to make the most valuable contribution to total output. We should avoid allocating astrophysicists to farming and experienced farmers to our space research centers! Nor do we want Iowa's farmland planted to cotton and Alabama's to corn when experience indicates that the opposite assignment would provide the nation substantially more of both products from the same amount of land. Full production also implies that the best-available technologies are employed. We don't want our farmers harvesting wheat with scythes or picking corn by hand.

In Part 2 we shall find that the level at which resources are employed depends directly upon the level of total spending. Similarly, Chapter 5 and Part 5 are concerned with achieving full production or efficient resource allocation in a market economy.

### △   Production Possibilities Table

The nature of the economizing problem can be brought into even clearer focus by the use of a production possibilities table.[3] This ingenious device reveals the core of the economizing problem: *A full-employment, full-production economy cannot have an unlimited output of goods and services.*

**Assumptions**   We make several specific assumptions to set the stage for our illustration.

1   The economy is operating at full employment and achieving full production.

2   The available supplies of the factors of production are fixed. But, of course, they can be shifted or reallocated, within limits, among different uses; for example, a relatively unskilled laborer can work on a farm, on an automobile assembly line, or in a gas station.

3   The state of the technological arts is constant; that is, technology does not change during the course of our analysis.

The second and third assumptions are another way of saying that we are looking at our economy at some specific point in time, or over a very short period of time. Over a relatively long period it would clearly be unrealistic to rule out technological advances and the possibility that resource supplies might vary.

4   To simplify our illustration further, suppose our economy is producing just two products—drill presses and bread—instead of the innumerable goods and services actually produced. Bread is symbolic of *consumer goods,* that is, those goods which directly satisfy our wants; drill presses are symbolic of *capital goods,* that is, those goods which satisfy our wants *indirectly* by permitting more efficient production of consumer goods.

**Necessity of Choice**   Now, is it not evident from the assumptions we have made that our economy is faced with a very fundamental choice? Our total supplies of resources are limited. Thus the total amounts of drill presses and bread that our economy is capable of producing are limited. *Limited resources mean a limited output.* A choice must be made as to what quantities of each product society wants produced. Since resources are limited in supply and fully employed, any increase in the production of drill presses will necessitate the shifting of resources away from the production of bread. And the reverse holds true: If we choose to step up the production of bread, needed resources must come at the expense of drill-press production. *Society cannot have its cake and eat it, too.* Facetiously put, there's no such thing as a "free lunch." This is the essence of the economizing problem.

[3]Paul A. Samuelson, *Economics,* 11th ed. (New York: McGraw-Hill Book Company, 1980), pp. 18–20.

**TABLE 2-1**
Production Possibilities of Bread and Drill Presses
with Full Employment, 1981 (*hypothetical data*)

| Type of product | Production alternatives | | | | |
|---|---|---|---|---|---|
| | A | B | C | D | E |
| Bread (in hundred thousands) | 0 | 1 | 2 | 3 | 4 |
| Drill presses (in thousands) | 10 | 9 | 7 | 4 | 0 |

Let us generalize by noting in Table 2-1 some alternative combinations of drill presses and bread which our economy might conceivably choose. Though the data in this and the following tables are hypothetical, the points illustrated are of tremendous practical significance. At alternative A, our economy would be devoting all its resources to the production of drill presses, that is, capital goods. At alternative E, all available resources would be devoted to the production of bread, that is, consumer goods. Both these alternatives are clearly unrealistic extremes; any economy typically strikes a balance in dividing its total output between capital and consumer goods. As we move from alternative A to E, we step up the production of consumer goods (bread). How? By shifting resources away from capital goods production. When we remember that consumer goods directly satisfy our wants, any movement toward alternative E looks tempting. In making this move, society increases the current satisfaction of its wants. But there is a cost involved. This shift of resources catches up with society over time as its stock of capital goods dwindles—or at least ceases to expand at the current rate—with the result that the efficiency of future production is impaired. In short, in moving from alternative A toward E, society is in effect choosing "more now" at the expense of "much more later." In moving from E toward A, society is choosing to forgo current consumption. This sacrifice of current consumption frees resources which can now be used in stepping up the production of capital

goods. By building up its stock of capital in this way, society can anticipate more efficient production and, therefore, greater consumption in the future.

The critical idea is this: *At any point in time, a full-employment, full-production economy must sacrifice some of product X to obtain more of product Y.* The basic fact that economic resources are scarce prohibits such an economy from having more of both X and Y.

△  **Production Possibilities Curve**

To ensure our understanding the production possibilities table, let us view these data graphically. We employ a simple two-dimensional graph, putting the output of drill presses (capital goods) on the vertical axis and the output of bread (consumer goods) on the horizontal axis, as in Figure 2-1. Following the plotting procedure discussed in Chapter 1, we can locate the "production possibilities" or "transformation"[4] curve, as shown in Figure 2-1.

△  **Optimum Product-Mix**

We know that each point on the production possibilities curve represents some maximum output of the two products. To realize the various combinations of bread and drill presses which fall on the production possibilities curve, society must achieve full employment and full production. All combinations of bread and drill presses on the curve represent maximum quantities attainable only as the result of the most efficient use of all available resources.

But now a final question arises: If all outputs on the production possibilities curve reflect full employment and full production, which combination will society prefer? This is a subjective question—a moral issue—and the economist as a social scientist possesses no

---

[4] Why "transformation"? Because in moving from one alternative to another, say from *B* to *C,* we are in effect transforming drill presses into bread by shifting resources from the production of the former to the production of the latter.

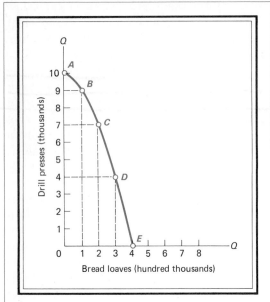

**FIGURE 2-1   THE PRODUCTION POSSIBILITIES CURVE**

Each point on the production possibilities curve represents some maximum output of any two products. Society must choose which product-mix it desires: more drill presses means less bread, and vice versa.

superior judgment or insight on this matter. Consider, for example, points $B$ and $D$ in Figure 2-1. Which output-mix is superior or "best"? This, to repeat, is a nonscientific matter; it reflects the values of society as expressed by its control group—the dictatorship, the party, the electorate, the citizenry, the individual institutions, or some combination thereof. What the economist can say is that if a society's production possibilities are as in Table 2-1 *and* if that society seeks the product-mix indicated by, say, alternative $B$, it is using its resources inefficiently if it realizes a total output comprised only of $8\frac{7}{8}$ units of drill presses and $\frac{9}{10}$ unit of loaves of bread. And the economist can also say that the society cannot hope to achieve a national output of $9\frac{1}{2}$ units of drill presses and $1\frac{3}{8}$ units of loaves of bread with its available resources. These are quantitative, objective, matters. But, although he or she

may have opinions as an individual, the economist as a social scientist cannot say that combination $B$ is "better" or "worse" than combination $D$. This is purely a qualitative matter.

### △ Law of Increasing Costs

We have stressed that resources are scarce relative to the virtually unlimited wants which these resources can be used to satisfy. As a result, choices among alternatives must be made. Specifically, more of X (bread) means less of Y (drill presses). *The amount of other products which must be forgone or sacrificed to obtain a unit of any given product is called the opportunity cost of that good.* In our case the amount of Y (drill presses) which must be forgone or given up to get another unit of X (bread) is the *opportunity cost,* or simply the *cost,* of X. Hence, in moving from possibility $A$ to $B$ in Table 2-1, we find that the cost of 1 unit of bread is 1 unit of drill presses. But, as we now pursue the concept of cost through the additional production possibilities—$B$ to $C$, $C$ to $D$, and so forth—an important economic principle is revealed to us. In moving from alternative $A$ to alternative $E$, the sacrifice or cost of drill presses involved in getting each additional unit of bread *increases*. Hence, in moving from $A$ to $B$, just 1 unit of drill presses is sacrificed for 1 more unit of bread; but going from $B$ to $C$ involves the sacrifice of 2 units of drill presses for 1 more of bread; then 3 of drill presses for 1 of bread; and finally 4 for 1.

**Concavity**   Graphically, the law of increasing costs is reflected in the shape of the production possibilities curve. Specifically, the curve is *concave* or bowed out from the origin. Why? Because, as verified by the dashed lines in Figure 2-1, when the economy moves from $A$ toward $E$, it must give up successively larger amounts of drill presses (1, 2, 3, 4) as shown on the vertical axis to acquire equal increments of bread (1, 1, 1, 1) as shown on the horizontal axis. Technically, this means that the slope of the production possibilities curve becomes steeper as we move from $A$ to $E$ and such a curve, by definition, is concave as viewed from the origin.

**Rationale**  What is the economic rationale for the law of increasing costs? *Why* does the sacrifice of drill presses increase as we get more bread? The answer to this query is rather complex. But, simply stated, it amounts to this: *Economic resources are not completely adaptable to alternative uses.* As we attempt to step up bread production, resources which are less and less adaptable to agriculture must be induced, or "pushed," into that line of production. If we start at A and move to B, we can first pick resources whose productivity of bread is greatest in relation to their productivity of drill presses. But as we move from B to C, C to D, and so on, those resources which are highly productive of bread become increasingly scarce. To get more bread, resources whose productivity in drill presses is great in relation to their productivity in bread will be needed. It will obviously take more and more of such resources—and hence an increasingly great sacrifice of drill presses—to achieve a given increase of 1 unit in the production of bread. This lack of perfect flexibility, or interchangeability, on the part of resources and the resulting increase in the sacrifice of one good that must be made in the acquisition of more and more units of another good are sometimes termed the *law of increasing costs,* costs in this case being stated as sacrifices of goods and not in terms of dollars and cents.

The reader should verify that (1) under the unrealistic assumption of perfect adaptability of resources the production possibilities would be a straight line, implying *constant* opportunity costs, and (2) in Table 2-1 and Figure 2-1 the law of increasing costs holds true in moving from alternative E to alternative A.

## □ UNEMPLOYMENT, GROWTH, AND THE FUTURE

It is important to understand what happens when the first three assumptions underlying the production possibilities curve are released.

### △ Unemployment and Underemployment

The first assumption was that our economy is characterized by full employment and full production. How would our analysis and conclusions be altered if idle resources were available (unemployment) or if employed resources were used inefficiently (underemployment)? With full employment and full production, our five alternatives represent a series of maximum outputs; that is, they illustrate what combinations of drill presses and bread might be produced when the economy is operating at its full capacity. With *un*employment or *under*employment, the economy would obviously be producing less than each alternative shown in Table 2-1.

Graphically, a situation of unemployment or underemployment can be illustrated by a

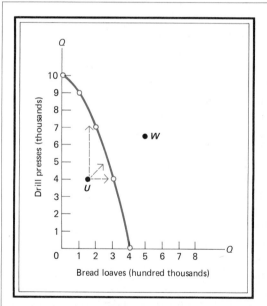

**FIGURE 2-2  UNEMPLOYMENT AND THE PRODUCTION POSSIBILITIES CURVE**

Any point inside the production possibilities curve, such as *U*, indicates unemployment or underemployment. By moving toward full employment and full production, the economy can produce more of either or both of the two products, as the arrows indicate. Point *W* is unattainable.

point *inside* the original production possibilities curve, which has been reproduced in Figure 2-2. Point *U* is such a point. Here the economy is obviously falling short of the various maximum combinations of bread and drill presses reflected by all the points *on* the production possibilities curve. The broken arrows in Figure 2-2 indicate three of the possible paths back to full employment and full production. A movement toward full employment and full production will obviously entail a greater output of one or both products. And there are points *outside* the production possibilities curve, like point *W,* which would be superior to any point on the curve; but such points are unobtainable, given the current supplies of resources and technology. The production barrier of full employment prohibits the production of any combination of capital and consumer goods lying outside the production possibilities curve.

△  **A Growing Economy**

What happens to the production possibilities curve when we drop the remaining assumptions that the quantity and quality of resources and technology are fixed? The answer is: The production possibilities curve will shift position; that is, the potential total output of the economy will change.

**Expanding Resource Supplies**   Now let us abandon the simplifying assumption that our total supplies of land, labor, capital, and entrepreneurial ability are fixed. Common sense tells us that over a period of time the growing population in the United States will bring about increases in the supplies of labor and entrepreneurial ability.[5] Historically, our stock of capital has increased at a significant, though unsteady, rate. And although we are

[5]This is not to say that population growth as such is always desirable. In Chapter 21 we shall discover that overpopulation can be a constant drag upon the living standards of many underdeveloped countries. In advanced countries overpopulation can have adverse effects upon the environment and the quality of life.

**TABLE 2-2**
Production Possibilities of Bread and Drill Presses with Full Employment, 2001 (*hypothetical data*)

| Type of product | Production alternatives | | | | |
|---|---|---|---|---|---|
| | A′ | B′ | C′ | D′ | E′ |
| Bread (in hundred thousands) | 0 | 2 | 4 | 6 | 8 |
| Drill presses (in thousands) | 14 | 12 | 9 | 5 | 0 |

depleting some of our energy and mineral resources, new sources are constantly being discovered. The drainage of swamps and the development of irrigation programs add to our supply of arable land. Assuming continuous full employment and full production, the net result of these increased supplies of the factors of production will be the ability to produce more of both drill presses and bread. Thus in, say, the year 2001, the production possibilities of Table 2-1 for 1981 may be obsolete, having given way to those shown in Table 2-2. Observe that the greater abundance of resources results in a greater output of one or both products at each alternative; economic growth, in the sense of an expanded total output, has occurred.

But note this important point: Such a favorable shift in the production possibilities curve does not guarantee that the economy will operate at a point on that new curve. The economy might fail to realize fully its new potentialities. Some 100 million jobs will give us full employment at the present time, but ten or twenty years from now our labor force, because of a growing population, will be larger, and 100 million jobs will not be sufficient for full employment. In short, the production possibilities curve may shift, but the economy may fail to produce at a point on that new curve.

**Technological Advance**   Our other simplifying assumption is a constant or unchanging technology. Observation tells us that technology has progressed with amazing rapidity over a long period. What does an advancing technology entail? New and better goods and improved ways of producing these goods. For the moment, let us think of technological advance as entailing merely improvements in capital facilities—more efficient machinery and equipment. How does such technological advance alter our earlier discussion of the economizing problem? In this way: Technological advance, by improving productive efficiency, allows society to produce more goods with a fixed amount of resources. As with increases in resource supplies, technological advance permits the production of more drill presses *and* more bread.

What happens to the production possibilities curve of Figure 2-2 when the supplies of resources increase or an improvement in technology occurs? The curve shifts outward and to the right, as illustrated by the orange curve in Figure 2-3. *Economic growth—the ability to produce a larger total output—is reflected in a rightward shift of the production possibilities curve; it is the result of increases in resource supplies and technological progress.* The consequence of growth is that our full-employment economy can enjoy a greater output of both bread and drill presses.

On Figure 2-2 the student should pencil in two new production possibilities curves: one to show the situation where a better technique for producing drill presses has been developed, the technology for producing bread being unchanged, and the other to illustrate an improved technology for bread, the technology for producing drill presses being constant.

### △  Present Choices and
### Future Possibilities

You may have anticipated this important point in the foregoing paragraphs: *An economy's current choice of position on its production possibilities curve is a basic determinant of the future location of that curve.* To illustrate this notion, let us designate the two axes of the production possibilities curve as "goods for the future" and "goods for the present," as

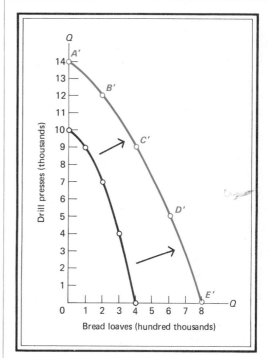

**FIGURE 2-3  ECONOMIC GROWTH AND THE PRODUCTION POSSIBILITIES CURVE**

The expanding resource supplies and technological advances which characterize a growing economy move the production possibilities curve outward and to the right. This permits the economy to enjoy larger quantities of both types of goods.

in Figure 2-4a and b. By "goods for the future" we refer to such things as capital goods, research and education, and preventive medicine, which obviously tend to increase the quantity and quality of property resources, enlarge the stock of technological information, and improve the quality of human resources. It is, as we have already seen, "goods for the future" which are the ingredients of economic growth. By "goods for the present" we mean pure consumer goods in the form of foodstuffs, clothing, transistor radios, automobiles, power mowers, and so forth.

Now suppose there are two economies, Alphania and Betania, which at the moment are identical in every respect except that Al-

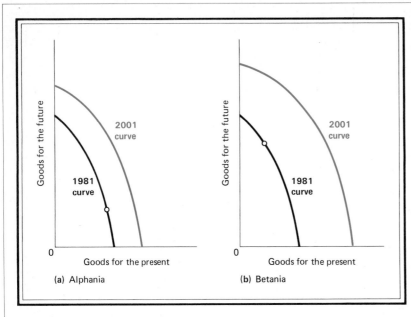

**FIGURE 2-4  AN ECONOMY'S PRESENT CHOICE OF POSITION ON ITS PRODUCTION POSSIBILITIES CURVE HELPS DETERMINE THE CURVE'S FUTURE LOCATION**

A current choice favoring "present goods," as rendered by Alphania in **(a)**, will cause a modest rightward shift of the curve. A current choice favoring "future goods," as rendered by Betania in **(b)**, will result in a greater rightward shift of the curve.

phania's current (1981) choice of position on its production possibilities curve strongly favors "present goods" as opposed to "future goods." The dot in Figure 2-4a indicates this choice. Betania, on the other hand, renders a current (1981) choice which stresses large amounts of "future goods" and lesser amounts of "present goods" (Figure 2-4b). Now, all other things being the same, we can expect the future (2001) production possibilities curve of Betania to be farther to the right than that of Alphania. That is, by currently choosing an output which is more conducive to technological advance and to increases in the quantity and quality of property and human resources, Betania will tend to achieve greater economic growth than will Alphania, whose current choice of output places less emphasis upon those goods and services which cause the production possibilities curve to shift rightward.

△  **Real World Applications**

Let us consider several of many possible applications of the production possibilities curve.

**1**  Many students are faced with the problem of allocating a fixed amount of time between studying and working to finance their education. The implied production possibilities type of trade-off is that more hours spent working obviously mean more income, but also indicate less study time and a lower grade average.

**2**  An historical illustration: In beginning to produce war goods for World War II, the United States found itself with considerable unemployment. Hence, our economy was able to accomplish the production of an almost unbelievably large quantity of war goods and at the same time increase the volume of consumer goods output (Figure 2-2).[6] The Russians, on the other hand, entered World War II at almost capacity production; that is, they were operating close to full employment. Therefore, their military preparations entailed a considerable shifting of resources from the

[6]There did occur, however, rather acute shortages of specific types of consumer goods.

production of civilian goods and a concomitant drop in the standard of living.

**3**   The much-publicized "tax revolt" of recent years is in essence an assertion that less resources should be allocated to public or governmental goods and services and more to private goods and services. If we go back to Figure 2-1 and put private goods on the vertical axis and public goods on the horizontal axis, we can say that supporters of the tax revolt seek a northwest shift along the production possibilities curve. This is to be achieved by passing legislation like California's Proposition 13 which will limit tax collections, government spending, or both, thereby freeing resources currently used in the public sector. Private households and businesses, now having larger after-tax incomes, will increase their spending and reabsorb these resources in the private sector.

**4**   Since the mid-1960s the United States has experienced a rather alarming decline in the rate of growth of labor productivity; that is, the growth of output per worker hour has diminished (Chapter 19). Many economists feel a major cause of this decline is that the rate of increase in the mechanization of labor has slowed because of insufficient investment. The proposed remedy is to increase investment as compared to consumption. That is, a *D* to *C* type of shift in Figure 2-1 is recommended. Special tax incentives to make business investment more profitable is an appropriate policy to facilitate this shift. The expectation is that the restoration of a more rapid rate of productivity growth will accelerate the growth of the economy (that is, the rightward shift of the production possibilities curve) through time.

**5**   This chapter's Last Word, about the war goods–civilian goods trade-off for India, is recommended reading at this point.

## □  ECONOMIZING: FIVE FUNDAMENTAL QUESTIONS

In order to provide a broad understanding of the essence of the economizing problem, the preceding discussion was pitched at a fairly abstract level. Let us now be more practical and examine some of the specific questions or problems that any economic system must answer in attempting to use its scarce resources to achieve the maximum satisfaction of society's material wants. Basically, there are Five Fundamental Questions which must be answered in attempting to achieve and maintain efficiency in the use of scarce resources.

### △  Level of Resource Use

*At what level—to what degree—should resources be utilized in the production process?* Society must first decide the extent to which resources should be available for current production. For human resources we must decide when workers should enter the labor force, when they should retire, the length of the work week, the number and length of holidays and vacations, and so on. The trade-off here is obviously between work and leisure. Work yields money income and, ultimately, want-satisfying goods and services. But leisure also satisfies wants. What good is a stereo set or a tennis racket if one has no time to use them? For property resources the problem of conservation is relevant. The current rapid exploitation of such nonrenewable natural resources as petroleum and natural gas is conducive to a large output *now,* but at the same time may lessen the economy's ability to produce in the *future.* What is the optimum rate of natural resource utilization?

Having determined the level of resource utilization which it desires, society must then achieve that level of resource use. Society must avoid the involuntary idleness of its human and property resources. Involuntary idleness is the height of economic inefficiency. To be efficient, any economic system must somehow provide for high and stable levels of employment.

### △  What Is to Be Produced

*Society must decide what collection of goods and services will most fully satisfy its wants.* What specific goods and services are to be produced? And in what quantities do we want each produced? In our discussion of the production possibilities curve we assumed a two product economy. But as a stroll through any supermarket or department store makes abundantly clear, the problem is much more complex! Do we want to produce Fords? Textbooks? Pink Floyd records? Football stadiums? Neutron bombs? Drill presses? And what amounts of each? Keep in mind that this decision has a time dimension: In deciding upon the relative amounts of capital and consumer goods to produce, society is weighing the relative merits of future, as opposed to current, want fulfillment. More resources devoted to the expansion of capital facilities means less consumption now, but much more consumption later.

### △   Organizing Production

Having determined the desired composition of total output, we must ask: *How should this total output be produced?* What is the best combination of resources—that is, the best technology—to use in producing any given output? Agricultural products, for example, can be produced with varying combinations of resources. Why is it that in the United States we use a great deal of land and relatively little labor? And why do the Japanese use a great deal of labor and relatively little land? The answer, as you might anticipate, depends upon the relative scarcities of available resources.

### △   Distributing Output

*How should the output of the economy be shared among the various economic units which comprise it?* How should the total output of consumer goods be shared by the various households in our economy? Should output be distributed on the basis of need? Or on the basis of one's contribution to production? What degree of inequality in the sharing of output is necessary or desirable? Similarly, how should any additions to our stock of capital equipment included in our total output be apportioned to the various industries and the individual firms in those industries? What part of total output should be given over to government? Obviously, these questions involve not only economics but also politics and ethics.

### △   Accommodating Change

*Can the economic system make the appropriate responses required to remain efficient over time?* Modern industrial societies are dynamic, changing things. What changes? Several things: consumer tastes, the supplies of resources, and technology. All these changes imply the need for significant reallocations of resources in order to preserve efficiency in their use. The collection of goods and services which pleased your parents in the 1940s or 1950s will not be acceptable to you in the 1980s. You will want resources allocated to hand calculators, not to slide rules. Similarly, changing resource supplies and the development of new techniques of production will call for new resource alignments if efficiency is to be preserved. It would be grossly inefficient to produce automobiles or harvest corn by the same methods used in, say, the 1920s.

Keep in mind that scarcity of economic resources lurks behind all five of these Fundamental Questions and their component parts. The Five Questions are merely a breakdown of the basic economizing problem of scarce resources and unlimited wants. Also, the apparent interrelatedness of these questions is almost self-evident; it is difficult to treat the Five Questions independently of one another—they demand simultaneous treatment.

### ☐   THE "ISMS"

We must now recognize that a variety of different institutional arrangements and coordinating mechanisms may be used by a society in responding to the Five Fundamental Questions. Generally speaking, the industrially advanced economies of the world differ essentially on two grounds: (1) the ownership of the means of production, and (2) the method by which economic activity is coordinated and directed. Let us briefly examine the main characteristics of the two "polar" types of economic systems.

### △  Pure Capitalism

*Pure,* or *laissez faire, capitalism* is characterized by the private ownership of resources and the use of a system of markets and prices to coordinate and direct economic activity. In such a system each participant is motivated by his or her own selfish interests; each economic unit seeks to maximize its income through individual decision making. The market system functions as a mechanism through which individual decisions and preferences are communicated and coordinated in responding to the Five Fundamental Questions. The fact that goods and services are produced and resources are supplied under competitive conditions means there are many independently acting buyers and sellers of each product and resource. As a result, economic power is widely dispersed. Advocates of pure capitalism argue that such an economy is conducive to efficiency in the use of resources, output and employment stability, and sufficient economic growth. Hence, there is no need for government planning, control, or intervention. Indeed, governmental interference will simply disturb the efficiency with which the market system functions. Government's role is therefore limited to the protection of private property and establishing an appropriate legal framework to facilitate the functioning of free markets (Chapter 5).

### △  The Command Economy

The polar alternative to pure capitalism is the *command economy* or *communism,* characterized by public ownership of all property resources and collective determination of economic decisions through central economic planning. All major decisions concerning the level of resource use, the composition and distribution of output, and the organization of production are determined by a central planning board. Business firms are governmentally owned and produce according to state directives. That is, production targets are determined by the planning board for each enterprise and the plan specifies the amounts of resources to be allocated to each enterprise so that it might realize its production goals. Workers are assigned to occupations and perhaps even allocated geographically by the plan. The division of output between capital and consumer goods is centrally decided as is the allocation of consumer goods among the citizenry. Capital goods are allocated among industries in terms of the central planning board's long-term priorities.

### △  Mixed Systems

Real world economies are arrayed between the extremes of pure capitalism and the command economy. The United States economy leans toward pure capitalism, but with important differences. Government plays an active role in our economy in promoting economic stability and growth, in providing certain goods and services which would be underproduced or not produced at all by the market system, in modifying the distribution of income, and so forth. In contrast to the wide dispersion of economic power among many small units which characterizes pure capitalism, American capitalism has spawned powerful economic organizations in the form of huge corporations and strong labor unions. The ability of these power blocs to manipulate and distort the functioning of the market system to their advantage provides a further reason for governmental involvement in the economy. While the Soviet Union approximates the command economy, it relies to some extent upon market-determined prices and has some remnants of private ownership.

But it must be emphasized that private ownership and reliance on the market system do not always go together, nor do central planning and public ownership. For example, the *fascism* of Hitler's Nazi Germany has been dubbed *authoritarian capitalism* because the economy was subject to a high degree of governmental control and direction, but property was privately owned. In contrast the Yugoslavian economy of *market socialism* is characterized by public ownership of resources coupled with increasing reliance upon free markets to organize and coordinate economic activity. The Swedish economy is also a hybrid system. Although over 90 percent of business activity is in private hands, government is deeply involved in achieving economic stability and in redistributing income. Table 2-3 summarizes the various ways economic systems can be categorized on the basis of the two criteria we are using. Keep in mind that the real world examples we have plugged into this framework are no more than approximations.

△   **The Traditional Economy**
     Table 2-3 is couched in terms of industrially advanced or at least semideveloped economies. Many of the underdeveloped countries of

the world have *traditional* or *customary economies* (Chapter 21). Production methods, exchange, and the distribution of income are all sanctioned by custom. Heredity and caste circumscribe the economic roles of individuals and socioeconomic immobility is pronounced. Technological change and innovation are closely constrained because they clash with tradition and threaten the social fabric. Economic activity is secondary to religious and cultural values and society's desire to perpetuate the status quo. In making the decision to pursue economic development, traditional economies must face the question as to which model in Table 2-3 will result in growth and simultaneously be the least incompatible with other economic and noneconomic goals valued by that society.

     The basic point to be emphasized is that there are no unique or universally accepted answers to the Five Fundamental Questions. Various societies, having different cultural and historical backgrounds, different mores and customs, and contrasting ideological frameworks—not to mention resources which differ both quantitatively and qualitatively—supply significantly different answers to the Five Questions. Russia, the United States, and Great Britain, for example, are all—in terms of their accepted goals, ideology, technologies, resources, and culture—attempting to achieve efficiency in the use of their respective resources. The best method for answering the Five Questions in one economy may be inappropriate for another economic system.

**TABLE 2-3**
Comparative Economic Systems

|  |  | Coordinating mechanism | |
|---|---|---|---|
|  |  | Market system | Central planning |
| Ownership of resources | Private | United States | Nazi Germany |
|  | Public | Yugoslavia | Soviet Union |

## Summary

     **1**   The science of economics centers upon two basic facts: First, human material wants are virtually unlimited; second, economic resources are scarce.
     **2**   Economic resources may be classified as property resources—materials and capital—or as human resources—labor and entrepreneurial ability.
     **3**   Economics is concerned with the problem of administering scarce resources in the production of goods and services for the fulfillment of the material wants of society. Both the full employment and the full production of available resources are essential if this administration is to be efficient.

4   At any point in time a full-employment, full-production economy must sacrifice the output of some types of goods and services to achieve increased production of others. Because resources are not equally productive in all possible uses, the shifting of resources from one use to another gives rise to the law of increasing costs; that is, the production of additional units of product X entails the sacrifice of increasing amounts of product Y.

5   Over time, technological advance and increases in the quantity and quality of human and property resources permit the economy to produce more of all goods and services. Society's choice as to the composition of current output is a determinant of the future location of the production possibilities curve.

6   The Five Fundamental Questions are an elaboration of the economizing problem.

7   The various economic systems of the world differ in their ideologies and also in their approaches in answering the Five Fundamental Questions. Critical differences center upon *a.* private versus public ownership of resources, and *b.* the use of the market system versus central planning as a coordinating mechanism.

## Questions and Study Suggestions

1   Terms and concepts to remember: economizing problem; land, labor, capital, the entrepreneurial ability; full employment; full production; production possibilities table (curve); law of increasing costs; economic growth; the Five Fundamental Questions; pure or laissez faire capitalism; command economy or communism; authoritarian capitalism; market socialism; traditional economy.

2   "Economics is the study of the principles governing the allocation of scarce means among competing ends when the objective of the allocation is to maximize the attainment of the ends."[7] Explain. Why is the problem of unemployment a part of the subject matter of economics?

3   "Wants aren't insatiable. I can prove it. I get all the coffee I want to drink every morning at breakfast." Critically analyze. Explain: "Goods and services are scarce because resources are scarce." Analyze: "It is the nature of all economic problems that absolute solutions are denied us."

4   What are economic resources? What are the major functions of the entrepreneur? "Economics is . . . neither capitalist nor socialist: it applies to every society. Economics would disappear only in a world so rich that no wants were unfulfilled for lack of resources. Such a world is not imminent and may be impossible, for time is always limited."[8] Carefully evaluate and explain these statements. Do you agree that, conceptually, time is an economic resource?

5   Comment on the following statement from a newspaper article: "Our junior high school serves a splendid hot meal for 55 cents without costing the taxpayers anything, thanks in part to a government subsidy."

6   The following is a production possibilities table for war goods and civilian goods:

| Type of product | Production alternatives | | | | |
| --- | --- | --- | --- | --- | --- |
| | A | B | C | D | E |
| Automobiles (in millions) | 0 | 2 | 4 | 6 | 8 |
| Guided missiles (in thousands) | 30 | 27 | 21 | 12 | 0 |

[7] George J. Stigler, *The Theory of Price* (New York: The Macmillan Company, 1947), p. 12.
[8] Joseph P. McKenna, *Intermediate Economic Theory* (New York: Holt, Rinehart and Winston, Inc., 1958), p. 2.

*a.*  Show these production possibilities data graphically. What do the points on the curve indicate? How does the curve reflect the law of increasing costs? Explain. If the economy is currently at point *C,* what is the cost of 1 million more automobiles? Of one thousand more guided missiles?

*b.*  Label point *G* inside the curve. What does it indicate? Label point *H* outside the curve. What does this point indicate? What must occur before the economy can attain the level of production indicated by point *H?*

*c.*  Upon what specific assumptions is the production possibilities curve based? What happens when each of these assumptions is released?

*d.*  Suppose improvement occurs in the technology of producing guided missiles but not in the production of automobiles. Draw the new production possibilities curve. Now assume that a technological advance occurs in producing automobiles but not in producing guided missiles. Draw the new production possibilities curve. Finally, draw a production possibilities curve which reflects technological improvement in the production of both products.

**7**  "The present choice of position on the production possibilities curve is a major factor in economic growth." Explain.

**8**  State the Five Fundamental Questions which all economies face. Why must an economy be adaptable to change in order to maintain efficiency in the use of scarce resources? Contrast the means by which pure capitalism, market socialism, and a command economy attempt to answer the Five Questions.

## Selected References

Heilbroner, Robert L.: *The Worldly Philosophers,* 4th ed.(New York: Simon & Schuster, Inc., 1972), chap. 2.

Knight, Frank H.: *The Economic Organization* (New York: Harper & Row, Publishers, Incorporated, 1965), chap. 1.

Mundell, Robert A.: *Man and Economics* (New York: McGraw-Hill Book Company, 1968), chap. 1.

# LAST WORD
## Bombs or Bread for India?

India illustrated vividly the economizing problem in the form of the "guns or butter" issue by exploding its first atomic bomb in May of 1974.

The Indian government woke up Sunday as the sixth nation in the world with a nuclear capability. Rakhal and millions of his countrymen woke up hungry.

The 40-year-old laborer hadn't even heard of his country's first atomic test blast. When he was told the device exploded Saturday in the Rajastan Desert, he showed little interest.

"It's beyond my intelligence to know anything about a bomb," he told a visitor to his streetside camp. "My only ambition is to feed my children and my wife."

Some of the higher levels of Indian society were jubilant over the underground explosion, which put India alongside the United States, the Soviet Union, Britain, France and China as nations which have exploded nuclear devices.

Politicians and newspapers from the Moscow-leaning Patriot to the right-wing Motherland hailed the blast as a grand national achievement. "Indian genius triumphs," headlined the middle-of-the-road Hindustan Times. "Nation is thrilled."

But some young educated Indians, speaking at a Saturday night gathering, questioned the wisdom of Prime Minister Indira Gandhi's decision to devote resources to nuclear explosions when millions of Indian poor like Rakhal can't get enough to eat.

There are about 580 million people in India; an estimated 30% live in poverty, earning less than $30 a year. Nearly 80% of the nation's children are said to be malnourished; more than 70% of the country's people are illiterate.

"We may be hungry," one young Indian celebrant said in a typical comment. "But now at least we're someone to be reckoned with."

The Hindustan Times said the nuclear test proves "India has the talent, the resources and the infrastructure that makes for high achievement capability."

"Our knowledge in nuclear science has raised our status not only in Southeast Asia but in the whole world," said defense minister Jagjivan Ram.

But as newspaper readers were learning details of the explosion, Rakhal and his wife were giving their five children a chunk of bread for breakfast.

"Look at the oven there," Rakhal said, gesturing at a small hole flanked by rocks. "There is no fire in it because there is nothing to cook. The children are crying because they don't have enough to eat."

Rakhal brought his family to New Delhi from Bihar in eastern India on a public promise of land redistribution.

That was four months ago. Since then he's been working as a day laborer when he can. When there is no work, he goes to government offices to claim the land he thinks he is due.

"They don't give me any hope," he said. "For the past four days I have not had any jobs. If this continues I will go back home."

Accurate estimates are unavailable of how much was spent for the blast, which the government insists will not be used to develop nuclear weapons. But experts say the cost of equipping the country with a modest nuclear retaliatory force would range from $3 billion over 10 years to $1 billion over five years.

"Atomic Test Raises India's Clout; Poor Remain Hungry," *Lincoln Evening Journal*, May 29, 1974.

# Pure Capitalism and the Circular Flow

chapter 3

The task of the present chapter is to describe the capitalist ideology and to explain how pure, or laissez faire, capitalism would operate. Strictly speaking, pure capitalism has never existed and probably never will. Why, then, do we bother to consider the operation of such an economy? Because it gives us a very rough *first approximation* of how modern American capitalism functions. And approximations or models, when properly handled, can be very useful. In other words, pure capitalism constitutes a simplified model which we shall then modify and adjust to correspond more closely to the reality of American capitalism.

In explaining the operation of pure capitalism, we shall discuss:

**1** The institutional framework and basic assumptions which make up the capitalist ideology.

**2** Certain institutions and practices common to all modern economies.

**3** Capitalism and the circular flow of income.

**4** How product and resource prices are determined.

**5** The market system and the allocating of economic resources.

The first three topics constitute the present chapter; the latter two will be the subject matter of Chapters 4 and 5.

## ☐ CAPITALIST IDEOLOGY

Unfortunately, there is no neat and universally accepted definition of capitalism. We are therefore required to examine in some detail the basic tenets of capitalism to acquire a comprehensive understanding of what pure capitalism entails. In short, the framework of capitalism embodies the following institutions and assumptions: (1) private property, (2) freedom of enterprise and choice, (3) self-interest as the dominant motive, (4) competition, (5) reliance upon the price system, and (6) a limited role for government.

△ **Private Property**

Under a capitalistic system, property resources are owned by private individuals and private institutions rather than by government. Private property, coupled with the freedom to negotiate binding legal contracts, permits private persons or businesses to obtain, control, employ, and dispose of economic resources as they see fit. The institution of private property is sustained over time by the *right to bequeath,* that is, by the right of a property owner to designate the recipient of this property at the time of death.

Needless to say, there are broad legal limits to this right of private ownership. For example, the use of one's resources for the production of narcotics is prohibited by law. Nor is public ownership nonexistent. Even in pure capitalism, recognition is given to the fact that public ownership of certain "natural monopolies" may be essential to the achievement of efficiency in the use of resources.

△ **Freedom of Enterprise and Choice**

Closely related to private ownership of property is freedom of enterprise and choice. Capitalism charges its component economic units with the responsibility of making certain choices, which are registered and made effective through the free markets of the economy. *Freedom of enterprise* means that under pure capitalism, private business enterprises are free to obtain economic resources, to organize these resources in the production of a good or service of the firm's own choosing, and to sell it in the markets of their choice. No artificial obstacles or restrictions imposed by government or other producers block an entrepreneur's choice to enter or leave a particular industry.

*Freedom of choice* means that owners of property resources and money capital can employ or dispose of these resources as they see fit. It also means that laborers are free to enter any of those lines of work for which they are qualified. Finally, it means that consumers are at liberty, within the limits of their money incomes, to buy that collection of goods and services which they feel is most appropriate in satisfying their wants. Freedom of consumer choice may well be the most profound of these freedoms. The consumer is in a particularly strategic position in a capitalistic economy; in a sense, the consumer is sovereign. The range of free choices for suppliers of human and property resources is circumscribed by the choices of consumers. The consumer ultimately decides what the capitalistic economy should produce, and resource suppliers must make their free choices within the boundaries thereby delineated. Resource suppliers and businesses are not really "free" to produce goods and services consumers do not desire.

Again, broad legal limitations prevail in the expression of all these free choices.

△ **Role of Self-Interest**

Since capitalism is an individualistic system, it is not surprising to find that the primary driving force of such an economy is the promotion of one's self-interest; each economic unit attempts to do what is best for itself. Hence, entrepreneurs aim at the maximization of their firms' profits or, as the case might be, the minimization of losses. And, other things being equal, owners of property resources attempt to achieve the highest price obtainable from the rent or sale of these resources. Given the amount and irksomeness of the effort involved, those who supply human resources will also attempt to obtain the highest possible incomes from their employment. Consumers, in purchasing a given product, will seek to obtain it at the lowest price. In short, capitalism presumes self-interest as the fundamental *modus operandi* for the various economic units as they express their free choices. The motive of self-interest gives direction and consistency to what might otherwise be an extremely chaotic economy.

Although self-interest is the basic motive underlying the functioning of capitalism, there are exceptions to the rule: Businesses and individuals do not always act in their own self-interest. Altruistic motives are part of the makeup of economic units. Yet, self-interest is the best single statement of how economic units actually behave.

△  **Competition**

Freedom of choice exercised in terms of promoting one's own monetary returns provides the basis for competition, or economic rivalry, as a fundamental feature of capitalism. Competition, as economists see it, entails:

①  The presence of large numbers of independently acting buyers and sellers operating in the market for any particular product or resource.

②  The freedom of buyers and sellers to enter or leave particular markets.

Let us briefly explore these two related aspects of competition:

**Large Numbers**  The essence of competition is the widespread diffusion of economic power within the two major aggregates—businesses and households—which comprise the economy. When a large number of buyers and sellers are present in a particular market, no one buyer or seller will be able to demand or offer a quantity of the product sufficiently large to noticeably influence its price. Let us examine this statement in terms of the selling or supply side of the product market.

We have all observed that when a product becomes unusually scarce, its price will rise. For example, an unseasonable frost in Florida may seriously curtail the output of citrus crops and sharply increase the price of orange juice. Similarly, *if* a single producer, or a small group of producers acting together, can somehow control or restrict the total supply of a product, then price can be raised to the seller's advantage. By controlling supply, the producer can "rig the market" on his or her own behalf. Now the essence of competition is that

there are so many sellers that each, *because he or she is contributing an almost negligible fraction of the total supply,* has virtually no control over the supply or, therefore, over the product price.

For example, suppose there are 10,000 farmers, each of whom is supplying 100 bushels of corn in the Kansas City grain market at some particular time when the price of corn happens to be $4 per bushel. Could a single farmer who feels dissatisfied with the existing price cause an artificial scarcity of corn and thereby boost the price above $4? The answer is obviously "No." Farmer Jones, by restricting output from 100 to 75 bushels, exerts virtually no effect upon the total supply of corn. In fact, total supply is reduced only from 1,000,000 to 999,975 bushels. This obviously is not much of a shortage! Supply is virtually unchanged, and, therefore, the $4 price persists. In brief, competition means that each seller is providing a drop in the bucket of total supply. Individual sellers can make no noticeable dent in total supply; hence, a seller cannot *as an individual producer*[1] manipulate product price. This is what is meant when it is pointed out that an individual competitive seller is "at the mercy of the market."

The same rationale applies to the demand side of the market. Buyers are plentiful and act independently. Thus single buyers cannot manipulate the market to their advantage.

The important point is this: *The widespread diffusion of economic power underlying competition controls the use and limits the potential abuse of that power.* Economic rivalry prevents economic units from wreaking havoc upon one another as they attempt to further their self-interests. Competition imposes limits upon expressions of self-interest by buyers and sellers. Competition is a basic regulatory force in capitalism.

---

[1]Of course, if a number of farmers simultaneously restricted their production, the resulting change in total supply could no longer be ignored, and price would rise. Competition (a large number of sellers) implies the impossibility of such collusion.

**Entry and Exit**   Competition also assumes that it is a simple matter for producers to enter (or leave) a particular industry; there are no artificial legal or institutional obstacles to prohibit the expansion (or contraction) of specific industries. This aspect of competition is prerequisite to the flexibility which is essential if an economy is to remain efficient over time. Freedom of entry is necessary if the economy is to adjust appropriately to changes in consumer tastes, technology, or resource supplies. This matter will receive detailed treatment in Chapter 5.

△   **Markets and Prices**

The basic coordinating mechanism of a capitalist economy is the market or price system. *Capitalism is a market economy.* The decisions rendered by the buyers and sellers of products and resources are made effective through a system of markets. The preferences of sellers and buyers are registered on the supply and demand sides of various markets, and the outcome of these choices is a system of product and resource prices. These prices are guideposts upon which resource owners, entrepreneurs, and consumers make and revise their free choices in furthering their self-interests. Just as competition is the controlling mechanism, so a system of markets and prices is a basic organizing force. The price system is an elaborate communication system through which innumerable individual free choices are recorded, summarized, and balanced against one another. Those who obey the dictates of the price system are rewarded; those who ignore them are penalized by the system. Through this communication system, society renders its decisions concerning what the economy should produce, how production can be efficiently organized, and how the fruits of productive endeavor are to be distributed among the individual economic units which make up capitalism.

Not only is the price system the mechanism through which society renders decisions concerning how it allocates its resources and distributes the resulting output, but it is through the price system that these decisions are carried out. However, a word of caution: Economic systems based upon the ideologies of socialism and communism also depend upon price systems, but not to the same degree or in the same way as does pure capitalism. Socialistic and communistic societies use markets and prices primarily to implement the decisions made wholly or in part by a central planning authority. In capitalism, the price system functions both as a device for registering innumerable choices of free individuals and businesses *and* as a mechanism for carrying out these decisions.

In Chapters 4 and 5 we shall analyze the mechanics and the operation of a capitalistic price system.

△   **Limited Government**

A competitive capitalist economy is thought to be conducive to a high degree of efficiency in the use or allocation of its resources. Hence, there is allegedly little real need for governmental intervention in the operation of such an economy beyond its aforementioned role of imposing broad legal limits upon the exercise of individual choices and the use of private property. The concept of pure capitalism as a self-regulating and self-adjusting type of economy precludes any significant economic role for government. As we shall see shortly, capitalism in practice has not been self-regulating to the degree economists once supposed. But for the moment, at least, our analysis will exclude government. Chapter 6 will elaborate the functions of government in present-day mixed capitalism.

☐   **OTHER CHARACTERISTICS**

Private property, freedom of enterprise and choice, self-interest as a motivating force, competition, and reliance on a price system are all institutions and assumptions which are more or less exclusively associated with pure capitalism. In addition, there are certain institutions and practices which are characteristic of all modern economies. They are ① the use of an advanced technology and large amounts of capital goods, ② specialization, and ③ the use of money. Specialization and an advanced technology are prerequisites to the efficient employment of any economy's resources. The use of money is a permissive characteristic which allows society more easily to practice and reap the benefits of specialization and of the employment of advanced productive techniques.

### △ Extensive Use of Capital Goods

All modern economies—whether they approximate the capitalist, socialist, or communist ideology—are based upon an advanced technology and the extensive use of capital goods. Under pure capitalism it is competition, coupled with freedom of choice and the desire to further one's self-interest, which provides the means for achieving a rapid rate of technological advance. The capitalistic framework is felt to be highly effective in harnessing incentives to develop new products and improved techniques of production. Why? Because the monetary rewards derived therefrom accrue directly to the innovator. Pure capitalism therefore presupposes the extensive use and rapid development of complex capital goods: tools, machinery, large-scale factories, and facilities for storage, transportation, and marketing.

Why are the existence of an advanced technology and the extensive use of capital goods important? Because the most direct method of producing a product is usually the least efficient.[2] Even Robinson Crusoe avoided the inefficiencies of direct production in favor of "roundabout production." It would be ridiculous for a farmer—even a backyard farmer—to go at production with bare hands. Obviously, it pays huge dividends in terms of

---

[2]Remember that consumer goods satisfy wants directly, while capital goods do so indirectly through the more efficient production of consumer goods.

more efficient production and, therefore, a more abundant output, to fashion tools of production, that is, capital equipment, to aid in the productive process. There is a better way of getting water out of a well than to dive in after it!

But there is a catch involved. As we recall our discussion of the production possibilities curve and the basic nature of the economizing problem, it is evident that, with full employment and full production, resources must be diverted from the production of consumer goods in order to be used in the production of capital goods. We must currently tighten our belts as consumers in order to free resources for the production of capital goods which will increase productive efficiency and permit us to have a greater output of consumer goods at some future date.

### △ Specialization

The extent to which society relies upon specialization is astounding. The vast majority of consumers produce virtually none of the goods and services they consume and, conversely, consume little or nothing of what they produce. The hammer-shop laborer who spends a lifetime stamping out parts for jet engines may never "consume" an airplane trip. The assembly-line worker who devotes eight hours a day to the installation of windows in Chevrolets may own a Ford. Few households seriously consider any extensive production of their own food, shelter, and clothing. Many farmers sell their milk to the local creamery and then buy oleomargarine at the Podunk general store. Society learned long ago that self-sufficiency breeds inefficiency. The jack-of-all-trades may be a very colorful individual, but is certainly lacking in efficiency.

In what specific ways might human specialization—*the division of labor*—enhance productive efficiency? First, specialization permits individuals to take advantage of existing differences in their abilities and skills. If caveman A is strong, swift afoot, and accurate with a spear, and caveman B is weak and slow, but patient, this distribution of talents can be most efficiently utilized by making A a hunter and B a fisherman. Second, even if the abilities of A and B are identical, specialization may prove to be advantageous. Why? Because by devoting all one's time to a single task, the doer is more likely to develop the appropriate skills and to discover improved techniques than when apportioning time among a number of diverse tasks. One learns to be a good hunter by hunting! Finally, specialization—devoting all one's time to, say, a single task—obviously avoids the loss of time which is entailed in shifting from one job to another. For all these reasons the division of labor results in greater productive efficiency in the use of human resources.

Specialization also is desirable on a regional basis. Oranges could be grown in Nebraska, but because of the unsuitability of the land, rainfall, and temperature, the costs involved would be exceedingly high. Florida could achieve some success in the production of wheat, but for similar reasons such production would be a relatively costly business. As a result, Nebraskans produce those products—wheat in particular—for which their resources are best adapted, and Floridians do the same, producing oranges and other citrus fruits. In so doing, both produce surpluses of their specialties. Then, very sensibly, Nebraskans and Floridians swap some of their surpluses. Specialization permits each area to put its best foot forward, that is, to turn out those goods which its resources can most efficiently produce. In this way both Nebraska and Florida can enjoy a larger amount of both wheat and oranges than would otherwise be the case. In short, human and geographical specialization are both essential in achieving efficiency in the use of resources.

Despite these advantages, specialization does entail certain drawbacks. For example, the monotony and drudgery of specialized work are well known. Imagine the boredom of our previously mentioned assembly-line worker who is still putting windows in Chevro-

lets. The Last Word segment of this chapter dramatizes this point. Second, specialization and mutual interdependence vary directly with one another. The less each of us produces for oneself, the more we are dependent upon the output of others. A railroad or truckers' strike very quickly results in product shortages. A third problem centers upon the exchanging of the surpluses which specialization entails. An examination of this problem leads us into a discussion of the use of money in the economy.

△  **Use of Money**

Virtually all economies, advanced or primitive, are money-using. Money performs a variety of functions (see Chapter 14), but first and foremost it is a medium of exchange.

In our Nebraska-Florida example, it is necessary for Nebraskans to trade or exchange wheat for Florida's oranges if both states are to share in the benefits of specialization. If trade was highly inconvenient or prohibited for some reason, gains from specializing according to comparative advantage would be lost to society. Why? Because consumers want a wide variety of products and, in the absence of trade, would tend to devote their human and material resources to many diverse types of production. If exchange could not occur or was very inconvenient to transact, Nebraska and Florida would be forced to be more self-sufficient, and the advantages of specialization would not be realized. *In short, a convenient means of exchanging goods is a prerequisite of specialization.*

Now exchange can, and sometimes does, occur on the basis of *bartering,* that is, swapping goods for goods. But bartering as a means of exchange can pose serious problems for the economy. Specifically, exchange by barter requires a *coincidence of wants* between the two transactors. In our example, we assumed that Nebraskans had excess wheat to trade and that they wanted to obtain oranges. And we assumed Floridians had excess oranges to swap and that they wanted to acquire wheat. So

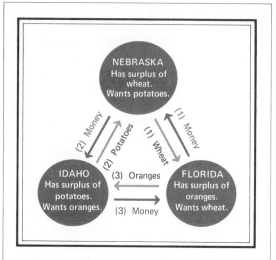

**FIGURE 3-1  MONEY FACILITATES TRADE WHERE WANTS DO NOT COINCIDE**

By the use of money as a medium of exchange, trade can be accomplished, as indicated by the arrows, despite a noncoincidence of wants. By facilitating exchange, the use of money permits an economy to realize the efficiencies of specialization.

exchange occurred. But if this coincidence of wants did not exist, trade would be stymied. Let us pose such a problem.

Suppose Nebraska does not want any of Florida's oranges but is interested in buying potatoes from Idaho. Ironically enough, Idaho wants Florida's oranges but not Nebraska's wheat. And, to complicate matters, suppose that Florida wants some of Nebraska's wheat but none of Idaho's potatoes. The situation is summarized in Figure 3-1.

In no case do we find a coincidence of wants. Trade by barter obviously would be difficult. To overcome such a stalemate, modern economies use *money,* which is simply a convenient social invention for facilitating the exchange of goods and services. Historically, cattle, cigarettes, shells, stones, pieces of metal, and many other diverse commodities have been used, with varying degrees of success, as a medium for facilitating exchange. But to be

money, an item needs to pass only one test: *It must be generally acceptable by buyers and sellers in exchange.* Money is socially defined; whatever society accepts as a medium of exchange is money. Most modern economies, for reasons made clear in Chapter 14, find it convenient to use pieces of paper as money. We shall assume that this is the case with the Nebraska-Florida-Idaho economy; they use pieces of paper which they call "dollars" as money. Can the use of paper dollars as a medium of exchange overcome the stalemate we have posed?

Obviously it can, with trade occurring as shown in Figure 3-1:

**1**  Floridians can exchange money for some of Nebraska's wheat.

**2**  Nebraskans can take the money realized from the sale of wheat and exchange it for some of Idaho's potatoes.

**3**  Idahoans can then exchange the money received from the sale of potatoes for some of Florida's surplus oranges.

The willingness to accept paper money (or any other kind of money, for that matter) as a medium of exchange has permitted a three-way trade which allows each state to specialize in one product and obtain the other product(s) its residents desire, despite a noncoincidence of wants. Barter, resting as it does upon a coincidence of wants, would have impeded this exchange and in so doing would have induced the three states not to specialize. Of course, the efficiencies of specialization would then have been lost to those states. Strange as it may first seem, two exchanges—surplus product for money and then money for a wanted product—are simpler than the single product-for-product exchange which bartering entails! Indeed, in this example, product-for-product exchange would not be likely to occur at all.

A final example: Imagine a Detroit laborer producing crankshafts for Oldsmobiles. At the end of the week, instead of receiving a brightly colored piece of paper endorsed by the company comptroller, or a few pieces of paper neatly engraved in green and black, the laborer receives from the company paymaster four Oldsmobile crankshafts. Inconvenient as this is, and with no desire to hoard crankshafts, the laborer ventures into the Detroit business district, intent upon spending this hard-earned income on, say, a bag of groceries, a pair of jeans, and a movie. Obviously, the worker is faced with some inconvenient and time-consuming trading, and may not be able to negotiate any exchanges at all. Finding a clothier who has jeans and who happens to be in the market for an Oldsmobile crankshaft can be a formidable task. And, if the jeans do not trade evenly for crankshafts, how do the transactors "make change"? Examples such as this demonstrate that money is one of the great social inventions of civilization!

To recapitulate: The use of technologically advanced capital goods, a high degree of specialization in production, and the use of money are basic institutional characteristics of all modern economies.

## □   THE CIRCULAR FLOW MODEL

Our discussion of specialization and the related need for a monetary system to facilitate exchange puts us in a position to reemphasize the role of markets and prices in a capitalistic economy. The remainder of this chapter is devoted to a general overview of the market system for the purpose of pinpointing the two basic types of markets of pure capitalism and noting the character of the transactions which occur therein. Chapter 4 presents a rather detailed examination of how specific prices are actually determined in pure capitalism. Then Chapter 5 provides a more rigorous discussion of how pure capitalism goes about answering the Five Fundamental Questions through the workings of the price system.

### △   Two Markets

Figure 3-2 provides the simple overview we seek. The upper half of the diagram portrays *resource markets*. Here, households, which

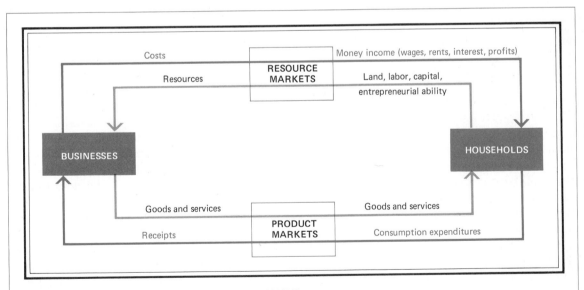

FIGURE 3-2 THE CIRCULAR FLOW OF OUTPUT AND INCOME

The prices paid for the use of land, labor, capital, and entrepreneurial ability are determined in the resource market shown in the upper loop. Businesses are on the demand side and households on the supply side of this market. The prices of finished goods and services are determined in the product market located in the lower loop. Households are on the demand side and businesses on the supply side of this market.

directly or indirectly (through their ownership of business corporations) own all economic resources, *supply* these resources to businesses.[3] Businesses, of course, will *demand* resources because they are the means by which firms produce goods and services. The coming together of demand and supply for the immense variety of human and property resources establishes the price of each (Chapter 4). The payments which businesses make in obtaining resources are costs to businesses, but simultaneously constitute flows of wage, rent, interest, and profit income to the households supplying these resources.

Now consider the *product markets* shown in the bottom half of the diagram. The money income received by households from the sale of resources does not, as such, have real value. Consumers cannot eat or wear coins and paper money. Hence, through the expenditure of money income, households express their *demand* for a vast array of goods and services. Simultaneously, businesses combine the resources they have obtained to produce and *supply* goods and services in these same markets. The interaction of these demand and supply decisions determines product prices (Chapter 4). Note, too, that the flow of consumer expenditures for goods and services constitutes sales revenues or receipts from the viewpoint of businesses.

The circular flow model implies a complex, interrelated web of decision making and economic activity. Note that households and businesses participate in both basic markets, but on different sides of each. Businesses are on the buying or demand side of the resource markets, and households, as resource owners and suppliers, are on the selling or supply side. In the product market, these positions are reversed; households, as consumers, are on the buying or demand side, and businesses are on the selling or supply side. Each group of economic units both buys and sells.

Furthermore, the specter of scarcity haunts these transactions. Because households have only limited amounts of resources to supply to businesses, the money incomes of consumers will be limited. This means that each consumer's income will go only so far. A limited number of dollars obviously will not permit the purchase of all the goods and services which the consumer might like to buy. Similarly, because resources are scarce, the output of finished goods and services is also necessarily limited. Scarcity permeates our entire discussion.

To summarize: In a monetary economy, households, as resource owners, sell their resources to businesses and, as consumers, spend the money income received therefrom in buying goods and services. Businesses must buy resources in order to produce goods and services; their finished products are then sold to households in exchange for consumption expenditures or, as businesses view it, receipts. The net result is a counterclockwise *real* flow of economic resources and finished goods and services, and a clockwise *money* flow of income and consumption expenditures. These flows are simultaneous and repetitive.

△   **Limitations**

There are certain noteworthy shortcomings and omissions inherent in the circular flow overview of the workings of pure capitalism:

**1**   The circular flow model does not reflect the myriad facts and details relevant to specific households, specific businesses, and specific resource and product markets. Nor does it show transactions *within* the business and household sectors. Indeed, the main virtue of the circular flow model is that it lays bare the fundamental operations of pure capitalism without ensnaring the viewer in a maze of details. We seek here a view of the whole forest; the examination of specific trees will come later.

---

[3]For present purposes think of businesses simply as organizational charts, that is, institutions on paper apart from the capital, raw materials, labor, and entrepreneurial ability which breathe life into them and make them "going concerns."

**2** The circular flow model makes no mention of the economic role of government. The reason? The institutions of pure capitalism would allegedly give rise to a self-contained, self-regulating economy in which government's role would be minor. In Chapter 6 the circular flow will be modified to reflect the economic functions of government in the mixed capitalism which now characterizes the American economy.

**3** This model assumes that households spend exactly all their money income and that,

therefore, the flows of income and expenditure are constant in volume. In real terms this means that the levels of output and employment are constant. Part 2 of this book is concerned with the causes and effects of fluctuations in income and output flows.

**4** Our discussion of the circular flow does not explain how resource and product prices are actually determined. This is the task to which we turn in the ensuing chapter: How are resource and product prices determined in a purely capitalistic economy?

## Summary

**1** The capitalistic system is characterized by private ownership of resources and the freedom of individuals to engage in the economic activities of their choice as a means for advancing their material well-being. Self-interest is the driving force of such an economy, and competition functions as a regulatory or control mechanism. Capitalistic production is not organized in terms of a government plan, but rather features the price system as a means of organizing and making effective the myriad individual decisions which determine what is produced, the methods of production, and the sharing of output. Indeed, government plays a minor and relatively passive role.

**2** Specialization and an advanced technology based on the extensive use of capital goods are features common to all modern economies. Functioning as a medium of exchange, money circumvents problems entailed in bartering and thereby permits greater specialization.

**3** An overview of the operation of the capitalistic system can be gained through the circular flow of income. This simplified model locates the product and resource markets and presents the major income-expenditure flows and resources-output flows which constitute the lifeblood of the capitalistic economy.

## Questions and Study Suggestions

**1** Key terms and concepts to remember: private property; freedom of choice; freedom of enterprise; self-interest; competition; roundabout production; specialization and division of labor; barter; money as a medium of exchange; circular flow of income; resource and product markets.

**2** "Capitalism may be characterized as an automatic self-regulating system motivated by the self-interest of individuals and regulated by competition."[4] Explain and evaluate.

**3** Explain how the price system is a means of communicating and implementing decisions concerning allocation of the economy's resources.

**4** What advantages result from "roundabout" production? What problem is involved in increasing a full-employment, full-production economy's stock of capital goods? Illustrate this problem in terms of the production possibilities curve. Does an economy with unemployed resources face the same problem?

[4]Howard R. Bowen, *Toward Social Economy* (New York: Holt, Rinehart and Winston, Inc., 1948), p. 249.

**5**   What are the advantages of specialization in the use of human and material resources? The disadvantages?

**6**   What problems does barter entail? Indicate the economic significance of money as a
medium of exchange. "Money is the only commodity that is good for nothing but to be gotten
rid of. It will not feed you, clothe you, shelter you, or amuse you unless you spend or invest
it. It imparts value only in parting."[5] Explain this statement.

**7**   Describe the operation of pure capitalism as portrayed by the circular flow of income.
Locate resource and product markets and emphasize the fact of scarcity throughout your
discussion.

## Selected References

Bowen, Howard, R.: *Toward Social Economy* (New York: Holt, Rinehart and Winston, Inc., 1948),
    chaps. 1–5.
Ebenstein, William: *Today's Isms,* 8th ed. (Englewood Cliffs, N.J.: Prentice-Hall, Inc., 1980), chap. 3.
Loucks, William N., and William G. Whitney: *Comparative Economic Systems,* 9th ed. (New York: Harper
    & Row, Publishers, Incorporated, 1973), chap. 2.
Monsen, R. Joseph, Jr.: *Modern American Capitalism: Ideologies and Issues* (Boston: Houghton Mifflin
    Company, 1963).
Romano, Richard, and Melvin Leiman (eds.): *Views on Capitalism,* 2d ed. (Beverly Hills, Calif.: Glencoe
    Press, 1975).

[5]Federal Reserve Bank of Philadelphia, "Creeping Inflation," *Business Review,* August 1957, p. 3.

# LAST WORD
## Specialization and the Alienated Worker

Although specialization is a fundamental means of increasing productivity, it makes for monotonous and boring jobs. Gary Brynner, President of UAW Local 1112 at GM's Lordstown, Ohio, automobile assembly plant, airs his views.

"Alienation" is, I guess, a good term. There are symptoms of the alienated worker in our plant where we specialize, where I am president. Absentee rate has gone continually higher. Turnover rate is enormous. The use and turning to alcohol and drugs is becoming a bigger and bigger problem, and apathy—apathy within our union movement toward union leaders and to the Government.

I think those lead from the alienation of the worker. In our plant we make 101.6 cars an hour, the fastest line speed in the country. A guy has about 36 seconds to do an operation. The jobs are so fragmented that he is offered very little as far as input to that project. He cannot associate with it or he does not realize what he is doing to it.

Conveyor lines in our plant, the heights, and every movement of the conveyor line is determined to make the guy a little more efficient, to take movement of the bending and stretching, to make him more efficient.

The arbitrary rights of management tend to alienate the worker. The number of hours he works in a day, the number of days he works in a week, are all determined by arbitrary management, their decision, no recourse by the employee.

The job assignments within the plant in the same classification are solely the right of management, no say for the employee. The job content, and there is not much to that because when you have 36 seconds you do not have much of a job to do, and all we are left with is the dead end jobs, jobs that offer little challenge to the more educated worker, little chance for advancement, and hardly any chance to participate as a worker. We have more educated workers, as everybody knows, and that creates a problem in our plant. He is brought into the plant and his orientation session ends and starts with his papers on insurance and his assignment to a foreman who immediately puts his warm body on the line. He is introduced to a gentleman or a brother and told this is your operation and in 15 or 20 minutes or an hour or 3 hours, whatever, as quickly as they can get away, that is his job. That is what he looks forward to day in and day out, 10 hours a day, 11 hours a day, 6 or 7 days a week, as in our case.

From *Worker Alienation, 1972:* Hearings before the Subcommittee on Employment, Manpower, and Poverty, U.S. Senate, 92d Congress, 2d Session, Washington, p. 10, abridged.

# The Mechanics of Individual Prices: Demand and Supply

chapter 4

"Teach a parrot to say, 'Demand and supply,' and you have an economist!" There is a strong element of truth in this quip because, in fact, the simple tools of demand and supply can take one far in understanding not only specific economic issues, but also the operation of the entire economic system.

The much-simplified analysis of the operation of pure capitalism presented at the conclusion of Chapter 3 assumed that resources and goods and services sell for certain given prices. This permitted us to sidestep the fundamental question to which we now turn: How are prices "set," or determined, in pure capitalism? The answer is easy to state but a bit more difficult to understand. In short, prices are determined in the product market by the interaction of the supply decisions of competing businesses and the demand decisions of competing households. In the resource market, the demand decisions of competing businesses, coupled with the supply decisions of competing households, determine prices (Figure 3-2). Our immediate objective is to verify these answers. In doing so, we shall concentrate on the product market, then shift our attention later in the chapter to the resource market. The task is to explain the mechanics of prices. How does the interaction of demand and supply decisions determine product and resource prices?

## ☐ DEMAND

The term "demand" has a very definite meaning to the economist. _Demand_ is defined as _a schedule which shows the various amounts of a product which consumers are willing and able to purchase at each specific price in a set of possible prices during some specified period of time._[1] Demand simply portrays a series of alternative possibilities which can be set down

[1] In adjusting this definition to the resource market, merely substitute the word "resources" for "product" and "businesses" for "consumers."

**TABLE 4-1**
**An Individual Buyer's Demand for Corn**
(*hypothetical data*)

| Price per bushel | Quantity demanded per week |
|---|---|
| $5 | 10 |
| 4 | 20 |
| 3 | 35 |
| 2 | 55 |
| 1 | 80 |

in tabular form. As our definition indicates, we usually view demand from the vantage point of price; that is, we read demand as showing the amounts consumers will buy at various possible prices. It is equally correct and sometimes more useful to view demand from the reference point of quantity. That is, instead of asking what quantities can be sold at various prices, we can ask what prices can be gotten from consumers for various quantities of a good. Table 4-1 is a hypothetical demand schedule for a single consumer who is purchasing bushels of corn.

This tabular portrayal of demand reflects the relationship between the price of corn and the quantity that our mythical consumer would be willing and able to purchase at each of these prices. Note that we say willing and *able,* because willingness alone is not effective in the market. I may be willing to buy a Cadillac, but if this willingness is not backed by the ability to buy, that is, by the necessary dollars, it will not be effective and, therefore, not reflected in the market. In Table 4-1, if the price of corn in the market happened to be $5 per bushel, our consumer would be willing and able to buy 10 bushels per week; if it were $4, the consumer would be willing and able to buy 20 bushels per week; and so forth.

The demand schedule in and of itself does not tell us which of the five possible prices will actually exist in the corn market. As we have already said, this depends on demand *and supply.* Demand, then, is simply a tabular statement of a buyer's plans, or intentions, with respect to the purchase of a product.

Note that, to be meaningful, the quantities demanded at each price must relate to some specific time period—a day, a week, a month, and so forth. To say that "a consumer will buy 10 bushels of corn at $5 per bushel" is vague and meaningless. To say that "a consumer will buy 10 bushels of corn *per week* at $5 per bushel" is clear and very meaningful.

△ **Law of Demand**

A fundamental characteristic of demand is this: As price falls, the corresponding quantity demanded rises, or, alternatively, as price increases, the corresponding quantity demanded falls. In short, there is an *inverse* relationship between price and quantity demanded. Economists have labeled this inverse relationship the *law of demand.* Upon what foundation does this law rest? There are several levels of sophistication upon which to argue the case.

**1** Common sense and simple observation are consistent with a downsloping demand curve. People ordinarily *do* buy more of a given product at a low price than they do at a high price. To consumers, price is an obstacle which deters them from buying. The higher this obstacle, the less of a product they will buy; the lower the price obstacle, the more they will buy. In other words, a high price discourages consumers from buying, and a low price encourages them to buy. The plain fact that businesses have "sales" is concrete evidence of their belief in the law of demand. "Bargain days" are based on the law of demand.

**2** In any given time period each buyer of a product will derive less satisfaction or benefit or "utility" from each successive unit of a product. For example, the second "Big Mac" will yield less satisfaction than the first; the third still less added benefit or utility than the second; and so forth. Hence, because consumption is subject to *diminishing marginal utility*—successive units of a given product yield less and less extra satisfaction—consumers will only buy additional units if price is reduced.

**3**  At a slightly more sophisticated level the law of demand can be explained in terms of income and substitution effects. The *income effect* simply indicates that, at a lower price, one can afford more of the good without giving up any alternative goods. In other words, a decline in the price of a product will increase the purchasing power of one's money income; hence, you are able to buy more of the product than before. A higher price will have the opposite effect. The *substitution effect* suggests that, at a lower price, one has the incentive to substitute the cheaper good for similar goods which are now relatively more expensive. Consumers tend to substitute cheap products for dear products. To illustrate: A decline in the price of beef will increase the purchasing power of consumer incomes, making them able to buy more beef (the income effect). At a lower price, beef is relatively more attractive and it is substituted for pork, mutton, chicken, and fish (the substitution effect). The income and substitution effects combine to make consumers able and willing to buy more of a product at a low price than at a high price.

△  **The Demand Curve**

This inverse relationship between product price and quantity demanded can be presented on a simple two-dimensional graph measuring quantity demanded on the horizontal axis and price on the vertical axis.[2] From Chapter 1 we recall that the process involved is merely that of locating on the graph those five price-quantity possibilities shown in Table 4-1. We do this by drawing perpendiculars from the appropriate points on the two axes. Thus, in plotting the "$5-price–10-quantity-demanded" possibility, we must draw a perpendicular from the horizontal (quantity) axis at 10 to meet a perpendicular drawn from the vertical (price) axis at $5. If this is done for all five possibilities, the result is a series of points as shown in Figure 4-1. Each of these points represents a specific price and the corresponding quantity which the consumer will choose to purchase at that price. Now, assuming the same inverse

[2] Putting price on the vertical axis and quantity demanded on the horizontal axis is a matter of convention; we do it for the same reason that a red traffic light means "Stop" and a green one means "Go."

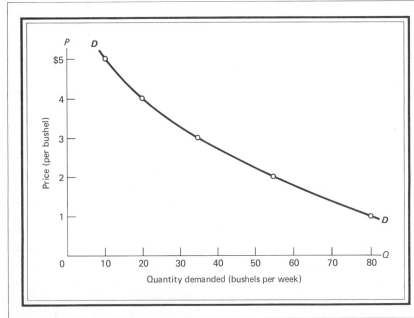

**FIGURE 4-1  AN INDIVIDUAL BUYER'S DEMAND CURVE FOR CORN**

An individual's demand schedule graphs as a downsloping curve such as *DD*, because price and quantity demanded are inversely related. Specifically, the law of demand generalizes that consumers will buy more of a product as its price declines.

relationship between price and quantity demanded at all points between the ones graphed, we can generalize on the inverse relationship between price and quantity demanded by drawing a curve to represent *all* price-quantity-demanded possibilities within the limits shown on the graph. The resulting curve is called a *demand curve* and is labeled *DD* in Figure 4-1. It slopes downward and to the right because the relationship it portrays between price and quantity demanded is inverse. The law of demand—people buy more at a low price than they do at a high price—is reflected in the downward slope of the demand curve.

What is the advantage of graphing our demand schedule? After all, Table 4-1 and Figure 4-1 contain exactly the same data and reflect the same relationship between price and quantity demanded. The advantage of graphing is that it permits us to represent clearly a given relationship—in this case the law of demand—in a much simpler way than we could if we were forced to rely upon verbal and tabular presentation. A single curve on a graph, if understood, is simpler to state *and to manipulate* than tables and lengthy verbal presentations would be. Graphs are invaluable tools in economic analysis. They permit clear expression and handling of ofttimes complex relationships.

△ **Individual and Market Demand**

Until now we have been dealing in terms of just one consumer. The assumption of com-

petition obligates us to consider a situation in which a large number of buyers are in the market. The transition from an *individual* to a *market* demand schedule can be accomplished easily by the process of summing the quantities demanded by each consumer at the various possible prices. If there were just three buyers in the market, as is shown in Table 4-2, it would be an easy chore to determine the total quantities demanded at each price. Figure 4-2 shows the same summing procedure graphically, using only the $3 price to illustrate the adding-up process. Note that we are simply summing the three individual demand curves *horizontally* to derive the total demand curve.

Competition, of course, entails many more than three buyers of a product. So—to avoid a lengthy addition process—let us suppose there are 200 buyers of corn in the market, each of whom chooses to buy the same amount at each of the various prices as our original consumer does. Thus, we can determine market demand by multiplying the quantity-demanded data of Table 4-1 by 200, as in Table 4-3. Curve $D_1$ in Figure 4-3 indicates this market demand curve for the 200 buyers.

△ **Determinants of Demand**

When the economist constructs a demand curve such as $D_1$ in Figure 4-3, the assumption is made that price is the most important determinant of the amount of any product purchased. But the economist is aware that fac-

**TABLE 4-2**
Market Demand for Corn, Three Buyers (*hypothetical data*)

| Price per bushel | Quantity demanded, first buyer | | Quantity demanded, second buyer | | Quantity demanded, third buyer | | Total quantity demanded per week |
|---|---|---|---|---|---|---|---|
| $5 | 10 | + | 12 | + | 8 | = | 30 |
| 4 | 20 | + | 23 | + | 17 | = | 60 |
| 3 | 35 | + | 39 | + | 26 | = | 100 |
| 2 | 55 | + | 60 | + | 39 | = | 154 |
| 1 | 80 | + | 87 | + | 54 | = | 221 |

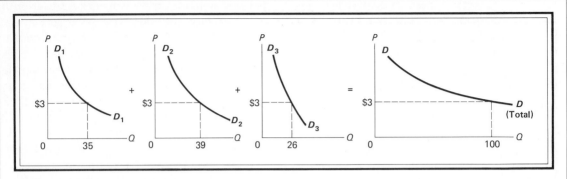

FIGURE 4-2   THE MARKET DEMAND CURVE IS THE SUM OF THE INDIVIDUAL DEMAND CURVES

Graphically the market demand curve ($D$ total) is found by summing horizontally the individual demand curves ($D_1$, $D_2$, and $D_3$) of all consumers in the market.

**TABLE 4-3**
**Market Demand for Corn, 200 Buyers (*hypothetical data*)**

| (1)<br>Price<br>per<br>bushel | (2)<br>Quantity<br>demanded<br>per week,<br>single buyer | | (3)<br>Number of<br>buyers<br>in the market | | (4)<br>Total<br>quantity<br>demanded<br>per week |
|---|---|---|---|---|---|
| $5 | 10 | × | 200 | = | 2,000 |
| 4 | 20 | × | 200 | = | 4,000 |
| 3 | 35 | × | 200 | = | 7,000 |
| 2 | 55 | × | 200 | = | 11,000 |
| 1 | 80 | × | 200 | = | 16,000 |

tors other than price can and do affect purchases. Thus, in locating a given demand curve such as $D_1$, it must also be assumed that "other things are equal"; that is, the *nonprice determinants*[3] of the amount demanded are conveniently assumed to be constant. When these nonprice determinants of demand do in fact change, the location of the demand curve will shift to some new position to the right or left of $D_1$.

What are the major nonprice determinants of market demand? The basic ones are (1) the tastes or preferences of consumers, (2) the number of consumers in the market,

(3) the money incomes of consumers, (4) the prices of related goods, and (5) consumer expectations with respect to future prices and incomes.

△   **Changes in Demand**

What happens if one or more of the determinants of demand should change? We know the answer: A change in one or more of the determinants will change the demand schedule data in Table 4-3 and therefore the location of the demand curve in Figure 4-3. Such a change in the demand schedule data, or, graphically, a shift in the location of the demand curve, is designated as a *change in demand*.

More specifically, if consumers become willing and able to buy more of this particular good at each possible price than is reflected in column 4 of Table 4-3, an *increase in demand*

[3] By nonprice determinants we mean factors other than the price of the specific product under consideration. We shall find that changes in the prices of *other* goods may affect the demand for the specific product.

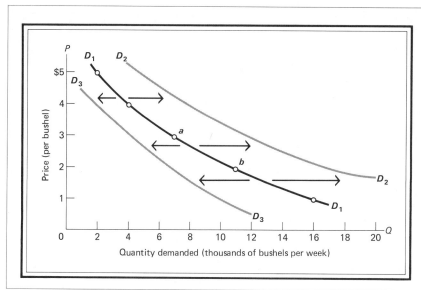

**FIGURE 4-3  CHANGES IN THE DEMAND FOR CORN**

A change in one or more of the determinants of demand—consumer tastes, the number of buyers in the market, money incomes, the prices of other goods, or consumer expectations—will cause a change in demand. An increase in demand shifts the demand curve to the right, as from $D_1 D_1$ to $D_2 D_2$. A decrease in demand shifts the demand curve to the left, as from $D_1 D_1$ to $D_3 D_3$. A change in the quantity demanded involves a movement, caused by a change in the price of the product under consideration, from one point to another—as from $a$ to $b$—on a fixed demand curve.

has occurred. In Figure 4-3, this increase in demand is reflected in a shift of the demand curve to the *right,* for example, from $D_1$ to $D_2$. Conversely, a *decrease in demand* occurs when, because of a change in one or more of the determinants, consumers buy less of the product at each possible price than is indicated in column 4 of Table 4-3. Graphically, a decrease in demand entails a shift of the demand curve to the *left,* for example, from $D_1$ to $D_3$ in Figure 4-3.

Let us now examine the effect upon demand of changes in each of the aforementioned nonprice determinants.

**1  Tastes**  A change in consumer tastes favorable to this product—possibly prompted by advertising or fashion changes—will mean that more will be demanded at each price; that is, demand will increase. An unfavorable change in consumer preferences will cause demand to decrease, shifting the curve to the left.

**2  Number of Buyers**  It is equally obvious that an increase in the number of consumers in a market—brought about perhaps by improvements in transportation or by pop-

ulation growth—will constitute an increase in demand. Fewer consumers will be reflected by a decrease in demand.

**3  Income**  The impact of changes in money income upon demand is a bit more complex. For most commodities, a rise in income will cause an increase in demand. Consumers typically buy more steaks, stereos, and Scotch as their incomes increase. Conversely, the demand for such products will decline in response to a fall in incomes. Commodities whose demand varies *directly* with money income are called *superior,* or *normal,* goods.

Although most products are normal goods, there are a few exceptions. Examples: As incomes increase beyond some point, the amounts of bread or potatoes or cabbages purchased at each price may diminish because the higher incomes now allow consumers to buy more high-protein foods, such as dairy products and meat. Similarly, rising incomes may cause the demands for hamburger and oleomargarine to decline as wealthier consumers switch to T-bones and butter. Goods whose demand varies *inversely* with a change in money income are called *inferior* or "poor man's" goods.

**4  Prices of Related Goods**  Whether a given change in the price of a related good will increase or decrease the demand for the product under consideration will depend upon whether the related good is a substitute for, or a complement to, it. For example, butter and oleomargarine are *substitute,* or competing, goods. When the price of butter rises, consumers will purchase a smaller amount of butter, and this will cause the demand for oleomargarine to increase. Conversely, as the price of butter falls, consumers will buy larger quantities of butter, causing the demand for oleomargarine to decrease. To generalize: When two products are substitutes, the price of one good and the demand for the other are *directly* related. So it is with Schlitz and Budweiser, sugar and saccharin, Chevrolets and Fords, tea and coffee, and so forth.

But other pairs of products are *complementary* goods; they "go together." If the price of gasoline falls and, as a result, you drive your car more, this extra driving will increase your demand for motor oil. Conversely, an increase in the price of gasoline will diminish the demand for motor oil. Thus gas and oil are jointly demanded; they are complements. And so it is with ham and eggs, Scotch and soda, phonographs and records, golf clubs and golf balls, cameras and rolls of film, and so forth. When two commodities are complements, the price of one good and the demand for the other are *inversely* related.

Many pairs of goods, of course, are not related at all—they are *independent* goods. For such pairs of commodities as, for example, butter and golf balls, potatoes and automobiles, bananas and wristwatches, we should expect that a change in the price of one would have little or no impact upon the demand for the other.

**5  Expectations**  Consumer expectations of higher future prices may prompt them to buy now in order to "beat" the anticipated price rises, and, similarly, the expectation of rising incomes may induce consumers to be less tightfisted in their current spending. Conversely, expectations of falling prices and income will tend to decrease the current demand for products.

We might summarize by saying that an increase in the demand for product X—the decision of consumers to buy more of X at each possible price—can be caused by (1) a favorable change in consumer tastes, (2) an increase in the number of buyers in the market, (3) a rise (fall) in income if X is a normal (inferior) good, (4) an increase (decrease) in the price of related good Y if Y is a substitute for (complement to) X, and (5) expectations of future increases in prices and incomes. Conversely, a decrease in the demand for X can be associated with (1) an unfavorable change in tastes, (2) a decrease in the number of buyers in the market, (3) a rise (fall) in income if X is an inferior (normal) good, (4) an increase (decrease) in the price of related good Y if Y is complementary to (a substitute for) X, and (5) expectations of future price and income declines.

△  **Changes in Quantity Demanded**

A "change in demand" must not be confused with a "change in the quantity demanded." We have noted that a *change in demand* refers to a shift in the entire demand curve either to the right (an increase in demand) or to the left (a decrease in demand). The consumer's state of mind concerning purchases of this product has been altered. The cause: a change in one or more of the determinants of demand. As used by economists, the term "demand" refers to a schedule or curve; therefore, a "change in demand" must mean that the entire schedule has changed and that graphically the curve has shifted its position.

In contrast, a *change in the quantity demanded* designates the movement from one point to another point—from one price-quantity combination to another—on a fixed demand curve. The cause of a change in the quantity demanded is a change in the price of the product under consideration. In Table 4-3 a decline in the price asked by suppliers of corn from $5 to $4 will increase the quantity of corn demanded from 2000 to 4000 bushels.

Figure 4-3 is helpful in making the distinction between a change in demand and a change in the quantity demanded. The shift of the demand curve $D_1$ to either $D_2$ or $D_3$ entails changes in demand. But the movement from point $a$ to point $b$ on curve $D_1$ is a change in the quantity demanded.

The reader should decide whether a change in demand or a change in the quantity demanded is involved in each of the following illustrations:

**1**   Consumer incomes rise, with the result that more jewelry is purchased.

**2**   A barber raises the price of haircuts and experiences a decline in volume of business.

**3**   The price of Fords goes up, and, as a consequence, the sales of Chevrolets increase.

☐  **SUPPLY**

*Supply* may be defined as *a schedule which shows the various amounts of a product which a producer is willing and able to produce and make available for sale in the market at each specific price in a set of possible prices during some specified time period.*[4] This schedule portrays a series of alternative possibilities, such as those shown in Table 4-4 for a single producer. Let us suppose, in this case, that our producer is a farmer producing corn, the demand for which we have just considered. Our definition of supply indicates that supply is usually viewed from the vantage point of price. That is, we read supply as showing the amounts producers will offer at various possible prices. It is more useful and quite correct in some instances to view supply from the reference point of quantity. Instead of asking

**TABLE 4-4**
**An Individual Producer's Supply of Corn**
(*hypothetical data*)

| Price per bushel | Quantity supplied per week |
|---|---|
| $5 | 60 |
| 4 | 50 |
| 3 | 35 |
| 2 | 20 |
| 1 | 5 |

what quantities will be offered at various prices, we can ask what prices will be required to induce producers to offer various quantities of a good.

△  **Law of Supply**

It will be immediately noted that Table 4-4 shows a *direct* relationship between price and quantity supplied. As price rises, the corresponding quantity supplied rises; as price falls, the quantity supplied also falls. This particular relationship is called the *law of supply*. It simply tells us that producers are willing to produce and offer for sale more of their product at a high price than they are at a low price. Why? This again is basically a commonsense matter.

Price, we recall, is a deterrent from the consumer's standpoint. The obstacle of a high price means that the consumer, being on the paying end of this price, will buy a relatively small amount of the product; the lower the price obstacle, the more the consumer will buy. The supplier, on the other hand, is on the receiving end of the product's price. To a supplier, price is revenue per unit and therefore is an inducement or incentive to produce and sell a product. The higher the price of the product, the greater the incentive to produce and offer it in the market.

Consider a farmer whose resources are shiftable within limits among alternative products. As price moves up in Table 4-4, the farmer will find it profitable to take land out of wheat, oats, and soybean production and put it into corn. Furthermore, higher corn prices will

[4] In talking of the resource market, our definition of supply reads: a schedule which shows the various amounts of a resource which its owners are willing to supply in the market at each possible price in a series of prices during some specified time.

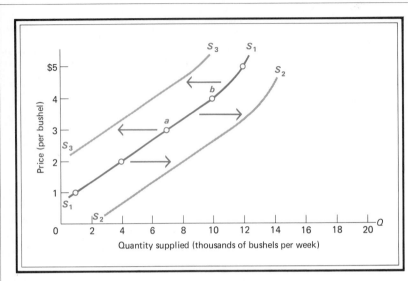

**FIGURE 4-4  CHANGES IN THE SUPPLY OF CORN**

A change in one or more of the determinants of supply—productive techniques, resource prices, the prices of other goods, price expectations, or the number of sellers in the market—will cause a change in supply. An increase in supply shifts the supply curve to the right, as from $S_1S_1$ to $S_2S_2$. A decrease in supply is shown graphically as a movement of the curve to the left, as from $S_1S_1$ to $S_3S_3$. A change in the quantity supplied involves a movement caused by a change in the price of the product under consideration, from one point to another—as from $a$ to $b$—on a fixed supply curve.

make it possible for the farmer to cover the costs associated with more intensive cultivation and the use of larger quantities of fertilizers and pesticides. All these efforts result in more output of corn. Consider a manufacturing concern. Beyond some point manufacturers usually encounter increasing production costs per unit of output. Therefore, a higher product price is necessary to cover these rising costs. But why do costs rise? They rise because certain productive resources—in particular, the firm's plant and machinery—cannot be expanded in a short period of time. Hence, as the firm increases the amounts of more readily variable resources such as labor, materials, and component parts, the fixed plant will at some point become crowded or congested with the result that productive efficiency declines and the cost of successive units of output increases. Producers must receive a higher price to produce these more costly units.[5]

△   **The Supply Curve**

As in the case of demand, it is convenient to present graphically the concept of supply.

[5] Chapters 25 and 26 provide a more sophisticated explanation of the relationship between costs and supply.

Our axes in Figure 4-4 are the same as those in Figure 4-3, except for the obvious change of "quantity demanded" to "quantity supplied." The graphing procedure is the same as that previously explained, but of course the quantity data and relationship involved are different. The market supply data graphed in Figure 4-4 as $S_1$ are shown in Table 4-5, which assumes there are 200 suppliers in the market having the same supply schedules as the producer previously portrayed in Table 4-4.

△   **Determinants of Supply**

In constructing a supply curve, the economist assumes that price is the most significant determinant of the quantity supplied of any product. But, as with the demand curve, the supply curve is anchored on the "other things are equal" assumption. That is, the supply curve is drawn on the supposition that certain nonprice determinants of the amount supplied are given and do not change. If any of these nonprice determinants of supply do in fact change, the location of the supply curve will be altered.

The basic nonprice determinants of supply are (1) the technique of production, (2) resource prices, (3) taxes and subsidies, (4) prices

**TABLE 4-5**
**Market Supply of Corn, 200 Producers (*hypothetical data*)**

| (1)<br>Price<br>per<br>bushel | (2)<br>Quantity<br>supplied<br>per week,<br>single<br>producer | | (3)<br>Number of<br>sellers<br>in the market | | (4)<br>Total<br>quantity<br>supplied<br>per week |
|---|---|---|---|---|---|
| $5 | 60 | × | 200 | = | 12,000 |
| 4 | 50 | × | 200 | = | 10,000 |
| 3 | 35 | × | 200 | = | 7,000 |
| 2 | 20 | × | 200 | = | 4,000 |
| 1 | 5 | × | 200 | = | 1,000 |

of other goods, (5) price expectations, and (6) the number of sellers in the market. To repeat: A change in any one or more of these determinants will cause the supply curve for a product to shift to either the right or the left. A shift to the *right,* from $S_1$ to $S_2$ in Figure 4-4, designates an *increase in supply:* Producers are now offering more of the product at each possible price. A shift to the *left,* $S_1$ to $S_3$ in Figure 4-4, indicates a *decrease in supply:* Suppliers are offering less at each price.

△ **Changes in Supply**

Let us consider the effect of changes in each of these determinants upon supply.

**1** and **2**   The first two determinants of supply—technology and resource prices—are the two major components of production costs. As indicated in our explanation of the law of supply, the relationship between production costs and supply is an intimate one. The critical point for present purposes is that anything which serves to lower production costs, that is, a technological improvement or a decline in resource prices, will increase supply. With lower costs, businesses will find it profitable to offer a larger amount of the product at each possible price. An increase in the price of resources (a deterioration of technology being unlikely) will raise costs and cause a decrease in supply; that is, the supply curve will shift to the left.

**3**   We will discover later (Chapters 6 and 23) that certain taxes, such as sales taxes, add to production costs and therefore reduce supply. Conversely, subsidies lower costs and increase supply.

**4**   Changes in the prices of other goods can also shift the supply curve for a product. A decline in the price of wheat may cause a farmer to produce and offer more corn at each possible price. Conversely, a rise in the price of wheat may make farmers less willing to produce and offer corn in the market.

**5**   Expectations concerning the future price of a product can also affect a producer's current willingness to supply that product. It is difficult, however, to generalize concerning the way the expectation of, say, higher prices will affect the present supply curve of a product. Farmers might withhold some of their current corn harvest from the market, anticipating a higher corn price in the future. This will cause a decrease in the current supply of corn. On the other hand, in many types of manufacturing, expected price increases may induce firms to expand production immediately, causing supply to increase.

**6**   Given the scale of operations of each firm, the larger the number of suppliers, the greater will be market supply. As more firms enter an industry, the supply curve will shift to the right. The smaller the number of firms in an industry, the less the market supply will be. This means that as firms leave an industry, the supply curve will shift to the left.

### △  Changes in Quantity Supplied

The distinction between a "change in supply" and a "change in the quantity supplied" parallels that between a change in demand and a change in the quantity demanded. A *change in supply* is involved when the entire supply curve shifts. An increase in supply shifts the curve to the right; a decrease in supply shifts it to the left. The cause of a change in supply is a change in one or more of the determinants of supply. The term "supply" is used by economists to refer to a schedule or curve. A "change in supply" therefore must mean that the entire schedule has changed or that the curve has shifted.

A *change in the quantity supplied,* on the other hand, refers to the movement from one point to another point on a stable supply curve. The cause of such a movement is a change in the price of the specific product under consideration. In Table 4-5 a decline in the price of corn from $5 to $4 decreases the quantity of corn supplied from 12,000 to 10,000 bushels.

Shifting the supply curve from $S_1$ to $S_2$ or $S_3$ in Figure 4-4 obviously entails changes in supply. The movement from point $a$ to point $b$ on $S_1$, however, is merely a change in the quantity supplied.

The reader should determine which of the following involves a change in supply and which entails a change in the quantity supplied:

1  Because production costs decline, producers sell more automobiles.

2  The price of wheat declines, causing the number of bushels of corn sold per month to increase.

3  Fewer oranges are offered for sale because their price has decreased in retail markets.

**TABLE 4-6**
**Market Supply and Demand for Corn**
(*hypothetical data*)

| (1)<br>Total quantity supplied per week | (2)<br>Price per bushel | (3)<br>Total quantity demanded per week | (4)<br>Surplus (+) or shortage (−) (arrows indicate effect on price) |
|---|---|---|---|
| 12,000 | $5 | 2,000 | +10,000↓ |
| 10,000 | 4 | 4,000 | + 6,000↓ |
| 7,000 | 3 | 7,000 | 0 |
| 4,000 | 2 | 11,000 | − 7,000↑ |
| 1,000 | 1 | 16,000 | −15,000↑ |

### ☐  SUPPLY AND DEMAND: MARKET EQUILIBRIUM

We may now bring the concepts of supply and demand together to see how the interaction of the buying decisions of households and the selling decisions of producers will determine the price of a product and the quantity which is actually bought and sold in the market. In Table 4-6, columns 1 and 2 reproduce the market supply schedule for corn (from Table 4-5), and columns 2 and 3, the market demand schedule for corn (from Table 4-3). Note that in column 2 we are using a common set of prices. We assume competition—the presence of a large number of buyers and sellers.

Now the question to be faced is this: Of the five[6] possible prices at which corn might sell in this market, which will actually prevail as the market price for corn? Let us derive our answer through the simple process of trial and error. For no particular reason, we shall start with an examination of $5. Could this be the prevailing market price for corn? The answer is "No," for the simple reason that producers are willing to produce and supply to the market some 12,000 bushels of corn at this price while buyers, on the other hand, are willing to take only 2000 bushels off the market at this price. In other words, the relatively high price of $5 encourages farmers to produce a great

---

[6]Of course, there are many possible prices; our example shows only five of them.

deal of corn, but that same high price discourages consumers from taking the product off the market. Other products appear as "better buys" when corn is high-priced. The result in this case is a 10,000-bushel *surplus* of corn in the market. This surplus, shown in column 4, is the excess of quantity supplied over quantity demanded at the price of $5. Practically put, corn farmers would find themselves with unwanted inventories of output.

Could a price of $5—even if it existed temporarily in the corn market—persist over a period of time? Certainly not. The very large surplus of corn would prompt competing sellers to bid down the price in order to encourage buyers to take this surplus off their hands. Suppose price gravitates down to $4. Now the situation has changed considerably. The lower price has encouraged buyers to take more of this product off the market and, at the same time, has induced farmers to use a smaller amount of resources in producing corn. The surplus, as a result, has diminished to 6000 bushels. However, a surplus still exists and competition among sellers will once again bid down the price of corn. We can conclude, then, that prices of $5 and $4 will be unstable because they are "too high." The market price for corn must be something less than $4.

To avoid letting the cat out of the bag before we fully appreciate how supply and demand determine product price, let us now jump to the other end of our price column and examine $1 as the possible market price for corn. It is evident that at this price, quantity demanded is in excess of quantity supplied by 15,000 units. This relatively low price discourages farmers from devoting their resources to corn production; the same low price encourages consumers to attempt to buy more corn than would otherwise be the case. Corn is a "good buy" when its price is relatively low. In short, there is a 15,000-bushel *shortage* of corn. Can this price of $1 persist as the market price? No. Competition among buyers will bid up the price to something greater than $1. In other words, at a price of $1, many consumers

who are willing and able to buy at this price will obviously be left out in the cold. Many potential consumers, in order to ensure that they will not have to do without, will express a willingness to pay a price in excess of $1 to ensure getting some of the available corn. Suppose this competitive bidding up of price by buyers boosts the price of corn to $2. This higher price obviously has reduced, but not eliminated, the shortage of corn. For $2, farmers are willing to devote more resources to corn production, and some buyers who were willing to pay $1 for a bushel of corn will choose not to buy corn at a price of $2, deciding to use their incomes to buy other products or maybe to save more of their incomes. But a shortage of 7000 bushels still exists at a price of $2. We can conclude that competitive bidding among buyers will push market price to some figure greater than $2.

By trial and error we have eliminated every price but $3. So let us now examine it. At a price of $3, *and only at this price,* the quantity which farmers are willing to produce and supply in the market is identical with the amount consumers are willing to buy. As a result, there is neither a shortage nor a surplus of corn at this price. We have already seen that a surplus causes price to decline and a shortage causes price to rise. With neither a shortage nor a surplus at $3, there is no reason for the actual price of corn to move away from this price. The economist calls this price the *equilibrium price,* equilibrium meaning "in balance" or "at rest." At $3, quantity supplied and quantity demanded are in balance; hence $3 is the only stable price of corn under the supply and demand conditions shown in Table 4-6. Or, stated differently, the price of corn will be established where the supply decisions of producers and the demand decisions of buyers are mutually consistent. Such decisions are consistent with one another only at a price of $3. At any higher price, suppliers want to sell more than consumers want to buy; at any lower price, consumers want to buy more than producers are willing to offer for sale. Discrep-

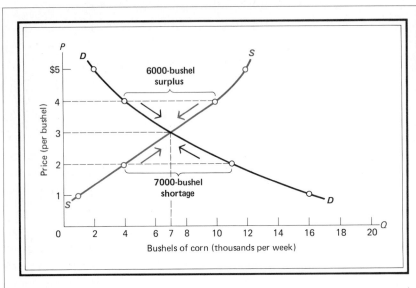

**FIGURE 4-5   THE EQUILIBRIUM PRICE AND QUANTITY FOR CORN AS DETERMINED BY MARKET DEMAND AND SUPPLY**

The intersection of the down-sloping demand curve $D$ and the upsloping supply curve $S$ indicates the equilibrium price and quantity, $3 and 7000 bushels in this instance. The shortages of corn which would exist at below equilibrium prices, for example, 7000 bushels at $2, drive price up, and in so doing, increase the quantity supplied and reduce the quantity demanded until equilibrium is achieved. The surpluses which above-equilibrium prices would entail, for example 6000 bushels at $4, push price down and thereby increase the quantity demanded and reduce the quantity supplied until equilibrium is achieved.

ancies between supply and demand intentions of sellers and buyers, respectively, will prompt price changes which subsequently will bring these two sets of plans into accord with one another.

A graphic analysis of supply and demand should yield the same conclusions. Figure 4-5 puts the market supply and market demand curves for corn on the same graph, the horizontal axis now reflecting both quantity demanded and quantity supplied. A close examination of this diagram clearly indicates that at any price above the equilibrium price of $3, quantity supplied will exceed quantity demanded. This surplus will cause a competitive bidding down of price by sellers eager to relieve themselves of their surplus. The falling price will cause less corn to be offered and will simultaneously encourage consumers to buy more. Any price below the equilibrium price will entail a shortage; that is, quantity demanded will exceed quantity supplied. Competitive bidding by buyers will push the price up toward the equilibrium level. And this rising price will simultaneously bring forth a greater supply from producers and ration buy-

ers out of the market, thereby causing the shortage to vanish. Graphically, the intersection of the supply curve and the demand curve for the product will indicate the equilibrium point. In this case, as we know, equilibrium price and quantity are $3 and 7000 bushels.

△   **Rationing Function of Prices**

The ability of the competitive forces of supply and demand to establish a price where supply and demand decisions are synchronized is sometimes called the *rationing function* of prices. In this case, the equilibrium price of $3 clears the market, leaving no burdensome surplus for the sellers and no inconvenient shortage for the potential buyers. The composite of freely made individual buying and selling decisions sets this price which clears the market. In effect, the market mechanism of supply and demand says this: Any buyer who is willing and able to pay $3 for a bushel of corn will be able to acquire one; those who are not, will not. Similarly, any seller who is willing and able to produce bushels of corn and offer them for sale at a price of $3 will be able to do so successfully; those who are not, will not. As we will see shortly, were it not that competitive prices automatically bring supply and demand decisions into consistency with one another, some type of administrative control by government would be necessary to avoid or control the shortages or surpluses which might otherwise occur.

### △  Changes in Supply and Demand

It was noted earlier that demand might change because of fluctuations in consumer tastes or incomes, changes in consumer expectations, or variations in the prices of related goods. On the other hand, supply might vary in response to changes in technology, resource prices, or taxes. Our analysis would be incomplete if we did not stop to consider the effect of changes in supply and demand upon equilibrium price.

**Changing Demand**   Let us first analyze the effects of a change in demand, assuming that supply is conveniently constant. Suppose now that demand increases, as shown in Figure 4-6a. What is the effect upon price? Noting that the new intersection of the supply and

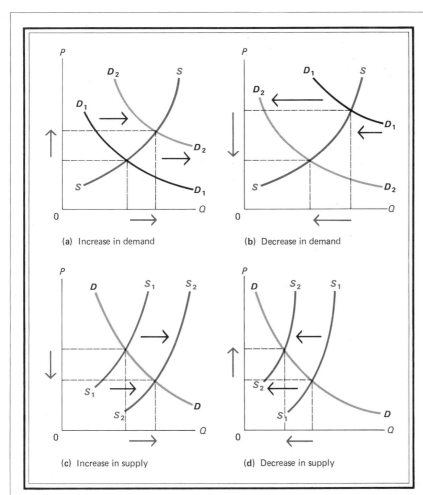

**FIGURE 4-6  CHANGES IN DEMAND AND SUPPLY AND THE EFFECTS ON PRICE AND QUANTITY**

The increase in demand of **(a)** and the decrease in demand of **(b)** indicate a direct relationship between a change in demand and the resulting changes in equilibrium price and quantity. The increase in supply of **(c)** and the decrease in supply of **(d)** show an inverse relationship between a change in supply and the resulting change in equilibrium price, but a direct relationship between a change in supply and the accompanying change in equilibrium quantity.

(a) Increase in demand

(b) Decrease in demand

(c) Increase in supply

(d) Decrease in supply

demand curves is at a higher point on both the price and quantity axes, we can conclude that an increase in demand, other things (supply) being equal, will have a *price-increasing effect* and a *quantity-increasing effect.* (The value of graphic analysis now begins to become apparent; we need not fumble with columns of figures in determining the effect on price and quantity but only compare the new with the old point of intersection on the graph.) A decrease in demand, as illustrated in Figure 4-6*b*, reveals *price-decreasing* and *quantity-decreasing effects.* Price falls, and quantity also declines. *In brief, we find a direct relationship between a change in demand and the resulting changes in both equilibrium price and quantity.*

**Changing Supply**   Let us reverse the procedure and analyze the effect of a change in supply on price, assuming that demand is constant. If supply increases, as in Figure 4-6*c*, the new intersection of supply and demand is obviously at a lower price; equilibrium price falls. Equilibrium quantity, however, increases. If supply decreases, on the other hand, this will tend to increase product price. Figure 4-6*d* illustrates this situation. Here, price increases but quantity declines. In short, an increase in supply has a *price-decreasing* and a *quantity-increasing effect.* A decrease in supply has a *price-increasing* and a *quantity-decreasing effect. There is an inverse relationship between a change in supply and the resulting change in equilibrium price, but the relationship between a change in supply and the resulting change in equilibrium quantity is direct.*

**Complex Cases**   Obviously, a host of more complex cases might arise, involving changes in both supply and demand. Two cases are possible when it is supposed that supply and demand change in *opposite directions.* Assume first that supply increases and demand decreases. What effect does this have upon equilibrium price? This example couples

two price-decreasing effects, and the net result will be a price fall greater than that which would result from either change taken in isolation. How about equilibrium quantity? Here the effects of the changes in supply and demand are opposed: The increase in supply tends to increase equilibrium quantity, but the decrease in demand tends to reduce the equilibrium quantity. The direction of the change in quantity depends upon the relative sizes of the changes in supply and demand. The second possibility is for supply to decrease and demand to increase. Two price-increasing effects are involved here. We can predict an increase in equilibrium price greater than that caused by either change taken separately. The effect upon equilibrium quantity is again indeterminate, depending upon the relative size of the changes in supply and demand. If the decrease in supply is relatively larger than the increase in demand, the equilibrium quantity will be less than it is initially. But if the decrease in supply is relatively smaller than the increase in demand, the equilibrium quantity will increase as a result of these changes. The reader should trace through these two cases graphically to verify the conclusions we have outlined.

What if supply and demand change in the *same direction?* Suppose first that supply and demand both increase. What is the effect upon equilibrium price? It depends. Here we must compare two conflicting effects on price—the price-decreasing effect of the increase in supply and the price-increasing effect of the increase in demand. If the increase in supply is of greater magnitude than the increase in demand, the net effect will be for equilibrium price to decrease. If the opposite holds true, equilibrium price will increase. The effect upon equilibrium quantity is certain: Increases in supply and in demand both have quantity-increasing effects. This means that equilibrium quantity will increase by an amount greater than that which either change would have entailed in isolation. Secondly, a decrease in both supply and demand can be subjected to similar analysis. If the decrease in supply is greater than the decrease in demand, equilibrium price will rise. If the reverse holds true, equilibrium price will fall. Because decreases in supply and demand both have quantity-decreasing effects, it can be predicted with certainty that equilibrium quantity will be less than that which prevailed initially.

Incidentally, the possibility that supply and demand will both change in a given period of time is not particularly unlikely. As a matter of fact, a single event might simultaneously affect both supply and demand. For example, a technological improvement in cheese production might lower both the supply of, and the demand for, fluid milk.

Needless to say, special cases might arise where a decrease in demand and a decrease in supply, on the one hand, and an increase in demand and an increase in supply, on the other, cancel out. In both these cases, the net effect upon equilibrium price will be zero; price will not change. The reader should again work out these more complex cases in terms of supply and demand curves to verify all these results.

### ⬧ The Resource Market

What about the shape of the supply and demand curves in the resource market? As in the product market, resource supply curves are typically upsloping, and resource demand curves are typically downsloping. Why?

Resource supply curves generally slope upward; that is, they reflect a *direct* relationship between resource price and quantity supplied, because it is in the interest of resource owners themselves to supply more of a particular resource at a high price than at a low price. High income payments in a particular occupation or industry encourage households to supply more of their human and property resources. Low income payments discourage resource owners from supplying resources in this particular occupation or industry and, as a matter of fact, encourage them to supply their resources elsewhere.

On the demand side, businesses tend to buy less of a given resource as its price rises, and they tend to substitute other relatively low-priced resources for it. Entrepreneurs will find it profitable to substitute low- for high-priced resources. More of a particular resource will be demanded at a low price than at a high price. The result? A downsloping demand curve for the various resources.

In short, just as the supply decisions of businesses and the demand decisions of consumers determine prices in the product market, so the supply decisions of households and demand decisions of businesses set prices in the resource market.

### △ "Other Things Equal" Revisited

Recall from Chapter 1 that as a substitute for their inability to conduct controlled experiments, economists invoke the "other things being equal" assumption in their analyses. We have seen in the present chapter that a number of forces bear upon both supply and demand. Hence, in locating specific supply and demand curves, such as $D_1$ and $S$ in Figure 4-6a, economists are isolating the impact of what they judge to be the most important determinant of the amounts supplied and demanded—that is, product price. In thus representing the laws of demand and supply by downsloping and upsloping curves respectively, the economist assumes that all the nonprice determinants of demand (incomes, tastes, and so forth) and supply (resource prices, technology, and other factors) are constant or unchanging. That is, price and quantity demanded are inversely related, *other things being equal*. And price and quantity supplied are directly related, *other things being equal*.

By failing to remember that the "other things equal" assumption is requisite to the laws of demand and supply, one can encounter confusing situations which *seem* to be in conflict with these laws. For example: Suppose General Motors sells 200,000 Chevettes in 1980 at an average price of $4,000; 300,000 at an average price of $4,500 in 1981; and 400,000 in

1982 at an average price of $5,000. Price and the number purchased vary *directly,* and these real-world data seem to be at odds with the law of demand. But is there really a conflict here? The answer, of course, is "No." These data do *not* refute the law of demand. The catch is that the law of demand's "other things equal" assumption has been violated with the passage of time. Specifically, because of, for example, growing incomes, population growth, and rising gasoline prices which increase the attractiveness of compact cars, the demand curve for Chevettes has simply increased over the years—shifted to the right as from $D_1$ to $D_2$ in Figure 4-6a—causing price to rise and, simultaneously, a larger quantity to be purchased.

Conversely, consider Figure 4-6d. Comparing the original $S_1D$ and the new $S_2D$ equilibrium positions, we note that *less* of the product is being sold or supplied at a higher price; that is, price and quantity supplied seem to be *inversely* related, rather than *directly* related as the law of supply indicates. The catch again is that the "other things equal" assumption underlying the upsloping supply curve has been violated. Perhaps production costs have gone up or a special tax has been levied on this product, shifting the supply curve from $S_1$ to $S_2$. These examples emphasize the importance of our earlier distinction between a "change in the quantity demanded (or supplied)" and a "change in demand (supply)."

## ☐ A POWERFUL TOOL

It should be stressed that the competitive market, or "supply and demand," model is an extremely powerful and versatile tool for economic understanding. Anticipating a number of topics which will be considered in more detail in later chapters, let us briefly note (1) the wide applicability of the model, (2) some implications of governmental interference with the competitive market, and (3) some novel applications of the model to current problems.

### △ Applicability

We have seen in the present chapter that the supply and demand model applies to both product and resource markets. But our treatment of resource markets has been most general. Later we will discover how the model can be applied in modified forms to explain wage rates, rents, and interest rates (see Figures 31-3, 32-1, and 16-1a and the accompanying discussions). The model is also very helpful in explaining exchange rates among foreign currencies (Figure 43-3) and in predicting the effects of sales taxes (Figures 23-7 and 23-8). It would not be difficult to cite additional examples.

### △ Interference: Legal Prices

A thorough understanding of the market model is helpful in forecasting the effects of legal prices, that is, of governmentally established prices which are higher (price supports) or lower (price ceilings or controls) than equilibrium prices. Consider, first, *price supports*. In the product market, price supports for certain agricultural products result in surpluses. Price supports—designed to subsidize farm incomes—rob the price mechanism of its rationing ability, making it necessary for government to buy and store surplus output (Figure 35-5 and accompanying discussion). In the labor market, the minimum wage creates surpluses of labor; that is, the minimum wage tends to cause unemployment (Figure 31-7 and discussion). Conversely, *price ceilings* upset the rationing function of prices in the opposite direction by causing product and resource shortages (see Chapter 18's discussion of wage-price controls). In this case, government must introduce some sort of bureaucratic mechanism to ration products and resources which are in short supply at the controlled (below-equilibrium) prices.

The tone of the above comments suggests that legal prices are undesirable. Actually, their desirability is a matter of debate. Proponents of price supports in agriculture, the minimum wage, and wage-price controls make forceful equity or income distribution arguments to justify the use of such legal prices. Perhaps the most telling criticism is that interference with the competitive market model to achieve equity objectives may be in conflict with the efficiency of the free market in bringing buyers and sellers together, that is, in assuring that the market is cleared. Let us look at a further example to underscore this point. Some economists have pointed out that the equity-efficiency trade-off is dramatically evident in the case of rent controls as practiced in New York City since World War II. Controls were originally imposed to deal with the equity aspects of the wartime housing shortage, that is, to prevent landlords from "gouging" tenants. But as the general price level has increased since the war and rent controls have persisted, landlords have found it increasingly unprofitable to maintain their buildings and private construction has declined sharply. This has contributed to blighted and decaying neighborhoods and, ironically, to an intensification of the housing shortage. In brief, free-market proponents contend that rent controls have been counterproductive; rent controls have intensified the housing shortage and, curiously, the persistence of the shortage has tended to "justify" and perpetuate the application of rent controls![7] Chapter 23's Last Word is recommended reading at this point.

### △  Novel Uses

Some economists advocate new applications of the market model to solve problems which we are currently trying—with varying degrees of success—to resolve through the public bureaucracy. Consider two illustrations. First, it is argued that the imposition of legal prohibitions or special taxes upon pollutors gives rise to endless legal wrangling and costly bureaucracies for enforcement. It would allegedly be more efficient (less costly) and more effective to establish a market for "pollu-

tion rights." The supply of these rights should be equal to the amount of pollutants that, say, a lake can recycle or absorb naturally. Demand will then determine the price of these rights. Potential pollutors will now be confronted with a direct monetary incentive *not* to pollute. Desirable side effects may also occur: The market price for pollution rights may stimulate incentives to develop more efficient (cheaper) means for waste disposal; the revenue from the sale of the rights may be used to finance environmental improvements; conservationists may buy up and not use some of the rights, thereby contributing to an even cleaner environment; and so forth. (For details consult Figure 36-2 and the accompanying discussion.)

Second example: Some economists hold that the use of "peak pricing" might effectively deal with temporary problems of congestion. (Congestion, by the way, is one form of pollution.) To illustrate, on certain days and at certain hours, airports become congested with the landings and takeoffs of unusually large numbers of aircraft. This congestion problem during peak traffic hours can be dealt with in several ways. One solution is to expand airport facilities (increase supply). But critics say this is an overly costly and therefore inefficient solution because the new facilities, not to mention a portion of existing facilities, will be underutilized during off-peak hours. Another option is queuing, that is, forcing planes to be stacked in a circling pattern until landing space becomes available. This imposes costs upon passengers in the form of delays in reaching their destinations and increased risk of accidents. The final solution—of particular interest to us—is to use peak pricing, that is, to increase landing fees during the peak hours and thereby create a monetary incentive for some airlines to shift their flights away from peak hours. In the short run, this shift will obviously decrease the demand for airport facilities during peak periods—the peaks will tend to be evened out—*and* airports will realize additional revenue to expand facilities as justified by the long-term growth of air travel.

[7]Milton Friedman, *An Economist's Protest* (New Jersey: Thomas Horton and Company, 1972), pp. 157–158.

## Summary

**1**  Demand refers to a schedule which summarizes the willingness of buyers to purchase a given product during a specific time period at each of the various prices at which it might be sold. According to the law of demand, consumers will ordinarily buy more of a product at a low price than they will at a high price. Therefore, the relationship between price and quantity demanded is inverse and demand graphs as a downsloping curve.

**2**  Changes in one or more of the basic determinants of demand—consumer tastes, the number of buyers in the market, the money incomes of consumers, the prices of related goods, and consumer expectations—will cause the market demand curve to shift. A shift to the right is an increase in demand; a shift to the left, a decrease in demand. A change in demand is to be distinguished from a change in the quantity demanded, the latter involving the movement from one point to another point on a fixed demand curve because of a change in the price of the product under consideration.

**3**  Supply is a schedule showing the amounts of a product which producers would be willing to offer in the market during a given time period at each possible price at which the commodity might be sold. The law of supply says that producers will offer more of a product at a higher price than they will at a low price. As a result, the relationship between price and quantity supplied is a direct one, and the supply curve is upsloping.

**4**  A change in production techniques, resource prices, taxes, the prices of other goods, price expectations, or the number of sellers in the market will cause the supply curve of a product to shift. A shift to the right is an increase in supply; a shift to the left, a decrease in supply. In contrast, a change in the price of a given product will result in a change in the quantity supplied, that is, a movement from one point to another on a given supply curve.

**5**  Under competition, the interaction of market demand and market supply will adjust price to that point at which the quantity demanded and the quantity supplied are equal. This is the equilibrium price. The corresponding quantity is the equilibrium quantity.

**6**  The ability of market forces to synchronize selling and buying decisions so as to eliminate potential surpluses or shortages is sometimes termed the "rationing function" of prices.

**7**  A change in either demand or supply will cause equilibrium price and quantity to change. There is a direct relationship between a change in demand and the resulting changes in equilibrium price and quantity. Though the relationship between a change in supply and the resulting change in equilibrium price is inverse, the relationship between a change in supply and equilibrium quantity is direct.

**8**  The concepts of supply and demand are also applicable to the resource market.

## Questions and Study Suggestions

**1**  Key terms and concepts to remember: demand schedule (curve); law of demand; diminishing marginal utility; income and substitution effects; normal (superior) good; inferior good; complementary goods; substitute (competing) goods; supply schedule (curve); law of supply; change in demand (supply) versus change in the quantity demanded (supplied); equilibrium price and quantity; rationing function of prices.

**2**  Explain the law of demand. Why does a demand curve slope downward? What are the determinants of demand? What happens to the demand curve when each of these determinants changes? Distinguish between a change in demand and a change in the quantity demanded, noting the cause(s) of each.

**3**  Critically evaluate: "In comparing the two equilibrium positions in Figure 4-6a, I note that a larger amount is actually purchased at a higher price. This obviously refutes the law of demand."

**4**   Explain the law of supply. Why does the supply curve slope upward? What are the determinants of supply? What happens to the supply curve when each of these determinants changes? Distinguish between a change in supply and a change in the quantity supplied, noting the cause(s) of each.

**5**   Explain the following news dispatch from Hull, England: "The fish market here slumped today to what local commentators called 'a disastrous level'—all because of a shortage of potatoes. The potatoes are one of the main ingredients in a dish that figures on almost every café menu—fish and chips."

**6**   Suppose the total demand for wheat and the total supply of wheat per month in the Kansas City grain market are as follows:

| Thousands of bushels demanded | Price per bushel | Thousands of bushels supplied | Surplus (+) or shortage (−) |
|---|---|---|---|
| 85 | $4.60 | 72 | −13 |
| 80 | 4.80 | 73 | −7 |
| 75 | 5.00 | 75 | equilibrium |
| 70 | 5.20 | 77 | +7 |
| 65 | 5.40 | 79 | +14 |
| 60 | 5.60 | 81 | +21 |

*a.*   What will be the market or equilibrium price? What is the equilibrium quantity? Using the surplus-shortage column, explain why your answers are correct.

*b.*   Using the above data, graph the demand for wheat and the supply of wheat. Be sure to label the axes of your graph correctly. Label equilibrium price "*P*" and equilibrium quantity "*Q*."

*c.*   Why will $4.60 not be the equilibrium price in this market? Why not $5.60? "Surpluses drive prices up; shortages drive them down." Do you agree?

*d.*   Now suppose that the government establishes a ceiling price of, say, $4.80 for wheat. Explain carefully the effects of this ceiling price. Demonstrate your answer graphically. What might prompt government to establish a ceiling price?

*e.*   Assume now that the government establishes a supported price of, say, $5.40 for wheat. Explain carefully the effects of this supported price. Demonstrate your answer graphically. What might prompt the government to establish this price support?

*f.*   "Legally fixed prices strip the price mechanism of its rationing function." Explain this statement in terms of your answers to 6d and 6e.

**7**   What effect will each of the following have upon the demand for product B?
*a.*   Product B becomes more fashionable.
*b.*   The price of product C, a good substitute for B, goes down.
*c.*   Consumers anticipate declining prices and falling incomes.
*d.*   There is a rapid upsurge in population growth.

**8**   What effect will each of the following have upon the supply of product B?
*a.*   A technological advance in the methods of producing B.
*b.*   A decline in the number of firms in industry B.
*c.*   An increase in the prices of resources required in the production of B.
*d.*   The expectation that the equilibrium price of B will be lower in the future than it is currently.
*e.*   A decline in the price of product A, a good whose production requires substantially the same techniques and resources as does the production of B.

   *f.*   The levying of a special sales tax upon B.

  **9**   Explain and illustrate graphically the effect of:

   *a.*   An increase in income upon the demand curve of an inferior good.

   *b.*   A drop in the price of product S upon the demand for substitute product T.

   *c.*   A decline in income upon the demand curve of a normal good.

   *d.*   An increase in the price of product J upon the demand for complementary good K.

  **10**   "In the corn market, demand often exceeds supply and supply sometimes exceeds demand." "The price of corn rises and falls in response to changes in supply and demand." In which of these two statements are the terms "supply" and "demand" used correctly? Explain.

  **11**   How will each of the following changes in demand and/or supply affect equilibrium price and equilibrium quantity in a competitive market; that is, do price and quantity *rise, fall,* or *remain unchanged,* or are the answers *indeterminate,* depending upon the magnitudes of the shifts in supply and demand? You should rely on a supply and demand diagram to verify answers.

   *a.*   Supply decreases and demand remains constant.

   *b.*   Demand decreases and supply remains constant.

   *c.*   Supply increases and demand is constant.

   *d.*   Demand increases and supply increases.

   *e.*   Demand increases and supply is constant.

   *f.*   Supply increases and demand decreases.

   *g.*   Demand increases and supply decreases.

   *h.*   Demand decreases and supply decreases.

  **12**   "Prices are the automatic regulator that tends to keep production and consumption in line with each other." Explain.

  **13**   Explain: "Even though parking meters yield little or no net revenue, they should nevertheless be retained because of the rationing function they perform."

  **14**   Many states have usury laws which stipulate the maximum interest rate which lenders (commercial banks, savings and loan associations, and so forth) can charge borrowers. Indicate in some detail what would happen in the loan market during those periods when the equilibrium interest rate exceeds the stipulated maximum. On the basis of your analysis, do you favor usury laws?

  **15**   *Advanced analysis:* Assume that the demand for a commodity is represented by the equation $Q_d = 12 - 2P$ and supply by the equation $Q_s = 2P$, where $Q_d$ and $Q_s$ are quantity demanded and quantity supplied respectively and $P$ is price. Using the equilibrium condition $Q_s = Q_d$, solve the equations to determine equilibrium price. Now determine equilibrium quantity. Graph the two equations to substantiate your answers.

## Selected References

Boulding, Kenneth E.: *Economic Analysis: Microeconomics,* 4th ed. (New York: Harper & Row, Publishers, Incorporated, 1966), chaps. 8, 10, 11.

Brue, Stanley L., and Donald R. Wentworth: *Economic Scenes: Theory in Today's World,* 2d ed. (Englewood Cliffs, N.J.: Prentice-Hall, Inc., 1980), chap. 4.

Henderson, Hubert: *Supply and Demand* (Chicago: The University of Chicago Press, 1958), chap. 2.

# LAST WORD
# The Demand for Basketball Games

Given an average ticket price of $4.50, what non-price factors are most important in determining the number of tickets that will be demanded for professional basketball games?

It is important to be able to assess quantitatively the effect on team attendance of factors such as the quality of the team, the size of the team's home city, ticket prices, competition from alternative forms of entertainment, and the number of games played. From knowledge of the importance of these factors, one can predict the likely success of a team, and whether teams in certain areas are likely to be much more financially successful than teams in other areas . . .

(1) Population is a significant factor in team success. Each additional 1 million population in a team's home area is worth 58,000 additional spectators. At the average ticket price of $4.50, this translates into at least $250,000 in revenues, not including income from concessions.

(2) The playing success of the team is also important. Winning 60 percent of the games played is worth nearly 100,000 fans more than winning 40 percent.

(3) Competition from other sports is also a factor in attendance. For every professional sports team in the city, regardless of the sport, basketball attendance declines by 66,000.

(4) If every team in both leagues played one more home game during a season, the average increase in team attendance for the season would be 4,000; the actual attendance at the extra game might be higher, of course, but some of this attendance would be a switch from other games.

(5) All other things being equal (including the playing record of the teams), a team that has played in a city 10 years will draw 7,000 fewer fans during the season than a team playing its first year in a new city.

(6) We define a superstar as any player who has made a league all-star team five times or, in the case of players with only a few years of professional experience, one who is obviously a dominant player in the game—e.g., a Kareem Abdul-Jabbar or an Issel. Using this definition, having a superstar on the team is worth 25,000 attendance during the season. This figure, of course, is an average for all teams and for all 17 players in the two leagues classified as superstars by our criteria. Still using the $4.50 average ticket price, this means that about 17 professional basketball players produce about $100,000 a year in gross revenues for their teams beyond whatever contribution these talented athletes make to the won-lost record of the team.

Including the contribution a superstar makes to his team's winning percentage, the results suggest that basketball superstars are worth salaries exceeding $100,000 a year, as measured by the contribution they make to team revenues. Furthermore, a player such as Kareem Abdul-Jabbar is probably worth much more. If he is the difference between winning and losing in 20 percent of his team's games and if he is twice the fan attraction of the average of our 17 superstars, then, by himself, he accounts for nearly $500,000 a year in gate receipts. . .

Statement of Dr. Roger G. Noll in *Professional Basketball*, Hearings before the Subcommittee on Antitrust and Monopoly of the Committee on the Judiciary, U.S. Senate, 92d Congress, 1st Session, Washington, 1971, pp. 343–345, abridged.

# The Price System and the Five Fundamental Questions

# chapter 5

We saw in Chapter 3 that the capitalist ideology makes clear the importance of freedom of enterprise and choice. Consumers are at liberty to buy what they choose; businesses, to produce and sell what they choose; and resource suppliers, to make their property and human resources available in whatever occupations they choose. Upon reflection, we might wonder why such an economy does not collapse in complete chaos. If consumers want bread, businesses choose to produce automobiles, and resource suppliers want to offer their services in manufacturing shoes, production would seem to be deadlocked because of the obvious inconsistency of these free choices.

Fortunately, two other features of capitalism—a system of markets and prices and the force of competition—provide the coordinating and organizing mechanisms which overcome the potential chaos posed by freedom of enterprise and choice. *The competitive price system is a mechanism both for communicating the decisions of consumers, producers, and resource suppliers to one another and for synchronizing those decisions toward consistent production objectives.*

Armed with an understanding of individual markets and prices gained from Chapter 4, we are now in a position to analyze the operation of the price system. More specifically, in this chapter we first want to understand how the price system operates as a mechanism for communicating and coordinating individual free choices. Deferring the full-employment question until Part 2, we want to see how the price system answers the other four Fundamental Questions. How does the price system (1) determine what is to be produced, (2) organize production, (3) distribute total output, and (4) accommodate change? Then, secondly, we want to evaluate the operation of the market economy.

# ☐ OPERATION OF THE PRICE SYSTEM

The setting for our discussion is provided by Chapter 3's circular flow diagram (Figure 3-2). In examining how the price system answers the Fundamental Questions we must add demand and supply diagrams as developed in Chapter 4 to represent the various product and resource markets embodied in the circular flow model.

## △ Determining What Is to Be Produced

Given the product and resource prices established by competing buyers and sellers in both the product and resource markets, how would a purely capitalistic economy decide the types and quantities of goods to be produced? Remembering that businesses are motivated to seek profits and avoid losses, we can generalize that those goods and services which can be produced at a profit will be produced and those whose production entails a loss will not. And what determines profits or the lack of them? Two things:

**1** The total receipts which a firm gets from selling a product.

**2** The total costs of producing it.

Both total receipts and total costs are price-times-quantity figures. Total receipts are found by multiplying product price by the quantity of the product sold. Total costs are found by multiplying the price of each resource used by the amount employed and summing the costs of each.

**Economic Profits**   To say that those products which can be produced profitably will be produced and those which cannot will not is only an accurate generalization if the meaning of economic costs is clearly understood. In order to grasp the full meaning of costs, let us once again think of businesses as simply organizational charts, that is, businesses "on paper," distinct and apart from the capital, raw materials, labor, and entrepreneurial ability which make them going concerns. In order to become actual producing concerns, these "on paper" businesses must secure all four types of

resources. The payments which must be made to secure and retain the needed amounts of these resources are *economic costs.* The per unit size of these costs—that is, resource prices—will be determined by supply and demand conditions in the resource market. The point to note is that—like land, labor, and capital—entrepreneurial ability is a scarce resource and consequently has a price tag on it. Costs therefore must include not only wage and salary payments to labor and interest and rental payments for capital and land, but also payments to the entrepreneur for the functions he or she performs in organizing and combining the other resources in the production of some commodity. The cost payment for these contributions by the entrepreneur is called a *normal profit.* Hence, a product will be produced only when total receipts are large enough to pay wage, interest, rental, and normal profit costs. Now if total receipts from the sale of a product more than cover all production costs, including a normal profit, the remainder will accrue to the entrepreneur as the risk taker and organizing force in the going concern. This return above costs is called a *pure,* or *economic, profit.* It is *not* an economic cost, because it need not be realized in order for the business to acquire and retain entrepreneurial ability.

**Profits and Expanding Industries**   A few hypothetical examples will explain more concretely how the price system determines what is to be produced. Suppose that the most favorable relationship between total revenue and total cost in producing product X occurs when the firm's output is 15 units. Assume, too, that the best combination of resources to use in producing 15 units of X entails 2 units of labor, 3 units of land, 1 of capital, and 1 of entrepreneurial ability, selling at prices of $2, $1, $3, and $3, respectively. Finally, suppose that the 15 units of X which these resources produce can be sold for $1 per unit. Will firms enter into the production of product X? Yes, they will. A firm producing product X under these conditions will be able to pay wage, rent, interest, and normal profit costs of $13 [= (2 × $2) + (3 × $1) + (1 × $3) + (1 × $3)]. The difference between total revenue of $15 and total costs of $13 will be an economic profit of $2.

This economic profit is evidence that industry X is a prosperous one. Such an industry will tend to expand as new firms, attracted by these above-normal profits, are created or shift from less profitable industries. But the entry of new firms will be a self-limiting process. As new firms enter industry X, the market supply of X will increase relative to the market demand. This will lower the market price of X to the end that economic profits will in time disappear. The market supply and demand situation prevailing when economic profits become zero will determine the total amount of X produced.

**Losses and Declining Industries**   But what if the initial market situation for product X were less favorable? Suppose conditions in the product market initially were such that the firm could sell the 15 units of X at a price of just 75 cents per unit. Total revenue would be $11.25 (= 15 × 75 cents). After paying wage, rental, and interest costs of $10, the firm would yield a below-normal profit of $1.25. In other words, *losses* of $1.75 (= $11.25 − $13) would be incurred. Certainly, firms would not be attracted to this unprosperous industry. On the contrary, if these losses persisted, entrepreneurs would seek the normal or economic profits offered by more prosperous industries. This means that, in time, existing firms in industry X would go out of business entirely or migrate to other industries where normal or better profits prevail. However, as this happens, the market supply of X will fall relative to the market demand, thereby raising product price to the end that losses will eventually disappear. Industry X will then stabilize itself in size. The market supply and demand situation that prevails at that point where economic profits are zero will determine the total output of product X.

**"Dollar Votes"**   The important role of consumer demand in determining the types and quantities of goods produced must be emphasized. Consumers, unrestrained by government and possessing money incomes from the sale of resources, spend their dollars upon those goods which they are most willing and able to buy. These expenditures are in effect *dollar votes* by which consumers register their wants through the demand side of the product market. If these votes are great enough to provide a normal profit, businesses will produce that product. An increase in consumer demand, that is, an increase in the dollar votes cast for a product, will mean economic profits for the industry producing it. These profits will signal the expansion of that industry and increases in the output of the product. A decrease in consumer demand, that is, fewer votes cast for the product, will result in losses and, in time, contraction of the adversely affected industry. As firms leave the industry, the output of the product declines. In short, the dollar votes of consumers play a key role in determining what products profit-seeking businesses will produce. As noted in Chapter 3, the capitalistic system is sometimes said to be characterized by *consumer sovereignty* because of the strategic role of consumers in determining the types and quantities of goods produced.

**Market Restraints on Freedom**   From the viewpoint of businesses, we now see that firms are not really "free" to produce what they wish. The demand decisions of consumers, by making the production of some products profitable and others not, restrict the choice of businesses in deciding what to produce. Businesses must synchronize their production choices with consumer choices or face the penalty of losses and eventual bankruptcy.

Much the same holds true with respect to resource suppliers. The demand for resources is a *derived demand*—derived, that is, from the demand for the goods and services which the resources help produce. There is a demand for auto workers only because there is a demand for automobiles. More generally, in seeking to maximize the returns from the sale of their human and property resources, resource suppliers are prompted by the price system to make their choices in accord with consumer demands. If only those firms which produce goods wanted by consumers can operate profitably, only those firms will demand resources. Resource suppliers will not be "free" to allocate their resources to the production of goods which consumers do not value highly. The reason? There will be no firms producing such products, because consumer demand is not sufficient to make it profitable. In short, consumers register their preferences on the demand side of the product market, and producers and resource suppliers respond appropriately in seeking to further their own self-interests. The price system communicates the wants of consumers to business and resource suppliers and elicits appropriate responses.

△   **Organizing Production**

How is production to be organized in a market economy? This Fundamental Question is composed of three subquestions:

**1**   How should resources be allocated among specific industries?

**2**   What specific firms should do the producing in each industry?

**3**   What combinations of resources— what technology—should each firm employ?

**Production and Profits**   The preceding section has answered the first subquestion. The price system steers resources to those industries whose products consumers want badly enough to make their production profitable. It simultaneously deprives unprofitable industries of scarce resources. If all firms had sufficient time to enter prosperous industries and to leave unprosperous industries, the output of each industry would be large enough for the firms to just make normal profits. If total industry output at this point happens to be 1500 units and the most profitable output for each firm is 15 units, as in our previous example, the industry will obviously be made up of 100 competing firms.

The second and third subquestions are closely intertwined. In a competitive market economy, the firms which do the producing are those which are willing and able to employ the economically most efficient technique of production. And what determines the most efficient technique? Economic efficiency depends upon:

**1**   Available technology, that is, the alternative combinations of resources or inputs which will produce the desired output.

**2**   The prices at which the needed resources can be obtained.

**Least-Cost Production**   The combination of resources which is most efficient economically depends not only upon the physical or engineering data provided by available technology but also upon the relative worth of the required resources as measured by their market prices. Thus, a technique which requires just a few physical inputs of resources to produce a given output may be highly *inefficient* economically if the required resources are valued very highly in the market. In other words, *economic efficiency entails getting a given output of product with the smallest input of scarce resources, when both output and resource inputs are measured in dollars-and-cents terms.* In short, that combination of resources which will produce, say, $15 worth of product X at the lowest possible money cost is the most efficient.

Table 5-1 will help illustrate these points. Suppose there are three different techniques by which the desired $15 worth of product X can be produced. The quantity of each resource required by each technique and the prices of the required resources are shown in Table 5-1. By multiplying the quantities of the various resources required by the resource prices in each of the three techniques, the total cost of producing $15 worth of X by each technique can be determined. It can be concluded that technique No. 2 is economically the most efficient of the three, for the simple reason that it is the least costly way of producing $15 worth of X. Technique No. 2 permits society to

**TABLE 5-1**
Techniques for Producing $15 Worth of Product X (*hypothetical data*)

| Resource | Technique No. 1 | Technique No. 2 | Technique No. 3 | Price per unit of resource |
|---|---|---|---|---|
| Labor | 4 | 2 | 1 | $2 |
| Land | 1 | 3 | 4 | 1 |
| Capital | 1 | 1 | 2 | 3 |
| Entrepreneurial ability | 1 | 1 | 1 | 3 |
| Total cost of $15 worth of X | $15 | $13 | $15 | |

obtain $15 worth of output by using up a smaller amount of resources—$13 worth—than would be used up by the two alternative techniques. Technique No. 2 is the most efficient, because it gives society $15 worth of output for an input of $13 worth of resources; the alternative techniques entail an input of $15 worth of resources for the same amount of output.

But what guarantee is there that technique No. 2 will actually be used? The answer obviously is that firms will want to use the most efficient technique because it yields the greatest profit.

We must emphasize that a change in *either* technology *or* resource prices may cause the firm to shift from the technology now employed. For example, if the price of labor falls to 50 cents, technique No. 1 will be superior to technique No. 2. That is, businesses will find that they can lower their costs by shifting to a technology which involves the use of more of that resource whose price has fallen. The reader also should verify that a new technique involving 1 unit of labor, 4 of land, 1 of capital, and 1 of entrepreneurial ability will be preferable to all three techniques listed in Table 5-1, assuming the resource prices given there.[1]

[1]There is a geographic or locational aspect to the question of organizing production which we ignore at this point. The question "*Where* to produce?" will be considered in detail in Chapter 36.

△   **Distributing Total Output**

The price system enters the picture in two ways in solving the problem of distributing total output. Generally speaking, any given product will be distributed to consumers on the basis of their ability and willingness to pay the existing market price for it. If the price of X is $1 per unit, those buyers who are able and willing to pay that price will get a unit of this product; those who are not, will not. This, we recall, is the rationing function of equilibrium prices.

What determines a consumer's ability to pay the equilibrium price for X and other available products? The size of one's money income. And money income in turn depends upon the quantities of the various property and human resources which the income receiver supplies and the prices which they command in the resource market. Thus, resource prices play a key role in determining the size of each household's claim against the total output of society. Within the limits of a consumer's money income, his or her willingness to pay the equilibrium price for X determines whether or not some of this product is distributed to that person. And this willingness to buy X will depend upon one's preference for X in comparison with available close substitutes for X and their relative prices. Thus, product prices play a key role in determining the expenditure patterns of consumers.

We should emphasize that there is nothing particularly ethical about the price system as a mechanism for distributing output. Those households which manage to accumulate large amounts of property resources by inheritance, through hard work and frugality, through business acumen, or by crook will receive large incomes and thus command large shares of the economy's total output. Others, offering unskilled and relatively unproductive labor resources which elicit low wages, will receive meager money incomes and small portions of total output.

## △ Accommodating Change

Industrial societies are dynamic: Consumer preferences, technology, and resource supplies all change. This correctly implies that the particular allocation of resources which is *now* the most efficient for a *given* pattern of consumer tastes, for a *given* range of technological alternatives, and for *given* supplies of resources can be expected to become obsolete and inefficient as consumer preferences change, new techniques of production are discovered, and resource supplies alter over time. Can the market economy negotiate adjustments in resource uses appropriate to such inevitable changes and thereby remain efficient?

**Guiding Function of Prices**  Let us suppose a change occurs in consumer tastes. Specifically, let us say that consumers decide they want more hand calculators and fewer slide rules than the economy is currently providing. Will the price system communicate this change to businesses and resource suppliers and prompt appropriate adjustments?

The assumed change in consumers' tastes will be communicated to producers through an increase in the demand for calculators and a decline in the demand for slide rules. This means that calculator prices will rise and slide rule prices will fall. Now, assuming firms in both industries are enjoying precisely normal profits prior to these changes in consumer demand, higher calculator prices will mean economic profits for the calculator industry,

and lower slide rule prices will entail losses for the slide rule industry. Self-interest induces new competitors to enter the prosperous calculator industry. Losses will in time force firms to leave the depressed slide rule industry.

But these adjustments, we recall, are both self-limiting. The expansion of the calculator industry will continue only to the point at which the resulting increase in the market supply of calculators brings calculator prices back down to a level at which normal profits again prevail. Similarly, contraction in the slide rule industry will persist until the accompanying decline in the market supply of slide rules brings slide rule prices up to a level at which the remaining firms can receive a normal profit. The crucial point to note is that these adjustments in the business sector are completely appropriate to the assumed changes in consumer tastes. Society—meaning consumers—wants more hand calculators and fewer slide rules, and that is precisely what it is getting as the calculator industry expands and the slide rule industry contracts. These adjustments, incidentally, portray the concept of consumer sovereignty at work.

This analysis proceeds on the assumption that resource suppliers are agreeable to these adjustments. Will the price system prompt resource suppliers to reallocate their human and property resources from the slide rule to the calculator industry, thereby permitting the output of calculators to expand at the expense of slide rule production? The answer is "Yes."

The economic profits which initially follow the increase in demand for calculators will not only provide that industry with the inducement to expand but will also give it the added receipts with which to obtain the resources essential to its growth. Higher calculator prices will permit firms in that industry to pay higher prices for resources, thereby drawing resources from what are now less urgent alternative employments. Willingness and ability to employ more resources in the calculator industry will be communicated back into the resource market through an increase in the demand for resources. Substantially the reverse occurs in the adversely affected slide rule industry. The losses which the decline in consumer demand initially entails will cause a decline in the demand for resources in that industry. Workers and other resources released from the contracting slide rule industry can now find employment in the expanding calculator industry. Furthermore, the increased demand for resources in the calculator industry will mean higher resource prices in that industry than those being paid in the slide rule industry, where declines in resource demand have lowered resource prices. The resulting differential in resource prices will provide the incentive for resource owners to further their self-interests by reallocating their resources from the slide rule to the calculator industry. And this, of course, is the precise shift needed to permit the calculator industry to expand and the slide rule industry to contract.

The ability of the price system to communicate changes in such basic data as consumer tastes and to elicit appropriate responses from both businesses and resource suppliers is sometimes called the *directing* or *guiding function* of prices. By affecting product prices and profits, changes in consumer tastes direct the expansion of some industries and the contraction of others. These adjustments carry through to the resource market as expanding industries demand more resources and contracting industries demand fewer. The resulting changes in resource prices guide resources from the contracting to the expanding industries. In the absence of a price system, some administrative agency, presumably a governmental planning board, would have to undertake the task of directing business institutions and resources into specific lines of production.

Analysis similar to that just outlined would indicate that the price system would adjust appropriately to similar fundamental changes—for example, to changes in technology and changes in the relative supplies of various resources.

**Initiating Progress**   Adjusting to given changes is one thing; initiating changes, particularly desirable changes, is something else again. Is the competitive price system congenial to technological improvements and capital accumulation, the interrelated changes which lead to greater productivity and a higher level of material well-being for society? This is not an easy question to answer. We state our reply at this point without stopping for qualifications and modifications (see Chapter 29).

*Technological advance*   The competitive price system would seem to contain the incentive for technological advance. The introduction of cost-cutting techniques provides the innovating firm with a temporary advantage over its rivals. Lower production costs mean economic profits for the pioneering firm. By passing a part of its cost reduction on to the consumer through a lower product price, the innovating firm can achieve a sizable increase in sales and lucrative economic profits at the expense of rival firms. Furthermore, the competitive price system would seem to provide an environment conducive to the rapid diffusion of a technological advance. Rivals *must* follow the lead of the most progressive firm or suffer the immediate penalty of losses and the eventual pain of bankruptcy.

We should note that the lower product price which the technological advance permits will cause the innovating industry to expand. This expansion may be the result of existing firms' expanding their rates of output or of new firms entering the industry under the lure of the economic profits initially created by a technological advance. This expansion, that is, the diversion of resources from less progressive to more progressive industries, is as it should be. Sustained efficiency in the use of scarce resources demands that resources be continually reallocated from industries whose productive techniques are relatively less efficient to those whose techniques are relatively more efficient.

*Capital accumulation*   But technological advance typically entails the use of increased amounts of capital goods. Can the price system provide the capital goods upon which technological advance relies? More specifically, can the entrepreneur as an innovator command through the price system the resources necessary to produce the machinery and equipment upon which technological advance depends?

Obviously, the entrepreneur can. If society registers dollar votes for capital goods, the product market and the resource market will adjust to these votes by producing capital goods. In other words, the price system acknowledges dollar voting for both consumer and capital goods. But who, specifically, will register votes for capital goods? First, the entrepreneur as a receiver of profit income can be expected to apportion a part of his or her income to the accumulation of capital goods. By so doing, an even greater profit income can be achieved in the future if the innovation proves successful. Furthermore, by paying a rate of interest, entrepreneurs can borrow portions of the incomes of other households and use these borrowed funds in casting dollar votes for the production of more capital goods.

△  **Competition and Control:**
   **The "Invisible Hand"**
Though the price system is the organizing mechanism of pure capitalism, it is essential to recognize the role of competition as the mechanism of control in such an economy. The market mechanism of supply and demand communicates the wants of consumers (society) to businesses and through businesses to resource suppliers. It is competition, however, which forces businesses and resource suppliers to make appropriate responses. To illustrate: The impact of an increase in consumer demand for some product will raise that good's price above the wage, rent, interest, and normal profit costs of production. The resulting economic profits in effect are a signal to producers that society wants more of the product. It is competition—in particular, the ability of new firms to enter the industry—that simultane-

ously brings an expansion of output and a lowering of price back to a level just consistent with production costs. However, if the industry was not competitive, but was dominated by, say, one huge firm which was able to prohibit the entry of potential competitors, that firm could continue to enjoy economic profits by preventing the expansion of the industry.

But competition does more than guarantee responses appropriate to the wishes of society. It is competition which forces firms to adopt the most efficient productive techniques. In a competitive market, the failure of some firms to use the least costly production technique means their eventual elimination by other competing firms who do employ the most efficient methods of production. Finally, we have seen that competition provides an environment conducive to technological advance.

A very remarkable aspect of the operation and the adjustments of a competitive price system is that a curious and important identity is involved—the identity of private and social interests. That is, firms and resource suppliers, seeking to further their own self-interest and operating within the framework of a highly competitive market system, will simultaneously, as though guided by an "invisible hand,"[2] promote the public or social interest. For example, we have seen that given a competitive environment, business firms use the least costly combination of resources in producing a given output because it is in their self-interest to do so. To act otherwise would be to forgo profits or even to risk bankruptcy over a period of time. But, at the same time, it is obviously also in the social interest to use scarce resources in the least costly, that is, most efficient, manner. Not to do so would be to produce a given output at a greater cost or sacrifice of alternative goods than is really necessary. Furthermore, in our more-calculators–fewer-slide rules illustration, it is self-interest, awakened and guided by the competi-

[2] Adam Smith, *The Wealth of Nations* (New York: Modern Library, Inc., originally published in 1776), p. 423.

tive price system, which induces the very responses appropriate to the assumed change in society's wants. Businesses seeking to make higher profits and to avoid losses, on the one hand, and resource suppliers pursuing greater monetary rewards, on the other, negotiate the very changes in the allocation of resources and therefore the composition of output which society now demands. The force of competition, in other words, controls or guides the self-interest motive in such a way that it automatically, and quite unintentionally, furthers the best interests of society.

## ☐  AN EVALUATION OF THE PRICE SYSTEM

Is the price system the best means of responding to the Fundamental Questions? This is a complex question; any complete answer necessarily leaps the boundary of facts and enters the realm of values. This means there is no scientific answer to the query. The very fact that there exist many competing ways of allocating scarce resources—that is, many different kinds of economic systems (Table 2-3)—is ample evidence of disagreement as to the effectiveness of the price system.

### △  The Case for the Price System

The virtues of the price system are implicit in our discussion of its operation. Two merit emphasis.

**Allocative Efficiency**  The basic economic argument for the price system is that it leads to an efficient allocation of resources. The competitive price system, it is argued, guides resources into the production of those goods and services most wanted by society. It forces the use of the most efficient techniques in organizing resources for production, and it is conducive to the development and adoption of new and more efficient production techniques. In short, proponents of the price system argue that the "invisible hand" will in effect harness self-interest so as to provide society with the greatest output of wanted goods from its available resources. This, then, suggests the maximum economic efficiency. It is this presumption of allocative efficiency which makes most economists hesitant to advocate governmental interference with, or regulation of, free markets.

**Freedom**  The major noneconomic argument for the price system is its great emphasis upon personal freedom. One of the fundamental problems of social organization is how to coordinate the economic activities of large numbers of individuals and businesses. We recall from Chapter 2 that there are basically two ways of providing this coordination: one is central direction and the use of coercion; the other is voluntary cooperation through the price system. Only the price system can coordinate economic activity without coercion. The price system permits—indeed, it thrives upon—freedom of enterprise and choice. Entrepreneurs and workers are not herded from industry to industry to meet the production targets established by some omnipotent governmental agency. On the contrary, they are free to further their own self-interests, subject, of course, to the rewards and penalties imposed by the price system itself.

> So long as effective freedom of exchange is maintained, the central feature of the market organization of economic activity is that it prevents one person from interfering with another in respect of most of his activities. The consumer is protected from coercion by the seller because of the presence of other sellers with whom he can deal. The seller is protected from coercion by the consumer because of other consumers to whom he can sell. The employee is protected from coercion by the employer because of other employers for whom he can work, and so on. And the market does this impersonally and without centralized authority.[3]

[3] Milton Friedman, *Capitalism and Freedom* (Chicago: The University of Chicago Press, 1962), pp. 14–15.

To summarize: the competitive price system is allegedly conducive to both allocative efficiency and freedom.

△ **The Case against the Price System**

The case against the price system is somewhat more complex. Critics of the market economy base their position on the following points.

**Demise of Competition**   Critics argue that capitalistic ideology is permissive of, and even conducive to, the demise of its main controlling mechanism—competition. The alleged weakening of competition as a control mechanism comes from two basic sources.

**1**   Though desirable from the social point of view, competition is most irksome to the individual producer subject to its rigors. It is allegedly inherent in the free, individualistic environment of the capitalistic system that profit-seeking entrepreneurs will attempt to break free of the restraining force of competition in trying to better their position. Combination, conspiracy, and cutthroat competition are all means to the end of reducing competition and escaping its regulatory powers. As Adam Smith put the matter two centuries ago: "People of the same trade seldom meet together but the conversation ends in a conspiracy against the public, or in some diversion to raise prices."

**2**   Some economists believe that the very technological advance which the price system fosters has contributed to the decline of competition. Modern technology typically requires (*a*) the use of extremely large quantities of real capital; (*b*) large markets; (*c*) a complex, centralized, and closely integrated management; and (*d*) large and reliable sources of raw materials. Such an operation implies the need for producers who are large-scale not only in the absolute sense but also in relation to the size of the market. In other words, the achievement of maximum productive efficiency through the employment of the best available technology often requires the existence of a small number of large firms rather than a large number of small ones.

To the degree that competition declines, the price system will be weakened as a mechanism for efficiently allocating resources. Producers and resource suppliers will be less subject to the will of consumers; the sovereignty of producers and resource suppliers will then challenge and weaken the sovereignty of consumers. The "invisible hand" identity of private and social interests will begin to lose its grip. Furthermore, the protection from coercion which the market system provides is predicated upon the widespread dispersion of economic power. The concentration of economic power which accompanies the decline of competition permits the possessors of that power to engage in coercive acts.

**Wasteful and Inefficient Production**   Critics also challenge the assertion that the price system provides the goods most wanted by society. We have just encountered one facet of the critics' position: To the extent that a weakening of competition lessens consumer sovereignty, the price system becomes less proficient in allocating resources in precise accord with the wishes of consumers. But there are other reasons for questioning its efficiency.

*Unequal income distribution*   Critical socialists contend that the price system allows the more efficient, or more cunning, entrepreneurs to accumulate vast amounts of property resources, the accumulation process being extended through time by the right to bequeath. This, in addition to differences in the amount and quality of human resources supplied by various households, causes a highly unequal distribution of money incomes in a market economy. The result is that families differ greatly in their ability to express their wants in the market. The wealthy have more dollar votes than the poor. Hence, it is concluded that the price system allocates resources to the production of frivolous luxury goods for the rich at the expense of the output of necessities for the poor. A country that

. . . spends money on champagne before it has provided milk for its babies is a badly managed, silly, vain, stupid, ignorant nation. . . . The only way in which such a nation can make itself wealthy and prosperous is by good housekeeping: that is by providing for its wants in order of their importance, and allowing no money to be wasted on whims and luxuries until the necessities have been thoroughly served.[4]

The point is that the claim of "efficiency" in the allocation of resources has a hollow ring if the distribution of income and therefore of output does not meet some reasonable standards of fairness or equity. We shall pursue the debate over income inequality in Chapter 37.

**Market failure: externalities**   Critics cite two important cases of market failure. First, the price system may fail to register all the benefits and costs associated with the production and consumption of certain goods and services. That is, some benefits and costs are external to the market in that they accrue to parties other than the immediate buyer and seller. Such benefits and costs are called *spillover* or *external* benefits and costs. For example, consumer demand as registered in the market embodies only the satisfactions which accrue to individual consumers who purchase goods and services; it does not reflect the fact that the purchase of such services as polio shots and chest x-rays yields widespread benefits or satisfactions to the community (society) as a whole. Similarly, the supply decisions of producers are based upon the costs which the market obligates them to bear and do not reflect external costs, that is, costs borne by society at large as various forms of environmental pollution. The point is this: Where demand and supply do *not* accurately reflect all the benefits and all the costs of production, that is, where external benefits and costs exist, the price system cannot be expected to bring

about an allocation of resources which best satisfies the wants of society. In Chapter 6 we examine policies to correct such malallocations of resources.

**Market failure: social goods**   Second, the price system tabulates only individual wants. There are many wants involving goods and services which cannot be financed by individuals through the market. For example, such goods and services as education, highways, flood-control programs, and national defense cannot be purchased in desired amounts by households on an individual basis. They can only be consumed economically on a social, or collective, basis. The price system, it is argued, is incapable of registering such social, or collective, wants.

**Instability**   Finally, it is recognized that the price system is an imperfect mechanism for achieving full employment and price level stability. The problems of unemployment and inflation will be analyzed in detail in Part 2.

Which of these two positions—one for, and the other against, the price system—is correct? To a degree both are. The several criticisms of the market economy are reasonably accurate and certainly too serious to ignore. On the other hand, we cannot judge an issue by the number of arguments pro and con. The basic economic argument for the price system—that it tends to provide an efficient allocation of resources—is not easily undermined. In practice, the price system is—or at least can be—reasonably efficient.

△ **Relevance, Realism, and the Price System**

Does the price system of American capitalism function in the same fashion as the price system discussed in this chapter? In principle, yes; in detail, no. Our discussion of the price system provides us with a working model—a rough approximation—of the actual price system of our economy. Our analysis presents a much simplified, yet useful, picture of the real thing. The competitive price system also gives

[4]George Bernard Shaw, *The Intelligent Woman's Guide to Socialism and Capitalism* (New York: Brentano's, Inc., 1928), pp. 50–55. Used by permission of the Public Trustee and the Society of Authors.

us a norm, or standard, against which the real-world economy can be compared.

Specifically, there are two basic differences between the price system as pictured in this chapter and the actual price system of American capitalism.

**Bigness**   In many product and resource markets, competition clearly has been supplanted by a few giant business corporations and huge labor unions. Competition is simply not as vigorous in practice as our discussion of the price system assumed. This means that the decisions of businesses and resource suppliers are less than perfectly synchronized with those of consumers, and that changes in the production goals of society are less precisely communicated throughout the economy. Giant business and labor groups in American capitalism have the power to resist the dictates of consumer sovereignty and, as a matter of fact, will usually find it personally advantageous to do so.

**Government**   Another major difference between our model price system and the market system of American capitalism lies in the economic role of government in the latter. In contrast with the passive, limited government envisioned in the ideology of pure capitalism, the public sector is an active and integral com-

ponent of our economy. In particular, the economy of the United States has taken cognizance of the important elements of truth which permeate the noted criticisms of the price system. Through government, society has taken steps to correct these shortcomings. Therefore, government pursues policies designed not only to preserve and bolster competition, but also to adjust certain inequities fostered by the price system, to hasten the reallocation of resources, to meet collective wants, and to help maintain full employment. It is with these and related economic functions of government that the ensuing chapter is concerned.

Is our analysis of the price system realistic? Does it provide a workable description of the price system of American capitalism? One scholar has responded to these questions as follows:

> For all the new quality of twentieth-century industrial society, the great principles of self-interest and competition, however watered down or hedged about, still provide basic rules of behavior which no economic organization can afford to disregard entirely . . . the laws of the market can be discerned . . . if we look beneath the surface.[5]

[5] Robert L. Heilbroner, *The Worldly Philosophers,* 3d ed. (New York: Simon & Schuster, Inc., 1967), pp. 53–54.

## Summary

**1**   In a market economy, the interacting decisions of competing buyers and sellers will determine a system of product and resource prices at any given point in time.

**2**   Those products whose production and sale yield total receipts sufficient to cover all costs, including a normal profit, will be produced. Those whose production will not yield a normal profit will not be produced.

**3**   Economic profits designate an industry as prosperous and signal its expansion. Losses mean an industry is unprosperous and result in a contraction of that industry. Industrial expansion and contraction are self-limiting processes. As expansion increases market supply relative to market demand, the price of a product falls to the point where all economic profits disappear. As contraction decreases market supply relative to market demand, the resulting increase in product price eliminates losses and makes the industry normally profitable once again.

**4**   Consumer sovereignty dominates a competitive market economy. The penalty of losses and the lure of profits force both businesses and resource suppliers to channel their efforts in accordance with the wants of consumers.

**5**   Competition forces firms to use the least costly, and therefore the most economically efficient, productive techniques.

**6**   The price system plays a dual role in distributing total output among individual households. The prices commanded by the quantities and types of resources supplied by each household will determine the number of dollar claims against the economy's output each household receives. Given consumer tastes, product prices are of fundamental importance in determining consumer expenditure patterns. Within the limits of each household's money income, consumer preferences and the relative prices of products determine the distribution of total output.

**7**   The competitive price system can communicate changes in consumer tastes to resource suppliers and entrepreneurs, thereby prompting appropriate adjustments in the allocation of the economy's resources. The competitive price system also provides an environment conducive to technological advance and capital accumulation.

**8**   Competition, the primary mechanism of control in the market economy, will foster an identity of private and social interests; as though directed by an "invisible hand," competition harnesses the self-interest motives of businesses and resource suppliers so as to simultaneously further the social interest.

**9**   The basic economic virtue of the price system is its continuing emphasis upon efficiency. It produces what consumers want through the use of the most efficient techniques. Operation and adjustments of the price system are automatic in the sense that they are the result of individual, decentralized decisions, not the centralized decisions of government.

**10**   Criticisms of the price system are several: ***a.*** The controlling mechanism, competition, tends to weaken over time; ***b.*** inherent income inequalities, inability to register collective wants, and the presence of external benefits and costs prevent the price system from producing that collection of goods most wanted by society; ***c.*** the competitive price system does not guarantee full employment or price level stability.

**11**   The price system of American capitalism differs from the competitive price system in that the former is characterized by ***a.*** giant corporations and unions in certain product and resource markets, and ***b.*** government intervention in the economy to correct the major defects of the price system. Yet, the competitive price system does provide a working model whereby we can understand the price system of American capitalism.

## Questions and Study Suggestions

**1**   Key terms and concepts to remember: economic versus normal profits; expanding versus declining industries; "dollar votes"; derived demand; consumer sovereignty; least-cost production technique; directing (guiding) function of prices; "invisible hand"; market failure.

**2**   Describe in detail how the price system answers the Fundamental Questions. Why must economic choices be made? Explain: "The capitalistic system is a profit and loss economy."

**3**   "Production methods which are inferior in the engineering sense may be the most efficient methods in the economic sense." Explain.

**4**   Evaluate and explain the following statements:

  ***a.***   "The most important feature of capitalism is the absence of a central economic plan."

  ***b.***   "Competition is the indispensable disciplinarian of the market economy."

**5**  Explain fully the meaning and implications of the following quotation.[6]

The beautiful consequence of the market is that it is its own guardian.  If output prices or certain kinds of remuneration stray away from their socially ordained levels, forces are set into motion to bring them back to the fold.  It is a curious paradox which thus ensues: the market, which is the acme of individual economic freedom, is the strictest taskmaster of all.  One may appeal the ruling of a planning board or win the dispensation of a minister; but there is no appeal, no dispensation, from the anonymous pressures of the market mechanism.  Economic freedom is thus more illusory than at first appears.  One can do as one pleases in the market.  But if one pleases to do what the market disapproves, the price of individual freedom is economic ruination.

**6**  Assume that a business firm finds that its profits will be at a maximum when it produces $40 worth of product A.  Suppose also that each of the three techniques shown in the following table will produce the desired output.

| Resource | Technique No. 1 | Technique No. 2 | Technique No. 3 | Price per unit of resource |
|---|---|---|---|---|
| Labor | 5 | 2 | 3 | $3 |
| Land | 2 | 4 | 2 | 4 |
| Capital | 2 | 4 | 5 | 2 |
| Entrepre- neurial ability | 4 | 2 | 4 | 2 |

*a.*  Given the resource prices shown, which technique will the firm choose?  Why?

*b.*  Assume now that a new technique, technique No. 4, is developed.  It entails the use of 2 units of labor, 2 of land, 6 of capital, and 3 of entrepreneurial ability.  Given the resource prices in the table, will the firm adopt the new technique?  Explain your answer.

*c.*  Suppose now that the price of labor falls to $1.50 per unit, all other resource prices being unchanged.  Which technique will the producer now choose?  Explain.

*d.*  "The price system causes the economy to conserve most in the use of those resources which are particularly scarce in supply.  Resources which are scarcest relative to the demand for them have the highest prices.  As a result, producers use these resources as sparingly as is possible."  Evaluate this statement.  Does your answer to question 6c bear out this contention?  Explain.

**7**  Foreigners frequently point out that, comparatively speaking, Americans are very wasteful of food and material goods and very conscious, and overly economical, in their use of time.  Can you provide an explanation for this observation?

**8**  Interpret and explain the following quotation in terms of Table 5-1.[7]

Soviet industrialization has taken place against the background of an abundance of manpower. . . .  It was therefore economically sensible for them to use labor lavishly, substituting it whenever possible for capital goods, and bringing in more workers when-

[6]Ibid., p. 42.
[7]Robert W. Campbell, "Problems of United States–Soviet Economic Comparisons," in Joint Economic Committee, *Comparisons of the United States and Soviet Economies* (Washington: Government Printing Office, 1960), p. 26.

ever it was possible by doing so to squeeze a bit more output out of existing enterprises. The result of such a policy was to make output per worker low, but it was still the correct thing to do in the light of the abundance of labor.

Output per Soviet worker is considerably lower than output per American worker. Does this necessarily mean that the Soviet economy is inefficient and wasteful as compared with the United States economy? Explain.

**9** What are the major criticisms of the price system? Carefully evaluate these criticisms. Analyze in detail: "No allocation of resources can be termed 'efficient' unless we define the 'optimum' distribution of income."

## Selected References

Boulding, Kenneth E.: *Economic Analysis: Microeconomics,* 4th ed. (New York: Harper & Row, Publishers, Incorporated, 1966), chap. 6.

Fels, Rendigs, and Robert G. Uhler: *Casebook of Economic Problems and Cases* (St. Paul: West Publishing Company, 1976), parts 1–3.

Heilbroner, Robert L.: *The Worldly Philosophers,* 4th ed. (New York: Simon & Schuster, Inc., 1972), chap. 3.

Klaasen, Adrian (ed.): *The Invisible Hand* (Chicago: Henry Regnery Company, 1965).

Leeman, Wayne A. (ed.): *Capitalism, Market Socialism, and Central Planning* (Boston: Houghton Mifflin Company, 1963), chaps. 1, 2, 9–11.

# LAST WORD
## Nasty Profits and Wholesome Subsidies

In this excerpt a conservative economist criticizes governmental actions which interfere with the functioning of the price system.

The media have been heavily preoccupied with two items in recent weeks. One is concern with the *abundance*—or overabundance, whatever that might mean—of oil industry profits; the other is concern with the *absence* of profits in the case of Chrysler Corporation.

The response of policymakers in Washington has been, in effect, to squeeze both sides toward the middle. They are trying to apply the finishing touches to a so-called "windfall profits" tax to take all but a small fraction of increased oil industry revenue resulting from the rise in world-wide energy prices. Presumably, the managements of the firms and the thousands of shareholders of the firms are not to be entrusted with their own money. As for Chrysler, the White House has proposed a taxpayer guarantee of $1.5 billion in loans—a bailout twice what the company dared to ask for.

Apparently, nothing fails like success, and nothing succeeds like failure. It is a monstrous subversion of freedom and efficiency alike to deny both the right to succeed and the right to fail. We can reasonably wonder how far our society expects to travel on an incentive scheme which singles out the profitable for "punitive" tax increases and pours revenues into enterprises which flunk the market test. This will promote investment, not in productive capacity and consumer satisfaction, but in political dealing. Thus we actually encourage the dreaded "special interest" through further politicizing economic decisionmaking.

If a firm makes a profit, the community has demonstrated that it puts a higher value on the output of the firm than on the resources used by the firm. That firm has an incentive to expand its operations, and, by expanding, it is responding to consumer preferences. Conversely, a firm making a loss is using resources more valuable than its output. It should reduce output—perhaps all the way to zero—thereby releasing resources to be used in ways the community deems more valuable.

Neither the oil companies nor Chrysler got an order writ on tablets of stone to put their money where they did. Investors in each case attempted to cash in on their educated assessments as to where they could maximize their revenues vis-à-vis their costs. That the petroleum industry has experienced a profit is cause for consumers to cheer—not for joy over the good fortune of the (ugh) oil producers, but because those efficient people, out of greed, have served the community so well.

William R. Allen, *Midnight Economist: Radio Essays* (Los Angeles: International Institute for Economic Research, 1980), pp. 22–23, abridged. Reprinted by permission.

# Mixed Capitalism and the Economic Functions of Government

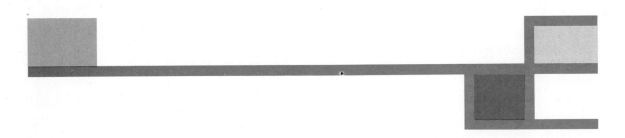

# chapter 6

We now begin the move from our abstract working model of pure capitalism to a discussion of American capitalism. In so doing we inject a significant dose of reality into our analysis.

All real-life economies are "mixed"; government and the price system share the function of answering the Five Fundamental Questions. Yet, the various economies of the world differ drastically in the particular blend of government direction and market direction which they embody (see Table 2-3). The economy of Soviet Russia, the topic of the final chapter of this book, leans heavily toward a centrally planned economy. American capitalism, on the other hand, is predominantly a market economy. At the same time, the economic functions of government—Federal, state, and local—are of very considerable significance.

It is not an easy matter to quantify the economic role of government. A rough indica-

tor of the relative importance of the market and government is the fact that currently about four-fifths of the total output of our economy is provided by the market system, the remaining one-fifth being produced under the sponsorship of government. But in addition to sponsoring production, government is also involved in a variety of so-called welfare programs designed to redistribute income within the private sector of the economy. Data indicate that taxes and total government disbursements—for the purchase of goods and services *and* for welfare activities—are approximately 33 percent of the national output. Finally, a variety of difficult-to-quantify programs designed to protect the environment, improve worker health and safety, protect consumers from unsafe products, provide equal access to employment opportunities, and regulate the pricing behavior of certain industries, impose government into virtually every aspect of economic activity. Government's economic role is clearly large and pervasive. Instead of Chapter 3's pure capitalism, our economy can be better described as *mixed capitalism.* The functioning of the private sector through the price system (Chapters 4 and 5) is modified in a variety of significant ways by the public sector.

## ☐ ECONOMIC FUNCTIONS OF GOVERNMENT

The economic functions of government are many, and they are varied. In fact, the economic role of government is so broad in scope that it is virtually impossible to establish an all-inclusive list of its economic functions. We shall employ the following breakdown of government's economic activities as a pattern for our discussion, recognizing that some overlapping is unavoidable.

First, some of the economic functions of government are designed to strengthen and facilitate the operation of the price system. The two major activities of government in this area are:

① Providing the legal foundation and a social environment conducive to the effective operation of the price system.

② Maintaining competition.

Through a second group of functions, government supplements and modifies the operation of the price system. There are three major functions of government here. They involve:

③ Redistributing income and wealth.

④ Adjusting the allocation of resources so as to alter the composition of the national output.

⑤ Stabilizing the economy, that is, controlling unemployment and inflation caused by the business cycle, and promoting economic growth.

While this fivefold breakdown of government's functions is a useful way of analyzing its economic role, we shall find that most government activities and policies have *some* impact in all these areas. For example, a program to redistribute income to the poor affects the allocation of resources to the extent that the poor buy somewhat different goods and services from those that wealthier members of society buy. A decline in, say, government military spending for the purpose of lessening inflationary pressures also tends to reallocate resources from public to private uses.

Let us briefly consider the first two functions of government and then analyze the redistributive, allocative, and stabilization roles of government in more detail.

## ☐ LEGAL AND SOCIAL FRAMEWORK FOR THE PRICE SYSTEM

Government assumes the task of providing the legal framework and certain basic services prerequisite to the effective operation of a market economy. The necessary legal framework involves such things as providing for the legal status of business enterprises, defining the rights of private ownership, and providing for the enforcement of contracts. Government also establishes legal "rules of the game" to govern the relationships of businesses, resource suppliers, and consumers with one another. Through legislation, government is enabled to referee economic relationships, detect foul play, and exercise authority in imposing appropriate penalties. The basic services provided by government include the use of police powers to maintain internal order, provision of a system of standards for measuring the weight and quality of products, and establishment of a monetary system to facilitate the exchange of goods and services.

The Pure Food and Drug Act of 1906 and its various amendments provide an excellent example of how government has strengthened the operation of the price system. This act sets rules of conduct to govern producers in their relationships with consumers. It prohibits the sale of adulterated and misbranded foods and drugs, requires the net weights and ingredients of products to be specified on their containers, establishes quality standards which must be stated on the labels of canned foods, and prohibits deceptive claims on patent-medicine labels. All these measures are designed to prevent fraudulent activities on the part of producers and, simultaneously, to increase the public's confidence in the integrity of the price system. In later chapters we shall discuss similar legislation pertaining to labor-management relations and the relations of business firms to one another.

It is worth noting that resource allocation will be altered and, in general, improved upon by this type of government activity. Supplying a medium of exchange, ensuring the quality of products, defining ownership rights, and enforcing contracts tend to increase the volume of exchange. This widens markets and permits greater specialization in the use of both property and human resources. Such specialization, we saw in Chapter 3, means a more efficient allocation of resources.

## ☐   MAINTAINING COMPETITION

Competition is the basic regulatory mechanism in a capitalistic economy. It is the force which subjects producers and resource suppliers to the dictates of buyer or consumer sovereignty. With competition, it is the supply and demand decisions of *many* sellers and buyers which determine market prices. This means that individual producers and resource suppliers can only adjust to the wishes of buyers as tabulated and communicated by the price system. Profits and survival await the competitive producers who obey the price system; losses and eventual bankruptcy are the lot of those who deviate from it. With competition, buyers are the boss, the market is their agent, and businesses are their servant.

The growth of monopoly drastically alters this situation. What is monopoly? Broadly defined, it is the situation wherein the number of sellers becomes small enough for each seller to influence total supply and therefore the price of the commodity being sold. What is its significance? Simply this: When monopoly supplants competition, sellers can influence, or

"rig," the market in terms of their own self-interests and to the detriment of society as a whole. Through their ability to influence total supply, monopolists can create artificial shortages of products and thereby enjoy higher prices and, very frequently, persistent economic profits. This is obviously in direct conflict with the interests of consumers. Monopolists are not regulated by the will of society as competitive sellers are. Producer sovereignty supplants consumer sovereignty to the degree that monopoly supplants competition. The result is that resources are allocated in terms of the profit-seeking interests of monopolistic sellers rather than in terms of the wants of society as a whole. In short, monopoly tends to cause a misallocation of economic resources.

In the United States the government has attempted to control monopoly primarily in two ways. First, in the case of "natural monopolies"—that is, in industries wherein technological and economic realities rule out the possibility of competitive markets—the government has created public commissions to regulate prices and service standards. Transportation, communications, and electric and other utilities are illustrations of regulated industries. At local levels of government, public ownership of electric and water utilities is quite common. But, second, in the vast majority of markets, efficient production can be attained with a high degree of competition. The Federal government has therefore enacted a series of antimonopoly or antitrust laws, beginning with the Sherman Act of 1890, for the purpose of maintaining and strengthening competition as an effective regulator of business behavior. The regulatory commissions and antitrust laws will be examined critically in Chapter 34. Even if the legal foundation of capitalistic institutions is assured and competition is maintained, there will still be a need for certain additional economic functions on the part of government. *The market economy at its best has certain biases and shortcomings which compel government to supplement and modify its operation.*

# ☐ REDISTRIBUTION OF INCOME

The price system is an impersonal mechanism, and the distribution of income to which it gives rise may entail more inequality than society desires. The market system yields very large incomes to those whose labor, by virtue of inherent ability and acquired education and skills, commands high wages. Similarly, those who possess—by virtue of hard work or easy inheritance—valuable capital and land receive large property incomes. But others in our society have less ability and have received modest amounts of education and training. And these same people typically have accumulated or inherited no property resources. Hence, their incomes are very low. Furthermore, many of the aged, the physically and mentally handicapped, and husbandless women with dependent children earn only very small incomes or, like the unemployed, no incomes at all through the price system. In short, the price system entails considerable inequality in the distribution of money income and therefore in the distribution of total output among individual households. Although progress has been made, poverty amidst overall plenty in American capitalism persists as a major economic and political issue.

Government has assumed the responsibility for ameliorating income inequality in our society. This responsibility is reflected in a variety of policies and programs. First, *public assistance or welfare programs* provide relief to the destitute, aid to the dependent and handicapped, and unemployment compensation to the unemployed. Similarly, our social security and Medicare programs provide financial support for the retired and aged sick. All these programs bring income to households which would otherwise have little or none. Secondly, government also alters the distribution by *market intervention,* that is, by modifying the prices established by market forces. Price supports for farmers and minimum-wage legislation are illustrations of government price fixing designed to raise the incomes of specific groups. Finally, the Federal *income tax* is designed to take a greater proportion of the incomes of the rich than of the poor and therefore has a kind of Robin Hood effect upon income distribution. As a result, the after-tax distribution of income tends to be more equal than the before-tax distribution. Redistributional policies are explored in detail in Chapter 37.

# ☐ REALLOCATION OF RESOURCES

Economists are cognizant of two major cases of *market failure,* that is, situations in which the competitive price system would either (1) produce the "wrong" amounts of certain goods and services, or (2) fail to allocate any resources to the production of certain goods and services whose output is economically justified. The first case involves "spillovers" or "externalities" and the second "social" or "public" goods.

## △ Spillovers or Externalities

We found in Chapter 5 that one of the virtues of a competitive market system is that it would result in an efficient allocation of resources. That is, the "right" or optimum amount of resources would be allocated to each of the various goods and services produced. Hence, for the competitive market shown in Figure 6-1a, the equilibrium output $Q_e$ is also identified as the optimum output $Q_o$.

But the conclusion that competitive markets automatically bring about allocative efficiency rests upon the hidden assumption that all the benefits and costs associated with the production and consumption of each product are fully reflected in the market demand and supply curves. Stated differently, it is assumed that there are no *spillovers* or *externalities* associated with the production or consumption of any good or service. A *spillover*[1] occurs when some of the benefits or costs associated

---

[1]Spillovers may go by other names—for example, external economies and diseconomies, neighborhood effects, and social benefits and costs.

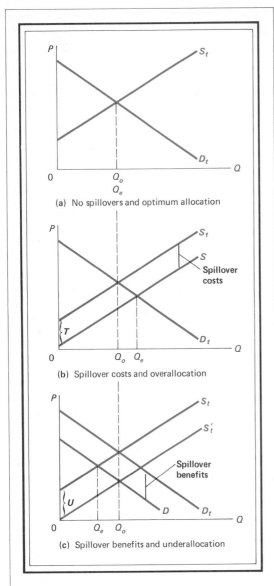

**FIGURE 6-1 SPILLOVERS AND THE ALLOCATION OF RESOURCES**

Without spillovers (a) the equilibrium output $Q_e$ is also the most efficient, or optimal, output $Q_o$. But with spillover costs (b) resources are overallocated to production; that is, the equilibrium output exceeds the optimum output. Conversely, spillover benefits (c) cause an underallocation of resources in that the optimum output exceeds the equilibrium output. A specific tax of $T$ per unit in (b) can correct the overallocation of resources. Similarly, a specific subsidy per unit of $U$ in (c) can correct the underallocation of resources.

with the production or consumption of a good "spill over" onto third parties, that is, to parties other than the immediate buyer or seller. Spillovers are also termed *externalities* because they are benefits and costs accruing to some individual or group external to the market transaction.

**Spillover Costs** When the production or consumption of a commodity inflicts costs upon some third party without compensation, there exists a spillover cost. The most obvious examples of spillover costs involve environmental pollution. When a chemical manufacturer or meat-packing plant dumps its wastes into a lake or river, swimmers, fishermen, and boaters—not to mention communities which seek a usable water supply—suffer spillover costs. When a petroleum refinery pollutes the air with smoke or a paint factory creates distressing odors, the community bears spillover costs for which it is not compensated.

How do spillover or social costs affect the allocation of resources? Figure 6-1*b* tells the story. When spillover costs occur—when producers shift some of their costs onto the community—their production costs are lower than would otherwise be the case. That is, the supply curve does not include or "capture" all the costs which can be legitimately associated with the production of the good. Hence, the producer's supply curve, $S$, understates the total costs of production and therefore lies below the supply curve which would include all costs, $S_t$. By polluting, that is, by creating spillover costs, the firm enjoys lower production costs and the supply curve $S$. The result, as shown in Figure 6-1*b*, is that the equilibrium output $Q_e$ is larger than the optimum output $Q_o$. Stated differently, resources are *overallocated* to the production of this commodity.

**Spillover Benefits** But spillovers may also take the form of benefits. The production or consumption of certain goods and services may confer social or spillover benefits on third parties or the community at large for which payment or compensation is not required. For example, chest x-rays and polio immunization shots result in direct benefits to the immediate consumer. But an early diagnosis of tuberculosis and the prevention of a contagious disease yield widespread and substantial spillover benefits to the entire community. Education is another standard example of spillover benefits. Education entails benefits to individual consumers: "More educated" people generally achieve higher incomes than do "less educated" people. But education also confers sizable benefits upon society; for example, the economy as a whole benefits from a more versatile and more productive labor force, on the one hand, and smaller outlays in the areas of crime prevention, law enforcement, and welfare programs, on the other. Significant, too, is the fact that political participation correlates positively with the level of education; for example, the percentage of persons who vote increases with educational attainment.

Figure 6-1c shows the impact of spillover benefits upon resource allocation. The existence of spillover benefits simply means that the market demand curve, which reflects only private benefits, understates total benefits. The market demand curve fails to capture all the benefits associated with the provision and consumption of goods and services which entail spillover benefits. Thus $D$ in Figure 6-1c indicates the benefits which private individuals derive from education; $D_t$ is drawn to include these private benefits *plus* the additional spillover benefits accruing to society at large. Thus, while market demand $D$ and supply $S_t$ would yield an equilibrium output of $Q_e$, this output would be less than the optimum output $Q_o$. The market system would not produce enough education; that is, resources would be *underallocated* to education.

Our discussion of spillover costs and benefits yields two generalizations:

**1**   When spillover *costs* are significant, the market will *overallocate* resources to the production of that good or service. The equilibrium output will exceed that output which entails allocative efficiency.

**2**   When spillover *benefits* are important, the market will *underallocate* resources to that commodity. The equilibrium output will fall short of the optimum output.

**Corrective Government Policy**   What actions might government take to correct the overallocations and underallocations of resources associated with spillover costs and benefits? In both instances government attempts to "internalize" the external costs and benefits; that is, government follows certain policies designed to cause the market to take into account spillover costs and benefits.

Consider, first, the case of spillover costs. Two basic courses of action are common: corrective legislation and special taxes.

**1**   Looking at our examples of air and water pollution, we find that the most direct action is simply to pass *legislation* which prohibits or limits pollution. Such legislation forces potential polluters to bear the costs of more properly disposing of industrial wastes; for example, firms must buy and install smoke-abatement equipment or facilities to purify water which has been contaminated by manufacturing processes. Such action forces potential offenders, under the threat of legal action, to bear *all* the costs associated with their production. In short, legislation can shift the supply curve $S$ toward $S_t$ in Figure 6-1b, tending to bring the equilibrium and optimum outputs into equality.

**2**   A second and less direct action is for government to levy a *special tax* which approximates the spillover costs per unit of output. Through this tax, government attempts to shove back onto the offending firm those external or spillover costs which private industry would otherwise avoid. Specifically, a special tax equal to $T$ per unit in Figure 6-1b will increase the firm's costs, shifting the supply curve from $S$ to $S_t$. The result is that the equilibrium output $Q_e$ will decline so that it corresponds with the optimum output $Q_o$ and the overallocation of resources will be eliminated.[2]

[2] Another option, discussed in Chapter 36, is designed to curtail pollution by creating a market for pollution rights.

What policies are appropriate for the case of spillover benefits? In the first place, assuming that the spillover or social benefits are not inordinately large when compared with the benefits received by individual purchasers, government can encourage the production of such goods and services by subsidizing their output. *Subsidies* are simply special taxes in reverse; taxes impose an extra cost on producers, whereas subsidies reduce their costs. In Figure 6-1c a subsidy of $U$ per unit to producers will shift the supply curve from $S_t$ to $S_t'$ and increase the equilibrium output $Q_e$ to bring it into correspondence with the optimum output $Q_o$. Hence, the underallocation of resources will be corrected.[3] Public subsidization of education, mass immunization programs, and public health clinics are cases in point.

A second policy option arises if spillover benefits are extremely large: Government may simply choose to finance or, in the extreme, to own and operate such industries. This option leads us into a discussion of social goods and services.

### △  Social Goods and Services

Consider the characteristics of *private goods* which are produced through the price system. These goods are *divisible* in that they come in units small enough to be afforded by individual buyers. Furthermore, private goods are subject to the *exclusion principle* in that those who are willing and able to pay the equilibrium price get the product, but those who are unable or unwilling to pay are excluded from the benefits provided by that product.

There are certain kinds of goods and services—called *social* or *public goods*—which would not be produced at all by the price system because their characteristics are essentially opposite those of private goods. Public goods are *indivisible,* involving such large units that they cannot be sold to individual buyers.

In addition, the exclusion principle does *not* apply; that is, there is no effective way of excluding individuals from the benefits of social goods once those goods come into existence. Obtaining the benefits of private goods is predicated upon *purchase;* the benefits from public goods accrue to society from the *production* of such goods.

The classic public goods example is a lighthouse on a treacherous coast or harbor. The construction of a lighthouse might be economically justified in that benefits (fewer shipwrecks) exceed production costs. But the benefit accruing to each individual user would not justify the purchase of such a large and indivisible product. (Do you know anyone who owns a lighthouse?) In any event, once in operation, its warning light is a guide to *all* ships. There is no practical way to exclude certain ships from its benefits. And why should any ship owner voluntarily pay for the benefits received from the light? The light is there for all to see, and a ship captain cannot be excluded from seeing it if the ship owner chooses not to pay. Economists call this the *free-rider problem.* Furthermore, given the inapplicability of the exclusion principle, there is obviously no economic incentive for private enterprises to supply lighthouses. If the services of the lighthouse cannot be priced and sold, it will clearly be unprofitable for private firms to devote resources to lighthouses. In short, here is a service which yields substantial benefits but for which the market would allocate no resources. National defense, flood-control and insect-abatement programs are other public goods. Hence, if society is to enjoy such goods and services, they must be provided by the public sector and financed by compulsory charges in the form of taxes.

**Large Spillover Benefits**   While the inapplicability of the exclusion principle rather sharply sets off public from private goods, a variety of other goods and services are provided by government even though the exclusion principle *could* be applied. In particular, such

[3]Government might choose to subsidize consumers, shifting the demand curve from $D$ to $D_t$. However, in practice it is usually more convenient to subsidize producers.

goods and services as education, streets and highways, police and fire protection, preventive medicine, and sewage disposal could be subject to the exclusion principle, that is, they could be priced and provided by private producers through the market system. But, as noted earlier, these are all services which entail substantial spillover benefits and therefore would be grossly underproduced by the market system. Therefore, government undertakes or sponsors their provision to avoid the underallocation of resources which would otherwise occur. Such goods and services are sometimes called *quasi-public goods.* One can understand the long-standing controversies surrounding the status of medical care and housing. Are these private goods to be provided through the market system, or are they quasi-public goods to be provided by government?

△ **Allocating Resources to Social Goods**
     Given that the price system would fail to allocate resources for public goods and would underallocate resources for quasi-public goods, what is the mechanism by which such goods get produced?
     Social goods are purchased through the government on the basis of group, or collective, choices, in contrast to private goods, which are purchased from private enterprises on the basis of individual choices. More specifically, the types and quantities of the various social goods produced are determined in a democracy by political means, that is, by voting. The quantities of the various social goods consumed are a matter of public policy.[4] These group decisions, made in the political arena, supplement the choices of households and businesses in answering the Five Fundamental Questions.

[4]There are obvious differences between *dollar voting,* which dictates output in the private sector of the economy, and *political voting,* which determines output in the public sector. The rich person has many more votes to cast in the private sector than does the poor person. In the public sector, each—at least in theory—has an equal say. Furthermore, the children who cast their votes for bubble gum and comic books in the private sector are banned by virtue of their age from the registering of social choices.

Assuming these group decisions have been rendered, precisely how are resources reallocated from the production of private goods to the production of social goods? In a full-employment economy, government is faced with the task of freeing resources from private employment to make them available for the production of social goods. The obvious means of releasing resources from private uses is to reduce private demand for them. This is accomplished by levying taxes on businesses and households, thereby diverting some of their incomes—some of their potential purchasing power—out of the income-expenditure streams. With lower incomes, businesses and households will be forced to curtail their investment and consumption spending. *In short, taxes tend to diminish private demand for goods and services, and this decrease in turn prompts a drop in the private demand for resources.* By diverting purchasing power from private spenders to government, taxes free resources from private uses. *Government expenditure of the tax proceeds can then reabsorb these resources and provide social goods and services.* For example, corporation and personal income taxes release resources from the production of investment goods—drill presses, boxcars, warehouses—and consumer goods—food, clothing, and television sets. Government expenditures tend to reabsorb these resources in the production of guided missiles, military aircraft, and new schools and highways. Government purposely reallocates resources to bring about significant changes in the composition of the economy's total output.

□ **STABILIZATION**
Historically, the most recent and in some ways the most important function of government is that of stabilizing the economy—assisting the private economy to achieve both the full employment of resources and a stable price level. Part 2 of this book examines in detail the determinants of employment and the price level in a capitalistic economy. Hence, at this point

we pause only to outline and assert (rather than fully explain) the stabilization function of government.

The key point is that the level of output depends directly upon total spending or aggregate demand. A high level of total demand means it will be profitable for the various industries to produce large outputs, and this condition, in turn, will necessitate that both property and human resources be employed at high levels. But we shall find in Part 2 that there are no mechanisms in the capitalistic system to ensure that aggregate demand will be at that particular level which will provide for full employment. Two unhappy possibilities might arise:

**1 Unemployment** The level of total demand in the private sector may be too low for full employment. The government's obligation is to augment private demand so that total demand—private *and* public—will be sufficient to generate full employment. How can government do this? One answer[5] is, by using the same techniques—government spending and taxes—as it uses to reallocate resources to the production of social goods. Specifically, government should increase its own spending on social goods and services on the one hand, and reduce taxes in order to stimulate private spending on the other.

**2 Inflation** The second possibility is that the economy may attempt to spend in excess of its productive capacity. If aggregate demand exceeds the full-employment output, the excess demand will have the effect of pulling up the price level. Excessive aggregate demand is inflationary. Government's obligation here is to eliminate the excess spending. It does this primarily by cutting its own expenditures and by raising taxes so as to curtail private spending.

[5] We will find in later chapters that government has means other than its expenditure-tax policies to help achieve economic stability.

Caution: The real world, unfortunately, is more complex than our discussion implies. Hence, the lamentable situation of simultaneous unemployment and inflation which plagued the 1970s is not susceptible to such simple and self-evident remedies. We deal with these complexities in Chapter 18.

## ☐ EVALUATING GOVERNMENT'S ROLE

Thus far we have been content to state the major economic functions of government and to indicate the overall impact of their performance upon the economy. We now turn to the problem of evaluating the economic role of government. Unfortunately, government's economic role is extremely difficult to assess. There are no simple quantitative standards by which the scope and quality of government's performance can be gauged. Any evaluation of the public sector quickly pushes us beyond the boundaries of economic science and into the larger realms of political theory and philosophy. Nevertheless, let us consider the following three questions:

**1** To what extent is there agreement upon the legitimacy of the five stated governmental functions?

**2** Do guidelines exist for determining the appropriate scope of public sector activities?

**3** Given that there are certain deficiencies or failures in private decision making through the market system, are there analogous failures involved in collective decision making in the public sector?

### △ Desirability of Functions

Should government perform the five economic functions we have just discussed? All things considered, there is general and widespread agreement that these functions entail tasks which legitimately devolve on government. And, in fact, with the exception of the stabilization function, government has performed all these functions to a greater or lesser degree throughout American economic history. True, a small minority within the United States espouses the philosophy of "that government is best which governs least." At the other extreme, there are those who look upon an expansion of the functions of government as a panacea for any and all the ills of society. Though these groups are often highly vocal, it must be emphasized that they are small minorities. The vast majority of people is in fairly close agreement that government has some obligation in each of the areas we have discussed.

People of goodwill may agree that all five of the stated functions of government are legitimate, but they may seriously disagree about the extent to which these functions should be pursued and whether a specific project or program falls within the public sector. Few would question that government has *some* role to play in providing national defense, education, and highways. But there may be substantial disagreement about the size of the public budget for each of these purposes. And there may be controversy about whether certain particular projects—the provision of medical care or electric power, for example—should be within the public sector at all.

△ **Benefit-Cost Analysis**

Economics can provide some guidance to efficient decision making in the public sector. This guidance takes the form of *benefit-cost analysis.*

Suppose government is contemplating some specific project, for example, a flood-control project. The basic nature of the economizing problem (Chapter 2) tells us that any decision to use more resources in, say, the public sector will involve both a benefit and a cost. The benefit is the extra satisfaction resulting from the output of more social goods; the cost is the loss of satisfaction associated with the concomitant decline in the production of private goods. Should the resources under consideration be shifted from the private to the public sector? The answer is "Yes" *if* the bene-

fits from the extra social goods exceed the cost resulting from having fewer private goods. The answer is "No" *if* the value or cost of the forgone private goods is greater than the benefits associated with the extra social goods.

But benefit-cost analysis can do more than merely indicate whether a public program is worth undertaking. It can also provide guidance concerning the extent to which a given project should be pursued. Economic questions, after all, are not simply questions to be answered by "Yes" or "No," but rather, matters of "how much" or "how little." Consider the case of flood control. We note first that the benefits from a flood-control project are largely spillovers and that the exclusion principle is not readily applicable. That is, a flood-control project is basically a social good. Now, should government undertake a flood-control project in a given river valley? And, if so, what is the proper size or scope for the project?

Table 6-1 provides us with the answers. Here we list a series of increasingly ambitious and increasingly costly flood-control plans. To what extent, if at all, should government undertake flood control? The answers depend upon costs and benefits. Costs in this case are largely the capital costs of constructing and maintaining levees and reservoirs; benefits take the form of reduced flood damage.

In the first place, a quick glance at all the plans indicates that in each instance total benefits (column 4) exceed total costs (column 2), indicating that a flood-control project on this river is economically justifiable. But a second question remains: What is the optimum size or scope for this project? The answer is determined by comparing the additional, or *marginal,* costs and the additional, or *marginal,* benefits associated with each plan. The guideline is formalized common sense: Pursue an activity or project so long as the marginal benefits (column 5) exceed the marginal costs (column 3). Stop the activity or project at, or as close as possible to, that point at which marginal benefits equal marginal costs. In this case Plan C—the medium-sized reservoir—is

**TABLE 6-1**
Benefit-Cost Analysis For a Flood-Control Project

| (1)<br>Plan | (2)<br>Total annual cost of project | (3)<br>Extra or marginal cost | (4)<br>Total annual benefit (reduction in damage) | (5)<br>Extra or marginal benefit |
|---|---|---|---|---|
| Without protection | $ 0 | | $ 0 | |
| | | $ 3,000 | | $ 6,000 |
| A: Levees | 3,000 | | 6,000 | |
| | | 7,000 | | 10,000 |
| B: Small reservoir | 10,000 | | 16,000 | |
| | | 8,000 | | 9,000 |
| C: Medium reservoir | 18,000 | | 25,000 | |
| | | 12,000 | | 7,000 |
| D: Large reservoir | 30,000 | | 32,000 | |

*Source:* Adapted from Otto Eckstein, *Public Finance,* 3d ed. (Englewood Cliffs, N.J.: Prentice-Hall, Inc., 1973), p. 23. Used with permission.

the best plan. Plans A and B are too modest; in both cases marginal benefits exceed marginal costs. Plan D entails marginal costs ($12,000) in excess of marginal benefits ($7000) and therefore cannot be justified. Plan D isn't economically justifiable; it involves an overallocation of resources to this flood-control project. Plan C is closest to the optimum; it "pushes" flood control so long as marginal benefits exceed marginal costs. Regarded from a slightly different vantage point, the marginal benefit–marginal cost rule will determine which plan entails the maximum excess of total benefits over total costs or, in other words, the plan which yields the largest *net* gain to society.

It is worth noting that benefit-cost analysis explodes the myth that "economy in government" and "reduced government spending" are synonymous. "Economy" is concerned with efficiency in resource use. If a government program yields marginal benefits which are less than the marginal benefits attainable from alternative private uses—that is, if costs exceed benefits—then the proposed public program should *not* be undertaken. But if the reverse is true—if benefits exceed costs—then it would be uneconomical or "wasteful" *not* to spend on that governmental program. Economy in government does *not* mean the minimization of public spending; rather, it means allocating resources between the private and public sectors until no net benefits can be realized from additional reallocations.

△ **Limitations and Problems**

Benefit-cost analysis is extremely helpful in promoting clear thinking about the public sector and is in fact very useful in actual studies involving projects such as flood control and highway construction. But we must acknowledge that many attempts to apply benefit-cost analysis encounter severe problems and limitations.

**Measurement**  In the first place, benefit-cost analysis—as demonstrated in Table 6-1—assumes that benefits and costs can be measured with reasonable accuracy. To the extent that this is not the case, the reliability of benefit-cost analysis as a guide to public spending is diminished. Now the problem is that most of the programs appropriate for the public sector are those which entail large spillover effects, the values of which are very difficult to accurately quantify.

Consider the possible benefits and costs associated with the construction of a new freeway in a major metropolitan area. In addition to estimating the obvious costs—land purchase and costs of construction—the responsible agency must also estimate the spillover cost of additional air pollution which results from an enlarged flow of traffic. Furthermore, more traffic may call for increased expenditures for traffic police. What about benefits? Improved transportation means a widening of markets, more competition, and a greater opportunity for the community to specialize and improve economic efficiency. But what is the monetary value of this benefit? And the freeway may help make more jobs accessible to the central city poor. Again, what is the dollar value of these benefits? Given the suggested difficulties in estimating all the costs and benefits associated with such relatively tangible undertakings as highway and reservoir construction, one can imagine the enormous obstacles in applying benefit-cost analysis to space exploration, foreign aid, or a vocational training program for disadvantaged youths. The point is that the full costs and benefits associated with government programs are not easily calculated, and benefit-cost analysis is frequently difficult to apply.

**Interactions**  Secondly, we must recognize that in practice the allocative, redistributional, and stabilization functions of government are all closely intertwined. A government policy or action specifically designed, say, to reallocate resources from private to public uses will almost invariably affect the distribution of income and have implications for output and price level stabilization. These interactions complicate the making of rational decisions. Consider, once again, our flood-control project. Its purpose is primarily allocative—to increase the output of a specific social good which is worth more than alternative private goods. But the project might have adverse effects in terms of society's distributional and stabilization objectives. Suppose that the taxes to be collected in financing the project are of such a kind that they are paid disproportionately by low-income people. And suppose that the resulting benefits accrue chiefly to wealthy farmers and prosperous business executives. *If* greater equality in income distribution is a high-priority policy objective of society, then presumably the adverse redistributional effects of the project should be taken into account. But how? How can the "cost" of the redistributional impact be measured?

A similar conflict might arise with respect to the stabilization function. Assume the economy is experiencing quite severe inflation as a result of excess aggregate spending. Now, despite the desirability of the flood-control project as indicated by benefit-cost analysis, should the project be initiated in view of the fact that the added spending on flood control will intensify inflationary pressures? The point is that if a social goods project has adverse implications with respect to society's distributional and stabilization goals, the case for the project is less clear than if these implications were favorable or, at least, substantially neutral. In the context of such possible dilemmas, the rendering of rational public policy decisions becomes complex indeed.

## ☐ PUBLIC SECTOR FAILURE?[6]

It would be incorrect to assume that the economic functions of government are performed effectively and efficiently. Indeed, the recent "taxpayers' revolt" (Chapter 8) reflects considerable public disenchantment with, and distrust of, government. This antigovernment sentiment has diverse roots, but it stems in part from the apparent failure of costly government programs to resolve socioeconomic ills. For example, it is argued that foreign aid programs have contributed little or nothing to the economic growth of the less developed nations. Similarly, critics of the war on poverty programs point to the persistence of poverty, particularly in the urban ghettos. We hear reports that well-financed state and Federal school enrichment programs have had no perceptible impact upon the educational attainment of students. Some programs have allegedly fostered the very problems they were

[6]This section is based upon the excellent discussion of public sector failure found in James D. Gwartney and Richard Stroup, *Economics: Private and Public Choice,* 2d ed. (New York: Academic Press, 1980), chap. 32. The interested reader should also consult Richard B. McKenzie and Gordon Tullock, *Modern Political Economy* (New York: McGraw-Hill Book Company, 1978).

designed to solve: Our farm programs were originally designed to save the family farm, but in fact have heavily subsidized large corporate farms which in turn have driven family farms out of business. There are also charges that government agencies have become mired in a blizzard of paperwork. The popular press tells us that social workers in New York City spend 70 to 80 percent of their time doing paperwork, leaving only 20 to 30 percent of their time for their clients. It is alleged that the public bureaucracy embodies great duplication of effort; that obsolete programs persist; that various agencies work at cross purposes, and so on. The apparent inability of government to come to grips with inflation is also an important factor in the public's skepticism towards government.

Coincident with this popular disenchantment, there has evolved a body of literature on the *theory of public choice* which alleges that, just as certain limitations or failures are embodied in the private sector's price system, so there are also more-or-less inherent deficiencies in the political processes and bureaucratic agencies which comprise the public sector. Hence, we might agree that government has a legitimate role to play in dealing with instances of market failure; that is, government should make adjustments for spillover costs and benefits, provide social goods and services, temper income inequality, and so forth. We might also accept benefit-cost analysis as an important guide to economically efficient decision making in the public sector. But a more fundamental question remains: Are there inherent problems or shortcomings within the public sector which constrain governmental decision making as a mechanism for promoting economic efficiency? In fact, casual reflection suggests that there may be significant divergence between "sound economics" and "good politics." We know that the former calls for the public sector to pursue various programs so long as marginal benefits exceed marginal costs. Good politics, however, suggests that politicians should support those

programs and policies which will maximize their chances of getting elected and retained in office.

Let us now briefly consider some possible reasons for public sector failure, that is, some reasons why the public sector may function inefficiently in an economic sense.

△  **Special Interests**

Ideally, public decisions promote the general welfare or, at least, the interests of the vast majority of the citizenry. But it is contended that, in fact, government often promotes the goals of small special-interest groups to the detriment of the public at large. Stated differently, efficient public decision making is often impaired by a *special-interest effect.*

How can this happen? In part the answer is inherent in the definition of a special-interest issue: This is an issue, program, or policy from which a small number of people individually will receive *large* gains at the expense of a large number of persons who individually suffer *small* losses. The small group of potential beneficiaries will be well informed and highly vocal on this issue, pressing politicians for approval. The large numbers who face small losses will generally be uninformed and indifferent on this issue; after all, they have little at stake. Crudely put, politicians feel they will clearly lose the support of the small special-interest group which supports the program if they vote against it. But the politicians will *not* lose the support of the large group of uninformed voters who will evaluate them on other issues in which voters have a stronger interest. Furthermore, the politicians' inclination to support special-interest legislation is enhanced by the fact that such groups are often more than willing to help finance the campaigns of "right-minded" politicians. The result is that the politician will support the special-interest program, even though that program may *not* be economically desirable from a social point of view.

Examples of special-interest groups realizing legislation and policies which are unjustified on the basis of efficiency or equity considerations are manifold: tariffs on foreign products which limit domestic competition and raise prices to consumers (Chapter 42); tax loopholes which benefit the very rich (Chapter 8); "pork-barrel" public works programs; and so forth.

### △ Clear Benefits, Hidden Costs

It is also contended that the vote-seeking politician will not *objectively* weigh all the costs and benefits of various programs, as economic rationality demands, in deciding which to support and which to reject. Rather, the vote-seeking politician will tend to favor programs which entail immediate and clear-cut benefits, on the one hand, and vague, difficult-to-identify, or deferred, costs, on the other. Conversely, politicians will look askance at programs which embody immediate and easily identifiable costs along with future benefits which are diffuse and vague. The point here is that such biases in the area of public choice can lead politicians to reject economically justifiable programs and to accept programs which are economically irrational. Example: A proposal to construct and expand mass transit systems in large metropolitan areas may be economically rational on the basis of objective benefit-cost analysis of the sort illustrated in Table 6-1. But if (1) the program is to be financed by immediate increases in highly visible income taxes *and* (2) benefits will accrue only a decade hence when the project is completed, the vote-seeking politician may decide to oppose the program. Assume, on the other hand, that a proposed program of Federal aid to municipal police forces is *not* justifiable on the basis of objective benefit-cost analysis. But if costs are concealed and deferred through deficit financing, the program's modest benefits may loom so large that it gains political approval.

### △ Nonselectivity

Public-choice theorists also argue that the nature of the political process is such that

citizens are forced to be less selective in the choice of public goods and services than they are in the choice of private goods and services. In the market sector, the citizen *as consumer* can reflect personal preferences very precisely by buying certain goods and forgoing others. However, in the public sector the citizen *as voter* is confronted with two or more candidates for office, each of whom represents different "bundles" of programs (social goods and services). The critical point is that in no case is the bundle of social goods represented by any particular candidate likely to fit precisely the wants of the particular voter. For example, voter Smith's favored candidate for office may endorse national health insurance, the development of nuclear energy, subsidies to tobacco farmers, and tariffs on imported automobiles. Citizen Smith votes for this candidate because the bundle of programs he endorses comes closest to matching Smith's preferences, even though Smith may oppose tobacco subsidies and tariffs on foreign cars. The voter, in short, must take the good with the bad; in the public sector, one is forced to "buy" goods and services one does not want. It is as if, in going to a clothing store, you were forced to buy an unwanted pair of slacks to get a wanted pair of shoes. This is obviously a situation wherein resources are *not* being allocated efficiently so as best to satisfy consumer wants. In this sense, the provision of social goods and services is held to be inherently inefficient.

### △ Bureaucracy and Inefficiency

Finally, it is contended that private businesses are inherently more efficient than public agencies. The reason for this is *not* that lazy and incompetent workers somehow end up in the public sector, while the ambitious and capable gravitate to the private sector. Rather, it is held that the market system creates incentives and pressures for internal efficiency which are absent in the public sector. More specifically, the managers of private enterprises have a strong personal incentive—increased profit income—to be efficient in their operation. Whether a private firm is in a competitive or monopolistic environment, lower costs through efficient management contribute to enlarged profits. There is no tangible personal gain—a counterpart to profits—for the bureau chief who achieves efficiency within his or her domain. In brief, there is simply less incentive to be cost-conscious in the public sector. Indeed, in a larger sense the market system imposes an explicit test of performance of private firms—the test of profits and losses. A firm which is efficient is profitable and therefore successful; it survives, prospers, and grows. An enterprise which is inefficient is unprofitable and unsuccessful; it declines and in time goes bankrupt and ceases to exist. But there is no similar, clear-cut test by which one can assess the efficiency or inefficiency of public agencies. How can one determine whether TVA, a state university, a local fire department, the Department of Agriculture, or the Bureau of Indian Affairs is operating efficiently?

Cynics argue that, in fact, a public agency which uses its resources inefficiently may be in line for a budget increase! In the private sector, inefficiency and monetary losses lead to the abandonment of certain activities—the discontinuing of certain products and services. But government, it is contended, is loath to abandon activities in which it has failed. "Indeed, the typical response of government to the failure of an activity is to double its budget and staff."[7] This obviously means that public sector inefficiency may be sustained on a larger scale. Furthermore, returning to our earlier comments regarding special-interest groups, it has been pointed out that public programs spawn new constituencies of bureaucrats and beneficiaries whose political clout causes programs to be sustained or expanded after they have fulfilled their goals or, alternatively, even if they have failed miserably in their mission. Relevant bureaucrats, school administrators,

and teachers may become a highly effective special-interest group for sustaining inefficient programs of Federal aid to education or for causing these programs to be expanded beyond the point at which marginal benefits equal marginal costs.

Postscript: Some specific suggestions have been offered recently to deal with the problems of bureaucratic inefficiency. Benefit-cost analysis, of course, is one suggested approach. It has also been proposed that all legislation establishing new programs contain well-defined performance standards so the public can better judge efficiency. Further, the suggestion has been made that expiration dates—so-called "sunset laws" be written into all new programs, thereby forcing a thorough periodic evaluation which might indicate the need for program abandonment.

△   **Imperfect Institutions**

One might argue that these criticisms of public sector efficiency are overdrawn and too cynical. Perhaps this is so. On the other hand, they are sufficiently persuasive to shake one's faith in a simplistic concept of a benevolent government responding with precision and efficiency to the wants of its citizenry. We have seen that the market system of the private sector is by no means perfectly efficient; indeed, government's economic functions are attempts to correct the price system's shortcomings. But now we find that the public sector may also be subject to important deficiencies in fulfilling its economic functions. "The relevant comparison is not between perfect markets and imperfect governments, nor between faulty markets and all-knowing, rational, benevolent governments, but between inevitably imperfect institutions."[8]

One of the important implications of the fact that the market system and public agencies are both imperfect institutions is that, in practice, it can be exceedingly difficult to de-

[7] Peter F. Drucker, "The Sickness of Government," *The Public Interest,* Winter 1969, p. 13.

[8] Otto Eckstein, *Public Finance,* 3d ed. (Englewood Cliffs, N.J.: Prentice-Hall, Inc., 1973), p. 17.

termine whether some particular activity can be performed with greater success in the private or the public sector.[9] It is easy to reach agreement on polar cases: National defense must lie in the public sector, whereas wheat production can best be accomplished in the private sector. But what about health insurance? The provision of parks and recreation areas? Fire protection? Housing? Education? The point is that it is very hard to assess each type of good or service and to say unequivocally that its provision should be assigned to either the public or the private sector. Evidence that this is so is reflected in the fact that all the goods and services mentioned above are provided in part by both private enterprises and public agencies.

## ☐ THE ISSUE OF FREEDOM

Finally, let us consider an important, but elusive, question: What is the nature of the relationship between the role and size of the public sector, on the one hand, and freedom, on the other? Although no attempt is made here to explore this issue in depth, it is relevant to indicate the outlines of two divergent views on this question.

### △ The Conservative Position

Many conservative economists feel that, in addition to the economic costs involved in any expansion of the public sector, there is also a cost in the form of diminished individual freedom. Two basic points constitute this position. First, there is the "power corrupts" argument.[10] "Freedom is a rare and delicate plant. . . . history confirms that the great threat to freedom is the concentration of power. . . . by concentrating power in political hands, [government] is . . . a threat to freedom." Secondly, one can practice selectivity in the market system of the private sector, using

one's income to buy precisely what one chooses and rejecting unwanted commodities. But in the public sector—even assuming a high level of political democracy—conformity and coercion are inherent. If the majority decides in favor of certain governmental actions—to build a reservoir, to establish an old-age insurance program, to provide a guaranteed annual income—the minority must conform. Hence, the "use of political channels, while inevitable, tends to strain the social cohesion essential for a stable society."[11] To the extent that decisions can be rendered selectively by individuals through markets, the need for conformity and coercion is lessened and this "strain" reduced. Proponents of this view argue that (1) the scope of government should be strictly limited, and (2) government power should be decentralized.

### △ The Liberal Stance

But liberal economists are skeptical of the conservative position. They hold that the conservative view is based upon what we shall call the *fallacy of limited decisions*. That is, the conservatives implicitly assume that during any particular period of time there is a limited, or fixed, number of decisions to be made in connection with the operation of the economy. Hence, if government makes more of these decisions in performing its stated functions, the private sector of the economy will necessarily have fewer "free" decisions or choices to make. This is held to be fallacious reasoning. By sponsoring the production of social goods, government is, in fact, *extending* the range of free choice by permitting society to enjoy goods and services which would not be available in the absence of governmental provision. One can cogently argue that it is in large measure through the economic functions of government that we have been striving to free ourselves in some measure from ignorance, unemployment, poverty, disease, crime, discrimination, and other ills. Note, too, that in

---

[9] Our survey of the "isms" in Chapter 2 is indicative of the diversity of judgments on this question internationally.
[10] Milton Friedman, *Capitalism and Freedom* (Chicago: The University of Chicago Press, 1962), p. 2.

[11] Ibid., p. 23.

providing most social goods, government does not typically undertake production itself, but rather, purchases these goods through private enterprise. When government makes the decision to build an interstate highway, private concerns are given the responsibility for making a myriad of specific decisions and choices in connection with the carrying out of this decision.

Finally, it should be noted that during a depression, the number of choices made by private businesses and households is greatly restricted. Why? Because production has been slowed and incomes have been drastically curtailed. The business executive has fewer choices to make concerning, for example, the types of products and combinations of resources he or she may use. Indeed, some firms will have to close down and make no decisions at all. Consumers have fewer decisions to make in disposing of their incomes, because their incomes are now very small or conceivably nonexistent. Now if government, by increased participation and intervention in the economy, can correct or even alleviate a depression, the number of decisions and choices open to both businesses and consumers will increase. That is, government, by making

more decisions concerning the operation of the economy, might restore prosperity, permitting the number of private decisions to increase also. Hence, the number of private and public decisions made in the operation of the economy may, *within limits,* vary in the same direction. A larger number of governmental decisions may or may not mean a smaller number of private decisions.

One of America's leading economists has summarized the liberal view in these pointed words:[12]

> Traffic lights coerce me and limit my freedom. Yet in the midst of a traffic jam on the unopen road, was I really "free" before there were lights? And has the algebraic total of freedom, for me or the representative motorist or the group as a whole, been increased or decreased by the introduction of well-engineered stop lights? Stop lights, you know, are also go lights. . . . When we introduce the traffic light, we have, although the arch individualist may not like the new order, by cooperation and coercion created for ourselves greater freedom.

[12] Paul A. Samuelson, "Personal Freedoms and Economic Freedoms in the Mixed Economy," in Earl F. Cheit (ed.), *The Business Establishment* (New York: John Wiley & Sons, Inc., 1964), p. 219.

## Summary

1   The American economy can be described as mixed capitalism.  It is primarily a market economy, yet government influences the operation of the price system in a variety of ways.

2   The basic economic functions of government entail *a.* providing a legal and social framework appropriate to the effective operation of the price system, *b.* maintaining competition, *c.* redistributing income, *d.* reallocating resources to adjust for spillovers and provide social goods and services, and *e.* stabilizing the economy.

3   Society generally condones government activity in the five areas outlined above. Benefit-cost analysis can provide useful guidance as to the economic desirability and most efficient scope of social goods output.

4   Public choice theorists cite a number of reasons why government might be inefficient in providing social goods and services.  *a.* There are strong reasons for politicians to support special-interest legislation.  *b.* Public choice may be biased in favor of programs with immediate and clear-cut benefits and difficult-to-identify costs *and* against programs with immediate and easily identified costs and vague or deferred benefits.  *c.* Citizens as voters have less

selectivity with respect to social goods and services than they do as consumers in the private sector. **d.** Government bureaucracies have less incentive to operate efficiently than do private businesses.

**5** There is substantial disagreement as to the relationship between the size of the public sector and individual freedom.

## Questions and Study Suggestions

**1** Key terms and concepts to remember: mixed capitalism; monopoly; spillover costs and benefits; social good; exclusion principle; free-rider problem; benefit-cost analysis; public choice theory; special-interest effect; nonselectivity of social goods; bureaucracy; fallacy of limited decisions.

**2** Why is the American economy called "mixed capitalism"? Enumerate and briefly discuss the main economic functions of government.

**3** Explain why, in the absence of spillovers, equilibrium and optimum outputs are identical in competitive markets. What divergences arise between equilibrium and optimum output when **a.** spillover costs and **b.** spillover benefits are present? How might government correct for these discrepancies? "The presence of spillover costs suggests an underallocation of resources to that product and the need for governmental subsidies." Do you agree? Explain how zoning laws might be used to deal with the problem of spillover costs.

**4** What are the basic characteristics of social goods? Explain the significance of the exclusion principle. By what means does government provide social goods?

**5** Use your understanding of the characteristics of private and public goods to determine whether the following should be produced through the market system or by government: **a.** bread; **b.** street lighting; **c.** bridges; **d.** parks; **e.** swimming pools; **f.** medical care; **g.** mail delivery; **h.** housing; **i.** air traffic control.

**6** The following table shows the total costs and total benefits in billions for four different antipollution programs of increasing scope. Which program should be undertaken? Why?

| Program | Total cost | Total benefit |
|---------|-----------|---------------|
| A | $ 3 | $ 7 |
| B | 7 | 12 |
| C | 12 | 16 |
| D | 18 | 19 |

**7** Carefully evaluate this statement: "The public, as a general rule . . . gets less production in return for a dollar spent by government than from a dollar spent by private enterprise." [13]

**8** "The conclusion seems inescapable that pure capitalism . . . would be subject to grave deficiencies and inconsistencies. Such a system would have little chance of survival." [14] Do you agree? Why?

**9** "It is conceivable that the Federal government can contribute materially to economic stability and greater efficiency in the use of resources without interfering in the details of business and personal life." Do you agree? Explain.

---

[13] National Association of Manufacturers, *The American Individual Enterprise System* (New York: McGraw-Hill Book Company, 1946), p. 952.
[14] Howard R. Bowen, *Toward Social Economy* (New York: Holt, Rinehart and Winston, Inc., 1948), p. 321.

**10**   Carefully evaluate the following statement, and contrast its philosophy with that in question 7.[15]

> The admitted functions of government embrace a much wider field than can be easily included within the ring fence of a restrictive definition . . . it is hardly possible to find any ground of justification common to them all, except the comprehensive one of general expediency; nor to limit the interference of government by any universal rule, save the simple and vague one that it should never be admitted but when the case of expediency is strong.

## Selected References

Eckstein, Otto: *Public Finance,* 4th ed. (Englewood Cliffs, N.J.: Prentice-Hall, Inc., 1979), chaps. 1, 2.

Gwartney, James D., and Richard Stroup: *Economics: Private and Public Choice,* 2d ed. (New York: Academic Press, 1980), chaps. 30–32.

Haveman, Robert Henry: *The Economics of the Public Sector* (New York: John Wiley & Sons, Inc., 1970), chaps. 1–5.

McKenzie, Richard B., and Gordon Tullock: *Modern Political Economy* (New York: McGraw-Hill Book Company, 1978), chaps. 21 and 22.

Musgrave, Richard A., and Peggy B. Musgrave: *Public Finance in Theory and Practice,* 3d ed. (New York: McGraw-Hill Book Company, 1980), chaps. 1–6.

Schultze, Charles L.: *The Public Use of Private Interest* (Washington, D. C.: The Brookings Institution, 1977).

---

[15] John Stuart Mill, *Principles of Political Economy* (New York: Appleton-Century-Crofts, Inc., 1878), vol. II, p. 392.

# LAST WORD
## Government and Freedom

Milton Friedman, America's best-known conservative economist, considers the relationship between government and economic freedom.

Freedom is a rare and delicate plant. Our minds tell us, and history confirms, that the great threat to freedom is the concentration of power. Government is necessary to preserve our freedom, it is an instrument through which we can exercise our freedom; yet by concentrating power in political hands, it is also a threat to freedom. Even though the men who wield this power initially be of good will and even though they be not corrupted by the power they exercise, the power will both attract and form men of a different stamp.

How can we benefit from the promise of government while avoiding the threat to freedom? Two broad principles embodied in our Constitution give an answer that has preserved our freedom so far, though they have been violated repeatedly in practice while proclaimed as precept.

First, the scope of government must be limited. Its major function must be to protect our freedom both from the enemies outside our gates and from our fellow-citizens: to preserve law and order, to enforce private contracts, to foster competitive markets. Beyond this major function, government may enable us at times to accomplish jointly what we would find it more difficult or expensive to accomplish severally. However, any such use of government is fraught with danger. We should not and cannot avoid using government in this way. But there should be a clear and large balance of advantages before we do. By relying primarily on voluntary co-operation and private enterprise, in both economic and other activities, we can insure that the private sector is a check on the powers of the governmental sector and an effective protection of freedom of speech, of religion, and of thought.

The second broad principle is that government power must be dispersed. If government is to exercise power, better in the county than in the state, better in the state than in Washington. If I do not like what my local community does, be it in sewage disposal, or zoning, or schools, I can move to another local community, and though few may take this step, the mere possibility acts as a check. If I do not like what my state does, I can move to another. If I do not like what Washington imposes, I have few alternatives in this world of jealous nations.

# The Facts of American Capitalism: The Private Sector

chapter 7

This and the next chapter are designed to put meat on our bare-boned model of mixed capitalism. We have discussed the three major aggregates of mixed capitalism—business, households, and government—on a very general and somewhat abstract basis. We must now add color to our crude sketch by painting in the factual characteristics of these transactors as they function in our American brand of mixed capitalism. In short, we must breathe reality into our abstract model by adding "the facts" of American economic life. The present chapter contributes factual information pertinent to the *private sector,* that is, households and businesses. The following chapter does the same for the governmental, or *public, sector.*

## ☐ HOUSEHOLDS AS INCOME RECEIVERS

The household sector of American capitalism is currently composed of some 82 million households. These households play a dual role: They are the ultimate suppliers of all economic resources and simultaneously the major spending group in the economy. Hence, we shall consider households first as income receivers and second as spenders.

There are two related approaches to studying the facts of income distribution.

**1** The *functional distribution* of income is concerned with the manner in which society's money income is divided among wages, rents, interest, and profits. Here total income is distributed according to the function performed by the income receiver. Wages are paid to labor, rents and interest compensate property resources, and profits flow to the owners of corporations and unincorporated businesses.

**2** The *personal distribution* of income has to do with the way in which the total money income of society is apportioned among individual households. A basic understanding of both the functional and the personal distribution of income is essential to understanding the role of households in American capitalism.

## △  Functional Distribution of Income

The distributive shares of the national income for 1979 were as shown in Table 7-1.

Clearly the largest source of income for households are the wages and salaries paid to workers by the businesses and governmental units hiring them. Proprietors' income—that is, the incomes of doctors, lawyers, small business owners, farmers, and other unincorporated enterprises—is in fact a combination of wage, profit, rent, and interest incomes. Corporate profits are virtually self-defining; these are the earnings of incorporated businesses. Interest and rent have constituted relatively small shares of total income over an extended period. The reader might consult the section on income shares at the end of Chapter 32 to gain some insight as to how and why these functional shares have changed historically.

Perhaps the remarkable thing about the functional distribution of income in our capitalistic system is that the bulk of the national income goes to labor and not to "capital." If we make the reasonable estimate that about two-thirds of proprietors' income is, in fact, wages and salaries and the remainder is capitalist income, we find that approximately four-fifths of total income is received by labor resources and only about one-fifth as capitalist (profit, rent, and interest) incomes.

**TABLE 7-1**
**The Sources of Income, 1979**

|  | Billions of dollars | Percent of total |
|---|---|---|
| Wages and salaries . . . . . . | $1459 | 76 |
| Proprietors' income . . . . . . | 130 | 7 |
| Corporate profits. . . . . . . . | 178 | 9 |
| Interest . . . . . . . . . . . . . | 129 | 7 |
| Rents . . . . . . . . . . . . . . . | 27 | 1 |
| Total income . . . . . . . . | $1923 | 100 |

*Source:* U.S. Department of Commerce, *Survey of Current Business,* March 1980. Details may not add to totals because of rounding.

## △  Personal Distribution of Income

A quick glance ahead at Table 37-1 will reveal that there is considerable inequality in the distribution of income among individual households. But we defer examination of empirical details and policy issues relevant to the personal distribution of income until Chapter 37 to concentrate on this question: Why is the personal distribution of money income—the way income is apportioned among households—important in understanding the operation of American capitalism? What impact does the distribution of money income among households have upon the operation of the economy? The answer is that the manner in which income is distributed among families affects both the *size* and the *composition* of output.

**1   Size of Output**   The personal distribution of income is a major determinant of how society divides its money income between consumption and saving. We will discover in Chapters 11 and 12 that this division is of utmost significance in determining the levels of output and employment in the economy. Consumption, being a form of spending, induces production and employment. Saving, defined by economists as that part of current income which is not consumed, does not account for production and employment. It follows that a distribution of income which results in a large volume of saving in relation to consumption *may* be conducive to low levels of production and employment. On the other hand, a distribution which entails a very small volume of saving in relation to consumption will promote high levels of production and employment.

**2   Composition of Output**   The personal distribution of money income goes a long way toward determining the pattern of consumer spending in the economy. A highly unequal distribution of income among individual households results in an expenditure pattern much different from that entailed in a more nearly equal distribution. Generally speaking, the more unequal the distribution of a given total money income, the greater will be the demand for, and the output of, luxury goods. Businesses, as we have seen, usually find it to their advantage to adjust their outputs to consumer demands. As a consequence, the economy's product-mix is largely geared to the composition of consumer expenditures. And in turn, the economy's product-mix obviously determines the manner in which scarce resources are allocated.

To repeat, the personal distribution of income has direct and significant consequences for the two major aspects of economics: (1) the level of resource use, and (2) the allocation of resources among alternative uses.

**Determinants** What determines the amount of money income received by an individual household in, say, a year? Common sense tells us that (1) the quantities of the various human and property resources which a household is able and willing to supply to businesses, (2) the prices which these resources command in the resource market, and (3) the actual level of employment of these resources are the immediate determinants of a household's money income. For the majority of American households, labor service is the only resource supplied. Thus by taking, for example, 2000 hours of labor service at a wage rate of $5 per hour, total money income for the year is found to be $10,000. But the third determinant poses a possible qualification: Though the household may be willing and able to supply 2000 hours of labor service per year, there is no guarantee that businesses will purchase this amount. If businesses are only able to use profitably 1500 of the hours offered, the workers' money income will obviously decline accordingly.

**Income and Productivity** In capitalistic economies, money income is roughly based upon the contribution which a household's

resources make to the total production of the economy. Households earn money incomes which are generally in accord with the value of their contributions to total output. If the resources in a household's possession are capable of efficiently producing goods which consumers want, the income earned will be high; if not, it will be low. The prices established by the forces of supply and demand in the resource market roughly gauge the relative worth or "productivity" of the various resources. If a business enterprise pays $8 an hour for unskilled labor and $16 an hour for highly skilled labor, it implies that the skilled labor is twice as productive as unskilled labor. If the market places a high value on the contributions of a resource to production, the supplying household receives a large income. If the market puts a low value on a resource's contribution, the supplying household's income tends to be low.

It is obvious that a distribution of income based upon productivity can result in considerable inequality. The quantity and quality of resources owned by various households and the prices they can command in the resource market can and do vary quite widely. Furthermore, the relationship between income and productivity is in fact only a very rough approximation. Some resource suppliers receive incomes substantially in excess of, and others receive incomes substantially less than, their productivity. Why is this so? Because monopolistic forces in both product and labor markets in the form of huge corporations and strong labor unions can distort prices so they do not accurately reflect productivity. Similarly, barriers to mobility—for example, discrimination on the basis of race and sex which arbitrarily keeps qualified blacks and women out of high-productivity–high-wage occupations—also distort the link between productivity and incomes. Hence, the personal distribution of income is actually more unequal than it would be if the economy were more competitive and discrimination because of race and sex did not exist.

**TABLE 7-2**

**The Disposition of Income, 1979**

|  | Billions of dollars | Percent of total |
|---|---|---|
| Personal taxes . . . . . . . . . | $ 300 | 15 |
| Personal consumption expenditures* . . . . . . . . . | 1550 | 81 |
| Personal saving . . . . . . . . . | 73 | 4 |
| Total income . . . . . . . . . | $1923 | 100 |

* Includes interest paid to businesses.

*Source:* U.S. Department of Commerce, *Survey of Current Business.*

## ☐ HOUSEHOLDS AS SPENDERS

How do households dispose of the income which they receive? In general terms, the answer is simple: A part is given to government in the form of personal taxes, and the remainder is divided between personal consumption expenditures and personal saving. Specifically, the way in which households disposed of their total income in 1979 is shown in Table 7-2.

### △ Personal Taxes

Personal taxes, of which the Federal personal income tax is the major component, have risen sharply in both absolute and relative terms since World War II. In 1941, households paid $3.3 billion, or about 3 percent of their $95.3 billion personal income, in personal taxes. In 1979, $300 billion, or about 15 percent of that year's $1,923 billion total income, flowed to government as personal taxes.

Economists define saving as "that part of after-tax income which is *not* consumed;" hence, households have just two choices with their incomes after taxes—to consume or to save.

### △ Personal Saving

Let us first consider the saving component of after-tax income. Saving is defined as that portion of current (this year's) income which is not paid out in taxes or in the purchase of consumer goods, but rather, flows into bank accounts, insurance policies, bonds and stocks, and other financial assets.

Why do households want to save? After all, it is ultimately goods and services which satisfy consumer wants, not the pieces of paper which we call checkbooks, savings account books, certificates of deposit, and bonds. The reasons for saving are many and diverse, but they center around *security* and *speculation.* Households save to provide a nest egg for unforeseen contingencies—sickness, accident, unemployment—for retirement from the work force, or simply for the overall financial security of one's family. On the other hand, saving might well occur for speculation. One might channel a part of one's income to the purchase of securities, speculating as to increases in their monetary value.

The desire or willingness to save, however, is not enough. This willingness must be accompanied by the *ability* to save. And, as we shall discover later (Table 11-1), the ability to save depends basically upon the size of one's income. If income is very low, households may *dissave;* that is, they may consume in excess of their after-tax incomes. They manage to do this by borrowing and by digging into savings which they may have accumulated in years when their incomes were higher. However, both saving and consumption vary directly with income; as households get more income, they divide it between saving and consumption. Actually, the bulk of the personal saving that occurs in our economy is done by those households in the $50,000, $100,000, or higher income brackets. The top 10 percent of the income receivers account for most of the personal saving in our society.

### △ Personal Consumption Expenditures

Table 7-2 clearly suggests that the bulk of total income flows from income receivers back into the business sector of the economy as personal consumption expenditures.

Since the size and composition of the economy's total output depend to a very considerable extent upon the size and composition of the flow of consumer spending, it is imperative that we examine how households divide their expenditures among the various goods and services competing for their dollars. Consumer expenditures may be classified in several ways. For example, they may be divided into services and products; and products in turn may be subdivided on the basis of their durability. Thus the U.S. Department of Commerce classifies consumer spending as (1) expenditures on nondurables, (2) expenditures on durables, and (3) expenditures on services. If a product generally has an expected life of one year or more, it is called a *durable good;* if its life is less than one year, it is labeled *nondurable.* Automobiles, refrigerators, washing machines, television sets, and most furniture are good examples of consumer durables. Most food and clothing items are nondurables. *Services,* of course, refer to the services which lawyers, barbers, mechanics, and others provide to consumers.

This threefold breakdown, detailed in Table 7-3, is of considerable importance because it implies that a good many consumer outlays are discretionary or postponable. During prosperity, durable, or "hard," goods

are typically traded in or scrapped before they become utterly useless. This is ordinarily the case with automobiles and most major household appliances. But if a recession threatens or begins to materialize, consumers may forgo expenditures on durables, choosing to put up with an old model car and outdated household appliances. The desire to conserve dollars for the nondurable necessities of food and clothing may cause a radical shrinkage of expenditures on durables. Much the same is true of many services. True, one cannot postpone an operation for acute appendicitis. But education, dental work, and a wide variety of less pressing services can be deferred or, if necessary, forgone entirely. In brief, the durable goods and services segments of personal consumption expenditures are subject to considerably more variation over time than are expenditures on nondurables.

## ☐  THE BUSINESS POPULATION

Businesses constitute the second major aggregate of the private sector.

**TABLE 7-3**
**The Composition of Personal Consumption Expenditures, 1979***

| Types of consumption | Amount (billions of dollars) | | Percent of total |
|---|---|---|---|
| Durable goods | | $ 213 | 14 |
| Motor vehicles and parts | $ 91 | | 6 |
| Furniture and household equipment | 86 | | 6 |
| All others | 36 | | 2 |
| Nondurable goods | | 597 | 40 |
| Clothing and shoes | 100 | | 7 |
| Food | 302 | | 20 |
| Gasoline and oil | 65 | | 4 |
| Fuel oil and coal | 18 | | 1 |
| All others | 112 | | 8 |
| Services | | 700 | 46 |
| Household operations | 102 | | 7 |
| Housing | 241 | | 16 |
| Transportation | 59 | | 4 |
| Personal services, recreation, and others | 298 | | 19 |
| Personal consumption expenditures | | $1510 | 100 |

*Excludes interest paid to businesses.
*Source:* U.S. Department of Commerce, *Survey of Current Business.* Details may not add to totals because of rounding.

## △  Plants, Firms, and Industries

To avoid any possible confusion, we preface our discussion of the business population with some comments concerning terminology. In particular, one must distinguish among a plant, a firm, and an industry.

**1**  A *plant* is a physical establishment in the form of a factory, farm, mine, retail or wholesale store, or warehouse which performs one or more specific functions in the fabrication and distribution of goods and services.

**2**  A business *firm,* on the other hand, is the business organization which owns and operates these plants. Although most firms operate only one plant, many firms own and operate a number of plants. Multiplant firms may be "horizontal," "vertical," or "conglomerate" combinations. For example, without exception each of the large steel firms of our economy—United States Steel, Bethlehem Steel, Republic Steel, and the others—are *vertical combinations* of plants; each firm owns ore and coal mines, limestone quarries, coke ovens, blast furnaces, rolling mills, forge shops, foundries, and, in some cases, fabricating shops. The large chain stores in the retail field—for example, A&P, Kroger, Safeway, J. C. Penney—are *horizontal combinations* in that each plant is at the same stage of production. Other firms are *conglomerates; that is,* they comprise plants which operate across many different markets and industries. For example, International Telephone and Telegraph, apart from operations implied by its name, is involved through affiliated plants on a large-scale basis in such diverse fields as automobile rentals, hotels, baking products, educational materials, and insurance (Chapter 34).

**3**  An *industry* is a group of firms producing the same, or at least similar, products. Though an apparently uncomplicated concept, industries are usually difficult to identify in practice. For example, how are we to identify the automobile industry? The simplest answer is, "All firms producing automobiles." But automobiles are heterogeneous products.

While Cadillacs and Buicks are similar products, and Buicks and Fords are similar, and Fords and Chevettes are similar, it is clear that Chevettes and Cadillacs are very dissimilar. At least most buyers think so. And what about trucks? Certainly, small pickup trucks are similar in some respects to station wagons. Is it better to speak of the "motor vehicle industry" rather than of the "automobile industry"? This matter of delineating an industry becomes all the more complex when it is recognized that most enterprises are multiproduct firms. American automobile manufacturers are also responsible for such diverse products as diesel locomotives, buses, refrigerators, guided missiles, and air conditioners. We pose these questions, not with a view to resolving them, but merely to note that industry classifications are rarely clear-cut and always somewhat arbitrary.

## ☐  LEGAL FORMS OF BUSINESS ENTERPRISES

The business population is extremely diverse, ranging from giant corporations like Exxon with 1979 sales of $79 billion and 169,000 employees to neighborhood specialty shops and "mom and pop" groceries with one or two employees and sales of only $100 or $150 per day. This diversity makes it desirable to classify business firms by some criterion such as legal structure, industry or product, or size. Table

**TABLE 7-4**

**The Business Population By Form of Legal Organization**

| Form | Number of firms | Percent of total |
|------|-----------------|------------------|
| Sole proprietorships* | 11,358,000 | 78 |
| Partnerships | 1,096,000 | 8 |
| Corporations | 2,105,000 | 14 |
| Total | 14,559,000 | 100 |

*Includes farmers and professional people in business for themselves.
*Source: Statistical Abstract of the United States.* Data are for 1976.

7-4 shows how the business population is distributed among the three major legal forms: (1) the sole proprietorship, (2) the partnership, and (3) the corporation. Let us define and outline the advantages and disadvantages associated with each.

△  **Sole Proprietorship**

A sole proprietorship is literally an individual in business for himself or herself. The proprietor owns or obtains the materials and capital equipment used in the operation of the business and personally supervises its operation. Responsibility for the efficient coordination of the resources owned or commanded rests directly upon the proprietor's shoulders.

**Advantages**   Obviously, this extremely simple type of business organization has certain distinct advantages:

**1**  A sole proprietorship is very easy to organize—there is virtually no legal red tape or expense.

**2**  The proprietor is his or her own boss and has very substantial freedom of action. Since the proprietor's profit income depends upon the enterprise's success, there is a strong and immediate incentive to manage the affairs of the business wisely.

**Disadvantages**   But the disadvantages of this form of business organization are great:

**1**  With rare exceptions, the financial resources of a sole proprietorship are insufficient to permit the firm to grow into a large-scale enterprise. Specifically, finances are usually limited to what the proprietor has in his or her bank account and to what he or she is able to borrow. Since the mortality rate is relatively great for proprietorships, commercial banks are not overly eager to extend much credit to them.

**2**  Being in complete control of an enterprise forces the proprietor to carry out all basic management functions. A proprietor must make all basic decisions concerning, for example, buying, selling, and the acquisition and maintenance of personnel, not to mention the technical aspects which might be involved in producing, advertising, and distributing the product. In short, the potential benefits of specialization in business management are usually inaccessible to the typical small-scale proprietorship.

**3**  Most important of all, the proprietor is subject to *unlimited liability.* This means that individuals in business for themselves risk not only the assets of the firm but also their personal assets. Should the assets of an unsuccessful proprietorship be insufficient to satisfy the claims of creditors, those creditors can file claims against the proprietor's personal property. The stakes are high insofar as individual proprietorships are concerned.

△  **Partnership**

The partnership form of business organization is more or less a natural outgrowth of the sole proprietorship. As a matter of fact, partnerships were developed in an attempt to overcome some of the major shortcomings of proprietorships. A partnership is almost self-defining. It is a form of business organization wherein two or more individuals agree to own and operate a business. Usually they pool their financial resources and their business acumen. Similarly, they share the risks and the profits or losses which may accrue to them. There are innumerable variations. In some cases, all partners are active in the functioning of the enterprise; in others, one or more partners may be "silent"—that is, they contribute their finances but do not actively participate in the management of the firm.

**Advantages**   What are the advantages of a partnership arrangement?

**1**  Like the sole proprietorship, it is easy to organize. Although a written agreement is almost invariably involved, legal red tape is not great.

**2**  Greater specialization in management is made possible, because there are more participants.

**3** Again, because there are several participants, the odds are that the financial resources of a partnership will be less limited than those of a sole proprietorship. Partners can pool their money capital and are usually somewhat better risks in the eyes of bankers.

**Disadvantages** The partnership often does less to overcome the shortcomings of the proprietorship than first appears and, indeed, raises some new potential problems which the sole proprietorship does not entail.

**1** Whenever there are several people participating in management, this division of authority can lead to inconsistent, divided policies or to inaction when action is required. Worse yet, partners may flatly disagree on basic policy. For all these reasons, management in a partnership may be very unwieldy and cumbersome.

**2** The finances of partnerships are still limited, although generally superior to those of a sole proprietorship. The financial resources of three or four partners may be such as to restrict severely the potential growth of a successful enterprise.

**3** The continuity of a partnership is very precarious. The withdrawal or death of a partner generally entails the dissolution and complete reorganization of the firm, severely disrupting its operations.

**4** Finally, unlimited liability plagues a partnership, just as it does a proprietorship. In fact, each partner is liable for all business debts incurred, not only as a result of each partner's own management decisions, but also as a consequence of the actions of any other partner. A wealthy partner risks money on the prudence of less affluent partners.

△ **Corporation**

Corporations are legal entities, distinct and separate from the individuals who own them. As such, these governmentally designated "legal persons" can acquire resources, own assets, produce and sell products, incur debts, extend credit, sue and be sued, and carry on all those functions which any other type of enterprise performs.

**Advantages** The advantages of the corporate form of business enterprise have catapulted this type of firm into a dominant position in modern American capitalism. Although corporations are relatively small in numbers (Table 7-4), they are frequently large in size and scale of operations. In fact, they account for about two-thirds of the output of all private businesses.

**1** The corporation is by far the most effective form of business organization for raising money capital. The corporation features new methods of finance—the selling of stocks and bonds—which allow the firm to tap the savings of untold thousands of households. Through the securities market, corporations can pool the financial resources of extremely large numbers of people. Financing by the sale of securities also has decided advantages from the viewpoint of the purchasers of these securities. First, households can now participate in enterprise and share the expected monetary reward therefrom without having to assume an active part in management. And, in addition, an individual can spread any risks by buying the securities of a variety of corporations. Finally, it is usually easy for the holder of corporate securities to dispose of these holdings. Organized stock exchanges facilitate the transfer of securities among buyers and sellers. Needless to say, this increases the willingness of savers to buy corporate securities. Furthermore, corporations ordinarily have easier access to bank credit than do other types of business organization. This is the case not only because corporations are better risks but also because they are more likely to provide banks with profitable accounts.

**2** Corporations have the distinct advantage of *limited liability*. The owners (stockholders) of a corporation risk only what they paid for the stock purchased. Their personal assets are not at stake if the corporation founders on the rocks of bankruptcy. Creditors can sue the corporation as a legal person, but not the owners of that corporation as individuals. Limited liability eases the corporation's task in acquiring money capital.

**3** As a legal entity, the corporation has a life independent of its owners and, for that matter, of its individual officials. Proprietorships are subject to sudden and unpredictable demise, but, legally at least, corporations are immortal. The transfer of corporate ownership through the sale of stock will not disrupt the continuity of the corporation. In short, corporations have a certain permanence, lacking in other forms of business organization, which is conducive to long-range planning and growth.

**4** Corporations, because of their strategic position in acquiring money capital, typically have the ability to obtain more specialized, and therefore more efficient, management than can proprietorships and partnerships.

**5** Last but not least is the possible tax advantage which incorporation may give for an enterprise whose net profits are sizable. As we shall find in Chapter 8, the maximum 46 percent marginal tax rate facing a corporation is preferable to the maximum 70 percent marginal rate of the personal income tax.

**Disadvantages** The corporation's advantages are of tremendous significance and typically override any accompanying disadvantages. Yet the drawbacks of the corporate form of organization merit mentioning.

**1** There are some red tape and legal expense in obtaining a corporate charter.

**2** From the social point of view, it must be noted that the corporate form of enterprise lends itself to certain abuses. Because the corporation is a legal entity, unscrupulous business owners sometimes can avoid personal responsibility for questionable business activities by adopting the corporate form of enterprise. And, despite legislation to the contrary, the corporate form of organization has been a cornerstone for the issue and sale of worthless securities. Note, however, that these are potential abuses of the corporate form, not inherent defects.

**3** A further possible disadvantage of corporations has to do with the taxation of corporate income. Briefly, there is a problem of *double taxation;* that part of corporate income which is paid out as dividends to stockholders is taxed twice—once as a part of corporate profits and again as a part of the stockholders' personal incomes. This disadvantage must be weighed against the previously noted fact that the maximum tax rates on corporate enterprises are less than those which may apply to unincorporated firms.

**4** In the sole proprietorship and partnership forms, those who own the real and financial assets of the firm also directly manage or control those assets.[1] Most observers agree that this is as it should be. But, in larger corporations where the ownership of common stock is widely diffused over tens or hundreds of thousands of stockholders, a fundamental cleavage between ownership and control will arise. The roots of this cleavage lie in the lethargy of the typical stockholder. Most stockholders simply do not exercise their voting rights or, if they do, merely sign these rights over by proxy to the corporation's present officers. And why not? Average stockholders know little or nothing about the efficiency with which "their" corporation is being managed. Because the typical stockholder may own only 1000 of 15,000,000 shares of common stock outstanding, one vote "really doesn't make a bit of difference"! Not voting, or the automatic signing over of one's proxy to current corporate officials, has the effect of making those officials self-perpetuating.

The separation of ownership and control is of no fundamental consequence so long as the actions of the control (management) group and the wishes of the ownership (stockholder) group are in accord. The catch lies in the fact that the interests of the two groups are not always identical. For example, management, seeking the power and prestige which accompanies control over a *large* enterprise, may favor unprofitable expansion of the firm's op-

---

[1]The silent-partner arrangement is the exception.

erations.  Or a conflict of interest can easily develop with respect to current dividend policies.  What portion of corporate earnings after taxes should be paid out as dividends, and what amount should be retained by the firm as undistributed profits?  More obviously, corporation officials may vote themselves large salaries, pensions, bonuses, and so forth, out of corporate earnings which might otherwise be used for increased dividend payments.  In short, the separation of ownership and control raises important and intriguing questions about the distribution of power and authority, the accountability of corporate managers, and the possibility of intramural conflicts between managers and shareholders.

△   **Incorporate or Not?**

What determines whether or not a firm incorporates?  As our discussion of the corporate form implies, the need for money capital is a critical determinant.  The money capital required to establish and operate a barbershop, a shoe-shine stand, or a small gift shop is mod-

est, making incorporation unnecessary.  In contrast, modern technology and a much larger dollar volume of business make incorporation imperative in many lines of production.  For example, in most branches of manufacturing—automobiles, steel, fabricated metal products, electrical equipment, household appliances, and so forth—very substantial money requirements for investment in fixed assets and for working capital are involved.  Given these circumstances, there is no choice but to incorporate.  To exist is to incorporate.

☐   **INDUSTRIAL DISTRIBUTION AND BIGNESS**

What do the 14.5 million firms which compose the business sector of our economy produce?  Table 7-5 measures in several different ways the significance of the various industry classifications.  Column 2 indicates the numerical and percentage distribution of the business population among the various industries.  Column 3 shows in both absolute and relative terms the portion of the national income origi-

**TABLE 7-5**
Industry Classes: Number of Firms, National Income Originating, and Employment Provided*

| (1) Industry | (2) Number of private businesses | | (3) Contribution to national income | | (4) Full-time workers employed | |
|---|---|---|---|---|---|---|
| | Thousands | Percent | Billions | Percent | Thousands | Percent |
| Agriculture, forestry, and fisheries | 3,653 | 25 | $  66.6 | 3 | 1,486 | 2 |
| Mining | 93 | 1 | 55.1 | 3 | 858 | 1 |
| Construction | 1,221 | 8 | 95.3 | 4 . | 4,048 | 5 |
| Manufacturing | 468 | 3 | 509.1 | 24 | 19,995 | 24 |
| Wholesale and retail trade | 3,123 | 22 | 360.5 | 17 | 16,672 | 20 |
| Finance, insurance, and real estate | 1,688 | 12 | 298.7 | 14 | 4,445 | 5 |
| Transportation, communications, and public utilities | 444 | 3 | 190.8 | 9 | 4,692 | 6 |
| Services | 3,833 | 26 | 268.7 | 13 | 15,109 | 18 |
| Government | | | 258.9 | 12 | 15,820 } | 19 |
| Rest of world | | | 20.5 | 1 | | |
| Total | 14,523 | 100 | $2127.6 | 100 | 83,125 | 100 |

*Column 2 is for 1976; 3 for 1978; and 4 for 1978.
*Source: Statistical Abstract of the United States, 1979*, pages 442, 553, and *Survey of Current Business*.

nating in the various industries. Column 4 indicates the absolute and relative amounts of employment provided by each industry. Several points in Table 7-5 are noteworthy:

**1** The wholesale and retail industries and the service industries (hotels, motels, personal services, and so forth) are heavily populated with firms and are simultaneously very important sources of employment and incomes in the economy.

**2** A large number of firms are engaged in agriculture, but agriculture is relatively insignificant as a provider of incomes and jobs. This implies that agriculture is comprised of a large number of small, competitive producers (Chapter 35).

**3** Table 7-5 reminds us that not all the economy's income and employment originate in private domestic enterprises. Government and foreign enterprises account for about 13 percent of the economy's national income and employ about 19 percent of the labor force.

**4** The relatively small number of firms in manufacturing account for about one-fourth of national income and total employment. These figures correctly suggest that the American capitalist economy is highly industrialized, characterized by gigantic business corporations in its manufacturing industries. This point merits brief elaboration.

To what degree does big business prevail in our economy? Casual evidence suggests that many of our major industries are dominated by corporate giants which enjoy assets and annual sales revenues calculated in billions of dollars, employ hundreds of thousands of workers, have a hundred thousand or more stockholders, and earn annual profits after taxes running into hundreds of millions of dollars. We have already cited the vital statistics of Exxon, America's largest corporation, for 1979: sales, about $79 *billion;* assets, about $49 *billion;* employees, about 169,000. Remarkably, there are only 18 or 20 nations in the world with annual national outputs in excess of Exxon's annual sales!

In 1979 some 173 industrial corporations enjoyed annual sales of over $2 billion; a total of 285 industrial firms realized sales in excess of $1 billion. By comparison, only 25 state governments had revenues in excess of $2 billion in the same year. More generally, the fact that corporations, constituting only 14 percent of the business population, produce two-thirds of total business output hints at the dominant role of large corporations in our economy.

But the dominance of giant corporations varies significantly from industry to industry. Big business dominates manufacturing and is pronounced in the transportation, communications, power utilities, and banking and financial industries. At the other extreme are some 3 million farmers whose total sales are less than the economy's four largest industrial corporations! In between are a wide variety of retail and service industries wherein relatively small firms are characteristic.[2] More specifically, a look ahead at Table 28-1 reveals a list of industries wherein economic concentration is quite modest. Table 29-1, on the other hand, indicates a number of very basic manufacturing industries wherein economic power is highly concentrated.

**TABLE 7-6**
**Share of Manufacturing Assets Held by the 100 Largest and 200 Largest Corporations**

| Year | Share of 100 largest corporations | Share of 200 largest corporations |
|------|-----------------------------------|-----------------------------------|
| 1929 | 38.2% | 45.8% |
| 1941 | 38.2 | 45.1 |
| 1950 | 38.4 | 46.1 |
| 1955 | 43.0 | 51.6 |
| 1960 | 45.5 | 55.2 |
| 1965 | 45.9 | 55.9 |
| 1968 | 48.8 | 60.4 |
| 1974 | 44.4 | 56.7 |
| 1978 | 45.5 | 58.3 |

*Source:* Senate Subcommittee on Antitrust and Monopoly, *Economic Concentration,* part 8a (Washington, 1969), p. 173, and *Statistical Abstract of the United States.*

[2] See John Kenneth Galbraith, *Economics and the Public Purpose* (New York: New American Library, 1973), pp. 42–43.

Historical data on the concentration of economic power do not reveal an unambiguous trend. For example, we note in Table 7-6 that the share of manufacturing assets held by the 100 largest manufacturing firms rose from about 38 percent in 1929 to 46 percent in 1978. In fact, today the 100 largest firms hold about the same share of total manufacturing assets as the 200 largest firms did some forty-five years ago. Observe, however, that concentration seems to have diminished in the 1968–1978 period. It should be emphasized that economists debate the meaning and relevance of these and similar data to the issue of concen-tration; some highly respected economists believe that concentration has not been in-creasing or, if it has, the increase has been "at the pace of a glacial drift." It is generally agreed that the American economy is highly concentrated and that this concentration will persist.

We shall consider the economic issues posed by big businesses in Chapters 27, 29, and 34. Let it suffice to say at this point that large corporations do dominate the American busi-ness landscape and reasonable grounds do exist for labeling the United States a "big business" economy.

## Summary

**1** The functional distribution of income shows how society's total income is divided among wages, rents, interest, and profits; the personal distribution of income shows how total income is divided among individual households. The distribution of income is an important determinant of the level and composition of total output.

**2** Households divide their total incomes among personal taxes, saving, and consumer goods. Consumer expenditures on durables and some services are discretionary and there-fore postponable.

**3** Sole proprietorships, partnerships, and corporations are the major legal forms which business enterprises may assume. Though proprietorships dominate numerically, the bulk of total output is produced by corporations. Corporations have grown to their position of dominance in the business sector primarily because they are **a.** characterized by limited liability, and **b.** in a superior position to acquire money capital for expansion.

**4** Manufacturing accounts for a larger percentage of national income and employment in American capitalism than does any other industrial classification. The wholesale, retail, and service industries are also major sources of income and employment.

**5** Ours is a "big business" economy in the sense that many industries are dominated by a small number of large corporations.

## Questions and Study Suggestions

**1** Key terms and concepts to remember: functional and personal distribution of income; durable and nondurable goods; horizontal and vertical combinations; conglomerates; sole proprietorship; partnership; corporation; limited liability; separation of ownership and control.

**2** What implications does the personal distribution of income have for the size and composition of the economy's total output? For resource allocation? Explain.

**3** What happens to the volumes of consumption and saving as disposable income rises? What is "dissaving"? When is dissaving most likely to occur?

**4** Why is the demand for consumer durable goods less stable than that for nondurables?

**5**  Distinguish clearly between a plant, a firm, and an industry. Why is an "industry" often difficult to define in practice?

**6**  What are the major legal forms of business organization? Briefly state the advantages and disadvantages of each. How do you account for the dominant role of corporations in our economy?

**7**  Explain and evaluate the separation of ownership and control which characterizes the corporate form of business enterprise.

**8**  What are the major industries in American capitalism in terms of *a.* the number of firms in operation, and *b.* the amount of income and employment provided?

**9**  Explain and evaluate the following statements:

*a.*  "It is the consumer, and the consumer alone, who casts the vote that determines how big any company should be."

*b.*  "The very nature of modern industrial society requires labor, government, and businesses to be 'big' and their bigness renders impossible the functioning of the older, small-scale, simpler, and more flexible capitalist system."[3]

*c.*  "The legal form which an enterprise assumes is dictated primarily by the financial requirements of its particular line of production."

*d.*  "If we want capitalism, we must also accept inequality of income distribution."

## Selected References

Baratz, Morton S.: *The American Business System in Transition* (New York: Thomas Y. Crowell Company, 1970).

Boulding, Kenneth E.: *Economic Analysis: Microeconomics,* 4th ed. (New York: Harper & Row, Publishers, Incorporated, 1966), chaps. 15, 16.

Cheit, Earl F. (ed.): *The Business Establishment* (New York: John Wiley & Sons, Inc., 1964).

Davis, Keith, William C. Frederick, and Robert L. Blomstrom: *Business and Society,* 4th ed. (New York: McGraw-Hill Book Company, 1980).

Green, Mark, and Robert Massie, Jr. (eds.): *The Big Business Reader* (New York: The Pilgrim Press, 1980).

Reid, Samuel Richardson: *The New Industrial Order* (New York: McGraw-Hill Book Company, 1976), introduction and part 1.

Steiner, George A., and John F. Steiner (eds.): *Issues in Business and Society,* 2d ed. (New York: Random House, 1977).

Swagler, Roger M.: *Caveat Emptor!* (Lexington, Mass.: D. C. Heath and Company, 1975).

Trebing, Harry M. (ed.): *The Corporation in the American Economy* (Chicago: Quadrangle Books, Inc., 1970).

[3] Eugene O. Golob, *The Isms* (New York: Harper & Row, Publishers, Incorporated, 1954), p. 53.

# LAST WORD
# Big Corporations:
# The View from West Virginia

Big business—good or bad? Here a coal miner sets forth his views on the impact of large coal corporations on life in his state.

I, and other citizens I have talked with from West Virginia, indict the big corporations which have come into our State and have virtually destroyed its beauty and the dignity of its people. I have learned the hard way that these corporations do not worry or care about treating people fairly. They take millions of dollars worth of coal, timber, and gas out of the State and leave nothing in return except barren mountains, bad roads, polluted streams, and people who have been robbed of their birthright.

The people of West Virginia are determined to use whatever means they can to stop this and to see that a fair share of the extracted wealth is left in the State. Up to the present time, all we have been getting is the refuse. Our State is being used as a garbage dump for out-of-State interests who could not care less for the State or its people. These big corporations make coal a curse rather than an asset to the State. As they operate now, West Virginia would be better off if coal had never been discovered there.

Following are some of the ways in which these corporations are destroying West Virginia:

**1.** Destruction of the environment. Land is stripped that is impossible to reclaim. Steep mountains are stripped of timber and coal with no regard as to where they are located in relation to people's homes, private property, and streams. Thus, homes are destroyed, streams are polluted, and mountainsides are eroded, causing slides and floods.

**2.** Cutting down the job market. These corporations feel no obligation to the people. Their sole purpose is to make money. The first way they think of is to cut down on jobs and keep production high. They do this through mechanization. They are willing to spend large sums of money on upkeep and repairs, but they never feel obligated to make more money by employing more people.

**3.** The use of discriminatory practices. The companies would hire white workers who lived 50 to 60 miles away in order not to hire local black workers. This has happened in some instances that I know of personally. My own father was denied a job because of this practice.

**4.** Unfair labor practices. In some instances, local people are hired, but the main work force usually lives in other communities some distance away or even in other States. This cuts down on union activity by keeping the men apart.

**5.** Absentee land ownership. The corporations buy up the land and the mineral rights and hold it in reserve. They will not sell it for homesites, and they do not let others develop it. They also pay very low taxes on it. If this land could be obtained by other people, perhaps small local industries could be started and developed, thus helping the economic development of the area.

**6.** They tend to control agencies. I have known mines that were unsafe and whenever the mine inspectors would come around they would be notified beforehand so they could get things seemingly safe for one day and when they did not get them safe, the mining inspector would not go inside but certify the mine as being safe anyway. They would cause people to not receive unemployment compensation by saying there was work available when there was not. They try to stop pensions connected with the coal industry such as black lung, social security, and miner's welfare, and workmen's compensation. They conspire to shut down small businesses. With their money and power they make a joke of the free enterprise system. They finance political campaigns, and in a lot of instances get their own people elected to office.

I know that the beauty of bygone days is lost forever, but I feel that there is something still left to salvage. Therefore, I ask that the plunder and pillage of large corporations stop now.

From *Controls or Competition,* Hearings before the Subcommittee on Antitrust and Monopoly of the Committee on the Judiciary, 92d Congress, 1st Session, Washington, 1972, pp. 143–144.

# The Facts of American Capitalism: The Public Sector

# chapter 8

The basic goal of this chapter is to get acquainted with some factual aspects of the public sector. Specifically, what kinds of taxes are used by Federal, state, and local governments? For what purposes and programs are their tax revenues disbursed? Persistent controversy surrounding the scope of government's economic role makes it particularly important that the facts of government be clearly understood and placed in proper perspective. Two points must be made at the outset.

**1** It is with the public sector's role as a receiver and disposer of "income" that this chapter is concerned. While it is through taxation and expenditures that government's impact upon the economy is most directly felt, there are many other ways in which government affects economic life (Chapter 6). For example, government's regulatory activities have increased very significantly in the past two decades (Chapter 34). These activities entail many important implications for output,

employment, productivity, the price level, and resource allocation which go far beyond those measured by the tax collections and expenditures involved in the financing of regulatory agencies. In short, a mere examination of public spending and tax revenues does not yield an accurate impression of the economic significance of the public sector.

**2** There is a significant difference between the transactions of the private and public sectors of the economy: The former are *voluntary,* and the latter *compulsory.* The receipts and expenditures of households and businesses are the result of voluntary decisions by those two aggregates in buying and selling goods and resources. Government tax revenues are the result of compulsory levies: households and businesses have no choice but to pay taxes. To a lesser degree, this compulsion appears on the expenditure side of government's transactions. While no one is compelled to use governmentally provided highways, libraries, or health clinics, all physically and mentally capable children who are within stated age brackets must consume public education or its equivalent.

## □  PUBLIC SECTOR GROWTH

By any reasonable measure, the public sector's role in the economy has expanded both *absolutely* and *relatively.* Figure 8-1 portrays the absolute increases in government spending since 1929. In relative terms, government expenditures claimed only 8 percent of total output in 1929; by 1979 government spending was about 21 percent of national output!

As with the business and household sectors of the economy, the receipt and the expenditure of government income need not match in any particular year or period of years. Surpluses and deficits—the latter in particular—are not at all uncommon insofar as public finance is concerned. Nevertheless, with the exception of large-scale deficit financing during World War II, a graph of government tax collections would rather closely follow the trend of spending shown in Figure 8-1. In 1978, public spending was financed by an average tax bill of $2594 presented to every man, woman, and child in the United States. Or, from a slightly different vantage point, in 1980 the average taxpayer will spend 2 hours and 52 minutes of an 8-hour workday to pay taxes!

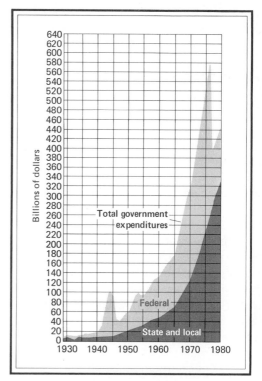

**FIGURE 8-1  FEDERAL, STATE, AND LOCAL EXPENDITURES, 1929-1979**

Government expenditures have grown both absolutely and as a percentage of total output. Hot and cold wars, population growth, urbanization, income maintenance programs, and inflation are some of the more important factors underlying this growth. Government tax collections have also increased significantly over time, roughly matching the increases in government spending. (*Economic Report of the President, 1979.*)

### △  Some Causes

Recall from Chapter 6 that the desire of the citizenry to correct or alleviate the instability, inefficiency, and inequities which the price system may foster provides a basic rationale for the public sector. Consider now an admittedly incomplete list of some specific factors which account for the spectacular growth of government spending and taxes.

**1   War and Defense**  Hot and cold wars have tended to sustain Federal expenditures at high levels for the past four decades. War, national defense, and military-space research are among the major causes of the phenomenal growth of government spending and taxation which has occurred since 1940. In 1979, expenditures for national defense were on the order of $118 billion.

**2   Population Growth**  The growth of population has been rapid; there are about twice as many Americans today as there were a scant sixty years ago. This obviously means there are more people for whom social goods and services must be provided. Stated differently, even with a constant level of government spending per person, total government spending would have increased dramatically in recent decades.

**3  Urbanization and the Demand for Social Goods**  Not only has the size of our population been an important factor underlying the growth of government, but so has the geographic location of the population. In particular, the increasing urbanization of our economy has necessitated massive expenditures on streets, public transportation facilities, police and fire protection, sewers, and so forth. Furthermore, the public has demanded more and better social goods and services to "match" the rising standard of living provided by the private sector of the economy. We want bigger and better highways to accommodate more and better automobiles. We seek more and better educational facilities to upgrade the labor force for the more demanding jobs of private industry.

**4  Environmental Quality**  Population growth and urbanization have contributed to serious and well-publicized problems of environmental quality. In particular, society has become highly aware that the production and consumption of vast quantities of goods can give rise to serious social or spillover costs in the form of air, water, and land pollution. Government has inherited a central role in coping with these environmental problems.

**5  Egalitarianism**  Since the mid-1960s there has occurred a sharp expansion of programs designed to alleviate poverty and reduce income inequality. Social security, unemployment compensation, welfare, Medicare, food stamps, and public housing are examples. These programs accounted for about 3 percent of national output twenty years ago; now they require over 10 percent.

**6  Inflation**  A rising price level accounts for a considerable portion of the historical rise in government spending. Because of inflation,

government has had to spend larger and larger amounts for given quantities of goods and services. Indeed, the prices of the goods and services purchased by government have increased more rapidly than have the prices of private consumer and investment goods.

△  **Purchases versus Transfers**

Going beyond the trend of government spending, we must also distinguish between two fundamentally different types of governmental outlays.

**Purchases**  *Government purchases* of goods and services are virtually self-defining. This concept refers to such ordinary governmental purchases as paper clips, typewriter ribbons, automobiles, and school buildings, as well as to such uniquely social goods as jet fighters, atomic submarines, superhighways, and space capsules. Purchases of services include the hiring of clerks, schoolteachers, judges, military personnel, and so forth. Government purchases are often called *exhaustive* in that they directly absorb or employ resources, and the resulting production contributes to the national output.

**Transfers**  *Transfer payments,* on the other hand, are disbursements for which government currently receives no products or services in return. Most government insurance and income-maintenance programs fall in this classification: for example, social security payments to the aged, unemployment compensation, welfare payments, and aid to the handicapped. Some transfer payments, called *subsidies,* go to businesses: for example, certain payments to farmers under our agricultural programs. Because transfer payments rechannel tax revenues back to households and businesses, these payments in effect are "negative taxes." Transfers are frequently labeled *nonexhaustive* because, as such, they do not directly absorb resources or account for production.

**A Distinction**   There is a noteworthy difference between transfer payments and government purchases of goods and services. Through government spending on goods, society tends to reallocate resources from private to social goods consumption. Through transfers, government changes the composition of the output of private goods. If government taxes amount to $10, we can expect purchases of private goods and services to decline by roughly that amount. In purchasing social goods and services with this $10 worth of tax revenue, individuals or groups within the economy, working through government, are in effect negotiating a substitution of social for private goods. Transfer payments are different: Instead of increasing social goods at the expense of private goods, transfers merely tend to "rearrange" private consumption. Though $10 in tax revenues will reduce the private goods consumption of taxpayers by about that amount, households to whom this $10 is transferred can be expected to increase their expenditures on private goods by about $10. But, in all probability, the recipients will purchase somewhat different goods from those bought by the taxpayers. Hence, transfers alter the composition of private goods production.

This distinction between government purchases and transfer payments is relevant for our discussion of the growth of government. One can argue that transfer payments involve a lesser degree of government intervention in the economy than do government purchases. Because transfers in recent years have been growing more rapidly than government purchases, Figure 8-1 may tend to overstate in a sense the expanding role of the public sector.

☐   **FEDERAL FINANCE**

Let us now disaggregate the public sector into Federal, state, and local units of government in order to compare the character of their expenditures and taxes. Table 8-1 tells the story for the Federal government.

△   **Federal Expenditures**

Although Table 8-1 reveals a wide variety of Federal expenditures, two important areas of spending stand out: *income security and health* and *national defense*. The first cate-

**TABLE 8-1**
**The Federal Budget, 1978**

| Tax receipts | Billions of dollars | Percent of total | Expenditures | Billions of dollars | Percent of total |
|---|---|---|---|---|---|
| Personal income tax . . . . .$181 | | 45 | Income security and health . . .$190 | | 42 |
| Payroll taxes . . . . . . . . . . 124 | | 31 | National defense . . . . . . . . . . 105 | | 23 |
| Corporate income taxes . . . 60 | | 15 | Veterans' benefits . . . . . . . . . . 19 | | 4 |
| Excise taxes . . . . . . . . . . . 18 | | 4 | Interest on public debt . . . . . . 44 | | 10 |
| Customs duties . . . . . . . . . 7 | | 2 | International affairs . . . . . . . . 6 | | 1 |
| Estate and gift taxes . . . . . 5 | | 1 | Science, space, and | | |
| All other . . . . . . . . . . . . 7 | | 2 | technology . . . . . . . . . . . . . 5 | | 1 |
| | | | Education, training, and | | |
| | | | social services . . . . . . . . . . 26 | | 6 |
| | | | Commerce and | | |
| | | | transportation . . . . . . . . . . 19 | | 4 |
| | | | Natural resources, | | |
| | | | environment, and energy . . . 16 | | 4 |
| | | | All other . . . . . . . . . . . . . . . 21 | | 5 |
| Total receipts . . . . . . .$402 | | 100 | Total expenditures . . . . . .$451 | | 100 |

*Source: Economic Report of the President.* Because of rounding, figures may not add up to totals. Data are estimates.

**TABLE 8-2**
A Progressive Personal Income Tax (*hypothetical data*)

| (1)<br>Total<br>taxable<br>income | (2)<br>Total<br>tax | (3)<br>Average<br>tax rate,<br>(2) ÷ (1) | (4)<br>Change in<br>income,<br>Δ(1) | (5)<br>Change<br>in taxes,<br>Δ(2) | (6)<br>Marginal<br>tax rate,<br>(5) ÷ (4) |
|---|---|---|---|---|---|
| $     1,000 | $        0 | 0% | | | |
| 3,000 | 150 | 5 | $    2,000 | $    150 | 7.5% |
| 6,000 | 600 | 10 | 3,000 | 450 | 15 |
| 10,000 | 1,500 | 15 | 4,000 | 900 | 22.5 |
| 20,000 | 5,000 | 25 | 10,000 | 3,500 | 35 |
| 50,000 | 20,000 | 40 | 30,000 | 15,000 | 50 |
| 100,000 | 50,000 | 50 | 50,000 | 30,000 | 60 |
| 500,000 | 300,000 | 60 | 400,000 | 250,000 | 62 |
| 1,000,000 | 650,000 | 65 | 500,000 | 350,000 | 70 |

gory reflects the myriad previously mentioned income-maintenance programs which assist the aged, the disabled, the unemployed, the handicapped, the medically indigent, families with no breadwinner, and so forth. The national defense category understates the economic costs of wars and military preparedness because the ensuing four classifications are closely associated with the military. *Veterans' services*—which include GI Bill payments, medical care, disability pay, and pensions to veterans and their dependents—obviously are expenditures associated with past wars. And, since a large portion of the Federal debt was incurred in financing past wars, a sizable portion of the annual payment of *interest on the public debt* also can be considered as a war-born outlay. Furthermore, *international affairs* involve expenditures for the economic and technological development of foreign countries and the costs of administering our foreign affairs. In part, these outlays stem from altruistic motives. But a selfish reason dominates: These expenditures are designed to keep foreign countries from turning to communism. Finally, outlays for *science and space research* clearly have important implications for national security. As a group, these five expenditure categories account for about $179 billion, or about 39 percent, of total Federal outlays. War and military preparedness

carry extremely high price tags. The remaining categories of spending listed in Table 8-1 are largely self-explanatory.

△   **Federal Receipts**

The receipts side of Table 8-1 makes it clear that the personal income tax, payroll taxes, and the corporate income tax are the basic Federal revenue getters, accounting for 45, 31, and 15 cents of each tax dollar collected.

**Personal Income Tax**   The personal income tax is the kingpin of our national tax system and it therefore deserves rather extended comment. This tax is levied on *taxable income,* that is, on the incomes of households and unincorporated businesses after certain exemptions and deductions have been taken into account.[1]

*Mechanics*   Table 8-2 gives us a general picture of the mechanics of the personal income tax. Although the figures are hypothetical, the actual tax rates shown correspond closely to those which now prevail. Column 2 shows the absolute amount of taxes which

---

[1]The major deductions and exemptions from gross income in determining taxable income are (1) business costs and expenses incurred in earning income, (2) gifts to charitable institutions, (3) interest payments, (4) certain state and local tax payments, and (5) a $1000 exemption for the taxpayer and each dependent.

must be paid at each income level shown in column 1. The *average tax rate* in column 3 is merely the total tax paid divided by taxable income. Thus, at a taxable income of $3000, the average tax rate is 5 percent (= $150 ÷ $3000); at $6000, it is 10 percent (= $600 ÷ $6000); and so on. By definition, any tax—such as our personal income tax— whose average tax *rate* increases as income increases is called a *progressive tax.*

The *marginal tax rate* is the tax rate paid on additional or incremental income. By definition, it is the *increase* in taxes paid as additional income is obtained divided by that increase in income. Columns 4 and 5 provide the data needed to calculate the marginal tax rate. Thus we observe that if a family's taxable income is $1000, it pays no taxes. But if its income rises to $3000, it will be required to pay $150 (column 5) on the $2000 increase in its income (column 4). The marginal tax rate is therefore 7.5 percent (= $150 ÷ $2000). On the next $3000 increment of taxable income which takes the family from the $3000 to the $6000 level, it must pay additional taxes of $450, so the marginal tax rate on this extra income is 15 percent (= $450 ÷ $3000). Note that as income increases, the marginal tax rate rises rather sharply. Indeed, it is the fact that each increment of income is taxed at a higher marginal tax rate which pulls up the average tax rate.[2] For the United States, the top marginal tax rate is 70 percent. This obviously means that you can never be made worse off by earning an extra dollar; at least 30 cents of it will be yours to keep.[3]

*Economic aspects*   The economic implications of the personal income tax merit brief comment. Recall from Chapter 6 that three basic functions of government are to provide social goods and services, redistribute income, and stabilize the economy. The personal income tax can be employed very effectively in pursuing these goals.

**1**   It is obviously capable of bringing in large amounts of revenue to finance social goods and services, as Table 8-1 clearly indicates. Indeed, the progressive tax rates make tax collections very responsive to the long-run growth of the national income.

**2**   The personal income tax obviously has considerable potential for redistributing income. Given its progressivity as revealed by Table 8-2, the tax contributes to greater income equality. But we must be cautious on this point: We shall find momentarily that a variety of tax loopholes have eroded the income tax base and that its progressivity is substantially less than the table suggests.

**3**   A final and less obvious point is that a progressive income tax can help to stabilize the economy. For example, during prosperity, money incomes rise and total demand tends to outrun productive capacity so that inflation occurs. The fact that income tax rates are progressive means that tax collections will rise at a more rapid rate than incomes. These rising tax collections have the effect of diverting income from the expenditures stream, thereby lessening inflationary pressures. Conversely, as the economy backslides into recession and total demand is inadequate to maintain full employment, tax collections decline at a more rapid rate than does income. This decrease tends to bolster the income-expenditures stream and to cushion the recession. In short, the *automatic* changes in tax collections which accompany a progressive income tax add an element of *built-in stability* to the economy (Chapter 13).

But a caveat is in order. During the 1970s we have encountered periods wherein unemployment and inflation have occurred simultaneously. Under these unfortunate conditions, the progressive income tax can have a destabilizing effect. Inflation pushes households into

[2]The theory is the same as one you may have encountered in school. You must get a score on an additional or "marginal" examination which is higher than your existing average grade in order to pull your average up!
[3]Maybe more! If all the family's income is "earned" income (from wages, salaries, and professional fees), the maximum marginal tax rate is 50 percent, rather than 70 percent.

higher tax brackets without increasing their real incomes and their higher tax payments come largely at the expense of consumer spending. This decline in spending contributes to more unemployment!

Despite these virtues, critics of the personal income tax contend that its high marginal tax rates may discourage incentives to work, invest, and assume risks. But it is difficult to determine whether these harmful effects have in fact occurred. Consider work. A rising marginal tax rate means a worker gets a smaller after-tax wage rate for each hour of work. Hence, because work is less and less rewarding, the worker may decide to work *fewer* hours. On the other hand, if he or she is motivated to earn a target income of, say, $15,000 per year, the progressive tax rates may spur a person to work *more* hours to achieve that income. The consensus of empirical studies on this matter is that the effect of income taxes on work habits is small.

**Payroll Taxes**   Social security contributions, or payroll taxes, are the premiums paid on the compulsory insurance plans, for example, old age insurance and Medicare, provided for by existing social security legislation. These taxes are paid by both employers and employees. Improvements in, and extensions of, our social security programs, plus growth of the labor force, have resulted in very significant increases in payroll taxes in recent years.

**Corporate Income Tax**   The corporate income tax has a relatively simple structure. The first $25,000 of taxable profits is taxed at 17 percent; the second $25,000 is taxed at 20 percent; and the third and fourth $25,000 increments of profits are taxed at 30 and 40 percent respectively. All taxable profits above $100,000 are taxed at 46 percent.

Recall from Chapter 7 that the corporate income tax entails a problem of "double taxation." That part of corporate income which is paid out as dividends is taxed twice. It is first taxed under the corporate income tax as de-

scribed in the last paragraph and it is taxed again as personal income to stockholders.

**Sales, Excise, and Other Taxes**   Commodity or consumption taxes may take the form of sales taxes or excise taxes. The difference between the two is basically one of coverage. Sales taxes fall on a wide range of products, whereas excises are taxes on a small, select list of commodities.

As Table 8-1 indicates, the Federal government collects excise taxes imposed upon such commodities as alcoholic beverages, tobacco, gasoline, and tires. However, the Federal government does *not* levy a general sales tax; sales taxes are the bread and butter of most state governments.

△ **Federal Tax Loopholes**

The progressive rates of the personal and corporate income taxes imply that the Federal tax system makes the distribution of income more nearly equal. But in fact, these taxes contain a number of important legal loopholes, that is, provisions which give favorable tax treatment to certain kinds of income. Because these loopholes generally favor high-income recipients, the after-tax distribution is less nearly equal than would otherwise be the case. In particular, the personal income tax in practice is significantly less progressive than Table 8-2 suggests. For example, Treasury Department data show that people falling in tax brackets where the average tax rate of Table 8-2 is, say, 40 or 50 percent, actually pay taxes at a rate of 30 or 35 percent.

Skirting technical details, let us briefly mention a few of the more important loopholes.

**1  Tax-exempt Securities**   Interest income on the bonds of state and local governments is exempt from the Federal income tax. Many high-income people can reduce their income tax liabilities very substantially by availing themselves of this loophole. For example, people in the highest personal income tax bracket can reduce the tax rate on their interest income from 70 to zero percent by switching from savings deposits or corporate bonds to state and local bonds.

**2  Capital Gains**  An individual realizes a capital gain when either securities or property are sold at a higher price than the person paid for them.  Provided the gain is long term, that is, that the securities or property have been held for a year or more, only 40 percent of the gain need be reported as taxable income.  Thus for an individual in, say, the 50 percent tax bracket, only 20 percent ($\frac{1}{2}$ of 40 percent) of any income from long-term capital gains will be taxed away.

**3  Other Tax Breaks**  A variety of other means exist by which the taxable portion of personal and corporate incomes can be reduced.  Homeowners—who increasingly are upper-income people—can deduct interest charges and property taxes in determining their taxable incomes.  By making deposits in certain retirement programs, high-income people can defer tax payments on those deposits until retirement when their incomes—and therefore their tax rates—will probably be lower.  Corporations currently enjoy an investment tax credit by which they can deduct 10 percent of their expenditures for capital

goods from their tax bills.  Business executives can receive compensation in several forms—for example, annuities and pension funds—which are not currently taxable.  Multinational corporations pay no taxes on the profits of their overseas subsidiaries until (and if) these profits are brought home to the United States.

The basic point to be emphasized is that these and other tax loopholes are means by which high-income people are able to reduce their tax liabilities.  The result is that the Federal personal and corporate income taxes are, in practice, much less effective in leveling incomes than might first appear.

☐  **STATE AND LOCAL FINANCE**
While the Federal government finances itself largely through personal and corporate income taxation and payroll taxes, state and local governments rely heavily upon sales and property taxes, respectively.  And although there is considerable overlapping in the types of expenditures made by the three levels of government, income security and national defense account for the majority of Federal expenditures, whereas education, highways, and public welfare lead at state and local levels.

△  **State Expenditures and Receipts**
Note in Table 8-3 that the basic sources of tax revenue at the state level are sales and

**TABLE 8-3**
**Consolidated Budget of All State Governments 1978**

| Tax receipts | Billions of dollars | Percent of total | Expenditures | Billions of dollars | Percent of total |
|---|---|---|---|---|---|
| Sales, excise, and gross receipts taxes | $ 58.3 | 51 | Education | $29.6 | 26 |
| Personal income taxes | 29.1 | 26 | Public welfare | 25.7 | 23 |
| Corporate income taxes | 10.7 | 9 | Highways | 14.7 | 13 |
| Property taxes | 2.4 | 2 | Health, hospitals | 13.5 | 12 |
| Death and gift taxes | 1.8 | 2 | Public safety | 6.4 | 6 |
| Licenses, permits, and others | 11.0 | 10 | All others | 22.6 | 20 |
| Total receipts | $113.3 | 100 | Total expenditures | $112.5 | 100 |

*Source:* Bureau of the Census, *State Government Finances in 1978*. Because of rounding, figures may not add up to totals.

excise taxes, which account for about 51 percent of all state tax revenues. State personal income taxes, which entail much more modest rates than those employed by the Federal government, run a poor second. Taxes on corporate income, property, inheritances, and a variety of licenses and permits constitute the remainder of state tax revenue. On the expenditure side of the picture, the major outlays of state governments are for (1) education, (2) public welfare, and (3) highway maintenance and construction.

It is important to note that the budget statement shown in Table 8-3 contains aggregated data and therefore tells us little about the finances of individual states. States vary tremendously in the types of taxes employed. Thus, although sales and personal income taxes are the major sources of revenue for all state governments combined, four states have no general sales tax and six do not use the personal income tax. Furthermore, great variations in the size of tax receipts and disbursements exist among the states.

△  **Local Expenditures and Receipts**

The receipts and expenditures shown in Table 8-4 are for all units of local government, including counties, municipalities, townships, and school districts. One major source of revenue and a single basic use of revenue stand out:

The bulk of the revenue received by local government comes from property taxation; the bulk of local revenue is spent for education. Other, less important sources of funds and types of disbursements are self-explanatory.

The gaping deficit shown in Table 8-4 is largely removed when nontax resources of income are taken into account: In 1978 the tax revenues of local governments were supplemented by some $84 billion in intergovernmental grants from Federal and state governments. Furthermore, local governments received an additional $17 billion as proprietary income, that is, as revenue from government-owned liquor stores and utilities.

☐  **REVENUE SHARING**

A fiscal mismatch has evolved in recent years between the Federal government, on the one hand, and state and local governments, on the other. Federal tax revenues, derived heavily from personal and corporate income taxes, are very sensitive to changes in the economy. As growth increases the national income, sizable increases in Federal tax revenues automatically occur. State and local tax revenues, based primarily on sales and property taxes, are less responsive to growth. At the same time, population growth and urbanization have necessitated substantial increases in state

**TABLE 8-4**
Consolidated Budget of All Local Governments, 1978

| Tax receipts | Billions of dollars | Percent of total | Expenditures | Billions of dollars | Percent of total |
|---|---|---|---|---|---|
| Property taxes . . . . . . . . . . . . | $64.1 | 80 | Education . . . . . . . . . . . . . | $81.2 | 44 |
| Sales and excises. . . . . . . . . . . | 9.3 | 11 | Police, fire, and general | | |
| Personal income taxes . . . . . . . | 4.1 | 5 | government. . . . . . . . . . | 24.0 | 13 |
| Licenses, permits, and others . . | 2.9 | 4 | Housing, parks, sanitation . | 17.4 | 10 |
| | | | Health and hospitals. . . . . | 12.6 | 7 |
| | | | Public welfare . . . . . . . . | 11.9 | 7 |
| | | | Highways. . . . . . . . . . . . | 10.0 | 5 |
| | | | All others . . . . . . . . . . . | 25.9 | 14 |
| Total receipts . . . . . . . . . . | $80.4 | 100 | Total expenditures . . . . | $183.0 | 100 |

*Source:* Bureau of the Census, *Government Finances in 1977–1978.* Because of rounding, figures may not add up to totals.

and local expenditures for education, streets and highways, public welfare, police protection, and other public services. Furthermore, the costs of state and local governments have been pushed up rapidly as a result of the unionization of many state and municipal workers. In short, despite substantial increases in sales and property tax rates, state and local governments have been faced with serious fiscal problems. The well-publicized financial problems of New York City and Cleveland are dramatic cases in point.

Historically, this fiscal imbalance has been redressed by a growing volume of intergovernmental grants flowing from the Federal government to state and local governments. Until 1972 this aid took the form of *categorical grants,* that is, grants which are earmarked to such specific programs as highway construction, education, and health care *and* are contingent upon matching state and local funds. A major departure from this pattern came in 1972 with the passage of the State and Local Fiscal Assistance Act, more commonly known as the *Revenue Sharing Act.* The essence of this act is that the Federal government will make unrestricted or "block" grants without the requirement of matching funds. The states retain one-third of their grants and must pass the remaining two-thirds on to local units of government. The formula for allocating Federal monies to the states takes into account such factors as (1) state and local tax efforts, (2) per capita incomes, and (3) population. Inclusion of the first factor is to provide relatively more aid to those states which display an interest in meeting their own problems *and* to discourage states from using the grants to "finance" tax cuts. Per capita income and population size are used in the grant formula to provide relatively more aid to states with large populations and low per capita incomes, thereby tending to redistribute income among the states. The act, as extended by 1976 congressional action, provides approximately $6 billion of aid per year to states and localities. When added to categorical grants of some $69 billion, overall Federal aid to state and local governments was about $75 billion in 1978.

## ☐  APPORTIONING THE TAX BURDEN

The very nature of social goods and services (see Chapter 6) makes it exceedingly difficult to measure precisely the manner in which their benefits are apportioned among individuals and institutions in the economy. It is virtually impossible to determine accurately the amount by which John Doe benefits from military installations, a network of highways, a public school system, and local police and fire protection.

The situation is a bit different on the taxation side of the picture. Statistical studies reveal rather clearly the manner in which the overall tax burden is apportioned. Needless to say, this is a question which affects each of us in a vital way. Although the average citizen is concerned with the overall level of taxes, chances are he or she is even more interested in exactly how the tax burden is allocated among individual taxpayers.

### △  Benefits Received versus Ability to Pay

There are two basic philosophies on how the economy's tax burden should be apportioned.

**Benefits-received Principle**   The *benefits-received principle* of taxation asserts that households and businesses should purchase the goods and services of government in basically the same manner in which other commodities are bought. It is reasoned that those who benefit most from government-supplied goods or services should pay the taxes necessary for their financing. Some social goods are financed essentially on the basis of the benefits principle. For example, gasoline taxes are typically earmarked for the financing of highway construction and repairs. Those who benefit from good roads pay the cost of those roads. Difficulties immediately arise, however, when an accurate and widespread application of the benefits principle is considered:

**1**  How does one go about determining the benefits which individual households and businesses receive from national defense, education, and police and fire protection? Recall (Chapter 6) that social goods entail widespread social or spillover benefits and that the exclusion principle is inapplicable. Even in the seemingly tangible case of highway finance we find it difficult to measure benefits. Individual car owners benefit in different degrees from the existence of good roads. And those who do not own cars also benefit. Businesses would certainly benefit greatly from any widening of their markets which good roads will encourage.

**2**  Government efforts to redistribute income would be self-defeating if financed on the basis of the benefits principle. It would be absurd to ask poor families to pay the taxes needed to finance their welfare payments! It would be equally ridiculous to think of taxing unemployed workers to finance the unemployment compensation payments which they receive.

**Ability-to-pay Principle**  The *ability-to-pay principle* of taxation stands in sharp contrast to the benefits principle. Ability-to-pay taxation rests on the idea that the tax burden should be geared directly to one's income and wealth. As the ability-to-pay principle has come to be applied in the United States, it contends that individuals and businesses with larger incomes should pay more taxes—both absolutely and relatively—than those with more modest incomes.

What is the rationale of ability-to-pay taxation? Proponents argue that each additional dollar of income received by a household will yield smaller and smaller increments of satisfaction. It is argued that, because consumers act rationally, the first dollars of income received in any period of time will be spent upon basic high-urgency goods; that is, upon those goods which yield the greatest benefit or satisfaction. Successive dollars of income will go for less urgently needed goods and finally for trivial goods and services. This means that a dollar taken through taxes from a poor person who has few dollars constitutes a greater sacrifice than does a dollar taken by taxes from the rich person who has many dollars. Hence, in order to balance the sacrifices which taxes impose on income receivers, it is contended that taxes should be apportioned according to the amount of income one receives.

This is appealing, but problems of application exist here, too. In particular, although we might agree that the household earning $25,000 per year has a greater ability to pay taxes than the household receiving a paltry $5000, exactly *how much more* ability to pay does the first family have as compared with the second? Should the rich person simply pay the *same percentage* of his or her larger income—and hence a larger absolute amount—as taxes? Or should the rich man or woman be made to pay a *larger fraction* of this income as taxes? The problem is that there is no scientific way of measuring one's ability to pay taxes. Thus, in practice, the answer hinges upon guesswork, the tax views of the political party in power, expediency, and the urgency with which government needs revenue. As we shall discover in a few moments, the tax structure of our economy is much more in tune with the ability-to-pay principle than with the benefits-received principle.

△  **Progressive, Proportional, and Regressive Taxes**

Any discussion of the ability-to-pay and the benefits-received principles of taxation leads ultimately to the question of tax rates and the manner in which tax rates change as one's income increases.

**Definitions**  Taxes are ordinarily classified as being progressive, proportional, or regressive. These designations focus upon the relationship between tax rates and *income* for the simple reason that all taxes—regardless of whether they are levied upon income or upon a product or building or parcel of land—are ultimately paid out of someone's income.

**1**   A tax is *progressive* if its rate *increases as income increases.* Such a tax claims not only a larger absolute amount, but also a larger fraction or percentage of income as income increases.

**2**   A *regressive* tax is one whose rate *declines as income increases.* Such a tax takes a smaller and smaller proportion of income as income increases. A regressive tax may or may not take a larger absolute amount of income as income expands.

**3**   A tax is *proportional* when its rate *remains the same,* regardless of the size of income.

Let us illustrate in terms of the personal income tax. Suppose the tax rates are such that a household pays 10 percent of its income in taxes, regardless of the size of its income. This would obviously be a proportional income tax. But suppose the rate structure is such that the household with an annual taxable income of less than $1000 pays 5 percent in income taxes, the household realizing an income of $1000 to $2000 pays 10 percent, $2000 to $3000 pays 15 percent, and so forth.[4] This, as we have already explained, would obviously be a *progressive* income tax. The final case is where the rates decline as taxable income rises: You pay 15 percent if you earn less than $1000; 10 percent if you earn $1000 to $2000; 5 percent if you earn $2000 to $3000; and so forth. This is a *regressive* income tax. Generally speaking, progressive taxes are those which bear down most heavily on the rich; regressive taxes are those which hit the poor hardest.

**Applications**   What can we say about the progressivity, proportionality, or regressivity of

the major kinds of taxes used in the United States? We have already stressed the progressive features of the Federal *personal income tax.* Recall, however, that in practice various exemptions, deductions, and tax loopholes dampen its overall progressivity.

At first glance a *general sales tax* with, say, a 3 percent rate would seem to be proportional. But in fact it is regressive with respect to income. The reason for its regressivity is that a larger portion of a poor person's income is exposed to the tax than is the case with a rich person; the latter avoids the tax on the part of income which is saved, whereas the former is unable to save. Example: "Poor" Smith has an income of $12,000 and spends it all. "Rich" Jones has an income of $24,000 but spends only $16,000 of it. Assuming a 3 percent sales tax applies to the expenditures of each individual, Smith will obviously pay $360 (3 percent of $12,000) in sales taxes, and Jones will pay $480 (3 percent of $16,000). Note that whereas *all* of Smith's $12,000 income is subject to the sales tax, only two-thirds of Jones's $24,000 income is taxed. Thus, while Smith pays $360, or 3 percent, of a $12,000 income as sales taxes, Jones pays $480, or just 2 percent, of a $24,000 income. Hence, we conclude that the general sales tax is regressive.

The Federal *corporate income tax* appears to be mildly progressive and is generally regarded as such; after all, tax rates rise from 17 to 46 percent as corporate profits rise up to the $100,000 level.[5] But this assumes that corporation owners (shareholders) bear the tax. Some tax experts argue that at least a part of the tax is passed through to consumers in the form of higher product prices. To the extent that this occurs, the tax tends to be regressive, like a sales tax.

*Payroll taxes* are regressive because they apply to only a fixed absolute amount of one's income. For example, in 1980, payroll tax rates were 6.13 percent, but this figure applies only

---

[4] We refer here to average or effective tax rates, not to marginal tax rates.

[5] For larger corporations who count their profits in terms of millions of dollars the tax is virtually proportional.

to the first $25,900 of one's wage income. Thus a person earning exactly $25,900 would pay $1,587.67, or 6.13 percent of his or her wage income, while someone with twice that income, or $51,800, would also pay $1,587.67—only 3.07 percent of his or her wage income. Note, too, that this regressivity is enhanced because the payroll tax excludes nonwage income. If our individual with the $51,800 wage income also received $25,900 in nonwage (dividend, interest, rent) income, then the payroll tax would only be 2.04 percent ( = $1,587.67 ÷ $77,700) of the total income.

There is considerable uncertainty and debate surrounding *property taxes*. The traditional view holds that property taxes are regressive for essentially the same reasons as are sales taxes. First, property owners add the tax to the rents which tenants are charged. Second, property taxes, as a percentage of income, are higher for poor families than for rich families because the poor must spend a larger proportion of their incomes for housing.[6] The alleged regressivity of the property tax may be reinforced by the fact that property tax rates are not likely to be uniform as between various political subdivisions. For example, if property values decline in, say, a decaying central city area, property tax rates must be increased in the city to bring in a given amount of revenue. But in a wealthy suburb, where the market value of housing is rising, a given amount of tax revenue can be maintained with lower property tax rates.

△  **Shifting and Incidence of Taxes**

Taxes do not always stick where the government levies them. Some taxes can be *shifted* among various parties in the economy. It is therefore necessary to locate as best we

[6]Controversy arises in part because empirical research, which compares the value of housing to lifetime (rather than a single year's) income, suggests that this ratio is approximately the same for all income groups. Students interested in this controversy should consult Henry J. Aaron, *Who Pays the Property Tax? A New View* (Washington: Brookings Institution, 1975).

can the final resting place or *incidence* of the major types of taxes.

**Personal Income Tax**  The incidence of the personal income tax generally falls on the individual upon whom the tax is levied; little chance exists for shifting. But there might be exceptions to this. Individuals and groups who can effectively control the price of their labor services may be able to shift a part of the tax. For example, doctors, dentists, lawyers, and other professional people who can readily increase their fees may do so because of the tax. Unions might regard personal income taxes as part of the cost of living and, as a result, bargain for higher wages. If they are successful, they may shift a portion of the tax from workers to employers. Generally, however, we can conclude that the individual upon whom the tax is initially levied bears the burden of the personal income tax. The same ordinarily holds true of inheritance taxes.

**Corporate Income Tax**  We have already suggested that the incidence of the corporate income tax is much less certain. The traditional view has it that a firm which is currently charging the profit-maximizing price and producing the profit-maximizing output will have no reason to change price or output when a corporate income tax is imposed. That price and output combination which yields the greatest profit before the tax will still be the most profitable after government takes a fixed percentage of the firm's profits in the form of income taxes. According to this view, the company's stockholders (owners) must bear the incidence of the tax in the form of lower dividends or a smaller amount of retained earnings. On the other hand, some economists argue that the corporate income tax is shifted in part to consumers through higher prices and to resource suppliers through lower prices. In modern industry, where a small number of firms may control a market, producers may not be in the profit-maximizing position initially. The reason? By fully exploiting their market position currently, monopolistic firms might elicit adverse public opinion and governmental censure. Hence, they may await such events as increases in tax rates or wage increases by unions to provide an "excuse" or rationale for price increases with less fear of public criticism. When this actually occurs, a portion of the corporate income tax may be shifted to consumers through higher prices.

Both positions are plausible. Indeed, the incidence of the corporate income tax may well be shared by stockholders and the firm's customers and resource suppliers.

**Sales and Excise Taxes**   Sales and excise taxes are the "hidden taxes" of our economy. They are hidden because such taxes are typically shifted by sellers to consumers through higher product prices. There may be some difference in the shiftability of sales taxes and excises, however. Because a sales tax covers a much wider range of products than an excise, there is little chance for consumers to resist the price boosts which sales taxes entail by reallocating their expenditures to untaxed products.

Excises, however, fall on a relatively short, select list of goods. Therefore, the possibility of consumers turning to substitute goods and services is greater. For example, an excise tax on theater tickets which does not apply to other types of entertainment might be difficult to pass on to consumers via price increases. Why? Because price boosts might result in considerable substituting of alternative types of entertainment by consumers. The higher price will cause such a marked decline in sales that a seller will be better off to bear all, or a large portion of, the excise rather than the sharp decline in sales. With many excises, however, modest price increases have little or no effect on sales. Excises on gasoline, cigarettes, and alcoholic beverages are cases in point. Here there are few good substitute products to which consumers can turn as prices rise. For these commodities, the seller is in a better position to shift the tax.

In general, it is safe to say that the bulk of a sales or excise tax will generally be shifted to the consumer through higher product prices.[7]

**Property Taxes**   Many property taxes are borne by the property owner for the simple reason that there is no other party to whom they can be shifted. This is typically true in the case of taxes on land, personal property, and owner-occupied residences. For example, even when land is sold, the property tax is not likely to be shifted. The buyer will tend to discount the value of the land to allow for the future taxes which must be paid on it, and this expected taxation will be reflected in the price a buyer is willing to offer for the land.

Taxes on rented and business property are a different story. Taxes on rented property can be, and usually are, shifted wholly or in part from the owner to the tenant by the simple process of boosting the rent. Business property taxes are treated as a business cost and therefore are taken into account in establishing product price; thus such taxes are ordinarily shifted to the firm's customers.

Table 8-5 summarizes this discussion of the shifting and incidence of taxes.

△   **The American Tax Structure**

As we have seen, the Federal, state, and local governments of the United States employ a variety of taxes. We have concluded that some of these taxes—the personal and corporate income taxes and inheritance taxes—are progressive, whereas others—sales taxes, excises, and property taxes—are for the most part regressive. What is the total picture? One estimate—and these figures must be very rough because of the uncertainty of tax incidence—is shown in Table 8-6.

Employing family income as the tax base, column 2 of this table tells us the percentage of income taken by Federal taxes in each of the

---

[7] Later (Chapter 23) we will employ supply and demand analysis as a basis for more sophisticated generalizations as to the shifting and incidence of sales taxes.

**TABLE 8-5**
**The Probable Incidence of Taxes**

| Type of tax | Probable incidence |
|---|---|
| Personal income tax | The household or individual upon which it is levied. |
| Corporate income tax | Disagreement. Some economists feel the firm on which it is levied bears the incidence; others conclude the tax is shifted, wholly or in part, to consumers. |
| Sales and excise taxes | With exceptions, consumers who buy the taxed products. |
| Property taxes | Owners in the case of land and owner-occupied residences; tenants in the case of rented property; consumers in the case of business property. |

nine income classes. The progressivity found here reflects the important role of the personal and corporate income taxes at the Federal level. Note, however, that the progressivity of the income tax is dampened by tax loopholes and the regressivity of the payroll tax. Column 3 presents similar data for state and local taxes. Regressivity is evident here, reflecting the predominance of sales and property taxes at the state and local levels. Column 4 sums the two preceding columns and shows the percentage of income taken in Federal, state, and local taxes combined from each of the listed income groups.

Column 4 tells us that aside from the highest and lowest income classes, the overall tax structure is roughly proportional. Only for the highest "$50,000 and over" income class do we find strong evidence of progressivity. And, conversely, for the very poor "under $2000" class, the tax structure is highly regressive. Given that the overall tax system takes roughly one-third of income in taxes from a very large proportion of income receivers, we can conclude that, except for the noted extremes, the tax system per se is generally neutral in its impact upon the distribution of income.

But columns 5 and 6 remind us that tax revenues are used in part to finance transfer payments. Transfers are in effect "taxes in reverse" or "negative taxes." While taxes flow

**TABLE 8-6**
**Estimated Tax Rate By Income Levels** (*taxes as a percentage of income*)

| (1)<br>Family<br>income | (2)<br>Federal<br>taxes | (3)<br>State and<br>local taxes | (4)<br>All taxes,<br>or (2) + (3) | (5)<br>Government<br>transfer<br>payments | (6)<br>Net taxes,<br>or (4) − (5) |
|---|---|---|---|---|---|
| Under $2,000 | 22.7% | 27.2% | 50.0% | 106.5% | −56.5% |
| $2,000–$4,000 | 18.7 | 15.7 | 34.6 | 48.5 | −13.9 |
| $4,000–$6,000 | 19.0 | 12.1 | 31.0 | 19.6 | 11.4 |
| $6,000–$8,000 | 19.4 | 10.7 | 30.1 | 8.6 | 21.5 |
| $8,000–$10,000 | 19.1 | 10.1 | 29.2 | 5.5 | 23.7 |
| $10,000–$15,000 | 19.9 | 9.9 | 29.8 | 3.9 | 25.9 |
| $15,000–$25,000 | 20.7 | 9.4 | 30.0 | 3.0 | 27.0 |
| $25,000–$50,000 | 25.0 | 7.8 | 32.8 | 2.1 | 30.7 |
| $50,000 and over | 38.4 | 6.7 | 45.0 | 0.4 | 44.7 |
| Total tax<br>on all income | 21.7% | 9.9% | 31.6% | 6.9% | 24.6% |

*Source:* Roger A. Herriot and Herman P. Miller, "The Taxes We Pay," *Conference Board Record,* May 1971, p. 40.

from households to government, transfers flow from government to households. We note in columns 5 and 6 that direct government transfers to families are highly progressive. For example, although the families in the "under $2000" class pay 50 percent of their income as taxes, they receive transfer benefits equal to 106 percent of their incomes. Hence, net taxes—that is, taxes and transfers combined—augment the incomes of these families by 56 percent. Similarly, families in the "$2000–$4000" class receive transfers in excess of their taxes, so that their incomes are supplemented by about 14 percent. All higher-income classes pay taxes in excess of transfers and therefore are "net contributors" to, rather than "net recipients" from, the total tax-transfer system. The conclusion to be drawn from column 6 is that the impact of the combined tax-transfer system is quite progressive.

A final point: Table 8-6 is an incomplete picture of the redistributive effect of total governmental activities for the simple reason that it excludes government purchases of goods and services. As mentioned earlier in regard to households and businesses, determining the extent to which each income class benefits from the various types of Federal, state, and local expenditures shown in Tables 8-1, 8-3, and 8-4 is extremely difficult. Therefore, the overall progressivity or regressivity of total public sector activity—including taxes, transfers, *and* government purchases of goods and services—is anything but clear.[8]

☐ **THE TAXPAYERS' REVOLT**
The late 1970s spawned an extensive reexamination of government spending and taxes. The landmark event was voter approval of California's *Proposition 13* which severely restricted the level and growth of property taxes in that state. Although only a few other states have

adopted proposals similar to Proposition 13, others have limited state expenditures to a fixed percentage of state incomes or have tied the growth of government spending to the economic growth of the state. At the Federal level Congress has debated, but not passed, the *Kemp–Roth bill* which proposes to cut personal income taxes by 30 percent over a three-year period.

Why now? Why have taxpayers become interested in imposing lids on taxes and government spending at this time? The reasons are manifold and intertwined. First, serious concerns have evolved about the overall fairness of the tax-transfer system. In the case of Proposition 13 the issue centered upon the apparent injustices embodied in property taxation and, in particular, the fact that such taxes are not a good indicator of ability to pay. The classic case is that of the fixed-income homeowner who finds that the market value of his or her home—and hence property tax payments—has increased substantially since the time of purchase. But the appreciated value of one's home cannot be realized unless it is sold. In short, strong opposition developed to soaring tax bills based on unrealized gains in housing values. Secondly, the tax revolt has been spurred by the combination of sharp inflation and slow growth of output and productivity during the 1970s. Inflation means not only an increase in the cost of living, but it pushes families into higher income tax brackets. For example, a 7 percent increase in personal incomes will increase Federal tax collections by about 10 or 11 percent as people move into higher tax brackets. At the same time the taxpayer realizes no real benefit from the 7 percent increase in money income because prices are going up by 7 percent or more! Feeling a standard-of-living crunch, households have joined the tax revolt to seek relief through lower tax bills. Finally, as noted at the outset of this chapter, the sheer size and role of government expanded greatly in the decades since World War II. Hence, the tax revolt is also a protest against not merely

[8]The ambitious reader should consult Richard A. Musgrave and Peggy B. Musgrave, *Public Finance in Theory and Practice,* 3d ed., (New York: McGraw-Hill Book Company, 1980), chap. 13.

growing overall tax burdens but also alleged government waste, inefficiency, and power.

Critics of the tax revolt remind us that "there's no free lunch" and that lids on taxes or government spending will inevitably mean declines in the quantity and quality of public goods and services. But supporters of the tax revolt contend this need not be the case. They take the position that taxes are now so high that incentives to invest, to innovate, and to work have been seriously impaired. Tax relief, it is argued, will unshackle the economy and spur economic growth, to the end that the resulting increases in personal and corporate incomes, payrolls, and sales will increase the overall tax base and yield *more* tax revenues. Critics reply that there is no evidence to suggest that current tax levels have seriously affected incentives and, therefore, lower tax rates will not induce increases in tax collections.

Opponents of the tax revolt also feel that tax and spending lids comprise a "meat-ax approach" to our tax problems and fail to address the critical issue of which public goods and services are justifiable and worthy of retention or expansion and which are not. Finally, critics of the revolt point out that restricting the size of government growth (and thereby the overall tax burden), reducing government inefficiency, and reforming state and local tax systems to make them more equitable are quite distinct goals which call for different policies and legislative initiatives. Supporters of the tax revolt, critics contend, have failed to grasp this distinction. While the overall magnitude and consequences of the tax revolt are unclear at this point in time, there can be no doubt that a thorough reassessment of the relative roles of public and private sectors is now underway.

## Summary

**1** Historically, government tax receipts and expenditures have grown rapidly, both in absolute amounts and in relation to the size of the national income. Wars and national defense, population growth, urbanization, environmental problems, egalitarianism, and inflation have been among the more important causes underlying the growth of government.

**2** The main categories of Federal spending are for "income security and health" and "national defense"; revenues come primarily from the personal income, payroll, and corporate income taxes. The primary sources of revenue for the states are sales and excise taxes; education, welfare, and highways are the major state expenditures. At the local level, most revenue comes from the property tax, and education is the most important expenditure. State and local tax revenues are supplemented by Federal revenue sharing.

**3** The ability-to-pay principle of taxation is more evident in the American tax structure than is the benefits-received philosophy.

**4** Taxes on personal income and inheritance taxes are progressive. The corporate income tax is probably progressive. General sales, excise, payroll, and property taxes tend to be regressive.

**5** Sales and excise taxes are likely to be shifted; personal income taxes are not. There is disagreement as to whether corporate income taxes are shifted. The incidence of property taxes depends primarily upon whether the property is owner- or tenant-occupied.

**6** Over the income range which includes the bulk of American households, the overall tax structure is roughly proportional. The combined tax-transfer system, however, is quite progressive.

7   The recent "taxpayers' revolt" reflects citizen concern regarding tax equity, the impact of inflation upon living standards, and government waste and inefficiency.

## Questions and Study Suggestions

1   Key terms and concepts to remember: government purchases; transfer payments; personal income tax; marginal and average tax rates; payroll tax; corporate income tax; double taxation; sales and excise taxes; property tax; revenue sharing; benefits-received principle; ability-to-pay principle; progressive tax; proportional tax; regressive tax; tax shifting; tax incidence; taxpayers' revolt; Proposition 13; Kemp–Roth bill.

2   Describe and account for the historical growth of the public sector of the economy. Why might it be significant to distinguish between "transfer payments" and "government purchases of goods and services" in evaluating the impact of the growth of government expenditures?

3   What are the most important source of revenue and the major type of expenditure at the Federal level? At the state level? At the local level?

4   Briefly describe the mechanics of the Federal personal income tax. Explain why the average or effective personal income tax rate is less than the marginal tax rate.

5   What is revenue sharing? Why has it occurred? Briefly describe the State and Local Fiscal Assistance Act of 1972. If you were in charge of distributing $10 billion per year among the states, what considerations would you include in your distribution formula?

6   Distinguish clearly between the benefits-received and the ability-to-pay principles of taxation. Which philosophy is more evident in our present tax structure? Justify your answer. To which principle of taxation do you subscribe? Why?

7   Precisely what is meant by a progressive tax? A regressive tax? A proportional tax? Comment upon the progressivity or regressivity of each of the following taxes, indicating in each case your assumption concerning tax incidence:
   a.   The Federal personal income tax
   b.   A 3 percent state general sales tax
   c.   A Federal excise tax on playing cards
   d.   A municipal property tax on real estate
   e.   The Federal corporate income tax

8   Comment in detail on the overall progressivity or regressivity of a. the American tax system and b. the tax-transfer system.

9   Explain and evaluate each of the following statements:
   a.   "No tax on income can be a just tax unless it leaves individuals in the same relative condition in which it found them."
   b.   "Because there is no sure definition of the limits to progression, no firm basis of its 'reasonable' use, no protection against its unconscionable abuse, those who uphold the system as a revenue device are playing into the hands of the group that would use progressive taxation as the means of destroying private capitalism and ushering in the collectivist state."
   c.   "Even tho it be an open question whether all inequality in wealth and income be unjust, such great degrees of inequality as the modern world shows are regarded as not consonant with canons of justice. Very rich persons should be called to pay taxes not only in proportion to their incomes but more than in proportion."

10   It has been proposed that a special excise tax be placed on new autos with rates structured so that the tax on high gas-mileage cars is small, while the tax on low gas-mileage cars is high. Do you favor this proposal?

# Selected References

Break, George F., and Joseph A. Pechman: *Federal Tax Reform: The Impossible Dream?* (Washington: The Brookings Institution, 1975).

Laffer, Arthur B., and Jan P. Seymour (eds.): *The Economics of the Tax Revolt: A Reader* (New York: Harcourt Brace Jovanovich, Inc., 1979).

Maxwell, James A., and J. Richard Aronson: *Financing State and Local Government,* 3d ed. (Washington: The Brookings Institution, 1977).

Musgrave, Richard A., and Peggy B. Musgrave: *Public Finance in Theory and Practice,* 3d ed. (New York: McGraw-Hill Book Company, 1980), particularly parts 3 and 4.

Pechman, Joseph A.: *Federal Tax Policy,* 3d ed. (Washington: The Brookings Institution, 1977).

# LAST WORD
## The American Way of Tax

Our tax system has tried to further many goals: raising revenue, regulating the overall level of demand, promoting greater socioeconomic equality, rewarding desirable and punishing undesirable behavior, and so on. The following article is a humorous look at the curious effects the tax system may have upon behavior and decision-making.

The Tax Man was very cross about Figg. Figg's way of life did not conform to the way of life several governments wanted Figg to pursue.

"What's the idea of living in a rental apartment over a delicatessen in the city, Figg?" he inquired.

Figg explained that he liked urban life. In that case, said the Tax Man, he was raising Figg's city sales and income taxes. "If you want them cut, you'll have to move out to the suburbs," he said.

Figg gave up the city and rented a suburban house but the Tax Man was not satisfied. He squeezed Figg until beads of blood popped out along the seams of Figg's wallet.

"Mercy, good Tax Man," Figg gasped. "Tell me how to live so that I may please my government, and I shall obey."

The Tax Man told Figg to quit renting and buy a house. The government wanted everyone to accept large mortgage loans from bankers. If Figg complied, it would cut his taxes.

Figg bought a house, which he did not want, in a suburb where he did not want to live, and he invited his friends and relatives to attend a party celebrating his surrender to a way of life that pleased his governments.

"I have had enough of this, Figg," the Tax Man declared. "Your government doesn't want you entertaining friends and relatives. This will cost you plenty."

Figg immediately threw out all his friends and relatives, then asked the Tax Man what sort of people his government wished him to entertain. "Business associates," said the Tax Man. "Entertain plenty of business associates, and I shall cut your taxes."

To make the Tax Man and his government happy, Figg began entertaining people he didn't like in the house he didn't want in the suburb where he didn't want to live.

Then was the Tax Man enraged indeed. "Figg!" he thundered, "I will not cut your taxes for entertaining straw bosses, truck drivers and pothole fillers."

"Why not?" said Figg. "These are the people I associate with in my business."

"Which is what?" asked the Tax Man.

"Earning my pay by the sweat of my brow," said Figg.

"Your government is not going to bribe you for performing salaried labor," said the Tax Man. "Don't you know, you imbecile, that tax rates on salaried income are higher than on any other kind?"

And he taxed the sweat of Figg's brow at a ferocious rate.

"Get into business, or minerals, or international oil," warned the Tax Man, "or I shall make your taxes as the taxes of 10."

Figg went into business, which he hated, and entertained people he didn't like in the house he didn't want in the suburb where he did not want to live, and the Tax Man and all the governments and the nation were happy, except for a rising incidence of divorce, tax forms, madness, fatuity, loneliness and suicide.

At length the Tax Man summoned Figg for an angry lecture. He demanded to know why Figg had not bought a new plastic factory to replace his old metal and wooden plant. "I hate plastic," said Figg.

"Your government is sick and tired of metal, wood and everything else that smacks of the real stuff, Figg!" roared the Tax Man, seizing Figg's purse. "Your depreciation is all used up."

There was nothing for Figg to do but go to plastic, and the Tax Man rewarded him with a brand new depreciation schedule plus an investment credit deduction from the bottom line.

Thanks to the money the Tax Man granted him for living in a suburb where he didn't want to live and for entertaining people he didn't like in a house he didn't want while engaging in work he wasn't interested in with plastic equipment he hated, Figg began to make a profit. The Tax Man was outraged.

"What's the idea of making a profit, Figg?" he demanded, placing his iron grip on Figg's bank account.

"Spare me," Figg pleaded.

"Only if you sell your business!" roared the Tax Man.

"After forcing me to get into business, the Government now wants me to get out of business?" asked Figg.

"Exactly," said the Tax Man. "Sell, and I'll tax the profit from the sale at a delightfully low capital-gain rate of only 25 percent. Otherwise, I'll take the meat ax to those profits."

Figg sold. Having nothing to do with his time, he decided to die. The Tax Man was furious. "Just try it," he said, "and I'll strip your estate down to the stalk." So Figg changed his mind.

This is why people are living so much longer nowadays. The government needs a large supply of people over 65 to keep the Social Security tax rising.

Russell Baker, "The American Way of Tax," *The New York Times*, April 12, 1977. Copyright © 1977 by The New York Times Company. Reprinted by permission.

# NATIONAL INCOME, EMPLOYMENT, AND FISCAL POLICY

PART TWO

# National Income Accounting

chapter **9**

Throughout Part 1 of this book we have made the flat statement that American capitalism does not consistently provide for the full employment of available resources. It has also been noted that the levels of employment and production depend upon the size of certain flows of expenditures and income. Part 2 now deals at length with the problem of measuring, explaining, and using public policy to manage, if need be, the volumes of employment, production, and income in the economy. Specifically, in this chapter we seek an understanding of certain accounting techniques which assist us in gauging the level of production achieved by the economy. In Chapter 10 we examine the economic fluctuations which have characterized our economy, emphasizing the effects of unemployment and inflation. Then in Chapters 11 and 12 we seek to explain those factors which determine the levels of employment and production in our economy. Finally, in Chapter 13 we will explore how fiscal policy—the

altering of government expenditures and tax collections—might be used to help stabilize output, employment, and the price level.

## ☐ MEASURING THE ECONOMY'S PERFORMANCE

The present task is that of defining and understanding a group of so-called social or national income accounting concepts which have been designed to measure the overall production performance of the economy. Why do we bother with such a project? Because social accounting does for the economy as a whole what private accounting does for the individual business enterprise or, for that matter, for the household. The business executive is vitally interested in knowing how well his or her firm is doing, but the answer is not always immediately discernible.

Measurement of the firm's flows of income and expenditures is needed to assess the firm's operations for the current year. With this information available, the executive can gauge the economic health of the firm. If things are going well, the accounting data can be used to explain this success. It may be that costs are down or sales and product prices are up, resulting in large profits. If things are going badly, accounting measures can be employed to discover immediate causes. And by examining the accounts over a period of time, the executive can detect growth or decline for the firm and indications of the immediate causes. All this information is invaluable in helping the executive make intelligent policy decisions.

A system of national income accounting does much the same thing for the economy as a whole: It allows us to keep a finger on the economic pulse of the nation. The various measures which make up our social accounting system permit us to measure the level of production in the economy at some point in time and explain the immediate causes of that level of performance. Further, by comparing the national income accounts over a period of time, we can plot the long-run course which the economy has been following; the growth or stagnation of the economy will show up in the national income accounts. Finally, the information supplied by the national income accounts provides a basis for the formulation and application of public policies designed to improve the performance of the economy; without the national income accounts, economic policy would be based upon guesswork. In short, national income accounting allows us to keep tab on the economic health of society and to formulate intelligently policies which will improve that health.

## ☐  GROSS NATIONAL PRODUCT

There are many conceivable measures of the economic well-being of society. It is generally agreed, however, that the best available indicator of an economy's health is its annual total output of goods and services or, as it is sometimes called, the economy's aggregate output.

The basic social accounting measure of the total output of goods and services is called the *gross national product* or, simply, GNP. It is defined as *the total market value of all final goods and services produced[1] in the economy in one year.* Our definition of GNP is very explicit and merits considerable comment.

### △   GNP is a Monetary Measure

Note, first, that GNP measures the market value of annual output. GNP is a monetary measure. Indeed, it must be if we are to compare the heterogeneous collections of goods and services produced in different years and get a meaningful idea of their relative worth. Put simply, if the economy produces three oranges and two apples in year 1 and two oranges and three apples in year 2, in which year is society better off? There is no answer to this question until price tags are attached to the various products as indicators of society's evaluation of their relative worth. The problem is resolved in Table 9-1, where it is assumed that the money price of the oranges is 10 cents and the price of apples is 15 cents. It can be concluded that year 2's output is superior to that of year 1. Why? Because society values year 2's output more highly; society is willing to pay more for the collection of goods produced in year 2 than of goods produced in year 1.

### △   Avoiding Double Counting

To measure total output accurately, all goods and services produced in any given year must be counted once, but not more than once. Most products go through a series of production stages before reaching a market. As a result, parts or components of most products are bought and sold many times. Hence, to avoid counting several times the parts of

---

[1] We shall see that all goods *produced* in a particular year may not be *sold;* some may be added to inventories. Any increase in inventories must be included in determining GNP, since GNP measures all current production regardless of whether or not it is sold.

**TABLE 9-1**
Comparing Heterogeneous Outputs By Using Money Prices (*hypothetical data*)

| Year | Annual outputs | Market value |
|---|---|---|
| 1 | 3 oranges and 2 apples | 3 at 10 cents + 2 at 15 cents = 60 cents |
| 2 | 2 oranges and 3 apples | 2 at 10 cents + 3 at 15 cents = 65 cents |

products that are sold and resold, GNP includes only the market value of final goods and ignores transactions involving intermediate goods.

By *final goods* we mean goods and services which are being purchased for final use and not for resale or further processing or manufacturing. Transactions involving *intermediate goods*, on the other hand, refer to purchases of goods and services for further processing and manufacturing or for resale. The sale of *final* goods is *included* and the sale of intermediate goods is *excluded* from GNP. Why? Because the value of final goods includes all the intermediate transactions involved in their production. The inclusion of intermediate transactions would involve double counting and an exaggerated estimate of GNP.

An example will clarify this point. Suppose there are five stages of production in getting a Hart, Schaffner & Marx suit manufactured and into the hands of a consumer who, of course, is the ultimate or final user. As Table 9-2 indicates, firm A, a sheep ranch, provides $50 worth of wool to firm B, a wool processor.

Firm A pays out the $50 it receives in wages, rents, interest, and profits. Firm B processes the wool and sells it to firm C, a suit manufacturer, for $75. What does firm B do with this $75? As noted, $50 goes to firm A, and the remaining $25 is used by B to pay wages, rents, interest, and profits for the resources needed in processing the wool. And so it goes. The manufacturer sells the suit to firm D, a clothing wholesaler, who in turn sells it to firm E, a retailer, and then, at last, it is bought for $200 by a consumer, the final user of the product. At each stage, the difference between what a firm has paid for the product and what it receives for its sale is paid out as wages, rent, interest, and profits for the resources used by that firm in helping to produce and distribute the suit.

The basic question is this: How much should we include in GNP in accounting for the production of this suit? Just $200, the value of the final product! Why? Because this figure includes all the intermediate transactions leading up to the product's final sale. It would be a gross exaggeration to sum all the

**TABLE 9-2**
Value Added in a Five-Stage Productive Process (*hypothetical data*)

| (1)<br>Stage of production | (2)<br>Sales value of<br>materials or product | (3)<br>Value<br>added |
|---|---|---|
| Firm A, sheep ranch | $ 50 | $ 50 |
| Firm B, wool processor | 75 | 25 |
| Firm C, suit manufacturer | 100 | 25 |
| Firm D, clothing wholesaler | 140 | 40 |
| Firm E, retail clothier | 200 | 60 |
| Total sales values | $565 | |
| Value added (total income) | | $200 |

intermediate sales figures and the final sales value of the product in column 2 and add the entire amount, $565, to GNP. This would be a serious case of double counting, that is, counting the final product and the sale and resale of its various parts in the multistage productive process.

There is an alternative means of determining the $200 figure which is to be included in GNP. And this is by the *value-added* method—that is, by summing the value added to the total worth of the product at each step in the productive process. Column 3 summarizes this procedure. Note that this measures the total income derived from the production and sale of the suit. As you might expect, it is easier for the national income accountants to count only final goods than to pursue the value-added method of deriving GNP.

△　**GNP Excludes Nonproductive Transactions**

GNP attempts to measure the annual production of the economy. In so doing, the many nonproductive transactions which occur each year must be carefully excluded. Nonproductive transactions are of two major types: (1) purely financial transactions, and (2) secondhand sales.

 **Financial Transactions**　Purely financial transactions in turn are of three general types: public transfer payments, private transfer payments, and the buying and selling of securities. We have already mentioned public transfer payments (Chapter 8). These are the social security payments, welfare payments, and veterans' payments which government makes to particular households. The basic characteristic of these disbursements is that recipients make no contribution to *current* production in return for them. Thus, to include them in GNP would be to overstate this year's production. Private transfer payments—for example, a university student's monthly subsidy from home or an occasional gift from a wealthy relative—do not entail

production but simply the transfer of funds from one private individual to another. Security transactions, that is, the buying and selling of stocks and bonds, are also excluded from GNP. Stock market transactions involve merely the swapping of paper assets. As such, these transactions do not directly involve current production. It should be noted, however, that by getting money from the hands of savers into the hands of spenders, some of these security transactions may indirectly give rise to spending which does account for output.

**Secondhand Sales**　The reason for excluding secondhand sales from GNP is fairly obvious: Such sales either reflect no *current production*, or they involve double counting. For example, suppose you sell your 1976 Ford to a neighbor. This transaction would be excluded in determining GNP because no current production is involved. The inclusion of the sales of goods produced some years ago in this year's GNP would be an exaggeration of this year's output. Similarly, if you purchased a brand new Ford and resold it a week later to your neighbor, we should still want to exclude the resale transaction from the current GNP. Why? Because when you originally bought the new car, its value was included in GNP. To include its resale value would be to count it twice.

△　**Two Sides to GNP**

Given a general understanding of the meaning of GNP, we now raise this question: How can the market value of total output—or for that matter, any single unit of output—be measured? How can we measure, for example, the market value of a cashmere sweater?

In two ways: First, we can just look at how much a consumer, as the final user, spends in obtaining it. Second, we can add up all the wage, rental, interest, and profit incomes created in the production of the sweater. This is simply the value-added approach we spoke of earlier. These are, indeed, two ways of looking at the same thing. *What is spent on a product*

**TABLE 9-3**
The Income and Output Approaches to GNP

| Output, or expenditures, approach | Income, or allocations, approach |
|---|---|
| Consumption expenditures by households<br> plus<br>Government purchases of goods and services<br> plus<br>Investment expenditures by businesses<br> plus<br>Expenditures by foreigners | = GNP = | Wages<br> plus<br>Rents<br> plus<br>Interest<br> plus<br>Profits<br> plus<br>Nonincome charges or allocations |

*is received as income by those who contributed to its production.* Indeed, Chapter 3's circular flow model is based upon this notion. If $90 is spent on the sweater, that is necessarily the total amount of income derived from its production. This equality of the expenditure for a product and the income derived from its production is guaranteed, because profit income serves as a balancing item. Profit—or loss—is the income which remains after wage, rent, and interest incomes have been paid by the producer. If the wage, rent, and interest incomes which the firm must pay in getting the sweater produced are less than the $90 expenditure for the sweater, the difference will be the firm's profits.[2] Conversely, if wage, rent, and interest incomes exceed $90, profits will be negative, that is, losses will be realized, to balance the expenditure on the product and the income derived from its production.

The same line of reasoning is also valid for the output of the economy as a whole. There are two different ways of looking at GNP: One is to look at GNP as the sum of all the expenditures involved in taking that total output off the market. This is called the *output,* or *expenditures, approach.* The other is to look at it in terms of the income derived or created from the production of the GNP. This is called

the *earnings, or income, or allocations, approach* to the determination of GNP. A closer analysis of these two approaches will reveal that they amount to this: *GNP can be determined either by adding up all that is spent on this year's total output or by summing up all the incomes derived from the production of this year's output.* Putting this in the form of a simple equation, we can say that

| The amount spent on this year's total output | = | the money income derived from the production of this year's output |
|---|---|---|

As a matter of fact, this is more than an equation: It is an identity. Buying—that is, spending money—and selling—that is, receiving money income—are actually two aspects of the same transaction. *What is spent on a product is income to those who have contributed their human and property resources in getting that product produced and to market.*

For the economy as a whole, we can expand the above identity to read as in Table 9-3. This summary statement simply tells us that all final goods produced in the American economy are purchased either by the three domestic sectors—households, government, and businesses—or by foreign nations. It also shows us that the total receipts which businesses acquire from the sale of total output are allocated among the various resource suppliers as wage, rent, interest, and profit income.

---

[2]The term "profits" is used here in the accounting sense so as to include both normal profits and economic profits as defined in Chapter 5.

Later we shall explain two additional nonincome allocations of total receipts. Using this summary as a point of reference, let us point out in some detail the meaning and significance of the various types of expenditures and the incomes derived therefrom.

## ☐ THE EXPENDITURES APPROACH TO GNP

To determine GNP through the expenditures approach, one must add up all types of spending on finished or final goods and services. But our national income accountants have much more sophisticated terms for the different types of spending than the ones we have employed in Table 9-3. We must therefore familiarize ourselves with these terms and their meanings.

### ▲ Personal Consumption Expenditures (C)

What we have called "consumption expenditures by households" is "personal consumption expenditures" to the national income accountants. It entails expenditures by households on durable consumer goods (automobiles, refrigerators, gas ranges, and so forth), nondurable consumer goods (bread, milk, beer, cigarettes, shirts, toothpaste), and consumer expenditures for services (of lawyers, doctors, mechanics, barbers). We shall use the letter $C$ to designate the total of these expenditures.

### Government Purchases of Goods and Services (G)

This classification of expenditures includes all governmental spending, Federal, state, and local, on the finished products of businesses and all direct purchases of resources—labor, in particular—by government. However, it excludes all government transfer payments, because such outlays, as previously noted, do not reflect any current production but merely transfer governmental receipts to certain specific households. The letter $G$ will be used to indicate government purchases of goods and services.

### Gross Private Domestic Investment ($I_g$)

This seemingly complicated term refers to all investment spending by American business firms. What is included as investment spending? Basically three things: (1) all final purchases of machinery, equipment, and tools by business enterprises; (2) all construction; and (3) changes in inventories. This obviously entails more than we have imputed to the term "investment" thus far. Hence, we must explain why each of these three items is included under the general heading of gross private domestic investment.

The reason for inclusion of the first group of items is apparent. This is simply a restatement of our original definition of investment spending as the purchase of tools, machinery, and equipment. The second item—all construction—merits some explanation. It is clear that the building of a new factory, warehouse, or grain elevator is a form of investment. But why include residential construction as investment rather than consumption? The reason is this: Apartment buildings are clearly investment goods because, like factories and grain elevators, they are income-earning assets. Other residential units which are rented are for the same reason investment goods. Furthermore, owner-occupied houses are classified as investment goods because they could be rented out to yield a money income return, even though the owner does not choose to do so. For these reasons all residential construction is considered as investment. Finally, why are changes in inventories counted as investment? Because an increase in inventories is, in effect, "unconsumed output," and that precisely is what investment is!

**Inventory Changes as Investment** Remembering that GNP is designed to measure total current output, we must certainly make an effort to include in GNP any products which are produced but not sold this year. In short, if GNP is to be an accurate measure of total output, it must include the market value of any additions to inventories which accrue during the year. Were we to exclude an increase in inventories, GNP would understate the current year's total output. If businesses have more goods on their shelves and in their warehouses at the end of the year than they had at the start, the economy has produced more than it has consumed during this particular year. This increase in inventories obviously must be added to GNP as a measure of *current* production.

What about a decline in inventories? This must be subtracted in figuring GNP, because in such a situation the economy sells a total output which exceeds current production, the difference being reflected in an inventory reduction. Some of the GNP taken off the market this year reflects not current production but, rather, a drawing down of inventories which were on hand at the beginning of this year. And the inventories on hand at the start of any year's production represent the production of previous years. Consequently, a decline in inventories in any given year means that the economy has consumed more than it has produced during the year; that is, society has consumed all of this year's output plus some of the inventories inherited from previous years' production. Remembering that GNP is a measure of the *current* year's output, we must omit any consumption of past production, that is, any drawing down of inventories, in determining GNP.

**Noninvestment Transactions**    We have discussed what investment is; it is equally important to emphasize what investment is not. Specifically, investment does not refer to the transfer of paper assets or secondhand tangible assets. The buying of stocks and bonds is excluded from the economist's definition of investment, because such purchases merely transfer the ownership of existing assets. The same holds true of the resale of existing assets. Investment is the construction or manufacture of *new* capital assets. It is the creation of such earning assets that gives rise to jobs and income, not the exchange of claims to existing capital goods.

**Gross versus Net Investment**    We have broadened our concepts of investment and investment goods to include purchases of machinery and equipment, all construction, and changes in inventories. Now let us focus our attention on the three modifiers, "gross," "private," and "domestic," which national income accountants see fit to use in describing investment. The second and third terms simply tell us, respectively, that we are talking about spending by private business enterprises as opposed to governmental (public) agencies and that the firms involved are American—as opposed to foreign—firms.

The term "gross," however, cannot be disposed of so easily. *Gross private domestic investment* includes the production of *all* investment goods—those which are to replace the machinery, equipment, and buildings used up in the current year's production plus any net additions to the economy's stock of capital. In short, gross investment includes both replacement and added investment. On the other hand, we reserve the term *net private domestic investment* to refer only to the added investment which has occurred in the current year. A simple example will make the distinction clear. In 1979 our economy produced about $386 billion worth of capital goods. However, in the process of producing the GNP in 1979, the economy used up some $243 billion worth of machinery and equipment. As a result, our economy added $143 (or $386 minus $243) billion to its stock of capital in 1979. Therefore, *gross* investment was $386 billion in 1979, but *net* investment was only $143 billion. The difference between the two is the value of the capital used up or depreciated in the production of 1979's GNP.

**Net Investment and Economic Growth**    The relationship between gross investment and depreciation (replacement investment) provides a good indicator of whether our economy is expanding, static, or declining. Figure 9-1 illustrates these three cases.

*1  Expanding economy*    When gross investment exceeds depreciation, as in Figure

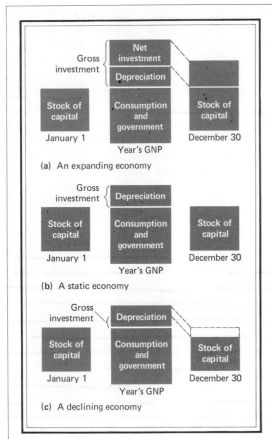

**FIGURE 9-1  EXPANDING, STATIC, AND DECLINING ECONOMIES**

In an expanding economy (a), gross investment exceeds depreciation, which means that the economy is making a net addition to its stock of capital facilities. In a static economy (b), gross investment precisely replaces the capital facilities depreciated in producing the year's output, leaving the stock of capital goods unchanged. In a declining economy (c), gross investment is insufficient to replace the capital goods depreciated by the year's production. As a result, the economy's stock of capital declines.

9-1a, the economy is obviously expanding in the sense that its productive capacity—as measured by its stock of capital goods—is growing. More simply, net investment is a positive figure in an expanding economy. For example, as noted above, in 1979 gross investment was $386 billion, and $243 billion worth

of capital goods were consumed in producing that year's GNP. This meant that our economy ended 1979 with $143 billion more capital goods than it had on hand at the start of the year. More bluntly stated, we made a $143 billion addition to our "national factory" in 1979. Increasing the supply of capital goods, you will recall, is a basic means of expanding the productive capacity of the economy (see Figures 2-3 and 2-4).

② **Static economy**   A stationary or static economy reflects the situation in which gross investment and depreciation are equal. This means the economy is standing pat; it is producing just enough capital to replace what is consumed in producing the year's output—no more and no less. This happened in 1942 during World War II. Investment was purposely restricted by governmental action to free resources for war goods production. Hence, in 1942 gross investment and depreciation (replacement investment) were approximately equal at $10 billion. This meant that at the end of 1942 our stock of capital was about the same as at the start of that year. In other words, *net* investment was about zero. Our economy was a stationary one in the sense that its productive facilities failed to expand. Figure 9-1*b* represents the case of a static economy.

③ **Declining economy**   The unhappy case of a declining economy arises whenever gross investment is less than depreciation, that is, when the economy consumes more capital in a year than it manages to produce. Under such circumstances net investment will be a negative figure—the economy will be "disinvesting." Depressions foster such circumstances. During bad times, when production and employment are at a low ebb, the nation has a greater productive capacity than it is currently utilizing. Hence, there is little or no incentive to replace depreciated capital equipment, much less add to the existing stock. Depreciation is likely to exceed gross investment, with the result that the nation's stock of capital is less at the end of the year than it was at the start. This was the case during the heart of the Great Depression. In 1933, for example, gross investment was only $1.4 billion, while the capital consumed during that year was $6.9 billion. Net disinvestment was therefore $5.5 billion. Figure 9-1c illustrates the case of a disinvesting, or declining, economy.

We shall use the symbol $I$ to refer to domestic investment spending and attach the subscript $g$ when referring to gross and $n$ when referring to net investment.

$I_g$   $I_n$

## Net Exports ($X_n$)

How do American international trade transactions enter into national income accounting? We can best explain it in this way: First, remember that we are trying to add up all spending in American markets which accounts for or induces the production of goods and services in the American economy. A bit of reflection will lead you to the conclusion that spending by foreigners on American goods will account for American output just as will spending by Americans. Hence, we want to add in what foreigners spend on American goods and services—that is, we want to add in the value of American exports—in determining GNP by the expenditures approach. On the other hand, we must recognize that a portion of consumption, investment, and government purchases are for goods which have been imported, that is, produced abroad, and therefore do *not* reflect productive activity in the United States. The value of imports is estimated and subtracted to avoid an overstatement of total production in the United States.

Rather than treat these two items—American exports and imports—separately, our national income accountants merely take the difference between the two. Hence, *net exports of goods and services* or, more simply, *net exports, is the amount by which foreign spending on American goods and services exceeds American spending on foreign goods and services.* For example, should foreigners

buy $9 billion worth of American exports and Americans buy $7 billion worth of foreign imports in a given year, net exports would be *plus* $2 billion. It must be emphasized that our definition of net exports might result in a negative figure. If foreigners spend $10 billion on American exports and Americans spend $12 billion on foreign imports, our "excess" of foreign spending over American spending is *minus* $2 billion.

The letter $X_n$ will be used to designate net exports.

$$C + I_g + G + X_n = GNP$$

The four categories of expenditures that we have discussed—personal consumption expenditures ($C$), government expenditures on goods and services ($G$), gross private domestic investment ($I_g$), and net exports ($X_n$)—are comprehensive. They include all possible types of spending. Added together, they measure the market value of the year's output or, in other words, the GNP. That is,

$$C + I_g + G + X_n = GNP$$

For 1979 (Table 9-4):

$$\$1510 + \$386 + \$476 + (-\$4) = \$2369$$

## □ THE INCOME APPROACH TO GNP[3]

How was this $2369 billion of expenditures allocated or distributed as income? It would be most convenient if we could simply say that the total expenditures upon the economy's annual output flow to households as wage, rent, interest, and profit incomes. Unfortunately, the picture is complicated somewhat by two nonincome charges against the value of total output, that is, against GNP. These are (1) a capital consumption allowance, and (2) indirect business taxes.

---

[3]Some instructors may choose to omit this section because the expenditures approach is more relevant for the analysis of Chapters 11–13.

**TABLE 9-4**
**The Income Statement for the Economy, 1979 (*in billions of dollars*)**

| Receipts: expenditures approach | | Allocations: income approach | |
|---|---|---|---|
| Personal consumption expenditures $(C)$ | $1510 | Capital consumption allowance | $ 243 |
| Government purchases of goods and | | Indirect business taxes | 201 |
| services $(G)$ | 476 | Compensation of employees | 1459 |
| Gross private domestic investment $(I_g)$ | 386 | Rents | 27 |
| Net exports $(X_n)$ | −4 | Interest | 130 |
| | | Proprietors' income | 130 |
| | | Corporate income taxes | 93 |
| | | Dividends | 53 |
| | | Undistributed corporate profits | 33 |
| Gross national product | $2369 | Gross national product | $2369 |

*Source:* U.S. Department of Commerce data. Because of rounding, figures may not add up to totals.

△ **Depreciation: Capital Consumption Allowance**

The useful life of most capital equipment extends far beyond the year of purchase. Actual expenditures for capital goods and their productive life are not synchronized in the same accounting period. Hence, to avoid gross understatement of profit and therefore of total income in the year of purchase and overstatement of profit and of total income in succeeding years, individual businesses estimate the useful life of their capital goods and allocate the total cost of such goods more or less evenly over the life of the machinery. The annual charge which estimates the amount of capital equipment used up in each year's production is called "depreciation." Depreciation is essentially a bookkeeping entry designed to provide a more accurate statement of profit income and hence total income provided by a firm in each year.

If profits and total income for the economy as a whole are to be stated accurately, a gigantic depreciation charge for the economy as a whole must be made against the total receipts of the business sector. This depreciation charge is called a "capital consumption allowance." Why? Because that is exactly what it is—an allowance for capital goods which have been "consumed" in the process of

producing this year's GNP. It is this huge depreciation charge which constitutes the previously noted difference between $I_g$ and $I_n$. For present purposes, the significance of this charge lies in the fact that it claims a part of the business sector's receipts which is, therefore, not available for income payments to resource suppliers. In real terms, that is, in terms of physical goods and services, the capital consumption allowance tells us in effect that a portion of this year's GNP must be set aside to replace the machinery and equipment used up in accomplishing its production. In other words, all of GNP cannot be consumed as income by society without impairing the economy's stock of productive facilities.

△ **Indirect Business Taxes**

The second complicating nonincome charge arises from the presence of government. Government levies certain taxes, called "indirect business taxes," which business firms treat as costs of production and therefore add to the prices of the products they sell. Such taxes include general sales taxes, excises, business property taxes, license fees, and custom duties. We can think of it in this way: A firm produces a product designed to sell at, say, $1. As we have seen, the production of this item creates an equal amount of wages, rental, interest, and profit income. But now government, in need of revenue to finance its activities, imposes a 3 percent sales tax on all products sold at retail. The retailer merely adds this 3 percent to the price of the product, raising its price from $1 to $1.03 and thereby shifting the burden of the sales tax to consumers.[4]

Obviously, this 3 percent of total receipts which reflects the tax must be paid out to government before the remaining $1 can be paid to households as wage, rent, interest, and profit incomes. Government, in effect, is a preferred creditor. Furthermore, this flow of indirect business taxes to government is not earned income, because government contributes nothing directly to the production of the good in return for these sales tax receipts. As a matter of fact, in the cases of sales and excise taxes the finished product is being handed to the consumer at the time the tax is levied. In short, we must be careful to exclude indirect business taxes when figuring the total income earned in each year by the factors of production.

Capital consumption allowances and indirect business taxes account for the nonincome allocations listed in Table 9-3. As just noted, what remains is wages, rents, interest, and profits. But, for a variety of reasons, national income statisticians need a more sophisticated breakdown of wages and profits than we have employed thus far in this discussion.

△ **Compensation of Employees**

This largest income category comprises primarily the wages and salaries which are paid by businesses and government to suppliers of labor. It also includes an array of wage and salary supplements, in particular payments by employers into social insurance and into a variety of private pension, health, and welfare funds for workers. These wage and salary supplements are a part of the employer's cost of

obtaining labor and therefore are treated as a component of the firm's total wage payments.

△ **Rents**

Rents are almost self-explanatory. They consist of income payments received by households which supply property resources.

△ **Interest**

Interest refers to money income payments which flow from private businesses to the suppliers of money capital. For reasons to be noted later, interest payments made by government are excluded from interest income.

△ **Proprietors' Income**

What we have loosely termed "profits" is also broken into two basic accounts by national income accountants: One part is called *proprietors' income* or income of unincorporated businesses, and the other, *corporate profits*. The former account is largely self-defining. It refers to the net income of sole proprietorships, partnerships, and cooperatives. On the other hand, corporate profits cannot be dismissed so easily, because corporate earnings may be distributed in several ways.

△ **Corporate Profits**

Generally speaking, three things can be done with corporate profits: First, a part will be claimed by, and therefore flow to, government as *corporate income taxes*. Second, a part of the remaining corporate profits will be paid out to stockholders as *dividends*. Such payments flow to households, which, of course, are the ultimate owners of all corporations. What remains of corporate profits after both corporate income taxes and dividends have been paid is called *undistributed corporate profits*. These retained corporate earnings, along with capital consumption allowances, are invested currently or in the future in new plants and equipment, thereby increasing the real assets of the investing businesses.

Table 9-4 summarizes our detailed discus-

---

[4] In Chapter 23 we shall use supply and demand analysis to find that the shifting of a sales tax is not quite this simple.

sions of both the expenditure and income approaches to GNP. The reader will recognize that this is merely a gigantic income statement for the economy as a whole. The left-hand side tells us what the economy produced in 1979 and the total receipts derived from that production. The right-hand side indicates how the income derived from the production of 1979's GNP was allocated. One can determine GNP either by adding up the four types of expenditures on final goods and services or by adding up the nine categories of income and nonincome charges which stem from that output's production. Because output and income are two sides of the same coin, the two sums will necessarily match.

## ☐  OTHER SOCIAL ACCOUNTS

Our discussion has centered upon GNP as a measure of the economy's annual output. However, there are certain related social accounting concepts of equal importance which can be derived from GNP. To round out our understanding of social accounting, it is imperative that we trace through the process of deriving these related concepts. This procedure will also enhance our understanding of how the expenditure and income approaches to GNP dovetail one another. Our plan of attack will be to start with GNP and make a series of adjustments—subtractions and additions—necessary to the derivation of the related social accounts.

### △  Net National Product (NNP)

GNP as a measure of total output has an important defect: It tends to give us a somewhat exaggerated picture of this year's production. Why? *Because it fails to make allowance for that part of this year's output which is necessary to replace the capital goods consumed in the year's production.*

Two examples will help make this point clear: First, suppose a farmer starts the year by planting 20 bushels of wheat, realizing a total output of 400 bushels at the end of the year. Is it correct to represent his output for the year

as 400 bushels? Certainly not. He would have had 20 bushels available if he had planted nothing at all. His *net* output for the year is 400 minus 20, or 380 bushels. This is a more accurate measure of the production that has actually occurred this year than is 400 bushels. Second, using hypothetical figures, suppose that on January 1, 1981, the economy had $100 billion worth of capital goods on hand. Assume also that during 1981, $40 billion worth of this equipment and machinery is used up in producing a GNP of $800 billion. Thus, on December 31, 1981, the stock of capital goods on hand stands at only $60 billion. Is it fair to say that the GNP figure of $800 billion accurately measures this year's output? No. It would be much more accurate to subtract from the year's GNP the $40 billion worth of capital goods which must be used to replace the machinery and equipment consumed in producing that GNP. This leaves a *net* output figure of $800 minus $40, or $760 billion.

In short, a figure for *net* output is a more accurate measure of a year's production than is *gross* output. In our system of social accounting, we derive a figure for *net national product* (NNP) by subtracting the capital consumption allowance, which measures replacement investment or the value of the capital used up in a year's production, from GNP. Hence, in 1979:

|                                       | Billions |
|---------------------------------------|----------|
| Gross national product  . . . . . . . . . . . . . | $2369 |
| Capital consumption balance  . . . . . . . . . | −243 |
|   Net national product  . . . . . . . . . . . . . | $2126 |

NNP, then, is GNP adjusted for depreciation charges. It measures the total annual output which the entire economy—households, businesses, and governments—might consume without impairing our capacity to produce in ensuing years.

It is a simple matter, by the way, to adjust Table 9-4 from GNP to NNP. On the income side we just strike out capital consumption allowance. The other eight allocations should add up to a NNP of $2126 billion. On the expenditure side, one must change *gross* private domestic investment to *net* private domestic investment by subtracting replacement investment as measured by the capital consumption allowance from the former figure. In 1979, a gross investment figure of $386 billion less a depreciation charge of $243 billion results in a net private domestic investment figure of $143 billion and therefore a NNP of $2126 billion.

### △  National Income (NI)

In analyzing certain problems, we are vitally interested in how much income is *earned* by resource suppliers for their contributions of land, labor, capital, and entrepreneurial ability which go into the year's net production or, alternatively stated, how much it costs society in terms of economic resources to produce this net output. The only component of NNP which does not reflect the current productive contributions of economic resources is indirect business taxes. It will be recalled that government contributes nothing directly to production in return for the indirect business tax revenues which it receives; government is *not* considered to be a factor of production. Hence, to get a measure of total wage, rent, interest, and profit incomes earned from the production of the year's output, we must subtract indirect business taxes from NNP. The resulting figure is called the *national income*. From the viewpoint of resource suppliers, it measures the incomes they have earned for their current contributions to production. From the viewpoint of businesses, national income measures factor or resource costs; national income reflects the market costs of the economic resources which have gone into the creation of this year's output. In 1979:

|                              | Billions |
|------------------------------|---------:|
| Net national product         | $2126    |
| Indirect business taxes      | −202     |
| National income              | $1924    |

A glance at Table 9-4 shows that national income can also be obtained through the income approach by simply adding up all the allocations with the exception of capital consumption allowances and indirect business taxes. The seven allocations of GNP which remain after the two nonincome charges have been subtracted constitute the national income.

### △  Personal Income (PI)

Income *earned* (national income) and income *received* (personal income) are likely to differ for the reason that some income which is earned—social security contributions (payroll taxes), corporate income taxes, and undistributed corporate profits—is not actually received by households, and, conversely, some income which is received—transfer payments—is not currently earned. Transfer payments, you may recall, are made up of such items as (1) old age and survivors' insurance payments and unemployment compensation, both of which stem from our social security program, (2) welfare payments, (3) a variety of veterans' payments, for example, GI Bill of Rights and disability payments, (4) payments out of private pension and welfare programs, and (5) interest payments paid by government and by consumers.[5]

Obviously, in moving from national income as a measure of income earned to personal income as an indicator of income actually received, we must subtract from national income those three types of income which are earned but not received and add in income received but not currently earned. This is done as follows:

---

[5] Why include interest payments on government bonds as income *not* currently earned, particularly when interest on the bonds of private firms is included in national income as earned income? The rationale underlying the exclusion is this: Much of the debt has been incurred in connection with (1) war and defense and (2) recessions. Furthermore, unlike public deficits to finance airports or highways, deficits stemming from the military and recessions yield no productive assets (services) to the economy. Hence, interest paid on such debt does *not* reflect the generation of any current output or income. Similar reasoning underlies the inclusion of interest payments by consumers as a part of transfer payments.

| | Billions |
|---|---|
| National income (income earned) | $1924 |
| Social security contributions | −190 |
| Corporate income taxes | −93 |
| Undistributed corporate profits | −33 |
| Transfer payments | +315 |
| Personal income (income received) | $1923 |

### △ Disposable Income (DI)

*Disposable income* is simply personal income less personal taxes. *Personal taxes* are comprised of personal income taxes, personal property taxes, and inheritance taxes, the first of the three being by far the most important. This adjustment is as follows:

$$DI = PI - PT$$

| | Billions |
|---|---|
| Personal income (income received before personal taxes) | $1923 |
| Personal taxes | −300 |
| Disposable income (income received after personal taxes) | $1623 |

Disposable income is the amount of income which households have to dispose of as they see fit. Basically, the choices are two. Remembering that economists conveniently define saving as "not spending," or better, "that part of disposable income which is not spent on consumer goods," it follows that households divide their disposable income between consumption and saving.

### △ Relationships between Major Social Accounts

We have derived four new social accounting concepts from GNP: (1) net national product (NNP), the market value of the annual output net of capital consumption allowances; (2) national income (NI), income *earned* by the factors of production for their current contributions to production, or the factor costs entailed in getting the year's total output produced; (3) personal income (PI), income *re-*

*ceived* by households before personal taxes; and (4) disposable income (DI), income received by households less personal taxes. The relationships between these concepts are summarized in Table 9-5.

### ☐ MONEY VERSUS REAL GNP

Recall that GNP, by definition, is the *money* or *market value* of all goods and services produced in a year. Money values necessarily are used as a common denominator in order to sum a heterogeneous output into a meaningful total. But this raises a problem: The value of different years' outputs (GNPs) can be compared only if the value of money itself does not change because of inflation or deflation.

Stated differently, inflation or deflation complicates gross national product because GNP is a prices-times-quantity figure. The raw data from which the national income accountants estimate GNP are the total sales figures of business firms; these figures obviously embody changes in *both* the quantity of output *and* the level of prices. This means that a change in either the quantity of total physical output or the price level will affect the size of GNP. However, it is the quantity of

**TABLE 9-5**
The Relationships between GNP, NNP, NI, PI, and DI in 1979

| | Billions |
|---|---|
| Gross national product (GNP) | $2369 |
| Capital consumption allowance | −243 |
| Net national product (NNP) | $2126 |
| Indirect business taxes | −202 |
| National income (NI) | $1924 |
| Social security contributions | −190 |
| Corporate income taxes | −93 |
| Undistributed corporate profits | −33 |
| Transfer payments | +315 |
| Personal income (PI) | $1923 |
| Personal taxes | −300 |
| Disposable income (DI) | $1623 |

goods produced and distributed to households which affects their standard of living and not the size of the price tags which these goods bear. The hamburger of 1965 which sold for 30 cents yielded the same satisfaction as will an identical hamburger selling for 95 cents in 1980. The problem, then, is one of adjusting a price-times-quantity figure so it will accurately reflect changes in physical output, not changes in prices.

Fortunately, national income accountants have been able to resolve this difficulty: They *deflate* GNP for rising prices and *inflate* it when prices are falling. These adjustments give us a picture of GNP for various years *as if* prices and the value of the dollar were constant. A GNP figure which reflects current prices, that is, which is *not* adjusted for changes in the price level, is called *unadjusted* or *money GNP*. Similarly, GNP figures which are inflated or deflated for price level changes measure *adjusted* or *real GNP*.

△  **The Adjustment Process**

Some examples will help us understand how GNP figures are adjusted for price changes. First, an exceedingly simple example: Assume our economy produces only one good, product X, and in the amounts indicated in Table 9-6 for years 1, 2, and 3. An examination of columns 1 and 2 tells us that the *money* GNPs for years 2 and 3, as shown in column 4, greatly overstate the increases in *real* output occurring in those two years. That is, the

monetary measure of production (money GNP) does not accurately reflect the actual changes which have occurred in physical output (real GNP). Considerable portions of the sharp increases in money GNP in years 2 and 3 are due to the drastic inflation shown in column 2, the remainder being due to the changes in physical output shown in column 1. Both increases in physical output and price increases are reflected in the money GNP.

Now the situation facing our social accountants is this: In gathering statistics from the financial reports of businesses and deriving GNP for years 1, 2, and 3, governmental accountants come up with the figures for money GNP shown in column 4. They will *not* know directly to what extent changes in price, on the one hand, and changes in quantity of output, on the other, have accounted for the given increases in money GNP. Social accountants will not have before them the data of columns 1 and 2, but only the data of column 4. Being resourceful individuals, they attempt to adjust the money GNP figure for price changes. They do this by deriving a general price index which estimates overall changes in the price level. By expressing this price index as a decimal and dividing it into money GNP, one can obtain real GNP. In our example, wherein we are dealing with only one product, a simple single-price index number is all that is required. Such a price index is nothing more than *a percentage comparison from a fixed point of reference*. This point of reference, or bench

**TABLE 9-6**
Deflating Money GNP *(hypothetical data)*

| Year | (1) Units of output | (2) Price of X | (3) Price index, percent (Year 1 = 100) | (4) Unadjusted, or money, GNP (1) × (2) | (5) Adjusted, or real, GNP |
|------|------|------|------|------|------|
| 1 | 5 | $10 | 100 | $ 50 | $50 ( = $ 50 ÷ 1.00) |
| 2 | 7 | 20 | 200 | 140 | 70 ( = 140 ÷ 2.00) |
| 3 | 8 | 25 | 250 | 200 | 80 ( = 200 ÷ 2.50) |
| 4 | 10 | 30 | ____ | ____ | ____ |
| 5 | 11 | 28 | ____ | ____ | ____ |

mark, is called the *base year*. By comparing prices in previous and ensuing years with prices in the base year, we can tell how much prices have increased or decreased *relative to* what they were in the base year. Suppose product X sells for $10 in year 1, $20 in year 2, and $25 in year 3, as shown in Table 9-6. Selecting year 1 as the base year, we can express the prices of product X in years 2 and 3 relative to X's price in year 1 through the formula

$$\text{Price index} = \frac{\text{price in any given year}}{\text{price in base year}} \times 100$$

We multiply the price comparison by 100 in order to express it as a percentage. Using year 2 as the given year, we find that

$$\text{Price index} = \frac{\$20}{\$10} \times 100 = 200 \text{ percent}$$

and for year 3,

$$\text{Price index} = \frac{\$25}{\$10} \times 100 = 250 \text{ percent}$$

For year 1 the index must be 100 percent, since the given year and the base year are identical. In this case,

$$\text{Price index} = \frac{\$10}{\$10} \times 100 = 100 \text{ percent}$$

These index numbers tell us that the price of product X in the year 2 was 200 percent of what it was in year 1 and in year 3 it was 250 percent of year 1's price. The index numbers of column 3 can now be used to deflate the inflated money GNP figures of column 4. As already noted, *the simplest and most direct method of deflating is to express these index numbers as hundredths, that is, in decimal form, and divide them into the corresponding money GNP.*[6] That is,

$$\frac{\text{money GNP}}{\text{price index (as decimal)}} = \text{real GNP}$$

Column 5 shows the results with the relevant calculations in parentheses. These real GNP figures measure the value of total output in years 1, 2, and 3 *as if* the price of product X had been constant at $10 throughout the three-year period. Real GNP thus shows the market value of each year's output measured in terms of constant dollars, that is, dollars which have the same value, or purchasing power, as in the base year. Real GNP is clearly superior to money GNP as an indicator of the economy's productive performance over a period of time.

To ensure your understanding of the deflating process, you are urged to complete Table 9-6 for years 4 and 5. Second, it is recommended that you rework the entire deflating procedure, using year 3 as the base year. You will find, by the way, that in this case you must inflate some of the money GNP data, just as we have deflated it in our examples.

△   **Inflating and Deflating**

Table 9-7 provides us with a "real-world" illustration of the inflating and deflating process. Here we are taking actual money GNP figures for selected years and adjusting them with an index of the general price level to obtain real GNP. Note that the base year is 1972. Because the long-run trend has been for the price level to rise, the problem is one of increasing, or *inflating,* the pre-1972 figures. This upward revision of money GNP acknowledges that prices were lower in years prior to 1972 and, as a result, money GNP figures understated the real output of those years. Column 4 indicates what GNP would have been in all these selected years if the 1972 price level had prevailed. However, the rising price level has caused the money GNP figures for the post-1972 years to overstate real output; hence, these figures must be reduced, or *deflated,* as in column 4 in order for us to gauge

---

[6]This yields the same result as the more complex procedure of dividing money GNPs by the corresponding index number and multiplying the quotient by 100.

**TABLE 9-7**
Adjusting GNP for Changes in the Price Level
(*selected years, in billions of dollars*)

| (1)<br>Year | (2)<br>Money, or<br>unadjusted,<br>GNP | (3)<br>Price level<br>index,*<br>percent<br>(1972 = 100) | (4)<br>Real, or<br>adjusted, GNP,<br>1972 dollars |
|---|---|---|---|
| 1946 | $ 209.6 | 44.06 | $ 475.7 (= 209.6 ÷ 0.4406) |
| 1951 | 330.2 | 57.27 | _____ |
| 1958 | 448.9 | 66.06 | $ 679.5 (= 448.9 ÷ 0.6606) |
| 1964 | 635.7 | 72.71 | _____ |
| 1968 | 868.5 | 82.57 | $1051.8 (= 868.5 ÷ 0.8257) |
| 1972 | 1171.1 | 100.00 | $1171.1 (= 1171.1 ÷ 1.0000) |
| 1974 | 1406.9 | 116.20 | _____ |
| 1977 | 1899.5 | 141.70 | $1340.5 (= 1899.5 ÷ 1.4170) |
| 1979 | 2368.5 | 165.50 | $1431.1 (= 2368.5 ÷ 1.6550) |

*U.S. Department of Commerce implicit price deflators.
*Source:* U.S. Department of Commerce data.

what GNP would have been in 1974, 1977, and so on, if 1972 prices had actually prevailed. In short, while the *money* GNP figures reflect both output and price changes, the *real* GNP figures allow us to estimate changes in real output, because the real GNP figures, in effect, hold the price level constant. The reader should trace through the computations involved in deriving the real GNP figures given in Table 9-7 and also determine real GNP for years 1951, 1964, and 1974, for which the figures have been purposely omitted.[7]

☐  **GNP AND SOCIAL WELFARE**
GNP is a reasonably accurate and extremely useful measure of national economic performance. It is not, and was never intended to be, an index of social welfare. GNP is merely a measure of the annual volume of market-

---

[7]Technical footnote: While this discussion of Table 9-7 provides an intuitive understanding of the process of inflating or deflating GNP with appropriate index numbers, a thorough grasp of the rationale for dividing money GNP by an appropriate index to get real GNP calls for further comment. Suppose we want to adjust money GNP for 1981 to real GNP (in 1972 prices) so we can determine the growth of real GNP between 1972 and 1981. We know, first, that money GNP for 1981 ($GNP_{1981}$) is equal to the physical output in 1981 ($Q_{1981}$) times the prices ($P_{1981}$) at which the output sold. That is,

$$GNP_{1981} = Q_{1981} \cdot P_{1981}$$

We also know from the text's discussion of index numbers that the price index for 1981, using 1972 as the base year, equals the ratio of prices in 1981 to prices in 1972. Thus

$$\text{1981 price index} = P_{1981}/P_{1972}$$

The text also directs us to divide money GNP for 1981 by this 1981 price index to get real GNP for 1981, that is, 1981's output measured at 1972 prices:

$$\frac{GNP_{1981}}{P_{1981}/P_{1972}} = \frac{Q_{1981} \cdot P_{1981}}{P_{1981}/P_{1972}}$$

Inverting and multiplying by the fraction or ratio which represents the 1981 index, we get

$$\frac{GNP_{1981}}{P_{1981}/P_{1972}} = (Q_{1981} \cdot P_{1981}) \cdot \frac{P_{1972}}{P_{1981}}$$

The $P_{1981}$ expressions cancel, leaving

$$\frac{GNP_{1981}}{P_{1981}/P_{1972}} = Q_{1981} \cdot P_{1972}$$

That is to say, by dividing the 1981 money GNP ($GNP_{1981}$) by the 1981 price index ($P_{1981}/P_{1972}$) we derive real GNP for 1981 or, more specifically, the 1981 output ($Q_{1981}$) measured in terms of 1972 prices ($P_{1972}$).

oriented activity. And, while GNP may yield a workable impression of material well-being, it is a far cry from being a meaningful indicator of social welfare:[8]

> . . . any number of things could make the Nation better off without raising its real GNP as measured today: we might start the list with peace, equality of opportunity, the elimination of injustice and violence, greater brotherhood among Americans of different racial and ethnic backgrounds, better understanding between parents and children and between husbands and wives, and we could go on endlessly.

There is, nevertheless, a widely held assumption that there should be a strong positive correlation between real GNP and social welfare, that is, greater production should move society toward "the good life." Hence, it is important to understand some of the shortcomings of GNP—some reasons why GNP might understate or overstate real output and why more output will not necessarily make society better off.

### △　Nonmarket Transactions

There are certain productive transactions which do not appear in the market. Hence, GNP as a measure of the market value of output fails to include these productive transactions. Standard examples include the productive services of the wife, the efforts of the carpenter who repairs his or her own home, or the work of the erudite professor who writes a scholarly but nonremunerative article. Such transactions are *not* reflected in the profit and loss statements of business firms and therefore escape the national income accountants, causing GNP to be understated. However, some very important nonmarket transactions, such as that portion of farmers' output which farm-

ers consume themselves, are estimated by national income accountants.

### △　Leisure

Over a long period of years, leisure has increased very significantly. The current average workweek is about 39 hours, as compared with 53 hours at the turn of the century. The expanded availability of paid vacations and holidays, particularly since World War II, has significantly reduced work time. Increased leisure has added immeasurably to our well-being. Hence, our system of social accounting understates our well-being by not directly taking cognizance of this. Nor do the accounts reflect the satisfaction—the "psychic income"—which one might derive from one's work.

### △　Improved Product Quality

GNP is a quantitative rather than a qualitative measure. It does not accurately reflect improvements in the quality of products. This is a shortcoming: Quality improvement obviously affects economic well-being every bit as much as does the quantity of goods. To the extent that product quality has improved over time, GNP understates improvement in our material well-being.

### △　The Composition and Distribution of Output

Changes in the composition and the allocation of total output among specific households may influence economic welfare. GNP, however, reflects only the size of output and does not tell us anything about whether this collection of goods is "right" for society. A switchblade knife and a Beethoven LP record, both selling for $6.95, are weighted equally in the GNP. And, although the point is a matter for vigorous debate (see Chapter 37), some economists feel that a more equal distribution of total output would increase national economic well-being. If these economists are correct, a future trend toward a more nearly equal

[8]Arthur M. Okun, "Social Welfare Has No Price Tag," *The Economic Accounts of the United States: Retrospect and Prospect* (U.S. Department of Commerce, July 1971), p. 129.

distribution of GNP would enhance the economic welfare of society. A less nearly equal future distribution would have the reverse effect. In short, GNP measures the size of total output but does not reflect changes in the composition and distribution of output which might also affect the economic well-being of society.

△  **GNP and the Environment**

There are undesirable and much publicized "gross national by-products" which accompany the production and growth of the GNP. These take the form of dirty air and water, automobile junkyards, congestion, noise, and various other forms of environmental pollution. Although we shall defer detailed discussion of the economics of pollution to Chapter 36, it is quite clear that the costs of pollution affect our economic well-being adversely. These spillover costs associated with the production of the GNP are not now deducted from total output and, hence, GNP overstates our national economic welfare. Ironically, as GNP increases, so does pollution and the extent of this overstatement. As put by one economist, "The ultimate physical product of economic life is garbage."[9] A rising GNP means more garbage—more environmental pollution. In fact, under existing accounting procedures, when a manufacturer pollutes a river and government spends to clean it up, the cleanup expense is added to the GNP while the pollution is not subtracted! This line of thought is explored further in the Last Word segment of the present chapter.

△  **The Underground Economy**

Some economists contend that the underground or illegal sector of our economy has been expanding in relative importance with the result that the national income accounts are understating our output and growth rates by increasing amounts. GNP data simply do not pick up information for such illegal activities as gambling, loan-sharking, prostitution, and the narcotics trade. These may well be "growth industries." Furthermore, inflation has squeezed real incomes directly and by pushing families into higher income-tax brackets (Chapter 8), strengthens the incentive to receive income in forms (for example, barter or cash) which cannot be readily traced by the Internal Revenue Service. Finally, increasing government regulations, prohibitions, and reporting burdens provide a growing incentive for businesses to engage in unreported activities.

Although there is considerable dispute as to the size and growth of the underground economy, there is some evidence that it is sizeable and expanding. If so, our national income accounts not only understate the economy's performance, but also provide an increasingly questionable factual basis for policy formation.[10]

△  **Per Capita Output**

For many purposes the most meaningful measure of economic well-being is per capita output. Because GNP measures the size of total output, it may conceal or misrepresent changes in the standard of living of individual households in the economy. For example, GNP may rise significantly, but if population is also growing rapidly, the per capita standard of living may be relatively constant or may even be declining.

We will find in Chapter 21 that this is the plight of many of the less developed countries. Consider India. Its national output grew at about 3.3 percent per year over the 1966–1977 period. But annual population growth exceeded 2 percent, resulting in a meager annual increase in per capita output of only 1.3 percent.

---

[9]See the delightful and perceptive essay "Fun and Games with the Gross National Product" by Kenneth E. Boulding, in Harold W. Helfrich, Jr. (ed.), *The Environmental Crisis* (New Haven: Yale University Press, 1970), p. 162.

[10]The interested student should consult Edgar L. Feige, "How Big is the Irregular Economy?" and Peter M. Gutmann, "Statistical Illusions, Mistaken Policies," both of which appear in *Challenge*, November–December, 1979.

# Summary

Figure 9-2 embodies a comprehensive summary and synthesis of all the social accounting measures discussed in this chapter. As a more realistic and more complex expression of the circular flow model of the economy (discussed in Chapter 3), this figure merits careful study by the reader. Starting at the GNP rectangle in the upper left-hand corner, the expenditures side of GNP is shown to the left. For simplicity's sake, we have assumed net exports to be zero. Immediately to the right of the GNP rectangle are the nine income components of GNP and then the various additions and subtractions which are needed in the derivation of NNP, NI, and PI. In the household sector we see the flow of personal taxes out of PI and the division of DI between consumption and personal saving. In the government sector the flows of revenue in the form of four basic types of taxes are denoted on the right; on the left, government disbursements take the form of purchases of goods and services and transfers. To simplify, a balanced budget is assumed in the public sector. The position of the business sector is such as to emphasize, on the left, investment expenditures and, on the right, the three major sources of funds for business investment.

    The major virtue of Figure 9-2 is that it simultaneously portrays the expenditure and income aspects of GNP, fitting the two approaches to one another. This figure correctly indicates that these flows of expenditure and income are part of a continuous, repetitive

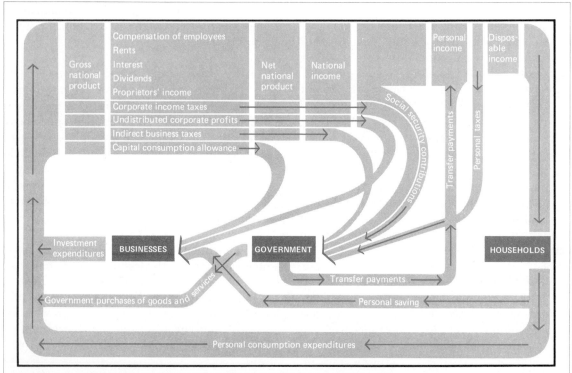

FIGURE 9-2   NATIONAL OUTPUT AND THE FLOWS OF EXPENDITURE AND INCOME

This figure is an elaborate circular flow diagram which fits the expenditures and allocations sides of GNP to one another. The reader should trace through the income and expenditures flows, relating them to the five basic national income accounting measures.

process.  Cause and effect are intermingled: Expenditures give rise to income, and out of this income arise expenditures which again flow to resource owners as income, and so forth.

Finally, the following concise definitions of the most important measures of the economy's performance should be thoroughly understood in studying Figure 9-2:

1  *Gross national product* (GNP) refers to the market value of all final goods and services produced in the economy in a given year.

2  *Net national product* (NNP) is gross national product minus capital consumption allowances (depreciation).  NNP may also be found by summing personal consumption expenditures, *net* private domestic investment, government purchases of goods and services, and *net* exports.

3  *National income* (NI) is the total income *earned* by resource suppliers for their contributions to the production of GNP.  National income also measures the costs of the resources used up in producing GNP.  Its magnitude can be derived by subtracting indirect business taxes from NNP or by summing compensation of employees, rents, interest, proprietors' income, corporate income taxes, dividends, and undistributed corporate profits.

4  *Personal income* (PI) is the total income *received* by households during a given year.  PI is determined by subtracting from national income that income which is earned but not received (social security contributions, corporate income taxes, and undistributed corporate profits) and adding that income which is received but not earned (transfer payments).

5  *Disposable income* (DI) is the portion of personal income which remains after the payment of personal taxes.

*NNP =*
*GNP-CCA*
*(dep)*

*PI = NI -*
*Income which*
*is earned but*
*Not received*

## Questions and Study Suggestions

1  Key terms and concepts to remember: gross national product; final and intermediate goods; double counting; value added; expenditure and income approaches; gross and net private domestic investment; net exports; net national product; national income; personal income; disposable income; inflating and deflating.

2  "National income statistics are a powerful tool of economic understanding and analysis."  Explain.  "An economy's output is its income."  Do you agree?

3  Why do national income accountants include only final goods in measuring total output?  How do GNP and NNP differ?

4  What is the difference between gross private domestic investment and net private domestic investment?  If you were to determine net national product through the expenditures approach, which of these two measures of investment spending would be appropriate?  Explain.

5  Why are changes in inventories included as a part of investment spending?  Suppose inventories declined by $1 billion during 1981.  How would this affect the size of gross private domestic investment and gross national product in 1981?  Explain.

6  Use the concepts of gross and net investment to distinguish between an expanding, a static, and a declining economy.  "In 1933 net private domestic investment was minus $5.5 billion.  This means in that particular year the economy produced no capital goods at all."  Do you agree?  Explain: "Though net investment can be positive, negative, or zero, it is quite impossible for gross investment to be less than zero."

7  Define net exports.  Suppose foreigners spend $7 billion on American exports in a given year and Americans spend $5 billion on imports from abroad in the same year.  What is the amount of America's net exports?

is a list of national income figures for a given year.  All figures are in
uestion will ask you to determine the major national income measures
and income methods.  The answers derived by each approach should

| | |
|---|---|
| ...ption expenditures. . . . . . . | $245 |
| ...er payments . . . . . . . . . . . . . . . . . | 12 |
| Rents . . . . . . . . . . . . . . . . . . . . . . . . | 14 |
| Capital consumption allowance (depreciation) | 27 |
| Social security contributions . . . . . . . . . . | 20 |
| Interest . . . . . . . . . . . . . . . . . . . . . . | 13 |
| Proprietors' income . . . . . . . . . . . . . . . . | 31 |
| Net exports . . . . . . . . . . . . . . . . . . . . | 3 |
| Dividends. . . . . . . . . . . . . . . . . . . . . . | 16 |
| Compensation of employees . . . . . . . . . . . | 221 |
| Indirect business taxes. . . . . . . . . . . . . . | 18 |
| Undistributed corporate profits. . . . . . . . . | 21 |
| Personal taxes . . . . . . . . . . . . . . . . . . . | 26 |
| Corporate income taxes . . . . . . . . . . . . . | 19 |
| Corporate profits. . . . . . . . . . . . . . . . . . | 56 |
| Government purchases of goods and services | 72 |
| Net private domestic investment. . . . . . . . | 33 |
| Personal saving. . . . . . . . . . . . . . . . . . . | 16 |

$$GNP = C + I_g + G + EX_N$$

$$GNP = 245$$
$$+ 172$$
$$+ 3$$
$$\underline{33}$$
$$(353)$$

$$NNP = 353$$

$$-27$$
$$= NNP$$

*a.* Using the above data, determine GNP and NNP by both the expenditure and income methods.

*b.* Now determine NI (1) by making the required subtractions from GNP, and (2) by adding up the types of income which comprise NI.

*c.* Make those adjustments for NI required in deriving PI.

*d.* Make the required adjustments from PI (as determined in 8c) to obtain DI.

**9** Given the following national income accounting data, compute *a.* GNP, *b.* NNP, and *c.* NI. All figures are in billions.

| | |
|---|---|
| Compensation of employees . . . . . . . . . . . | $194.2 |
| U.S. exports of goods and services. . . . . . . | 13.4 |
| Capital consumption allowance. . . . . . . . . | 11.8 |
| Government purchases of goods and services | 59.4 |
| Indirect business taxes. . . . . . . . . . . . . . | 12.2 |
| Net private domestic investment. . . . . . . . | 52.1 |
| Transfer payments . . . . . . . . . . . . . . . . . | 13.9 |
| U.S. imports of goods and services . . . . . . | 16.5 |
| Personal taxes . . . . . . . . . . . . . . . . . . . | 40.5 |
| Personal consumption expenditures. . . . . . | 219.1 |

**10** Why do national income accountants compare the market value of the total outputs in various years rather than actual physical volumes of production?  Explain.  What problem is posed by any comparison over time of the market values of various total outputs?  How is this problem resolved?

**11** The following table shows money GNP and an appropriate price index for a group of selected years.  Compute real GNP.  Indicate in each calculation whether you are inflating or deflating the money GNP data.

| Year | Money GNP, billions | Price level index, percent (1972 = 100) | Real GNP, billions |
|---|---|---|---|
| 1947 | $ 232.8 | 49.70 | $ _____ |
| 1956 | 420.7 | 62.90 | $ _____ |
| 1967 | 796.3 | 79.02 | $ _____ |
| 1973 | 1306.3 | 105.92 | $ _____ |
| 1978 | 2127.6 | 152.05 | $ _____ |

**12** Which of the following are actually included in deriving this year's GNP? Explain your answer in each case.

*a.* Interest on an AT&T bond
*b.* Social security payments received by a retired factory worker
*c.* The services of a painter in painting the family home
*d.* The income of a dentist
*e.* The money received by Smith when he sells a 1978 Chevrolet to Jones
*f.* The monthly allowance which a college student receives from home
*g.* Rent received on a two-bedroom apartment
*h.* The money received by Wilson when he resells this year's model Plymouth to Wilcox
*i.* Interest received on government bonds
*j.* A two-hour decline in the length of the workweek
*k.* The purchase of an AT&T bond
*l.* A $2 billion increase in business inventories
*m.* The purchase of 100 shares of GM common stock
*n.* The purchase of an insurance policy
*o.* Wages paid to a domestic servant
*p.* The market value of a homemaker's services
*q.* The purchase of a Renaissance painting by a public art museum

**13** Explain: "A man diminishes the national income by marrying his cook."

## Selected References

Abraham, William I.: *National Income and Economic Accounting* (Englewood Cliffs, N.J.: Prentice-Hall, Inc., 1969).

Dernburg, Thomas F., and Duncan M. McDougall: *Macroeconomics,* 6th ed. (New York: McGraw-Hill Book Company, 1980), chap. 2.

Shapiro, Edward: *Macroeconomic Analysis,* 4th ed. (New York: Harcourt Brace Jovanovich, Inc., 1978), chap. 2 and appendix.

U.S. Department of Commerce: *The Economic Accounts of the United States: Retrospect and Prospect* (Washington, 1971).

———: *The National Income and Product Accounts of the Uni ed States, 1929–1974* (Washington, 1976).

———: *Survey of Current Business.* July issues contain annual national income data.

# LAST WORD
## National Income: Voluntary and Involuntary Expenditures

Professor Robert Lekachman of City University of New York contends that our voluntary expenditures on national output often necessitate involuntary expenditures. While the former enhance our economic well-being, the latter clearly do not.

At its simplest, my argument claims that current conventions in vogue among the income estimators suffer from an aggregative fallacy: the requirement that the statistician lump together voluntary and involuntary expenditures. In the realm of common sense at least, is it not strange to count according to their respective dollar values both the market sales of cigarettes and the medical expenditures by the victims of cigarette-induced maladies such as lung cancer, emphysema, tuberculosis, and coronaries? With an equally weird agnosticism, the national income expert totals not only the value of the oil pumped up from the Santa Barbara channel or the Gulf coast but also the expenses of cleaning up beaches and salvaging fishing grounds in the wake of oil-well blowouts. There are other peculiar triumphs of theory over reality. The statistician joins together the value of Consolidated Edison's sales of electrical energy in metropolitan New York and its customers' additional spending upon soaps and cleansers to restore their clothing, windows, household goods, and persons from the damage caused by air pollution. By current criteria, gross national product rises when auto sales increase, regardless of what may be happening to the quality of the enjoyments that these arrogant chariots generate or the variety of adverse side effects for which they are responsible. The gross national product records the sales of distilled liquor and the expenditures upon the treatment of alcoholics. And so on and on. Generically, the fault is a refusal to distinguish between spending that implements the tastes and desires of the spender and defensive expenditures forced upon him by his environment.

Probably the best that can be said for conventional statistics is that so long as the composition of output between the pluses of pleasure and the minuses of repair and treatment remains roughly the same, intertemporal comparisons convey meaning. That is to say, if in 1981 as in 1971 two-thirds of what Americans buy represents uncoerced choice and the remaining third is an effort to defend themselves against the side effects of harmful goods and careless misuse of the environment, sensible comparisons are possible of such magnitudes as per capita gross national product. Totally unanswered, however, because unmeasured, is the central query about the key assumption: Have these percentages in fact remained constant? Many believe that they have not, that in truth defensive spending is steadily rising both in absolute amount and as a share of total expenditure.

Robert Lekachman, *National Income and the Public Welfare* (New York: Random House, Inc., 1972), pp. 7–8.

# The Business Cycle: Unemployment and Inflation

chapter **10**

Emphasis in Part 1 of this book was upon the essentially microeconomic problem of full production. To facilitate our discussion of how American capitalism allocates resources, we assumed that resources would be fully employed. But actual experience indicates that full employment cannot be taken for granted. Hence, in Parts 2 and 3 we seek to explore the problem of achieving and maintaining full employment in our economy.

The goals of the present chapter are these: First, we seek an overview of the business cycle—the periodic fluctuations in output, employment, and price levels which have characterized our economy. Second, we will look in more detail at unemployment. What are the various types of unemployment? How is unemployment measured? Why is unemployment an economic problem? Third, we turn our attention to inflation—the big problem which has plagued us since the late 1960s. What are inflation's causes? And consequences?

## ☐ OVERVIEW OF THE BUSINESS CYCLE

Our society seeks economic growth *and* full employment *and* price level stability along with other less quantifiable goals (Chapter 1). The broad spectrum of American economic history reflects quite remarkable economic growth. Technological progress, rapid increases in productive capacity, and a standard of living which is among the highest in the world are strategic facets of the dynamic character of our economy.

### △ The Historical Record

But our long-run economic growth has not been steady. Rather, it has been interrupted by periods of economic instability as Figure 10-1 reveals. Periods of rapid economic expansion have sometimes been marred by inflation, that is, price instability, and at other times, expansion has given way to recession and depression, that is, low levels of employment and

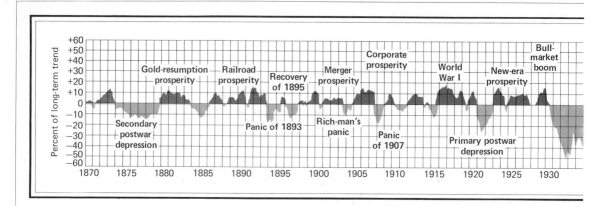

output. Indeed, on a few occasions—most notably in the 1970s—we have had the unhappy experience of a rising price level and abnormally high unemployment simultaneously. In short, secular economic growth has been interrupted and complicated by both unemployment and inflation.

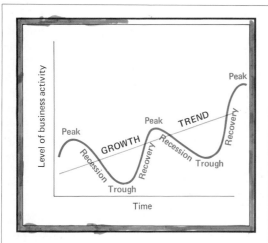

**FIGURE 10-2  THE BUSINESS CYCLE**

Economists distinguish between four phases of the business cycle and recognize that the duration and strength of each phase is highly variable. A recession, for example, need not always entail serious and prolonged unemployment. Nor need a cyclical peak always entail full employment.

△  **Phases of the Cycle**

Generally speaking, the term *business cycle* refers to the recurrent ups and downs in the level of economic activity which extend over a period of several years. Individual business cycles vary tremendously in duration and intensity. Yet all embody common phases which are variously labeled by different economists. Figure 10-2 shows us an idealized business cycle. We begin with a cyclical *peak* where the economy is at full employment and the national output is also at, or very close to, capacity. The price level is likely to be rising during this cyclical phase. In the ensuing *recession* output and employment both decline, but prices in our economy tend to be inflexible or "sticky" in a downward direction. The price level is likely to fall only if the recession is severe and prolonged (that is, a "depression").[1] The *trough* is where output and employment "bottom out" at their lowest levels. Finally, in the *recovery* phase the economy's levels of output and employment expand toward full employment. As recovery intensifies, the price level may begin to rise prior to the realization of full employment and capacity production.

Despite common phases, specific business cycles vary greatly in duration and intensity.

[1] An old one-liner is that "A recession is when a neighbor loses his job; a depression is when *you* lose *your* job!"

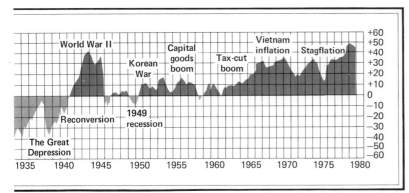

**FIGURE 10-1 AMERICAN BUSINESS-CYCLE EXPERIENCE**

The American economy has encountered periods of prosperity and depression. Only minor recessions have occurred since World War II. (Cleveland Trust Company.)

(Indeed, some economists prefer to talk of business *fluctuations,* rather than *cycles,* because the latter term implies regularity and the former does not.) The Great Depression of the 1930s seriously undermined the level of business activity for an entire decade. By comparison, the business declines of 1924 and 1927 were minor in both intensity and duration, as most of our post-World War II recessions also have been.

### △ Causation: A First Glance

Historically, economists have suggested a variety of theories to explain fluctuations in business. Some theories center upon innovation, contending that major innovations such as the railroad, the automobile, or synthetic fibers have a great impact upon investment and consumption spending and therefore upon output, employment, and the price level. But these major innovations occur irregularly and thus contribute to the variability of economic activity. Other economists have explained the business cycle in terms of political and random events as is suggested by some of the labeling in Figure 10-1. Wars, for example, can be economically very disruptive. A virtually insatiable demand for war goods during hostilities can generate a period of overfull employment and sharp inflation, only to be followed by an economic slump when peace returns and military

spending plummets. Still other economists view the cycle as a purely monetary phenomenon. When government creates too much money, an inflationary boom is generated; a relative paucity of money will precipitate a declining output and unemployment.

Despite this diversity of opinion, most economists concede that the immediate determinant of the levels of national output and employment is the level of total spending or aggregate demand. In an economy that is largely market-directed, businesses produce goods and services only if they can be sold profitably. Crudely stated, if total demand is low, many businesses will not find it profitable to produce a large volume of goods and services. Hence, output, employment, and the level of incomes will all be low. A higher level of total demand will mean that more production will be profitable; hence, output, employment, and incomes will all be higher also. Later in this chapter we will find that the relationship between aggregate demand and the price level is more complex and that, in fact, inflation may arise from causes other than a change in total spending.

### △ Noncyclical Fluctuations

It must not be concluded that all changes in business activity are due to the business cycle. On the one hand, there are *seasonal variations* in business activity. For example, the pre-Christmas and pre-Easter buying rushes cause considerable fluctuations each year in the tempo of business activity, particularly in the retail industry. Agriculture, the automobile industry, construction—indeed, virtually all industries are subject to some degree of seasonality.

Business activity is also subject to a *secular trend.* The secular trend of an economy is its expansion or contraction over a long period of years, for example, 25, 50, or 100 years. We simply note at this juncture that the long-run secular trend for American capitalism has been one of rather remarkable expansion (Chapter 20). For present purposes, the importance of this long-run expansion is that the business cycle involves fluctuations in business activity around a long-run growth trend. Note that in Figure 10-1 cyclical fluctuations are measured as deviations from the secular growth trend and that the idealized cycle of Figure 10-2 is drawn against a trend of growth.

△ **Cyclical Impact: Durables
and Nondurables**

The business cycle is pervasive; it is felt in virtually every nook and cranny of the economy. The interrelatedness of the economy allows few, if any, to escape the cold hand of depression or the fever of inflation. Yet we must keep in mind that various individuals and various segments of the economy are affected in different ways and in different degrees by the business cycle.

Insofar as production and employment are concerned, those industries producing capital goods and consumer durables are typically hit hardest by recession. The construction industry is particularly vulnerable. Output and employment in nondurable consumer goods industries are less sensitive to the cycle. Industries producing housing and commercial buildings, heavy capital goods, farm implements, automobiles, refrigerators, gas ranges, and similar products bear the brunt of bad times. Conversely, these "hard goods" industries seem to be stimulated most by expansion. Two facts go far to explain the vulnerability of these industries to the cycle.

**1 Postponability**   Within limits, the purchase of hard goods is postponable. Hence, as the economy slips into bad times, producers forestall the acquisition of more modern productive facilities and the construction of new plants. The business outlook simply does not warrant increases in the stock of capital goods. In all probability the firm's present capital facilities and buildings will still be usable and in excess supply. Except in bad times, capital goods are usually replaced before they are completely depreciated; when recession strikes, however, business firms will patch up their outmoded equipment and make it do. As a result, investment in capital goods will decline sharply. Chances are that some firms, having excess plant capacity, will not even bother to replace all the capital which they are currently consuming. Net investment may be a negative figure. Much the same holds true for consumer durables. When recession rolls around and the family budget must be trimmed, it is likely that plans for the purchases of durables will first feel the ax. You decide to make repairs on your old car rather than buy a new model.

Food and clothing—consumer nondurables—are a different story. A family must eat and must clothe itself. These purchases are much less postponable. True, to some extent the quantity and most certainly the quality of these purchases will decline. But not so much as is the case with durables.

**2 Monopoly Power**   Most industries producing capital goods and consumer durables are industries of high concentration, wherein a relatively small number of firms dominate the market. As a result, these firms have sufficient monopoly power to resist lowering prices by restricting supply in the face of a declining demand. Consequently, the impact of a fall in demand centers primarily upon production and employment. The reverse holds true in nondurable, or soft, goods industries, which are for the most part highly competitive and characterized by low concentration. Price declines cannot be resisted in such industries, and the impact of a declining demand falls to a greater extent on prices than upon the levels of production. Figure 10-3 is informative on this point. It shows the percentage declines in price and quantity which occurred in ten selected industries as the economy fell from peak prosperity in 1929 to the depth of depression in 1933. Speaking very generally, high-concentration industries make up the top half of the table and low-concentration industries the bottom half. Note the drastic production declines and relatively modest price declines of the high-concentration industries on the one hand, and the large price declines and relatively small output declines which took place in the low-concentration industries on the other.

Armed with this thumbnail sketch of the business cycle, let us now examine unemployment and inflation in more detail.

## □ UNEMPLOYMENT

"Full employment" is an elusive concept to define. One might initially interpret it to mean that everyone who is in the labor market—100 percent of the labor force—is employed. But such is not the case. Some unemployment is regarded as normal or warranted.

### △ Types of Unemployment

Let us approach the task of defining full employment by distinguishing between several different types of unemployment.

**Frictional Unemployment**  Given freedom of occupational and job choice, at any point in time some workers will be "between jobs." That is, some workers will be in the process of voluntarily switching jobs. Others

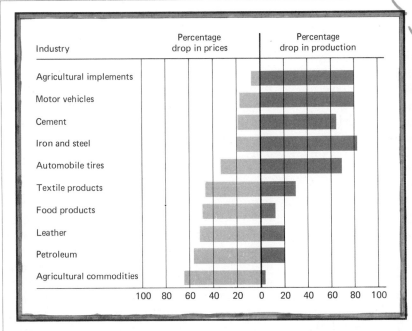

FIGURE 10-3 | RELATIVE PRICE AND PRODUCTION DECLINES IN TEN INDUSTRIES, 1929-1933

The high-concentration industries shown in the top half of this figure were characterized by relatively small price declines and large declines in output when the economy entered the Great Depression. In the low-concentration industries of the bottom half, price declines were relatively large, and production fell by relatively small amounts. [Gardiner C. Means, *Industrial Prices and Their Relative Flexibility* (Washington, 1953), p. 8.]

| Industry | Percentage drop in prices | Percentage drop in production |
|---|---|---|
| Agricultural implements | | |
| Motor vehicles | | |
| Cement | | |
| Iron and steel | | |
| Automobile tires | | |
| Textile products | | |
| Food products | | |
| Leather | | |
| Petroleum | | |
| Agricultural commodities | | |

100  80  60  40  20  0  20  40  60  80  100

will have job connections but will be temporarily laid off because of seasonality (for example, bad weather in the construction industry) or model changeovers (as in the automobile industry). And there will be some workers, particularly young people, looking for their first jobs.

Economists use the term *frictional unemployment* for the group of workers who are unemployed for these kinds of reasons. Frictional unemployment is regarded as inevitable and, at least in part, desirable. Why desirable? Because those workers who are voluntarily "between jobs" are typically moving from low-paying, low-productivity jobs to higher-paying, higher-productivity positions. This means more income for the workers and a better allocation of labor resources—and therefore a larger real output—for the economy as a whole.

**Structural Unemployment**  Frictional unemployment shades into a second category, called *structural unemployment.* Important changes occur over time in the structure of consumer demand and in technology, which in turn alter the structure or the composition of the total demand for labor. Unemployment results because the composition of the labor force does not respond quickly or completely to the new structure of job opportunities. As a result, some workers find that they have no readily marketable talents; their skills and experience have been rendered obsolete and unwanted by changes in technology and consumer demand. Examples: Years ago, highly skilled glassblowers were thrown out of work by the invention of bottlemaking machines. More recently, unskilled and inadequately educated blacks have been dislodged from agriculture in the South as a result of the mechanization of agriculture. Many of these workers have migrated to the ghettos of northern cities and have suffered prolonged unemployment because of insufficient skills.

The distinction between frictional and structural unemployment is hazy. The difference essentially is that frictionally unemployed workers have salable skills, whereas structurally unemployed workers are not readily reemployable without retraining, additional education, and possibly geographic movement.

**Cyclical Unemployment**  By cyclical unemployment we obviously mean unemployment caused by the business cycle, that is, by a deficiency of aggregate or total demand. As the overall level of business activity decreases, unemployment increases; as business activity increases, unemployment declines. Cyclical unemployment at the depth of the Great Depression in 1933 reached about 25 percent of the labor force!

△  **Defining "Full Employment"**

Economists regard some frictional and structural unemployment as unavoidable; hence, "full employment" is defined as something less than employment of 100 percent of the labor force. In the 1960s it was commonly held that this unavoidable minimum of frictional and structural unemployment was about 4 percent of the labor force. In other words, full employment was said to exist when 96 percent of the labor force was employed.

But this 4 percent *full-employment unemployment rate* was challenged by the economic advisers of both the Ford and Carter administrations. They have argued that, for several reasons, this figure should be revised upward to 5, 5½, or even 6 percent. First, they point out that certain groups, in particular women and young workers who traditionally have quite high unemployment rates, are becoming relatively more important in the labor force. Second, our unemployment compensation program, which has expanded both in terms of numbers of workers covered and size of benefits, allows unemployed workers to seek reemployment at a more leisurely pace, thereby increasing the unemployment rate. Finally, substantial increases in the minimum wage have boosted unemployment among teenage and other inexperienced workers. Many employers have simply found that the legal minimum wage exceeds the value of the output of many young workers and, therefore, it is not profitable to employ them (Chapter 31).

△ **Measuring Unemployment**

The controversy over the full-employment unemployment rate is complicated by problems encountered in the actual measurement of the rate of unemployment. Table 10-1 is a helpful starting point. The total population is divided into three broad groups. One group is comprised of (1) those under 16 years of age, (2) the armed forces, and (3) people who are institutionalized, for example, in mental hospitals or correctional institutions. This group is comprised of people who are not considered to be potential members of the civilian labor force. A second group, labeled "not in labor force," are adults who are potential workers, but for some reason—they are homemakers, in school, or retired—are not employed and are not seeking work. The remaining group is the *civilian labor force*, which constituted about 47 percent of the total population in 1979. The *unemployment rate* is simply the percentage of the civilian labor force which is unemployed. In 1979 the rate was 5.8 percent (= 5,963 ÷ 102,908).

The Bureau of Labor Statistics (BLS) attempts to determine who is employed and who is not by conducting a nationwide random survey of some 55,000 households each month. A series of questions are asked regarding what members of the household are working, unemployed and looking for work, not looking for work, and so on. Despite the fact that very sophisticated sampling and interview techniques are used, the data collected from this survey have been subjected to a number of criticisms.

**1  Part-Time Employment**  The official data include all part-time workers as fully employed. Many part-timers want to work full time, but can't find suitable full-time work or are on short hours because of a temporary slack in consumer demand. These workers are really partially employed and partially unemployed. By counting them as fully employed the official BLS data tend to *understate* the unemployment rate.

**2  Discouraged Workers**  One must be actively seeking work in order to be counted as unemployed. That is, an unemployed individual who is not actively seeking employment is simply classified as "not in the labor force." The problem is that there exists a sizable number of workers who, after unsuccessfully seeking employment for a time, become discouraged and drop out of the labor force. While the number of *discouraged workers* is larger during recession than during prosperity, estimates suggest that 1 million or more may fall into this category. By not counting discouraged workers as unemployed, official data tend to *understate* the unemployment rate.

**3  False Information**  On the other hand, the unemployment rate may be *overstated* in that some respondents who are not working may claim they are looking for work, even though that is not the case. Hence, these individuals will be classified as "unemployed," rather than "not in the labor force." The motivation for giving this false information is that

**TABLE 10-1**
**The Civilian Labor Force, Employment, and Unemployment, 1979 (*in thousands*)**

| | |
|---|---:|
| Total population . . . . . . . . . . . . . . . . . . | 220,584 |
| Under 16, armed forces, and institutionalized . . . . . . . . . . . . . . . . | 59,053 |
| Not in labor force . . . . . . . . . . . . . . . . | 58,623 |
| Civilian labor force . . . . . . . . . . . . . | 102,908 |
| Employed . . . . . . . . . . . . . . . . . . | 96,945 |
| Unemployed . . . . . . . . . . . . . . . | 5,963 |

$$\text{Unemployment rate} = \frac{\text{unemployed}}{\text{civilian labor force}} = \frac{5,963}{102,908} = 5.8\%$$

*Source:* Bureau of Labor Statistics.

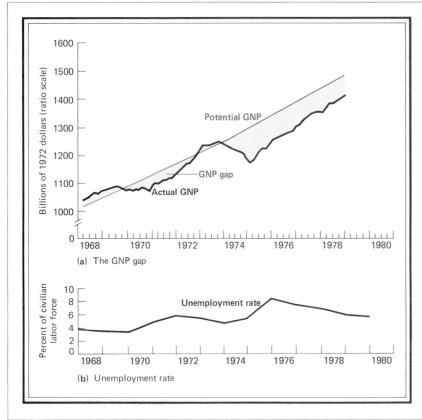

FIGURE 10-4 POTENTIAL AND
ACTUAL GNP (a)  AND THE
UNEMPLOYMENT RATE (b)

The difference between potential
and actual GNP is the GNP gap.
The GNP gap measures the
output which the economy
sacrifices because it fails to utilize fully its productive potential.
Note that a high unemployment
rate means a large GNP gap.
(*Economic Report of the
President and Business
Conditions Digest.*)

an individual's unemployment compensation
or welfare benefits may be contingent upon
professed job pursuit.

The overall point to be made is that, although the unemployment rate is a basic consideration in policymaking, it is subject to certain shortcomings. While the unemployment
rate is one of the best measures of the economic condition of the nation, it is not an
infallible barometer of our economic health.[2]

△  **Economic Cost of Unemployment**
Regardless of the problems associated
with measuring the unemployment rate and

defining the full-employment unemployment
rate, above-normal unemployment entails
great economic and social costs.

**GNP Gap**   The basic economic cost of
unemployment is forgone output. *When the
economy fails to generate enough jobs for all
who are able and willing to work, potential
production of goods and services is irretrieva-
bly lost.* Economists measure this sacrificed
output in terms of the *GNP gap.* This gap is
simply the amount by which the *actual GNP*
falls short of *potential GNP.* Potential GNP is
determined by assuming that full employment
is achieved and projecting the economy's "normal" growth rate. Figure 10-4 shows the GNP
gap for recent years and underscores the close
correlation between the unemployment rate
and the GNP gap. We are dealing here with
very large numbers. For example, Figure 10-4

[2]To pursue this topic one might consult the Bureau of
Labor Statistics, *How the Government Measures Unem-
ployment* (Department of Labor, 1977); and Stewart
Schwab and John J. Seater, "The Unemployment Rate:
Time to Give it a Rest?", *Business Review* (Federal Re-
serve Bank of Philadelphia), May–June, 1977, pp. 11–18.

indicates that 1975 was a year of serious recession with an unemployment rate of $8\frac{1}{2}$ percent. The corresponding GNP gap in 1975 was $115 billion!

**Unequal Burdens**   Aggregate figures conceal the fact that the cost of unemployment is unequally distributed. An increase in the unemployment rate from 4 to, say, 6 percent would be more tolerable if every worker's hours of work and wage income were reduced proportionately. But, in fact, unemployment is borne heavily by teenagers, by women workers, and particularly by minority groups. For example, data show that in 1979 the unemployment rate was 5.8 percent for the labor force as a whole. But the breakdown of this figure revealed startling inequities. The unemployment rate for blacks and other minorities was 11.3 percent, compared with 5.1 percent for whites. Unemployment among male workers 20 years of age and over was only 4.1 percent, compared with 5.7 for females. Among all teenagers of labor-force age, the unemployment rate was 16 percent. For black teenagers, the figure was about 33 percent.

The reader may derive some comfort from the fact that the unemployment rate varies inversely with education: More schooling reduces the likelihood of unemployment. For example, in 1978 the unemployment rate for high school dropouts was 12.4 percent, as compared to 6.2 percent and 2.5 percent for high school and college graduates respectively.

△ **Noneconomic Costs**

Unemployment is much more than an economic catastrophe; it is a social catastrophe as well. Depression means idleness. And idleness means loss of skills, loss of self-respect, a plummeting of morale, family disintegration, and sociopolitical unrest. Consider the following two commentaries on the Great Depression from Studs Terkel's revealing book *Hard Times*.[3]   First, the comments of a young

[3]Studs Terkel, *Hard Times* (New York: Avon Books, 1971), pp. 131, 398.

woman who was fortunate enough to attend college:

> When I attended Berkeley in 1936, so many of the kids had actually lost their fathers. They had wandered off in disgrace because they couldn't support their families. Other fathers had killed themselves, so the family could have the insurance. Families had totally broken down. Each father took it as his personal failure. These middle-class men apparently had no social sense of what was going on, so they killed themselves.
>
> It was still the Depression. There were kids who didn't have a place to sleep, huddling under bridges on the campus. I had a scholarship, but there were times when I didn't have food. The meals were often three candy bars.

Second, the reminiscences of a craftsman's son:

> One of the most common things—and it certainly happened to me—was this feeling of your father's failure. That somehow he hadn't beaten the rap. Sure things were tough, but why should I be the kid who had to put a piece of cardboard into the sole of my shoe to go to school? It was not a thing coupled with resentment against my father. It was simply this feeling of regret, that somehow he hadn't done better, that he hadn't gotten the breaks. Also a feeling of uneasiness about my father's rage against the way things are. . . .
>
> Remember, too, the shock, the confusion, the hurt that many kids felt about their fathers not being able to provide for them. This reflected itself very often in bitter quarrels between father and son. . . .
>
> We had bitter arguments about new ideas. Was Roosevelt right in making relief available? Was the WPA a good idea? Did people have the right to occupy their farms and hold them by force? The old concept that there was something for everybody who worked in America went down the drain with the Great Depression. This created family strains. A lot of parents felt a sense of guilt. . . .
>
> My father led a rough life: he drank. During the Depression, he drank more. There was more conflict in the home. A lot of fathers—mine, among them—had a habit of taking off. They'd

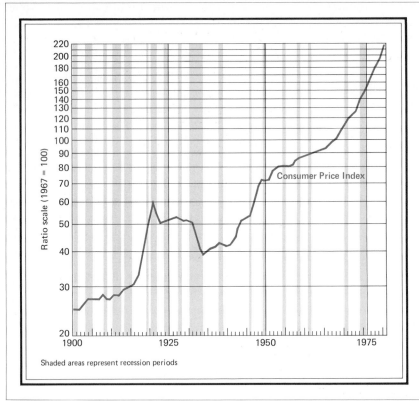

**FIGURE 10-5 PRICE LEVEL BEHAVIOR IN THE UNITED STATES SINCE 1900**

The price level has generally risen since the turn of the century. Three particularly sharp periods of increase are evident: the World War I period, the immediate post-World War II period (1945-1948), and the period 1966 to the present. Note that periods of deflation generally correspond with recession years as shown by the shaded areas.

Consumer Price Index

Ratio scale (1967 = 100)

Shaded areas represent recession periods

go to Chicago to look for work. To Topeka. This left the family at home, waiting and hoping that the old man would find something. And there was always the Saturday night ordeal as to whether or not the old man would get home with his paycheck. Everything was sharpened and hurt more by the Depression.

It is no exaggeration to say that:[4]

> A job gives hope for material and social advancement. It is a way of providing one's children a better start in life. It may mean the only honorable way of escape from the poverty of one's parents. It helps to overcome racial and other social barriers. In short . . . a job is the passport to freedom and to a better life. To deprive people of jobs is to read them out of our society.

History makes it all too clear that severe

[4]Henry R. Reuss, *The Critical Decade* (New York: McGraw-Hill Book Company, 1964), p. 133.

unemployment is conducive to rapid and sometimes violent social and political change. Witness the movement to the left of American political philosophy during the Depression of the 1930s. The Depression-inspired New Deal was a veritable revolution in American political and economic thinking. Witness also Hitler's ascent to power against a background of unemployment. Furthermore, there can be no question that the heavy concentration of unemployment among blacks and other minorities has been an important cause of the unrest and violence which periodically has plagued American cities.

☐ **INFLATION**

Now let us turn to inflation as an aspect of economic instability. The problems posed by inflation are more subtle than those of unemployment and hence are somewhat more difficult to grasp.

What is inflation? Why is it to be feared? *Inflation is a rising general level of prices.* This does not mean, of course, that *all* prices are necessarily rising. Even during periods of acute inflation, some specific prices may be relatively constant and others actually falling. Nor does inflation mean that prices rise evenly or proportionately. Indeed, one of the major sore spots of inflation lies in the fact that prices tend to rise very unevenly. Some spring upward; others rise at a more leisurely pace; others do not rise at all. Figure 10-5 gives us an historical overview of inflation in the United States. Note that we have been living in an age of inflation since the start of World War II.

The so-called *rule of 70* provides us with a convenient formula for gaining a quantitative appreciation of inflation. Specifically, the rule allows one to quickly calculate the number of years required for a doubling of the price level. All one need do is divide the number 70 by the annual rate of inflation. For example, a 3 percent annual rate of inflation will double the price level in about 23 (=70 ÷ 3) years. Inflation of 8 percent per year will double the price level in about 9 (=70 ÷ 8) years. Inflation at 12 percent will double the price level in only about 6 years!

Our plan of attack is to survey the causes of inflation and then to consider its consequences.

△  **Causes: Theories of Inflation**

Economists distinguish between three types of inflation.

**1  Demand-Pull Inflation** Traditionally, changes in the price level have been attributed to an excess of total demand. The economy may attempt to spend beyond its capacity to produce; that is, it may seek some point like $W$ in Figure 2-2. The business sector cannot respond to this excess demand by expanding real output for the obvious reason that all available resources are already fully employed. Therefore, this excess demand will bid up the prices

of the fixed real output, causing *demand-pull inflation.* The essence of demand-pull inflation is often crudely expressed in the phrase "too much money chasing too few goods."

But the relationship between total demand, on the one hand, and output, employment, and the price level, on the other, is more complex than these terse comments suggest. Figure 10-6 is helpful in unraveling these complications.

In range 1 total spending—the sum of consumption, investment, and government spending—is so low that the national output is far short of its maximum, full-employment level. In other words, a substantial GNP gap exists. Unemployment rates are high and businesses have a great deal of idle productive capacity. Now assume that aggregate demand increases. National output will rise and the unemployment rate will fall, but there will be little or no increase in the price level. The reason is that there are large amounts of idle human and property resources which can be put back to work at their *existing* prices. An unemployed worker does not ask for a wage

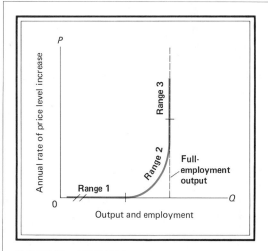

**FIGURE 10-6  THE PRICE LEVEL AND THE LEVEL OF EMPLOYMENT**

The price level generally begins to rise before full employment is reached. At full employment, additional spending tends to be purely inflationary.

increase during a job interview! In terms of Chapter 4's demand and supply analysis, the price-raising effects of the assumed increases in demand are offset by the price-reducing effects of increases in supply. The increases in supply are possible because idle resources are available and the additional production is profitable. The net result is large output-increasing effects and no price-increasing effects.

As demand continues to rise, the economy enters range 2 wherein it is approaching full employment and is closer to fully utilizing its available resources. But we note that, before full employment is achieved, the price level begins to rise. Why so? As production expands, supplies of idle resources do not vanish simultaneously in all sectors and industries of the economy. That is, bottlenecks begin to develop. Some industries are fully utilizing their productivity capacity before others and cannot respond to further increases in demand for their products by increasing supply. So their prices rise. As labor markets tighten, some types of labor become fully employed and their money wages rise. This increases production costs and prompts businesses to increase their prices. Tight labor markets enhance the bargaining power of unions and increase their ability to obtain sizable wage increases. Businesses are less likely to resist union wage demands because they do not want to be faced with a strike at a time when the economy is becoming increasingly prosperous. Furthermore, with aggregate demand rising, higher costs can be quite easily passed along to consumers through price increases. Finally, as full employment is approached, firms will be forced to employ less efficient (less productive) workers and this contributes to rising costs and prices. The inflation which occurs in range 2 is sometimes called "premature inflation" because it occurs before the economy reaches full employment.

Finally, as aggregate demand increases into range 3, full employment will be realized in all sectors of the economy. Industries in the aggregate can no longer respond to increases in demand with increases in supply. National output is now at a maximum and further increases in demand will merely cause demand-pull inflation. Total demand in excess of society's capacity to produce pulls the price level upward.

Reprise: Chapter 9 drew a distinction between money and real GNP that is helpful at this point. So long as the price level is constant (range 1), increases in money and real GNP are identical. But with premature inflation (range 2), money GNP is rising faster than real GNP, so money GNP must be "deflated" to measure changes in physical output. With pure inflation (range 3), money GNP is rising—perhaps rapidly—but real GNP is constant.

The relationship expressed in Figure 10-6 is only partially reversible. That is, many product and resource prices which are flexible upward as the economy approaches the full-employment output become relatively rigid and inflexible when declines in total spending result in reductions in output and employment. This is primarily the result of monopolistic power—the ability to influence prices—which many businesses and unions possess. Unions can usually resist wage cuts and sometimes secure wage boosts even though the total level of spending and therefore output and employment are falling. Monopolistic businesses are equally able to forestall reductions in product prices (Figure 10-3). Prices that go up during periods of full employment do not necessarily come down—at least all the way—when spending declines and unemployment ensues. It is not surprising that the long-run trend of the price level in American capitalism has been upward.[5]

**Cost-Push Inflation** Inflation may also arise on the supply or cost side of the market. There have been a number of periods in our

[5]Range 2 of Figure 10-6 will reappear in a slightly altered form in Chapter 18. There we will explore some of the controversy surrounding its shape and location.

recent economic history wherein the price level has risen despite rather widespread evidence that aggregate demand was not excessive. We have experienced periods wherein output and employment were both *declining* (evidence of a deficiency of total demand), while at the same time the general price level was *increasing.*

The *cost-push* or *market power* theory of inflation explains rising prices as follows. Unions have considerable control over wage rates; that is, they possess considerable market power. Indeed, they have enough market power that even with a moderate deficiency of total demand, some unemployment, and some unutilized industrial capacity, the stronger unions can obtain wage increases. Large corporate employers, faced now with increased costs but also in the possession of considerable market power, push their increased wage costs and "something extra" on to consumers by raising the prices of their products. This theory is obviously based upon the presumption that both unions and businesses typically possess a significant degree of market power and therefore, within limits, can manipulate wages and prices independent of overall conditions of total demand. Thus it is that we find cost-push inflation sometimes labeled "administered price" inflation or simply "seller's inflation."

Not surprisingly, management contends that wage increases initiate price increases and therefore unions are obviously the villains in the cost-push inflation scenario. This is the "wage-push" variant of cost-push inflation. Labor counters by charging that big businesses have the power to adjust or administer price increases which are neither initiated nor justified by increases in wage costs. This constitutes the "profit-push" variant of cost-push inflation. A final variant of cost-push inflation, labeled "commodity inflation," traces rising product prices to increases in the costs of raw material inputs or energy. Thus the substantial price level increases which have occurred in the past decade because of the decisions of the Organization of Petroleum Exporting

Countries (OPEC) to raise oil prices are a dramatic example of cost-push inflation.

**Structural Inflation**   A less widely cited explanation of inflation centers upon the effects of a change in the structure, though not the level, of aggregate demand. The rationale for *structural* or *demand-shift inflation* is based on the fact that for a number of reasons—a basic one of which is the market power of big businesses and unions—prices and wages tend to be flexible upward but inflexible downward. Let us assume that total demand is not excessive, but that a rather sharp change in the structure or composition of total demand occurs. This structural change in demand means that prices and wages will rise in those segments of the economy experiencing an expanding demand. However, because of their downward stickiness, wages and prices will *not* fall in those sectors of the economy wherein demand has declined. The result is a *net* increase in price and wage levels; that is, inflation will occur.

It must be emphasized that these three theories—demand-pull, cost-push, and structural inflation—are not unrelated or mutually exclusive. All three can operate simultaneously. For example, an excessive level of total demand whose composition is significantly changing can cause both demand-pull and structural inflation simultaneously. And the exertion of market power may cause cost-push forces to accentuate this inflation, particularly in those industries where unions are strong and businesses concentrated.

△   **Redistributive Effects of Inflation**

Let us now shift our attention from causes to effects. We first consider how inflation capriciously redistributes income; secondly, we examine possible effects upon the national output.

In practice, output and the price level may move together; inflation is often, but certainly not always, associated with an expanding real output. And, on those infrequent occasions wherein deflation occurs, it is typically accompanied by a shrinking real output. But in order to isolate the effects of a changing price level upon the distribution of income, let us for the moment imagine that real output is constant and at the full-employment level. Assuming the size of the income pie is fixed, how does inflation affect the size of the slices going to different income receivers? Later we will release this fixed output assumption and examine possible output effects of inflation.

Any analysis of the redistributive impact of inflation and deflation demands that we first distinguish carefully between real and money income. *Money income* is simply the number of dollars one receives in his or her pay envelope. *Real income,* on the other hand, is the amount of goods and services which a consumer can obtain with this money income. A moment's reflection will make clear that your real income depends upon (1) your money income, and (2) the prices which you must pay for the goods and services you purchase.

**Fixed Money Income Groups**  With this distinction in mind, it is easy to see why *inflation arbitrarily penalizes people living on relatively fixed money incomes.* Those households whose money incomes lag behind the rising level of product prices will find that their real incomes will deteriorate because of inflation. The purchasing power of each dollar's worth of income they receive will fall as prices rise. And, because they receive about the same number of dollars in their pay envelopes, their standard of living must decline accordingly.

Who are these people? The most obvious cases are pensioners, white-collar workers, some public employees, and people living on welfare and other transfer payments which remain fixed over substantial periods. In particular, elderly people who receive modest and inflexible pensions are the victims of inflation. Note, however, that the adverse redistributive effect of inflation upon social security recipients has been offset in recent years by substantial increases in the size of benefits; in fact,

social security benefits are now *indexed,* that is, tied to the consumer price index to prevent erosion from inflation.

People living on flexible incomes *may* benefit from inflation. The money incomes of such households may spurt ahead of the price level, or cost of living, with the result that their real incomes are enhanced. Workers employed in expanding industries and represented by vigorous unions may keep their wage incomes apace with, or ahead of, the rate of inflation. However, some wage earners are hurt by inflation. Those situated in declining industries or without the benefit of strong, aggressive unions may find that the price level skips ahead of their money incomes. Business executives and other profit receivers *might* benefit from inflation. *If* product prices rise faster than resource prices, business receipts then will grow at a faster rate than will costs. Thus some profit incomes will outdistance the rising tide of inflation.

**Savers**  Inflation also casts its evil eye upon savers. *As prices rise, the real value, or purchasing power, of a nest egg of savings will deteriorate.* People who have idle dollars in their pockets and demand deposits in banks will be hit hard by inflation. Similarly, savings accounts, insurance policies, annuities, and other fixed-value paper assets which were once adequate to meet rainy-day contingencies or to provide for a comfortable retirement decline in real value during inflation. Example: A household may save $1000 and "lend" it to a commercial bank or savings and loan association at, say, 6 percent interest. But if inflation is 13 percent (as in 1979), the real value or purchasing power of that $1000 will be cut to about $938 at the end of the year. That is, the saver will receive $1060 (equal to $1000 plus $60 of interest), but deflating that $1060 for 13 percent inflation means that the real value of that $1060 is only about $938 (equal to $1060 divided by 1.13). Mortgage holders and bondholders will also be adversely affected. A household's accumulated claims upon the economy's output are worth less and less as prices rise.

**Debtors and Creditors**   Inflation also redistributes income by altering the relationship between debtors and creditors. Specifically, *inflation tends to benefit debtors (borrowers) at the expense of creditors (lenders)*. Suppose you borrow $1000 from a bank, which you are to repay in two years. If in that period of time the general level of prices were to double, the $1000 which you repay will have only half the purchasing power of the $1000 originally borrowed. True, if we ignore interest charges, the same number of dollars is repaid as was borrowed. But because of inflation, each of these dollars will now buy only half as much as it did when the loan was negotiated. As prices go up, the value of the dollar comes down. Thus, because of inflation, the borrower is given "dear" dollars but pays back "cheap" dollars.

But an important amendment is in order. Our comments assume that inflation is unexpected; inflation just happened, to the surprise of both lender and borrower. The stated redistribution of income from lender to borrower might be altered *if* inflation is anticipated. For example, suppose that a lender (perhaps a commercial bank or a savings and loan) and a borrower (a household) both agree that 5 percent is a fair rate of interest on a one-year loan, *provided* the price level is stable. But assume inflation has been occurring and both lender and borrower agree it is reasonable to anticipate a 6 percent increase in the price level over the next year. If the bank lends the household $100 at 5 percent, the bank will be paid back $105 at the end of the year. But if 6 percent inflation does occur during the year, the purchasing power of that $105 will have been reduced to about $99. The *lender* will in effect have paid the *borrower* $1 to use the lender's money for a year! The lender can avoid this curious subsidy by simply increasing the interest rate by the amount of the anticipated inflation. That is, by charging 11 percent the

lender will receive back $111 at the end of the year which, adjusted for the 6 percent inflation, has the real value or purchasing power of about $105. In this instance there is a mutually agreeable transfer of purchasing power from borrower to lender of $5 or 5 percent for the use of $100 for one year.

This example implies several points. First, the redistribution effects of inflation depend upon whether that inflation is unexpected or anticipated. If unanticipated, inflation will entail a transfer of real income from lender to borrower. But if inflation is anticipated, creditors will be inclined to demand higher interest rates to compensate for the fact that they will be paid back in terms of dollars of diminished purchasing power. (The reader might work out an example to indicate that an actual rate of inflation which is less than anticipated will result in a larger than intended real income payment to the lender at the end of the year.) Second, this analysis also implies that, rather than being a cause of inflation, high interest rates are a consequence of inflation. Third—and less obvious—uncertainty over future rates of inflation add an element of risk to long-term contracts which can have a harmful effect upon investment spending and the level of national output.

**Empirical Evidence**   Empirical research suggests that, since World War II, inflation has brought about a massive redistribution of wealth from the household to the public sector of the economy. There are two reasons for this. First, governments have incurred very large debts and, to a considerable extent, government bonds have been held by households. That is, governments are large debtors and households have been their creditors. The postwar inflation has consequently shifted wealth from households to government. Secondly, recall from Chapter 8 that Federal income tax rates are progressive. Hence, during inflationary periods people pay more taxes, not only because their money incomes are higher, but also because they move into higher tax brackets and therefore pay a higher percentage of their incomes to government. Progressive taxes transfer real income from households to the public sector. Given these redistributive consequences, some economists have wondered out loud whether society can really expect government to be particularly zealous in its efforts to halt inflation.

Debtor status is undoubtedly important in assessing the redistributive impact of inflation upon the various income classes. Data suggest that inflation seems to hit the very poor and the very rich the hardest, while providing some benefit for middle and upper-middle income receivers. Explanation: The poor have few debts because no one will lend to them; the rich have relatively few debts because they are rich! Thus, neither the poor nor the rich benefit as debtors from inflation. But the middle and upper-middle income classes are heavily in debt and they do benefit from inflation. Finally, the relative importance of indebtedness suggests that inflation tends to transfer wealth from the elderly to the young. The former owe little, whereas the latter are heavily in debt as the result of "setting up households, borrowing heavily to buy houses, cars, furniture, and the like, and to finance their children's education."[6]

**Recap and Addenda**   To summarize: Inflation arbitrarily "taxes" those who receive relatively fixed money incomes and "subsidizes" those who receive flexible money incomes. Inflation arbitrarily penalizes savers. Finally, unanticipated inflation benefits debtors at the expense of creditors. It should come as no surprise that the effects of deflation are substantially the reverse. *Assuming no change in total output,* those with fixed money incomes will find their real incomes enhanced. Creditors will benefit at the expense of debtors. And savers will find that the purchasing power of

their savings has grown as a result of falling prices.

Two final points must be appended to this discussion. First, the fact that any given family is likely to be an income earner, a holder of financial assets, and an owner of real assets simultaneously is likely to cushion the redistributive impact of inflation. For example, if the family owns fixed-value monetary assets (savings accounts, bonds, and insurance policies), inflation will lessen their real value. But that same inflation is likely to increase the real value of any property assets (a house, land) which the family owns. In short, many families are simultaneously hurt and benefited by inflation. All these effects must be considered before we are able to conclude that the family's net position is better or worse because of inflation.

The second point to be reemphasized is that the redistributive effects of inflation are *arbitrary* in that they occur without regard to society's goals and values. Inflation lacks a social conscience and takes from some and gives to others, regardless of whether they be rich, poor, young, old, healthy, or infirm.

△ **Output Effects of Inflation**

We have assumed thus far that the economy's real output is fixed at the full-employment level. As a result, the redistributive effects of inflation and deflation have been in terms of some groups gaining absolutely at the expense of others. *If* the size of the pie is fixed and inflation causes some groups to get larger slices, other groups must necessarily get smaller slices. But, in fact, the level of national output may vary as the price level changes.

There is, frankly, much uncertainty and disagreement as to whether inflation is likely to be accompanied by a rising or a falling real national output. Let us briefly consider three scenarios, the first of which associates inflation with an expanding output and the remaining two with a declining output.

[6]See G. L. Bach, "Inflation: Who Gains and Who Loses?" *Challenge,* July–August 1974, pp. 48–55. The above two paragraphs are based upon Bach's research.

**1   Stimulus of Demand-Pull Inflation** Many economists have argued that mild demand-pull inflation tends to have a stimulating effect upon national output and employment. Imagine an increase in aggregate demand which is generating an economic recovery (Figure 10-2) and creating a modest demand-pull inflation. Under such conditions, product prices will tend to increase ahead of wages and other resource prices, thereby expanding business profits. Increased profits will prompt businesses to expand production, increasing national output and reducing unemployment. This scenario implies that any capricious redistributive effects of inflation are likely to be more than offset by the gains associated with more jobs and more output. The fact that the price level may be 2 or 3 percent higher will be only a minor irritant to an unemployed worker who is able to find a new job.

**2   Cost-Push Inflation and Unemployment** Let us now detail an equally plausible set of circumstances wherein inflation might cause output and employment to both *decline*. Suppose the level of aggregate demand is initially such that the economy is enjoying full employment *and* price level stability. If cost-push inflation now occurs, the amount of real output which the existing level of total demand will buy will be reduced. That is, a given level of aggregate demand will only be capable of taking a smaller real output off the market when cost-push pressures boost the price level. Hence, real output will fall and unemployment will rise.

Economic events of the 1970s lend support to this scenario. In late 1973 the Organization of Petroleum Exporting Countries (OPEC) became effective and exerted its market power to quadruple the price of oil. The cost-push inflationary effects generated rapid price level increases in the 1973–1975 period. At the same time the unemployment rate rose from slightly less than 5 percent in 1973 to 8.5 percent in 1975!

**3   Hyperinflation and Breakdown** Still other economists express anxiety over our first scenario. They are fearful that the mild, "creeping" inflation which might initially accompany economic recovery may snowball into a more severe "hyperinflation" whose ultimate impact upon national output and employment can be devastating. The contention is that, as prices persist in creeping upward, households and businesses will come to expect them to rise further. So, rather than let their idle savings and current incomes depreciate, people are induced to "spend now" to beat anticipated price rises. Businesses do the same in buying capital goods. Action on the basis of this "inflationary psychosis" intensifies the pressure on prices, and inflation feeds upon itself. Furthermore, as the cost of living rises, labor demands and gets higher money wages. Indeed, unions may seek wage increases sufficient not only to cover last year's price level increase but also to compensate for the inflation anticipated during the future life of their new collective bargaining agreement. Prosperity is not a good time for business firms to risk strikes by resisting such demands. Business managers recoup their rising labor costs by boosting the prices they charge consumers. And for good measure, businesses are likely to jack prices up an extra notch or two to be sure that profit receivers keep abreast or ahead of the inflationary parade. As the cost of living skips merrily upward as a result of these price increases, labor once again has an excellent excuse to demand another round of substantial wage increases. But this triggers another round of price increases. The net effect is a cumulative *wage-price inflationary spiral.* Money-wage and price rises feed upon each other, and this helps creeping inflation burst into galloping inflation.

Aside from disruptive redistributive effects, it is alleged that hyperinflation can precipitate economic collapse. Severe inflation encourages a diversion of effort toward speculative, and away from productive, activity. Businesses may find it increasingly profitable to hoard both materials and finished products in anticipation of further price increases. But, by restricting the availability of materials and products relative to the demand for them, such actions will tend to intensify inflationary pressures. Rather than invest in capital equipment, businesses and individual savers may purchase nonproductive wealth—jewels, precious metals, real estate, and so forth—as hedges against inflation.

In the extreme, as prices shoot up sharply and unevenly, normal economic relationships are disrupted. Business owners do not know what to charge for their products. And consumers do not know what to pay. Resource suppliers will want to be paid in kind, rather than with rapidly depreciating money. Creditors will avoid debtors to escape the repayment of debts with cheap money. Money becomes virtually worthless and ceases to do its job as a standard of value and medium of exchange. The economy may literally be thrown into a state of barter. Production and exchange grind toward a halt, and the net result is economic, social, and very possibly political chaos. Hyperinflation has precipitated monetary collapse, depression, and sociopolitical disorder.

Unfortunately, history reveals a number of examples which fit this gloomy scenario. These are typically instances of wartime or war-associated inflation which accelerated into galloping inflation with disastrous results. Consider the effects of World War II upon price levels in Hungary and Japan:

The inflation in Hungary exceeded all known records of the past. In August, 1946, 828 octillion (1 followed by 27 zeros) depreciated pengös equaled the value of 1 prewar pengö. The price of the American dollar reached a value of $3 \times 10^{22}$ (3 followed by 22 zeros) pengös. Fishermen and farmers in 1947 Japan used scales to weigh currency and change, rather than

bothering to count it. Prices rose some 116 times in Japan, 1938 to 1948.[7]

The German inflation of the 1920s was also catastrophic:[8]

The German Weimar Republic is an extreme example of a weak government which survived for some time through inflationary finance. On April 27, 1921, the German government was presented with a staggering bill for reparations payments to the Allies of 132 billion gold marks. This sum was far greater than what the Weimar Republic could reasonably expect to raise in taxes. Faced with huge budget deficits, the Weimar government simply ran the printing press to meet its bills.
During 1922, the German price level went up 5,470 percent. In 1923, the situation worsened; the German price level rose 1,300,000,000,000 times. By October of 1923, the postage on the lightest letter sent from Germany to the United States was 200,000 marks. Butter cost 1.5 million marks per pound, meat 2 million marks, a loaf of bread 200,000 marks, and an egg 60,000 marks. Prices increased so rapidly that waiters changed the prices on the menu several times during the course of a lunch. Sometimes customers had to pay double the price listed on the menu when they ordered.
Photographs of the period show a German housewife starting the fire in her kitchen stove with paper money and children playing with bundles of paper money tied together into building blocks!

What can be concluded from this discussion of the output effects of inflation? Only that the relationship between inflation and unemployment is uncertain, depending upon the cause and the rapidity of the inflationary process.

[7]Theodore Morgan, *Income and Employment,* 2d ed. (Englewood Cliffs, N.J.: Prentice-Hall, Inc., 1952), p. 361.
[8]Raburn M. Williams, *Inflation! Money, Jobs, and Politicians* (Arlington Heights, Ill.: AHM Publishing Corporation, 1980), p. 2.

# Summary

**1**   Our economy has been characterized by fluctuations in national output, employment, and the price level. Although characterized by common phases—peak, recession, trough, recovery—business cycles vary greatly in duration and intensity.

**2**   Although the business cycle has been explained in terms of such ultimate causal factors as innovations, political events, and money creation, it is generally agreed that the level of aggregate demand is the immediate determinant of national output and employment.

**3**   All sectors of the economy are affected by the business cycle, but in varying ways and degrees. The cycle has greater output and employment ramifications in the capital goods and durable consumer goods industries than it does in nondurable goods industries. Over the cycle, price fluctuations are greater in competitive than in monopolistic industries.

**4**   Some economists specify a full-employment unemployment rate as low as 4 percent, while others consider it to be as high as 6 percent. The accurate measurement of unemployment is complicated by the existence of part-time and discouraged workers.

**5**   The economic cost of unemployment, as measured by the GNP gap, consists of the goods and services which society forgoes when its resources are involuntarily idle. Unemployment is also conducive to a deterioration of national morale and to social and political unrest.

**6**   Inflation may have various causes, as is suggested by the demand-pull, cost-push, and structural theories of inflation.

**7**   Inflation tends to arbitrarily redistribute income at the expense of fixed-income receivers, creditors, and savers.

**8**   Economists disagree as to the output effect of inflation. Some argue that mild demand-pull inflation is a stimulus to output and employment. Others point out that cost-push inflation can cause the national output to fall and the unemployment rate to rise. Still others are fearful of "hyperinflation" which might undermine the monetary system and precipitate economic collapse.

# Questions and Study Suggestions

**1**   Key terms and concepts to remember: business cycle; seasonal variations; secular trend; frictional, structural, and cyclical unemployment; full-employment unemployment rate; discouraged workers; GNP gap; demand-pull, cost-push, and structural inflation; rule of 70; money and real income; hyperinflation.

**2**   What are the major phases of the business cycle? How long do business cycles last? How do seasonal variations and secular trends complicate measurement of the business cycle? Why does the business cycle affect output and employment in durable goods industries more severely than industries producing nondurables?

**3**   Why is it difficult to determine the full-employment unemployment rate? Why is it difficult to distinguish between frictional, structural, and cyclical unemployment? Why is unemployment an economic problem? What are the consequences of the "GNP gap"? What are the noneconomic effects of unemployment? How is the unemployment rate calculated?

**4**   Given that there exists an unemployment compensation program which provides income for those who are out of work, why worry about unemployment?

**5**   Explain how an *increase* in your money income and a *decrease* in your real income might occur simultaneously. Who loses from inflation? From unemployment? If you had to choose between *a.* full employment with a 6 percent annual rate of inflation or *b.* price stability with a 7 percent unemployment rate, which would you select? Why?

**6** Carefully describe the relationship between total spending and the levels of output and employment. Explain the relationship between the price level and increases in total spending as the economy moves from substantial unemployment to moderate unemployment and, finally, to full employment.

**7** Explain how a severe "hyperinflation" might lead to a depression.

**8** Evaluate as accurately as you can the manner in which each of the following individuals would be affected by fairly rapid inflation:

  **a.** a pensioned railroad worker

  **b.** a department-store clerk

  **c.** a UAW assembly-line worker

  **d.** a heavily indebted farmer

  **e.** a retired business executive whose current income comes entirely from interest on government bonds

  **f.** the owner of an independent smalltown department store

**9** A noted television comedian once defined inflation as follows: "Inflation? That means your money today won't buy as much as it would have during the depression when you didn't have any." Is his definition accurate?

## Selected References

Bach, G. L.: "Inflation: Who Gains and Who Loses?" *Challenge,* July–August 1974, pp. 48–55.

*Economic Report of the President* (Washington, D.C.) Published annually.

Gordon, Robert Aaron: *Economic Instability & Growth: The American Record* (New York: Harper & Row, Publishers, Incorporated, 1974).

Heilbroner, Robert L.: *Beyond Boom and Crash* (New York: W. W. Norton & Company, Inc., 1978).

Lekachman, Robert: *Inflation: The Permanent Problem of Boom and Bust* (New York: Random House, Inc., 1973).

U.S. Department of Commerce: *Survey of Current Business.* January issues survey the economy's performance in the preceding year.

# LAST WORD
## The Ravages of "Taxflation"

(Reprinted from *U.S. News & World Report.*)

A new term has crept into the vocabulary used to portray the burdens that inflation places on many Americans: "Taxflation."

Simply put, at the same time that inflation boosts salaries and wages without increasing buying power, it also pushes people into higher income-tax brackets. With each step up the ladder, an individual stands to pay a heftier bill, with the federal government coming out a big winner. . . .

The accompanying table shows in dollars and cents how, despite wage hikes equal to inflation over the past five years, a worker is worse off in real terms. Behind the problem: The one-two punch of bigger income-tax payments and higher Social Security taxes that result from a salary hike.

For many, the squeeze is more like a bear hug because wage boosts have been outstripped by the inflation rate, leaving workers even further behind than the table shows.

Hard hit, too, are the many families in which both husband and wife work. These people are affected doubly by higher income and Social Security taxes. If each spouse earned as much as the maximum wage taxed by Social Security, the couple's combined payroll tax would have increased a whopping $1,263 between 1974 and now. . . .

What can be done to provide relief from taxflation? The major suggestion is to "index" the income-tax system. While proposals vary in their details, the gist of the plan is this:

Tax brackets, exemptions, deductions and other aspects of the tax code would rise automatically each year in line with inflation. For instance, if the cost of living rose 10 percent in 1979, the personal exemption on 1979 income would be increased 10 percent—from $1,000 to $1,100. Brackets also would be widened. Thus, the 28 percent rate, now applied to taxable incomes in the $20,200–$24,600 bracket on joint returns, would be applied to taxable incomes of $22,220–$27,060. . . .

### How Inflation Robs the Taxpayer—An Example

A married worker with a nonworking spouse and two children had income of $20,000 in 1974. Pay rose just as fast as inflation, so that in 1979 it will total $29,380. But—

|  | 1974 | 1979 |
|---|---|---|
| Gross Income | $20,000 | $29,380 |
| Federal income tax | $ 2,510 | $ 4,030 |
| Social Security tax | $ 772 | $ 1,404 |
| After-tax income | $16,718 | $23,946 |
| After-tax income in 1974 dollars | $16,718 | $16,301 |

Thus, the tax bite is up from 16.4 percent of gross income to 18.5 percent, and purchasing power has fallen $417.

"Catch-Up Raises That Don't Quite Catch Up," *U.S. News & World Report*, October 1, 1979, p. 52, abridged. Copyright © 1979 U.S. News & World Report, Inc.

# The Background and Analytical Tools of Employment Theory

## chapter 11

This and the following chapter are concerned with assessing the ability of a capitalistic economy to achieve the full employment of its resources. If the price system can provide for a reasonably efficient allocation of resources, what is to prevent it from providing for the full utilization of society's available resources?

More specifically, the objectives of the present chapter are threefold: In the first place, we want to understand why for many years economists thought capitalism was capable of providing for virtually uninterrupted full employment. Involved here is a discussion of the so-called classical theory of employment. Second, the shortcomings of the classical theory will be noted and analyzed. Then, finally, the tools of modern employment theory will be introduced and explained. In Chapters 12 and 13 we shall employ these tools to analyze the equilibrium levels of output and employment and extend our analysis to indicate the effects of government policies upon output and employment.

Three simplifying assumptions will greatly facilitate achievement of these objectives:

1  A "closed economy" will be assumed. That is, our discussion will deal with the domestic economy, deferring the complications arising from international trade transactions until later chapters.

2  Government will be ignored until Chapter 13, thereby permitting us in Chapters 11 and 12 to determine whether or not laissez faire capitalism is capable of achieving full employment.

3  Although saving actually occurs in both the business and household sectors of the economy, we shall for convenience speak as if all saving were personal saving.[1]

[1]When using NNP as our measure of total output, it is accurate to assume that the bulk of the economy's saving is done by households. Personal saving was $113 billion and undistributed corporate profits were $33 million in 1979. If GNP were employed, however, capital consumption allowances of $243 billion would have to be included as a part of business saving, making business saving almost three times as great as personal saving.

Two implications of these assumptions are noteworthy. First, assumptions 1 and 2 mean that we are omitting net exports, $X_n$, and government purchases, $G$, from our total spending equation of Chapter 9. Thus, for the time being, total spending or "aggregate demand" is comprised simply of consumption, $C$, and investment, $I$. Second, assumptions 2 and 3 permit us to treat NNP, NI, PI, and DI as being equal to one another for the simple reason that all the items which in practice distinguish them from one another are due to government (taxes and transfer payments) and business saving (see Table 9-5). This means that we can readily shift our discussion among these various output and income measures without encountering serious complications which would otherwise arise.

Now the ground is cleared to rephrase our basic question: Is capitalism able to achieve and maintain a full-employment, noninflationary total output?

## ☐  THE CLASSICAL THEORY OF EMPLOYMENT

Answers to this question have varied historically. Until the Great Depression of the 1930s, many prominent economists—now called classical economists[2]—felt that the price system was capable of providing for the full employment of the economy's resources. It was acknowledged that now and then abnormal circumstances would arise in such forms as wars, political upheavals, droughts, speculative crises, gold rushes, and so forth, to push the economy from the path of full employment (see Figure 10-1). But it was contended that when these deviations occurred, automatic adjustments within the price system would soon restore the economy to the full-employment level of output. Although it is not now generally accepted, an analysis of the classical theory of employment is important for at least

two reasons. First, an understanding of the classical theory will lay a firm foundation for understanding modern employment theory. Second, classical theory is the intellectual antecedent of the monetarist view of macroeconomics which will be considered in Chapter 17.

The classical theory of employment was grounded on two basic notions. First, it was argued that underspending—that is, a level of spending insufficient to purchase a full-employment output—was most unlikely to occur. Second, even if a deficiency of total spending were to arise, price-wage adjustments would occur so as to ensure that the decline in total spending would *not* entail declines in real output, employment, and real incomes.

### △  Say's Law

The classical economists' denial of the possibility of underspending was based upon their faith in Say's Law. *Say's Law* is the disarmingly simple notion that the very act of producing goods generates an amount of income exactly equal to the value of the goods produced. That is, the production of any output would automatically provide the wherewithal to take that output off the market. *Supply creates its own demand.*[3] The essence of Say's Law can be envisaged most easily in terms of a barter economy. A shoemaker, for example, produces or *supplies* shoes as a means of buying or *demanding* the shirts and stockings produced by other craftsmen. The shoemaker's supply of shoes *is* his demand for other goods. And so it allegedly is for other producers and for the entire economy: Demand must be the same as supply! In fact, the circular flow model of the economy and national income accounting both suggest something of this sort. The income generated from the production of any level of total output would, *when spent,* be just sufficient to provide a matching total demand. Assuming that the composition of output is in accord with con-

[2]Most notable among the classical economists are John Stuart Mill, F. Y. Edgeworth, Alfred Marshall, and A. C. Pigou.

[3]Attributed to the nineteenth-century French economist J. B. Say.

sumer preferences, all markets would be cleared of their outputs. It would seem that all that business owners need do to sell a full-employment output is to produce that output; Say's Law guarantees that there will be sufficient consumption spending for its successful disposal.

**Saving: A Complicating Factor**   However, there is one obvious omission in this simple application of Say's Law. Although it is an accepted truism that output gives rise to an identical amount of money income (Chapter 9), there is no guarantee that the recipients of this income will spend it all. Some income might be saved (not spent) and therefore not reflected in product demand. Saving would constitute a break, or "leakage," in the income-expenditure flows and therefore would undermine the effective operation of Say's Law. Saving is a withdrawal of funds from the income stream which will cause consumption expenditures to fall short of total output. If households saved some portion of their incomes, supply would not create its own demand. Saving would cause a deficiency of consumption. The consequences? Unsold goods, cutbacks in production, unemployment, and falling incomes.

**Saving, Investment, and the Interest Rate**   But the classical economists were reluctant to bow to those economists who suggested that such a virtuous act as saving could give rise to underspending and the calamity of depression. Instead, they argued that saving would not really result in a deficiency of total demand, because each and every dollar saved would be invested by businesses. Investment would allegedly occur to compensate for any deficiency of consumer spending; that is, investment would fill any consumption "gap" caused by saving. Business firms, after all, do not plan to sell their entire output to consumers but, rather, to produce a considerable portion of total output in the form of capital goods for sale to one another. In other words,

investment spending by businesses is a supplement or an addition to the income-expenditure stream which may fill any consumption gap arising from saving. Thus, if businesses as a group intend to invest as much as households want to save, Say's Law will hold and the levels of national output and employment will remain constant. Whether or not the economy could achieve and sustain a level of spending sufficient to provide a full-employment level of output and income therefore would depend upon whether businesses were willing to invest enough to offset the amount households want to save.

The classical economists argued that capitalism contained a very special market—the *money market*—which would guarantee an equality of saving and investment plans and therefore full employment. That is, the money market—and, more specifically, the *interest rate* (the price paid for the use of money)— would see to it that dollars which leaked from the income-expenditure stream as saving would automatically reappear as dollars spent on investment goods. The rationale underlying the saving and investment equating adjustments of the interest rate was simple and, if not too carefully scrutinized, very plausible. The classical economists contended that, other things being equal, households normally prefer to consume rather than to save. The consumption of goods and services satisfies human wants; idle dollars do not. Hence, it was reasoned that consumers would save only if someone would pay them a rate of interest as a reward for their thriftiness. The greater the interest rate, the more dollars saved; that is, the saving (supply-of-dollars) curve of households would be upsloping, as shown by $S$ in Figure 11-1. And who would be inclined to pay for the use of saving? None other than investors—business owners who seek (demand) money capital to replace and enlarge their plants and their stocks of capital equipment. Because the interest rate is a cost to borrowing businesses, they will be more willing to borrow and invest at low than at high interest rates.

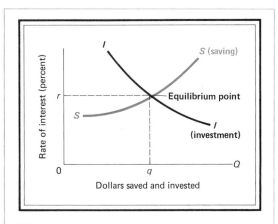

**FIGURE 11-1  CLASSICAL VIEW OF THE MONEY MARKET**

The classical economists believed that the saving plans of households would be reflected in a supply-of-dollars curve *S* and the investment plans of businesses in a demand-for-dollars curve *I* in the money market. The equilibrium interest rate *r*, the price paid for the use of money, would equate the amounts households and businesses planned to save and invest, thereby guaranteeing a full-employment level of spending.

est rate down to a new and lower equilibrium level. And this lower interest rate will expand the volume of investment spending until it again equals the amount of saving, thereby preserving full employment. In short, changes in the interest rate would guarantee the operation of Say's Law even in an economy in which substantial saving occurs. As the classical economists saw it, the economy was analogous to a gigantic bathtub wherein the volume of water measured the levels of output and employment. Any leakage down the drain of saving would be returned to the tub through the spigot of investment. This had to be the case, because the interest rate connected the drainpipe and the spigot!

△  **Price-Wage Flexibility**

The classical economists bolstered their conclusion that full employment is the norm of capitalism with a second basic argument. They argued that the level of output which business producers can sell depends not only upon the level of total spending but also upon the level of product prices. This meant that even if the interest rate should somehow temporarily fail to equate the amounts which households wanted to save with the investment intentions of businesses, any resulting decline in total spending would be offset by proportionate declines in the price level. That is, $20 will buy four shirts at $5, but $10 will buy the same number of shirts provided their price falls to $2.50. Hence, if households somehow managed to succeed in saving more than businesses were willing to invest, the resulting decline in total spending would not result in a decline in real output, real income, and the level of employment *if* product prices declined in proportion to the decline in expenditures.

And, according to the classical economists, this is precisely what would happen. Competition among sellers would ensure price flexibility! As declines in product demand became general, competing producers would lower their prices to dispose of accumulating sur-

This means that the investment (demand-for-dollars) curve of businesses is downsloping, as shown by *I* in Figure 11-1.

Classical economists concluded that the money market, wherein savers supply dollars and investors demand dollars, would establish an equilibrium price for the use of money—an equilibrium interest rate—at which the quantity of dollars saved (supplied) would equal the number of dollars invested (demanded). Saving, said the classicists, does not really constitute a break in the income-expenditure stream or a fatal flaw in Say's Law, because the money market or, more specifically, the interest rate will necessitate that each and every dollar saved will get into the hands of investors and be spent on capital equipment. Therefore, an increase in thriftiness is not a cause for social concern, because this simply shifts the supply-of-saving curve to the right. Although saving will momentarily exceed investment and perhaps cause some temporary unemployment, the surplus of saving will drive the inter-

pluses. In other words, the result of "excess" saving would be to lower prices; and lower prices, by increasing the value of the dollar, would permit nonsavers to obtain more goods and services with their current money incomes. Saving would therefore lower prices, but not output and employment.

"But," ever-present skeptics have asked, "doesn't this ignore the resource market? Although businesses can sustain their sales in the face of a declining demand by accepting lower product prices, won't they find it unprofitable to do so? As product prices decline, won't resource prices—particularly wage rates—have to decline significantly to permit businesses to produce *profitably* at the now lower prices?" The classical economists replied that wage rates must and would decline. General declines in product demand would be mirrored in declines in the demand for labor and other resources. The immediate result would be a surplus of labor, that is, unemployment, at the wage rate prevailing prior to these declines in the demand for labor. However, though not willing to employ all workers at the original wage rates, producers would find it profitable to employ additional workers at lower wage rates. The demand for labor, in other words, is downsloping; those workers unable to locate employment at the old higher wage rates could find jobs at the new lower wage rates.

Would workers be willing to accept lower wage rates? Competition among unemployed workers, according to the classical economists, would guarantee it. In competing for scarce jobs, idle workers would bid down wage rates until these rates (wage costs to employers) were so low that employers would once again find it profitable to hire all available workers. This would happen at the new lower equilibrium wage rate. The classical economists therefore concluded that *involuntary unemployment* was impossible. Anyone who was willing to work at the market-determined wage rate could readily find employment. Competition in the labor market ruled out involuntary idleness.

△  **Classical Theory and Laissez Faire**

Strictly speaking, each of these price system adjustments—fluctuations in the interest rate on the one hand, and price-wage flexibility on the other—seemed fully capable of maintaining full employment in a capitalistic economy. Working together, the classical economists felt, the two adjustment mechanisms made full employment a forgone conclusion. The classical economists came to embrace capitalism as a self-regulating economy wherein full employment was regarded as the norm. Capitalism was capable of "running itself." Government assistance in the operation of the economy was deemed unnecessary—nay, harmful. In an economy capable of achieving both full production and full employment, governmental interference could only be a detriment to its efficient operation.

☐  **KEYNESIAN ECONOMICS**

One embarrassing fact persistently denied the validity of the classical theory of employment—recurring periods of prolonged unemployment and inflation. While one might explain a minor depression, such as the brief downswings of 1924 and 1927, in terms of wars and similar external considerations, serious and prolonged downswings, such as the Great Depression of the 1930s, were not so easily rationalized. There is a remarkable inconsistency between a theory which concludes that unemployment is virtually impossible and the actual occurrence of a ten-year siege of very substantial unemployment.[4] And so various economists came to criticize both the rationale and the underlying assumptions of classical employment theory. They tried to find a bet-

[4]It is interesting to note that most of the classical economists stuck to their theoretical guns during the 1930s, arguing that (1) the reluctance of union and business monopolies to accept price and wage cuts, (2) misguided New Deal policies which sought to prevent price-wage declines, and (3) government policies in the area of money and banking which interfered with the operation of the interest rate prevented a quick recovery from the cyclical downswing of the early 1930s.

ter, more realistic explanation of those forces which determine the level of employment.

Finally, in 1936 the renowned English economist John Maynard Keynes (pronounced "canes") came forth with a new explanation of the level of employment in capitalistic economies. In his *General Theory of Employment, Interest, and Money,*[5] Keynes virtually knocked the props out from under the classical view and, in doing so, touched off a major revolution in economic thinking on the question of unemployment. Although Keynes fathered modern employment theory, many others have since refined and extended his work. In this and the following chapters, we are concerned with modern employment theory, or "Keynesian economics," as it stands today.

Keynesian employment theory contrasts sharply with the classical position. Its blunt conclusion is that capitalism simply does not contain any mechanisms capable of guaranteeing full employment. The economy, it is argued, might come to rest—that is, reach an aggregate output equilibrium—with either considerable unemployment or substantial inflation. Full employment accompanied by a relatively stable level of prices is more of an accident than a norm. Capitalism is *not* a self-regulating system capable of perpetual prosperity; capitalism cannot be depended upon to "run itself." Furthermore, depressions should not be associated exclusively with external forces such as wars, droughts, and similar abnormalities. Rather, the causes of unemployment and inflation lie to a very considerable degree in the failure of certain fundamental economic decisions—in particular, saving and investment decisions—to be completely synchronized in a capitalistic system. Internal, in addition to external, forces contribute to economic instability.

Keynesians back these sweeping contentions by rejecting the very mechanisms upon which the classical position is grounded—the interest rate and price-wage adjustments.

[5] New York: Harcourt, Brace & World, Inc., 1936.

## △  The Unlinking of Saving and Investment Plans

Keynesian theory rejects Say's Law by seriously questioning the ability of the interest rate to synchronize the saving and investment plans of households and businesses. The fact that modern capitalism is amply endowed with an elaborate money market and a wide variety of financial institutions does not diminish this skepticism about the interest rate as a mechanism capable of connecting the saving drain and the investment spigot. Most untenable is the classical contention that business firms would invest more when households increased their rates of saving. After all, does not more saving mean less consumption? Can we really expect business planners to expand their capital facilities as the markets for their products shrink? More generally, the modern view holds that savers and investors are essentially distinct groups that formulate their saving and investment plans for different reasons which, in each instance, are largely unrelated to the rate of interest.

**1  Savers and Investors Are Different Groups**  Who decides the amounts to be saved and invested in a capitalistic economy? (We continue to ignore government in our discussion.) Business organizations of all kinds and descriptions, and, in particular, corporations, make the vast majority of investment decisions. And who makes the saving decisions? Here the picture is a bit more cluttered. In a wealthy economy such as that of American capitalism, households save substantial amounts—at least when prosperity prevails. It is true, of course, that business corporations also do a considerable amount of saving in the form of undistributed corporate profits. The important point is that to a significant degree, saving and investment decisions are made by different groups of individuals (see footnote 1 of this chapter).

**2  Savers and Investors Are Differently Motivated**  The nonidentity of savers and investors would not necessarily be fatal to the classical theory if their decisions were motivated and synchronized by some common factor such as the interest rate. But Keynesians contend this is not the case. Saving decisions are motivated by diverse considerations. Some save in order to make large purchases which exceed any single paycheck; households save to make down payments on houses and to buy automobiles or television sets. Some saving is solely for the convenience of having a pool of liquid funds readily available to take advantage of any extraordinarily good buys which one may chance upon. Or saving may occur to provide for the future needs of individuals and their families: households save to provide for the future retirement of the family breadwinner or to expose the offspring to the rigors of a college education. Or saving may be a precautionary, rainy-day measure—a means of protecting oneself against such unpredictable events as prolonged illness and unemployment. Or saving may be merely a deeply ingrained habit that is practiced on an almost automatic basis with no specific purposes in mind. Much saving is highly institutionalized or contractual: for example, payments for life insurance and annuities or participation in a "bond-a-month" program. The basic point is that none of these diverse motives for saving is particularly sensitive to the interest rate. In fact, Keynesians argue that one can readily pose a situation wherein, contrary to the classical conception (Figure 11-1), saving is *inversely* related to the interest rate. To illustrate: If a family requires an annual retirement income of $6000 from saving, it will need to save $100,000 if the interest rate is 6 percent, but only $50,000 if the interest rate is 12 percent!

What, in the Keynesian view, does determine the level of saving? The primary determinant is the level of national income. In particular, a higher level of income will mean a high volume of both saving and consumption for households individually and as a group. When income is low, households must spend

their entire incomes to achieve an acceptable standard of living; indeed, low incomes may give rise to dissaving. Higher incomes, however, permit households to increase both consumption and the level of saving.

Why do businesses purchase capital goods? The motivation for investment spending, as we shall discover in a few pages, is complex. The interest rate—the cost of obtaining money capital with which to invest—undoubtedly is a consideration in formulating investment plans. But the interest rate is not the most important factor. The rate of profit which business firms expect to realize on the investment is the really crucial determinant of the amounts they desire to invest. In fact, some economists argue that the investment plans of businesses are generally rather insensitive to changes in the interest rate. Furthermore, during the downswing of the business cycle, profit expectations will be so bleak that the level of investment will be low and possibly declining despite substantial reductions in the interest rate. Interest rate reductions are not likely to stimulate investment spending when it is most sorely needed.

**3  Money Balances and Banks**  Keynesian employment theory envisions the classical conception of the money market (Figure 11-1) as being oversimplified and therefore incorrect in another sense. Specifically, the classical money market assumes that current saving is the only source of funds for the financing of investment. Keynesian economics holds that there are two other sources of funds which can be made available in the money market: (1) the accumulated money balances held by households, and (2) commercial banks. Keynesian theory stipulates that the public holds money balances not merely to negotiate day-to-day transactions, but also as a form of accumulated wealth. Now the important point for present purposes is that, by drawing down or decumulating a portion of these money balances and offering these dollars to investors, a supply of funds in excess of current saving can be made available in the money market. Similarly, as we will find in Chapter 15, when commercial banks make loans, they add to the money supply. Bank lending, therefore, is also a means of augmenting current saving as a source of funds for investment. The consequence is that a reduction in the money balances held by households *and* bank lending can give rise to an amount of investment which is in excess of current saving. This implies that Say's Law is invalid and that output, employment, and the price level can fluctuate. More specifically, we shall soon see that an excess of investment over saving results in an increase in total spending which has an expansionary effect on the economy. If the economy is initially in a recession, output and employment will increase; if the economy is already at full employment, the added spending will cause demand-pull inflation.

Conversely, classical theory is incorrect in assuming that all current saving will appear in the money market. If (1) households add some of their current saving to their money balances

rather than channel it into the money market, or (2) some current saving is used to retire outstanding bank loans, then the amount of funds made available in the money market will be less than that shown by the classical saving curve in Figure 11-1. This suggests that the amount of current saving will exceed the amount invested. Again, Say's Law does not hold and macroeconomic instability will result. In this case the excess of saving over investment will mean a decline in total demand which is contractionary; output and employment will tend to fall.[6]

To summarize: The Keynesian position is that saving and investment plans can be at odds and thereby can result in fluctuations in total output, total income, employment, and the price level. It is largely a matter of chance that households and businesses will desire to save and invest identical amounts. Keynesian economists feel they are better plumbers than their classical predecessors by recognizing that the saving drain and the investment spigot are *not* connected.

---

[6]Technical footnote: It is a relatively simple matter to portray these Keynesian criticisms in terms of the classical conception of the money market. In the first case (Figure *a*), funds are shifted by households from their accumulated money balances to the money market *and* banks create funds (money) by lending. Adding these amounts horizontally to current saving $S$, we get the supply-of-funds curve $F_1$. At the resulting equilibrium interest rate $r_1$, investment is $I_1$ and obviously in excess of current saving $S_1$. In the second case (Figure *b*), the supply-of-funds curve, $F_2$, is

less than current saving $S$, because portions of current saving have been added to the money balances of households *and* used to retire bank debt. These portions of current saving have been subtracted horizontally from the $S$ curve to derive the $F_2$ curve. At the relevant equilibrium interest rate $r_2$, investment is only $I_2$ while current saving is obviously more at $S_2$. The conclusion is that the money market does *not* ensure the equality of saving and investment; Say's Law is therefore invalid; and the economy is subject to macroeconomic instability.

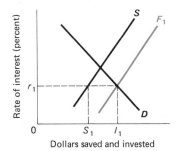

(a) Decreased money balances and
bank lending

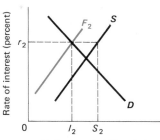

(b) Increased money balances and
bank loan retirement

## △  The Discrediting of
## Price-Wage Flexibility

But what of the second aspect of the classical position—the contention that downward price-wage adjustments will eliminate the unemployment effects of a decline in total spending?

**1**  Price-wage flexibility, Keynesians argue, simply does not exist to the degree necessary for ensuring the restoration of full employment in the face of a decline in total spending. The price system of capitalism has never been perfectly competitive and now it is riddled by market imperfections and circumscribed by practical and political obstacles which work against downward price-wage flexibility. To be specific, monopolistic producers, dominating many important product markets, have both the ability and the desire to resist falling product prices as demand declines. And in the resource markets, strong labor unions are equally persistent in holding the line against wage cuts. In this endeavor they are ably assisted by minimum-wage legislation, public opinion as to what are reasonable and "customary" wage rates, and practical-minded politicians who are well aware of the power of labor at the polls. Even employers might be wary of wage cuts, recognizing possible adverse effects upon worker morale and productivity. In short, as a practical matter, downward price-wage flexibility cannot be expected to offset the unemployment effects of a decline in total spending.

**2**  Furthermore, even if price-wage declines accompanied a contraction of total spending, it is doubtful that these declines would help reduce unemployment. The reason? The volume of total money demand cannot remain constant as prices and wages decline. That is, lower prices and wages necessarily mean lower money incomes, and lower money incomes in turn entail further reductions in total spending. The net result is likely to be little or no change in the depressed levels of output and employment.

Keynesians point out that the classicists were tripped up in their reasoning by the fallacy of composition. Because any particular group of workers typically buys only a small amount of what they produce, the product and therefore labor demand curves of a single firm can be regarded as independent of any wage (income) changes accorded its own workers. In other words, it is correct to reason that a decline in its wage rate will move a *single firm* down its stable labor demand curve and result in more workers hired, that is, more employment. But this reasoning, argue Keynesian economists, is not applicable to the economy as a whole, to general wage cuts. Why? Because wages are the major source of income in the economy. Widespread wage declines will therefore result in declines in incomes and in the demand for both products and the labor used in producing them. The result is that employers will hire little or no additional labor after the general wage cuts. What holds true for a single firm—a wage cut for its employees will not adversely affect labor demand—is not true for the economy as a whole—general wage cuts *will* lower money incomes and cause the demand for products and labor to decline generally.

Recapitulation: Keynesians argue, in the first place, that prices and wages are in fact not flexible downward and, second, even if they were, that it is highly doubtful that price-wage declines would alleviate widespread unemployment.

## □  TOOLS OF MODERN
## EMPLOYMENT THEORY

By rejecting the analysis of the classical economists, we are in effect recognizing that there is no automatic mechanism with the capacity to make full employment the normal state of affairs in a capitalistic system. Yet the question remains: How are the levels of output and employment determined in modern capitalism?

The touchstone of any meaningful answer is that *the amount of goods and services pro-*

*duced and therefore the level of employment depend directly upon the level of total spending or "aggregate demand."* Subject to the economy's productive potential as determined by the scarce resources available to it, businesses will produce that level of output which they can profitably sell. Workers and machinery are idled when there are no markets for the goods and services they are capable of producing. Total spending, on the one hand, and total output and employment, on the other, vary directly. Therefore, in explaining the economy's output-employment levels, we must obviously begin by examining the consumption and investment components of total spending.

## □ CONSUMPTION AND SAVING

In terms of absolute size, consumption is the main component of total spending (Chapter 9). It is therefore of obvious importance to understand the major determinants of consumption spending. You may also recall that economists define personal saving as "not spending" or "that part of DI which is not consumed"; in other words, disposable income equals consumption plus saving. Hence, in examining the determinants of consumption we are also simultaneously exploring the determinants of saving.

### △ Income-consumption and Income-saving Relationships

There are many considerations which influence the level of consumer spending. But common sense and available statistical data both suggest that the most important determinant of consumer spending is income—in particular, disposable income. And, of course, since saving is that part of disposable income which is not consumed, DI is also the basic determinant of personal saving.

Consider some recent historical data. In Figure 11-2 each dot indicates the consumption–disposable income relationship for each year since 1960 and the thick line is fitted to these points. Note, most obviously, that con-

sumption is directly related to disposable income and, indeed, households clearly spend most of their income. But we can say more. The thin 45-degree line is added to the diagram as a point of reference. Because this line bisects the 90-degree angle formed by the vertical and horizontal axes of the graph, each point on the 45-degree line must be equidistant from the two axes. We can therefore regard the vertical distance from any point on the horizontal axis to the 45-degree line as either consumption *or* disposable income. If we regard it as disposable income, then the amount (the vertical distance) by which the actual amount consumed in any given year falls short of the 45-degree guideline indicates the amount of saving in any particular year. For example, in 1979 consumption was $1510 billion, and disposable income was $1623; hence, saving in 1979 was $113 billion. That is, disposable income less consumption equals saving. By observing these vertical distances as we move to the right on Figure 11-2, we note that saving also varies directly with the level of disposable income. In fact, not shown on Figure 11-2 is the fact that in years of very low income, for example, some of the worst years of the Great Depression, consumption exceeded disposable income. The dots for these years would obviously be located *above* the 45-degree line. Households actually consumed in excess of their current incomes by *dissaving,* that is, by going into debt and liquidating previously accumulated wealth.

To summarize: Figure 11-2 suggests that (1) households consume most of their disposable income and (2) both consumption and saving are directly related to the level of income.

### △ The Consumption Schedule

Figure 11-2 embodies historical data; it shows us how much households *actually did consume* (and save) at various levels of DI over a period of years. For analytical purposes we need an income-consumption relationship—a consumption schedule—which shows the various amounts households *plan* to consume at

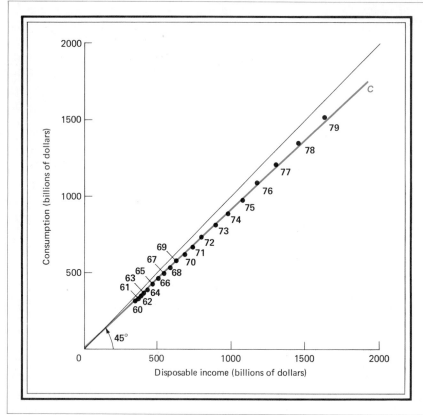

FIGURE 11-2 CONSUMPTION
AND DISPOSABLE INCOME,
1960–1979

Each dot in this figure shows
consumption and disposable
income in a given year. The
*C* line generalizes upon the
relationship between
consumption and disposable
income. It indicates a direct
relationship and that households consume the bulk of
their incomes.

various possible levels of disposable income
which might conceivably prevail at some specific *point in time*. A hypothetical *consumption schedule* of the type we require for analysis is shown in columns 1 and 2 of Table 11-1.
It is plotted in Figure 11-3*a*. This consumption
schedule reflects the consumption-disposable
income relationship suggested by the empirical
data of Figure 11-2, and it is consistent with a
variety of empirical family budget studies. The
relationship is direct—as common sense certainly would suggest—and, in addition, we
note that households will spend a larger *proportion* of a small disposable income than of a
large disposable income.

△   **The Saving Schedule**

It is a simple task to derive a *saving
schedule*. Because disposable income equals
consumption plus saving (DI = C + S), we

need only subtract consumption from disposable income to find the amount saved at each
level of DI. That is, DI − C = S. Hence, columns 1 and 3 of Table 11-1 constitute the
saving schedule. This schedule is plotted in
Figure 11-3*b*. Note that there is a direct relationship between saving and DI but that saving constitutes a smaller proportion (fraction)
of a small DI than it does of a large DI. If
households consume a smaller and smaller
proportion of DI as DI goes up, they must save
a larger and larger proportion.

Remembering that each point on the 45-
degree line indicates an equality of DI and
consumption, we see that dissaving would
occur at the relatively low DI of $370 billion;
that is, households will consume in excess of
their current incomes by drawing down accumulated savings or by borrowing. Graphically,
the vertical distance of the consumption

**TABLE 11-1**
**The Consumption and Saving Schedules** (*hypothetical data; columns 1 through 3 in billions*)

| (1) Level of output and income (NNP = D1) | (2) Consumption | (3) Saving (1) − (2) | (4) Average propensity to consume (APC) (2)/(1) | (5) Average propensity to save (APS) (3)/(1) | (6) Marginal propensity to consume (MPC) Δ(2)/Δ(1) | (7) Marginal propensity to save (MPS) Δ(3)/Δ(1) |
|---|---|---|---|---|---|---|
| $370 | $375 | $−5 | 1.01 | −.01 | | |
| | | | | | .75 | .25 |
| 390 | 390 | 0 | 1.00 | .00 | | |
| | | | | | .75 | .25 |
| 410 | 405 | 5 | .99 | .01 | | |
| | | | | | .75 | .25 |
| 430 | 420 | 10 | .98 | .02 | | |
| | | | | | .75 | .25 |
| 450 | 435 | 15 | .97 | .03 | | |
| | | | | | .75 | .25 |
| 470 | 450 | 20 | .96 | .04 | | |
| | | | | | .75 | .25 |
| 490 | 465 | 25 | .95 | .05 | | |
| | | | | | .75 | .25 |
| 510 | 480 | 30 | .94 | .06 | | |
| | | | | | .75 | .25 |
| 530 | 495 | 35 | .93 | .07 | | |
| | | | | | .75 | .25 |
| 550 | 510 | 40 | .93 | .07 | | |

schedule *above* the 45-degree line is equal to the vertical distance of the saving schedule *below* the horizontal axis at the $370 billion level of output and income (see Figure 11-3*a* and *b*). In this instance, each of these two vertical distances measures the $5 billion of *dissaving* which occurs at the $370 billion income level. The *break-even income* is at the $390 billion income level; this is the level at which households consume their entire incomes. Graphically, the consumption schedule cuts the 45-degree line, and the saving schedule cuts the horizontal axis at the break-even income level. At all higher incomes, households will plan to save a portion of their income. The vertical distance of the consumption schedule *below* the 45-degree line measures this saving, as does the vertical distance of the saving schedule *above* the horizontal axis. For example, at the $410 billion level of income, both these distances indicate $5 billion worth of saving (see Figure 11-3*a* and *b*).

△ **Average and Marginal Propensities**

Columns 4 to 7 of Table 11-1 point up additional characteristics of the consumption and saving schedules.

**APC and APS**   That fraction, or percentage, of any given total income which is consumed is called the *average propensity to consume* (APC), and that fraction of any total income which is saved is called the *average propensity to save* (APS). That is,

$$APC = \frac{consumption}{income}$$

and

$$APS = \frac{saving}{income}$$

For example, at the $470 billion level of income in Table 11-1, the APC is 45/47, or about 96 percent, while the APS is obviously 2/47, or about 4 percent. By calculating the APC and APS at each of the nine levels of DI shown in Table 11-1, we find that the APC falls and the APS rises as DI increases. This quantifies a point made a moment ago: The fraction of total DI which is consumed declines as DI rises, a movement that makes it necessary for the fraction of DI which is saved to rise as DI rises. Indeed, because disposable income is ei-

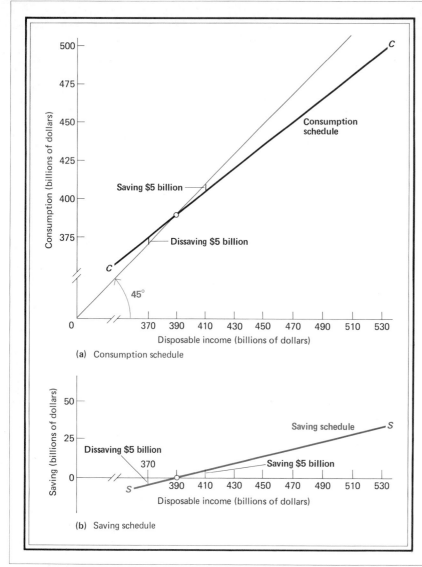

**FIGURE 11-3 CONSUMPTION (a) AND SAVING (b) SCHEDULES**

The two parts of this figure show the income-consumption and income-saving relationships graphically. Each point on the 45-degree line in (a) indicates an equality of DI and consumption. Therefore, because saving equals DI minus consumption, the saving schedule in (b) is found by subtracting the consumption schedule vertically from the 45-degree guideline. Consumers "break even," that is, consumption equals DI (and saving therefore equals zero) at $390 billion for these hypothetical data.

ther consumed or saved, the sum of the fraction of any level of DI which is consumed plus the fraction which is saved (not consumed) must exhaust that level of income. In short, APC + APS = 1. Columns 4 and 5 of Table 11-1 illustrate this point.

**MPC and MPS**   The fact that households consume a certain portion of some given total income—for example, 45/47 of a $470 billion disposable income—does not guarantee that they will consume the same proportion of any *change* in income which they might receive. The proportion, or fraction, of any change in income which is consumed is called the *marginal propensity to consume* (MPC), marginal meaning "extra" or "a change in." Or, alternatively stated, the MPC is the ratio of a *change* in consumption to the *change* in income which brought the consumption change about; that is,

$$MPC = \frac{\text{change in consumption}}{\text{change in income}}$$

Similarly, the fraction of any change in income which is saved is called the *marginal propensity to save* (MPS). That is, MPS is the ratio of a *change* in saving to the *change* in income which brought it about:

$$MPS = \frac{\text{change in saving}}{\text{change in income}}$$

Thus, if disposable income is currently $470 billion and household incomes rise by $20 billion, we find that they will consume $15/20$, or $3/4$, and save $5/20$, or $1/4$, of that increase in income (see columns 6 and 7 of Table 11-1). In other words, the MPC is $3/4$, or .75, and the MPS is $1/4$, or .25. *The sum of the MPC and the MPS for any given change in disposable income must always be 1*. That is, consuming and saving out of extra income is an either-or proposition; that fraction of any change in income which is not spent is, by definition, saved. Therefore the fraction consumed (MPC) plus the fraction saved (MPS) must exhaust the whole increase in income:

$$MPC + MPS = 1$$

In our example .75 plus .25 equals 100 percent, or 1.

Economists are not in complete agreement as to the exact behavior of the MPC and MPS as income increases. For many years it was assumed that the MPC declined and the MPS increased as income increased. That is, it was felt that a smaller and smaller fraction of increases in income would be consumed and a larger and larger fraction of these increases would be saved. Many economists now feel that the MPC and MPS for the economy as a whole are relatively constant. Statistical data such as those of Figure 11-2 are consistent with this position. We will assume the MPC and MPS to be constant, not only because of this

statistical evidence, but also because a constant MPC and MPS will simplify our analysis considerably. You will note that for each of the nine $20 billion income increases shown in Table 11-1, consumption increases by $15 billion, that is, by $15/20$, or $3/4$, of the increase in income, and saving increases by $5 billion, that is, by $5/20$, or $1/4$, of the increase in income. We assume the MPC and MPS to be constant at $3/4$ and $1/4$, respectively.[7]

△   **Nonincome Determinants of Consumption and Saving**

The level of disposable income is the basic determinant of the amounts households will consume and save, just as price is the basic determinant of the quantity demanded of any product. You will recall that changes in determinants other than price, such as consumer tastes, incomes, and so forth (Chapter 4), will cause the demand curve for a given product to

[7]The mathematically inclined reader will recognize that the MPC is the numerical value of the slope of the consumption schedule and the MPS is the numerical value of the slope of the saving schedule. The slope of any line can be measured by the ratio of the vertical change to the horizontal change involved in moving from one point to another point on that line. Thus, in the accompanying diagram, if the vertical change is 15 and the horizontal change is 20 between points $A$ and $B$, the slope of the line is $15/20 = 3/4$. Now it is evident in the figure that the slope of the consumption schedule between any two points is measured by the change in consumption (the vertical change) relative to the change in income (the horizontal change). And this ratio, change in consumption/change in income, is the fraction of any change in income that is spent; that is, it measures the MPC. Similar reasoning tells us that the MPS measures the slope of the saving schedule.

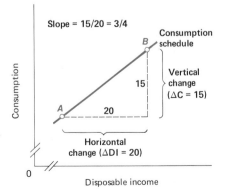

shift location. Similarly, there are certain determinants other than income which might cause households to consume more or less at each possible level of DI and thereby change the locations of the consumption and saving schedules.

**1  Stocks of Liquid Assets**  Generally speaking, the greater the amounts of liquid assets—money, saving accounts, private and public bonds, stocks, insurance policies, and so forth—owned by consumers, the greater will be their willingness to consume at each possible level of DI. The ownership of liquid assets makes households feel more secure financially and hence more willing to spend out of current disposable income. Hence, an increase in the stocks of liquid assets held by households will tend to shift the consumption schedule upward (and the saving schedule downward) and vice versa.

**2  Stocks of Durable Goods on Hand**  If the economy has enjoyed an extended period of prosperity, consumers may find themselves well supplied with various durable goods. That is, the majority of families may own late-model cars, television sets, refrigerators, and other household appliances, all worthy of years of future service. Hence, for a time many households will be "out of the market" for such products, with the result that consumers are willing to spend less and save more at each possible level of disposable income.

**3  Expectations**  Household expectations concerning future prices, money incomes, and the availability of goods may have a significant impact upon current spending and saving. Expectations of rising prices and product shortages tend to trigger more spending and less saving currently, that is, to shift the consumption schedule upward and the saving schedule downward. Why? Because it is natural for consumers to seek to avoid paying higher prices or having to "do without." Expected inflation and expected shortages induce

people to "buy now" to escape higher future prices and bare shelves. The expectation of rising money incomes in the future also tends to make consumers more footloose in their current spending. Conversely, expected price declines, anticipations of shrinking incomes, and the feeling that goods will be abundantly available may induce consumers to retrench on their consumption and build up their savings.

**4  Consumer Indebtedness**  The level of consumer credit can also be expected to affect the willingness of households to consume and, save out of current income. If households are in debt to the degree that, say, 20 or 25 percent of their current incomes are committed to installment payments on previous purchases, consumers may well be obliged to retrench on current consumption in order to reduce their indebtedness. Conversely, if consumer indebtedness is relatively low, households may consume at an unusually high rate by increasing this indebtedness.

**5  Attitudes toward Thrift**  Next, a catchall item: An economy's general attitude toward frugality will help determine the amounts of consumption and saving forthcoming at each possible level of DI. Attitudes toward thrift are governed as much by social and psychological considerations as they are by economic factors. If a society accepts the belief that saving is very virtuous and that "a dollar saved is a dollar earned," saving will tend to be greater and consumption less at each level of disposable income than would be the case where saving was held in lower esteem. There is some evidence to suggest that in the underdeveloped countries attitudes toward thrift are relatively weak, as most households are very anxious to consume in order to emulate the higher living standards of the more advanced nations.

Attitudes toward thrift can be influenced by government policies. During World War II the Federal government waged intensive propaganda campaigns to encourage households to

save by buying war bonds. These campaigns—coupled with the hard fact that many
consumer durables were unavailable or in
scant supply—were fairly successful in boosting the saving schedule and therefore in lowering the consumption schedule. Peacetime government policies may also affect the
consumption and saving schedules. By com-
mitting itself to policies designed to promote
full employment, government may diminish
the fear of unemployment and thereby weaken
an important motive to save.

**6   Taxation**   In Chapter 13, where consumption will be plotted against before-tax
income, we will find that changes in taxes will
shift the consumption and saving schedules.
Specifically, we will discover that taxes are
paid partly at the expense of consumption *and*
partly at the expense of saving. Therefore, an
*increase* in taxes will shift *both* the consumption and saving schedules *downward*. Conversely, a tax reduction will be partly consumed and partly saved by households. Thus a
tax *decrease* will shift *both* the consumption
and saving schedules *upward*.

△   **Shifts and Stability**

Three final and related points are relevant
to our discussion of the consumption and saving schedules.

**1**   The movement from one point to another on a given stable consumption schedule
(for example, $A$ to $B$ on $C_0$ in Figure 11-4a) is
called a *change in the amount consumed*. The
sole cause of this change is a change in the
level of disposable income. On the other hand,
a *change in the consumption schedule* refers to
an upward or downward shift of the entire
schedule—for example, from $C_0$ to $C_1$ or $C_2$ in
Figure 11-4a. A relocation of the consumption
schedule is obviously caused by changes in any
one or more of the nonincome determinants
just discussed. A similar terminological distinction applies to the saving schedule in Figure 11-4b.

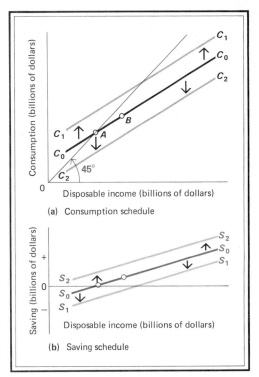

**FIGURE 11-4   SHIFTS IN THE CONSUMPTION (a)
AND SAVING (b) SCHEDULES**

A change in any one or more of the nonincome
determinants will cause the consumption and saving
schedules to shift. If households consume more at
each level of DI, they are necessarily saving less.
Graphically this means that an upshift in the consumption schedule ($C_0$ to $C_1$) entails a downshift
in the saving schedule ($S_0$ to $S_1$). Conversely, if
households consume less at each level of DI, they
are saving more. A downshift in the consumption
schedule ($C_0$ to $C_2$) is reflected in an upshift of
the saving schedule ($S_0$ to $S_2$).

**2**   A related point is that, insofar as the
first five nonincome determinants of consumption are concerned, the consumption and saving schedules will necessarily shift in opposite
directions. If households decide to consume
*more* at each possible level of disposable income, this means that they want to save *less,*
and vice versa. Graphically, if the consumption schedule shifts upward from $C_0$ to $C_1$ in
Figure 11-4, the saving schedule will shift

downward from $S_0$ to $S_1$. Similarly, a down-shift in the consumption schedule from $C_0$ to $C_2$ means an upshift in the saving schedule from $S_0$ to $S_2$. The exception to this involves the sixth nonincome determinant—taxation. We shall discover in Chapter 13 that households will consume less *and* save less in order to pay higher taxes. Hence, a tax increase will lower *both* the consumption and saving schedules, whereas a tax cut will shift *both* schedules upward.

**3** Economists are in general agreement that, aside from deliberate governmental actions designed to shift them, the consumption and saving schedules are quite stable. This may be because consumption-saving decisions are strongly influenced by habit or because the nonincome determinants are diverse and changes in them frequently work in opposite directions and therefore tend to be self-canceling.

## ☐ INVESTMENT

Let us now turn to investment, the second component of private spending. Recall that investment refers to expenditures on new plants, capital equipment, machinery, and so forth. What determines the level of net investment spending? There are two basic determinants: (1) the expected rate of net profits which businesses hope to realize from investment spending, and (2) the rate of interest.

### △ Expected Rate of Net Profit

The level of investment spending is guided by the profit motive; the business sector buys capital goods only when it expects such purchases to be profitable. Consider a simplified example. Suppose the owner of a small cabinetmaking shop is considering investing in a new sanding machine which costs $1000 and has a useful life of only one year. The new machine will presumably increase the firm's output and sales revenue. Specifically, let us suppose that the *net* expected revenue (that is, net of such operating costs as power, lumber,

labor, certain taxes, and so forth) from the machine is $1100. In other words, after operating costs have been accounted for, the remaining expected net revenue is sufficient to cover the $1000 cost of the machine and leave a return of $100. Comparing this $100 return or profit with the $1000 cost of the machine, we find that the expected *rate* of net profit on the machine is obviously 10 percent ($= \$100/\$1000$).

### △ The Interest Rate

But there is one important cost associated with investing which our example has ignored. And that, of course, is the interest rate—the financial cost the firm must pay to borrow the *money* capital required for the purchase of the *real* capital (the sanding machine).[8] Our generalization is this: If the expected rate of net profits (10 percent) exceeds the interest rate (say, 7 percent), it will be profitable to invest. But if the interest rate (say, 12 percent) exceeds the expected rate of net profits (10 percent), it will obviously be unprofitable to invest.

### △ Investment-Demand Curve

We must now move from micro to macro, that is, from a single firm's investment decision to an understanding of the total demand for investment goods by the entire business sector. Assume every firm in the economy has estimated the expected rate of net profits from all relevant investment projects and these data have been collected. These estimates can now be *cumulated* by asking: How many dollars' worth of investment projects entail an expected rate of net profit of, say, 16 percent or more? Of 14 percent or more? Of 12 percent or more? And so on.

---

[8]The role of the interest rate as a cost in investing in real capital is valid even if the firm does not borrow but, rather, finances the investment internally out of funds saved from past profits. By using this money to invest in the sander, the firm incurs an opportunity cost (Chapter 2) in the sense that it forgoes the interest income which it could have realized by lending the funds to someone else.

Suppose we find that there are no prospective investments which will yield an expected net profit of 16 percent or more. But there are $5 billion of investment opportunities with an expected rate of net profits between 14 and 16 percent; an *additional* $5 billion yielding between 12 and 14 percent; still an *additional* $5 billion yielding between 10 and 12 percent; and an *additional* $5 billion in each successive 2 percent range of yield down to and including the 0 to 2 percent range. By *cumulating* these figures we obtain the data of Table 11-2, which are shown graphically by the *investment-demand* curve in Figure 11-5. Note in Table 11-2 that the figure opposite 12 percent, for example, tells us there are $10 billion worth of investment opportunities which will yield an expected net profit of 12 percent *or more;* the $10 billion, in other words, includes the $5 billion of investment which will yield an expected return of 14 percent or more *plus* the $5 billion which is expected to yield between 12 and 14 percent.

Given this cumulated information on expected net profit rates of all possible investment projects, we again introduce the interest rate or financial cost of investing. We know from our sanding machine example that an investment project will be undertaken provided its expected net profit rate exceeds the interest rate. Let us apply this reasoning to

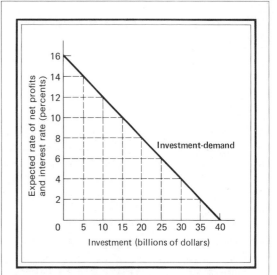

**FIGURE 11-5   THE INVESTMENT-DEMAND CURVE**

The investment-demand curve for the economy is derived by arraying all relevant investment projects in descending order of their expected rate of net profitability and applying the rule that investment should be undertaken up to the point at which the interest rate is equal to the expected rate of net profits. The investment-demand curve is downsloping, reflecting an inverse relationship between the interest rate (the financial price of investing) and the aggregate quantity of capital goods demanded.

**TABLE 11-2**
**Profit Expectations and Investment (*hypothetical data*)**

| Expected rate of net profit (in percent) | Amount of investment (billions of dollars per year) |
| --- | --- |
| 16% | $ 0 |
| 14 | 5 |
| 12 | 10 |
| 10 | 15 |
| 8 | 20 |
| 6 | 25 |
| 4 | 30 |
| 2 | 35 |
| 0 | 40 |

Figure 11-5. If we assume that rate of interest is 12 percent, we find that $10 billion of investment spending will be profitable, that is, $10 billion worth of investment projects entail an expected net profit rate of 12 percent or more. Stated differently, at a financial "price" of 12 percent, $10 billion worth of investment goods will be demanded. Similarly, if the interest rate were lower at, say, 10 percent, then an additional $5 billion of investment projects would become profitable and the total amount of investment goods demanded would be $15 billion (= $10 + $5). At an interest rate of 8 percent, a further $5 billion of investment would become profitable and the total demand for investment goods would be $20 billion. At 6 percent, investment would be $25 billion. And so forth. *By applying the rule that all investment projects should be undertaken up to the*

*point at which the expected rate of net profit equals the interest rate, we discover that the curve of Figure 11-5 is the investment-demand curve.* That is, various possible financial prices of investing (various interest rates) are shown on the vertical axis and the corresponding quantities of investment goods demanded are revealed on the horizontal axis. By definition, any line or curve embodying such data is the investment-demand curve. Consistent with our product and resource demand curves of Chapter 4, observe the *inverse* relationship between the interest rate (price) and the amount of spending on investment goods (quantity demanded).

This conception of the investment decision allows us to anticipate an important aspect of macroeconomic policy. We shall find in our discussion of monetary policy in Chapter 16 that by changing the supply of money, government can alter the interest rate. This is done primarily to change the level of investment spending. Think of it in this way: At any point in time, business firms in the aggregate have a wide variety of investment projects under consideration. If interest rates are high, only those projects with the highest expected rate of net profit will be undertaken. Hence, the level of investment will be small. As the interest rate is lowered, projects whose expected rate of net profit is less will also become commercially feasible and the level of investment will rise.

△   **Shifts in Investment Demand**

In discussing the consumption schedule, we noted that, although disposable income is the key determinant of the amount consumed, there are other factors which affect consumption. These "nonincome determinants," you will recall, cause shifts in the consumption schedule. So it also is with the investment-demand schedule. Figure 11-5 portrays the interest rate as the main determinant of investment. But other factors or variables determine the location of the investment-demand curve. Let us briefly consider several

of the more important "noninterest determinants" of investment-demand, noting how changes in these determinants might shift the investment-demand curve. We observe at the outset that any factor which increases the expected net profitability of investment will shift the investment-demand curve to the right. Conversely, anything which decreases the expected net profitability of investment will shift the investment-demand curve to the left.

**1   Acquisition, Maintenance, and Operating Costs**   As our sanding machine example revealed, the initial costs of capital goods, along with the estimated costs of operating and maintaining those goods, are obviously important considerations in gauging the expected rate of net profitability of any particular investment. To the extent that these costs rise, the expected rate of *net* profit from prospective investment projects will fall, shifting the investment-demand curve to the left. Conversely, if these costs decline, expected net profit rates will rise, shifting the investment-demand curve to the right. Note that the wage policies of unions may affect the investment-demand curve because wage rates are a major operating cost for most firms.

**2   Business Taxes**   Business owners look to expected profits *after taxes* in making their investment decisions. Hence, an increase in business taxes will lower profitability and tend to shift the investment-demand curve to the left; a tax reduction will tend to shift it to the right.

**3   Technological Change**   Technological progress—the development of new products, improvements in existing products, the creation of new machinery and new production processes—is a basic stimulus to investment. The development of a more efficient machine, for example, will lower production costs or improve product quality, thereby increasing the expected rate of net profit from investing in the machine. Profitable new products—such as hand calculators, citizen-band radios, digital watches, and so on—induce a flurry of investment as firms tool up for expanded production. In short, a rapid rate of technological progress shifts the investment-demand curve to the right, and vice versa.

**4   The Stock of Capital Goods on Hand** Just as the stock of consumer goods on hand affects household consumption-saving decisions, so the stock of capital goods on hand influences the expected profit rate from additional investment in a given industry. To the extent that a given industry is well stocked with productive facilities and inventories of finished goods, investment will be retarded in that industry. The reason is obvious: Such an industry will be amply equipped to fulfill present and future market demand at prices which yield mediocre profits. If an industry has enough, or even excessive, productive capacity, the expected rate of profit from further investment in the industry will be low, and therefore little or no investment will occur. To summarize: Excess productive capacity tends to shift the investment-demand curve to the left; a relative scarcity of capital goods shifts it to the right.

**5   Expectations** We noted earlier that business investment is based upon *expected* profits. Capital goods are durable—they may have a life expectancy of ten or twenty years—and thus the profitability of any capital investment will depend upon business planners' expectations of the *future* sales and *future* profitability of the product which the capital helps produce. Business expectations may be based upon elaborate forecasts of future business conditions which incorporate a number of "business indicators." Nevertheless, such elusive and difficult-to-predict factors as changes in the domestic political climate, the thrust of foreign affairs, population growth, stock market conditions, and so on, must be taken into account on a subjective or intuitive basis. For present purposes we note that, if business ex-

ecutives are optimistic about future business conditions, the investment-demand curve will shift to the right; a pessimistic outlook will shift it to the left.

△   **Investment and Income**
In order to add the investment decisions of businesses to the consumption plans of households (Chapter 12), we need to express investment plans in terms of the level of disposable income, or NNP. That is, we want to construct an *investment schedule* showing the amounts which business firms as a group plan or intend to invest at each of the various possible levels of income or output. Such a schedule will mirror the investment plans or intentions of business owners and managers in the same way the consumption and saving schedules reflect the consumption and saving plans of households.

We shall assume in our analysis that business investment is geared to long-term profit expectations as influenced by such considerations as technological progress, population growth, and so forth, and therefore is *autonomous* or independent of the level of current income. More specifically, let us suppose that the investment-demand curve is as shown in Figure 11-5 *and* that the current rate of interest is 8 percent. This means that the business sector will find it profitable to spend $20 billion on investment goods. In Table 11-3, columns 1 and 2, we are assuming that this level of investment will be forthcoming at every level of income. The $I_n$ line in Figure 11-6 shows this graphically.

This assumed independence of investment and income is admittedly a simplification. A higher level of business activity may *induce* additional spending on capital facilities, as suggested by columns 1 and 3 of Table 11-3 and $I'_n$ in Figure 11-6. There are at least two reasons why investment might vary directly with income. First, investment is related to profits; much investment is financed internally out of business profits. Therefore, it is very plausible to suggest that as disposable income rises, so

**TABLE 11-3**
The Investment Schedule (*hypothetical data; in billions*)

| (1) Level of output and income | (2) Investment, $I_n$ | (3) Investment, $I'_n$ |
|---|---|---|
| $370 | $20 | $10 |
| 390 | 20 | 12 |
| 410 | 20 | 14 |
| 430 | 20 | 16 |
| 450 | 20 | 18 |
| 470 | 20 | 20 |
| 490 | 20 | 22 |
| 510 | 20 | 24 |
| 530 | 20 | 26 |

will business profits and therefore the level of investment. Second, at low levels of income and output, the business sector will tend to have unutilized, or excess, productive capacity; that is, many industries will have idle machinery and equipment and therefore little incentive to purchase additional capital goods. But, as the level of income rises, this excess capacity disappears and firms are inclined to add to their stock of capital goods. Our simplification, however, is not too severely at odds with reality and will greatly facilitate later analysis.

△  **Instability of Investment**

In contrast to the consumption schedule, the investment schedule is unstable. Proportionately, investment is the most volatile component of private spending. Some of the more important factors which explain this variability are as follows:

**1  Durability**  Because of their durability, capital goods have a rather indefinite useful life. Within limits, purchases of capital goods are discretionary and therefore postponable. Older equipment or buildings can be scrapped and entirely replaced, on the one hand, or patched up and used for a few more years, on the other. Optimism about the future may prompt business planners to replace their older facilities, that is, to modernize their plants, and this obviously means a high level of investment. A slightly less optimistic view, however, may lead to very small amounts of investment as older facilities are repaired and kept in use.

**2  Irregularity of Innovation**  We have noted that technological progress is a major determinant of investment. New products and new processes provide a major stimulus to investment. However, history suggests that

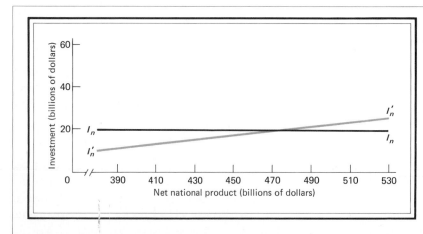

**FIGURE 11-6 THE INVESTMENT SCHEDULE: TWO POSSIBILITIES**

Our discussion will be facilitated by employing the investment schedule $I_n$, which assumes that the investment plans of businesses are independent of the current level of income. Actually, the investment schedule may be slightly upsloping, as suggested by $I'_n$.

major innovations—railroads, electricity, automobiles, and so forth—occur quite irregularly, and when they do occur, these innovations induce a vast upsurge or "wave" of investment spending which in time recedes. A classic illustration: The widespread acceptance of the automobile in the 1920s not only brought about substantial increases in investment in the automobile industry itself, but also induced tremendous amounts of investment in such related industries as steel, petroleum, glass, and rubber, not to mention public investment in streets and highways. But when investment in these related industries was ultimately completed—that is, when they had created capital facilities sufficient to meet the needs of the automobile industry—total investment leveled off.

**3  Variability of Profits**  We know that business owners and managers invest only when they feel it will be profitable to do so and that, to a significant degree, the expectation of future profitability is influenced by the size of current profits. Current profits, however, are themselves highly variable (line 12 of the table on the inside covers). Hence the variability of profits contributes to the volatile nature of the incentive to invest. Furthermore, the instability of profits may also cause investment fluctuations, because profits are a major source of funds for business investment. American businesses tend to prefer this internal source of financing to increases in external debt or stock issue. In short, expanding profits give business planners both greater incentives and greater means to invest; declining profits have the reverse effects. The fact that actual profits are variable adds to the instability of investment.

**4  Variability of Expectations**  We have already discussed how the durability of capital equipment results in the making of investment decisions upon the basis of *expected* net profit. Now, while there is a tendency for business firms to project current business conditions into the future, it is equally true that expectations are sometimes subject to radical revision when some event or combination of events suggests a significant change in future business conditions. What kinds of events make business confidence so capricious? Changes in the domestic political climate, cold-war or energy developments, changes in population growth and therefore in anticipated market demand, court decisions in key labor or antitrust cases, legislative actions, strikes, changes in governmental economic policies, and a host of similar considerations may give rise to waves of business optimism or pessimism.

The stock market merits specific comment in this regard. Business planners frequently look to the stock market as an index or barometer of the overall confidence of society in future business conditions; a rising "bull" market signifies public confidence in the business future, whereas a falling "bear" market implies a lack of confidence. The stock market, however, is a highly speculative market, and initially modest changes in stock prices can be seriously intensified by participants who jump on the bandwagon by buying when prices begin to rise and by selling when stock prices start to fall. Furthermore, by affecting the relative attractiveness of new capital as opposed to purchasing ownership claims (stock) to existing capital facilities, upsurges and slumps in stock values also affect the level of investment.

For these and similar reasons, it is quite correct to associate most fluctuations in output and employment with changes in investment. In terms of Figure 11-6, we can think of this volatility as being reflected in frequent and substantial upward and downward shifts in the investment schedule.

# Summary

**1**   Classical employment theory envisioned laissez faire capitalism as being capable of providing virtually continuous full employment. This analysis was based on Say's Law and the assumption of price-wage flexibility.

**2**   The classical economists argued that because supply creates its own demand, general overproduction was impossible. This conclusion was held to be valid even when saving occurred, because the money market, or more specifically, the interest rate, would automatically synchronize the saving plans of households and the investment plans of businesses.

**3**   Classical employment theory also held that even if temporary declines in total spending were to occur, these declines would be compensated for by downward price-wage adjustments to the end that real output, employment, and real income would not decline.

**4**   Keynesian employment theory rejects the notion that the interest rate would equate saving and investment by pointing out that savers and investors are substantially different groups who make their saving and investment decisions for different reasons—reasons which are largely unrelated to the interest rate. Furthermore, because of changes in *a.* the public's holdings of money balances, and *b.* bank loans, the supply of funds may exceed or fall short of current saving to the end that saving and investment will not be equal.

**5**   Keynesian economists discredit price-wage flexibility on both practical and theoretical grounds. They argue that *a.* union and business monopolies, minimum-wage legislation, and a host of related factors have virtually eliminated the possibility of substantial price-wage reductions, and *b.* price-wage cuts will lower total income and therefore the demand for labor.

**6**   The basic tools of Keynesian employment theory are the consumption, saving, and investment schedules, which show the various amounts that households intend to consume and save and that businesses plan to invest at the various possible income-output levels.

**7**   The locations of the consumption and saving schedules are determined by such factors as *a.* the amounts of liquid assets owned by households; *b.* the stocks of durables consumers have on hand; *c.* expectations of future income, future prices, and product availability; *d.* the relative size of consumer indebtedness; *e.* overall attitudes toward thrift; and *f.* taxation. The consumption and saving schedules are relatively stable.

**8**   The *average* propensities to consume and save show the proportion or fraction of any level of *total* income that is consumed and saved. The *marginal* propensities to consume and save show the proportion or fraction of any *change* in total income that is consumed or saved.

**9**   The immediate determinants of investment are *a.* the expected rate of net profit and *b.* the rate of interest. The economy's investment-demand curve can be determined by arraying investment projects in descending order according to their expected net profitability and applying the rule that investment will be profitable up to the point at which the interest rate equals the expected rate of net profit. The investment-demand curve reveals an inverse relationship between the interest rate and the level of aggregate investment.

**10**   Shifts in the investment-demand curve can occur as the result of changes in *a.* the acquisition, maintenance, and operating costs of capital goods; *b.* business taxes; *c.* technology; *d.* the stocks of capital goods on hand; and *e.* expectations.

**11**   We make the simplifying assumption that the level of investment determined by projecting the current interest rate off the investment-demand curve does not vary with the level of aggregate income.

**12**   The durability of capital goods, the irregular occurrence of major innovations, profit volatility, and the variability of expectations all contribute to the high degree of instability of investment spending.

# Questions and Study Suggestions

1   Key terms and concepts to remember: classical theory of employment; Say's Law; price-wage flexibility; Keynesian economics; consumption and saving schedules; break-even income; average propensities to consume and save; marginal propensities to consume and save; investment-demand curve; investment schedule.

2   Explain the classical economists' conclusion that Say's Law would prevail even in an economy where substantial saving occurred.  What arguments have Keynesian economists used to undermine the classical view that Say's Law would result in sustained full employment?

3   "Unemployment can be avoided so long as businesses are willing to accept lower product prices, and workers to accept lower wage rates."   Critically evaluate.

4   Precisely how are the APC and the MPC different?  Why must the sum of the MPC and the MPS equal 1?  What are the basic determinants of the consumption-saving schedules?  Of your own level of consumption?

5   Explain precisely what relationships are shown by **a.** the consumption schedule, **b.** the saving schedule, **c.** the investment-demand curve and **d.** the investment schedule.

6   Complete the following table:

| Level of output and income (NNP = DI) | Consumption | Saving |
|---|---|---|
| $240 | $_____ | $ − 4 |
| 260 | _____ | 0 |
| 280 | _____ | 4 |
| 300 | _____ | 8 |
| 320 | _____ | 12 |
| 340 | _____ | 16 |
| 360 | _____ | 20 |
| 380 | _____ | 24 |
| 400 | _____ | 28 |

   **a.**   Show the consumption and saving schedules graphically.
   **b.**   Determine the APS and APC for each level of income.
   **c.**   Now determine the MPC and MPS for each change in the income level.
   **d.**   Locate the break-even level of income.  How is it possible for households to dissave at very low income levels?
   **e.**   If the proportion of total income which is consumed decreases and the proportion which is saved increases as income rises, explain both verbally and graphically how the MPC and MPS can be relatively constant at various levels of income.

7   Explain how each of the following will affect the consumption and saving schedules or the investment schedule:
   **a.**   A decline in the amount of government bonds which consumers are holding
   **b.**   The threat of limited, nonnuclear war, leading the public to expect future shortages of consumer durables
   **c.**   A decline in the interest rate
   **d.**   A sharp decline in stock prices
   **e.**   An increase in the rate of population growth
   **f.**   The development of a cheaper method of manufacturing pig iron from ore

**g.** The announcement that the social security program is to be expanded in both coverage and size of benefits

**h.** The expectation that mild inflation will persist in the next decade

**i.** Expected petroleum shortages

**8** Explain why an upshift in the consumption schedule typically involves an equal downshift in the saving schedule. What is the exception?

**9** What are the basic determinants of investment? Explain the relationship between the interest rate and the level of investment. Why is the investment schedule less stable than the consumption-saving schedules?

**10** Assume there are no investment projects in the economy which yield an expected rate of net profit of 25 percent or more. But suppose there are $10 billion of investment projects yielding expected net profit of between 20 and 25 percent; another $10 billion yielding between 15 and 20 percent; another $10 billion between 10 and 15 percent; and so forth. Cumulate these data and present them graphically, putting the expected rate of net profit on the vertical axis and the amount of investment on the horizontal axis. What will be the equilibrium level of aggregate investment if the interest rate is **a.** 15 percent, **b.** 10 percent, and **c.** 5 percent? Explain why this curve is the investment-demand curve.

**11** *Advanced analysis:* Linear equations for the consumption and saving schedules take the general form $C = a + bY$ and $S = -a + (1 - b)Y$, where $C$, $S$, and $Y$ are consumption, saving, and national income respectively. The constant $a$ represents the vertical intercept, and $b$ is the slope of the consumption schedule.

**a.** Use the following data to substitute specific numerical values into the consumption and saving equations.

| National income (Y) | Consumption (C) |
|---|---|
| $ 0 | $ 80 |
| 100 | 140 |
| 200 | 200 |
| 300 | 260 |
| 400 | 320 |

**b.** What is the economic meaning of $b$? Of $(1 - b)$?

## Selected References

Dernburg, Thomas F., and Duncan M. McDougall: *Macroeconomics*, 6th ed. (New York: McGraw-Hill Book Company, 1980), chaps. 3, 5.

Dillard, Dudley: *The Economics of John Maynard Keynes* (Englewood Cliffs, N.J.: Prentice-Hall, Inc., 1948), chaps. 1, 2, 12.

Lekachman, Robert: *The Age of Keynes* (New York: Random House, Inc., 1966).

Lindauer, John: *Macroeconomics*, 3d ed. (Santa Barbara, Calif.: John Wiley & Sons, Inc., 1976), chaps. 3, 4.

Peterson, Wallace C.: *Income, Employment, and Economic Growth*, 4th ed. (New York: W. W. Norton & Company, Inc., 1978), chap. 4.

# LAST WORD
## Poverty Amidst Plenty

Before Keynes' *General Theory* economists did not have a convincing explanation of depression. But intelligent laymen understood that deficient demand was the crux of the problem. Consider the testimony of Mr. Oscar Ameringer, an Oklahoma City newspaper editor, before a Congressional Committee in 1932.

During the last three months I have visited . . . some 20 States of this wonderfully rich and beautiful country. Here are some of the things I heard and saw: In the State of Washington I was told that the forest fires raging in that region all summer and fall were caused by unemployed timber workers and bankrupt farmers in an endeavor to earn a few honest dollars as fire fighters. The last thing I saw on the night I left Seattle was numbers of women searching for scraps of food in the refuse piles of the principal market of that city. A number of Montana citizens told me of thousands of bushels of wheat left in the fields uncut on account of its low price that hardly paid for the harvesting. In Oregon I saw thousands of bushels of apples rotting in the orchards. Only absolute flawless apples were still salable, at from 40 to 50 cents a box containing 200 apples. At the same time, there are millions of children who, on account of the poverty of their parents, will not eat one apple this winter.

While I was in Oregon the Portland Oregonian bemoaned the fact that thousands of ewes were killed by the sheep raisers because they did not bring enough in the market to pay the freight on them. And while Oregon sheep raisers fed mutton to the buzzards, I saw men picking for meat scraps in the garbage cans in the cities of New York and Chicago. I talked to one man in a restaurant in Chicago. He told me of his experience in raising sheep. He said that he had killed 3000 sheep this fall and thrown them down the canyon, because it cost $1.10 to ship a sheep, and then he would get less than a dollar for it. He said he could not afford to feed the sheep, and he would not let them starve, so he just cut their throats and threw them down the canyon.

As a result of this appalling overproduction on the one side and the staggering underconsumption on the other side, 70 percent of the farmers of Oklahoma were unable to pay the interest on their mortgages. Last week one of the largest and oldest mortgage companies in that State went into the hands of the receiver. In that and other States we have now the interesting spectacle of farmers losing their farms by foreclosure and mortgage companies losing their recouped holdings by tax sales.

The farmers are being pauperized by the poverty of industrial populations and the industrial populations are being pauperized by the poverty of the farmers. Neither has the money to buy the product of the other, hence we have overproduction and underconsumption at the same time and in the same country.

. . . I am of the opinion that all this talk about speedy recovery and prosperity being just around the corner is bosh and nonsense. What we are confronted with is not a mere panic like those of 1873 and 1883, but a world-wide economic catastrophe that may spell the end of the capitalistic era—for the cause of it is production for profit instead of production for consumption. The masses can not buy what they have themselves produced; and unless ways and means are found to make cash customers out of some 20,000,000 of unemployed wage earners and bankrupt farmers, there can be no recovery.

I do not believe I have anything further to say.

From *Unemployment in the United States:* Hearings before a Subcommittee of the House Committee on Labor, 72d Congress, 1st Session, Washington, 1932, pp. 98–99, 104–105, abridged.

# The Equilibrium Levels of Output, Employment, and Income

# chapter 12

This chapter is both a continuation and an expansion of Chapter 11. We seek, first, to use the consumption, saving, and investment schedules developed in Chapter 11 to explain the equilibrium levels of output, income, and employment. Next, we analyze changes in the equilibrium level of NNP. Until government is added to our discussion in Chapter 13, we retain the simplifying assumptions of Chapter 11 which permitted us to equate NNP and DI.

We now have before us all the analytical tools necessary to explain the equilibrium levels of output, employment, and income. By *equilibrium output* we refer to that level of total output which, once achieved, will be sustained. It exists where the flow of income created by the production of the output gives rise to a level of total spending sufficient to clear the product market of that output. In pursuing the important task of determining and explaining the equilibrium level of output, two closely interrelated approaches—the *aggregate*

*demand–aggregate supply* (or $C + I_n = \text{NNP}$ approach) and the *leakages-injections* (or, in the simplified discussion of this chapter, the $S = I_n$ approach)—will be employed. Both will be discussed tabularly and graphically.

Precautionary note: In this and the next chapter we deal with a *model* of the economy which is designed to convey an understanding of the basic determinants of the levels of output and employment. The specific numbers employed are only illustrative; they are not intended to measure the real world.

## ☐ AGGREGATE DEMAND-AGGREGATE SUPPLY APPROACH

Let us first discuss the aggregate demand–aggregate supply approach, using both simple arithmetic data and graphic analysis.

### △ Tabular Analysis

Table 12-1 merely brings together the income-consumption and income-saving data of

**TABLE 12-1**
**Determination of the Equilibrium Levels of Employment, Output, and Income: The Private Sector** (*hypothetical data*)

| (1) Possible levels of employment,* millions | (2) Aggregate supply (output and income) (NNP = DI),† billions | (3) Consumption, billions | (4) Saving, billions | (5) Investment, billions | (6) Aggregate demand $(C + I_n)$, billions | (7) Unintended investment $(+)$ or disinvestment $(-)$ in inventories | (8) Tendency of employment, output, and incomes |
|---|---|---|---|---|---|---|---|
| 40 | $370 | $375 | $−5 | $20 | $395 | $−25 | Increase |
| 45 | 390 | 390 | 0 | 20 | 410 | −20 | Increase |
| 50 | 410 | 405 | 5 | 20 | 425 | −15 | Increase |
| 55 | 430 | 420 | 10 | 20 | 440 | −10 | Increase |
| 60 | 450 | 435 | 15 | 20 | 455 | −5 | Increase |
| 65 | 470 | 450 | 20 | 20 | 470 | 0 | Equilibrium |
| 70 | 490 | 465 | 25 | 20 | 485 | +5 | Decrease |
| 75 | 510 | 480 | 30 | 20 | 500 | +10 | Decrease |
| 80 | 530 | 495 | 35 | 20 | 515 | +15 | Decrease |
| 85 | 550 | 510 | 40 | 20 | 530 | +25 | Decrease |

* In later chapters on economic growth we will find that employment need not vary proportionately with output.
† If government is ignored and it is assumed that all saving occurs in the household sector of the economy, NNP as a measure of aggregate supply is equal to NI, PI, and DI. This means that households receive a DI equal to the value of total output.

Table 11-1 and the simplified income-investment data of columns 1 and 2 in Table 11-3.

This table is in many respects similar to Table 4-6, the supply and demand table for a specific product. You will recall that the demand schedule shows the amount consumers plan to purchase, and the supply schedule, the amount producers plan to offer at various prices. The equilibrium price was located at the point where the quantity demanded and the quantity supplied were equal. Barring revisions in the buying plans of consumers or the selling plans of producers, price and the corresponding amount exchanged would not vary from their equilibrium levels. This same general type of reasoning can be applied to *aggregate* demand and *aggregate* supply with three notable differences. First, because total output is composed of heterogeneous goods, it is essential to state total supply in money terms rather than physical units. Second, the equilibrating factor is obviously the level of output and income rather than price. Third, and most important, it is quite accurate to regard the forces of supply and demand as playing equally

important roles in determining the price of an individual product; changes in either supply or demand can alter equilibrium price. But in the case of aggregate equilibrium, it is correct to envision aggregate demand as the crucial determining variable or force to which the level of aggregate supply (NNP) adjusts. We should regard the aggregate supply schedule—the set of production intentions of businesses—as fixed and the actual amount produced by businesses as responding to shifts in aggregate demand.

**Aggregate Supply**   Column 2 of Table 12-1 is in effect the total, or aggregate, supply schedule for the economy. It indicates the various possible levels of total output—that is, the various possible NNPs—which the business sector of the economy might produce. *Producers are willing to offer each of these ten levels of output on the expectation that they will receive an identical amount of receipts of income from its sale.* That is, the business sector will produce $370 billion worth of output, thereby incurring $370 billion worth of wage, rent, interest, and profit costs, only if they expect that this output can be sold for $370 billion worth of receipts. Some $390 billion worth of output will be offered if businesses feel this output can be sold for $390 billion. And so it is for all the other possible levels of output.

**Aggregate Demand**    The total, or aggregate, demand schedule is shown in column 6 of Table 12-1. It shows the total amount which will be spent at each possible output-income level. In dealing with the private sector of the economy, the aggregate demand schedule simply shows the amount of consumption and voluntary net investment spending $(C + I_n)$ which will be forthcoming at each output-income level. We use net rather than gross investment because we are employing NNP rather than GNP as a measure of total output.

**Equilibrium NNP**    Now the question is this: Of the ten possible levels of NNP indicated in Table 12-1, which will be the equilibrium level? That is, which level of total output will the economy be capable of sustaining? The answer is: The equilibrium level of output is that output whose production will create total spending just sufficient to purchase that output. In other words, the equilibrium level of NNP is where the total quantity of goods supplied (NNP) is precisely equal to the total quantity of goods demanded $(C + I_n)$. Examination of the aggregate supply schedule of column 2 and the aggregate demand schedule of column 6 indicates that this equality exists only at the $470 billion level of NNP. This is the only level of output at which the economy is willing to spend precisely the amount necessary to take that output off the market. Here the annual rates of production and spending are in balance. There is no overproduction, which results in a piling up of unsold goods and therefore cutbacks in the rate of production, nor is there an excess of total spending, which draws down inventories and prompts increases in the rate of production. In short, there is no

reason for businesses to vary from this rate of production; $470 billion is therefore the equilibrium NNP.

**Disequilibrium**    To enhance our understanding of the meaning of the equilibrium level of NNP, let us examine other possible levels of NNP to see why they cannot be sustained. For example, at the $410 billion level of NNP, businesses would find that if they produced this output, the income created by this production would give rise to $405 billion in consumer spending. Supplemented by $20 billion of investment, the total quantity demanded $(C + I_n)$ would be $425 billion, as shown in column 6. The economy obviously provides an annual rate of spending more than sufficient to purchase the current $410 billion rate of production. Because businesses are producing at a lower rate than buyers are taking goods off the shelves, an unintended decline in business inventories of $15 billion would occur (column 7) if this situation were sustained. But businesses will adjust to this aggregate demand–aggregate supply imbalance by stepping up production. And a higher rate of output will mean more jobs and a higher level of total income. In short, if the total quantity of goods demanded exceeds the total quantity supplied, the latter will be driven upward. By making the same comparisons of NNP (column 2) and $C + I_n$ (column 6) at all other levels of NNP below the $470 billion equilibrium level, it will be found that the economy wants to spend in excess of the level at which businesses are willing to produce. The excess of total spending at all these levels of NNP will drive NNP upward to the $470 billion level.

The reverse holds true at all levels of NNP above the $470 billion equilibrium level. That is, businesses will find that the production of these total outputs fails to generate the levels of spending needed to take them off the market. Being unable to recover the costs involved in producing these outputs, businesses will cut back on their production. To illustrate: At the

$510 billion level of output, business managers will be disappointed to find that there is insufficient spending to permit the sale of that output. Of the $510 billion worth of income which this output creates, $480 billion is received back by businesses as consumption spending. Though supplemented by $20 billion worth of investment spending, the total quantity demanded ($500 billion) falls $10 billion short of the $510 billion quantity supplied. If this imbalance persisted, $10 billion of inventories would pile up (column 7). But businesses will react to this unintended accumulation of unsold goods by cutting back on the rate of production. This decline in NNP will mean fewer jobs and a decline in total income. The reader should verify that deficiencies of total spending exist at all other levels of NNP in excess of the $470 billion level.

*The equilibrium level of NNP exists where the total quantity supplied, measured by NNP, and the aggregate quantity demanded, $C + I_n$, are equal.* Any excess of total spending over total output will drive the latter upward. Any deficiency of total spending will pull NNP downward.

△   **Graphic Analysis**

The same analysis can be readily envisioned through a simple graph. In Figure 12-1 the 45-degree line (which was merely a guideline in Chapter 11's discussion of consumption and saving) now represents the economy's aggregate supply schedule. Let us see why this is so. By definition, each point on the aggregate supply schedule will indicate (on the vertical axis) the amount which the business community must receive back as total spending, or

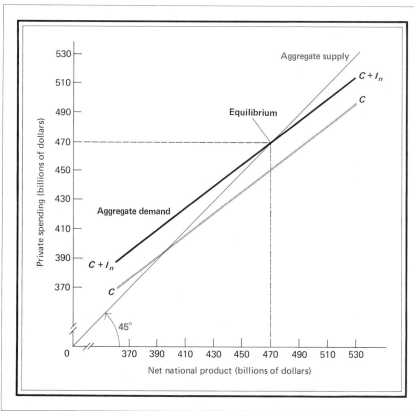

FIGURE 12-1  THE AGGREGATE DEMAND–AGGREGATE SUPPLY APPROACH TO THE EQUILIBRIUM NNP

The aggregate supply schedule is the 45-degree line, because business will produce any given level of NNP only when they expect a level of total spending $(C + I_n)$ just sufficient to dispose of that output.  The equilibrium level of NNP is determined by the intersection of this aggregate supply schedule with the $C + I_n$, or aggregate demand, schedule. Only at this point are the production and purchasing plans of the economy consistent with one another.

total revenue from business's point of view, in order to be induced or motivated to produce the corresponding level of national output (on the horizontal axis). Now, if we make the quite obvious and realistic assumption that the business sector will produce or supply that national output whose value is equal to anticipated spending (receipts), we get a series of points equidistant from the two axes of Figure 12-1—that is, we get the 45-degree line for the aggregate supply schedule. We are simply saying that profit-seeking businesses in the aggregate will be willing to undertake the production of, for example, a $430 billion national output only if anticipated expenditures are $430 billion. That is, businesses will offer any level of NNP only if they expect $C + I_n$ to be just sufficient to clear that output off the national market. Similarly, businesses will produce and offer a $450 billion output if they expect $C + I_n$ to be $450. If businesses expected total spending to be greater or less than $450 billion, they would find it profitable to offer an equally larger or smaller national output.[1] Thus, a series of points—a line—equidis-

[1] Quite nonsensical results follow if one experiments with lines lying below or above the 45-degree line. In the accompanying figure, line 1 suggests that the business sector would be willing to produce, for example, a $430 billion national output if total expenditures were expected to be only $390 billion! Surely it is ridiculous to suggest that businesses will purposely produce $40 billion of output in

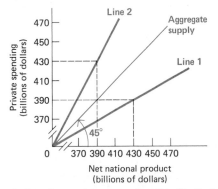

excess of what they anticipate can be sold. Similarly, line 2 implies that businesses will produce, for example, only $390 billion of national output when they anticipate total expenditures of $430 billion. This suggests that the business sector will purposely forgo the production of $40 billion of saleable output.

tant from the total output (NNP) axis and the total spending $(C + I_n)$ axis will summarize the aggregate supply plans of the business sector. Being equidistant from the two axes, this line is necessarily the 45-degree line. We conclude that *the 45-degree line is the aggregate supply schedule.* This schedule shows the various outputs which businesses will offer at each of the various levels of spending that might prevail.

To get the $C + I_n$ or aggregate demand schedule in Figure 12-1, we simply graph the consumption schedule of Figure 11-3a and add to it *vertically* the constant $20 billion amount from Figure 11-6, which, we assume, businesses will want to invest at each possible level of NNP. More directly, we can plot the $C + I_n$ data of column 6 in Table 12-1.

The question: What is the equilibrium level of NNP? The answer: That NNP at which the aggregate quantity demanded and the aggregate quantity supplied are equal. And this must be where the aggregate supply schedule (the 45-degree line) and the aggregate demand schedule $(C + I_n)$ intersect. Because our graphed schedules are based on the data of Table 12-1, we once again find the equilibrium output to be at the $470 billion level. It is evident from Figure 12-1 that no levels of NNP above the equilibrium level are sustainable, because $C + I_n$ falls short of NNP. For example, at the $510 billion NNP level, $C + I_n$ is only $500 billion. Inventories of unsold goods rise to undesired levels. This unhappy state of affairs will prompt businesses to readjust their production sights downward in the direction of the $470 billion output level. Conversely, at all possible levels of NNP less than the $470 billion level, the economy desires to spend in excess of what businesses are producing. $C + I_n$ exceeds the value of the corresponding output. At the $410 billion NNP, for example, $C + I_n$ totals $425 billion. Inventories decline as the rate of spending exceeds the rate of production, prompting businesses to raise their production sights in the direction of the $470 billion NNP. Unless there is some change in the consumption-saving plans of households or the investment plans of businesses, the $470 billion level of NNP will be sustained indefinitely.

The aggregate demand–aggregate supply approach to the determination of NNP has the advantage of spotlighting total spending as the immediate determinant of the levels of output, employment, and income. Though the leakages-injections approach is less direct, it does have the advantage of giving emphasis to the reason $C + I_n$ and NNP are unequal at all levels of output except the equilibrium level.

The essence of the leakages-injections approach is this: Under our simplifying assumptions we know that the production of any level of national output or aggregate supply will generate an identical amount of income. But we also know a part of that income may be saved—that is, *not* consumed—by households. Saving therefore represents a *leakage,* withdrawal, or diversion of potential spending or demand from the income-expenditures stream. The obvious consequence of saving is that consumption falls short of aggregate output or NNP; hence, by itself consumption is insufficient to take aggregate supply off the market, and this fact would seem to set the stage for a decline in total output. However, the business sector does not intend to sell its entire output to consumers; some of the national output will take the form of capital or investment goods which will be sold within the business sector. Investment can therefore be thought of as an *injection* of spending into the income-expenditure stream which supplements consumption; stated differently, investment is a potential offset to, or replacement for, the leakage of saving.

If the leakage of saving exceeds the injection of investment, then $C + I_n$ will fall short of NNP—aggregate demand will fall short of aggregate supply—and this level of NNP will be too high to be sustainable. In other words, any NNP where saving exceeds investment will

be an above-equilibrium NNP. Conversely, if the injection of investment exceeds the leakage of saving, then $C + I_n$ will be greater than NNP and NNP will be driven upward. To repeat: Any NNP where investment exceeds saving will be a below-equilibrium NNP. Only where $S = I_n$—where the leakage of saving is exactly offset by the injection of investment—will aggregate demand equal aggregate supply. And we know that the equality of aggregate demand and aggregate supply defines the equilibrium NNP.

It is important to keep in mind that in the very simple private economy of this chapter, there are only one leakage (saving) and one injection (investment) to worry about. In general terms, a *leakage* is any use of income other than its expenditure on domestically produced output. Hence, in the more realistic models which follow (Chapters 13 and 41), we shall find that the additional leakages of taxes and imports will have to be incorporated into our analysis. Similarly, an *injection* is any supplement to consumer spending on domestic production. So, again, in later models we must add injections of government purchases and exports to our discussion. But for the present, in putting the leakages-injections approach to work, we need only compare the single leakage of saving with the sole injection of investment to assess the impact upon NNP.

△ **Tabular Analysis**

The saving schedule (columns 2 and 4) and the investment schedule (columns 2 and 5) of Table 12-1 are pertinent. Our $C + I_n =$ NNP approach has just led us to conclude that all levels of NNP that are less than $470 billion are unstable because the corresponding $C + I_n$ exceeds these NNPs, driving NNP upward. A comparison of the amounts households and businesses want to save and invest at each of the below-equilibrium NNP levels explains the excesses of total spending. In particular, at each of these relatively low NNP levels, businesses plan to invest more than households want to save. For example, at the $410 billion level of NNP, households will save only $5 billion, thereby spending $405 of their $410 billion incomes. Supplemented by $20 billion of business investment, total spending $(C + I_n)$ is obviously $425 billion. Total spending exceeds NNP by $15 billion ($= \$425 - \$410$) *because* the amount businesses plan to invest at this level of NNP exceeds the amounts households save by $15 billion. It is the fact that a very small "leakage" of saving at this relatively low income level will be more than compensated for by the relatively large injection of investment spending which causes $C + I_n$ to exceed NNP and induce the latter upward.

Similarly, all levels of NNP above the $470 billion level are also unstable, because here NNP exceeds $C + I_n$. The reason for this insufficiency of total spending lies in the fact that at all NNP levels above $470 billion, households will want to save in excess of the amount businesses plan to invest. That is, the saving leakage is not replaced or compensated for by the injection of investment. For example, households will choose to save at the high rate of $30 billion at the $510 billion NNP. Businesses, however, will plan to invest only $20 billion at this NNP. This $10 billion excess of saving over planned investment will cause total spending to fall $10 billion short of the value of total output. And this deficiency will cause NNP to decline.

Again we verify that the equilibrium NNP is at the $470 billion level. It is only at this point that the saving desires of households and the investment plans of businesses are equal. And only when businesses and households attempt to invest and save at equal rates—where the leakages and injections are equal—will $C + I_n = $ NNP. Only here will the annual rates of production and spending be in balance; only here will unplanned changes in inventories be absent. One can think of it in this way: If saving were zero, consumer spending would always be sufficient to clear the market of any given NNP; that is, consumption would equal NNP. But saving can and does occur, causing consumption to fall short of NNP. Hence, only when businesses are willing to invest at the same rate at which households save will the amount by which consumption falls short of NNP be precisely compensated for.

△  **Graphic Analysis**

The leakages-injections approach to determining the equilibrium NNP can be readily demonstrated graphically. In Figure 12-2 we have merely combined the saving schedule of Figure 11-3*b* and the simplified investment schedule of Figure 11-6. The numerical data for these schedules are repeated in columns 2, 4, and 5 of Table 12-1. It is evident that the

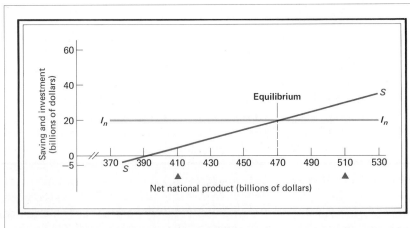

**FIGURE 12-2  THE LEAKAGES–INJECTIONS APPROACH TO THE EQUILIBRIUM NNP**

A second approach is to view the equilibrium NNP as determined by the intersection of the saving ($S$) and investment ($I_n$) schedules. Only at the point of equilibrium will households plan to save the amount businesses want to invest. It is the consistency of these plans which causes NNP and $C + I_n$ to be equal.

equilibrium level of NNP is at $470 billion, where the saving and investment schedules intersect. Only here do businesses and households invest and save at the same rates; therefore, only here will NNP and $C + I_n$ be equal. At all higher levels of NNP, households will save at a rate higher than businesses plan to invest. The fact that the saving leakage exceeds the investment injection causes $C + I_n$ to fall short of NNP, driving the latter downward. At the $510 billion NNP, for example, saving of $30 billion will exceed investment of $20 billion by $10 billion, with the result that $C + I_n$ is $500 billion—$10 billion short of NNP. At all levels of NNP below the $470 billion equilibrium level, businesses will plan to invest at a rate in excess of the amount households save. Here the injection of investment exceeds the leakage of saving so that $C + I_n$ exceeds NNP, driving the latter upward. To illustrate: At the $410 billion level of NNP the $5 billion leakage of saving is more than compensated for by the $20 billion that businesses plan to invest. The result is that $C + I_n$ exceeds NNP by $15 billion, inducing businesses to produce a larger NNP.

□ **PLANNED VERSUS ACTUAL INVESTMENT**

We have emphasized that because savers and investors are essentially different groups and are differently motivated, discrepancies in saving and investment can occur and these differences bring about changes in the equilibrium NNP. Now we must recognize that, in another sense, saving and investment must always be equal to one another! This apparent contradiction concerning the equality of saving and investment is resolved when we distinguish between *planned* investment and saving (which need not be equal) and *actual* investment and saving (which by definition must be equal). The catch essentially is that *actual investment consists of both planned and unplanned investment (unplanned changes in inventory investment), and the latter functions*

*as a balancing item which always equates the actual amounts saved and invested in any period of time.*

△ **Disequilibrium and Inventories**

Consider, for example, the $490 billion above-equilibrium NNP (Table 12-1). What would happen if businesses produced this output, thinking they could sell it? At this level, households save $25 billion of their $490 billion DI, so consumption is only $465 billion. *Planned* investment (column 5) is $20 billion; that is, businesses want to buy $20 billion worth of capital goods. This means aggregate demand $(C + I_n)$ is $485 billion, and sales therefore fall short of production by $5 billion. This extra $5 billion of goods is obviously retained by businesses as an *unintended* or unplanned increase in inventories (column 7). It is unintended because it results from the failure of total spending to take total output off the market. Remembering that, by definition, changes in inventories are a part of investment, we note that *actual* investment of $25 billion ($20 planned *plus* $5 unintended or unplanned) equals saving of $25 billion, even though saving exceeds *planned* investment by $5 billion. Businesses, obviously not anxious to accumulate unwanted inventories at this annual rate, will react by cutting back on production.

Now look at the below-equilibrium $450 billion output (Table 12-1). Because households save only $15 billion of their $450 billion DI, consumption is $435 billion. Planned investment by businesses is $20 billion, so aggregate demand is $455 billion. That is, sales exceed production by $5 billion. How can this be? The answer is that an unplanned decline in business inventories has occurred. More specifically, businesses have unintentionally *dis*invested $5 billion in inventories (column 7). Note once again that *actual* investment is $15 billion ($20 planned *minus* $5 unintended or unplanned) and equal to saving of $15 billion, even though *planned* investment exceeds saving by $5 billion. This unplanned decline in investment in inventories due to the excess of sales over production will induce businesses to increase the NNP by expanding production.

To summarize: At all *above-equilibrium* levels of NNP (where saving exceeds planned investment), actual investment and saving are equal because of unintended increases in inventories which, by definition, are included as a part of actual investment. Graphically (Figure 12-2), the unintended inventory increase is measured by the vertical distance by which the saving schedule lies above the (planned) investment schedule. At all *below-equilibrium* levels of NNP (where planned investment exceeds saving), actual investment will be equal to saving because of unintended decreases in inventories which must be subtracted from planned investment to determine actual investment. These unintended inventory declines are shown graphically as the vertical distance by which the (planned) investment schedule lies above the saving schedule.

### △  Achieving Equilibrium

These distinctions are important because they correctly suggest that *it is the equality of planned investment and saving which determines the equilibrium level of NNP*. We can think of the process by which equilibrium is achieved as follows:

1  A difference between saving and planned investment causes a difference between the production and spending plans of the economy as a whole.

2  This difference between aggregate production and spending plans results in unintended investment or disinvestment in inventories.

3  As long as unintended investment in inventories persists, businesses will revise their production plans downward and thereby reduce the NNP. Conversely, as long as unintended disinvestment in inventories exists, firms will revise their production plans upward and increase the NNP. Both types of movements in NNP are toward equilibrium in that they tend to bring about the equality of planned investment and saving.

4  Only where planned investment and saving are equal will the level of NNP be stable or in equilibrium; that is, only where planned investment equals saving will there be no unintended investment or disinvestment in inventories to drive the NNP downward or upward. Note in column 7 of Table 12-1 that only at the $470 billion equilibrium NNP is there no unintended investment or disinvestment in inventories.

### □  CHANGES IN EQUILIBRIUM NNP AND THE MULTIPLIER

Thus far, we have been concerned with explaining the equilibrium levels of total output and income. But we saw in Chapter 10 that actually the NNP of American capitalism is seldom stable; rather, it is characterized by long-run growth and punctuated by cyclical fluctuations. Let us turn to the questions of *why* and *how* the equilibrium level of NNP fluctuates.

The equilibrium level of NNP will change in response to changes in the investment schedule or the saving-consumption schedules. Because investment spending generally is less stable than the consumption-saving schedules, we shall assume that changes in the investment schedule occur. The impact of changes in investment can be readily envisioned through Figure 12-3a and b. Suppose the expected rate of net profit on investment rises (shifting the investment-demand curve of Figure 11-5 to the right) *or* the interest rate falls (moving down the stable curve). As a result, investment spending increases by, say, $5 billion. This is indicated in Figure 12-3a by an upward shift in the aggregate demand schedule from $(C + I_n)_0$ to $(C + I_n)_1$, and in Figure 12-3b by an upward shift in the investment schedule from $I_{n0}$ to $I_{n1}$. In each of these portrayals the consequence is a rise in the equilibrium NNP from $470 to $490 billion.

Conversely, if the expected rate of net profit from investment decreases *or* the interest rate rises, a decline in investment spending

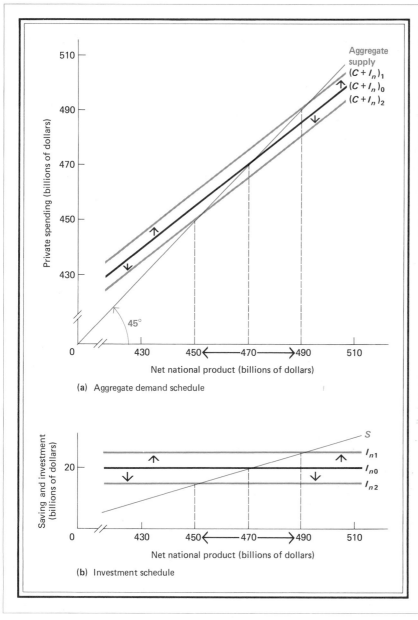

**FIGURE 12-3  CHANGES IN THE EQUILIBRIUM NNP CAUSED BY SHIFTS IN (a) THE AGGREGATE DEMAND SCHEDULE AND (b) THE INVESTMENT SCHEDULE**

An upshift in the aggregate demand schedule from, say, $(C + I_n)_0$ to $(C + I_n)_1$ will increase the equilibrium NNP. Conversely, a downshift in the aggregate demand schedule from, say, $(C + I_n)_0$ to $(C + I_n)_2$ will lower the equilibrium NNP. In the saving-investment figure an upshift in the investment schedule $(I_{n0}$ to $I_{n1})$ will raise, and downshift $(I_{n0}$ to $I_{n2})$ will lower, the equilibrium NNP.

**(a)  Aggregate demand schedule**

**(b)  Investment schedule**

of, say, $5 billion will occur. This is shown by the downward shift of the investment schedule from $I_{n0}$ to $I_{n2}$ in Figure 12-3b and the aggregate demand schedule from $(C + I_n)_0$ to $(C + I_n)_2$ in Figure 12-3a. In each case, these shifts cause the equilibrium NNP to fall from the original $470 billion level to $450 billion.

The reader should verify these conclusions in terms of Table 12-1 by substituting $25 billion and then $15 billion for the $20 billion planned investment figure in column 5 of the table.

Incidentally—and at the risk of getting ahead of ourselves—the indicated $5 billion changes in investment may be the direct result of economic policy. Looking back at Table 11-2, we find that the initial $20 billion level of investment is associated with an 8 percent interest rate. *If* the economy is in a recession, the monetary authorities may purposely negotiate a reduction in the interest rate to 6 percent (by increasing the money supply), causing a $5 billion increase in investment and thereby in aggregate demand to stimulate the economy. Conversely, *if*, with the initial $20 billion of investment, the economy faces a demand-pull inflation problem, the monetary authorities may increase the interest rate to 10 percent (by reducing the money supply), thereby reducing investment and aggregate demand to constrain the inflation. Monetary policy—changing the money supply for the purpose of altering interest rates and aggregate demand—is the subject of Chapter 16.

When changes in the consumption-saving schedules occur, they will have similar effects. If households want to consume more (save less) at each level of NNP, the aggregate demand schedule will shift upward and the saving schedule downward in Figure 12-3a and b, respectively. In either portrayal these shifts will mean an increase in the equilibrium NNP. If households want to consume less (save more) at each possible NNP, the resulting drop in the consumption schedule and the increase in the saving schedule will in turn reduce the equilibrium NNP.

△  **The Multiplier Effect**

You have undoubtedly detected a curious feature of these examples: A $5 billion change in investment spending has given rise to a $20 billion change in the output-income level. This surprising result is called the *multiplier effect* or, more simply, the *multiplier*. Specifically, the multiplier is the ratio of a change in equilibrium NNP to the original change in (investment) spending which caused that change in NNP. That is:

$$\text{Multiplier} = \frac{\text{change in NNP}}{\text{change in investment}}$$

The multiplier is based upon two seemingly innocent facts. On the one hand, the economy is characterized by repetitive, continuous flows of expenditures and income wherein the dollars spent by Smith are received as income by Jones. On the other hand, any change in income will cause both consumption and saving to vary in the same direction as, and by a fraction of, the change in income. It follows from these two facts that an initial change in the rate of spending will cause a spending chain reaction which, although of diminishing importance at each successive step, will cumulate to a multiple change in NNP.

**Illustration**   The multiplier effect is illustrated numerically in Table 12-2 for a $5 billion

**TABLE 12-2**
The Multiplier: A Tabular Illustration (*hypothetical data; in billions*)

|  | (1)<br>Change in<br>income | (2)<br>Change in<br>consumption<br>(MPC = ¾) | (3)<br>Change in<br>saving<br>(MPS = ¼) |
|---|---|---|---|
| Assumed increase in investment | $ 5.00 | $ 3.75 | $1.25 |
| Second round | 3.75 | 2.81 | 0.94 |
| Third round | 2.81 | 2.11 | 0.70 |
| Fourth round | 2.11 | 1.58 | 0.53 |
| Fifth round | 1.58 | 1.19 | 0.39 |
| All other rounds | 4.75 | 3.56 | 1.19 |
| Totals | $20.00 | $15.00 | $5.00 |

increase in investment spending. We continue to assume that the MPC is three-fourths; the MPS is therefore one-fourth. Also assume that the economy is initially in equilibrium at $470 billion.

The initial increase in investment generates an equal amount of wage, rent, interest, and profit income for the simple reason that spending and receiving income are two sides of the same transaction. How much consumption will be induced by this $5 billion increase in the incomes of households? We find the answer by applying the marginal propensity to consume of three-fourths to this change in income. Thus, the $5 billion income increase causes consumption to rise by $3.75 (= $\frac{3}{4}$ of $5) billion and saving by $1.25 (= $\frac{1}{4}$ of $5) billion. The $3.75 billion which is spent is received by other households as income. They in turn consume three-fourths, or $2.81 billion, of this $3.75 billion and save one-fourth, or $0.94 billion. The $2.81 billion which is consumed flows to still other households as income. Though the spending and respending effects of the initial increase in investment diminish with each successive round of spending, the cumulative increase in the output-income level will be $20 billion if the process is carried through to the last dollar. The assumed $5 billion increase in investment will therefore increase the equilibrium NNP by $20 billion, from $470 to $490 billion.

It is no coincidence that the multiplier effect ends at the point where exactly enough saving has been generated to offset the initial $5 billion increase in investment spending. It is only then that the disequilibrium created by the investment increase will be corrected. In this case, NNP and total incomes must rise by $20 billion to create $5 billion in additional saving to match the $5 billion increase in investment spending. Income must increase by 4 times the initial excess of investment over saving, because households save one-fourth of any increase in their incomes (that is, the MPS is one-fourth). In this example the multiplier— the number of times the ultimate increase in

income exceeds the initial increase in investment spending—is 4.

**Characteristics of the Multiplier**   Two noteworthy characteristics of the multiplier are not sufficiently emphasized by mere illustrations of its mechanics:

**1**   Remember that a change in any of the components of the aggregate demand schedule will give rise to a multiplier effect. In practice, economists usually associate the multiplier with changes in investment because of the relative instability of the investment schedule as compared with the consumption schedule. But keep in mind that a shift in the consumption schedule or, as we shall see in Chapter 13, a shift in the schedule of government spending will also prompt a similar chain reaction.

**2**   Keep in mind too that the multiplier works in both directions. That is, a small increase in spending can give rise to a multiple increase in NNP, or a small decrease in spending can be magnified into a much larger decrease in NNP by the multiplier. Note carefully the effects of the shift in $(C + I_n)_0$ to $(C + I_n)_1$ or $(C + I_n)_2$ and $I_{n0}$ to $I_{n1}$ or $I_{n2}$ in Figure 12-3a and b.

**The Multiplier and the Marginal Propensities**   You may have sensed from Table 12-2 that a relationship of some sort must exist between the MPS and the size of the multiplier. There is such a relationship: the fraction of an increase in income which is saved—that is, the MPS—determines the cumulative respending effects of any initial change in $I_n$, $G$, or $C$, and therefore the multiplier. More specifically, *the size of the MPS and the size of the multiplier are inversely related.* The smaller the fraction of any change in income which is saved, the greater the respending at each round and, therefore, the greater the multiplier. If the MPS is one-fourth, as in our example, the multiplier is 4. If the MPS were one-third, the multiplier would be 3. If the MPS were one-fifth, the multiplier would be 5. Look again at Table 12-2 and Figure 12-3b. Initially the economy is in equilibrium at the $470 billion level of NNP. Now businesses increase investment by $5 billion so that planned investment of $25 billion exceeds saving of $20 billion at the $470 billion level. That is, $470 billion is obviously no longer the equilibrium NNP. The question is: By how much must net national product or income rise to restore equilibrium? The answer is: By enough to generate $5 billion of additional saving to offset the $5 billion increase in investment. Because households save $1 out of every $4 of additional income they receive (MPS = $\frac{1}{4}$), NNP must obviously rise by $20 billion—4 times the assumed increase in investment—to create the $5 billion of extra saving necessary to restore equilibrium. Hence, a multiplier of 4. If the MPS was one-third, NNP would only have to rise by $15 billion (3 times the increase in investment) to generate $5 billion of additional saving and restore equilibrium, and the multiplier therefore would be 3. But if the MPS were one-fifth, NNP would have to rise by $25 billion in order for an extra $5 billion of saving to be forth-

coming and equilibrium to be restored, yielding a multiplier of 5.

We can summarize these and all other possibilities by merely saying that *the multiplier is equal to the reciprocal of the MPS.* The reciprocal of any number is the quotient you obtain by dividing 1 by that number. In short, we can say:

$$\text{The multiplier} = \frac{1}{\text{MPS}}$$

This formula provides us with a shorthand method of determining the multiplier. All we need to know is the MPS to calculate the size of the multiplier quickly. Recall, too, from Chapter 11 that since MPC + MPS = 1, it follows that MPS = 1 − MPC. Therefore, we can also write our multiplier formula as[2]

$$\text{The multiplier} = \frac{1}{1 - \text{MPC}}$$

While we have developed our two multiplier formulas intuitively, the underlying arithmetic is easily understood.[3]

---

[2]Furthermore, the importance of footnote 7 in Chapter 11 now becomes clear. There we noted that the MPS measures the slope of the saving schedule. In terms of the leakages-injections ($S = I_n$) approach, this means that if the MPS is relatively large (say, one-half) and the slope of the saving schedule is therefore relatively steep (one-half), any given upward shift in investment spending will be subject to a relatively small multiplier. For example, a $5 billion increase in investment will entail a new point of intersection of the $S$ and $I_n$ schedules only $10 billion to the right of the original equilibrium NNP. The multiplier is only 2. But if the MPS is relatively small (say, one-sixth), the slope of the saving schedule will be relatively gentle. Therefore, a $5 billion upward shift in the investment schedule will provide a new intersection point some $30 billion to the right of the original equilibrium NNP. The multiplier is 6 in this case. The reader should verify these two examples by drawing appropriate saving and investment diagrams.

[3]The algebra underlying the multiplier is that of an "infinite geometric progression" or, simply stated, an infinite series of numbers, each of which is a fixed *fraction* of the previous number. If we designate the fixed fraction as $b$, the geometric progression is:

$$k = 1 + b + b^2 + b^3 + \cdots + b^n \qquad (1)$$

where $k$ is the sum of the progression.

This equation can be readily manipulated to prove

that $k = \dfrac{1}{1 - b}$. Multiplying both sides of equation (1) by $b$ we get:

$$bk = b + b^2 + b^3 + b^4 + \cdots + b^{n+1} \qquad (2)$$

Now by subtracting equation (2) from equation (1) we find that all the terms on the right side of equation (1) drop out except the first (the "1") *and* that only the last term on the right side of equation (2) remains. Thus we have:

$$k - bk = 1 - b^{n+1}$$

Factor $k$ on the left side:

$$k(1 - b) = 1 - b^{n+1}$$

Now divide by $(1 - b)$:

$$k = \frac{1 - b^{n+1}}{(1 - b)}$$

Since $n$ is very large, the value of $b^{n+1}$ approaches zero and can be dropped, resulting in:

$$k = \frac{1}{1 - b}$$

In terms of economic content, $k$ indicates the size of the multiplier and $b$ is the MPC. The reader should experiment with equation (1), using MPC's of, say, .5, .6, and .8, to show that a $1 increase in spending will generate $2, $2.50, and $5 of income, respectively.

**Significance of the Multiplier**   The significance of the multiplier is self-evident. A relatively small change in the investment plans of businesses or the consumption-saving plans of households can trigger a much larger change in the equilibrium level of NNP. The multiplier magnifies the fluctuations in business activity initiated by changes in spending.

Note that the larger the MPC (the smaller the MPS), the greater will be the multiplier. For example, if the MPC is $3/4$ and the multiplier is therefore 4, a $10 billion decline in investment will reduce the equilibrium NNP by $40 billion. But if the MPC is only $2/3$ and the multiplier is thereby 3, the same $10 billion drop in investment will cause the equilibrium NNP to fall by only $30 billion. This makes sense intuitively: A large MPC means the chain of induced consumption shown in column 2 of Table 12-2 dampens down slowly and thereby cumulates to a large change in income. Conversely, a small MPC (a large MPS) causes induced consumption to decline quickly so the cumulative change in income is small.

Incidentally, we will find, in discussing the so-called built-in stabilizers in Chapter 13, that one of the major goals of public policy is to structure a system of taxes and transfer payments which will reduce the MPC and diminish the size of the multiplier, thereby lessening the destabilizing effect of a given change in investment, consumption, or government expenditures.

**Generalizing the Multiplier**   The multiplier concept as presented here is sometimes called the *simple multiplier* for the obvious reason that it is based upon a very simple model of the economy. In terms of the $\dfrac{1}{\text{MPS}}$ formulation, the simple multiplier reflects only the leakage of saving. But, as noted earlier, in the real world successive rounds of income and spending can also be dampened down by other leakages in the form of taxes and imports. That is, in addition to the leakage into saving, some portion of income at each round would be siphoned off as additional taxes, and another part would be used to purchase additional goods from abroad. The result of these additional leakages is that the $\dfrac{1}{\text{MPS}}$ statement of the multiplier can be generalized by changing the denominator to read "fraction of the change in income which is not spent on domestic output" or "fraction of the change in income which leaks, or is diverted, from the income-expenditure stream." The more realistic multiplier which results when all these leakages—saving, taxes, and imports—are taken into account is called the *complex multiplier*. The Council of Economic Advisers has estimated the complex multiplier for the United States to be about 2.

△   **Paradox of Thrift**

A curious paradox is suggested by the leakages-injections approach to NNP determination and by our analysis of the multiplier. The paradox is that if society attempts to save more, it may end up actually saving the same amount, or even less. Figure 12-4 is relevant. Suppose $I_n$ and $S_1$ are the current investment and saving schedules which determine a $470 billion equilibrium NNP. Now assume that households, perhaps anticipating a recession, attempt to save, say, $5 billion more at each income level in order to provide a nest egg against the expected bad times. This attempt to save more is reflected in an upward shift of the saving schedule from $S_1$ to $S_2$. But this very upshift creates an excess of saving over planned investment at the current $470 billion equilibrium output. And we know that the multiplier effect will cause this small increase in saving (decline in consumption) to be reflected in a much larger—$20 billion ($5 × 4) in this case—*decline* in equilibrium NNP.

There is a paradox here in several different senses. First, note that at the new $450 billion equilibrium NNP, households are saving the same amount they did at the original $470 billion NNP. Society's attempt to save more has been frustrated by the multiple decline in

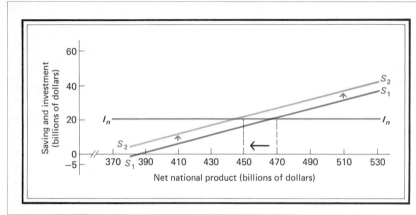

**FIGURE 12-4  THE PARADOX OF THRIFT**

Unless offset by an upshift in the investment schedule, any attempt by households to save more ($S_1$ to $S_2$) will be frustrated by a multiple decline in the equilibrium NNP.

the equilibrium NNP which that attempt itself caused. Second, this analysis suggests that thrift, which has always been held in high esteem in our economy, can be something of a social vice. From the individual point of view, a penny saved may be a penny earned. But from the social point of view, a penny saved is a penny not spent and therefore causes a decline in someone's income. The act of thrift may be virtuous from the individual's viewpoint but disastrous from the social standpoint because of its undesirable effects upon total output and employment.[4] Third, it is ironic, if not paradoxical, that households may be most strongly induced to save more (consume less) at the very time when increased saving is most inappropriate and economically undesirable, that is, when the economy seems to be backsliding into a recession. An individual fearing the loss of his or her job will hardly be inclined to go on a spending spree.

The reader should pursue this analysis of the paradox of thrift and the multiplier by substituting an upsloping investment schedule (Table 11-3 and Figure 11-6) for the simplified investment schedule we have employed. In the case of the paradox of thrift, you should conclude that the attempt of households to save

[4] Recall from Chapter 2, however, that an economy which saves *and* invests a large proportion of its *full-employment output* will tend to achieve a high rate of growth.

more will not merely be frustrated but will actually give rise to a *decline* in the amount saved. You should also find that a positively sloped investment schedule will increase the size of the multiplier and in effect make it a "supermultiplier."[5]

### ☐  EQUILIBRIUM VERSUS FULL-EMPLOYMENT NNP

We now turn from the task of explaining to that of evaluating the equilibrium NNP.

[5] *Hints:* (1) Substitute the investment schedule of columns 1 and 3 in Table 11-3 in column 5 of Table 12-1; (2) assume a $5 billion increase in saving; (3) compute (estimate) the new equilibrium point at which planned investment equals saving; (4) compare the original and the new amounts saved; and (5) calculate the size of the multiplier. Note that the size of the multiplier is larger because, for each successive round of income, there will occur not only additional consumption as in our simple multiplier, but also additional investment. Not only does the multiplier process involve a marginal propensity to consume (MPC) of .75, but also a marginal propensity to invest (MPI) of .10, the latter defined as the ratio of a change in investment relative to the change in NNP which induced or resulted in that change in investment. Hence, we must add the MPI to the denominator of our $\dfrac{1}{1 - \text{MPC}}$ formulation of the multiplier, making it $\dfrac{1}{1 - (\text{MPC} + \text{MPI})}$. In this case the multiplier equals $\dfrac{1}{1 - (.75 + .10)} = \dfrac{1}{.15} = 6\tfrac{2}{3}$. Question 8 at the end of this chapter provides a further opportunity to work with the "supermultiplier."

Too much emphasis cannot be placed upon the fact that the $470 billion equilibrium NNP embodied in our analysis (Table 12-1 and Figures 12-1 and 12-2) may or may not entail full employment. Remember: The basic theme of Keynesian economics is that capitalism contains no mechanisms capable of automatically creating that particular level of aggregate demand which will induce businesses to produce a full-employment noninflationary level of output. The aggregrate demand schedule might well lie above or below that which would intersect aggregate supply at the full-employment noninflationary level of output.

△ **Recessionary Gap**

Assume in Figure 12-5a that the full employment noninflationary level of national output is $490 billion. Suppose, too, that the aggregate demand schedule is at $(C + I_n)_1$, which, incidentally, happens to be the aggre-

gate demand schedule developed and employed in this chapter. This schedule intersects aggregate supply to the left of the full-employment output, causing the economy's aggregate production to fall $20 billion short of its capacity production. In terms of Table 12-1, the economy is failing to employ 5 million of its 70 million available workers and, as a result, is sacrificing $20 billion worth of output.

The amount by which aggregate demand falls short of the full-employment level of NNP is called the *recessionary gap* simply because this deficiency of spending has a contractionary or depressing impact upon the economy. In this case, note in Table 12-1 that, assuming the full-employment NNP to be $490 billion, the corresponding level of total demand is only $485 billion. Hence, the recessionary gap is $5 billion. Graphically, the recessionary gap is the *vertical* distance by which the aggregate demand schedule $(C + I_n)_1$ falls short of

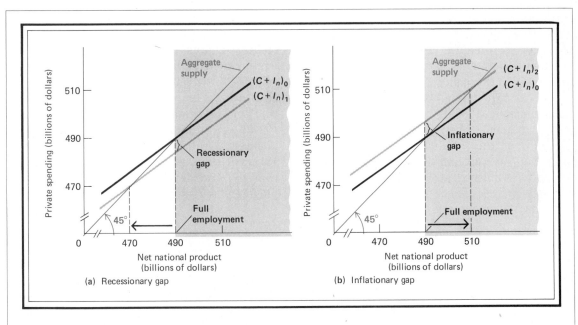

**FIGURE 12-5 RECESSIONARY AND INFLATIONARY GAPS**

The equilibrium and full-employment NNPs may not coincide. A recessionary gap, shown in (a), is the amount by which aggregate demand falls short of the full-employment level of aggregate supply. It will cause a multiple decline in real NNP. The inflationary gap in (b) is the amount by which aggregate demand exceeds the full-employment level of aggregate supply. This gap will cause a multiple increase in money NNP.

the full-employment point on the aggregate supply schedule. Caution: The recessionary gap is *not* the $20 billion difference between the equilibrium and the full-employment NNP; this $20 billion difference is the $5 billion recessionary gap *times* the multiplier of 4.

△  **Inflationary Gap**

If aggregate demand happens to be at $(C + I_n)_2$ in Figure 12-5b, a demand-pull inflationary gap will exist. Specifically, the amount by which aggregate demand exceeds the full-employment level of NNP is called an *inflationary gap*. In this case, a $5 billion inflationary gap is assumed to exist, as shown by the *vertical* distance between $(C + I_n)_2$ and the full-employment point on the aggregate supply schedule.

The effect of this inflationary gap—this excess demand—will be to pull up the prices of the economy's fixed physical volume of production. Businesses as a whole cannot respond to the $5 billion in excess demand by expanding their real outputs, so *demand-pull inflation* will occur. Now Figure 12-5b suggests that the $5 billion inflationary gap, subject to a multiplier of 4, will cause *money* NNP to rise by $20 billion (to $510 billion) while *real* NNP remains unchanged at $490. This is, in fact, one possible outcome. But the reader should be warned that the inflationary process is dynamic and complex and that equilibrium need not be reestablished at $510 billion. Specifically, the process of inflation may have a feedback effect upon the aggregate demand schedule. For example, the occurrence and anticipation of inflation may shift the consumption schedule upward; rising prices will expand money profits and tend to increase investment spending. In short, inflation might "feed upon itself" and accelerate in a way which cannot be visualized by the simple

point-in-time analytics of Figure 12-5b. Let us settle for this generalization: NNP changes to the left of the full-employment output (the white area of Figure 12-5a) are *real* changes; NNP changes to the right of full-employment output (the orange area) in Figure 12-5b are merely monetary or "paper" changes in NNP. The main purpose of Chapter 13 is to explain how government might alter its expenditures and tax collections so as to eliminate recessionary and inflationary gaps.

△  **Premature Inflation**

Complication: There is substantial evidence to suggest that in advanced capitalist economies the transition from the white (real changes) area to the orange (price changes) area is not abrupt, as in Figure 12-5, but is actually rather blurred. That is, as aggregate demand rises and the economy *approaches* full employment, *both* real NNP *and* the price level will increase (Figure 10-6). If the price level does indeed rise *before* the economy is at full-employment or capacity output, this increase suggests that the ideal goal of "full employment without inflation" may be unattainable. Instead, society may be forced to choose between "full employment with inflation" or "price stability with unemployment." Premature inflation and possible policies to alleviate it will be the focal point of Chapter 18; until then, we embrace the simplification that the price level is constant until full employment is realized.[6]

---

[6]Our discussion ignores another complication: Full employment (or capacity production) itself is something of an elastic concept because a given number of workers can increase their hours of work just by working overtime, or, as a matter of fact, persons who are not ordinarily in the labor force may be induced to offer their services when job opportunities are abundant. The general validity of our analysis is not impaired by ignoring this refinement.

# Summary

**1**   For a no-government economy the equilibrium level of NNP is that at which the aggregate quantity demanded and the aggregate quantity supplied are equal or, graphically, where the $C + I_n$ line intersects the 45-degree line. At any NNP greater than the equilibrium NNP, aggregate quantity supplied will exceed the aggregate quantity demanded, resulting in unintended investment in inventories, depressed profits, and eventual declines in output, employment, and income. At any below-equilibrium NNP, the aggregate quantity demanded will exceed the aggregate quantity supplied, thereby resulting in unintended disinvestment in inventories, substantial profits, and eventual increases in NNP.

**2**   A complementary leakages-injections approach determines the equilibrium NNP at the point where the amount households save and the amount businesses plan to invest are equal. This is at the point where the saving and investment schedules intersect. Any excess of saving over planned investment will cause a shortage of total spending, forcing NNP to fall. Any excess of planned investment over saving will cause an excess of total spending, inducing NNP to rise. These changes in NNP will in both cases correct the indicated discrepancies in saving and planned investment.

**3**   Shifts in the saving-consumption schedules or in the investment schedule will cause the equilibrium output-income level to change by several times the amount of the initial change in spending. This phenomenon, which accompanies both increases and decreases in spending, is called the *multiplier effect*. The simple multiplier is equal to the reciprocal of the marginal propensity to save.

**4**   The *paradox of thrift* is the notion that the attempt of society to save more, as reflected in an upshift of the saving schedule, may be frustrated by the multiple decline in the equilibrium NNP which will ensue.

**5**   The equilibrium level of NNP and the full-employment noninflationary NNP need not coincide. The amount by which aggregate demand falls short of the full-employment NNP is called the recessionary gap; this gap prompts a multiple decline in real NNP. The amount by which aggregate demand exceeds the full-employment NNP is the inflationary gap; it causes demand-pull inflation.

# Questions and Study Suggestions

**1**   Key terms and concepts to remember: aggregate demand; aggregate supply; leakages-injections approach; equilibrium NNP; planned and actual investment; multiplier effect; paradox of thrift; supermultiplier; recessionary and inflationary gaps.

**2**   Explain graphically the determination of the equilibrium NNP by *a.* the aggregate demand–aggregate supply approach and *b.* the leakages-injections approach for the private sector of the economy. Why must these two approaches always yield the same equilibrium NNP?

**3**   "Planned investment is equal to saving at all levels of NNP; actual investment equals saving only at the equilibrium NNP." Do you agree? Explain. Explain the paradox of thrift and indicate its significance.

**4**   Critically evaluate:

*a.*   "It is socially desirable for households to attempt to increase their rate of saving whenever a recession begins. In this way households will be able to accumulate the financial resources to pay their way through bad times."

*b.*   "The fact that households may save more than businesses want to invest is of no consequence, because events will in time force households and businesses to save and invest at the same rates."

**5**   What is the multiplier effect? What relationship does the MPC bear to the size of the multiplier? The MPS? What will the multiplier be when the MPS is 0, 0.4, 0.6, and 1? When the MPC is 1, $\%_9$, $\frac{2}{3}$, $\frac{1}{2}$, and 0? How much of a change in NNP will result if businesses increase their level of investment by $8 billion and the MPC in the economy is $\frac{4}{5}$? If the MPC is $\frac{2}{3}$? Explain the difference between the simple and the complex multiplier.

**6**   What effect will each of the changes designated in question 7 at the end of Chapter 11 have upon the equilibrium level of NNP? Explain your answers.

**7**   Assuming the level of investment is $16 billion and independent of the level of total output, complete the following table and determine the equilibrium level of output and income which the private sector of the economy would provide.

| Possible levels of employment, millions | Aggregate supply (NNP = DI), billions | Consumption, billions | Saving, billions |
|---|---|---|---|
| 40 | $240 | $244 | $ _____ |
| 45 | 260 | 260 | _____ |
| 50 | 280 | 276 | _____ |
| 55 | 300 | 292 | _____ |
| 60 | 320 | 308 | _____ |
| 65 | 340 | 324 | _____ |
| 70 | 360 | 340 | _____ |
| 75 | 380 | 356 | _____ |
| 80 | 400 | 372 | _____ |

**a.**   If this economy has a labor force of 70 million, will there exist an inflationary or a recessionary gap? Explain the consequences of this gap.

**b.**   Will an inflationary or a recessionary gap exist if the available labor force is only 55 million? Trace the consequences.

**c.**   What are the sizes of the MPC and the MPS?

**d.**   Use the multiplier concept to explain the increase in the equilibrium NNP which will occur as the result of an increase in planned investment spending from $16 to $20 billion.

**8**   Using the consumption and saving data given in question 7, what will the equilibrium level of income be if planned investment is $2 billion at the $240 billion level of NNP and increases by $2 billion for every $20 billion increase in NNP? Assuming that businesses want to invest $4 billion more at each level of NNP, what will be the new equilibrium NNP? What is the size of the "supermultiplier"? Explain why it is larger than the multiplier derived in question 7.

**9**   Using the consumption and saving data given in question 7 and assuming the level of investment is $16 billion, what are the levels of saving and planned investment at the $380 billion level of aggregate supply? What are the levels of saving and actual investment? What are saving and planned investment at the $300 billion level of aggregate supply? What are the levels of saving and actual investment? Use the concept of unintended investment to explain adjustments toward equilibrium from both the $380 and $300 billion levels of aggregate supply.

**10**   *Advanced analysis:* Assume the consumption schedule for the economy is such that $C = 50 + 0.8Y$. Assume further that investment is autonomous or exogenous (indicated by $I_0$); that is, planned investment is independent of the level of income and in the amount $I = I_0 = 30$. Recall also that in equilibrium the aggregate amount of output supplied ($Y$) is equal to the aggregate amount demanded ($C + I$), or $Y = C + I$.

**a.**   Calculate the equilibrium level of income for this economy. Check your work by putting the consumption and investment schedules in tabular form and determining the equilibrium income.

**b.**   What will happen to equilibrium $Y$ if $I = I_0 = 10$? What does this tell you about the size of the multiplier?

**11**   *Advanced analysis:* If $I = I_0 = 50$ and $C = 30 + 0.5Y$, what is the equilibrium level of income? If $I = 10 + 0.1Y$ and $C = 50 + 0.6Y$, what is the equilibrium level of income? What is the multiplier for this economy?

## Selected References

Campagna, Anthony S.: *Macroeconomics: Theory and Policy* (Boston: Houghton Mifflin Company, 1974), chaps. 3–5, 8, 9.

Hansen, Alvin: *A Guide to Keynes* (New York: McGraw-Hill Book Company, 1953).

Makin, John H.: *Macroeconomics* (Hinsdale, Ill.: The Dryden Press, 1975), chap. 4.

Peterson, Wallace C.: *Income, Employment, and Economic Growth,* 4th ed. (New York: W. W. Norton & Company, Inc., 1978), chaps. 5–7.

Shapiro, Edward: *Macroeconomic Analysis,* 4th ed. (New York: Harcourt, Brace, Jovanovich, Inc., 1978), chaps. 4–5.

# LAST WORD
## Squaring the Economic Circle

Humorist Art Buchwald examines the functioning of the multiplier.

WASHINGTON—The recession hit so fast that nobody knows exactly how it happened. One day we were the land of milk and honey and the next day we were the land of sour cream and food stamps.

This is one explanation.

Hofberger, the Chevy salesman in Tomcat, Va., a suburb of Washington, called up Littleton, of Littleton Menswear & Haberdashery, and said, "Good news, the . . . Impalas have just come in and I've put one aside for you and your wife."

Littleton said, "I can't, Hofberger. My wife and I are getting a divorce."

"I'm sorry," Littleton said, "but I can't afford a new car this year. After I settle with my wife, I'll be lucky to buy a bicycle."

Hofberger hung up. His phone rang a few minutes later.

"This is Bedcheck the painter," the voice on the other end said. "When do you want us to start painting your house?"

"I changed my mind," said Hofberger. "I'm not going to paint the house."

"But I ordered the paint," Bedcheck said. "Why did you change your mind?"

"Because Littleton is getting a divorce and he can't afford a new car."

That evening when Bedcheck came home his wife said, "The new color television set arrived from Gladstone's TV Shop."

"Take it back," Bedcheck told his wife.

"Why?" she demanded.

"Because Hofberger isn't going to have his house painted now that the Littletons are getting a divorce."

The next day Mrs. Bedcheck dragged the TV set in its carton back to Gladstone. "We don't want it."

Gladstone's face dropped. He immediately called his travel agent, Sandstorm. "You know that trip you had scheduled for me to the Virgin Islands?"

"Right, the tickets are all written up."

"Cancel it. I can't go. Bedcheck just sent back the color TV set because Hofberger didn't sell a car to Littleton because they're going to get a divorce and she wants all his money."

Sandstorm tore up the airline tickets and went over to see his banker, Gripsholm. "I can't pay back the loan this month because Gladstone isn't going to the Virgin Islands."

Gripsholm was furious. When Rudemaker came in to borrow money for a new kitchen he needed for his restaurant, Gripsholm turned him down cold. "How can I loan you money when Sandstorm hasn't repaid the money he borrowed?"

Rudemaker called up the contractor, Eagleton, and said he couldn't put in a new kitchen. Eagleton laid off eight men.

Meanwhile, General Motors announced it was giving a rebate on its new models. Hofberger called up Littleton immediately. "Good news," he said, "even if you are getting a divorce, you can afford a new car."

"I'm not getting a divorce," Littleton said. "It was all a misunderstanding and we've made up."

"That's great," Hofberger said. "Now you can buy the Impala."

"No way," said Littleton. "My business has been so lousy I don't know why I keep the doors open."

"I didn't know that," Hofberger said.

"Do you realize I haven't seen Bedcheck, Gladstone, Sandstorm, Gripsholm, Rudemaker or Eagleton for more than a month? How can I stay in business if they don't patronize my store?"

Art Buchwald, "Squaring the Economic Circle," *Cleveland Plain Dealer*, February 22, 1975. Reprinted by permission.

# Fiscal Policy and the Public Debt

chapter **13**

The basic task of Chapter 13 is to add the public sector to the analysis of the equilibrium NNP developed in the two preceding chapters. It is crucial to recall at the outset that the consumption and investment decisions of households and businesses are based upon private self-interest and that the sum of these decisions may result in either a recessionary or an inflationary gap. In contrast, government is an instrument of society as a whole; hence, within limits government's decisions with respect to spending and taxing are designed to influence the equilibrium NNP in terms of the general welfare. In particular, we saw in Chapter 6 that a fundamental function of the public sector is to stabilize the economy. This stabilization is achieved in part through *fiscal policy,* that is, through the manipulation of the public budget—government spending and tax collections—for the expressed purpose of achieving the full-employment, noninflationary level of NNP.

More specific goals of this chapter are to (1) analyze the impact of government purchases and taxes upon the equilibrium NNP; (2) survey some basic problems in the application of fiscal policy; (3) explain how some degree of economic stability is built into our tax system; (4) discuss briefly several contrasting budget philosophies; and (5) assess the quantitative and nonquantitative aspects of the public debt.

## ☐ EMPLOYMENT ACT OF 1946 AND THE CEA

The notion that governmental fiscal actions can exert an important stabilizing influence upon the economy began to gain widespread acceptance during the Depression crisis of the 1930s. Keynesian employment theory played a major role in emphasizing the importance of remedial fiscal measures. In 1946, when the end of World War II recreated the specter of

unemployment, the Federal government formalized in law its area of responsibility in promoting economic stability. The *Employment
Act of 1946* proclaims:

> The Congress hereby declares that it is the con-
> tinuing policy and responsibility of the Federal
> Government to use all practicable means con-
> sistent with its needs and obligations and other
> essential considerations of national policy, with
> assistance and cooperation of industry, agricul-
> ture, labor and State and local governments, to
> coordinate and utilize all its plans, functions, and
> resources for the purpose of creating and main-
> taining, in a manner calculated to foster and
> promote free competitive enterprise and the
> general welfare, conditions under which there
> will be afforded useful employment opportuni-
> ties, including self-employment, for those able,
> willing, and seeking to work and to promote
> maximum employment, production, and pur-
> chasing power.

The Employment Act of 1946 is a landmark in American socioeconomic legislation in
that it commits the Federal government to
take positive action through monetary and
fiscal policy to maintain economic stability.

Responsibility for fulfilling the purposes of
the act rests with the executive branch; the
President must submit an annual Economic
Report which describes the current state of the
economy and makes appropriate policy recommendations. The act also established a *Council of Economic Advisers* (CEA) to assist and
advise the President on economic matters, and
a *Joint Economic Committee* (JEC) of the
Congress, which has investigated a wide range
of economic problems of national interest. In
its advisory capacity as "the President's intelligence arm in the eternal war against the
business cycle," the CEA and its staff gather
and analyze relevant economic data and use
them to make forecasts; to formulate programs
and policies designed to fulfill the goals of the
Employment Act; and to "educate" the President, the Congress, and the general public on

problems and policies relevant to the nation's
economic health.[1]

The *Full Employment and Balanced
Growth Act of 1978,* popularly known as the
*Humphrey–Hawkins Act,* reaffirms and extends the stabilization goals of the Federal
government. The act requires the government
to establish five-year goals for the economy
and to formulate a program or plan to achieve
these goals. The attainment of a 4 percent
unemployment rate and a 3 percent inflation
rate by 1983 are explicitly identified in the
legislation as national economic objectives.
Other priorities include the improving of the
United States' position in international markets, encouraging the growth of private investment, and reducing the size of the public
sector.[2]

## ☐ DISCRETIONARY FISCAL POLICY

Let us first focus attention upon discretionary
fiscal policy. *Discretionary fiscal policy* is the
deliberate manipulation of taxes and government spending by the Congress for the purpose
of offsetting cyclical fluctuations in output
and employment and stimulating economic
growth.

### △ Simplifying Assumptions

To keep a potentially complex discussion
as clear as possible, four simplifying assumptions are invoked.

**1** We continue to employ the simplified
investment schedule, wherein the level of in-

---

[1] Walter W. Heller's *New Dimensions of Political Economy*
(New York: W. W. Norton & Company, Inc., 1967) pro-
vides an incisive explanation of the functions of CEA and
an intriguing account of the Council's operation under Dr.
Heller's chairmanship during the 1961–1964 period. Arthur
M. Okun's *The Political Economy of Prosperity* (New
York: W. W. Norton & Company, Inc., 1970) is also highly
recommended.

[2] See the *Economic Report of the President, 1979,* pp.
106–134. Given the poor performance of our economy in
the 1970s, the 4 percent unemployment rate and the 3
percent inflation rate are generally regarded to be unrealistic goals.

vestment is independent of the level of NNP, in our analysis.

**2** We shall suppose that the initial impact of government purchases is such that they neither depress nor stimulate private spending. That is, government purchases will not cause any upward or downward shifts in the consumption and investment schedules.

**3** It will be presumed that the government's net tax revenues[3] are derived entirely from personal taxes. The significance of this is that, although DI will fall short of PI by the amount of government's tax revenues, NNP, NI, and PI will remain equal.

**4** Finally, we assume initially that a fixed amount of taxes is collected regardless of the level of NNP. This assumption will be dropped later.

In our discussion of the private sector of the economy, we implicitly assumed that government purchases of goods and services ($G$) and tax revenues ($T$) were both zero. Now let us suppose that $G$ and $T$ both increase from zero to, say, $20 billion, and note the impact of each and then the combined impact of the

two. As before, we pursue our analysis both tabularly and graphically.

△ **Government Purchases and Equilibrium NNP**

Suppose that government decides to purchase $20 billion worth of goods and services regardless of what the level of NNP might be. Table 13-1 shows the impact upon the equilibrium NNP in terms of simple arithmetic data. Columns 1 through 4 are carried over from Table 12-1 for the private economy, wherein, you might recall, the equilibrium NNP was $470 billion. The only new wrinkle is the addition of government purchases in column 5. By adding government purchases to private spending ($C + I_n$), we get a new higher level of aggregate demand as shown in column 6. Comparing columns 1 and 6, we find that aggregate demand and aggregate supply are equal at a higher level of NNP; specifically, equilibrium NNP has increased from $470 to $550 billion.[4] *Increases in public spending, like increases in private spending, will boost the aggregate demand schedule in relation to*

---

[3]By net taxes we mean total tax revenues less negative taxes in the form of transfer payments.

[4]Given our assumption that the full-employment noninflationary NNP is $490 billion, most of this increase will be in *money* rather than *real* NNP.

**TABLE 13-1**
The Impact of Government Purchases on Equilibrium NNP

| (1) Aggregate supply (output and income) (NNP = DI), billions | (2) Consumption, billions | (3) Saving, billions | (4) Investment, billions | (5) Government purchases, billions | (6) Aggregate demand ($C + I_n + G$), billions, or (2) + (4) + (5) |
|---|---|---|---|---|---|
| $370 | $375 | $−5 | $20 | $20 | $415 |
| 390 | 390 | 0 | 20 | 20 | 430 |
| 410 | 405 | 5 | 20 | 20 | 445 |
| 430 | 420 | 10 | 20 | 20 | 460 |
| 450 | 435 | 15 | 20 | 20 | 475 |
| 470 | 450 | 20 | 20 | 20 | 490 |
| 490 | 465 | 25 | 20 | 20 | 505 |
| 510 | 480 | 30 | 20 | 20 | 520 |
| 530 | 495 | 35 | 20 | 20 | 535 |
| **550** | **510** | **40** | **20** | **20** | **550** |

*the aggregate supply schedule and result in a higher equilibrium NNP.* Note, too, that government spending is subject to the multiplier. A $20 billion increase in government purchases has increased equilibrium NNP by $80 billion.

In terms of the leakages-injections approach, government purchases—like investment—are an injection of spending. Recall that the leakage of saving causes consumption to fall short of disposable income, causing a potential spending gap. This gap may be filled by injections of both investment and government purchases. Observe in Table 13-1 that the $550 billion equilibrium level of NNP occurs where $S = I_n + G$.

Figure 13-1 shows the impact of government purchases graphically. In Figure 13-1$a$ we simply add government purchases, $G$, vertically to the level of private spending, $C + I_n$. As a result, the aggregate demand schedule (private plus public) has been increased to $C + I_n + G$, resulting in the indicated $80 billion

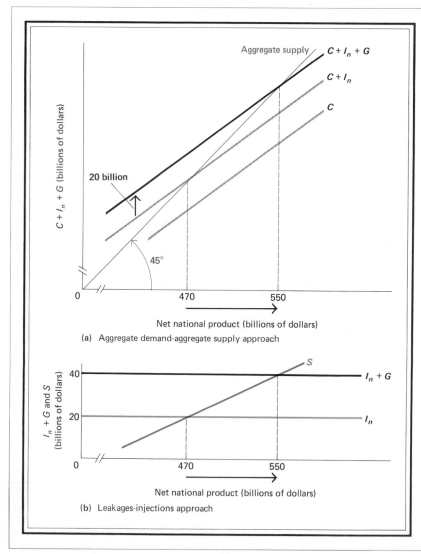

(a) Aggregate demand-aggregate supply approach

(b) Leakages-injections approach

**FIGURE 13-1 GOVERNMENT SPENDING AND THE EQUILIBRIUM NNP**

**(a)** *The aggregate demand-aggregate supply approach.* The addition of government expenditures $G$ to our analysis raises the aggregate demand $(C + I_n + G)$ schedule and increases the equilibrium level of NNP as would an increase in $C$ or $I_n$. Note that changes in government spending are subject to the multiplier effect. **(b)** *Leakages-injections approach.* In terms of the leakages-injections approach, government spending supplements private investment spending $(I_n + G)$, increasing the equilibrium NNP.

increase in equilibrium NNP. Figure 13-1*b* shows the same change in the equilibrium NNP in terms of the leakages-injections approach. Like investment, government spending is an offset to the leakage of saving. Hence, with *G* added to our discussion, the equilibrium level of NNP is now determined at the point where the amount households plan to save is offset exactly by the amount which businesses plan to invest *plus* the amount government desires to spend on goods and services. That is, the equilibrium NNP is determined by the intersection of the *S* schedule and the $I_n + G$ schedule. Note that either approach indicates the same new equilibrium NNP.

What of the effect of a *decline* in government spending? Obviously, a decline in *G* will cause aggregate demand to fall in Figure 13-1*a* and the $I_n + G$ schedule to fall in Figure 13-1*b*. In either case the result is a multiple *decline* in the equilibrium NNP.

△  **Taxation and Equilibrium NNP**

But government also collects tax revenues. How do tax collections affect the equi-

librium level of NNP?  To answer this question in the simplest way, we will assume that government imposes a lump-sum tax of $20 billion on NNP; that is, government now collects $20 billion of taxes at each and every level of NNP.[5] What is the impact of government's increasing tax collections from zero to $20 billion at each level of NNP?

Table 13-2 is relevant. Taxes are inserted as column 2 and we note in column 3 that DI (after-tax income) is obviously less than NNP by the amount of the taxes. DI has been reduced by $20 billion—the amount of the taxes—at each level of NNP. And, because DI is made up of consumer spending and saving, we can expect a decline in DI to lower both consumption and saving. But by how much will each decline? The MPC and the MPS hold the answer: The MPC tells us what fraction of a decline in DI will come at the expense of consumption, and the MPS indicates what

[5] This is clearly a regressive tax system because the average tax rate, $T/\text{NNP}$, falls as NNP rises. Most industrially advanced economies have proportional or progressive tax systems. The important modifications to which these latter two systems give rise will be noted shortly.

**TABLE 13-2**
Determination of the Equilibrium Levels of Employment, Output, and Income: Private and Public Sectors (*hypothetical data*)

| (1) Possible levels of aggregate supply (NNP = NI = PI), billions | (2) Taxes, billions | (3) Possible levels of disposable income, billions, or (1) − (2) | (4) Consumption, billions | (5) Saving, billions, or (3) − (4) | (6) Investment, billions | (7) Government expenditures, billions | (8) Aggregate demand $(C_a + I_n + G)$, billions, or (4) + (6) + (7) |
|---|---|---|---|---|---|---|---|
| $370 | $20 | $350 | $360 | $ −10 | $20 | $20 | $400 |
| 390 | 20 | 370 | 375 | −5 | 20 | 20 | 415 |
| 410 | 20 | 390 | 390 | 0 | 20 | 20 | 430 |
| 430 | 20 | 410 | 405 | 5 | 20 | 20 | 445 |
| 450 | 20 | 430 | 420 | 10 | 20 | 20 | 460 |
| 470 | 20 | 450 | 435 | 15 | 20 | 20 | 475 |
| 490 | 20 | 470 | 450 | 20 | 20 | 20 | 490 |
| 510 | 20 | 490 | 465 | 25 | 20 | 20 | 505 |
| 530 | 20 | 510 | 480 | 30 | 20 | 20 | 520 |
| 550 | 20 | 530 | 495 | 35 | 20 | 20 | 535 |

fraction of a drop in DI will come at the expense of saving. Observing that the MPC equals three-fourths and the MPS equals one-fourth, we can conclude that if government collects $20 billion in taxes at each possible level of NNP, the amount of consumption forthcoming at each level of NNP will drop by $15 billion (three-fourths of $20 billion), and the amount of saving at each level of NNP will fall by $5 billion (one-fourth of $20 billion). Observe in columns 4 and 5 of Table 13-2 that the amounts of consumption and saving *at each level of NNP* are $15 and $5 billion smaller, respectively, than in Table 13-1. Thus, for example, before the imposition of taxes, where NNP equaled DI, consumption was $420 billion and saving $10 billion at the $430 billion level of NNP (Table 13-1). After taxes are imposed, DI is $410 billion, obviously $20 billion short of the $430 billion NNP, with the result that consumption is only $405 billion and saving is $5 billion.

To summarize: Taxes cause DI to fall short of NNP by the amount of the taxes. This decline in DI in turn causes both consumption and saving to be less at each level of NNP. The sizes of the declines in $C$ and $S$ are determined by the MPC and the MPS.

What is the effect upon equilibrium NNP? We calculate aggregate demand once again as shown in column 8. Note that aggregate demand is $15 billion less at each level of aggregate supply than it was in Table 13-1. The reason, of course, is that after-tax consumption, $C_a$, is $15 billion less at each level of NNP. Comparing aggregate supply and aggregate demand in columns 1 and 8, it is apparent that the aggregate amounts supplied and demanded are equal only at the $490 billion NNP. Observe that the imposition of a $20 billion lump-sum tax has caused equilibrium NNP to fall from $550 billion (Table 13-1) to $490 billion.

Our alternative leakages-injections approach confirms this result. Taxes, like saving, are a leakage from the income-expenditures stream. Saving and paying taxes are both

nonconsumption uses of income. Consumption will now fall short of aggregate supply—thereby creating a potential spending gap—in the amount of after-tax saving *plus* taxes. This gap may be filled by planned investment and government purchases. Hence, our new equilibrium condition for the leakages-injections approach is: After-tax saving plus taxes equals investment plus government purchases. Symbolically, $S_a + T = I_n + G$. You should verify in Table 13-2 that this equality of leakages and injections is fulfilled *only* at the $490 billion NNP.

The impact of the $20 billion increase in taxes is shown graphically in Figure 13-2a and b. In Figure 13-2a the $20 billion *increase* in taxes shows up as a $15 (*not* $20) billion *decline* in the aggregate demand $(C_a + I_n + G)$ schedule. Under our simplifying assumption that all taxes are personal income taxes, this decline in aggregate demand is solely the result of a decline in the consumption component of the aggregate demand schedule. The equilibrium NNP shifts from $550 billion to a $490 billion level as a result of this tax-caused drop in consumption. To generalize: *Increases in taxes will lower the aggregate demand schedule relative to the aggregate supply schedule and cause the equilibrium NNP to fall.*

Consider now the leakages-injections approach: The analysis here is slightly more complex because the imposition of $20 billion in taxes has a twofold effect in Figure 13-2b. First, the taxes reduce DI by $20 billion and, with the MPS at one-fourth, cause saving to fall by $5 billion at each level of NNP. In Figure 13-2b this is shown as a shift from $S$ (saving before taxes) to $S_a$ (saving after taxes). Then the $20 billion in taxes as such appear as a $20 billion additional leakage at each NNP level which must be added to $S_a$, giving us $S_a + T$. Equilibrium now exists at the $490 billion NNP, where the total amount which households save plus the amount of taxes government intends to collect are equal to the total amount businesses plan to invest plus the amount of government purchases. The equilibrium condition for the leakages-injections approach now is $S_a + T = I_n + G$. Graphically, it is the intersection of the $S_a + T$ and the $I_n + G$ schedules which determines the equilibrium NNP.

A *decrease* in existing taxes will cause the aggregate demand schedule to rise as a result of an upward shift in the consumption schedule in Figure 13-2a. In terms of Figure 13-2b a

tax cut will cause a decline in the $S_a + T$ schedule. The result in either case is a multiple *increase* in the equilibrium NNP.

△ **Balanced-budget Multiplier**

Note an important and curious thing about our tabular and graphic illustrations. *Equal increases in government spending and taxation increase the equilibrium NNP. That*

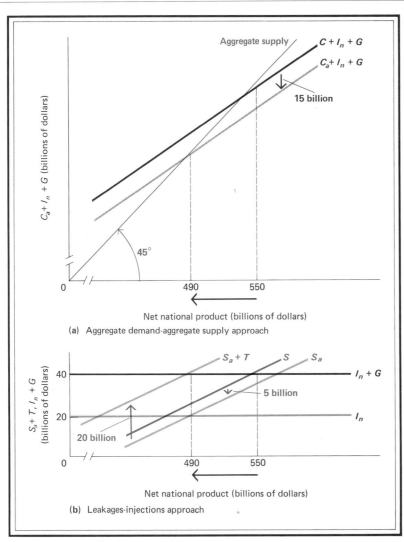

(a) Aggregate demand-aggregate supply approach

(b) Leakages-injections approach

**FIGURE 13-2 TAXES AND THE EQUILIBRIUM NNP**

(a) *The aggregate demand-aggregate supply approach.* If the MPC is three-fourths, the imposition of $20 billion of taxes will lower the consumption schedule by $15 billion and thereby cause a decline in the equilibrium NNP. (b) *The leakages-injections approach.* Here taxes have a twofold effect. First, with an MPS of one-fourth, the imposition of taxes of $20 billion will reduce disposable income by $20 billion and saving by $5 billion at each level of NNP. This is shown by the shift from $S$ (saving before taxes) to $S_a$ (saving after taxes). Second, the $20 billion of taxes constitute an additional $20 billion leakage at each NNP level, giving us $S_a + T$. By adding government, the equilibrium condition changes from $S = I_n$ to $S_a + T = I_n + G$.

*is, if G and T are both increased by $X, the equilibrium level of national output will rise by $X.* The $20 billion increase in *G* and *T* causes the equilibrium NNP to increase from $470 to $490 billion. The rationale for this so-called *balanced-budget multiplier* is revealed in our example. A change in government spending has a more powerful effect upon aggregate demand than does a tax change of the same size. Government spending has a *direct* and unadulterated impact upon aggregate demand. Government spending is a component of aggregate demand and, when government purchases increase by $20 billion as in our example, aggregate demand shifts upward by the entire $20 billion. But a change in taxes affects aggregate demand *indirectly* by changing disposable income and thereby changing consumption. Specifically, our lump-sum tax increase shifts the aggregate demand schedule downward only by the amount of the tax *times* the MPC. That is, a $20 billion tax increase shifts aggregate demand downward by $15 billion (= $20 billion × ¾). The overall result is *net* upward shift of the aggregate demand schedule of $5 billion which, subject to a multiplier of 4, boosts NNP by $20 billion. *Equal increases in G and T are expansionary.* The reader should experiment to verify that the balanced-budget multiplier is valid regardless of the sizes of the marginal propensities to consume and save.

△ **Fiscal Policy over the Cycle**

Our discussion clearly suggests how fiscal policy might be used to help stabilize the economy. The fundamental purpose of fiscal policy is to eliminate a recessionary or an inflationary gap. When a recessionary gap (Figure 12-5a) exists, an *expansionary* fiscal policy is in order. This obviously entails (1) increased government spending, *or* (2) lower taxes, *or* (3) a combination of the two. In other words, if the budget is balanced at the outset, fiscal policy should move in the direction of a government budget *deficit* during a recession or depression to close the existing recessionary

gap. Conversely, when an inflationary gap (Figure 12-5b) is present, and demand-pull inflation stalks the land, a restrictive or *contractionary* fiscal policy is appropriate. A contractionary policy is composed of (1) decreased government spending, *or* (2) higher taxes, *or* (3) a combination of these two policies. Fiscal policy should move toward a *surplus* in the government's budget when the economy is faced with the problem of closing an inflationary gap.

These statements of the nature of expansionary and contractionary fiscal policies merit two further comments, both of which involve the balanced-budget multiplier. First, a qualification: In our numerical and graphic illustrations, the balanced-budget multiplier closed a $5 billion recessionary gap and moved the economy from the unemployment NNP of $470 billion to the full-employment noninflationary NNP of $490 billion. Because a change in government spending has a more powerful effect on aggregate demand than does an equal change in taxes, an increased budget which results in a relatively small surplus might be slightly expansionary. Hence, if a contractionary fiscal policy is desired, the required surplus must be large enough to offset the balanced-budget multiplier.

Second, the balanced-budget multiplier indicates that equal increases in government spending and taxes will boost the equilibrium NNP by the amount of those increases. This correctly implies that not only does the difference between government spending and taxes (the size of a deficit or surplus) affect the NNP, but so does the absolute size of the budget. In our illustration, increases in *G* and *T* of $20 billion increased NNP by $20 billion. If *G* and *T* had both increased by only $10 billion, equilibrium NNP would only have risen by $10 billion.

△ **Financing Deficits and Disposing of Surpluses**

Given the size of a deficit, its expansionary effect upon the economy will depend upon the method by which it is financed. Similarly, given the size of a surplus, its deflationary impact will depend upon its disposition.

**Borrowing versus New Money**  There are two different ways by which the Federal government can finance a deficit: by borrowing from (selling interest-bearing bonds to) the public, or by issuing new money to its creditors.[6] The impact upon aggregate demand will be somewhat different in each case.

*1  Borrowing*  If the government goes into the money market and borrows, it will obviously be competing with private business borrowers for funds. This added demand for funds will drive the equilibrium interest rate upward. We know from Chapter 11 that investment spending is inversely related to the interest rate. Hence, government borrowing will have a *crowding-out effect;* that is, as government borrows, the interest rate will rise and thereby choke off some private investment spending. The astute reader will note that we are abandoning the second simplifying assumption made at the start of this chapter: the assumption that government spending would neither depress nor stimulate private spending. We are now noting that if government spending is financed by borrowing, the resulting increase in the interest rate can be expected to depress private investment.

*2  Money creation*  If deficit spending is financed by issuing new money, the crowding-out effect can be avoided. Federal spending can increase without any adverse effect upon investment. Our conclusion is that *the creation of new money is a more expansionary way of financing deficit spending than is borrowing.*

---

[6]This statement implies that government merely prints up new dollar bills to finance its expenditures. Although it could do this, the Treasury accomplishes the same result more subtly by borrowing (obtaining loans) from central (Federal Reserve) banks. The Treasury draws checks against these loans to finance its expenditures and, when the recipients deposit these checks in their own accounts at commercial banks, the supply of demand-deposit or checking account money is increased. The details of this process will be explained in Chapter 16.

**Debt Retirement versus an Idle Surplus**
Demand-pull inflation calls for fiscal action by government which will result in a budget surplus. However, the anti-inflationary effect of this surplus depends upon what government does with it. Generally speaking, government can dispose of a surplus in one of two ways. Let us assess these options.

*1  Debt reduction*  Since the Federal government has an outstanding debt of some $826 billion, it is logical that government should use a surplus to retire outstanding debt. The anti-inflationary impact of a surplus, however, may be reduced somewhat by this. In retiring debt held by the general public, the government transfers its surplus tax revenues into the hands of households and businesses that *might* in turn spend these funds on consumer and capital goods. But this potential increase in private spending should not be exaggerated. In all probability, a sizable portion of the surplus funds received by households and businesses as their bonds mature will be used to purchase private securities rather than goods and services.

*2  Impounding*  On the other hand, government can realize a greater anti-inflationary impact from its budgetary surplus by simply impounding the surplus funds, that is, by allowing them to stand idle. An impounded surplus means that the government is extracting and withholding purchasing power from the income-expenditure stream. If surplus tax revenues are not reinjected into the economy, there is no possibility of the surplus being spent. That is, there is no chance that the funds will create inflationary pressure to offset the deflationary impact of the surplus itself. We conclude that *the impounding of a budgetary surplus is more contractionary than the use of the surplus to retire public debt.*

△  **Policy Options: *G* or *T*?**

Is it preferable to use government spending or taxes in eliminating recessionary and inflationary gaps? The answer depends to a considerable extent upon one's view as to whether the public sector is too large or too small. Hence, those "liberal" economists, who think that the public sector needs to be enlarged to meet various failures of the market system (Chapter 6), can recommend that aggregate demand should be expanded during recessions by increasing government purchases *and* that aggregate demand should be constrained during inflationary periods by increasing taxes. Conversely, "conservative" economists, who contend that the public sector is overly large and inefficient, can advocate that aggregate demand be increased during recessions by cutting taxes *and* that aggregate demand be reduced during inflation by cutting government spending. It is significant that an active fiscal policy designed to stabilize the economy can be associated with either an expanding or a contracting public sector.

## ☐ PROBLEMS AND COMPLICATIONS

Unfortunately, there is a great deal of difference between fiscal policy on paper and fiscal policy in practice. It is therefore imperative that we examine some specific problems which may be encountered in enacting and applying appropriate fiscal policy.

### △ Problems of Timing

Several problems of timing may arise in connection with fiscal policy.

**1  Recognition Lag**  It is extremely difficult to predict accurately the future course of economic activity. The recognition lag refers to the time which elapses between the beginning of a recession or an inflation and the recognition that it is in fact occurring. The economy may be four or six months into a recession or an inflation before this fact shows up in relevant statistics and is acknowledged.

**2  Administrative Lag**  The wheels of democratic government are often slow in turning. There will inevitably be a lag between the time that the need for fiscal action is recognized and the time that action is actually taken. The $11 billion tax cut which became law in February of 1964 was first proposed to President Kennedy by the Council of Economic Advisers in 1961, and in turn proposed by him in late 1962! The 1968 surcharge on personal and corporate incomes was enacted approximately a year after it was requested by President Johnson. Indeed, Congress has on occasion consumed so much time in adjusting fiscal policy that the economic situation has taken a turnabout in the interim, thereby rendering the policy action completely inappropriate.

A frequent proposal is that Congress give the President limited authority to alter tax rates for purposes of countercyclical fiscal policy and thereby circumvent time-consuming congressional debate. Opponents argue that the proposal transfers an important function of the legislative branch to the executive branch of government and disturbs the "balance of power" between the two.

**3  Operational Lag**  There will also be a lag between the time that fiscal action is taken by Congress and the time that action has an impact upon output, employment, or the price level. Although changes in tax rates can be put into effect quickly, government spending on public works—the construction of dams, interstate highways, and so forth—entails long planning periods and even longer periods of construction. Such spending is of questionable usefulness in offsetting short—for example, six- or eighteen-month—periods of recession.

### △ Political Problems

Fiscal policy is created in the political area and this greatly complicates its use in stabilizing the economy.

**1  Other Goals**  Recall that economic stability is *not* the sole objective of government spending and taxing policies. Government is also concerned with the provision of social goods and services and the redistribution of income (Chapter 6). Classic example: During World War II government spending for military goods rose dramatically, causing strong and persistent inflationary pressures in the early 1940s. The defeat of Nazi Germany and Japan was simply a higher priority goal than achieving price level stability. More generally, state and local governments do not assume it is their obligation to help stabilize the economy. In fact, state and local finance often tends to reinforce, rather than alleviate, cyclical fluctuations. State and local governments do most of their spending for schools, libraries, and streets and highways during prosperity. As is true of households and private businesses, they often cut expenditures and sometimes even retire debt during recessions. During the Great Depression of the 1930s, most of the increase in Federal spending was canceled by declines in state and local spending. At the other extreme, state and local governments may cut taxes during periods of inflationary pressure. Recall from Chapter 8 that the tax revolt is partially in response to inflation eroding real incomes.

**2   Expansionary Bias?**   Rhetoric to the contrary, deficits tend to be politically attractive and surpluses politically painful. That is, there may well be a political bias in favor of deficits; in other words, fiscal policy may embody an expansionary-inflationary bias. Why so? Tax reductions tend to be politically popular. And so are increases in government spending, provided that the given politician's constituents share liberally in the benefits. But higher taxes upset voters and reducing government expenditures can be politically precarious. For example, it might well be political hara-kiri for a farm-state senator to vote for tax increases and against agricultural subsidies.

**3   A Political Business Cycle?**   In Chapter 6's section on public sector failure (p. 101), it was suggested that the overriding goal of politicians is to get reelected. A few

economists have recently put forth the notion of a *political business cycle.* That is, they have argued that politicians might manipulate fiscal policy to maximize voter support, even though their fiscal decisions tend to *destabilize* the economy. According to this view, fiscal policy, as we have described it, may be corrupted for political purposes and thereby be a cause of economic fluctuations.

The suggested scenario goes something like this. The populace, it is assumed, takes economic conditions into account in voting. Incumbents are penalized at the polls if economic conditions are depressed; they are rewarded if the economy is prosperous. Hence, as an election approaches, the incumbent administration (aided by an election-minded Congress) will invoke tax cuts and increases in government spending. Not only will these actions be popular per se, but the resulting stimulus to the economy will push all the critical economic indicators in proper directions. Output and real incomes will rise; unemployment will fall; and the price level will be relatively stable (see range 1 of Figure 10-6). As a result, incumbents will enjoy a very cordial economic environment in which to stand for reelection.

But after the election, continued expansion of the economy is reflected increasingly in a rising price level and less in growing real incomes (ranges 2 and 3 of Figure 10-6). Growing public concern over inflation will prompt politicians to invoke a contractionary fiscal policy. Crudely put, a "made-in-Washington" recession will be engineered by trimming government spending and increasing taxes in order to restrain inflation. Won't this recession hurt incumbents? Not really, because the next election is still two or three years away and the critical consideration for most voters is the performance of the economy in the year or so prior to the election. Indeed, the recession provides a new starting point from which fiscal policy can again be used to generate another expansion in time for the next election campaign!

This possible perversion of fiscal policy is

both highly disturbing and inherently difficult to document. Although empirical evidence is mixed and inconclusive, there is some evidence in support of this political theory of the business cycle.[7]

## ☐ NONDISCRETIONARY FISCAL POLICY: BUILT-IN STABILIZERS

Given various obstacles to the successful application of discretionary fiscal policy, it is reassuring to note that to some degree appropriate fiscal policy occurs automatically! This so-called automatic or *built-in stability* is not embodied in our discussion of discretionary fiscal policy because we assumed a simple lump-sum tax whereby the same amount of tax revenue was collected at each level of NNP. Built-in stability arises because in reality our net tax system (net taxes equal taxes minus transfers and subsidies) is such that *net tax revenues*[8] *vary directly with NNP*. Virtually all taxes will yield more tax revenue as NNP rises. In particular, personal and corporate income taxes have progressive rates and result in more than proportionate increases in tax collections as NNP expands. Furthermore, as NNP increases and more goods and services are purchased, revenues from sales and excise taxes will increase. And, similarly, payroll tax payments increase as economic expansion creates more jobs. Obviously, when NNP declines, tax receipts from all these sources will decline. Transfer payments (or "negative taxes") behave in precisely the opposite way. Unemployment compensation payments, welfare payments, and subsidies to farmers all *decrease* during economic expansion and *increase* during a contraction. On the table on the inside covers of this book, observe, for example, the declines in personal and corporate

income tax receipts (lines 15 and 11) and the increases in transfer payments (line 13) during the 1949, 1954, 1958, and 1970 recessions.

### △  Automatic or Built-in Stabilizers

Figure 13-3 is helpful in understanding how the tax system gives rise to built-in stability. Government expenditures $G$ are given and assumed to be independent of the level of NNP; expenditures are decided upon at some fixed level by the Congress. But Congress does *not* determine the *level* of tax revenues; rather, it establishes tax *rates*. Tax revenues then vary directly with the level of NNP which the economy actually realizes. The direct relationship between tax revenues and NNP is shown in the upsloping $T$ line.

The economic importance of this direct relationship between tax receipts and NNP comes into focus when we remember two things. First, taxes are a leakage or withdrawal of potential purchasing power from the economy. Second, it is desirable from the standpoint of stability to increase leakages or withdrawals of purchasing power when the economy is moving toward inflation and to diminish these withdrawals when the economy is tending to slump. In other words, the kind of tax system portrayed in Figure 13-3 builds some stability into the economy by automatically bringing about changes in tax revenues and therefore in the public budget which tend to counter both inflation and unemployment. Generally speaking, a *built-in stabilizer is anything which tends to increase the government's deficit (or reduce its surplus) during a recession and to increase its surplus (or reduce its deficit) during inflation without requiring explicit action by policy makers*. And, as Figure 13-3 clearly reveals, this is precisely what our tax system tends to do. As NNP rises during prosperity, tax revenues *automatically* increase and, because they are a leakage, restrain the economic expansion. Stated differently, as the economy moves toward a higher NNP, tax revenues automatically rise and tend to move the budget from a deficit to a surplus.

---

[7]The interested reader should consult Edward R. Tufte, *Political Control of the Economy* (Princeton, N.J.: Princeton University Press, 1978).

[8]From now on, we shall use the term "taxes" in referring to net taxes.

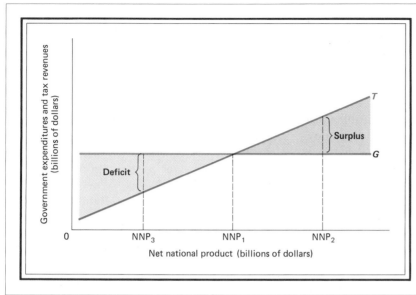

FIGURE 13-3 BUILT-IN STABILITY

If tax revenues vary directly with NNP, then the deficits which will tend to occur automatically during recession will help alleviate that recession. Conversely, the surpluses which tend to occur automatically during expansion will assist in offsetting possible inflation.

Conversely, as NNP falls during recession, tax revenues *automatically* decline and this reduction in leakages cushions the economic contraction. That is, with a falling NNP, tax receipts decline and tend to move the public budget from a surplus to a deficit. In terms of Figure 13-3, the low level of income $NNP_3$ will automatically give rise to an expansionary budget deficit; the high and perhaps inflationary income level $NNP_2$ will automatically generate a contractionary budget surplus.

Discretionary fiscal policy can be used to alter the degree of built-in stability. For example, if Congress should alter our tax system so as to make tax revenues even more sensitive to changes in NNP than presumed in Figure 13-3—and this could be done, for example, by putting greater relative dependence upon taxes with progressive rates or by increasing the progressivity of the overall tax structure—then the tax line would be steeper and built-in stability would be more pronounced.

△  **Qualifications and Subtleties**

There is no question but that the built-in stability provided by our tax system has served the economy well. Yet three significant points must be appended to our discussion.

1  **Amelioration, not Correction**  The built-in stabilizers are *not* capable of correcting an undesirable change in the equilibrium NNP. All that the stabilizers do is reduce the magnitude or severity of economic fluctuations. Hence, discretionary fiscal action—that is, changes in tax rates, tax structure, and expenditures—by Congress is required to correct an inflation or a recession of any appreciable magnitude. It is estimated that in the United States the built-in stabilizers are currently strong enough to reduce fluctuations in national income by one-third or more. One recent study suggests that the built-in stabilizers during recent recessions prevented an average of 36 to 52 percent of the income declines which would have occurred in their absence. On the other hand, during recent expansions potential income increases were reduced by as much as 25 to 42 percent.[9]

[9] Peter Eilbott, "The Effectiveness of the Automatic Stabilizers," *American Economic Review,* June 1966, pp. 450–465.

**2 "Fiscal Drag"** The presence of a tax system wherein tax revenues vary directly with NNP is not an unmitigated good. Such a tax system may tend to produce a *fiscal drag* in the form of budgetary surpluses which make it difficult to achieve and sustain full employment.

Built-in stability is clearly desirable *if* the economy fluctuates around the full-employment level of NNP. But if the economy is initially in a recession, the same degree of built-in stability can make it more difficult to move to full employment. Consider Figure 13-3 once again. If NNP$_1$ is the full-employment level of output and the economy is currently enjoying full employment, the built-in stability provided by the $T$ line is clearly desirable in that the tax system will dampen any tendency for the economy to deviate from full employment. But what if the actual output is at some recessionary level, such as NNP$_3$? In this case the expansionary impact of any increase in $C$, $I$, or $G$ will be blunted by the presence of the built-in stabilizers. Some of the stimulating impact of an increase in spending will leak into expanding tax revenues. In short, just as built-in stability is helpful in maintaining full employment once it is achieved, so that same built-in stability tends to maintain unemployment once it exists.

There is also a long-run aspect to the fiscal drag problem. Suppose the full-employment output is at NNP$_1$ and the economy is actually operating at this level. The budget, you will note, is currently in balance. Now the catch is that ours is a growing economy (Part 3) and that, through time, the full-employment output will shift toward NNP$_2$. But this growth automatically generates a budget surplus which tends to precipitate a recession and choke off growth. (For example, if the full-employment output expands by 4 percent per year, tax revenues will automatically increase by some $25 to $30 billion per year!) In short, when a time dimension is added to Figure 13-3 to allow for growth, built-in stability may make it difficult to sustain full employment through time. During periods of substantial growth, significant budget surpluses automatically appear and have a contractionary impact. The remedy? The Federal government must use discretionary fiscal policy to cut taxes, or increase expenditures, to eliminate fiscal drag (Chapter 8).

**3 Full-Employment Budget** Built-in stability—the fact that tax revenues vary directly with NNP—makes it hazardous to use the *actual* budget surplus or deficit in any given year as an index of the government's fiscal stance. To illustrate: Suppose the economy is at full employment at NNP$_1$ in Figure 13-3 and, as we note, the budget is in balance. Now, assume that, during the year, $C$ or $I_n$ declines, causing a recession at NNP$_3$. The government, let us assume, takes no discretionary fiscal action; therefore, the $G$ and $T$ lines remain in the positions shown in the diagram. Obviously, as the economy moves to NNP$_3$, tax revenues fall and, with government expenditures unaltered, a deficit occurs. But this deficit is clearly *not* the result of positive countercyclical fiscal actions by the government; rather it is the by-product of fiscal inaction as the economy slides into a recession. The basic point is that one cannot say anything very meaningful about the government's fiscal posture—whether Congress was appropriately manipulating taxes and expenditures—by looking at the historical record of budgetary deficits or surpluses. The actual budget surplus or deficit reflects not only possible discretionary decisions about spending and taxes (as shown in the locations of the $G$ and $T$ lines in Figure 13-3), but also the level of equilibrium NNP (where the economy is operating on the horizontal axis of Figure 13-3). Hence, given that tax revenues vary with NNP, the fundamental problem of comparing deficits or surpluses in year 1 and year 2 is that the level of NNP may be vastly different in each of the two years.

Economists have resolved this problem through the notion of a full-employment budget. Simply stated, the *full-employment budget indicates what the Federal budgetary*

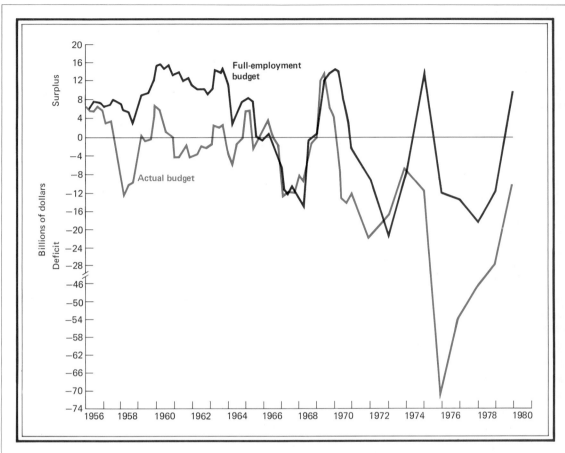

FIGURE 13-4   THE FULL-EMPLOYMENT BUDGET AND THE ACTUAL BUDGET

The full-employment budget surplus or deficit is a better indicator of the government's fiscal posture than is the actual surplus or deficit.  The actual budget has been in deficit with much greater frequency than the full-employment budget because NNP has been at less than full employment.

*surplus or deficit would be if the economy were to operate at full employment throughout the year.* Figure 13-4 compares the full-employment budget and the actual budget over approximately two decades.  Note that, although the actual budget has usually been in deficit, the full-employment budget typically is in surplus.  Consider 1961 and 1962, years of above-normal unemployment and sluggish economic growth.  A look at the actual budget deficits in these years implies that government was appropriately engaged in an expansionary fiscal policy.  But the full-employment budget data tell us that this was *not* the case.  The full-employment budget data indicate that, if the economy had been at full employment, there would have been a budgetary surplus.  Our fiscal policy in 1961 and 1962 was in fact contractionary, and this was partially responsible for the less-than-full-employment levels of NNP, the consequent poor tax harvests, and the deficits which occurred in the actual budgets for 1961 and 1962.  Our fiscal policy stance in those years?  Contractionary as suggested by the full-employment budget, not expansionary as implied by the actual budget.

## ☐ BUDGET PHILOSOPHIES

The essence of countercyclical fiscal policy is that the Federal budget should move toward a deficit during recession and toward a surplus during inflation. This correctly suggests that the use of an activist fiscal policy is unlikely to result in a balanced budget in any particular year. Is this a matter for concern? Let us approach this question by examining the economic implications of several contrasting budget philosophies.

### △  Annually Balanced Budget

Until the Great Depression of the 1930s, the *annually balanced budget* was generally accepted without question as a desirable goal of public finance. Upon examination, however, it becomes evident that an annually balanced budget largely rules out government fiscal activity as a countercyclical, stabilizing force. Worse yet, an annually balanced budget actually intensifies the business cycle. To illustrate: Suppose that the economy encounters a siege of unemployment and falling incomes. As Figure 13-3 indicates, in such circumstances tax receipts will automatically decline. In seeking to balance its budget, government must either (1) increase tax rates, (2) reduce government expenditures, or (3) employ a combination of these two. It is obvious that all these policies are contractionary; each one further dampens, rather than stimulates, the level of aggregate demand.

Similarly, an annually balanced budget will intensify inflation. Again, Figure 13-3 tells us that, as money incomes rise during the course of inflation, tax collections will automatically increase. To avoid the impending surplus, government must either (1) cut tax rates, (2) increase government expenditures, or (3) adopt a combination of both. It is clear that all three of these policies will add to inflationary pressures.

The basic conclusion, then, is evident: *An annually balanced budget is not economically neutral; the pursuit of such a policy is procyclical, not countercyclical.*

### △  Cyclically Balanced Budget

The notion of a *cyclically balanced budget* envisions government exerting a countercyclical influence and at the same time balancing its budget. In this case, however, the budget would not be balanced annually—after all, there is nothing sacred about twelve months as an accounting period—but rather, over the course of the business cycle.

The rationale of this budget philosophy is simple, plausible, and appealing. To offset recession, government should lower taxes and increase spending, thereby purposely incurring a deficit. During the ensuing inflationary upswing, taxes would be raised and government spending slashed. The resulting surplus could then be used to retire the Federal debt incurred in financing the recession. In this way government fiscal operations would exert a positive countercyclical force, and the government could still balance its budget—not annually, but over a period of years.

The basic problem with this budget philosophy is that the upswings and downswings of the business cycle may not be of equal magnitude and duration (Figure 10-1), and hence the goal of stabilization comes into conflict with balancing the budget over the cycle. For example, a long and severe slump, followed by a modest and short period of prosperity, would mean a large deficit during the slump, little or no surplus during prosperity, and therefore a cyclical deficit in the budget.

### △  Functional Finance

According to *functional finance,* the question of a balanced budget—either annually or cyclically—is of secondary importance. The primary purpose of Federal finance is to provide for noninflationary full employment, that is, to balance the economy, not the budget. If the attainment of this objective entails either persistent surpluses or a large and growing public debt, so be it. The problems involved in government deficits or surpluses are relatively minor compared with the highly undesirable alternatives of prolonged recession or persistent inflation. The Federal budget is first and foremost an instrument for achieving and maintaining macroeconomic stability. Government should not hesitate to incur any deficits and surpluses required in achieving this goal. In response to those who express concern about the large Federal debt which the pursuit of functional finance might entail, proponents of this budget philosophy offer three arguments. First, our tax system is such that tax revenues automatically increase as the economy expands. Hence, given government expenditures, a deficit which is successful in stimulating equilibrium NNP will be partially self-liquidating (Figure 13-3). Second, given its taxing powers and the ability to create money, the government's capacity to finance deficits is virtually unlimited. Finally, it is contended that the problems of a large Federal debt are substantially less burdensome than most people think. It is to the matter of the public debt that we now turn.

## □ THE PUBLIC DEBT

Because modern fiscal policy endorses unbalanced budgets for the purpose of stabilizing the economy, its application will quite possibly lead to a growing public debt. Let us now briefly consider the public debt—its causes, its characteristics, its size, and the burdens and benefits associated with it.

### △ Dimensions of Debt

Growth of the public debt, as Table 13-3 indicates, has been substantial since 1929. The public debt is, of course, the accumulation of all past deficits, minus surpluses, of the Federal budget.

**Causes** Why have these deficits occurred? As Table 13-3 makes clear, a considerable portion of the public debt is attributable to war finance. The public debt grew more than fivefold during World War II and it also increased substantially during the Korean and Vietnam wars. Some deficits have been the

**TABLE 13-3**
Quantitative Significance of the Public Debt: The Public Debt and Interest Payments in Relation to GNP, 1929–1979

| (1) Year | (2) Public debt, billions | (3) Gross national product,* billions | (4) Interest payments, billions | (5) Public debt as percentage of GNP, (2) ÷ (3) | (6) Interest payments as percentage of GNP, (4) ÷ (3) | (7) Per capita public debt |
|---|---|---|---|---|---|---|
| 1929 | $ 16.3 | $ 103.1 | $ 0.7 | 16% | 0.7% | $ 134 |
| 1940 | 50.9 | 99.7 | 1.1 | 51 | 1.1 | 382 |
| 1946 | 259.5 | 208.5 | 4.2 | 124 | 2.0 | 1827 |
| 1950 | 256.7 | 284.8 | 4.5 | 90 | 1.6 | 1689 |
| 1954 | 278.8 | 364.8 | 5.0 | 76 | 1.4 | 1404 |
| 1958 | 283.0 | 447.3 | 5.6 | 63 | 1.3 | 1617 |
| 1962 | 304.0 | 560.3 | 7.2 | 54 | 1.3 | 1626 |
| 1967 | 322.9 | 796.3 | 12.6 | 41 | 1.6 | 1625 |
| 1972 | 426.4 | 1171.1 | 20.6 | 36 | 1.8 | 2042 |
| 1976 | 620.4 | 1691.6 | 34.6 | 37 | 2.0 | 2884 |
| 1979 | 826.5 | 2368.5 | 52.6 | 35 | 2.2 | 3747 |

*In current dollars.
*Source: Economic Report of the President* (Washington, 1980).

result of discretionary fiscal policy designed to offset recession or stimulate growth. At other times, deficits have been the consequence of built-in stability; for example, above-normal unemployment rates in the 1970s—particularly in the 1974–1976 period—automatically reduced tax collections and tended to cause deficits. Furthermore, in the past ten years or so various income-maintenance programs—social security, unemployment compensation, food stamps, aid to dependent children, and so forth—have expanded sharply in terms of numbers, coverage, and levels of benefits and have been one of the causes of unbalanced budgets.

**Public Debt, Public Credit**   To whom do we owe the public debt? The answer is: For the most part, we owe it to ourselves! About three-fourths of our government bonds are held internally, that is, they are owned and held by citizens and institutions—banks, businesses, insurance companies, governmental agencies, and trust funds—within the United States. Thus the public debt is also a public credit. While the public debt is a liability to the American people (as taxpayers), most of that same debt is simultaneously an asset to the American people (as bondholders). Retirement of the public debt would therefore call for a gigantic transfer payment whereby American individuals and institutions would pay higher taxes and the government in turn would pay out most of those tax revenues to those same taxpaying individuals and institutions in the aggregate in redeeming the bonds which they hold. Although a redistribution of wealth would result from this gigantic financial transfer, it need not entail any immediate decline in the economy's aggregate wealth or standard of living. The repayment of an internally held public debt entails no leakage of purchasing power from the economy of the country as a whole.

**Quantitative Aspects**   There is no denying it: The absolute size of the public debt is so

large—$826 billion in 1979—as to be almost beyond comprehension. But we must not fear large numbers per se. Let us therefore put the size of the public debt in better perspective.

*1   Debt and GNP*   A bald statement of the absolute size of the debt glosses over the fact that the wealth and productive ability of our economy have also increased tremendously over the years. It is safe to say that a wealthy nation has greater ability to incur and carry a large public debt than does a poor nation. In other words, it seems more realistic to measure changes in the public debt *in relation to* changes in the economy's GNP. Column 5 in Table 13-3 presents such data. Note that instead of the sixteenfold increase in the debt between 1940 and 1979 shown in column 2, we now find that the *relative* size of the debt has *declined* considerably since 1946. And this ratio of Federal debt to GNP, incidentally, is small when compared with similar ratios for other advanced nations. Note, too, in column 7, that the per capita size of the public debt has not increased spectacularly.

*2   Interest charges*   Many economists feel that the primary burden of the debt is the annual interest charge that accrues as a result of the debt. The absolute size of these interest payments is shown in column 4. Interest on the debt is now the third largest item of expenditures in the Federal budget (Table 8-1). Interest charges as a percentage of GNP are presented in column 6. In these terms, the burden of the debt is about the same as it was in 1946. The failure of this ratio to fall significantly in the past twenty years reflects the phenomenon of rising interest rates much more than a rising debt.

*3   Private debt*   Although the size and growth of public debt are looked upon with awe and alarm, private debt has grown much faster. Private and public debt were of about equal size in 1947. But private debt has grown much faster and is now about four times as large as the public debt. If you insist upon worrying about debt, you will do well to concern yourself with private as well as public indebtedness.

### △ Two Myths

Both the existence and the expansion of the public debt can entail problems. But prior to a discussion of its disadvantages and advantages, let us lay to rest two rather widely held myths.

**Going Bankrupt**  Can a large public debt somehow "bankrupt" the government, making it unable to meet its financial obligations? Given the fact that the government has the power to tax, it is extremely difficult to conceive of a situation wherein the government could become bankrupt. Indeed, there is no reason why the public debt need be reduced, much less eliminated. In practice, as portions of the debt fall due each month, government does not typically cut expenditures or raise taxes to provide funds to *retire* the maturing bonds. (We know that with depressed economic conditions, this would be unwise fiscal policy.) Rather, the government simply *refinances* the debt, that is, it sells new bonds and uses the proceeds to pay off holders of the maturing bonds.

**Shifting Burdens**  Does the public debt impose a burden upon future generations? Was some of the economic burden of World War II, for example, shifted to future generations by the decision to finance military purchases through the sale of government bonds? Again, the answer is "No." Recalling the production possibilities curve, we can see that the economic cost of World War II consisted of the civilian goods which society had to forgo in shifting scarce resources to war goods production. Regardless of whether the financing of this reallocation was achieved through higher taxes or borrowing, the real economic burden of the war would have been essentially the same. In short, the burden of the war was borne by the persons who lived during the war; they were the ones who did without a multi-

tude of consumer goods to permit the United States to arm itself and its allies.[10]

### △ Real Burden of the Debt

But we must be careful not to whitewash the public debt. The existence of a large public debt does pose real and potential problems.

**External Debt**  Externally held debt is a burden. This part of the public debt obviously is not "owed to ourselves," and in real terms the payment of interest and principal requires the transfer of a portion of our real output to other nations. It is worth noting that foreign ownership of the public debt has increased dramatically in recent years. In 1960 only about 5 percent of the debt was foreign-owned; currently foreign ownership is about 25 percent! The $8 billion paid as interest each year to foreign bond owners contributes to our balance of payments deficit (Chapter 44). The assertion that "we owe the debt to ourselves" and the implication that the debt should be of little or no concern is much less accurate than it was a scant decade or two ago.

**Incentives**  Table 13-3 indicates that the present public debt necessitates an annual interest payment of almost $53 billion. With no increase in the size of the debt, this annual interest charge must be paid out of tax revenues. These added taxes may tend to dampen incentives to bear risk, to innovate, to invest, and to work. In this indirect way, the existence of a large debt can impair economic growth.

**Crowding-out Effect**  We have already called attention to the crowding-out effect, that is, the possibility that deficit financing (or

---

[10] Wartime production may cause a nation's stock of capital to cease to grow or to dwindle as precious resources are shifted from the production of capital goods and to the production of war goods. As a result, future generations inherit a smaller stock of capital goods than they otherwise would. This occurred in the United States during World War II (see table on inside covers, line 2). But, again, this shifting of costs is independent of how a war is financed.

the refinancing of existing public debt) will increase the interest rate and reduce private investment spending. If this occurs, future generations will inherit a smaller stock of private capital.

**Income Redistribution** Bond ownership is concentrated among the wealthier groups in society and the Federal tax structure is basically proportional (Table 8-6). Therefore, interest payments on the debt tend to contribute to income inequality.[11]

**Debt, Liquidity, and Inflation** The very existence of a large debt tends to be inflationary. This is so for the following reasons:

**1** Because they are highly liquid assets, the possession of government bonds makes consumers feel wealthy. This feeling of wealth leads to greater consumption out of their incomes. In short, the existence of a large public debt tends to shift the consumption schedule upward. *If* the economy is already at full employment, this shift will be inflationary.

**2** Furthermore, government bonds can be converted into money easily and with little or no risk of loss. Government bonds, therefore, constitute a potential backlog of purchasing power which can add materially to inflationary fires. During periods of inflation, it is very tempting for consumers to dig into this reserve of purchasing power in an attempt to beat rising prices. Such an attempt to beat inflation will cause more inflation. Something like this happened at the end of World War II; the inflation-causing buying spree of 1946–1947 was financed partially by the cashing in of bonds purchased during the war.

**3** Finally, we stressed in Chapter 10 that, because inflation entails a redistribution of income from creditors to debtors, the public

debt makes the Federal government a major beneficiary of inflation. Given these circumstances, it is reasonable to raise the question as to whether government will pursue vigorously anti-inflationary policies.

But the contention that a large public debt has an inflationary bias must be qualified. First, *changes* in the size of the public debt have a much greater impact upon employment, output, and the price level than does the *absolute size* of the existing debt. Thus a $15 billion increase in the debt can be expected to exert a much greater expansionary or inflationary effect on the economy than the mere presence of an existing debt of, say, $826 billion. Moreover, remember that deficit spending is inflationary only if it is inappropriate fiscal policy. Deficit spending under full-employment conditions is inflationary; but this is ill-advised fiscal policy. Deficit spending during recession is expansionary; it increases employment and output and is therefore well advised.

**Wasteful Government Spending** It is frequently argued that wasteful government expenditures are more likely to creep into the Federal budget when deficit financing is readily available. Politicians are motivated to screen expenditures more carefully when they are faced with the delicate problem of financing such programs out of tax increases. The fact that deficit financing gives the illusion of deferring the costs of government expenditures makes it easier for projects of questionable merit to find their way into the budget.

△ **Positive Role of Debt**

But there is a brighter side to the public debt.

**Debt Creation, Stability, and Growth** We must not forget that debt—both public and private—plays a positive role in a prosperous and growing economy. We know that as income expands, so does saving. Keynesian employment theory and fiscal policy tell us that if

---

[11] However, at least one empirical study suggests that the redistributional impact is not evident and in fact may favor lower income groups. See Donald F. Vitaliano, "The Payment of Interest on the Public Debt and the Distribution of Income," *Journal of Economics and Business,* Spring–Summer 1973, pp. 175–186.

aggregate demand is to be sustained at the full-employment level, this expanding volume of saving or its equivalent must be obtained and spent by consumers, businesses, or government. The process by which saving is transferred to spenders is debt creation. Now, in fact, consumers and businesses do borrow and spend a great amount of saving. Private debt has increased spectacularly—much faster than public debt—since World War II. But if households and businesses are not willing to borrow and thereby to increase private debt sufficiently fast to absorb the growing volume of saving, an increase in public debt must absorb the remainder or the economy will falter from full employment and fail to realize its growth potential.

**Other Advantages**  Apart from debt creation, in at least three respects the very *existence* of a large debt can be desirable.

**1**  Because government bonds are highly liquid and virtually risk-free securities, they make an excellent purchase for small and conservative savers. To the extent that the availability of government bonds encourages saving, more resources are freed for investment and economic growth tends to be enhanced.

**2**  It should also be noted that although a large debt may pose inflationary problems in a full-employment economy, the same debt can cushion a cyclical downswing. A condition that is potentially undesirable in a full-employment economy may be very desirable in a less-than-full-employment economy. A large public debt may prove to be a kind of built-in stabilizer insofar as recessions are concerned.

**3**  Finally, Chapter 16 will reveal the important role which government bonds play in putting monetary policy into effect. The sale and purchase of government bonds by the economy's central banks influence the money supply, the level of spending, hence the level of economic activity.

## Summary

**1**  Government responsibility for achieving and maintaining full employment is set forth in the Employment Act of 1946. The Council of Economic Advisers (CEA) was established to advise the President on policies appropriate to fulfilling the goals of the act.

**2**  Increases in government spending expand, and decreases contract, the equilibrium NNP. Conversely, increases in taxes reduce, and decreases expand, the equilibrium NNP. Appropriate fiscal policy therefore calls for increases in government spending and decreases in taxes—that is, for a budget deficit—to correct for unemployment. Decreases in government spending and increases in taxes—that is, a budget surplus—are appropriate fiscal policy for correcting inflation.

**3**  The balanced-budget multiplier indicates that equal increases in government spending and taxation will increase the equilibrium NNP.

**4**  Financing a government deficit through the creation of new money is more expansionary than financing the same deficit by borrowing. A surplus is more deflationary when impounded by government than it is when used to retire outstanding public debt.

**5**  The enactment and application of appropriate fiscal policy are subject to certain problems and questions. Some of the most important are these: **a.** Can the enactment and application of fiscal policy be better timed so as to maximize its effectiveness in heading off economic fluctuations? **b.** Can the economy rely upon Congress to enact appropriate fiscal policy?

**6**  Built-in stability refers to the fact that net tax revenues vary directly with the level of NNP. Therefore, during a recession, the public budget automatically tends toward a stabilizing deficit; conversely, during expansion, the budget automatically tends toward an anti-inflationary surplus.  Built-in stability ameliorates, but does not correct, undesired changes in the NNP.  Furthermore, the existence of built-in stability may create a "fiscal drag" problem.

**7**   The full-employment budget indicates what the Federal budgetary surplus or deficit would be *if* the economy operated at full employment throughout the year.  The full-employment budget is a more meaningful indicator of the government's fiscal posture than is its actual budgetary surplus or deficit.

**8**   Budget philosophies include the annually balanced budget, the cyclically balanced budget, and functional finance.

**9**   The public debt is now $826 billion or about 35 percent of the GNP.  A large public debt may **a.** impair incentives to innovate and invest, **b.** "crowd out" private investment, **c.** enhance income inequality, **d.** add to inflationary pressures, and **e.** be conducive to wasteful government spending.  Debt creation transfers saving to spenders and thereby plays a positive function in maintaining high levels of output and employment.


## Questions and Study Suggestions

**1**   Key terms and concepts to remember: Employment Act of 1946; Council of Economic Advisers; Full Employment and Balanced Growth Act of 1978 (Humphrey–Hawkins Act); discretionary fiscal policy; expansionary and contractionary fiscal policy; balanced-budget multiplier; political business cycle; built-in stabilizers; fiscal drag; actual and full-employment budgets; annually balanced budget; cyclically balanced budget; functional finance; public debt.

**2**   Explain graphically the determination of equilibrium NNP through both the aggregate demand–aggregate supply approach and the leakages-injections approach for the private sector.  Now add government spending and taxation, showing the impact of each upon the equilibrium NNP.  Explain how discretionary fiscal policy can be used to close inflationary and recessionary gaps.

**3**   Refer to the tabular data for question 7 at the end of Chapter 12.  Now, assuming investment is $16 billion, incorporate government into the table by assuming that it plans to tax and spend $20 billion at each possible level of NNP.  Assume all taxes are personal taxes and that government spending does not entail shifts in the consumption and investment schedules.  Explain the changes in the equilibrium NNP which the addition of government entails.

**4**   What is the balanced-budget multiplier?  Demonstrate the balanced-budget multiplier in terms of your answer to question 3.  Explain: "Equal increases in government spending and tax revenues of *n* dollars will increase the equilibrium NNP by *n* dollars."  Does this hold true regardless of the size of the MPS?

**5**   Explain the functioning of the built-in stabilizers.  How might the effect of "fiscal drag" be offset?  Define the "full-employment budget" and explain its significance.

**6**   What is the best method of financing a government deficit during depression?  What is the best means of disposing of a surplus during inflation?  Explain your answers.  "If the economy needs $10 billion with which to finance the expansion and improvement of its highways, it should simply print up the needed money to finance the undertaking.  In this way we'll get the roads, and no one will be hurt by having to pay higher taxes."  Evaluate this suggestion, first under conditions of full employment, and second under depressed conditions.

**7**   Briefly state and evaluate the major problems encountered in enacting and applying fiscal policy.  Which do you feel are the most significant?  How might you determine whether a political business cycle exists?

**8**   Explain how both "conservative" and "liberal" economists might support an activist fiscal policy.

**9**   Comment upon the size and causes of the public debt.  How does an internally held public debt differ from an externally held public debt?  What would be the effects of retiring an internally held public debt?  Distinguish between refinancing and retiring public debt.

**10**   In what ways might the mere existence of a large public debt contribute to inflationary pressures?  "Incurring a public debt is more inflationary than carrying an existing public debt."  Do you agree?

**11**   Explain or evaluate each of the following statements:

**a.**   "Rising prices cause real incomes to fall.  In such circumstances all levels of government should cut taxes.  This will permit the American people to maintain their standard of living."

**b.**   "A national debt is like a debt of the left hand to the right hand."

**c.**   "As a society becomes wealthier, saving increases.  If prosperity is to be sustained, the private and public sectors together must borrow and spend an amount sufficient to offset this saving.  The expansion of debt is therefore a prerequisite of full employment."

**d.**   "Difficulties in applying stabilization policy are imbedded in the political rather than in the economic system and the main obstacle to successful policy is the government itself."

**12**   Use Figure 13-3 to explain why a deficit increase which causes the economy to expand might be partly self-liquidating.  In requesting a tax cut in the early 1960s President Kennedy said "It is a paradoxical truth that tax rates are too high today and tax revenues are too low and the soundest way to raise tax revenues in the long run is to cut tax rates now."  Was his rationale correct?

**13**   *Advanced analysis.*  Assume that, in the absence of any taxes, the consumption schedule for an economy is as follows:

| NNP, billions | Consumption, billions |
|---|---|
| $100 | $120 |
| 200 | 200 |
| 300 | 280 |
| 400 | 360 |
| 500 | 440 |
| 600 | 520 |
| 700 | 600 |

**a.**   Graph this consumption schedule and note the size of the MPC.

**b.**   Assume now a lump-sum (regressive) tax system is imposed in such a way that the government collects $10 billion in taxes at all levels of NNP.  Calculate the tax rate at each level of NNP.  Graph the resulting consumption schedule and compare the MPC and the multiplier with that of the pretax consumption schedule.

**c.**   Now suppose a proportional tax system with a 10 percent tax rate is imposed instead of the regressive system.  Calculate the new consumption schedule, graph it, and note the MPC and the multiplier.

**d.**   Finally, impose a progressive tax system such that the tax rate is zero percent when NNP is $100, 5 percent at $200, 10 percent at $300, 15 percent at $400, and so forth.  Determine and graph the new consumption schedule, noting the effect of this tax system on the MPC and the multiplier.

**e.**   Explain why the proportional and progressive tax systems contribute to greater economic stability, while the regressive system does not.  Demonstrate graphically.

**14**   *Advanced analysis.*  We can add the public sector to the private economy model of question 10 at the end of Chapter 12 as follows.  Assume $G = G_0 = 28$ and $T = T_0 = 30$.  Because of the presence of taxes, the consumption schedule, $C = 50 + 0.8Y$, must be modified to read $C = 50 + 0.8(Y - T)$, where the term $(Y - T)$ is disposable (after-tax) income. Assuming all taxes are on personal income, investment remains $I = I_0 = 30$. Using the equilibrium condition $Y = C_a + I + G$, determine the equilibrium level of income. Explain why the addition of the public budget with a slight surplus *increases* the equilibrium income. Now substitute $T = 0.2Y$ for $T = T_0 = 30$, and solve again for the level of income.

## Selected References

Blinder, Alan S.: *Fiscal Policy in Theory and Practice* (Morristown, N.J.: General Learning Press, 1973).
Carson, Robert B.: *Macroeconomic Issues Today: Alternative Approaches* (New York: St. Martin's Press, 1980), chaps. 2–4.
Committee on the Judiciary: *Balancing the Budget* (Washington, 1975).
*Economic Report of the President* (Washington, published annually).
Gordon, Robert J.: *Macroeconomics* (Boston, Mass.: Little, Brown and Company, 1978), chaps. 17 and 18.
Heilbroner, Robert L., and Peter L. Bernstein: *A Primer on Government Spending,* 2d ed. (New York: Vintage Books, Random House, Inc., 1970).
Okun, Arthur (ed.): *The Battle against Unemployment,* rev. ed. (New York: W. W. Norton & Company, Inc., 1972), parts 2 and 4.

# LAST WORD
## The Impotence of Fiscal Policy

Some economists feel that fiscal policy is an impotent and unpredictable stabilization tool.

The real question is whether or not conventional fiscal policy works as advertised.

If fiscal policy works, and its impact is properly measured by the size of the full employment deficit, then it should be possible to find some correlation between either the level or direction of the full employment budget and some measure of current or subsequent economic activity. George Terborgh tried to find some such link back in 1968, in *The New Economics,* but found only a weak correlation that turned out to be perverse. That is, larger full employment surpluses were associated with faster economic growth. More rigorous tests by economists at the St. Louis Fed, and again at Citibank, had no more luck in uncovering the magical properties of the full employment budget. A sharp shift toward larger full employment deficits did not prevent the recession of 1953–54, for example, nor the mini-recession of 1967. In 1946, a $60 billion reduction of Federal spending (equivalent to $400 billion today) was followed by a vigorous boom, and a combination of tax cuts and higher spending in 1948 (the equivalent of $75 billion today) was followed by a sharp recession.

The theory of fiscal policy is almost as messy as the evidence. If deficit spending is financed by borrowing from the private sector, there is no obvious stimulus—even to that undifferentiated thing called "demand." Whoever buys the government securities surrenders exactly as much purchasing power as is received by the beneficiaries of Federal largess. There would be a net fiscal stimulus only if there were no private demand for the funds needed to cover the added Treasury borrowing. Otherwise, lendable funds are just diverted from market-determined uses to politically-determined uses.

There *may* be a stimulus in some circumstances if the deficit is financed by a more rapid increase in the money supply, but this is really a monetary stimulus, not a purely fiscal effect.

In the long run, resources allocated through the government must displace those allocated through markets, and growth of government spending must be at the expense of the private sector. The government has only three sources of revenue—taxes, borrowing, and printing money—and increasing any one of those must reduce the private sector's command over real resources. Although deficit spending may at times be a short-run stimulus to nominal demand, it is also a long-run drag on real supply—siphoning resources from uses that would otherwise augment the economy's productive capacity, and instead diverting those resources into hand-to-mouth consumption through government salaries, subsidies, and transfer payments.

So, the theory and evidence suggests that fiscal policy is essentially impotent, or at least unpredictable, except as a device to promote inflationary monetary policy and/or to reduce investment and growth.

Alan Reynolds, "Full Employment Budget: How Good a Guide to Public Policy?" *Tax Review,* April 1977, pp. 14–15, abridged. Reprinted by permission of the Tax Foundation, Inc.

# MONEY,
# MONETARY POLICY,
# AND
# ECONOMIC STABILITY

# PART THREE

# Money and Banking in American Capitalism

chapter 14

Money—one of the truly great inventions of man—constitutes a most fascinating aspect of economic science.[1]

> Money bewitches people. They fret for it, and they sweat for it. They devise most ingenious ways to get it, and most ingenuous ways to get rid of it. Money is the only commodity that is good for nothing but to be gotten rid of. It will not feed you, clothe you, shelter you, or amuse you unless you spend it or invest it. It imparts value only in parting. People will do almost anything for money, and money will do almost anything for people. Money is a captivating, circulating, masquerading puzzle.

Money is also one of the most crucial elements of economic science. It is much more than a passive component of the economic system—a mere tool for facilitating the econo-

my's operation. When operating properly, the monetary system is the lifeblood of the circular flows of income and expenditure which typify all economies. A well-behaved money system is conducive to both full production and full employment. Conversely, a malfunctioning monetary system can make major contributions to severe fluctuations in the economy's levels of output, employment, and prices.

In this chapter we are concerned with the nature and functions of money and the basic institutions of the American banking system. Chapter 15 looks into the methods by which individual commercial banks and the banking system as a whole can vary the money supply. In Chapter 16 we discuss how the central banks of the economy attempt to regulate the supply of money so as to promote full employment and price level stability. Finally, Chapter 17 is devoted to *monetarism*—an alternative to the Keynesian macroeconomics of Chapters 11 through 13—which contends that

[1]Federal Reserve Bank of Philadelphia, "Creeping Inflation," *Business Review,* August 1957, p. 3.

267

the money supply is *the* key determinant of output, employment, and the price level.

The structure of the present chapter is as follows. We begin with a review of the functions of money and a discussion of the demand for money. Next, attention shifts to the supply of money as we pose a complicated question: What constitutes money in our economy? Third, we consider what "backs" the money supply in the United States. Finally, the institutional structure and the basic functions of the American banking system will be described.

## □   THE FUNCTIONS OF MONEY

What is money? Money is what money does. Anything that performs the functions of money is money. There are three functions of money:

**1**   First and foremost, money is a *medium of exchange;* that is, money is usable in buying and selling goods and services. As a medium of exchange, money allows society to escape the complications of barter and thereby to reap the benefits of geographic and human specialization (see Chapter 3).

**2**   Money is also a *standard of value.* Society finds it convenient to use the monetary unit as a yardstick for measuring the relative worth of heterogeneous goods and resources. This has obvious advantages. With a money system, we need not state the price of each product in terms of all other products for which it might possibly be exchanged; that is, we need not state the price of cows in terms of corn, cream, cigars, Chevrolets, cravats, or some other product. This use of money as a common denominator means that the price of each product need be stated *only* in terms of the monetary unit. By dramatically reducing the number of prices in the economy, this use of money permits transactors to readily compare the relative worth of various commodities and resources. Such comparisons facilitate

rational decision making. Recall from Chapter 9 the necessity of using money as a standard of value in measuring the GNP. Money is also used as a standard of value for transactions involving future payments. Debt obligations of all kinds are measured in terms of money.

**3**   Finally, money serves as a *store of value.* Because money is the most liquid of all assets, it is a very convenient form in which to store wealth. Though it does not yield monetary returns such as one gets by storing wealth in the form of real assets (property) or paper assets (stocks, bonds, and so forth), money does have the advantage of being immediately usable by a firm or a household in meeting any and all financial obligations.

## □   THE DEMAND FOR MONEY

These comments on the functions of money suggest two basic reasons why there is a demand for money, that is, why the public wants to hold money.

### △   Transactions Demand

The first reason, of course, is that people want money as a medium of exchange—as a means of conveniently negotiating the purchase of goods and services. Households must have enough money on hand to buy groceries and to pay mortgage and utility bills until the next paycheck is received. Similarly, businesses need money to pay for labor, materials, power, and so on. Money demanded for these purposes is simply called the *transactions demand* for money. Not surprisingly, the basic determinant of the amount of money demanded for transaction purposes is the level of money GNP. The larger the total money value of all goods and services exchanged in the economy, the larger will be the amount of money needed to negotiate these transactions. *The transactions demand for money varies directly with money GNP.* Note that we specify *money* GNP. Households and firms will want more money for transactions purposes if *either* prices rise *or* real output increases. In both instances there will be a larger dollar volume of transactions to negotiate.

△  **Asset Demand**

The second reason for holding money is rooted in the fact that money functions as a store of value. People may hold their financial assets in a variety of forms—for example, as corporate stocks, private or government bonds, or as money. (We will find momentarily that "money" is comprised of coins, paper currency, and bank checking accounts). Hence, there is an *asset demand* for money.

What determines the asset demand for money? To get at an answer we must first recognize that each of the various forms in which one's financial assets may be held has associated advantages and disadvantages. To simplify, let us compare holding bonds with holding money as an asset. The advantage of holding money is its liquidity; money is the most liquid of all assets in that it is immediately usable in the making of purchases. Obviously, money is an especially attractive asset to be holding when the prices of goods, services, and other financial assets are expected to decline. When the price of a bond falls, the bondholder suffers a loss. But lower prices mean that the money holder's dollars have increased in purchasing power. The disadvantage of holding money as an asset is that, in comparison with holding bonds, one does *not* earn interest income. Faced with this information, the problem is to decide how much of your financial assets to hold as bonds and how much as money. The solution depends primarily upon the rate of interest. Think of it this way: By holding money a household or business incurs an opportunity cost (Chapter 2). That is, by holding money one forgoes or sacrifices interest income. If a bond pays 9 percent interest, then it costs you $9 per year of forgone income to hold $100 as cash. It is no surprise that *the asset demand for money varies inversely with the rate of interest.* When the interest rate or opportunity cost of holding

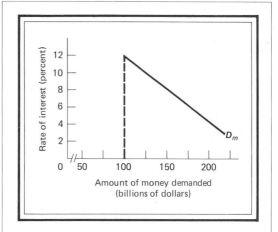

**FIGURE 14-1 THE DEMAND FOR MONEY**

The total demand for money is comprised of the transactions and asset demands. The transactions demand, which depends upon the money GNP rather than the interest rate, is represented by the dashed vertical line. The asset demand, which varies inversely with the interest rate, is added horizontally to the transactions demand to obtain total money demand, $D_m$.

money as an asset is low, the public will choose to hold a large amount of money as assets. Conversely, when the interest rate is high, it is costly to "be liquid" and the amount of assets held in the form of money will be small. Stated differently, when it is expensive to hold money as an asset, people will hold less of it; when money can be held cheaply, people will hold more of it.

△  **Total Money Demand**

Look now at Figure 14-1 where we bring together the two components of the demand for money. Here we portray the relationship between the total amount of money demanded *and the interest rate.* Because the transactions demand for money depends upon the level of money GNP and is independent of the interest rate, we show the transactions demand as a dashed vertical line. The amount of money demanded for transactions is assumed to be unrelated to changes in the rate of interest. Why have we located the transactions demand at $100 billion? While the specific choice of that amount is arbitrary, a rationale can be easily provided. For example, if each dollar held for transactions purposes is spent on the average three times per year *and* money GNP is assumed to be $300 billion, then the public would obviously need $100 billion of money to purchase that GNP.

We have just explained that the asset demand for money varies inversely with the interest rate. This relationship is reflected in the downsloping solid line in Figure 14-1. Note that we have added the asset demand horizontally to the dashed transactions demand for money. Therefore, the solid line labeled $D_m$ represents the *total* demand for money. This line represents the total amount of money the public will want to hold for transactions and as an asset at each possible interest rate. Further note that a change in the money GNP—working through the transactions demand for money—will cause the total money demand curve to shift. Specifically, an increase in money GNP will mean that the public will want to hold a larger amount of money for transactions purposes and this will shift the money demand curve to the right. For example, if the money GNP increases from $300 to $450 billion and we continue to suppose that the average dollar held for transactions is spent three times per year, then the transactions demand line will shift from $100 to $150 billion. As a result, the total money demand curve will lie $50 billion further to the right at each possible interest rate than was formerly the case. Conversely, a decline in money GNP will shift the total money demand curve to the left.

We will return to the demand for money later (Chapter 16) for reasons you might have already anticipated. After developing the concept of the supply of money in this and the following chapter, the demand for and the supply of money will be brought together to explain the functioning of the money market and the determination of the equilibrium rate of interest.

**TABLE 14-1**
Money in the United States, November 1979

| Money | Billions of dollars | Percent of total |
|---|---|---|
| Coins and paper money | $106 | 28 |
| Demand deposits | 273 | 72 |
| Total $M_1$ | $379 | 100 |

*Source: Federal Reserve Bulletin,* January 1980.

## □  THE SUPPLY OF MONEY

Let us now consider the supply of money. Historically, such diverse items as whales' teeth, elephant tail bristles, circular stones, nails, slaves, cattle, beer, cigarettes, and pieces of metal have functioned as media of exchange. Currently, in our economy the debts of governments and of banks are employed as money.

### △  Money Defined: $M_1$

Economists are not in agreement as to what specific items constitute the economy's money supply. Narrowly defined—and designated as $M_1$—the money supply is composed of three items: (1) coins, (2) paper money, and (3) demand deposits, or checking accounts. The first two items are debts of government and governmental agencies; the third represents a debt of commercial banks. Table 14-1 gives us an idea of the quantitative importance of these items in both absolute and relative terms. Let us comment briefly on each of these components of the money supply.

**Coins**  Ranging from copper pennies to silver dollars, coins constitute the "small change" of our money supply. Coins are a very small portion of our total money supply. Currently, about $9 or $10 billion worth of coins are in circulation, amounting to only 2 or 3 percent of the total money supply. Coins are essentially "convenience money" in that they permit us to make all kinds of very small purchases.

It is notable that all coins in circulation in

the United States are *token money*. This simply means that the *intrinsic value*—that is, the value of the bullion contained in the coin itself—is less than the face value of the coin. This is purposely the case so as to avoid the melting down of token money for profitable sale as bullion. If our 50-cent pieces each contained, say, 75 cents' worth of silver bullion, it would be highly profitable to melt these coins for sale as bullion. Despite the illegality of such a procedure, 50-cent pieces would tend to disappear from circulation. This is one of the potential defects of commodity money: Its worth as a commodity may come to exceed its worth as money, causing it to cease functioning as a medium of exchange.

**Paper Money**  Much more significant than coins, paper money constitutes about 25 or 26 percent of the economy's money supply. Virtually all this $96 or $97 billion of paper currency is in the form of *Federal Reserve Notes,* that is, notes which have been issued by the Federal Reserve Banks with the authorization of Congress. The coin and paper money components of the money supply are frequently lumped together and simply labeled *currency.*

**Demand Deposits**  The safety and convenience of using checks, or bank money, have made demand deposits (checking accounts) the most important type of money in the United States. Despite the integrity of our postal employees, one would not think of stuffing, say, $4,896.47 in an envelope and dropping it in a mailbox to pay a debt; but to write and mail a check for a large sum is commonplace. A check must be endorsed by the person cashing it; the drawer of the check subsequently receives the canceled check as an endorsed receipt attesting to the fulfillment of the obligation. Similarly, because the writing of a check requires endorsement by the drawer, the theft or loss of one's bankbook is not nearly so ca-

lamitous as would be the loss of an identical amount of currency. It is, furthermore, more convenient to write a check in many cases than it is to transport and count out a large sum of currency. For all these reasons, checkbook money has come to be the dominant form of money in American capitalism. Even Table 14-1 belittles the significance of bank money; it is estimated that in dollar value, about 90 percent of all transactions are carried out by the use of checks.

It might seem strange that demand deposits or checking accounts are a part of the money supply. But the reason for their inclusion is clear: Checks, which are nothing more than a means for transferring the ownership of demand deposits, are generally acceptable as a medium of exchange.[2] Furthermore, demand deposits can be immediately converted into paper money and coins on demand; checks drawn upon demand deposits are for all practical purposes the equivalent of currency.

To summarize:

Money, $M_1$ = demand deposits + currency

Currency is essentially government-created money, and demand deposits, we shall discover in Chapter 15, are bank-created money.

**Qualification**  A technical qualification of our definition of money must be added: Currency and demand deposits owned by government (the Treasury) and by Federal Reserve or commercial banks are excluded. This exclusion is partly to avoid overstating the money supply and partly because money in the possession of households and businesses—that is, "in circulation"—is more relevant to the level of spending in the economy.[3]

△ **Near-Monies and $M_2$**

But the line between what we have de-

---

[2]As a stop at any gas station will verify, checks are somewhat less generally acceptable as a medium of exchange than is currency!

fined as money and certain other highly liquid assets called "near-monies" is a fine one. *Near-monies* are certain financial assets such as time deposits and certain government bonds which, although they do not directly function as a medium of exchange, can be readily converted into currency or demand deposits. The most important near-money is commercial bank time deposits (savings accounts). By adding these deposits to our $M_1$ definition we obtain a broader and quantitatively enlarged definition of the money supply which we will label $M_2$. In November of 1979 these time deposits amounted to $564 billion. Adding these to $M_1$ yields an $M_2$ money supply of $943 billion.

Proponents of the $M_1$ definition reject the inclusion of time deposits on the grounds that an asset, to be money, must be *directly and immediately* usable as a medium of exchange. On the other hand, the case for the broader $M_2$ definition has been strengthened in recent years both by legislative action and technological innovations which have blurred the distinction between time and demand deposits. With the customer's authorization, a bank can now automatically transfer funds from the customer's time deposit to his or her demand deposit when the latter falls below some agreed-upon level. Thus, the "moneyness" of time deposits has been increased. Similarly, savings and loan associations have developed

what are called *NOW* (negotiable order of withdrawal) *accounts* which in effect are checking accounts based upon the time deposits held by those associations. These same thrift institutions have developed telephone bill–paying services which perform essentially the same medium of exchange function as checks, except disbursements are made out of savings accounts rather than checking accounts.

We will adopt and employ the traditional narrow $M_1$ in our ensuing discussion and analysis. But it is recognized that (1) the definition of money is controversial, and (2) as the relatively new innovations outlined above become more widely used the case for a broader definition of money becomes stronger.

Near-monies are important to our discussion for several related reasons.

**1**  The fact that people have such highly liquid assets available affects their consuming-saving habits. Generally speaking, the greater the amount of financial wealth people have in the form of near-monies, the greater is their willingness to spend out of their money incomes.

**2**  The conversion of near-monies into money or vice versa can affect the stability of the economy. For example, during the prosperity-inflationary phase of the business cycle, a significant conversion of time deposits into demand deposits or currency adds to the money supply and, if not offset, could enhance inflationary pressures.

**3**  The specific definition of money adopted is important for purposes of monetary policy. For example, the money supply as measured by $M_1$ might be constant, while money defined as $M_2$ might be increasing. Now, if the monetary authorities feel it is appropriate to have an expanding supply of money, acceptance of our narrow $M_1$ definition would call for specific actions to increase currency and demand deposits. But acceptance of the broader $M_2$ definition would suggest that the desired expansion of the money supply is

---

[3] A paper dollar in the hands of John Doe obviously constitutes just $1 of the money supply. But, if we were to count dollars held by banks as a part of the money supply, that same $1 would count for $2 when deposited in a commercial bank. It would count for a $1 demand deposit owned by Doe and also for $1 worth of currency resting in the bank's vault. This problem of double counting can be avoided by excluding currency resting in commercial banks (and currency redeposited in the Federal Reserve Banks or other commercial banks) in determining the total money supply. The exclusion of currency held by, and demand deposits owned by, government is somewhat more arbitrary. The major reason for this exclusion is that it permits us better to gauge the money supply and rate of spending which occurs in the private sector of the economy apart from spending initiated by government policy.

already taking place and that no specific policy action is required.

## ☐ WHAT "BACKS" THE MONEY SUPPLY?

This is a slippery question; any reasonably complete answer is likely to be at odds with the preconceptions many of us hold with respect to money.

### △ Money as Debt

The first point to recognize is that the major components of the money supply—paper money and demand deposits—are debts, or promises to pay. Paper money is the circulating debt of the Federal Reserve Banks. Demand deposits are the debts of commercial banks.

Furthermore, paper currency and demand deposits have no intrinsic value. A $5 bill is just a piece of paper, and a demand deposit is merely a bookkeeping entry. And coins, we already know, have an intrinsic value less than their face value. Nor will government redeem the paper money you hold for anything tangible, such as gold. In effect, we have wisely chosen to "manage" our money supply in seeking to provide the amount of money needed for that particular volume of business activity which one hopes will foster full employment, price level stability, and a healthy rate of economic growth. Such management of the money supply is eminently more sensible than linking the money supply to gold or any other commodity whose supply might arbitrarily and capriciously change. After all, a substantial increase in the nation's gold stock as the result of mining or importation might increase the money supply far beyond that amount needed to transact a full-employment level of business activity and therefore might result in sharp inflation. Conversely, the historical decline in domestic gold production or the loss of gold in settling international transactions (Chapters 43 and 44) could reduce the domestic money supply to the point where economic activity was choked off and unemployment and a retarded growth rate resulted. The important point is that paper money cannot be converted into a fixed amount of gold or some other precious metal but is exchangeable only for other pieces of paper money. The government will swap one paper $5 bill for another bearing a different serial number. That is all you can get should you ask the government to redeem some of the paper money you hold. Similarly, demand-deposit money cannot be exchanged for gold but only for paper money, which, as we have just seen, will not be redeemed by the government for anything tangible. The Last Word segment of this chapter merits a careful reading at this point.

### △ Value of Money

If currency and demand deposits have no intrinsic characteristics which give them value *and* if they are not backed by gold or other precious metals, then why are they money? A reasonably complete answer to this question involves three points.

**1  Acceptability**  Currency and demand deposits are money for the simple reason they are accepted as such. By virtue of long-standing business practice, currency and demand deposits perform the basic function of money; they are acceptable as a medium of exchange. Suppose you swap a $10 bill for a shirt or blouse at a clothing store. Why does the merchant accept this piece of paper in exchange for some product? The answer is curious: The merchant accepts paper money because he or she is confident that others will also be willing to accept it in exchange for goods and services. The merchant knows that one can purchase the services of clerks, acquire products from wholesalers, pay the rent on one's store, and so forth. Each of us accepts paper money in exchange because we have confidence that it will be exchangeable for real goods and services when we choose to spend it.

**2  Legal Tender**  Our confidence in the acceptability of paper money is partly a matter of law; currency has been designated as *legal tender* by government. This means that paper currency must be accepted in the payment of a debt or the creditor forfeits the privilege of charging interest and the right to sue the debtor for nonpayment. Put more bluntly, the acceptability of paper dollars is bolstered by the fact that government says these dollars are money. The paper money in our economy is basically *fiat money;* it is money because the government says it is, not because of redeemability in terms of some precious metal. The general acceptability of currency is also bolstered by the willingness of government to accept it in the payment of taxes and other obligations due the government.

Lest we be overimpressed by the power of government, it should be noted that the fact that paper currency is generally accepted in exchange is decidedly more important than government's legal tender decree in making these pieces of paper function as money. Indeed, the government has *not* decreed checks to be legal tender, but they nevertheless successfully perform the vast bulk of the economy's exchanges of goods, services, and resources.

**3  Relative Scarcity**  At a more fundamental level, the value of money, like the economic value of anything else, is essentially a supply and demand phenomenon. That is, money derives its value from its scarcity relative to its usefulness. The usefulness of money, of course, lies in its unique capacity to be exchanged for goods and services, either now or in the future. The economy's demand for money thus depends upon its total dollar volume of transactions in any given time period plus the amount of money individuals and businesses want to hold for possible future transactions. Given a reasonably constant demand for money, the value or "purchasing power" of the monetary unit will be determined by the supply of money. Let us see why this is so.

△  **Money and Prices**

The real value or purchasing power of money is the amount of goods and services a unit of money will buy. It is obvious, furthermore, that the amount a dollar will buy varies inversely with the price level; stated differently, a reciprocal relationship exists between the general price level and the value of the dollar. Figure 14-2 allows us to visualize this inverse relationship.[4] When the consumer price index or "cost-of-living" index goes up, the purchasing power of the dollar necessarily goes down, and vice versa. Higher prices lower the value of the dollar because more dollars will now be needed to command a given amount of goods and services. Conversely, lower prices increase the purchasing power of the dollar because you will now need fewer dollars to obtain a given quantity of goods and services. If the price level doubles, the value of the dollar will decline by one-half, or 50 percent. If the price level falls by one-half, or 50 percent, the purchasing power of the dollar will double.[5]

You have probably heard or read of situations wherein a nation's currency became worthless and unacceptable in exchange. Indeed, we noted several in Chapter 10. With few exceptions these were situations where government issued so many pieces of paper currency that the value of each of these units of money was almost totally undermined. The infamous post-World War I inflation in Germany is a notable example. In December of 1919 there

---

[4] Figure 14-2 is called a "ratio" or "semi-log" chart because equal vertical distances measure equal percentage changes rather than equal absolute changes.
[5] The arithmetic of this relationship is slightly more complex than these examples suggest. If we let $P$ equal the price level expressed as an index number and $D$ equal the value of the dollar, then our reciprocal relationship is

$$D = \frac{1}{P}$$

*If $P$ equals 1.00, then $D$ obviously is 1.00. But if the price level rises to 1.20, then $D$ will be .83⅓. Hence, a 20 percent *increase* in the price level will cause a 16⅔ percent *decline* in the value of the dollar.

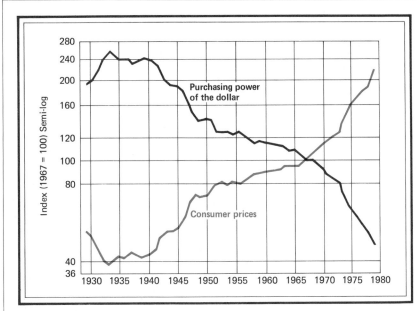

**FIGURE 14-2 THE PRICE LEVEL AND THE VALUE OF MONEY**

A reciprocal or inverse relationship exists between the general price level and the purchasing power of the dollar.

were about 50 billion marks in circulation. Exactly four years later this figure had expanded to 496,585,345,900 billion marks! The result? The German mark in 1923 was worth an infinitesimal fraction of its 1919 value.[6] Inflation, you will recall, is frequently the consequence of society's spending beyond its capacity to produce. Other things being equal, increases in the money supply tend to increase total spending. Once full employment is reached and total output becomes virtually fixed, this added spending can only serve to make prices spiral up. The shirt which sold for $10 in our earlier illustration may, after severe inflation, cost $100. This means that the dollar, which was formerly worth one-tenth of a shirt, is now worth just one-hundredth of a shirt. The dollar's value, or purchasing power, has obviously been reduced to 10 percent of its former value by inflation.

How might inflation and the accompanying decreases in the value of the dollar affect

[6] Frank G. Graham, *Exchange, Prices and Production in Hyperinflation Germany, 1920–1923* (Princeton, N.J.: Princeton University Press, 1930), p. 13.

the acceptability of paper dollars as money? Households and businesses are willing to accept paper currency as a medium of exchange so long as they know it can in turn be spent by them without any noticeable loss in its purchasing power. But, with spiraling inflation, this is not the case. Runaway inflation, such as Germany faced in the early 1920s, may significantly depreciate the value of money between the time of its receipt and its expenditure. Money will be "hot" money. It is as if the government were constantly taxing away the purchasing power of dollars. Rapid depreciation of the value of the dollar may cause it to cease functioning as a medium of exchange. Businesses and households may refuse to accept paper money in exchange because they do not want to bear the loss in its value which will occur while it is in their possession. (All this despite the fact that government says the paper currency is legal tender!) Without an acceptable medium of exchange, the economy will revert to inefficient barter.

Similarly, people are willing to use money as a store of value so long as there is no unreasonable deterioration in the value of those stored dollars because of inflation. And the economy can effectively employ the monetary unit as a standard of value only when its purchasing power is relatively stable. A yardstick of value which is subject to drastic shrinkage no longer permits buyers and sellers to establish clearly the terms of trade. When the value of the dollar is declining rapidly, sellers will not know what to charge and buyers will not know what to pay for the various goods and services.

△  **Managing Money**

The overriding implication of this discussion of the value of money is this: The major "backing" of paper money is the government's ability to keep the value of money reasonably stable. This entails (1) appropriate fiscal policy, as explained in Chapter 13, and (2) intelligent management or regulation of the money supply, as noted above. The acceptability of paper money depends in part upon sound management of the monetary system and in part upon the pursuit of appropriate fiscal measures by government. Businesses and households accept paper money in exchange for goods and services so long as it will command a roughly equivalent amount of goods and services when they in turn spend it. In our economy a blending of legislation, government policy, and social practice serves as a bulwark against any imprudent expansion of the money supply which might jeopardize money's value in exchange.

What we have said with respect to paper currency also applies to demand-deposit money. In this case money is the debt of the commercial banks. If you have a checking account worth $100, this merely means that your commercial bank is indebted to you for that number of dollars. You can collect this debt in one of two ways. You can go to the bank and demand paper currency for your demand deposit; this simply amounts to changing the debts you hold from bank debts to government-issued debts. Or, and this is

more likely, you can "collect" the debt which the bank owes you by transferring this claim by check to someone else. For example, if you buy a $100 suit from your clothier, you can pay for it by writing a check, which transfers the bank's indebtedness from you to your clothier. The bank now owes your clothier the $100 which it previously owed to you. Why does the clothier accept this transfer of indebtedness (the check) as a medium of exchange? Because the clothier can convert it into currency on demand or can in turn transfer the debt to others in making purchases of his or her choice. Thus checks, as means of transferring bank debts, are acceptable as money because of the commercial banks' ability to honor these claims.

In turn, the ability of commercial banks to honor claims against them depends upon their not creating too many of these claims. We shall find in a moment that a decentralized system of private, profit-seeking banks does not contain sufficient safeguards against the creation of too much check money. Hence, the American banking system has a substantial amount of centralization and governmental control to guard against the imprudent creation of check money by commercial banks.

Caution: These comments are not to be interpreted to mean that in practice the supplies of currency and demand-deposit money have been judiciously controlled so as to achieve a high degree of economic stability. Indeed, some economists allege that our inflationary woes of the past ten or fifteen years are largely the consequence of imprudent increases in the money supply!

△  **Recap**

Let us summarize the major points of this section:

**1**  In the United States and other advanced economies, all money is essentially the debts of government and commercial banks.

**2**  These debts efficiently perform the functions of money so long as their value, or purchasing power, is relatively stable.

**3** The value of money is no longer rooted in carefully defined quantities of precious metals, but rather, in the amount of goods and services money will purchase in the marketplace.

**4** Government's responsibility in stabilizing the value of the monetary unit involves (1) the application of appropriate fiscal policies, and (2) effective control over the supply of money.

## □ INSTITUTIONAL FRAMEWORK OF THE AMERICAN BANKING SYSTEM

We have noted that the major component of the money supply, demand deposits, is created by commercial banks and that government-created money, coins and paper currency, typically comes into circulation through the commercial banks. It is essential, then, that we take a thorough look at the framework of the American banking system prior to a detailed analysis in Chapter 15 of how commercial banks create money.

### △ Need for Centralization

It became painfully apparent rather early in American history that, like it or not, centralization and public control were prerequisites of an efficient banking system. Congress became increasingly aware of this about the turn of the twentieth century. Decentralized banking fostered the inconvenience and confusion of a heterogeneous currency, monetary mismanagement, and an inflexible supply of money. The last-mentioned problem was particularly acute. A dynamic and growing economy demands a flexible money supply—one which will respond to the economy's varying needs. The volume of trade expands and contracts unevenly and irregularly; hence, the supply of money must be elastic in meeting the needs of the economy. "Too much" money can precipitate dangerous inflationary problems; "too little" money can stunt the economy's

growth by hindering the production and exchange of goods and services. The United States and innumerable foreign countries have learned through bitter experience that a decentralized banking system is not likely to provide that particular money supply which is most conducive to the welfare of the economy as a whole.

An unusually acute money panic in 1907 was the straw that broke Congress's back. A National Monetary Commission was established to study the monetary and banking problems of the economy and to outline a course of action for Congress. The end result was the Federal Reserve Act of 1913.

### △ Structure of the Federal Reserve System

The banking system which has developed under the frequently amended Federal Reserve Act is sketched in Figure 14-3. It is important

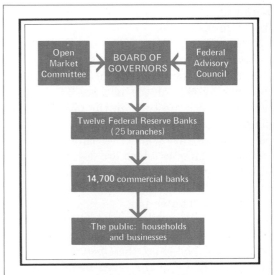

**FIGURE 14-3 FRAMEWORK OF THE FEDERAL RESERVE SYSTEM AND ITS RELATIONSHIP TO THE PUBLIC**

With the advice and counsel of the Open Market Committee and the Federal Advisory Council, the Board of Governors makes the basic policy decisions which regulate our money and banking systems. These decisions are made effective through the twelve Federal Reserve Banks.

that we understand the nature and functions of the various segments which compose the banking system and the relationships which the parts bear to one another.

**Board of Governors**  The kingpin of our money and banking system is the Board of Governors of the Federal Reserve System. The seven members of this Board are appointed by the President with the confirmation of the Senate. Terms are long—fourteen years—and staggered so that one member is replaced every two years. The intention is to provide the Board with continuity and experienced membership. The Board is staffed by appointment rather than elections in an attempt to divorce monetary policy from partisan politics. An important argument for this philosophy of independence currently is that it is politically expedient for the administration in power to invoke expansionary fiscal policies—tax cuts and pork-barrel spending tend to win votes—and the monetary authorities can offset the resulting inflation only if it is independent of the administration.

The Board of Governors has the responsibility of exercising general supervision and control over the operation of the money and banking system of the nation. The Board's actions, which are to be in the public interest and designed to promote the general economic welfare, are made effective through certain control techniques which are designed to alter the money supply. The character and functioning of these control mechanisms will be detailed in Chapter 16.

Two important bodies assist the Board of Governors in determining basic banking policy. On the one hand, the *Open Market Committee,* made up of the seven members of the Board plus five of the presidents of the Federal Reserve Banks, sets the System's policy with respect to the purchase and sale of government bonds in the open market. These open-market operations constitute the most significant technique by which the monetary authorities can affect the money supply (Chapter 16). On the other hand, the *Federal Advisory Council* is composed of twelve prominent commercial bankers, one selected annually by each of the twelve Federal Reserve Banks. The Council meets periodically with the Board of Governors to voice its views on banking policy. However, as its name indicates, the Council is purely advisory; it has no policy-making powers.

**The Twelve Federal Reserve Banks**  The twelve Federal Reserve Banks have three major characteristics. They are (1) central banks, (2) quasi-public banks, and (3) bankers' banks.

*1   Central banks*  Most Americans are blessed with a more-or-less inherent fear of centralization. As a result, our banking system is less centralized than most of the other advanced economies of the world. As a matter of fact, the Federal Reserve Act was a compromise between exponents of centralization and advocates of decentralization. Hence, instead of creating a single central bank, the act divided the nation into twelve districts and provided for a Federal Reserve Bank to function as a central bank in each of these districts. Figure 14-4 shows these twelve Federal Reserve districts. Geographic considerations were also of significance in the creation of the Federal Reserve Banks. It was felt that a single central bank would be unresponsive to the peculiar economic problems faced by the various regions of the economy. In any event, the net result is that the twelve Federal Reserve Banks make up the central banking system of the economy. It is through these central banks that the basic policy directives of the Board of Governors are made effective. The Federal Reserve Bank of New York City is by far the most important of these central banks. The development of modern communication and transportation facilities has undoubtedly lessened the geographic need for a system of regional banks.

*2   Quasi-public banks*  The twelve Federal Reserve Banks are quasi-public banks.

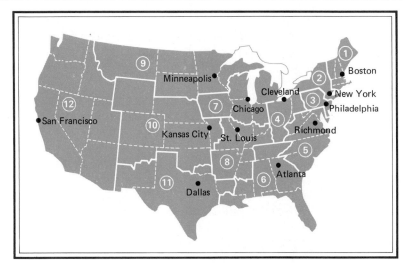

**FIGURE 14-4  THE TWELVE SERVE DISTRICTS**

The Federal Reserve System divides the United States into twelve districts, each of which has one central bank and in some instances one or more branches of the central bank. Hawaii and Alaska are included in the twelfth district. (*Federal Reserve Bulletin.*)

They reflect an interesting blend of private ownership and public control. The Federal Reserve Banks are owned by the member banks in their districts. Upon joining the Federal Reserve System, commercial banks are required to purchase shares of stock in the Federal Reserve Bank in their district. But the basic policies which the Federal Reserve Banks pursue are set by a public body—the Board of Governors. The central banks of American capitalism are privately owned but governmentally controlled.

The fact that the Federal Reserve Banks are essentially public institutions is vitally important to an understanding of their operation. In particular, it must be emphasized that the Federal Reserve Banks are not motivated by profits, as are private enterprises. The policies followed by the central banks are those designed to promote the economic well-being of the economy as a whole. Hence, the activities of the Federal Reserve Banks will frequently be at odds with the profit motive.[7]

[7]Though it is not their basic goal, the Federal Reserve Banks have actually operated profitably, largely as the result of Treasury debts held by them. A part of the profits has been used to pay 6 percent dividends to member banks on their holdings of stock; the bulk of the remaining profits has been turned over to the United States Treasury.

Furthermore, the Federal Reserve Banks are not in competition with commercial banks. With rare exceptions, the Federal Reserve Banks do not deal with the public, but rather, with the government and the commercial banks.

*3  Bankers' banks*  Finally, the Federal Reserve Banks are frequently called "bankers' banks." This is a shorthand way of saying that the Federal Reserve Banks perform essentially the same functions for commercial banks as commercial banks perform for the public. Just as commercial banks accept the deposits of and make loans to the public, so the central banks accept the deposits of and make loans to commercial banks. But the Federal Reserve Banks have a third function which commercial banks no longer perform: the function of issuing currency. Congress has authorized the Federal Reserve Banks to put into circulation Federal Reserve Notes, which constitute the economy's paper money supply.

**The Commercial Banks**  The workhorses of the American banking system are its 14,698 commercial banks. The majority of these are *state banks,* that is, private banks operating under state charters. But a good many have received their charters from the Federal government; that is, they are *national banks.* Less than 40 percent of all existing commercial banks are members of the Federal Reserve System. The 4616 national banks of our economy are required by law to join the Federal Reserve System; the remaining 10,082 state banks have the option of joining or declining to do so. As Figure 14-5 indicates, 1005 of the state banks have chosen to join the Federal Reserve System.

These statistics, however, tend to underestimate grossly the significance of the Federal Reserve System. Virtually all the larger commercial banks are members of the System, nonmembers being the smaller "country banks," for the most part. Thus, about 75 percent of all deposits held by the commercial banking system rest in member banks. In addition, nonmember banks can participate on a limited basis in the functioning of the Federal Reserve System. For example, nonmember banks can avail themselves of the Federal Reserve System's program for the efficient collection of checks.

Commercial banks, as already noted, have two basic functions. First, they hold the money deposits of businesses and households. Second, commercial banks make loans to the public, and in so doing, increase the economy's supply of money. Detailed analysis of these functions is the main objective of Chapter 15.

**Financial Intermediaries**   Although the present analysis will be concerned only with ordinary commercial banks, it is important to recognize that the commercial banking system is thoroughly supplemented by a diverse group of specialized banking and financial institutions. For example, savings banks and savings and loan associations accept the funds of relatively small savers as time deposits and make these funds available to investors by extending mortgage loans or by purchasing marketable securities. Investment banks, on the other hand, perform the task of marketing the newly issued bonds and stocks of corporations which desire funds for capital expansion. Insurance companies accept huge volumes of savings in the form of premiums on insurance policies and annuities and use these funds, wholly or in part, to buy a variety of private, corporate, and government securities. This listing of banking and financial institutions is not exhaustive.

All banking and financial institutions, including commercial banks, have one point in common: They are all dealers in credit or debt. *These individual institutions lend the funds deposited with them or acquired by them, receiving credit instruments—bonds, stocks, mortgages, or promissory notes—in return.* These institutions play a significant role in the economy, functioning as *financial intermediaries* between savers and investors. But, as we saw in Part 2, their operation falls short of perfection. These financial intermediaries do *not* provide for an exact and continuing

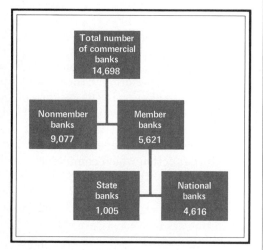

**FIGURE 14-5  THE CLASSIFICATION OF COMMERCIAL BANKS, JUNE 1978**

Less than half of all commercial banks are members of the Federal Reserve System. However, these member banks hold about 75 percent of all commercial bank deposits. (*Federal Reserve Bulletin.*)

balance of investment spending and the full-employment volume of saving.

**A Critical Distinction** Commercial banks, accepting both time and demand deposits and using the proceeds wholly or in part to acquire income-earning securities, function as intermediaries between savers and investors. But commercial banks also perform an additional function which other banking and financial institutions do not. That unique function is *to create money by extending bank credit—that is, by making loans—to businesses and households.* Other financial institutions can only *transfer* money from savers to spenders. In doing so they do not affect the total supply of money available. Commercial banks, however, can *create* demand-deposit money and make it available for use by potential spenders. Banks are by no means totally dependent upon the deposits of savers in making money available to spenders. Within limits, commercial banks can create the money which spenders desire. Generally speaking, it works this way: Banks accept the credit of borrowing individuals and businesses (their promissory notes) and give these borrowers bank credit (demand deposits) in return. By exchanging debts that are not money (promissory notes) for debts that are money (demand deposits), commercial banks perform the unique function of increasing the money supply. In retiring bank credit, commercial banks decrease the money supply. The mechanics of these transactions will be studied in some detail in the ensuing chapter. At this juncture, the basic point to recognize is this: *Because of their money-creating and money-destroying abilities, commercial banks are unique and highly strategic institutions in our economy.* Commercial banks play a particularly vital role in affecting the volume of money and hence the levels of spending, output, employment, and prices. Therefore, our attention is centered upon the functioning of commercial banks as opposed to the other financial intermediaries mentioned earlier.

△ **Functions of the Federal Reserve System**[8]

The Federal Reserve System—in particular, the twelve Federal Reserve Banks and the Board of Governors—was established to achieve certain definite objectives. These goals stem largely from the defects inherent in the system of uncoordinated state and national banks which prevailed prior to the passage of the Federal Reserve Act.

**Holding the Deposits of Member Banks** Federal Reserve Banks hold the deposits, or *reserves,* of member banks. Private businesses and individuals find it convenient to establish checking accounts at commercial banks. These accounts are simply reserves of funds which the owner more or less regularly draws upon and occasionally replenishes. In the same manner, member banks keep reserves—that is, money deposits—with the Federal Reserve Bank of their district. When in need of currency, the commercial banks can, within limits, draw upon these reserves. When in possession of surplus cash, commercial banks may deposit this extra currency in their reserves. Much of the daily work of the Federal Reserve Banks is concerned with increasing and decreasing the reserves of commercial banks as routine banking transactions occur.

**Supplying the Economy with Paper Currency** It is also the responsibility of the Federal Reserve Banks to supply the economy with needed paper currency or, more specifically, Federal Reserve Notes. As the fountainhead of the economy's paper money supply, the Federal Reserve Banks function as a reservoir of cash. When the economy needs more currency, the reservoir is opened and currency spills into the economy. When the economy has more currency than it desires to hold, the excess is channeled back into the reservoir.

[8] For a more detailed look at the service functions of the Federal Reserve Banks, see Board of Governors of the Federal Reserve System, *The Federal Reserve System: Purposes and Functions,* 6th ed. (1974), chaps. 1, 2, 7.

The commercial banks act as intermediaries between the public and the Federal Reserve Banks in each case. Specifically, it works something like this: During the Christmas buying rush, for example, the public wants more currency in circulation. To get this additional cash, individuals and businesses cash checks at the commercial banks. This lowers the amounts of currency resting in bank vaults. Commercial banks then turn to the bankers' banks and draw checks against their deposits (reserves) with the Federal Reserve Banks to replenish their vault cash. After the Christmas rush has subsided, less currency is needed. The public deposits this extra currency in their bank accounts. As a result, commercial banks find they have an overabundant stock of currency in their vaults. They deposit their surplus cash in the Federal Reserve Banks, thereby increasing their reserves.

### Providing for the Collection of Checks

As previously noted, a check is merely a written order which the drawer may use in making a purchase or paying a debt. A check is collected, or "cleared," when one or more banks negotiate a transfer of part of the drawer's checking account, or demand deposit, to the demand deposit of a recipient of the check. If Jones and Smith have checking accounts in the same commercial bank and Jones gives Smith a $10 check, Smith can collect this check by taking it to the commercial bank, where his account will be increased by $10 and Jones's reduced by $10. In many cases, however, the drawer and the receiver of a check will be located in different towns or different states and therefore have their accounts in commercial banks far distant from one another. An important function of the Federal Reserve Banks is to provide facilities for the rapid collection of checks where the banks of the drawer and the receiver are geographically remote. The mechanics of check collecting and its effect upon the financial position of commercial banks will be outlined in detail in the next chapter.

### Acting as Fiscal Agents for Government

The Federal Reserve Banks act as bankers and fiscal agents for the Federal government. The Federal government collects huge sums through taxation, spends equally astronomical amounts, and sells and redeems bonds. Naturally, the government wants to avail itself of banking facilities in carrying out these functions. Hence, the bankers' banks hold a part of the Treasury's checking accounts, aid the government in collecting various tax revenues, and administer the sale and redemption of government bonds.

### Supervising Member Banks

The Federal Reserve Banks supervise the operations of member banks. A banking system stands or falls on the financial soundness of the individual commercial banks of which it is composed. Unsound banking practices can have widespread repercussions, to the point of threatening the financial structure of the entire economy. Since commercial banking is "vested with a public interest," it has been subject to government supervision.

The Federal Reserve has supervisory powers over all member commercial banks.[9] This supervision usually takes the form of periodic, unannounced examinations of the commercial banks. Banks which do not conform to the standards set forth by the Federal Reserve authorities may be denied the privilege of borrowing from the Federal Reserve Banks, and in extreme cases the officers and directors of offending banks may be removed by the Board of Governors.

### Regulating the Supply of Money

Finally—and most important of all—the Federal

[9]The Federal Reserve is not alone in the task of supervision. The individual states supervise all banks which they charter. The Comptroller of the Currency supervises all national banks. Finally, the Federal Deposit Insurance Corporation has the power to supervise all banks whose deposits it insures. Hence, a member national bank which belongs to the FDIC will be subject to three supervisory agencies—the Federal Reserve, the Comptroller of the Currency, and the FDIC.

Reserve System has ultimate responsibility for regulating the supply of money. *The major task of the Federal Reserve authorities is to manage the money supply in accordance with the needs of the economy as a whole.* In the normally dynamic and expanding economy of American capitalism, this task entails making that amount of money available which is consistent with high and steadily rising levels of output and employment and a relatively constant price level.

Whereas all the other functions are of a more-or-less routine or service nature, the goal of correctly managing the money supply entails the making of basic and unique policy decisions of a nonroutine character. Chapter 16 discusses Federal Reserve monetary policy and its effectiveness in achieving economic stability in a growing economy. But before we turn to that subject we must understand how banks create money.

## Summary

1   Anything that functions as *a.* a medium of exchange, *b.* a standard of value, and *c.* a store of value is money.

2   The total demand for money is comprised of the transactions and asset demands for money. The transactions demand varies directly with money GNP; the asset demand varies inversely with the interest rate.

3   Most economists define money as demand deposits plus currency (coins and paper money) in circulation ($M_1$). Demand deposits, the largest component of the money supply, are money because they can be spent by writing checks against them. Some economists feel that time deposits (savings accounts) are also money and should be added to currency and demand deposits ($M_2$).

4   Money, which is essentially the debts of government and commercial banks, has value because of the goods and services which it will command in the market. Maintenance of the purchasing power of money depends to a considerable degree upon the effectiveness with which government manages the money supply.

5   The American banking system is composed of *a.* the Board of Governors of the Federal Reserve System, *b.* the twelve Federal Reserve Banks, and *c.* some 14,700 commercial banks. The Board of Governors is the basic policy-making body for the entire banking system. The directives of the Board are made effective through the twelve Federal Reserve Banks, which are simultaneously *a.* central banks, *b.* quasi-public banks, and *c.* bankers' banks. The commercial banks of the economy perform the tasks of accepting money deposits and making loans. In lending, commercial banks create demand deposits, and are, therefore, money-creating institutions.

6   The major functions of the Federal Reserve System are *a.* to hold the deposits or reserves of commercial banks, *b.* to supply the economy's needs for paper currency, *c.* to provide facilities for the rapid collection of checks, *d.* to act as fiscal agent for the Federal government, *e.* to supervise the operations of member banks, and *f.* to regulate the supply of money in terms of the best interests of the economy as a whole.

## Questions and Study Suggestions

1   Key terms and concepts to remember: medium of exchange; standard of value; store of value; transactions, asset, and total demands for money; token money; intrinsic value; Federal Reserve Notes; demand deposits; near-monies; $M_1$ and $M_2$; fiat money; legal tender;

Federal Reserve Banks; Board of Governors; Open Market Committee; Federal Advisory Council; commercial banks; financial intermediaries.

**2**  What is the basic determinant of *a.* the transactions demand, and *b.* the asset demand for money? Explain how these two demands might be combined graphically to determine total money demand. How might *a.* the expanded use of credit cards, and *b.* a shortening of worker pay periods affect the transactions demand for money?

**3**  Describe how drastic inflation can undermine the ability of money to perform its three basic functions.

**4**  What are the disadvantages of commodity money? What are the advantages of *a.* paper money and *b.* check money as compared with commodity money?

**5**  "Money is only a bit of paper or a bit of metal that gives its owner a lawful claim to so much bread or beer or diamonds or motorcars or what not. We cannot eat money, nor drink money, nor wear money. It is the goods that money can buy that are being divided up when money is divided up." [10] Evaluate and explain.

**6**  Fully evaluate and explain the following statements:

*a.*  "The invention of money is one of the great achievements of the human race, for without it the enrichment that comes from broadening trade would have been impossible."

*b.*  "Money is whatever society says it is."

*c.*  "When prices of everything are going up, it is not because everything is worth more, but because the dollar is worth less."

*d.*  "The difficult questions concerning paper [money] are . . . not about its economy, convenience or ready circulation but about the amount of the paper which can be wisely issued or created, and the possibilities of violent convulsions when it gets beyond bounds." [11]

**7**  What items constitute the money supply in American capitalism? What is the most important component of the money supply? Why is the face value of a coin greater than its intrinsic value? Distinguish between $M_1$ and $M_2$. What are near-monies? Of what significance are they? What arguments can you make for including time deposits in a definition of money?

**8**  "In most modern industrial economies of the world the debts of government and of commercial banks are used as money." Explain.

**9**  What "backs" the money supply in the United States? What determines the value of money? Who is responsible for maintaining the value of money? Why is it important for the money supply to be elastic, that is, capable of increasing or decreasing in size? What is meant by *a.* "sound money" and *b.* a "52-cent dollar"?

**10**  What is the major responsibility of the Board of Governors? Discuss the major characteristics of the Federal Reserve Banks. Of what significance is the fact that the Federal Reserve Banks are quasi-public?

**11**  What are the two basic functions of commercial banks? How do commercial banks differ from other financial intermediaries? State and briefly discuss the major functions of the Federal Reserve System.

---

[10] George Bernard Shaw, *The Intelligent Woman's Guide to Socialism and Capitalism* (New York: Brentano's, Inc., 1928), p. 9. Used by permission of the Public Trustee and the Society of Authors.
[11] F. W. Taussig, *Principles of Economics,* 4th ed. (New York: The Macmillan Company, 1946), pp. 247–248.

# Selected References

Board of Governors of the Federal Reserve System: *The Federal Reserve System: Purposes and Functions,* 6th ed. (1974), particularly chaps. 1, 2, 7.

Chandler, Lester V., and Stephen M. Goldfeld: *The Economics of Money and Banking,* 7th ed. (New York: Harper & Row, Publishers, Incorporated, 1977), chaps. 1–5, 8, 9.

Gambs, Carl M.: "Money—A Changing Concept in a Changing World," *Monthly Review,* Federal Reserve Bank of Kansas City, January 1977.

Robertson, D. H.: *Money,* 6th ed. (New York: Pitman Publishing Corporation, 1948).

Thomas, Lloyd B., Jr.: *Money, Banking, and Economic Activity* (Englewood Cliffs, N. J.: Prentice-Hall, Inc., 1979), chaps. 1–6, and 14.

Thorn, Richard S.: *Introduction to Money and Banking* (New York: Harper & Row, Publishers, Incorporated, 1976), chaps. 1–6.

Wenninger, John, and Charles M. Sivesind: "Defining Money for a Changing Financial System," *Quarterly Review* (Federal Reserve Bank of New York), Spring, 1979, pp. 1–8.

# LAST WORD
## A Dialogue on Money

The British monetary system, as it has emerged from the furnace of the last eight years, is . . . a somewhat eccentric contraption. Between some enquiring Socrates from another planet and an economist instructed to explain its nature some such dialogue as the following might well take place:

*Socrates:* I see that your chief piece of money carries a legend affirming that it is a promise to pay the bearer the sum of one pound. What is this thing, a pound, of which payment is thus promised?

*Economist:* A pound is the British unit of account.

*Socrates:* So there is, I suppose, some concrete object which embodies more firmly that abstract unit of account than does this paper promise?

*Economist:* There is no such object, O Socrates.

*Socrates:* Indeed? Then what your Bank promises is to give me another promise stamped with a different number in case I should regard the number stamped on this promise as in some way ill-omened?

*Economist:* It would seem, indeed, to be promising something of that kind.

*Socrates:* So that in order to be in a position to fulfil its promises all the Bank has to do is to keep a store of such promises stamped with all sorts of different numbers?

*Economist:* By no means, Socrates—that would make its balance-sheet a subject for mockery, and in the eyes of our people there resides in a balance-sheet a certain awe and holiness. The Bank has to keep a store of Government securities and a store of gold.

*Socrates:* What are Government securities?

*Economist:* Promises by the Government to pay certain sums of money at certain dates.

*Socrates:* What are sums of money? Do you mean Bank of England notes?

*Economist:* I suppose I do.

*Socrates:* So these promises to pay promises are thought to be in some way solider and more sacred than the promises themselves?

*Economist:* They are so thought, as it appears.

*Socrates:* I see. Now tell me about the gold. It has to be of certain weight, I suppose.

*Economist:* Not of a certain weight, but of a certain value in terms of the promises.

*Socrates:* So that the less each of its promises is worth, the more promises the Bank can lawfully make?

*Economist:* It seems, indeed, to amount to something of that kind.

*Socrates:* Do you find that your monetary system works well?

*Economist:* Pretty well, thank you, Socrates, on the whole.

*Socrates:* That would be, I suppose, not because of the rather strange rules of which you have told me, but because it is administered by men of ability and wisdom?

*Economist:* It would seem that that must be the reason, rather than the rules themselves, O Socrates.

Dennis H. Robertson, *Essays in Monetary Theory* (London: Staples Press, Ltd., 1939), pp. 158–159. Reprinted by permission.

# How Banks Create Money

# chapter 15

In Chapter 14 we saw that the Federal Reserve Banks are the primary source of the economy's paper money. However, we shall find in the present chapter that commercial banks are the fountainhead of the major component of the money system—demand deposits.

More specifically, in this chapter we want to explain and compare the money-creating abilities of (1) a *single* commercial bank which is part of a multibank system, and (2) the commercial banking *system* as a whole.

It will be convenient for us to seek these objectives through the commercial bank's balance sheet. An understanding of the basic items which make up a bank's balance sheet, and of the manner in which various transactions change these items, will provide us with a valuable analytical tool for grasping the workings of our monetary and banking systems.

## ☐ THE BALANCE SHEET OF A COMMERCIAL BANK

What is a *balance sheet*? It is merely a statement of assets and claims which portrays or summarizes the financial position of a firm—in this case a commercial bank—at some specific point in time. Every balance sheet has one overriding virtue: By definition, it must balance. Why? Because each and every known *asset,* being something of economic value, will be claimed by someone. Can you think of an asset—something of monetary value—which no one claims? A balance sheet balances because assets equal claims. The claims shown on a balance sheet are divided into two groups: the claims of the owners of a firm against the firm's assets, called *net worth,* and the claims of nonowners, called *liabilities.* Thus, it can be said that a balance sheet balances because

Assets = liabilities + net worth

A balance-sheet approach to our study of the money-creating ability of commercial banks is invaluable in two specific respects: On the one hand, a bank's balance sheet provides us with a convenient point of reference from which we can introduce new terms and concepts in a more or less orderly manner. On the other hand, the use of balance sheets will allow us to quantify certain strategic concepts and relationships which would defy comprehension if discussed in verbal terms alone.

## ☐ HISTORY AS PROLOGUE: THE GOLDSMITHS

We are about to use balance sheets to explain how a *fractional reserve system* of banking operates. The characteristics and functioning of such a system can be anticipated and more fully understood by pausing to consider a bit of economic history.

When the ancients began to use gold in making transactions, it soon became apparent that it was both unsafe and inconvenient for consumers and merchants to carry gold and to have it weighed and assessed for purity every time a transaction was negotiated. Hence, it became commonplace to deposit one's gold with goldsmiths who possessed vaults or strongrooms which, for a fee, they were willing to make available. Upon receiving a gold deposit, the goldsmith would issue a receipt to the depositor. Soon goods were traded for the goldsmiths' receipts and the receipts became an early form of paper money.

At this point the goldsmiths—now embryonic bankers—utilized a 100 percent reserve system, that is, their circulating paper money (receipts) were fully backed by gold. But, given the public's acceptance of the goldsmiths' receipts as paper money, the goldsmiths became aware that the gold they stored was rarely redeemed. In fact, the goldsmiths found themselves in charge of "going concerns" wherein the amount of gold deposited in any week or month was likely to exceed the amount redeemed. Hence, it was only a matter of time until some particularly adroit goldsmith hit upon the idea that paper money could be issued *in excess of* the amount of gold held! The goldsmith would put this additional paper money into circulation by making interest-earning loans to merchants, producers, and consumers. At this juncture a *fractional reserve system* of banking came into being. If, for example, our ingenious goldsmith made loans equal to the amount of gold stored, then the total value of paper money in circulation would be twice the value of the gold so that reserves would be 50 percent of outstanding paper money.

A system of fractional reserve banking—which is the kind of system we have today—embodies two significant characteristics.

**1   Money Creation and Reserves**   Banks in such a system can *create money*. When the goldsmith of our illustration made loans by giving borrowers paper money which was not fully backed by gold reserves, money was being created. Obviously, the quantity of such money the goldsmith could create would depend upon the amount of reserves it was deemed prudent to keep on hand. The smaller the amount of reserves, the larger the amount of paper money the goldsmith could create. Although gold is no longer used to "back" our money supply (Chapter 14), bank lending (money creation) today is constrained by the amount of reserves banks feel obligated, or are required, to keep.

**2   Bank Panics and Regulation**   Banks which operate on the basis of fractional reserves are vulnerable to bank "panics" or "runs." Our goldsmith who has issued paper money equal to twice the value of gold reserves obviously cannot convert all that paper money into gold in the unlikely event that all the holders of that paper money appear simultaneously demanding gold. In fact, there are innumerable instances of European and American banks ruined by this unfortunate circumstance. On the other hand, a bank panic is highly unlikely *if* the banker's reserve and lending policies are prudent. Indeed, the prevention of bank runs is a basic reason why banking systems are highly regulated industries.

## ☐ A SINGLE COMMERCIAL BANK IN A BANKING SYSTEM

Our goal now is to understand the money-creating potential of a single bank which is part of a multibank banking system. What accounts constitute a commercial bank's balance sheet? How does a single commercial bank create and destroy money? What factors govern the money-creating abilities of such a bank?

### △ Formation of a Commercial Bank

The answers to these questions demand that we understand the ins and outs of a commercial bank's balance sheet and how certain rather elementary transactions affect that balance sheet. We start with the organization of a local commercial bank.

**Transaction 1: The Birth of a Bank**  Let us start from scratch. Suppose some farsighted citizens of the metropolis of Wahoo, Nebraska, decide that their town is in need of a new commercial bank to provide all the banking services needed by that growing community. Assuming these enterprising individuals are able to secure a state charter for their bank, they then turn to the task of selling, say, $250,000 worth of capital stock to buyers, both in and out of the community. These financing efforts having met with success, the Merchants and Farmers Bank of Wahoo now exists—at least on paper. How does the Wahoo bank's balance statement appear at its birth?

The new owners of the bank have sold $250,000 worth of shares of stock in the bank—some to themselves, some to other people. As a result, the bank now has $250,000 in cash on hand and $250,000 worth of capital stock outstanding. Obviously the cash is an asset to the bank. The cash held by a bank is sometimes dubbed *vault cash* or *till money*. The outstanding shares of stock, however, constitute an equal amount of claims which the owners have against the bank's assets. That is, the shares of stock are obviously the net worth of the bank, though they are assets from the viewpoint of those who possess these shares. The bank's balance sheet would read:

**Balance Sheet 1: Wahoo Bank**

| Assets | | Liabilities and net worth | |
|---|---|---|---|
| Cash | $250,000 | Capital stock | $250,000 |

**Transaction 2: Becoming a Going Concern**  The newly established board of directors must now get the newborn bank off the drawing board and make it a living reality. The first step will be to acquire property and equipment. Suppose the directors, confident of the success of their venture, purchase a building for $220,000 and some $20,000 worth of office equipment. This simple transaction merely changes the composition of the bank's assets. The bank now has $240,000 less in cash and $240,000 worth of new property assets. Using an asterisk to denote those accounts which are affected by each transaction, we find that the bank's balance sheet at the conclusion of transaction 2 appears as follows:

**Balance Sheet 2: Wahoo Bank**

| Assets | | Liabilities and net worth | |
|---|---|---|---|
| Cash* | $ 10,000 | Capital stock | $250,000 |
| Property* | 240,000 | | |

Note that the balance sheet still balances, as indeed it must.

**Transaction 3: Accepting Deposits**  We have already emphasized that commercial banks have two basic functions: to accept deposits of money and to make loans. Now that our bank is in operation, let us suppose that the citizens and businesses of Wahoo decide to deposit some $100,000 in the Merchants and Farmers Bank. What happens to the bank's balance sheet?

The bank receives cash, which we have already noted is an asset to the bank. Suppose this money is placed in the bank in the form of demand deposits (checking accounts), rather than time deposits (savings accounts). These newly created demand deposits constitute claims which depositors have against the assets of the Wahoo bank. Thus the depositing of money in the bank creates a new liability account—demand deposits. The bank's balance sheet now looks like this:

**Balance Sheet 3: Wahoo Bank**

| Assets | | Liabilities and net worth | |
|---|---|---|---|
| Cash* | $110,000 | Demand | |
| Property | 240,000 | deposits* | $100,000 |
| | | Capital stock | 250,000 |

You should note that, although there is no direct change in the total supply of money, a change in the composition of the economy's money supply has occurred as a result of transaction 3. Bank money, or demand deposits, have *increased* by $100,000 and currency in circulation has *decreased* by $100,000. Currency held by a bank, you will recall (Chapter 14, footnote 3) is *not* considered to be a part of the economy's money supply.

It is obvious that a withdrawal of cash will reduce the bank's demand-deposit liabilities and its holdings of cash by the amount of the withdrawal. This, too, changes the composition, but not the total supply, of money.

**Transaction 4: Joining the Federal Reserve System**  Being a state bank, the Merchants and Farmers Bank of Wahoo will have the option of joining or not joining the Federal Reserve System. Suppose the directors of the bank weigh the costs and benefits involved and decide in favor of joining. To accomplish this, the bank must meet a very specific requirement: It must keep a *legal reserve deposit* in the Federal Reserve Bank of its particular district.

This legal reserve deposit is *an amount of funds equal to a specified percentage of its own deposit liabilities which a member bank must keep on deposit with the Federal Reserve Bank in its district.* Although banks are permitted to count vault cash as a part of reserves, the vast bulk of bank reserves is in the form of deposits in the Federal Reserve Banks. We shall simplify our discussion by supposing that our bank keeps its legal reserve *entirely* in the form of deposits in the Federal Reserve Bank of its district.

The "specified percentage" of its deposit liabilities which the commercial bank must deposit in the central bank is known as the *reserve ratio*. Why? Because that is exactly what it is—a ratio between the size of the deposits which the commercial bank must keep in the Federal Reserve Bank and the commercial bank's own outstanding deposit liabilities. This ratio is as follows:

$$\text{Reserve ratio} = \frac{\text{commercial bank's required deposit in Federal Reserve Bank}}{\text{commercial bank's demand-deposit liabilities}}$$

Hence, if the reserve ratio were 10 percent, our bank, having accepted $100,000 in deposits from the public, would be obligated to keep $10,000 as a deposit, or reserve, in the Federal Reserve Bank in Kansas City. If the ratio were 20 percent, $20,000 would have to be deposited in the Federal Reserve Bank. If 50 percent, $50,000, and so forth.

How is the exact size of the reserve ratio determined? Upper and lower limits have been legislated by Congress. Within these limits the actual required reserve ratio is established by the Board of Governors of the Federal Reserve

**TABLE 15-1**
Reserve Requirements of Member Banks, March 1980

| Demand deposits | Reserve requirement |
|---|---|
| $0–2 million | 7 % |
| $2–10 million | $9\frac{1}{2}$ |
| $10–100 million | $11\frac{3}{4}$ |
| $100–400 million | $12\frac{3}{4}$ |
| Over $400 million | $16\frac{1}{4}$ |

*Source: Federal-Reserve Bulletin.*

System.[1] As Table 15-1 indicates, the Board has set the reserve ratio on a graduated scale based upon the size of a bank's demand deposits. For example, a bank with demand deposits of $10 million would be required to have reserves of $900,000 (= 7 percent of $2 million *plus* $9\frac{1}{2}$ percent of $8 million). To avoid a lot of tedious computations, we shall suppose that the reserve ratio for all banks is 20 percent. This is a nice round figure and is reasonably close to reality. It is to be emphasized that reserve requirements are *fractional,* that is, less than 100 percent. This consideration will be vital in the ensuing analysis of the lending ability of the banking system.

The Wahoo bank will just be meeting the required 20 percent ratio between its deposit in the Federal Reserve Bank and its own deposit liabilities by depositing $20,000 in the Federal Reserve Bank. To distinguish this deposit from the public's deposits in commercial banks, we shall use the term *reserves* in referring to those funds which commercial banks deposit in the Federal Reserve Banks.

But let us suppose that the directors of the Wahoo bank anticipate that their holdings of the public's demand deposits will grow in the future. Hence, instead of sending just the minimum amount, $20,000, they send an extra $90,000, making a total of $110,000. In so

[1]State nonmember banks are required by state laws to keep reserves. These reserves usually take the form of cash and deposits in other commercial banks. Though the reserve ratio varies considerably among the states, 15 percent is about the average.

doing, the bank will avoid the inconvenience of sending additional reserves to the Federal Reserve Bank each time its own demand-deposit liabilities increase. And we shall see shortly that it is upon the basis of extra reserves that banks can lend and thereby earn interest income.

Actually, of course, the bank would not deposit *all* its cash in the Federal Reserve Bank. However, because (1) banks as a rule hold vault cash only in the amount of $1\frac{1}{2}$ or 2 percent of their total assets, and (2) vault cash can be counted as reserves, we shall find it expedient to assume that all the bank's cash is deposited in the Federal Reserve Bank and therefore constitutes the commercial bank's total reserves. The cumbersome process of adding two assets—"cash" and "deposits in the Federal Reserve Bank"—to determine "reserves" is thereby avoided.

At the completion of this transaction, the balance sheet of the Merchants and Farmers Bank will appear as follows:

**Balance Sheet 4: Wahoo Bank**

| Assets | | Liabilities and net worth | |
|---|---|---|---|
| Cash* | $      0 | Demand | |
| Reserves* | 110,000 | deposits | $100,000 |
| Property | 240,000 | Capital stock | 250,000 |

There are several points relevant to this transaction which must still be explained:

*1  Excess reserves* A note on terminology: The amount by which the bank's actual reserves exceed its required reserves is the bank's *excess* reserves. In this case,

| Actual reserves | $110,000 |
|---|---|
| Required reserves | −20,000 |
| Excess reserves | $ 90,000 |

The only reliable way of computing excess reserves is to multiply the bank's demand-deposit liabilities by the reserve ratio ($100,000 times 20 percent equals $20,000) to obtain required reserves, then to subtract this figure from the actual reserves listed on the asset side of the bank's balance sheet. To ensure an understanding of this process, the reader should compute excess reserves for the bank's balance sheet as it stands at the end of transaction 4 on the assumption that the reserve ratio is (a) 10 percent, (b) $33\frac{1}{3}$ percent, and (c) 50 percent.

Because the ability of a commercial bank to make loans depends upon the existence of excess reserves, this concept is of vital importance in grasping the money-creating ability of the banking system.

**2   *Control*** What is the rationale underlying the requirement that member banks deposit a reserve in the Federal Reserve Bank of their district? One might think that the basic purpose of reserves is to enhance the liquidity of a bank and thereby protect commercial bank depositors from losses; that is, it would seem that reserves constitute a ready source of funds from which commercial banks can meet large and unexpected withdrawals of cash by depositors. But this reasoning does not hold up under close scrutiny. Although, historically, reserves were looked upon as a source of liquidity and therefore protection for depositors, *legal,* or required, reserves cannot be used for the purpose of meeting unexpected cash withdrawals. If the banker's nightmare should materialize—that is, if everyone having a demand deposit in the bank appeared on the same morning to demand these deposits in cash—the banker could not draw upon required reserves to meet this "bank panic" without violating the legal reserve ratio and thereby incurring the wrath and penalties of the Federal Reserve authorities. In practice, legal reserves are *not* an available pool of liquid funds upon which commercial banks can rely in times of emergency.[2] As a matter of fact,

even if legal reserves were accessible to commercial banks, they would not be sufficient to meet a serious "run" on a bank. Why? Because, as already noted, reserves are *fractional;* that is, demand deposits may be 3, 4, or 5 times as large as a bank's required reserves.

It is not surprising that commercial bank depositors are protected by other means. As noted in Chapter 14, periodic bank examinations are an important device for promoting prudent commercial banking practices. Furthermore, the Federal Deposit Insurance Corporation exists to insure the deposit liabilities of member banks and qualified nonmember banks that voluntarily become members of the FDIC.

If the purpose of reserves is not to provide for commercial bank liquidity, what is their function? *Control* is the basic answer. Legal reserves are a means by which the Board of Governors can influence the lending ability of commercial banks. The next chapter will explain in detail how the Board of Governors can invoke certain policies which either increase or decrease commercial bank reserves and thereby affect the ability of banks to grant credit. The objective is to prevent banks from *over*extending or *under*extending bank credit. To the degree that these policies are successful in influencing the volume of commercial bank credit, the Board of Governors can help the economy avoid the business fluctuations which give rise to bank runs, bank failures, and collapse of the monetary system. It is in this indirect way—as a means of controlling commercial bank credit and thereby stabilizing the economy—that reserves protect depositors, not as a source of liquidity. As we shall see in a moment, another function of reserves is to facilitate the collection or "clearing" of checks.

**3   *Asset and liability*** Let us pause to

---

[2] This amendment must be added: As depositors withdraw cash from a commercial bank, the bank's demand-deposit liabilities will obviously decline. This lowers the absolute amount of required reserves which the bank must keep, thereby freeing some of the bank's actual reserves for use in meeting cash withdrawals by depositors. To illustrate: Suppose a commercial bank has reserves of $20 and demand-deposit liabilities of $100. If the legal reserve ratio is 20 percent, all the bank's reserves are obviously required.

Now, if depositors withdraw, say, $50 worth of their deposits as cash, the bank will only need $10 as required reserves to support the remaining $50 of demand-deposit liabilities. Thus $10 of the bank's actual reserves of $20 are no longer required. The bank can draw upon this $10 in helping to meet the cash withdrawals of its depositors. And, of course, if a bank goes out of business, all its reserves will be available to pay depositors and other claimants.

note a rather obvious accounting matter which transaction 4 entails. Specifically, *the reserve created in transaction 4 is an asset to the depositing commercial bank but a liability to the Federal Reserve Bank receiving it.* To the Wahoo bank the reserve is an asset. Why? Because it is a claim which this commercial bank has against the assets of another institution—the Federal Reserve Bank. To the Federal Reserve Bank this reserve is a liability, that is, a claim which another institution—the Wahoo bank—has against it. Just as the demand deposit you get by depositing money in a commercial bank is an asset to you and a liability to your commercial bank, so the deposit or reserve which a commercial bank establishes by depositing money in a banker's bank is an asset to the commercial bank and a liability to the Federal Reserve Bank. An understanding of this relationship is necessary in pursuing transaction 5.

**Transaction 5: A Check Is Drawn against the Bank**   Now let us tackle a very significant and somewhat more complicated transaction. Suppose that Clem Bradshaw, a Wahoo farmer who deposited a substantial portion of the $100,000 in demand deposits which the Wahoo bank received in transaction 3, purchases $50,000 worth of farm machinery from the Ajax Farm Implement Company of Beaver Crossing, Nebraska. Bradshaw very sensibly pays for this machinery by writing a $50,000 check, against his deposit in the Wahoo bank, in favor of the Ajax company. We want to determine (1) how this check is collected or cleared, and (2) the effect that the collection of the check has upon the balance sheets of the banks involved in the transaction.

To accomplish this, we must consider the Wahoo bank, the Beaver Crossing bank, and the Federal Reserve Bank of Kansas City.[3] Let us suppose that both the commercial banks are members of the Federal Reserve System. And

to keep our illustration as clear as possible, we shall deal only with the changes which occur in those specific accounts affected by this transaction.

Let us trace this transaction in three related steps, keying the steps by letters to Figure 15-1.

*a.*   Mr. Bradshaw gives his $50,000 check, drawn against the Wahoo bank, to the Ajax company. The Ajax company in turn deposits the check in its account with the Beaver Crossing bank. The Beaver Crossing bank increases the Ajax company's demand deposit by $50,000 when it deposits the check. (The Ajax company is now paid off.) Bradshaw is elated over his new machinery, for which he has now paid.

*b.*   Now the Beaver Crossing bank has Bradshaw's check in its possession. This check is simply a claim against the assets of the Wahoo bank. How will the Beaver Crossing bank collect this claim? By sending this check—along with checks drawn on other banks—to the Federal Reserve Bank of Kansas City. Here a clerk will clear, or collect, this check for the Beaver Crossing bank by *increasing* its reserve in the Federal Reserve Bank by $50,000 and by *decreasing* the Wahoo bank's reserve by a like amount. The check is collected merely by making bookkeeping notations to the effect that the Wahoo bank's claim against the Federal Reserve Bank has been reduced by $50,000 and the Beaver Crossing bank's claim increased accordingly. Note these changes on the balance sheets in Figure 15-1.[4]

---

[3] Actually, the Omaha branch of the Federal Reserve Bank of Kansas City would handle the process of collecting this check.

[4] Here is an interesting sidelight: The collection of Bradshaw's check by the Beaver Crossing bank through the Federal Reserve Bank involves the same type of procedure as the collection of a check between two individuals who have deposits in the same commercial bank. Suppose you and I both have checking accounts in the Wahoo bank. I owe you $10 and I pay this debt by check. You deposit the $10 check in the bank. Here a bank clerk collects the check for you by noting a "+$10" in your account and a "−$10" in my account. And that's that. The same thing happens at the Federal Reserve Bank of Kansas City when the Beaver Crossing bank clears a $50,000 check against the Wahoo bank. The banker's bank increases the Beaver Crossing bank's deposit in the Federal Reserve Bank—that is, its reserve—by $50,000 and lowers the Wahoo bank's reserve by the same amount. The check is then cleared.

*c.* Finally, the cleared check is sent back to the Wahoo bank, and for the first time the Wahoo bank discovers that one of its depositors has drawn a check for $50,000 against his demand deposit. Accordingly, the Wahoo bank reduces Mr. Bradshaw's demand deposit by $50,000 and recognizes that the collection of this check has entailed a $50,000 decline in its reserves at the Federal Reserve Bank. Note that the balance statements of all three banks will still balance. The Wahoo bank will have reduced both its assets and its liabilities by $50,000. The Beaver Crossing bank will have $50,000 more in reserves and in demand deposits. The ownership of reserves at the Federal Reserve Bank will have changed, but total reserves will stay the same.

The point we are making is this: *Whenever a check is drawn against a bank and deposited in another bank, the collection of that check will entail a loss of both reserves and deposits by the bank upon which the check is drawn.* Conversely, if a bank receives a check drawn on another bank, the bank receiving the check will, in the process of collecting it, have its reserves and deposits increased by the amount of the check. In our example, the Wahoo bank loses $50,000 in both reserves and deposits to the Beaver Crossing bank. But there is no loss of reserves or deposits for the banking system as a whole. What one bank loses another bank gains.

Bringing all the other assets and liabilities back into the picture, the Wahoo bank's balance sheet looks like this at the end of transaction 5:

**Balance Sheet 5: Wahoo Bank**

| Assets | | Liabilities and net worth | |
|---|---|---|---|
| Reserves* | $ 60,000 | Demand | |
| Property | 240,000 | deposits* | $ 50,000 |
| | | Capital stock | 250,000 |

The reader should verify that with a 20 percent reserve requirement, the bank's *excess* reserves now stand at $50,000.

Transaction 5 is obviously reversible. If a check drawn against another bank is deposited in the Wahoo bank, the Wahoo bank will receive both reserves and deposits equal to the amount of the check as it is collected.

△ **Recap**

Let us summarize the salient conclusions from the first five transactions we have analyzed:

**1** When a bank accepts deposits of cash, the composition of the money supply is changed, but the total supply of money is not directly altered.

**2** Commercial banks which are members of the Federal Reserve System are required to keep legal reserve deposits, or simply "reserves," equal to a specified percentage of their own deposit liabilities on deposit with the Federal Reserve Bank of their district. The reserve ratio indicates the size of this "specified percentage." Reserves are primarily a means by which the monetary authorities can control the lending policies of commercial banks.

**3** The amount by which a bank's actual reserves exceed its required reserves is called "excess reserves."

**4** Commercial bank reserves are an asset to the commercial bank but a liability to the Federal Reserve Bank holding them.

**5** A bank which has a check drawn and collected against it will lose both reserves and deposits equal to the value of the check to the bank receiving the check.

△ **Money-creating Transactions of a Commercial Bank**

The next two transactions are particularly crucial because they explain how a single commercial bank can literally create money by making loans and by purchasing government bonds from the public. Though these transactions are similar in many respects, we treat them separately.

**Transaction 6: Granting a Loan**  You will recall that in addition to accepting deposits,

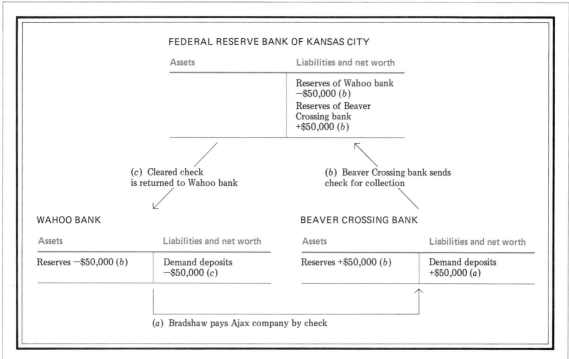

FEDERAL RESERVE BANK OF KANSAS CITY

| Assets | Liabilities and net worth |
|---|---|
| | Reserves of Wahoo bank −$50,000 (b) |
| | Reserves of Beaver Crossing bank +$50,000 (b) |

(c) Cleared check is returned to Wahoo bank

(b) Beaver Crossing bank sends check for collection

WAHOO BANK

| Assets | Liabilities and net worth |
|---|---|
| Reserves −$50,000 (b) | Demand deposits −$50,000 (c) |

BEAVER CROSSING BANK

| Assets | Liabilities and net worth |
|---|---|
| Reserves +$50,000 (b) | Demand deposits +$50,000 (a) |

(a) Bradshaw pays Ajax company by check

**FIGURE 15-1  THE COLLECTION OF A CHECK THROUGH A FEDERAL RESERVE BANK**

The bank against which a check is drawn and cleared loses both reserves and deposits; the bank in which the check is deposited acquires reserves and deposits.

commercial banks have a basic function of granting loans to borrowers. What effect does commercial bank lending have upon the balance sheet of a commercial bank?

Suppose that the Grisley Meat Packing Company of Wahoo decides that the time is ripe to expand its facilities. Suppose, too, that the company needs exactly $50,000—which, by some unexplained coincidence, just happens to be equal to the Wahoo bank's excess reserves—to finance this project.

The company approaches the Wahoo bank and requests a loan for this amount. The Wahoo bank is acquainted with the Grisley company's fine reputation and financial soundness and is convinced of its ability to repay the loan. So the loan is granted. The president of the Grisley company hands a promissory note—a high-class IOU—to the

Wahoo bank. The Grisley company, like all other modern firms, is interested in paying its obligations by check. Hence, instead of receiving a bushel basket full of cash from the bank, the Grisley company will get a $50,000 increase in its demand deposit in the Wahoo bank. From the Wahoo bank's standpoint it has acquired an interest-earning asset (the promissory note) and has created demand deposits to pay for this asset.

In short, the Grisley company has swapped an IOU for the right to draw an additional $50,000 worth of checks against its demand deposit in the Wahoo bank. Both parties are pleased with themselves. The Wahoo bank now possesses a new asset—an interest-bearing promissory note which it happily files under the general heading of "Loans." The Grisley company, sporting a fattened demand deposit, is now in a position to expand its operations.

*At the moment the loan is negotiated,* the Wahoo bank's position is shown by balance sheet 6a.

**Balance Sheet 6a: Wahoo Bank** (*when loan is negotiated*)

| Assets | | Liabilities and net worth | |
|---|---|---|---|
| Reserves | $ 60,000 | Demand | |
| Loans* | 50,000 | deposits* | $100,000 |
| Property | 240,000 | Capital stock | 250,000 |

All this looks innocent enough. But a closer examination of the Wahoo bank's balance statement will reveal a startling fact: *When a bank makes loans, it creates money.* The president of the Grisley company went to the bank with something which is *not* money—his IOU—and walked out with something that *is* money—a demand deposit.[5] When banks lend, they create demand deposits which are money. By extending credit the Wahoo bank has "monetized" an IOU. The Grisley company and the Wahoo bank have created and then swapped claims. The claim created by the Grisley company and given to the bank is not money; an individual's IOU is not generally acceptable as a medium of exchange. But the claim created by the bank and given to the Grisley company is money; checks drawn against a demand deposit are acceptable as a medium of exchange. It is through the extension of credit by commercial banks that the bulk of the money used in our economy is created.

But there are important forces which circumscribe the ability of a commercial bank to create demand deposits—that is, "bank money"—by lending. In the present case, the Wahoo bank can expect the newly created demand deposit of $50,000 to be a very active account. The Grisley company would not bor-

[5] In transaction 3, demand deposits were created, but only by currency going out of circulation. Hence, there was a change in the composition of the money supply but no change in the total supply of money.

row $50,000 at, say, 12, 14, or 20 percent interest for the sheer joy of knowing the funds were available if needed. Let us assume that the Grisley company awards a $50,000 contract to the Quickbuck Construction Company of Omaha. Quickbuck, true to its name, completes the expansion job and is rewarded with a check for $50,000 drawn by the Grisley company against its demand deposit in the Wahoo bank. The Quickbuck company, having its headquarters in Omaha, does not deposit this check back in the Wahoo bank but instead deposits it in the Fourth National Bank of Omaha. The Fourth National Bank now has a $50,000 claim against the Wahoo bank. This check is collected in the manner described in transaction 5. As a result, the Wahoo bank *loses* both reserves and deposits equal to the amount of the check; the Fourth National Bank *acquires* $50,000 of reserves and deposits. In short, assuming a check is drawn by the borrower for the entire amount of the loan ($50,000) and given to a firm which deposits it in another bank, the Wahoo bank's balance sheet will read as follows *after the check has been cleared against it:*

**Balance Sheet 6b: Wahoo Bank** (*after a check drawn on the loan has been collected*)

| Assets | | Liabilities and net worth | |
|---|---|---|---|
| Reserves* | $ 10,000 | Demand | |
| Loans | 50,000 | deposits* | $ 50,000 |
| Property | 240,000 | Capital stock | 250,000 |

You will note immediately that after the check has been collected, the Wahoo bank is just barely meeting the legal reserve ratio of 20 percent. The bank has *no excess reserves.* This poses an interesting question: Could the Wahoo bank have lent an amount greater than $50,000—an amount greater than its excess reserves—and still have met the 20 percent reserve requirement if a check for the full amount of the loan were cleared against it? The answer is "No." For example, suppose the

Wahoo bank had loaned $55,000 to the Grisley company. Collection of the check against the Wahoo bank would have lowered its reserves to $5,000 (= $60,000 − $55,000) and deposits would once again stand at $50,000 (= $105,000 − $55,000). The ratio of actual reserves to deposits would now be only $5,000/$50,000, or 10 percent. The Wahoo bank could thus *not* have lent $55,000. By experimenting with other figures in excess of $50,000, the reader will find that the maximum amount which the Wahoo bank could lend at the outset of transaction 6 is $50,000. This figure is identical with the amount of excess reserves which the bank had available at the time the loan was negotiated. We can conclude that *a single commercial bank in a multibank banking system can lend only an amount equal to its initial pre-loan excess reserves.* Why? Because when it lends, it faces the likelihood that checks for the entire amount of the loan will be drawn and cleared against the lending bank. A lending bank can anticipate the loss of reserves to other banks equal to the amount it lends.[6]

If commercial banks create demand deposits—that is, money—when they make loans, it seems logical to inquire whether money is destroyed when the loans are repaid. The answer is "Yes." Using balance sheet 6b, let us see what happens when the Grisley company repays the $50,000 it borrowed.

To simplify, we shall (1) suppose that the loan is repaid not in installments but rather in one lump sum three years after the date of negotiation, and (2) ignore interest charges on the loan. The Grisley company will write a check for $50,000 against its demand deposit, which presumably has been fattened by extra profits resulting from the company's expanded operations. As a result, the Wahoo bank's demand-deposit liabilities decline by $50,000;

the Grisley company has given up $50,000 worth of its claim against the bank's assets. In turn, the bank will surrender the Grisley company's IOU which it has been patiently holding these many months. The bank and the company have reswapped claims. But the claim given up by the Grisley company is money; the claim it is repurchasing—its IOU—is not. The supply of money has therefore been reduced by $50,000; that amount of demand deposits has been destroyed, unaccompanied by any increase in the money supply elsewhere in the economy. The Grisley company's IOU has been "demonetized." On the Wahoo bank's balance sheet, demand deposits and loans both fall by $50,000. You will note that the decline in demand deposits increases the bank's holdings of excess reserves; this provides the basis for new loans to be made.

In the highly unlikely event the Grisley company repays the loan with cash, the supply of money will still decline by $50,000. In this case, the Grisley company would repurchase its IOU by handing over $50,000 in cash to the bank. This causes loans to fall on the bank's balance sheet by $50,000 and, obviously, cash to increase by $50,000. Remember that we specifically excluded currency held by banks from the money supply on the ground that to include such cash would be double counting; it is apparent that this constitutes a $50,000 reduction in the supply of money.

**Transaction 7: Buying Government Securities**  When a commercial bank buys government bonds from the public,[7] the effect is substantially the same as that of lending. New money is created. To illustrate, let us assume that the Wahoo bank's balance sheet initially stands as it did at the end of transaction 5. Now assume that, instead of making a $50,000 loan, the bank buys $50,000 of government

---

[6]Qualification: If some of the checks written on a loan are redeposited back in the lending bank by their recipients, then that bank will be able to lend an amount somewhat greater than its initial excess reserves.

[7]Commercial banks are restrained by law in their purchase of private securities. It is felt that banks should be restricted to the performance of recognized banking functions and not permitted to become holding companies or speculative institutions.

securities from a securities dealer. The bank receives the interest-bearing bonds which appear on its balance statement as the asset "Securities" and gives the dealer an increase in its demand deposit account. The Wahoo bank's balance sheet would appear as follows:

**Balance Sheet 7: Wahoo Bank**

| Assets | | Liabilities and net worth | |
|---|---|---|---|
| Reserves | $ 60,000 | Demand | |
| Securities* | 50,000 | deposits* | $100,000 |
| Property | 240,000 | Capital stock | 250,000 |

The important point is that demand deposits, that is, the supply of money, have been increased by $50,000, as in transaction 6. *Commercial bank bond purchases from the public increase the supply of money in the same way as does lending to the public.* The bank accepts government bonds—which are not money—and gives the securities dealer an increase in its demand deposits—which is money.

Of course, when the securities dealer draws and clears a check for $50,000 against the Wahoo bank, the bank will lose both reserves and deposits in that amount and therefore will just be meeting the legal reserve requirement. Its balance sheet will now read precisely as in 6b except that "Securities" is substituted for "Loans" on the asset side.

Finally, as you undoubtedly suspect, the selling of government bonds to the public by a commercial bank—like the repayment of a loan—will reduce the supply of money. The securities buyer will pay by check and both "Securities" and "Demand deposits" (the latter being money) will decline by the amount of the sale.

△  **Profits and Liquidity**

The relative importance of the various asset items on a commercial bank's balance sheet is the result of the banker's pursuit of two conflicting goals. One goal is profits. Commercial banks, like any other business, are

seeking profits. To this end the bank is desirous of holding loans and securities. These two items are the major earning assets of commercial banks. On the other hand, a commercial bank must seek safety. For a bank, safety lies in liquidity—specifically such liquid assets as cash and excess reserves. Banks must be on guard for depositors' transforming their demand deposits into cash. Similarly, the possibility exists that more checks will be cleared against a bank than are cleared in its favor, causing a net outflow of reserves. Bankers are thus seeking a proper balance between prudence and profits. The compromise that is achieved determines the relative size of earning assets as opposed to highly liquid assets.

☐  **THE BANKING SYSTEM: MULTIPLE-DEPOSIT EXPANSION**

Thus far we have discovered that a single bank in a banking system can lend dollar for dollar with its excess reserves. Now what of the lending ability of all commercial banks taken as a group? Jumping to our conclusions, we shall find that *the commercial banking system can lend, that is, can create money, by a multiple of its excess reserves. This multiple lending is accomplished despite the fact that each bank in the system can only lend dollar for dollar with its excess reserves.* The immediate task is to uncover how these seemingly paradoxical conclusions come about.

To do this, it is necessary that we keep our analysis as clear as possible. Therefore, we shall rely upon three simplifying assumptions. First, suppose that the reserve ratio for all commercial banks is 20 percent. Second, assume initially that all banks are exactly meeting this 20 percent reserve requirement. No excess reserves exist; all banks are "loaned up." Third, we shall suppose that if any bank becomes able to increase its loans as a result of acquiring excess reserves, an amount equal to these excess reserves will be loaned to one borrower, who will write a check for the entire amount of the loan and give it to someone else, who deposits the check in another bank. This

Tom 9:00

assumption merely means that we are assuming the worst thing possible that can happen to any lending bank—a check for the entire amount of the loan is drawn and cleared against it and in favor of another bank.

## △  The Banking System's Lending Potential

To get the ball rolling, suppose that someone deposits $100 in currency in bank A. Having ample till money, bank A adds this $100 to its reserves. Since we are recording only *changes* in the balance sheets of the various commercial banks, bank A's balance sheet will now appear as follows ($a_1$):

**Balance Sheet: Commercial Bank A**

| Assets | | Liabilities and net worth | |
|---|---|---|---|
| Reserves | $+100 ($a_1$) | Demand | |
| | − 80 ($a_3$) | deposits | $+100 ($a_1$) |
| Loans | + 80 ($a_2$) | | + 80 ($a_2$) |
| | | | − 80 ($a_3$) |

Recall from transaction 3 that this $100 deposit of currency does *not* alter the money supply; while $100 of demand deposit money comes into being, an offsetting $100 of currency has gone out of circulation. What *has* happened is that bank A has acquired *excess reserves* of $80. Of the newly acquired $100 in reserves, 20 percent or $20 must be earmarked to offset the new $100 deposit and the remaining $80 is excess reserves. Remembering that a single commercial bank, such as bank A, can lend only an amount equal to its excess reserves, we conclude that bank A can lend a maximum of $80. When a loan for this amount is negotiated, bank A's loans will increase by $80, and the borrower will get an $80 demand deposit. Let us add these figures to bank A's balance sheet ($a_2$).

But now we must invoke our third assumption: The borrower draws a check for $80—the entire amount of the loan—and gives it to someone who deposits it in another bank, bank B. As we saw in transaction 6, bank A *loses* both reserves and deposits equal to the

amount of the loan ($a_3$). The net result of all the transactions is that bank A's reserves now stand at $20 (= $100 − $80), loans at $80, and demand deposits at $100 (= $100 + $80 − $80). Note that when the dust has settled, bank A is just meeting the 20 percent reserve ratio.

Recalling transaction 5, bank B *acquires* both the reserves and the deposits which bank A has lost. Bank B's balance sheet looks like this ($b_1$):

**Balance Sheet: Commercial Bank B**

| Assets | | Liabilities and net worth | |
|---|---|---|---|
| Reserves | $+80 ($b_1$) | Demand | |
| | −64 ($b_3$) | deposits | $+80 ($b_1$) |
| Loans | +64 ($b_2$) | | +64 ($b_2$) |
| | | | −64 ($b_3$) |

When the check is drawn and cleared, bank A *loses* $80 in reserves and deposits and bank B *gains* $80 in reserves and deposits. But 20 percent, or $16, of bank B's newly acquired reserves must be kept as required reserves against the new $80 in demand deposits. This means that bank B has $64 (= $80 − $16) in excess reserves. It can therefore lend $64 ($b_2$). When the borrower draws a check for the entire amount and deposits it in bank C, the reserves and deposits of bank B both fall by the $64 ($b_3$). As a result of these transactions, bank B's reserves will now stand at $16 (= $80 − $64), loans at $64, and demand deposits at $80 (= $80 + $64 − $64). Note that after all this has occurred, bank B is just meeting the 20 percent reserve requirement.

We are off and running again. Bank C has acquired the $64 in reserves and deposits lost by bank B. Its balance statement appears as follows ($c_1$):

**Balance Sheet: Commercial Bank C**

| Assets | | Liabilities and net worth | |
|---|---|---|---|
| Reserves | $+64.00 ($c_1$) | Demand | |
| | −51.20 ($c_3$) | deposits | $+64.00 ($c_1$) |
| Loans | +51.20 ($c_2$) | | +51.20 ($c_2$) |
| | | | −51.20 ($c_3$) |

Exactly 20 percent, or $12.80, of this new reserve will be required, the remaining $51.20 being excess reserves. Hence, bank C can safely lend a maximum of $51.20. Suppose it does $(c_2)$. And suppose the borrower draws a check for the entire amount and gives it to someone who deposits it in another bank $(c_3)$.

Bank D—the bank receiving the $51.20 in reserves and deposits—now notes these changes on its balance sheet $(d_1)$:

**Balance Sheet: Commercial Bank D**

| Assets | | Liabilities and net worth | |
|---|---|---|---|
| Reserves | $+51.20 $(d_1)$ | Demand | |
| | $-40.96$ $(d_3)$ | deposits | $+51.20 $(d_1)$ |
| Loans | $+40.96$ $(d_2)$ | | $+40.96$ $(d_2)$ |
| | | | $-40.96$ $(d_3)$ |

It can now lend $40.96 $(d_2)$. The borrower draws a check for the full amount and deposits it in another bank $(d_3)$.

Now, if we wanted to be particularly obnoxious, we could go ahead with this procedure by bringing banks E, F, G, H, . . . , N into the picture. We shall merely suggest that you check through computations for banks E, F, and G, to ensure that you have the procedure firmly in mind.

The nucleus of this analysis is summarized in Table 15-2. Data for banks E through N are supplied so you may check your computations. Our conclusion is a rather startling one: On the basis of the $80 in excess reserves (acquired by the banking system when someone deposited $100 of currency in bank A), the *commercial banking system* is able to lend $400. Lo and behold, the banking system is able to lend by a multiple of 5 when the reserve ratio is 20 percent! Yet you will note that each single bank in the banking system is lending only an amount equal to its excess reserves. How do we explain these seemingly conflicting conclusions? Why is it that the *banking system* can lend by a multiple of its excess reserves, but *each individual bank* can only lend dollar for dollar with its excess reserves?

**TABLE 15-2**
Expansion of the Money Supply by the Commercial Banking System

| Bank | (1) Acquired reserves and deposits | (2) Required reserves | (3) Excess reserves, or (1) – (2) | (4) Amount which the bank can lend; new money created = (3) |
|---|---|---|---|---|
| Bank A | $100.00 $(a_1)$ | $20.00 | $80.00 | $ 80.00 $(a_2)$ |
| Bank B | 80.00 $(a_3, b_1)$ | 16.00 | 64.00 | 64.00 $(b_2)$ |
| Bank C | 64.00 $(b_3, c_1)$ | 12.80 | 51.20 | 51.20 $(c_2)$ |
| Bank D | 51.20 $(c_3, d_1)$ | 10.24 | 40.96 | 40.96 $(d_2)$ |
| Bank E | 40.96 | 8.19 | 32.77 | 32.77 |
| Bank F | 32.77 | 6.55 | 26.22 | 26.22 |
| Bank G | 26.22 | 5.24 | 20.98 | 20.98 |
| Bank H | 20.98 | 4.20 | 16.78 | 16.78 |
| Bank I | 16.78 | 3.36 | 13.42 | 13.42 |
| Bank J | 13.42 | 2.68 | 10.74 | 10.74 |
| Bank K | 10.74 | 2.15 | 8.59 | 8.59 |
| Bank L | 8.59 | 1.72 | 6.87 | 6.87 |
| Bank M | 6.87 | 1.37 | 5.50 | 5.50 |
| Bank N | 5.50 | 1.10 | 4.40 | 4.40 |
| Other banks | 21.97 | 4.40 | 17.57 | 17.57 |
| Total amount of money created | | | | $400.00 |

*The answer lies in the fact that reserves lost by a single bank are not lost to the banking system as a whole.* The reserves lost by bank A are acquired by bank B. Those lost by B are gained by C. C loses to D, D to E, E to F, and so forth. Hence, although reserves can be, and are, lost by *individual* banks in the banking system, there can be no loss of reserves for the banking *system* as a whole. Hence, we reach the curious conclusion that an individual bank can only safely lend an amount equal to its excess reserves, but the commercial banking system can lend by a multiple of its excess reserves. This contrast, incidentally, is a fine illustration of why it is imperative that we keep the fallacy of composition firmly in mind. Commercial banks *as a group* can create money by lending in a manner much different from that of the *individual banks* in that system.

△  **The Monetary Multiplier**

The rationale involved in this *demand-deposit,* or *monetary, multiplier* is not unlike that underlying the income multiplier discussed in Chapter 12. The income multiplier was based on the fact that the expenditures of one household are received as income by another; the deposit multiplier rests on the fact that the reserves and deposits lost by one bank are received by another bank. And, just as the size of the income multiplier is determined by the reciprocal of the MPS, that is, by the leakage into saving which occurs at each round of spending, so the deposit multiplier $m$ is the reciprocal of the required reserve ratio $R,$ that is, of the leakage into required reserves which occurs at each step in the lending process. In short,

$$\text{Monetary multiplier} = \frac{1}{\text{required reserve ratio}}$$

or, symbolically:

$$m = \frac{1}{R}$$

In this formula, $m$ tells us the maximum number of new dollars of demand deposits which can be created for a *single dollar* of excess reserves, given the value of $R$. To determine the maximum amount of new demand deposit money, $D$, which can be created by the banking system on the basis of any given amount of excess reserves, $E$, we simply multiply the excess reserves by the monetary multiplier. That is,

Maximum demand deposit expansion
$$= \text{excess reserves} \times \text{monetary multiplier}$$

or, more simply,

$$D = E \times m$$

Thus, in our example of Table 15-2:

$$\$400 = \$80 \times 5$$

But keep in mind that, despite the similar rationale underlying the income and deposit multipliers, the former has to do with changes in income and the latter with changes in the supply of money.

Readers might experiment with these two teasers in testing their understanding of multiple credit expansion by the banking system:

**1**  Rework the preceding analysis (at least three or four steps of it) on the assumption that the reserve ratio is 10 percent. What is the maximum amount of money the banking system could create upon acquiring $100 in new reserves and deposits? (No, the answer is not $800!)

**2**  Explain how a banking system which is "loaned up" and faced with a 20 percent reserve ratio might be forced to *reduce* its outstanding loans by $400 as a result of a $100 cash withdrawal from a demand deposit which forces the bank to draw down its reserves by $100 in order to replenish its till money.

△  **Some Modifications**

Our discussion of credit expansion has

been conducted in a somewhat rarefied atmosphere. There are certain complications which might modify the quantitative preciseness of our analysis.

**Other Leakages**   Aside from the leakage of required reserves at each step of the lending process, two other leakages of money from the commercial banks might occur, thereby dampening the money-creating potential of the banking system.

*1   Currency drains*   A borrower may request that a part of his or her loan be paid in cash. Or the recipient of a check drawn by a borrower may present it at the bank to be redeemed partially or wholly in currency rather than added to the borrower's account. Thus, if the person who borrowed the $80 from bank A in our illustration asked for $16 of it in cash and the remaining $64 as a demand deposit, bank B would receive only $64 in new reserves (of which only $51.20 would be excess) rather than $80 (of which $64 was excess). This decline in excess reserves reduces the lending potential of the banking system accordingly. As a matter of fact, if the first borrower had taken the entire $80 in cash and if this currency remained in circulation, the multiple expansion process would have stopped then and there. But the convenience and safety of demand deposits make this unlikely.

*2   Excess reserves*   Our analysis of the commercial banking system's ability to expand the money supply by lending is based on the supposition that commercial banks are willing to meet precisely the legal reserve requirement. In practice, bankers are more prudent than this and arrange to have a "safety margin" of excess reserves to avoid the embarrassment of falling below the legal reserve ratio in the event that an unusually large amount of checks is cleared against them. Therefore bank A, upon receiving $100 in new cash, might choose to add $25, rather than the legal minimum of $20, to its reserves, the extra $5 serving as a buffer, or cushion, against adverse check

clearings. The overall credit expansion potential of the banking system would obviously be reduced by such additions to a bank's excess reserves.[8]

**Willingness versus Ability to Lend**   It is only fair to emphasize that our illustration of the banking system's ability to create money rests upon the assumption that commercial banks are willing to exercise their abilities to create money by lending and that households and businesses are willing to borrow. In practice, this need not be the case. Bankers, you will recall, seek a proper balance between prudence and profits. When prosperity reigns, banks may expand credit to the maximum of their ability. Why not? Loans are interest-earning assets, and in good times there is little fear of borrowers' defaulting. But if depression clouds appear on the economic horizon, bankers may hastily withdraw their invitations to borrow, seeking the safety of liquidity even if it involves the sacrifice of potential interest income. Bankers may fear the large-scale withdrawal of deposits by a panicky public and simultaneously doubt the ability of borrowers to repay. It is not too surprising that during some years of the Great Depression of the 1930s, banks had considerable excess reserves but lending was at a low ebb. Obviously, if the amount actually loaned by each commercial bank falls short of its excess reserves, the resulting multiple expansion of credit will be curtailed.

**The Need for Control**   The fact that bankers may not expand the supply of money to their maximum ability is of more than passing interest. It may be a factor which contrib-

---

[8]Specifically, in our $m = \dfrac{1}{R}$ monetary multiplier, we now add to $R$, the required reserve ratio, the additional excess reserves which bankers choose to keep. For example, if banks want to hold additional excess reserves equal to 5 percent of any newly acquired demand deposits, then the denominator becomes .25 (equal to the .20 reserve ratio plus the .05 addition to excess reserves). The monetary multiplier is reduced from 5 to 1/.25, or 4.

utes significantly to business fluctuations. By holding back on credit expansion as the economy begins to slip into a depression, commercial banks may further inhibit total spending and intensify that cyclical downswing. Indeed, a rapid shrinkage of the money supply contributed to the Great Depression of the 1930s. Conversely, by lending and thereby creating money to the maximum of their ability during prosperity, commercial banks may contribute to an excess of total spending and to the resulting inflationary pressures. Chapter 16 will explore the means by which the Board of Governors attempts to influence the lending policies of commercial banks so that they will offset rather than enforce cyclical fluctuations.

## Summary

**1** Commercial banks create money—that is, demand deposits, or bank money—when they make loans. The creation of demand deposits by bank lending is the most important source of money in our economy.

**2** The ability of a single commercial bank to create money by lending depends upon the size of its *excess* reserves. Generally speaking, a commercial bank can lend only an amount equal to the size of its excess reserves. It is thus limited because, in all likelihood, checks drawn by borrowers will be deposited in other banks, causing a loss of reserves and deposits to the lending bank equal to the amount which it has loaned.

**3** The commercial banking system as a whole can lend by a multiple of its excess reserves because the banking *system* cannot lose reserves, although individual banks can lose reserves to other banks in the system. The multiple by which the banking system can lend on the basis of each dollar of *excess* reserves is the reciprocal of the reserve ratio. This multiple credit expansion process is reversible.

## Questions and Study Suggestions

**1** Key terms and concepts to remember: balance sheet; fractional reserve system of banking; vault cash; legal (required) reserve deposit; reserve ratio; actual and excess reserves; monetary multiplier; and leakages.

**2** Why must a balance sheet always balance? What are the major assets and claims on a commercial bank's balance sheet?

**3** Why are commercial banks required to have reserves? Explain why reserves are assets to commercial banks but liabilities to the Federal Reserve Banks. What are excess reserves? How do you calculate the amount of excess reserves held by a bank? What is their significance?

**4** "Whenever currency is deposited in a commercial bank, cash goes out of circulation and, as a result, the supply of money is reduced." Do you agree? Explain.

**5** "When a commercial bank makes loans, it creates money; when loans are retired, money is destroyed." Explain.

**6** Explain why a single commercial bank can safely lend only an amount equal to its excess reserves but the commercial banking system can lend by a multiple of its excess reserves. Why is the multiple by which the banking system can lend equal to the reciprocal of its reserve ratio?

**7** Assume that Jones deposits $500 in currency in the First National Bank. A half-hour later Smith negotiates a loan for $750 at this bank. By how much and in what direction has the money supply changed? Explain.

**8** Suppose the Continental Bank has the following simplified balance sheet. The reserve ratio is 20 percent.

| Assets |  | (1) | (2) | Liabilities and net worth |  | (1) | (2) |
|---|---|---|---|---|---|---|---|
| Reserves | $22,000 | ___ | ___ | Demand | | | |
| Securities | 38,000 | ___ | ___ | deposits | $100,000 | ___ | ___ |
| Loans | 40,000 | ___ | ___ | | | | |

    ***a.*** What is the maximum amount of new loans which this bank can make? Show in column 1 how the bank's balance sheet will appear after the bank has loaned this additional amount.

    ***b.*** By how much has the supply of money changed? Explain.

    ***c.*** How will the bank's balance sheet appear after checks drawn for the entire amount of the new loans have been cleared against this bank? Show this new balance sheet in column 2.

    ***d.*** Answer questions *a, b,* and *c* on the assumption that the reserve ratio is 15 percent.

**9** Suppose the National Bank of Commerce has excess reserves of $8000 and outstanding demand deposits of $150,000. If the reserve ratio is 20 percent, what is the size of the bank's actual reserves?

**10** Suppose the following is a simplified consolidated balance sheet for the commercial banking system. All figures are in billions. The reserve ratio is 25 percent.

| Assets |  | (1) | Liabilities and net worth |  | (1) |
|---|---|---|---|---|---|
| Reserves | $ 52 | ___ | Demand | | |
| Securities | 48 | ___ | deposits | $200 | ___ |
| Loans | 100 | ___ | | | |

    ***a.*** How much excess reserves does the commercial banking system have? How much can the banking system lend? Show in column 1 how the consolidated balance sheet would look after this amount has been lent.

    ***b.*** Answer question 10*a* on the assumption that the reserve ratio is 20 percent. Explain the resulting difference in the lending ability of the commercial banking system.

**11** The Third National Bank has reserves of $20,000 and demand deposits of $100,000. The reserve ratio is 20 percent. Households deposit $5000 in currency in the bank. This $5000 is added by the bank to its reserves. How much excess reserves does the bank now have?

**12** Suppose again that the Third National Bank has reserves of $20,000 and demand deposits of $100,000. The reserve ratio remains at 20 percent. The bank now sells $5000 in securities to the Federal Reserve Bank in its district, receiving a $5000 increase in reserves in return. How much excess reserves does the bank now have? Why does your answer differ (yes, it does!) from the answer to question 11?

**13** What are "leakages"? How might they affect the money-creating potential of the banking system? Be specific.

# Selected References

Chandler, Lester V., and Stephen M. Goldfeld: *The Economics of Money and Banking,* 7th ed. (New York: Harper & Row, Publishers, Incorporated, 1977), chaps. 6, 7.

Duesenberry, James S.: *Money and Credit: Impact and Control,* 3d ed. (Englewood Cliffs, N.J.: Prentice-Hall, Inc., 1972).

Hutchingson, Harry D.: *Money, Banking, and the United States Economy,* 4th ed. (Englewood Cliffs, N.J.: Prentice-Hall, Inc., 1980), chaps. 7–9.

Klein, John J.: *Money and the Economy,* 4th ed. (New York: Harcourt Brace Jovanovich, Inc., 1978), chaps. 5–7.

Ritter, Lawrence S., and William L. Silber: *Principles of Money, Banking, and Financial Markets,* 3d ed. (New York: Basic Books, Inc., Publishers, 1980), chap. 2.

Thomas, Lloyd B., Jr.: *Money, Banking, and Economic Activity* (Englewood Cliffs, N.J.: Prentice-Hall, Inc., 1979), chaps. 6–9.

# LAST WORD
## The Day the Bank Closed

The use of bank checks as money is taken for granted. It is "the next thing to a natural disaster" when the system breaks down.

Towner, N.D. (UPI)—The closing of the Pioneer State Bank of Towner—which wasn't federally insured—has brought business to a near standstill in the community of 900 and threatens its future.

Ivan Schiele, owner of the Towner Coast-To-Coast store, sat in the Keyhole Bar "drowning my worries." His life savings were in the Pioneer State Bank of Towner before it closed for an investigation.

"I've got everything invested in there—$60,000 to $80,000," he said.

The effects of the closing are widespread. The government of the county, the town of 900, and businesses are facing problems getting out their payrolls. Housewives can't write checks for groceries. Business has dropped off to almost nothing.

"I feel very, very sorry for the people of Towner," Governor Arthur Link said.

It was reminiscent of the "bank holiday" declared by President Franklin D. Roosevelt in the early days of the New Deal.

The Pioneer State Bank of Towner was closed last Friday for a state investigation of its financial health, especially the prospect of getting repayment of some questionable loans.

Officials hope they can find out just what the bank's status is within a week or so.

"I think people feel that things like this happen to somebody else," the governor said. "But just imagine it's happening to us. We're used to writing checks for groceries, utilities, clothes, just about everything, and suddenly we can't write a check for anything because our bank is closed up."

Link added, "It's the next thing to a natural disaster like a tornado or flood except this doesn't threaten people's lives. But it could if the impact continues and people can't buy the necessities of life."

"If this keeps up," said businesswoman Mrs. Avis Schwenke, "it's going to close up the city."

"Bank Closure Threatens Town's Future," *Lincoln Evening Journal,* December 3, 1976.

# The Federal Reserve Banks and Monetary Policy

# chapter 16

In Chapter 15 our attention was focused upon the money-creating ability of individual banks and the commercial banking system. Our discussion ended on a disturbing note: Unregulated commercial banking might contribute to cyclical fluctuations in business activity. That is, commercial banks will find it profitable to expand the supply of money during inflationary prosperity and to restrict the money supply in seeking liquidity during depression. It is the task of this chapter to see how the monetary authorities of American capitalism attempt to reverse the procyclical tendencies of the commercial banking system through a variety of control techniques.

More specifically, the goals of the present chapter are these: First, the objectives of monetary policy, the roles of participating institutions, and the route by which monetary policy affects the operation of the economy are detailed. Next, the balance sheet of the Federal Reserve Banks is surveyed, because it is through these central banks that monetary policy is largely implemented. Third, the techniques of monetary control are analyzed in considerable detail. What are the major instruments of monetary control and how do they function? Fourth, the cause-effect chain through which monetary policy functions is restated graphically and the effectiveness of monetary policy is evaluated. Finally, a brief, but important, recapitulation of Keynesian employment theory and policy is presented.

## □ OBJECTIVES OF MONETARY POLICY

Before analyzing the techniques through which monetary policy is put into effect, it is essential that we clearly understand the objectives of monetary policy and locate the institutions responsible for the formulation and implementation of that policy.

Certain key points made in Chapter 14

merit reemphasis at the outset of our discussion. The Board of Governors of the Federal Reserve System has the responsibility of supervising and controlling the operation of our monetary and banking systems. It is this Board which formulates the basic policies which the banking system follows. Because it is a public body, the decisions of the Board of Governors are made in what it perceives to be the public interest. The twelve Federal Reserve Banks—the central banks of American capitalism—have the responsibility of implementing the policy decisions of the Board. You will recall that as quasi-public banks, the Federal Reserve banks are not guided by the profit motive, but rather, they pursue those measures which the Board of Governors recommends.

However, to say that the Board follows policies which "promote the public interest" is not enough. We must pinpoint the goal of monetary policy. It will come as no great surprise that *the fundamental objective of monetary policy is to assist the economy in achieving a full-employment, noninflationary level of total output.* Monetary policy consists in altering the economy's money supply for the purpose of stabilizing aggregate output, employment, and the price level. More specifically, monetary policy entails increasing the money supply during a recession to stimulate spending and, conversely, restricting the money supply during inflation to constrain spending.

### △   Cause-Effect Chain

But precisely how does monetary policy work toward this goal? The process is complicated, but essentially it boils down to this:[1]

**1   Excess Reserves**   By invoking certain control techniques, the Board of Governors and the Federal Reserve Banks can influence the size of both actual and required reserves—and therefore the excess reserves—of commercial banks.

**2   Money Supply**   Because excess reserves are the basis upon which commercial banks can expand the money supply by lending, any manipulations of excess reserves through the control techniques of the Board of Governors will affect the supply of money, that is, the amounts which commercial banks will be able and willing to lend at various possible interest rates.

**3   Interest Rate**   Given Chapter 14's downsloping demand for money curve, changes in the supply of money will affect the cost and availability of money. That is, changes in the supply of money will affect the interest rate and the amount of credit bankers are willing to make available to borrowers.

**4   Aggregate Demand**   Changes in the cost and availability of bank credit will in turn have an impact upon the spending decisions of society, particularly upon investment decisions, and therefore upon the levels of output, employment, income, and prices.

The cause-effect chain between monetary policy and output and employment is summarized in this outline:

Federal monetary policy influences the size of commercial bank excess reserves
   *which*
Influence the supply of money
   *which*
Influences the interest rate (the cost) and the availability of bank credit
   *which*
Influences investment spending, output, employment, and the price level

Let us examine the operation of monetary policy through a simple example. Suppose the economy is operating below the full-employ-

---

[1] We present here the Keynesian interpretation of how monetary policy works. Chapter 17 is devoted to the significantly different "monetarist" view of how monetary policy functions.

ment mark. Sidestepping troublesome complications and qualifications for the moment, we find that monetary policy would work something like this:

**1**   The Board of Governors will direct the Federal Reserve Banks to pursue certain policies designed to *increase* the (excess) reserves of commercial banks.

**2**   Finding themselves with abundant excess reserves, commercial banks are now in a position to make available a greater supply of money by granting bank credit. The banking *system* can *expand* the supply of money by a multiple of its excess reserves.

**3**   With an increase in the supply of money relative to the demand for it, interest rates will *decline,* and the quantity of bank credit (money) taken by borrowers will *increase.*

**4**   Low interest rates and the greater availability of bank credit will induce *increases* in spending. These increases will be subject to the multiplier effect, driving the equilibrium NNP upward by a multiple of the initial increases in total spending.

These four comments detail the ideal operation of an *easy money policy.* A *tight money policy* follows the same route, but the procedure is to lower commercial bank reserves, reduce the supply of money, raise the cost and lessen the availability of bank credit, and thereby curtail spending. Tight money should obviously be invoked when an excess of total spending is causing inflation in the economy.

△   **Monetary Policy and Investment**

Economists are in general agreement that the investment component of total spending is more likely to be affected by changes in the interest rate than is consumer spending. The interest rate does not seem to be a very crucial factor in determining how households divide their disposable income between consumption and saving. Indeed, it is not clear whether decreases in the interest rate will tend to increase or decrease the amount of consumption. On the one hand, a lower interest rate may

induce some households, particularly those operating small businesses, to save less, because it is now cheap to finance by borrowing. On the other hand, we have noted that those who save to provide a given retirement income or to accumulate funds for the education of their children find that a lower interest rate will mean that a larger volume of saving will be required to earn the needed income. Then, too, the effect of higher interest rates on consumer installment buying is not great, because considerable increases or decreases in the interest rate have little impact on the size of each monthly payment; that is, the consumer is not impressed by the total interest charge but only by how much interest must be paid per month. Furthermore, any tendency for higher interest charges to diminish consumer installment buying can be largely canceled by extending the repayment period from, say, twenty-four to thirty-six months.

The impact of changing interest rates upon investment spending is greater because of the size and long-term nature of such purchases. Capital equipment, factory buildings, warehouses, and so forth, are tremendously expensive purchases. In absolute terms the interest charges on funds borrowed for these purchases will be considerable. Similarly, the interest cost on a house purchased on a long-term contract will be very large: A $\frac{1}{2}$ percent change in the interest rate could easily amount to thousands of dollars on the total cost of a home. It is important to note as well that changes in the interest rate may also affect investment spending by changing the relative attractiveness of capital equipment purchases and bond purchases. If the interest rate rises on bonds, then, given the profit expectations on capital good purchases, businesses will be more inclined to use business savings to purchase securities than to buy capital equipment. Conversely, given profit expectations on investment spending, a fall in the interest rate makes capital goods purchases more attractive than bond ownership. In short, the impact of changing interest rates will be primarily upon investment spending and, through this channel, upon output, employment, and the level of prices.

So much for the objectives of monetary policy and the cause-effect chain which its application entails. We now seek an understanding of the techniques by which the Board of Governors can manipulate the size of commercial bank reserves.

## □ CONSOLIDATED BALANCE SHEET OF THE FEDERAL RESERVE BANKS

Because monetary policy is implemented by the twelve Federal Reserve Banks, it is essential to consider the nature of the balance sheet of these banks. Some of the assets and liabilities found here are considerably different from those found on the balance sheet of a commercial bank. Table 16-1 is a consolidated balance sheet which shows all the pertinent assets and liabilities of the twelve Federal Reserve Banks as of January 31, 1979.

### △  Assets

**Gold Certificates**  Gold certificates are warehouse receipts for the gold bullion held by the Treasury. In settling international payments, the United States Treasury may buy gold from foreign monetary authorities. The Treasury pays for such gold by drawing checks against its deposit in the Federal Reserve Banks. The clearing of these checks reduces Treasury deposits in the Federal Reserve

Banks. To replenish these deposits, the Treasury issues gold certificates—claims or warehouse receipts against the newly obtained gold—and deposits them in the Federal Reserve Banks. Treasury sales of gold to foreign monetary authorities have the opposite effect, reducing the Federal Reserve Banks' holdings of gold certificates.

**Securities**  These securities are the government bonds which the Federal Reserve Banks have purchased. Some of these bonds may have been purchased directly from the Treasury, but most are bought in the open market from commercial banks or the public. Although these bonds are an important source of income to the Federal Reserve Banks, they are not bought and sold purposely for income. Rather, as we shall see, they are bought and sold primarily to influence the size of commercial bank reserves and therefore their ability to create money by lending.

**Loans to Commercial Banks**  Commercial banks occasionally borrow from the Federal Reserve Banks. The IOUs which the commercial banks give to the bankers' banks in negotiating loans are listed as loans to commercial banks. From the Federal Reserve Banks' point of view, these IOUs are assets, that is, claims against the commercial banks which have borrowed from them. To the commercial banks, these IOUs are liabilities. In borrowing, the commercial banks obtain increases in their reserves in exchange for IOUs.

**TABLE 16-1**
Twelve Federal Reserve Banks' Consolidated Balance Sheet, January 31, 1979 (*in millions*)

| Assets | | Liabilities and net worth | |
|---|---|---|---|
| Gold certificates . . . . . . . . . . . . . . . . . . | $ 11,112 | Reserves of member banks . . . . . . . . . . | $ 29,520 |
| Securities . . . . . . . . . . . . . . . . . . . . . . . | 116,239 | Treasury deposits . . . . . . . . . . . . . . . . | 4,075 |
| Loans to commercial banks | 1,454 | Federal Reserve Notes (outstanding) . . . | 113,355 |
| All other assets . . . . . . . . . . . . . . . . . . | 31,054 | All other liabilities and net worth . . . . . | 12,909 |
| Total . . . . . . . . . . . . . . . . . . . . . . . | $159,859 | Total . . . . . . . . . . . . . . . . . . . . . . . | $159,859 |

*Source: Federal Reserve Bulletin,* January 1980.

△ **Liabilities**

On the liability side we find three major items:

**Reserves of Member Banks**  We are already familiar with this account. It is an asset from the viewpoint of the member banks but a liability to the Federal Reserve Banks.

**Treasury Deposits**  Just as businesses and private individuals find it convenient and desirable to pay their obligations by check, so does the United States Treasury. It keeps deposits in the various Federal Reserve Banks and draws checks on them in paying its obligations. To the Treasury such deposits are obviously assets; to the Federal Reserve Banks, liabilities. The Treasury creates and replenishes these deposits by depositing tax receipts, money borrowed from the public or the banks through the sale of bonds, and gold certificates.

**Federal Reserve Notes**  Virtually all our paper money supply is Federal Reserve Notes. These notes are issued by the Federal Reserve Banks. When in circulation, these pieces of paper money constitute circulating claims against the assets of the Federal Reserve Banks and are therefore treated by them as liabilities. Just as your own IOU is neither an asset nor a liability to you when it is in your own possession, so Federal Reserve Notes resting in the vaults of the various Federal Reserve Banks are neither an asset nor a liability. Only those notes in circulation are liabilities to the bankers' banks. These notes, which come into circulation through commercial banks, are not a part of the money supply until they are in the hands of the public.

□ **THE TOOLS OF MONETARY POLICY**

With this cursory understanding of the Federal Reserve Banks' balance sheet, we are now in a position to explore how the Board of Governors of the Federal Reserve System can influence the money-creating abilities of the commercial banking system. What tools or techniques can be employed at the discretion of the Board of Governors to influence commercial bank reserves?

The general, or quantitative, controls of the monetary authorities are three in number: (1) open-market operations, (2) changing the reserve ratio, and (3) changing the discount rate. These controls are general, or quantitative, in that they seek to manipulate the total quantity of bank credit. Later, we shall briefly mention selective, or qualitative, controls, which are aimed at influencing the volume of specific types of credit.

△ **Open-Market Operations**

Open-market operations are the most important means by which the money supply is controlled. The term *open-market operations* simply refers to the buying and selling of government bonds by the Federal Reserve Banks in the open market—that is, the buying and selling of bonds from or to commercial banks and the general public. How do these bond purchases and sales affect the excess reserves of commercial banks?

**Buying Securities**  Suppose the Board of Governors orders the Federal Reserve Banks to buy government bonds in the open market. From whom may these securities be purchased? In general, from commercial banks and the public. In either case the overall effect is basically the same—commercial bank reserves are increased.

Let us trace through the process by which the Federal Reserve Banks buy government bonds *from commercial banks*. This transaction is a simple one.

*a.*  The commercial banks give up a part of their holdings of securities to the bankers' banks.

*b.*  The Federal Reserve Banks pay for these securities by increasing the reserves of the commercial banks by the amount of the purchase.

Just as the commercial bank may pay for a bond bought from a private individual by increasing the seller's demand deposit, so the bankers' bank may pay for bonds bought from commercial banks by increasing the banks' reserves. In short, the consolidated balance sheets of the commercial banks and the Federal Reserve Banks will change as shown below.

**Federal Reserve Banks**

| Assets | Liabilities and net worth |
|---|---|
| + Securities (*a*) | + Reserves of member banks (*b*) |
| (*a*) Securities | (*b*) + Reserves |

**Commercial Banks**

| Assets | Liabilities and net worth |
|---|---|
| − Securities (*a*) <br> + Reserves (*b*) |  |

The most important aspect of this transaction is that, when Federal Reserve Banks purchase securities from commercial banks, the reserves—and therefore the lending ability—of the commercial banks are increased.

If the Federal Reserve Banks should purchase securities *from the general public*, the effect on commercial bank reserves would be substantially the same. Suppose that the Grisley Meat Packing Company possesses some negotiable government bonds which it sells in the open market to the Federal Reserve Banks. The transaction goes like this:

*a.* The Grisley company gives up securities to the Federal Reserve Banks and gets in payment a check drawn by the Federal Reserve Banks on themselves.

*b.* The Grisley company promptly deposits this check in its account with the Wahoo bank.

*c.* The Wahoo bank collects this check against the Federal Reserve Banks by sending it to the Federal Reserve Banks for collection. As a result the Wahoo bank receives an increase in its reserves.

Balance sheet changes are as shown below.

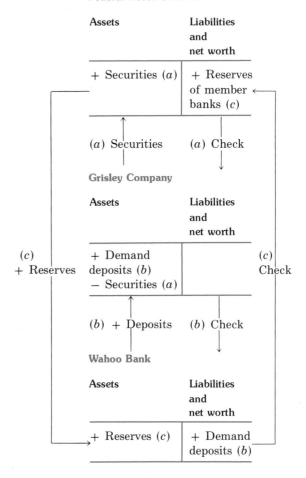

Two aspects of this transaction are noteworthy. First, as with Federal Reserve purchases of securities directly from commercial banks, the reserves and lending ability of the commercial banking system have been increased. Second, in this instance the supply of money is directly increased by the central banks' purchase of government bonds, aside from any expansion of the money supply which may occur as the result of the increase in commercial bank reserves.

You may detect a slight difference between the Federal Reserve Banks' purchases of securities from the commercial banking system and from the public. Assuming all commercial banks are "loaned up" initially, Federal Reserve bond purchases from commercial banks will increase the actual reserves and excess reserves of the commercial banks by the entire amount of the bond purchases. Thus a $1000 bond purchase from a commercial bank would increase both the actual and excess reserves of the commercial bank by $1000. On the other hand, Federal Reserve Bank purchases of bonds from the public increase actual reserves but also increase demand deposits. Thus a $1000 bond purchase from the public would increase actual reserves of the "loaned up" banking system by $1000; but with a 20 percent reserve ratio, the excess reserves of the banking system would only amount to $800. In the case of bond purchases from the public, it is *as if* the commercial banking system had already used one-fifth, or 20 percent, of its newly acquired reserves to support $1000 worth of new demand deposit money.

However, in each transaction the basic conclusion is the same: *When the Federal Reserve Banks buy securities in the open market, commercial banks' reserves will be increased.*

**Selling Securities**    We should now be highly suspicious that Federal Reserve Bank sales of government bonds will reduce commercial bank reserves. Let us confirm these suspicions.

Suppose the Federal Reserve Banks sell securities in the open market to *commercial banks:*

*a.*    The Federal Reserve Banks give up securities which the commercial banks obviously acquire.

*b.*    The commercial banks pay for these securities by drawing checks against their deposits—that is, their reserves—in the Federal Reserve Banks. The Federal Reserve Banks collect these checks by reducing the commercial banks' reserves accordingly.

In short, the balance sheet changes appear as follows:

**Federal Reserve Banks**

| Assets | Liabilities and net worth |
|---|---|
| − Securities (*a*) | − Reserves of member banks (*b*) |
| (*a*) Securities | (*b*) − Reserves |

**Commercial Banks**

| Assets | Liabilities and net worth |
|---|---|
| − Reserves (*b*) <br> + Securities (*a*) | |

Note specifically the reduction in commercial bank reserves.

Should the Federal Reserve Banks sell securities *to the public,* the overall effect would be substantially the same. Let us put the Grisley company on the buying end of government bonds which the Federal Reserve Banks are selling.

*a.*    The Federal Reserve Bank sells government bonds to the Grisley company, the latter paying for these securities by a check drawn on the Wahoo bank.

*b.*    The Federal Reserve Banks clear this check against the Wahoo bank by reducing its reserves.

*c.*    The Wahoo bank returns the Grisley company's check to it, reducing the company's demand deposit accordingly.

The balance sheets change as shown at the top of page 314:

Note that Federal Reserve bond sales of

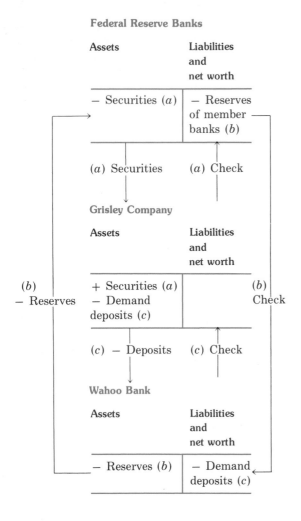

Federal Reserve Banks

| Assets | Liabilities and net worth |
|--------|---------------------------|
| − Securities (a) | − Reserves of member banks (b) |
| (a) Securities | (a) Check |

Grisley Company

| Assets | Liabilities and net worth |
|--------|---------------------------|
| + Securities (a) <br> − Demand deposits (c) | |
| (c) − Deposits | (c) Check |

Wahoo Bank

| Assets | Liabilities and net worth |
|--------|---------------------------|
| − Reserves (b) | − Demand deposits (c) |

(b) − Reserves

(b) Check

## △   The Reserve Ratio

How can the Board of Governors influence the ability of commercial banks to lend through manipulation of the legal reserve ratio? A simple example will supply a clear answer to this query. Starting with row 2 of Table 16-2, suppose a commercial bank's balance sheet shows that reserves are $5000 and demand deposits $20,000. If the legal reserve ratio stands at 20 percent, the bank's *required* reserves are $4000. Since *actual* reserves are $5000, it is apparent that the *excess* reserves of this bank are $1000. On the basis of this $1000 of excess reserves, we have seen that this single bank can lend $1000, but the banking system as a whole could create a maximum of $5000 in new bank money by lending. Now, what if the Board of Governors raised the legal reserve ratio from 20 to 25 percent (row 3)? Required reserves would jump from $4000 to $5000, shrinking excess reserves from $1000 to zero. It is obvious that *raising the reserve ratio increases the amount of required reserves banks must keep. Either banks lose excess reserves, diminishing their ability to create money by lending, or else they find their reserves deficient and are forced to contract the money supply.* In the case just cited, excess reserves are transformed into required reserves, and the money-creating potential of our *single bank* is reduced from $1000 to zero. The *banking system's* money-creating capacity declines from $5000 to zero.

What if the Board of Governors announced a forthcoming increase in the legal reserve requirement to 30 percent (row 4)? The commercial bank would be faced with the embarrassing prospect of failing to meet this requirement. To protect itself against such an eventuality, the bank would be forced to lower its outstanding demand deposits and at the same time to increase its reserves. To reduce its demand deposits, the bank would be disposed to let outstanding loans mature and to be repaid without extending new credit. To increase reserves, the bank might sell some of its holdings of securities, adding the proceeds

$1000 to the commercial banking system reduce the system's actual and excess reserves by $1000. But a $1000 bond sale to the public reduces excess reserves by $800 because demand-deposit money is also reduced by $1000 by the sale. In the case of bond sales to the public, it is *as if* the commercial banking system had reduced its outstanding demand deposits by $1000 to cushion the decline in excess reserves to the extent of $200.

In both variations of the Federal Reserve bond sale transaction, however, the basic conclusion is the same: *When the Federal Reserve Banks sell securities in the open market, commercial bank reserves are reduced.*

**TABLE 16-2**

**The Effects of Changes in the Reserve Ratio Upon the Lending Ability of Commercial Banks (*hypothetical data*)**

| (1) Legal reserve ratio, percent | (2) Demand deposits | (3) Actual reserves | (4) Required reserves | (5) Excess reserves, or (3) − (4) | (6) Money-creating potential of single bank, = (5) | (7) Money-creating potential of banking system |
|---|---|---|---|---|---|---|
| (1) 10 | $20,000 | $5000 | $2000 | $ 3000 | $ 3000 | $ 30,000 |
| (2) 20 | 20,000 | 5000 | 4000 | 1000 | 1000 | 5,000 |
| (3) 25 | 20,000 | 5000 | 5000 | 0 | 0 | 0 |
| (4) 30 | 20,000 | 5000 | 6000 | −1000 | −1000 | −3,333 |

to its reserves. Both courses of action will reduce the supply of money (see Chapter 15, transactions 6 and 7).

What would be the effect if the Board of Governors lowered the reserve ratio from the original 20 to 10 percent (row 1)? In this case, required reserves would decline from $4000 to $2000, and as a result, excess reserves would jump from $1000 to $3000. We can conclude that *lowering the reserve ratio changes required reserves to excess reserves, thereby enhancing the ability of banks to create new money by lending.*

Table 16-2 reveals that a change in the reserve ratio affects the money-creating ability of the *banking system* in two ways. First, it affects the size of excess reserves. Second, it changes the size of the monetary multiplier. Thus, for example, in raising the legal reserve ratio from 10 to 20 percent, excess reserves are reduced from $3000 to $1000, on the one hand, and the demand deposit multiplier is reduced from 10 to 5. Hence, the money-creating potential of the banking system declines from $30,000 (= $3000 × 10) to $5000 (= $1000 × 5).

Although changing the reserve ratio is a potentially powerful technique of monetary control, it is actually used infrequently. For example, reserve requirements have not been changed since December of 1976.

△ **The Discount Rate**

One of the traditional functions of a central bank is to be a "lender of last resort." That is, central banks will lend to commercial banks which are financially sound, but which have unexpected and immediate needs for additional funds. Thus it is that each Federal Reserve Bank will make short-term loans to commercial banks in its district.

When a commercial bank borrows, it turns over to the Federal Reserve Bank a promissory note or IOU drawn against itself and secured by acceptable collateral—typically United States government securities. Just as commercial banks charge interest on their loans, so do the Federal Reserve Banks charge interest on the loans they grant to commercial banks. This interest rate is called the *discount rate.*

Being a claim against the commercial bank, the borrowing bank's promissory note is an asset to the lending Federal Reserve Bank and appears on its balance sheet as "loans to commercial banks." To the commercial bank the IOU is a liability, appearing as "Loans from the Federal Reserve Banks" on the commercial bank's balance sheet. In payment of the loan the Federal Reserve Bank will *increase* the reserves of the borrowing commercial bank. Since no required reserves need be kept against loans from the Federal Reserve Banks, *all* new reserves acquired by borrowing from the Federal Reserve Banks would be excess reserves. These changes are reflected in the balance sheets of the commercial banks and the bankers' banks as follows:

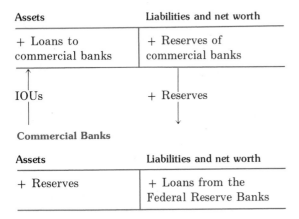

**Federal Reserve Banks**

| Assets | Liabilities and net worth |
|---|---|
| + Loans to commercial banks | + Reserves of commercial banks |
| IOUs | + Reserves |

**Commercial Banks**

| Assets | Liabilities and net worth |
|---|---|
| + Reserves | + Loans from the Federal Reserve Banks |

It is interesting to note that this transaction is analogous to a private person's borrowing from a commercial bank (see Chapter 15, transaction 6).

The important point, of course, is that *commercial bank borrowing from the Federal Reserve Banks increases the reserves of commercial banks, thereby enhancing their ability to extend credit to the public.*

The Board of Governors of the Federal Reserve System has the power to establish and manipulate the discount rate at which commercial banks can borrow from the Federal Reserve Banks. From the commercial banks' point of view, the discount rate obviously constitutes a cost entailed in acquiring reserves. Hence, when the discount rate is decreased, commercial banks are encouraged to obtain additional reserves by borrowing from the Federal Reserve Bank. Commercial bank lending based upon these new reserves will constitute an increase in the money supply. Conversely, an increase in the discount rate discourages commercial banks from obtaining

additional reserves through borrowing from the central banks. An increase in the discount rate is obviously consistent with the monetary authorities' desire to restrict the supply of money.

△ **Easy Money and Tight Money**

Suppose the economy is faced with unemployment and deflation. The monetary authorities correctly decide that an increase in the supply of money is needed to stimulate the volume of spending in order to help absorb the idle resources. To induce an increase in the supply of money, the Board of Governors must see to it that the excess reserves of commercial banks are expanded. What specific policies will bring this about?

**1** The Board of Governors should order the Federal Reserve Banks to buy securities in the open market. These bond purchases will be paid for by increases in commercial bank reserves.

**2** The reserve ratio should be reduced, automatically changing required reserves into excess reserves.

**3** The discount rate should be lowered to induce commercial banks to add to their reserves by borrowing from the Federal Reserve Banks.

For obvious reasons, this set of policy decisions is called an *easy money policy*. Its purpose is to make credit cheaply and easily available, so as to increase the volumes of spending and employment.

Suppose, on the other hand, excessive spending is pushing the economy into an inflationary spiral. The Board of Governors should attempt to reduce total spending by limiting or contracting the supply of money. The key to this goal lies in reducing the reserves of commercial banks. How is this done?

**1** The Federal Reserve Banks should sell government bonds in the open market to tear down commercial bank reserves.

**2** Increasing the reserve ratio will automatically strip commercial banks of excess reserves.

**3** A boost in the discount rate will discourage commercial banks from building up their reserves by borrowing at the Federal Reserve Banks.

This group of directives is appropriately labeled a *tight money policy*. The objective is to tighten the supply of money in order to reduce spending and control inflationary pressures.

△ **Relative Importance**

Of the three major monetary controls, open-market operations clearly have evolved as the most important control mechanism. The reasons for this development are worth noting.

The discount rate is less important than open-market operations for two interrelated reasons. First, in fact the amount of commercial bank reserves obtained by borrowing from the central banks is typically very small. On the average only 3 or 4 percent of bank reserves are acquired in this way. Indeed, it is often the effectiveness of open-market operations which induces the commercial banks to borrow from the Federal Reserve Banks. That is, to the extent that central bank bond sales make commercial banks temporarily short of reserves, the commercial banks will be prompted to borrow from the Federal Reserve Banks. Hence, rather than being a primary tool of monetary policy, discounting occurs largely in response to monetary policy as carried out by open-market operations.

A second consideration is that, while the manipulation of commercial bank reserves through open-market operations and the changing of reserve requirements are accomplished at the initiative of the Federal Reserve System, the discount rate depends upon the initiative of the commercial banks to be effective. For example, if the discount rate is lowered at a time when very few banks are inclined to borrow from the Federal Reserve Banks, the lower rate will have little or no impact upon bank reserves or the money supply.[2]

What about changes in reserve requirements?[3]

Because the impact is so powerful, so blunt, so immediate, and so widespread, the Federal Reserve uses its authority to change reserve requirements only sparingly, particularly during tight money periods when increases in reserve requirements would be appropriate. An increase in reserve requirements reduces commercial bank profitability, since banks then must hold a larger percentage of their assets in reserve balances that earn no interest. As membership in the Federal Reserve System is voluntary (except for banks with national charters), the Federal Reserve is not eager to discourage membership by raising reserve requirements too frequently. The "harsh hand of the Fed" is most evident when tight money is executed through higher reserve requirements. Since 1951, reserve requirements against demand deposits have been increased only five times, whereas they have been lowered on nine occasions.

But there are more positive reasons why open-market operations have evolved as the primary technique of monetary policy. This mechanism of monetary control has the advantage of flexibility—government securities can be purchased or sold in large or small amounts—and the impact upon bank reserves is quite prompt. Yet, compared with reserve-requirement changes, open-market operations work subtly and less directly. Furthermore, quantitatively there is no question about the potential ability of the Federal Reserve Banks to affect commercial bank reserves through bond sales and purchases. A glance at the

---

[2]Some economists point out that a change in the discount rate may have an important "announcement effect"; that is, a discount rate change may be a very clear and explicit way of communicating to the financial community and the economy as a whole the intended direction of monetary policy. Other economists doubt this, arguing that changes in the discount rate are often "passive" in that the rate is changed to keep it in line with other short-term interest rates, rather than to invoke a policy change.

[3]Lawrence S. Ritter and William L. Silber, *Money,* 2d ed. (New York: Basic Books, Inc., Publishers, 1973), p. 112.

consolidated balance sheet for the Federal Reserve Banks (Table 16-1) reveals very large holdings of government bonds ($116 billion), the sales of which could theoretically reduce commercial bank reserves from $30 billion to zero!

△ **Minor Qualitative Controls**

The three major instruments of monetary policy are supplemented periodically by certain other, less important credit controls in the form of qualitative, or selective, controls which pertain to the stock market, installment purchases, and moral suasion.

**Margin Requirement**  In some instances the overall flow of money and credit in the economy has been fairly serene, and at the same time speculative stock market purchases threaten to precipitate economic difficulties. To thwart this possibility, the Board of Governors has the authority to specify the *margin requirement,* or minimum percentage down payment which purchasers of stock must make. Thus, the current margin requirement of 50 percent means that only 50 percent of the purchase price of a security may be borrowed, the remaining 50 percent being paid "cash on the barrelhead." This rate will be raised when it is deemed desirable to restrict speculative stock purchases and lowered to revive a sluggish market. In fact, the 50 percent requirement has applied since 1974.

**Consumer and Real Estate Credit**  Congress occasionally has authorized the Board of Governors to invoke specific restraints on consumer credit. During World War II, money incomes were increasing at a time when the output of civilian goods was declining because of the drastic rechanneling of resources to the production of war goods. The result was sharp inflationary pressure in certain consumer goods industries. To dampen this pressure, Congress gave the Board of Governors temporary authority to specify minimum down payments and maximum repayment periods on loans involving the purchase of real estate and a variety of consumer durables.

Current example: Using legislative authority available to him, President Carter ordered the Federal Reserve in the spring of 1980 to impose new restrictions upon consumer borrowing as a part of his anti-inflation program. Specifically, lenders are required to make a "special deposit" in the Federal Reserve banks equal to 15 percent of any *increase* in the total amount of credit outstanding in the form of credit card purchases or unsecured personal loans. Because these special deposits earn no interest, they will increase the costs of lenders and discourage further expansions of consumer credit.

**Moral Suasion**  The monetary authorities sometimes use the less tangible technique of moral suasion to influence the lending policies of commercial banks. Moral suasion simply means the employment by the monetary authorities of "friendly persuasion"—policy statements, public pronouncements, or outright appeals—warning that excessive expansion or contraction of bank credit might involve serious consequences for the banking system and the economy as a whole. Such pronouncements are not limited to bank credit in general; they may call for the curtailment of specific types of bank credit. For example, in 1966 the Federal Reserve urged banks to limit the expansion of loans to businesses as rising military expenditures began to intensify inflationary pressures. Second example: In March of 1980 the Federal Reserve "strongly recommended" that banks restrict their lending to an annual growth rate of 6 to 9 percent, a figure substantially below the 20 percent growth rate otherwise anticipated.

☐ **MONETARY POLICY AND EQUILIBRIUM NNP: A RESTATEMENT**
At the beginning of this chapter the cause-effect chain through which monetary policy operates was outlined in a simplified fashion.

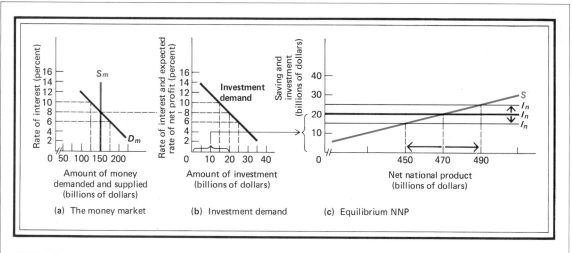

**FIGURE 16-1  MONETARY POLICY AND THE EQUILIBRIUM NNP**

An easy money policy will lower the interest rate, increase the investment component of aggregate demand, and thereby increase the equilibrium level of NNP.  Conversely, a tight money policy will raise the rate of interest, reduce the investment component of aggregate demand, and restrain demand-pull inflation.

We are now in a position to restate the relevant cause-effect relationships at a more sophisticated level.

### △  The Money Market, Investment, and NNP

Figure 16-1 is the focal point for this restatement. The diagram at the left shows the *money market,* wherein the demand for money curve, $D_m$, and the supply of money curve, $S_m$, are brought together. Recall from Chapter 14[4] that the total demand for money is comprised of the transactions and the asset demands. The former is directly related to the level of economic transactions as reflected in the size of the money NNP. The latter is inversely related to the interest rate. Recall too that the interest rate is the opportunity cost of holding money as an asset; the higher the cost, the smaller the amount of money the public wants

to hold.  In Figure 16-1a the total demand for money is related to the interest rate. In this presentation an increase in money NNP will shift $D_m$ to the right; a decline in money NNP will shift $D_m$ to the left.

We complete our portrayal of the money market by adding the money supply, $S_m$. The money supply is shown as a vertical line on the assumption that it is some fixed amount determined by the Board of Governor's policy independently of the rate of interest. In other words, while monetary policy (the supply of money) helps determine the interest rate, the interest rate does not in turn determine monetary policy. Figure 16-1a tells us that, given the demand for money, if the supply of money is $150 billion, the equilibrium interest rate will be 8 percent.

This 8 percent interest rate is projected off the investment-demand curve of Figure 16-1b. We find that at this 8 percent interest rate it will be profitable for businesses to invest $20 billion. Finally, in Figure 16-1c this $20 billion

---

[4]You might find it helpful to reread the section entitled "The Demand for Money" in Chapter 14 at this point.

of investment is plugged into the simple leak-ages-injections model for the private economy to determine the equilibrium level of NNP. *If this $470 billion equilibrium level of NNP en-tails unemployment, an easy money policy will increase the money supply, lower the interest rate, make a larger volume of investment spending profitable, and thereby expand the equilibrium NNP to, or at least toward, full employment.* More concretely, if the full-employment NNP is $490 billion, an increase in the money supply from $150 to $175 billion will reduce the interest rate from 8 to 6 percent and increase investment from $20 to $25 bil-lion, as shown in Figure 16-1b. This $5 billion upshift of the investment schedule from $I_{n1}$ to $I_{n2}$ in Figure 16-1c, subject to the relevant multiplier of 4, will increase equilibrium NNP from $470 billion to the desired $490 billion full-employment level. Conversely, *if* the orig-inal $470 billion NNP generates demand-pull inflation, a *tight money* policy will reduce the supply of money, increase the interest rate, cause a decline in investment, and thereby eliminate the inflationary gap. To illustrate: If the full-employment, noninflationary NNP is $450 billion, an inflationary gap of $5 billion will exist. That is, at the $450 billion level of NNP, planned investment exceeds saving—and therefore aggregate demand exceeds aggregate supply—by $5 billion. A decline in the money supply from $150 to $125 billion will increase the interest rate from 8 to 10 percent and re-duce investment from $20 to $15 billion in Figure 16-1b. The consequent $5 billion down-shift in Figure 16-1c's investment schedule from $I_{n1}$ to $I_{n3}$ will equate planned investment and saving—and therefore aggregate demand and aggregate supply—at the $450 billion NNP, thereby eliminating the initial $5 billion inflationary gap.

△ **Refinements and Feedbacks**

The components of Figure 16-1 allow us to (1) appreciate some of the factors which deter-mine the effectiveness of monetary policy and (2) note the existence of a "feedback" or

"circularity" problem which complicates mon-etary policy.

**Policy Effectiveness**   Figure 16-1 cor-rectly indicates the *directions* in which an easy or tight money policy will change the interest rate, investment, and the equilibrium NNP. It tells us little about the *magnitude* of the indi-cated changes and therefore about the effec-tiveness of monetary policy. What determines whether a given change in the money supply has a large or a small impact upon equilibrium NNP? The answer is: The shapes of the demand-for-money and investment-demand curves. You might pencil in alternative curves to convince yourself that *the steeper the $D_m$ curve, the larger will be the effect of any given change in the money supply upon the equilib-rium rate of interest. Furthermore, any given change in the interest rate will have a larger impact upon investment—and hence upon equilibrium NNP—the flatter the investment-demand curve.* In other words, monetary pol-icy will be most effective when the demand for money curve is relatively steep and the invest-ment-demand curve is relatively flat. Mone-tary policy will tend to be relatively ineffective when the money demand curve is flat and the investment demand curve is steep. As we shall find in Chapter 17, there is considerable con-troversy as to the precise shapes of these curves.

**Feedback Effects**   The alert reader may have sensed in Figure 16-1 a feedback or circu-larity problem which complicates and influ-ences the effectiveness of monetary policy. Bluntly stated, the nature of the circularity problem is as follows: By reading Figure 16-1 from left to right (as we have) we discover that the interest rate, working through the invest-ment-demand curve, is an important determi-nant of the equilibrium NNP. Now we must recognize that causation also runs the other way. The level of NNP is a determinant of the equilibrium interest rate! This link comes about because the transactions component of the money demand curve depends directly upon the level of money NNP.

How does this feedback from Figure 16-1*c* to 16-1*a* affect monetary policy? It means that the increase in the NNP which an easy money policy brings about will in turn *increase* the demand for money, tending to partially offset or blunt the interest-reducing effect of the easy money policy. Conversely, a tight money policy will tend to reduce the NNP. But this in turn will *decrease* the demand for money and tend to dampen the initial interest-increasing effect of the tight money policy.

## □ EFFECTIVENESS OF MONETARY POLICY

How well does monetary policy work? Actually, the effectiveness of monetary policy is subject to considerable debate.

### △ Shortcomings and Problems

It must be recognized that monetary policy entails certain limitations and encounters a number of real-world complications.

**1  Cyclical Asymmetry**   If pursued vigorously enough, tight money can actually destroy commercial bank reserves to the point where banks are *forced* to contract the volume of loans. As tight money eliminates excess reserves, banks will be obliged to allow outstanding loans to mature without making offsetting loans to other borrowers. This means a contraction in the money supply. But an easy money policy suffers from a "You can lead a horse to water, but you can't make him drink" kind of problem. An easy money policy can do no more than see to it that commercial banks have the ability—that is, the excess reserves needed—to make loans. It cannot guarantee, however, that loans will actually be negotiated and the supply of money increased. If the public does not want to borrow, or if commercial banks, seeking liquidity, are unwilling to lend, the easy money efforts of the Board of Governors will be to little avail. An easy

money policy can do no more than create excess reserves upon which loans may or may not be made.[5]

Caution: We are *not* suggesting that an easy money policy will not work. Rather, the point is that the power of a tight money policy may be greater than that of an easy money policy. Hence, it might be necessary to increase bank reserves by, say, $2 billion to achieve a given increase in the money supply, whereas only a $1 billion decrease in reserves would bring about an equal decline in the money supply.

**2  Changes in Velocity**   From a monetary point of view (Chapter 17), total spending or aggregate demand may be regarded as the money supply *multiplied* by the velocity of money, that is, the number of times per year the average dollar is spent on goods and services. Hence, if the money supply is $150 billion, total demand will be $600 billion if velocity is 4, but only $450 billion if velocity is 3.

Although the issue is controversial, some economists feel that velocity has a habit of changing in the opposite direction from the money supply, thereby tending to offset or frustrate policy-instigated changes in the money supply. That is, during inflation, when the money supply is restrained by policy, velocity tends to increase. Conversely, when policy measures are taken to increase the money supply during a recession, velocity may very well fall!

Postponing details until Chapter 17, velocity might behave in this manner because of the asset demand for money. We know that an easy money policy, for example, means an increase in the supply of money relative to the demand for it and therefore a reduction in the interest rate (Figure 16-1*a*). But now that the interest rate—the opportunity cost of holding

[5] *Qualification:* Remember that Federal Reserve purchases of securities *from the public* directly increase the supply of money apart from any expansion of bank credit which commercial banks may make available on the basis of the reserves they acquire as the result of these bond purchases.

money as an asset—is lower, the public will hold larger money balances. This means dollars move from hand to hand—from households to businesses and back again—less rapidly. In technical terms, the velocity of money has declined. A reverse sequence of events allegedly causes a tight money policy to induce an increase in velocity.

**3  Membership Erosion**  Although all banks holding national charters are required by law to belong to the Federal Reserve System and to meet its reserve requirements, each bank is free to choose whether it wants to operate under a national charter or under one granted by the state in which it is located. Since World War II many banks have been opting for state charters and choosing not to be members of the System. Hence, in 1947 some 49 percent of all banks were members and these banks accounted for about 85 percent of all deposits. Currently only 37 percent of all banks belong to the System and their share of total deposits is only 71 percent. Some 600 banks have dropped from the System in the past decade and the exodus seems to be accelerating. The basic reason for this erosion of membership is quite simple: Members must keep a reserve at the Federal Reserve which does *not* earn interest income. In current times of very high interest rates this opportunity cost of membership is particularly great. The consequence of declining membership is equally obvious. Declining membership means that the control which the Board of Governors exerts over the banking system—and therefore the effectiveness of monetary policy—is diminished.[6]

---

[6]The new *Depository Institutions Deregulation and Monetary Control Act of 1980* is designed to reverse this membership erosion. It requires *nonmember* banks to maintain reserves in the Federal Reserve equal to 10 percent of any *increase* in certain specified liabilities. This legislation also stipulates that the required reserve ratios for *all* commercial banks, savings and loan associations, mutual savings banks, and credit unions will be equalized over an eight-year period.

**4  Cost-Push Inflation**  As is the case with fiscal policy, monetary policy is designed to control inflation by restraining excess total spending. That is, an anti-inflationary monetary policy is geared to alleviate or correct demand-pull inflation. It is less effective in controlling cost-push inflation, the causes of which lie on the supply or cost side of the market. This issue will reappear in Chapter 18.

**5  The Investment Impact**  Some economists doubt that monetary policy has as much impact upon investment as Figure 16-1 implies. Their position is based upon several points.

First, we have already noted that the combination of a relatively flat money-demand curve and a relatively steep investment-demand curve will mean that a given change in the money supply will *not* elicit a very large change in investment and, hence, in the equilibrium NNP (Figure 16-1).

Second, the operation of monetary policy as portrayed may be complicated, and at least partially offset, by unfavorable changes in the location of the investment-demand curve. For example, the purpose of a tight money policy is to increase the interest rate, move businesses up the investment-demand curve, and thereby restrain aggregate demand and the rate of inflation. However, the very inflationary prosperity which the tight money policy is designed to control may well be accompanied by increasing business optimism or a rapid rate of technological progress which has the effect of *shifting* the investment-demand curve of Figure 16-1b to the *right*. This poses the possibility that investment spending will increase *despite* the higher interest rate. In short, the forces which cause inflation may also generate increases in the demand for investment goods which tend to counter a tight money policy. Conversely, a recessionary environment may undermine business confidence, shift the investment-demand curve to the left, and thereby tend to frustrate an easy money policy.

Finally, large monopolistic firms—the very firms which do the bulk of the investing—are in a position to pass on any increase in interest costs to consumers in the form of higher product prices. Indeed, in many cases monopolistic firms are able to finance substantial portions of their investment programs internally and therefore will not be hindered by the unavailability of credit for investment purposes. However, tight money is likely to have a considerable impact upon smaller firms in competitive industries. This is another criticism of tight money: It discriminates against such firms.

### △ Strengths of Monetary Policy

Despite these limitations and problems, most economists regard monetary policy as an essential component of our national stabilization policy. Indeed, several specific points can be made on behalf of monetary policy.

**1 Speed and Flexibility** In comparison with fiscal policy, monetary policy can be quickly altered. We have seen (Chapter 13) that the application of appropriate fiscal policy may be seriously delayed by congressional deliberations. In contrast, the Open Market Committee of the Federal Reserve Board can literally buy or sell securities on a daily basis and thereby influence the money supply and interest rates.

**2 Political Acceptability** Monetary policy is a more subtle and more politically conservative measure than is fiscal policy. Changes in government spending directly affect the allocation of resources, and, of course, tax changes can have extensive political ramifications. By contrast, monetary policy works by a more subtle route and therefore seems to be more politically palatable.

**3 Monetarism** In the next chapter we will examine in some detail the current debate over the relative effectiveness of monetary and fiscal policy. Let us merely note here that, although most economists view fiscal policy as a more powerful stabilization technique than monetary policy, there is a group of respected economists who feel that changes in the money supply are the key determinant of the level of economic activity and that fiscal policy is ineffective.

### □ EMPLOYMENT THEORY AND POLICY: RECAPITULATION

This is an opportune point at which to recapitulate and synthesize Keynesian employment theory and associated stabilization policies. We want to gain a better understanding of how the many analytical and policy aspects of macroeconomics discussed in this and the seven preceding chapters fit together. Figure 16-2 provides the "big picture" we seek. The overriding virtue of this diagram is that it shows how the many concepts and principles we have discussed relate to one another and how they constitute a coherent theory of what determines the level of resource use in a market economy.

Now let us review the substance of Figure 16-2. Reading from left to right, the key point, of course, is that the levels of output, employment, income, and prices are all directly related to the level of aggregate demand.[7] The decisions of business firms to produce goods and therefore to employ resources depend upon the total amount of money spent on these goods. To discover what determines the level of aggregate spending, we must examine its three major components.[8]

### △ Consumption

The absolute level of consumption spending depends upon the position of the consumption schedule and the level of net national

---

[7]In Chapter 18 we modify this statement in discussing stagflation, that is, inflation accompanied by *rising* unemployment.
[8]We assume a closed economy, that is, net exports are zero. In Chapter 42 we will analyze the effects of exports and imports upon output, income, and employment.

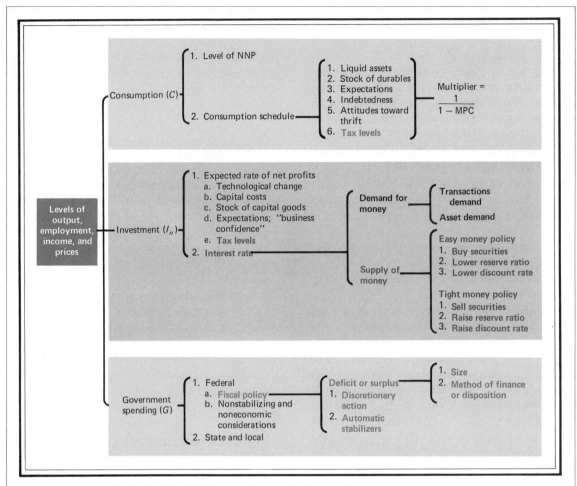

FIGURE 16-2  THE THEORY OF EMPLOYMENT AND STABILIZATION POLICIES

This figure integrates the various components of employment theory and stabilization policy. Note that determinants which constitute, or are strongly influenced by, public policy are shown in orange.

product or disposable income. Most economists are convinced that the consumption schedule is quite stable. Therefore, the absolute level of consumption spending usually can be thought of as changing in response to changes in NNP brought about by fluctuations in other components in aggregate demand. Furthermore, the slope of the consumption schedule, measured by the MPC (the marginal propensity to consume), is critical in determining the size of the multiplier.

△  **Investment**

Investment spending is a highly volatile component of aggregate demand and therefore likely to be a cause of fluctuations in the levels of output, employment, and prices. The instability of investment lies in its determinants: Business confidence is subject to frequent and substantial revision; technological progress occurs at an uneven rate; and the durability of capital goods makes their purchase postponable. Furthermore, business profits—an increasingly important source of funds for investment—are highly variable.

## △ Government Spending

The government purchases component of aggregate demand differs from consumption and investment in that it is determined by public policy. Consumption and investment decisions are made in the self-interest of the household and business sectors, respectively. Government spending decisions, on the other hand, are made, at least in part, to fulfill society's interest in high levels of output and employment and a stable price level. With this motivational distinction in mind, let us examine the major components and characteristics of stabilization policy.

## △ Fiscal and Monetary Policy

Fiscal policy refers, of course, to changes in government spending and tax revenues which are designed to eliminate either an inflationary or a recessionary gap. Figure 16-2 makes the potential stabilizing role of government quite evident; government spending, as one of the three major components of aggregate demand, directly affects output, employment, and the price level. Tax policy, on the other hand, works indirectly through the other two major components of total spending; taxation is a determinant of both consumption and investment.[9] In particular, reductions in the personal income tax tend to shift the consumption schedule upward; tax increases tend to shift it downward. Cuts in the corporation income tax or other business taxes tend to improve profit expectations, shift the investment-demand curve to the right, and stimulate investment; tax increases weaken profit expectations and reduce the willingness to invest.

Fiscal policy is both *discretionary* and *automatic*. The automatic or built-in stabiliz-

ers—the progressiveness of the net tax structure—causes tax collections to vary directly with the level of national income. Discretionary policy consists of the changing of spending levels and the manipulation of tax rates or the tax structure by Congress for the explicit purpose of achieving greater stability in the economy.

The functioning of monetary policy was just detailed in the discussion of Figure 16-1.

## △ Complexities and Problems

Although Figure 16-2 is a revealing overview of Keynesian theory and policy, it conceals a number of complexities and problems which merit at least brief comment.

**1   Employment–Price Level Trade-off** Recall (Figure 10-6) that unemployment and inflation may occur simultaneously. Chapter 18 will be concerned with this trade-off problem and the possibility that unemployment and inflation may have causes other than an inappropriate level of aggregate demand.

**2   Noneconomic and Microeconomic Factors** Figure 16-2 presents a *macroeconomic* theory and, as such, fails to consider the possible impacts of noneconomic and microeconomic considerations. For example, an unfortunate turn of international politics can create serious and prolonged macroeconomic disturbances. The OPEC oil cartel and the Vietnam war immediately come to mind. Furthermore, government spending and taxing decisions are *not* made on purely macroeconomic grounds. For example, a political party's commitment to relieve certain social problems—to mitigate economic inequality and poverty—may call for changes in spending or the tax structure that destabilize the economy. More generally stated, government expenditure and taxation policies are used not only to achieve macroeconomic stability, but also to achieve reallocations of resources and to redistribute income.

---

[9] In our earlier tabular (Table 13-1) and graphic (Figure 13-2) models of the economy, we made the simplifying assumption that all taxes were personal taxes and, therefore, tax changes only affected consumption.

**3   Quantification**   Aside from the troublesome stagflation problem, it is usually quite simple to identify the appropriate direction for changes in fiscal and monetary policy. Recession, for example, calls for a public deficit and an easy money policy. What we do *not* know—or at least do not know with great accuracy—is the *size* of the deficit needed or the *amount* by which the money supply should be increased. An important consequence is that it is simply not realistic to expect stabilization policy to work perfectly so as to provide continuous full employment and price stability. "Fine tuning" of the economy through stabilization policies has proven most difficult to achieve.

**4   Policy Coordination**   Although we have treated fiscal and monetary policy separately, they are in fact interrelated and should be coordinated. This can be illustrated by reference once again to Figure 16-1 and the feedback effects it embodies. The quantitative significance of, say, a given increase in government spending will depend upon whether it is accompanied by a "congenial" change in the money supply. Suppose it is determined that the actual NNP is $25 billion short of the full employment level and that the multiplier is 5. Hence, other things being equal, a $5 billion increase in government purchases will move the economy to full employment. But in fact, other things—in particular, the interest rate—cannot be expected to remain unchanged as the economy begins to expand under the impetus of the additional spending (Figure 16-1*c*). As production and NNP expand, the transactions demand for money will increase and, given the supply of money, interest rates will rise (Figure 16-1*a*). The higher interest rates will tend to "crowd out" some investment (Figure 16-1*b*) and thereby partially offset the expansionary impact of the increase in government spending. Unless the money supply is increased to keep the interest rate constant, the multiplier effect of Chapters 12 and 13 will be diminished because of money market feedbacks which curtail investment spending. The point is that fiscal and monetary policies do not operate in isolation; effective stabilization policy presumes their careful coordination.

## Summary

1   Like fiscal policy, the goal of monetary policy is to stabilize the economy. The route, or cause-effect chain, through which monetary policy functions is complex: *a.* Policy decisions affect commercial bank reserves; *b.* changes in reserves affect the supply of money; *c.* changes in the supply of money alter the interest rate; and *d.* changes in the interest rate affect investment, the equilibrium NNP, and the price level.

2   For a consideration of monetary policy, the most important assets of the Federal Reserve Banks are gold certificates, securities, and loans to commercial banks. The basic liabilities are the reserves of member banks, Treasury deposits, and Federal Reserve Notes.

3   Table 16-3 (page 327) draws together all the basic notions relevant to the application of easy and tight money policies.

4   Monetary policy is subject to a number of limitations and problems. *a.* The excess reserves which an easy money policy provides may not be used by banks to expand the supply of money. *b.* Policy-instigated changes in the supply of money may be partially offset by changes in the velocity of money. *c.* The decline in Federal Reserve membership has reduced the effectiveness of monetary policy. *d.* A tight money policy is of questionable relevance in correcting cost-push inflation. *e.* The impact of monetary policy will be lessened if the

**TABLE 16-3**
**A Summary of Monetary Policy**

| | |
|---|---|
| I. Problem: unemployment and deflation | I. Problem: inflation |
| II. Remedy: to induce an expansion in the supply of money, and therefore spending, by reducing the interest rate | II. Remedy: to induce a contraction in the supply of money, and therefore spending, by increasing the interest rate |
| III. Techniques of an easy money policy | III. Techniques of a tight money policy |
|   1. Buy bonds in the open market |   1. Sell bonds in the open market |
|   2. Lower reserve ratio |   2. Raise reserve ratio |
|   3. Lower discount rate |   3. Raise discount rate |

money-demand curve is flat and the investment-demand curve is steep. The investment-demand curve may also shift so as to negate monetary policy.

5   The advantages of monetary policy include its flexibility and political acceptability. Further, the monetarists feel that the supply of money is the single most important determinant of the level of national output.

6   Figure 16-2, which provides a summary statement of Keynesian employment theory and policy, merits careful study by the reader.

## Questions and Study Suggestions

1   Key terms and concepts to remember: monetary policy; quantitative controls; open-market operations; reserve ratio; discount rate; easy and tight money policies; qualitative (selective) controls; margin requirement; moral suasion; money market; feedback effects; velocity of money.

2   What is the basic objective of monetary policy? Describe the cause-effect chain through which monetary policy is made effective. Using Figure 16-1 as a point of reference, discuss how *a.* the shapes of the demand-for-money and investment-demand curves and *b.* the size of the MPS influence the effectiveness of monetary policy. How do feedback effects influence the effectiveness of monetary policy?

3   Suppose you are a member of the Board of Governors of the Federal Reserve System. The economy is experiencing a sharp and prolonged inflationary trend. What changes in *a.* the reserve ratio, *b.* the discount rate, and *c.* open-market operations would you recommend? Explain in each case how the change you advocate would affect commercial bank reserves and influence the money supply.

4   Use commercial bank and Federal Reserve Bank balance sheets in each case to demonstrate the impact of each of the following transactions upon commercial bank reserves:

   *a.*   The Federal Reserve Banks purchase securities from private businesses and consumers.

   *b.*   Commercial banks borrow from the Federal Reserve Banks.

   *c.*   The Board of Governors reduces the reserve ratio.

5   Evaluate the overall effectiveness of monetary policy. Why have open-market operations evolved as the primary means of controlling commercial bank reserves? Discuss the specific limitations of monetary policy.

6   In the following table you will find simplified consolidated balance sheets for the commercial banking system and the twelve Federal Reserve Banks. In columns 1 through 3, indicate how the balance sheets would read after each of the three ensuing transactions is

completed.  Do not cumulate your answers; that is, analyze each transaction separately, starting in each case from the given figures.  All accounts are in billions of dollars.

**Consolidated Balance Sheet:**
**All Commercial Banks**

|  | | (1) | (2) | (3) |
|---|---|---|---|---|
| Assets: | | | | |
| Reserves . . . . . . . . . . | $ 33 | ———— | ———— | ———— |
| Securities . . . . . . . . . . | 60 | ———— | ———— | ———— |
| Loans . . . . . . . . . . . . | 60 | ———— | ———— | ———— |
| Liabilities and net worth: | | | | |
| Demand deposits . . . . . | $150 | ———— | ———— | ———— |
| Loans from the Federal | | | | |
|   Reserve Banks . . . . . | 3 | ———— | ———— | ———— |

**Consolidated Balance Sheet:**
**Twelve Federal Reserve Banks**

|  | | (1) | (2) | (3) |
|---|---|---|---|---|
| Assets: | | | | |
| Gold certificates. . . . . . . | $20 | ———— | ———— | ———— |
| Securities . . . . . . . . . . | 40 | ———— | ———— | ———— |
| Loans to commercial | | | | |
|   banks . . . . . . . . . . . | 3 | ———— | ———— | ———— |
| Liabilities and net worth: | | | | |
| Reserves of commercial | | | | |
|   banks . . . . . . . . . . . | $33 | ———— | ———— | ———— |
| Treasury deposits . . . . . . | 3 | ———— | ———— | ———— |
| Federal Reserve Notes . . | 27 | ———— | ———— | ———— |

   *a.*   Suppose a decline in the discount rate prompts commercial banks to borrow an additional $1 billion from the Federal Reserve Banks.  Show the new balance sheet figures in column 1.

   *b.*   The Federal Reserve Banks sell $3 billion in securities to the public, who pay for the bonds with checks.  Show the new balance-sheet figures in column 2.

   *c.*   The Federal Reserve Banks buy $2 billion of securities from commercial banks. Show the new balance sheet figures in column 3.

   *d.*   Now review each of the above three transactions, asking yourself these three questions: (1) What change, if any, took place in the money supply as a direct and immediate result of each transaction?  (2) What increase or decrease in commercial banks' reserves took place in each transaction?  (3) Assuming a reserve ratio of 20 percent, what change in the money-creating potential of the commercial banking *system* occurred as a result of each transaction?

   **7**   Summarize the theory of employment, using the aggregate demand–aggregate supply approach.  Show in detail how monetary and fiscal policies might affect the various components of aggregate demand.

   **8**   Why is it unrealistic to expect fiscal and monetary policies to result in complete economic stability?  What might be done to improve monetary and fiscal policies?

   **9**   Design an antirecession stabilization policy, involving both fiscal and monetary policies, which is consistent with **a.** a relative decline in the public sector, **b.** greater income equality, and **c.** a high rate of economic growth.  Explain: "Truly effective stabilization policy presumes the coordination of fiscal and monetary policy."

   **10**   Some observers of monetary policy contend that the monetary authorities can control the supply of money *or* the interest rate, but not *both*.  Can you demonstrate this point?  (*Hint:* Assume in Figure 16-1*a* that the equilibrium interest rate and the money supply are those desired by the monetary authorities.  Now suppose that, because of expansionary fiscal policy, money GNP increases and therefore the demand for money increases.)

## Selected References

Board of Governors of the Federal Reserve System: *The Federal Reserve System: Purposes and Functions,* 6th ed. (1974), particularly chaps. 1, 4, 5.

Cargill, Thomas F.: *Money, the Financial System, and Monetary Policy* (Englewood Cliffs, N.J.: Prentice-Hall, Inc., 1979), chaps. 10–13.

Chandler, Lester V., and Stephen M. Goldfeld: *The Economics of Money and Banking,* 7th ed. (New York: Harper & Row, Publishers, Incorporated, 1977), chaps. 21–26.

Klein, John J.: *Money and the Economy,* 4th ed. (New York: Harcourt Brace Jovanovich, Inc., 1978), chaps. 11–13.

Ritter, Lawrence S., and William L. Silber: *Money,* 3d ed. (New York: Basic Books, Inc., 1977).

Thorn, Richard S.: *Introduction to Money and Banking* (New York: Harper & Row, Publishers, Incorporated, 1976), chaps.18–25.

# LAST WORD
## High Interest Rates Hit Home ·

Although the contractionary effects of a tight money policy are pervasive, the homebuilding and construction industries are most adversely affected.

(Reprinted from *U.S. News & World Report.*)

Record-high interest rates have forced builders to scrap plans for construction projects of every sort—offices, stores, apartments.

Homes already built are going begging as buyers shy away from mortgage rates that have skyrocketed to 17 percent in some parts of the country.

Manufacturers, rather than getting locked into high rates for long-term financing, are postponing plant expansion and equipment purchases.

Even the ordinary costs of doing business—maintaining inventories, for example—are straining company resources to the limit. The prime rate, which banks charge their best customers, has hit $18\frac{1}{2}$ percent and is expected to move still higher.

Together, these developments point to a massive slowing of economic activity and the loss of thousands of jobs. Says Albert H. Cox, Jr., president of Merrill Lynch Economics in New York, "With every passing day, the odds of a deep, long recession get stronger."

Biggest victim in the growing list of business casualties is construction. With builders paying interest rates of 20 percent or more on construction loans, economist Michael Sumichrast of the National Association of Home Builders predicts few more than 1 million housing starts for 1980—the lowest level since 1946. . . .

With each upward tick in mortgage rates, more people are cut out of the market. Paul Sposato of Long Island, N.Y., is typical. The 33-year-old salesman had hoped to buy a bigger home for his growing family but says: "Interest rates are so high that if I took out a mortgage for the same amount I own on my current house, my payments would be an extra $125 a month. A new home is totally out of the question now.". . .

That reaction, multiplied thousands of times across the country, explains why so many builders are scaling back.

Other sectors of the industry are suffering, too. In Bergen County, N.J., Peter Tucci, president of Tucci Enterprises, has shelved a 15-million-dollar office project. "I'm not going to get a 20 percent return on my investment," he explains, "so I have to put it aside.". . .

# Monetarism: An Alternative View

chapter 17

The Keynesian conception of employment theory and stabilization policy, summarized in the discussion regarding Figure 16-2, presents the view of macroeconomics which has dominated the thinking of most economists since World War II. In the past decade or so, however, this theory has been challenged by an alternative conception of macroeconomics in the form of *monetarism*. Both schools of thought are led by distinguished scholars. MIT's Paul Samuelson, Yale's James Tobin, and Minnesota's Walter Heller are among the distinguished spokesmen for the Keynesian position. The University of Chicago's Milton Friedman is the intellectual leader of the monetarist school. Winner of the 1976 Nobel prize in economics, his pioneering empirical and theoretical research asserts that the role of money in determining the level of economic activity and the price level is much greater than suggested by Keynesian thought.

The overall purpose of this chapter is to outline the monetarist view and to contrast it philosophically, analytically, and in terms of policy implications with the Keynesian view.

## □ PHILOSOPHICAL-IDEOLOGICAL DIFFERENCES

Explicit recognition of important philosophical and ideological differences between Keynesians and monetarists is most helpful in appreciating their disagreements in the areas of theory and policy.

### △ Keynesians: Political Liberalism

Keynesians believe that capitalism and, more particularly, the free-market system suffer from inherent shortcomings. The market system does not provide public goods; it seriously misallocates resources where externalities and monopolies exist; and it yields a highly unequal distribution of income (Chapter 6). More important for the present debate is the contention that capitalism contains no mechanism to guarantee macroeconomic stability. Imbalances of planned investment and saving *do* occur and the result is business fluctuations—periodic episodes of inflation or unemployment. Government, therefore, can and should play a positive, activist role in stabilizing the economy; discretionary fiscal and monetary policies are needed to alleviate the severe economic ups and downs which would otherwise characterize capitalism's course.

For two reasons Keynesians are especially enamored of fiscal policy. First, for reasons to be specified later, they believe it is a much more powerful stabilizing tool than is monetary policy. Second, fiscal policy—the manipulation of taxes and government spending—can also be used to achieve microeconomic goals in the areas of resource allocation and income distribution which Keynesians think are desirable and meritorious in their own right. For example, a tax cut or an increase in government spending can be used, not only to pull the economy out of a current recession, but also to increase the share of the national income going to the poor or to expand currently underproduced social goods and services.

△ **Monetarists: Laissez Faire and Conservatism**

In contrast, monetarists have a strong *laissez faire* or free-market orientation. They emphasize the capacity of the competitive market system automatically to allocate resources efficiently. Conversely, governmental decision making is held to be bureaucratic, inefficient, harmful to individual incentives, and frequently characterized by policy mistakes. Furthermore, centralized decision making by government inevitably erodes individual freedoms.[1]

[1]Friedman's conservative philosophy is effectively expounded in two of his books: *Capitalism and Freedom* (Chicago: The University of Chicago Press, 1962), and with Rose Friedman, *Free to Choose* (New York: Harcourt Brace Jovanovich, 1980).

Perhaps more important for present purposes is the monetarist view that the market system can potentially be the source of a high degree of macroeconomic stability. That is, the market system would tend to provide substantial stability in output, employment, and the price level *were it not for ill-advised governmental interference with the functioning of the economy.* Most monetarists would be sympathetic to the classical theory's contention that downward wage-price flexibility would greatly cushion, if not eliminate, the adverse effects of a decline in aggregate demand upon the levels of real output and employment (Chapter 11). The problem, as the monetarists see it, is that government has fostered and promoted downward wage-price inflexibility through the minimum-wage law, pro-union legislation, farm price supports, pro-business monopoly legislation, and so forth. The free-market system could provide substantial macroeconomic stability, but, despite good intentions, government interference has undermined this capability. Furthermore, as we shall detail momentarily, the monetarists argue that government has contributed to the instability of the system—to the business cycle—through its clumsy and mistaken attempts to achieve greater stability through discretionary fiscal and monetary policies.

Note that Keynesians and monetarists are almost diametrically opposed in their conceptions of the private and public sectors. To the Keynesian, the instability of private investment causes the economy to be unstable. Government plays a positive role by applying appropriate stabilization medicine. To the monetarist, government has harmful effects upon the economy. Government creates rigidities which weaken the capacity of the market system to provide substantial stability and it embarks upon monetary and fiscal measures which, although well intentioned, aggravate the very instability they are designed to cure.

☐ **THE BASIC EQUATIONS**

Keynesian economics focuses upon aggregate

demand and its components. The basic equation of the Keynesian model is:

$$C_a + I_n + G = \text{NNP} \qquad (1)$$

This theory says in essence that the aggregate amount spent by buyers is equal to the total value of the goods and services sold. In equilibrium, $C_a + I_n + G$ (aggregate demand) is equal to NNP (aggregate supply).

△ **Equation of Exchange**

Monetarism, as the label suggests, focuses upon money. The basic equation of monetarism is the *equation of exchange:*

$$MV = PQ \qquad (2)$$

where $M$ is the supply of money; $V$ is the income or circuit velocity of money, that is, the number of times per year the average dollar is spent on final goods and services; $P$ is the price level or, more specifically, the average price at which each unit of physical output is sold; and $Q$ is the physical volume of goods and services produced.

It should be emphasized at the outset that both approaches are useful and insightful to the understanding of macroeconomics.

The difference between the two approaches can be compared with two ways of looking at the flow of water through a sewer pipe—say, at the rate of 6000 gallons per hour. A neo-Keynesian investigator might say that the flow of 6000 gallons an hour consisted of 3000 gallons an hour from a paper mill, 2000 gallons an hour from an auto plant, and 1000 gallons an hour from a shopping center. A monetarist investigator might say that the sewer flow of 6000 gallons an hour consisted of an average of 200 gallons in the sewer at any one time with a complete turnover of the water 30 times every hour.[2]

In fact, the Keynesian equation can be quite readily "translated" into monetarist terms.

[2] Werner Sichel and Peter Eckstein, *Basic Economic Concepts* (Chicago: Rand McNally College Publishing Company, 1974), p. 344.

According to the monetarist approach, total spending or aggregate demand is simply the supply of money multiplied by its velocity. In short, $MV$ is the monetarist counterpart of $C_a + I_n + G$. Because $MV$ is the total amount spent on final goods in one year, it is obviously equal to NNP. Furthermore, we know from Chapter 9 that NNP is the sum of the physical outputs of various goods and services ($Q$) multiplied by their respective prices ($P$). That is, $\text{NNP} = PQ$. Thus, we can restate the Keynesian $C_a + I_n + G = \text{NNP}$ equation as the monetarist equation of exchange, $MV = PQ$. In a very real sense, the two approaches are two ways of looking at the same thing. But the critical question remains: Which theory is the more accurate portrayal of macroeconomics and therefore the better basis for economic policy?

△ **Spotlight on Money**

The Keynesian equation clearly puts money in a secondary role. Indeed, you will recall (Chapter 16) that the Keynesian conception of monetary policy entails a rather lengthy transmission mechanism:

Change in    Change in
monetary  → commercial →
policy        bank
            reserves

Change in    Change in    Change
money   → the interest → in
supply      rate       investment

Keynesians contend there are many loose links in this cause-effect chain with the result that monetary policy is an uncertain, unreliable, and weak stabilization tool when compared with fiscal policy. Remember some of the weaknesses of monetary policy cited in the previous chapter. For example, recall from Figure 16-1 that monetary policy will be relatively ineffective if the demand-for-money curve is relatively flat and the investment-demand curve is relatively steep. Furthermore, the investment-demand curve may shift adversely so that the impact of a change in the interest rate upon investment spending is muted or offset. Nor will an easy money policy be very effective if banks are not anxious to lend or the public eager to borrow.

The monetarists believe that money and monetary policy are much more important in determining the level of economic activity than do the Keynesians. In fact, *monetarists hold that changes in the money supply are the single most important factor in determining the levels of output, employment, and prices.* They believe that the cause-effect chain between the supply of money and the level of economic activity is short, direct, and tight. Specifically, *if V, the velocity of money, is stable or nearly so, the equation of exchange suggests that changes in the money supply will have a direct and predictable effect upon the level of NNP ( = PQ).* That is, if $V$ is constant, an increase in $M$ will obviously increase $P$ or $Q$ or *both P* and $Q$. The precise effects on $P$ and $Q$ will depend upon whether the economy is experiencing recession or full employment at the time $M$ is increased. If the economy is in a severe recession, an increase in $M$ will raise $Q$ more or less proportionately, with virtually no change in $P$. But if the economy is at full employment, $Q$ becomes constant because the economy is producing its capacity or maximum output; hence, increases in $M$ will be purely inflationary and will cause $P$ to increase proportionately. Or, as range 2 of Figure 10-6 reminds us, $P$ and $Q$ may both rise in response to an increase in $M$ as the economy approaches full employment.

Monetarism implies a simpler and much more direct transmission mechanism than does the Keynesian model. In the monetarist view:

Change in        Change
money     $\longrightarrow$   in
supply          NNP

## ☐  VELOCITY: STABLE OR UNSTABLE?

The critical theoretical issue involved in the Keynesian-monetarist debate centers on the question of whether the velocity of money, $V$, is stable. If it is, the equation of exchange tells us that the monetarists are indeed correct in claiming that a direct and dependable relationship exists between the money supply and the money NNP ( = $PQ$). In the extreme case of an absolutely constant $V$, a 10 percent increase (decrease) in the money supply will result in a proportionate 10 percent increase (decrease) in $PQ$ or money NNP. But if $V$ is *not* stable, the Keynesian contention that money plays a secondary role in macroeconomics is valid. That is, if $V$ is quite variable, the link between $M$ and $PQ$ will be loose and uncertain. (This chapter's Last Word section is a minidebate on this very issue.)

### △  Monetarists: V is Stable

What rationale do the monetarists offer for their contention that $V$ is stable? Basically, they argue that money is primarily a medium of exchange; the store of value function of money is inconsequential. In other words, there is a transactions demand for money, but *not* an asset demand. Furthermore, the amount of money the public will want to hold will depend upon the volume of transactions, that is, upon the level of NNP. Consider a simple example. Suppose that, when the level of NNP is $400 billion, the amount of money which the public wants or *desires* to hold in order to negotiate the purchase of this output is $100 billion.[3] If we further assume that the *actual* supply of money is $100 billion, we can say that the economy is in equilibrium with respect to money. That is, the *actual* amount of money supplied is equal to the amount the public *desires* to hold.

In the monetarist view an increase in the money supply of, say, $10 billion will upset this equilibrium in that the public will now be holding more money or liquidity than it wants to hold; the actual amount of money being held exceeds the desired amount. What happens? According to the monetarists, the excess

---

[3]This implies that $V$ is 4.

money balances will be spent on *real assets*—that is, on consumer and investment goods. This obviously means that NNP will rise. By how much? By $40 billion. The rationale is that when NNP reaches $440 billion, the *actual* money supply will again be the amount which the public *desires* to hold and, by definition, equilibrium will be reestablished. The basic point is that spending on goods and services will increase until NNP has increased to the extent that the original equilibrium relationship between NNP and the money supply is the same as it was prior to the increase in the money supply. In fact, that relationship—NNP/*M*—defines *V*! A stable relationship between NNP and *M* means a stable *V*.

△   **Keynesians: *V* is Unstable**

In the Keynesian view the velocity of money is intimately tied to the demand for money.[4] The Keynesian conception, you will recall, is that money is demanded, not only to use in negotiating transactions, but also to hold as an asset. Money demanded for *transactions* purposes will be "active" money, that is, money which is changing hands and circulating through the income-expenditures stream. In other words, transactions dollars have some positive velocity; for example, the average transactions dollar may be spent, say, six times per year and thereby negotiate $6 worth of transactions. In this case *V* is 6 for each transactions dollar. But money demanded and held as an *asset* is "idle" money; these dollars do *not* flow through the income-expenditures stream and therefore their velocity is zero. It follows that the overall velocity of the entire money supply will depend upon how it is divided between transaction and asset balances. Obviously, the greater the relative importance of "active" transactions balances, the larger will be *V*. Conversely, the greater the relative significance of "idle" asset balances, the smaller will be *V*.

Given this framework, Keynesians discredit the monetarist transmission mechanism—the allegedly tight and dependable relationship between changes in *M* and changes in NNP—by arguing that a substantial portion of any increase in the money supply may go into asset balances, *causing V to fall*. In the very extreme case, assume *all* the increase in the money supply is held by the public as additional asset balances. That is, the public simply hoards the additional money and uses none of it for transactions. The money supply will have increased, but velocity will decline by an offsetting amount so that there will be no effect whatsoever upon the size of NNP!

We can consider the Keynesian position at a slightly more sophisticated level by referring back to Figure 14-1. We note that the relative importance of the asset demand for money varies inversely with the rate of interest. Hence, an increase in the money supply will lower the interest rate. Because it is now less expensive to hold money as an asset, the public will hold larger zero-velocity asset balances. Therefore, the overall velocity of the money supply will fall. Conversely, a reduction in the money supply will raise the interest rate, making it more costly to hold money as an asset. The resulting decline in asset balances will increase the overall velocity of money. *In the Keynesian view velocity varies (1) directly with the rate of interest and (2) inversely with the supply of money.* If this analysis is correct, the tight relationship between *M* and NNP embodied in the monetarist's transmission mechanism does *not* exist because *V* will vary whenever *M* changes.

Incidentally, at this juncture we can more fully appreciate a point made at the end of Chapter 16 in discussing possible shortcomings of monetary policy. It was indicated that *V* has the bad habit of changing in the opposite direction than *M*. Our present discussion reveals the cause-effect chain through which this might occur.

△   **Empirical Evidence**

The stability of *V* is obviously an empiri-

---

[4]It might be a good idea to reread Chapter 14's "The Demand for Money" section at this point.

cal question and an appeal to "the facts" would seem sufficient to settle the issue. But, unfortunately, the facts are not easy either to discern or to interpret.

Monetarists think that the weight of empirical evidence clearly supports their position. In Figure 17-1 the money supply and the money national output (*PQ*) are both plotted.

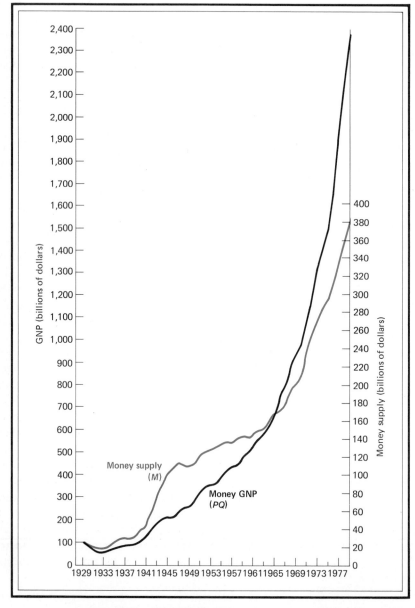

**FIGURE 17-1 THE MONEY SUPPLY AND THE GNP, 1929-1979**

Monetarists cite the close positive correlation between the money supply and money GNP as evidence in support of their position that money is the critical determinant of economic activity and the price level. They assume that the money supply is the "cause" and the GNP is the "effect," an assumption which Keynesians question. Monetarists also feel that the close correlation between *M* and money GNP indicates that the velocity of money is stable. (*Economic Report of the President.*)

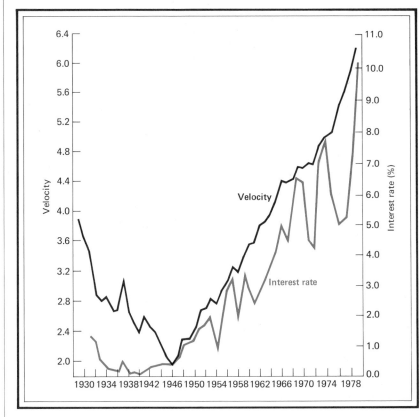

**FIGURE 17-2 THE VELOCITY OF MONEY AND THE INTEREST RATE, 1929-1979**

Keynesians argue that the velocity of money varies both cyclically and secularly. Hence, they conclude that any link between a change in the money supply and the subsequent change in NNP is tenuous and uncertain. More specifically, Keynesians contend that velocity varies directly with the rate of interest because a lower interest rate will increase the size of zero-velocity asset balances and therefore lower the overall velocity of money. (*Economic Report of the President.*)

Given that $MV = PQ$, the close correlation between $M$ and $PQ$ obviously suggests that $V$ is quite stable. Monetarists reason that the money supply is the critical causal force in determining the NNP; causation runs from $M$ to NNP.

But Keynesians are unimpressed with such data. They offer two arguments by way of rebuttal. First, they point out that by simple manipulation of $MV = PQ$, we find that $V = PQ/M = \text{NNP}/M$. That is, we can empirically calculate the value of $V$ by dividing each year's money output (NNP) by the money supply. Keynesians contend that the resulting data, shown in Figure 17-2, repudiate the monetarist contention that $V$ is stable. It appears that over the past fifty years velocity

has varied between 2 and 6. Keynesians also point out that the close correlation between the velocity of money and the interest rate shown in Figure 17-2 supports their analytical conclusion that velocity varies directly with the rate of interest.[5] Velocity, in the Keynesian view, is variable both cyclically and secularly and these variations seriously downgrade the role of money as a determinant of output, employment, and the price level. Keynesians add this reminder: Given the large size of the money supply, a small variation in velocity can have a very substantial impact on NNP. For

[5]Technical note: The short-term interest rate used here is the rate on three-month Treasury bills.

example, assume $M$ is \$300 billion and $V$ is 5. A modest 10 percent increase in $V$ will cause a \$150 billion increase in money NNP! That is, $MV$—and therefore $PQ$—are initially \$1500 billion ($= \$300 \cdot 5$). Now, if $V$ increases by 10 percent to 5.5, $PQ$ will be \$1650 billion ($= MV = 300 \cdot 5.5$). Stated in terms of the issue at hand, a very small variation in $V$ can offset a large change in $M$.

Secondly, Keynesians respond to Figure 17-1 by noting that *correlation* and *causation* are quite different things. Is it not possible that the changes in money GNP portrayed in Figure 17-1 were in fact caused by changes in aggregate demand, that is, in $C_a + I_n + G$, as suggested by the Keynesian model? Perhaps a favorable change in business expectations increased investment. And is it not also possible that the indicated growth in the national output prompted—indeed, necessitated—that businesses and consumers borrow more money over time from commercial banks in order to finance this rising volume of economic activity? In other words, Keynesians claim that causation may in fact run from aggregate demand *to* national output *to* the money supply, rather than from the money supply *to* national output as the monetarists contend. The important point, argue the Keynesians, is that the data of Figure 17-1 are as consistent with the Keynesian view as they are with the monetarist position.

The question of the stability of $V$ remains a crucial point of conflict between Keynesians and monetarists.

□  POLICY DEBATES

The differences in the Keynesian and monetarist theories spill over into the area of stabilization policy.

△  The Fiscal Policy Debate

Keynesians favor fiscal measures as the cornerstone of stabilization policy. There are two reasons for this. First and foremost, they contend that fiscal policy is a much more pow-

erful stabilization device than is monetary policy. This is implied by the basic equation of Keynesianism. Government spending, after all, is a direct component of aggregate demand. And taxes are only one short step removed in that tax changes allegedly affect consumption and investment in dependable and predictable ways. Second, fiscal policy can be used to remedy the microeconomic deficiencies which Keynesians perceive in the economy, but monetary policy cannot. Thus, as previously noted, an increase in government spending can simultaneously stimulate the economy *and* provide currently underproduced public goods and services. Similarly, a tax increase imposed on the very rich can simultaneously restrain demand-pull inflation and ameliorate the degree of income inequality.

Monetarists seriously downgrade or, in the extreme, reject fiscal policy as both a reallocative and a stabilization device. First, as suggested earlier, they contend that the use of fiscal policy to do "good deeds" is usually ill-advised. For example, tax changes to promote greater income equality tend to affect adversely incentives to work, invest, and bear risks, so that the total national income "pie" is decreased to the detriment of all. Similarly, increased government spending typically results in the production of public goods and services of dubious need *or* in the public sector's usurping production which could be achieved more efficiently through the private sector's price system.

Second and more important for present purposes, monetarists believe that fiscal policy is weak and ineffectual because of the *crowding-out effect* (Chapter 13). Monetarists' reasoning goes like this: Suppose government runs a budgetary deficit by selling bonds, that is, by borrowing from the public. By borrowing, they argue, government is obviously competing with private businesses for funds; that is, government borrowing will increase the demand for money, raise the interest rate, and thereby crowd out a substantial amount of private investment which otherwise would have been profitable. Hence, the net effect of a budget deficit upon aggregate demand is unpredictable and, at best, modest.

Alternatively, the workings of the crowding-out effect can be seen from a more analytical perspective by referring back to Figure 16-1. The financing of the government's deficit will increase the demand for money, shifting the $D_m$ curve of Figure 16-1a to the right. Given the money supply, $S_m$, the equilibrium interest rate will rise. This increase in the interest rate will be relatively large, according to the monetarists, because the $D_m$ curve is relatively steep. Furthermore, monetarists believe that the investment-demand curve of Figure 16-1b is relatively flat; that is, investment spending is very sensitive to changes in the interest rate. In short, the initial increase in the demand for money causes a relatively large rise in the interest rate which, projected off an interest-sensitive investment-demand curve, causes a large decline in the investment component of aggregate demand. The resulting large contractionary effect offsets the expansionary impact of the fiscal deficit and, on balance, the equilibrium NNP is unaffected. So sayeth Friedman: ". . . in my opinion, the state of the budget by itself has no significant effect on the course of nominal [money] income, on inflation, on deflation, or on cyclical fluctuations."[6] Admittedly, if a deficit was financed by the issuing of new money,[7] the crowding-out effect could be avoided and the deficit would be followed by economic expansion. *But,* the monetarists point out, the expansion would be due, *not* to the fiscal deficit per se, but rather, to the creation of additional money!

Keynesians, for the most part, do not deny that some investment may be crowded out. But they perceive the amount as being small and, hence, they conclude that the net impact

of an expansionary fiscal policy upon equilibrium NNP will be substantial. In terms of Figure 16-1 the Keynesian view is that the demand for money curve is relatively flat and the investment-demand curve is steep. (You may recall that this combination tends to make monetary policy relatively weak and ineffective.) Hence, the increase in $D_m$ will cause a very modest increase in the interest rate which, when bounced off a steep investment-demand curve, will result in a very small decrease in the investment component of aggregate demand. In other words, very little investment will be crowded out. It *is* acknowledged by Keynesians that a deficit financed by creating new money will have a greater stimulus than one financed by borrowing. In terms of Figure 16-1a, for any given increase in $D_m$ there is some increase in $S_m$ which will leave the interest rate, and therefore the volume of investment, unchanged.

It will come as no surprise that recent stabilization efforts are accorded vastly different interpretations by Keynesians and monetarists. Consider the 1964 tax cut and the 1968 tax increase.

> The Keynesians claim that the power of fiscal policy was demonstrated by the success of the 1964 tax cut in bringing the economy up to a high level of employment. The monetarists contend . . . that it was the rapid expansion of the money supply during the months preceding the tax cut that did the job. They also point to the failure of the 1968 tax surcharge to stop inflation. The Keynesians respond by asserting that acceleration of the war in Vietnam undid the impact of the 1968 tax increase.[8]

△ **Monetary Policy:**
**Discretion or Rules?**

The Keynesian conception of monetary policy is, of course, that portrayed in Figure 16-1. As just noted, Keynesians believe that the demand for money curve is relatively flat

[6]Statement by Friedman in Milton Friedman and Walter Heller, *Monetary vs. Fiscal Policy* (New York: W. W. Norton & Company, Inc., 1969), p. 51.
[7]See Chapter 13, footnote 6.

[8]Lawrence S. Ritter and William L. Silber, *Money,* 2d ed. (New York: Basic Books, Inc., Publishers, 1973), p. 150.

and the investment-demand curve relatively steep, causing monetary policy to be a comparatively weak stabilization tool. We have also seen that, in contrast, monetarists contend that the money demand curve is very steep and the investment-demand curve quite flat, a combination which means that a change in the money supply has a powerful effect upon equilibrium NNP. This is obviously in keeping with monetarism's fundamental contention that the money supply is the critical determinant of the level of economic activity and the price level.

However, most monetarists do *not* advise the use of easy and tight money policies to modify the "downs" and "ups" of the business cycle. Professor Friedman contends that, historically, the *discretionary* changes in the money supply made by the monetary authorities have in fact been a *destabilizing* influence in the economy. Examining the monetary history of the United States from the Civil War up to the establishment of the Federal Reserve System in 1913 and comparing this with the post-1913 record, Friedman concludes that, even if World War II and immediate postwar periods are ignored, the latter period was clearly more unstable. Much of this decline in economic stability after the Federal Reserve System became effective is attributed to faulty decisions on the part of the monetary authorities; *in the monetarist view economic instability is more a product of monetary mismanagement than it is of any inherent destabilizers in the economy.*

**Irregular Time Lags**   According to the monetarists, there are two important sources of monetary mismanagement. First, there is the matter of *time lags*. Although the monetary transmission mechanism is direct and straightforward, changes in the money supply have their impact upon NNP only after a rather long and variable time period. Friedman's empirical work suggests that a change in the money supply may significantly change NNP in as short a period as six to eight

months or in as long a period as two or two and a half years! Because it is virtually impossible to predict the time lag involved in a given policy action, there is little chance of determining accurately when specific policies should be invoked or, in fact, which policy measure— easy or tight money—is appropriate. Indeed, given the uncertain duration of this time lag, the use of discretionary monetary policy to "fine-tune" the economy for cyclical "ups" and "downs" may backfire and intensify these cyclical changes. For example, suppose an easy money policy is invoked because the various economic indicators suggest a mild recession. But assume now that within the ensuing six months the economy, for reasons quite unrelated to public policy actions, reverses itself and moves into the prosperity-inflationary phase of the cycle. At this point in time the easy money policy becomes effective and reinforces the inflation.

**Interest Rate: Wrong Target**   Second, monetarists argue that the monetary authorities have fallen into a trap by using the current level of interest rates as a guide to policy decisions. More specifically, it is argued that the Board of Governors has often tried to stabilize interest rates and in so doing they have actually made decisions of a *destabilizing* nature. Consider an example. Suppose the economy is coming out of a recession and is currently approaching full employment; that is, the economy is in range 2 of Figure 10-6 with aggregate demand, output, employment, and the price level all increasing. This expanding volume of economic activity will cause the demand for money to increase and therefore cause the interest rate to rise. Now, if the monetary authorities reason that their task is to stabilize interest rates, they will embark upon an easy money policy. But this expansionary monetary policy will add to aggregate demand at a time when the economy is already on the verge of an inflationary boom. That is, the attempt to stabilize interest rates will fan existing inflationary fires and tend to make the economy less stable. A similar scenario is applicable to an economy moving into a recession.

**The Monetary Rule**   Monetarist moral: The monetary authorities should stabilize, not the interest rate, but the rate of growth of the money supply. Specifically, Friedman advocates legislating the *monetary rule* that the money supply be expanded each year at the same annual rate as the potential growth of our real GNP; that is, the supply of money should be increased steadily at 3 to 5 percent per year.[9]

> Such a rule, it is claimed, would eliminate . . . the major cause of instability in the economy—the capricious and unpredictable impact of countercyclical monetary policy. As long as the money supply grows at a constant rate each year, be it 3, 4, or 5 percent, any decline into recession will only be temporary. The liquidity provided by a constantly growing money supply will cause aggregate demand to expand. Similarly, if the supply of money does not rise at a more than average rate, any inflationary increase in spending will burn itself out for lack of fuel.

Keynesian response: Despite a somewhat spotty record, it would be foolish to replace discretionary monetary policy with a monetary rule. Arguing that *V* is variable both cyclically and secularly, Keynesians contend that a constant annual rate of increase in the money supply could contribute to substantial fluctuations in aggregate demand and promote economic instability. As one Keynesian has quipped, the trouble with the monetary rule is that it tells the policy maker: "Don't do something, just stand there."

△ **Rational Expectations Theory**
The controversy over whether stabilization policy should be discretionary or based upon rules has been intensified by a new line of thought called *rational expectations theory.*

[9] Ibid., pp. 134–135.

This theory is based upon the long-recognized point that any theory's predicted outcome depends upon what it assumes about expectations. Consider, for example, a simple supply and demand model. Suppose an unusually large crop of sugar beets causes the supply of sugar to increase. What will be the predicted impact upon price? *If* consumers expect the increase in supply to be recurring and *permanent,* the demand for sugar will be unchanged and the price of sugar will fall. But *if* consumers anticipate that the increase in supply is *temporary,* they may decide to "stock up" on sugar. The resulting increase in demand may offset the increase in supply, leaving the price of sugar more or less unchanged. The important point is that different expectations trigger different kinds of economic decisions and, therefore, different outcomes.

**Policy Frustration**   The rational expectations theory suggests that, when households and businesses anticipate economic change, including those caused by discretionary fiscal and monetary policies, they will respond rationally in their own self-interest. Furthermore—and this is critical to our discussion of macroeconomic policy—it is argued that *the aggregated responses of the public to its expectations will tend to render discretionary stabilization policies ineffective!* Consider monetary policy. Suppose the economy is sluggish and the monetary authorities make pronouncements to the effect that an easy money policy is in the offing. Purpose: To increase real output and employment. But based upon past experience, the public anticipates that this expansionary policy will be accompanied by inflation (recall range 2 of Figure 10-6). As a result, the public will take self-protective actions. Workers will press for higher money wages. Businesses will increase the prices of their products. Lenders will raise their interest rates. All these responses are designed to prevent inflation from having anticipated adverse effects upon the real incomes of workers, businesses, and lenders. But collectively this behavior raises wage and price levels. Hence, the increase in aggregate demand brought about by the easy money policy is dissipated in higher prices and wages; therefore, real output and employment do *not* expand. In Keynesian terms, the higher wage costs (which shift the investment-demand curve to the left) and higher interest rates (which move investors up the investment-demand curve) choke off the increase in investment which the easy money policy was designed to generate (Figure 16-1). In terms of the monetarists' equation of exchange, the easy money policy increases $M$ and therefore increases aggregate demand, $MV$. But the public's expectation of inflation elicits an increase in $P$ of such an amount that, despite the increased $MV$, real output, $Q$, and employment are substantially unchanged.

Note carefully what has occurred here. The decision to increase $M$ was made for the purpose of increasing output and employment. But the public, acting upon the expected effects of easy money, has taken actions which have frustrated or nullified the policy's goal. Easy money has been translated into inflation, rather than into increases in output and employment. One can plausibly argue that the economy would have been better off if it had followed a steady money growth policy as suggested by the monetary rule. It was, after all, the government's discretionary easy money policy which prompted unions, businesses, and lenders to raise wages, prices, and interest rates. Why blame these groups for inflation, when the blame should be placed upon government?

**Procyclical Policy?**   Rational expectations theorists claim that discretionary policy may reinforce economic instability. Consider the following scenario. Suppose once again that the economy is sliding into a recession. Government's policy response is to cut taxes by enacting, say, an investment tax credit which allows businesses to subtract 10 percent of their investment expenditures from their taxable incomes. This unexpected windfall

will boost anticipated profits on investment projects and thereby stimulate investment spending. In short, fiscal policy works effectively in the fashion described in Chapter 13. But if this scenario occurs on several occasions, businesses will come to expect that, whenever the economy falls into a recession, policy makers will respond with an investment tax credit or some other form of tax relief. Hence, when recession occurs, businesses will postpone investment in anticipation of a forthcoming tax cut which will increase the profitability of that investment. But the decision to defer investment intensifies the cyclical downswing. When the tax cut is actually put into effect, there will occur an unusually large spurt of investment. Government tax policy has exaggerated the variability of investment and has intensified both the recession and recovery phases of the cycle. Conclusion: Discretionary policy tends to be procyclical rather than countercyclical. A much better alternative, according to the rational expectations theorists, would be to abandon discretionary policy in favor of rules.

**Relevance**   Several other points are pertinent with respect to the theory of rational expectations. First, while the theory provides support for the monetarists in the rules versus discretionary policy debate, the rationale for this conclusion is different than that of monetarism. According to the rational expectations theory, policy is ineffective, not because of policy errors or the inability to time decisions properly, but because of the reaction of the public to the expected effects of these policies. Second, if correct, the rational expectations theory helps explain the rather disappointing record of stabilization policy in the 1970s. (Indeed, the burgeoning interest in rational expectations theory stems partly from the fact that economists are uncertain as to why stabilization policy has not worked very well in recent years.) Perhaps discretionary policies have enjoyed differing degrees of effectiveness at different points in time for the simple reason that the public's expectations have been different! Finally, it must be emphasized that rational expectations theory is the new theory on the block and many questions and uncertainties surround it. Does the public garner and digest policy decisions as intelligently as the theory implies? Does the public act *that* rationally on the basis of this information? Keynesians might challenge our easy money example. To them an easy money policy results in more investment, increased productive capacity, and a larger aggregate supply. And the larger aggregate supply tends to be deflationary, not inflationary. Why, then, is it rational to associate easy money with inflation? While the jury will be out for some time on the rational expectations theory, there is little doubt that the theory has provided additional reasons to question whether stabilization policies can work as effectively and smoothly as Chapters 13 and 16 imply.

### △ A Continuing Debate

Our discussion of the theoretical and policy issues raised by the Keynesian-monetarist debate only skims the surface; vigorous pursuit of these analytical and policy questions soon takes one to the murky frontiers of economic knowledge. For several reasons we can be quite certain that this "great debate" will persist for some time to come. First, both positions are inherently plausible. "Each theory . . . provides a sensible framework for the orderly investigation of economic developments."[10] Second, the late 1960s and the 1970s have proven to be an extraordinarily turbulent "laboratory" for the testing of the two views. For example, the simultaneous inflation and unemployment of the 1970s and the external

shocks caused by the OPEC oil cartel have generated an unusually complex "real world" in which to trace and verify or reject the policy prescriptions of either school of thought. Finally, recall that the two views are imbedded in fundamentally different ideological stances; that is, differences relate not only to facts and theories, but also to subjective value judgments.

The controversy has been healthy in the sense that it has forced economists of all persuasions to rethink some of the very fundamental aspects of macroeconomics. And, as is true of most debates, some compromise and revision of positions has occurred. There are very few economists today who would embrace the extreme view that "money doesn't matter" or the opposite extreme that "only money matters." Stated differently, despite important differences between Keynesianism and monetarism, we must not lose sight of the fundamental fact that in both models money affects NNP in the same direction. In both theories an increase in the money supply will increase money NNP and vice versa. The debate centers upon the quantitative significance of these changes. Furthermore, thanks to the monetarists' emphasis upon the crowding-out effect, economists and policy makers have become more fully aware of the need to coordinate fiscal and monetary policies. If fiscal policy generates a crowding-out effect of some magnitude which diminishes the effectiveness of fiscal policy, then it is obviously imperative that an appropriate monetary policy be applied simultaneously to negate any potential crowding out of private investment. In summary, monetarists have had a great impact upon macroeconomic theory and policy, even though the majority of economists remain in the Keynesian camp.

[10]Paul Wonnacott, *Macroeconomics,* rev. ed. (Homewood, Ill.: Richard D. Irwin, Inc., 1978), p. 41.

# Summary

The following statements contrast the Keynesian and monetarist positions on a number of critical points.

   **1** *Ideological orientation.* The *Keynesian* view is that the price system is conducive to macroeconomic instability, the misallocation of resources, and income inequality. An activist public policy, centered upon fiscal policy, is required to remedy these shortcomings. The *monetarist* view is that public sector activities have tended to undermine the stabilizing potential of the price system and to result in wasteful, counterproductive programs for the purpose of remedying largely imagined socioeconomic ills.

   **2** *Analytical framework.* To *Keynesians* the basic determinant of real output, employment, and the price level is the level of aggregate demand. Hence, their basic equation is $C_a + I_n + G = \text{NNP}$. The components of aggregate demand are determined by a wide variety of factors which, for the most part, are unrelated to the supply of money. The basic equation of *monetarism* is the equation of exchange: $MV = PQ$. Because velocity $V$ is basically stable, the critical determinant of real output and employment $(Q)$ and the price level $(P)$ is the supply of money $M$.

   **3** *Monetary policy.* *Keynesians* argue that monetary policy entails a lengthy transmission mechanism, involving monetary policy decisions, bank reserves, the interest rate, investment, and finally the NNP. Uncertainties at each step in the mechanism limit the effectiveness and dependability of monetary policy. Money matters, but its manipulation through monetary policy is not a powerful stabilization device. More specifically, the combination of a relatively flat demand-for-money curve and a relatively steep investment-demand curve makes monetary policy relatively ineffective. *Monetarists* believe that the relative stability of $V$ indicates a rather tight and dependable link between the money supply and the money NNP. However, monetarists think that because of **a.** variable time lags in becoming effective and **b.** the incorrect use of the interest rate as a guide to policy, the application of discretionary monetary policy to "fine-tune" the economy is likely to fail. In practice, monetary policy has tended to destabilize the economy. Monetarists therefore recommend a monetary rule whereby the money supply is increased in accordance with the long-term growth of real NNP. The theory of *rational expectations* supports the case for rules as opposed to discretionary policy. This new theory holds that, when the public reacts in its own self-interest to the expected effects of discretionary policy, the effectiveness of such policy will be undermined.

   **4** *Fiscal policy.* The *Keynesian* position is that because **a.** government spending is a component of aggregate demand and **b.** tax changes have direct and dependable effects upon consumption and investment, fiscal policy is a powerful stabilization tool. *Monetarists* argue that fiscal policy is weak and uncertain in its effects. In particular, unless financed by an increase in the money supply, deficit spending will raise the interest rate and thereby crowd out private investment spending.

# Questions and Study Suggestions

   **1** Key terms and concepts to remember: Keynesianism; monetarism; equation of exchange; velocity of money; crowding-out effect; monetary rule; rational expectations theory.
   **2** Explain: "The debate between Keynesians and monetarists is an important facet of the larger controversy over the role of government in our lives."
   **3** State and explain the basic equations of Keynesianism and monetarism. Can you "translate" the Keynesian equation into the monetarist equation?

**4**   What is the transmission mechanism for monetary policy according to ***a.*** Keynesians and ***b.*** monetarists? What significance do the two schools of thought apply to money and monetary policy as a determinant of economic activity? According to monetarism, what happens when the actual supply of money exceeds the amount of money which the public wants to hold?

**5**   Why do monetarists recommend that a "monetary rule" be substituted for discretionary monetary policy? Explain: "One cannot assess what monetary policy is doing by just looking at interest rates." Indicate how an attempt to stabilize interest rates can be destabilizing.

**6**   Explain why monetarists assert fiscal policy is weak and ineffective. What specific assumptions do ***a.*** monetarists and ***b.*** Keynesians make with respect to the shapes of the demand-for-money and investment-demand curves? Why are the differences significant?

**7**   Indicate the precise relationship between the demand for money and the velocity of money. Discuss in detail: "The crucial issue separating Keynesians from monetarists is whether or not the demand for money is sensitive to changes in the rate of interest." Explain the Keynesian contention that a change in $M$ is likely to be accompanied by a change in $V$ in the opposite direction.

**8**   Explain and evaluate these statements in terms of the Keynesian-monetarist controversy:

***a.***   "If the national goal is to raise income, it can be achieved only by raising the money supply."

***b.***   "The size of a Federal budget deficit is not important. What is important is how the deficit is financed."

***c.***   "There is no reason in the world why, in an equation like $MV = PQ$, the $V$ should be thought to be independent of the rate of interest. There is every plausible reason for the velocity of circulation to be a systematic and increasing function of the rate of interest."

***d.***   "Monetarists assume that the $PQ$ side of the equation of exchange is 'passive'; Keynesians assume it is 'active'."

**9**   Explain how rational expectations might be an impediment to discretionary stabilization policies. Do you favor discretionary policies or rules? Justify your position.

## Selected References

Friedman, Milton, and Walter W. Heller: *Monetary vs. Fiscal Policy* (New York: W. W. Norton & Company, Inc., 1969).

Gordon, Robert J.: *Macroeconomics* (Boston: Little, Brown and Company, 1978), chap. 12.

Humphrey, Thomas M.: "The Quantity Theory of Money: Its Historical Evolution and Role in Policy Debates," *Economic Review* (Federal Reserve Bank of Richmond), May–June 1974, pp. 2–19.

Hutchinson, Harry D.: *Money, Banking, and the United States Economy,* 4th ed. (Englewood Cliffs, N.J.: Prentice-Hall, Inc., 1980), chap. 17.

Kreinin, Mordechai E.: "What Have We Learned and Not Learned about Economic Stabilization Policies?", *MSU Business Topics,* Winter 1978, pp. 34–53.

Lindert, Peter H.: *Prices, Jobs, and Growth: An Introduction to Macroeconomics* (Boston: Little, Brown and Company, 1976), chap. 10.

Poole, William: *Money and the Economy: A Monetarist View* (Reading, Mass.: Addison-Wesley Publishing Company, 1978).

Ritter, Lawrence S., and William L. Silber: *Money,* 2d ed. (New York: Basic Books, Inc., Publishers, 1973), chaps. 2, 4.

Wonnacott, Paul: *Macroeconomics,* rev. ed. (Homewood, Ill.: Richard D. Irwin, Inc., 1978), chap. 12.

# LAST WORD
## Inflation: A Monetary Phenomenon?

How "tight" is the relationship between the money supply and the price level? The monetarist view, expressed here by Milton Friedman, is that the relationship is tight and dependable. The second and more eclectic view, stated by Lawrence S. Ritter and William L. Silber, is that the relationship is loose and undependable.

*Monetarist view:* . . . the central fact is that inflation is always and everywhere a monetary phenomenon. Historically, substantial changes in prices have always occurred together with substantial changes in the quantity of money relative to output. I know of no exception to this generalization, no occasion in the United States or elsewhere when prices have risen substantially without a substantial rise in the quantity of money relative to output or when the quantity of money has risen substantially relative to output without a substantial rise in prices. And there are numerous confirming examples. Indeed, I doubt that there is any other empirical generalization in economics for which there is as much organized evidence covering so wide a range of space and time.

Some confirming examples are extremely dramatic and illustrate vividly how important the quantity of money is by comparison with everything else. After the Russian Revolution of 1917, there was a hyperinflation in Russia when a new currency was introduced and printed in large quantities. Ultimately, it became almost valueless. All the time, some currency was circulating which had been issued by the prerevolutionary Czarist government. The Czarist government was out of power. Nobody expected it to return to power. Yet, the value of the Czarist currency remained roughly constant in terms of goods and rose sharply in terms of the Bolshevik currency. Why? Because there was nobody to print any more of it. It was fixed in quantity and therefore it retained its value. Another story has to do with the United States Civil War. Toward the end of the war, the Union troops overran the place where the Confederates had been printing paper money to finance the war. In the course of moving to a new location, there was a temporary cessation of the printing of money. As a result, there was also a temporary interruption in the price rise that had been proceeding merrily.

*Eclectic view:* . . . money is not so clearly and uniquely the culprit when it comes to the real problem of our times, creeping inflation. The "fit" between the money supply and the cost of living exists, but it is rather loose and a bit baggy.

Take, for example, the last four decades:

**1** From the end of 1930 to the end of 1940, the money supply increased by 70 percent, but prices, instead of rising, fell 15 percent.

**2** From 1940 to 1950, the money supply increased by 175 percent, but prices rose by only 80 percent, less than half as much.

**3** From the end of 1950 to the end of 1960 provides the best fit; the money supply grew by about 25 percent and the consumer price index rose by about 20 percent.

**4** However, from 1960 through 1970 the relationship sags again; the money supply increased by 40 percent, but prices by just 20 percent.

Even the close relationship during the 1950s turns out to be less impressive upon further examination. During the first half of the decade the money supply increased twice as fast as prices, while during the second half prices increased twice as rapidly as the money supply. At the end of the 1960s, the money supply was about 4½ times larger than it had been in 1940, but prices were "only" about 2½ times higher. . . .

Over the long run, an increase in the money supply is a *necessary* condition for the continuation of inflation, creeping or otherwise.

But it is not a *sufficient* condition. Increases in the money supply do not always result in inflation.

Milton Friedman, "What Price Guideposts?" in George P. Shultz and Robert Z. Aliber, eds., *Guidelines, Informal Controls, and the Market Place* (Chicago: The University of Chicago Press, 1966), pp. 25–26, © 1966 by The University of Chicago; Lawrence S. Ritter and William L. Silber, *Money,* 2d ed. (New York: Basic Books, Inc., Publishers, 1973), pp. 67–68, abridged.

# Stagflation: New Problems and New Policies    chapter 18

In the mid-1960s the American economy was healthy and expanding. Furthermore, political leaders and the public had great confidence in the knowledge and policy prescriptions of economists. The tax cut of 1964 had increased output and employment and accelerated the growth of real GNP as Keynesian economists had predicted. In 1965 inflation was virtually absent; the price level increased that year by only 1.9 percent. Furthermore, the economy was practically at full employment. But the past twelve or fifteen years have been turbulent for the economy. In the 1970s and early 1980s we have been faced with the worst of all possible macroeconomic worlds. Specifically, *stagflation*—the stagnation of output and employment coupled with inflation—has been the paramount problem. The inability of economists to satisfactorily explain this problem—much less resolve it through policy recommendations—has shaken the public's confidence in economists and their policy recommendations.

The present chapter attempts to explain this turnabout. Specific goals are as follows:

**1** The so-called Phillips Curve is introduced as a possible explanation of the coexistence of unemployment and inflation.

**2** We next consider policies other than traditional fiscal and monetary policies which might be invoked to deal with cost-push inflation. Emphasis is upon incomes policies, that is, wage-price guideposts and controls.

**3** The economic developments of the past decade are surveyed to indicate the challenges which these events have posed for traditional macroeconomic theory and policy.

Warning: This chapter deals with important, unsettled questions in modern economics; therefore, although opinions and judgments are plentiful, unassailable evidence and clear-cut policy prescriptions are scarce.

## ☐ DEMAND-PULL INFLATION

Inflation has been regarded traditionally as the consequence of excess total demand. Recall our aggregate demand–aggregate supply approach to income determination in terms of Figure 12-5a. We reasoned that if aggregate demand is initially deficient at $(C + I_n)_1$, the economy will experience unemployment. But the use of expansionary fiscal and monetary policies can be used to shift the aggregate demand schedule upward to $(C + I_n)_0$, closing the recessionary gap and establishing full employment. Our *assumption* has been that the expansion of aggregate demand up to the full-employment level would increase employment and real output, *but leave the price level unchanged.* Hence, the "right" level of aggregate demand—$(C + I_n)_0$ in Figure 12-5a—would give us the best of all possible macroeconomic worlds wherein society enjoyed full employment *and* price level stability simultaneously.

Demand-pull inflation occurs when the economy attempts to spend beyond its capacity to produce. In popular jargon, demand-pull inflation occurs when "too much money is chasing too few goods." If aggregate demand is in excess of the economy's full-employment output (as valued at current or existing prices), an *inflationary gap* will exist; $(C + I_n)_2$ entails such a gap in Figure 12-5b. Because the economy already is at full employment and operating at a point on its production possibilities curve, real output is fixed and cannot be expanded in response to this excess demand; hence, the excess of total demand will have the effect of pulling up the price level.[1]

These comments can be succinctly restated in terms of the monetarists' equation of exchange ($MV = PQ$). Assuming unemployment initially, an expanding aggregate demand ($MV$) will cause real output ($Q$) to rise but leave the price level ($P$) unchanged. But once

full employment is reached, $Q$ becomes constant or fixed and any further expansion of $MV$ will simply pull up $P$.

The assumed compatibility of full employment and price level stability can be demonstrated graphically in Figure 18-1. Here we show the annual rate of inflation on the left vertical axis[2] and the unemployment rate on the horizontal axis. We assume, for reasons given in Chapter 10, that "full employment" exists when no more than 4 percent of the labor force is unemployed. The blue L-shaped line with the right-angle kink at full employment reflects the assumption that full employment and price level stability are compatible.[3] Hence, starting with a severe recession where unemployment is 8 or 9 percent, increases in aggregate demand would have the

[2] Ignore the right vertical axis for the moment.
[3] This assumption has been implicit throughout all our earlier analysis with the exception of the brief discussion surrounding Figure 10-6 and the concluding section of Chapter 12.

[1] Recall from Chapter 12 the dynamic character of the inflationary process. In particular, a rising price level *may* have feedback effects on both consumption and investment spending and thereby accelerate through time. This means that a new equilibrium with price level stability may *not* be realized at $510 billion, as Figure 12-5b implies.

**FIGURE 18-1 PRICE LEVEL-UNEMPLOYMENT RELATIONSHIPS**

The blue curve is drawn on the assumption that full employment and price level stability are compatible goals. The orange Phillips Curve, which is fitted to data for the 1960s, suggests there is a trade-off between unemployment and inflation.

sole effect of *reducing* the unemployment rate and thereby *increasing* real output ($Q$) until full employment is achieved; the price level ($P$) would remain constant up to the 4 percent full-employment point. As aggregate demand rises beyond that required for full employment and thereby becomes excess demand, the sole consequence would be increases in the price level ($P$); real output ($Q$) would remain constant at the full-employment level.

The demand-pull theory of inflation is widely accepted by economists, and over the years it has provided a useful and reasonably accurate explanation of many of our inflationary experiences. For example, the inflationary pressures of World War II, although partially suppressed by wage and price controls, were explainable in terms of demand-pull. So were most of the postwar inflation of the late 1940s, the inflation associated with the Korean war, and the inflation of 1966–1968.

☐   THE PHILLIPS CURVE:
PREMATURE INFLATION
Unfortunately, the experience of the United States and other advanced capitalistic nations suggests that this simplistic demand-pull scenario is an incomplete explanation of inflation. At times the economy has encountered significant increases in the price level *before* full employment has been achieved; that is, inflation has occurred *before* aggregate demand became excessive.

These events prompted economists to reexamine the problem of inflation in an effort to determine whether such episodes were "special cases" or whether "premature inflation" was a fact of economic life. The resulting pioneering empirical work of the late 1950s and 1960s on the relationship between the rate of unemployment and the rate of inflation yielded the so-called Phillips Curve,[4] which seemed to

confirm that the price level typically does rise *before* full employment is achieved.

Consider again Figure 18-1 wherein the rate of increase in the price index and the corresponding unemployment rate in the United States have been plotted for the 1960s. The orange Phillips Curve fitted to these data points suggests an unfortunate relationship: Low rates of unemployment seem to be associated with high rates of inflation and, conversely, price stability or low rates of inflation apparently are associated with high rates of unemployment. In short, there seems to be a trade-off between employment and the price level.[5] Specifically, these data suggested that to achieve full employment—defined as 4 percent of the labor force unemployed (Chapter 10)—society must endure an accompanying inflation on the order of a 3 or 3½ percent annual increase in the price level. Conversely, the achievement of near price level stability required the existence of an unemployment rate of about 6 or 7 percent. Most importantly, note that the Phillips Curve provides an explanation of the simultaneous existence of inflation and unemployment.

△   **Logic of the Phillips Curve**
How can the Phillips Curve be explained? What causes the unfortunate trade-off between full employment and price level stability? Basically, there are two sets of complementary considerations which explain premature inflation.

**1   Labor Market Imbalances**   A partial explanation lies in certain imbalances—"bottlenecks" and structural problems—which arise in labor markets as the economy expands toward full employment. The basic point here is that "the" labor market in the United States in fact comprises an extremely large number of individual labor markets which are stratified and distinct both occupationally and geo-

---

[4] Named after the British economist A. W. Phillips, who developed this concept. See his "The Relationship between Unemployment and the Rate of Change in Money Wage Rates in the United Kingdom, 1862–1957," *Economica*, November 1958, pp. 283–299.

[5] You may remember the notion of premature inflation as presented earlier in Figure 10-6, which is simply the Phillips Curve trade-off "flopped over" graphically.

graphically. This labor market diversity suggests that, as the economy expands, full employment will *not* be realized simultaneously in each individual labor market. While full employment and labor shortages may exist for some occupations and some areas, unemployment will persist for other occupations and regions. To illustrate: In 1979 the overall unemployment rate was 5.8 percent. But the unemployment rate for professional and technical workers was only 2.4 percent, while the rate for all blue-collar workers was 6.9 percent. Furthermore, within the blue-collar classification, common laborers experienced an unemployment rate of almost 11 percent, while the rate for craftsmen and foremen was only 4.5 percent. Similarly, unemployment was unusually high in Modesto, California (11.8 percent), Flint, Michigan (9.0 percent), but very low in Wichita Falls, Texas (2.4 percent). These disparities mean that in an expanding economy, even though the overall unemployment rate may be 5 or 6 percent, scarcities will develop for specific kinds of labor and for labor in certain geographic areas, and the wage rates of such workers will rise. Rising wage rates mean higher costs and necessitate higher prices. The net result is rising prices even though overall unemployment persists.

It is fair to ask why labor market adjustments do not eliminate these bottleneck problems. Why, for example, do not unemployed laborers become craftworkers? The answer, of course, is that such shifts cannot be made with sufficient speed to eliminate labor market bottlenecks. The training for a new occupation is costly in terms of both time and money. Furthermore, even if one has the ability, time, and money to acquire the needed skills and to relocate, an unemployed laborer in Kalamazoo may just not be aware of the shortage of skilled craftworkers in Kenosha. Then, too, artificial restrictions upon the shiftability of workers sustain structural imbalances. For example, discrimination on the basis of race, ethnic background, or sex can keep qualified workers from acquiring available positions. Similarly,

licensing requirements and union restrictions upon the number of available apprenticeships inhibit the leveling out of imbalances between specific labor markets. An unemployed real estate salesman or beautician in Kankakee may be unable to take an available job a relatively short distance away in Keokuk, if licensing requirements in Illinois and Iowa are significantly different. In brief, labor market adjustments are neither sufficiently rapid nor complete enough to prevent production costs and product prices from rising *before* overall full employment is achieved.

**2   Market Power: Cost-Push Inflation**
A complementary explanation of the Phillips Curve is based upon the assumption that labor unions and big businesses both possess significant amounts of monopoly or market power with which to raise wages and prices and that this power becomes easier to exert as the economy approaches full employment. Hence, the "wage-push" or "cost-push" inflationary scenario goes something like this: As the economy moves toward full employment, labor markets tighten and unions become more aggressive in their wage demands. Furthermore, increasing prosperity will tend to enhance the willingness of businesses to grant union wage demands. On the one hand, firms will hesitate to resist union demands and risk a costly strike at the very time when business activity is becoming increasingly profitable. On the other hand, economic expansion provides a favorable environment in which monopoly power can be used to pass wage increases on to consumers in the form of higher product prices.

Alternatively, market-power inflation may be "profit-push"; that is, inflation may be initiated by businesses as they seek higher profit margins. Large corporations which have the ability to manipulate or administer their prices may decide to increase prices to expand profits. Whether wage-push, profit-push, or some combination of the two is responsible, the result is a rising price level in the absence of excess aggregate demand.

### △  The Wage Rate–Productivity Nexus

It is important to recognize at this point that not all increases in money wage rates are destined to be inflationary. *Only money wage increases which are greater than average productivity increases will cause labor costs per unit of output to rise.* This becomes clear once it is recognized that labor cost per unit of output, $L$, is equal to the money wage rate, $W$, divided by the average productivity of labor, $P_L$. That is, $L$, equals $W/P_L$. Consider a simple example. Suppose that the productivity (output) of labor per hour is 10 units. If the wage rate is $5.00 per hour, the labor cost *per unit of output* is obviously $0.50 ($=$ \$5.00/10$). If both $W$ and $P_L$ now increase at the same percentage rate, $L$ will be constant. If productivity and wage rates both rise, say, by 10 percent, labor cost per unit of output will remain at $0.50 ($=$ \$5.50/11$). However, if the wage rate increases by, say, 20 percent while productivity rises by only 10 percent, then labor cost per unit of output will rise to approximately $0.55 ($=$ \$6.00/11$). The important point for immediate purposes is that increases in wage rates must exceed productivity increases in order to increase labor costs per unit of output and be inflationary.

Look back at Figure 18-1 once again and consider the right-hand vertical axis which measures the annual percentage increase in wage rates. Observe that the difference in the left-hand (price) scale and the right-hand (wage rate) scale is the assumed 3 percent annual average increase in labor productivity. Hence, as our example indicates, a 3 percent increase in wage rates (right axis) translates into a constant, or "0 percent change," in the price level (left axis). Why? Because the assumed 3 percent average increase in labor productivity "absorbs" the 3 percent increase in wage rates; therefore, unit labor costs and product prices remain unchanged. Similarly, a 5 percent average increase in wage rates is only partially offset by the 3 percent labor productivity increase, so unit labor costs and prices will rise by 2 percent, and so on. All this as-sumes that firms do *not* attempt to expand their profit margins but merely allow higher unit labor costs to "pass through" to the consumer.

### △  Stabilization Policy Dilemma

The Phillips Curve embodies a serious policy dilemma because traditional fiscal and monetary policies merely alter aggregate demand and therefore do nothing to correct the labor market imbalances and the market power which bring forth premature inflation. More specifically, the manipulation of aggregate demand through fiscal and monetary measures simply has the effect of moving the economy *along* the given Phillips Curve. Hence, the expansionary fiscal policy and the easy money policy which combine to boost aggregate demand and bring full employment will simultaneously entail inflation. Point $A$ on the Phillips Curve of Figure 18-2 is illustrative. Conversely, a restrictive fiscal policy and a tight money policy can be used to achieve price level stability, but only at the cost of excessive unemployment and forgone production. Point $B$ in Figure 18-2 is relevant. *Traditional macroeconomic policies can be used to manipulate aggregate demand and thereby to choose a point on the Phillips Curve, but such policies do not improve upon the "unemployment rate–rate of inflation" menu embodied in the Phillips Curve.* What has eluded recent United States fiscal and monetary policies is the outcome suggested by point $C$ in Figure 18-2 where full employment and price stability are simultaneously attained.

### ☐  NEW POLICY OPTIONS

These circumstances have led most of the advanced capitalist nations, including the United States, to supplement traditional macroeconomic policy with additional policies designed to shift the Phillips Curve leftward to a more desirable position, that is, to a position wherein full employment and price level stability are more compatible. The broken Phillips Curve

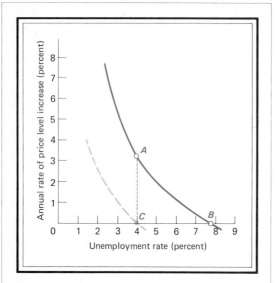

**FIGURE 18-2  THE PHILLIPS CURVE AND PUBLIC POLICY**

The Phillips Curve poses a cruel dilemma in that fiscal and monetary policies force society to accept inflation in order to achieve full employment (point A) or to accept unemployment to achieve price level stability (point B). As a result, many societies have experimented with market policies and wage-price policies designed to shift the Phillips Curve leftward, as indicated by the broken curve, so as to make full employment and price level stability compatible goals (point C).

in Figure 18-2 is illustrative. Generally speaking, two categories of policies have been proposed: *market policies* and *wage-price, or incomes, policies.*

△  **Market Policies**

Market policies are designed to eliminate the underlying causes of the Phillips Curve. Two kinds of market policies can be distinguished. *Manpower policy* is intended to reduce or eliminate imbalances and bottlenecks in labor markets. A *procompetition policy* attempts to reduce the market power of unions and large corporations.

**Manpower Policy**  The goal of manpower policy is to improve the efficiency of labor markets so that any given level of aggregate demand will be associated with a lower level of

unemployment. In other words, the purpose of manpower policy is to achieve a better matching of workers to jobs, thereby reducing labor market imbalances. Successful manpower policies will shift the Phillips Curve to the left. Several different kinds of programs will provide a better matching of workers to jobs.

*1  Vocational training*  Programs of vocationally oriented education and training will permit marginal and displaced workers to be more quickly reemployed. The Manpower Development and Training Act (MDTA) of 1962 is the landmark piece of legislation in this area in that it provides for both institutional and on-the-job training for the unemployed, for disadvantaged youth, and for older workers whose skills are meager or obsolete.[6]

*2  Job information*  A second type of manpower policy is concerned with improving the flow of job information between unemployed workers and potential employers and with enhancing the geographic mobility of workers. For example, a number of proposals have been made in recent years to modernize the United States Employment Service in order to increase its effectiveness in bringing job seekers and employers together.

*3  Nondiscrimination*  Another facet of manpower policy is concerned with the reduction or elimination of artificial obstacles to employment. Prejudice and discrimination have been an important roadblock in the matching of workers and jobs; discrimination is a basic factor in explaining why unemployment rates for blacks are roughly twice as high as for whites. The Civil Rights Act of 1964 attempts to improve manpower utilization by removing discrimination because of race, religion, sex, or ethnic background as an obstacle to employment or union membership.

**Procompetition Policy**  A second avenue for improving the unemployment rate–rate of

[6]The Act also requires the publication of an annual *Employment and Training Report of the President* which discusses labor force developments and problems and contains descriptions of major manpower programs.

inflation trade-off is to reduce the monopoly or market power of unions and businesses. The contention here is that the monopoly power of unions must be reduced so that they will be less able to push up wage rates ahead of average productivity increases. Similarly, more competition in the product market will reduce the discretionary power of large corporations to raise prices.

How can the economy be made more competitive? A basic recommendation is to apply our existing antitrust (antimonopoly) laws much more vigorously to big businesses and to remove existing legal restrictions upon entry to certain regulated industries (Chapter 34). Similarly, the elimination of tariffs and other restrictions upon foreign imports will tend to increase the competitiveness of American markets. On the labor front, it is periodically argued that the antimonopoly laws should be applied to unions or that collective bargaining should be less centralized.

But serious questions can be raised about such proposals. In the first place, political realities are such that any administration is unlikely to undertake a vigorous antimonopoly or antiunion crusade. Antitrust legislation has been a fact of life in the United States for almost a century, yet there is no clear answer on whether it has significantly retarded the growth of monopoly, much less increased competition. Indeed, some economists feel that large monopolistic corporations are necessary if the economy is to enjoy the economies of mass production and a high rate of technological progress. Hence, although an effective antimonopoly policy might be helpful in containing cost-push inflation, it might also entail diminished productive efficiency now and in the future. Nor is it at all clear that antitrust policies can be applied to labor without virtually destroying unions and the institution of collective bargaining. Unions and collective bargaining perform a number of desirable functions for workers which would be largely sacrificed by a campaign that reduces the bargaining power of unions.

△  **Wage-Price (Incomes) Policies**

A second general approach to the Phillips Curve dilemma accepts the existence of monopoly power and labor market imbalances as more-or-less inevitable facts of economic life, and seeks to alter the behavior of labor and product-market monopolists so as to make their wage and price decisions more compatible with the twin goals of full employment and price level stability. Although they differ primarily in degree, it is meaningful to distinguish between wage-price *guideposts* and wage-price *controls*. In essence, guideposts and controls differ in that the former rely upon the voluntary cooperation of labor and business, whereas the latter have the force of law.

Wage-price guideposts and wage-price controls are sometimes called *incomes policies*. The reason for this label is that a person's real income—the amount of goods and services one can obtain with one's money income—obviously depends upon the size of that money income and the prices of the goods and services he or she buys. Guideposts and controls are designed to constrain both money incomes and prices paid, thereby affecting real incomes.

**Wage-Price Guideposts: Kennedy–Johnson Version**   In the period from 1962 to 1966, the Kennedy and Johnson administrations attempted to shift the Phillips Curve to the left by setting forth "guideposts for noninflationary wage and price behavior."[7] The guideposts were essentially a set of wage and price rules which, if followed by labor and management, would prevent the occurrence of premature inflation.

*1  Wage guidepost*   The basic wage guidepost was that wage rates in all industries should rise in accordance with the rate of increase in labor productivity for the nation as a whole. The rationale of this guidepost is that if the average hourly output of workers increases by, say, 3 percent, then employers can raise

---

[7] *Economic Report of the President, 1962* (Washington), pp. 185–190.

money wage rates by 3 percent without experiencing any overall increase in labor costs per unit of output. Of course, the productivity increases of some industries will exceed, while those of others will fall short of, the overall or average increase in national productivity. Hence, for an industry whose productivity rises by less than national productivity, unit labor costs will rise. For example, if national productivity rose by 3 percent while productivity rose by only 1 percent in industry X, then, with money wage rates increasing by 3 percent, that industry would experience approximately a 2 percent *increase* in its unit labor costs. Conversely, if productivity rose by 5 percent in industry Y, then the 3 percent increase in money wages would *decrease* unit labor costs by about 2 percent.

   **2 Price guidepost**   *The basic price guidepost was that prices should change to compensate for changes in unit labor costs.* This meant that in industries whose rate of productivity was equal to the national average, prices would be constant because unit labor costs would be unchanged. For industries where productivity rose by less than the national average, prices could be increased by enough to cover the resulting increase in unit labor costs. Industry X, cited earlier, could increase its prices by 2 percent. For industries wherein productivity increases exceeded the national average, prices would be expected to fall in accordance with the resulting decline in unit labor costs. Industry Y should lower its prices by 2 percent. These price increases and decreases would cancel out and leave the overall price level unchanged.

   **Carter Guideposts**   The Kennedy–Johnson guideposts came to be largely irrelevant in the latter half of the 1960s as rising military spending on the Vietnam War changed inflation from cost-push to demand-pull. But in 1978 the Carter Administration established a new guidepost program. Against a background of accelerating inflation, the Carter program called for maximum wage increases of 7 percent and price increases $\frac{1}{2}$ percent below a

firm's average price increases for the 1976–1977 period. Prices were subject to a maximum $9\frac{1}{2}$ percent increase. An innovative aspect of the new program was a *real-wage insurance* proposal which promised tax rebates to workers who limited themselves to 7 percent money wage increases only to find themselves faced with price inflation in excess of 7 percent. For example, if a worker earning $10,000 received a 7 percent ($700) money wage increase and inflation occurred at 9 percent, the worker would get a special $200 tax rebate to prevent his or her real income from falling. The Carter program was accompanied by promises to reduce government deficits, cut Federal employment through attrition, and reduce cost-increasing government regulations.

   The guidepost approach is implemented through the use of moral suasion, or what skeptics have labeled an "open mouth" or "jawbone" policy. The President, the Secretary of Labor, and other high administration officials address appeals and admonitions to labor and business leaders, urging them to be "socially responsible" by exercising self-restraint in reaching wage-price decisions. In practice, moral suasion was sometimes supplemented by ad hoc measures: for example, threats of antitrust investigation or the abolition of protective tariffs for potential offenders.

   **Wage-Price Controls: Mandatory Restraints**   Wage-price controls have typically been a wartime phenomenon in the United States. Thus, during World War II, controls were widely used to repress inflationary pressures. In 1971, however, peacetime controls were introduced as a part of President Nixon's *New Economic Policy.* Faced with stagflation—an unfortunate combination of unemployment and rising prices—taxes were cut by some $7 to $8 billion to stimulate aggregate demand and, it was hoped, output and employment. The problem, however, was to prevent this expansionary fiscal policy from being translated into additional inflation rather than into increases in employment and real output.

The Nixon response was to invoke authority, given him under the Economic Stabilization Act of 1970, in ordering a freeze on wages, prices, and rents. More precisely, the President's Executive order made it illegal to (1) increase wages or salaries, (2) charge more for a product than the highest price charged in the 30-day period prior to the freeze, and (3) raise the rents landlords charged tenants. Although the Nixon freeze was phased out in 1974, inflation rates on the order of 18 percent in early 1980 have rekindled interest in the imposition of comprehensive wage-price controls.

**The Wage-Price Policy Debate**  There has been heated and prolonged debate in the United States as to the desirability and efficacy of incomes policies. The debate centers on three points.

*1  Workability and compliance*  Critics argue that the voluntary *guideposts* approach is doomed to failure because it asks business and labor leaders to abandon their primary functions and to forgo the goals of maximum profits and higher wages. A union leader will not gain favor with the rank and file by not insisting on attainable wage increases; nor does a corporate official become endeared to stockholders by bypassing potentially profitable price increases. For these reasons little voluntary cooperation can be expected from labor and management.

Wage and price *controls* have the force of law and, therefore, labor and management can be forced to obey. Nevertheless, problems of enforcement and compliance can be severe, particularly if wage and price controls are quite comprehensive and if they are maintained for an extended time. The basic problem is that, over time, strong economic incentives develop to evade controls. For example, it can be highly profitable to violate controls upon products and resources which are particularly scarce. The reason is that to be effective, the maximum legal price will be less than the free-market price; therefore, it will be profitable to violate the controls. Hence, it is not surprising that, despite strong patriotic moti-

vation for compliance and the sizable enforcement bureaucracy which accompanied the World War II controls, illegal *black markets*—wherein prices were above legal limits—flourished for many products. Furthermore, firms can effectively circumvent price controls by lowering the quality or size of their product. If the price of a candy bar is frozen at 15 cents, its price can be effectively doubled by reducing its size by one half!

Proponents of incomes policies respond that available evidence suggests such policies have been workable. Admittedly, the problem of measuring empirically the effectiveness of guidelines or controls is complex. Nevertheless, some important statistical studies suggest that the guideposts did make at least a modest contribution to wage-price stability in the middle 1960s.[8] Furthermore, the rate of inflation did decline perceptibly after the imposition of the wage-price freeze in 1971. And most economists would agree that the use of direct wage-price controls during World War II did contain—or at least defer—the serious inflation which would otherwise have occurred. In general, although wage-price policies may encounter problems of compliance and workability when applied over an extended period, proponents contend there is reason to believe that such policies can be helpful in controlling short-term episodes of premature inflation.

*2  Allocative efficiency*  Opponents of incomes policies contend that effective guideposts or controls interfere with the allocative function of the price system. The crucial point is that product and resource prices must be allowed to fluctuate freely and fully in response to changing market conditions—that is, to changes in demand, changes in resource supplies, and changes in technology—in order for allocative efficiency to be sustained through time (Chapter 5). Effective price controls would prohibit the market system from making these adjustments. For example, if an increase in the demand for some product

[8]John Sheahan, *The Wage-Price Guideposts* (Washington: The Brookings Institution, 1967), chap. 7.

should occur, its price could *not* rise to signal society's wish for more output and therefore more resources in this area of production. In fact, controls strip the market mechanism of its rationing function, that is, of its ability to equate quantity demanded and quantity supplied, and product shortages will result. Question: Which buyers are to obtain the product and which are to do without? One possibility is that the product can be rationed on a first-come-first-serve basis or by favoritism. But this is likely to be highly arbitrary and inequitable; those who are first in line or those able to cultivate a friendship with the seller get as much of the product as they want while others get none at all. In the interest of equity, government may have to undertake the task of rationing the product to consumers. This was done for a wide variety of products during World War II by issuing ration coupons to buyers on an equitable basis. Note, however, that governmental rationing contributes to the compliance-bureaucracy problem noted earlier.

Defenders of incomes policies respond as follows: If effective guideposts or controls are imposed upon a competitive economy, then in time the resulting rigidities will undoubtedly impair allocative efficiency. But is it correct to assume that resource allocation will be efficient in the absence of a wage-price policy? After all, cost-push inflation arises *because* big labor and big businesses possess monopoly power and consequently have the capacity to distort the allocation of resources. In short, it is not at all clear that a wage-price policy would further distort resource allocation in an economy already characterized by monopoly and allocative inefficiency. In fact, if guideposts or controls are specifically applied to those industries characterized by monopoly, it can be plausibly argued that allocative efficiency may be improved.[9]

**3   The freedom issue**   Libertarians are quick to point out that guideposts and controls

seriously conflict with freedom of action. Restraints upon wage and price decisions are obviously coercive and therefore at odds with the capitalistic ideology's insistence upon free markets and prices. Guideposts and controls move society "in an authoritarian direction" and in effect create a new and more crucial trade-off problem between the goal of full employment with price stability, on the one hand, and freedom of choice, on the other.

Proponents of incomes policies respond that free economic decision making is not an unmitigated good. Certainly, free choices which promote socially desirable ends are to be protected. Hence, freedom of choice is virtuous within the context of a competitive price system because the "invisible hand" is effectively at work to translate free choices based upon self-interest into socially desirable outcomes (Chapter 5). But the discretionary decisions of unions and business monopolists which are the target of wage-price policies are clearly not of this type. When the market system is characterized by monopoly, the "invisible hand" fumbles the ball so that decisions made on the basis of self-interest are at odds with the social interest. More specifically, free decisions by monopolists in the pursuit of private gain may come at the expense of price level stability and allocative efficiency. Incomes policy proponents contend that social control of such antisocial decision making makes sense both economically and philosophically.[10]

A final point: The validity of the criticisms of wage-price policy depends upon the rigidity, comprehensiveness, and duration of such a policy. A "loose," informal, flexible policy applied to a few key sectors of the economy for a relatively short period should wreak little havoc on resource allocation and economic freedom. But an inflexible, "no exceptions" system applied comprehensively to the entire economy for an extended time would clearly raise serious problems. The dilemma, of course, is that the informal and flexible system

[9]This assertion will be explained in Chapter 27 in the section on "Regulated Monopoly."

[10]Jerry E. Pohlman, *Inflation Under Control?* (Reston, Va.: Reston Publishing Company, Inc., 1976), pp. 154–156.

may be inadequate to the task of effectively improving upon the unemployment rate–rate of inflation options available to society.

**Tax-based Incomes Policies (TIP)**   How effective have incomes policies been? The evidence, in a word, is "mixed."[11]   Some economists have argued that incomes policies should be accompanied by a system of special tax penalties *or* tax rebates for compliance in order to improve their effectiveness. For example, one widely discussed *tax-based income policy (TIP)* envisions that a special penalty should be added to the basic 46 percent corporate income tax of any firm which grants a money wage increase in excess of the guidepost figure. For example, if the wage guidepost is 5 percent and a firm grants a 7 percent increase, then the firm's tax will be increased by some multiple of the excessive 2 percent. If the multiple is, say, 2, then the corporate income tax will be increased by 4 percentage points ($2 \times 2$ percent), from the usual 46 percent rate to 50 percent. The purpose of the extra tax would be to stiffen management's resistance to union wage demands and thus to result in collective bargaining agreements more conducive to price stability. The authors of this particular plan argue that, because wages are the largest cost in most industries *and* product prices are a "remarkably constant" percentage markup over unit labor costs, there is no need for a separate control over prices.

Proponents of the plan argue that it could be made effective without the need for a new and costly administrative bureaucracy; that it does not call for radical institutional surgery on either unions or businesses; that it is quite compatible with the market system; and, even more important, that it would work.[12]   Perhaps the most damaging criticism is the argument that the corporate income tax may ultimately

be shifted to consumers through price increases; if so, the special tax penalty will simply add to the rate of inflation.

☐   **STAGFLATION:
THE AWKWARD SEVENTIES**
Although data for the 1950s and particularly the 1960s (Figure 18-1) seemed to confirm the notion of the Phillips Curve, the data points for the 1970s suggest that the curve has shifted to the right (or upward) as indicated by the thin curves in Figure 18-3. It is important to

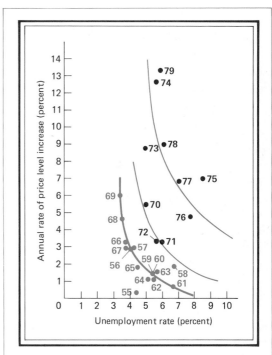

FIGURE 18-3 THE APPARENT INSTABILITY OF THE PHILLIPS CURVE.

While data for the 1955–1969 period generally conform to the conventional concept of the Phillips Curve, data for the 1970s suggest that the curve is unstable and has shifted to the right. Most Keynesians attribute these shifts to such factors as random shocks, inflationary expectations, and changes in the composition of the labor force. "Supply-side economists" envision an increasing tax wedge, declining productivity and efficiency caused by weakened economic incentives, and the cost-increasing impact of government regulation as factors underlying such shifts. "Accelerationists" argue that the conventional Phillips Curve does not exist.

[11] The interested reader should see ibid., particularly chaps. 10–12.
[12] For details, see Sidney Weintraub, "An Incomes Policy to Stop Inflation," *Lloyds Bank Review,* January 1971, pp. 1–12; and Henry C. Wallich and Sidney Weintraub, "A Tax-based Incomes Policy," *Journal of Economic Issues,* June 1971, pp. 1–19.

observe that such a shift of the Phillips Curve is consistent with the occurrence of stagflation, that is, with simultaneous *increases* in the price level and the rate of unemployment.

Why might the curve have shifted upward in the 1970s? A number of specific explanations have been put forth. A first set of reasons, which might be regarded as appendages to Keynesian economics, relates the worsening of the Phillips Curve tradeoff to random shocks, inflationary expectations, and changes in the composition of the labor force. A second group of reasons, which we shall label "supply-side economics," relates the unfavorable shift of the curve to such factors as the impact of rising taxes and transfer payments upon production incentives and the effect of growing public regulation of businesses upon costs. A final "accelerationist view" will contend that the Phillips Curve tradeoff as portrayed in Figure 18-1 simply does not exist!

## ☐ KEYNESIANISM EXTENDED

It was not too difficult for Keynesian and other economists to detect some special forces at work in the 1970s which could account for an upward shift of the Phillips Curve.

### △ Random Shocks

In the early 1970s the economy was subject to a series of more-or-less random shocks which tended to generate a pervasive boost in costs and prices.

**1** A severe worldwide agricultural shortfall occurred, reflecting poor harvests, particularly in Asia and the Soviet Union. American agricultural exports expanded sharply, thereby reducing domestic supplies of foodstuffs. Result? Domestic food prices rose by a dramatic 35 percent during 1973–1974.

**2** Worldwide shortages of certain strategic raw materials developed, causing substantial increases in material prices.

**3** In the 1971–1973 period, the dollar was devalued to help ease the United States' chronic balance of payments deficits (Chap-

ter 44). Devaluation means that it now takes more dollars to buy units of foreign monies; this in turn causes the prices of all American imports to rise. In brief, devaluation sharply boosted American import prices.

**4** Most importantly, the effective formation of the Organization of Petroleum Exporting Countries (OPEC) in late 1973 resulted in the dramatic quadrupling of the world price of oil. There ensued price increases for a whole range of petroleum products and energy in general which quickly permeated the entire economy. Indeed, repeated increases in the price of imported oil buffeted the economy throughout the 1970s.

While these shocks suggest a worsening of the Phillips Curve and stagflation, it is important to understand the process by which stagflation occurs. The equation of exchange, $MV = PQ$, serves us well in this regard. Assume that cost-push forces (rising oil prices, material shortages, agricultural shortfalls) cause the price level $P$ to rise. Now, if $MV$ (aggregate demand) is constant, $Q$ (real output and, implicitly, employment) must fall. A given level of aggregate demand will take a smaller real output off the market when cost-push pressures increase the price level. Stated differently, cost-side increases in the price level reduce the spendable incomes of consumers and investors. Hence, unemployment is not merely a coincidental accompaniment of inflation, but rather unemployment occurs *because* of a higher price level. The dramatic oil price increase was tantamount to a gigantic excise tax paid by American consumers and businesses to the OPEC nations. Like any other "tax" increase, the effect was contractionary with respect to output and employment. And, ironically, the built-in stability feature of our tax system worked perversely during this period. As the *money* incomes of households and businesses inflated rapidly, so did personal and corporate income tax payments. In short, the OPEC "tax" and higher domestic tax bills left consumers and businesses with less to spend on domestic consumer and investment goods.

Results? Falling real output and rising unemployment.

△ **Inflationary Expectations**

The Phillips Curve may also have shifted upward in the 1970s because of changes in inflationary expectations. If the public—workers and businesses—expect substantial inflation in the future, these expectations will be included in their wage demands and price policies. And, if so, the position of the Phillips Curve may worsen. *Scenario 1:* Assume a 5 percent unemployment rate and a recent history of price level stability. Given this past price stability, there are no expectations of future inflation. Unions therefore bargain for, say, a 3 percent increase in money wages. If productivity also increases by this amount, we know that unit labor costs will be constant and there will be no wage-push pressure for the price level to rise. Assuming businesses exert no effort to increase their profit margins, prices will remain constant. In this case a 5 percent unemployment rate is associated with a zero rate of inflation. *Scenario 2:* Suppose a 5 percent unemployment rate once again, but a recent history of rather substantial inflation. Unions, anticipating continuing inflation, demand and obtain, say, a 6 percent increase in money wages. Given a 3 percent increase in productivity, this wage increase translates into a 3 percent increase in unit labor costs. Businesses anticipate that continuing inflation will erode their real profits and therefore boost their prices by 4 percent, that is, by 3 percent to cover their high labor costs and by 1 percent to help preserve their real profits. Result: A 5 percent unemployment rate is now associated with a 4 percent rate of inflation. Scenario 2 obviously implies a point on a Phillips Curve which is higher, or to the right of, the curve suggested by Scenario 1. Conclusion: Other things being equal, the development or strengthening of inflationary expectations can result in higher wage costs and thereby shift the Phillips Curve to a less desirable position. Recalling that the mild inflation of the early 1960s gave way to increasingly strong demand-pull inflation in the late 1960s, it is reasonable to argue that inflationary expectations were aroused and the Phillips Curve for the 1970s therefore shifted to the right (Figure 18-3).

△ **Changing Labor-Force Composition**

Another view is that the Phillips Curve has been shifting to the right in the 1960s and 1970s because of important changes which have occurred in the composition of the labor force. In particular, in the past decade or so teenagers and women have come to constitute larger and larger proportions of the total labor force. This is significant because the unemployment rates associated with teenage and women workers are substantially above those for the labor force as a whole. Hence, with these high-unemployment groups more dominant in the labor force, the level of aggregate demand which would previously yield, say, 4 percent inflation and $3\frac{1}{2}$ percent unemployment, now results in 4 percent inflation and $5\frac{1}{2}$ percent unemployment. This obviously implies a worse inflation-unemployment rate trade-off, that is, a rightward shift of the Phillips Curve.

□ **SUPPLY-SIDE ECONOMICS**

In the past five or ten years a number of economists—many of them with conservative leanings—have called to attention a variety of more subtle and fundamental changes in the structure of our economy which allegedly have contributed to a worsening Phillips Curve and stagflation. These so-called *supply-side economists* believe that Keynesian economics has been greatly weakened by the modifications and extensions needed to interpret the economic events of the 1970s. First, the Phillips Curve was appended to the Keynesian model to explain the simultaneous *existence* of inflation and unemployment. Then adverse shifts in the curve needed to be rationalized in terms of such factors as random shocks, inflationary expectations, and changes in the composition of the labor force, in order to understand simultaneous *increases* in inflation and unemployment rates. Hence, supply-side economists contend that stagflation has become a problem in search of a theory and, needless to say, also in search of a remedy. After so many patches, we must discard the old fabric and weave a new one! While supply-side economists do not purport to have a full-blown theory to supplant Keynesianism, they do believe they have developed some new perspectives, interpretations, and policy insights which are highly relevant to the macroeconomic problems of the 1970s and 1980s.

Supply-side economists assert that Keynesian economics does not come to grips with stagflation because its focal point is aggregate demand. Writing in the 1930s against the background of the Great Depression, Keynes focused upon the problems of unemployment and excess productive capacity. As you are well aware, his basic conclusion was that depressions are the result of a deficiency of aggregate demand and, therefore, the expansion of demand through appropriate fiscal and monetary policies would restore full employment. Production costs and aggregate supply play an essentially passive role in the Keynesian model. Given the availability of idle resources, aggregate supply would simply respond to an increase in aggregate demand. It is the contention of supply-side economists that changes in supply (costs) must be recognized as an "active" force in determining both the levels of inflation *and* unemployment. Economic disturbances can be generated on the supply side, as well as on the demand side. Furthermore, by emphasizing the demand side, Keynesians have neglected certain supply-side policies which might alleviate stagflation.

### △ Rising Costs and the Public Sector

While supply-side economists recognize that such forces as OPEC-sponsored increases in oil prices and inflationary expectations can shift the Phillips Curve and generate stagfla-

tion, they see additional and more basic structural changes at work. These structural changes, which have increased production costs and therefore product prices, are related to the expanding role of the public sector.

**The Tax "Wedge"** Supply-side economists begin by noting that the historical growth of the public sector has increased the nation's tax bill both absolutely and as a percentage of the national income. In the Keynesian view higher taxes represent a withdrawal of purchasing power from the economy and therefore have a contractionary or anti-inflationary effect (Chapter 13). Supply-siders argue to the contrary: They contend that sooner or later most taxes are incorporated into business costs and shifted forward to consumers in the forms of higher prices.[13] Taxes, in short, entail a cost-push effect. Supply-side economists point out that in the 1970s state and local governments negotiated substantial increases in sales and excise taxes and that the Federal government has boosted dramatically payroll (social security) taxes. These are precisely the kinds of taxes which are incorporated in business costs and reflected in higher prices. The point is that most taxes constitute a "wedge" between the costs of resources and the price of a product. As government has grown, this tax wedge has increased, shifting the Phillips Curve upward and thereby contributing to stagflation.

**Tax-transfer Disincentives** But supply-side economists contend that taxes have even more important adverse effects. The spectacular growth of our tax-transfer system in the past two decades has had highly negative effects upon incentives to work, invest, innovate, and assume entrepreneurial risks. In short, the tax-transfer system has eroded the productiv-

---

[13] A similar argument may be made with respect to interest rates. That is, while a high interest rate (tight) money policy is designed to restrain inflation, businesses may treat the higher rates as any other business cost and build them into higher prices.

ity of our economy and the decline in efficiency has meant higher production costs and stagflation. The argument essentially is that higher taxes will obviously reduce the after-tax rewards of workers and producers, thereby making work, innovations, investing, and risk-bearing less financially attractive.

Consider a worker. He or she is less inclined to put forth maximum effort as taxes cut into wages and salaries. Furthermore, the existence of unemployment compensation and welfare programs has made the loss of one's job less of an economic crisis than formerly. The fear of being unemployed and therefore the need to be a disciplined, productive worker is simply less acute than previously. Indeed, most transfer programs are designed to discourage work. Our social security and aid to families with dependent children programs are such that transfers are reduced sharply if recipients earn income. These programs simply encourage recipients *not* to be productive.

Similarly, the sacrifices and risks associated with saving and investing do not "pay" to the extent they did when taxes were lower. As a result, saving and investing are discouraged, workers find themselves less well-equipped with technologically advanced machinery and equipment, and therefore labor productivity languishes.[14]

The overall conclusion, according to the supply-side economists, is that the growth and character of our tax-transfer system has had negative effects upon productive efficiency. The consequence is similar to an increase in the price of OPEC oil or an increase in inflationary expectations—a worsening Phillips Curve and stagflation.

**Overregulation**  Government involvement in the economy in the form of regulation has also had adverse effects upon productivity and costs. Although we defer any detailed discussion until Chapter 34, two points should

be noted. First, it is held that "industrial" regulation—government regulation of specific industries such as transportation or communications—frequently has the effect of providing firms in the regulated industry with a kind of legal monopoly or cartel. That is, governmental regulation in effect protects such firms from the rigors of competition with the result that these firms tend to be less efficient and incur higher costs of production than otherwise. Second, there has occurred a substantial increase in the "social" regulation of industry in the past decade or so. A new array of government regulations has been imposed upon industry in response to the problems of pollution, product safety, worker health and safety, and equal access to job opportunities. Supply-side economists point out that social regulation has increased significantly the costs of doing business. The overall impact of both varieties of regulation is higher costs and prices and a tendency toward stagflation.

△ **Supply-side Policies: Tax Cuts**

Remedies and policies to deal with stagflation are implicit in our discussion of causes. It would, indeed, be very helpful if the OPEC cartel dissolved and energy prices declined or, at least, ceased to rise. And we might wish that workers and businesses would purge the Great Inflation of the 1970s from their minds so as to eliminate the impact of inflationary expectations. And supply-side economists strongly endorse reduced government regulation on the grounds that deregulation will reduce production costs and tend to alleviate stagflation. But supply-side economists believe that a substantial tax cut is the most critical policy which can be used to alleviate stagflation. The *Kemp–Roth bill* (Chapter 8) which proposes to cut personal and corporate income taxes by 30 percent—an estimated $110 to $120 billion—over a three-year period is the focal point for supply-side policy. Lower taxes mean, on the one hand, a direct reduction in the tax wedge and, on the other hand, increases in productive efficiency which reduce costs per

[14]At this point you might want to look ahead to the section entitled "Case Study: The U.S. Productivity Slowdown" in Chapter 19.

unit of output. Both results reverse the cost-increasing tendencies which have been causing stagflation. Stated differently, by lowering production costs the tax cut will shift the Phillips Curve downward to a better position wherein society enjoys greater price stability *and* less unemployment.

The notion of tax cuts—especially a mammoth cut such as that proposed by the Kemp–Roth bill—in a time of inflation has generated considerable controversy. Keynesian and other economists flatly object. The demand-side orientation of Keynesians leads them to contend that the Kemp–Roth tax cut would generate very large budget deficits which would greatly accelerate the rate of inflation. Stated differently, tax cuts will increase the consumption and investment components of aggregate demand and seriously aggravate our inflationary woes.

But Arthur Laffer, a prominent supply-side economist at the University of Southern California, argues that lower tax *rates* are quite compatible with constant or even enlarged tax *revenues*. A tax cut need not result in inflationary deficits. His position is based on what has come to be known as the *Laffer curve* which, as shown in Figure 18-4, depicts the relationship between tax rates and tax revenues. The basic notion is that, as tax rates increase from zero to 100 percent, tax revenue will increase from zero to some maximum level (at *M*) and then decline to zero. Tax revenues decline beyond some point because higher tax rates presumably discourage economic activity and the tax base (national output and income) diminishes. This is easiest to envision at the extreme where tax rates are 100 percent. Tax revenues here are reduced to zero because the 100 percent confiscatory tax rate has brought production to a halt. A 100 percent tax rate applied to a tax base of zero yields no revenue! Professor Laffer's contention is that we are now at some point such as *N* where tax rates are so high that production has been discouraged to the extent that tax revenues are below the maximum at *M*. If the economy is at *N*, then it is obvious that lower tax *rates* are quite

compatible with constant tax *revenues*. In Figure 18-4 we simply lower tax rates, moving from point *N* to point *L*, and government will collect an unaltered amount of tax revenue! Laffer's reasoning obviously is that lower tax rates will stimulate incentives to work, save and invest, innovate, and accept business risks, thereby triggering a substantial expansion of national output and income. This enlarged tax base will sustain tax revenues even though tax rates are now lower.[15]

[15]The avoidance of a deficit will be abetted in two additional ways. First, tax avoidance and evasion will decline. High marginal tax rates prompt taxpayers to avoid taxes through the use of various tax shelters (for example, buying municipal bonds the interest on which is tax free) or to conceal income from the Internal Revenue Service. Lower tax rates will reduce the inclination to engage in such activities. Second, the stimulus to production and employment which a tax cut provides will reduce government transfer payments. For example, more job opportunities will reduce unemployment compensation payments and thereby tend to reduce a budget deficit.

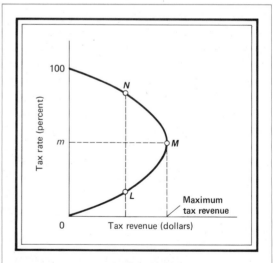

**FIGURE 18-4 THE LAFFER CURVE**

The Laffer Curve suggests that up to point *M* higher tax rates will result in larger tax revenues. But still higher rates will have adverse effects upon incentives to produce, reducing the size of the national income tax base to the extent that tax revenues decline. It follows that, if tax rates are above *Om*, tax reductions will result in increases in tax revenues. The controversial empirical question is to determine at what actual tax rates will tax revenues begin to fall.

△ **Criticisms**

The Kemp–Roth tax cut proposal and the Laffer Curve on which it is based have been subject to considerable criticism.

**1 Position on Curve** Skeptics note that the Laffer Curve is merely a logical proposition which asserts that there must be some level of tax rates between zero and 100 percent at which tax revenues will be maximized. Economists of all persuasions can agree with this statement. But the issue at hand is an empirical question: Where is our economy now located on that curve? If it is *assumed*—as Professor Laffer does—that we are at $N$ in Figure 18-4, then the tax cut proposal must be given serious consideration. But critics contend that where the United States is located on the curve is undocumented and unknown. If the economy is actually at any point southwest of $M$, then lower tax rates will *reduce* tax revenues and create a budget deficit which will intensify inflation.

**2 Incentives and Taxes** A related criticism has to do with the question of the sensitivity of economic incentives to changes in tax rates. Skeptics point out that there is ample empirical evidence to suggest that the impact of a tax reduction upon incentives will be small, of uncertain direction, and relatively slow to emerge. For example, with respect to incentives to work:

> . . . the major empirical studies of the impact of income taxation on the supply of labor have found quite mixed results: some individuals work harder if the tax burden is eased and others work less because their after-tax income goals are achieved with less effort.[16]

Furthermore, any positive effects which tax cuts may have upon real output may be slow to appear:

In the long run, most tax changes that increase total capital formation and thereby raise the rate of economic growth will eventually raise revenues. However, the long run is likely to be very long indeed since a major proportionate increase in savings and investment will cause only a tiny proportionate increase in the capital stock every year, and it is the latter which is important to economic growth. Consequently, the long run must be measured in terms of decades rather than years.[17]

**3 Reinforcing Inflation** Most economists take the position that the demand-side effects of a tax cut exceed the supply-side effects. Hence, they predict the Kemp–Roth tax cut will generate large increases in demand which will overwhelm any increase in productive capacity, resulting in large budget deficits and soaring inflation.

△ **Evaluation**

While the majority of economists seem to be skeptical of supply-side economics and policy, there is reluctance to reject the supply-side position out of hand. Supply-side economists have performed a service in pointing out certain less obvious cost considerations which may be of significance in explaining the presence and persistence of stagflation. Furthermore, it is important to be reminded that the supply side is not passive in macroeconomic theory and policy. We may be assured that, as a result of the debate surrounding supply-side economics, policymakers will be more alert to the incentive effects inherent in changing either tax rates or the tax structure. Future tax changes will be designed to achieve, not merely short-run alterations in aggregate demand to counter cyclical fluctuations, but also to promote the long-run expansion of real output. It is worth noting that the most recent annual report of the Joint Economic Committee of Congress embodies a clearcut reorientation from demand-side to supply-side policy recommendations. "The Joint Economic Committee is now on record in support of the view that tax

[16]Testimony of Otto Eckstein in Senate Budget Committee, *Leading Economists' Views of Kemp–Roth* (Washington, 1978), p. 53.

[17]Testimony of R. G. Penner in ibid., p. 139.

policy can and should be directed toward improving the productivity performance of the economy over the long term and need not be enacted only to counter a recession."[18] Finally, economists of various persuasions are just beginning to subject supply-side analysis and policy to serious empirical testing. Hopefully, we will know a great deal more about the validity of supply-side economics and policy in a few years than we do now.

## ☐ THE ACCELERATIONIST VIEW

One might legitimately examine *all* the points plotted in Figure 18-3 and proclaim that the Phillips Curve trade-off simply does not exist! Considering the entire 1955–1979 period, one can argue that a vertical line located at the 5

[18] Joint Economic Committee, *The 1980 Joint Economic Report: Plugging in the Supply Side* (Washington, 1980), p. 1.

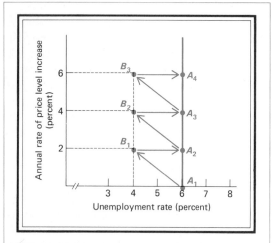

**FIGURE 18-5 THE ACCELERATIONIST VIEW**

The accelerationists note that an expansion of aggregate demand may temporarily increase profits and therefore output and employment ($A_1$ to $B_1$). But money wages will soon rise, reducing profits and thereby negating the short-run stimulus to production and employment ($B_1$ to $A_2$). Consequently, in the long run there is no trade-off between the rates of inflation and unemployment; the long-run Phillips Curve is vertical. This suggests that Keynesian expansionary policies will generate accelerating inflation rather than a lower rate of unemployment.

or 6 percent rate of unemployment summarizes the unemployment-inflation "relationship" as well as, or perhaps better than, the heavy Phillips Curve.

At this point our monetarist-Keynesian debate of Chapter 17 resurfaces. The Phillips Curve is an extension of, or amendment to, Keynesian economics. Therefore, it is not surprising to find monetarists like Milton Friedman taking the position that the Phillips Curve does *not* exist as a stable, "long-run" phenomenon. This stance is labeled the *accelerationist view* because, as we shall discover momentarily, it concludes that Keynesian full-employment policies, based on the incorrect assumption that the Phillips Curve *does* exist, will result in an accelerating rate of inflation.

**Analysis**  A simplified explanation of the accelerationist theory is as follows. Assume that the "normal" or full-employment rate of unemployment is higher than believed. Suppose it is, say, 6 percent (as shown by point $A_1$ in Figure 18-5) rather than 4 percent.[19] But government decides that a 6 percent rate of unemployment is economically and politically intolerable and therefore invokes expansionary fiscal and monetary policies. The resulting increase in aggregate demand pulls up the price level and, *given the level of money wages,* business profits increase. Firms respond to expanded profits by increasing output and therefore hiring additional workers. In the short run the economy thus moves to point $B_1$, which, in contrast with $A_1$, obviously entails a higher level of employment along with a higher rate of inflation. This $A_1$ to $B_1$ shift, you will note, is consistent with our earlier conception

[19] There may be a number of reasons why the full-employment rate of unemployment has increased in recent years. For example, the composition of the labor force has changed so that women and youths—demographic groups characterized by above-normal unemployment rates—now constitute larger proportions of the labor force. Furthermore, there is evidence that our unemployment compensation system allows unemployed workers to seek reemployment at a more leisurely pace.

of the Phillips Curve. The economy has simply accepted some inflation as the "cost" of achieving a reduced level of unemployment.

But according to the accelerationist view, point $B_1$ is *not* a stable equilibrium position. And the reason, according to Friedman, is that workers will recognize that their *real* wages and incomes have fallen; that is, their *money* wages have been constant at a time when the level of product prices has increased. Workers will therefore demand and receive money wage increases to restore the purchasing power they have lost. But, as money wages rise to restore the previous level of real wages which existed at $A_1$, business profits will be reduced to their earlier level. This profit reduction means that the original motivation of businesses to increase output and employ more workers will disappear. Consequence? Unemployment returns to its original 6 percent level at point $A_2$. Note, however, that the economy is now faced with a higher rate of inflation—2 percent rather than zero percent. That is, the higher level of aggregate demand which originally moved the economy from $A_1$ to $B_1$ still exists and, hence, the inflation which it created persists. In brief, as Friedman sees it, an along-the-Phillips-Curve kind of shift from $A_1$ to $B_1$ is merely a "short-run" or transient phenomenon. In the "long run"—that is, after money wages catch up with price level increases—unemployment will return to the normal rate at $A_2$.

The process may now be repeated. Government may reason that certain extraneous, chance events have frustrated its expansionist policies. Hence, government tries again. Policy measures are used to increase aggregate demand and the scenario repeats itself. Prices rise momentarily ahead of money wages, profits expand, and output and employment increase ($A_2$ to $B_2$). But, in time, workers now press for, and are granted, higher money wages to restore their level of real wages. Profits, therefore, fall to their original level, causing employment to gravitate back to the normal rate at $A_3$. Government's "reward" for trying

to force the actual rate of unemployment below the natural rate is the perverse one of a still higher (4 percent) rate of inflation!

If we conceive of $A_1B_1, A_2B_2, A_3B_3$, and so forth as indicating a series of "short-run" Phillips Curves, the accelerationist view can be interpreted as saying that, ironically, governmental attempts through policy to move along the short run Phillips Curve ($A_1B_1$) *cause* the curve to shift to a *less* favorable position ($A_2B_2$, then $A_3B_3$, and so on). In other words, a stable Phillips Curve with the dependable series of unemployment rate–inflation rate trade-offs which it implies simply does not exist. There is, in fact, no *stable* rate of inflation (such as 2 percent at $B_1$) which can be accepted as the "cost" of reduced unemployment (6 percent to 4 percent) in the *long run*. To keep unemployment at the desired 4 percent level, government must continuously expand the level of aggregate demand. The "cost" of a 4 percent unemployment rate is *not* a constant 2 percent annual rate of inflation at $B_1$, but rather an accelerating rate of inflation, that is, an annual rate of inflation that increases from 2 percent ($B_1$) to 4 percent ($B_2$) to 6 percent ($B_3$), and so forth. Stated differently, the *long-run relationship* between unemployment and inflation is shown by the vertical line through $A_1, A_2, A_3$ and $A_4$. The Phillips Curve as portrayed earlier in Figure 18-1 does not exist.

**Rational Expectations Revisited**  This explanation assumes that increases in money wages lag behind increases in the price level. This lag gives rise to temporary increases in profits which in turn temporarily stimulate employment. But recall Chapter 17's theory of rational expectations which suggests that, when government invokes expansionary fiscal and monetary policies, labor will anticipate inflation and a subsequent decline in real wages. Workers will incorporate this expected inflation into their wage demands. If we make the assumption that workers correctly and fully anticipate the amount of price inflation and adjust their current money wage demands accordingly so as to maintain their real wages, then even the temporary increases in profits, output, and employment will *not* occur. In this case, instead of the temporary increase in employment shown by the movement from $A_1$ to $B_1$ in Figure 18-5, the movement will be directly from $A_1$ to $A_2$. Fully anticipated inflation by labor means there will be no short-run decline in unemployment. Price inflation which is fully anticipated in the money wage demands of workers will generate a vertical line through $A_1$, $A_2$, $A_3$ and $A_4$ in Figure 18-5. Policy implication: Keynesian measures to achieve a (misspecified) full-employment rate of unemployment will generate an accelerating rate of inflation, not a lower rate of unemployment. Note, incidentally, that Friedman's accelerationist theory is consistent with his philosophy that government's attempts to do good deeds typically fail and at considerable cost to society. In this instance the "cost" is in the form of accelerating inflation.

## ☐ LESSONS AND ISSUES

What observations or lessons, if any, have emerged from our economic experiences of the past ten or fifteen years? And what salient issues remain to be decided?

### △ Lessons of Stagflation

Several important observations have evolved from the economic turbulence of recent years.

**1 Interdependence** The United States has become increasingly linked to the world economy, and this growing international interdependence can be an added source of macroeconomic instability. Recall that rising foreign oil prices, worldwide shortages of strategic raw materials, and the devaluation of the dollar were all key forces in the 1973–1975 stagflation. Increasing economic interdependence means that our domestic economy may be subject to more and more destabilizing "shocks" which we cannot directly control.

**2 Supply, Demand, and Policy** The distinction between inflation resulting from excessive demand and that caused by cost or supply-side phenomena is critical for policy. In particular, the application of the aggregate demand management tools of Keynesian economics to an inflation problem derived from cost or supply considerations may not only be ineffective, but harmful.

The equation of exchange, $MV = PQ$, is useful once again in illustrating this point. Assume that random shocks or the cost-increasing forces cited by supply-side economists cause $P$ to rise. Given the level of aggregate demand, $MV$, real output and employment, $Q$, must fall. In short, we have stagflation. Note the policy dilemma. On the one hand, unemployment can be countered by an expansionary demand policy, but this will tend to validate and aggravate inflation. The other option is obviously a restrictive demand policy for the purpose of dampening inflation, but this will promote further reductions in real output and employment. *There is no demand-side policy which will simultaneously decrease both the rate of unemployment and the rate of inflation.* It is at this juncture that policy makers—often with reluctance and trepidation—turn to incomes and procompetition policies.

**3 Institutional-Structural Factors** Economists have become increasingly interested in structural-institutional changes and their possible impacts upon the economy and upon public policies. That is, considerations which economists have typically ignored or regarded as "given" in their theories are now being scrutinized to determine whether the overall economic environment has changed sufficiently so that accepted theories and policies must be revised. Consider some far-ranging examples.

First, has the market power of giant corporations and huge labor unions evolved to the stage wherein cost-push inflation—and perhaps stagflation—will become increasingly common and severe problems?

Second, have changes occurred in the economy which call for an upward revision of the "full employment rate of unemployment" from 4 percent to, say, 5 or 6 percent?[20] Note, on the one hand, the composition of the labor force has changed so that certain demographic groups which are characterized by high unemployment rates—youths and women, in particular—now bulk larger proportionately in the labor force. Observe, furthermore, that there is mounting evidence that our unemployment insurance system prompts workers to seek new jobs at a more leisurely pace, thus increasing the unemployment rate. This is an important matter because full-employment policies based on a full-employment rate of unemployment which is "too low" will inject an inflationary bias into the economy as implied by the accelerationist view.

Third, should expectations be accorded a more integral role in macroeconomic theory and policy? Some economists feel that the stubbornness of inflation in the 1970s is related to the intensification of inflationary expectations. After a decade of continuous inflation, expectations of continuing inflation came to be widely held and built into labor contracts, consumption and investment decisions, interest rates, and so on. These actions generated continued inflationary pressures, even in the face of constraints on aggregate demand and the application of incomes policies. It is relevant

to recall Chapter 17's rational expectations theory, that is, the disturbing possibility that policy decisions may be negated by the expectations which those policies generate.

### △  A New Model?

Perhaps the fundamental question evolving from the awkward decade of the 1970s is whether Keynesian economics (Figure 16-2) is losing its relevance as an analytical model and as a basis for policy. Does the stagflation of the 1970s and early 1980s reflect the fortuitous convergence of a series of "random shocks" which, although temporarily disruptive to the economy, do *not* invalidate Keynesian economics and its policy prescriptions? Having absorbed these shocks, are we once again returning to a "Keynesian world" wherein the traditional fiscal and monetary policies are applicable and effective? Or are the 1970s and early 1980s an indication that certain fundamental changes have occurred in the institutional and structural framework of the economy which undermine the validity of Keynesian economics? Are we now operating in a new environment wherein the old generalizations no longer apply? Do we need a new model of the economy as a framework for understanding and policy formation? Economists are now deeply involved in various aspects of this great debate, and it will undoubtedly be some time before a clear consensus emerges.

[20] This upward revision is suggested in the *Economic Report of the President, 1977* (Washington), pp. 48–51.

## Summary

**1**  The simple theory of demand-pull inflation is based upon the implicit assumption that full employment and price level stability are compatible goals. However, recent inflationary episodes suggest that premature inflation occurs as the economy approaches full employment.

**2**  Empirical studies of premature inflation have yielded the Phillips Curve, which suggests that society must accept inflation to realize full employment or accept unemployment to achieve price level stability. Although labor market imbalances and monopoly power underlie the Phillips Curve, it is significant that only wage rate increases in excess of average labor productivity increases are inflationary.

**3**  Traditional macro policy—fiscal and monetary policies—allows society to select a position on the Phillips Curve, but does not improve upon the unemployment-versus-inflation trade-offs implicit in the curve itself. Hence, other policies designed to provide a more desirable Phillips Curve have been developed. These consist of *a.* market policies—manpower policies designed to reduce labor market imbalances and procompetition policies which reduce the market power of unions and corporations—and *b.* wage-price policies in the form of voluntary guideposts or mandatory controls.

4 Economists have evaluated wage-price policies in terms of their workability and compliance, impact upon resource allocation, and compatibility with freedom of choice.

5 In the 1970s the Phillips Curve seems to have shifted upward (rightward), a shift which is consistent with stagflation.

6 Keynesians explain this worsening Phillips Curve in terms of random shocks, inflationary expectations, and changes in the composition of the labor force.

7 Supply-side economists trace stagflation to the growth of the public sector and, more specifically, to the growing tax "wedge" between production costs and product prices, the adverse effects of the tax-transfer system upon incentives, and government overregulation of businesses. Based upon the Laffer Curve, supply-side adherents advocate a sizable tax cut such as proposed by the Kemp–Roth bill as a remedy for stagflation.

8 Proponents of the accelerationist view argue that in the long run the traditional Phillips Curve trade-off does not exist. Expansionary demand-management policies will result in accelerating inflation with no permanent decline in the unemployment rate.

## Questions and Study Suggestions

1 Key terms and concepts to remember: demand-pull inflation; Phillips Curve; stagflation; cost- (wage-, profit-) push inflation; stabilization policy dilemma; incomes policy; wage-price guideposts; wage-price controls; tax-based incomes policy (TIP); real wage insurance proposal; random shocks; inflationary expectations; supply-side economics; tax "wedge"; Kemp–Roth bill; Laffer Curve; accelerationist view.

2 Compare the causes and implications of *a.* demand-pull inflation and *b.* premature inflation. Draw a Phillips Curve and explain its shape. Illustrate and explain the dilemma which the Phillips Curve poses for traditional stabilization policy. "There is no way to make full employment, price stability, and free markets compatible." Do you agree? Explain.

3 Assume the following information is relevant for an industrially advanced economy in the 1980–1982 period:

| Year | Price level index | Rate of increase in labor productivity | Index of industrial production | Unemployment rate | Average hourly wage rates |
|------|-------------------|----------------------------------------|--------------------------------|-------------------|---------------------------|
| 1980 | 167 | 4  % | 212 | 4.5% | $6.00 |
| 1981 | 174 | 3 | 208 | 5.2 | $6.50 |
| 1982 | 181 | 2.5 | 205 | 5.8 | $7.10 |

Describe in detail the macroeconomic situation faced by this society. Is cost-push inflation in evidence? What policy proposals would you recommend?

4 Distinguish between market policies and wage-price policies as means of shifting the Phillips Curve to a more desirable position.

5 Explain the Kennedy–Johnson wage-price guideposts, indicating in detail the relationship between money wages, productivity, and unit labor costs. What specific problems are associated with the use of wage-price guideposts and controls? Evaluate these problems and note the arguments in favor of guideposts and controls. Would you favor a special tax on firms which grant wage increases in excess of productivity increases?

**6** "Controlling prices to halt inflation is like breaking a thermometer to control the heat. In both instances you are treating symptoms rather than causes." Do you agree? Does the correctness of the statement vary when applied to demand-pull and to cost-push inflation? Explain.

**7** Discuss the causes of inflation in the early 1970s. Why was the inflation of the 1970s accompanied by rising unemployment?

**8** Why is the issue of the stability or the existence of the Phillips Curve important for public policy? Explain and evaluate: "Monetary and fiscal policy are more likely to guarantee inflation without full employment than they are to provide full employment without inflation."

**9** What reasons do supply-side economists give to explain upward shifts in the Phillips Curve? Using the Laffer Curve, explain why they recommend a tax cut to remedy stagflation.

**10** Use an appropriate diagram to explain the accelerationist's rationale for concluding that the Phillips Curve is a vertical line. Explain how expectations might frustrate public policy.

**11** Explain and evaluate: "Keynesian economics is a topsy-turvy view of the world. Keynesians advocate higher interest rates and tax boosts to restrain inflation. But both policies contribute to cost-push inflation directly by increasing production costs and indirectly by impairing productivity."

## Selected References

Colander, David C. (ed.): *Solutions to Inflation* (New York: Harcourt Brace Jovanovich, Inc., 1979).

Fuller, Robert: *Inflation: The Rising Cost of Living on a Small Planet* (Washington: Worldwatch Institute, 1980).

Hotson, John M.: *Stagflation and the Bastard Keynesians* (Waterloo, Canada: University of Waterloo Press, 1976).

Humphrey, Thomas M.: "Changing Views of the Phillips Curve," *Monthly Review* (Federal Reserve Bank of Richmond, July 1973), pp. 2–13.

Joint Economic Committee: *The 1980 Joint Economic Report* (Washington, 1980), particularly chaps. 1–4.

Pohlman, Jerry E.: *Inflation Under Control?* (Reston, Va.: Reston Publishing Company, Inc., 1976).

Senate Budget Committee: *Leading Economists' Views of Kemp–Roth* (Washington, 1978).

Williams, Raburn M.: *Inflation: Money, Jobs, and Politicians* (Arlington Heights, Ill.: AHM Publishing Corporation, 1980).

# LAST WORD
## The Slow Road to Full Employment

Okun's Law suggests that large changes in real output are required to achieve small changes in the unemployment rate.

One fundamental limitation on what economic managers can accomplish is the ornery fact that it takes a lot of economic growth to produce even a small reduction in the unemployment rate. The relationship between growth and unemployment is summed up in what has come to be called Okun's Law, worked out by economist Arthur M. Okun.

Okun's Law begins with the proposition that the economy has to grow in line with the long-term trend rate, about 4 percent a year, just to keep the unemployment rate from going higher. In other words, with normal improvements in productivity it takes normal growth of output to create enough additional jobs to offset the normal yearly growth in the labor force. This much is obvious enough, but now comes the surprising part. Okun's Law holds that for each percentage point by which real GNP growth falls below the 4 percent trend, the unemployment rate increases by only one-third of a point. And for each percentage point of growth above the trend, the unemployment rate declines by only one-third of a point. In brief, the unemployment rate is "sticky" both on the downside and on the upside.

Obviously intended as a rough rule of thumb rather than as a rigorous formula, Okun's Law has worked out remarkably well over the years. It works because of the varying sensitivity of the underlying factors to turns in the business cycle. In a recession, employers do not lay off workers as rapidly as they scale down output. (As a result, productivity worsens.) The increased difficulty of finding a job induces some workers to leave the labor force or discourages others from entering it; these effects help to hold down the official unemployment rate.

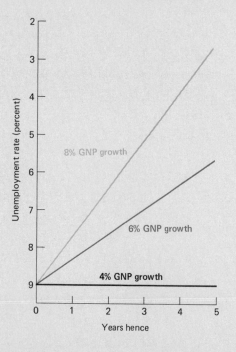

The bleak outlook for jobs is indicated by these three lines showing what various rates of growth in real GNP would do to the unemployment rate over the next five years. Growth at the long-term trend rate of 4 percent would leave unemployment unchanged from its expected average of 9 percent this year [1975]. A long stretch of 6 percent growth—exceeding the fastest pace the U.S. has sustained for more than two years in a row since World War II—would still leave unemployment above 5.5 percent in 1980. Even if output grew at 8 percent, a rate that the U.S. has achieved only in brief spurts, it would take four years to bring unemployment down to the 4 percent rate that used to be considered "full employment." All three lines are plotted in accord with "Okun's Law." (*Fortune Art Department/Vahe Kirishjian*)

During upturns, of course, the reverse happens: output increases faster than employment, with the result that productivity rises rapidly. And people are pulled into the labor force as prospects for employment improve.

As the chart makes plain, Okun's Law spells bad news about unemployment in years ahead. According to his formula, a year of 6 percent real growth would reduce the unemployment rate by only two-thirds of 1 percent. So it would take six years of 6 percent growth to reduce unemployment by four points—from, say, 9.5 to 5.5. And by the standards of the past, six years of 6 percent growth would be an extraordinary economic performance.

Lewis Beman, "The Slow Road Back to Full Employment," *Fortune,* June 1975. Reprinted by permission from *Fortune* magazine.

# ECONOMIC GROWTH: ANALYSIS AND POLICY

# PART FOUR

# The Economics of Growth

chapter 19

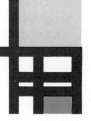

In the past 200 years our economy has grown from an industrial infant to a vigorous, productive giant. This long-run growth has not occurred at a steady pace. On the contrary, it has been punctuated by periods of instability—unemployment and inflation. Parts 2 and 3 of this book have dealt with the causes and potential cures of short-run economic instability. The business cycle, the theory of employment, and fiscal and monetary policy have been the focal points of our analysis.

The task of Part 4 is to take a searching look at economic growth. In Chapter 19 we are concerned primarily with the basic theory of economic growth. Chapter 20 summarizes the growth record of the United States and analyzes recent debate over the desirability of economic growth. In Chapter 21 we shall look at the problem of economic growth from the viewpoint of the developing countries.

## ☐ GROWTH ECONOMICS

Employment theory—detailed along with stabilization policy in Parts 2 and 3—is of a static or short-run character. That is, it assumes the economy has fixed amounts of resources or inputs available and therefore is capable of producing some capacity or full-employment level of national output. The central question of employment theory is: What must be done to utilize fully the nation's *existing* productive capacity? The essence of Keynes's answer, of course, is that aggregate demand should be adjusted through fiscal and monetary measures to the full-employment level of output at which actual NNP will equal capacity or potential NNP (Figure 10-4).

In contrast, growth economics is concerned with the question of how to *increase* the economy's productive capacity or full-employment NNP. Whereas employment theory is couched in terms of a fixed-capacity output, the economics of growth takes a long-run perspective and seeks to uncover the forces that alter the economy's capacity to produce over time.

### △  Two Definitions

Economic growth is defined and measured in two related ways. Specifically, economic growth may be defined (1) as the increase in real GNP or NNP which occurs over a period of time, or (2) as the increase in real GNP or NNP *per capita* which occurs over time. Both definitions are useful. For example, if one is concerned with the question of military potential, the first definition is more relevant. But per capita output is obviously superior for comparisons of living standards among nations or regions. While India's GNP is about 40 percent larger than Switzerland's, the latter's standard of living is about 70 times as great as India's. Our attention in this chapter is primarily upon the growth of real output and income per capita.

### △  Importance of Growth

Why is growth a widely held economic goal? The answer is self-evident: The growth of total output relative to population means a higher standard of living. An expanding real output means greater material abundance and implies a more satisfactory answer to the economizing problem. Our question can be answered from a slightly different perspective. *A growing economy is in a superior position to meet new needs and resolve socioeconomic problems both domestically and internationally.* A growing economy, by definition, enjoys an increment in its annual real output which it can use to satisfy existing needs more effectively or to undertake new projects. An expanding real wage or salary income makes new opportunities available to any given family—a trip to Europe, a new stereo, a college education for each child, and so forth—without the sacrifice of other opportunities and enjoyments. Similarly, a growing economy can, for example, undertake new programs to alleviate poverty and clean up the environment *without* impairing existing levels of consumption, investment, and social goods production. *Growth lessens the burden of scarcity.* A growing economy, unlike a static one, *can* have its cake and eat it too. By easing the burden of scarcity—by relaxing society's production constraints—economic growth allows a nation to realize existing economic goals more fully and to undertake new output-absorbing endeavors.

### △  Arithmetic of Growth

People sometimes wonder why economists get so excited about seemingly minuscule changes in the rate of growth. Does it really matter very much whether our economy grows at 4 percent or 3 percent? It matters a great deal! For the United States, which has a current real GNP of about $1,431 billion, the difference between a 3 and a 4 percent growth rate is over $14 billion worth of output per year. For a very poor country, a .5 percent change in the growth rate may well mean the difference between starvation and mere hunger.

Furthermore, when envisioned over a period of years, an apparently small difference in the rate of growth becomes exceedingly important because of the "miracle" of compound interest. Example: Suppose Alphania and Betania have identical GNPs. But Alphania begins to grow at a 4 percent annual rate, while Betania grows at only 2 percent. Recalling our "rule of 70" of Chapter 10, Alphania would find that its GNP would double in only about eighteen years ($= 70 \div 4$); Betania would take thirty-five years ($= 70 \div 2$) to accomplish the same feat. The importance of the growth rate is undeniable.

### ☐  CAUSES: A FIRST LOOK

What are the sources of economic growth? Basically, there are six strategic ingredients in the growth of any economy. Four of these factors relate to the physical ability of an economy to grow. They are (1) the quantity and quality of its natural resources, (2) the quantity and quality of its human resources, (3) the supply or stock of capital goods, and (4) technology. These four items may be termed the *supply factors* in economic growth. These are the physical agents of greater production. It is the availability of more and better resources, including the stock of technological knowledge, which permits an economy to produce a greater real output.

But the ability to grow and the actual realization of growth may be quite different things. Specifically, two additional considerations contribute to growth. First, there is a *demand factor* in growth. To realize its growing productive potential, a nation must obviously provide for the full employment of its expanding supplies of resources. This requires a growing level of aggregate demand. Second, there is the *allocative factor* in growth. To achieve its productive potential, a nation must provide not only for the full employment of its resources, but also for full production from them. The ability to expand production is not a sufficient condition for the expansion of total output; the actual employment of expanded resource supplies *and* the allocation of those resources in such a way as to get the maximum amount of useful goods produced are also required.

It is notable that the supply and demand factors in growth are related. For example, unemployment tends to retard the rate of capital accumulation and may slow expenditures for research. And, conversely, a low rate of innovation and investment can be a basic cause of unemployment.

These factors can be placed in proper perspective by recalling Chapter 2's production possibilities curve, reproduced in Figure 19-1. This is a best-performance curve in that it indicates the various *maximum* combinations of products the economy can produce, given the quantity and quality of its natural, human, and capital resources, and its stock of technological know-how. Obviously, an improvement in any of the supply factors will push the pro-

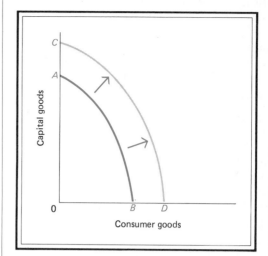

FIGURE 19-1 ECONOMIC GROWTH AND THE PRODUCTION POSSIBILITIES CURVE

Economic growth is indicated by an outward shift of the production possibilities curve, as from *AB* to *CD*. Increases in the quantity and quality of resources and technological advance permit this shift; full employment and allocative efficiency are essential to its realization.

duction possibilities curve to the right, as indicated by the shift from *AB* to *CD* in Figure 19-1. Increases in the quantity or quality of resources and technological progress push the curve to the right. But the demand and allocative factors remind us that the economy need not realize its maximum productive potential; the curve may shift to the right and leave the economy behind at some level of operation *inside* the curve. In particular, the economy's enhanced productive *potential* will not be *realized* unless (1) aggregate demand increases sufficiently to sustain full employment, and (2) the additional resources are employed efficiently, that is, so they make the maximum possible contribution to the national output.

Example: The net increase in the labor force of the United States is roughly 2½ million workers per year. As such, this increment raises the productive capacity, or potential, of the economy. But the realization of the extra output these additional workers are capable of producing presumes they are able to find jobs and that these jobs are in those firms and industries where their talents are fully utilized. Society doesn't want new labor force entrants to be unemployed; nor does it want pediatricians working as plumbers.

## ☐ GROWTH: THE CLASSICAL MODEL

British "classical" economists of the late eighteenth and early nineteenth centuries—in particular, David Ricardo and Thomas Malthus—made substantial contributions to our understanding of growth which remain relevant today. Let us survey their ideas which centered upon the interaction of (1) population growth and (2) the law of diminishing returns.

### △   Law of Diminishing Returns

If *all* of a nation's resources increased, we would expect a more-or-less proportionate increase in its national output. That is, if a nation's supplies of land, labor, and capital all doubled, we would anticipate a doubling of total output.

But an economy may find it extremely difficult to increase *all* its resources in a balanced or proportionate manner. Land, in particular, is a relatively fixed resource. Typically, the mineral deposits and amount of arable land available to a nation can be increased only within narrow limits. What will happen to total output when inputs are increased *disproportionately*, that is, when property resources (land) are held constant and more labor is applied to them? The answer to this question has its roots in the famous *law of diminishing returns,*[1] which has applications both to the economy as a whole and to individual firms and industries (Chapters 25 and 30).

[1] This law goes by other names: for example, the principle of diminishing marginal productivity and the law of variable proportions. At this point we consider the law in an intuitive fashion; a more precise presentation is found in Chapter 25.

The concept of diminishing returns can best be understood by performing an easy mental experiment. Imagine an economy whose property resources (land and real capital) are absolutely fixed. In particular, visualize a primitive, underdeveloped economy whose stock of capital goods is negligible and whose supply of arable land is fixed. Assume, too, that technology—the stock of technological knowledge—is fixed; this means that the *quality* of both capital and labor is given. Assuming its population is growing, this simple agrarian society is concerned primarily with adding labor to a fixed amount of land and a few rudimentary farm tools to produce the food and fiber needed by its population. What happens to total output as equal increments—equal doses—of labor are added to a fixed amount of property (primarily land) resources? The law of diminishing returns indicates that *as successive equal increments of one resource* (*labor, in this case*) *are added to a fixed resource* (*land and property*), *beyond some point the resulting output per worker or average product will diminish in size.*

Qualification: Note we say "beyond some point." The initial increments or doses of labor may be subject to *increasing returns*—average product may rise for a time. The reason for this is that initially, with a very small labor force, property resources will be grossly underutilized. The fixed supplies of land and capital will be seriously understaffed. A very small amount of labor combined with a very large amount of land will result in relatively inefficient production. As equal increments or doses of labor are added to the fixed amount of land, the problem of underutilization is overcome and the resulting average product will increase for a time.

But this stage of increasing returns will inevitably reverse itself. As more and more labor is added to the fixed amount of property resources, a point will be reached where land and capital come to be overstaffed or overutilized. That is, *each* worker will be equipped with smaller and smaller amounts of land and capital. In our simple agrarian society, more and more workers will be farming each acre of arable land and *each* worker will have fewer tools with which to work. Hence, output per worker will tend to decline.

Figure 19-2 portrays the law of diminishing returns and embodies both a phase of increasing and decreasing worker productivity as labor is added (on the horizontal axis) to presumably fixed quantities of land and capital.

### △ Optimum Population

Average product is obviously an important indicator of growth because *output per worker and real income per worker are essentially the same thing.* That is, an increase in output per worker *is* our second definition of economic growth.

That particular population size at which real output or income per person is at a maximum is called the *optimum population* for society. The optimum population is that population which, given the economy's property resources and technology, will yield the greatest income per person. This concept reinforces an earlier point: Population growth may be a mixed blessing insofar as growth is concerned. In Figure 19-2 the expansion of the population and labor force up to $Q$ will be accompanied by

a rising real output and income per person; a larger population will reduce real income per worker as labor productivity declines. Hence, $OQ$ is the optimum population.

### △ Malthus and Misery

Diminishing returns correctly suggest that the relationship between the size of a country's population (labor force) and its property resources is highly relevant in determining both its total output and its output per person or standard of living. Indeed, this fact was perceived by the English economist Thomas R. Malthus at the close of the eighteenth century and enunciated in his famous *Essay on the Principle of Population* (1798). Malthus's explicit purpose was "to account for much of that poverty and misery observable among the lower classes of every nation," and his explanation of this misery was rooted firmly in the law of diminishing returns.

The essence of Malthus's thesis is quite simple: *The population of a nation tends to outrun its capacity to produce the food and fiber needed to sustain itself.* Population tends to increase at a constant geometric rate (2, 4, 8, 16, 32, 64, 128, 256, and so on). But the output of food, on the other hand, increases *at best* only at a constant arithmetic rate (1, 2, 3, 4, 5,

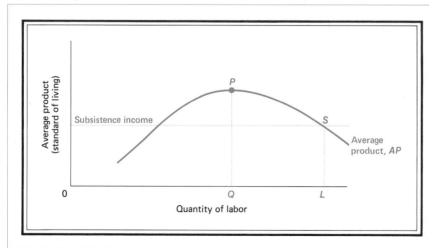

**FIGURE 19-2 DIMINISHING RETURNS AND THE CLASSICAL GROWTH MODEL**

In the classical growth model, as labor is added to fixed amounts of land and capital, output per worker and the standard of living will eventually decline in accordance with the law of diminishing returns. In this instance output per worker is maximized at $QP$ and thereafter diminishes. Expansion of the labor force to $OL$ will reduce the standard of living to the subsistence level, $LS$. The optimum population size is at $OQ$ where output per worker is at a maximum.

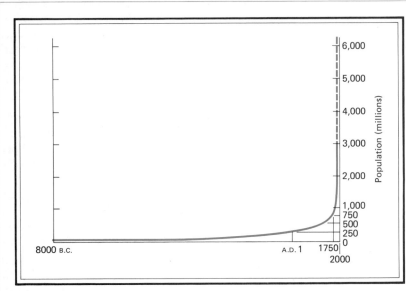

FIGURE 19-3  THE LONG-RUN TREND OF WORLD POPULATION GROWTH

A dramatic acceleration of world population growth has been experienced in modern times. (*John D. Durand, "A Long-range View of World Population Growth," The Annals, January 1967 p. 3.*)

6, and so forth).  Given these different rates of increase, population will in time inevitably press upon the food supply and the results will be subsistence living levels, misery, and, in the extreme, starvation.  But why won't the food supply increase at a more rapid rate?  Because of diminishing returns.  As the growing population puts more and more laborers to work on a fixed amount of arable land, output per worker will diminish (Figure 19-2).  Each worker is combined with less and less land, so worker productivity declines.

We have just seen that a society's output per worker is its income per worker.  A diminishing average product therefore means a falling standard of living.  In short, the pressure of an expanding population and labor force upon fixed land resources invokes the law of diminishing returns.  Total output increases less than proportionately to population, so the standard of living necessarily declines.  In the eighteenth century, the result was the widespread misery and poverty which Malthus readily observed.  We might draw a subsistence level-of-living line in Figure 19-2 and summarize Malthus's position by saying that, given

the reality of diminishing returns, persistent and substantial population growth (a rightward movement along the horizontal axis) will keep the level of living (vertical axis) perilously close to the bare subsistence level (point $S$).  Only the gloomy team of disease, malnutrition, and famine will bring population growth to a halt at $OL$.  (It was this pessimistic prediction, incidentally, which caused economics to become known as the "dismal science.")

We are all well aware that mankind has been undergoing an extraordinary expansion of numbers.  The magnitude of this unparalleled population explosion is portrayed vividly in Figure 19-3.  World population growth in just the last two centuries has been 3 times larger than the cumulated expansion of mankind during all the previous millennia of man's existence!  Given this incredible growth of population and its projected continuance, *and* given the hard fact that only a finite amount of land exists on our planet, it is highly relevant to inquire as to the extent to which Malthus's gloomy forecast has (or will) come to pass.  Is the Malthusian prediction being realized in any of today's nations?

Clearly the specter of Malthus stalks many of the so-called underdeveloped nations of the world. In India, for example, rapid population growth has been a basic factor in making malnutrition, famine, and disease a way of life—and of death. Indeed, many of the nations of Africa, South America, and Asia are finding it extremely difficult to raise their living standards, because rapid population growth means that year after year there are more mouths to feed and more bodies to clothe and shelter. While Egypt's Aswan Dam makes a substantial contribution to that nation's output of food, the growth in population which occurred during the period of construction has had the effect of leaving per capita food production substantially unchanged!

## ☐ IMPROVING LABOR PRODUCTIVITY

In contrast, the "advanced" nations of the world—the United States, Canada, the countries of Western Europe, Australia, New Zealand, and Japan—enjoy high and rising standards of living despite considerable population growth. The question is: Why the differences? Why poverty in India and plenty in Indiana? From a policy standpoint, how can a nation improve its standard of living?

The answer is implicit in classical growth theory: Reduce the size of the population and labor force *or* increase the productivity of labor *or* do both! If the economy is at the subsistence income level of $SL$ in Figure 19-2, the standard of living can be increased by reducing the size of the labor force and thereby moving toward the optimum population of $OQ$. But population growth can be difficult to control through government policy as many of the underdeveloped countries have discovered. In fact, virtually all nations are experiencing significant population growth. The second option—increasing labor's productivity—is the one typically pursued through public policy.

But how can labor productivity be increased? In terms of Figure 19-2, how can the average product curve be shifted upward so as to realize more output per worker for any given population size? A moment's reflection suggests the answer: by altering the assumptions upon which the law of diminishing returns—and hence the given average product curve—is based.

Let us perform a second mental experiment similar to that underlying Figure 19-2. Again we add a growing labor force to a constant conglomerate of property resources and technical knowledge, as before. But now let us assume that these property resources are fixed at a higher level both quantitatively and qualitatively.[2] Specifically, suppose each worker, instead of being equipped with a negligible amount of capital, is aided in his or her productive efforts with, say, $100 worth of machinery and equipment. Suppose, too, that technology is better than in our first experiment; for example, farmers now have discovered the contribution which contour plowing and crop rotation can make to output. And let us assume the labor force itself is qualitatively superior—physically and mentally—to that of our first experiment.

Would these changes revoke the law of diminishing returns? Although "revoke" is perhaps too strong a word, these factors can offset or forestall diminishing returns. We can envision what happens by looking at the curves in Figure 19-4. The average-product curve designated as $AP_1$ is taken from Figure 19-2 and merely repeats the results of our original experiment. $AP_2$ portrays the results of our second experiment. Note that this new curve still reflects the law of diminishing returns but is at a higher level, and the point at which worker productivity begins to fall corresponds with a larger population or labor force. Why? Because each level of labor input is now equipped with more capital and better technological know-how, the labor force itself is supe-

[2]In Chapter 21 we shall find that less tangible "resources"—for example, attitudes and institutional arrangements—must often be changed if growth is to occur.

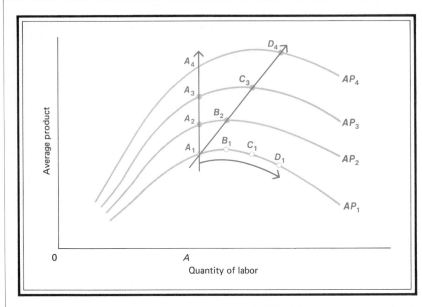

FIGURE 19-4   RISING
PRODUCTIVITY AND
ECONOMIC GROWTH

The "forces of growth"—
increases in the stock of capital,
technological progress, and
improvements in the quality of
labor—may offset diminishing
returns by shifting the average-
product curve upward. A
growing economy with a
constant population will follow
the $A_1A_2A_3A_4$ path. A
growing economy with an
expanding population will
achieve a higher output per
worker along the $A_1B_2C_3D_4$
path. A nongrowing economy
whose population is expanding
will follow the $A_1B_1C_1D_1$
path on an unchanging average-
product curve and will be
subject to a declining output
per worker.

rior, and all resources are better managed. For all these reasons, any given number of workers will produce a larger total output, and hence a larger output per worker, than under the inferior conditions of our first experiment. A third experiment involving still more capital, a further advanced technology, and a labor force and managerial talent of even higher quality will again raise the productivity curve and locate its maximum point further to the right, as indicated by $AP_3$. Still further improvements in the quantity of capital, technology, management techniques, and labor force would yield $AP_4$.

A bit of reflection reveals that, for any nation with a growing population and labor force, we can think of the course of its standard of living through time as the net result of two opposed forces. On the one hand, diminishing returns cause the application of successive inputs of labor to result eventually in declining labor productivity and a falling standard of living. On the other hand, we have the "forces of growth"—increases in the stock of capital, technological progress, and qualitative im-

provements in the labor force and in management—tending to offset diminishing returns by violating the very assumptions or conditions upon which the functioning of the law depends.

Now, and at the hazard of oversimplification, what has happened in the less developed countries is that the forces of growth have been absent or, at best, present in only modest degrees, so that diminishing returns have prevailed. And, as Malthus envisioned, population has indeed tended to press upon the food supply, to the end that living standards have remained pitifully low (Table 21-1). In Figure 19-4 this case can be envisioned as the movement down a stable average-product curve, as from $A_1$ to $B_1$ to $C_1$ and so forth, on curve $AP_1$. As our diagram suggests, such an economy is literally going "over the hill."

At the other extreme, suppose population and the labor force are constant at, say, $OA$ in Figure 19-4 and the forces of growth are strongly evident. In this case the average-productivity curve shifts upward and traces the path suggested by $A_1$, $A_2$, $A_3$, and $A_4$. In general, the developed countries of the world have been experiencing growth in their populations and labor forces. But at the same time, the forces of growth have been pushing their $AP$ curves upward. Hence, the advanced nations have been following the kind of path suggested by $A_1$, $B_2$, $C_3$, and $D_4$. Diminishing returns have *tended* to be at work, but these nations, by adding to their stocks of capital and of knowledge and by improving the quality of labor and management, have been able to more than offset diminishing returns and to achieve a higher and higher standard of living over time.

### □   CASE STUDY: THE UNITED STATES' PRODUCTIVITY SLOWDOWN

Let us pause to apply our analysis of productivity growth to a troublesome problem—the recent slowdown in the rate of United States' productivity growth which began in the mid-1960s. First, some facts. In the 1948–1966 period productivity—measured as output per worker per hour—rose at an average annual rate of 3.3 percent. That figure fell to 2.1 percent in the 1966–1973 period and then to only 1.1 percent in 1972–1978. In short, the decline in our productivity growth has been alarmingly large. Furthermore, as Table 19-1 indicates, all the major industrial nations have been experiencing more rapid productivity growth since the mid-1960s than we have.[3] Let us examine this slowdown in terms of the kinds of factors just discussed.

**1   Investment**   It is agreed that investment—more precisely the amount of machinery and equipment which each worker uses—is a critical determinant of productivity growth. A worker using a bulldozer can move more dirt

**TABLE 19-1**
Productivity Growth in Selected Countries, 1966–1976 (*average annual percent change*)

| Country | Productivity increase |
|---|---|
| United States | 2.2% |
| United Kingdom | 3.1 |
| Canada | 3.5 |
| Switzerland | 5.1 |
| France | 5.8 |
| Sweden | 5.2 |
| Italy | 5.3 |
| Germany | 5.8 |
| Netherlands | 7.4 |
| Belgium | 8.1 |
| Denmark | 8.0 |
| Japan | 8.9 |

*Source:* Bureau of Labor Statistics. Data are for manufacturing workers.

per hour than can that same worker equipped with an ordinary shovel. Figure 19-5 shows a very high correlation between the percentage of a nation's GNP devoted to investment goods and its realized increase in productivity.

Why has investment been a smaller proportion of GNP in the United States than elsewhere? Experts cite the following reasons. First, the uncertain stagflation environment of the 1970s has tended to dampen business incentives to invest. Indeed, the fact that stock prices have been depressed while construction costs have been soaring tends to induce firms to expand by buying *existing* businesses rather than by building *new* plants and equipment. Inflation has depressed investment in other ways. Inflation squeezes *real* after-tax profits and impinges upon the ability to invest. And recall from Chapter 10 that inflation adds to the riskiness of long-term contracts associated with investment. Secondly, the recent expansion of government regulation of businesses in the areas of pollution control and worker health and safety have absorbed business resources which might otherwise have been used to invest in new and better capital goods. Third, high marginal tax rates may have dis-

---

[3]The *levels* of labor productivity in other countries remain below that of the United States. The unfavorable productivity growth comparisons of Table 19-1 mean that other nations are closing the gap between our level of labor productivity and theirs.

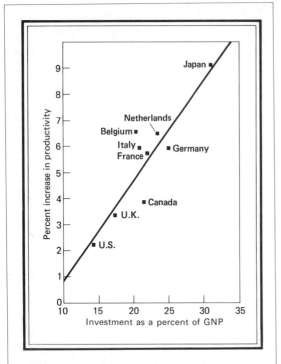

**FIGURE 19-5 INVESTMENT AND THE GROWTH OF PRODUCTIVITY**

Data for a variety of industrialized nations indicate that the larger the proportion of GNP which a nation invests, the higher will be its rate of productivity growth. (Michael K. Evans testimony in Joint Economic Committee, *Special Study on Economic Change, Part 2,* 1978, p. 603. Data for 1960–1976.)

couraged the undertaking of new investment projects.

2  **Quality of Labor**  A variety of considerations relating to the quality of labor may be contributing to the slower rate of productivity growth. First, important changes have taken place in the age–sex composition of the labor force. In particular, unusually large numbers of young workers—workers having less experience and training and thus lower-than-average productivity—have been entering the labor force as the result of the post-World War II "baby boom." Simultaneously, early retirements, prompted by liberalized social security benefits and the option to obtain partial bene-

fits at age 62, have removed substantial numbers of experienced, high-productivity workers from the labor force. Similarly, the labor force participation of women has increased significantly since the mid-1960s. Many of these entrants are married women who have little or no labor force experience. Also, because of sex discrimination, women traditionally have been assigned to less productive jobs. A second and more subtle point is that historically the overall productivity of the labor force has grown because of the long-term shift of workers from agriculture (where average productivity is low) to industry (where average productivity is high). In recent years agricultural workers have become a small and relatively stable proportion of the total labor force, essentially ending productivity gains from this agriculture-to-industry reallocation. Third, the fact that the level of educational attainment of the labor force has been increasing at a slower rate than in years past has undoubtedly reinforced the productivity slowdown. A final and less tangible point is that there may have occurred a decline in the "work ethic." The contention is that, given the overall affluence of our society and the presence of such income maintenance programs as unemployment compensation, workers feel under less pressure to work hard and to discipline themselves on the job. Furthermore, many workers allegedly feel alienated and "turned off" by highly specialized assembly-line jobs and this discontent precipitates productivity declines.

3  **Technological Progress**  Technological advance—usually reflected in improvements in the *quality* of capital goods—and improvements in the efficiency with which inputs are combined may also have faltered. Technological progress is fueled by expenditures for formal research and development (R & D) programs and we know that R & D spending in the United States has been declining as a percentage of GNP since the mid-1960s. Specifically, R & D outlays rose steadily in the postwar period to a peak of 3 percent of

GNP by the mid-1960s, only to decline to about 2 percent by the late 1970s. This decline is partly the consequence of decreased Federal support and partly the result of businesses' reaction to the economic instability and uncertainty associated with the 1970s. In addition, the new flood of regulatory legislation having to do with pollution, worker health and safety, equal employment opportunities, and so on, have undoubtedly absorbed a great deal of management's time in understanding the new regulations and complying with them. While the goals of such legislation are laudable, the opportunity cost of compliance is that managers have less time to devote to the development of more efficient means of combining resources (Chapter 35).

What are the implications of the productivity slowdown? First and most obviously, our standard of living cannot rise as rapidly as it has in the past. It is partly because of our poor productivity performance that Americans no longer enjoy the highest per capita GNP in the world. Secondly, we discovered in our discussion of incomes policies in Chapter 18 that productivity increases tend to offset increases in money wage rates and thereby have an ameliorating effect on cost-push inflationary pressures. Our decline in the rate of productivity growth therefore contributes to rapidly rising unit labor costs and a higher rate of inflation. A third and related point is that our slow rate of productivity growth as compared to our major international trading partners tends to increase the relative prices of American goods in world markets. The result is a loss of international markets for American producers, an intensification of our balance of payments deficits, and a weakening of the international value of the dollar.

## ☐ AGGREGATE DEMAND AND GROWTH

Classical theory focuses upon the supply side of economic growth, that is, upon those factors which determine the productive capacity of the economy. We now want to consider the demand side of economic growth within the context of Keynesian employment theory.

### △ Keeping Pace with Capacity

The essence of the problem is that in an economy whose productive capacity is expanding, the full-employment noninflationary NNP will obviously be increasing over time. As noted earlier, the realization or achievement of that desired output clearly depends upon an expanding level of aggregate demand. Figure 19-6 is based upon the simple income-determination model of Figure 12-5 wherein we assume the full-employment NNP in year 1 is $490 billion and that, fortunately, aggregate demand is at $(C_a + I_n + G)_1$, so that full employment is being realized. But now, in a growth context, we must acknowledge that the economy's productive capacity—its full-employment NNP—will be increasing through time. That is, increases in the quantity and quality of resources and technological advances will make it possible for the economy to produce a larger full-employment NNP in year 2. Suppose these supply factors in growth permit a 4 percent increase in real output so that the full-employment NNP is approximately $510 billion in year 2. The obvious point is that, in order for this enhanced productive potential to be realized, aggregate demand must expand at a rate sufficient to maintain full employment. In this instance, aggregate demand must shift upward to $(C_a + I_n + G)_2$. If aggregate demand grows less or not at all, the consequence will be underutilized productive capacity, unemployed resources, and a retarded growth rate. On the other hand, if aggregate demand shifts above $(C_a + I_n + G)_2$, the economy will realize its increased capacity to produce but it will also incur inflation. Note that fiscal and monetary policies must now be manipulated to hit a moving target!

### △ Full-Employment Growth Model

More sophisticated growth models focus

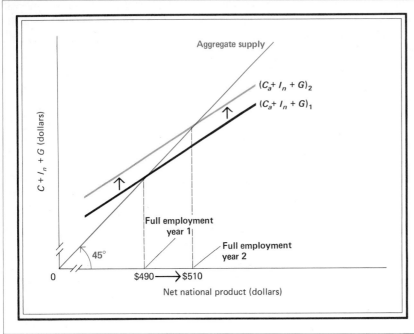

**FIGURE 19-6  AGGREGATE DEMAND AND FULL EMPLOYMENT IN A GROWING ECONOMY**

As the result of increases in the quantity and quality of resources and technological progress, the full-employment NNP will increase over time, for example, from $490 in year 1 to $510 in year 2. To utilize this expanded productive capacity, aggregate demand must increase from $(C_a + I_n + G)_1$ to $(C_a + I_n + G)_2$.

attention upon the investment component of aggregate demand. Figure 19-6 stresses the *income-creating* aspect of net investment; that is, investment is regarded solely as a generator of output, income, and employment. But we must now recognize that net investment also has a *capacity-creating* aspect. Net investment represents an addition to the nation's stock of capital goods and this enhances the productive capacity of the economy. An economy which engages in net investment in year 1 is expanding its "national factory" and will

thereby have the capacity to produce a larger full-employment NNP in year 2.

**Assumptions**  Table 19-2 embodies a simple macroeconomic growth model which highlights the capacity-creating role of net investment and allows us to isolate certain crucial factors which determine an economy's full-employment growth rate. We begin by making several simplifying assumptions which are reflected in the first row of the table. Assume, first, a private economy wherein aggregate

**TABLE 19-2**
**Full-Employment Growth Rates** (*hypothetical data, in billions*)

| (1) Year | (2) Full-employment NNP | (3) Full-employment level of saving | (4) Full-employment level of investment | (5) Increase in full-employment NNP |
|---|---|---|---|---|
| 1 | $100 | $20 | $20 | |
| 2 | 105 | 21 | 21 | $5      $(= 20 \div 4)$ |
| 3 | 110.25 | 22.05 | 22.05 | 5.25 $(= 21 \div 4)$ |
| 4 | 115.76 | 23.15 | 23.15 | 5.51 $(= 22.05 \div 4)$ |
| 5 | ____ | ____ | ____ | ____ |

demand is composed of only consumption and investment. Suppose, too, the economy is currently (year 1) in equilibrium at the full-employment NNP of $100 billion. Third, assume that the average propensity to save (APS) is .20.[4] Now, noting that saving is $20 billion (.20 × $100 billion), we know that the level of investment required to achieve full employment is also $20 billion ($S = I_n$). In short, the year 1 figures of Table 19-2 represent a very simple income-determination model a la Chapter 12.

**Capital-Output Ratio**  But now we must introduce the capacity-creating aspect of net investment and observe that this economy will be able to produce a larger full-employment NNP in year 2. The question is: How much larger? This depends upon the *capital-output ratio,* that is, the ratio or relationship between net investment and the resulting increase in productive or output capacity of the economy. Let us suppose this ratio is 4:1 or, more simply, 4. This means that every $4 of net investment in year 1 makes the economy capable of producing $1 of additional output in year 2 and succeeding years. Knowing that it takes $4 worth of net investment to increase productive capacity by $1, we can simply divide year 1's $20 billion of net investment by the capital-output ratio of 4 to find the increase in the economy's full-employment NNP as the result of year 1's investment. In column 5 of Table 19-2 we find that the answer is $5 billion; full-employment output in year 2 is $105 billion, compared with year 1's $100 billion.

Succeeding rows in Table 19-2 merely repeat this procedure. We find that in year 2 the full-employment level of saving will be $21 billion (= $105 billion × .20). It is assumed in column 3 that net investment is just sufficient to offset this saving leakage so that full employment is again realized. Same question: By how much will year 2's net investment increase

productive capacity in year 3? Again, in column 5 we get the answer by dividing net investment by the capital-output ratio. Year 2's net investment will permit the economy to produce an extra $5.25 billion (= $21 billion ÷ 4) in year 3. The reader is urged to follow through on this procedure for years 3 and 4 and to calculate the omitted figures for year 5.

**The Growth Rate**  It is important to stress that Table 19-2 traces through the growth scenario of an economy wherein aggregate demand grows by just that amount necessary to sustain full employment through time. The figures of the table therefore reflect the *full-employment* growth rate for this economy. Inspection of column 2 indicates that the full-employment NNP is growing by 5 percent per year. Similarly, by inspecting column 4 we find that the growth in net investment which is required to sustain full employment is also 5 percent. Furthermore, although the growth *rates* of NNP and net investment are constant, this obviously means that the *absolute* increases in NNP and net investment are larger and larger each year.

*Formula*  Let us now generalize: Column 5 of Table 19-2 tells us that each year NNP increases by the proportion of the NNP which is saved and invested (determined by the APS) *divided by* the capital-output ratio. Hence, we can say that:

The full-employment growth rate

$$= \frac{\text{average propensity to save}}{\text{capital-output ratio}}$$

For the illustrative data of Table 19-2:

$$5\% \text{ or } .05 = \frac{.20}{4}$$

Obviously, any alteration in the basic data of our model—any change in the APS or the capital-output ratio—will change the full-employment growth rate. Specifically, from our formula it is clear that, *given the APS, a decline in the capital-output ratio will increase*

[4]To avoid complications, we assume the APS is constant at various levels of NNP.

*the growth rate.* For example, with an APS of .20, a decline in the capital-output ratio from 4 to 2 will increase the growth rate from 5 to 10 percent. On reflection this is not at all surprising: A lower capital-output ratio implies that the productivity of capital or investment goods has increased. That is, when the capital-output ratio declines from 4 to 2, it means that now, because of, say, technological progress, only one-half as much additional capital goods are required to increase NNP by $1 as were necessary before. Similarly, *given the capital-output ratio, an increase in the APS will increase the full-employment growth rate.* Given our capital-output ratio of 4, an increase in the APS to, say, .40 would increase the economy's full-employment growth rate from 5 to 10 percent. The rationale for this generalization is rooted in Figure 2-4; other things being equal, an economy which saves and invests a larger proportion of its national output will grow more rapidly. Question 8 at the end of the chapter provides an opportunity for further confirmation of these generalizations.

## □ ALLOCATIVE EFFICIENCY AND GROWTH

The forces of growth—both the supply factors and an appropriately expanding level of aggregate demand—will call for changes in the allocation of the economy's resources over time. If these changes in resource use do not occur with reasonable speed and completeness, the economy will fail to realize fully its capacity for growth.

On the supply side, if we were to disaggregate the economy's overall growth, we would find that the productive capacities of some industries and firms are expanding rapidly while those of others are growing slowly or perhaps even contracting. Such changes obviously imply appropriate adjustments in the allocation of resources. Where, for example, do expanding industries obtain the resources which their growth requires? In part, they may be obtained from current increases in our total supplies of resources. Thus, an expanding industry may get a part of the additional labor it needs from new labor force entrants. It may obtain the remainder of its added labor from other, declining industries. In either event some mechanism is needed to guide new resources into their most productive uses or, as the case may be, to direct currently employed resources from low-productivity to high-productivity employments. In short, changes in technology (as reflected in either new productive techniques or new goods) and changes in the relative scarcities, and therefore prices, of resources which are germane to growth call for constant reallocations of human and property resources among alternative uses. As noted earlier, if these resource realignments do not occur with reasonable rapidity and completeness, the economy's capacity for growth may be underfulfilled.

The need for sustained allocative efficiency also has roots on the demand side. We already know that aggregate demand must expand appropriately if the full-capacity output of an expanding economy is to be realized. This generalization, however, conceals the fact that as total demand grows, its composition or structure will change. The demands for some goods will be highly sensitive to increases in income. For other goods, demand might be quite insensitive to income growth. For example, the demands for potatoes, soap, and wheat grow very modestly as income expands, but the demands for steak, education, jewelry, and automobiles tend to increase sharply as income rises. In any event, extensive shifts in the allocation of resources will again be necessary.

# Summary

**1** Economic growth may be defined either in terms of **a.** an expanding real national output (income) or **b.** an expanding per capita real output (income).  Growth lessens the burden of scarcity and provides increases in the national output which can be used in the resolution of domestic and international socioeconomic problems.

**2** The supply factors in economic growth are **a.** the quantity and quality of a nation's natural resources, **b.** the quantity and quality of its human resources, **c.** its stock of capital facilities, and **d.** its technology.  Two other factors—a sufficient level of aggregate demand and allocative efficiency—are essential if the economy is to realize its growth potential.

**3** The principle of diminishing returns exercises a constraint upon growth where one or more resources are fixed in supply.  This law tells us that with a given technology, the addition of successive units of one resource (labor) to fixed amounts of other resources (land and capital) will ultimately result in diminishing output per worker or, in other words, declining labor productivity.

**4** Thomas Malthus used the law of diminishing returns over a century and a half ago to explain the widespread poverty which then existed.  In particular, he argued that rapid population growth, coupled with diminishing returns in agricultural production, was tending to keep real income per capita at the subsistence level.

**5** Technological progress, increases in the stock of capital, and improvements in the quality of labor and management have the effect of offsetting diminishing returns by increasing the productivity of labor (Figure 19-4).

**6** The rate of growth of the productivity of American labor has declined since the mid-1960s, causing a slowdown in the rise of our living standards and contributing to inflation.

**7** An expanding productive potential will not be achieved unless aggregate demand expands at an appropriate rate.  Growth models emphasize the capacity-creating aspect of net investment and demonstrate that the economy's full-employment growth rate can be calculated by dividing the APS by the capital-output ratio.  The APS and the growth rate are directly related; the capital-output ratio and the growth rate are inversely related.

**8** The realization of the growth potential of an economy presumes that appropriate reallocations of resources are achieved.

# Questions and Study Suggestions

**1** Key terms and concepts to remember: economic growth; supply, demand, and allocative factors in growth; law of diminishing returns; average product; labor productivity; optimum population; productivity slowdown; income-creating and capacity-creating aspects of investment; capital-output ratio; full-employment growth rate.

**2** What difficulties are involved in measuring economic growth?  Why is economic growth important?  Explain why the difference between a 3.5 percent and a 3.0 percent annual growth rate might be of great importance.

**3** What are the major causes of economic growth?  "There are both a demand and a supply side to economic growth."  Explain.  Illustrate the operation of both sets of factors in terms of the production possibilities curve.

**4** State the law of diminishing returns.  Why are diminishing returns significant for a nation's economic growth?

**5** Explain: "Rapid population growth may both contribute to, and detract from, a nation's economic progress."  What is meant by an "optimum population"?

**6** How did Malthus explain the extremely low levels of income which were so common in the eighteenth century?  To what extent, if any, is Malthus's explanation of poverty relevant today? How can an economy with a rapidly growing population and labor force effectively offset diminishing returns?

    **7** Account for the recent slowdown in the United States' rate of productivity growth. What are the consequences of this slowdown? Will it persist? Explain.

    **8** What is the full-employment growth rate? How can it be calculated? If the capital-output ratio is 3, what will the full-employment growth rate be when the APS is .10, .20, and .30? If the APS is .30, what will the full-employment growth rate be when the capital-output ratio is 5, 4, and 3? What two generalizations can you derive from these examples?

## Selected References

Fabricant, Solomon: *A Primer on Productivity* (New York: Random House, 1969).

Gill, Richard T.: *Economic Development: Past and Present,* 3d ed. (Englewood Cliffs, N.J.: Prentice-Hall, Inc., 1972), particularly chaps. 1–4.

Joint Economic Committee: *Special Study on Economic Change, Part 2* (Washington, D.C., 1978).

Joint Economic Committee: *U.S. Economic Growth from 1976 to 1986: Prospects, Problems, and Patterns, Vol. 1* (Washington, D.C., 1976).

Kendrick, John W.: *Understanding Productivity* (Baltimore: The Johns Hopkins University Press, 1977).

McConnell, Campbell R.: "Why is U.S. Productivity Slowing Down?", *Harvard Business Review,* March–April, 1979, pp. 36–60.

New York Stock Exchange: *Reaching A Higher Standard of Living* (NYSE, 1979).

Rostow, W. W.: *The Stages of Economic Growth,* 2d ed. (New York: Cambridge University Press, 1971).

# LAST WORD
# Population and the
# Growth Mystique

The national Commission on Population Growth argues that there is no convincing economic argument for continued population growth in the United States.

. . . we find no convincing economic argument for continued national population growth. On the contrary, most of the plusses are on the side of slower growth. This finding is at variance with much opinion, especially in the business community and among many civic leaders. We have sought to find the reason for this seeming contradiction.

Periods of rapid population growth in this country have generally been periods of rapid economic expansion as well. It is not surprising, therefore, that we associate population growth with economic progress. However, the historical association of population growth with economic expansion would be an erroneous guide to the formulation of population policy for the future.

This connection reflects in large part the fact that periods of rapid expansion attracted immigrants to our shores and thus quickened population growth as a result. Additions to population through immigration are far more stimulating to economic growth than are additions by natural increase. This is because, while babies remain dependent for many years before beginning to contribute to output, many immigrants are of working age and thus become immediately productive. . . .

This answer may not satisfy the gas station owner, local food retailer, or banker, to whom it seems obvious that "more people" means more customers or more savings accounts. Once again, however, we need to examine the *kind* of growth that means more business, and its relationship to local economic expansion. The rapid local population growth that means more business results chiefly from other people moving in, not more people being born and raised. Adults moving in make ready customers and ready employees. They have grown up elsewhere, their education has been paid for elsewhere, and being young, they impose few of the demands of the dependent aged. Since mobile people are, on the average, better qualified than those who do not move, it is no surprise that they provide an extra boost to local establishments.

We have studied the effects of lower national population growth rates on the economic well-being of urban and rural areas within the nation. Is there reason to fear that the ills typical of areas of population decline today would become more serious or widespread if national population growth rates declined? We conclude that there is not; such fears are based on a mistaken belief that population decline causes economic decline. In reality, the chain of causation in distressed areas runs from (1) the decline of regional competitive capability to (2) unemployment to (3) net outmigration to (4) population loss. Accordingly, there is little reason to suppose that local problems of unemployment or obsolescence of physical facilities would be more serious in a situation of zero or negative national population growth than they would be at any positive level of national population growth. In the future, as in the past, areas of relatively high unemployment will tend to be areas of relative population loss; but the relative population loss will be the consequence and not the cause of local unemployment.

The diminished burden of providing for dependents, and for the multiplication of facilities to keep up with expanding population, should make more of our national output available for many desirable purposes: new kinds of capital formation, including human resources investment; public expenditure involving qualitative improvement and modernization; and greater attention to environmental and amenity objectives. Thus, whatever the future problems of urban areas and regions may be, we should have more ample per capita resources to attack them in a situation with a lower rate of population growth than we would have with a higher rate.

Report of the Commission on Population Growth and the American Future, *Population and the American Future* (Washington, 1972), pp. 51–53, abridged.

# Economic Growth: Fact and Controversy

This chapter has three main objectives. The first is to state and explain the growth record of the United States. Secondly, we will outline the current debate over the *desirability* of growth as an economic goal. Thirdly, we will examine the question: Is continued economic growth *feasible?* In dealing with this question we will present and critically discuss the so-called Doomsday models of economic growth.

## ☐ GROWTH RECORD OF THE UNITED STATES

Table 20-1 gives us a rough idea of economic growth in the United States over past decades as viewed through our two definitions of growth. Column 2 summarizes the economy's growth as measured by increases in real GNP. Although not steady, the growth of real GNP has been quite remarkable. *The real GNP has increased fourfold since 1940.* It is remarkable

**TABLE 20-1**
Real GNP and Per Capita GNP, 1929–1979

| (1) Year | (2) GNP, billions of 1972 dollars | (3) Population, millions | (4) Per capita GNP, 1972 dollars (2) ÷ (3) |
|---|---|---|---|
| 1929 | $ 315 | 122 | $2584 |
| 1933 | 221 | 126 | 1768 |
| 1940 | 344 | 132 | 2601 |
| 1945 | 559 | 140 | 3995 |
| 1950 | 534 | 152 | 3504 |
| 1955 | 655 | 166 | 3946 |
| 1960 | 737 | 181 | 4078 |
| 1965 | 926 | 194 | 4765 |
| 1970 | 1075 | 205 | 5248 |
| 1975 | 1202 | 214 | 5631 |
| 1979 | 1431 | 221 | 6487 |

*Source: Economic Report of the President.*

that the growth in the real GNP since 1965 is roughly equal to its total growth in the entire period between 1776 and 1940!

**TABLE 20-2**
Growth of Real GNP and Real GNP Per Capita in Selected Countries

| | Growth rates of real GNP | | Growth rates of real GNP per capita | |
|---|---|---|---|---|
| | 1870–1969 | 1960–1977 | 1870–1969 | 1960–1977 |
| United States | 3.7% | 3.6% | 2.0% | 2.4% |
| Japan | 4.2 | 8.7 | — | 7.4 |
| Germany | 3.0 | 3.8 | 1.9 | 3.2 |
| United Kingdom | 1.9 | 2.4 | 1.3 | 2.1 |
| France | 2.0 | 4.9 | 1.7 | 4.0 |
| Italy | 2.2 | 4.4 | 1.5 | 3.7 |
| Canada | 3.6 | 5.1 | 1.8 | 3.4 |

*Source:* U.S. Department of Commerce, *Historical Statistics of the United States: Colonial Times to 1970* (Washington, 1975), p. 225; and *Statistical Abstract of the United States, 1979,* p. 437.

But our population has also grown significantly. Hence, using our second definition of growth, we find in column 4 that *real per capita GNP was two and one-half times larger in 1979 than it was in 1940.*

What about our *rate* of growth? Statistical data (Table 20-2) suggest that the long-term growth rate of the United States' real GNP has been on the order of $3\frac{1}{2}$ percent per year, while real GNP per capita has grown at about 2 to $2\frac{1}{2}$ percent per year.

For at least two reasons these quantitative conclusions understate the economic growth which the American economy has actually experienced.

**1** The figures of Tables 20-1 and 20-2 do *not* fully take into account improvements in product quality. Purely quantitative data do not provide an accurate comparison between an era of crystal sets and one of stereophonic phonographs.

**2** The increases in real GNP and per capita GNP shown in Table 20-1 were accomplished despite very sizable increases in leisure. The seventy-hour workweek is a thing of the distant past. The standard workweek is now less than forty hours.

On the other hand, in our discussion of the growth controversy we shall find that these measures of growth do *not* take into account adverse effects upon the physical environment or upon the quality of life itself.

While impressive, the United States' growth record has been less dramatic than those achieved by some other developed countries. As Table 20-2 indicates, in recent years Japan and a number of countries of Western Europe—not to mention the Soviet Union (Chapter 45)—have reached comparable or superior rates of growth.

□ **SOURCES OF UNITED STATES GROWTH**

There are two fundamental ways by which any society can increase its real output and income: (1) by increasing its inputs of resources and (2) by increasing the productivity of those inputs. Let us build upon the framework of the previous chapter (see Figures 19-2 and 19-4 in particular) and focus our attention upon inputs of labor. By so doing we can say that *our real GNP in any year depends upon the input of labor (measured in worker hours) multiplied by the productivity of labor (measured as real output per worker per hour).* That is,

Total output = worker hours
$\qquad\qquad\times$ labor productivity

Hypothetical illustration: Assume an economy with 10 workers, each of whom works 2000 hours per year (50 weeks at 40 hours per week) so that total input of worker hours is 20,000 hours. If productivity—average real output per worker hour—is $5, then total output or real GNP will be $100,000 (=20,000 × $5).

What determines the number of hours worked each year? And, more importantly, what determines labor productivity? Figure 20-1 provides us with a framework for answering these questions. The hours of labor input depend upon the size of the employed labor force and the length of the average workweek. Labor force size in turn depends upon the size of the working age population and labor force participation rates, that is, the percentage of the working age population which is actually in the labor force. The average workweek is governed by legal and institutional considera-

tions and by collective bargaining. Productivity is determined by such factors as the quality of labor, the property resources with which workers are equipped, and technology as reflected in the quality of capital goods and the efficiency with which the various inputs are allocated, combined, and managed. Stated differently, productivity increases when the health, training, education, and motivation of workers are improved; when workers have more and better machinery and natural resources with which to work; when production is better organized and managed; and when labor is reallocated from less efficient industries to more efficient industries.

Incidentally, Figure 20-1 complements Figure 16-2. The latter figure outlines the determinants of the *demand* for national output. Figure 20-1 summarizes those factors which determine a nation's capacity to *supply* or produce aggregate output. By locating Figure 20-1 to the left of Figure 16-2 one obtains a more complete model of the economy which sketches the determinants of both the demand for, and the supply of, national output.

Employing the organizational framework of Figure 20-1, let us consider a variety of points which help to explain long-term economic growth in the United States. We first consider some of the major influences upon labor inputs.

△   **Labor Inputs**

Figure 20-2 indicates that our population and labor force have both expanded through time. A quite high birthrate, a declining death rate, and—for a time—heavy immigration have teamed to provide the United States with substantial population growth throughout much of its history. Our population quadrupled during the first half of the nineteenth century, it more than trebled during the last half, and has increased almost threefold since 1900. Our population and civilian labor force were 221 million and 103 million, respectively, in 1979 and continue to grow. Historical declines in the length of the average workweek have

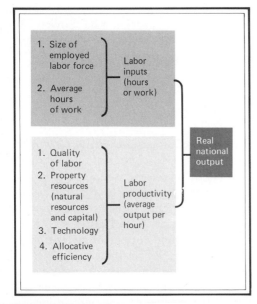

FIGURE 20-1 THE DETERMINANTS OF REAL OUTPUT

Real GNP can be usefully viewed as the product of the quantity of labor inputs multiplied by labor productivity.

**FIGURE 20-2 POPULATION AND LABOR FORCE GROWTH, 1928–1979**

Since 1929 both the population and the labor force have roughly doubled. (*Bureau of Census data.*)

Perhaps the simplest measure of labor force quality is the level of educational attainment. Figure 20-3 reflects the impressive gains which have been realized. Currently almost three-fourths of the labor force has received at least a high school education. Of this group about 17 percent have acquired a college education or more. Only about a tenth of the civilian labor force has received no more than an elementary school education. Indeed, it is possible that Americans may be "overeducating" themselves relative to anticipated job openings. In particular, we may be building up a surplus of workers with bachelor and advanced degrees who will encounter difficulties in finding jobs which utilize fully their training and skills.[1] On the other hand, school attendance and educational achievement are *not* identical. A recent Ford Foundation study concluded that some 23 million adults are too

[1]See Richard B. Freeman, *The Overeducated American* (New York: Academic Press, Inc., 1976).

tended to reduce labor inputs, but the workweek has declined very modestly since World War II. Declining birthrates in the past 20 years have brought about a decline in the rate of population growth. However, largely because of increased participation of women in labor markets, our civilian labor force continues to grow by 2 to 3 million workers per year.

△ **Productivity Increases**

Consider now the main factors which have tended to increase the productivity of labor.

**Quality of Labor**   Ben Franklin once said that "He that hath a trade hath an estate." This is an archaic way of saying that education and training improve a worker's productivity and result in higher earnings. Like investment in real capital, investment in human capital is an important means of increasing labor productivity. Worker for worker, the quality of the United States labor force is among the highest in the world.

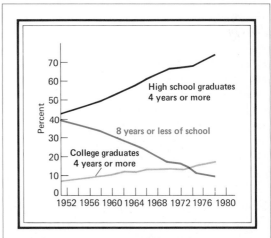

**FIGURE 20-3  RECENT CHANGES IN THE EDUCATIONAL ATTAINMENT OF THE LABOR FORCE**

The percentage of the labor force completing high school and college has been rising steadily in recent years, while the percentage who did not go to high school or complete elementary school has been falling. (*Employment and Training Report of the President.*)

illiterate to function competently in our society! And college entrance examinations for the past decade or so indicate declines in the verbal and quantitative skills of college-bound students.

**Property Resources: Land and Capital Goods**   To a very great extent workers, regardless of their skills and training, are no better than the property resources with which they are combined. Other things being equal, a farmer will obviously be more productive when the land being cultivated is fertile and receives an appropriate amount of rainfall. And recall from Chapter 3 that the indirect or roundabout production which capital goods afford is a basic means of increasing worker productivity. Our farmer's output per hour of cultivation will be substantially greater with a tractor than with a hoe.

*Natural resources*   There is no doubt that the generous and varied supplies of natural resources with which the United States has been blessed have been an important contributor to our economic growth. We enjoy an abundance of fertile soil, quite desirable climatic and weather conditions, ample quantities of most mineral resources, generous sources of power, and so forth. It is generally agreed that, with the possible exception of the Soviet Union, the United States has a larger variety and greater quantity of natural resources than any other nation. This is not to deny the existence of problem areas, for example, our increasing dependence upon foreign oil.

While an abundant natural resource base is very helpful to the growth process, we must not conclude that a meager resource base dooms a nation to slow growth. Although Japan's natural resources are severely constrained, its post-World War II growth has been remarkable (Table 20-2). Japan has improved its productivity by relying upon imported raw materials. On the other hand, some of the very underdeveloped countries of Africa and South America have substantial amounts of natural resources.

*Stock of capital*   Recall from Table 19-2 that increases in a nation's stock of capital goods depend upon the saving-investment process. This process has resulted in an historical trend toward the use of more and more real capital per worker. For example, in the 1889 to 1969 period the stock of capital goods increased sixfold and, over this same period, labor-hours doubled. Hence, the quantity of capital goods per labor-hour was roughly three times as large in 1969 than it was in 1889.[2] Data also show that the average factory worker was equipped with about $5200 of capital equipment in 1939. This figure quadrupled to $20,400 in 1963 and then doubled in the next decade to $41,100 in 1973.

Having said all this, a glance back at Figure 19-5 reminds us that investment spending in the United States has *not* compared favorably with other nations as a percent of GNP. This fact is important in explaining why the real GNPs of such countries as Japan and West Germany have been expanding faster than that of the United States (Table 20-2).

**Technological Progress**   Generally speaking, technological progress involves the more efficient use of resources, that is, combining or employing given resources in new ways so as to result in a larger output. In practice, technological advance and capital formation (investment) are closely related processes; technological advance often entails investment in new machinery and equipment. The idea that there is a more efficient way to catch a rabbit than running it down led to investment in the bow and arrow. And it is obviously necessary to construct new nuclear power plants in order to apply nuclear power technology. However, modern crop-rotation practices and contour plowing are ideas which contribute greatly to output, although they do not necessarily entail the use of new kinds or increased amounts of capital equipment.

[2] Solomon Fabricant, *A Primer on Productivity* (New York: Random House, Inc., 1969), chap. 5.

What has been the rate of technological advance in the United States? Casual observation suggests that, historically, it has been both rapid and profound. Gas and diesel engines, conveyer belts, and assembly lines come to mind as obviously significant developments of the past. More recently, the lamp of technology has freed the automation jinni and with it the potential wonders of the push-button factory. Supersonic jets, the transistor and integrated circuitry, computers, xerography, containerized shipping, and nuclear power—not to mention space travel—are technological achievements which were in the realm of fantasy a mere generation ago.

Although it is difficult to measure unambiguously a nation's scientific output, total expenditures on research and development (R & D) constitute a rather widely accepted indicator of a nation's effort to advance technologically. The overall picture for the United States since World War II has been one of dramatic expansion of private and public R & D spending. Real expenditures on R & D were approximately $10 billion in 1955, but have grown steadily so that they were in excess of $30 billion in 1978. However, recall from Chapter 19 that R & D spending has been declining as a percentage of GNP. In the mid-1960s these expenditures reached a high of about 3 percent of GNP, but subsequently declined and are now slightly in excess of 2 percent of GNP. The United States is ploughing back a declining fraction of its output into the development of new technological knowledge, and in recent years this cutback has tended to slow the growth of productivity and real GNP.

**Allocative Efficiency**    The social environment of an economy can be every bit as significant as its physical environment in influencing economic growth. The social environment of any society must meet two requirements to facilitate economic growth. First, it must encourage those changes in products, productive techniques, and capital facilities which are vital to economic growth. Second, it must provide a suitable mechanism for negotiating with reasonable efficiency the reallocations of resources which are appropriate to the development of new products, new productive techniques, and changes in resource supplies and the structure of demand.

*Social environment*    The overall social-cultural-political environment of the United States generally has been conducive to economic growth. Several interrelated factors contribute to this favorable environment. First, as opposed to many other nations, there are virtually no social or moral taboos upon production and material progress. Indeed, American social philosophy has embraced the notion that material advance is an attainable and highly desirable economic goal. The inventor, the innovator, and the business executive are accorded high degrees of prestige and respect in American society. Second, Americans have traditionally possessed healthy attitudes toward work and risk taking; our society has benefited from a willing labor force and an ample supply of entrepreneurs. Third, our economy has been characterized by a stable political system wherein internal order, the right of property ownership, the legal status of enterprise, and the enforcement of contracts have been fostered. Though not subject to quantification, this bundle of characteristics has undoubtedly provided an excellent foundation for American economic growth.

*Resource realignments*    New methods, new products, and changes in resource supplies and consumer demand all call for realignments of resources. And the price system, we have seen, provides the carrot of profits and the stick of losses to induce the expansion of innovating industries and to force the contraction of those industries whose products have been rendered obsolete or less desirable by these changes. How effectively have these realignments been negotiated? This is not an easily answered question. However, some evidence of the reallocative capacity of the economy is shown in Figure 20-4. Over the years, rather

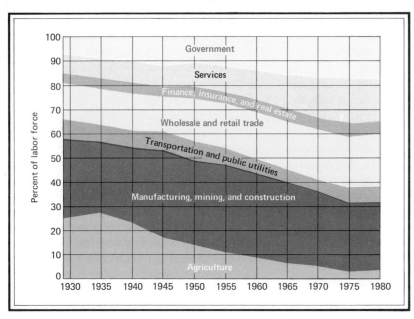

**FIGURE 20-4 THE CHANGING OCCUPATIONAL STRUCTURE OF THE LABOR FORCE, 1929–1979**

Long-term occupational shifts suggest that the price system has worked quite effectively in reallocating labor among alternative uses.

massive shifts have occurred in the industrial-occupational allocation of the labor force.

*Obstacles*    This is not to deny that there have been important impediments to the resource realignments necessitated by growth and change. Specific businesses and resource suppliers caught in declining industries have often sought—frequently with government help—to impede the reallocations of resources essential to economic growth. Monopolies in both product and resource markets have retarded the reallocations of resources required for economic growth. Business monopolies may find it more profitable to suppress a newly discovered product or productive technique than to have their present capital facilities rendered obsolete before they have been fully depreciated. Some labor unions have followed similar policies, resisting new work methods which threaten to cause unemployment by making workers more productive. To illustrate: Unions in the building trades have frequently resisted the use of spray guns, fearing that workers will paint themselves out of jobs.

And some unions, following restrictive membership policies, such as those of limiting the number of apprentices or charging high initiation fees, have created an artificial obstacle to labor mobility and have therefore limited the reallocation of human resources demanded by economic growth. Similarly, discrimination based upon race, sex, or ethnic background remains an important obstacle to allocative efficiency.

These contrived impediments to growth are enforced by certain inherent resource immobilities. Apart from union and business monopolies, resources are far from perfectly mobile. The obstacles to labor mobility, for example, are many and varied. Geographic immobility stems from the reluctance of workers to break existing social ties, move to a new community, meet new people, and take roots. Moreover, insofar as occupational mobility is concerned, it is no easy chore to abandon one's life work at, say, middle age and assume the responsibility, costs, and inconvenience of learning a new trade.

## △   Relative Importance

Table 20-3 summarizes the findings of a pioneering study by Edward F. Denison which attempts to assess the relative importance of the factors shown in Figure 20-1. While these data are rough approximations and do not perfectly dovetail with our discussion, the resulting estimates are highly informative. In particular, these data underscore the fact that *productivity growth has been the overwhelming force underlying the growth of our real GNP.* Note that increases in labor inputs accounted for about one-fourth of the growth of GNP over the 1948–1969 period; the remaining three-fourths was attributable to rising labor productivity. Department of Labor data yield very similar results. Real GNP increased at an average annual rate of 3.5 percent per year over the 1947–1977 period. During this period labor productivity increased by 2.8 percent per year, while worker-hours of labor increased by 0.7 percent per year.

## △   Demand, Instability, and Growth

Thus far our discussion of growth has been confined to supply factors, that is, to factors which determine the full-employment or potential output. However, an expanding productive capacity as such does not guarantee growth in the real GNP. We know from Chapter 19 that aggregate demand must expand by an appropriate amount in order for an expanded productive capacity to be utilized.

Figure 10-4 reminds us vividly of the extent to which the actual performance of our economy frequently falls short of its potential output. The result? A wasteful GNP gap and a rate of growth substantially less than that which higher levels of aggregate demand would have brought about. Looking back into history, we find that the Great Depression of the 1930s was a serious blow to the United States' long-run growth record. Between 1929 and 1933 our real GNP (measured in 1972 prices) actually *declined* from $315 to $222 billion! In 1939 the real GNP was approximately at the same level as in 1929 (see line 17 on table inside front cover).

But this is only a part of the picture. Cyclical *un*employment can have certain harmful "carry-over" effects upon the growth rate in subsequent years of full employment through the adverse effects it may have upon the supply factors in growth. For example, unemployment depresses investment and capital accumulation. The case is similar for investment in human capital: Families simply do not have sufficient financial resources to spend on additional education and training. Furthermore, why spend time and money on college training for teaching or engineering when these job markets are slack? The expansion of research budgets may be slowed by recession; union resistance to technological change may stiffen, and so forth. Though it is impossible to quantify the impact of these considerations upon the growth rate, they undoubtedly can be of considerable importance.

## △   Reprise

Our discussion of United States economic growth suggests that increases in labor productivity have been decidedly more important than increases in labor inputs in expanding real GNP. But growth in labor productivity does not just happen. It is brought about by

**TABLE 20-3**

The Sources of Growth in U.S. Real National Income, 1948–1969

| Source of growth | | Percent of total growth |
|---|---|---|
| Increase in inputs | | 24% |
| Increase in quantity of labor | 24% | |
| Increase in productivity | | 76 |
| Improved education and training | 12 | |
| Increase in quantity of capital | 21 | |
| Improved technology | 34 | |
| Improved resource allocation | 9 | |
| | | 100% |

*Source:* Edward F. Denison, *Accounting for United States Economic Growth, 1929–1969* (Washington: The Brookings Institution, 1974), p. 130.

improvements in the physical and mental abilities of the labor force itself, by increasing the quantity of real capital per worker, by improving technology, and by shifting resources from low- to high-productivity uses. Nor can productivity growth and the expansion of real output be taken for granted. As we shall find in Chapter 21, many of the so-called underdeveloped countries of the world have put forth substantial efforts to achieve economic growth but have realized little or no success. Similarly, growth rates for the industrially advanced nations are erratic. You are urged at this point to reread Chapter 19's case study of the recent slowdown of productivity growth in the United States.

## ☐  IS GROWTH DESIRABLE?

So much for the facts and causes of American economic growth. We now turn to the task of evaluation. Two related questions arise. First, is economic growth *desirable?* Is the United States' growth record to be envied or avoided? Second, is future growth *possible?* Are there unavoidable limits upon the process of economic growth? Let us treat these two questions in the order stated.

### △  The Case against Growth

In recent years serious questions have been raised as to the desirability of continued economic growth for already affluent nations. A number of interrelated arguments comprise this antigrowth sentiment.

**1  Pollution**  Concern with environmental deterioration is an important component of the antigrowth position. The basic point here is that industrialization and growth result in serious problems of air, water, and land pollution. Furthermore, economic growth means industrial noise and stench, ugly cities, traffic jams, and many other of the disamenities of modern life. These adverse social or spillover costs are held to be the consequence of the obvious fact that the production of the GNP

changes the form of resources, but does not destroy them. Virtually all inputs in the productive process are eventually returned to the environment in some form of waste. For example, in the United States each person accounts for an estimated 2000 pounds of solid wastes per year. The more rapid our growth and the higher our standard of living, the more waste there is for the environment to absorb—or attempt to absorb. An economic policy designed to maximize the GNP is allegedly a policy which maximizes resource depletion and environmental pollution. In an already wealthy society, further growth may mean only the satisfaction of increasingly trivial wants at the cost of mounting threats to our ecological system.

Antigrowth economists feel that a more rational policy should be based upon the proposition that future growth should be purposely constrained. A few economists would recommend a policy of zero growth—both *zero economic growth* (ZEG) and *zero population growth* (ZPG). Others merely argue that the GNP should be constrained to some socially acceptable standard of living which is significantly below the maximum attainable.

**2  Problem Resolution?**  There is little compelling evidence that economic growth has been a solvent for socioeconomic problems, as its proponents claim. Antigrowth economists assert, for example, that the domestic problem of poverty—income inequality—is essentially a problem of distribution, not production. The United States, it is argued, has possessed for many years the productive capacity to provide all its citizens with a decent standard of living, but it has not been willing to do so. The requisites for solving the poverty problem are commitment and political courage, not further increases in output. In general, there is no compelling evidence that growth has been, or will be, a palliative for domestic problems.

**3  Human Obsolescence and Insecurity**  Antigrowth economists contend that rapid growth—and in particular the changing technology which is the core of growth—poses new anxieties and new sources of insecurity for workers. Both high-level and low-level workers face the prospect of having their hard-earned skills and experience rendered obsolete by an onrushing technology.[3]

> Since change today is faster and more thorough than it was, say, a generation ago, and the generation hence will be faster yet, every one of us, manager, workman or scientist, lives closer to the brink of obsolescence. Each one of us that is adult and qualified feels menaced in some degree by the push of new developments which establish themselves only by discarding the methods and techniques and theories that he has learned to master.

**4   Growth and Human Values**   Critics of growth also offer a group of related arguments which say, in effect, that while growth may permit us to "make a living," it does not provide us with "the good life." We may, in fact, be producing more, but enjoying it less. Indeed, the requisites of growth may preclude attainment of the good life. For example, growth focuses upon the quantitative relationship between inputs and outputs. Output satisfies wants. Therefore, any increase in output from a given quantity of inputs means growth and presumably an improvement in human welfare. Antigrowth economists retort that one must also recognize that human welfare depends upon the character of the inputs. Must not the "loss of aesthetic and instinctual gratification suffered by ordinary working men over two centuries of technological innovation that changed them from artisans and craftsmen into machine-minders and dial-readers" be entered on the liability side of the balance sheet of economic growth? More specifically, it is charged that growth means industrialization, uncreative and unsatisfying mass-production jobs, and workers who are alienated in

that they have little or no control over the decisions which affect their lives.

At a more philosophical level it is argued that a growth-oriented society confers a "sweat-and-strain, look-to-the-future" conception of life upon its members.

> Less than fifty years ago a person could reach the economic goals of his life when he married, bought and furnished a house, educated his children, and accumulated some savings for his old age. Today he is lured further and further away from rest and satisfaction by more and more new goods and gadgets; they keep him tied to the leash of work and acquisition until he is buried without ever having reached a moment of peace where he could look back to his work and say: It is good.[4]

△   **In Defense of Growth**

But many economists defend growth as a high-priority goal, making such arguments as follow.

**1   Living Standards**   The primary defense of economic growth is the obvious one that it is the basic path to material abundance and rising standards of living (Table 20-1). *Growth makes the unlimited wants–scarce resources dilemma less acute.* Recalling the "rule of 70," an increase in worker productivity of 3 percent per year will double real output (income) per worker in about 23 years. To be sure, the realization of the benefits of growth necessarily entails costs. A society cannot be relatively wealthy in terms of material goods and services without accepting the costs and disamenities which that wealth inevitably entails. The defender of growth says, in effect, "Show me a pastoral society with an untouched environment, an abundance of leisure, and nonsecular values, and I will show you an underdeveloped, poverty-ridden country."

---

[3] E. J. Mishan, *Technology and Growth* (New York: Frederick A. Praeger, Inc., 1970), p. 115.

[4] Walter A. Weisskopf, "Economic Growth and Human Well-being," *Quarterly Review of Economics and Business,* Summer 1964, p. 20.

## 2   Growth   and   the   Environment

Growth proponents feel that the connection between growth, on the one hand, and the environment, on the other, is overdrawn. To a considerable degree these are separable issues. If society should flatly abandon the goal of growth and produce a constant real output every year, it would still have to make choices about the composition of output which would affect the environment and the quality of life. Society would still have to weigh the relative merits of enjoying the natural beauty of a forest or cutting the timber for productive uses. And, if the timber were cut, society would have to decide whether it would be used for housing or billboards. And, as one defender of growth has quipped, even in a zero-growth society "some people would still bring transistor radios to the beach."

Pollution is not so much a by-product of growth as it is a shortcoming of the price system. Specifically, much of the environment—streams, lakes, oceans, and the air—are treated as "common property" and no charge is made for their use.

> Factories, power plants, municipal sewers, drivers of cars, strip-miners of coal and deep-miners of coal, and all sorts of generators of waste are allowed to dump that waste into the environment, into the atmosphere and into running water and the oceans, without paying the full cost of what they do.[5]

Hence, our environmental resources are overused and debased. Recalling Chapter 6's terminology, environmental pollution is a case of spillover or external costs, and the correction of this problem entails regulatory legislation or the imposition of special taxes ("effluent charges") to remedy the price system's flaw and eliminate the misuse of the environment. There are, to be sure, serious pollution problems. But limiting growth is the wrong response. "The way to control pollution is to control pollution, not growth."[6]

Finally, one need not be a growth fanatic to point out that programs to clean up the environment are going to make substantial demands upon the national output. If we decide on a zero-growth policy, the required output must come at the expense of our current standard of living. But with growth—with an expanding income pie—we can simultaneously sustain or even increase per capita income *and* devote a larger slice of the national output to antipollution endeavors.

## 3   Income Inequality

Growth is the only practical way of achieving a more equitable distribution of income in our society. "It is inevitably less likely that a middle-class electorate will vote to redistribute part of its own income to the poor than it will be willing to allocate a slightly larger share of a growing total."[7] In fact, the distribution of income in the United States has been basically stable since World War II (Chapter 37); it follows that the basic means for improving the economic position of the poor is to move the entire distribution of income upward through economic growth. This argument is even more compelling for the underdeveloped countries of the world. The basic means by which the people of Asia, Africa, and Latin America can achieve a decent standard of living is through a rising real GNP. A no-growth policy would substantially eliminate the prospect for the world's poor to improve their economic positions.

## 4   Nonmaterial   Considerations

Defenders of growth argue that its retardation or cessation will not automatically foster humanistic goals nor promote "the good life."

---

[5] Robert M. Solow, "Is the End of the World at Hand?" *Challenge,* March–April 1973, p. 49.

[6] Marc J. Roberts, "On Reforming Economic Growth," in Mancur Olson and Hans H. Landsberg (eds.), *The No-Growth Society* (New York: W. W. Norton & Company, Inc., 1973), p. 125.

[7] Solow, op. cit., p. 41.

Indeed, we should expect the contrary. For example, the ending of growth will not mean the elimination of production-line work; historically, growth has been accompanied by a *decline* in the fraction of the labor force so employed. Nor has growth uniformly made labor more unpleasant or hazardous. New machinery is usually less taxing and less hazardous than the machinery it replaces. Furthermore, why would the retardation or prohibition of growth reduce materialism or alienation? Would we not expect the results to be quite the opposite? The loudest protests against materialism are heard in those nations and from those groups who now enjoy the highest levels of material security! More positively, it is the high standards of living which growth provides that make it possible for more people "to take the time for education, reflection, and self-fulfillment."[8]

## ☐ THE DOOMSDAY MODELS

Out of the debate over the *desirability* of growth a more sobering controversy has evolved as to whether or not continued growth is *possible*. The cornerstone of this controversy is the notion that resources are ultimately finite on "spaceship earth." Pessimists worry about both the availability of resources or *inputs* and the effects of *outputs*. Modern productive technology is heavily dependent upon exhaustible natural resources; it also employs the environment—the absorptive capacity of which is limited—for waste disposal. Hence, on the one hand, there is concern that we must ultimately run out of certain kinds of natural resources—oil, coal, copper, manganese, arable land—which are obviously critical to the productive process. On the other hand, there is fear that the increased waste which inevitably results from economic growth will overwhelm the absorptive capacity of the ecological system.

Using elaborate computer models developed at MIT, the Club of Rome—a group of some one hundred scientists, businessmen, and academicians—triggered a worldwide controversy with its conclusion that continued economic growth is impossible. According to their scenario, the current growth paths of population, output, and pollution are on a catastrophic collision course with production limits imposed by natural resources and the pollution-absorbing capacity of the environment.

> If the present growth trends in world population, industrialization, pollution, food production, and resource depletion continue unchanged, the limits to growth on this planet will be reached sometime within the next one hundred years. The most probable result will be a rather sudden and uncontrollable decline in both population and industrial capacity.[9]

Figure 20-5 shows the "standard run" Doomsday model. Data for 1900 through 1970 are actual historical trends; the data for 1971 through 2100 are computerized forecasts of these trends based upon the assumption that "there will be in the future no great changes in human values nor in the functioning of the global population-capital system as it has operated for the last one hundred years." The Club of Rome concludes that:[10]

> The behavior mode of the system . . . is clearly that of overshoot and collapse . . . the collapse occurs because of nonrenewable resource depletion. The industrial capital stock grows to a level that requires an enormous input of resources. In the very process of that growth it depletes a large fraction of the resource reserves available. As resource prices rise and mines are depleted,

[8]Roberts, op. cit., p. 133.

[9]Dennis L. Meadows and others, *The Limits to Growth* (Washington: Potomac Associates, 1972), p. 29. The interested reader should also consult E. F. Schumacher, *Small Is Beautiful* (New York: Harper & Row, Publishers, Incorporated, 1973), and Paul R. Ehrlich and Anne H. Ehrlich, *The End of Affluence* (New York: Ballantine Books, Inc., 1974).
[10]Meadows, op. cit., pp. 131–132.

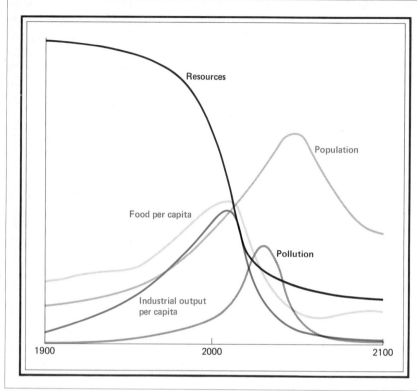

FIGURE 20-5  GROWTH AND
COLLAPSE:  A DOOMSDAY
MODEL

This computer model "assumes
no major change in the physical,
economic, or social relationships
that have historically governed
the development of the world
system. . . . Food, industrial
output, and population grow
exponentially until the rapidly
diminishing resource base
forces a slowdown in industrial
growth.  Because of natural
delays in the system, both
population and pollution
continue to increase for some
time after the peak of industrialization.  Population growth
is finally halted by a rise in the
death rate due to decreased
food and medical services."
[*Dennis L. Meadows and others,
The Limits to Growth (Washington:
Potomac Associates, 1972),
p. 129.*]

more and more capital must be used for obtaining resources, leaving less to be invested for
future growth.  Finally investment cannot keep
up with depreciation, and the industrial base
collapses, taking with it the service and agricultural systems, which have become dependent on
industrial inputs (such as fertilizers, pesticides,
hospital laboratories, computers, and especially
energy for mechanization).  For a short time the
situation is especially serious because population,
with the delays inherent in the age structure and
the process of social adjustment, keeps rising.
Population finally decreases when the death rate
is driven upward by lack of food and health
services.

The exact timing of these events is not meaningful, given the great aggregation and many uncertainties in the model.  It is significant, however,
that growth is stopped well before the year 2100.
We have tried in every doubtful case to make the
most optimistic estimate of unknown quantities,

and we have also ignored discontinuous events
such as wars or epidemics, which might act to
bring an end to growth even sooner than our
model would indicate.  In other words, the model
is biased to allow growth to continue longer than
it probably can continue in the real world.  *We
can thus say with some confidence that, under
the assumption of no major change in the present
system, population and industrial growth will
certainly stop within the next century, at the
latest.*

Other Club of Rome computer runs entail
much more optimistic assumptions, but the
end result is always a dramatic collapse of the
system. The dismal conclusion of all the Club
of Rome models is: "The basic behavior mode
of the world system is exponential growth of
population and capital, followed by collapse."[11]  If natural resource limits do not pre-

[11]Ibid., p. 149.

cipitate collapse, then famine or pollution will.

If the Doomsday models are at all meaningful, what policies can be recommended to avoid their "overshoot-and-collapse" prophecies? The road to survival calls for a stop to both economic and population growth. That is, top-priority policies entail zero economic growth (ZEG) and zero population growth (ZPG). For example, the Club of Rome concludes that a no-growth "stationary state" can be achieved in the next century *if* (1) population growth is zero; (2) there is no net investment in real capital; (3) technology reduces resource consumption per unit of industrial output to one-fourth of its 1970 level; (4) pollution is reduced to one-fourth of its 1970 level; and (5) real capital is shifted from industrial production to food and services. The result is a no-growth equilibrium—a state of stagnation—which can be extended more or less indefinitely through time. The projected worldwide average income per capita figure would be about one-half the United States' current level.

## □  NEW HORIZONS?

The Doomsday models have sparked an ongoing controversy and, in the process, considerable criticism. Consider the following overlapping arguments.

### △  Fun and Games with Numbers?

The Club of Rome, it is contended, has *assumed* exponential or geometric growth for population and production and has *assumed* certain absolute limits upon natural resources and technological capabilities. The overshoot-collapse outcome of the resulting computer runs is then merely the inevitable consequence of these assumptions. The fundamental question is: Are these assumptions—and therefore the predictions drawn from them—realistic? To paraphrase an old joke, one can project the reproduction rate of alligators and conclude that in X years we will be up to our eyeballs, or thereabouts, in alligators. The

point is that a different—and perhaps more plausible—set of assumptions would yield a much happier portrayal of mankind's future. Recall that Malthus's model (Chapter 19) is not unlike the Doomsday models in that it forecasts subsistence living levels as the result of geometric expansion of the population and arithmetic expansion of the food supply. And, while the simple projection of these assumptions does inevitably lead to the indicated conclusion, the assumptions of the model have not been accurate for the United States, Canada, Western Europe, Japan, the Soviet Union, and a number of other advanced and semi-advanced nations.

### △  Role of Technology

The Doomsday pessimists may have grossly underestimated the capabilities of technological progress. Specifically, technological progress—which has been highly instrumental in botching Malthus's dismal predictions—may offset the predictions of the Doomsday models in a variety of ways.

**1  Applying Existing Knowledge**  There are potentially great benefits to be realized by the wider application of *existing* technology. For example, British economist-journalist Norman Macrae has recently argued that "if all the land now cultivated were brought up to Dutch standards of efficiency, then the world could feed 60 billion people, 15 times today's population."[12] This great potential increase in food production is alleged to be an understatement because it does not take into account that, currently, only 3 percent of the earth's surface is farmed or the fact that much of the agricultural output of poor countries is now eaten by easily destroyable pests. Macrae predicts that we shall "find ourselves swimming in food gluts" within the next three decades.

**2  New Resource Discoveries**  The Doomsday models fail to recognize adequately

[12] Norman Macrae, *America's Third Century* (New York: Harcourt Brace Jovanovich, Inc., 1976), p. 49.

that the supply of natural resources should not be regarded as fixed, but rather as resources the supplies of which increase as the result of technological advance. Specifically, technological progress can "create new uses for formerly worthless substances, make available heretofore inaccessible stocks, and make feasible the extraction of formerly high-cost, low-quality materials."[13] The impact of technological advance over time is thus to continually raise resource ceilings and forestall the production-resource collision embodied in the Doomsday models. Is this reality or wishful thinking? According to one expert, "in the United States, technology has kept ahead of increased use, and the relative costs of resource inputs have declined."[14]

**3  New Resources and Resource Productivity**  It must also be recognized that technological progress entails a history of substituting newly discovered or newly developed resources for old ones. Many of the industrial materials used today—for example, plastics— were not even conceptually recognized a short time ago. Similarly, in our early history wood was the basic source of energy. But, aided by technological advances, society has shifted to coal, petroleum, and natural gas, thereby greatly expanding our supplies of energy resources. Optimists now envision solar, geothermal, and nuclear power on the horizon. Thus one recent authoritative estimate indicates that known reserves of fossil fuels are sufficient to last over 500 years at current consumption rates. But by adding *known* nuclear technology, energy resources become sufficient to last for over 8000 years. "With breeder reactors, and more dramatically with a fusion technology, there is virtually unlimited energy available."[15]

Equally significant is the possibility of using technology to increase the productivity of natural resources. Because, historically, labor has been the largest component of production costs, technological advances have been designed to increase the productivity of labor. But if future growth increases the relative scarcity and therefore the relative cost of natural resources, we can expect technological advances to become increasingly oriented toward achieving greater output per input of natural resources. And, in fact, one can point to some remarkably resource-saving innovations.

> . . . microminiaturisation with integrated circuits means that it is going to be increasingly economic to put on a chip the size of a postage stamp properly connected electrical circuits which would previously have required assemblies of machinery that fill a room.[16]

The point is that technological progress holds the potential for greatly expanding the output obtainable from a given amount of natural resource inputs.

**4  Increasing Returns to Technology**  Most important and with obviously crucial implications for the previous three points, technological knowledge—the ability to solve the problems associated with the geometric expansion of population and industrial production—may also expand at a geometric rate. Indeed, the "knowledge explosion" of the post–World War II era suggests that this has been the case. If technology does, or can be made to, expand at a geometric rate, output could continue to grow as new technology is substituted for labor, capital, and nonaugmentable natural resources.

Barnett and Morse have argued that technological progress is self-generating and is therefore subject to increasing, rather than diminishing, returns:

[13]Thomas M. Humphrey, "The Dismal Science Revisited," *Monthly Review of the Federal Reserve Bank of Richmond,* March 1973, p. 11.
[14]Roberts, op. cit., p. 121.
[15]William D. Nordhaus, "Resources as a Constraint on Growth," *American Economic Review,* May 1974, p. 25.

[16]Macrae, op. cit., p. 52.

. . . a strong case can be made for the view that the cumulation of knowledge and technological progress is automatic and self-reproductive in modern economies, and obeys a law of increasing returns. Every cost-reducing innovation opens up possibilities of application in so many new directions that the stock of knowledge, far from being depleted by new developments, may even expand geometrically.[17]

If this observation is reasonably realistic, it makes sense—despite the indisputable finiteness of the earth—to think in terms of unrestrained economic progress.

### △ Feedback Mechanisms

Critics also contend that the Doomsday models make inadequate allowance for various feedback mechanisms which can function so as to prevent the occurrence of the predicted overshoot-collapse scenario.

**The Price System**   The price system is, of course, the basic mechanism by which market economies signal and react to changes in relative scarcity. As reserves of, say, copper or aluminum become increasingly scarce, their prices will rise. Two responses automatically occur. On the one hand, resource users become more strongly motivated to conserve such resources either by employing substitutes (for example, plastic for copper pipes in new housing) or by developing new resource-saving production techniques. On the other hand, higher resource prices provide an incentive for resource producers to expand output by mining lower-grade ores or by recycling, both of which may have been economically unfeasible at lower prices. The point is that the price mechanism automatically induces responses which tend to alleviate resource shortages. "The economy is not a mindless glutton that will devour the last morsel before it notices that the plate is empty."[18]

[17]Harold Barnett and Chandler Morse, *Scarcity and Growth* (Baltimore: The Johns Hopkins University Press, 1963), p. 236.
[18]Roberts, op. cit., p. 121.

**Behavioral Patterns**   Critics of the Doomsday position argue that in the long run alterations in human behavior may be more important than the finiteness of the world's resources in determining our materialistic future.

There is evidence, for example, that people can and will adjust behavioral patterns with respect to procreation so that we will not breed ourselves into economic oblivion. In the United States the "baby boom" of the late 1940s has more recently become a "birth dearth." This change is attributable to improved birth control techniques, wider acceptance of family planning to achieve an "ideal" family size, changed attitudes toward abortion, and the greater participation of women in the labor force. Birthrates in the United States are currently at, or slightly below, zero population growth levels! It is highly relevant for the present discussion to note that economic growth *may* be a prerequisite for the control of population growth. That is, the opportunity cost of children rises as growth increases average incomes. In wealthy nations high wage rates mean that more income is forgone when parents spend time rearing children. It is therefore economically rational to have fewer children. Conversely, in poor nations the opportunity cost of children is low and, indeed, a large family is hopefully regarded as a substitute for the inability of parents to accumulate savings for retirement.

Consider how the so-called world food problem might be remedied by changes in human behavior designed to correct existing inefficiencies. According to Macrae, the world's pig population consumes seven times more primary protein than do North Americans. The world's horses, used primarily for recreation, consume more than the Chinese people. Cows, a third of which are located in Africa and Asia and serve no nutritive purpose, consume more grain than the entire world population. The point is that the potential exists through the altering of human decisions to discontinue highly inefficient practices in converting grain into meat and thereby greatly to alleviate the "food problem."[19]

Finally, there is growing evidence of behavioral changes which have dealt effectively with the problem of pollution. The reclamation of Germany's once-polluted Ruhr valley is a classic example of pollution problems getting better, not worse. Furthermore, "the pollution level in London has been reduced by 85 percent in the last 15 years, doubling the hours of winter sunshine and adding 55 species of fish to the once-moribund Thames."[20]

Whether one comes down on the side of the Doomsday pessimists or the technology-to-the-rescue optimists, certain important messages and questions do emerge from the growth debate. We are reminded, for example, that the fundamental question of scarcity has a time dimension. Absolutely exhaustible resources which are used today will obviously not be available tomorrow. What is the optimum way to allocate such resources through time? Can this optimum allocation be more effectively achieved via the market mechanism or government decision making, for example, by some sort of national or international planning? The debate also emphasizes that growth is not an unmitigated good. The impact of an ever-expanding output upon the environment and, more elusively, upon "life-styles" must be taken into account in any comprehensive evaluation of future growth. Finally, the debate points out that factors which fall essentially outside the pale of economics—in particular, population growth—have a critical bearing upon economic well-being.

[19]See Macrae, op. cit., p. 50.
[20]Roger Leroy Miller, *The Economics of Macro Issues* (San Francisco: Canfield Press, 1976), p. 169.

## Summary

1   The long-term growth rate of real GNP for the United States has been about 3½ percent; real GNP per capita has grown at about 2 percent.

2   The real GNP of the United States has grown, partly because of increased inputs of labor, and primarily because of increases in the productivity of labor. Improvements in the quality of labor, increases in the quantity of capital, technological progress, and improved allocative efficiency are among the more important factors which increase labor productivity.

3   Critics of economic growth *a.* cite adverse environmental effects; *b.* argue that domestic and international problems are essentially matters of distribution, not production; *c.* contend that growth is a major source of human obsolescence and insecurity; and *d.* argue that growth is frequently in conflict with certain human values.

4   Proponents of growth stress that *a.* growth means a better solution to the wants-means dilemma; *b.* environmental problems are only loosely linked to growth; *c.* growth is the only feasible means by which greater income equality can be realized; and *d.* growth is more consistent with "the good life" than is stagnation.

5   Recent Club of Rome computer models portray an "overshoot-collapse" scenario as the result of the collision between current growth paths of population, production, and pollution and output limits imposed by natural resources and nature's pollution-absorbing capacity. Zero economic and population growth—ZEG and ZPG—are recommended policies for avoiding overshoot and collapse.

6   Critics argue that the Doomsday models *a.* are based upon unrealistic assumptions, *b.* fail to emphasize sufficiently the scarcity-offsetting capacity of technological progress, and *c.* neglect the role of such feedback mechanisms as the price system and changes in human behavior.

## Questions and Study Suggestions

**1**   Key terms and concepts to remember: labor productivity; Club of Rome; Doomsday models; zero economic growth; zero population growth; feedback mechanisms.

**2**   Briefly describe the growth record of the United States in this century.  Compare the rates of growth in real GNP and real GNP per capita, explaining any differences.  To what extent might these figures understate or overstate economic well-being?

**3**   To what extent have increases in our real GNP been the result of more labor inputs? Of increasing labor productivity?  Are the United States data of Table 20-2 generally consistent with the data of Table 20-3?  Explain.

**4**   Describe the Doomsday models.  "Our prime national goal . . . should be to reach a zero growth rate as soon as possible.  Zero growth in people, in GNP, and in our consumption of everything.  That is the only hope of attaining a stable economy: that is, of halting deterioration of the environment on which our lives depend."  Do you agree?  What programs and policies might be used if we sought to decelerate our rate of growth?

**5**   "If we want economic growth in a free society, we may have to accept a measure of instability."  Evaluate.  The noted philosopher Alfred North Whitehead once remarked that "the art of progress is to preserve order amid change and to preserve change amid order." What did he mean?  Is this contention relevant for economic growth?  What implications might this have for public policy?  Explain.

**6**   Comment on the following statements:

*a.*   "The price mechanism is the greatest conserver of scarce natural resources."

*b.*   "Technological advance is destined to play a more important role in economic growth in the future than it has in the past."

*c.*   "Income inequality is a matter of redistribution, not of further growth."

*d.*   "The issues of economic growth and environmental pollution are separable and distinct."

*e.*   "Nature imposes particular scarcities, not an inescapable general scarcity."

## Selected References

Allvine, Fred C., and Fred A. Tarpley, Jr.: *The New State of the Economy* (Cambridge, Mass.: Winthrop Publishers, Inc., 1977).

Heilbroner, Robert L.: *The Economic Transformation of America* (New York: Harcourt Brace Jovanovich, Inc., 1977).

Interfutures: *Facing the Future* (Paris: Organization for Economic Cooperation and Development, 1979).

Macrae, Norman: *America's Third Century* (New York: Harcourt Brace Jovanovich, Inc., 1976).

Meadows, Dennis, and others: *The Limits to Growth* (Washington: Potomac Associates, 1972).

Olson, Mancur, and Hans H. Landsberg (eds.): *The No-Growth Society* (New York: W. W. Norton & Company, Inc., 1973).

Schumacher, E. F.: *Small is Beautiful* (New York: Harper & Row, Publishers, Incorporated, 1973).

Scientific American: *The Human Population* (San Francisco: W. H. Freeman and Company, 1974), particularly chaps. 1, 2, 6–11.

Thurow, Lester: "The Implications of Zero Economic Growth," *Challenge,* March–April 1977, pp. 36–43.

# LAST WORD
## Productivity and Jobs

Do workers lose their jobs as a consequence of becoming more productive?

One of the most significant sources of resistance to productivity improvement is the widespread association of the concept with the loss of jobs and unemployment. The question of labor displacement has troubled people since the early days of the machine age. A decade ago automation and the possibility of mass unemployment (which did not materialize) caused intense concern.

There is no doubt that automation, mechanization, or any advance which makes for higher labor productivity can wipe out jobs. The immediate effect of increases in output per man-hour is to reduce employment per unit of output. If output is unchanged and hours of work remain the same, this reduction in employment per unit makes for a reduction in the industry's aggregate employment. However, if output is increased, employment can remain the same or be expanded.

Important indirect effects of productivity increases can result in such output increases. A rise in an industry's productivity also presses down on the price of the industry's product. If productivity rises rapidly, reduction in production costs and in selling prices will follow. With demand responding to the reduction in price, output will rise and thus partially or wholly offset the effect of higher output per man-hour on employment. If demand is sufficiently responsive to the decline in price, the resulting rise in output could even exceed the rise in output per man-hour. The number of man-hours worked in the industry would then go up, not down.

The historical record shows that this event is not infrequent. In the long run, industries whose productivity has risen more rapidly than in the whole economy have often raised their employment by a larger percentage than industry generally, and not by a smaller percentage, as might be supposed. Correspondingly, industries whose productivity has seriously lagged, such as footwear, have often raised their employment less than industry generally or have actually cut employment.

Another important fact stands out in the historical records. While output per man-hour rose more rapidly after than before World War II, the rate of unemployment of the labor force as a whole averaged less after the war than before it. It is also noteworthy that Japan and many European countries have substantially lower rates of unemployment but faster rates of productivity increase.

National Commission on Productivity and Work Quality, *Annual Report* (Washington, 1975).

# Growth and the Underdeveloped Nations

chapter 21

It is exceedingly difficult for the typical American family, whose 1978 average income was $15,060, to grasp the hard fact that some two-thirds of the world's population persistently lives at, or perilously close to, the subsistence level. Ironically, most Americans are too preoccupied with problems associated with affluence—pollution, rapid urban growth, the monotony and alienation which often accompany employment in large-scale enterprises—to acknowledge the abject poverty which characterizes much of our planet. But, in fact, hunger, squalor, and disease prevail in most nations of the world.

## ☐ UNDERSTANDING UNDERDEVELOPMENT

The purposes of this chapter are to identify the underdeveloped nations, to understand why they are underdeveloped, and to discuss policies and strategies by which they might achieve more rapid growth.

## △ Low per Capita Income

The underdeveloped nations of the world bear a common brand: poverty—low per capita incomes as compared with such industrially advanced countries as the United States, Great Britain, and Canada. Table 21-1 identifies most of the underdeveloped nations. Of course, where one draws the line between "developed," "semideveloped," and "underdeveloped" is an arbitrary matter. Nevertheless, in Table 21-1 we can roughly envision these three classifications. Looking at the 1977 data, we might tag those nations with per capita incomes of $3000 or more as developed, or advanced, nations. Included here, primarily, are the United States, Canada, Australia, New Zealand, most countries of Western Europe, Japan, Israel, and the Soviet Union. We are also struck by the high incomes of some of the oil rich countries such as Kuwait, Saudi Arabia, and Libya, although these countries are not "developed" in the sense of being highly industrialized. Next is the semideveloped

**TABLE 21-1**

Per Capita GNP, 1977, and Average Annual Growth Rate, 1970-1977, for Countries With Populations of 1 Million or More

| Country | GNP per capita | | Country | GNP per capita | | Country | GNP per capita | |
|---|---|---|---|---|---|---|---|---|
| | Amount (US$), 1977 | Growth rate (%), 1970-77 | | Amount (US$), 1977 | Growth rate (%), 1970-77 | | Amount (US$), 1977 | Growth rate (%), 1970-77 |
| Kuwait | 12,690 | −0.9 | Chile | 1250 | −1.8 | Yemen, People's Dem. Rep. of | 350 | 11.2 |
| Switzerland | 11,080 | 0.1 | Panama | 1200 | −0.1 | Egypt, Arab Rep. of | 340 | 5.2 |
| Sweden | 9340 | 1.2 | China, Rep. of | 1180 | 5.5 | Sudan | 330 | 2.5 |
| Denmark | 9160 | 2.3 | Mexico | 1160 | 1.2 | Indonesia | 320 | 5.7 |
| United States | 8750 | 2.0 | Algeria | 1140 | 2.1 | Kenya | 290 | 0.9 |
| Germany, Fed. Rep. of | 8620 | 2.2 | Turkey | 1110 | 4.5 | Angola | 280 | −3.4 |
| Norway | 8570 | 3.9 | Jamaica | 1060 | −2.0 | Togo | 280 | 5.3 |
| Canada | 8350 | 3.4 | Korea, Rep. of | 980 | 7.6 | Mauritania | 270 | −0.1 |
| Belgium | 8280 | 3.5 | Malaysia | 970 | 4.9 | Lesotho | 250 | 9.9 |
| Netherlands | 7710 | 2.2 | Jordan | 940 | 6.5 | Central African Rep. | 240 | 0.9 |
| France | 7500 | 3.1 | Mongolia | 870 | 1.6 | Haiti | 230 | 2.1 |
| Australia | 7290 | 1.6 | Nicaragua | 870 | 2.5 | Madagascar | 230 | −2.7 |
| Saudi Arabia | 7230 | 13.0 | Syrian Arab Rep. | 860 | 6.1 | Afghanistan | 220 | 2.7 |
| Libya | 6520 | −4.5 | Dominican Republic | 840 | 4.6 | Benin | 210 | 0.5 |
| Japan | 6510 | 3.6 | Tunisia | 840 | 6.5 | Tanzania | 210 | 2.1 |
| Austria | 6450 | 3.8 | Guatemala | 830 | 3.3 | Zaire | 210 | −1.4 |
| Finland | 6190 | 2.8 | Ecuador | 820 | 6.1 | Guinea | 200 | 2.5 |
| German Dem. Rep. | 5070 | 4.9 | Ivory Coast | 770 | 1.1 | Pakistan | 200 | 0.8 |
| United Kingdom | 4540 | 1.6 | Colombia | 760 | 3.8 | Sierra Leone | 200 | −1.3 |
| New Zealand | 4480 | 0.9 | Cuba | 750 | −1.2 | Niger | 190 | −1.8 |
| Czechoslovakia | 4240 | 4.3 | Paraguay | 750 | 4.3 | India | 160 | 1.1 |
| Israel | 3760 | 2.0 | Peru | 720 | 1.8 | Rwanda | 160 | 1.3 |
| Italy | 3530 | 2.0 | Korea, Dem. People's Rep. of | 680 | 5.3 | Sri Lanka | 160 | 1.3 |
| USSR | 3330 | 4.4 | Albania | 660 | 4.1 | Malawi | 150 | 3.1 |
| Poland | 3290 | 6.3 | Morocco | 610 | 4.2 | Burma | 140 | 1.3 |
| Spain | 3260 | 3.6 | El Salvador | 590 | 2.1 | Mozambique | 140 | −4.3 |
| Hungary | 3100 | 5.1 | Nigeria | 510 | 4.4 | Upper Volta | 140 | 1.6 |
| Ireland | 3060 | 2.1 | Papua New Guinea | 510 | 2.5 | Burundi | 130 | 0.6 |
| Greece | 2950 | 4.0 | Yemen Arab Republic | 510 | n.a. | Chad | 130 | −1.0 |
| Bulgaria | 2830 | 5.7 | Congo, People's Rep. of the | 500 | 0.8 | Mali | 120 | 1.9 |
| Singapore | 2820 | 6.6 | Bolivia | 480 | 2.9 | Somalia | 120 | −1.1 |
| Venezuela | 2630 | 3.2 | Philippines | 460 | 3.7 | Ethiopia | 110 | 0.2 |
| Hong Kong | 2620 | 5.8 | Rhodesia | 460 | −0.1 | Nepal | 110 | 2.4 |
| Trinidad and Tobago | 2620 | 1.5 | Zambia | 460 | −0.2 | Bhutan | 90 | −0.3 |
| Puerto Rico | 2450 | 0.1 | Thailand | 430 | 4.1 | Lao People's Dem. Rep. | 90 | n.a. |
| Yugoslavia | 2100 | 5.1 | Cameroon | 420 | 1.0 | Bangladesh | 80 | −0.2 |
| Argentina | 1870 | 1.8 | Honduras | 420 | 0.0 | Iran | n.a. | n.a. |
| Portugal | 1840 | 3.1 | China, People's Rep. of | 410 | 4.5 | Lebanon | n.a. | n.a. |
| Iraq | 1570 | 7.1 | Liberia | 410 | 1.1 | Kampuchea, Dem. | n.a. | n.a. |
| Romania | 1530 | 9.9 | Senegal | 380 | 0.4 | Uganda | n.a. | n.a. |
| Uruguay | 1450 | 1.3 | Ghana | 370 | −2.0 | Viet Nam | n.a. | n.a. |
| Brazil | 1410 | 6.7 | | | | | | |
| South Africa | 1400 | 1.1 | | | | | | |
| Costa Rica | 1390 | 3.2 | | | | | | |

*Source:* World Bank, *World Bank Atlas,* 1979. Countries with populations of one million or more. GNP per capita rounded to nearest US $10.

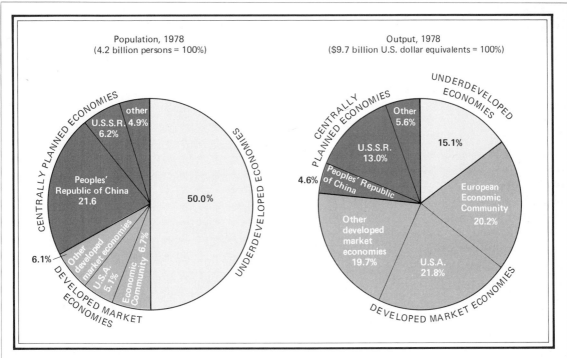

**FIGURE 21-1 GLOBAL POPULATION AND OUTPUT**

The industrially advanced nations produce about two-thirds of world output, although their population is only 18 percent of the total. In contrast the underdeveloped nations, with over half the world's population, generate only about one-eighth of global output. (*World Bank and CIA data*).

group, whose per capita incomes vary from, say, $1000 to $2999 per year. This heterogeneous group is largely composed of several Central and South American countries plus several more European nations. The rest of the world—including most of Asia, Africa, and Latin America—bear the designation "underdeveloped," or "less developed."

△   **Dimensions of Inequality**

The vast income disparities between the advanced and the underdeveloped countries are further dramatized in Figure 21-1. Here the world is divided into three groups of nations: (1) the industrially advanced market economies, dominated by the United States, the European Economic Community (the "Common Market"), and Japan; (2) the centrally planned economies, comprising mainly the Soviet Union, her satellites, and the People's Republic of China; and (3) the so-called *Third World* countries—the semideveloped and underdeveloped countries. Note that in 1978 the industrialized market economies, with less than 18 percent of the world population, generated about 62 percent of world output! Although the United States embodies about 6 percent of the world's population, it enjoyed about 22 percent of world output. The Third World, with about half the world's population, generated only about 15 percent of world output. The Indian subcontinent, with over 15 percent of the world's population, produced about 1 percent of the world's output.

Furthermore, a closer examination of Table 21-1 reveals very significant differences in the progress of the Third World nations. Some have achieved substantial growth of per capita GNP while many others—sometimes labeled Fourth World nations—have made minuscule progress or no progress at all. Whether or not a Third World nation achieves some degree of development depends upon a variety of factors including the presence of strategic raw materials, rates of population growth, foreign aid, and the degree of internal political stability. It is important to note that aggregated figures suggest that the income gap between rich and poor nations has been widening; in terms of per capita GNP the advanced nations as a group are growing at about 3.5 percent annually, while Third World nations are growing at 2.5 percent per year.

## △ Implications

But statistics both reveal and conceal. The human implications of the poverty which characterizes so much of our planet merits emphasis:[1]

> The poverty of underdeveloped countries means that their people, on a broad average, have a life expectancy only about half that of the people of the highly developed countries. They suffer much of the time from malaria, dysentery, tuberculosis, trachoma, or other ills. . . . Their food supply is about one-third less, measured in calories, than that of the developed countries, and when account is taken of the needs of the human body for the relatively expensive "protective" foods, such as milk and meat, the extent of malnutrition is found to be very great indeed. The opportunity to attend school is limited to a small minority. . . . Only one person in four or five, again on a broad average of underdeveloped countries, knows how to read or write. The supply of cloth for clothing, home furnishing, and other purposes is about one-fourth as great per person in underdeveloped as in highly developed

countries. Nonhuman energy to supplement the labor of human beings in industry, agriculture, transport, and household tasks is less than one-twentieth as plentiful, measured in horsepower-hours per person. Incomes, on the average, are less than one-tenth as high.

In Table 21-2 various socioeconomic indicators for selected Third World nations are contrasted with those for the United States and Japan. These data clearly verify the major points stressed in the above quotation.

## △ Viewpoint of Underdeveloped Nations

The bulk of the people in the underdeveloped nations are not resigned to their fate. Far from it. Most seek and feel they have a right to a better life. As they see it, poverty is not inescapable.

Two recent developments—one economic and the other political—have fanned the desire of the underdeveloped nations for material and social betterment:

**1** As noted, the per capita income gap between the economically advanced nations and the underdeveloped nations has not merely persisted, but has widened. Among nations, the rich have been getting richer and the poor have been getting relatively poorer.

This widening has intensified the discontent of the peoples of the underdeveloped countries. The "equation" for social unrest is no secret:

Aspirations − standard of living
$$= \text{social unrest}$$

As the living standards of the advanced nations have improved, the economic goals and aspirations of the underdeveloped nations have increased accordingly. But their actual standard of living in most instances has shown meager growth. The differential—social unrest—has clearly been on the increase. Witness the chronic political instability in many of the underdeveloped nations.

[1] Eugene Staley, *The Future of Underdeveloped Countries* (New York: Harper & Row, Publishers, Incorporated, for the Council on Foreign Relations, 1954), pp. 15–18.

**TABLE 21-2**
Selected Socioeconomic Indicators of Development

| Country | (1) Per capita GNP, 1977 | (2) Life expectancy at birth, 1977 | (3) Infant mortality per 1000 live births* | (4) Adult literacy rate, 1975 | (5) Daily per capita calorie supply, 1974 | (6) Per capita energy consumption, 1976† |
|---|---|---|---|---|---|---|
| United States | $8520 | 73 years | 18 | 99% | 3504 | 11,554 |
| Japan | 5670 | 76 | 26 | 99 | 2835 | 3679 |
| Brazil | 1360 | 62 | 94 | 76 | 2516 | 731 |
| Mauritania | 270 | 42 | 189 | 17 | 1663 | 102 |
| India | 150 | 51 | 139 | 36 | 1976 | 218 |
| Upper Volta | 130 | 42 | 182 | 5 | 1859 | 18 |
| Ethiopia | 110 | 39 | 181 | 10 | 1914 | 27 |
| Bangladesh | 90 | 47 | 132 | 22 | 2024 | 33 |

*Various years.
†Kilogram coal equivalent.
*Source: World Development Report, 1979.*

**2** It has been only since World War II that many of the underdeveloped lands have achieved political independence. Accompanying this freedom from colonial status has been a tremendous upsurge of nationalistic spirit. The less developed countries seek the economic independence, respect, and social status which they feel are due them as independent nations.

△ **Dubious Lessons of History**
It is disarmingly tempting for the advanced nations to offer less fortunate nations a simple formula for economic development: "Do what we did." Such a formula is glib, inaccurate, and, to the informed citizens of poor nations, insulting. The truth is that the now advanced nations initiated their development in an environment vastly different from that currently faced by the underdeveloped countries. Witness the favorable setting for American economic development: abundant and diverse mineral resources, opulent sources of power, navigable rivers, fertile and free farmland, a temperate climate, a small but energetic and (for that time) intelligent labor force, and finally, the virtual absence of social

and moral taboos on business and commerce. This is an environment ripe for economic growth. Throw these characteristics into reverse and you have the typical underdeveloped nation: a niggardly resource base, a lack of power, low-quality land, a teeming and untrained population, a tropical climate, and a host of fetishes narrowly circumscribing any existing spirit of enterprise. The more-or-less spontaneous growth arising from the favorable environs of the North American continent is not likely to blossom in such a briar patch.

□ **BREAKING THE POVERTY BARRIER**
The avenues of economic growth are essentially the same for both advanced and underdeveloped nations:

**1** Existing supplies of resources must be used more efficiently. This entails not only the elimination of unemployment but also the achievement of greater efficiency in the allocation of resources.

**2** The supplies of productive resources must be altered—typically, increased. By expanding the supplies of raw materials, capital equipment, effective manpower, and technological knowledge, a nation can push its production possibilities curve to the right (Chapter 19).

Why have some nations been so successful in pursuing these avenues of growth while other countries have lagged far behind? The answer, as noted above, lies in differences in the physical and sociocultural environments of the various nations. Our plan of attack is to examine the obstacles in the underdeveloped countries to altering the quantities and improving efficiency in the use of (1) natural resources, (2) human resources, (3) capital goods, and (4) technological knowledge. Emphasis here will be upon the private sector of the economy. In addition, social, institutional, and cultural impediments to growth will be illustrated. And finally, the roles of government and foreign aid in the development process will be analyzed.

△  **Natural Resources**

There is no simple generalization with respect to the role of natural resources in the economic development of Third World nations. This is true mainly because the distribution of natural resources among these nations is very uneven. Some underdeveloped nations encompass valuable deposits of bauxite, tin, copper, tungsten, nitrates, petroleum, and so forth. In a few instances the underdeveloped countries have been able to use their natural resource endowments to achieve rapid growth and a significant redistribution of income from the rich to the poor nations. The Organization of Petroleum Exporting Countries (OPEC), of course, is the outstanding example. On the other hand, we must recognize that in many cases natural resources are owned or controlled by the huge multinational corporations of the industrially advanced countries to the end that the economic benefits from these resources are largely diverted abroad. Other Third World nations simply lack mineral deposits, face a paucity of arable

land, and have few sources of power. It is important to note that the vast majority of the less developed countries are located in Central and South America, Africa, the Indian subcontinent, and Southeast Asia where tropical climates prevail. The hot, humid climate is not conducive to productive labor; crop and livestock diseases are widespread; and weed and insect infestations plague agriculture.

In a very real sense a weak resource base can pose a particularly serious obstacle to growth. Real capital can be accumulated and the quality of the labor force can be improved through education and training. But the natural resource base is largely unaugmentable. Hence, it is unrealistic for many of the underdeveloped nations to envision an economic destiny comparable with that of the United States, Canada, or the Soviet Union. Automated steel, automobile, and aluminum plants are not a part of their foreseeable economic futures. But, again, we must be careful in generalizing: Switzerland, Israel, and Japan, for example, have achieved relatively high levels of living *despite* restrictive natural resource bases.

△  **Employment of Human Resources**

Three statements describe the typical underdeveloped nation's circumstances with respect to human resources:

1  It is overpopulated.
2  Underemployment is widespread.
3  The quality of the labor force is exceedingly low.

**Overpopulation**  Figure 21-1 suggests that many of the nations with the most meager natural and capital resources have the largest populations to support. Table 21-3 compares population densities and population growth rates of a few selected nations with those of the United States and the world as a whole. Most important for the long run is the vivid contrast of population growth rates: In the past twenty years the underdeveloped nations have experienced about a 2.5 percent annual increase in

**TABLE 21-3**
**Population Statistics for Selected Countries**

| Country | Population per square kilometer, 1977 | Annual rate of population increase, 1970–1977 |
|---|---|---|
| United States | 23 | 0.8% |
| Hong Kong | 4320 | 2.0 |
| Bangladesh | 559 | 2.5 |
| Sri Lanka | 213 | 1.7 |
| India | 190 | 2.1 |
| Haiti | 171 | 1.7 |
| Kenya | 25 | 3.8 |
| Philippines | 150 | 2.7 |
| World | 30 | 1.9 |

Source: United Nations, *Demographic Yearbook, 1977.*

population as compared with a 0.7 percent annual rate for the advanced countries. Recalling the "rule of 70," the current rate suggests that the Third World's total population will double in about 28 years! These simple statistics are a significant reason why the per capita income gap between underdeveloped and advanced nations has tended to widen. In some of the underdeveloped countries, the Malthusian population doctrine, rooted in the law of diminishing returns, is all too apparent. Population actually presses upon the food supply to the extent that per capita food consumption is pulled down perilously close to the subsistence level. In the worst instances, it is only the despicable team of malnutrition and disease and the high death rate they engender which keeps incomes near subsistence.

It would seem at first glance that, since

Per capita standard of living

$$= \frac{\text{consumer goods (food) production}}{\text{population}}$$

the standard of living could be raised merely by boosting consumer goods—particularly food—production. But in reality the problem is much more complex than this, because any increase in consumer goods production which initially raises the standard of living is likely to

induce a population increase. This increase, if sufficient in size, will dissipate the improvement in living standards, and subsistence living levels will again prevail.

But why does population growth tend to accompany increases in output? First, the nation's *death* or *mortality rate* will decline with initial increases in production. This decline is the result of (1) a higher level of per capita food consumption, and (2) the basic medical and sanitation programs which almost invariably accompany the initial phases of economic development. Second, the *birthrate* will remain high or may even increase, particularly so as the medical and sanitation programs cut the rate of infant mortality. The cliché that "the rich get richer and the poor get children" is uncomfortably accurate for many of the underdeveloped nations of the world. In short, an increase in the per capita standard of living may give rise to a population upsurge which will cease only when the standard of living has again been reduced to the level of bare subsistence.

In addition to the fact that rapid population growth can translate an expanding GNP into a stagnant or slow-growing GNP per capita, there are less obvious reasons why population expansion is an obstacle to development. On the one hand, large families reduce the capacity of households to save, and this inability restricts the economy's capacity to accumulate capital. On the other hand, high birthrates result in a larger proportion of children in the population or, in other words, a smaller productive work force relative to total population.

Most authorities advocate birth control as the obvious and most effective means for breaking out of this dilemma. And breakthroughs in contraceptive technology in the past three decades have made this solution increasingly relevant. But the obstacles to population control are great. Low literacy rates make it difficult to disseminate information on the use of contraceptive devices. In peasant agriculture, large families are a major source of labor. Furthermore, adults may look upon having many children as a kind of informal social security system; the more children one has, the greater the probability of having a relative to care for one during old age. Finally, many nations which stand to gain the most through birth control are often the least willing, for religious and sociocultural reasons, to embrace contraception programs. Population growth in Latin America, for example, is among the most rapid in the world.

*Caution:* Not all underdeveloped nations suffer from overpopulation, nor may one conclude that a large population necessarily means underdevelopment. The points to note are: (1) A large and rapidly growing population may pose a special obstacle to economic development; and (2) many of the underdeveloped and semideveloped nations are so burdened.[2]

**Unemployment**　Aside from the drag of overpopulation, the underdeveloped countries are faced with serious unemployment problems. In contrast to the unemployment in advanced nations, the problem is not so much cyclical fluctuations—most underdeveloped nations are too poor to afford a business cycle!—but rather, a chronic and large-scale overallocation of labor to agriculture.

How has this problem of disguised unemployment come about? The predominance of agriculture is common to virtually all the underdeveloped nations. It is very likely that two-thirds, four-fifths, or more of an underdeveloped nation's labor force are engaged in agricultural pursuits. Much—possibly 25 to 30 percent—of this farm labor is underemployed,

or surplus, labor,[3] that is, labor which contributes little or nothing to total agricultural output. In Chapter 19's discussion of the principle of diminishing returns, the agricultural "plant" (the fixed supply of arable land) of most underdeveloped nations is grossly overstaffed, to the extent that one-fourth or one-third of the nation's agricultural labor force contributes little or nothing to total output! This means that a large fraction of an underdeveloped nation's labor force might be reallocated from agricultural to industrial pursuits with little or no decline, and possibly an increase, in food production.

But the opportunity for such productivity-increasing reallocation of labor has not been realized in most countries. It is true that rural population pressures have often caused substantial migrations to the cities. However, the lack of industrial growth means that relatively few jobs are available in urban areas. And, even when jobs are available, the transplanted workers frequently do not possess the minimum levels of training and education to qualify for the jobs. Hence, unemployment is often extremely high in the seemingly endless slums which surround the cities of the underdeveloped countries.

**Quality of the Labor Force**　Though long on numbers, the populations of the underdeveloped nations are pitifully short on quality. Poor countries have simply not been able to invest sufficiently in their human capital (Table 21-2, columns 4 and 5); that is, expenditures on health and education have been meager. Low levels of literacy, malnutrition, the absence of proper medical care, and insufficient educational facilities all contribute to populations ill equipped for economic development and industrialization. Particularly vital is the absence of a vigorous entrepreneurial class willing to bear risks, accumulate capital, and provide the organizational requisites essential to economic growth. Closely related is the dearth of labor that is prepared to handle the

---

[2]The interested reader should consult Clifford M. Hardin (ed.), *Overcoming World Hunger* (Englewood Cliffs, N.J.: Prentice-Hall, Inc., 1969), and The Editors of Scientific American, *The Human Population* (San Francisco: W. H. Freeman and Company, 1974), particularly chaps. 1, 2, 9, and 10.
[3]See Ragnar Nurkse, *Problem of Capital Formation in Underdeveloped Countries* (Fair Lawn, N.J.: Oxford University Press, 1967), p. 35.

routine supervisory functions basic to any program of development.

△  **Capital Accumulation**

Most economists feel that an important focal point of economic development is the accumulation of capital goods. There are several reasons for this emphasis upon capital formation:

**1**  All underdeveloped countries do suffer from a critical shortage of capital goods—factories, machinery and equipment, public utilities, and so forth. There can be no doubt that better-equipped labor forces would greatly enhance the productivity of the underdeveloped nations and help to boost the per capita standard of living.

**2**  Increasing the stock of capital goods is crucial because of the very limited possibility of increasing the supply of arable land. If there is little likelihood of offsetting the law of diminishing returns in agriculture by increasing the supply of land, the obvious alternative is to counter its operation by better equipping the available agricultural work force or by providing industrial capital to which this labor can be reallocated. In terms of Figure 19-4, the accumulation of capital may permit a nation to achieve the $A_1B_2C_3D_4$ path to development as opposed to following the $A_1B_1C_1D_1$ route to stagnation.

**3**  Once initiated, the process of capital accumulation can be cumulative. If capital accumulation can increase output ahead of population growth, a margin of saving may arise which permits further capital formation. In a sense, capital accumulation can feed upon itself.

Let us first consider the prospects for underdeveloped nations to accumulate capital domestically. Then we shall examine the possibility of foreign capital flowing into them. In each of these cases we are concerned with private capital; public investment will be considered later.

**Domestic Capital Formation**  How does an underdeveloped nation—or any nation for that matter—accumulate capital? The answer: through the processes of saving and investing. A nation must save, that is, refrain from consumption, to release resources from consumer goods production. Investment spending must then occur to absorb these released resources in the production of capital goods. But the impediments to saving and investing are much greater in a low-income nation than in an advanced economy.

*The savings potential*  Consider first the savings side of the picture. The savings potential of the underdeveloped countries is low. Statistics indicate that they manage to save at best some 5 percent of their national incomes, whereas the advanced nations save 10 percent or more. In explaining this point, it is important to distinguish between (1) the masses of people, who are unable or unwilling to save, and (2) the very wealthy, who can save, but who do not make their savings available for the accumulation of productive capital goods.

**1**  Saving is a luxury far beyond the reach of the masses of people in the underdeveloped nations; most consume their entire incomes to keep body and soul intact. Incomes are just too low to permit the masses to save. But this is only half the picture. There is serious doubt as to whether significant increases in per capita incomes would generate much saving. Most experts agree that the propensities of underdeveloped nations to consume—that is, their willingness to spend—depend not only upon their own levels of income but also upon the relationship of their income levels to those of the advanced nations. Better communications, increased literacy, expanding hordes of affluent tourists, and, in some instances, the presence of foreign troops have made the peoples of the underdeveloped nations increasingly aware of the superior consumption levels of the advanced nations. This whets the appetites of the poverty-ridden and intensifies their dissatisfaction with their own standard of living.

New wants and higher aspirations lead to a high propensity to consume.[4] The peoples of the underdeveloped nations, in short, are most eager to consume, not save, any forthcoming increases in their national incomes.

**2**   This is not to say that no one saves in an underdeveloped nation. We have noted that saving might be as high as 5 percent of the national income. This saving stems from the highly unequal distribution of income which characterizes most of the underdeveloped nations. Ironically, both the poorest and the richest families of the world reside in the least developed countries. Those fortunate few with astronomical incomes—the tribal chieftains, the kings, the large landowners, the oil-rich sheiks, and the political leaders—do have ample capacity to save. Unfortunately, these high-income receivers frequently dispense their wealth on luxury goods, trivialities, foreign travel, the hoarding of precious metals, or the purchase of existing properties in the form of land or urban real estate. The monetary saving which does occur often flows abroad for safekeeping or to take advantage of the more convenient saving outlets provided by the securities markets of the advanced nations. The important point is that those few who have the ability to save are often unwilling to do so or, if they are willing, do not make their savings available domestically for investment in productive facilities.

**Investment obstacles**   The investment side of the capital formation process abounds with equally serious obstacles. These obstacles undermine the rate of capital formation even when a sufficient volume of savings is available to finance the needed investment. *The major obstacles to investment fall into two categories: the lack of investors and the lack of incentives to invest.*

Oddly enough, in some underdeveloped countries—Turkey and Pakistan, for example—the major obstacle to investment is basically the lack of business executives who are willing to assume the risks associated with investment. This, of course, is a special case of qualitative deficiencies of the labor force previously discussed.

But even if substantial savings and a vigorous entrepreneurial class are present, an essential ingredient in capital formation—the incentive to invest—may be weak. And clearly a host of factors may combine in an underdeveloped nation to cripple investment incentives. Political and social instability—in particular, the fear of nationalization of industry—may dampen the incentive to invest. Similarly, very low incomes mean a limited domestic market—a lack of demand—for most nonagricultural goods. This factor is especially crucial when one recognizes that the chances of successfully competing with the mature industries of the advanced nations in international markets are meager. Then, too, the previously cited lack of trained administrative and operating personnel may be a vital factor in retarding investment. Finally, many of the underdeveloped countries simply do not have a sufficient accumulation of the *basic social capital,* that is, the public utilities, which is prerequisite to private investment of a productive nature. Poor roads, inadequate railways, little gas and electricity production, antiquated communications, unsatisfactory housing, and meager educational and public health facilities scarcely provide an inviting environment for investment spending.

The absence of basic social capital presents more of a problem than one might first surmise. The dearth of social capital means that a great deal of investment spending which does not *directly* result in the production of goods and which may not be capable of bearing profits must take place prior to, and simultaneously with, productive investment in manufacturing machinery and equipment. Statistics for the advanced nations indicate that about 60 percent of gross investment goes for housing, public works, and public utilities, leaving about 40 percent for directly productive investment in manufacturing, agriculture, and

[4] Ibid., p. 58.

commerce.[5] These figures probably understate the percentage of total investment which must be devoted to social capital in the emerging nations. The volume of investment required to initiate economic development may be much greater than it first appears.

There is one potential bright spot in this otherwise dismal picture: the possibility of accumulating capital through *nonfinancial* or *in-kind investment*. Given the prerequisite leadership and willingness to cooperate, capital can be accumulated by transferring surplus agricultural labor to the improvement of agricultural facilities or to the construction of basic social capital. If each agricultural village would allocate its surplus labor to the construction of irrigation canals, wells, schools, sanitary facilities, and roads, significant amounts of capital might be accumulated at no sacrifice of consumer goods production. Nonfinancial investment simply bypasses the problems embodied within the financial aspects of the capital accumulation process. Such investment does not require consumers to save portions of their money income, nor does it presume the presence of an entrepreneurial class anxious to invest. In short, provided the leadership and cooperative spirit are present, nonfinancial investment is a promising avenue for the accumulation of basic capital goods.

△  **Technological Advance**

Technological advance and capital formation are frequently part of the same process. Yet, there are advantages in treating technological advance, or the accumulation and application of new ideas concerning methods of producing, and capital formation, or the accumulating of capital goods, as separate processes.

This is particularly so in discussing the underdeveloped countries. We view technological advance in the industrially advanced na-

tions as an essentially evolutionary process wherein researchers first inch forward the boundaries of technological knowledge. Then follow the financing and construction of the ever larger amounts of complex capital equipment which the technological advance demands. But this picture is not accurate for the less developed countries. The rudimentary state of their current technology puts these nations far from the frontiers of technological advance. There already exists an enormous body of technological knowledge accumulated by the advanced nations which the underdeveloped countries might adopt and apply without undertaking the expensive task of research. For example, the adoption of modern crop-rotation practices and the introduction of contour plowing require no additional capital equipment, and they may contribute very significantly to productivity. By raising grain storage bins a few inches above the ground, a large amount of grain spoilage can be avoided. Such changes may sound minor to people of advanced nations. However, the resulting gains in productivity can mean the difference between subsistence and starvation in some poverty-ridden nations.

In most instances the application of either existing or new technological knowledge entails the use of new and different capital goods. But, within limits, this capital can be obtained without an increase in the rate of capital formation. That is, if the annual flow of replacement investment is rechanneled from technologically inferior to technologically superior capital equipment, productivity can be increased out of a constant level of investment spending. Actually, some technological advances may be *capital-saving* rather than *capital-using*. A new fertilizer, better adapted to a nation's topography and climate, might be cheaper than that currently employed. A seemingly high-priced metal plow which will last ten years may be cheaper in the long run than an inexpensive but technologically inferior wooden plow which requires annual replacement.

[5]W. Arthur Lewis, *The Theory of Economic Growth* (Homewood, Ill.: Richard D. Irwin, Inc., 1955), p. 210.

All this is not to deny that, before a nation's development program is far along, further technological process will call for an expanding flow of investment in capital goods. However, even here we must keep in mind that the productivity increases which the most fundamental technological advances permit may provide an increase in the standard of living sufficient to generate a part of the saving prerequisite to meeting the nation's expanding capital goods requirements. By boosting incomes, technological advances may provide for the capital accumulation upon which still further technological progress depends. To a degree, technological advance and capital formation may feed upon one another.

### △  Sociocultural and Institutional Factors

Purely economic considerations are not sufficient to explain the occurrence or the absence of economic growth. Massive social and institutional readjustments are usually an integral part of the growth process. Economic development entails not only changes in a nation's physical environment (that is, new transportation and communications facilities, new schools, new housing, new plants and equipment), but also drastic changes in the ways in which people think, behave, and associate with one another. Emancipation from custom and tradition is frequently the fundamental prerequisite of economic development. Possibly the most crucial but least tangible ingredient in economic development is *the will to develop.* Economic growth may hinge upon "what individuals and social groups *want,* and *whether they want it badly enough to change their old ways of doing things* and to work hard at installing the new."[6]

Sociocultural impediments to growth are numerous and varied. Consider a few examples.

1  Some of the least developed countries have failed to achieve the preconditions for a national economic unit. Tribal allegiances take precedence over national identity. Warring tribes confine all economic activity within the tribe, eliminating any possibility for production-increasing specialization and trade.

2  Religious beliefs and observances may seriously restrict the length of the work day and divert resources which might otherwise have been used for investment to ceremonial uses. In rural India, for example, total ceremonial expenditures are estimated at about 7 percent of per capita income.[7] More generally, religious and philosophical beliefs may be dominated by the *capricious universe view,* that is, the notion that there is little or no correlation between an individual's activities and endeavors, on the one hand, and the outcomes or experiences which that person encounters, on the other.

> If the universe is deemed capricious, the individual will learn to expect little or no correlation between actions and results. This will result in a fatalistic attitude. . . .
>
> These attitudes impinge on all activities including saving, investment, long-range perspective, supply of effort, and family planning. If a higher standard of living and amassing of wealth is treated as the result of providence rather than springing from hard work and saving, there is little rationale for saving, hard work, innovations, and enterprise.[8]

3  The existence of a caste system—formal or informal—causes labor to be allocated to occupations on the basis of caste or tradition rather than on the basis of skill or merit.

Consider now some growth obstacles of an institutional character. Political corruption and bribery are commonplace in many Third World nations. School systems and public service agencies are often ineptly administered

[6] Staley, op. cit., p. 218.

[7] Inder P. Nijhawan, "Socio-Political Institutions, Cultural Values, and Attitudes: Their Impact on Indian Economic Development," in J. S. Uppal (ed.), *India's Economic Problems* (New Delhi: Tata McGraw-Hill Publishing Company, Ltd., 1975), p. 31.

[8] Ibid., p. 33.

and their functioning impaired by petty politics. Tax systems are frequently arbitrary, unjust, cumbersome, and detrimental to incentives to work and invest. Political decisions are often motivated by the desire to enhance the nation's international prestige, rather than to foster development. For example, India's explosion of a nuclear bomb in 1974 (Last Word section of Chapter 2) created a substantial controversy over societal priorities.

Because of the predominance of farming in the underdeveloped nations, the problem of achieving that institutional environment in agriculture which is most conducive to increasing production must be a vital consideration in any growth program. More specifically, the institutional problem of *land reform* demands attention in virtually all underdeveloped nations. But the needed reform may vary tremendously between specific nations. In some underdeveloped countries the problem assumes the form of excessive concentration of land ownership in the hands of a few wealthy families. This situation is demoralizing for the tenants, weakening their incentive to produce, and is typically not conducive to capital improvements. At the other extreme is the absurd arrangement whereby each and every

family owns and farms a minute fragment of land far too small for the application of modern agricultural technology. An important complication to the problem of land reform lies in the fact that political considerations often push reform in that direction which is least defensible on economic grounds. For many nations, land reform may well be the most acute institutional problem to be resolved in initiating the process of economic development.

☐   THE VICIOUS CIRCLE:
A SUMMING UP

It is important to recognize that many of the characteristics of the underdeveloped countries just described are simultaneously causes and consequences of their poverty. These countries are caught in a vicious circle: They are poor because they are poor! Consider Figure 21-2. The fundamental feature of an underdeveloped nation is low per capita income. Being poor, a family has little ability or incentive to save. Furthermore, low incomes mean low levels of demand. As a result, there are few available resources, on the one hand, and no strong incentives, on the other, for investment in real or

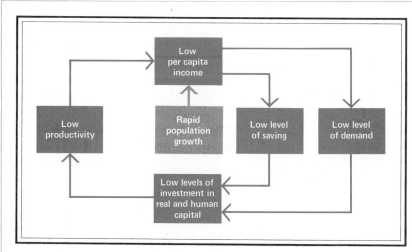

FIGURE 21-2  THE VICIOUS CIRCLE OF UNDERDEVELOPMENT

Low per capita incomes make it extremely difficult for poor nations to save and invest, a condition that perpetuates low productivity and low incomes. Furthermore, rapid population growth may quickly absorb increases in per capita real income and thereby may negate the possibility of breaking out of the underdevelopment circle.

human capital. This means that labor productivity is low. And, since output per person is real income per person, it follows that per capita income is low.

Many experts feel that the key to breaking out of this vicious circle is to increase the rate of capital accumulation, that is, to achieve a level of investment of, say, 12 percent of the national income. But Figure 21-2 reminds us that the real villain for many underdeveloped nations—rapid population growth—may be waiting in the wings to undo the potentially beneficial effects of this higher rate of capital accumulation. Recall our macro growth model based upon Table 19-2. Suppose an underdeveloped country manages to increase its average propensity to save to 12 percent, and that all this saving is absorbed as investment in real capital. Now, if we assume, not unrealistically, that the capital-output ratio is, say, 4, then real output will rise by 3 percent per year.[9] Given a stable population, real income per person will also rise by 3 percent per year. If this per capita growth rate persists, the standard of living will *double* in about twenty-three years. But what if population grows at, say, the Latin American rate of about 3 percent per year? Then real income per person is unchanged and the vicious circle persists!

More optimistically, *if* population can be kept constant or constrained to some growth rate significantly below 3 percent, then real income per person will rise. And this implies the possibility of still further enlargement in the flows of saving and investment, continued advances in productivity, and the continued growth of per capita real income. In short, if a process of self-sustaining expansion of income, saving, investment, and productivity can be achieved, the self-perpetuating vicious circle of poverty can be transformed into a self-regen-

erating, beneficent circle of economic progress. The trick, obviously, is to make effective those policies and strategies which will accomplish this transition.

## ☐ CRUCIAL ROLE FOR GOVERNMENT

Economists agree that, at least during the initial stages of growth, government can be expected to play a major role. The reasons for this stem from the character of the obstacles facing these nations.

**1   Law and Order**   Some of the poorest countries are plagued by widespread banditry and intertribal warfare which divert both attention and resources from the task of development. A strong and stable national government is needed to establish domestic law and order and to achieve peace and unity.

**2   Lack of Entrepreneurship**   The absence of a sizable and vigorous entrepreneurial class, ready and willing to accumulate capital and initiate production, indicates that in many cases private enterprise is intrinsically not capable of spearheading the growth process.

**3   Public Goods**   Many of the basic obstacles to economic growth center upon deficiencies of public goods and services. Sanitation and basic medical programs, education, irrigation and soil conservation projects, and the construction of highways and transportation-communication facilities are all essentially nonmarketable goods and services yielding widespread spillover benefits. Government is the sole institution in a position to provide these goods and services in required quantities.

**4   Forced Saving and Investment**   Government action may also be required to break through the saving-investment dilemma which impedes capital formation in the underdeveloped nations. We have noted that when the ability to save does exist, the desire to emulate

---

[9] Recall from Chapter 19 that:

$$\text{Growth rate} = \frac{\text{average propensity to save}}{\text{capital-output ratio}}$$

Hence, in this case, $.12/4 = .03$, or 3 percent.

the consumption standards of the advanced nations may make an underdeveloped nation's citizenry unwilling to save. And, when an entrepreneurial class exists, the deficiency of domestic markets and the temptation to invest in the advanced nations may similarly slow capital formation.

It may well be that only governmental fiscal action can provide a solution by forcing the economy to accumulate capital. The alternatives here are essentially twofold. One is to force the economy to save by increasing taxes. These tax revenues can then be channeled into top-priority investment projects. The problems of honestly and efficiently administering the tax system and achieving a relatively high degree of compliance with tax laws are frequently very great.

The other alternative is to force the economy to save through inflation; that is, the government can finance capital accumulation by creating and spending new money or by selling bonds to banks and spending the proceeds. The resulting inflation, you will recall, is the equivalent of an arbitrary tax upon the economy. There are serious arguments against the advisability of saving through inflation. In the first place, inflation tends to distort the composition of investment away from productive facilities to such items as luxury housing, precious metals and jewels, or foreign securities, which provide a better hedge against rising prices. Furthermore, significant inflation may reduce voluntary saving as potential savers become less willing to accumulate depreciating money or securities payable in money of declining value. Internationally, inflation may boost the nation's imports and retard its flow of exports, creating balance of payments difficulties.

**5   Social-Institutional Problems**   Government is obviously in the key position to deal effectively with the social-institutional obstacles to growth. Population growth and land reform are basic problems which call for the broad approach that only government can provide. And government is in an advantageous position to stimulate the will to develop, to change a philosophy of "Heaven and faith will determine the course of events" to one of "God helps those who help themselves."

But all this must not blind us to certain potential problems and disadvantages which a governmentally directed development program may entail. If entrepreneurial talent is lacking in the private sector, can we expect leaders of quality to be present in the ranks of government? Is there not a real danger that government bureaucracy, not to mention outright maladministration and corruption, will prove an impediment, not a stimulus, to much-needed social and economic change? And, too, what of the tendency of centralized economic planning to favor the spectacular "showpiece" projects at the expense of less showy but more productive programs? Might not political objectives take precedence over the economic goals of a governmentally directed development program?

It must also be emphasized strongly that we are not here advocating socialism or communism as the most likely path to opulence. The point is that government might well be obligated by the environmental characteristics of an underdeveloped country to provide the incentive and the means of *initially* breaking the poverty barrier. With economic growth there may evolve a price system, an entrepreneurial class, and all the institutions and attitudes prerequisite to a strong private economy. Government may then relinquish its key role, assured that the private sector of the economy is capable of sustaining the growth process.

□ **ROLE OF THE ADVANCED NATIONS**

What are the ways by which the advanced nations can help the less developed countries in their quest for growth? To what degree have these avenues of assistance been pursued?

Generally speaking, underdeveloped nations can benefit from (1) an expanding volume of trade with advanced nations; (2) flows of private capital from the more affluent nations; and (3) foreign aid, that is, grants and loans from the governments of advanced nations. Let us consider these possibilities in the order stated.

△   **Expanding Trade**

Some authorities maintain that the simplest and most effective means by which the United States and other advanced nations can aid the underdeveloped nations is by lowering international trade barriers, thereby enabling Third World nations to expand their national incomes through an increased volume of trade.

Though there is undoubtedly some truth in this view, lowered trade barriers are not a panacea. It is true that some Third World nations need only large foreign markets for their raw materials to achieve growth. But the problem for most of the developing nations is not that of obtaining markets for the utilization of existing productive capacity or the sale of relatively abundant raw materials, but rather, the more fundamental one of getting the capital and technical assistance needed to produce something for export!

Furthermore, it must be recognized that close trade ties with advanced nations is not without disadvantages. The old quip, "When Uncle Sam gets his feet wet, the rest of the world gets pneumonia," contains considerable truth for many less developed nations. In particular, a recession in the First World can have disastrous consequences for the prices of raw materials and the export earnings of Third World nations. For example, in mid–1974 the price of copper was $1.52 per pound; by the end of 1975 it had fallen to $.53 per pound! Stability and growth in the industrially advanced nations are clearly important to progress in the underdeveloped countries.

△   **Private Capital Flows**

Our vicious circle of underdevelopment emphasizes the importance of capital accumu-

lation in achieving economic growth. Foreign capital—both private and public—can obviously supplement an emerging country's saving and investment efforts and play a crucial role in breaking the circle of underdevelopment.

The underdeveloped countries have in fact received substantial flows of private capital from the advanced nations. In the 1960s these flows amounted to $3 or $4 billion per year. Inspired undoubtedly by an intensified search for oil, private flows grew dramatically in the 1970s. The figure for 1977 was about $26 billion.

The advanced nations and their huge multinational corporations contend that the flow of private capital would be much larger if conditions in the Third World nations were more receptive. That is, in addition to all the previously mentioned deterrents to domestic capital accumulation in the poor nations, there are special obstacles to foreign investment. For example, foreign capital is often subject to (1) discriminatory taxation, (2) limitations or prohibitions upon the withdrawal of profits, (3) cumbersome governmental regulations and red tape, and (4) the ever-present danger of nationalization without compensation.

△   **Foreign Aid: Public Loans and Grants**

Many obstacles to economic development cannot be overcome by private capital alone. In particular, most of the underdeveloped nations are sadly lacking in the basic social capital—irrigation and public health programs and educational, transportation, and communications systems—prerequisite to the attraction of either domestic or foreign private capital. Foreign public aid is needed to tear down this major roadblock to the flow of private capital to the underdeveloped countries.

**Direct Aid**   The United States has assisted the underdeveloped nations directly through a variety of programs and through participation in international institutions designed to stimulate economic development. Over the past decade, American economic aid—including both loans and grants—has averaged $4 to $5 billion per year. The bulk of this aid is administered by our Agency for International Development (AID). A significant amount, however, takes the form of grants of surplus food under the Food for Peace program. Other advanced nations have also embarked upon substantial foreign aid programs. In 1977 foreign aid from all noncommunist nations was about $20 billion.

**The World Bank Group** The United States is a major participant in the World Bank, the major objective of which is to assist underdeveloped nations in achieving growth. Supported by some 134 member nations, the World Bank not only lends out of its capital funds, but also (1) sells bonds and lends the proceeds, and (2) guarantees and insures private loans.

Several characteristics of the World Bank merit comment.

**1** The World Bank is in a sense a "last resort" lending agency; that is, its loans are limited to productive projects for which private funds are not readily available.

**2** Because many World Bank loans have been for basic development projects—multipurpose dams, irrigation projects, health and sanitation programs, communications and transportation facilities—it has been hoped that the Bank's activities will provide the basic social capital prerequisite to substantial flows of private capital.

**3** The Bank has played a significant role in providing technical assistance to underdeveloped nations by helping them discover what avenues of growth seem most appropriate for their economic development.

In recent years two World Bank affiliates have come into existence, functioning in areas where the World Bank has been weak. The International Finance Corporation (IFC) has the primary function of investing in *private* enterprises in underdeveloped nations. The International Development Association (IDA) makes "soft loans"—that is, loans which may not be self-liquidating—to the very poorest of the underdeveloped countries on more liberal terms than does the World Bank.

## ☐ NEOCOLONIALISM?

Despite these flows of private investment and foreign aid, the Third World nations are far from content with their relationships vis-à-vis the industrially advanced nations. The feeling is widespread among Third World nations that their economies are being dominated by the business interests of the United States and Europe. The advanced nations, it is argued, are not genuinely interested in the economic progress of the Third World, but rather in exploiting the natural resources, the raw materials, the cheap labor, and the markets which exist there. Many of the underdeveloped nations have emerged from colonial status only since World War II. Despite political independence, they feel that an economically based *neocolonialism* persists. Both private investment and public aid, it is contended, have tended to exploit the Third World economies and keep them dependent upon, and subservient to, the rich nations.

### △ Dependence

Consider private capital flows. Underdeveloped countries seek to make their economies more diversified. They want to develop home markets on the one hand, and to reduce their dependence upon world markets and the economic well-being of the advanced nations on the other. Foreign private capital, however, seeks out those industries which are currently the most profitable, that is, the ones which are now producing for the export market. In brief, while the underdeveloped nations strive for less dependence on world markets, flows of foreign private capital often tend to enhance that dependence. Exxon, Alcoa, United Fruit, British Shell, and the rest are after profits and they allegedly have no particular interest in the overall progress of the less developed countries. Indeed, progress in the form of industrialization might in time mean unwanted competition in world markets.

### △ Aid: How Effective?

Third World nations are skeptical of foreign aid on several grounds.

**1  Amount**  The Third World countries argue that the flow of foreign aid has been grossly inadequate. True, on the surface the United States' $6 billion of aid in 1978 seems like an impressive amount. But in fact it is only one-fourth of 1 percent of its GNP! In comparative terms, at least, one cannot say that American economic aid to the underdeveloped nations has been extravagant. As one authority has put it,[10]

> There is practically no danger that the United States government will spend more than our national interest requires on economic aid to underdeveloped countries. The danger is all the other way. Underdeveloped countries are not represented in Congress where the appropriation logs are rolled, and the compelling American interest in the advancement of the underdeveloped parts of the free world is less easy for statesmen to explain than for narrowmindedness and shortsightedness to obscure.

**2  Effectiveness**  Several factors diminish the effectiveness of foreign aid. (1) Much aid is "tied" to the granting or lending country; for example, "tied" American loans and grants must be spent by the recipient nation upon American goods and services. This means that underdeveloped nations are denied the opportunity to "shop around" in world markets for potentially better buys on capital goods and technological assistance. (2) Inflation in the United States and other aid-giving countries

has acted to erode the real value of aid dollars to recipient nations. (3) The current foreign debt of the Third World is on the order of $260 billion. Hence, a large portion of the foreign aid received by many underdeveloped countries must go to pay interest on outstanding debt, rather than to finance development.

**3  Politics**  A third complaint is that the size and the direction of foreign aid are strongly influenced by the national interests of the donor country, rather than based upon need or the prospects for development. The United States, for example, is continuously redirecting its aid to promote its political, military, and economic interests overseas. At best, aid is viewed as a device for sustaining pro-American and pro-capitalistic governments, even though those governments may be undemocratic, unprogressive, and unpopular. At worst, aid is held to be part of a larger overall imperialistic strategy which encompasses political-military pressure, far-flung military bases, "imperialistic wars," and the clandestine subversion of revolutionary movements which might lead to the establishment of "unfriendly" political regimes.[11]

### ☐ THE FUTURE

What next? What will be the fate of the Third World nations over, say, the remainder of this century and beyond? Will substantial progress be made? Or, with perhaps a few exceptions, will stagnation and poverty prevail? Obviously, the forecasts required to respond to these questions cannot be made with any reasonable degree of certainty. Yet a number of intriguing and plausible scenarios have been offered.

### △ Progress

The most optimistic view is this: In the past decade or so the overall growth of the

---

[10]Staley, op cit., p. 372. For a highly critical view of foreign aid see C. R. Hensman, *Rich Against Poor: The Reality of Aid* (Baltimore, Md.: Penguin Books, Inc., 1971).

[11]The section entitled "Imperialism" in Chap. 40 expands upon these arguments.

GNPs of the Third World nations has been on the order of 5 or 6 percent, quite comparable to many of the more advanced nations. Given important breakthroughs in birth-control technology and a rapidly expanding awareness of the need to control populations, this growth of GNP will be translated into an improving standard of living. Furthermore, the potentialities of the "Green Revolution," that is, the important technological breakthroughs in agriculture which have created new high-yield strains of rice and wheat, may be realized on an expanded scale to resolve basic food and nutritional problems within the foreseeable future.

## △   Forced Redistribution

Another scenario envisions the Third World improving its economic status through the exercise of greater economic muscle in its relationships with the advanced countries. Inspired by the success of the OPEC oil cartel and the apparent vulnerability of the industrialized nations to raw material embargoes, it is envisioned that various groups of less developed nations will form cartels (monopolies) to control the worldwide supply of some particular raw material. Following the OPEC lead, the cartels will increase the prices of their raw materials sharply and thereby significantly redistribute world income and wealth from the rich to the poor countries. Given the substantial contribution of OPEC's higher oil prices to the worldwide stagflation of the 1970s, there is no doubt that this scenario has the potential for the serious disruption of the international economic system which now exists.

## △   Confrontation

A final scenario envisions a rich nations–poor nations confrontation of frightening proportions. Assume that the population problem perseveres; that is, that Malthus's grim prognosis is realized in many Third World countries and population expands at unmanageable rates. Suppose, too, that nuclear capability spreads to the underdeveloped nations. The result, it is argued, is the horrendous possibility of "wars of redistribution." That is, as the rich nations get richer and the economic situation of the underdeveloped countries deteriorates under the burden of population pressures, it becomes increasingly possible that radical poor nations will threaten a nuclear holocaust as a means of blackmailing rich nations into sharing their wealth.[12]

---

[12] See Robert L. Heilbroner, *An Inquiry into the Human Prospect, Updated and Reconsidered for the 1980s* (New York: W. W. Norton & Company, Inc., 1980).

## Summary

1   Most nations of the world are underdeveloped (low per capita income) nations. Spurred by *a.* the widening gap between their incomes and those of the advanced nations, and *b.* the rising spirit of nationalism, people of the underdeveloped nations are far from content with their current economic status.

2   Initial scarcities of natural resources and the limited possibility of augmenting existing supplies may impose a rigid limitation upon a nation's capacity to develop.

3   The presence of large populations in underdeveloped countries contributes to low per capita incomes. In particular, increases in per capita incomes frequently induce rapid population growth, to the end that per capita incomes again deteriorate to near-subsistence levels.

4   Disguised unemployment in the form of surplus agricultural labor exists in most underdeveloped nations. This underemployment stems from the absence of alternative job opportunities on the one hand, and the occupational and geographic immobility of agricultural labor on the other.

**5** In underdeveloped nations both the saving and investment aspects of the capital formation process are impeded by formidable obstacles. The vast majority of households in underdeveloped nations receive incomes too small to permit them to save. The very wealthy have considerable ability to save but prefer to spend lavishly or to invest their savings in socially unproductive ways.

**6** The absence of a vigorous entrepreneurial class and the weakness of investment incentives are the major obstacles to capital accumulation when money capital is readily available. Political and social instability, the lack of large domestic markets, shortages of operating and administrative personnel, and deficiencies of basic social capital all contribute to an uninviting environment for private investment. Some degree of capital accumulation can usually be achieved, however, through nonfinancial investment.

**7** Appropriate social and institutional changes and, in particular, the presence of "the will to develop" are essential ingredients in economic development.

**8** The vicious circle of underdevelopment brings together many of the obstacles to growth and says in effect that "poor countries are poor because of their poverty." Low incomes inhibit saving and the accumulation of real and human capital, making it difficult to increase productivity and incomes. Rapid population growth can offset otherwise promising attempts to break the vicious circle.

**9** The role of government in the development of the underdeveloped nations is likely to be considerable. The nature of the obstacles to growth—the absence of an entrepreneurial class, the dearth of social capital, the saving-investment dilemma, and the presence of social-institutional obstacles to growth—suggest the need for government action in initiating the growth process.

**10** The advanced nations can assist in development by reducing trade barriers and by providing both private and public capital. However, many underdeveloped nations feel their trade, investment, and aid relationships with advanced nations are such that they constitute a new form of economic colonialism.

## Questions and Study Suggestions

**1** Key terms and concepts to remember: underdeveloped nation; Third World; investment in human capital; nonfinancial investment; basic social capital; capital-saving and capital-using technological advance; the "will to develop"; vicious circle of poverty; World Bank; the "Green Revolution"; neocolonialism.

**2** What are the major characteristics of an underdeveloped nation? List the major avenues of economic development available to such a nation. State and explain the obstacles which face the underdeveloped nations in breaking the poverty barrier. Use the "vicious circle of underdevelopment" to outline in detail the steps which an underdeveloped country might take to initiate economic development.

**3** Discuss and evaluate:

*a.* "The path to economic development has been clearly blazed by American capitalism. It is only for the underdeveloped nations to follow this trail."

*b.* "Economic inequality is conducive to saving, and saving is the prerequisite of investment. Therefore, greater inequality in the income distribution of the underdeveloped countries would be a spur to capital accumulation and growth."

*c.* "The spirit of nationalism sometimes aids and sometimes impedes the process of economic growth."

*d.* "The advanced economies fear the complications which stem from oversaving; the underdeveloped countries bear the yoke of undersaving."

   ***e.***   "The core of the development process involves changing human beings more than it does altering a nation's physical environment."

   ***f.***   "America's 'foreign aid' program is a sham.  In reality it represents neocolonialism—a means by which the underdeveloped nations can be nominally free in a political sense but remain totally subservient in an economic sense."

   ***g.***   "Poverty and freedom cannot persist side by side; one must triumph over the other."

   **4**   Much of the initial investment in an underdeveloped country must be devoted to basic social capital which does not directly or immediately lead to a greater production of goods and services.  What bearing might this have upon the degree of inflation which results as government finances capital accumulation through the creating and spending of new money?

   **5**   "The nature of the problems faced by the underdeveloped nations creates a bias in favor of a governmentally directed as opposed to a decentralized development process."  Do you agree?  Substantiate your position.

   **6**   Assume an underdeveloped country saves and invests 16 percent of its national income each year and that its capital-output ratio is 4.  What does this mean for the growth of per capita incomes if population is increasing by 6 percent per year?  By 4 percent per year?  By 1 percent per year?  What, if anything, does this example suggest with respect to growth policies?

## Selected References

Hagen, Everett E.: *The Economics of Development,* 3d ed. (Homewood, Ill.: Richard D. Irwin, Inc., 1980).

Higgins, Benjamin, and Jean Downing Higgins: *Economic Development of a Small Planet* (New York: W. W. Norton & Company, Inc., 1979).

McLaughlin, Martin M.: *The United States and World Development: Agenda 1979* (New York: Praeger Publishers, 1979).

Meier, Gerald M. (ed.): *Leading Issues in Economic Development,* 3d ed. (New York: Oxford University Press, 1976).

Morgan, Theodore: *Economic Development: Concept and Strategy* (New York: Harper & Row, Publishers, Incorporated, 1975).

Schachter, Oscar: *Sharing the World's Resources* (New York: Columbia University Press, 1977).

Thompson, W. Scott (ed.): *The Third World: Premises of U.S. Policy* (San Francisco: Institute for Contemporary Studies, 1978).

Wriggins, W. Howard, and Gunnar Adler-Karlsson: *Reducing Global Inequities* (New York: McGraw-Hill Book Company, 1978).

Zuvekas, Clarence, Jr.: *Economic Development: An Introduction* (New York: St. Martin's Press, 1979).

# LAST WORD
# Starving in a Land of Plenty

The following newspaper article outlines how a series of problems converged in 1978 and 1979 to bring Zaire to the brink of starvation.

In the sprawling but poorly equipped Mama Yemo Hospital, long lines of expressionless women sit clutching children with distended bellies, hollow eyes and protruding ribs—signs of malnutrition. According to statistics, half the children admitted in this condition die.

Plagued by drought, disease, rampant corruption and disintegration of government services, many people here and in the countryside of one of Africa's most richly endowed countries are starving.

In Kinshasa, malnutrition in children has been rated "chronic" by a team of U.S. doctors. East of the capital, in the country's normally most productive and populous rural province, Lower Zaire, doctors have diagnosed a famine comparable to that of the drought of 1973-74 in the Sahel region of sub-Sahara Africa.

Inland, plant diseases have ravaged crops while deteriorated roads and soaring fuel prices have made land transport prohibitive. Bands of low-paid and ill-fed soldiers prey on farmers and their dwindling stocks.

Unless protein-rich food comes soon, the doctors said, the children are threatened, at the least, with retardation of body and brain growth. At the worst, their hungry bodies succumb to common afflictions such as parasites, measles, cholera, pneumonia and malaria.

In Kinshasa, the shortfall of food from Lower Zaire has been aggravated by quadrupling of fuel prices, a 100 percent devaluation of the nation's currency and soaring food prices.

An average income of 80-100 zaires a month—$62-$78 at the official rate and $16-$20 at the more realistic black market rate—is less than half the amount needed to feed a family of four.

The immediate cause of the famine was an 18-month drought. It ended in November with rains that came with such fury new plantings were washed away. Food production fell by 60 percent.

Conditions for famine existed years before the drought: rapid population growth, the collapse of government services and economic crisis under President Mobutu Sese Seko's allegedly "corrupt" regime, widespread pillaging by soldiers and a flood of refugees from neighboring Angola.

Hunger and corruption, educated Zaireans point out, are not limited to Zaire. But what embitters and demoralizes the blacks is that they are starving in a land of plenty, a country, which before independence from Belgium in 1960, exported food.

Serge Schmemann, "Zaireans Are Starving in a Land of Plenty," *Lincoln Journal*, February 25, 1979.

# THE ECONOMICS OF THE FIRM AND RESOURCE ALLOCATION

PART FIVE

# The Market Structures of American Capitalism

chapter **22**

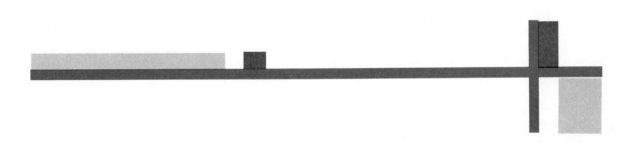

Scarce resources and unlimited wants, you will recall, are the foundation of economic science. The efficient management of scarce resources is a major goal of our economic system. Furthermore, there are two major facets to the problem of achieving efficient resource use. The first, which we have examined in Parts 2 and 3 and, to some degree, in Part 4 of this book, centers upon the full employment of available resources. The second aspect of the economizing problem—the one to which we now turn—has to do with allocating employed resources among alternative uses in the most efficient manner. Stated differently, Parts 2, 3, and 4 focused upon the first of the Five Fundamental Questions posed in Chapter 2: "Can the economy achieve the full employment of its available resources?" Part 5 deals with the remaining four questions: "Can the economy produce that output most desired by society?" "Will the production of that output be orga-

nized in the most efficient manner?" "Can the economy satisfactorily distribute that output?" "Is the economy capable of maintaining efficiency in the use of its resources in the face of changes in the relative supplies of resources, changes in consumer tastes, and changes in technology?" All four of these questions obviously have an important bearing on the problem of achieving and maintaining an efficient allocation of available resources.

We are well aware that one of the major characteristics of capitalistic economies is their heavy reliance upon a price system as a means for allocating resources (Chapter 5). Our major topics of discussion, then, are prices and the price system. Specifically, our basic goal in the ensuing chapters is to acquire a comprehensive understanding of the operation and relative efficiency of the *price system* in allocating resources within the framework of American capitalism. As a means to achieving this primary goal, we also seek a thorough analysis of *individual prices* under a variety of contrasting market arrangements.

Using the product market as a point of reference, the present chapter defines and describes the various market arrangements we propose to examine. In the subsequent chapters in Part 5, we shall review and apply our previous analysis of demand and supply, enhance our understanding of the demand side of the market, explore the production (supply) side of the market through a discussion of production costs—the major determinant of a firm's willingness to supply a given product—and examine in some detail the interaction of supply and demand under the various market arrangements described in the present chapter. Our attention will then shift to the functioning of prices in the resource market. Finally, the overall operation of the price system is examined.

## ☐ FOUR BASIC MARKET MODELS

There is no such thing as an "average" or "typical" industry. Detailed examination of the business sector of American capitalism reveals an almost infinite number of different market situations; no two industries are alike. At one extreme we may find a single producer completely dominating a particular market. At the other we discover thousands upon thousands of firms, each of which supplies a minute fraction of market output. Between these extremes lies an almost unlimited variety of market arrangements, most of which shade into one another.

Obviously, any attempt to examine each specific industry would be an endless and impossible task. There are simply too many of them. Hence, we seek a more realistic objective—to define and discuss several basic market structures, or models. In so doing, we shall acquaint ourselves with the *general* way in which price and output are determined in most of the market types which characterize our economy.

But the use of a few market models as typifying most of American industries calls for a word or two of caution.

**1** The market models to be considered are necessarily abstractions. They are merely first approximations and, as such, do not purport to present a complete picture of reality (see Chapter 1). In no case will these models we are about to define provide a *detailed* explanation of the functioning of any specific firm. Yet they will do a reasonably good job of outlining the operation of many firms.

**2** Some firms and industries will not fall neatly within any of the market models we are about to outline; rather, they will bear characteristics of two or more of these models. This means that the classification of a given firm or industry might entail an element of arbitrariness. This is the same type of problem which other scientists encounter. The botanist, for example, classifies all plants under three family groups—algae and fungi (thallophytes), moss plants (bryophytes), and vascular plants (tracheophytes). Yet many forms of plant life do not neatly fit into any one of these families, but rather are borderline cases. So it is with the economist in classifying industries.

**3** Finally, it is important to recognize at the outset that the economist's definitions of the basic market models do not coincide with those typically employed by business managers and laymen. The definitions which follow are not of commonsense vintage. "Competition," for example, has a much more precise meaning to the economist than it does to the average business executive.

Economists envision four relatively distinct market situations. These are (1) pure competition, (2) pure monopoly, (3) monopolistic competition, and (4) oligopoly. The immediate task is to describe the major characteristics of each of these four market models. In doing so, we shall use the seller's side of the product market as a point of reference. We shall see later that the same general models also are relevant for the buying side of the market.

## △ Pure Competition

A purely competitive market has several distinct characteristics which set it off from other market structures.

**1  Very Large Numbers**  A main feature of a purely competitive market is the presence of a large number of independently acting sellers, usually offering their products in a highly organized market.

**2  Standardized Product**  Competitive firms are producing a standardized or virtually standardized product. Given price, the consumer is indifferent as to the seller from which the product is purchased. In a competitive market the products of firms B, C, D, E, and so forth are looked upon by the buyer as perfect substitutes for that of firm A.

**3  "Price Taker"**  In a purely competitive market *individual firms* exert no significant control over product price. This characteristic follows from the preceding two. Under pure competition each firm produces such a small fraction of total output that increasing or decreasing its output will have no perceptible influence upon total supply or, therefore, product price. To illustrate, assume there are 10,000 competing firms, each of which is currently producing 100 units of output. Total supply is obviously 1,000,000. Now suppose one of these 10,000 firms cuts its output to 50 units. Will this affect price? No. And the reason is clear: This restriction of output by a single firm has an almost imperceptible impact on total supply—specifically, the total quantity supplied declines from 1,000,000 to 999,950. This is obviously not enough of a change in total supply to affect product price noticeably. In short, the individual competitive producer is a *price taker;* he or she cannot adjust market price, but can only adjust to it.

Stated differently, the individual competitive producer is at the mercy of the market; product price is a given datum over which the producer exerts no influence. The firm can get the same price per unit for a large output as it can for a small output. To ask a price higher than the going market price would be futile. Consumers will not buy anything from firm A at a price of $2.05 when its 9999 competitors are selling an identical, and therefore a perfect substitute product at $2 per unit. Conversely, because firm A can sell as much as it chooses at $2 per unit, there is no reason for it to charge some lower price, say, $1.95. Indeed, to do so would shrink its profits.

Finally, a subtle but highly important point: Although the *individual* firm cannot influence product price by varying its output, all firms in a competitive industry acting *as a group* can cause market price to vary. Should all 10,000 firms cut their outputs from 100 to 50 units, the total quantity supplied will decline from 1,000,000 to 500,000 units. This is most certainly a very significant change and can be expected to boost product price considerably. In brief, the individual firm cannot significantly influence price, but all firms as a group can. Although product price to an individual competitive seller is fixed, that price is free to move up or down in accordance with changes in either *total* demand or *total* supply.

**4  Free Entry**  New firms are free to enter and existing firms are free to leave purely competitive industries. In particular, no significant obstacles—legal, technical, financial, or other—exist to prohibit new firms from coming into being and selling their outputs in competitive markets.

**5  No Nonprice Competition**  Because purely competitive firms are producing a standardized product, there is virtually no room for *nonprice competition,* that is, competition on the basis of differences in product quality, advertising, or sales promotion. By definition each firm in a competitive market is producing an identical product. Hence, no firm has a quality edge over its rivals. Advertising by individual firms will be to no avail, because each firm's product has no distinguishing features to be advertised or promoted. Buyers will know that the products of all firms have the same features. Advertising has virtually no chance of convincing them otherwise.

**6   Examples**   Really precise examples of pure competition are few and far between. If we neglect the government's farm program, agriculture provides us with most of the good illustrations. Thus, we find, for example, that there are hundreds of thousands of farmers producing class I corn—a product which is obviously standardized or uniform. Class I corn is class I corn! Each firm supplies such a small fraction of the total that no single farmer has any control over the market price for class I corn. The individual farmer accepts the market price which exists in the highly organized market as a datum over which he or she has no influence; the farmer can sell as much or as little as he or she wants without affecting that price. Financial resources are not squandered on advertising or sales promotion. Farmer Jones knows that thousands upon thousands of other farmers are producing an identical product and that buyers are well aware of this. Hence, advertising would be futile, a sheer waste of time, effort, and money. The markets for wheat, cotton, barley, oats, the various types of livestock, and a good many other farm staples also fit rather well into the competitive mold we have outlined. Although few industries approximate pure competition, this model provides a norm against which less competitive markets can be evaluated.

△   **Pure Monopoly**

Now we turn to the other extreme of the spectrum. Pure monopoly provides us with the sharpest contrast to pure competition.

**1   Single Seller**   A pure, or absolute, monopolist is a one-firm industry. A single firm is the only producer of a given product or the sole supplier of a service; hence, the firm and the industry are synonymous.

**2   No Close Substitutes**   It follows from this first characteristic that the monopolist's product is unique in the sense that there are no good, or close, substitutes available. From the buyer's point of view, this means that there are no reasonable alternatives. The buyer must buy the product from the monopolist or do without.

A question arises at this point: When are products "good" substitutes? There is no clear answer to this query. In a very broad sense, all goods and services which compete for the consumer's dollar are substitutes. A down payment on a house may be a substitute for a new automobile. A two-week vacation may be a substitute for a television set. A pair of shoes may be a substitute for a new pair of slacks. A symphony concert may be a substitute for a fraternity dance. Yet, in a more restricted sense of the term, it is clear that some products and services simply do not have reasonably good substitutes. Candles and kerosene lamps are not good substitutes for electric lights. Spices are poor substitutes for salt. Bus or train transportation may be a poor substitute for owning one's own automobile. To some, a symphony concert is no substitute at all for the Signa Phi Nothing formal.

In our discussion we shall employ the idea of substitution in the narrower sense of the term. Hence, we can agree that, as most consumers see it, there are no good substitutes for the water piped into our homes by the municipal waterworks or the electric power provided by the local power company. Digging a well or importing water from a neighboring community is not a realistic substitute for running water in one's home. And few would regard kerosene lighting as an acceptable substitute for electric lights. In any event your television set will not run on kerosene. Up to World War II, manufacturers whose products entailed the need for a strong but lightweight metal had little choice but to purchase aluminum from Alcoa; no competing aluminum producers were in existence prior to the war.

**3 "Price Maker"** We have emphasized that the individual firm operating under pure competition exercises no influence over product price. This is so because it contributes only a negligible portion of total supply. In vivid contrast, the pure monopolist is a *price maker;* the firm exercises considerable control over price. And the reason is obvious: It is responsible for, and therefore controls, the total quantity supplied. Given a downsloping demand curve for its product, the monopolist can cause product price to change by manipulating the quantity of the product supplied. If it is advantageous, we can expect this power to be so used.

**4 Blocked Entry** If, by definition, a pure monopolist has no immediate competitors, there must be a reason for this lack of competition. And there is: The existence of monopoly depends upon the existence of barriers to entry. Be they economic, technological, legal, or other, certain obstacles must exist to keep new competitors from coming into the industry if monopoly is to persist. Entry is not easy under conditions of pure monopoly; on the contrary, it is blocked. More of this in Chapter 27.

**5 Goodwill Advertising** Depending upon the type of product or service involved, monopolists may or may not engage in extensive advertising and sales promotion activity. Local public utilities see no point in large expenditures for advertising; local citizens who want water, gas, and electric power and telephone service already know from whom they must buy.

If pure monopolists do advertise, such advertising is likely to be of a public relations, or goodwill, character rather than highly competitive, as is the advertising associated with, say, cigarettes, detergents, and beer. Because they have no immediate rivals, monopolists, in trying to induce more people to buy their products, need not invoke the ours-is-better-than-theirs type of advertising which characterizes radio and television. Rather, the monopolist's pitch is likely to be, "We're really nice fellows and certainly wouldn't do anything to exploit other firms, our beloved employees, or, heaven forbid, consumers." Or the monopolist may be anxious for the public to recognize that at least 90 percent of the firm's stock is held by destitute widows and orphans. Or, finally, the monopolist may be content merely to point out the technological progress for which the firm has been responsible.

**6 Examples** Because pure monopoly is admittedly an extreme market model, we once again find relatively few precise illustrations. Most local public utilities are pure monopolists for the municipalities which they serve. Thus, consumers either purchase their water, electricity, gas, and telephone service from the local utility or do without. Much the same may hold true of railway service in rural areas. On a nationwide basis, American Telephone and Telegraph approximates a pure monopoly. As we have said, Alcoa was a virtual monopolist in the production of most basic aluminum products until World War II; now it faces some competition from Reynolds and Kaiser. The United Shoe Machinery Company is the only manufacturer of certain equipment used in the production of shoes. IBM is the only source of certain calculating machines.

This is not to say that the pure monopolist will charge the highest price obtainable for its product or service. Consumers may find it impossible to do without some amount of water and highly inconvenient to do without some quantity of electricity. But the amounts they purchase will vary inversely with price. If the prices of electricity and water were extremely high, the poor (but cheap) substitutes of kerosene lamps and drawing water from a well would become relevant. And an extremely high price on office machines might even induce firms to substitute bookkeepers for the machines.

△  **Monopolistic Competition**

As its name indicates, monopolistic competition stands between the extremes of pure competition and pure monopoly. It embraces characteristics of both, but it stands closer to pure competition.

**1  Relatively Large Numbers**  As is the case with pure competition, monopolistic competition entails a large number of sellers acting independently. This does not mean that there need be 1,000, 10,000, or 1,000,000 firms in the industry; 30, 40, or 100 firms of more or less equal size may prevail. The important point is that each firm produces a fairly small share of the total output.

**2  Product Differentiation**  In contrast to pure competition, wherein the product is standardized, *product differentiation* is a major characteristic of monopolistically competitive industries. Product differentiation entails not only physical differences in the products of various producers or sellers in the industry, but also differences in such factors as the location and "snob appeal" of the seller's store, the packaging of the product, the cordiality of the firm's salespeople, the effectiveness of its advertising, the availability of credit, the company's reputation for servicing or "making good" on defective products, and so forth. The net result is that, although all firms in such an industry are producing the same general type or class of product, the particular product of each firm will have certain distinguishing features which set it off to some extent from those of other firms in the industry. In other words, the products of monopolistically competitive firms are close, but not perfect, substitutes. While the presence of a relatively large number of firms makes for competition, product differentiation gives rise to a measure of monopoly power. Indeed, monopolistic competition is sometimes called "the case of differentiation and large numbers."

**3  Limited Price Control**  Monopolistically competitive producers have a limited amount of control over product price. The control that exists depends essentially upon the degree of product differentiation and the number and proximity of competitors. The monopolistically competitive producer can raise price modestly without having sales fall to zero. Why? Because buyers recognize some differences between the products of various sellers. In the presence of product differentiation, consumers are likely to have definite preferences for the products of specific sellers, and relatively small price increases by one firm will not cause all buyers to seek out the close substitute products of rival firms in that industry. Generally, when the rivals of a monopolistically competitive firm are many in number and in close proximity, each firm's control over price will be less than would otherwise be the case.

**4  Relatively Easy Entry**  Entry into monopolistically competitive industries is typically easy. Nevertheless, entry may be a bit more difficult under monopolistically competitive conditions than when pure competition prevails. This is so because of product differentiation. A new firm must not only obtain the capital necessary to go into business but must also win clients away from existing firms. Securing a share of the market may entail considerable research and product development costs by the new firm to ensure that its product will have features which distinguish it from products already on the market. Similarly, considerable advertising outlays may be necessary to inform consumers of the existence of a new brand and to convince a number of them that it will be to their advantage to switch to the new product. In short, greater financial obstacles may face the potential newcomer under monopolistic competition than under pure competition.

**5 Nonprice Competition** Because products are differentiated, monopolistically competitive industries are ordinarily characterized by vigorous competition in areas other than price. Economic rivalry, as we have seen, may be based not only on price, but also on product quality, advertising, and conditions or services associated with the sale of a product. Great emphasis is placed upon trademarks and brand names as means for convincing the consumer that the products of one's rivals are not as good substitutes for brand X as they might first seem. Indeed, quality and advertising competition go hand in hand. Advertising proclaims and, if possible, magnifies real differences in product quality. While quality competition manipulates the firm's product, advertising and sales promotion attempt to manipulate the consumer.

**6 Examples** A considerable number of industries approximate the conditions of monopolistic competition (see Table 28-1). At the manufacturing level the women's dress industry provides a good example; New York City and a few other large metropolitan areas are the locations of the many small manufacturers which constitute this industry. The shoe industry also has features which make it reasonably close to being monopolistically competitive. A good many types of retail trade, particularly in cities of any size, occur under conditions which approximate monopolistic competition. Most cities contain a fairly large number of grocery stores, cleaning establishments, clothing shops, gasoline stations, restaurants, hairdressers, and so forth, all of which are providing differentiated products and services.

△ **Oligopoly**

The remaining market model—oligopoly—is less precisely defined by economists than are the three market structures just discussed. Two reasons go far to explain this lack of pre-

ciseness. On the one hand, oligopoly includes a wider range of market structures than do the other three market models; in effect it embraces all the remaining market situations which do not fit the rather clearly defined market models of pure competition, monopolistic competition, and pure monopoly. On the other hand, as we shall discover in a moment, oligopoly has certain characteristics which make it difficult to come up with hard and fast predictions about the behavior of oligopolistic industries.

**1 Fewness** The basic characteristic of oligopoly is "fewness." Oligopoly exists whenever a few firms dominate the market for a product. When we hear of the "Big Three," "Big Four," or "Big Six," we can be relatively certain that the industry is oligopolistic. This does not mean, of course, that the Big Three or Four necessarily share the total market. The dominant few may control, say, 70 or 80 percent of a market, with a competitive fringe—a group of smaller firms—sharing the remainder.

When a few firms dominate a market, each of these firms will have a share of the market sufficiently large so that its actions and policies will have repercussions on the other firms. Because each firm supplies a large portion of the total industry output, actions taken by any one firm to improve its share of the market will directly and immediately affect its rivals. Hence, each firm must carefully weigh the expected reactions of its rivals when considering changes in product price, advertising outlays, product quality, and so forth. Such clear-cut *mutual interdependence* is peculiar to oligopoly. It is not present in pure competition or monopolistic competition because of the large numbers of firms involved. The pure monopolist has no need to worry about the reactions of rivals, because there are none. Indeed, it can be said that oligopoly exists whenever the number of sellers is so few that the actions of one will have obvious and significant repercussions on the others. The firms of an oligopolistic industry are all in the same boat. If one rocks the boat, the others will be affected and in all probability will know the identity of the responsible firm and can retaliate.

**2   Standardized or Differentiated**   Oligopolists may be producing virtually standardized products or differentiated products. Speaking very generally, those oligopolistic industries which are producing raw materials or semifinished goods are typically offering virtually uniform products to buyers. For example, most metal products—steel, copper, zinc, lead, and aluminum—along with cement, rayon, explosives, industrial alcohol, and some building materials, are virtually uniform goods produced in markets in which a few large firms are dominant. On the other hand, oligopolistic industries producing finished consumer goods are typically offering differentiated products to buyers. Automobiles, tires, petroleum products, soap, cigarettes, ballpoint pens, breakfast foods, aircraft, farm implements, plus a host of electrical appliances—refrigerators, radios, electric razors, and so forth—are produced by oligopolistic industries wherein product differentiation is considerable.[1]

**3   Pricing Interdependence**   An individual oligopolistic firm's control over price tends to be closely circumscribed by the mutual interdependence which characterizes such markets. Specifically, if a given firm lowers price, it will initially gain sales at the expense of its several rivals. However, these adversely affected rivals will have little choice but to retaliate to recover their shrinking shares of the market; they will match or even undercut the given firm to preserve their market share. The result may be a price war and possibly losses for all firms. Conversely, if a given oli-

gopolist increases its price, rival firms stand to gain sales and profits by adhering to their present prices. That is, a price-boosting oligopolist runs the risk of "pricing itself out of the market" to the benefit of rivals. For both these reasons, there is a strong tendency for firms in oligopolist markets not to alter their prices very frequently.

The potentially adverse effects of price warring or pricing oneself out of the market can be largely avoided by a group of oligopolistic firms through the establishment of some sort of collusive agreement by which all firms either increase or decrease their prices as a group. Under such an arrangement the firms as a group can exert control over price in much the same way as can a pure monopolist.

**4   Difficult Entry**   Obstacles to entry are typically formidable in oligopolistic industries. The ownership of strategic patents or essential raw materials by existing firms may virtually prohibit the entry of new firms. Furthermore, the technology of heavy industry may demand that a new competitor be a large-scale producer from the outset, thus ruling out the possibility of a new firm starting on a small-scale basis and in time expanding into a significant rival of existing firms. In addition, certain advantages of being established—that is, the mere fact that existing firms are producing well-known, highly advertised products and selling them through long-established marketing outlets—may work against the successful entrance of new firms into the industry. Yet, in contrast to pure monopoly, entry is not usually blocked completely in oligopolistic industries. For example, the entry of Sylvania Electric into the electrical equipment industry after World War II presented a formidable rival for General Electric and Westinghouse. Entry into oligopolistic industries is very difficult, but by no means impossible.

**5   Advertising and Quality Competition**   Oligopolistic industries frequently channel considerable amounts of resources into

---

[1] Illustrations are from Joe S. Bain, *Pricing, Distribution, and Employment,* rev. ed. (New York: Holt, Rinehart and Winston, Inc., 1953), pp. 273–274, 333.

advertising and other promotional activities. But the type and amount of advertising will depend upon whether the firms are producing standardized or differentiated products.

Advertising competition is likely to be strong among oligopolists who are producing differentiated products. For example, each major automobile producer or cigarette manufacturer will have a large budget for convincing the consumer that its particular product is significantly superior to those of its rivals. Such advertising is likely to be of a highly competitive ours-is-better-than-theirs nature. On the other hand, public relations advertising is the bill of fare for oligopolists who are producing virtually standardized products. United States Steel does not try to convince the public that its sheet steel is superior to that produced by Republic, Bethlehem, or any of its other rivals. Skilled buyers who purchase the raw or fabricated steel products from these firms know that any differences are negligible. Hence, advertising in such industries is to keep the company in the public's eye, to convince the public that big business is an essential cog in the American economy, and so forth. It must be added that the producers of both standardized and differentiated products may engage in "social responsibility" advertising, for example, advertising which proclaims that the corporation is doing good deeds with respect to pollution, the hiring of minorities, and so forth.

Quality competition may be intense under oligopoly, particularly when product differentiation prevails. The research and design departments of many oligopolistic industries have become increasingly important over the years. Indeed, it is through research and rapid product development that the entry of potential rivals into the industry may be thwarted.

**6 Examples** A good many American industries fall under the heading of oligopoly. As a matter of fact, most of those industries which come to mind when we think of "big business" are some form or another of oligop-

oly. In addition to the specific examples previously mentioned, Table 29-1 contains a list of industries which are oligopolistic.

Table 22-1, which provides a convenient summary of the major characteristics of the four market models, merits your careful consideration.

△ **Imperfect Competition**

We shall find it convenient from time to time to distinguish between the characteristics of a purely competitive market and those of all other basic market arrangements—pure monopoly, monopolistic competition, and oligopoly. To facilitate such comparisons we shall employ *imperfect competition* as a generic term to designate all those market structures which deviate from the purely competitive market model.

□ **THE BUYER'S SIDE OF THE MARKET**

The preceding definitions of the four basic market models are couched in terms of the seller's side of the market. The same variety of market arrangements can and does exist on the buying or demand side. Here, however, the classification is almost exclusively based on the number of buyers. For example, a very large number of purchasers obviously means pure competition on the buying side of the market. *Monopsony* describes the situation in which there is only one buyer. When a few buyers dominate a market, *oligopsony* exists. *Monopsonistic competition* designates the presence of a fairly large number of buyers.

With the selling and buying sides of the market placed together as in Figure 22-1, it is easy to recognize that an almost infinite number of seller-buyer relationships can exist. A few representative examples will help underscore this point. The public utilities field is usually characterized by pure monopoly on the selling side and pure competition on the buying side. The market for raw tobacco links a great many purely competitive tobacco farm-

**TABLE 22-1**
**Characteristics of the Four Basic Market Models**

| Characteristic | Market model | | | |
| | Pure competition | Monopolistic competition | Oligopoly | Pure monopoly |
| --- | --- | --- | --- | --- |
| Number of firms | A very large number | Many | Few | One |
| Type of product | Standardized | Differentiated | Standardized or differentiated | Unique; no close substitutes |
| Control over price | None | Some, but within rather narrow limits | Circumscribed by mutual interdependence; considerable with collusion | Considerable |
| Conditions of entry | Very easy, no obstacles | Relatively easy | Significant obstacles present | Blocked |
| Nonprice competition | None | Considerable emphasis on advertising, brand names, trademarks, etc. | Typically a great deal, particularly with product differentiation | Mostly public relations advertising |
| Example | Agriculture | Retail trade, dresses, shoes | Steel, automobiles, farm implements, many household appliances | AT&T, local utilities |

ers on the selling side with a few large buyers—American, Liggett and Myers, Lorillard, and Reynolds—dominating the demand side. Where a strong union exists, specific labor markets often approximate *bilateral monopoly*—pure monopoly on one side and pure monopsony on the other. The local union is the "seller" of labor services, and the company is the single buyer. In the "original equipment" segment of the automobile tire market, we have oligopsonistic buyers—General Motors, Ford, and Chrysler—linked with oligop-

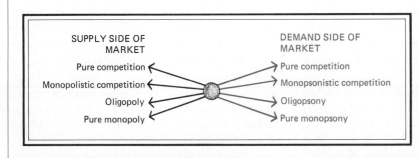

**FIGURE 22-1 SOME BASIC MARKET RELATIONSHIPS**

The four basic market models are pertinent to both the selling and buying sides of markets; this suggests the existence of a very large number of selling-buying relationships.

olistic sellers—Goodyear, Firestone, U.S. Rubber, and B. F. Goodrich. A similar arrangement exists in the market for tin plate—a few large steel companies are the sole producers, and two large tin-can manufacturers are the major buyers. In professional athletics team owners have established new player "drafts" which give employing teams the exclusive right—and therefore monopsony power—in bargaining a contract with a given player (Chapter 31). And so it goes. When all the hybrid cases falling between the four basic market models are taken into account, it is clear that the number of possible market arrangements can be and actually is extremely large.

## ☐ OTHER COMPETITIVE DIMENSIONS

It is important that we qualify and amend the foregoing definitions and explanations of the various market models in several ways.

### △ Geographic Factor

In practice the competitiveness of an industry or a firm is a geographic phenomenon. That is, the degree of competition in a particular industry depends upon the size of the market. Although a given city may have seventy or eighty grocery stores, a particular supermarket in a suburban area may, for all practical purposes, be competing only with three other chain stores and one or two independent corner groceries. Similarly, commercial banking appears to be highly competitive at first glance—after all, there are some 14,600 banks in our economy providing essentially identical services. But to the farmer in What Cheer, Iowa, borrowing from the Chase Manhattan Bank in New York or the Bank of America in California is out of the question. In negotiating a loan, Farmer Jones will look to the What Cheer State Bank or possibly one or two of the larger banks in a nearby city. These comments correctly imply that improved transportation and communication tend to strengthen competition; more efficient, lower-cost transporta-

tion and communication bring geographically remote producers into competition with one another.

In short, before hastily labeling an industry as "competitive" or "monopolistic," we must be very sure that we have properly delineated the geographic boundaries of the market. The number of firms alone is not a sufficient criterion by which to gauge the competitiveness of an industry; proximity is important, too.

### △ Interindustry Competition

It is important to recognize the significance of interindustry or interproduct competition. Although a few firms may be the only ones producing a specific product, they may face rather severe rivalry from other somewhat distinct products. Illustrations of such interproduct competition are numerous. The aluminum industry is a strong oligopoly with three firms—Alcoa, Reynolds, and Kaiser—dominating the market. Buyers who must use aluminum have no choice but to do business with one of these industrial giants. However, in many cases other materials—steel, copper, and even wood or plastics—are suitable substitutes for aluminum. Hence, steel competes with aluminum in the manufacturing of many automobile parts. Aluminum and copper contest the market for transmission lines. Aluminum battles both steel and wood in housing construction. These comments add up to the fact that the control over price which the Big Three of the aluminum industry possess is subject to limitations dictated by the prices of distinct but nevertheless competing products. Another example: The Big Two of the tin-can industry—American Can and Continental Group—dominate over 80 percent of their market. From within the industry they face little serious competition. But from without, they face the competition of glass, plastic, and paper containers.

### △ Nonprice Competition

This is a convenient juncture at which to

restate a point emphasized earlier: Competition is something more than the willingness and ability to cut prices. Competition in other areas than price may be vigorous and important in an industry. Variations in product quality, advertising and promotional activities, and so forth are important elements of competition which may supplement or, in some cases, supplant price competition.

### △  Technological Advance

The previous explanations of the four basic market models tend to classify the various markets at some particular *point* in time. Hence, they neglect an important competitive force which functions only over a *period* of time. That competitive force is technological advance. The development of new products and new techniques of production can result in new competition for producers who previously enjoyed a considerable degree of monopoly power.[2]

> In capitalist reality . . . it is . . . competition from the new commodity, the new technology, the new source of supply, the new type of organization (the largest-scale unit of control for instance)— competition which commands a decisive cost or quality advantage and which strikes not at the margins of the profits and the outputs of the existing firms but at their foundations and their very lives. This kind of competition is . . . so . . . important that it becomes a matter of comparative indifference whether competition in the ordinary sense functions more or less promptly; the powerful lever that in the long run expands output and brings down prices is in any case made of other stuff.
>
> . . . that competition of the kind we now have in mind acts not only when in being but also when it is merely an ever-present threat. It disciplines before it attacks. The businessman feels himself to be in a competitive situation even if he is alone in his field. . . . In many cases, though not in all, this will in the long run enforce behavior very similar to the perfectly competitive pattern.

Some examples may help to underscore this point. For over a decade a single firm enjoyed the position of a pure monopolist in the production of rayon. Its profits, enormous by any standard, were the result of the successful competition this innovation provided for other textiles. But more recently the development of acetates, nylon, acrylic, and other "miracle fibers" has in turn provided considerable competition for rayon.[3] In a similar manner, the rapid development of the dehydrated and quick-frozen food industries during World War II has permitted an intensification of the competition which paper, fiber, and plastic containers provide for the Big Two of the tin-can industry. Consider, finally, the widespread repercussions of the transistor. Its development spawned new firms—Texas Instruments, Fairchild, and Intel, among others—which have made serious inroads on the electronics components businesses once dominated by such giants as General Electric, Sylvania, and Westinghouse. Similarly, innovative Japanese firms used the transistor to undermine the leadership of such American firms as GE and RCA in the radio and television markets. And in the past few years the semiconductor technology which created the transistor has been applied to watchmaking, and, as a result, Switzerland's watchmaking industry has faced severe competition from the digital watches of American electronics firms.

### 🏛  DETERMINANTS OF MARKET STRUCTURE

Agriculture is an almost purely competitive industry. The clothing industry fits roughly into the mold of monopolistic competition. The steel and automobile industries are obviously oligopolistic. American Telephone and Telegraph nationally, and public utilities locally, approximate pure monopolies. What forces explain the emergence of these different market structures? What factors have caused

---

[2]Joseph A. Schumpeter, *Capitalism, Socialism, and Democracy,* 3d ed. (New York: Harper & Row, Publishers, Incorporated, 1950), pp. 84–85.

[3]A. D. H. Kaplan, *Big Enterprise in a Competitive System,* rev. ed. (Washington: The Brookings Institution, 1964), p. 185.

agriculture to remain highly competitive and the automobile industry, spiced in its infancy with seventy-odd producers, now to be a tight oligopoly dominated by the Big Three? Although there exists no short, easy answer to these questions, we can put our fingers on some of the more important forces which historically have played significant roles in determining the competitive structures of the various American industries. Generally speaking, such factors as (1) legislation and government policy, (2) the policies and practices of business firms, (3) technological considerations, and (4) institutions and characteristics inherent in the capitalistic ideology, go far to explain the variety of market structures which characterizes American capitalism.

## Legislation and Government Policy

Government has promoted both monopoly and competition. By issuing *exclusive franchises* to so-called natural monopolies (for example, public utilities), government has purposely created many pure monopolies in industries which might otherwise have attained some degree of competition. Federal government commissions—the Interstate Commerce Commission, for example, and the Federal Communications Commission—play the major role in determining the degree of competition in the land transportation and radio–television industries. Similarly, *patent laws* often have promoted monopoly by giving innovating firms the exclusive right to manufacture a product for extended periods of time. *Tariffs* and other artificial barriers to international trade have promoted and preserved monopoly power in some domestic industries. On the other hand, there is but little doubt that the liberal Homestead Act of 1862 provided a competitive base for American agriculture. *Antitrust legislation*—the Sherman and Clayton Acts—is explicitly designed to curb the abuses of monopoly power.

We find here seemingly inconsistent government policies; but this inconsistency can be at least partially explained. Although government has pursued a generally antimonopolistic social policy, it simultaneously seeks other social objectives. One of these goals is the promotion of technological advance—an aim which patent legislation tends to foster. And in the case of public utilities, competition has simply not functioned effectively; here government has condoned and promoted monopoly, but has then provided regulatory commissions designed to prevent the abuse of this government-sponsored monopoly power.

## Business Policies and Practices

The practices and policies pursued by various firms and industries can also be critical in determining the structure of industry. In some industries, mergers, consolidations, and the development of holding companies have pushed in the direction of oligopoly or monopoly. The evolution of the corporate form of business enterprise and collusive practices between legally independent firms have played a similar role. In other industries, cutthroat competition has resulted in some firms driving others from existence, thereby lowering the number of competitors in the industry. In still other instances, firms have acquired ownership or control over vital raw materials so as to eliminate present rivals and destroy the possibility of new firms coming into being. These practices and developments, however, have occurred unevenly among various industries, causing some to move in the direction of monopoly and others to remain quite highly competitive.

## Technology

Technology has undoubtedly been an important determinant of industrial structure. In a good many industries, technology has developed to the point where the existence of large industrial giants is necessary if efficient low-cost production is to be achieved. Technology has given rise to economies of mass production which only large producers can realize. This means that, given consumer demand, efficient production necessitates the existence of a few large producers rather than many small producers. It is thus that technological advance has "forced" the market structure of many "heavy" industries—for example, the automobile, steel, and aluminum industries—in the direction of oligopoly. Economists differ in evaluating the extent to which technological factors require bigness; we shall examine the conflicting views in greater detail in Chapter 34.

In some industries, technological advance has worked toward the same end but in a somewhat different manner. Superior research on product development has permitted some firms to outgrow and often eliminate less progressive rivals. Furthermore, this tendency is frequently cumulative; by gaining a larger share of the market through its superior research, a firm realizes the financial rewards that facilitate a widening of the technological advantages which it possesses over its rivals.

△  **Capitalistic Institutions**
We must be reminded that the institutions

of American capitalism are permissive of the concentration of economic power and the development of oligopoly and monopoly. The relatively free, individualistic economic environment of the economy is a fertile ground for the most efficient, the most courageous, the most fortunate, or the most crafty producer to conquer rivals in an effort to become free from the regulatory powers of competition. Freedom of contract, private property, and inheritance rights have also contributed to the concentration of economic power. And, too, the business cycle has probably abetted the tendency toward monopoly. As one scholar puts it:[4]

> Weaklings may still fail, and disappear, especially in more difficult times. Good times make it easy to finance consolidations, and tempting for the strong company to expand and the weak to sell out. Thus, both adversity and prosperity work alike to reduce the number of firms in an industry.

[4]John Kenneth Galbraith, *American Capitalism,* rev. ed. (Boston: Houghton Mifflin Company, 1956), p. 35.

## Summary

1   American industry is characterized by differing degrees of competition. The market models of ***a.*** pure competition, ***b.*** pure monopoly, ***c.*** monopolistic competition, and ***d.*** oligopoly are classifications into which most industries can be fitted with reasonable accuracy. These market models—the major features of which are summarized in Table 22-1—are merely first approximations of reality.

2   Similar market classifications, based essentially upon numbers, are applied to the buying, or demand, side of the market.

3   The economist's definitions of the four market models focus attention upon ***a.*** the number of firms, ***b.*** the degree of product differentiation, and ***c.*** the ease or difficulty encountered by new firms in entering the industry. However, certain other important factors which have a bearing upon the competitive nature of an industry must also be considered: ***a.*** In practice, any meaningful description of the market structure of an industry requires a proper definition of the geographic limits of the market. ***b.*** Interindustry or interproduct competition is a significant force in many markets which might otherwise appear to be lacking in competition. ***c.*** Nonprice competition may be an important supplement to price competition. ***d.*** Technological advance, working as a competitive force through time, often undermines existing industries characterized by strong monopolistic elements.

4   Legislation, government policies, research and technological development, industry practices, and a variety of other factors have all played significant roles in determining the present structure of American industry.

# Questions and Study Suggestions

**1**   Key terms and concepts to remember: pure competition; pure monopoly; monopolistic competition; oligopoly; imperfect competition; standardized product; product differentiation; pricetaker and pricemaker; nonprice competition; monopsony; monopsonistic competition; oligopsony; bilateral monopoly; interindustry competition.

**2**   Under which of the four market classifications discussed in the chapter does each of the following most accurately fit: ***a.*** a supermarket located in your home town; ***b.*** the steel industry; ***c.*** a Kansas wheat farm; ***d.*** the commercial bank in which you or your family has an account; ***e.*** the automobile industry.   In each case justify your classification.   Specify assumptions you have made about the geographic limits of the various markets.

**3**   "Purely competitive producers have no price policy, but monopolistically competitive, oligopolistic, and purely monopolistic firms do."   Explain.   Why doesn't a purely competitive producer advertise its product?

**4**   The president of E. I. du Pont de Nemours & Company once made the following statements:

> The difference between three and one [firms] is very substantial.   It is the difference between monopoly and no monopoly.   Oligopoly . . . to me is meaningless, because there is either competition or there is not.   If there is competition, the public interest is being served.

What differences, if any, can you detect between this definition of "competition" and the economist's definition of "pure competition"?   Do you feel that all industries can be meaningfully categorized as competitive or not competitive?   Explain your answers.

**5**   A single farmer is "at the mercy of the market" in that he must regard the market price for his products as being fixed.   Yet agricultural prices are very flexible.   Reconcile these two statements.

**6**   What is interindustry competition?   How important is it in each of the following industries?   In each case specify the competing products or industries: ***a.*** automobile; ***b.*** railway; ***c.*** cement; ***d.*** steel; ***e.*** coal; and ***f.*** glass container.

**7**   What is nonprice competition?   How prevalent do you think nonprice competition to be in the industries mentioned in questions 2 and 6?

**8**   "Competition should be judged solely on the basis of the number of firms in the industry; the larger the number, the greater the competition."   Critically evaluate.

**9**   What are some of the major forces which determine the market structure of industries?   Drawing on your knowledge of American history, evaluate the relative significance of these forces in explaining the market structures of the following industries: ***a.*** automobile; ***b.*** television; ***c.*** tobacco; ***d.*** steel; ***e.*** petroleum; and ***f.*** agriculture.   Be as specific as you can in your answers.

**10**   "Technological advance has both encouraged and limited the development of monopoly."   Do you agree?   Explain.

# Selected References

Averitt, Robert T.: *The Dual Economy: The Dynamics of American Industry Structure* (New York: W. W. Norton & Company, Inc., 1968).

Baird, Charles W.: *Prices and Markets: Microeconomics* (St. Paul: West Publishing Company, 1975), chap. 6.

Galbraith, John Kenneth: *Economics and the Public Purpose* (Boston: Houghton Mifflin Company, 1973).

Weiss, Leonard W.: *Economics and American Industry* (New York: John Wiley & Sons, Inc., 1961), chap. 1.

# LAST WORD
# The Changing Automobile
# Market

Escalating gasoline prices have threatened the preeminence of American firms in the
automobile market.

(Reprinted from *U.S. News & World Report*.)

Caught short in the clamor for small cars, U.S. auto makers are mounting a major effort to convince import-hungry motorists to "buy American."

Hoping to break a profit-sapping sales slump that has hounded them for months, the Big Three auto manufacturers have launched a broad offensive in recent days. Among the steps they have taken:

Factory rebates. Ford's rebate is $300 to $500 on some 1979 and 1980 models. General Motors is giving $500 on some '79s, and Chrysler $200 to $700 on all '79s.

A novel money-back guarantee at Chrysler, coupled with a $50 "rebate" for purchasing any U.S. car after test driving a Chrysler.

A campaign to convince Japanese firms to build cars in the U.S.—with threats of import quotas, tariffs or other trade restrictions if they refuse. . . .

At the heart of the problem for the U.S. firms: A customer desire for fuel-efficient small cars, which are in short supply from domestic factories. In increasing numbers, potential car buyers are being put off by long waits for fuel-stingy American cars and are finding imports in abundance.

Retailers of American cars say that their lots are glutted with less-efficient full-size cars and trucks—some of them 1979-model carry-overs—that have sold poorly since the first gas lines appeared last spring. . . .

Results have been disastrous for many dealers. High interest rates make it hard, if not impossible, to carry huge inventories of unsold cars. In the past year, more than 500 dealerships have failed—five times the normal rate.

But American dealers selling imported cars are faring well. They don't take quietly the criticism being heaped on Japanese manufacturers.

"In the eyes of our competitors, we are too successful in providing for the needs of our customers," said Robert McElwaine, president of the American International Automobile Dealers Association. He said that U.S. car makers have been slow in moving to more-fuel-efficient cars while "our manufacturers have been willing to make the kind of expenditures needed to produce state-of-the-art vehicles and respond quickly to the market. The wounds of the domestic automobile industry are largely self-inflicted.". . .

"Detroit's Hard Sell to Lure Back Customers," *U.S. News & World Report,* February 25, 1980, pp. 71–72, abridged. Copyright © 1980 U.S. News & World Report, Inc.

# Demand, Supply, and Elasticity: Some Applications

chapter **23**

In Chapter 4 we familiarized ourselves with the rudiments of demand and supply analysis. In the present chapter we seek a more sophisticated understanding of demand and supply. Specifically, the tasks of this chapter are threefold. First, a brief summary of the elements of demand and supply analysis is presented. Second, we shall consider the concept of elasticity as applied to both demand and supply. Third, some specific applications of demand and supply analysis are discussed.

## ☐ DEMAND, SUPPLY, AND MARKET PRICE[1]

Demand and supply both refer to schedules. The demand schedule shows the relationship between various possible prices of a product

---

**TABLE 23-1**
**The Demand For, and Supply of, Corn**
(*hypothetical data*)

| (1) Total quantity demanded per week | (2) Price per bushel | (3) Total quantity supplied per week | (4) Surplus (+) or shortage (−) (arrow indicates effect on price) |
|---|---|---|---|
| 2,000 | $5 | 12,000 | +10,000↓ |
| 4,000 | 4 | 10,000 | + 6,000↓ |
| 7,000 | 3 | 7,000 | 0 |
| 11,000 | 2 | 4,000 | − 7,000↑ |
| 16,000 | 1 | 1,000 | −15,000↑ |

and the quantities which consumers will purchase at each of these prices (Table 23-1, columns 1 and 2). The price–quantity-demand relationship thus portrayed is an inverse one. Consumers typically buy less at a high price than at a low price. This commonsense relationship is called the *law of demand*. Graphically the demand curve is downsloping (*DD* in Figure 23-1).

---

[1]This review is not a substitute for Chapter 4. The student is strongly urged to reread Chapter 4 at this point.

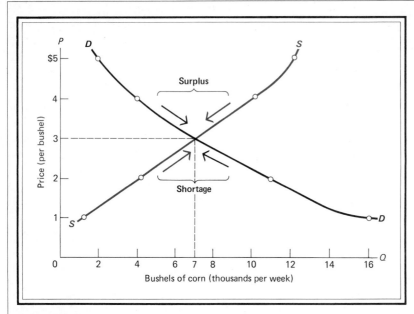

Equilibrium price and equilibrium quantity are determined by the intersection of demand *DD* and supply *SS*.

The supply schedule embodies the relationship between possible product prices and the quantities which producers will supply at each of those prices (Table 23-1, columns 2 and 3). The relationship between price and quantity supplied is a direct one. The *law of supply* states that producers will find it profitable to devote more resources to the production of a good when its price is high than they will when it is low. When graphed, this direct relationship results in an upsloping supply curve (*SS* in Figure 23-1).

The intersection of demand and supply determines the market, or equilibrium, price and quantity. Both Table 23-1 and Figure 23-1 clearly show that the demand and supply data here assumed result in an equilibrium price of $3 and an equilibrium quantity of 7000 units. Competition causes any other price to be unstable. The shortages which accompany *below*-equilibrium prices will prompt competing buyers to bid up the price, as consumers want to avoid doing without the product. A rising price will (1) induce firms to allocate more resources to the production of this good,

and (2) ration some consumers out of the market. These adjustments are illustrated in Figure 23-1 by the arrows moving up the supply curve and up the demand curve respectively. The surpluses which result at any *above*-equilibrium price will induce competing sellers to shade their prices to work off these excess stocks. The falling price will (1) prompt firms to allocate fewer resources to this line of production, and (2) ration some additional buyers into the market. These adjustments are shown by the arrows moving down the supply and demand curves respectively in Figure 23-1.

Changes in the determinants of either demand or supply can cause the demand and supply schedules (curves) to shift. Variations in consumer tastes, incomes, the prices of related goods, consumer expectations, and the number of buyers in the market all will account for shifts in demand. Changes in any of those factors which affect production costs—for example, technology or resource prices—will cause supply to shift. The relationship between a change in demand and the resulting changes in equilibrium price and quantity is a direct one. An inverse relationship exists between a change in supply and the ensuing change in price. However, the relationship between a change in supply and the ensuing change in quantity is direct.

## ☐ ELASTICITY OF DEMAND

The law of demand tells us that consumers will respond to a price decline by buying more of a product. But the degree of responsiveness of consumers to a price change may vary considerably from product to product. Furthermore, we will find that consumer responsiveness typically varies substantially between different price ranges for the same product.

Economists measure how responsive, or sensitive, consumers are to a change in the price of a product by the concept of *elasticity*. The demand for some products is such that consumers are relatively responsive to price changes; modest price changes give rise to very considerable changes in the quantity purchased. The demand for such products is said to be *elastic*. For other products, consumers are relatively unresponsive to price changes; that is, substantial price changes result only in modest changes in the amount purchased. In such cases demand is *inelastic*.

### △ The Elasticity Formula

Economists measure the degree of elasticity or inelasticity by the *elasticity coefficient,* or $E_d$, in this formula:

$$E_d = \frac{\text{percentage change in quantity demanded}}{\text{percentage change in price}}$$

One calculates these *percentage* changes, of course, by dividing the change in price by the original price and the consequent change in quantity demanded by the original quantity demanded. Thus, our formula restated:

$$E_d = \frac{\dfrac{\text{change in quantity demanded}}{\text{original quantity demanded}}}{\div \dfrac{\text{change in price}}{\text{original price}}}$$

**Use of Percentages**  But why use percentages rather than absolute amounts in measuring consumer responsiveness? The answer is that if we use absolute changes, our impression of buyer responsiveness will be arbitrarily affected by the choice of units. To illustrate: If the price of product X falls from $3 to $2 and consumers, as a result, increase their purchases from 60 to 100 pounds, we get the impression that consumers are quite sensitive to price changes and therefore that demand is elastic. After all, a price change of "one" has caused a change in the amount demanded of "forty." But by changing the monetary unit from dollars to pennies (why not?), we find a price change of "one hundred" causes a quantity change of "forty," giving the impression of inelasticity. The use of percentage changes avoids this problem. The given price decline is 33 percent whether measured in terms of dollars ($1/$3) or in terms of pennies (100¢/300¢).[2]

**Interpretations**  Now let us interpret our formula. Demand is *elastic* if a given percentage change in price results in a larger percentage change in quantity demanded. Example: If a 2 percent decline in price results in a 4 percent increase in quantity demanded, demand is elastic. In all such cases, where demand is elastic, the elasticity coefficient will obviously be greater than 1; in this case it will be 2. If a given percentage change in price is accompanied by a relatively smaller change in the quantity demanded, demand is *inelastic*. Illustration: If a 3 percent decline in price gives rise to a 1 percent increase in the amount de-

---

[2] The careful reader will note that the elasticity coefficient of demand will always be negative. This is so for the obvious reason that the demand curve is downsloping; that is, price and quantity are inversely related. Economists are generally inclined to ignore the minus sign (as we do here) in order to avoid an ambiguity which might otherwise arise. It can be confusing to say that an elasticity coefficient of −4 is greater than one of −2; this possible confusion can be avoided if we simply say a coefficient of 4 indicates greater elasticity than one of 2. This difficulty does not arise with supply because price and quantity are directly related.

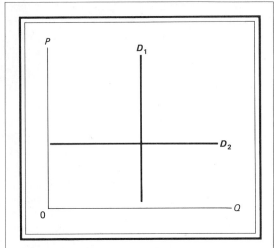

**FIGURE 23-2  PERFECTLY INELASTIC AND
ELASTIC DEMAND**

A perfectly inelastic demand curve, $D_1$, graphs as a line
parallel to the vertical axis; a perfectly elastic demand
curve, $D_2$, is drawn parallel to the horizontal axis.

manded, demand is inelastic. Specifically, the
elasticity coefficient is $\frac{1}{3}$ in this instance. It is
apparent that the elasticity coefficient will
always be less than 1 when demand is inelastic. The borderline case which separates elastic and inelastic demands occurs where a percentage change in price and the accompanying
percentage change in quantity demanded happen to be equal. For example, a 1 percent drop
in price causes a 1 percent increase in the
amount sold. This special case is termed *unit
elasticity,* because the elasticity coefficient is
exactly 1, or unity.

It must be emphasized that when economists say demand is "inelastic," they do not
mean consumers are completely unresponsive
to a price change. The term *perfectly inelastic*
demand designates the extreme situation
wherein a change in price results in no change
whatsoever in the quantity demanded. Approximate example: an acute diabetic's demand for insulin. A demand curve parallel
to the vertical axis—such as $D_1$ in Figure
23-2—shows this situation graphically. Con-

versely, when economists say demand is "elastic," they do not mean that consumers are
completely responsive to a price change. In the
extreme situation, wherein there is some small
price reduction which would cause buyers to
increase their purchases from zero to all they
could obtain, we say that demand is *perfectly
elastic.* A perfectly elastic demand curve is a
line parallel to the horizontal axis; $D_2$ in Figure 23-2 is illustrative. We shall find later in
Chapter 26 that such a demand curve applies
to a firm which is selling in a purely competitive market.

△  **Refinement: Midpoints Formula**

An annoying problem arises in applying
the elasticity formula. To illustrate: In calculating the elasticity coefficient for corn for the
$5–$4 price range in Table 23-2, should we use
the $5–2000-bushel price-quantity combina-
tion or the $4–4000-bushel combination as a
point of reference in calculating the percentage
changes in price and quantity which the elasticity formula requires? Our choice will influence the outcome. Using the $5–2000-bushel
reference point, we find that the percentage
decrease in price is 20 percent and the percentage increase in quantity is 100 percent. Substituting in the formula, the elasticity coefficient is 100/20, or 5. But, using the
$4–4000-bushel reference point, we find that
the percentage increase in price is 25 percent
and the percentage decline in quantity is 50
percent. The elasticity coefficient is therefore
50/25, or 2, in this case. Although the formula
indicates that demand is elastic in both cases,
the two solutions involve a considerable difference in the degree of elasticity. In other instances—experiment, for example, with the
$3–$2 price range—the formula may indicate a
slightly elastic demand for one price-quantity
combination and slight inelasticity of demand
for the other.

Economists have reached a workable compromise to this problem by using the *averages*
of the two prices and the two quantities under

**TABLE 23-2**
**Elasticity of Demand as Measured by the Total-Receipts Test and the Elasticity**
**Coefficient (*hypothetical data*)**

| (1)<br>Total quantity demanded per week | (2)<br>Price per bushel | (3)<br>Total revenue (expenditures) | (4)<br>Total-revenue test | (5)<br>Elasticity coefficient, $E_d$ (approximate) |
|---|---|---|---|---|
| 2,000 | $5 | $10,000 | | |
| | | | Elastic | $\dfrac{2,000}{6,000/2} \div \dfrac{1}{9/2} = 3.00$ |
| 4,000 | 4 | 16,000 | | |
| | | | Elastic | $\dfrac{3,000}{11,000/2} \div \dfrac{1}{7/2} = 1.91$ |
| 7,000 | 3 | 21,000 | | |
| | | | Elastic | $\dfrac{4,000}{18,000/2} \div \dfrac{1}{5/2} = 1.11$ |
| 11,000 | 2 | 22,000 | | |
| | | | Inelastic | $\dfrac{5,000}{27,000/2} \div \dfrac{1}{3/2} = 0.56$ |
| 16,000 | 1 | 16,000 | | |

consideration for reference points. In the $5–$4 price-range case, the price reference is $4.50 and the quantity reference 3000 bushels. The percentage change in price is now about 22 percent and the percentage change in quantity about 67 percent, giving us an elasticity coefficient of 3. Instead of gauging elasticity at either one of the extremes of this price-quantity range, this solution estimates elasticity at the midpoint of the $5–$4 price range. More positively stated, we can refine our earlier statement of the elasticity formula to read

$$E_d = \frac{\text{change in quantity}}{\text{sum of quantities}/2} \div \frac{\text{change in price}}{\text{sum of prices}/2}$$

Substituting data for the $5–$4 price range, we get

$$E_d = \frac{2000}{6000/2} \div \frac{1}{9/2} = 3.00$$

In column 5 of Table 23-2 we have calculated the elasticity coefficients for the demand data of Table 23-1, using the midpoints formula. The reader should verify each of these calculations.

△   **The Total-Revenue Test**

Perhaps the easiest way to gauge whether demand is elastic or inelastic is to note what happens to total revenue or receipts—total expenditures from the buyer's viewpoint—when product price changes.

**1** If demand is *elastic,* a decline in price will result in an increase in total revenue. Why? Because even though a lesser price is being received per unit, enough additional units are now being sold to more than make up for the lower price. This is illustrated in Figure 23-3 for the $5–$4 price range of our demand curve from Table 23-1. Total revenue, of course, is price times quantity. Hence, the area shown by the rectangle $OP_1AQ_1$ is total revenue ($10,000) when price is $P_1$ ($5) and quantity demanded is $Q_1$ (2000 bushels). Now when price declines to $P_2$ ($4), causing the quantity demanded to increase to $Q_2$ (4000 bushels), total revenue changes to $OP_2BQ_2$ ($16,000), which is obviously larger than $OP_1AQ_1$. It is larger because the *loss* in revenue due to the lower price per unit (area $P_2P_1AC$) is *less* than the *gain* in revenue due to the larger sales (area $Q_1CBQ_2$) which accompanies the lower price. This reasoning is reversible: If demand is elastic, a price increase will reduce total revenue. Why? Because the *gain* in total revenue caused by the higher unit price (area $P_2P_1AC$) is less than the *loss* in revenue associated with the accompanying fall in sales ($Q_1CBQ_2$).

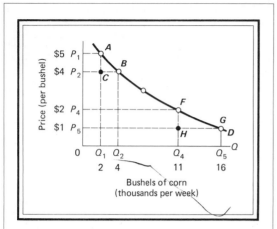

**FIGURE 23-3   ELASTICITY AND TOTAL REVENUE**

If demand is elastic, as in the $5-$4 price range, a change in price will cause total revenue to change in the opposite direction. Conversely, if demand is inelastic, as in the $2-$1 price range, price and total revenue will move in the same direction.

will cause total revenue to change in the same direction.

**3**   In the special case of *unit elasticity*, an increase or decrease in price will leave total revenue unchanged. The loss in revenue due to a lower unit price will be exactly offset by the gain in revenue brought about by the accompanying increase in sales. Conversely, the gain in revenue due to a higher unit price will be exactly offset by the loss in revenue associated with the accompanying decline in the amount demanded.

Columns 3 and 4 of Table 23-2 apply the total-revenue test to the entire demand curve for corn.

△   **Characteristics**

The alert reader may have detected two subtle but notable characteristics of elasticity from our applications of the elasticity formula and the total-revenue tests.

**Elasticity and Price Range**   First, elasticity typically varies over the different price ranges of the same demand schedule or curve. For most demand curves—including our illustrative demand for corn in Table 23-2 —demand tends to be more elastic in the upper-left portion than in the lower-right portion. This is essentially a consequence of the arithmetic properties of the elasticity measure. Specifically, in the upper-left portion the percentage change in quantity tends to be large because the original quantity from which the percentage quantity change is derived is small. Similarly, in this portion the percentage change in price tends to be small because the original price from which the percentage price change is calculated is large. The relatively large percentage change in quantity divided by the relatively small change in price yields an elastic demand. The reverse holds true for the lower-right portion of the demand curve. Here the percentage change in quantity tends to be small because the original quantity from which the percentage change is determined is large. Similarly, the percentage change in price tends

Generalization: *If demand is elastic, a change in price will cause total revenue to change in the opposite direction.*

**2**   If demand is *inelastic,* a price decline will cause total revenue to fall. The modest increase in sales which occurs will be insufficient to offset the decline in revenue per unit, and the net result is that total revenue declines. This situation exists for the $2–$1 price range of our demand curve, as shown in Figure 23-3.   Initially, total revenue is $OP_4FQ_4$ ($22,000) when price is $P_4$ ($2) and quantity demanded is $Q_4$ (11,000 bushels). If we reduce price to $P_5$ ($1), quantity demanded will increase to $Q_5$ (16,000 bushels). Total revenue will change to $OP_5GQ_5$ ($16,000), which is obviously less than $OP_4FQ_4$. It is smaller because the loss in revenue due to the lower unit price (area $P_5P_4FH$) is larger than the *gain* in revenue due to the accompanying increase in sales (area $Q_4HGQ_5$). Again our analysis is reversible: If demand is inelastic, a price increase will increase total revenue. Generalization: *If demand is inelastic, a change in price*

to be large because the original price from which the relative price change is calculated is small. The relatively small percentage change in quantity divided by the relatively large percentage change in price results in an inelastic demand.

**Elasticity versus Slope**   In the second place, the graphic appearance, that is, the slope, of a demand curve is *not* a sound basis upon which to judge its elasticity. For example, in Figure 23-3 we find that because the demand curve has a steeper slope at relatively higher prices and a flatter slope at relatively lower prices, one is tempted to associate an inelastic demand with high prices and an elastic demand with low prices. But this is dangerous reasoning. Have we not just discovered that the elasticity formula and the total-revenue test indicate that the reverse is true? The catch lies in the fact that the slope—the flatness or steepness—of a demand curve is based upon *absolute* changes in price and quantity, while elasticity has to do with *relative* changes in price and quantity. The difference between slope and elasticity can also be made quite clear by calculating elasticity for various price-quantity combinations on a straight-line demand curve. You will find that, although the slope is obviously constant throughout, demand tends to be elastic in the high-price range and inelastic in the low-price range. Question 18 at the end of this chapter is relevant.

△   **Determinants of Elasticity of Demand**

There are no iron-clad, exceptionless generalizations concerning the determinants of the elasticity of demand. The following points, however, are usually accepted as valid and helpful.

**1   Substitutability**   Generally speaking, the larger the number of good substitute products available, the greater the elasticity of demand. We shall find in Chapter 26 that in a purely competitive market, where by definition there is an extremely large number of perfect substitutes for the product of any given seller, the demand curve to that single seller will be perfectly elastic (Figure 26-1). If one competitive seller of wheat or corn raises its price, buyers will turn to the readily available perfect substitutes of its many rivals. At the other extreme, the diabetic's demand for insulin is undoubtedly highly inelastic. It is worth noting that the elasticity of demand for a product depends upon how narrowly the product is defined. The demand for Texaco motor oil is more elastic than is the overall demand for motor oil. A number of other brands are readily substitutable for Texaco's oil, but there is no good substitute for motor oil per se.

**2   Proportion of Income**   Other things being equal, the larger a good bulks in one's budget the greater will tend to be the elasticity of demand for it. A 10 percent increase in the price of pencils or chewing gum will amount to only a few pennies and elicit little response in terms of amount demanded. A 10 percent increase in the price of automobiles or housing means price increases of, say, $600 and $5,000 respectively. These latter increases are significant fractions of the annual incomes of many families, and quantities purchased could be expected to diminish significantly.

**3   Luxuries versus Necessities**   The demand for "necessities" tends to be inelastic; the demand for "luxuries" tends to be elastic. Bread and electricity are generally regarded as necessities; we "can't get along" without them. A price increase will not reduce significantly the amount of bread consumed or the amounts of lighting and power used in a household. A more extreme case: One does not decline an operation for acute appendicitis because the physician's fee has just gone up! On the other hand, French cognac and emeralds are luxuries which, by definition, can be forgone without undue inconvenience. If the price of cognac or emeralds rises, one need not purchase and, in so deciding, one will encounter no great hardship. The demand for salt tends to be highly inelastic on several counts. It is a "necessity"; unsalted cooking leaves much to be desired. There are no good substitutes available. Finally, salt is a negligible item in the family budget.

**4  Time**  Generally speaking, the demand for a product tends to be more elastic the longer the time period under consideration. One aspect of this generalization has to do with the fact that many consumers are creatures of habit. When the price of a product rises, it takes time to seek out and experiment with other products to see if they are acceptable to us. The social drinker may not immediately reduce his purchases to any significant degree when the price of bourbon rises by, say, 10 percent. But, given time, he may shift his affections to Scotch or vodka for which he has now "developed a taste." Another facet of this generalization has to do with product durability. Studies show that the "short-run" demand for gasoline is more inelastic at .2 than is the "long-run" demand at .7. Why so? Because in the long run, large, gas-guzzling automobiles wear out and, in a context of rising gasoline prices, are replaced by smaller, higher-mileage cars.

Table 23-3 shows estimated price elasticities of demand for a variety of products. It is recommended that you use the elasticity determinants just discussed to explain or rationalize each of these elasticity coefficients.

△  **Some Practical Applications**
The concept of elasticity of demand is something more than a theoretical notion designed to confuse unwary students. It is a notion of great practical significance. Some examples will make this evident.

**1  Wage Bargaining**  The United Automobile Workers once contended that automobile manufacturers should raise wages and

**TABLE 23-3**
**Selected Price Elasticities of Demand**

| Product | Price elasticity |
|---|---|
| Bread | .15 |
| Beef | .64 |
| Lamb and mutton | 2.65 |
| Eggs | .32 |
| Restaurant meals | 2.27 |
| Jewelry and watches | .41 |
| Electricity (household) | .13 |
| Medical care | .31 |
| Tobacco products | .46 |
| Automobile tires | .86 |
| Newspapers and magazines | .42 |

*Sources:* H. S. Houthakker and Lester D. Taylor, *Consumer Demand in the United States: Analyses and Projections,* 2d ed. (Cambridge, Mass.: Harvard University Press, 1970); and P. S. George and G. A. King, *Consumer Demand for Food Commodities in the United States with Projections for 1980* (Berkeley: University of California, 1971).

simultaneously cut automobile prices. Arguing that the elasticity of demand for automobiles was about 4, the UAW concluded that a price cut would help check inflation, boost the total receipts of manufacturers, and preserve or even increase the profits of producers. A spokesman for the Ford Motor Company, however, claimed that available studies suggest an elasticity of demand for automobiles in the 0.5–1.5 range. He held that price cuts would therefore shrink profits or result in losses for manufacturers. In this case, the elasticity of demand for automobiles was a strategic factor in labor-management relations and wage bargaining.[3]

**2  Bumper Crops**  Another example: Studies indicate that the demand for most farm products is highly inelastic. As a result, increases in the output of farm products due to a good growing season or to productivity in-

[3]See the statement by Theodore Yntema, vice president of finance, Ford Motor Company, before the Subcommittee on Antitrust and Monopoly of the Committee on the Judiciary, United States Senate, Feb. 4–5, 1958.

creases depress both the prices of farm products and the total receipts (incomes) of farmers. For farmers as a group, the inelastic nature of the demand for their products means that a bumper crop may be a mixed blessing. For policy makers it means that higher farm incomes depend upon the restriction of farm output.

**3  Automation**  The impact of automation, that is, of rapid technological advance, upon the level of employment depends in part upon the elasticity of demand for the product being manufactured. Suppose a firm installs new laborsaving machinery, resulting in the technological unemployment of, say, 500 workers. Suppose too that a part of the cost reduction resulting from this technological advance is passed on to consumers in the form of reduced product prices. Now, the effect of this price reduction upon the firm's sales and therefore the quantity of labor it needs will obviously depend upon the elasticity of product demand. An elastic demand might increase sales to the extent that some of, all, or even more than, the 500 displaced workers are reabsorbed by the firm. An inelastic demand will mean that few, if any, of the displaced workers will be reemployed, because the increase in the volume of the firm's business will be small.

**4  Deregulation**  Recent governmental deregulation of the airlines has resulted in increased profits for many carriers. The reason is that deregulation has increased price competition among the airlines, thereby lowering air fares. Lower fares, coupled with an elastic demand for air travel,[4] have increased revenues. Because the additional costs associated with flying full, as opposed to partially empty, aircraft are minimal, revenues have increased

[4]For a summary of studies on the elasticity of demand for air travel, see George W. Douglas and James C. Miller, III, *Economic Regulation of Domestic Air Transport* (Washington, D.C.: The Brookings Institution, 1974), pp. 34-38.

ahead of costs and profits have increased. In time, of course, these increased profits may be competed away by new firms entering the industry. And, unfortunately, in the past several years rapidly rising fuel costs have more than offset the tendency of fares to decline.

**5  Excise Taxes**  Government pays attention to the elasticity of demand when selecting goods and services upon which to levy excise taxes. Assume a $1 tax is currently levied upon some product and 10,000 units are sold. Tax revenue is obviously $10,000. If the tax is now raised to, say, $1.50, and sales decline to 5,000 because of an elastic demand, tax revenue will *decline* to $7,500. A higher tax on a product, the demand for which is elastic, will bring in less tax revenue. Hence, it behooves legislatures to seek out products for which demand is inelastic—for example, liquor and cigarettes—when levying excises.

These examples could be multiplied, but the main point is clear. Elasticity of demand is vitally important to businesses, farmers, labor, and government policy makers.

△ **Elasticity of Supply**

The concept of price elasticity can also be applied to supply. If producers are responsive to price changes, supply is elastic. If they are relatively insensitive to price changes, supply is inelastic.

The elasticity formula is pertinent in determining the degree of elasticity or inelasticity of supply. The only obvious alteration is the substitution of "percentage change in quantity *supplied*" for "percentage change in quantity *demanded.*"

The main determinant of the elasticity of supply is the amount of *time* which a producer has to respond to a given change in product price. Generally speaking, we can expect a greater output response—and therefore greater elasticity of supply—the longer the amount of time a producer has to adjust to a given price change. Why? Because a producer's response to an increase in the price of product X depends upon its ability to shift resources from the production of other products[5] to the production of X. And the shifting of resources takes time: the greater the time, the greater the resource "shiftability." Hence, the greater will be the output response and the elasticity of supply.

In analyzing the impact of time upon the elasticity of supply, economists find it useful to distinguish between the immediate market period, the short run, and the long run.

**1   The Market Period**   The immediate market period is so short a time that producers cannot respond to a change in demand and price. Example: Suppose a small truck farmer brings his entire season's output of tomatoes—one truckload—to market. The supply curve will be perfectly inelastic; the farmer will sell the truckload whether the price is high or low. Why? Because he cannot offer more tomatoes than his one truckload if the price of tomatoes should be higher than he had anticipated. Even though he might like to offer more, tomatoes cannot be produced overnight. It will take another full growing season to respond to a higher-than-expected price by producing more than one truckload. Similarly, because the product is perishable, the farmer cannot withhold it from the market. If the price is lower than he had anticipated, he will still sell the entire truckload. Costs of production, incidentally, will not be important in making this decision. Even though the price of tomatoes may fall far short of production costs, the farmer will nevertheless sell out to avoid a total loss through spoilage. In a very short time, then, our farmer's supply of tomatoes is fixed; he can offer one truckload no matter how high the price. The perishability of the product forces the farmer to sell all, no matter how low the price.

Figure 23-4a illustrates the truck farmer's perfectly inelastic supply curve in the market period. Note that he and other truck farmers are unable to respond to an assumed increase in demand; they do not have time to increase the amount supplied. The price increase from $P_o$ to $P_m$ simply rations a fixed supply to buyers, but elicits no increase in output.[6]

**2   The Short Run**   In the short run, the plant capacity of individual producers and of the industry is presumed to be fixed. But firms do have time to use their plants more or less intensively. Thus in the short run, our truck farmer's plant, which we shall consider as his land and farm machinery, is presumed fixed. But he does have time in the short run to cultivate tomatoes more intensively by applying more labor and more fertilizer and pesticides to his crop. The result is a greater output response to the presumed increase in demand; this greater output response is reflected in a more elastic supply of tomatoes, as shown by $S_S$ in Figure 23-4b. Note that the increase in demand is met by a larger quantity adjustment ($Q_o$ to $Q_s$) and a smaller price adjustment ($P_o$ to $P_s$) than in the market period; price is therefore lower than in the market period.

**3   The Long Run**   The long run is a time period sufficiently long so that firms can make all desired resource adjustments; individual firms can expand (or contract) their plant capacities, and new firms can enter (or existing firms can leave) the industry. In the "tomato industry" our individual truck farmer is able to acquire additional land and buy more machinery and equipment. Furthermore, more farmers may be attracted to tomato production by the increased demand and higher price. These adjustments mean an even greater supply re-

---

[5]The prices of which we assume to remain constant.

[6]The supply curve need not be perfectly inelastic (vertical) in the market period. If the product is not perishable, producers may choose, at low current prices, to store some of their product for future sale. This will cause the market supply curve to have some positive slope.

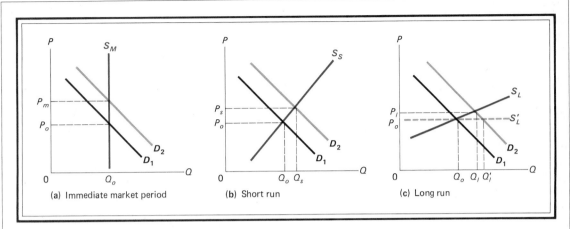

**FIGURE 23-4  TIME AND THE ELASTICITY OF SUPPLY**

The greater the amount of time producers have to adjust to a change in demand, the greater will be their output response. In the immediate market period **(a)** there is insufficient time to change output, and so supply is perfectly inelastic. In the short run **(b)** plant capacity is fixed, but output can be altered by changing the intensity of its use; supply is therefore more elastic. In the long run **(c)** all desired adjustments—including changes in plant capacity—can be made, and supply becomes still more elastic.

sponse, that is, an even more elastic supply curve $S_L$. The result, shown in Figure 23-4c, is a small price effect ($P_o$ to $P_l$) and a large output effect ($Q_o$ to $Q_l$) in response to the assumed increase in demand.

The solid supply curve in Figure 23-4c entails a new long-run equilibrium price $P_l$ which is somewhat higher than the original price, $P_o$, in Figure 23-4a. Why higher? The presumption is that tomato farming is an *increasing-cost industry,* meaning simply that the industry's expansion causes the prices of relevant resources to rise. The increased demand for fertilizer and farm equipment has pushed their prices up somewhat; the expanded demand for land has increased its value. In short, it is common and realistic to expect the expansion of an industry to result in "increasing costs." Hence, while $P_o$ was sufficient for profitable production in Figure 23-4a, a higher price, $P_l$, is required for profitable production in the enlarged industry. If the tomato industry hired very small or negligible portions of relevant resources, then its in-

creased demand for these inputs would leave their prices unchanged. In this *constant-cost industry* case the long-run supply curve would be perfectly elastic, as shown by the dashed curve $S'_L$ in Figure 23-4c. The new price would be equal to the original price, $P_o$, in Figure 23-4a. We shall discuss these cases more fully in Chapter 26.

A final point: You may have noted that no mention has been made of a total-revenue test for elasticity of supply. Indeed, there is none. Supply shows a direct relationship between price and the amount supplied; that is, the supply curve is upsloping. Thus, regardless of the degree of elasticity or inelasticity, price and total receipts will always move together.

## ☐ APPLICATIONS OF SUPPLY AND DEMAND ANALYSIS

Supply and demand analysis and the elasticity concept will be applied repeatedly in the remainder of this book. Let us strengthen our understanding of these analytical tools and their significance by examining two important applications: (1) legal prices, and (2) the incidence of sales taxes.

### △  Legal Prices

For the most part, the price system functions effectively in rationing goods and services and in allocating resources. Yet, under certain circumstances and in certain sectors of the economy, government has established by law prices which are above or below the equilibrium level. Let us briefly examine what happens to the functioning of the market when legal price fixing occurs.

**Price Ceilings and Shortages**  Price ceilings—maximum prices fixed by government which are *below* equilibrium prices—were used extensively during World War II and to a lesser extent during the Korean conflict as anti-inflationary devices. More recently, wage-price policies have been applied to alleviate the problem of premature inflation embodied in the Phillips Curve (Chapter 18).

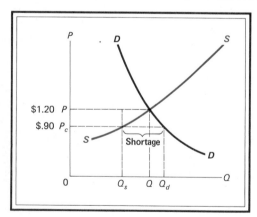

**FIGURE 23-5   CEILING PRICES RESULT IN PERSISTENT SHORTAGES**

Because the imposition of a price ceiling such as $P_c$ results in a persistent product shortage, as indicated by the distance $Q_s Q_d$, government must undertake the job of rationing the product in order to achieve an equitable distribution.

Let us turn back the clock to World War II and analyze the effects of a ceiling price upon, say, butter. The booming wartime prosperity of the early 1940s was shifting the demand for butter to the right so that, as in Figure 23-5, the equilibrium or market price $P$ was, say, $1.20 per pound. On the one hand, the rapidly rising price of butter was contributing to inflation and, on the other, rationing out of the butter market those families whose money incomes were not keeping pace with the soaring cost of living. Hence, to help stop inflation and to keep butter on the poor man's table, government imposed a ceiling price $P_c$ of, say, $.90 per pound.

What will be the effects of this ceiling price? The rationing ability of the free market will be rendered ineffective. At the ceiling price there will be a persistent shortage of butter. That is, the quantity of butter demanded at $P_c$ is $Q_d$ and the quantity supplied is only $Q_s$; hence, a persistent shortage in the amount $Q_s Q_d$ occurs. Stated differently, the legal price $P_c$ prevents the usual market adjustment wherein competition among buyers would bid up price, thereby simultaneously inducing more production and rationing some buyers out of the market until the shortage disappears at the equilibrium price and quantity, $P$ and $Q$.

Now, by preventing this free-market adjustment process from occurring, the ceiling price poses problems born of the market disequilibrium. First, how is the available supply $Q_s$ to be apportioned among buyers who want the amount $Q_d$? Should the supply be distributed on a first-come–first-served basis, that is, to those who are willing and able to stand in line the longest? Should the grocer distribute butter on the basis of favoritism? The point is that an unregulated shortage is hardly conducive to the equitable distribution of butter. Hence, to avoid catch-as-catch-can distribution, government must establish some formal system of rationing the product to consumers. This was accomplished during World War II by issuing ration coupons to individuals on an equitable basis. An effective rationing system entails the printing of ration coupons equal to $Q_s$ pounds of butter and the equitable distribution of these coupons among consumers so that, for example, the rich family of four and the poor family of four will both get the same number of coupons.

But the use of ration coupons does not prevent a second problem from arising. Specifically, the demand curve in Figure 23-5 tells us there are many buyers who are willing to pay more than the ceiling price. And, of course, it is more profitable for grocers to sell above the ceiling price. Hence, despite the sizable enforcement bureaucracy which accompanied World War II price controls, illegal *black markets*—markets wherein products were bought and sold at prices above the legal limits—flourished for many goods.

Finally, recall from Chapter 18 that ceiling prices entail the larger problem of prohibiting the price movements which are essential to preserve allocative efficiency through time. Example: Rent controls in New York City have contributed to a persistent housing shortage. Although the short-term effect of such controls may be to keep housing within reach of some of the poor, their longer-term impact is to inhibit alleviation of the housing shortage. Given low rents, investors are reluctant to construct new housing and investing in repairs tends to be unprofitable. The point is that rent controls prevent the rent increases needed to signal the profitable allocation of more resources to the construction of new housing and the renovation of old housing in New York City. This chapter's Last Word is relevant.

**Price Supports and Surpluses**   Price supports—minimum prices fixed by government which are *above* equilibrium prices—have generally been invoked when society has felt that the free functioning of the market system has failed to provide an equitable distribution of income. Minimum-wage legislation and the support of agricultural prices are the two most widely discussed examples of government price supports. Let us examine price supports as applied to a specific farm commodity.

Suppose the going market price for corn is $3 per bushel, and as a result of this price, farmers realize extremely low incomes. Government decides to lend a helping hand by establishing a legal support price of, say, $4 per bushel.

What will be the effects? At any price above the equilibrium price, quantity supplied will obviously exceed quantity demanded; there will be a persistent surplus of the product. Farmers will be willing to produce and offer for sale more than private buyers are willing to purchase at the supported price. The size of this surplus will vary directly with the elasticity of demand and supply. The greater the elasticity of demand and supply, the greater the resulting surplus. As is the case with a ceiling price, the rationing ability of the free market obviously has been disrupted by the imposition of a legal price.

Figure 23-6 provides us with a graphic illustration of the effect of a supported price. Let $SS$ and $DD$ be the supply and demand curves for corn. Equilibrium price and quantity are obviously $P$ and $Q$, respectively. If government imposes a supported price of $P_s$, farmers will be willing to produce $Q_s$, but private buyers will only take $Q_d$ off the market at that price. The surplus entailed is measured by the excess of $Q_s$ over $Q_d$.

Government inherits the task of coping with the surplus which a supported price entails. There are two general approaches open to government. First, it might invoke certain programs to restrict supply (for example, acreage allotments) or to increase demand (for example, research on new uses for agricultural products) in order to reduce the difference between the equilibrium price and the supported price and thereby the size of the resulting surplus. If these efforts are not wholly successful, then, secondly, government must purchase the surplus output (thereby subsidizing farmers) and store or otherwise dispose of it. We shall

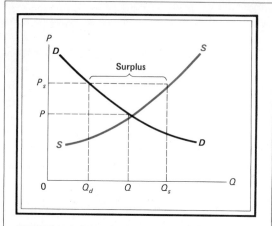

**FIGURE 23-6  SUPPORTED PRICES RESULT IN PERSISTENT SURPLUSES**

A price support such as $P_s$ gives rise to a persistent product surplus as indicated by the distance $Q_d Q_s$. Government must either purchase these surpluses or take measures to eliminate them by restricting product supply or increasing product demand.

have more to say about agricultural surpluses in Chapter 35.

The same reasoning as used in our agricultural price support example will lead us to conclude in Chapter 31 that, although the minimum wage is intended to improve the economic position of low-income workers, its actual effect may be to increase unemployment among such workers. The reader is urged to work through the implications of an above-equilibrium minimum wage in terms of Figure 23-6.

Recapitulation: Ceiling and supported prices rob the free-market forces of supply and demand of their ability to bring the supply decisions of producers and the demand decisions of buyers into accord with one another. Freely determined prices automatically ration products to buyers; legal prices do not. Therefore, government must accept the administrative problem of rationing which stems from price ceilings and the problem of buying or eliminating surpluses which price supports entail. Legal prices tend to break down unless

accompanied by programs to control consumption or production. But remember this: Although legal prices involve knotty problems for government by upsetting the rationing and allocation functions of the market mechanism, one must be careful not to prejudge ceilings or supports as undesirable. Legal prices are designed to correct alleged inequities which free-market prices entail.

### △  Tax Incidence

The concepts of supply and demand *and* the notion of elasticity are useful in determining who pays a sales or excise tax. Suppose that Figure 23-7 shows the market for a certain domestic wine and that the no-tax equilibrium price and quantity are $4 and 15 million bot-

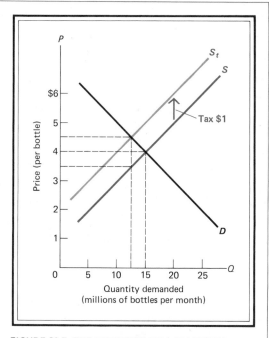

**FIGURE 23-7  THE INCIDENCE OF A SALES TAX**

The imposition of a sales tax of a specified amount, say $1 per unit, shifts the supply curve upward by the amount of the tax. This results in a higher price ($4.50) to the consumer and a lower after-tax price ($3.50) to the producer. In this particular case the burden of the tax is shared equally by consumers and producers.

tles. Now assume that government levies a specific sales or excise tax of $1 per bottle on this wine. Who actually pays this tax—producers or consumers? In technical terms (Chapter 8), what is the *incidence* of this tax?

**Division of Burden**  Assuming that government imposes the tax upon sellers (suppliers), it can be viewed as an addition to the supply price of the product. Therefore, the tax has the effect of shifting the supply curve upward by the amount of the tax. Thus, while sellers were willing to offer, for example, 6 million bottles of untaxed wine at $2 per bottle, they must now receive $3 per bottle—$2 plus the $1 tax—to offer the same 6 million bottles. Sellers must now get $1 more for each quantity supplied in order to receive the same per unit price as they were getting before the tax. The tax-caused upshift in the supply curve is shown in Figure 23-7, where $S$ is the "no-tax" supply curve and $S_t$ is the "after-tax" supply curve.

Careful comparison of after-tax supply and demand with the pretax equilibrium reveals that the new equilibrium price is $4.50, compared with the before-tax price of $4.00. In this particular case, one-half of the tax is paid by consumers and the other half by producers. Consumers obviously pay 50 cents more per bottle and, after remitting the $1 tax per unit to government, producers receive $3.50, or 50 cents less than the $4.00 before-tax price. In this instance, consumers and producers share the burden of the tax equally; producers shift half the tax forward to consumers in the form of a higher price and bear the other half themselves.

Note, incidentally, that the equilibrium quantity has fallen from 15 to $12\frac{1}{2}$ million bottles. This reduction in output may well have been an intended outcome of the imposition of the tax. That is, government may have reasoned that certain spillover or external costs result from the consumption of alcoholic beverages and therefore imposed an excise tax to adjust the market supply curve for these

costs and reduce the amount of resources allocated to wine production (Chapter 6).

**Elasticities**  If the elasticities of demand and supply were different from those shown in Figure 23-7, the incidence of the tax would also be different. Two generalizations are relevant.

**1**  *Given supply, the more inelastic the demand for the product, the larger the portion of the tax shifted forward to consumers.* The easiest way to verify this is to sketch graphically the extreme cases where demand is perfectly inelastic and perfectly elastic. In the first case the tax is shifted entirely to consumers; in the second instance the incidence of the tax is entirely upon sellers. Figure 23-8$a$ contrasts the more likely cases where demand might be relatively elastic ($D_e$) or relatively inelastic ($D_i$) in the relevant price range. In the elastic demand case, a small portion of the tax ($P_o P_e$) is shifted forward to consumers, and most of the tax is borne by producers. In the inelastic demand case, most of the tax ($P_o P_i$) is shifted to consumers, and only a small amount is paid by producers.

Note, too, that the decline in equilibrium quantity is smaller, the more inelastic the demand. This recalls an earlier application of the elasticity concept: Revenue-seeking legislatures tend to put heavy excise taxes upon liquor, cigarettes, automobile tires, and other products whose demand tends to be inelastic.

**2**  *Given demand, the more inelastic the supply the larger the portion of the tax borne by producers.* Figure 23-8$b$ explains this generalization. $S_e$ is a relatively elastic, and $S_i$ is a relatively inelastic, supply curve. $S_{et}$ and $S_{it}$ show these two curves after the imposition of an identical sales or excise tax. With the inelastic supply, we find that price rises by only $P_o P_i$; so a large portion of the tax must be borne by producers or sellers. But if supply is elastic, price will rise by the larger amount $P_o P_e$, so most of the tax is shifted to buyers and sellers bear only a small part of it. Quantity also declines less with an inelastic supply than it does with an elastic supply.

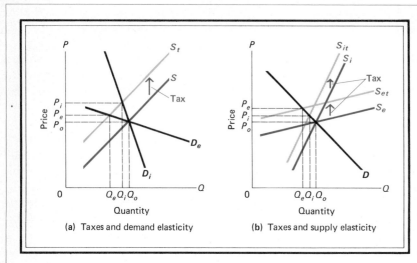

(a) Taxes and demand elasticity

(b) Taxes and supply elasticity

**FIGURE 23-8 ELASTICITY AND THE INCIDENCE OF A SALES TAX**

In **(a)** we find that if demand is elastic ($D_e$) in the relevant price range, price will rise modestly ($P_o$ to $P_e$) when a sales or excise tax is imposed; hence the producer bears most of the tax burden. But if demand is inelastic ($D_i$) in the relevant price range, price will increase substantially ($P_o$ to $P_i$) and most of the tax will be shifted to consumers. Part **(b)** demonstrates that a sales or excise tax of a given amount will fall primarily upon producers when supply is inelastic ($S_i$), but largely upon buyers when supply is elastic ($S_e$).

**Implications**   There are many additional implications which can be derived from this kind of analysis. For example, recall that subsidies are negative taxes. Therefore, a specific subsidy paid to a producer shifts the supply curve *downward* by the amount of the subsidy. What generalizations can you derive which relate the incidence of the benefits from a subsidy of some fixed amount per unit of output to the elasticity of demand? The elasticity of supply? Also, you might demonstrate graphically how excise taxes and subsidies can be used to adjust output and therefore improve the allocation of resources when substantial spillover costs and benefits are present in the production or consumption of certain goods (Chapter 6). The point to be stressed is that the tools of supply and demand and elasticity are of great significance in analyzing the full implications of taxes and subsidies.

## Summary

**1**   The present chapter extends the rudiments of demand and supply analysis developed in Chapter 4. The summarizing statements pertinent to that chapter should be reviewed at this point.

**2**   Elasticity of demand measures the responsiveness of consumers to price changes. If consumers are sensitive to price changes, demand is elastic. If consumers are unresponsive to price changes, demand is inelastic.

**3**   The price elasticity formula measures the degree of elasticity or inelasticity of demand. The formula is

$$E_d = \frac{\text{percentage change in quantity demanded}}{\text{percentage change in price}}$$

The averages of the prices and quantities under consideration are used as reference points in determining the percentage changes in price and quantity. If $E_d$ is greater than 1, demand is elastic. If $E_d$ is less than 1, demand is inelastic. Unit elasticity is the special case in which $E_d$ equals 1.

**4** Price elasticity of demand can be determined by observing the effect of a price change upon total receipts from the sale of the product. If price and total receipts move in opposite directions, demand is elastic. If price and total receipts move in the same direction, demand is inelastic.

**5** The number of available substitutes, the size of an item in one's budget, whether the product is a luxury or necessity, and the time period involved are all considerations which influence elasticity of demand.

**6** Elasticity varies at different price ranges on a demand curve. Furthermore, it is not correct to judge elasticity by the steepness or flatness of a demand curve on a graph.

**7** The elasticity concept is also applicable to supply. Elasticity of supply depends upon the shiftability of resources between alternative employments. This shiftability in turn varies with the amount of time producers have to adjust to a given price change.

**8** Legally fixed prices upset the rationing function of free-market prices. Effective price ceilings result in persistent product shortages, and if an equitable distribution of the product is sought, government will have to ration the product to consumers. Price supports give rise to product surpluses; government must purchase these surplus products *or* eliminate them by imposing restrictions on production or by increasing private demand.

**9** Sales and excise taxes affect supply and therefore equilibrium price and quantity. The more inelastic the demand for a product, the greater is the portion of the tax which is shifted to consumers. The greater the inelasticity of supply, the larger the portion of the tax borne by sellers.

## Questions and Study Suggestions

**1** Key terms and concepts to remember: elasticity formula; elastic versus inelastic demand; perfectly inelastic demand; perfectly elastic demand; total-revenue test; elasticity of supply; market period; the short run and long run; increasing- and constant-cost industries; price ceiling; price support; tax incidence.

**2** Answer questions 2, 4, and 11 at the end of Chapter 4.

**3** In many oligopolistic industries, for example, the petroleum industry, producers justify their reluctance to lower prices by arguing that the demand for their products is inelastic. Explain.

**4** How will the following changes in price affect total receipts (expenditures)—that is, will total receipts *increase, decline,* or *remain unchanged?*

    *a.* Price falls and demand is inelastic.↓

    *b.* Price rises and demand is elastic. ↓

    *c.* Price rises and supply is elastic. ↑

    *d.* Price rises and supply is inelastic.↑

    *e.* Price rises and demand is inelastic.↑

    *f.* Price falls and demand is elastic.↑

    *g.* Price falls and demand is of unit elasticity. Un

**5** Determine the elasticity of demand and supply for the following demand and supply schedules. Use the total-revenue test to check the answers given by the $E_d$ formula.

| $E_s$ | Quantity supplied | Product price | Quantity demanded | Total revenue | $E_d$ |
|---|---|---|---|---|---|
| | 28,000 | $10 | 10,000 | $_____ | |
| _____ | 22,500 | 9 | 13,000 | _____ | _____ |
| _____ | 17,000 | 8 | 17,000 | _____ | _____ |
| _____ | 13,000 | 7 | 22,000 | _____ | _____ |
| _____ | 11,000 | 6 | 25,000 | _____ | _____ |

**6** What are the major determinants of elasticity of demand? Use these determinants in judging whether the demand for the following products is elastic or inelastic: ***a.*** oranges; ***b.*** cigarettes; ***c.*** Winston cigarettes; ***d.*** gasoline; ***e.*** butter; ***f.*** salt; ***g.*** automobiles; ***h.*** football games; ***i.*** diamond bracelets; and ***j.*** this textbook.

**7** Why is it difficult to judge elasticity of demand or supply by merely observing the appearance of a demand or supply curve on a graph?

**8** Empirical estimates suggest the following demand elasticities: .6 for physicians' services; 4.0 for foreign travel; and 1.2 for radio and television receivers. Use the generalizations for the determinants of elasticity developed in this chapter to explain each of these figures.

**9** What effect may a rule that university students live in university dormitories have upon the elasticity of demand for dormitory space? What impact might this in turn have upon room rates?

**10** Suppose you are sponsoring an outdoor rock concert. Your major costs—for the band, land rent, and security—are largely independent of attendance. Use the concept of elasticity of demand to explain how you might go about establishing ticket prices.

**11** Why is it desirable for ceiling prices to be accompanied by government rationing? And for price supports to be accompanied by surplus-purchasing or output-restricting or demand-increasing programs? Show graphically why price ceilings entail shortages and price supports result in surpluses. What effect, if any, does the elasticity of demand and supply have upon the size of these shortages and surpluses? Explain.

**12** New York City has had rent controls since 1941. What effect do you think they have had upon the demand for housing? Upon the construction of new housing?

**13** How would you expect the elasticity of supply of product X to differ in a situation of full employment in industry X, on the one hand, and of considerable unemployment in the industry, on the other? Explain.

**14** "If the demand for farm products is highly inelastic, a bumper crop may reduce farm incomes." Evaluate and illustrate graphically.

**15** What is the incidence of ***a.*** a sales tax and ***b.*** a subsidy, when demand is highly inelastic? Elastic? What effect does the elasticity of supply have upon the incidence of a sales tax? A subsidy?

**16** Suppose you are chairperson of a state commission that is responsible for establishing a program to raise new revenue through the use of excise taxes. Would elasticity of demand be important to you in determining those products upon which excises should be levied? Explain.

**17** Explain the error in the following argument: "For the past four years the prices of automobiles have been rising and each year people have purchased more autos. Price and quantity are directly related and the economists' law of demand is obviously incorrect."

**18** *Advanced analysis.* The price-quantity data shown below constitute a straight-line demand curve. Use either the elasticity coefficient or the total-revenue test to determine the elasticity of demand for each possible price change. What can you conclude about the relationship between the slope of a curve and its elasticity?

| Product price | Quantity demanded |
|---|---|
| $5 | 1 |
| 4 | 2 |
| 3 | 3 |
| 2 | 4 |
| 1 | 5 |

# Selected References

Allen, Clark Lee: *The Framework of Price Theory* (Belmont, Calif.: Wadsworth Publishing Company, Inc., 1967), chaps. 2–4.

Boulding, Kenneth E.: *Economic Analysis: Microeconomics,* 4th ed. (New York: Harper & Row, Publishers, Incorporated, 1966), chaps. 7–12.

Brennan, Michael J.: *Theory of Economic Statics,* 2d ed. (Englewood Cliffs, N.J.: Prentice-Hall, Inc., 1970), chaps. 4–8.

Brue, Stanley L., and Donald R. Wentworth: *Economic Scenes: Theory in Today's World,* 2d ed. (Englewood Cliffs, N.J.: Prentice-Hall, Inc., 1980), chap. 5.

Kaish, Stanley: *Microeconomics: Logic, Tools, and Analysis* (New York: Harper & Row, Publishers, Incorporated, 1976), chap. 3.

# LAST WORD
## Rent Controls: A Self-Fulfilling Prophecy

Rent controls may aggravate the very problem they are designed to rectify.

To the Editor:

Your recent news article on rent control prompts some comments.

Rent control (or stabilization) may not be forever but it is likely to be for a very long time. Once installed, controls have an immediate and passionate constituency which virtually guarantees their continuance regardless of need. For example, in my own county of Westchester, some 80,000 units are now subject to either rent control or rent stabilization. This represents a bloc of over 100,000 voters out of a total population of somewhat under 900,000. No conceivable coalition of builders, apartment owners and other "interests" is going to be able to match that political muscle. New York City's controls were enacted in the midst of a world war and have now lasted one third of a century with no end in sight.

Rent controls will depress the construction of new rental housing. Since controls limit profit opportunities but not loss possibilities, this conclusion seems inevitable. Capital will be shifted from areas with controls to areas without controls. Controls are thus a self-fulfilling prophecy. Brought into being by a housing shortage, they depress construction, helping to perpetuate the shortage which justifies their existence. Controls will lead to lower housing quality. If a unit must be rented at below market rates (otherwise controls have no meaning) the motivation to improve it disappears. The rational course for the owner is to improve his short-term cash flow by disinvesting.

Controls will shift the property tax burden. Since property taxes on rental properties are paid out of rents, controlled rents mean less capacity to pay taxes. Thus the burden will be shifted from controlled properties to owner-occupied residences and commercial structures. As in other areas of life, "there is no free lunch."

As an instrument of income redistribution—from wealthy landlords to poor tenants—controls leave a lot to be desired because not all landlords are rich and not all tenants are poor. It would make more sense to subsidize poor tenants directly than to control the entire market to help those who cannot survive in it unassisted.

Rent control (or stabilization) is politically attractive because tenants far outnumber landlords and because it appears to protect the weak against the powerful. But like some other quick fixes, its short-term effects are much more pleasant than its long-term effects.

John M. Levy
Dobbs Ferry, N.Y.

# Further Topics in the Theory of Consumer Demand[1]

# chapter 24

In Chapter 23 we extended our understanding of demand and supply by introducing the concept of price elasticity and by discussing some specific applications of demand and supply analysis. The present chapter is devoted to further consideration of the demand side of the market. In Chapter 25 we shall discuss production costs, which, we shall discover, are the major determinant of supply. The goal of Chapters 26 to 29 is to use our understanding of demand and supply in analyzing pricing and output decisions under the various market structures which were outlined in Chapter 22.

Now for a more detailed look at the two main objectives of the present chapter. First, we seek a more sophisticated explanation of the law of demand. Second, we want to understand how consumers allocate their money incomes among various goods and services.

Why does a consumer buy some specific bundle of goods rather than any one of a number of other collections of goods which are available?

## ☐ TWO EXPLANATIONS OF THE LAW OF DEMAND

The law of demand may be treated as a commonsense notion. A high price usually does discourage consumers from buying; a low price typically does encourage them to buy. Now let us explore two complementary explanations of the downsloping nature of the demand curve which will back up our everyday observations.[2]

### △ Income and Substitution Effects

You may recall from Chapter 4 that the law of demand—the downsloping demand curve—can be explained in terms of the income

---

[1] To the instructor: This is an optional chapter which may be omitted without impairing the continuity and meaning of ensuing chapters.

[2] A third explanation, based upon *indifference curves,* is in some respects more precise and more sophisticated than the two we now discuss. An introduction to indifference curve analysis is provided in the appendix to this chapter.

and substitution effects. Whenever the price of a product decreases, two things happen to cause the amount demanded to increase.

**1  Income Effect**  If the price of a product—say, steak—declines, the real income or purchasing power of anyone buying that product will increase. This increase in real income will be reflected in increased purchases of a variety of products, including steak. For example, with a constant money income of, say, $20 per week you can purchase 10 pounds of steak at a price of $2 per pound. But if the price of steak falls to $1 per pound and you buy 10 pounds of steak, $10 per week is freed for buying more of this and other commodities. A decline in the price of steak increases the real income of the consumer, enabling him or her to purchase a larger quantity of steak. This is called the *income effect*.

**2  Substitution Effect**  The lower price of a product means that it is now cheaper relative to all other products. And consumers will tend to substitute the cheaper product for other products which are now relatively more expensive. In our example, as the price of steak falls—the prices of other products being unchanged—steak will become more attractive to the buyer. At $1 per pound it is a "better buy" than at $2 per pound. Consequently, the lower price will induce the consumer to substitute steak for some of the now less attractive items in the budget. Steak may well be substituted for pork, chicken, veal, and a variety of other foods. A lower price increases the relative attractiveness of a product and makes the consumer willing to buy more of it. This is known as the *substitution effect*.

The income and substitution effects combine to make a consumer able and willing to buy more of a specific good at a low price than at a high price.

△  **Law of Diminishing Marginal Utility**

A second explanation centers upon the notion that, although consumer wants in general may be insatiable, wants for specific commodities can be fulfilled. In a given span of time, wherein the tastes of buyers are unchanged, consumers can get as much of specific goods and services as they want. The more of a specific product consumers obtain, the less anxious they are to get more units of the same product. This can be most readily seen for durable goods. A consumer's want for an automobile, when he or she has none, may be very strong; the desire for a second car is much less intense; for a third or fourth, very weak. Even the wealthiest of families rarely have more than a half-dozen cars, despite the fact that their incomes would allow them to purchase and maintain a whole fleet of them.

Economists put forth the idea that specific consumer wants can be fulfilled with succeeding units of a commodity in the *law of diminishing marginal utility*. Let us dissect this law to see exactly what it means. A product has utility if it has the power to satisfy a want. *Utility* is want-satisfying power. Two characteristics of this concept must be emphasized: First, "utility" and "usefulness" are by no means synonymous. Paintings by Picasso may be useless in the functional sense of the term yet be of tremendous utility to art connoisseurs. Second—and implied in the first point—utility is a subjective notion. The utility of a specific product will vary widely from person to person. A bottle of muscatel wine may yield substantial utility to the Skid Row alcoholic, but zero or negative utility to the local WCTU president.

By *marginal* utility we simply mean the extra utility, or satisfaction, which a consumer gets from one additional unit of a specific product. In any relatively short time wherein the consumer's tastes can be assumed not to change, the marginal utility derived from successive units of a given product will decline.[3]

---

[3] For a time the marginal utility of successive units of a product may increase. A third cigarette may yield a larger amount of extra satisfaction than the first or second. But beyond some point, we can expect the marginal utility of added units to decline.

Why? Because a consumer will eventually become saturated, or "filled up," with that particular product. The fact that marginal utility will decline as the consumer acquires additional units of a specific product is known as the *law of diminishing marginal utility.*

We have noted that utility is a subjective concept. As a result, it is not susceptible to precise quantitative measurement. But for purposes of illustration, let us assume that we can measure satisfaction with units we shall call "utils." This mythical unit of satisfaction is merely a convenient pedagogical device which will allow us to quantify our thinking about consumer behavior. Thus, in Table 24-1, we can illustrate the relationship between the quantity obtained of a product—say, product A—and the accompanying extra utility derived from each successive unit. Here we assume that the law of diminishing marginal utility sets in with the first unit of A obtained. Each successive unit yields less and less extra utility than the previous one as the consumer's want for A comes closer and closer to fulfillment. Total utility can obviously be found for any number of units of A by cumulating the marginal-utility figures as indicated in Table 24-1. The third unit of A has a marginal utility of 7 utils; 3 units of A yields a total utility of 25 utils ( = 10 + 8 + 7).

Now, how does the law of diminishing marginal utility explain why the demand curve for a specific product is downsloping? If suc-cessive units of a good yield smaller and smaller amounts of marginal, or extra, utility, the consumer will buy additional units of a product only if its price falls. The consumer for whom these utility data are relevant may buy, say, 2 units of A at a price of $1. But, owing to diminishing marginal utility from additional units of A, a consumer will choose *not* to buy more at this price, because giving up money really means giving up other goods, that is, alternative ways of getting utility. Therefore, additional units of A are "not worth it" unless the price (sacrifice of other goods) declines. From the seller's viewpoint, diminishing marginal utility forces the producer to lower the price in order to induce buyers to take a larger quantity of the product. This rationale obviously supports the notion of a downsloping demand curve.

## ☐  THEORY OF CONSUMER BEHAVIOR

In addition to providing a basis for explaining the law of demand, the idea of diminishing marginal utility also plays a key role in explaining how consumers should allocate their money income among the many goods and services which are available for them to buy.

### △  Consumer Choice and Budget Restraint

We can picture the situation of the typical consumer as being something like this:

**1 Rational Behavior** The average consumer is a fairly rational person, and attempts to dispose of his or her money income in such a way as to derive the greatest amount of satisfaction, or utility, from it. The typical consumer wants to get "the most for his money."

**2 Preferences** We may suppose, too, that the average consumer has rather clear-cut preferences for various goods and services available in the market. We assume that buyers have a pretty good idea of how much mar-

**TABLE 24-1**
**The Law of Diminishing Marginal Utility as Applied to Product A** (*hypothetical data*)

| Unit of product A | Marginal utility, utils | Total utility, utils |
|---|---|---|
| First | 10 | 10 |
| Second | 8 | 18 |
| Third | 7 | 25 |
| Fourth | 6 | 31 |
| Fifth | 5 | 36 |
| Sixth | 4 | 40 |
| Seventh | 3 | 43 |

ginal utility they will get from successive units of the various products which they might choose to purchase.

**3　Budget Restraint**　The consumer's money income is limited in amount. Because a consumer supplies limited amounts of human and property resources to businesses, the money income received will be limited. With a few exceptions—the Rockefellers, Bob Hope, and Saudi Arabia's King Khalid—all consumers are subject to a *budget restraint.*

**4　Prices**　The goods and services available to consumers have price tags on them. Why? Because they are scarce in relation to the demand for them, or, stated differently, their production entails the use of scarce and therefore valuable resources. In the ensuing examples we shall suppose that product prices are not affected by the amounts of specific goods which the individual consumer buys; pure competition exists on the buying or demand side of the market.

Obviously, if a consumer has a limited number of dollars and the products he or she wants have price tags on them, the consumer will be able to purchase only a limited amount of goods. The consumer cannot buy everything wanted when each purchase exhausts a portion of a limited money income. It is precisely this obvious point which brings the economic fact of scarcity home to the individual consumer.[4]

> In making his choices, our typical consumer is in the same position as the Western prospector . . . who is restocking for his next trip into the back country and who is forced by the nature of the terrain to restrict his luggage to whatever he can carry on the back of one burro. If he takes a great deal of one item, say baked beans, he must necessarily take much less of something else, say bacon. His job is to find that collection of products which, in view of the limitations imposed on the total, will best suit his needs and tastes.

[4]E. T. Weiler, *The Economic System* (New York: The Macmillan Company, 1952), p. 89.

The consumer must make compromises; some choosing must be done among alternative goods to obtain with limited money resources the most satisfying mix of goods and services.

△　**Utility-maximizing Rule**

The question then boils down to this: Of all the collections of goods and services which a consumer can obtain within the limit of his or her budget, which specific collection will yield the greatest utility or satisfaction? Bluntly put, the rule to be followed in maximizing satisfactions is that *the consumer's money income should be allocated so that the last dollar spent on each product purchased yields the same amount of extra (marginal) utility.* We shall call this the *utility-maximizing rule.* When the consumer is "balancing his margins" in accordance with this rule, there will be no incentive to alter his or her expenditure pattern. The consumer will be in equilibrium and, barring a change in tastes, income, or the prices of the various goods, he or she will be worse off—total utility will decline—by any alteration in the collection of goods purchased.

Now a detailed illustration will help explain the validity of the rule. For simplicity's sake we limit our discussion to just two products. Keep in mind that the analysis can readily be extended to any number of goods. Suppose that consumer Brooks is trying to decide which combination of two products—A and B—she should purchase with her limited daily income of $10. Obviously, Brooks's preferences for these two products and their prices will be basic data determining the combination of A and B which will maximize her satisfactions. Table 24-2 summarizes Brooks's preferences for products A and B. Column 2a shows the amount of extra or marginal utility Brooks will derive from each successive unit of A. Column 3a reflects Brooks's preferences for product B. In each case the relationship between the number of units of the product obtained and the corresponding marginal utility reflects the law of diminishing marginal utility. Diminishing marginal utility is assumed to set in with the first unit of each product purchased.

**TABLE 24-2**
**The Utility-Maximizing Combination of Products A and B Obtainable with an Income of $10\* (*hypothetical data*)**

| (1) | (2) Product A: price = $1 | | (3) Product B: price = $2 | |
|---|---|---|---|---|
| Unit of product | (a) Marginal utility, utils | (b) Marginal utility per dollar (MU/price) | (a) Marginal utility, utils | (b) Marginal utility per dollar (MU/price) |
| First | 10 | 10 | 24 | 12 |
| Second | 8 | 8 | 20 | 10 |
| Third | 7 | 7 | 18 | 9 |
| Fourth | 6 | 6 | 16 | 8 |
| Fifth | 5 | 5 | 12 | 6 |
| Sixth | 4 | 4 | 6 | 3 |
| Seventh | 3 | 3 | 4 | 2 |

*It is assumed in this table that the amount of marginal utility received from additional units of each of the two products is independent of the quantity of the other product. For example, the marginal-utility schedule for product A is independent of the amount of B obtained by the consumer.

But before we can apply the utility-maximizing rule to these data, we must put the marginal-utility information of columns 2a and 3a on a per-dollar-spent basis. Why? Because a consumer's choices will be influenced not only by the extra utility which successive units of, say, product A will yield, but also by how many dollars (and therefore how many units of alternative good B) she must give up to obtain those added units of A. Example: Brooks may clearly prefer to own a Cadillac rather than a Ford; she may be twice as happy with a Cadillac than with a Ford. Yet she may buy a Ford because a Cadillac costs three or four times as much as a Ford. Brooks may feel that *per dollar spent,* a Ford is a better buy. The point is this: To make the amounts of extra utility derived from differently priced goods comparable, marginal utility must be put on a per-dollar-spent basis. This is done in columns 2b and 3b. These figures are obtained by dividing the marginal-utility data of columns 2a and 3a by the assumed prices of A and B—$1 and $2, respectively.

Now we have Brooks's preferences—on unit and per dollar bases—and the price tags of A and B before us. Brooks stands patiently with $10 to spend on A and B. In what order should she allocate her dollars on units of A and B to achieve the highest degree of utility within the limits imposed by her money income? And what specific combination of A and B will she have obtained at the time that she exhausts her $10?

Concentrating on columns 2b and 3b of Table 24-2, we find that Brooks should first spend $2 on the first unit of B. Why? Because its marginal utility per dollar of 12 utils is higher than A's. But now Brooks finds herself indifferent about whether she should buy a second unit of B or the first unit of A. Suppose she buys both of them: Brooks now has 1 unit of A and 2 of B. Note that with this combination of goods the last dollar spent on each yields the same amount of extra utility. Does this combination of A and B therefore represent the maximum amount of utility which Brooks can obtain? The answer is "No." This collection of goods only costs $5 [=(1 × $1) + (2 × $2)]; Brooks has $5 of income remaining, which she can spend to achieve a still higher level of total utility.

Examining columns 2b and 3b again, we find that Brooks should spend the next $2 on a third unit of B. But, now with 1 unit of A and 3 of B, we find she is again indifferent to a second unit of A and a fourth unit of B. Let us again assume Brooks purchases one more unit of each. Marginal utility per dollar is now the same for the last dollar spent on each product, *and* Brooks's money income of $10 is exhausted $[(2 \times \$1) + (4 \times \$2)]$. *The utility-maximizing combination of goods attainable by Brooks is 2 units of A and 4 of B.*[5]

It is to be emphasized that there are other combinations of A and B which are obtainable with $10. But none of these will yield a level of total utility as high as do 2 units of A and 4 of B. For example, 4 units of A and 3 of B can be obtained for $10. However, this combination violates the utility-maximizing rule; total utility here is only 93 utils, clearly inferior to the 96 utils yielded by 2 of A and 4 of B. Furthermore, there are other combinations of A and B (such as 4 of A and 5 of B *or* 1 of A and 2 of B) wherein the marginal utility of the last dollar spent is the same for both A and B. But such combinations are either unobtainable with Brooks's limited money income (as 4 of A and 5 of B) or fail to exhaust her money income (as 1 of A and 2 of B) and therefore do not yield her the maximum utility attainable.

△  **Algebraic Restatement**

We are now in a position to restate the utility-maximizing rule in simple algebraic terms. Our rule simply says that a consumer will maximize her satisfaction when she allocates her money income in such a way that the last dollar spent on product A, the last on product B, and so forth, yield equal amounts of additional, or marginal, utility. Now the marginal utility per dollar spent on A is indicated by MU of product A/price of A (column 2b of Table 24-2) and the marginal utility per dollar

spent on B by MU of product B/price of B (column 3b of Table 24-2). Our utility-maximizing rule merely requires that these ratios be equal. That is,

$$\frac{\text{MU of product A}}{\text{price of A}} = \frac{\text{MU of product B}}{\text{price of B}}$$

and, of course, the consumer must exhaust her available income. Our tabular illustration has shown us that the combination of 2 units of A and 4 of B fulfills these conditions in that

$$\frac{8}{1} = \frac{16}{2}$$

and the consumer's $10 income is spent.

If the equation is not fulfilled, there will be some reallocation of the consumer's expenditures between A and B, from the low to the high marginal-utility-per-dollar product, which will increase the consumer's total utility. For example, the consumer may spend $10 on 4 of A and 3 of B. But here we find that

$$\frac{\text{MU of A: 6 utils}}{\text{price of A: \$1}} < \frac{\text{MU of B: 18 utils}}{\text{price of B: \$2}}$$

The last dollar spent on A provides only 6 utils of satisfaction, and the last dollar spent on B provides 9. On a per dollar basis, units of B provide more extra satisfaction than units of A. The consumer will obviously increase her total satisfaction by purchasing more of B and less of A. As dollars are reallocated from A to B, the marginal utility from additional units of B will decline as the result of moving *down* the diminishing marginal-utility schedule for B, and the marginal utility of A will rise as the consumer moves *up* the diminishing marginal-utility schedule for A. At some new combination of A and B—specifically, 2 of A and 4 of B—the equality of the two ratios and therefore consumer equilibrium will be achieved. As we already know, the net gain in utility is 3 utils $(= 96 - 93)$.

---

[5]To simplify, we assume in this example that Brooks spends her entire income; she neither borrows nor saves. Saving can be regarded as a utility-yielding commodity and incorporated in our analysis. It is treated thus in question 5 at the end of the chapter.

## ☐ MARGINAL UTILITY AND THE DEMAND CURVE

It is a quite simple step from the utility-maximizing rule to the construction of an individual's downsloping demand curve. Recall from Chapters 4 and 23 that the basic determinants of an individual's demand curve for a specific product are (1) preferences or tastes, (2) money income, and (3) the prices of other goods. Now the utility data of Table 24-2 reflect our consumer's preferences. Let us continue to suppose that her money income is given at $10. And, concentrating upon the construction of a simple demand curve for product B, let us assume that the price of A—representing "other goods"—is given at $1. We should now be able to derive a simple demand schedule for B by considering alternative prices at which B might be sold and determining the corresponding quantity our consumer will choose to purchase. Of course, we have already determined one such price-quantity combination in explaining the utility-maximizing rule: Given tastes, income, and the prices of other goods, the rational consumer will purchase 4 units of B at a price of $2. Now assume the price of B falls to $1. This means that the marginal-utility-per-dollar data of column 3b will double, because the price of B has been halved; the new data for column 3b are in fact identical to those shown in column 3a. The purchase of 2 units of A and 4 of B is no longer an equilibrium combination. By applying the same reasoning used to develop the utility-maximizing rule, we now find Brooks's utility-maximizing position entails 4 units of A and 6 of B. That is, we can sketch Brooks's demand curve for B as in Table 24-3. This, of course, confirms the downsloping demand curve discussed in earlier chapters.

**TABLE 24-3**
**The Demand Schedule for Product B**

| Price per unit of B | Quantity demanded |
| --- | --- |
| $2 | 4 |
| 1 | 6 |

## ☐ THE TIME DIMENSION

The theory of consumer behavior has been generalized to take the economic value of *time* into account.[6] Both consumption and production activities have a common characteristic—they take time. And time is obviously a valuable economic resource; by working—by using an hour in productive activity—one may earn $6, $10, or $50, depending upon one's education, skills, and so forth. By using that hour for leisure or in consumption activities, one obviously incurs the opportunity cost of forgone income; you sacrifice the $6, $10, or $50 you could have earned by working.

### △ The Value of Time

In the marginal-utility theory of consumer behavior, economists traditionally have assumed that consumption is an instantaneous act. However, it is logical to argue that the "prices" of consumer goods should include, not merely the market price, but also the value of the time required in the consumption of the good. In other words, the denominators of our earlier marginal-utility/price ratios are inadequate because they do not reflect the "full price"—market price *plus* the value of the consumption time—of the product.

Imagine a consumer who is considering the purchase of a round of golf, on the one hand, and a concert, on the other. The market price of the golf game is $5 and the concert is $8. But the golf game is more time-intensive than the concert. Suppose you will spend four hours on the golf course, but only two hours at the concert. If your time is worth, say $4 per hour—as evidenced by the $4 wage rate you can obtain by working—then we must recognize that the "full price" of the golf game is $21 (the $5 market price *plus* $16 worth of time). Similarly, the "full price" of the concert is $16 (the $8 market price *plus* $8 worth of time). We find that, contrary to what market prices

[6]The classic article, Gary Becker's "A Theory of the Allocation of Time," *Economic Journal*, September 1965, pp. 493–517, is not easily digested by the beginning student.

alone would indicate, the "full price" of the concert is really *less* than the "full price" of the golf game. If we now invoke the simplifying assumption that the marginal utility derived from successive golf games and concerts are identical, traditional theory would indicate that one should consume more golf games than concerts because the market price of the former is lower ($5) than the latter ($8). But when time is taken into account, the situation is reversed and golf games are more expensive ($21) than are concerts ($16). Hence, it is rational to consume more concerts than golf games!

### △  Some Implications

By taking time into account, we can explain certain observable phenomena which the traditional theory does not. It may be rational for the unskilled worker or retiree whose time has little or no market value to ride a bus from New York to Chicago. But the corporate executive, whose time is very valuable, will find it cheaper to fly, even though bus fare is only a fraction of plane fare. It is sensible for the retiree, living on a modest social security check and having ample time, to spend many hours shopping for bargains. It is equally intelligent for the highly paid physician, working 55 hours per week, to patronize fast-food restaurants and to buy a new television set over the phone. Affluent Americans are observed by foreigners to be "wasteful" of food and other material goods, but "overly economical" in the use of time. Americans who visit less developed countries find that time is used casually or "squandered," while material goods are very highly prized and carefully used. These differences are not a paradox or a case of radically different temperaments. The differences are primarily a quite rational reflection of the fact that the high labor productivity which is characteristic of an advanced society gives time a high market value, whereas precisely the opposite is true in a less developed country.

A final point: As labor productivity has increased historically with the growth of our economy, time has become more valuable in the labor market. Or, stated differently, time used on pure leisure and various consumer activities has become more expensive. As a result, we make a great effort to use nonwork time more "productively." Where possible, we try to increase the pleasure or utility yield per hour by consuming more per unit of time. In some cases this means making consumption more goods-intensive; for example, by buying or renting a motorized golf cart, the time required for a round of golf can be reduced. One watches the news on television because it takes less time than reading the newspaper. In other instances, we consume two or more items simultaneously. After dinner, the consumer "may find himself drinking Brazilian coffee, smoking a Dutch cigar, sipping a French cognac, reading *The New York Times,* listening to a Brandenburg Concerto and entertaining his Swedish wife—all at the same time, with varying degrees of success."[7] But the yield from certain uses of time—pure idleness, cultural pursuits, and the "cultivation of mind and spirit"—cannot be readily increased, Hence, time tends to be shifted from these uses to areas where the yield is greater. This helps explain why, although economic development may bring affluence in the form of goods, it also increases the relative scarcity of time and creates a more hectic life-style. Economic growth, it is argued, cannot produce abundance in all respects; total affluence—an abundance of *both* goods and time—is a logical fallacy. Advanced economies are goods rich and time poor, while underdeveloped countries are time rich and goods poor!

---

[7] Staffan B. Linder, *The Harried Leisure Class* (New York: Columbia University Press, 1970), p. 79. This delightful book is required reading for the person who wants to pursue the many implications of the increasing value of time.

## Summary

**1**   The law of demand can be explained in terms of the income and substitution effects or the law of diminishing marginal utility.

**2**   The income effect says that a decline in the price of a product will enable the consumer to buy more of it with a fixed money income.  The substitution effect points out that a lower price will make a product relatively more attractive and therefore increase the consumer's willingness to substitute it for other products.

**3**   The law of diminishing marginal utility states that beyond some point, additional units of a specific commodity will yield ever-declining amounts of extra satisfaction to a consumer. It follows that a lower price will be needed to induce the consumer to increase purchases of such a product.

**4**   We may assume that the typical consumer is rational and acts on the basis of rather well-defined preferences; consumers act sensibly and know roughly the satisfaction they will derive from successive units of various products available to them.  Because income is limited and goods have prices on them, the consumer cannot purchase all the goods and services he or she might like to have.  The consumer should therefore select that attainable combination of goods which will maximize his or her utility or satisfaction.

**5**   The consumer's utility will be maximized when income is allocated so that the last dollar spent on each product purchased yields the same amount of extra satisfaction. Algebraically, the utility-maximizing rule is fulfilled when

$$\frac{\text{MU of product A}}{\text{price of A}} = \frac{\text{MU of product B}}{\text{price of B}}$$

and the consumer's income is spent.

**6**   The utility-maximizing rule and the demand curve are logically consistent.

**7**   The theory of consumer choice has been generalized by taking into account the time required in the consumption of various goods and services.

## Questions and Study Suggestions

**1**   Key terms and concepts to remember: income effect; substitution effect; utility; law of diminishing marginal utility; utility-maximizing rule.

**2**   Explain the law of demand through the income and substitution effects, using a price increase as a point of departure for your discussion.  Explain the law of demand in terms of diminishing marginal utility.

**3**   Mrs. Peterson buys loaves of bread and quarts of milk each week at prices of 50 cents and 40 cents, respectively.  At present she is buying these two products in amounts such that the marginal utilities from the last units purchased of the two products are 80 and 70 utils, respectively.  Is she buying the best, that is, the utility-maximizing, combination of bread and milk? If not, how should she reallocate her expenditures between the two goods?

**4**   "Nothing is more useful than water: but it will purchase scarce any thing; scarce any thing can be had in exchange for it.  A diamond, on the contrary, has scarce any value in use; but a very great quantity of other goods may frequently be had in exchange for it." [8]  Explain.

**5**   Columns 1 through 4 of the table show the marginal utility, measured in terms of utils,

[8] Adam Smith, *The Wealth of Nations* (New York: Modern Library, Inc., originally published in 1776), p. 28.

which Mr. Black would get by purchasing various amounts of products A, B, C, and D. Column 5 shows the marginal utility Black gets from saving. Assume that the prices of A, B, C, and D are $24, $4, $6, and $18, respectively, and that Black has a money income of $106.

| Column 1 | | Column 2 | | Column 3 | | Column 4 | | Column 5 | |
|---|---|---|---|---|---|---|---|---|---|
| Units of A | MU | Units of B | MU | Units of C | MU | Units of D | MU | No. of $ saved | MU |
| 1 | 36 | 1 | 15 | 1 | 24 | 1 | 72 | 1 | 5 |
| 2 | 30 | 2 | 12 | 2 | 15 | 2 | 54 | 2 | 4 |
| 3 | 24 | 3 | 8 | 3 | 12 | 3 | 45 | 3 | 3 |
| 4 | 18 | 4 | 7 | 4 | 9 | 4 | 36 | 4 | 2 |
| 5 | 13 | 5 | 5 | 5 | 7 | 5 | 27 | 5 | 1 |
| 6 | 7 | 6 | 4 | 6 | 5 | 6 | 18 | 6 | $\frac{1}{2}$ |
| 7 | 4 | 7 | $3\frac{1}{2}$ | 7 | 2 | 7 | 15 | 7 | $\frac{1}{4}$ |
| 8 | 2 | 8 | 3 | 8 | 1 | 8 | 12 | 8 | $\frac{1}{8}$ |

   *a.*   What quantities of A, B, C, and D will Black purchase in maximizing his satisfactions?
*b.*   How many dollars will Black choose to save? *c.*   Check your answers by substituting in the algebraic statement of the utility-maximizing rule.

   **6**   "In the long run it may be irrational to purchase goods on the basis of habit; but in the short run habitual buying may prove to be a very sensible means of allocating income." Do you agree? Explain.

   **7**   How can time be incorporated into the theory of consumer behavior? Foreigners frequently point out that, comparatively speaking, Americans are very wasteful of food and other material goods and very conscious of, and overly economical in, their use of time. Can you provide an explanation for this observation?

   **8**   Explain: *a.*   "Before economic growth, there were too few goods; after growth, there is too little time." *b.*   "It is irrational for an individual to take the time to be completely rational in economic decision making."

   **9**   *Advanced analysis.* Let $MU_a = z = 10 - x$ and $MU_b = z = 21 - 2y$, where $z$ is marginal utility measured in utils, $x$ is the amount spent on product A, and $y$ is the amount spent on product B. Assume the consumer has $10 to spend on A and B; that is, $x + y = 10$. How is this $10 best allocated between A and B? How much utility will the marginal dollar yield?

# Selected References

Ferguson, C. E., and S. Charles Maurice: *Economic Analysis*, 3d ed. (Homewood, Ill.: Richard D. Irwin, Inc., 1978), chaps. 3, 4.

Leftwich, Richard H.: *The Price System and Resource Allocation*, 6th ed. (Hinsdale, Ill.: The Dryden Press, Inc., 1976), chaps. 5–7.

Linder, Staffan B.: *The Harried Leisure Class* (New York: Columbia University Press, 1970).

Mansfield, Edwin: *Microeconomics: Theory and Applications*, 3d ed. (New York: W. W. Norton & Company, Inc., 1979), chaps. 3, 4.

Miller, Roger LeRoy: *Intermediate Microeconomics* (New York: McGraw-Hill Book Company, 1978), chaps. 2, 3.

# Appendix to Chapter 24

## ☐ INDIFFERENCE CURVE ANALYSIS

A more sophisticated explanation of consumer behavior and consumer equilibrium is based upon (1) budget lines and (2) indifference curves.

### △ The Budget Line: What Is Obtainable

*A budget line simply shows the various combinations of two products which can be purchased with a given money income.* For example, if the price of product A is $1.50 and the price of B is $1.00, then the consumer could purchase all the combinations of A and B shown in Table 24-4 with $12 of money income. We note that at one extreme the consumer might spend all of his or her income on 8 units of A and have nothing left to spend on B. Or, by giving up 2 units of A and thereby "freeing" $3, the consumer could have 6 units of A and 3 of B. And so on to the other extreme, at which the consumer could buy 12 units of B at $1.00 each, thereby expending his or her entire money income on B and having nothing left to spend on A.

Figure 24-1 shows the budget line graphically. Note that the slope of the budget line measures the ratio of the price of B to the price of A; that is, the slope is $P_B/P_A = \$1.00/\$1.50 = 2/3$. This is merely the mathematical way of saying that the consumer must forgo 2 units of A (measured on the vertical axis) at $1.50 each in order to make available $3

to spend on 3 units of B (measured on the horizontal axis). In other words, in moving down the budget or price line, 2 of A must be given up to obtain 3 of B. This obviously yields a slope of 2/3.

Two other characteristics of the budget line merit comment.

**1**   The location of the budget line varies with money income. Specifically, an *increase* in money income will shift the budget line to the *right;* a *decrease* in money income will move it to the *left.* To verify these statements, simply recalculate Table 24-4 on the assumption that money income is (*a*) $24 and (*b*) $6 and plot the new budget lines in Figure 24-1.

**2**   A change in product prices will also shift the budget line. A decline in the prices of both products—which is the equivalent of an income increase—will shift the curve to the right. You can verify this assertion by recalcu-

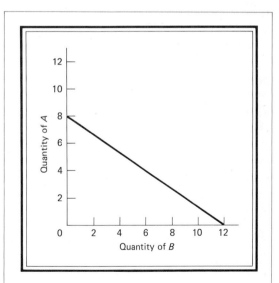

**FIGURE 24-1  A CONSUMER'S BUDGET LINE**

The budget line shows all of the various combinations of any two products which can be purchased, given the prices of the products and the consumer's money income.

**TABLE 24-4**
**The Budget Line: Combinations of A and B Obtainable with an Income of $12** (*hypothetical data*)

| Units of A (price = $1.50) | Units of B (price = $1.00) | Total expenditures |
|---|---|---|
| 8 | 0 | $12 (= $12 + $0) |
| 6 | 3 | $12 (= $9 + $3) |
| 4 | 6 | $12 (= $6 + $6) |
| 2 | 9 | $12 (= $3 + $9) |
| 0 | 12 | $12 (= $0 + $12) |

lating Table 24-4 and replotting Figure 24-1 on the assumption that $P_A = \$.75$ and $P_B = \$.50$. Conversely, an increase in the prices of A and B will shift the curve to the left. Again, assume $P_A = \$3$ and $P_B = \$2$ and rework Table 24-4 and Figure 24-1 to substantiate this statement. Note in particular what happens if we change $P_B$ while holding $P_A$ (and money income) constant. The reader should verify that, if we lower $P_B$ from $1.00 to $.50, the budget line will fan outward to the right. Conversely, by increasing $P_B$ from, say, $1.00 to $1.50, the line will fan inward to the left. In both instances the line remains "anchored" at 8 units on the vertical axis because $P_A$ has not changed.

△ **Indifference Curves:**
    **What Is Preferred**

Budget lines obviously reflect "objective" market data having to do with income and prices. The budget line reveals the combinations of A and B which are obtainable, given money income and prices. Indifference curves, on the other hand, embody "subjective" information about consumer preferences for A and B. By definition, *an indifference curve shows all combinations of products A and B which will yield the same level of satisfaction or utility to the consumer.* Table 24-5 and Figure 24-2 present a hypothetical indifference curve involving products A and B. The consumer's subjective preferences are such that he or she will realize the same total utility from each combination of A and B shown in the table or curve; hence, the consumer will be indifferent as to which combination is actually obtained.

**TABLE 24-5**
An Indifference Schedule (*hypothetical data*)

| Combination | Units of A | Units of B |
|---|---|---|
| *j* | 12 | 2 |
| *k* | 6 | 4 |
| *l* | 4 | 6 |
| *m* | 3 | 8 |

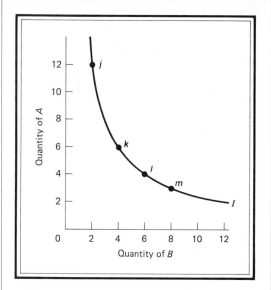

**FIGURE 24-2  A CONSUMER'S INDIFFERENCE CURVE**

Every point on an indifference curve represents some combination of products *A* and *B* which is equally satisfactory to the consumer; that is, each combination of *A* and *B* embodies the same level of total utility.

It is essential to understand several characteristics of indifference curves.

**1   Downsloping**  Indifference curves are downsloping for the obvious reason that both product A and product B yield utility to the consumer. Hence, in moving from combination *j* to combination *k,* the consumer is obtaining more of B and thereby increasing his or her total utility; therefore, some of A must be taken away to decrease total utility by a precisely offsetting amount. In brief, "more of B" necessitates "less of A" so that the quantities of A and B are inversely related. And any curve which reflects inversely related variables is downsloping.

**2   Convex to Origin**  But, as viewed from the origin, a downsloping curve can be concave (bowed outward) or convex (bowed inward). A concave curve has an increasing (steeper) slope as one moves down the curve, while a convex curve has a diminishing (flatter) slope as one moves down it. (Recall that the production possibilities curve of Figure 2-1 is concave, reflecting the law of increasing costs.) We note in Figure 24-2 that *the indifference curve is convex as viewed from the origin.* That is, the slope diminishes or becomes flatter as we move from *j* to *k,* to *l,* to *m* and so on down the curve.

What is the rationale for this convexity? The answer is that a consumer's subjective willingness to substitute B for A (or vice versa) will depend upon the amounts of B and A which he or she has to begin with. Consider Table 24-5 and Figure 24-2 once again, beginning at point *j.* Here, in relative terms, the consumer has a substantial amount of A and very little of B. This means that "at the margin" B is very valuable (that is, its marginal utility is high), while A is less valuable at the margin (its marginal utility is low). It follows that the consumer will be willing to give up a substantial amount of A to get, say, two more units of B. In this particular case, the consumer is willing to forgo 6 units of A to get 2 more units of B. But at point *k* the consumer now has less A and more B. This means that A will now be somewhat more valuable, and B somewhat less valuable, at the margin. Hence, considering the move from point *k* to point *l,* the consumer is only willing to give up 2 units of A to get 2 more units of B. Having still less of A and more of B at point *l,* the consumer is only willing to give up 1 unit of A in return for 2 more of B. In general, as the amount of B *increases,* the marginal utility of additional units of B *decreases.* Similarly, as the quantity of A *decreases,* its marginal utility *increases.* This means in Figure 24-2 that in moving down the curve the consumer will be willing to give up smaller and smaller amounts of A as an offset to acquiring each additional unit of B. The result is a curve with a diminishing slope, that is, one which is convex when viewed from the origin.

3  **Indifference Map**  The single indiffer-

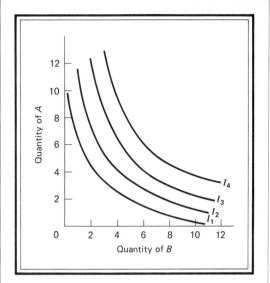

**FIGURE 24-3  AN INDIFFERENCE MAP**

An indifference map is comprised of a set of indifference curves. Each successive curve further from the origin indicates a higher level of total utility. That is, any combination of products A and B shown by a point on $I_4$ is superior to any combination of A and B shown by a point on $I_3, I_2,$ or $I_1$.

ence curve of Figure 24-2 reflects some constant (but unspecified) level of total utility of satisfaction. It is possible—and useful for our analysis—to sketch a whole series of indifference curves or, in other words, an *indifference map* as shown in Figure 24-3. Each curve reflects a different level of total utility. Specifically, each curve to the *right* of our original curve (labeled $I_3$ in Figure 24-3) reflects combinations of A and B which yield *more* utility than $I_3$. Each curve to the *left* of $I_3$ reflects *less* total utility than $I_3$. In other words, *as we move out from the origin each successive indifference curve entails a higher level of utility.* This can be simply demonstrated by drawing a line in a northeasterly direction from the origin and noting that its points of intersection with each successive curve entail larger amounts of *both* A and B and therefore a higher level of total utility.

## △ Equilibrium at Tangency

Noting that the axes of Figures 24-1 and 24-3 are identical, we can now determine the consumer's equilibrium position by combining the budget line and the indifference map as shown in Figure 24-4. Recall that, by definition, the budget line indicates all combinations of A and B which the consumer can obtain, given his or her money income and the prices of A and B. The question is: Of these obtainable combinations, which will the consumer most prefer? The answer is: That obtainable combination which yields the greatest satisfaction or utility. Specifically, *the utility-maximizing combination will be the one lying on the highest obtainable indifference curve.* In terms of Figure 24-4 the consumer's utility-maximizing or

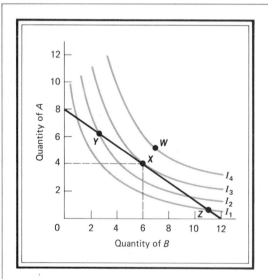

**FIGURE 24-4 THE CONSUMER'S EQUILIBRIUM POSITION**

The consumer's equilibrium position is at point $X$, where the budget line is tangent to the highest attainable indifference curve, $I_3$. In this case the consumer will buy 4 units of $A$ at \$1.50 per unit and 6 of $B$ at \$1 per unit with a \$12 money income. Points $Z$ and $Y$ also represent attainable combinations of $A$ and $B$, but yield less total utility as is evidenced by the fact they are on lower indifference curves. While $W$ would entail more utility than $X$, it is outside the budget line and therefore unobtainable.

equilibrium combination of A and B is at point $X$ where the budget line is *tangent* to $I_3$. Why not, for example, point $Y$? Because $Y$ is on a lower indifference curve, $I_2$. By trading "down" the budget line—by shifting dollars from purchases of A to purchases of B—the consumer can get on an indifference curve further from the origin and thereby increase total utility from the same income. Why not $Z$? Same reason: Point $Z$ is on a lower indifference curve, $I_1$. By trading "up" the budget line—by reallocating dollars from B to A—it is possible for the consumer to get on higher indifference curve $I_3$ and increase total utility. How about point $W$ on indifference curve $I_4$? While it is true that $W$ entails a higher level of total utility than does $X$, point $W$ is beyond (outside) the budget line and hence *not* obtainable to the consumer. Point $X$ is the best or optimum *obtainable* combination of products A and B.

## △ Deriving the Demand Curve

In our earlier comments on the characteristics of the budget line we noted that, given the price of A, an increase in the price of B will cause the budget line to fan inward to the left. This knowledge can now be used to derive a demand curve for product B. In Figure 24-5a we have simply reproduced Figure 24-4 showing our initial consumer equilibrium at point $X$. The budget line involved in determining this equilibrium position assumes a money income of \$12 and that $P_A = \$1.50$ and $P_B = \$1.00$. Let us examine what happens to the equilibrium position if we increase $P_B$ to \$1.50, holding money income and the price of A constant.

The result is shown in Figure 24-5a. The budget line fans to the left, yielding a new equilibrium point of tangency with indifference curve $I_2$ at point $X'$. At $X'$ we find the consumer is buying 3 units of B and 5 of A as compared to 4 of A and 6 of B at $X$. Our interest is in B and we note that we have sufficient information to locate the demand curve for product B. That is, we know that at equilibrium point $X$ the price of B is \$1.00 and 6 units are purchased; at equilibrium point $X'$ the

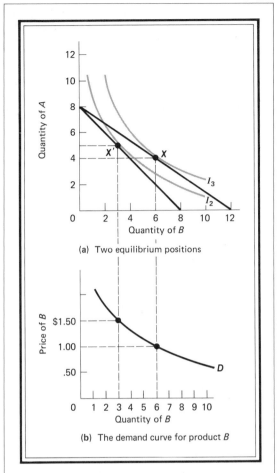

**FIGURE 24-5 DERIVING THE DEMAND CURVE**

When the price of *B* is increased from $1.00 to $1.50 in (a) the equilibrium position moves from *X* to *X'*, decreasing the quantity demanded from 6 to 3 units. The demand curve for *B* is determined in (b) by plotting the $1.00-6 units and the $1.50-3 units price-quantity combinations for *B*.

of B. Hence, we can simply drop dashed perpendiculars from Figure 24-5a down to the horizontal axis of Figure 24-5b. On the vertical axis of Figure 24-5b we merely locate the two chosen prices of B. Connecting these prices with the relevant quantities demanded, we locate two points on the demand curve for B. In drawing the demand curve as shown, we assume that all the "in-between" price-quantity points are similarly derived. The point is that, by simple manipulation of the price of B in an indifference curve-budget line context, a downsloping demand curve for B can be derived.

△ **The Measurement of Utility**

The alert reader may have sensed an important difference between the marginal utility theory and the indifference curve theory of consumer demand. The marginal utility theory assumes that utility is *numerically* measurable. That is, the consumer is assumed to be able to say *how much* extra utility he or she derives from an extra unit of A or B. Given the prices of A and B, the consumer must be able to measure the marginal utility derived from successive units of A and B in order to realize the utility-maximizing (equilibrium) position as previously indicated by

$$\frac{\text{Marginal utility of A}}{\text{Price of A}} = \frac{\text{marginal utility of B}}{\text{price of B}}$$

The indifference curve approach poses a less stringent requirement for the consumer: He or she need only be able to specify whether a given combination of A and B yields more, less, or the same amount of utility than some other combination of A and B. The consumer need only be able to say, for example, that 6 of A and 7 of B yield more (or less) satisfaction than 4 of A and 9 of B; indifference curve analysis does *not* require the consumer to specify *how much* more (or less) satisfaction will be realized.

price of B is $1.50 and 3 units are purchased. These data are shown graphically as a demand curve for B in Figure 24-5b. Note that the horizontal axes of Figures 24-5a and 5b are identical; both measure the quantity demanded

## Summary

1   The indifference curve approach to consumer behavior is based upon the consumer's budget line and indifference curves.

2   The budget line shows all combinations of two products which the consumer can purchase, given money income and the prices of the products.

3   A change in product prices or money income will shift the budget line.

4   An indifference curve shows all combinations of two products which will yield the same level of total utility to the consumer. Indifference curves are downsloping and convex to the origin.

5   An indifference map consists of a number of indifference curves; the further from the origin, the higher the level of utility associated with each curve.

6   The consumer will select that point on the budget line which puts him or her on the highest attainable indifference curve.

7   Changing the price of one product shifts the budget line and determines a new equilibrium position. A downsloping demand curve can be determined by plotting the price-quantity combinations associated with the old and new equilibrium positions.


## Questions and Study Suggestions

1   Key terms and concepts to remember: budget line; indifference curve; indifference map; equilibrium position.

2   What information is embodied in a budget line? What shifts will occur in the budget line as money income *a.* increases and *b.* decreases? What shifts will occur in the budget line as the price of the product shown on the horizontal axis *a.* increases and *b.* decreases?

3   What information is contained in an indifference curve? Why are such curves *a.* downsloping and *b.* convex to the origin? Why does total utility increase as the consumer moves to indifference curves further from the origin? Why can't indifference curves intersect?

4   Using Figure 24-4, explain why the point of *tangency* of the budget line with an indifference curve is the consumer's equilibrium position. Explain why any point where the budget line *intersects* an indifference curve will *not* be equilibrium.

5   Explain graphically how indifference analysis can be used to derive a demand curve.

# LAST WORD
## Does Money Buy Happiness?

The theory of consumer behavior tells us that more money expenditures mean more of the material benefits of life. But do these material benefits result in greater happiness?

The question simply is: Do the facts actually indicate that people who get more money typically feel happier?

The conclusions to which the evidence points, in brief, are these. *In all societies, more money for the individual typically means more individual happiness. However, raising the incomes of all does not increase the happiness of all.* The happiness-income relation provides a classic example of the logical fallacy of composition—*what is true for the individual is not true for society as a whole.*

The resolution of this paradox lies in the relative nature of welfare judgments. Individuals assess their material well-being, not in terms of the absolute amount of goods they have, but relative to a social norm of what goods they ought to have. At any given time, those above the norm typically feel happier than those below. Over time, however, the process of economic advance leads, not only to a general increase in incomes, but also to a corresponding rise in the social norm by which material well-being is judged. This increase in material aspirations in a society, itself produced by material progress, thus negates the positive impact of income growth on happiness that one might have expected from the happiness-income relation among individuals prevailing at any point of time. . . .

What do the data show on the comparative happiness of income groups within a country at a given time? Does greater happiness go with higher income? The answer is, quite clearly, yes. This does not mean that there are no unhappy people among the rich and no happy people among the poor. On the average, however, higher-income people are happier than the poor.

This positive relation between happiness and income appears in every single one of the 30 national population surveys studied. Eleven of these surveys relate to the United States between 1946 and 1970, and 19 other countries, including three communist nations (Poland, Yugoslavia, and Cuba) and 11 countries in Asia, Africa, and Latin America. Note that the association between greater individual happiness and more money appears without exception in widely different countries and social systems—in non-Western as well as Western societies, poor as well as rich countries, Communist as well as non-Communist nations. . . .

In simple comparisons within countries, there is a repeated positive association between income and happiness; but when one compares rich and poor countries, or higher and lower income situations in a given country at two different times, the happiness differences by income levels do not appear.

How can one explain this paradoxical result? If for the individual more money typically means more happiness, why not for society as a whole? The answer lies in the way that people form their welfare judgments. The satisfaction one gets from his material situation depends not on the absolute amount of goods he has, but on how this amount compares with what he thinks he needs. A lot of goods relative to perceived needs makes for a lot of material satisfaction and thus greater happiness; if goods are low compared with needs, the result is relatively less happiness.

A crucial question, then, is how are needs determined. If perceived needs were essentially the same for all people in all times and places, being determined, say, primarily by physiological considerations, then more money would mean more happiness, not only among individuals at a given time, but also in those societies which grow richer over time.

In fact, however, what people perceive as their needs is socially determined, and those who live in richer times and places perceive their needs in more ambitious terms than those in poorer societies. Needs, or material aspirations, are formed as the result of prior and on-going experience in a society—in the language of sociology, through the socialization experience of the individual. Thus what one "needs" as he reaches adulthood typically depends on the impressions he has formed of "how to live" from observing life around him and in his society while growing up.

Richard A. Easterlin, "Does Money Buy Happiness?" *The Public Interest,* No. 30, Winter, 1973, pp. 3–10, abridged. Copyright © by National Affairs, Inc., 1973. Reprinted by permission.

# The Costs of Production

chapter 25

Product prices are determined by the interaction of the forces of demand and supply. Preceding chapters have focused our attention upon the factors underlying demand. The basic factor underlying the ability and willingness of firms to supply a product in the market is the cost of production. The production of any good requires the use of economic resources which, because of their relative scarcity, bear price tags. The amount of any product which a firm is willing to supply in the market depends upon the prices (costs) and the productivity of the resources essential to its production, on the one hand, and the price which the product will bring in the market, on the other. The present chapter is concerned with the general nature of production costs. Product prices are introduced in the following several chapters, and the supply decisions of producers are then explained.

## □ ECONOMIC COSTS

The economist's notion of costs goes back to the basic fact that resources are scarce and have alternative uses. Thus, to use a bundle of resources in the production of some particular good means that certain alternative production opportunities have been forgone. *Costs in economics have to do with missed opportunities or sacrificed alternatives.* More specifically, the *opportunity cost* of any resource in producing some good is its value or worth in its best alternative use. This conception of costs is clearly embodied in the production possibilities curve of Chapter 2. Note, for example, that at point $C$ in Table 2-1 the opportunity cost of producing 100,000 *more* units of bread is the 3000 units of drill presses which must be forgone. The steel that is used for armaments is not available for the manufacture of automobiles or apartment buildings. And if an assembly-line worker is capable of producing automobiles or washing machines, then the cost to society in employing this worker in an automobile plant is the contribution the worker would otherwise have made in producing washing machines. The cost to you in reading this chapter is the alternative uses of your time which you must forgo.

## △   Explicit and Implicit Costs

Let us now consider costs from the viewpoint of an individual firm. Given the notion of opportunity costs, we can say that *economic costs are those payments a firm must make, or incomes it must provide, to resource suppliers in order to attract these resources away from alternative lines of production.* These payments or incomes may be either *explicit* or *implicit.* The monetary payments—that is, cash expenditures which a firm makes to those "outsiders" who supply labor services, materials, fuel, transportation services, power, and so forth—are called *explicit costs.* But, in addition, a firm may use certain resources which the firm itself owns. Our notion of opportunity costs tells us that, regardless of whether a resource is owned or hired by an enterprise, there is a cost involved in using that resource in a specific employment. The costs of such self-owned, self-employed resources are non-expenditure or *implicit costs.* To the firm, those implicit costs are the money payments which the self-employed resources could have earned in their best alternative employments. For example, suppose Brooks operates a corner grocery as a sole proprietor. She owns her store building and supplies all her own labor and money capital. Though her enterprise has no explicit rental or wage costs, implicit rents and wages are incurred. By using her own building for a grocery, Brooks sacrifices the $400 monthly rental income which she could otherwise have earned by renting it to someone else. Similarly, by using her money capital and labor in her own enterprise, Brooks sacrifices the interest and wage incomes which she otherwise could have earned by supplying

these resources in their best alternative employments. And, finally, by running her own enterprise, Brooks forgoes the earnings she could realize by supplying her managerial efforts in someone else's firm.

## △   Normal Profits as a Cost

The minimum payment required to keep Brooks's entrepreneurial talents engaged in this enterprise is called a *normal profit.* As is true of implicit rent or implicit wages, her normal return for the performing of entrepreneurial functions is an implicit cost. If this minimum, or normal, return is not realized, the entrepreneur will withdraw her efforts from this line of production and reallocate them to some alternative line of production. Or the individual may cease being an entrepreneur in favor of becoming a wage or salary earner.

In short, the economist includes as costs all payments—explicit and implicit, the latter including a normal profit—required to retain resources in a given line of production.

## △   Economic, or Pure, Profits

Our discussion of economic costs correctly suggests that economists and accountants use the term "profits" differently. By "profits" the accountant generally means total receipts less explicit costs. But to the economist, "profits" means total receipts less *all* costs (explicit and implicit, the latter including a normal profit to the entrepreneur). Therefore, when an economist says that a firm is just covering its costs, it is meant that all explicit and implicit costs are being met and that the entrepreneur is receiving a return just large enough to retain his or her talents in the present line of production. If a firm's total receipts exceed all its economic costs, any residual accrues to the entrepreneur. This residual is called an *economic,* or *pure, profit.* It is not a cost, because by definition it is a return in excess of the normal profit required to retain the entrepreneur in this particular line of production. In Chapter 32 we shall find that economic profits are associated with risk bearing and monopoly power.

△  **Short Run and Long Run**

The costs which a firm or an industry incurs in producing any given output will depend upon the types of adjustment it is able to make in the amounts of the various resources it employs. The quantities employed of many resources—labor, raw materials, fuel, power, and so forth—can be varied easily and quickly. Other resources require more time for adjustment. For example, the capacity of a manufacturing plant, that is, the size of the factory building and the amount of machinery and equipment therein, can only be varied over a considerable period of time. In some heavy industries it may take several years to alter plant capacity.

These differences in the time necessary to vary the quantities of the various resources used in the productive process make it essential to distinguish between the short run and the long run. The *short run* refers to a period of time too brief to permit an enterprise to alter its plant capacity, yet long enough to permit a change in the level at which the fixed plant is utilized. The firm's plant capacity is fixed in the short run, but output can be varied by applying larger or smaller amounts of labor, materials, and other resources to that plant. Existing plant capacity can be used more or less intensively in the short run.

From the viewpoint of existing firms, the *long run* refers to a period of time extensive enough to allow these firms to change the quantities of *all* resources employed, including plant capacity. From the viewpoint of an industry, the long run also encompasses enough time for existing firms to dissolve and leave the industry and for new firms to be created and to enter the industry. *While the short run is a "fixed-plant" time period, the long run is a "variable-plant" time period.*

Some examples will make clear the distinction between the short run and the long run. If a General Motors plant were to hire an extra 100 workers or to add an entire shift of workers, this would be a short-run adjustment. If the same GM plant were to add a new wing to its building and install more equipment, this would be a long-run adjustment.

It is important to note that the short run and the long run are conceptual rather than specific calendar time periods. In light manufacturing industries, changes in plant capacity may be negotiated almost overnight. A small firm making men's clothing can increase its plant capacity in a few days or less by ordering and installing a couple of new cutting tables and several extra sewing machines. But heavy industry is a different story. It may take Ford or General Motors several years to construct a new assembly plant and to install elaborate assembly-line equipment.

We turn now to the task of analyzing production costs in the short-run, or fixed-plant, period. Following this we consider costs in the long-run, or variable-plant, period.

## ☐  PRODUCTION COSTS IN THE SHORT RUN

A firm's costs of producing any output will depend not only upon the prices of needed resources, but also upon technology—the quantity of resources it takes to produce that output. It is the latter, technological aspect of costs with which we are concerned for the moment. In the short run a firm can change its output by adding variable resources to a fixed plant. Question: How does output change as more and more variable resources are added to the firm's fixed resources?

△  **Law of Diminishing Returns**

The answer is provided in general terms by the *law of diminishing returns.* You may recall that we discussed this famous law in aggregative terms in Chapter 19; we now examine it in more detail from the vantage point of an individual firm. This engineering law states that *as successive units of a variable resource (say, labor) are added to a fixed resource (say, capital or land), beyond some point the extra, or marginal, product attributable to each additional unit of the variable resource will de-*

*cline*. Stated somewhat differently, if additional workers are applied to a given amount of capital equipment, as is the case in the short run, eventually output will rise less than in proportion to the increase in the number of workers employed. A couple of examples will illustrate this law.

**Rationale** Suppose a farmer has a fixed amount of land—say, 80 acres—in which corn has been planted. Assuming the farmer does not cultivate the cornfields at all, yield will be, say, 40 bushels per acre. If the land is cultivated once, output may rise to 50 bushels per acre. A second cultivation may increase output to 57 bushels per acre, a third to 61, and a fourth to, say, 63. But further cultivations will add little or nothing to total output. Successive cultivations add less and less to the land's yield. If this were not the case, the world's needs for corn could be fulfilled by extremely intense cultivation of this single 80-acre plot of land. Indeed, if diminishing returns did not occur, the world could be fed out of a flowerpot.

The law of diminishing returns also holds true in nonagricultural industries. Assume a small planing mill is manufacturing wood furniture frames. The mill has a given amount of equipment in the form of lathes, planers, saws, sanders, and so forth. If this firm hired just one or two workers, total output and production per worker would be very low. These workers would have a number of different jobs to perform, and the advantages of specialization would be lost. Time would also be lost in switching from one job operation to another, and the machines would stand idle much of the time. In short, the plant would be understaffed, and production therefore would be inefficient. Production would be inefficient because there is too much capital relative to labor. These difficulties would disappear as more workers were added. Equipment would be more fully utilized, and workers could now specialize on a single job. Thus, as more workers are added to the initially understaffed plant, the extra or marginal product of each will tend to rise as a result of more efficient production. But this cannot go on indefinitely. As still more workers are added, problems of overcrowding will arise. Workers must wait in line to use the machinery, so now *workers* are underutilized. The extra, or marginal, product of additional workers declines because the plant is overstaffed. There is too much labor in proportion to the fixed amount of capital goods. In the extreme case, the con-

**TABLE 25-1**
**The Law of Diminishing Returns** (*hypothetical data*)

| (1) Inputs of the variable resource (labor) | (2) Total product | (3) Marginal product | (4) Average product |
|---|---|---|---|
| 0 | 0 |  | — |
| 1 | 10 | 10 | 10 |
| 2 | 25 | 15 | $12\frac{1}{2}$ |
| 3 | 37 | 12 | $12\frac{1}{3}$ |
| 4 | 47 | 10 | $11\frac{3}{4}$ |
| 5 | 55 | 8 | 11 |
| 6 | 60 | 5 | 10 |
| 7 | 63 | 3 | 9 |
| 8 | 62 | −1 | $7\frac{3}{4}$ |

tinuous addition of labor to the plant would use up all standing room, and production would be brought to a standstill.

**Numerical Example**   Table 25-1 presents a more explicit numerical illustration of the law of diminishing returns. Column 2 indicates the *total product* which will result from combining each level of labor input in column 1 with an assumedly fixed amount of capital goods. Column 3, *marginal product,* shows us the *change* in total output associated with each additional input of labor. Note that with no labor inputs, total product is zero; an empty plant will yield no output. The first two workers reflect increasing returns, their marginal products being 10 and 15 units of output respectively. But then, beginning with the third worker, marginal product—the increase in total product—diminishes continuously and actually becomes negative with the eighth worker. *Average product* or output per worker is shown in column 4. It is calculated simply by dividing total product (column 2) by the corresponding number of workers (column 1).

Figure 25-1*a* and *b* shows the law of diminishing returns graphically. The marginal product curve reflects the increases in total product associated with each successive dose of labor. Geometrically, marginal physical product is the slope of the total product curve. Note that so long as marginal product is positive, total product is increasing. And when marginal product is zero, total product is at its peak. Finally, when marginal product becomes negative, total product is necessarily declining. Increasing returns are reflected in a rising marginal physical product curve; diminishing returns, in a falling marginal physical product.

Average product also reflects the same general "increasing-maximum-diminishing" relationship between variable inputs of labor and output as does marginal product. But note this technical point concerning the relationship between marginal product and average product: Where marginal product exceeds average product, the latter must rise. And

wherever marginal product is less than average product, then average product must be declining. It follows that marginal product intersects average product where the latter is at a maximum. This relationship is a matter of mathematical necessity. You raise your average grade in a course only when your score on an additional (marginal) examination is greater than the average of all your past scores. If your grade on an additional exam is below your current average, your average will be pulled down.

△  **Fixed, Variable, and Total Costs**
The production data described by the law of diminishing returns must be coupled with resource prices to determine the total and per unit costs of producing various outputs. We have emphasized that in the short run some resources—those associated with the firm's plant—are fixed. Others are variable. This correctly suggests that in the short run, costs can be classified as either fixed or variable.

**Fixed Costs**   *Fixed costs are those costs which in total do not vary with changes in output.* Fixed costs are associated with the very existence of a firm's plant and therefore must be paid even if the firm's rate of output is zero. Such costs as interest on a firm's bonded indebtedness, rental payments, a portion of depreciation on equipment and buildings, insurance premiums, and the salaries of top management and key personnel are generally fixed costs. In column 2 of Table 25-2 we have assumed that the firm's total fixed costs are $100. Note that this fixed-cost figure prevails at all levels of output, including zero.

**Variable Costs**   *Variable costs are those costs which increase with the level of output.* They include payments for materials, fuel, power, transportation services, most labor, and similar variable resources. In column 3 of Table 25-2 we find that the total of variable costs changes with output; but note that the increases in variable costs associated with each one-unit increase in output are not constant. As production begins, variable costs will for a time increase by a decreasing amount; this is true through the fourth unit of output. Beyond the fourth unit, however, variable costs rise by increasing amounts for each successive unit of output. The explanation of this behavior of variable costs lies in the law of diminishing returns. Because of increasing marginal product, smaller and smaller increases in the amounts of variable resources will be needed for a time to get each successive unit of output produced. This means that total variable costs will increase by decreasing amounts. But when marginal product begins to decline as diminishing returns are encountered, it will be necessary to use larger and larger additional amounts of variable resources to produce each successive unit of output. Total variable costs will therefore increase by increasing amounts.

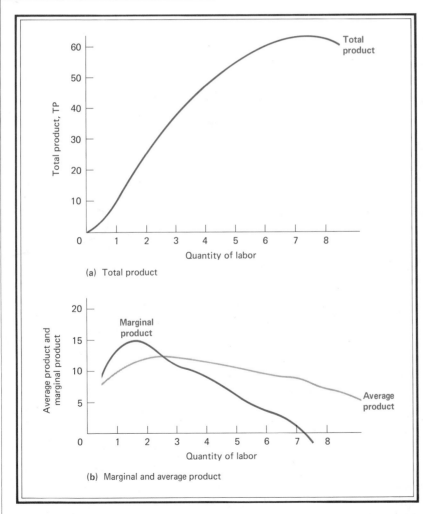

(a)  Total product

(b)  Marginal and average product

**FIGURE 25-1  THE LAW OF DIMINISHING RETURNS**

As a variable resource (labor) is added to fixed amounts of other resources (land or capital), the resulting total product will eventually increase by diminishing amounts, reach a maximum, and then decline as in (a).  Marginal product in (b) reflects the changes in total product associated with each input of labor.  Average product is simply output per worker. Note that marginal product intersects average product at the maximum average product.

**Total Cost**   *Total cost* is self-defining: It is the *sum of fixed and variable costs at each level of output.* It is shown in column 4 of Table 25-2. At zero units of output, total cost is equal to the firm's fixed costs. Then for each unit of production—1 through 10—total cost varies at the same rate as does variable cost.

Figure 25-2 shows graphically the fixed-, variable-, and total-cost data of Table 25-2. Note that total variable cost is measured vertically from the horizontal axis and total fixed cost is added vertically to total variable cost in locating the total-cost curve.

The distinction between fixed and variable costs is of no little significance to the business manager. Variable costs are those costs which businesses can control or alter in the short run by changing levels of production. On the other hand, fixed costs are clearly beyond the business executive's control; such costs are incurred and must be paid regardless of output level.

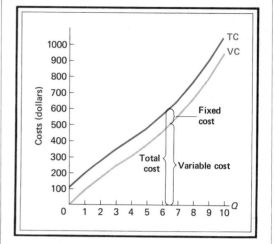

FIGURE 25-2  TOTAL COST IS THE SUM OF FIXED AND VARIABLE COSTS

Variable costs (VC) vary with output. Fixed costs are independent of the level of output. The total cost (TC) of any output is the vertical sum of the fixed and variable costs of that output.

**TABLE 25-2**
Total- and Average-Cost Schedules For an Individual Firm in the Short Run (*hypothetical data*)

| Total-cost data, per week | | | | Average-cost data, per week | | | |
|---|---|---|---|---|---|---|---|
| (1)<br>Total<br>product | (2)<br>Total<br>fixed<br>cost | (3)<br>Total<br>variable<br>cost | (4)<br>Total<br>cost | (5)<br>Average<br>fixed<br>cost | (6)<br>Average<br>variable<br>cost | (7)<br>Average<br>total<br>cost | (8)<br>Marginal<br>cost |
| (Q) | (TFC) | (TVC) | (TC)<br>$TC = TFC$<br>$+ TVC$ | (AFC)<br>$AFC = \dfrac{TFC}{Q}$ | (AVC)<br>$AVC = \dfrac{TVC}{Q}$ | (ATC)<br>$ATC = \dfrac{TC}{Q}$ | (MC)<br>$MC = \dfrac{\text{change in TC}}{\text{change in } Q}$ |
| 0 | $100 | $ 0 | $ 100 | | | | |
| 1 | 100 | 90 | 190 | $100.00 | $90.00 | $190.00 | $ 90 |
| 2 | 100 | 170 | 270 | 50.00 | 85.00 | 135.00 | 80 |
| 3 | 100 | 240 | 340 | 33.33 | 80.00 | 113.33 | 70 |
| 4 | 100 | 300 | 400 | 25.00 | 75.00 | 100.00 | 60 |
| 5 | 100 | 370 | 470 | 20.00 | 74.00 | 94.00 | 70 |
| 6 | 100 | 450 | 550 | 16.67 | 75.00 | 91.67 | 80 |
| 7 | 100 | 540 | 640 | 14.29 | 77.14 | 91.43 | 90 |
| 8 | 100 | 650 | 750 | 12.50 | 81.25 | 93.75 | 110 |
| 9 | 100 | 780 | 880 | 11.11 | 86.67 | 97.78 | 130 |
| 10 | 100 | 930 | 1030 | 10.00 | 93.00 | 103.00 | 150 |

△ **Per Unit, or Average, Costs**

Producers are certainly interested in their total costs, but they are equally concerned with their *per unit,* or *average, costs.* In particular, average-cost data are more usable for making comparisons with product price, which is always stated on a per unit basis. Average fixed cost, average variable cost, and average total cost are shown in columns 5 to 7 of Table 25-2. It is important that we know how these unit-cost figures are derived and how they vary as output changes.

**1   AFC**   *Average fixed cost* (AFC) is found by dividing total fixed cost (TFC) by the corresponding output (Q). That is,

$$\text{AFC} = \frac{\text{TFC}}{Q}$$

Whereas total fixed costs are, by definition, independent of output, AFC will decline as output increases. As output increases, a given total fixed cost of $100 is obviously being spread over a larger and larger output. When output is just 1 unit, total fixed costs and AFC are equal—$100. But at 2 units of output, total fixed costs of $100 become $50 worth of fixed costs per unit; then $33.33, as $100 is spread over 3 units; $25, when spread over 4 units; and so forth. This is what business executives commonly refer to as "spreading the overhead." We find in Figure 25-3 that AFC graphs as a continually declining figure as total output is increased.

**2   AVC**   *Average variable cost* (AVC) is calculated by dividing total variable cost (TVC) by the corresponding output (Q):

$$\text{AVC} = \frac{\text{TVC}}{Q}$$

AVC declines initially, reaches a minimum, and then increases again. Graphically, this provides us with a U-shaped or saucer-shaped AVC curve, as is shown in Figure 25-3.

Because total variable cost reflects the law of diminishing returns, so must the AVC fig-

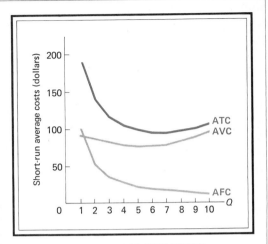

FIGURE 25-3  THE AVERAGE-COST CURVES

Average total cost (ATC) is the vertical sum of average variable cost (AVC) and average fixed cost (AFC). AFC necessarily falls as a given amount of fixed costs is apportioned over a larger and larger output. AVC initially falls because of increasing physical returns but then rises because of diminishing physical returns.

ures, which are derived from total variable cost. Because of increasing returns it takes fewer and fewer additional variable resources to produce each of the first 4 units of output. As a result, variable cost per unit will decline. AVC hits a minimum with the fifth unit of output, and beyond this point AVC rises as diminishing returns necessitate the use of more and more variable resources to produce each additional unit of output. In more direct terms, at low levels of output production will be relatively inefficient and costly, because the firm's fixed plant is understaffed. Not enough variable resources are being combined with the firm's plant; production is inefficient, and per unit variable costs are therefore relatively high. As output expands, however, greater specialization and a more complete utilization of the firm's capital equipment will make for more efficient production. As a result, variable cost per unit of output will decline. As more and more variable resources are added, some point will eventually be reached where diminishing returns are incurred. The firm's capital equipment will now be overstaffed, and the resulting overcrowding and overutilization of machinery impair efficiency. This means that AVC will increase.

You can verify the U or saucer shape of the AVC curve by returning to Table 25-1. Assume the price of labor is, say, $10 per unit. By dividing average product (output per worker) into $10 (price per worker), you will determine labor cost per unit of output. Because we have assumed labor to be the only variable output, labor cost per unit of output *is* variable cost per unit of output or AVC. By plotting average product and AVC data you will find they are mirror images of one another. When average product is initially low, AVC will be high. As workers are added, average product rises and this causes AVC to fall. Then, as still more workers are added and average product declines, AVC will rise. The "hump" of the average product curve is reflected in the saucer shape of the AVC curve.

**3  ATC**  *Average total cost* (ATC) can be found by dividing total cost (TC) by total output ($Q$) or, more simply, by adding AFC and AVC for each of the ten levels of output. That is,

$$ATC = \frac{TC}{Q} = AFC + AVC$$

These data are shown in column 7 of Table 25-2. Graphically, ATC is found by adding vertically the AFC and AVC curves, as in Figure 25-3. Thus the vertical distance between the ATC and AVC curves reflects AFC at any level of output.

△  **Marginal Cost**

There remains one final and very crucial cost concept—marginal cost. *Marginal cost (MC) is the extra, or additional, cost of producing one more unit of output.* MC can be determined for each additional unit of output simply by noting the change in total cost which that unit's production entails.

$$MC = \frac{\text{change in TC}}{\text{change in } Q}$$

In Table 25-2 we find that production of the first unit of output increases total cost from $100 to $190. Therefore, the additional, or marginal, cost of that first unit is $90. The marginal cost of the second unit is $80 (= $270 − $190); the MC of the third is $70 (= $340 − $270); and so forth. MC for each of the ten units of output is shown in column 8 of Table 25-2. MC can also be calculated from the total-variable-cost column. Why? Because the only difference between total cost and total variable cost is the constant amount of fixed costs. Hence, the change in total cost and change in total variable cost associated with each additional unit of output is the same.

Marginal cost is a strategic concept because it designates those costs over which the firm has the most direct control. More specifically, MC indicates those costs which are incurred in the production of the last unit of output and, simultaneously, the cost which can be "saved" by reducing total output by the last unit. Average-cost figures do *not* provide this information. For example, suppose the firm is undecided as to whether it should produce 3 or 4 units of output. At 4 units of output Table 25-2 indicates that ATC is $100. But the firm does not increase its total costs by $100 by producing, nor does it "save" $100 by not producing, the fourth unit. Rather, the change in costs involved here is only $60, as the MC column of Table 25-2 clearly reveals. A firm's decisions as to what output level to produce are typically marginal decisions, that is, decisions to produce a few more or a few less units. Marginal cost reveals the change in costs which one more unit or one less unit of output entails. When coupled with marginal revenue, which we will find in Chapter 26 indicates the change in revenue from one more or one less unit of output, marginal cost allows a firm to determine whether it is profitable to expand or contract its level of production. The analysis in the next four chapters centers upon these marginal calculations.

Marginal cost is shown graphically in Figure 25-4. Note that marginal cost declines sharply, reaches a minimum, and then rises rather sharply. This mirrors the fact that variable cost, and therefore total cost, increases first by decreasing amounts and then by increasing amounts (see Figure 25-2 and columns 3 and 4 of Table 25-2).

**MC and Marginal Product**   The shape of the marginal-cost curve is a reflection of, and the consequence of, the law of diminishing returns. The relationship between marginal product and marginal cost can be readily grasped by looking back to Table 25-1. If each successive unit of a variable resource (labor) is hired at a constant price, the marginal cost of each extra unit of output will *fall* so long as the marginal product of each additional worker is *rising*. This is so because marginal cost is simply the price or cost of an extra worker divided by his or her marginal product. Hence, in Table 25-1 suppose each worker can be hired at a cost of $10. Because the first worker's marginal product is 10 and the hire of this worker increases the firm's costs by $10, the marginal cost of each of these 10 extra units of output will be $1 ( =$10 ÷ 10). The second worker also increases costs by $10, but the marginal product is 15, so that the marginal cost of each of these 15 extra units of output is $.67 ( =$10 ÷ 15). In general, so long as marginal product is rising, marginal cost will be falling. But as diminishing returns set in—in this case, with the third worker—marginal cost will begin to rise. Thus, for the third worker, marginal cost is $.83 ( =$10 ÷ 12); $1.00 for the fourth worker; $1.25 for the fifth; and so on. The relationship between marginal product and marginal cost is evident. *Given the price (cost) of the variable resource, increasing returns (that is, a rising marginal product) will be reflected in a declining marginal cost and diminishing returns (that is, a falling marginal product) in a rising marginal cost.* The

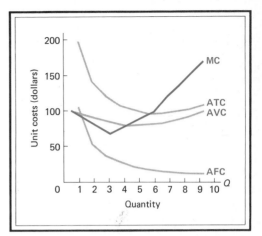

**FIGURE 25-4 THE RELATIONSHIP OF MARGINAL COST TO AVERAGE TOTAL COST AND AVERAGE VARIABLE COST**

Marginal cost (MC) cuts both ATC and AVC at their minimum points. This is so because whenever the extra or marginal amount added to total cost (or variable cost) is less than the average of that cost, the average will necessarily fall. Conversely, whenever the marginal amount added to total (or variable) cost is greater than the average of total cost, the average must rise.

MC curve is a mirror reflection of the marginal product curve. When marginal product is rising, marginal cost is falling. When marginal product is at a maximum, marginal cost is at a minimum. And when marginal product is falling, marginal cost is rising.

**Relation to AVC and ATC**   It is also notable that marginal cost cuts both AVC and ATC at their minimum points. This marginal-average relationship is a matter of mathematical necessity, which a commonsense illustration can make readily apparent. Suppose a baseball pitcher has allowed his opponents an average of 3 runs per game in the first three games he has pitched. Now, whether his average falls or rises as a result of pitching a fourth (marginal) game will depend upon whether the additional runs he allows in that extra game are fewer or more than his current 3-run average. If he allows fewer than 3 runs—for example, 1—in the fourth game, his total runs will rise from 9 to 10, and his average will fall from 3 to $2\frac{1}{2}$ ($=10 \div 4$). Conversely, if he allows more than 3 runs—say, 7—in the fourth game, his total will rise from 9 to 16 and his average from 3 to 4 ($=16 \div 4$). So it is with costs. When the amount added to total cost (marginal cost) is less than the average of total cost, ATC will fall. Conversely, when marginal cost exceeds ATC, ATC will rise. This means in Figure 25-4 that so long as MC lies below ATC, the latter will fall, and where MC is above ATC, ATC will rise. Therefore at the point of intersection where MC equals ATC, ATC has just ceased to fall but has not yet begun to rise. This, by definition, is the minimum point on the ATC curve. *The marginal cost curve cuts the average total cost curve at the latter's minimum point.* Because MC can be defined as the addition either to total cost *or* to total variable cost resulting from one more unit of output, this same rationale explains why MC also cuts AVC at the latter's minimum point. No such relationship exists for MC and average fixed cost, because the two are not related; marginal cost embodies only those costs which change with output, and fixed costs by definition are independent of output.

Let us now turn to the relationship between output and unit costs when all inputs are variable.

## ☐ PRODUCTION COSTS IN THE LONG RUN

In the long run all desired resource adjustments can be negotiated by an industry and the individual firms which it comprises. The firm can alter its plant capacity; it can build a larger plant or revert to a smaller plant than that assumed in Table 25-2. The industry can also change its plant size; the long run is an amount of time sufficient for new firms to enter or old firms to leave an industry. The impact of the entry and exodus of firms from an industry will be discussed in the next chapter; here we are concerned only with changes

in plant capacity made by a single firm. And in considering these adjustments, we couch our analysis in terms of ATC, making no distinction between fixed and variable costs for the obvious reason that all resources, and therefore all costs, are variable in the long run.

Suppose a single-plant manufacturing enterprise starts out on a small scale and then, as the result of successful operations, expands to successively larger plant sizes. What will happen to average total costs as this growth occurs? The answer is this: For a time successively larger plants will bring lower average total costs. However, eventually the building of a still larger plant will cause ATC to rise.

Figure 25-5 illustrates this situation for five possible plant sizes. ATC-1 is the average-total-cost curve for the smallest of the five plants, and ATC-5 for the largest. The relationship of the five plant sizes to one another is clearly that stated above. Constructing a larger plant will entail lower per unit costs through plant size 3. But beyond this point a larger plant will mean a higher level of average total costs.

The dotted lines perpendicular to the output axis are crucial. They indicate those points at which the firm should change plant size in order to realize the lowest attainable per unit costs of production. To illustrate in terms of Figure 25-5: For all outputs up to 20 units, the lowest per unit costs are attainable with plant size 1. However, if the firm's volume of sales expands to some level greater than 20 but less than 30 units, it can achieve lower per unit costs by constructing a larger plant—plant size 2. For any output between 30 and 50 units, plant size 3 will yield the lowest per unit costs. For the 50- to 60-unit range of output, plant size 4 must be built to achieve the lowest unit costs. Lowest per unit costs for any output in excess of 60 units demand the construction of the still larger plant of size 5.

Tracing these adjustments, we can conclude that the long-run ATC curve for the enterprise will comprise segments of the short-run ATC curves for the various plant

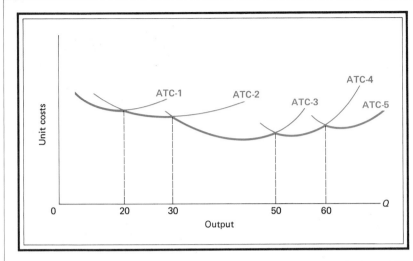

**FIGURE 25-5 THE LONG-RUN AVERAGE-COST CURVE: FIVE POSSIBLE PLANT SIZES**

The long-run average-cost curve is made up of segments of the short-run cost curves (ATC-1, ATC-2, etc.) of the various-sized plants from which the firm might choose. Each point on the bumpy planning curve shows the least unit cost attainable for any output when the firm has had time to make all desired changes in its plant size.

sizes which can be constructed. *The long-run ATC curve shows the least per unit cost at which any output can be produced after the firm has had time to make all appropriate adjustments in its plant size.* In Figure 25-5 the heavy, bumpy curve is the firm's long-run ATC curve or, as it is often called, the firm's planning curve. In most lines of production the choice of plant sizes is much wider than that assumed in our illustration. In fact, in

many industries the number of possible plant sizes is virtually unlimited. This means that in time, very small changes in the volume of output (sales) will prompt appropriate changes in the size of the plant. Graphically, this implies there is an unlimited number of short-run ATC curves, as suggested by Figure 25-6. The minimum ATC of producing each possible level of output is shown by the long-run ATC curve. Rather than being comprised of *segments* of

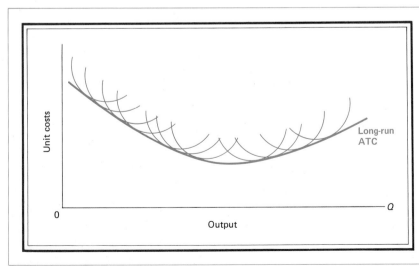

**FIGURE 25-6 THE LONG-RUN AVERAGE-COST CURVE: UNLIMITED NUMBER OF PLANT SIZES**

If the number of possible plant sizes is very large, the long-run average-cost curve approximates a smooth curve. Economies and diseconomies of scale cause the curve to be U-shaped.

short-run ATC curves as in Figure 25-5, the long-run ATC curve is made up of all the *points of tangency* of the theoretically unlimited number of short-run ATC curves from which the long-run ATC curve is derived. Hence, the planning curve is smooth rather than bumpy. Note that, with the exception of the minimum point on the long-run ATC curve, the long-run ATC curve is *not* tangent to the short-run ATC curves at the minimum points of the latter. Where the long-run ATC curve is diminishing, the points of tangency are to the left of the minimum points on the short-run ATC curves. Conversely, where long-run ATC is rising, the tangency points are to the right of the minimum points on the short-run ATC curves.

## △ Economies and Diseconomies of Scale

We have patiently accepted the contention that for a time a larger and larger plant size will entail lower unit costs but that beyond some point successively larger plants will mean higher average total costs. Now we must explain this point. Exactly why is the long-run ATC curve U-shaped? It must be emphasized, first of all, that the law of diminishing returns is *not* applicable here, because it presumes that one resource is fixed in supply and, as we have seen, the long run assumes that all resources are variable. Furthermore, our discussion assumes that resource prices are constant. What, then, is our explanation? The U-shaped long-run average-cost curve is explainable in terms of what economists call "economies and diseconomies" of large-scale production.

**Economies of Large Scale** Economies of scale or, more commonly, economies of mass production, explain the downsloping part of the long-run ATC curve. As the size of a plant increases, a number of considerations will for a time give rise to lower average costs of production.

**1 Labor Specialization** Increased specialization in the use of labor is feasible as a plant increases in size. The hire of more workers means that jobs can be divided and subdivided. Instead of performing five or six distinct operations in the productive process, each worker may now have just one task to perform. Workers can be used full time on those particular operations at which they have special skills. In a small plant skilled machinists may spend half their time performing unskilled tasks. This makes for high production costs. Further, the dividing of work operations which large scale allows will give workers the opportunity to become very proficient at the specific tasks assigned them. The jack-of-all-trades who is burdened with five or six jobs will not be likely to become very efficient in any of them. When allowed to concentrate on one task, the same worker may become highly efficient. Finally, greater specialization tends to eliminate the loss of time which accompanies the shifting of workers from one job to another.

**2 Managerial Specialization** Large-scale production also permits better utilization of, and greater specialization in, management. A supervisor capable of handling fifteen or twenty workers will be underutilized in a small plant hiring only eight or ten people. The production staff can be doubled with no increase in administrative costs. In addition, small firms will not be able to use management specialists to best advantage. In a small plant a sales specialist may be forced to divide his or her time between several executive functions—for example, marketing, personnel, and finance. A larger scale of operations will mean that the marketing expert can devote full time to supervising sales and product distribution while appropriate specialists are added to perform other managerial functions. Greater efficiency and lower unit costs are the net result.

**3 Efficient Capital** Small firms are often not able to utilize the most efficient productive equipment. In many lines of production the most efficient machinery is available only in very large and extremely expensive units. Furthermore, effective utilization of this equipment demands a high volume of production. This means only large-scale producers are able to afford and operate efficiently the best available equipment.

To illustrate: In the automobile industry the most efficient fabrication method entails the use of extremely elaborate assembly-line equipment. The efficient use of this equipment demands an annual output of an estimated 500,000 automobiles (Chapter 29). Only very large-scale producers can afford to purchase and use this equipment efficiently. The small-scale producer is between the devil and the deep blue sea. To fabricate automobiles with the use of other equipment is inefficient and therefore more costly per unit. The alternative of purchasing the most efficient equipment and underutilizing it with a small level of output is equally inefficient and costly.

**4  By-Products**  The large-scale producer is in a better position to utilize by-products than is a small firm. The large meatpacking plant makes glue, fertilizer, pharmaceuticals, and a host of other products from animal remnants which would be discarded by smaller producers.

All these technological considerations—greater specialization in the use of labor and management, the ability to use the most efficient equipment, and the effective utilization of by-products—will contribute to lower unit costs for the producer who is able to expand its scale of operations.

**Diseconomies of Large Scale**  But in time the expansion of a firm *may* give rise to diseconomies and therefore higher per unit costs.

The main factor causing diseconomies of scale has to do with certain managerial problems involved in efficiently controlling and coordinating a firm's operations as it becomes a large-scale producer. In a small plant a single key executive may render all the basic decisions relative to the plant's operation. Because of the firm's smallness, the executive is close to the production line and can, therefore, readily comprehend the various aspects of the firm's operations, easily digest the information gained from subordinates, and render clear and efficient decisions.

This neat picture changes, however, as a firm grows. The management echelons between the executive suite and the assembly line become many; top management is far removed from the actual production operations of the plant. It becomes impossible for one person to assemble, understand, and digest all the information essential to rational decision making in a large-scale enterprise. Authority must be delegated to innumerable vice-presidents, second vice-presidents, and so forth. This expansion in the depth and width of management entails problems of communication, coordination, and bureaucratic red tape and the possibility that the decisions of various subordinates will fail to mesh. The result is impaired efficiency and rising average costs.

The relevance of diseconomies of scale is not universally accepted by economists. Indeed, the existence and continued growth of such gigantic corporations as General Motors, AT&T, Exxon, and Prudential Life Insurance seem to cast doubt on the concept. In practice, computer-assisted communication systems have often been developed and applied for the purpose of overcoming or forestalling the decision-making problems embodied in the notion of diseconomies of scale. In cases where these efforts are successful, the long-run average-cost curve would fall and then become more or less constant as economies of scale are exhausted.

△  **Significance**

Economies and diseconomies of scale are something more than a plausible pipe dream of economic theorists. Indeed, in most American manufacturing industries economies of scale have been of great significance. Firms which have been able to expand their scale of operations to realize the economies of mass production have survived and flourished. Those unable to achieve this expansion have found themselves in the unenviable position of high-cost producers, doomed to a marginal existence or ultimate insolvency.

Diseconomies of scale, when encountered, can be equally significant. The organizational structure of General Motors, for example, is designed to avoid managerial diseconomies which its gigantic size would otherwise entail. This industrial colossus has subdivided itself into some thirty-six operating subdivisions, each of which is basically autonomous and in some cases—for example, its five automobile-producing divisions (Chevrolet, Buick, Oldsmobile, Pontiac, and Cadillac)—competing. A degree of decentralization has been sought which will allow full realization of the economies of mass production yet help to avoid diseconomies of scale.[1] Another example: Some economists feel that over the years U.S. Steel has declined in relative importance in the steel industry because of diseconomies of scale. One authority has described U.S. Steel as[2]

> . . . a big sprawling inert giant, whose production operations were improperly coordinated; suffering from a lack of a long-run planning agency; relying on an antiquated system of cost accounting; with an inadequate knowledge of the costs or of the relative profitability of the many thousands of items it sold; with production and cost standards generally below those considered everyday practice in other industries; with inadequate knowledge of its domestic markets and no clear appreciation of its opportunities in foreign markets; with less efficient production facilities than its rivals had; slow in introducing new processes and new products.

These comments correctly imply that economies and diseconomies of scale are a fundamental determinant of the structure of any industry. Where economies of scale are many and diseconomies are remote, the long-run

[1]See Leonard W. Weiss, *Economics and American Industry* (New York: John Wiley & Sons, Inc., 1961), pp. 347–350.
[2]Statement by George Stocking, cited in Walter Adams (ed.), *The Structure of American Industry*, 4th ed. (New York: The Macmillan Company, 1971), pp. 112–113.

ATC curve will decline over a long range of output, as in Figure 25-7a. Such is the case in the automobile, aluminum, steel, and a host of other heavy industries. This means that, given consumer demand, efficient production will be achieved only with a small number of large producers. On the other hand, where economies of scale are few and diseconomies quickly

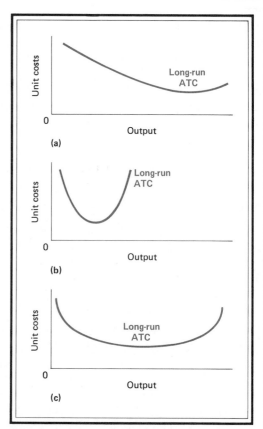

FIGURE 25-7 VARIOUS POSSIBLE LONG-RUN AVERAGE COST CURVES

(a) When economies of scale are many and diseconomies remote, the ATC will fall over a wide range of production. (b) If economies of scale are few and diseconomies are quickly incurred, minimum unit costs will be encountered at a relatively low output. (c) Where economies of scale are rather rapidly exhausted and diseconomies not encountered until a considerably large scale of output has been achieved, long-run average costs will be relatively constant over a wide range of output.

encountered, minimum unit costs will be achieved at a modest level of production. The long-run ATC curve for such a situation is shown in Figure 25-7b. In such industries a given level of consumer demand will support a large number of relatively small producers. Many of the retail trades and some types of farming fall into this category. So do certain types of light manufacturing, for example, the baking, clothing, and shoe industries. Fairly small firms are as efficient as, or more efficient than, large-scale producers in such industries.

In some industries we find a mixture of large and small producers operating with roughly the same degree of efficiency—the meat-packing, furniture, and some aspects of the household-appliance industries are representative. In such industries the long-run ATC curve may be such that there exists a wide range of output between the point at which available economies of scale are exhausted and the point at which diseconomies of scale are encountered. Or, alternatively, economies and diseconomies of scale may be largely self-canceling over an extended range of output. Figure 25-7c illustrates the situation in which average costs are relatively constant over a wide range of output.

Caution: We are not implying here that long-run unit costs are the only determinant of the structure of industry. Indeed, it was stressed in Chapter 22 that the major determinants of the competitiveness of industry are several and varied. We are saying that there is considerable evidence that cost considerations are one important force in determining the number and size of firms in a particular industry.

## Summary

1   Economic costs include all payments which must be received by resource owners in order to assure their continued supply in a particular line of production.  This definition includes explicit costs, which flow to resource suppliers who are separate from a given enterprise, and also implicit costs, which are the remuneration of self-owned and self-employed resources.  One of the implicit cost payments is a normal profit to the entrepreneur for functions performed.

2   In the short run a firm's plant capacity is fixed.  The firm can use its plant more or less intensively by adding or subtracting units of variable resources, but the firm does not have sufficient time to alter its plant size.

3   The law of diminishing returns describes what happens to output as a fixed plant is used more intensively.  The law states that as successive units of a variable resource such as labor are added to a fixed plant, beyond some point the resulting marginal product associated with each additional worker will decline.

4   Because some resources are variable and others fixed, costs can be classified as variable or fixed in the short run.  Fixed costs are those which are independent of the level of output.  Variable costs are those which vary with output.  The total cost of any output is the sum of fixed and variable costs at that output.

5   Average fixed, average variable, and average total costs are simply fixed, variable, and total costs per unit of output.  Average fixed costs decline continuously as output increases, because a fixed sum is being apportioned over a larger and larger number of units of production.  Average variable costs are U-shaped, reflecting the law of diminishing returns.  Average total cost is the sum of average fixed and average variable costs; it too is U-shaped.

6   Marginal cost is the extra, or additional, cost of producing one more unit of output.  Graphically, marginal cost cuts ATC and AVC at their minimum points.

**7** The long run is a period of time sufficiently long for a firm to vary the amounts of all resources used, including plant size. Hence, in the long run all costs are variable. The long-run ATC, or planning, curve is composed of segments of the short-run ATC curves, which represent the various plant sizes a firm is able to construct in the long run.

**8** The long-run ATC curve is generally U-shaped. Economies of scale are first encountered as a small firm expands. A number of considerations—greater specialization in the use of labor and management, the ability to use the most efficient equipment, and the more complete utilization of by-products—contribute to these economies of scale. Diseconomies of scale stem from the managerial complexities which accompany large-scale production. The relative importance of economies and diseconomies of scale in an industry is often a major determinant of the structure of that industry.

## Questions and Study Suggestions

**1** Key terms and concepts to remember: economic (opportunity) cost; explicit and implicit costs; normal and economic profits; short run and long run; law of diminishing returns; fixed costs; variable costs; total cost; average fixed cost; average variable cost; average total cost; marginal cost; economies and diseconomies of scale.

**2** Distinguish between explicit and implicit costs, giving examples of each. What are the explicit and implicit costs of going to college? Why does the economist classify normal profits as a cost? Are economic profits a cost of production?

**3** Which of the following are short-run and which are long-run adjustments? *a.* General Motors builds a new assembly plant; *b.* Acme Steel Corporation hires 200 more workers; *c.* a farmer increases the amount of fertilizer used on his corn crop; and *d.* an Alcoa plant adds a third shift of workers.

**4** Use the following data to calculate marginal physical product and average physical product. Plot total, marginal, and average physical product and explain in detail the relationship between each pair of curves.

| Inputs of labor | Total physical product | Marginal physical product | Average physical product |
|---|---|---|---|
| 1 | 15 | _____ | _____ |
| 2 | 34 | _____ | _____ |
| 3 | 51 | _____ | _____ |
| 4 | 65 | _____ | _____ |
| 5 | 74 | _____ | _____ |
| 6 | 80 | _____ | _____ |
| 7 | 83 | _____ | _____ |
| 8 | 82 | _____ | _____ |

What bearing does the law of diminishing returns have upon short-run costs? Be specific. "When marginal product is rising, marginal cost is falling. And when marginal product is diminishing, marginal cost is rising." Illustrate and explain graphically and through a numerical example.

**5** Why can the distinction between fixed and variable costs be made in the short run? Classify the following as fixed or variable costs: advertising expenditures, fuel, interest on company-issued bonds, shipping charges, payments for raw materials, real estate taxes, executive salaries, insurance premiums, wage payments, depreciation and obsolescence charges, sales taxes, and rental payments on leased office machinery. "There are no fixed costs in the long run; all costs are variable." Explain.

**6** Assume a firm has fixed costs of $60 and variable costs as indicated in the following table.  Complete the table.  When finished, check your calculations by referring to question 6 at the end of Chapter 26.

| Total product | Total fixed cost | Total variable cost | Total cost | Average fixed cost | Average variable cost | Average total cost | Marginal cost |
|---|---|---|---|---|---|---|---|
| 0 | $____ | $ 0 | $____ | $____ | $____ | $____ | |
| 1 | ____ | 45 | ____ | ____ | ____ | ____ | $____ |
| 2 | ____ | 85 | ____ | ____ | ____ | ____ | ____ |
| 3 | ____ | 120 | ____ | ____ | ____ | ____ | ____ |
| 4 | ____ | 150 | ____ | ____ | ____ | ____ | ____ |
| 5 | ____ | 185 | ____ | ____ | ____ | ____ | ____ |
| 6 | ____ | 225 | ____ | ____ | ____ | ____ | ____ |
| 7 | ____ | 270 | ____ | ____ | ____ | ____ | ____ |
| 8 | ____ | 325 | ____ | ____ | ____ | ____ | ____ |
| 9 | ____ | 390 | ____ | ____ | ____ | ____ | ____ |
| 10 | ____ | 465 | ____ | ____ | ____ | ____ | ____ |

*a.*   Graph fixed cost, variable cost, and total cost.  Explain how the law of diminishing returns influences the shapes of the variable-cost and total-cost curves.

*b.*   Graph AFC, AVC, ATC, and MC.  Explain the derivation and shape of each of these four curves and the relationships which they bear to one another.  Specifically, explain in nontechnical terms why MC cuts both AVC and ATC at their minimum points.

**7** Use the concepts of economies and diseconomies of scale to explain the shape of a firm's long-run ATC curve.  What bearing may the exact shape of this curve have upon the structure of an industry?

# Selected References

Bain, Joe S.: *Industrial Organization,* 2d ed. (New York: John Wiley & Sons, Inc., 1968), pp. 166–180.

Ferguson, C. E., and S. Charles Maurice: *Economic Analysis: Theory and Application,* 3d ed. (Homewood, Ill.: Richard D. Irwin, Inc., 1978), chaps. 5–6.

Kaish, Stanley: *Microeconomics: Logic, Tools, and Analysis* (New York: Harper & Row, Publishers, Incorporated, 1976), chap. 6.

Robinson, E. A. G.: *The Structure of Competitive Industry* (Chicago: The University of Chicago Press, 1958).

Stigler, George J.: *The Theory of Price,* 3d ed. (New York: The Macmillan Company, 1966), chaps. 6–8.

Watson, Donald S. (ed.): *Price Theory in Action,* 3d ed. (Boston: Houghton Mifflin Company, 1973), part 3.

# LAST WORD
## Economies of Scale at American Motors

The Chairman of the Board discusses economies of scale as they relate to American Motors.

A few years ago the Small Business Administration declared American Motors to be a small business. At the time, AMC had 40,000 employees, ranked as the 100th largest American corporation, and turned out 300,000 cars a year. *Small?* By the standards of its competition—General Motors with $36 billion in sales, Ford with $23 billion—AMC is small. But small on this scale doesn't have to mean inefficient.

"We all build cars the same way," says American Motors' Chairman Roy Chapin, "and we know that in the basic assembly structure of our vehicle—between the time the body starts and the time it comes off as a finished vehicle—our hours per car are *less* than some of our competitors'. Our return on equity is about the same as GM's. We think we've done a more efficient job of organizing our manpower, our tooling, the speeds at which we run our lines."

AMC's present prosperity is so impressive as to lend grist to the claims of Senator Philip Hart (Dem., Mich.) and others that medium-sized companies are just as efficient as huge ones and that GM, as a consequence, ought to be split up into as many as 12 independent companies.

"The one area where Senator Hart has validity," Chapin says, "is that when you get beyond a certain size, the economies of scale do not just continue *ad infinitum*. You can build a very profitable, viable automobile company on a volume of between 300,000 and 500,000 units a year. At American Motors we really have only two major product categories: the Matador/Ambassador and the Hornet/Gremlin. Both have basically the same tooling and use the same parts, but the vehicles look different and serve somewhat different purposes. If your volume, like ours, runs between 150,000 and 350,000 units in each of those categories, your cost per unit will be just a few dollars more than somebody making twice as many."

"Here's a quick lesson in automotive economics. You have a big block like this," Chapin says, shaping an invisible square with his hands. "That's your fixed costs. That's me, the building, utilities, amortization of your tooling—all the things that are constant whether you make a car or you don't. What you then have to do is make enough vehicles with enough marginal profit to cover that block. Let's say that marginal profit is $1,000 a vehicle. Once you get above that so-called break-even point, every extra $1,000 goes into your pocket. Since you don't have any additional fixed costs, those extra $1,000s are, in effect, free up to a certain point.

"At that point you have to build another assembly plant, fill another assembly line, buy another set of tools, put in another set of supervisors, hire more typists to fill out schedules. You have to duplicate almost all of your fixed costs. The trick is to get maximum productivity out of a given set of fixed costs, without having to add another set."

How soon those additional costs start paying for themselves depends on volume. "Say we want to build another 200,000 units to keep pace with demand," says Chapin. "Once you pass the 500,000 mark, the first 50,000 are going to cost you money; the next 100,000 will probably not leave you much better off, if any. Until you get to 650,000 you haven't really got your bait back for building all those new facilities. These are not our numbers, by the way, but the principle is correct."

"The Economies of Scale Do Not Just Continue." Reprinted by permission of *Forbes Magazine* from the May 15, 1974, issue.

# Price and Output Determination: Pure Competition

chapter 26

We now have at our disposal the basic tools of analysis needed to understand how product price and output are determined. These analytical tools are applicable to all four basic market models—pure competition, pure monopoly, monopolistic competition, and oligopoly. In this chapter we focus attention upon price and output determination in a purely competitive industry.

## □ PURE COMPETITION:
## CONCEPT AND OCCURRENCE

Pure competition, you will recall, presupposes that certain specific conditions are fulfilled.

**1** By definition, a purely competitive industry is composed of a large number of independent sellers.

**2** The firms offer a standardized product. This feature rules out nonprice competition, that is, advertising, sales promotion, and so forth.

**3** No individual firm supplies enough of the product to influence its market price noticeably.

**4** In a competitive industry no artificial obstacles prevent new firms from entering, or existing firms from leaving, the industry. Firms and the resources they employ are shiftable, or mobile.

Pure competition is rare in practice. This does not mean, however, that an analysis of how competitive markets work is a useless and irrelevant exercise in logic.

**1** In the first place, there are a few industries which more closely approximate the competitive model than they do any other market structure. For example, much can be learned about American agriculture by understanding the functioning of competitive markets.

**2** Moreover, pure competition provides the simplest context in which to apply the revenue and cost concepts developed in previous chapters. Pure competition is a clear and meaningful starting point for any discussion of price and output determination.

   **3** Finally, in the concluding section of this chapter we shall discover that the operation of a purely competitive economy provides us with a standard, or norm, against which the efficiency of the real-world economy can be compared and evaluated.

   Though pure competition is a relatively rare market structure in our economy, it is one of considerable analytical and some practical importance.

   Our analysis of pure competition centers upon four major objectives. First, we will examine demand from the competitive seller's viewpoint. Second, we seek an understanding of how a competitive producer adjusts to market price in the short run. Next, the nature of long-run adjustments in a competitive industry is explored. Finally, we seek to evaluate the efficiency of competitive industries from the standpoint of society as a whole.

## ☐  DEMAND TO A COMPETITIVE SELLER

Because each competitive firm offers a negligible fraction of total supply, the individual firm cannot perceptibly influence the market price which the forces of total demand and supply have established. The competitive firm does not have a price policy, that is, the ability to adjust price. Rather, the firm can merely *adjust to* the market price, which it must regard as a given datum determined by the market. The competitive seller is said to be a price *taker,* rather than a price *maker.*

### △  Perfectly Elastic Demand

   Stated technically, the demand curve facing the individual competitive firm is perfectly elastic. Columns 1 and 2 of Table 26-1 show a perfectly elastic demand curve where market price is assumed to be $131. Note that the firm cannot obtain a higher price by restricting

**TABLE 26-1**
**The Demand and Revenue Schedules For an Individual Purely Competitive Firm** (*hypothetical data*)

| Firm's demand or average-revenue schedule | | Revenue data | |
|---|---|---|---|
| (1) Product price (average revenue) | (2) Quantity demanded (sold) | (3) Total revenue | (4) Marginal revenue |
| $131 | 0 | $  0 | |
| 131 | 1 | 131 | $131 |
| 131 | 2 | 262 | 131 |
| 131 | 3 | 393 | 131 |
| 131 | 4 | 524 | 131 |
| 131 | 5 | 655 | 131 |
| 131 | 6 | 786 | 131 |
| 131 | 7 | 917 | 131 |
| 131 | 8 | 1048 | 131 |
| 131 | 9 | 1179 | 131 |
| 131 | 10 | 1310 | 131 |

output; nor need it lower price in order to increase its volume of sales.

   But a word of caution is in order. We are *not* saying that the *market* demand curve is perfectly elastic in a competitive market. Indeed, it is not, but rather, it is typically a downsloping curve as a glance ahead at Figure 26-7b indicates. As a matter of fact, the total-demand curves for most agricultural products are quite *ine*lastic, even though agriculture is the most competitive industry in our economy. We are saying that the demand schedule faced by the *individual firm* in a purely competitive industry is perfectly elastic. The distinction comes about in this way. For the industry—that is, for all firms producing a particular product—a larger volume of sales can be realized only by accepting a lower product price. All firms, acting independently but simultaneously, can and do affect total supply and therefore market price. But not so for the individual firm. If a single producer increases or decreases output, the outputs of all other competing firms being constant, the effect on total supply and market price is negligible. The single firm's demand or sales schedule is therefore perfectly elastic, as shown in Figures 26-1 and 26-7*a*. This is an instance in which the fallacy of composition is worth remembering. What is true for the group of firms (a downsloping, less than perfectly elastic, demand curve) is *not* true for the individual firm (a perfectly elastic demand curve).

△  **Average, Total, and Marginal Revenue**

A moment's reflection reveals that the firm's demand schedule is simultaneously a revenue schedule. What appears in column 1 of Table 26-1 as price per unit to the purchaser is obviously revenue per unit, or *average revenue,* to the seller. To say that a buyer must pay a price of $131 per unit is to say that the revenue per unit, or average revenue, received by the seller is $131. Price and average revenue are the same thing looked at from different points of view.

*Total revenue* for each level of sales can obviously be determined by multiplying price by the corresponding quantity which the firm can sell. Multiply column 1 by column 2, and the result is column 3. In this case, total receipts increase by a constant amount, $131, for each additional unit of sales. Each unit sold adds exactly its price to total revenue.

Whenever a firm is pondering a change in its output, it will be concerned with how its revenue will change as a result of that shift in output. What will be the additional revenue from selling another unit of output? *Marginal revenue* is the addition to total revenue, that is, the extra revenue, which results from the sale of one more unit of output. In other words, in Table 26-1, marginal revenue is simply the rate of change in total revenue. In column 3 we note that total revenue is obviously zero when zero units are being sold. The first unit of output sold increases total revenue from zero to $131. Marginal revenue—the increase in total revenue resulting from the sale of the first unit of output—is therefore $131. The

second unit sold increases total revenue from $131 to $262, so marginal revenue is again $131. Indeed, you will note in column 4 that marginal revenue is a constant figure of $131. Why? Because total revenue increases at a constant rate with every extra unit sold. Under purely competitive conditions, product price is constant to the individual firm; added units therefore can be sold without lowering product price. This means that each additional unit of sales adds exactly its price—$131 in this case—to total revenue. And marginal revenue *is* this rate of increase in total revenue. Marginal revenue is constant under pure competition because additional units can be sold at a constant price.

△  **Graphic Portrayal**

The competitive firm's demand curve and total- and marginal-revenue curves are shown graphically in Figure 26-1. The demand or average-revenue curve is perfectly elastic. The marginal-revenue curve coincides with the demand curve because the market is a purely competitive one, and as a result, product price is constant to the single firm. Each extra unit of sales increases total revenue by $131. Total revenue is a straight line up to the right. Its slope is constant—that is, it is a straight line—because marginal revenue is constant.

☐  **PROFIT MAXIMIZATION IN THE SHORT RUN: TWO APPROACHES**

In the short run the competitive firm has a fixed plant and is attempting to maximize its profits or, as the case may be, minimize its losses by adjusting its output through changes in the amounts of variable resources (materials, labor, and so forth) it employs. The economic profits it seeks are obviously the difference between total revenue and total costs. Indeed, this points out the direction of our analysis. The revenue data of the previous section and the cost data of Chapter 25 must be brought together in order that the profit-maximizing output for the firm can be determined.

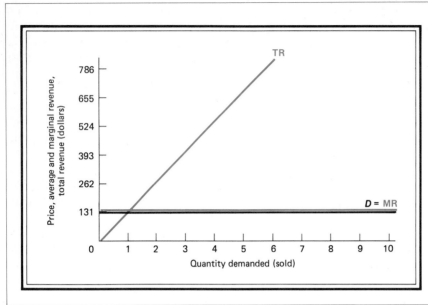

FIGURE 26-1 DEMAND,
MARGINAL REVENUE, AND
TOTAL REVENUE OF A
PURELY COMPETITIVE FIRM

Because it can sell additional
units of output at a constant
price, the marginal-revenue
curve (MR) of a purely competitive firm coincides with its
perfectly elastic demand curve
(D).  The firm's total-revenue
curve (TR) is a straight upsloping line.

There are two complementary approaches to determining the level of output at which a competitive firm will realize maximum profits or minimum losses. The first involves a comparison of total revenue and total costs; the second, a comparison of marginal revenue and marginal cost. Both approaches are applicable not only to a purely competitive firm but also to firms operating in any of the other three basic market structures. To ensure an understanding of output determination under pure competition, we shall invoke both approaches, emphasizing the marginal approach. Furthermore, hypothetical data in both tabular and graphic form will be employed to bolster our understanding of the two approaches.

△  **Total-Receipts–Total-Cost Approach**

Given the market price of its product, the competitive producer is faced with three related questions: (1) Should we produce? (2) If so, what amount? (3) What profit (or loss) will be realized?

At first glance, the answer to question 1 seems obvious: "You should produce if it is profitable to do so." But the situation is a bit more complex than this. In the short run a part of the firm's total costs is variable costs, and the remainder is fixed costs. The latter will have to be paid "out of pocket" even when the firm is closed down. In the short run a firm takes a loss equal to its fixed costs when it is producing zero units of output. This means that, although there may be no level of output at which the firm can realize a profit, the firm might still produce, provided that in so doing, it can realize a loss less than the fixed-cost loss it will face in closing down. In other words, the correct answer to the "Should we produce?" question is this: *The firm should produce in the short run if it can realize either an economic profit or a loss which is less than its fixed costs.*

Assuming the firm *will* produce, the second question becomes relevant: "How much should be produced?" The answer here is fairly obvious: *In the short run the firm should produce that output at which it maximizes profits or minimizes losses.*

Now let us examine three cases which will demonstrate the validity of these two generalizations and answer our third query by indicating how profits and losses can be readily calculated. In the first case the firm will maximize its profits by producing. In the second case it will minimize its losses by producing. In the third case the firm will minimize its losses by closing down. Our plan of attack is to assume given short-run cost data for all three cases and to explore the firm's production decisions when faced with three different product prices.

**Profit-Maximizing Case**  In all three cases we employ cost data with which we are already familiar. Columns 3 through 5 of Table 26-2 merely repeat the fixed-, variable-, and total-cost data which were developed in Table 25-2. Assuming that market price is $131, we can derive total revenue for each level of output by simply multiplying output times price, as we did in Table 26-1. These data are presented in column 2. Then in column 6 the profit or loss which will be encountered at each output is found by subtracting total cost from total rev-

enue. Now we have all the data needed to answer the three questions.

Should the firm produce? Yes, because it can realize a profit by doing so. How much? Nine units, because column 6 tells us that this is the output at which total economic profits will be at a maximum. The size of that profit? $299.

Figure 26-2a compares total revenue and total cost graphically. Total revenue is a straight line, because under pure competition each additional unit adds the same amount— its price—to total revenue (Table 26-1). Total costs increase with output; more production requires more resources. But the rate of increase in total costs varies with the relative efficiency of the firm. Specifically, the cost data reflect Chapter 25's law of diminishing returns. That is, for a time the rate of increase in total cost is less and less as the firm utilizes its fixed resources more efficiently. Then, after a time, total cost begins to rise by ever-increasing amounts because of the inefficiencies which accompany overutilization of the firm's plant. Comparing total cost with total revenue in Figure 26-2a, we note that a *break-even point*

**TABLE 26-2**
The Profit-Maximizing Output For a Purely Competitive Firm:
Total-Revenue–Total-Cost Approach (Price = $131) (*hypothetical data*)

| (1) Total product | (2) Total revenue | (3) Total fixed cost | (4) Total variable cost | (5) Total cost | (6) Total economic profit (+) or loss (−), = (2) − (5) |
|---|---|---|---|---|---|
| 0 | $    0 | $100 | $    0 | $  100 | $−100 |
| 1 | 131 | 100 | 90 | 190 | − 59 |
| 2 | 262 | 100 | 170 | 270 | −  8 |
| 3 | 393 | 100 | 240 | 340 | + 53 |
| 4 | 524 | 100 | 300 | 400 | +124 |
| 5 | 655 | 100 | 370 | 470 | +185 |
| 6 | 786 | 100 | 450 | 550 | +236 |
| 7 | 917 | 100 | 540 | 640 | +277 |
| 8 | 1048 | 100 | 650 | 750 | +298 |
| 9 | 1179 | 100 | 780 | 880 | +299 |
| 10 | 1310 | 100 | 930 | 1030 | +280 |

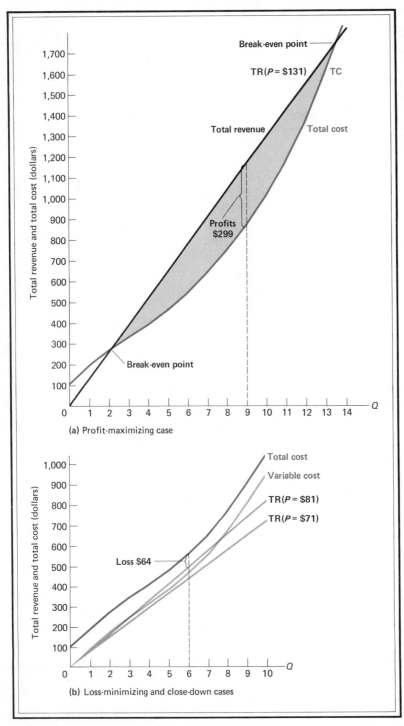

FIGURE 26-2  THE PROFIT-
MAXIMIZING (a), LOSS-
MINIMIZING, AND CLOSE-
DOWN CASES (b), AS SHOWN
BY THE TOTAL-REVENUE-
TOTAL-COST APPROACH

A firm's profits are maximized
in (a) at that output at which
total revenue exceeds total cost
by the maximum amount. A firm
will minimize its losses in (b) by
producing at that output at
which total cost exceeds total
revenue by the smallest amount.
However, if there is no output at
which total revenue exceeds
variable costs, the firm will
minimize losses in the short run
by closing down.

occurs at about 2 units of output. And, if our data were extended beyond 10 units of output, another such point would be incurred where total cost would catch up with total revenue, as is shown in Figure 26-2a. Any output outside these points will entail losses. Any output within these break-even points will entail an economic profit. The maximum profit is obviously achieved where the vertical difference between total revenue and total cost is greatest. For our data this is at 9 units of output and the resulting maximum profit is $299.

**Loss-Minimizing Case**   Assuming no change in costs, the firm may not be able to realize economic profits if the market yields a price considerably below $131. To illustrate: Suppose the market price is $81. As column 6 of Table 26-3 indicates, at this price all levels of output will entail losses. But the firm will not close down. Why? Because, by producing, the firm can realize a loss considerably less than the fixed-cost loss it would incur by closing down. Specifically, the firm will minimize its losses by producing 6 units of output. The

resulting $64 loss is clearly preferable to the $100 loss which closing down would involve. Stated differently, by producing 6 units the firm earns a total revenue of $486, sufficient to pay all the firm's variable cost ($450) and also a substantial portion—$36 worth—of the firm's $100 of fixed costs. There are, you will note, several other outputs which entail a loss less than the firm's $100 fixed costs; but at 6 units of output the loss is minimized.

**Close-Down Case**   Assume finally that the market price is a mere $71. Given short-run costs, column 9 of Table 26-3 clearly indicates that at all levels of output, losses will exceed the $100 fixed-cost loss the firm will incur by closing down. Obviously, then, the firm will minimize its losses by closing down, that is, by producing zero units of output.

Figure 26-2b demonstrates the loss-minimizing and close-down cases graphically. In the loss-minimizing case, the total-revenue line TR ($P = \$81$) exceeds total variable cost by the maximum amount at 6 units of output. Here total revenue is $486, and the firm recov-

**TABLE 26-3**
**The Loss-Minimizing Outputs For a Purely Competitive Firm: Total-Revenue–Total-Cost Approach (Prices = $81 and $71) (hypothetical data)**

| Product price = $81 | | | | | | Product price = $71 | | |
|---|---|---|---|---|---|---|---|---|
| (1) Total product | (2) Total revenue | (3) Total fixed cost | (4) Total variable cost | (5) Total cost | (6) Total economic profit (+) or loss (−), = (2) − (5) | (7) Total revenue | (8) Total cost | (9) Total economic profit (+) or loss (−), = (7) − (8) |
| 0 | $ 0 | $100 | $ 0 | $ 100 | $ −100 | $ 0 | $ 100 | $ −100 |
| 1 | 81 | 100 | 90 | 190 | −109 | 71 | 190 | −119 |
| 2 | 162 | 100 | 170 | 270 | −108 | 142 | 270 | −128 |
| 3 | 243 | 100 | 240 | 340 | − 97 | 213 | 340 | −127 |
| 4 | 324 | 100 | 300 | 400 | − 76 | 284 | 400 | −116 |
| 5 | 405 | 100 | 370 | 470 | − 65 | 355 | 470 | −115 |
| 6 | 486 | 100 | 450 | 550 | − 64 | 426 | 550 | −124 |
| 7 | 567 | 100 | 540 | 640 | − 73 | 497 | 640 | −143 |
| 8 | 648 | 100 | 650 | 750 | −102 | 568 | 750 | −182 |
| 9 | 729 | 100 | 780 | 880 | −151 | 639 | 880 | −241 |
| 10 | 810 | 100 | 930 | 1030 | −220 | 710 | 1030 | −320 |

ers all its $450 of variable costs and also $36 worth of its fixed costs. The firm's minimum loss is $64, clearly superior to the $100 fixed-cost loss involved in closing down. In the close-down case, the total-revenue line TR ($P = \$71$) lies below the total-variable-cost curve at all points; there is no output at which variable costs can be recovered. Therefore, the firm, by producing, would incur losses in excess of its fixed costs. The firm's best choice is to close down and pay its $100 fixed-cost loss out of pocket.

### △ Marginal-Revenue–Marginal-Cost Approach

An alternative means for determining the amounts which a competitive firm will be willing to offer in the market at each possible price is for the firm to determine and compare the amounts that each *additional* unit of output will add to total revenue, on the one hand, and to total cost, on the other. That is, the firm should compare the *marginal revenue* (MR) and the *marginal cost* (MC) of each successive unit of output. Any unit whose marginal revenue exceeds its marginal cost should obviously be produced. Why? Because on each such unit, the firm is gaining more in revenue from its sale than it adds to costs in getting that unit produced. Hence, the unit of output is adding to total profits or, as the case may be, subtracting from losses. Similarly, if the marginal cost of a unit of output exceeds its marginal revenue, the firm should avoid producing that unit. It will add more to costs than to revenue; such a unit will not "pay its way."

**MR = MC Rule**   In the initial stages of production, where output is relatively low, marginal revenue will usually (but not always) exceed marginal cost. It is therefore profitable to produce through this range of output. But at later stages of production, where output is relatively high, rising marginal costs will cause the reverse to be true. Marginal cost will exceed marginal revenue. Production of units of output falling in this range is obviously to be avoided in the interest of maximizing profits. Separating these two production ranges will be a unique point at which marginal revenue equals marginal cost. This point is the key to the output-determining rule: *The firm will maximize profits or minimize losses by producing at that point where marginal revenue equals marginal cost.* For convenience we shall call this profit-maximizing guide the MR = MC rule. For most sets of MR and MC data, there will be no nonfractional level of output at which MR and MC are precisely equal. In such instances the firm should produce the last complete unit of output whose MR exceeds its MC.

**Three Characteristics**   Three features of this MR = MC rule merit comment.

**1**   First, a qualification: The rule assumes that the firm will choose to produce rather than close down. Shortly, we shall note that marginal revenue must be equal to, or must exceed, average variable cost, or the firm will find it preferable to close down rather than produce the MR = MC output.

**2**   It is to be emphasized that the MR = MC rule is an accurate guide to profit maximization for all firms, be they purely competitive, monopolistic, monopolistically competitive, or oligopolistic. The rule's application is *not* limited to the special case of pure competition.

**3**   A third and related point is that the MR = MC rule can be conveniently restated in a slightly different form when being applied to a purely competitive firm. You will recall that product price is determined by the broad market forces of supply and demand, and although the competitive firm can sell as much or as little as it chooses at that price, the firm cannot manipulate the price itself. In technical terms the demand, or sales, schedule faced by a competitive seller is perfectly elastic at the going market price. The result is that product price and marginal revenue are equal; that is, each extra unit sold adds precisely its

**TABLE 26-4**
The Profit-Maximizing Output For a Purely Competitive Firm: Marginal-Revenue-Equals-Marginal-Cost Approach
(Price = $131) (*hypothetical data*)

| (1) Total product | (2) Average fixed cost | (3) Average variable cost | (4) Average total cost | (5) Marginal cost | (6) Price = marginal revenue | (7) Total economic profit (+) or loss − |
|---|---|---|---|---|---|---|
| 0 | | | | | | $−100 |
| | | | | $ 90 | $131 | |
| 1 | $100.00 | $90.00 | $190.00 | | | − 59 |
| | | | | 80 | 131 | |
| 2 | 50.00 | 85.00 | 135.00 | | | − 8 |
| | | | | 70 | 131 | |
| 3 | 33.33 | 80.00 | 113.33 | | | + 53 |
| | | | | 60 | 131 | |
| 4 | 25.00 | 75.00 | 100.00 | | | +124 |
| | | | | 70 | 131 | |
| 5 | 20.00 | 74.00 | 94.00 | | | +185 |
| | | | | 80 | 131 | |
| 6 | 16.67 | 75.00 | 91.67 | | | +236 |
| | | | | 90 | 131 | |
| 7 | 14.29 | 77.14 | 91.43 | | | +277 |
| | | | | 110 | 131 | |
| 8 | 12.50 | 81.25 | 93.75 | | | +298 |
| | | | | 130 | 131 | |
| 9 | 11.11 | 86.67 | 97.78 | | | +299 |
| | | | | 150 | 131 | |
| 10 | 10.00 | 93.00 | 103.00 | | | +280 |

price to total revenue as shown in Figure 26-1. Thus under pure competition—and *only* under pure competition—we may substitute price for marginal revenue in the rule, so that it reads as follows: *To maximize profits or minimize losses the competitive firm should produce at that point where price equals marginal cost (P = MC).* This *P* = MC rule is simply a special case of the MR = MC rule.

Now let us apply the MR = MC or, because we are considering pure competition, the *P* = MC rule, using the same three prices employed in our total-revenue–total-cost approach to profit maximization.

**Profit-Maximizing Case**   Table 26-4 reproduces the unit- and marginal-cost data derived in Table 25-2. It is, of course, the marginal-cost data of column 5 in Table 26-4 which we wish to compare with price (equal to marginal revenue) for each unit of output. Suppose first that market price, and therefore marginal revenue, is $131, as shown in column 6. What is the profit-maximizing output? It is readily seen that each and every unit of output up to and including the ninth adds more to total revenue than to total cost. That is, price,

or marginal revenue, exceeds marginal cost on all the first 9 units of output. Each of these units therefore adds to the firm's profits and should obviously be produced. The tenth unit, however, will not be produced, because it would add more to costs ($150) than to revenue ($131).

The level of economic profits realized by the firm can be readily calculated from the unit-cost data. Multiplying price ($131) times output (9), we find total revenue to be $1179. Total cost of about[1] $880 is found by multiplying average total cost ($97.78) by output (9). The difference of $299 is economic profits. An alternative means of calculating economic profits is to determine profit *per unit* by subtracting average total cost ($97.78) from product price ($131) and multiplying the difference (per unit profits of $33.22) by the level of output (9). By verifying the figures in column 7 of Table 26-4 the skeptical reader will find that

[1]In most instances the unit-cost data are rounded figures. Therefore, economic profits calculated from them will typically vary by a few cents from the profits determined in the total-revenue–total-cost approach. We here ignore the few-cents differentials and make our answers consistent with the results of the total-revenue–total-cost approach.

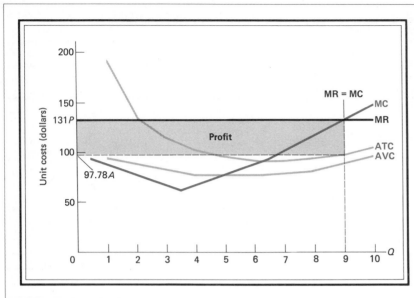

**FIGURE 26-3 THE SHORT-RUN PROFIT-MAXIMIZING POSITION OF A PURELY COMPETITIVE FIRM**

The $P$ = MC output allows the competitive producer to maximize profits or minimize losses. In this case price exceeds average total cost at the $P$ = MC output of 9 units. Economic profits per unit of $AP$ are realized; total economic profits are indicated by the orange rectangle.

any output other than that indicated to be most profitable by the MR $(P)$ = MC rule will entail either losses or profits less than $299.

Figure 26-3 makes the comparison of price and marginal cost graphically. Here per unit economic profit is indicated by the distance $AP$. When multiplied by the profit-maximizing output, the resulting total economic profit is shown by the orange rectangular area.

It should be noted that the firm is seeking to maximize its *total* profits, not its *per unit* profits. Per unit profits are largest at 7 units of output, where price exceeds average total cost by $39.57 ($131 minus $91.43). But by produc-

**TABLE 26-5**

The Loss-Minimizing Outputs For a Purely Competitive Firm: Marginal-Revenue-Equals-Marginal-Cost Approach (Prices = $81 and $71) (*hypothetical data*)

| (1) Total product | (2) Average fixed cost | (3) Average variable cost | (4) Average total cost | (5) Marginal cost | (6) $81 price = marginal revenue | (7) Profit (+) or loss (−), $81 price | (8) $71 price = marginal revenue | (9) Profit (+) or loss (−), $71 price |
|---|---|---|---|---|---|---|---|---|
| 0 | | | | | | $−100 | | $−100 |
| 1 | $100.00 | $90.00 | $190.00 | $ 90 | $81 | −109 | $71 | −119 |
| 2 | 50.00 | 85.00 | 135.00 | 80 | 81 | −108 | 71 | −128 |
| 3 | 33.33 | 80.00 | 113.33 | 70 | 81 | − 97 | 71 | −127 |
| 4 | 25.00 | 75.00 | 100.00 | 60 | 81 | − 76 | 71 | −116 |
| 5 | 20.00 | 74.00 | 94.00 | 70 | 81 | − 65 | 71 | −115 |
| 6 | **16.67** | **75.00** | **91.67** | 80 | 81 | − 64 | 71 | −124 |
| 7 | 14.29 | 77.14 | 91.43 | 90 | 81 | − 73 | 71 | −143 |
| 8 | 12.50 | 81.25 | 93.75 | 110 | 81 | −102 | 71 | −182 |
| 9 | 11.11 | 86.67 | 97.78 | 130 | 81 | −151 | 71 | −241 |
| 10 | 10.00 | 93.00 | 103.00 | 150 | 81 | −220 | 71 | −320 |

ing only 7 units, the firm would be forgoing the production of additional units of output which would clearly contribute to total profits. The firm is happy to accept lower per unit profits if the resulting extra units of sales more than compensate for the lower per unit profits.

**Loss-Minimizing Case**  Now let us apply the same reasoning on the assumption that market price is $81 rather than $131. Should the firm produce? If so, how much? And what will the resulting profits or losses be? The answers, respectively, are "Yes," "Six units," and "A loss of $64."

Column 6 of Table 26-5 shows the new price (equal to marginal revenue) alongside the same unit- and marginal-cost data presented in Table 26-4. Comparing columns 5 and 6, we find that the first unit of output adds $90 to total cost but only $81 to total revenue. One might be inclined to conclude: "Don't produce—close down!" But this would be hasty. Remember that in the very early stages of production, marginal physical product is low, making marginal cost unusually high. The price–marginal-cost relationship might im-

prove with increased production. And it does. On the next 5 units—2 through 6—price exceeds marginal cost. Each of these 5 units adds more to revenue than to cost, more than compensating for the "loss" taken on the first unit. Beyond 6 units, however, MC exceeds MR (P). The firm should therefore produce at 6 units. In general, the profit-seeking producer should always compare marginal revenue (or price under pure competition) with the *rising* portion of the marginal-cost schedule or curve.

Will production be profitable? No, it will not. At 6 units of output, average total costs of $91.67 exceed price of $81 by $10.67 per unit. Multiply by the 6 units of output, and the firm's total loss is about $64. Then why produce? Because this loss is less than the firm's $100 worth of fixed costs—the $100 loss the firm would incur in the short run by closing down. Looked at differently, the firm receives enough revenue per unit ($81) to cover its variable costs of $75 and also provide $6 per unit, or a total of $36, to apply against the payment of fixed costs. Therefore, the firm's loss is only $64 (= $100 − $36), rather than $100.

This case is shown graphically in Figure

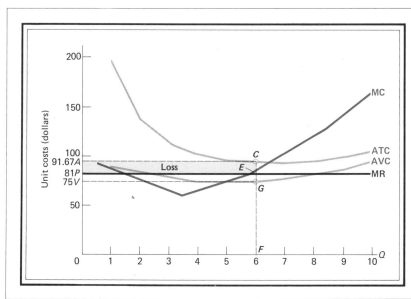

**FIGURE 26-4 THE SHORT-RUN LOSS-MINIMIZING POSITION OF A PURELY COMPETITIVE FIRM**

If price exceeds the minimum AVC but is less than ATC, the $P$ = MC output of 6 units will permit the firm to minimize its losses. In this instance losses are $AP$ per unit; total losses are shown by the area $APEC$.

26-4. Whenever price exceeds the minimum average variable cost but falls short of average total cost, the firm can pay a part of, but not all, its fixed costs by producing. In this instance total variable costs are shown by the area *OVGF*. Total revenue, however, is *OPEF*, greater than total variable costs by *VPEG*. This excess of revenue over variable costs can be applied against total fixed costs, represented by area *VACG*. Stated differently, by producing 6 units the firm's loss is only area *PACE*; by closing down, its loss would be its fixed costs shown by the larger area *VACG*.

**Close-Down Case**  Suppose now that the market yields a price of only $71. In this case it will pay the firm to close down, to produce nothing. Why? Because there is no output at which the firm can cover its average variable costs, much less its average total cost. In other words, the smallest loss it can realize by producing is greater than the $100 worth of fixed costs it will lose by closing down. The smart

thing is obviously to close down. This can be verified by comparing columns 3 and 8 of Table 26-5 and can be readily visualized in Figure 26-5. Price comes closest to covering average variable costs at the MR $(P)$ = MC output of 5 units. But even here, price or revenue per unit would fall short of average variable cost by $3 (= $74 − $71). By producing at the MR $(P)$ = MC output, the firm would lose its $100 worth of fixed costs *plus* $15 ($3 on each of the five units) worth of variable costs, for a total loss of $115. This clearly compares unfavorably with the $100 fixed-cost loss the firm would incur by choosing to close down. In short, it will obviously pay the firm to close down rather than operate at a $71 price or, for that matter, at any price less than $74.

The close-down case obligates us to modify our MR $(P)$ = MC rule for profit maximization or loss minimization. *A competitive firm will maximize profits or minimize losses in the short run by producing at that output at which MR $(P)$ = MC, provided that price exceeds the minimum average-variable-cost figure.*

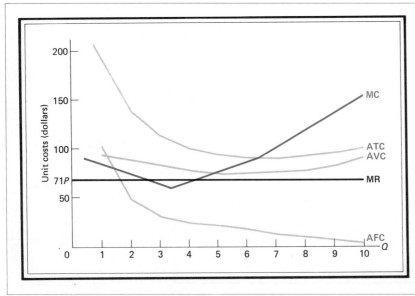

FIGURE 26-5 THE SHORT-RUN CLOSE-DOWN POSITION OF A PURELY COMPETITIVE FIRM

If price falls short of minimum AVC, the competitive firm will minimize its losses in the short run by closing down. There is no level of output at which the firm can produce and realize a loss smaller than its fixed costs.

**Marginal Cost and the Short-Run Supply Curve** Now the astute reader will recognize that we have simply selected three different prices and asked how much the profit-seeking competitive firm, faced with certain costs, would choose to offer or supply in the market at each of these prices. This information— price and corresponding quantity supplied— obviously constitutes the supply schedule for the competitive firm. Table 26-6 summarizes the supply-schedule data for the three prices we have chosen—$131, $81, and $71. The reader is urged to apply the MR ($P$) = MC rule (as modified by the close-down case) to verify the quantity-supplied data for the $151, $111, $91, and $61 prices and calculate the corresponding profits or losses. The supply schedule is obviously upsloping. In this instance, price must be $74 (equal to minimum average variable cost) or greater before any output is supplied. The profit-seeking firm is induced to offer more of the product as higher and higher prices are equated with the mar-ginal cost of larger and larger outputs in the cost table.

Figure 26-6 generalizes upon our application of the MR ($P$) = MC rule. Here we have drawn the appropriate cost curves. Then from the vertical axis we have extended a series of marginal-revenue lines from some of the various possible prices which the market might set for the firm. The crucial prices are $P_2$ and $P_4$. Our close-down case reminds us that at any

**TABLE 26-6**
The Supply Schedule of a Competitive Firm Confronted with the Cost Data of Table 26-4 (*hypothetical data*)

| Price | Quantity supplied | Maximum profit (+) or minimum loss (−) |
|---|---|---|
| $151 | 10 | $_____ |
| 131 | 9 | +299 |
| 111 | 8 | _____ |
| 91 | 7 | _____ |
| 81 | 6 | − 64 |
| 71 | 0 | −100 |
| 61 | 0 | _____ |

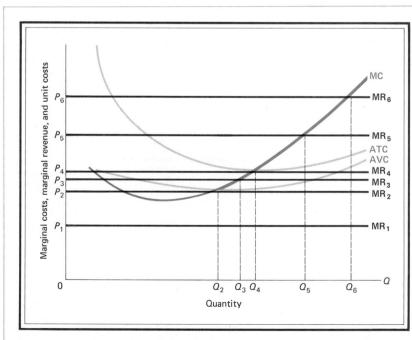

FIGURE 26-6 MARGINAL COST AND THE COMPETITIVE FIRM'S SHORT-RUN SUPPLY

Application of the $P$ = MC rule, as modified by the close-down case, reveals that the segment of the firm's MC curve which lies above AVC is its short-run supply curve. At any price between $P_2$ and $P_4$, such as $P_3$, losses will be minimized by producing the $P$ = MC output. At any price above $P_4$, such as $P_5$ or $P_6$, profits will be maximized at the $P$ = MC output.

price *below* $P_2$—that price equal to the minimum average variable cost—the firm should close down and supply nothing. Actually, by producing $Q_2$ units of output at a price of $P_2$, the firm will just cover its variable costs, and its losses will be equal to its fixed costs. The firm therefore would be indifferent as between closing down *or* producing $Q_2$ units of output. But at any price below $P_2$, such as $P_1$, the firm will close down and supply zero units of output. $P_4$ is strategic because it is the price at which the firm will just break even by producing $Q_4$ units of output, as indicated by the MR $(P) = $ MC rule. Here total revenue will just cover total costs (including a normal profit). At $P_3$ the firm supplies $Q_3$ units of output and, in so doing, minimizes its losses. At any other price between $P_2$ and $P_4$, the firm will minimize its losses by producing to the point where MR $(P) = $ MC. At any price above $P_4$, the firm will maximize its economic profits by producing to the point where MR $(P) = $ MC. Thus at $P_5$ and $P_6$ the firm will realize the greatest profits by supplying $Q_5$ and $Q_6$ units of output.

The basic point is this: Each of the various MR $(P) = $ MC intersection points shown in Figure 26-6 indicates a possible product price and the corresponding quantity which the profit-seeking firm would supply at that price.

These points, by definition, constitute the supply curve of the competitive firm. Because nothing would be produced at any price below the minimum average variable cost, we can conclude that *the portion of the firm's marginal-cost curve which lies above its average-variable-cost curve is its short-run supply curve.* The heavy segment of the marginal-cost curve is the short-run supply curve in Figure 26-6. This is the link between production costs and supply in the short run.

△   **Recapitulation**

Let us now pause to summarize the main points we have made concerning short-run competitive pricing. Table 26-7 provides a convenient check sheet on the total-revenue–total-cost and MR $= $ MC approaches to determining the competitive firm's profit-maximizing output. This table warrants careful study by the reader. In the MR $= $ MC approach it is noteworthy that in deciding whether or not to produce, it is the comparison of price with minimum average *variable* cost which is all-important. Then, in determining the profit-maximizing or loss-minimizing amount to produce, it is the comparison—or better yet, the equality—of MR $(P)$ and MC which is crucial. Finally, in determining the actual profit or loss

**TABLE 26-7**
Summary of Competitive Output Determination in the Short Run

|  | Total revenue–total cost approach | Marginal revenue–marginal cost approach |
|---|---|---|
| Should the firm produce? | Yes, if TR exceeds TC or if TC exceeds TR by some amount less than total fixed costs. | Yes, if price is equal to, or greater than, minimum average variable cost. |
| What quantity should be produced to maximize profits? | Produce where the excess of TR over TC is a maximum or where the excess of TC over TR is a minimum (and less than total fixed costs). | Produce where MR or price equals MC. |
| Will production result in an economic profit? | Yes, if TR exceeds TC. No, if TC exceeds TR. | Yes, if price exceeds average total cost. No, if average total cost exceeds price. |

associated with the MR $(P) = $ MC output, price and average *total* cost must be contrasted. A final basic conclusion implied in Table 26-7 is that the segment of the short-run marginal-cost curve which lies above the average-variable-cost curve is the competitive firm's short-run supply curve. This conclusion stems from the application of the MR $(P) = $ MC rule and the necessary modification suggested by the close-down case.

△ **Firm and Industry:**
   **Equilibrium Price**

Now one final wrap-up step remains. Having developed the competitive firm's short-run supply curve through the application of the MR $(P) = $ MC rule, we must determine which of the various price possibilities will actually be the equilibrium price. Recalling Chapter 4, we know that in a purely competitive market, equilibrium price is determined by *total,* or market, supply and total demand. To derive total supply, we know that the sales schedules or curves of the individual competitive sellers must be summed. Thus in Table 26-8, columns 1 and 3 repeat the individual competitive firm's supply schedule just derived in Table 26-6. Let us now conveniently assume that there are a total of 1000 competi-

tive firms in this industry, each having the same total and unit costs as the single firm we have been discussing. This allows us to calculate the total- or market-supply schedule (columns 2 and 3) by multiplying the quantity-supplied figures of the single firm (column 1) by 1000.

Now, in order to determine equilibrium price and output, this total-supply data must be compared with total-demand data. For purposes of illustration, let us assume total-demand data are as shown in columns 3 and 4 of Table 26-8. Comparing the total quantity supplied and total quantity demanded at the seven possible prices, we readily determine that the equilibrium price is $111 and that equilibrium quantity is 8000 units for the industry and 8 units for each of the 1000 identical firms.

Will these conditions of market supply and demand make this a prosperous or an unprosperous industry? Multiplying product price ($111) by output (8), we find the total revenue of each firm to be $888. Total cost is $750, found by multiplying average total cost of $93.75 by 8, or simply by looking at column 5 of Table 26-2. The $138 difference is the economic profit of each firm. Another way of calculating economic profits is to determine *per unit* profit by subtracting average total cost ($93.75) from product price ($111) and multiplying the difference (per unit profits of $17.25) by the firm's equilibrium level of output (8). For the industry, total economic profit is obviously $138,000. This, then, is a prosperous industry.

Figure 26-7a and b shows this analysis graphically. The individual supply curves of each of the 1000 identical firms—one of which is shown as ss in Figure 26-7a—are summed horizontally to get the total-supply curve SS of Figure 26-7b. Given total demand DD, equilibrium price is found to be $111, and equilibrium quantity for the industry is 8000 units. This equilibrium price is given and unalterable to the individual firm; that is, the typical firm's demand curve is perfectly elastic at the equilibrium price, as indicated by dd. Because

**TABLE 26-8**
**Firm and Market Supply and Market Demand**
*(hypothetical data)*

| (1)<br>Quantity supplied, single firm | (2)<br>Total quantity supplied, 1000 firms | (3)<br>Product price | (4)<br>Total quantity demanded |
|---|---|---|---|
| 10 | 10,000 | $151 | 4,000 |
| 9 | 9,000 | 131 | 6,000 |
| 8 | **8,000** | 111 | **8,000** |
| 7 | 7,000 | 91 | 9,000 |
| 6 | 6,000 | 81 | 11,000 |
| 0 | 0 | 71 | 13,000 |
| 0 | 0 | 61 | 16,000 |

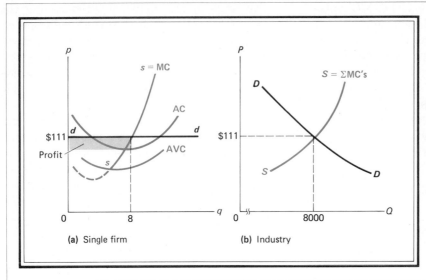

FIGURE 26-7  SHORT-RUN
COMPETITIVE EQUILIBRIUM
FOR A REPRESENTATIVE
FIRM (a)  AND THE
INDUSTRY (b)

The horizontal sum of the
1000 firms' supply curves
(*ss*) determines the industry
supply curve (*SS*). Given
industry demand (*DD*), the
short-run equilibrium price
and output for the industry
are $111 and 8000 units.
Taking the equilibrium
price as given datum, the
representative firm es-
tablishes its profit-maximizing output at 8 units and,
in this case, realizes the
economic profit shown
by the orange area.

price is given and constant to the individual firm, the marginal-revenue curve coincides with the demand curve. Price obviously exceeds average total cost at the firm's equilibrium MR ($P$) = MC output, resulting in a situation of economic profits similar to that already portrayed in Figure 26-3.

Assuming that no changes in costs or market demand occur, these diagrams reveal a genuine short-run equilibrium situation. There are no shortages or surpluses in the market to cause price or total quantity to change. Nor can any of the firms making up the industry improve their profits by altering their output. Note, too, that higher unit and marginal costs, on the one hand, or a weaker market demand situation, on the other, could have posed a loss situation similar to Figure 26-4. The student is urged to sketch, in Figure 26-7a and b, how higher costs and a less favorable demand could cause a short-run equilibrium situation entailing losses.

Figure 26-7a and b underscores a point made earlier: Product price is a given datum to the *individual* competitive firm, but at the same time, the supply plans of all competitive producers *as a group* are a basic determinant of product price. If we recall the fallacy of composition, we find there is no inconsistency here. Though each firm, supplying a negligible fraction of total supply, cannot affect price, the sum of the supply curves of all the many firms in the industry constitutes the industry supply curve, and this curve does have an important bearing upon price. In short, under competition, equilibrium price is a given datum to the individual firm and simultaneously is the result of the production (supply) decisions of all firms taken as a group.

☐  PROFIT MAXIMIZATION IN
THE LONG RUN
The long run permits firms to make certain adjustments which time does not allow in the short run. In the short run there are a given number of firms in an industry, each of which has a fixed, unalterable plant. True, firms may close down in the sense that they produce zero units of output in the short run; but they do not have sufficient time to liquidate their assets and go out of business. By contrast, in the

long run firms already in an industry have sufficient time either to expand or to contract their plant capacities, and, more important, the number of firms in the industry may either increase or decrease as new firms enter or old firms leave. We want to discover how these long-run adjustments modify our conclusions concerning short-run output and price determination.

It will facilitate our analysis greatly to make certain simplifying assumptions, none of which will impair the general validity of our conclusions.

1   We shall suppose that the only long-run adjustment is the entry and exodus of firms. Furthermore, for simplicity's sake we shall ignore the short-run adjustments already analyzed, in order to grasp more clearly the nature of long-run competitive adjustments.

2   It will also be assumed that all firms in the industry have identical cost curves. This allows us to talk in terms of an "average," or "representative," firm with the knowledge that all other firms in the industry are similarly affected by any long-run adjustments which occur.

3   We assume for the moment that the industry under discussion is a constant-cost

industry. This means simply that the entry and exodus of firms will *not* affect resource prices or, therefore, the locations of the unit-cost schedules of the individual firms.

Now our goal is to describe long-run competitive adjustments both verbally and through simple graphic analysis. It will be well to state in advance the basic conclusion we seek to explain: *After all long-run adjustments are completed, that is, when long-run equilibrium is achieved, product price will be exactly equal to, and production will occur at, each firm's point of minimum average total cost.* This conclusion follows from two basic facts: (1) Firms seek profits and shun losses, and (2) under competition, firms are free to enter and leave industries. If price initially exceeds average total costs, the resulting economic profits will attract new firms to the industry. But this expansion of the industry will increase product supply until price is brought back down into equality with average total cost. Conversely, if price is initially less than average total cost, the resulting losses will cause firms to leave the industry. As they leave, total product supply will decline, bringing price back up into equality with average total cost.

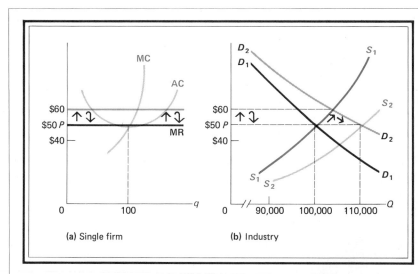

FIGURE 26-8 TEMPORARY PROFITS AND THE REESTABLISHMENT OF LONG-RUN EQUILIBRIUM IN A REPRESENTATIVE FIRM (a) AND THE INDUSTRY (b)

A favorable shift in demand $(D_1 D_1$ to $D_2 D_2)$ will upset the original equilibrium and cause economic profits. But profits will cause new firms to enter the industry, increasing supply $(S_1 S_1$ to $S_2 S_2)$ and lowering product price until economic profits are once again zero.

Our conclusion can best be demonstrated and its significance evaluated by assuming that the average or representative firm in a purely competitive industry is initially in long-run equilibrium. This is shown in Figure 26-8a, where price and minimum average total cost are equal at, say, $50. Economic profits here are zero; hence, the industry is in equilibrium or "at rest," because there is no tendency for firms to enter or leave the industry. As we know, the going market price is determined by total, or industry, demand and supply, as shown by $D_1D_1$ and $S_1S_1$ in Figure 26-8b. (The market supply schedule, incidentally, is a *short-run* schedule; the industry's long-run supply schedule will be developed in our discussion.) By examining the quantity axes of the two graphs, we note that if all firms are identical, there must be 1000 firms in the industry, each producing 100 units, to achieve the industry's equilibrium output of 100,000 units.

△   **Entry of Firms**
**Eliminates Profits**

Now our model is set up. Let us upset the serenity of this long-run equilibrium situation and trace the subsequent adjustments. Suppose that a change in consumer tastes increases product demand from $D_1D_1$ to $D_2D_2$. This favorable shift in demand obviously makes production profitable; the new price of $60 exceeds average total cost. *These economic profits will lure new firms into the industry.* Some of the entrants will be newly created firms; others will shift from less prosperous industries. But as the firms enter, the market supply of the product will increase, causing product price to gravitate downward from $60 toward the original $50 level. Assuming, as we are, that the entry of new firms has no effect upon costs, economic profits will persist, and entry will therefore continue until short-run market supply has increased to $S_2S_2$. At this point, price is again equal to minimum average total cost at $50. The economic profits caused by the boost in demand have been competed

away to zero, and as a result, the previous incentive for more firms to enter the industry has disappeared. Long-run equilibrium has been restored at this point.

Figure 26-8 tells us that upon the reestablishment of long-run equilibrium, industry output is 110,000 units and that each firm in the now expanded industry is producing 100 units. We can therefore conclude that the industry is now composed of 1100 firms; that is, 100 new firms have entered the industry.

△   **Exodus of Firms**
**Eliminates Losses**

To strengthen our understanding of long-run competitive equilibrium, let us throw our analysis into reverse. In Figure 26-9a and b, the heavy lines show once again the initial long-run equilibrium situation used as a point of departure in our previous analysis of how the entry of firms eliminates profits.

Now let us suppose that consumer demand falls from $D_1D_1$ to $D_3D_3$. This forces price down to $40, making production unprofitable. *In time these losses will force firms to leave the industry.* As capital equipment wears out and contractual obligations expire, some firms will simply toss in the sponge. As this exodus of firms proceeds, however, industry supply will decrease, moving from $S_1S_1$ toward $S_3S_3$. And as this occurs, price will begin to rise from $40 back toward $50. Assuming costs are unchanged by the exodus of firms, losses will force firms to leave the industry until supply has declined to $S_3S_3$, at which point price is again exactly $50, barely consistent with minimum average total cost. The exodus of firms continues until losses are eliminated and long-run equilibrium is again restored.

The reader will note from Figure 26-9a and b that total quantity supplied is now 90,000 units and each firm is producing 100 units. This obviously means that the industry is now populated by only 900 firms rather than the original 1000. Losses have forced 100 firms out of business.

Our prestated conclusion has now been

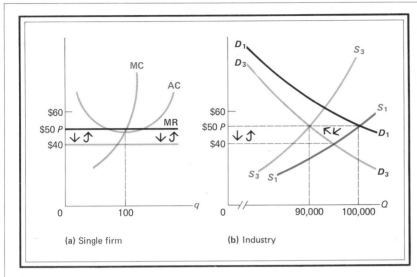

FIGURE 26-9 TEMPORARY LOSSES AND THE REESTABLISHMENT OF LONG-RUN EQUILIBRIUM IN A REPRESENTATIVE FIRM (a) AND THE INDUSTRY (b)

An unfavorable shift in demand ($D_1D_1$ to $D_3D_3$) will upset the original equilibrium and cause losses. But losses will cause firms to leave the industry, decreasing supply ($S_1S_1$ to $S_3S_3$) and increasing product price until all losses have disappeared.

(a) Single firm

(b) Industry

verified. Competition, as reflected in the entry and exodus of firms, forces price into equality with the minimum long-run average total cost of production, and each firm produces at the point of minimum long-run average total cost. Observe, too, that these expanding- and declining-industry cases comprise an explanation of the functioning of consumer sovereignty, a concept which we encountered at a less sophisticated level in Chapter 5.

### △ Long-Run Supply for a Constant-Cost Industry

We now ask: What is the nature of the long-run supply curve which evolves from this analysis of the expansion or contraction of a competitive industry? Even though our discussion is concerned with the long run, we have noted that the market supply curves of Figures 26-8b and 26-9b are short-run industry supply curves. However, the analysis itself permits us to sketch the nature of the long-run supply curve for this competitive industry. The crucial factor in determining the shape of the industry's long-run supply curve is the effect, if any, which changes in the number of firms in the industry will have upon the costs of the individual firms in the industry.

In the foregoing analysis of long-run competitive equilibrium we assumed the industry under discussion was a *constant-cost industry*. By definition, this means that the expansion of the industry through the entry of new firms will have no effect upon resource prices or, therefore, upon production costs. Graphically, the entry of new firms does *not* change the position of the long-run average-cost curves of the individual firms in the industry. When will this be the case? For the most part, when the industry's demand for resources is small in relation to the total demand for those resources. And this is most likely to be the situation when the industry is employing unspecialized resources which are being demanded by many other industries. In short, when the particular industry's demand for resources is a negligible component of the total demand, the industry can expand without significantly affecting resource prices and costs.

What will be the nature of the long-run supply curve for a constant-cost industry? The answer is contained in our previous discussion of the long-run adjustments toward equilibrium which profits or losses will initiate. Here we assumed that entrance or departure of firms would not affect costs. The result was that the entry or exodus of firms would alter industry output but always bring product price back to the original $50 level, where it is just consistent with the unchanging minimum average total cost of production. Specifically, we discovered that the industry would supply 90,000, 100,000, or 110,000 units of output, all at a price of $50 per unit. In technical terms, *the long-run supply curve of a constant-cost industry is perfectly elastic.*

This is demonstrated graphically in Figure 26-10, where the illustrative data from Figures 26-8 and 26-9 are retained. Suppose that industry demand is originally $D_1D_1$, industry output is $Q_1$ (100,000), and product price is $Q_1P_1$ ($50). This situation, referring to Figure 26-8, is one of long-run equilibrium. Now assume that demand increases to $D_2D_2$, upsetting this equilibrium. The resulting economic profits will attract new firms. Because this is a constant-cost industry, entry will continue and industry output will expand until price is

driven back down to the unchanged minimum average-total-cost level. This will be at price $Q_2P_2$ ($50) and output $Q_2$ (110,000).

This analysis, now using Figure 26-9 as a reference point, is reversible. A decline in short-run industry demand from $D_1D_1$ to $D_3D_3$ will cause an exodus of firms and ultimately a restoration of equilibrium at price $Q_3P_3$ ($50) and output $Q_3$ (90,000). A line which connects all points, such as these three, shows the various price–quantity supplied combinations which would be most profitable for the industry when it has had sufficient time to make *all* desired adjustments to assumed changes in industry demand. By definition, this line is the industry's long-run supply curve. In the case of a constant-cost industry we note that this line, $S_1S_1$ in Figure 26-10, is perfectly elastic.

### △ Long-Run Supply for an Increasing-Cost Industry

But constant-cost industries are a special case. In most instances the entry of new firms will affect resource prices and therefore unit costs for the individual firms in the industry. When an industry is using a significant portion of some resource whose total supply is not readily increased, the entry of new firms will increase resource demand in relation to supply and boost resource prices. This is particularly so in industries which are using highly specialized resources whose initial supply is not readily augmented. The result of higher resource prices will be higher long-run average costs for firms in the industry. These higher costs, it should be noted, take the form of an upward shift in the long-run average-cost curve for the representative firm.

The net result is that when an increase in product demand causes economic profits and attracts new firms to the industry, a two-way squeeze on profits will occur to eliminate those profits. On the one hand, the entry of new firms will increase market supply and lower product price, and, on the other, the entire average-total-cost curve of the representative firm will shift upward. This means that the

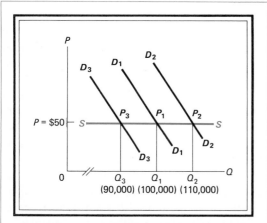

**FIGURE 26-10  THE LONG-RUN SUPPLY CURVE FOR A CONSTANT-COST INDUSTRY IS PERFECTLY ELASTIC**

Because the entry or exodus of firms does not affect resource prices or, therefore, unit costs, an increase in demand ($D_1D_1$ to $D_2D_2$) will cause an expansion in industry output ($Q_1$ to $Q_2$) but no alteration in price ($Q_1P_1 = Q_2P_2$). Similarly, a decrease in demand ($D_1D_1$ to $D_3D_3$) will cause a contraction of output ($Q_1$ to $Q_3$) but no change in price ($Q_1P_1 = Q_3P_3$). This means that the long-run industry supply curve ($SS$) will be perfectly elastic.

equilibrium price will now be higher than it was originally. The industry will only produce a larger output at a higher price. Why? Because expansion of the industry has increased average total costs, and in the long run product price must cover these costs. A greater industry output will be forthcoming at a higher price, or, more technically, the industry supply curve for an increasing-cost industry will be upsloping. Instead of getting either 90,000, 100,000, or 110,000 units at the same price of $50, in an increasing-cost industry 90,000 units might be forthcoming at $45; 100,000 at $50; and 110,000 at $55. The higher price is required to induce more production because costs per unit of output increase as the industry expands.

This can be seen graphically in Figure 26-11. Original market demand, industry output, and price are $D_1 D_1$, $Q_1$ (100,000) and $Q_1 P_1$ ($50) respectively. An increase in demand to $D_2 D_2$ will upset this equilibrium and give rise to economic profits. As new firms enter, (1) industry supply will increase, tending to drive price down, and (2) resource prices will rise, causing the average total costs of production to rise. Because of these average-total-cost increases, the new long-run equilibrium price will be established at some level above the original price, such as $Q_2 P_2$ ($55). Conversely, a decline in demand from $D_1 D_1$ to $D_3 D_3$ will make production unprofitable and cause an exodus of firms from the industry. The resulting decline in the demand for resources relative to their supply will lower resource prices and cause average total costs of production to decline. Hence, the new equilibrium price will be established at some level below the original price, such as $Q_3 P_3$ ($45).

Which situation—constant- or increasing-cost—is characteristic of American industry? Economists generally agree that increasing-cost industries are most common. Agriculture and extractive industries such as mining and lumbering are increasing-cost industries because each utilizes a very large portion of some basic resource—farmland, mineral

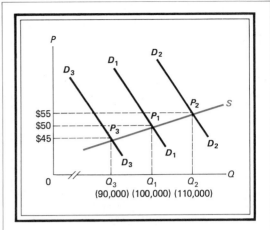

FIGURE 26-11  THE LONG-RUN SUPPLY CURVE FOR AN INCREASING-COST INDUSTRY IS UPSLOPING

In an increasing-cost industry the entry of new firms in response to increases in demand ($D_3 D_3$ to $D_1 D_1$ to $D_2 D_2$) will bid up resource prices and thereby increase unit costs. As a result, an increased industry output ($Q_3$ to $Q_1$ to $Q_2$) will be forthcoming only at higher prices ($Q_2 P_2 > Q_1 P_1 > Q_3 P_3$). The long-run industry supply curve (SS) is therefore upsloping.

deposits, and timberland. Expansion will significantly affect the demand for these resources and result in higher costs. It is less easy to generalize with respect to manufacturing industries. In their early stages of development, such industries may well be relatively constant-cost industries.[2] But as continued expansion increases the importance of these industries in resource markets, they may in time become increasing-cost industries.

---

[2]Under certain, very special circumstances, an industry may be for a time a *decreasing-cost industry*. For example, as more mines are established in a given locality, each firm's costs in pumping out water seepage may decline. With more mines pumping, the seepage into each is less, and pumping costs are therefore reduced. Furthermore, with only a few mines in an area, industry output might be so small that only relatively primitive and therefore costly transportation facilities are available. But as the number of firms and industry output expand, a railroad might build a spur into the area and thereby significantly reduce transportation costs. Under such special conditions, a firm's long-run supply curve may shift *downward*. We will have more to say about this kind of cost economy in Chapter 36.

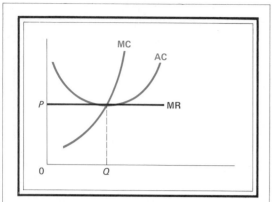

**FIGURE 26-12  FOR THE COMPETITIVE FIRM IN LONG-RUN EQUILIBRIUM, $P$ = AC = MC**

The equality of price and minimum average cost indicates that the firm is using the most efficient known technology and is charging the lowest price $P$ and producing the greatest output $Q$ consistent with its costs. The equality of price and marginal cost indicates that resources are being allocated in accordance with consumer preferences.

## ☐  AN EVALUATION OF COMPETITIVE PRICING

Whether a purely competitive industry is one of constant or increasing costs, the final long-run equilibrium position for each firm will have the same basic characteristics. As shown in Figure 26-12, price (and marginal revenue) will settle at the level where they are equal to minimum average cost. However, we discovered in Chapter 25 that the marginal-cost curve intersects, and is therefore equal to, average cost at the point of minimum average cost. In the long-run equilibrium position, "everything is equal." MR ($P$) = AC = MC. This triple equality is of more than geometric interest. It tells us that, although a competitive firm may realize economic profits or losses in the short run, it will barely break even by producing in accordance with the MR ($P$) = MC rule in the long run. Furthermore, this triple equality suggests certain conclusions concerning the efficiency of a purely competitive economy which are of great social significance. It is to an evaluation of competitive pricing from society's point of view that we now turn.

You will recall that the overview of the price system in Chapter 5 yielded some general conclusions with respect to the efficiency of any economy characterized by a competitive price system. Equipped now with a better understanding of costs and price-output determination under competition, we are in a position to sharpen our understanding of the efficiency of a competitive price economy. Specifically, we want to see how our analysis of long-run competitive equilibrium implies certain highly desirable features of a competitive price system.

### △  Efficient Allocation of Resources

Most economists argue that, subject to certain limitations and exceptions, a purely competitive economy will lead to the most efficient, or "ideal," allocation of resources. That is, *a competitive price economy will tend to allocate the fixed supplies of resources available to society in such a way as to maximize the satisfactions of consumers.* Actually, there are two related points which underlie this conclusion. First, it is argued that under pure competition firms will be forced to produce those goods which consumers want the most. Second, competition forces firms to use the most efficient, or least-cost, methods in the production of these goods. To facilitate our discussion, we shall examine the second point first.

**1  $P$ = AC**  We have just noted that in the long run, competition forces firms to produce at the point of minimum average total cost of production and to charge that price which is just consistent with these costs. This is obviously a most desirable situation from the consumer's point of view. It means that firms must use the best available (least-cost) technology or they will not survive. And, too, it means that consumers benefit from the highest volume of production and the lowest product price which are possible under the cost conditions which currently prevail. Furthermore, the costs involved in each instance are only those costs essential in producing a product.

Because products are standardized in competitive industries, there will be no selling or promotional costs which must be added to production costs in determining product price.

**2  $P = MC$**  But the competitive production of *any* collection of goods does not necessarily make for an efficient allocation of resources. Production must not only be technologically efficient, but it must also entail the "right goods," that is, the goods that consumers want the most. The competitive price system will see to it that resources are allocated so as to result in a total output whose composition best fits the preferences of consumers.

Let us see precisely how this comes about. We must first grasp the social meaning of competitive product and resource prices. The money price of any product—product X—is society's measure, or index, of the relative worth of that product at the margin. Similarly, recalling the notion of opportunity costs, we see that the marginal cost of producing X measures the value, or relative worth, of the other goods that the resources used in the production of an extra unit of X could otherwise have produced. In short, product price measures the benefit, or satisfaction, which society gets from additional units of X, and the marginal cost of an additional unit of X measures the sacrifice, or cost to society, of other goods in using resources to produce more of X. Now, under competition, the production of each product will occur up to that precise point at which price is equal to marginal cost (Figure 26-12). The profit-seeking competitor will realize the maximum possible profit only by equating price and marginal cost. To produce short of the MR $(P) = MC$ point will mean less than maximum profits to the individual firm and an *under*allocation of resources to this product from society's standpoint. The fact that price exceeds marginal cost indicates that society values additional units of X more highly than the alternative products which the appropriate resources could otherwise produce. For similar reasons, the production of X

should not go beyond the output at which price equals marginal cost. To do so would entail less than maximum profits for producers and an *over*allocation of resources to X from the standpoint of society. To produce X at some point at which marginal cost exceeds price means that resources are being used in the production of X at the sacrifice of alternative goods which society values more highly than the added units of X. In brief, *under pure competition, profit-motivated producers will produce each commodity up to that precise point at which price and marginal cost are equated. This means that resources are efficiently allocated under competition.* Each good is produced to the point at which the value of the last unit is equal to the value of the alternative goods sacrificed by its production. To alter the production of X would necessarily reduce consumer satisfactions. To produce X beyond the $P = MC$ point would result in the sacrifice of alternative goods whose value to society exceeds that of the extra units of X. To produce X short of the $P = MC$ point would involve the sacrifice of units of X which society values more than the alternative goods resources can produce.

A further attribute of the competitive price system is its ability to negotiate appropriate adjustments in resource use as changes occur in basic data of the economy. In a competitive economy, any changes in consumer tastes, resource supplies, or technology will automatically set in motion appropriate realignments of resources. As we have already explained, an increase in consumer demand for product X will increase its price. Disequilibrium will occur in that, at its present output, the price of X will now exceed its marginal cost. This will create economic profits in industry X and stimulate its expansion. Its profitability will permit the industry to bid resources away from less pressing uses. Expansion in this industry will end only when the price of X is again equal to its marginal cost, that is, when the value of the last unit produced is once again equal to the value of the alternative goods society forgoes in getting that last unit of X produced. Similarly, changes in the supplies of particular resources or in the techniques pertinent to various industries will upset existing price–marginal-cost equalities by either raising or lowering marginal cost. These inequalities will cause business executives, in either pursuing profits or shunning losses, to reallocate resources until price once again equals marginal cost in each line of production. In so doing, they correct any inefficiencies in the allocation of resources which changing economic data may temporarily impose upon the economy.

A final appealing feature of a purely competitive economy is that the highly efficient allocation of resources which it fosters comes about because businesses and resource suppliers freely seek to further their own self-interests. That is, the "invisible hand" (Chapter 5) is at work in a competitive market system. In a competitive economy, businesses employ resources until the extra, or marginal, costs of production equal the price of the product. This not only maximizes the profits of the individual producers but simultaneously results in a pattern of resource allocation which maximizes the satisfactions of consumers. The competitive price system organizes the private interests of producers along lines which are fully in accord with the interests of society as a whole.

△   **Shortcomings of the**
**Competitive Price System**
Despite these several virtues, economists acknowledge certain limitations of the price system which may impair its ability to allocate resources efficiently. Some of these criticisms have been previously noted in Chapters 5 and 6.

**The Income Distribution Problem** The contention that the competitive price system will allocate resources efficiently—that is, will produce the collection of goods and services which maximizes the satisfaction of consumer

wants—is predicated upon some given distribution of money income. In other words, money income is distributed among households in some specific way, and this distribution results in a certain structure of demand. The price system then brings about an efficient allocation of resources or, stated differently, an output of goods and services whose composition maximizes the fulfillment of these particular consumer demands. But what if the distribution of money income is altered so that the structure of demand changes? Would the competitive price system negotiate a new allocation of resources? The answer, of course, is "Yes"; the price system would reallocate resources and therefore change the composition of output to maximize the fulfillment of this new pattern of consumer wants. The problem, then, is, Which of these two "efficient" allocations of resources is the "most efficient"? Which allocation of resources yields the greatest level of satisfaction to society? There is no *scientific* answer to this question because we do not know how to measure and compare the satisfaction derived by various individuals from goods and services. If all people were precisely alike in their capacities to obtain satisfaction from income, economists could recommend that income be distributed equally and that the allocation of resources which would be appropriate to *that* distribution would be the "best" or "most efficient" of all. But, in fact, people are different by virtue of their education, experiences, and environment, not to mention their inherited mental and physical characteristics. Such differences can be used to argue for an unequal distribution of income.

The basic point for present purposes is that the distribution of income associated with the workings of the competitive price system is quite unequal and therefore may lead to the production of trifles for the rich while denying the basic needs of the poor. Hence, many economists believe that the distribution of income which pure competition provides should be modified by public action. They maintain that allocative efficiency is hardly a virtue if it comes in response to an income distribution which offends prevailing standards of equity. The question of income inequality will be accorded detailed treatment in Chapter 37.

**Market Failure: Spillovers and Social Goods**   The competitive price system does not accurately measure costs and benefits where spillover costs and benefits are significant. Under competition each producer will assume only those costs which it *must* pay. This correctly implies that in some lines of production there are significant costs which producers can and do avoid. Recall from Chapter 6 that these avoided costs accrue to society and are aptly called *spillover* or *external costs*. Firms may avoid the cost of properly disposing of waste materials or of buying smoke- and dust-abatement equipment. The result is significant spillover costs in the form of polluted rivers, smog, and a generally debased community. Similarly, unbridled competition may cause profit-seeking firms to brutally exploit farmland, timberland, and mineral deposits through the use of the cheapest production methods. The cost to society is the permanent loss of irreproducible natural resources. On the other hand, the consumption of certain goods and services, such as chest x-rays and polio shots, yields widespread satisfactions, or benefits, to society as a whole. These satisfactions are called *external* or *spillover benefits*.

Now the significance of spillover costs and benefits for present purposes is this: The profit-seeking activities of producers will bring about an allocation of resources which is efficient from society's point of view only if marginal cost embodies *all* the costs which production entails and product price accurately reflects *all* the benefits which society gets from a good's production (see Figure 6-1). Only in this case will competitive production at the MR $(P) =$ MC point balance the *total* sacrifices and satisfactions of society and result in an efficient allocation of resources. To the extent that price and marginal cost are not accu-

rate indexes of sacrifices and satisfactions—in other words, to the extent that spillover costs and benefits exist—production at the MR $(P) =$ MC point will *not* signify an efficient allocation of resources.

Remember, too, the point of the lighthouse example in Chapter 6: The market system does not provide for social or public goods, that is, for goods to which the exclusion principle does not apply. Despite its other virtues, the competitive price system ignores an important class of goods and services—national defense, flood-control programs, and so forth—which can and do yield satisfaction to consumers but which cannot be priced and sold through the market system.

**Productive Techniques**   The competitive price system may not always entail the use of the most efficient productive techniques or the development of improved techniques. There are both a static or "right now" aspect and a dynamic or "over time" aspect of this general criticism. The static aspect argues that in certain lines of production, existing technology may be such that a firm must be a large-scale producer in order to realize the lowest unit costs of production. Given consumer demand, this suggests that a relatively small number of efficient, large-scale producers is needed if production is to be carried on efficiently. In other words, existing mass-production economies might be lost if such an industry were populated by the large number of small-scale producers which pure competition requires. This point was discussed in some detail in Chapter 25.

The dynamic aspect of this criticism concerns the willingness and ability of purely competitive firms to undertake technological advance. The progressiveness of pure competition is debated by economists. For present purposes we merely call attention to the belief of some authorities that a purely competitive economy would *not* foster a very rapid rate of technological progress. They argue, first, that the incentive for technological advance may be weak under pure competition because the profit rewards accruing to an innovating firm as the result of a cost-reducing technological improvement will be quickly competed away by rival firms which readily adopt the new technique. Second, the small size of the typical competitive firm and the fact that it tends to "break even" in the long run raise serious questions as to whether such producers could finance substantial programs of organized research. We will return to this controversy in Chapter 29.

**Range of Consumer Choice** The competitive price system may not provide for a sufficient range of consumer choice or for the development of new products. This criticism, like the previous one, has both a static and a dynamic aspect. Pure competition, it is contended, entails product standardization, whereas other market structures—for example, monopolistic competition and, frequently, oligopoly—entail a wide range of types, styles, and quality gradations of any product. This product differentiation widens the consumer's range of free choice and simultaneously allows the buyer's preferences to be more completely fulfilled. Similarly, critics of pure competition point out that, just as pure competition is not likely to be progressive with respect to the development of new productive techniques, neither is this market structure conducive to the improvement of existing products or the creation of completely new ones.

The question of the progressiveness of the various market structures in terms of both productive techniques and product development will be a recurring one in the following three chapters.

## Summary

**1** A purely competitive industry comprises a large number of independent firms producing a standardized product. Pure competition assumes that firms and resources are mobile among different industries. No single firm can influence market price in a competitive industry; the firm's demand curve is perfectly elastic and price therefore equals marginal revenue.

**2** Short-run profit maximization by a competitive firm can be analyzed by a comparison of total revenue and total cost or through marginal analysis. A firm will maximize profits by producing that output at which total revenue exceeds total cost by the greatest amount. Losses will be minimized by producing where the excess of total cost over total revenue is at a minimum and less than total fixed costs.

**3** Provided price exceeds minimum average variable cost, a competitive firm will maximize profits or minimize losses by producing that output at which price or marginal revenue is equal to marginal cost. If price is less than average variable cost, the firm will minimize its losses by closing down. If price is greater than average variable cost but less than average total cost, the firm will minimize its losses by producing the $P = MC$ output. If price exceeds average total cost, the $P = MC$ output will provide maximum economic profits for the firm.

**4** Applying the MR $(P) = MC$ rule at various possible market prices leads to the conclusion that the segment of the firm's short-run marginal-cost curve which lies above average variable cost is its short-run supply curve.

**5** In the long run, competitive price will tend to equal the minimum average cost of production. This is so because economic profits will cause firms to enter a competitive industry until those profits have been competed away. Conversely, losses will force the exodus of firms from the industry until product price once again barely covers unit costs.

6   The long-run supply curve is perfectly elastic for a constant-cost industry, but upsloping for an increasing-cost industry.

7   In a purely competitive economy the profit-seeking activities of producers will result in an allocation of resources which maximizes the satisfactions of consumers. The long-run equality of price and minimum average cost indicates that competitive firms will use the most efficient known technology and charge the lowest price consistent with their production costs. The equality of price and marginal cost indicates that resources will be allocated in accordance with consumer tastes. The competitive price system will reallocate resources in response to a change in consumer tastes, technology, or resource supplies so as to maintain allocative efficiency over time.

8   Economists recognize four possible deterrents to allocative efficiency in a competitive economy. *a.* There is no reason why the competitive price system will result in an optimum distribution of income. *b.* In allocating resources, the price system does not allow for spillover costs and benefits or for the production of social goods. *c.* A purely competitive industry may preclude the use of the best-known productive techniques and foster a slow rate of technological advance. *d.* A competitive system provides neither a wide range of product choice nor an environment conducive to the development of new products.

## Questions and Study Suggestions

1   Key terms and concepts to remember: average, total, and marginal revenue; profit-maximizing case; break-even point; loss-minimizing case; close-down case; $MR(P) = MC$ rule; short-run supply curve; long-run supply curve; constant-cost industry; increasing-cost industry.

2   Strictly speaking, pure competition never has existed and probably never will. Then why study it?

3   Use the following demand schedule to determine total and marginal revenues for each possible level of sales.

| Product price | Quantity demanded | Total revenue | Marginal revenue |
|---|---|---|---|
| $2 | 0 | $_____ | $_____ |
| 2 | 1 | _____ | _____ |
| 2 | 2 | _____ | _____ |
| 2 | 3 | _____ | _____ |
| 2 | 4 | _____ | _____ |
| 2 | 5 | _____ | _____ |

   *a.*   What can you conclude about the structure of the industry in which this firm is operating? Explain.

   *b.*   Graph the demand, total-revenue, and marginal-revenue curves for this firm.

   *c.*   Why do the demand and marginal-revenue curves coincide?

   *d.*   "Marginal revenue is the rate of change in total revenue." Do you agree? Explain verbally and graphically, using the above data.

4   Why is the equality of marginal revenue and marginal cost essential for profit maximization in all market structures? Explain why price can be substituted for marginal revenue in the $MR = MC$ rule when an industry is purely competitive.

5   Explain: "A competitive producer must look to average variable cost in determining whether or not to produce in the short run, to marginal cost in deciding upon the best volume

of production, and to average total cost to calculate profits or losses." Why might a firm produce at a loss in the short run rather than close down?

6 Assume the following unit-cost data are for a purely competitive producer:

| Total product | Average fixed cost | Average variable cost | Average total cost | Marginal cost |
|---|---|---|---|---|
| 0 | | | | |
| 1 | $60.00 | $45.00 | $105.00 | $45 |
| 2 | 30.00 | 42.50 | 72.50 | 40 |
| 3 | 20.00 | 40.00 | 60.00 | 35 |
| 4 | 15.00 | 37.50 | 52.50 | 30 |
| 5 | 12.00 | 37.00 | 49.00 | 35 |
| 6 | 10.00 | 37.50 | 47.50 | 40 |
| 7 | 8.57 | 38.57 | 47.14 | 45 |
| 8 | 7.50 | 40.63 | 48.13 | 55 |
| 9 | 6.67 | 43.33 | 50.00 | 65 |
| 10 | 6.00 | 46.50 | 52.50 | 75 |

**a.**   At a product price of $32, will this firm produce in the short run? Why, or why not? If it does produce, what will be the profit-maximizing or loss-minimizing output? Explain. Specify the amount of economic profit or loss per unit of output.

**b.**   Answer the questions of 6a on the assumption that product price is $41.

**c.**   Answer the questions of 6a on the assumption that product price is $56.

**d.**   Complete the short-run supply schedule for the firm, and indicate the profit or loss incurred at each output (columns 1 to 3).

| (1) Price | (2) Quantity supplied, single firm | (3) Profit (+) or loss (−) | (4) Quantity supplied, 1500 firms |
|---|---|---|---|
| $26 | _____ | $ _____ | _____ |
| 32 | _____ | _____ | _____ |
| 38 | _____ | _____ | _____ |
| 41 | _____ | _____ | _____ |
| 46 | _____ | _____ | _____ |
| 56 | _____ | _____ | _____ |
| 66 | _____ | _____ | _____ |

**e.**   Explain: "That segment of a competitive firm's marginal-cost curve which lies above its average-variable-cost curve constitutes the short-run supply curve for the firm." Illustrate graphically.

**f.**   Now assume there are 1500 identical firms in this competitive industry; that is, there are 1500 firms, each of which has the same cost data as shown here. Calculate the industry supply schedule (column 4).

**g.**   Suppose the market demand data for the product are as follows:

| Price | Total quantity demanded |
|-------|-------------------------|
| $26   | 17,000 |
| 32    | 15,000 |
| 38    | 13,500 |
| 41    | 12,000 |
| 46    | 10,500 |
| 56    | 9,500 |
| 66    | 8,000 |

What will equilibrium price be? What will equilibrium output be for the industry? For each firm? What will profit or loss be per unit? Per firm?

   **7**   Using diagrams for both the industry and a representative firm, illustrate competitive long-run equilibrium. Employing these diagrams, show how **a.** an increase, and **b.** a decrease, in market demand will upset this long-run equilibrium. Trace graphically and describe verbally the adjustment processes by which long-run equilibrium is restored. Assume the industry is one of constant costs.

   **8**   Distinguish carefully between a constant-cost and an increasing-cost industry. Answer question 7 on the assumption that the industry is one of increasing costs. Compare the long-run supply curves of a constant-cost and an increasing-cost industry.

   **9**   Suppose a decrease in demand occurs in a competitive increasing-cost industry. Contrast the product price and industry output which exist after all long-run adjustments are completed with those which originally prevailed.

   **10**   In long-run equilibrium, $P = AC = MC$. Of what significance for the allocation of resources is the equality of $P$ and $AC$? The equality of $P$ and MC?

   **11**   Explain why some economists believe that an unequal distribution of income might impair the efficiency with which a competitive price system allocates resources. What other criticisms can be made of a purely competitive economy?

## Selected References

Leftwich, Richard H.: *The Price System and Resource Allocation,* 6th ed. (Hinsdale, Ill.: The Dryden Press, Inc., 1976), chap. 10.

Mansfield, Edwin: *Microeconomics: Theory and Applications,* 3d ed. (New York: W. W. Norton & Company, Inc., 1979), chap. 8.

Stigler, George J.: *The Theory of Price,* rev. ed. (New York: The Macmillan Company, 1952), chap. 10.

Stonier, Alfred W., and Douglas C. Hague: *A Textbook of Economic Theory,* 3d ed. (New York: Longmans, Green & Co., Inc., 1964), chaps. 6, 7.

Thompson, Arthur A., Jr.: *Economics of the Firm: Theory and Practice,* 2d ed. (Englewood Cliffs, N.J.: Prentice-Hall, Inc., 1977), chap. 10.

# LAST WORD
## Technology and Competition

Competitive pressures are often rooted in technological progress.

New electronic technology coupled with good, solid marketing should be the secret to successful business performance. But instead, this combination of functions has turned out to be disastrous for several industries.

Two prime examples are pocket calculators and digital watches.

The technology came first. Innovators were able to develop a calculator that you could hold in the palm of your hand, and a watch that flashed the time at the touch of a button.

The watches came out at $200 or more and the calculators at $100 or more. And they started to sell, even at these prices.

So the manufacturers pushed more money into marketing. And competitors saw the potential and rushed into the market place with new products.

But competition and rapid improvement in technology started pushing prices down dramatically. Retailers weren't about to stock up on $99.95 watches when they knew virtually the same watches would hit the market a month later at $79.95.

So the guy who made the $99.95 watch was stuck with it. Or he had to peddle it at a loss to keep up with the lower prices. And that forced several companies out of business and into bankruptcy.

During the holiday season, wristwatches bearing a nationally advertised name and containing the very same technology that sold for $200 a couple of years ago are available at about $16. Calculators are selling for less than $10.

And now, we can see the same thing happening all over again to some new industries: citizens band radios and electronic video games.

A year ago, these items generally were priced at $100 and up. Last week, stores were selling nationally advertised brands of CB radios and video games for as little as $39.95. And by next year, who knows?

One thing is sure, the technology-marketing combination has fractured several companies, but consumers are enjoying every minute of it.

"Watches That Sold for $200 Now Cost $16," *Lincoln Evening Journal,* Dec. 28, 1976. Reprinted by permission of the Chicago Daily News.

# Price and Output Determination: Pure Monopoly

Let us now jump to the opposite end of the industry spectrum and examine the characteristics, the bases, the price-output behavior, and the social desirability of pure monopoly.

## ☐ PURE MONOPOLY: CONCEPT AND OCCURRENCE

Pure or absolute monopoly exists when a single firm is the sole producer of a product for which there are no close substitutes. By the absence of close substitutes we mean that there are no other firms producing the same product or products varying only in very minor ways from that of the monopolist. For example, there is no close substitute for the electricity or water supplied by local utilities. Nor is there a good substitute for telephone service. On the international scene the De Beers diamond syndicate controls the noncommunist world's supply of diamonds. In small and geographically isolated towns the single local bookstore or movie theater may approximate pure monopoly. Of course, there is almost always *some* competition. Candles or kerosene lights are very imperfect substitutes for electricity; letters and carrier pigeons can be substituted for the telephone. Rubies, emeralds, and other precious stones are substitutable for diamonds. The important point arising out of all these cases is that the pure monopolist is the only supplier of a product or service for which there are no *close* substitutes available. Defined in this way, pure monopoly is admittedly a rare phenomenon.

Yet, a brief analysis of pure monopoly is important for two related reasons. First, some industries are reasonable approximations of pure monopoly. The behavior of firms with 80, 70, or even 60 percent of a market can often be explained with considerable accuracy through the pure monopoly market model. For all practical purposes the dominant firm *is* the industry in such instances. Second, a study of pure monopoly provides us with valuable insights concerning the more realistic market structures of monopolistic competition and oligopoly, which will be discussed in Chapters 28 and 29. These two market situations combine in differing degrees the characteristics of pure competition and pure monopoly.

### ☐ BARRIERS TO ENTRY

It was noted in Chapter 22 that the absence of competitors which characterizes pure monopoly is largely explainable in terms of barriers to entry, that is, considerations which prohibit additional firms from entering an industry. These barriers are also pertinent in explaining the existence of oligopoly and monopolistic competition between the market extremes of pure competition and pure monopoly. In the case of pure monopoly, entry barriers are sufficiently great to block completely all potential competition. Somewhat less formidable barriers permit the existence of oligopoly, that is, a market dominated by a few firms. Still weaker barriers result in the fairly large number of firms which characterizes monopolistic competition. The virtual absence of entry barriers helps explain the very large number of competing firms which is the basis of pure competition. The important point is this: Barriers to entry are pertinent not only to the extreme case of pure monopoly but also to the "partial monopolies" which are so characteristic of our economy. What forms do these entry barriers assume?

### △  Economies of Scale: Costs

Modern technology in many industries is such that efficient, low-cost production can be achieved only if producers are extremely large both absolutely and in relation to the market. Where economies of scale are very significant, a firm's average-cost schedule will decline over a wide range of output (Figure 25-7a). Given market demand, the achieving of low unit costs and therefore low unit prices for consumers depends upon the existence of a small number

of firms or, in the extreme case, only one firm. The automobile, aluminum, and steel industries are a few of many heavy industries which reflect such conditions. If three firms currently enjoy all available economies of scale and each has roughly one-third of a market, it is easy to see why new competitors may find it extremely difficult to enter this industry. On the one hand, new firms entering the market as small-scale producers will have little or no chance to survive and expand. Why? Because as small-scale entrants they will be unable to realize the cost economies enjoyed by the existing "Big Three" and therefore will be unable to realize the profits necessary for survival and growth. New competitors in the steel and automobile industries will not come about as the result of the successful operation and expansion of small "backyard" producers. They simply will not be efficient enough to survive. The other option is to start out big, that is, to enter the industry as a large-scale producer. In practice, this is virtually impossible. It is extremely unlikely that a new and untried enterprise will be able to secure the money capital needed to obtain capital facilities comparable to those accumulated by any of the Big Three in the automobile industry. The financial obstacles in the way of starting big are so great in many cases as to be prohibitive.

### △  Public Utilities: Natural Monopolies

In a few industries, economies of scale are particularly pronounced, and at the same time competition is impractical, inconvenient, or simply unworkable. Such industries are called *natural monopolies,* and most of the so-called public utilities—the electric and gas companies, bus firms, and water and communication facilities—can be so classified. These industries are generally given exclusive franchises by government. But in return for this sole right to supply electricity, water, or bus service in a given geographic area, government reserves the right to regulate the operations of such monopolies to prevent abuses of the monopoly power it has granted.

Let us examine some illustrations. It would be exceedingly wasteful for a community to have a number of firms supplying water or electricity. Technology is such in these industries that heavy fixed costs on generators, pumping and purification equipment, water mains, and transmission lines are required. This problem is aggravated by the fact that capital equipment must be sufficient to meet the peak demands which occur on hot summer days when lawns are being watered and air conditioners operated. These heavy fixed costs mean that unit costs of production decline with the number of cubic feet of water or kilowatt hours of electricity supplied by each firm. The presence of several water and electricity suppliers would divide the total market and reduce the sales of each competitor. Each firm would be pushed back up its declining average-cost curve. Firms would underutilize their fixed plants, with the result that unit cost and therefore electricity and water rates would be unnecessarily high. In addition, competition might prove to be extremely inconvenient. For example, the presence of a half-dozen telephone companies in a municipality would entail the inconvenience of having six telephones and six telephone books—not to mention six telephone bills—to ensure communications with all other residents in the same town.

Because firms are eager to spread their fixed costs and thereby achieve lower unit costs, cutthroat price competition tends to break out when a number of firms exist in these public utilities industries. The result may be losses, the bankruptcy of weaker rivals, and the eventual merger of the survivors. The evolving pure monopoly may be anxious to recoup past losses and to profit fully from its new position of market dominance by charging exorbitant prices for its goods or services.

To spare society from such disadvantageous results, government will usually grant an exclusive franchise to a single firm to supply water, natural gas, electricity, telephone service, or bus transportation. In return, government reserves the right to designate the mo-

nopolist's geographic area of operation, to regulate the quality of its services, and to control the prices which it may charge. The result is a regulated or government-sponsored monopoly—monopoly designed to achieve low unit costs but regulated to guarantee that consumers will benefit from these cost economies. We shall examine some of the problems associated with regulation later in this chapter.

△ **Ownership of Essential Raw Materials**

The institution of private property can be used by a monopoly as a means of achieving an effective obstacle to potential rivals. A firm owning or controlling a raw material which is essential in production can obviously prohibit the creation of rival firms. There are several classic examples. The Aluminum Company of America retained its monopoly position in the aluminum industry for many years by virtue of its control of all basic sources of bauxite, the major ore used in aluminum fabrication. At one time the International Nickel Company of Canada controlled approximately 90 percent of the world's known nickel reserves. As noted earlier, most of the world's known diamond mines are owned by the De Beers Company of South Africa.

△ **Patents and Research**

By granting an inventor the exclusive right to control a product for some seventeen years, American patent laws are aimed at protecting the inventor from having the product or process usurped by rival enterprises which have not shared in the time, effort, and money outlays which have gone into its development. By the same token, of course, patents may provide the inventor with a monopoly position for the life of the patent. Patent control figures prominently in the growth of many modern-day industrial giants—National Cash Register, General Motors, General Electric, du Pont, to name a few. The United Shoe Machinery Company provides a notable example of how patent control can be abused to achieve monopoly power. In this case United Shoe became the exclusive supplier of certain essential shoemaking machines through patent control. It extended its monopoly power to other types of shoemaking machinery by requiring all lessees of its patented machines to sign a "tying agreement" in which shoe manufacturers agreed also to lease all other shoemaking machinery from United Shoe. This allowed United Shoe to monopolize the market until partially effective antitrust action was taken by the government in 1955.

Research, of course, underlies the development of patentable products. Firms which gain a measure of monopoly power by their own research or by purchasing the patents of others are in a strategic position to consolidate and strengthen their market position. The profits provided by one important patent can be used to finance the research required to develop new patentable products. Monopoly power achieved through patents may well be cumulative.

△ **Unfair Competition**

A firm's rivals may be eliminated and the entry of new competitors blocked by aggressive, cutthroat tactics. Familiar techniques entail product disparagement, pressure on resource suppliers and banks to withhold materials and credit, the hiring away of strategic personnel, and aggressive price cutting designed to bankrupt competitors. Though many of these facets of unfair competition are now illegal or fringe upon illegality, they are of more than historical interest. For example, although Federal legislation prohibits price cutting intended to reduce competition, how is one to distinguish in practice between legitimate price competition based upon cost advantages and price competition designed to bankrupt rivals?

△ **Economies of Being Established**

A bit of reflection will reveal that for a variety of reasons an established, going con-

cern has numerous advantages over new, embryonic rivals. There are good reasons why existing firms should survive and prosper, whereas new firms have every reason to founder and fail. Established firms which have proved themselves by their continued existence and prosperity will have relatively easy access to the capital market, on favorable terms. This advantage is not unrelated to the fact that an established concern will tend to have a relatively efficient administrative framework staffed by competent and experienced personnel. The firm's longevity will have allowed it to eliminate inappropriate policies and to have screened the dolts from its administrative ranks. It must be added that going concerns will also be in a position to expand their size and market share by internal financing.

The new concern may have great difficulties in securing needed money capital. Its personnel and policies are untried and untested; it is an industrial question mark. If funds are available to newcomers, the added risks of investing in a new concern are likely to make the terms unattractive to the firm.

In addition, an established firm will be likely to have a widely known and highly advertised product, which it sells through well-established marketing channels to long-standing customers. A new firm faces serious financial obstacles in developing and advertising a product, in establishing marketing outlets, and in building up a clientele.

△ **Two Implications**

Our discussion of barriers to entry suggests two noteworthy points.

**1** Barriers to entry are rarely complete; indeed, this is merely another way of stating our earlier point that pure monopoly is rare. Although, as we have seen, research and technological advance may strengthen the market position of a firm, technology may also undermine existing monopoly power. Existing patent advantages may be circumvented by the development of new and distinct, yet substitutable, products. New sources of strategic raw materials may be found. It is probably not an overstatement to say that monopoly in the sense of a one-firm industry persists over time only with the sanction or aid of government— for example, the postal service.

**2** It is implied in our discussion that monopolies may be desirable or undesirable from the standpoint of economic efficiency. The public utilities and economies-of-scale arguments suggest that market demand and technology may be such that efficient low-cost production presupposes the existence of monopoly. On the other hand, our comments upon materials ownership, patents, and unfair competition as sources of monopoly imply more undesirable connotations of business monopoly.

With these points in mind, let us analyze the price-output behavior of a pure monopolist. Important insights with respect to the social desirability of monopoly will be revealed.

## □ PRICE AND OUTPUT DETERMINATION

Let us assume a pure monopolist which, through, say, patent and materials control, is able to block the entry of new firms to the market. Suppose, too, that the monopolist is unhampered by the existence or the prospect of a regulatory commission. In short, we have a monopolist which is ideally situated to exploit the market fully. The pure monopolist will determine its profit-maximizing output on the basis of its cost and demand data.

### △ Monopoly Demand

The crucial difference between a pure monopolist and a purely competitive seller lies on the demand side of the market. We recall from Chapter 26 that the purely competitive seller faces a perfectly elastic demand schedule at the market price determined by industry supply and demand. The competitive firm can sell as much or as little as it wants at the going market price. The competitive firm is a "price taker" and therefore must accept the market-

determined price. It follows that each additional unit sold will add a constant amount— its price—to the firm's total revenue. In other words, for the competitive seller marginal revenue is constant and equal to product price. This means that total revenue increases by a constant amount, that is, by the constant price of each unit sold. A glance back at Table 26-1 and Figure 26-1 will refresh you on the price, marginal revenue, and total revenue relationships for the purely competitive firm.

The monopolist's demand curve—indeed, the demand curve of *any* imperfectly competitive seller—is much different. Because the pure monopolist *is* the industry, its demand, or sales, curve is the industry demand curve. And the industry demand curve is not perfectly elastic, but rather, is downsloping. This is illustrated by columns 1 and 2 of Table 27-1. There are two implications of a downsloping demand curve which must be understood.

**Price Exceeds Marginal Revenue**   In the first place, a downsloping demand curve means that a pure monopoly can increase its sales only by charging a lower unit price for its product. *Furthermore, the fact that the monopolist must lower price to boost sales causes marginal revenue to be less than price (average revenue) for every level of output except the first.* The reason? Price cuts will apply not only to the extra output sold but also to all other units of output which otherwise could have been sold at a higher price. Each additional unit sold will add to total revenue its price *less* the sum of the price cuts which must be taken on all prior units of output. The marginal revenue of the second unit of output in Table 27-1 is $142 rather than its $152 price, because a $10 price cut must be taken on the first unit to increase sales from 1 to 2 units. Similarly, to sell 3 units the firm must lower price from $152 to $142. The resulting marginal revenue will be just $122—the $142 addition to total revenue which the third unit of sales provides less $10 price cuts on the first 2 units of output. It is this rationale which ex-

**TABLE 27-1**
Revenue and Cost Data of a Pure Monopolist (*hypothetical data*)

| Revenue data | | | | Cost data | | | |
|---|---|---|---|---|---|---|---|
| (1) Quantity of output | (2) Price (average revenue) | (3) Total revenue | (4) Marginal revenue | (5) Average total cost | (6) Total cost | (7) Marginal cost | (8) Profit (+) or loss (−) |
| 0 | $172 | $ 0 | | | $ 100 | | $−100 |
| | | | $162 | | | $ 90 | |
| 1 | 162 | 162 | | $190.00 | 190 | | − 28 |
| | | | 142 | | | 80 | |
| 2 | 152 | 304 | | 135.00 | 270 | | + 34 |
| | | | 122 | | | 70 | |
| 3 | 142 | 426 | | 113.33 | 340 | | + 86 |
| | | | 102 | | | 60 | |
| 4 | 132 | 528 | | 100.00 | 400 | | +128 |
| | | | 82 | | | 70 | |
| 5 | 122 | 610 | | 94.00 | 470 | | +140 |
| | | | 62 | | | 80 | |
| 6 | 112 | 672 | | 91.67 | 550 | | +122 |
| | | | 42 | | | 90 | |
| 7 | 102 | 714 | | 91.43 | 640 | | + 74 |
| | | | 22 | | | 110 | |
| 8 | 92 | 736 | | 93.73 | 750 | | − 14 |
| | | | 2 | | | 130 | |
| 9 | 82 | 738 | | 97.78 | 880 | | −142 |
| | | | −18 | | | 150 | |
| 10 | 72 | 720 | | 103.00 | 1030 | | −310 |

plains why the marginal-revenue data of column 4 of Table 27-1 fall short of product price in column 2 for all levels of output save the first. Because marginal revenue is, by definition, the increase in total revenue associated with each additional unit of output, the declining marginal revenue figures mean that total revenue will increase at a diminishing rate as shown in column 3 of Table 27-1. The relationships between the demand, marginal revenue, and total revenue curves are shown graphically in Figure 27-1.

**Price Maker** The second implication of a downsloping demand curve is this: In all imperfectly competitive markets in which such demand curves are relevant—that is, purely monopolistic, oligopolistic, and monopolistically competitive markets—firms have a price policy. By virtue of their ability to influence total supply, the output decisions of such firms necessarily affect product price. This is most evident, of course, in the present case of pure monopoly, where one firm controls total output. Faced with a downsloping demand curve, wherein each output is associated with some unique price, the monopolist unavoidably determines price in deciding what volume of output to produce. The monopolist simultaneously chooses both price and output. In columns 1 and 2 of Table 27-1 we find that the monopolist can sell only an output of 1 unit at

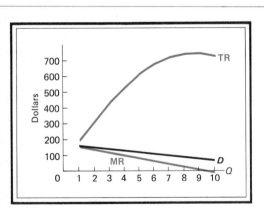

FIGURE 27-1 DEMAND, MARGINAL REVENUE, AND TOTAL REVENUE OF AN IMPERFECTLY COMPETITIVE FIRM

Because it must lower price to increase its sales, the marginal-revenue curve (MR) of an imperfectly competitive firm lies below its downsloping demand curve (*D*). Total revenue (TR) increases at a decreasing rate, reaches a maximum, and then declines.

a price of $162, only an output of 2 units at a price of $152 per unit, and so forth.[1]

But all this is not to imply that the monopolist is "free" of market forces in establishing price and output or that the consumer is somehow completely at the monopolist's mercy. In particular, the monopolist's downsloping demand curve means that high prices are associated with low volumes of sales and, conversely, low prices with larger outputs. The monopolist cannot raise price without losing sales or gain sales without charging a lower price. The question which now arises is this: What specific price-quantity combination on the demand curve will the pure monopolist choose? This depends not only upon demand and marginal-revenue data but also upon costs.

## △  Cost Data

On the cost side of the picture we shall assume that, although the firm is a monopolist in the product market, it hires resources competitively and employs the same technology as our competitive firm in the preceding chapter. This permits us to use the cost data developed in Chapter 25 and applied in Chapter 26, thereby facilitating a comparison of the price-output decisions of a pure monopoly with those of a pure competitor. Columns 5 through 7 of Table 27-1 merely restate the pertinent cost concepts of Table 25-2.

## △  Equating Marginal Revenue and Marginal Cost

A profit-seeking monopolist will employ the same rationale as a profit-seeking firm in a competitive industry. It will produce each successive unit of output so long as it adds

more to total revenue than it does to total costs. In technical language, the firm will produce up to that output at which marginal revenue equals marginal cost.

A comparison of columns 4 and 7 in Table 27-1 indicates that the profit-maximizing output is 5 units; the fifth unit is the last unit of output whose marginal revenue exceeds its marginal cost. What price will the monopolist charge? The downsloping demand curve of columns 1 and 2 in Table 27-1 indicates that there is only one price at which 5 units can be sold: $122.

This same analysis is presented graphically in Figure 27-2, where the demand, marginal-revenue, average-total-cost, and marginal-cost data of Table 27-1 have been drawn. A comparison of marginal revenue and marginal cost again indicates that the profit-maximizing output is 5 units or, more generally, $Q_m$. The unique price at which $Q_m$ can be sold is found by extending a perpendicular up from the profit-maximizing point on the output axis and then at right angles from the point at which it hits the demand curve to the vertical axis. The indicated price is $P_m$. By charging a price higher than $P_m$, the monopolist must move up the demand curve, and this means that sales will fall short of the profit-maximizing level $Q_m$. Specifically, the firm will be failing to produce units of output whose marginal revenue exceeds their marginal cost. If the monopolist charges less, it would involve a volume of sales in excess of the profit-maximizing output.

Columns 2 and 5 of Table 27-1 indicate that, at 5 units of output, product price of $122 exceeds average total cost of $94. Economic profits are therefore $28 per unit; total economic profits are then $140 (= 5 × $28). In Figure 27-2, per unit profit is indicated by the distance $AP_m$, and total economic profits—the orange area—are found by multiplying this unit profit by the profit-maximizing output $Q_m$.

The same profit-maximizing combination of output and price can also be determined by

---

[1] The notion of a supply curve does not apply in a purely monopolistic (or any other imperfectly competitive) market because of the ability of the seller to control product price. A supply curve shows the amounts producers will offer at various *given* prices which may confront them in the market. But prices are not "given" to the pure monopolist; it does not respond to a fixed price, but rather, sets the price itself.

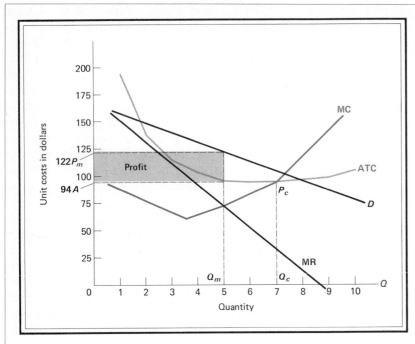

FIGURE 27-2  THE PROFIT-
MAXIMIZING POSITION OF
A PURE MONOPOLIST

The pure monopolist maximizes
profits by producing the MR =
MC output.  In this instance
profit is $AP_m$ per unit, total
profits are measured by the
orange rectangle.

comparing the total revenue and total costs incurred at each possible level of production. The reader should employ columns 3 and 6 of Table 27-1 to verify all the conclusions we have reached through the use of marginal-revenue–marginal-cost analysis. Similarly, an accurate graphing of total revenue and total cost against output will also show the greatest differential (the maximum profit) at 5 units of output.

### △  Misconceptions Concerning Monopoly Pricing

Our analysis explodes some popular fallacies concerning the behavior of monopolies.

**1  Not Highest Price**  Because a monopolist can manipulate output and price, it is often alleged that a monopolist "will charge the highest price it can get." This is clearly a misguided assertion. There are many prices above $P_m$ in Figure 27-2, but the monopolist shuns them solely because they entail a smaller than maximum profit. Total profits are the difference between total revenue and total costs, and each of these two determinants of profits depends upon the quantity sold as much as upon the price and unit cost.

**2  Total, Not Unit, Profits**  The monopolist seeks maximum *total* profits, not maximum *unit* profits. In Figure 27-2 a careful comparison of the vertical distance between average cost and price at various possible outputs indicates that per unit profits are greater at a point slightly to the left of the profit-maximizing output $Q_m$. This is more readily seen in Table 27-2, where unit profits are $32 at 4 units of output as compared with $28 at the profit-maximizing output of 5 units. In this instance the monopolist is accepting a lower-than-maximum per unit profit for the simple reason that the additional sales more than compensate for the lower unit profits. A profit-seeking monopolist would obviously rather sell 5 units at a profit of $28 per unit (for a total profit of $140) than 4 units at a profit of $32 per unit (for a total profit of only $128).

**3  Losses**  It must also be emphasized that pure monopoly does not guarantee economic profits. True, the likelihood of economic profits is greater for a pure monopolist than for a purely competitive producer. In the long run the latter is doomed by the free and easy entry of new firms to a normal profit; barriers to entry permit the monopolist to perpetuate economic profits in the long run. Of course, like the pure competitor, the monopolist cannot persistently operate at a loss. The firm must realize a normal profit or better in the long run or it will not survive. However, if the demand and cost situation faced by the monopolist is less favorable than that shown in Figure 27-2, short-run losses will be realized. Despite its dominance in the market, the monopolist shown in Figure 27-3 realizes a loss in

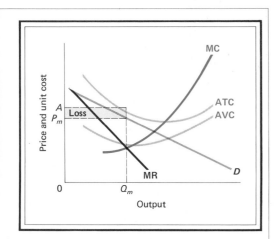

**FIGURE 27-3 THE LOSS-MINIMIZING POSITION OF A PURE MONOPOLIST**

If demand $D$ is weak and costs are high, the pure monopolist may be unable to make a profit. It will minimize losses in the short run by producing at that output where MR = MC. Loss per unit is $AP_m$, and total losses are indicated by the blue rectangle.

the short run by virtue of a weak demand and relatively high costs.

**4  Elastic Demand**  Because the demand curve facing a purely competitive firm is perfectly elastic, there is a temptation to assume a monopolist's demand curve is relatively, if not perfectly, inelastic. But this is not the case! A monopolist will always want to produce in the *elastic* range of its demand curve. The reason, recalling Chapter 23's total-revenue test for elasticity, is that by lowering price into the *inelastic* range of the curve, total revenue will decline. But the lower price is associated with a larger output and, therefore, increased production costs. Lower revenue and higher costs clearly indicate diminished profits (or increased losses). Hence, the monopolist will always want to avoid a price-output combination in the inelastic segment of its demand curve.

△  **Possible Restraints upon Profit Maximization**

The forgoing comments indicate that certain restraints are imposed upon the monopolist by the market. Cost and demand considerations set restrictions upon the monopolist's price-output behavior. Actually, certain other forces may cause the monopolist to exercise restraint; these forces may cause it purposely to charge a lower price and produce a greater output than are consistent with maximum profits. Two of these restraints merit further comment.

**Public Scrutiny**  In the first place, the monopolist does not have anonymity; the identity of monopolistic sellers is typically well known. It follows that the monopolist which fully exploits its market position may find itself the target of public criticism or the object of moral suasion designed to enforce a "voluntary" wage-price policy (Chapter 18). After all, in Figure 27-2 there are many prices less than $P_m$ which will entail outputs greater than $Q_m$ and still yield substantial economic profits to the monopolist. If criticism is widespread and persistent, it can lead to a loss of goodwill or, worse yet from the firm's viewpoint, some form of intervention by the government—antitrust action, rate regulation, government stimulation of new competitors, or, at the extreme, nationalization of the firm. Thus, from a very long-run standpoint it may be sensible for the monopolist to avoid unfavorable comment with respect to its market behavior, even at the sacrifice of some profits.

The "Long View"   Secondly, the monopoly may deliberately limit its profits so as not to attract new competitors. A highly profitable monopoly may cause potential rivals to double their efforts to overcome the monopolist's barriers. And remember: Barriers to entry are rarely insurmountable over time. Full exploitation of a monopolist's position in the short run may destroy that monopolistic position in the long pull.

The importance of these "voluntary" restraints is subject to heated debate. It would be a mistake to say that they undermine our profit-maximizing analysis; they probably cause minor deviations from the most profitable price-output combination.

## ☐   PRICE DISCRIMINATION

To this juncture we have assumed that the monopolist charges a uniform price to all buyers. Under certain conditions the monopolist might be able to exploit its market position more fully and thus increase profits by charging different prices to different buyers. In so doing the seller is engaging in price discrimination. *Price discrimination takes place when a given product is sold at more than one price and these price differences are not justified by cost differences.*

### △   Conditions

The opportunity to engage in price discrimination is not readily available to all sellers. In general, price discrimination is workable when three conditions are realized.

**1**   Most obviously, the seller must be a monopolist or, at least, possess some degree of monopoly power, that is, some ability to control price.

**2**   The seller must be able to segregate buyers into separate classes wherein each group has a different willingness or ability to pay for the product. This separation of buyers is usually based upon different elasticities of demand as later illustrations will make clear.

**3**   The original purchaser cannot resell the product or service. If those who buy in the low-price segment of the market can easily resell in the high-price segment, the resulting decline in supply would increase price in the low-price segment and the increase in supply would lower price in the high-price segment. The price discrimination policy would thereby be undermined. This correctly suggests that service industries—for example, the transportation industry or legal and medical services—are especially susceptible to price discrimination.

### △   How It Works

The simplest way to understand why price discrimination can yield additional profits is to look again at our monopolist's downsloping demand curve in Figure 27-2. We note that, although the profit-maximizing uniform price is $122, the segment of the demand curve lying above the profit area in Figure 27-2 tells us that there are buyers of the product who would be willing to pay *more than* $P_m$ ($122) rather than forgo the product. If the monopolist can somehow identify and segregate each of these buyers and thereby charge the maximum price each would pay, profits would be expanded considerably. In columns 1 and 2 of Table 27-1 we note that the buyers of the first 4 units of output would be willing to pay more than the equilibrium price of $122. If the seller could somehow extract the maximum price each would pay, total revenue would increase from $610 (= $122 × 5) to $710 (= $122 + $132 + $142 + $152 + $162) and profits would thereby increase from $140 (= $610 − $470) to $240 (= $710 − $470). Of course, price discrimination in practice is likely to be less definitive. At the most the monopolist may only be able to segment buyers into two or three groups rather than sell to each buyer at the highest price each will pay.

### △  Illustrations

Price discrimination is widely practiced in our economy. The sales representative who must communicate important information to corporate headquarters has a highly inelastic demand for long-distance telephone service and pays the high daytime rate. The college student making a periodic "reporting in" call to the folks at home has an elastic demand and defers the call to take advantage of lower evening or weekend rates. Electric utilities frequently segment their markets by end uses, such as lighting and heating. The absence of reasonable substitutes means that the demand for electricity for illumination is inelastic and the price per kilowatt hour for this use is high. But the availability of natural gas and petroleum as alternatives to electrical heating makes the demand for electricity elastic for this purpose and the price charged is therefore lower. Similarly, industrial users of electricity are typically charged lower rates than residential users because the former may have the alternative of constructing their own generating equipment while the individual household does not. Movie theaters and golf courses vary their charges on the basis of time (higher rates in the evening and on weekends when demand is strong) and age (ability to pay). Railroads vary the rate charged per ton mile of freight according to the market value of the product being shipped. The shipper of 10 tons of television sets or costume jewelry will be charged more than the shipper of 10 tons of gravel or coal. Physicians and lawyers frequently set their fees for a given service on the basis of ability to pay; a rich person may pay a higher fee for a divorce or to have an appendix removed than will a poor person. A manufacturer sells the same whiskey at a high price under a prestige label, but at a lower price under a different label. An appliance or tire

manufacturer sells its product directly to the public at one price and through Sears or Ward's at a lower price. Airlines charge high fares to traveling executives, whose demand for travel tends to be inelastic, and offer a variety of lower fares in the guise of "family rates" and "standby fares" to attract vacationers and others whose demands are more elastic.

### ☐  ECONOMIC EFFECTS OF MONOPOLY

Let us now evaluate pure monopoly from the standpoint of society as a whole. Our emphasis will be upon (1) price, output, and resource allocation; (2) the distribution of income; and (3) economic progress, that is, technological advance. To sharpen our analysis we ignore any possible restraints upon the monopolist's policies and presume that it seeks the maximum profit that its cost-revenue situation permits. We also assume that no price discrimination occurs.

### △  Price, Output, and Resource Allocation

In Chapter 26 we concluded that pure competition would result in a highly efficient, or "ideal," allocation of resources. In the long run the free entry and exodus of firms would force firms to operate at the optimum rate of output where unit costs of production would be at a minimum. Product price would be at the lowest level consistent with average total costs. To illustrate: In Figure 27-2 the competitive firm would sell $Q_c$ units of output at a price of $Q_cP_c$. Furthermore, long-run competitive equilibrium would also entail an efficient allocation of resources, in that production would occur up to that point at which price (the measure of a product's value to society) would equal marginal cost (the measure of the alternative products forgone by society in the production of any given commodity).

Figure 27-2 indicates that, *given the same costs,* a purely monopolistic firm will produce much less desirable results. As we have already discovered, the pure monopolist will maximize profits by producing an output of $Q_m$ and charging a price of $P_m$. It can be readily seen that *the monopolist will find it profitable to sell a smaller output and to charge a higher price than would a competitive producer.*[2] Furthermore, it is clear that, at $Q_m$ units of output, product price is considerably greater than marginal cost. This means that society values additional units of this monopolized

[2] In Figure 27-2 the price-quantity comparison of monopoly and pure competition is from the vantage point of the single purely competitive *firm* of Figure 26-7a. An equally illuminating approach is to start with the purely competitive *industry* of Figure 26-7b, which is reproduced below. Recall that the competitive industry's supply curve S is the horizontal sum of the marginal-cost curves of all the firms in the industry. Comparing this with industry demand D, we get the purely competitive price and output of $P_c$ and $Q_c$. Now suppose that this industry becomes a pure monopoly as a result of a wholesale merger or one firm's somehow buying out all its competitors. Assume, too, that no changes in costs or market demand result from this dramatic change in the industry's structure. What were formerly, say, 100 competing firms are now a pure monopolist consisting of 100 branch plants.

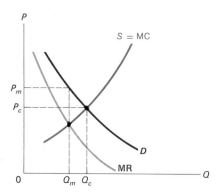

The industry supply curve is now simply the marginal-cost curve of the monopolist, the summation of the MC curves of its many branch plants. The important change, however, is on the market-demand side. From the viewpoint of each individual competitive firm, demand was perfectly elastic, and marginal revenue was therefore equal to price. Each firm equated MC to MR (and therefore to P) in maximizing profits (Chapter 26). But industry demand and individual demand are the same to the pure monopolist; the firm *is* the industry, and thus the monopolist correctly envisions a downsloping demand curve D. This means that marginal revenue MR will be less than price; graphically the MR curve lies below the demand curve. In choosing the profit-maximizing MC = MR position, the monopolist selects an output $Q_m$ which is smaller, and a price $P_m$ which is greater, than would be the case if the industry were organized competitively.

product more highly than it does the alternative products which resources could otherwise produce. In other words, the monopolist's profit-maximizing output results in an underallocation of resources; the monopolist finds it profitable to restrict output and therefore employ fewer resources than are justified from society's standpoint.

To summarize: *Given identical costs,* a purely monopolistic firm will find it profitable to charge a higher price, produce a smaller output, and foster an allocation of economic resources inferior to that of a purely competitive firm. These contrasting consequences are rooted in the barriers to entry which characterize monopoly.

There is one basic exception to these conclusions: The assumption that the unit costs available to the purely competitive and the purely monopolistic firm are the same may not hold in practice. Given production techniques and therefore production costs, consumer demand may not be sufficient to support a large number of competing firms producing at an output which permits each of them to realize all known economies of scale. In such instances a firm must be large in relation to the market—that is, it must be monopolistic—to produce efficiently (at low unit cost). Our previous discussion of economies of scale as a barrier to entry and the desirability of establishing public utilities in certain fields is based primarily upon such cost considerations (see Chapter 25).

How important is this exception? Most economists feel that it applies for the most part only to public utilities and is therefore not significant enough to undermine our general conclusions concerning the restrictive nature of monopoly. Evidence suggests that the giant corporations which populate many manufacturing industries now have more monopoly power than can be justified on the grounds that these firms are merely availing themselves of existing economies of scale.[3]

[3] See Joe S. Bain, "Economies of Scale, Concentration, and the Condition of Entry in Twenty Manufacturing Industries," *American Economic Review,* March 1954, pp. 15–39.

## △  Income Distribution

Business monopoly probably contributes to inequality in the distribution of income. By virtue of their market power, monopolists charge a higher price than would a purely competitive firm with the same costs; monopolists are in effect able to levy a "private tax" upon consumers and thereby to realize substantial economic profits. These monopolistic profits, it should be noted, are not widely distributed because corporate stock ownership is largely concentrated in the hands of upper income groups. The owners of monopolistic enterprises thereby tend to be enriched at the expense of the rest of society.

## △  Technological Advance

We have already qualified our condemnation of pure monopoly by noting that in a few instances *existing* mass-production economies may be lost if an industry comprises a large number of small, competing firms. There is also a dynamic aspect to this line of reasoning. To be specific, will competition or monopoly foster the more rapid improvement of products and productive techniques over time? This is fertile ground for honest differences of opinion.

**The Competitive Model**  Competitive firms certainly have the incentive—indeed, a market mandate—to employ the most efficient *known* productive techniques. We have seen that their very survival depends upon being efficient. But at the same time, competition tends to deprive firms of economic profit—an important means and a major incentive to develop *new* products and *new* improved productive techniques. The profits of technological advance may be short-lived to the innovating competitor. An innovating firm in a competitive industry will find that its many rivals will soon duplicate or imitate any technological advance it may achieve; rivals will share the rewards but not the costs of successful technological research.

**The Monopoly Model**  In contrast, we have seen that—thanks to entry barriers—a monopolist may persistently realize substantial economic profits. Hence, the pure monopolist will have greater financial resources for technological advance than will competitive firms. But what about the monopolist's incentives for technological advance? Here the picture is clouded.

There is one imposing argument which suggests that the monopolist's incentives to develop new products and new techniques will be weak: The absence of competitors means that there is no automatic stimulus to technological advance in a monopolized market. Because of its sheltered market position, the pure monopolist can afford to be inefficient and lethargic. The keen rivalry of a competitive market penalizes the inefficient; an inefficient monopolist does not face this penalty simply because it has no rivals. The monopolist has every reason to become satisfied with the status quo, to become complacent. It might well pay the monopolist to withhold or "file" technological improvements in both product and productive techniques in order to exploit existing capital equipment fully. New and improved products and techniques, it is argued, may be suppressed by monopolists to avoid any losses caused by the sudden obsolescence of existing machinery and equipment. And, even when improved techniques are belatedly introduced by monopolists, the accompanying cost reductions will accrue to the monopolist as increases in profits and only partially, if at all, to consumers in the form of lower prices and an increased output. Proponents of this view point out that in a number of industries which approximate pure monopoly—for example, steel and aluminum—the interest in research has been minimal. Such advances as have been realized have come largely from outside the industry or from the smaller firms which make up the "competitive fringe" of the industry.

Basically, there are at least two counterarguments:

**1**  Technological advance is a means of lowering unit costs and thereby expanding profits. As our analysis of Figure 27-2 implies, lower costs will give rise to a profit-maximizing position which involves a larger output and a lower price than previously. Furthermore, any expansion of profits will not be of a transitory nature; barriers to entry protect the monopolist from profit encroachment by rivals. In short, technological progress is profitable to the monopolist and therefore will be undertaken.

**2**  Research and technological advance may be one of the monopolist's barriers to entry; hence, the monopolist must persist and succeed in the area of technological advance or eventually fall prey to new competitors. Technological progress, it is argued, is essential to the maintenance of monopoly.

**A Mixed Picture**  Which view is more accurate? Frankly, economists are not sure. Most economists do not envision pure monopoly as a particularly progressive market structure. At the same time, they acknowledge that agriculture, the industry which most nearly fits the competitive model, has only on rare occasions provided itself with innovations in product and method. Government research and the oligopolistic firms which produce farm equipment have provided this competitive industry with most of its improvements in products and techniques. As we shall see in Chapter 29, one can make a case that oligopolistic industries, wherein firms are large enough to have the ability to finance research and at the same time are compelled to engage in such research because of the presence of a moderate number of rivals, may be more conducive to technological advance than any other market structure.

Now what can be offered by way of a summarizing generalization on the economic efficiency of pure monopoly? Simply this: In a static economy, wherein economies of scale are equally accessible to purely competitive and monopolist firms, pure competition will be superior to pure monopoly in that pure competition forces use of the best-known technology and allocates resources in accordance with the wants of society. On the other hand, when economies of scale available to the monopolist are not attainable by small competitive producers, or in a dynamic context in which changes in the rate of technological advance must be considered, the inefficiencies of pure monopoly are not so evident.

## ☐  REGULATED MONOPOLY

Most purely monopolistic industries are "natural monopolies" and therefore subject to social regulation. In particular, the prices or rates which public utilities—railroads, telephone companies, natural gas and electricity suppliers—can charge are determined by a Federal, state, or local regulatory commission or board.

Figure 27-4 shows the demand and cost conditions of a natural monopoly. Because of heavy fixed costs, demand cuts the average

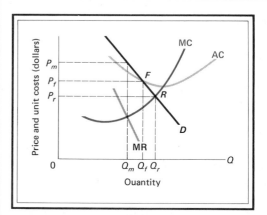

FIGURE 27-4 REGULATED MONOPOLY

Price regulation can improve the social consequences of a natural monopoly. The socially optimum price $P_r$ will result in an efficient allocation of resources but is likely to entail losses and therefore call for permanent public subsidies. The "fair-return" price $P_f$ will allow the monopolist to break even, but will not fully correct the underallocation of resources.

cost curve at a point where average cost is still falling. It would obviously be inefficient to have a number of firms in such an industry because, by dividing the market, each firm would move further to the left on its average cost curve so that unit costs would be substantially higher. In short, the relationship between market demand and costs is such that the attainment of low unit costs presumes only one producer.

We know that $P_m$ and $Q_m$ are the profit-maximizing price and output which the unregulated monopolist would choose. Because price exceeds average total cost, the monopolist enjoys a substantial economic profit which is likely to contribute to income inequality. Furthermore, price exceeds marginal cost, which indicates an underallocation of resources to this product or service. The question is: Can government regulation bring about better results from society's point of view?

△ **Socially Optimum Price**

If the objective of our regulatory commission is to achieve an efficient allocation of resources, it should obviously establish a legal (ceiling) price for the monopolist that is equal to marginal cost. Remembering that each point on the market demand curve designates a price-quantity combination, and noting that marginal cost cuts the demand curve only at point $R$, it is clear that $P_r$ is the only price which is equal to marginal cost. The imposition of this maximum or ceiling price causes the monopolist's effective demand curve to become $P_r RD$; the demand curve becomes perfectly elastic, and therefore $P_r =$ MR out to point $R$, where the regulated price ceases to be effective. The important point is that, given the legal price $P_r$, the monopolist will maximize profits by producing $Q_r$ units of output, because it is at this output that MR $(P_r) =$ MC. By making it illegal to charge more than $P_r$ per unit, the regulatory agency has eliminated the monopolist's incentive to restrict output in order to benefit from a higher price. In short, by imposing the legal price $P_r$ and letting the

monopolist choose its profit-maximizing output, the allocative results of pure competition can be simulated. Production takes place where $P_r =$ MC, and this equality indicates an efficient allocation of resources to this product or service. This reasoning, incidentally, is the basis for the argument made in Chapter 18 that mandatory price controls imposed in an imperfectly competitive economy might improve resource allocation.

△ **"Fair-Return" Price**

But the socially optimum price $P_r$ is likely to pose a problem of losses for the regulated firm. The price which equals marginal cost is likely to be so low that average total costs are not covered as is shown in Figure 27-4. The inevitable result is losses. The reason for this lies in the basic character of public utilities. Because they are required to meet "peak" demands (both daily and seasonally) for their product or service, they tend to have substantial excess productive capacity when demand is relatively "normal." This high level of investment in capital facilities means that unit costs of production are likely to decline over a wide range of output. In technical terms, the market demand curve in Figure 27-4 cuts marginal cost at a point to the left of the marginal-cost–average-total-cost intersection, so the socially optimum price is necessarily below AC. Therefore, to enforce a socially optimum price upon the regulated monopolist would mean short-run losses, and in the long run, bankruptcy for the utility.

What to do? One option would be a public subsidy sufficient to cover the loss which the socially optimum price would entail. Another possibility is to condone price discrimination in the hope that the additional revenue gained thereby will permit the firm to cover costs. In practice, regulatory commissions have pursued a third option; they have tended to back away somewhat from the objective of allocative efficiency and marginal-cost pricing. Most regulatory agencies in the United States are concerned with establishing a "fair-return" price.

This is so in no small measure because, as the courts have envisioned it, an unembellished socially optimum price would lead to losses and eventual bankruptcy and thereby deprive the monopoly's owners of their private property without "due process of law." Indeed, the Supreme Court has held that the regulatory agencies must permit a "fair return" to owners.

Remembering that total costs include a normal or "fair" profit, we see that the "fair" or "fair-return" price in Figure 27-4 would obviously be $P_f$, where price equals *average* cost. Because the demand curve cuts average cost only at point $F$, it is clear that $P_f$ is the only price which permits a fair return. The corresponding output at regulated price $P_f$ will be $Q_f$.

△  **Dilemma of Regulation**

A comparison of the results of the socially optimum price and the fair-return price suggests a policy dilemma. When price is set to achieve the most efficient allocation of resources ($P = MC$), the regulated utility is likely to suffer losses. Survival of the firm would presumably depend upon permanent public subsidies out of tax revenues. On the other hand, although a fair-return price ($P = AC$) allows the monopolist to cover costs, it only partially resolves the underallocation of resources which the unregulated monopoly would foster. That is, the fair-return price would only increase output from $Q_m$ to $Q_f$, whereas the socially optimum output is $Q_r$. Despite this knotty problem, the basic point is that regulation can improve upon the results of monopoly from the social point of view. Price regulation can simultaneously reduce price, increase output, and reduce the economic profits of monopolies.

## Summary

1   A pure monopolist is the sole producer of a commodity for which there are no close substitutes.

2   Barriers to entry, in the form of **a.** economies of scale, **b.** natural monopolies, **c.** the ownership or control of essential raw materials, **d.** patent ownership and research, **e.** unfair competition, and **f.** economies of being established, help explain the existence of pure monopoly and other imperfectly competitive market structures. Barriers to entry which are very formidable in the short run may prove to be surmountable in the long run.

3   The pure monopolist's market situation differs from that of a competitive firm in that the monopolist's demand curve is downsloping, causing the marginal-revenue curve to lie below the demand curve. Like the competitive seller, the pure monopolist will maximize profits by equating marginal revenue and marginal cost. Barriers to entry may permit a monopolist to acquire economic profits even in the long run. It is noteworthy, however, that **a.** the monopolist does not charge "the highest price it can get"; **b.** the maximum total profit sought by the monopolist rarely coincides with maximum unit profits; **c.** high costs and a weak demand may prevent the monopolist from realizing any profit at all; and **d.** the monopolist will want to avoid the inelastic range of its demand curve.

4   A monopolist can increase its profits by practicing price discrimination, provided it can segregate buyers on the basis of different elasticities of demand and the product or service cannot be readily transferred between the segregated markets.

5   Given the same costs, the pure monopolist will find it profitable to restrict output and charge a higher price than would a competitive seller. This restriction of output causes

resources to be misallocated, as is evidenced by the fact that price exceeds marginal cost in monopolized markets.

**6**   Monopoly tends to increase income inequality.

**7**   Economists disagree as to how conducive pure monopoly is to technological advance. Some feel that pure monopoly is more progressive than pure competition because its ability to realize economic profits provides for the financing of technological research. Others, however, argue that the absence of rival firms and the monopolist's desire to exploit fully its existing capital facilities weaken the monopolist's incentive to innovate.

**8**   Price regulation can be invoked to eliminate wholly or partially the tendency of monopolists to underallocate resources and to earn economic profits. The "socially optimum" price is determined where the demand and marginal cost curves intersect; the "fair return" price is determined where the demand and average cost curves intersect.

## Questions and Study Suggestions

**1**   Key terms and concepts to remember: pure monopoly; barriers to entry; natural monopoly; unfair competition; economies of being established; price discrimination; socially optimum price; fair-return price; the dilemma of regulation.

**2**   "No firm is completely sheltered from rivals; all firms compete for the dollars of consumers.  Pure monopoly, therefore, does not exist."  Do you agree?  Explain.

**3**   Discuss the major barriers to entry.  Explain how each barrier can foster monopoly or oligopoly.  Which barriers, if any, do you feel give rise to monopoly that is socially justifiable?

**4**   Critically evaluate and explain:

*a.*   "Because they can control product price, monopolists are always assured of profitable production by simply charging the highest price consumers will pay."

*b.*   "The pure monopolist seeks that output which will yield the greatest per unit profit."

*c.*   "An excess of price over marginal cost is the market's way of signaling the need for more production of a product."

*d.*   "The more profitable a firm, the greater its monopoly power."

*e.*   "The monopolist has a price policy; the competitive producer does not."

*f.*   "With respect to resource allocation, the interests of the seller and of society coincide in a purely competitive market but conflict in a monopolized market."

*g.*   "In a sense the monopolist makes a profit for not producing; the monopolist produces profits more than he does goods."

**5**   Carefully evaluate the following widely held viewpoint.  Can you offer any arguments to the contrary?[4]

> Competition is congenial to material progress.  It keeps the door open to new blood and new ideas.  It communicates to all producers the improvements made by any one of them.  Monopoly, as such, is not conducive to progress.  The large firm may engage in research and invent new products, materials, methods and machines.  But when it possesses a monopoly, it will be reluctant to make use of these inventions if they would compel it to scrap existing equipment or if it believes that their ultimate profitability is in doubt.  The monopolist may introduce innovations and cut costs, but instead of moving goods by reducing prices he is prone to spend large sums on alternative methods of promoting sales.  His refusal to cut prices deprives the community of any gain.

[4]Clair Wilcox, *Public Policies toward Business* (Homewood, Ill.: Richard D. Irwin, Inc., 1955), p. 12.

**6**   Suppose a pure monopolist is faced with the demand schedule shown below and the same cost data as the competitive producer discussed in question 6 at the end of

| Price | Quantity demanded | Total revenue | Marginal revenue |
|-------|-------------------|---------------|------------------|
| $100  | 1                 | $ _____     | $ _____        |
| 83    | 2                 | _____       | _____          |
| 71    | 3                 | _____       | _____          |
| 63    | 4                 | _____       | _____          |
| 55    | 5                 | _____       | _____          |
| 48    | 6                 | _____       | _____          |
| 42    | 7                 | _____       | _____          |
| 37    | 8                 | _____       | _____          |
| 33    | 9                 | _____       | _____          |
| 29    | 10                | _____       |                  |

Chapter 26.  Calculate total and marginal revenue and determine the profit-maximizing price and output for this monopolist.  What is the level of profits?  Verify your answer graphically and by comparing total revenue and total cost.  If this firm could engage in perfect price discrimination, that is, if it could charge each buyer the maximum acceptable price, what would be the level of profits?

**7**   Explain verbally and graphically how price (rate) regulation may improve the performance of monopolies.  What is the "dilemma of regulation"?

**8**   How does the demand curve faced by a purely monopolistic seller differ from that confronting a purely competitive firm?  Why does it differ?  Of what significance is the difference?  Why is the pure monopolist's demand curve not perfectly inelastic?

**9**   Assume a pure monopolist and a purely competitive firm have the same unit costs. Contrast the two with respect to **a.** price, **b.** output, **c.** profits, **d.** allocation of resources, and **e.** impact upon the distribution of income.  Since both monopolists and competitive firms follow the MC = MR rule in maximizing profits, how do you account for the different results?

**10**   No seller—not even a pure monopolist—will want to find itself in that range of its demand curve where demand is inelastic.  Can you explain why?

**11**   Assume a monopolistic publisher has agreed to pay an author 15 percent of the total revenue from the sales of a text.  Will the author and the publisher want to charge the same price for the text?  Explain.

## Selected References

Adams, Walter (ed.):*The Structure of American Industry,* 5th ed. (New York: The Macmillan Company, 1977), chaps. 9, 11.

Cox, Eli P.: "A Case for Price Discrimination," *Business Topics* (Michigan State University), Summer 1975, pp. 39–46.

Koch, James V.: *Microeconomic Theory and Applications* (Boston: Little, Brown and Company, 1976), chap. 9.

McKenzie, Richard B.: *Economic Issues in Public Policies* (New York: McGraw-Hill Book Company, 1980), chap. 5.

Robinson, E. A. G.: *Monopoly* (London: Nesbit and Company, 1941).

Schumpeter, Joseph A.: *Capitalism, Socialism, and Democracy,* 3d ed. (New York: Harper & Row, Publishers, Incorporated, 1950), chaps. 7, 8.

Weiss, Leonard W.: *Case Studies in American Industry,* 3d ed. (New York: John Wiley & Sons, 1980), chap. 3.

# LAST WORD
## Monopoly in Professional Basketball

Dr. Roger G. Noll analyzes monopoly pricing by professional basketball teams.

Basketball teams are organized into leagues which grant each club a franchise to provide its services in a designated geographic area. The franchise is a valuable economic asset because it not only gives the club the right to operate in an area, but grants it the privilege of being the sole provider of the service there. Thus, if anybody in the city wishes to see a live [professional] basketball game, he must buy it from the franchisee, or not at all. . . .

In the area of providing professional sports contests, we have in fact turned such monopoly power over to private interests to handle as they wish. . . .

One consequence of uncontrolled monopoly rights is monopoly pricing. In a competitive industry, prices tend to converge to the point where they equal the incremental [marginal] costs of providing one more consumer with output from the industry. If prices are above incremental costs, some firms will expand output or enter the industry in response to the potential for profit. This expansion will lower prices until costs and price fall into rough equality. If prices are below incremental costs, some firms will cut back on output or leave the industry to avoid losses on sales. In a noncompetitive market, the expansion of output to equate prices and incremental costs does not occur, for the monopolist can earn higher profits if prices are above—and output level below—the competitive level.

In basketball, the incremental cost of serving an additional spectator is almost solely the cost of improving team quality. [Data show that] improving the record of the team 10-percent increases attendance by 47,000 persons. And the teams who have done relatively better in winning games over the past few years, winning around 60 to 70 percent of their games, normally pay $10,000 to $20,000 more per player than average. This translates roughly to a cost of about $125,000 to increase attendance by 50,000. Since other costs—ushers, extra publicity, maintenance—are likely to be relatively small, the incremental cost of providing a live basketball game to an additional fan is certainly under $3, and probably not much above $2.50. However, [average ticket price is $4.50 and] many arenas have no seats at all priced as low as $2.50, the true incremental cost.

The preceding analysis indicates the following characterization of basketball operations. First, the handful of lucrative franchises exercise their full monopoly powers by charging very high prices. Then because the monopoly revenues in these cities are not significantly shared with other teams, the remaining borderline and losing franchises are also forced to charge monopoly prices to minimize losses. The result is a pricing structure that excludes many fans who are willing to pay the true incremental cost of letting them view a game. Yet, such pricing still does not prevent widespread financial losses . . . because the monopoly profits are retained by a small group of rich franchises.

Basketball has gone to the extreme of creating monopoly franchises and charging monopoly prices, but without equalization of the monopoly revenues to make the leagues economically viable. From the point of view of the fans, this is the worst possible arrangement. His own ticket prices are higher than the costs of providing him with the service, but the extra revenues he pays are not used to improve the financial position of weak teams and thereby make competition more even. Consequently, fans in the cities with poorer teams are, and will continue to be, faced with the unattractive alternatives of having no team at all or having a very highly priced poor team. . . . [they] also face high prices, and they can watch good teams—but they must watch their good teams play a large number of games against unnecessarily weak opposition because the very high profits of their own team are not shared.

From *Professional Basketball,* Hearings before the Subcommittee on Antitrust and Monopoly of the Committee on the Judiciary, U.S. Senate, 92d Congress, 1st Session, Washington, 1971, pp. 389–390, abridged.

# Price and Output Determination: Monopolistic Competition

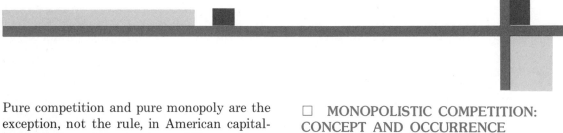

# chapter 28

Pure competition and pure monopoly are the exception, not the rule, in American capitalism. Most market structures fall somewhere between these two extremes. In Chapter 29 we shall discuss oligopoly, a market structure which stands close to pure monopoly. In the present chapter we are concerned with monopolistic competition. Monopolistic competition correctly suggests a blending of monopoly and competition; more specifically, monopolistic competition involves a very considerable amount of competition with a small dose of monopoly power intermixed.

Our basic objectives in this chapter are:

**1** To define and discuss the nature and prevalence of monopolistic competition.

**2** To analyze and evaluate the price-output behavior of monopolistically competitive firms.

**3** To explain and assess the role of nonprice competition, that is, competition based upon product quality and advertising, in monopolistically competitive industries.

□ **MONOPOLISTIC COMPETITION: CONCEPT AND OCCURRENCE**

First of all, let us recall, and also expand upon, the definition of monopolistic competition.

△ **Relatively Large Numbers**

Monopolistic competition refers to that market situation in which a relatively large number of small producers or suppliers are offering similar but not identical products. The contrasts between this and pure competition are important. Monopolistic competition does not require the presence of hundreds or thousands of firms but only a fairly large number—say 25, 35, 60, or 70.

Several important characteristics of monopolistic competition follow from the presence of relatively large numbers. In the first place, each firm has a comparatively small percentage of the total market, so each has a very limited amount of control over market price. Then too, the presence of a relatively large number of firms also ensures that collusion—concerted action by the firms to restrict output and rig price—is all but impossible. Finally, with numerous firms in the industry, there is no feeling of mutual interdependence among them; that is, each firm determines its policies without considering the possible reactions of rival firms. And this is a very reasonable way to act in a market in which one's rivals are very numerous. After all, the 10 or 15 percent increase in sales which firm X may realize by cutting price will be spread so thinly over its 20, 40, or 60 rivals that, for all practical purposes, the impact upon their sales will be imperceptible. Rivals' reactions can be ignored because the impact of one firm's actions upon each of its many rivals is so small that these rivals will have no reason to react.

△  **Product Differentiation**

Also in contrast to pure competition, monopolistic competition has the fundamental feature of *product differentiation.* Purely competitive firms produce a standardized product; monopolistically competitive producers turn out variations of a given product. A number of firms produce cosmetics, but the product of each differs from its rivals in one or more respects. Indeed, it must be emphasized that product differentiation has more dimensions than are immediately apparent. "Real," or physical, differences involving functional features, materials, design, and workmanship are obviously important aspects of product differentiation. But "imaginary" differences created through advertising, packaging, and the use of trademarks and brand names can be equally significant. Finally, the conditions of sale make for differentiation; the location of a store, the courteousness of its clerks, the firm's reputation for servicing its products, and the availability of credit are all facets of product differentiation.

The significance of product differentiation is basically twofold. On the one hand, despite the presence of a relatively large number of firms, monopolistically competitive producers do have limited amounts of control over the prices of their products because of differentiation. Consumers have preferences for the products of specific sellers and *within limits* will pay a higher price to satisfy those preferences. Sellers and buyers are no longer linked at random, as in a purely competitive market. On the other hand, product differentiation adds a new and complicating factor to our analysis: *nonprice competition.* Because products are differentiated, it can be supposed that they can be varied over time and that the differentiating features of each firm's product will be susceptible to advertising and other forms of sales promotion. In a monopolistically competitive market, economic rivalry centers not only upon price but also upon product variation and product promotion.

△  **Entry Conditions**

Entry into monopolistically competitive industries tends to be relatively easy. The fact that monopolistically competitive producers are typically small-sized firms, both absolutely and relatively, suggests that economies of scale and capital requirements are few. On the other hand, as compared with pure competition, there may be some added financial barriers posed by the need for deriving a product different from one's rivals and the obligation to advertise that product. Existing firms may hold patents on their products and copyrights on their brand names and trademarks, enhancing the difficulty and cost of successfully imitating them.

In short, monopolistic competition refers to industries that comprise a relatively large number of firms, operating noncollusively, in the production of differentiated products. Nonprice competition accompanies price competition. Ease of entry makes for competition by new firms in the long run.

△  **Illustrations**

Table 28-1 lists a group of manufacturing industries which approximate monopolistic competition. In addition, retail stores in metropolitan areas are generally monopolistically

**TABLE 28-1**
Percentage of Output* Produced by Firms in Selected Low-Concentration
Manufacturing Industries

| Industry | Four largest firms | Eight largest firms | Twenty largest firms |
|---|---|---|---|
| Book publishing | 19% | 31% | 56% |
| Men's and boys' suits and coats | 19 | 31 | 48 |
| Costume jewelry | 17 | 27 | 41 |
| Upholstered furniture | 14 | 23 | 36 |
| Wood furniture | 14 | 22 | 40 |
| Metal house furniture | 13 | 24 | 44 |
| Women's and misses' suits and coats | 13 | 18 | 26 |
| Paperboard boxes | 11 | 17 | 31 |
| Fur goods | 7 | 12 | 23 |
| Concrete block and brick | 5 | 18 | 24 |

*As measured by value of shipments. Data are for 1972.
*Source:* Bureau of the Census, *1972 Census of Manufacturers.*

competitive; grocery stores, gasoline stations, barber shops, dry cleaners, clothing stores, and so forth, operate under conditions similar to those we have described.

## ☐ PRICE AND OUTPUT DETERMINATION

Let us now analyze the price-output behavior of a monopolistically competitive firm. To facilitate this task we assume initially that the firms in the industry are producing *given* products and are engaging in a *given* amount of promotional activity. Later we shall note how product variation and advertising modify our discussion.

### △ The Firm's Demand Curve

Our explanation is couched in terms of Figure 28-1a. The basic feature of this diagram, which sets it off from our analyses of pure competition and pure monopoly, is the elasticity of the firm's individual demand, or sales, curve. The demand curve faced by a monopolistically competitive seller is highly, but not perfectly, elastic. It is much more elastic than the demand curve of the pure

monopolist, because the monopolistically competitive seller is faced with a relatively large number of rivals producing close-substitute goods. The pure monopolist, of course, has no rivals at all. Yet, for two reasons, the monopolistically competitive seller's sales curve is not perfectly elastic as is the purely competitive producer's: First, the monopolistically competitive firm has fewer rivals, and secondly, the products of these rivals are close but not perfect substitutes.

Generally speaking, the precise degree of elasticity embodied in the monopolistically competitive firm's demand curve will depend upon the exact number of rivals and the degree of product differentiation. The larger the number of rivals and the weaker the product differentiation, the greater will be the elasticity of each seller's demand curve, that is, the closer the situation will be to pure competition.

### △ The Short Run: Profits or Losses

The firm will maximize its profits or minimize its losses in the short run by producing that output designated by the intersection of marginal cost and marginal revenue, for reasons with which we are now familiar. The

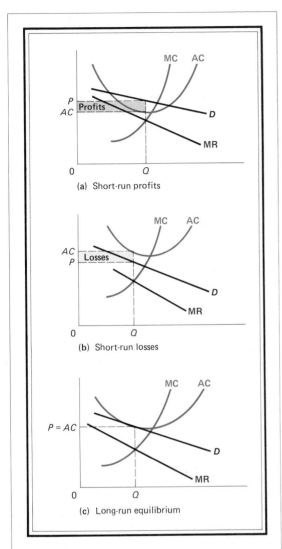

FIGURE 28-1 MONOPOLISTICALLY COMPETITIVE
FIRMS TEND TO REALIZE A NORMAL PROFIT IN
THE LONG RUN

The economic profits shown in (a) will induce new firms
to enter, causing the profits to be competed away. The
losses indicated in (b) will cause an exodus of firms until
normal profits are restored. Thus in (c), where price
just covers unit costs at the MR = MC output, the firm's
long-run equilibrium position is portrayed.

cated in orange. But a less favorable cost and
demand situation may exist, putting the monopolistically competitive firm in the position
of realizing losses in the short run. This is
illustrated by the light blue area in Figure
28-1*b*. In the short run the monopolistically
competitive firm may either realize an economic profit or be faced with losses.

△   **The Long Run: Break-Even**

In the long run, however, the tendency is
for monopolistically competitive firms to earn
a normal profit, that is, to break even. In the
short-run profits case, Figure 28-1*a*, we can
expect the economic profits to attract new
rivals, because entry is relatively easy. As new
firms enter, the demand curve faced by the
typical firm will fall (shift to the left) and
become more elastic. Why? Because each firm
has a smaller share of the total demand and
now faces a larger number of close-substitute
products. This in turn tends to cause the dis-
appearance of economic profits. When the
demand curve is tangent to the average-cost
curve at the profit-maximizing output, as
shown in Figure 28-1*c*, the firm is just breaking
even. Output $Q$ is the equilibrium output for
the firm; as Figure 28-1*c* clearly indicates, any
deviation from that output will entail average
costs which exceed product price and, therefore, losses for the firm. Furthermore, economic profits have been competed away, and
there is no incentive for more firms to enter. In
the short-run losses case, Figure 28-1*b*, we can
expect an exodus of firms to occur in the long
run. Faced with fewer substitute products and
blessed with an expanded share of total demand, surviving firms will find that their losses
disappear and gradually give way to approximately normal profits.[1]

Note that we have been very careful to say
that the representative firm in a monopolistically competitive market *tends* to break even

representative firm of Figure 28-1*a* produces an
output $Q$, charges a price $P$, and is fortunate
enough to realize a total profit of the size indi-

[1] For simplicity's sake we assume constant costs; shifts in
the cost curves as firms enter or leave would complicate
our discussion slightly, but would not alter the conclusions.

in the long run. There are certain complicating factors which prevent us from being more dogmatic. First, some firms may achieve a measure of product differentiation which cannot be duplicated by rivals even over a long span of time. A given gasoline station may have the only available location at the busiest intersection in town. Or a firm may hold a patent which gives it a slight and more-or-less permanent advantage over imitators. Such firms may realize a sliver of economic profits even in the long run. Second, remember that entry is not completely unrestricted. Because of product differentiation, there are likely to be greater financial barriers to entry than otherwise would be the case. This again suggests that some economic profits may persist even in the long run. A third consideration may work in the opposite direction, causing losses— below-normal profits—to persist in the long run. The proprietors of a corner delicatessen persistently accept a return less than they could earn elsewhere, because their business is a way of life to them. The suburban barber ekes out a meager existence, because cutting hair is "all he wants to do." With all things considered, however, the long-run profitless equilibrium of Figure 28-1c is probably a reasonable portrayal of reality.

## □ WASTES OF MONOPOLISTIC COMPETITION

Recalling our evaluation of competitive pricing in Chapter 26, we know that economic efficiency requires the triple equality of price, marginal cost, and average cost. The equality of price and marginal cost is necessary for a correct allocation of resources to the product. The equality of price with minimum average total cost suggests the use of the most efficient (least-cost) technology; this equality means that consumers will enjoy the largest volume of product and the lowest price which prevailing cost conditions will allow.

An examination of Figure 28-1c suggests that the monopolistic element in monopolistic competition causes a modest underallocation of resources to goods produced under this market structure. Price exceeds marginal cost in long-run equilibrium, thereby indicating that society values additional units of this commodity more than the alternative products which the needed resources can otherwise produce.

Furthermore, in contrast to purely competitive firms, as suggested in Figure 28-1c, monopolistically competitive firms produce somewhat short of the most efficient (least unit cost) output. Production entails higher unit costs than the minimum attainable. This in turn means a somewhat higher price than would result under pure competition. Consumers do *not* benefit from the largest output and lowest price which cost conditions permit. Indeed, monopolistically competitive firms must charge a higher than competitive price in the long run in order to manage a normal profit. Looked at differently, if each firm were able to produce at the most efficient output, a smaller number of firms could produce the same total output, and the product could be sold to consumers at a lower price. Monopolistically competitive industries tend to be overcrowded with firms, each of which is underutilized, that is, operating short of optimum capacity. This is typified by many kinds of retail establishments, for example, the thirty or forty gasoline stations, all operating short of capacity, that populate a medium-sized city. Underutilized plants, consumers penalized through higher than competitive prices for this underutilization, and producers just making a normal return in the long run—these are the so-called "wastes" of monopolistic competition.

But we must not be hypercritical of monopolistic competition. Some economists argue that in many monopolistically competitive industries the price and output results are not drastically different from those of pure competition. The highly elastic nature of each firm's demand curve guarantees that the results are nearly competitive. Furthermore, it must be kept in mind that any deviations from the purely competitive output and price may be offset by the fact that with monopolistic competition the consumer now can choose from among a number of variations of the product; he or she is not faced with a homogeneous commodity.

## ☐ NONPRICE COMPETITION

For reasons cited above, we can conclude that the situation portrayed in Figure 28-1c may not be the most beneficial to society. It can also be surmised that it is not very satisfying to the monopolistically competitive producer which barely captures a normal profit for its efforts. We can therefore expect monopolistically competitive producers to take steps to improve upon the long-run equilibrium position. But how can this be accomplished? The answer lies in product differentiation. Each firm has a product which is currently distinguishable in some more-or-less tangible way from those of its rivals. The product is presumably subject to further variation, that is, to product development. Then, too, the emphasis upon real product differences and the creation of imaginary differences may be achieved through advertising and related sales promotion. In short, the profit-realizing firm of Figure 28-1a is loath to stand by and watch new competitors encroach upon its profits by duplicating or imitating its product, copying its advertising, and matching its services to consumers. Rather, the firm will attempt to sustain these profits and stay ahead of competitors through further product development and by enhancing the quantity and quality of advertising. In this way it might prevent the long-run tendency of Figure 28-1c from becoming a reality. True, product development and advertising will add to the firm's costs. But they can also be expected to increase the demand for its product. If demand increases by more than enough to compensate for development and promotional costs, the firm will have improved its profit position. As Figure 28-1c suggests, the firm may have little or no

prospect of increasing profits by price cutting. So why not practice nonprice competition?

## △ Product Differentiation and Product Development

The likelihood that easy entry will promote product variety and product improvement is possibly a redeeming feature of monopolistic competition which may offset, wholly or in part, the "wastes" associated with this market structure. There are really two somewhat distinct considerations here: (1) product differentiation at a point in time, and (2) product improvement over a period of time.

**1   Differentiation**   Product differentiation means that at any point in time the consumer will be offered a wide range of types, styles, brands, and quality gradations of any given product. Compared with the situation under pure competition, this correctly suggests possible advantages to the consumer. The range of free choice is widened, and variations and shadings of consumer tastes are more fully met by producers. But skeptics warn that product differentiation is not an unmixed blessing. Product proliferation may reach the point where the consumer becomes confused and rational choice is then rendered time-consuming and difficult. Variety may add spice to the consumer's life, but only up to a point. Worse yet, some observers fear that the consumer, faced with a myriad of similar products, may rely upon such a dubious expedient as judging product quality by price; that is, the consumer may irrationally assume that price is necessarily an index of product quality.

**2   Development**   Product competition is an important avenue of technological innovation and product betterment over a period of time. Such product development may be cumulative in two different senses. (a) A successful product improvement by one firm obligates rivals to imitate or, if they can, improve upon this firm's temporary market advantage or suffer the penalty of losses. (b) Profits realized from a successful product improvement can be used to finance further improvements. Again, however, there are notable criticisms of the product development which may occur under monopolistic competition. Critics point out that many product alterations are more apparent than real, consisting of frivolous and superficial changes in the product which do not improve its durability, efficiency, or usefulness. A more exotic container, bright packaging, or "shuffling the chrome" is frequently the focal point for product development. It is argued, too, that particularly in the cases of durable and semidurable consumer goods, development seems to follow a pattern of "planned obsolescence," wherein firms improve their product only by that amount necessary to make the average consumer dissatisfied with last year's model.

Do the advantages of product differentiation, properly discounted, outweigh the "wastes" of monopolistic competition? It is difficult to say, short of examining specific cases; and even then, concrete conclusions are difficult to come by.

△  **Advertising**

A monopolistically competitive producer may gain at least a temporary edge on rivals by manipulating the product. The same result may be achieved by manipulating the consumer through advertising and sales promotion. While product differentiation adapts the product to consumer demand, advertising adapts consumer demand to the product.

There is considerable controversy as to the economic and social desirability of advertising. This controversy is not an unimportant one. Currently, advertising and promotional expenditures in the United States were estimated to be $44 billion in 1978. This exceeded the amount all state and local governments spent on public welfare. Hence, if advertising is generally wasteful, any potential virtues of monopolistically competitive markets are thereby dimmed, and the need for corrective public policies is indicated. Let us survey the basic claims for and the charges against advertising.

**The Case for Advertising**  Some of the arguments in favor of advertising follow:

**1**  Advertising allegedly provides the information which assists consumers in making rational choices. In a dynamic, complex economy there is an acute need for the consumer to be closely acquainted with new firms, new products, and improvements in existing products. Advertising is the medium which disperses such information.

**2**  Advertising supports national communications. Radio, television, magazines, and newspapers are financed in part through advertising.

**3**  Advertising is said to be a stimulant to product development. Successful advertising is frequently based upon unique and advantageous features of a firm's product. Hence, a firm is obligated to improve its product to provide "sales points" for competing successfully in the advertising sphere.

**4**  Through successful advertising a firm can expand its production and thereby realize greater economies of scale. As shown in Figure 28-2, by shifting the firm's demand curve to the right through advertising, production will expand from, say, $Q_1$ to $Q_2$. Despite the fact that advertising outlays will shift the firm's average-cost curve upward, unit costs will nevertheless decline from, say, $AC_1$ to $AC_2$. Greater productive efficiency resulting from economies of scale more than offsets the increase in unit costs due to advertising. Consumers will therefore get the product at a lower price with advertising than they would in its absence.

**5**  It is held that advertising is a force which promotes competition. By providing information about a wide variety of substitute products, advertising tends to diminish monopoly power. In fact, intensive advertising is frequently associated with the introduction of new products designed to compete with existing brands.

**6**  Advertising allegedly promotes full employment by inducing high levels of consumer spending. This is particularly crucial, it is argued, in a wealthy society such as ours, where much of total production takes the form

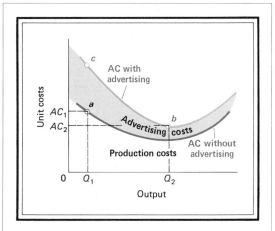

**FIGURE 28-2 THE POSSIBLE EFFECTS OF ADVERTISING UPON A FIRM'S OUTPUT AND AVERAGE COSTS**

Proponents of advertising contend that resulting economies of scale will expand the firm's production from, say, $a$ to $b$ and lower unit costs as economies of scale are realized. Some critics argue that advertising is more likely to increase costs and leave output largely unchanged, as is suggested by the movement from $a$ to $c$.

of luxury or semiluxury goods which fulfill no basic wants. One need not advertise to sell food to a hungry man, but advertising and sales promotion are essential in persuading families that they need a second car, a video recorder, or an automatic dishwasher. Stability in an opulent society calls for want-creating activities—in particular, advertising—or high levels of production and employment will not be sustainable.

**The Case against Advertising** Some of the arguments on the other side of the picture allegedly "debunk" the claims for advertising; others raise new points.

**1** Critics of advertising point out that the basic objective of advertising is to persuade, not to inform. Competitive advertising is based upon misleading and extravagant claims which confuse and frequently insult the intelligence of consumers, not enlighten them. Indeed, advertising may well persuade consumers in some cases to pay high prices for much-acclaimed but inferior products, forgoing better but unadvertised products selling at lower prices.

**2** Advertising expenditures as such are relatively unproductive; they add little or nothing to the well-being of society. Advertising diverts human and property resources from other more pressing areas. For example, lumber which is sorely needed in the production of housing is squandered on the construction of unsightly billboards. In short, advertising constitutes an inefficient use of scarce resources.

**3** Significant external costs are entailed by advertising. Billboards blot out roadside scenery and generally debase the countryside. Sound trucks disrupt suburban serenity. Of potentially greater importance are the effects which advertising's support of national communications may have upon the accuracy and quality of those communications. Will a newspaper present an unprejudiced report of the labor dispute in which its major advertiser is involved? Will a television newscast conveniently ignore the fact that antitrust action has been initiated against its sponsor?

**4** Much advertising tends to be self canceling. The million-dollar advertising campaign of one cigarette manufacturer is largely offset by equally expensive campaigns waged by its rivals. Few additional people smoke cigarettes. Each firm has about the same portion of the market as it had originally. And the cost, and therefore the price, of cigarettes is higher. In Figure 28-2 self-canceling advertising may move the firm from point $a$ to point $c$, not from $a$ to $b$.

**5** It is claimed that advertising promotes the growth of monopoly. On the one hand, extensive advertising creates financial barriers to entry and thereby intensifies the market power which firms already possess. This is held to be the case in the tobacco industry, where producers as a group may spend considerably in excess of $650 million per year on advertising and related promotional activities. The three major auto manufacturers—GM, Ford, and Chrysler—currently spend about $665 million for advertising per year. Furthermore, by creating brand loyalties, consumers become less responsive to price cutting by competitors, thereby enhancing the monopoly power possessed by the firm which is advertising its product.

**6**   Most economists are reluctant to accept advertising as an important determinant of the levels of output and employment. There has been little evidence of economic stagnation in the post-World War II years that would seem remediable by advertising and promotional outlays. Furthermore, the most volatile aspect of aggregate demand is not so much highly advertised consumer goods as it is little-advertised investment goods. The argument has also been made that advertising expenditures are procyclical, that is, they fluctuate *with* total spending, intensifying unemployment during bad times and adding to inflationary pressures during prosperous times.

### △   Empirical Evidence

Evidence on the economic effects of advertising is mixed. Such studies are usually plagued by data problems and difficulties in determining cause and effect. Suppose it is found that firms which do a great deal of advertising seem to have considerable monopoly power and large profits. Does this mean that advertising creates barriers to entry which in turn generate monopoly power and profits? Or do entry barriers associated with factors quite remote from advertising cause monopoly profits which in turn allow firms to spend lavishly in advertising their products? Given these difficulties, let us survey several conflicting studies.

Comanor and Wilson have recently examined the role of advertising in forty-one industries manufacturing consumer goods and reached the general conclusion that advertising is anticompetitive. Specifically, they report that "the heavy volume of advertising expenditures in some industries serves as an important barrier to new competition in the markets

served by these industries."[2] The prices of the heavily advertised goods exceed their marginal costs, reflecting a misallocation of resources. Furthermore, for many of the studied industries expenditures for advertising were found to be "excessive" and wasteful of scarce resources.

Other studies suggest that advertising enhances competition and has economically desirable results. For example, a study of the eyeglasses industry compared prices in states where professional codes of ethics permitted optometrists to advertise with those where codes prohibited or restricted advertising. The conclusion was that prices of eyeglasses were from 25 to 40 percent higher in states where advertising was restricted.[3] A similar study of retail drug prices, comparing states where advertising was permitted with those in which it was not, found that prescription drug prices were about 5 percent lower in states which permitted advertising.[4] Finally, a study of the toy industry yielded the conclusion that television advertising had the effect of bringing about substantial price reductions.

> Advertising cuts distribution margins on advertised brands for two reasons: *first,* advertising causes goods to turn over rapidly so they can be sold profitably with smaller markups; and *second,* advertising creates product identity—which, in differentiated products, permits the public to compare prices between stores, thus setting a limit on the retailer's freedom to mark up. Products which are both heavily advertised and are fast sellers will be pulled through the distribution channels with the lowest markups of all.[5]

---

[2] William S. Comanor and Thomas A. Wilson, *Advertising and Market Power* (Cambridge, Mass.: Harvard University Press, 1974), p. 239.
[3] Lee and Alexandra Benham, "Regulating Through the Professions: A Perspective on Information Control," *Journal of Law and Economics,* October 1975, pp. 421–447.
[4] John F. Cady, *Restricted Advertising and Competition: The Case of Retail Drugs* (Washington, D.C.: American Enterprise Institute, 1976).
[5] Robert L. Steiner, "Does Advertising Lower Consumer Prices?" *Journal of Marketing,* October 1973, p. 21.

### △ Monopolistic Competition and Economic Analysis

Our discussion of nonprice competition correctly implies that the equilibrium situation of a monopolistically competitive firm is actually much more complex than the previous graphic analysis indicates. Figure 28-1*a, b,* and *c assume* a given product and a given level of advertising expenditures. But we now know these are not given in practice. The monopolistically competitive firm must actually juggle three variable considerations—price, product, and promotion—in seeking maximum profits. What specific variety of product, selling at what price, and supplemented by what level of promotional activity, will result in the greatest level of profits attainable? This complex situation is not readily expressed in a simple, meaningful economic model. At best we can note that each possible combination of price, product, and promotion poses a different demand and cost (production plus promotion) situation for the firm, some one of which will allow it maximum profits. In practice, this optimum combination cannot be readily forecast but must be sought by the process of trial and error. And even here, certain limitations may be imposed by the actions of rivals. A firm may not risk the elimination of advertising expenditures for fear its share of the market will decline sharply, to the benefit of its rivals who do advertise. Similarly, patents held by rivals will rule out certain desirable product variations.

## Summary

**1**  The distinguishing features of monopolistic competition are: *a.* There is a large enough number of firms so that each has little control over price, mutual interdependence is absent, and collusion is virtually impossible; *b.* products are characterized by real and imaginary differences and by varying conditions surrounding their sale; and *c.* entry to the industry is relatively easy. Many aspects of retailing, and some industries wherein economies of scale are few, approximate monopolistic competition.

**2**  Monopolistically competitive firms may earn economic profits or incur losses in the short run. The easy entry and exodus of firms give rise to a long-run tendency for them to earn a normal profit.

**3**  The long-run equilibrium position of the monopolistically competitive producer is less socially desirable than that of a purely competitive firm. Under monopolistic competition, price exceeds marginal cost, suggesting an underallocation of resources to the product, and price exceeds minimum average total cost, indicating that consumers do not get the product at the lowest price which cost conditions would allow. However, because the firm's demand curve is highly elastic, these "wastes" of monopolistic competition should not be overemphasized.

**4**  Product differentiation provides a means by which monopolistically competitive firms can offset the long-run tendency for economic profits to approximate zero. Through product development and advertising outlays, a firm may strive to increase the demand for its product more than nonprice competition increases its costs.

**5**  Although subject to certain dangers and problems, product differentiation affords the consumer a greater variety of products at any point in time and improved products over time. Whether these features fully compensate for the "wastes" of monopolistic competition is a moot question.

6  There is sharp disagreement as to the economic benefits of advertising.  Proponents justify advertising on the grounds that it *a.* aids consumers in exercising rational choices, *b.* supports national communications, *c.* speeds product development, *d.* permits firms to realize economies of scale, *e.* promotes competition, and *f.* encourages spending and a high level of employment.  Critics assert that advertising *a.* confuses rather than informs, *b.* misallocates resources away from more urgent employments, *c.* involves a variety of external costs, *d.* results in higher, not lower, costs and prices, *e.* promotes monopoly, and *f.* is not a strategic determinant of spending and employment.

7  In practice the monopolistic competitor seeks that specific combination of price, product, and promotion which will maximize its profits.

## Questions and Study Suggestions

1  Key terms and concepts to remember: monopolistic competition; product differentiation; wastes of monopolistic competition; nonprice competition.

2  How does monopolistic competition differ from pure competition?  From pure monopoly?  Explain fully what product differentiation entails.

3  Compare the elasticity of the monopolistically competitive producer's demand curve with that of *a.* a pure competitor, and *b.* a pure monopolist.  Assuming identical long-run costs, compare graphically the prices and output which would result under pure competition and monopolistic competition.  Explain: "Monopolistically competitive industries are characterized by too many firms, each of which produces too little."

4  "Monopolistic competition is monopoly up to the point at which consumers become willing to buy close substitute products and competitive beyond that point."  Explain.

5  "Competition in quality and in service may be quite as effective in giving the buyer more for his money as is price competition."  Do you agree?  Explain why monopolistically competitive firms frequently prefer nonprice to price competition.

6  Critically evaluate and explain:

*a.*  "In monopolistically competitive industries economic profits are competed away in the long run; hence, there is no valid reason to criticize the performance and efficiency of such industries."

*b.*  "Monopolistic competition is merely a way station on the road to oligopoly."

*c.*  "In the long run monopolistic competition leads to a monopolistic price but not to monopolistic profits."

7  Do you agree or disagree with the following statements?  Why?

*a.*  "The amount of advertising which a firm does is likely to vary inversely with the real differences in its product."

*b.*  "If each firm's advertising expenditures merely tend to cancel the effects of its rivals' advertising, it is clearly irrational for these firms to maintain large advertising budgets."

8  Carefully evaluate the two views expressed in the following statements:

*a.*  "It happens every day.  Advertising builds mass demand.  Production goes up—costs come down.  More people can buy—more jobs are created.  These are the ingredients of economic growth.  Each stimulates the next in a cycle of productivity and plenty which constantly creates a better life for you."

*b.*  "Advertising constitutes 'inverted education'—a costly effort to induce people to buy without sufficient thought and deliberation and therefore to buy things they don't need.  Furthermore, advertising intensifies economic instability because advertising outlays vary directly with the level of consumer spending."

Which view do you feel is the more accurate?  Justify your position.

## Selected References

Adams, Walter (ed.): *The Structure of American Industry,* 5th ed. (New York: The Macmillan Company, 1977), chap. 2.

Bain, Joe S.: *Industrial Organization,* 2d ed. (New York: John Wiley & Sons, Inc., 1968), chaps. 7, 8.

Douglas, Edna: *Economics of Marketing* (New York: Harper & Row, Publishers, 1975), chap. 18.

Leftwich, Richard H.: *The Price System and Resource Allocation,* 6th ed. (Hinsdale, Ill.: The Dryden Press, Inc., 1976), chap. 13.

Meyer, Robert A.: *Microeconomic Decisions* (Boston: Houghton Mifflin Company, 1976), chap. 12.

Simon, Julian A.: *Issues in the Economics of Advertising* (Urbana: University of Illinois Press, 1970).

Weiss, Leonard W.: *Case Studies in American Industry,* 3d ed. (New York: John Wiley & Sons, Inc., 1980), chap. 5.

# LAST WORD
## Beer: Trouble Brewing

Some economists feel there is a tendency for monopolistically competitive industries to evolve into oligopoly. The following is a brief case study in accord with this view.

When the United States officially went wet again in 1933, 750 breweries across the country—most of them small, family-owned businesses—eagerly reopened their taps. But although beer consumption has grown from 40 million to 133 million barrels in the intervening 40 years, control of the industry has gradually consolidated into the hands of a few giant companies and the number of U.S. breweries has been drastically reduced to a mere 64. The local brewer seems on a path to extinction.

In Chicago, for instance, there is now only one brewery compared with 32 on the day of repeal. In the East, P. Ballantine & Sons was forced to shut down last year and sell its brand name to Falstaff; Piel Bros. plans to close one of its two breweries this fall and has the other up for sale. In a few years, says William M. O'Shea, head of the Brewers Association of America, "there won't be a dozen breweries left in the country."

Many of the locals, of course, fail simply because of poor management. "Many breweries did not keep up with manufacturing techniques and automation," says an official of Adolph Coors Co., the fourth-largest U.S. brewer and a dominant factor in Western markets. "They weren't fast-thinking enough." But the small brewers say their condition wouldn't be so precarious if it weren't for predatory price-cutting by the majors. The little companies have consistently pushed legal action against the three national giants, Anheuser-Busch, Schlitz and Pabst, which account for 44 per cent of all the beer sold in the U.S.

Whether their price-cutting is legal or not, the big brewers have other overpowering advantages. Their huge advertising expenditures create demand for their beer all over the country, a demand they meet from their strategically placed regional breweries. The only way the locals can compete is with low prices.

If the small beer companies could keep their prices a little below those of the majors, they could coexist. But they are often saddled with old, inefficient plants, and their costs keep rising while the majors keep automating and reducing theirs. "Schlitz in Winston-Salem can make beer and ship it into New York 33 cents a case cheaper than we can make it in Brooklyn," says Richard Fisher, Piel's controller.

All the locals aren't quite ready to surrender. G. Heileman of La Crosse, Wis., for instance, has grown right along with the majors, partly by acquiring other brands such as Blatz, and it is now felt something of a regional power. In the past year, two new beer companies have started up in Florida.

The small brewers also are starting to get some help from state legislatures. A New York law that is going into effect this month is designed to curtail the majors' price-cutting ploys. "But when you solve one problem, others always arise," Howard Jones, president of the New York State Brewers Association, says mournfully. "The big brewers could pour in advertising or hold tremendous sales contests, and put us right back where we were."

Indeed, short of a complete dismemberment of the Big Three, there seems little that can be done to protect most of the locals. John C. Maxwell Jr., a leading beer-industry analyst, concludes: "Today, there is no way for a local brewer to survive unless he gets a grant from the Ford Foundation."

# Price and Output Determination: Oligopoly

chapter 29

In many of our manufacturing, mining, wholesaling, and retailing industries, a few firms are dominant. Such industries are called *oligopolies*. It is with these industries that the present chapter is concerned. Specifically, we have four objectives. We seek first to define oligopoly, assess its occurrence, and note the reasons for its existence. The second and major goal is to survey the possible courses of price-output behavior which oligopolistic industries might follow. Third, the role of nonprice competition, that is, competition on the basis of product development and advertising, in oligopolistic industries is discussed. Next, some comments with respect to the economic efficiency and social desirability of oligopoly are offered. Finally, many of the salient points of the chapter are underscored in a brief case study of the automobile industry.

## ☐ OLIGOPOLY: CONCEPT AND OCCURRENCE

What are the basic characteristics of oligopoly? How frequently is it encountered in our economy? Why has this industry structure developed?

### △ Fewness

The outstanding feature of oligopoly is "fewness." When a relatively small number of firms dominate the market for a good or service, the industry is oligopolistic. But what specifically is meant by "a few" firms? This is necessarily vague, because the market model of oligopoly covers a great deal of ground, ranging from pure monopoly, on the one hand, to monopolistic competition, on the other. Thus oligopoly encompasses the tin-can industry, in which two firms tend to dominate an entire national market, and the situation in which, say; ten or fifteen gasoline stations may enjoy roughly equal shares of the petroleum products market in a medium-sized town. Table 29-1 lists a number of major industries in which fewness is present in varying degrees. This table correctly suggests that the market structure of oligopoly is very common and very important in American capitalism. At the local level, some aspects of the retail trades—particularly in small- and medium-sized towns—are characterized by oligopoly.

Oligopolies may be *homogeneous* or *differentiated;* that is, the firms in an oligopolistic industry may produce standardized or differentiated products. Many industrial products—steel, zinc, copper, aluminum, lead, cement, industrial alcohol, and so forth—are

virtually standardized products in the physical sense and are produced under oligopolistic conditions. Of course, even here slight physical differences may exist, and the service, credit, and speed of delivery may differ between sellers, making for a measure of differentiation. But for most practical purposes these are standardized products. On the other hand, many consumer goods industries—automobiles, tires, typewriters, soap, cigarettes, and a host of electrical appliances—are differentiated oligopolies.

△  **Underlying Causes**

Why are certain industries composed of only a few firms? Specific reasons are manifold, but two related factors—economies of scale and the advantages of merger—are perhaps of greatest importance.

**TABLE 29-1**
Percentage of Output* Produced by Firms in Selected High-Concentration Manufacturing Industries

| Industry | Percentage of industry output produced by first four firms |
|---|---|
| Locomotives and parts | 97 |
| Cellulose fibers | 96 |
| Telephone and telegraph equipment | 94 |
| Primary lead | 93 |
| Motor vehicles | 93 |
| Flat glass | 92 |
| Electric lamps (bulbs) | 90 |
| Turbines and generators | 90 |
| Chewing gum | 87 |
| Cigarettes | 84 |
| Sewing machines | 84 |
| Household laundry equipment | 83 |
| Typewriters | 81 |
| Gypsum products | 80 |
| Primary aluminum | 79 |
| Tires and inner tubes | 73 |
| Metal cans | 66 |
| Soap and detergents | 62 |

*As measured by value of shipments. Data are for 1972.
*Source:* Bureau of the Census, *Concentration Ratios in Manufacturing.*

**Economies of Scale**   We discovered in Chapter 25 that, where economies of scale are substantial (see Figure 25-7a), reasonably efficient production will be possible only with a small number of producers; in other words, efficiency requires that the productive capacity of each firm be large relative to the total market. Indeed, it is an unstable situation for an industry to have a large number of high-cost firms, each of which is failing to realize existing economies of scale. In Figure 25-5, for example, a firm currently operating with the small and inefficient plant size indicated by ATC-1 will recognize that this short-run position is unsatisfactory; it can realize substantially lower unit costs and a larger profit by expanding its plant to ATC-2. The same can be said for the move to ATC-3. However, given a reasonably stable market demand, all the many firms with small (ATC-1) plant sizes cannot now survive. The profitable expansion to larger plant sizes by some will necessarily come at the expense of rivals. The realization of economies of scale by some firms implies that the number of rival producers is simultaneously being reduced through failure or merger.

Historically, what has happened in many industries is that technological progress has made more and more economies of scale attainable over time. Thus many industries started out with a primitive technology, few economies of scale, and a relatively large number of competitors. But then, as technology improved and economies of scale became increasingly pronounced, the less alert or less aggressive firms fell by the wayside and a few producers emerged. For example, estimates suggest that over eighty firms populated the automobile industry in its infancy. Over the years, the development of mass-production techniques reduced the field through failure and combination. Now the Big Three— General Motors, Ford, and Chrysler—account for 98 percent of domestic automobile production.

But why, you may ask, aren't new firms created to enter the automobile industry? The answer, of course, is that to achieve the low unit costs essential to survival, any new entrants must necessarily start out as large producers. This may require hundreds of millions of dollars worth of investment in machinery and equipment alone. Economies of scale can be a formidable barrier to entry. They explain not only the evolution of oligopoly in many industries, but also why such industries are not likely to become more competitive.

We must note that the development or persistence of some oligopolies can be traced at least in part to other entry barriers. In the electronics, chemical, and aluminum industries, the ownership of patents and the control of strategic raw materials have been important. And perhaps prodigious advertising outlays may provide an added financial barrier to entry, as some economists argue has been the case in the cigarette industry. But in general, economies of scale are the dominant barrier in most oligopolies.

**The Urge to Merge**    The second factor in explaining oligopoly or fewness is merger. The motivation for merger has diverse roots. Of

immediate relevance is the fact that the combining of two or more formerly competing firms by merger may increase their market share substantially and enable the new and larger production unit to achieve greater economies of scale. Another significant motive underlying the "urge to merge" is the market power which may accompany merger. A firm that is larger both absolutely and relative to the market may have greater ability to control the market for, and the price of, its product than does a smaller, more competitive producer. Furthermore, the large size which merger entails may give the firm the advantage of being a "big buyer" and permit it to demand and obtain lower prices (costs) from input suppliers than previously.

△  **Mutual Interdependence**

Regardless of the means by which oligopoly evolves, it is clear that rivalry among a small number of firms interjects a new and complicating factor into our discussion: *mutual interdependence.* Imagine three firms, A, B, and C, each of which has about one-third of the market for a particular product. If A cuts price, its share of the market will increase. But B and C will be directly, immediately, and adversely affected by A's price cutting. Hence, we can expect some *reaction* on the part of B and C to A's behavior: B and C may match A's price cut or even undercut A, thereby precipitating a price war. This response correctly suggests that no firm in an oligopolistic industry will dare to alter its price policies without attempting to calculate the most likely reactions of its rivals. To be sure, cost and demand data are important to the oligopolist in establishing price, but to these we must add the reaction of rivals—a highly uncertain factor. The situation faced by oligopolistic producers resembles that of participants in games of strategy, such as poker, bridge, or chess. There is no means of knowing beforehand the best way to play your cards, because this depends upon the way other participants play theirs. Players must pattern their actions according to the actions and expected reactions of rivals.

It is to be emphasized that the mutual interdependence resulting from fewness, and the consequent need for a firm to weigh the possible reactions of rivals in altering its price policy, are unique features of oligopoly. The large number of rivals, which characterizes pure competition and monopolistic competition, and the absence of rivals, which is the earmark of pure monopoly, rule out mutual interdependence in these market structures. Indeed, a good, workable definition of oligopoly is this: Oligopoly exists when the number of firms in an industry is so small that each must consider the reactions of rivals in formulating its price policy.

## ☐ PRICE–OUTPUT BEHAVIOR

The theories of competitive, monopolistic, and monopolistically competitive markets as presented in prior chapters are quite standard and widely accepted segments of microeconomics. But economic analysis offers no standard portrait of oligopoly. In general, there are two major reasons why it is difficult to use formal economic analysis in explaining the price behavior of oligopolies.

**1**  The previously noted fact that oligopoly encompasses many specific market situations works against the development of a single, generalized explanation or model of how an oligopoly determines price and output. Pure competition, monopolistic competition, and pure monopoly all refer to rather clear-cut market arrangements; oligopoly does not. It includes the situation in which two or three firms dominate an entire market as well as the situation in which twelve or fifteen firms compete. It includes both product differentiation and standardization. It encompasses the cases in which firms are acting in collusion and those in which they are not. It embodies the situations in which barriers to entry are very strong and those in which they are not quite so strong. In short, the many breeds, or strains, of oligopoly preclude the development of any

simple market model which provides a general explanation of oligopolistic behavior.

**2**  The element of mutual interdependence which fewness adds to the analysis is a most significant complication. To be specific, the inability of a firm to predict with certainty the reactions of its rivals makes it virtually impossible to estimate the demand and marginal-revenue data faced by an oligopolist. And without such data, firms cannot determine their profit-maximizing price and output even in theory, as we shall presently make clear.

Despite these analytical difficulties, two interrelated characteristics of oligopolistic pricing stand out. On the one hand, oligopolistic prices tend to be inflexible, or "sticky." Prices change less frequently in oligopoly than they do under pure competition, monopolistic competition, and in some instances, pure monopoly. Figure 10-3 provides some interesting data on this point. On the other hand, when oligopolistic prices do change, firms are likely to change their prices together; that is, oligopolistic price behavior suggests the presence of incentives to act in concert or collusively in setting and changing prices.

## ☐ FOUR VARIANTS

To gain insight into oligopoly pricing we will examine four rather distinct models: (1) the kinked demand curve, (2) collusive pricing, (3) price leadership, and (4) cost-plus pricing.

### △ Kinked Demand:
### Noncollusive Oligopoly

Again imagine an oligopolistic industry comprised of just three firms, A, B, and C, each having about one-third of the total market for a differentiated product. Assume the firms are "independent" in the sense that they do not engage in collusive practices in setting prices. Suppose, too, that the going price for firm A's product is $QP$ and its current sales are $Q$, as shown in Figure 29-1. Now the question is, "What does the firm's demand, or sales, curve look like?" We have just noted that mutual interdependence, and the uncertainty of rivals' reactions which interdependence entails, make this question difficult to answer. The location and shape of an oligopolist's demand curve depend upon how the firm's rivals will react to a price change introduced by A. There are two plausible assumptions about the reactions of A's rivals with which we might experiment.

**Match or Ignore?**  One possibility is that firms B and C will exactly match any price change initiated by A. In this case, A's demand and marginal-revenue curves will look something like $D_1D_1$ and $MR_1MR_1$ in Figure 29-1. (Ignore the $MC_1$ and $MC_2$ curves for the moment.) If A cuts price, its sales will increase very modestly, because its two rivals will follow suit and thereby prevent A from gaining any price advantage over them. The small increase in sales which A (and its two rivals) will realize is at the expense of other industries; A will gain no sales from B and C. If A raises the going price, its sales will fall only modestly. Why? Because B and C match its price increase, so A does not price itself out of the market. The industry now loses some sales to other industries, but A loses no customers to B and C.

The other obvious possibility is that firms B and C will simply ignore any price change invoked by A. In this case, the demand and marginal-revenue curves faced by A will resemble $D_2D_2$ and $MR_2MR_2$ in Figure 29-1. The demand curve in this case is considerably more elastic than under the assumption that B and C will match A's price changes. The reasons are clear. If A lowers its price and its rivals do not, A will gain sales sharply at the expense of its two rivals because it will obviously be underselling them. Conversely, if A raises price and its rivals do not, A will be pricing itself out of the market and will lose many customers to B and C, which are now underselling it. Because of product differentiation, however, A's sales do not fall to zero when it raises price; some of A's customers will

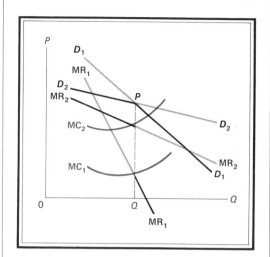

**FIGURE 29-1  THE KINKED DEMAND CURVE**

The nature of a noncollusive oligopolist's demand and marginal-revenue curves will depend upon whether its rivals will match ($D_1D_1$ and $MR_1MR_1$) or ignore ($D_2D_2$ and $MR_2MR_2$) any price changes which it may initiate from the current price $QP$. In all likelihood an oligopolist's rivals will ignore a price increase but follow a price cut. This causes the oligopolist's demand curve to be kinked (dark blue $D_2PD_1$) and his marginal-revenue curve to have a vertical break, or gap (dark blue $MR_2MR_1$). Furthermore, because any shift in marginal costs between $MC_1$ and $MC_2$ will cut the vertical (dashed) segment of the marginal-revenue curve, no change in either price $QP$ or output $Q$ will occur.

pay the higher price because they have strong preferences for A's product.

Now, which is the most logical assumption for A to make as to how its rivals will react to any price change it might initiate? The answer is "some of each"! Common sense and observation of oligopolistic industries suggest that price declines will be matched as a firm's competitors act to prevent the price cutter from taking their customers, but that price increases will be ignored, because rivals of the price-increasing firm stand to gain the business lost by the price booster. In other words, the dark blue $D_2P$ segment of the "rivals ignore" demand curve seems relevant for price increases, and the dark blue $PD_1$ segment of the "rivals follow" demand curve is more realistic for price cuts. It is logical, or at least a good guess, that an oligopolist's demand curve is "kinked" on the order of the dark blue $D_2PD_1$. The curve is highly elastic above the going price, but much less elastic or even inelastic below the current price. Note also that if it is correct to suppose that rivals will follow a price cut but ignore an increase, the marginal-revenue curve of the oligopolist will also have an odd shape. It, too, will be made up of two segments—the dark blue part of the marginal-revenue curve appropriate to $D_1D_1$ and the dark blue chunk of the marginal-revenue curve appropriate to $D_2D_2$. Because of the sharp differences in elasticity of demand above and below the going price, there occurs a gap, or what we can treat as a vertical segment, in the marginal-revenue curve. In Figure 29-1 the marginal-revenue curve is shown by the two dark blue lines connected by the dotted vertical segment, or gap.

**Price Inflexibility**  This analysis is important in that it goes far to explain why price changes are infrequent in noncollusive oligopolistic industries.

1  The kinked-demand schedule gives each oligopolist good reason to believe that any change in price will be for the worse. A firm's customers will desert it in quantity if it raises price. If it lowers price, its sales at best will increase very modestly. Even if a price cut increases its total revenue somewhat, the oligopolist's costs may well increase by a more-than-offsetting amount. Should the dark blue $PD_1$ segment of its sales schedule be *inelastic* in that $E_d$ is less than 1, the firm's profits will surely fall. A price decrease will lower the firm's total receipts, and the production of a somewhat larger output will increase total costs. Worse yet, a price cut by A may be *more* than met by B and C. That is, A's initial price cut may precipitate a *price war;* so the amount sold by A may actually decline as its rival firms charge still lower prices. These are all good reasons on the demand side of the picture why noncollusive oligopolies might seek "the quiet

life" and follow live-and-let-live, or don't-upset-the-applecart, price policies. More specifically, if the resulting profits are satisfactory to the several firms at the existing price, it may seem prudent to them not to alter that price.

2  The other reason for price inflexibility under noncollusive oligopoly works from the cost side of the picture. The broken marginal-revenue curve which accompanies the kinked demand curve suggests that within limits, substantial cost changes will have no effect upon output and price. To be specific, any shift in marginal cost between $MC_1$ and $MC_2$ as shown in Figure 29-1 will result in no change in price or output, because the oligopolist fears a price war, on the one hand, and that it may price itself out of the market, on the other.

**Shortcomings**  The kinked-demand analysis has been subjected to two major criticisms. First, the analysis *does not explain how the going price gets to be at PQ (Figure 29-1) in the first place.* Rather, it merely helps to explain why oligopolists may be reluctant to deviate from an existing price which yields them a "satisfactory" or "reasonable" profit. The kinked demand curve explains price inflexibility but not price itself. Second, oligopoly prices are not as rigid—particularly in an upward direction—as the kinked-demand theory indicates. In the 1970s many oligopolistic producers raised their prices frequently and substantially. Such price increases might be better explained in terms of collusive oligopoly.

△  **Collusive Oligopoly**

The conditions of oligopoly—a small number of mutually interdependent firms—is conducive to collusion. The disadvantages and uncertainties of the noncollusive, kinked-demand model to producers are obvious. There is always the danger of a price war breaking out. In particular, in a general business recession each firm will find itself with excess capacity and therefore it can reduce per unit costs by increasing its market share. Then, too, the possibility is always present that a new firm may surmount entry barriers and initiate aggressive price cutting to gain a foothold in the market. In addition, the kinked demand curve's tendency toward rigid prices may adversely affect profits if general inflationary pressures increase costs. Stated differently, collusive control over price may permit oligopolists to reduce uncertainty, increase profits, and perhaps even prohibit the entry of new rivals.

**Price and Output**   Where will price and output be established under collusive oligopoly? To answer this question we must construct a highly simplified situation. Assume once again there are three firms—A, B, and C—producing homogeneous products. Each firm has identical cost curves. Each firm's demand curve is indeterminate unless we know how its rivals will react to any price change. Therefore, let us suppose each firm assumes that its two rivals will match either a price cut or a price increase. In other words, each firm's demand curve is of the $D_1D_1$ type in Figure 29-1. Assume further that the demand curve for each firm is identical. Given identical cost and identical demand and marginal-revenue data, we can say that Figure 29-2 represents the position of each of our three oligopolistic firms.

What price-output combination should each firm choose? If firm A were a pure monopolist, the answer would be clear enough: Establish output at $Q$, where marginal revenue equals marginal cost, charge the corresponding price $PQ$, and enjoy the maximum profit attainable. However, firm A *does* have two rivals selling identical products, and if A's assumption that its rivals will match its price[1] proves to be incorrect, the consequences could be disastrous for A. Specifically, if B and C actually charge prices below $PQ$, then firm A's demand curve will shift quite sharply to the left as its potential customers turn to its rivals, which

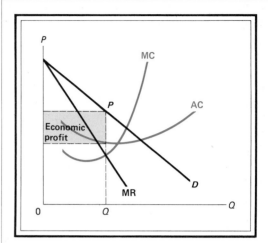

**FIGURE 29-2  COLLUSION AND THE TENDENCY TOWARD JOINT-PROFIT MAXIMIZATION**

If oligopolistic firms are faced with identical or highly similar demand and cost conditions, they will tend to behave collusively and maximize joint profits. The price and output results are essentially the same as those of pure (unregulated) monopoly; each oligopolist charges price $QP$ and produces output $Q$.

are now selling the same product at a lower price. Of course, A can retaliate by cutting its price too; but this will have the effect of moving all three firms down their demand curves, lowering their profits, and perhaps even driving them to some point where average cost exceeds price. So the question becomes, "Will B and C want to charge a price below $PQ$?" Under the assumptions we have made, and recognizing that A will have little choice except to match any price they may set below $PQ$, the answer is "No." Faced with the same demand and cost circumstances, B and C will find it in their interest to produce $Q$ and charge $PQ$. This is a curious situation; each firm finds it most profitable to charge the same price $PQ$, but only if its rivals will actually do so! How can the three firms realize the $PQ$-price and $Q$-quantity solution in which each is keenly interested? How can this be made a reality so that all three can avoid the less profitable outcomes associated with either higher or lower prices?

---

[1] Recall that this is the assumption upon which A's demand curve in Figure 29-2 is based.

The answer is obvious: The firms will all be motivated to collude—to "get together and talk it over"—and agree to charge the same price $PQ$. In addition to reducing the omnipresent possibility of price warring, each firm will realize the maximum profit. And for society, the result is likely to be about the same as if the industry were a pure monopoly composed of three identical plants (Chapter 27).

**Cartels and Such**   Collusion may assume a variety of forms. The most comprehensive form of collusion is the *cartel* which typically involves a formal written agreement with respect to both price and production. Output must be controlled—that is, the market must be shared—in order to maintain the agreed-upon price. The most spectacularly successful cartel of recent years has been OPEC (the Organization of Petroleum Exporting Countries) which raised the world price of oil from $2.50 to $11.00 per barrel within a six-month period in 1973–1974. By early 1980 price hikes had brought the per barrel price into the $30 to $32 range! The result has been enormous profits for cartel members, a substantial stimulus to worldwide inflation, and serious balance of payments problems for oil importers.

> OPEC is partly informal. . . . its rules are largely *ad hoc* and adjustable. "Agreed" prices are hammered out at lively, argumentative meetings. There are target prices and, for each country, planned output levels, but "enforcement" lacks clear powers and penalties. Some members depart (slightly) from the target prices. It is largely the Arab states' shared beliefs and willingness to make sacrifices that holds this "cartel" together. They are helped by the fact that the buyers are many and diverse. They [the buyers] lack a firm basis for exerting monopsony power. OPEC's future impact depends on the balance between the Arab solidarity on the one hand and (1) the new oil exporters (e.g., Britain or Mexico) as possible price-cutters and (2) the possible monopsony action by buyers on the other.[2]

[2] William G. Shepherd, *The Economics of Industrial Organization* (Englewood Cliffs, N.J.: Prentice-Hall, Inc., 1979), pp. 307–308.

Cartels are illegal in the United States and hence collusion has been less formal. For example, in 1960 an extensive price-fixing and market-sharing scheme involving heavy electrical equipment such as transformers, turbines, circuit breakers and switchgear was uncovered. Elaborate sub rosa schemes were developed by such participants as General Electric, Westinghouse, and Allis-Chalmers to rig prices and divide the market.

> The manner in which prices were fixed, bids controlled, and markets allocated may be illustrated by *power switch gear assemblies*. . . .five companies and twelve individuals were involved. It was charged that at least twenty-five meetings were held between the middle of November 1958 and October 1959 in various parts of the country. . . .
>
> At these periodic meetings, a scheme or formula for quoting nearly identical prices to electric utility companies, private industrial corporations and contractors was used by defendant corporations, designated by their representatives as a "phase of the moon" or "light of the moon" formula. Through cyclic rotating positioning inherent in the formula one defendant corporation would quote the low price, others would quote intermediate prices and another would quote the high price; these positions would be periodically rotated among the defendant corporations. This formula was so calculated that in submitting prices to these customers, the price spread between defendant corporations' quotations would be sufficiently narrow so as to eliminate actual price competition among them, but sufficiently wide so as to give an appearance of competition. This formula was designed to permit each defendant corporation to know the exact price it and *every* other defendant corporation would quote on each prospective sale.
>
> At these periodic meetings, a cumulative list of sealed bid business secured by all of the defendant corporations was also circulated and the representatives present would compare the relative standing of each corporation according to its agreed upon percentage of the total sales pursuant to sealed bids. The representatives present would then discuss particular future bid invitations and designate which defendant corporation should submit the lowest bid therefor, the

amount of such bid, and the amount of the bid to be submitted by others.[3]

Some twenty-nine manufacturers and forty-six company officials were indicted in this "great electrical conspiracy" which violated our antitrust laws. Substantial fines, jail penalties, and lawsuits by victimized buyers were the final outcome.

In innumerable other instances collusion is still less formal. *Gentlemen's agreements* frequently are struck at cocktail parties, on the golf course, or at trade association meetings where competing firms reach a verbal agreement on product price, leaving market shares to the ingenuity of each seller as reflected in nonprice competition. Although they too collide with the antitrust laws, their elusive character makes them more difficult to detect and prosecute successfully.

**Obstacles to Collusion** In practice cartels and similar collusive arrangements are difficult to establish and maintain. Let us briefly consider several important barriers to collusion.

*1 Demand and cost differences* When oligopolists' costs and product demands differ, it is more difficult to reach an agreement on price. Where products are differentiated, we would expect this to be the case. Indeed, even with highly standardized products, we would expect that firms might have somewhat different market shares and would operate with differing degrees of productive efficiency. Thus it is likely that even homogeneous oligopolists would have somewhat different demand and cost curves. In either event, differences in costs and demand will mean that the profit-maximizing price for each firm will differ; there will be no single price which is readily acceptable to all. Price collusion therefore depends upon the ability to achieve compromises and concessions—to arrive at a degree of "under-

standing" which in practice is often difficult to achieve. For example, the MR = MC positions of firms A, B, and C may call for them to charge $12, $11, and $10 respectively, but this price cluster or range may be unsatisfactory to one or more of the firms. Firm A may feel that differences in product quality justify only a $1.50, rather than a $2, price differential between its product and that of firm C. In short, cost and demand differences make it difficult for oligopolists to agree on a single price or a "proper" cluster of prices; these differentials are therefore an obstacle to collusion.

*2 Number of firms* Other things being equal, the larger the number of firms, the more difficult it is to achieve a cartel or some other form of price collusion. Agreement on price by three or four producers that control an entire market is much more readily accomplished than it is in the situation where ten firms each have roughly 10 percent of the market, or where the Big Three have, say, 70 percent of the market, while a "competitive fringe" of eight or ten smaller firms do battle for the remainder.

*3 Cheating* There is also a more-or-less persistent temptation for collusive oligopolists to engage in clandestine price cutting, that is, to make secret price concessions in order to get additional business. The technical aspects of cheating can be grasped by looking back at Figure 29-2 where the oligopolist is selling $OQ$ units at price $PQ$. At first glance it would seem that additional sales would violate the MR = MC rule and therefore *reduce* profits. But this is an instance of price discrimination where, through secrecy, the buyers of $OQ$ units and the buyers of additional units are separated into two markets. This separation through secrecy means that the sales of units beyond $OQ$ add their full price to marginal revenue; that is, additional sales through secret price concessions do *not* require a price cut on all prior units sold. Marginal revenue is equal to price for these additional units so that the sale of this extra output via cheating will be profitable out to the point at which *price* equals marginal cost.

[3]Jules Backman, *The Economics of the Electrical Machinery Industry* (New York: New York University Press, 1962), pp. 135–138, abridged. Reprinted by permission.

The difficulty with cheating is that buyers who are paying $PQ$ may get wind of the lower-priced sales and demand similar treatment. Or buyers receiving price concessions from one oligopolist may use this concession as a wedge to getting even larger price concessions from the firm's rivals. The attempt of buyers to play sellers against one another may precipitate price warring among the firms. In short, although it is potentially profitable, the use of secret price concessions is a threat to the maintenance of collusive oligopoly over time.

**4   Recession**   Recession is an enemy of collusion because slumping markets cause average costs to rise. In technical terms, as the oligopolists' demand and marginal-revenue curves shift to the left (Figure 29-2), each firm moves back to a higher point on its average-cost curve. The firms find they have substantial excess productive capacity, sales are down, unit costs are up, and profits are being squeezed. Under such conditions, businesses may feel they are in a better position to avoid serious profit reductions by price cutting in the hope of gaining sales at the expense of rivals.

**5   Legal obstacles: antitrust**   Our antitrust laws (Chapter 34) prohibit cartels and the kind of price-fixing collusion we have been discussing. It is for these reasons that less obvious means of price rigging—such as price leadership—has evolved in the United States.

△   **Price Leadership: Tacit Collusion**

*Price leadership* is still a less formal means by which oligopolists can coordinate their price behavior without engaging in outright collusion. Formal agreements and clandestine meetings are not involved.[4] Rather, a practice evolves whereby one firm—usually the largest or the most efficient in the industry—initiates price changes, and all other firms more-or-less automatically follow that price change. The importance of price leadership is

evidenced in the fact that such industries as farm machinery, anthracite coal, cement, copper, gasoline, newsprint, tin cans, lead, sulfur, rayon, fertilizer, glass containers, steel, automobiles, and nonferrous metals are practicing, or have in the recent past practiced, price leadership.

Consider the case of the cigarette industry which provides a classic example of tight price leadership. In this instance the Big Three, producing from 68 to 90 percent of total output, evolved a highly profitable practice of price leadership which resulted in virtually identical prices over the entire 1923 to 1941 period!

> In 1918 American Tobacco tried to lead a price rise, but Reynolds (the largest seller) refused to follow. In 1921, American cut its price and Reynolds retaliated with a further cut, which American and the other sellers were forced to match. This experience apparently had a profound educational impact on American and the other major brand sellers, none of whom challenged Reynolds' leadership again for a decade. Between 1923 and 1941, virtual price identity prevailed continuously among the "standard" brands. During this period there were eight list price changes. Reynolds led six of them, five upward and one downward, and was followed each time, in most cases within 24 hours of its announcement. The other two changes were downward revisions during 1933 led by American and followed promptly by the other standard brand vendors. American also attempted to lead a price increase in 1941, but Reynolds again refused to follow and the change was rescinded. Throughout this period, the return on invested capital realized by Reynolds, American, and Liggett & Myers averaged 18 per cent after taxes—roughly double the rate earned by American manufacturing industry as a whole.[5]

Since 1946 cigarette pricing has been somewhat less rigid, reflecting both successful

---

[4]A word of caution: Upon (legal) investigation what initially appears to be price leadership often turns out to be a more formal conspiracy.

[5]F. M. Scherer, *Industrial Pricing: Theory and Evidence* (Chicago: Rand McNally & Company, 1970), p. 38.

antitrust action and the development of in-creasingly heterogeneous product lines.

The examination of price leadership in a variety of industries suggests that the price leader is likely to observe the following tactics. First, because price changes always entail some risk that rivals will not follow, price adjust-ments will be made infrequently. The price leader will *not* respond pricewise to minuscule day-to-day changes in cost and demand condi-tions. Price will be changed only when cost and demand conditions have been altered sig-nificantly and on an industry-wide basis. That is, the price leader will typically revise price upward in response to industry-wide wage in-creases, an increase in taxes, or an increase in the price of some basic input such as energy. In the automobile industry price adjustments are made on the occasion of the introduction of new models each fall. Secondly, impending price adjustments are often communicated by the price leader to the industry through speeches by major executives, trade publica-tion interviews, and so forth. By publicizing "the need to raise prices" the price leader can elicit a consensus among its competitors for the actual increase.

△ **Cost-plus Pricing**

A final model of oligopolistic price behav-ior centers upon what is variously known as *cost-plus, markup,* or *rule-of-thumb* pricing. In this case the oligopolist uses a formula or pro-cedure to estimate cost per unit of output and a markup is applied to cost in order to deter-mine price. Unit costs, however, vary with output and therefore the firm must assume some typical or target level of output. For example, the firm's average cost figure may be that which is realized when the firm is operat-ing at, say, 75 or 80 percent of capacity. A markup, usually in the form of a percentage, is applied to average cost in determining price. For example, an appliance manufacturer may estimate unit costs of dishwashers to be $150, to which a 50 percent markup is applied. This yields a $225 price to retailers.

But why is the markup 50 percent, rather than 25 or 100 percent? The answer is that the firm is seeking some target profit or rate of return on its investment. To illustrate, Gen-eral Motors has been using cost-plus pricing for over forty years:

> GM begins its pricing analysis with an objective of earning, on the average over the years, a return of approximately 15 per cent after taxes on total invested capital. Since it does not know how many autos will be sold in a forthcoming year, and hence what the average cost per unit (in-cluding prorated overhead) will be, it calculates costs on the assumption of *standard volume*— that is, operation at 80 per cent of conservatively rated capacity. A *standard price* is next calcu-lated by adding to average cost per unit at stand-ard volume a sufficient profit margin to yield the desired 15 per cent after-tax return on capital. A top level price policy committee then uses the standard price as the initial basis of its price decision, making (typically small) adjustments upward or downward to take into account actual and potential competition, business conditions, long-run strategic goals, and other factors.[6]

Two final points. First, cost-plus pricing has obvious advantages for multiproduct firms which would otherwise be faced with the diffi-cult and costly process of estimating demand and cost conditions for perhaps hundreds of different products. In practice, it is virtually impossible to allocate correctly certain com-mon overhead costs such as power, lighting, insurance, and taxes to specific products. Sec-ondly, this method of pricing is *not* inconsist-ent with outright collusion or price leadership. If the several producers in an industry have roughly similar costs, adherence to a common pricing formula will result in highly similar prices and price changes. As we shall find in the case study which concludes this chapter, General Motors uses cost-plus pricing *and* is the price leader in the automobile industry.

[6] Ibid., p. 46.

☐ **ROLE OF NONPRICE COMPETITION**

We have noted that, for several reasons, oligopolists have an aversion to price competition. This aversion may lead to some more-or-less informal type of collusion on price. In the United States, however, price collusion is usually accompanied by nonprice competition. It is typically through nonprice competition that each firm's share of the total market is determined. This emphasis upon nonprice competition has its roots in two basic facts.

**1** Price cuts can be quickly and easily met by a firm's rivals. Because of this the possibility of significantly increasing one's share of the market through price competition is small; rivals will promptly cancel any potential gain in sales by matching price cuts. And, of course, the risk is always present that price competition will precipitate disastrous price warring. Nonprice competition is less likely to get out of hand. More positively stated, oligopolists seem to feel that more permanent advantages can be gained over rivals through nonprice competition because product variations, improvements in productive techniques, and successful advertising gimmicks cannot be duplicated so quickly and so completely as can price reductions.

**2** There is a more obvious reason for the tremendous emphasis which oligopolists put upon nonprice competition: Manufacturing oligopolists are typically blessed with substantial financial resources with which to support advertising and product development. Hence, although nonprice competition is a basic characteristic of both monopolistically competitive and oligopolistic industries, the latter are in a financial position to indulge more fully.

☐ **OLIGOPOLY AND ECONOMIC EFFICIENCY**

Is oligopoly an "efficient" market structure from society's standpoint? More specifically, how does the price-output behavior of the oli-

gopolist compare with that of a purely competitive firm? Given that there exists a variety of oligopoly models—kinked-demand, collusion, price leadership, and cost-plus pricing—it is difficult to make such a comparison.

△ **Two Views**

Two distinct views have evolved regarding the economic consequences of oligopoly. The *traditional view* holds that, because oligopoly is close to monopoly in structure, we should expect it to operate in a roughly similar way. Being characterized by barriers to entry, oligopoly can be expected, according to this view, to result in a restriction of output short of the point of lowest unit costs and a corresponding market price which yields substantial, if not maximum, economic profits. Indeed, one may even argue that oligopoly is actually less desirable than pure monopoly for the simple reason that pure monopoly in the United States is almost invariably subject to government regulation to mitigate abuses of such market power. Informal collusion among oligopolists may yield price and output results similar to pure monopoly, yet at the same time maintain the outward appearance of several independent and "competing" firms.

The traditional view is challenged by the *Schumpeter-Galbraith view,* which holds that large oligopolistic firms with market power are requisite to a rapid rate of technological progress. It is argued, first, that modern research to develop new products and new productive techniques is incredibly expensive. Therefore, only large oligopolistic firms are able to finance extensive research and development (R & D) activities. Secondly, the existence of barriers to entry gives the oligopolist some assurance that it will realize any profit rewards to which successful R & D endeavors may give rise. In Galbraith's words:

> The modern industry of a few large firms [is] an excellent instrument for inducing technical change. It is admirably equipped for financing technical development. Its organization provides

strong incentives for undertaking development and for putting it into use. . . . In the modern industry shared by a few large firms, size and the rewards accruing to market power combine to insure that resources for research and technical development will be available. The power that enables the firm to have some influence on prices insures that the resulting gains will not be passed on to the public by imitators (who have stood none of the costs of development) before the outlay for development can be recouped. In this way market power protects the incentive to technical development.[7]

Bluntly put, small competitive firms have neither the *means* nor the *incentives* to be technologically progressive; large oligopolists do.

If the Schumpeter-Galbraith view is correct, it suggests that over time oligopolistic industries will foster rapid product improvement, lower unit production costs, lower prices, and perhaps a greater output and more employment than would the same industry organized competitively. And there is anecdotal and case-study evidence which suggests that many oligopolistic manufacturing industries—for example, television and other electronics products, home appliances, automobile tires—have been characterized by substantial improvements in product quality, falling relative prices, and expanding levels of output and employment.

Those who embrace the traditional view are not without counterarguments. They contend that oligopolists have a strong incentive to impede innovation and restrain technological progress. The larger corporation wants to maximize profits by exploiting fully all its capital assets. Why rush to develop and introduce a new product (for example, fluorescent lights) when that product's success will render obsolete all equipment designed to produce an ex-

isting product (incandescent bulbs)?[8] Furthermore, it is not difficult to cite oligopolistic industries wherein it is generally agreed that interest in research and development has been modest at best: the steel, cigarette, and aluminum industries are cases in point.

△ **Technological Progress:
The Evidence**

Which view is more nearly correct? Unfortunately, empirical studies have yielded ambiguous results. The consensus, however, seems to be that giant oligopolies are probably *not* the fountainhead of technological progress. For example, a study[9] of sixty-one important inventions made during the 1880 to 1965 period indicates that over half were the work of independent inventors, quite disassociated from the industrial research laboratories of corporate enterprise. Such substantial advances as air conditioning, power steering, the ballpoint pen, cellophane, the jet engine, insulin, xerography, the helicopter, and the catalytic cracking of petroleum have this individualistic heritage. Other equally important advances have been provided by small- and medium-sized firms. According to this study, about two-thirds—forty out of sixty-one—of the basic inventions of this century have been fathered by independent inventors or the research activities of relatively small firms. This is not to deny that in a number of oligopolistic industries—for example, the aircraft, chemical, petroleum, and electronics industries—research activity has been pursued vigorously and fruitfully. But even here the picture is clouded by the fact that a very substantial portion of the research carried on in the aircraft-missile, electronics, and communications industries is heavily subsidized with public funds.

---

[7]John Kenneth Galbraith, *American Capitalism,* rev. ed. (Boston: Houghton Mifflin Company, 1956), pp. 86–88. Also see Joseph Schumpeter, *Capitalism, Socialism, and Democracy* (New York: Harper & Row Publishers, Inc., 1942).

[8]See Daniel Hamberg, "Invention in the Industrial Research Laboratory," *Journal of Political Economy,* April 1963, pp. 95–115.
[9]John Jewkes, David Sawers, and Richard Stillerman, *The Sources of Invention,* rev. ed. (New York: St. Martin's Press, Inc., 1968).

It is of interest that some leading researchers in this field have tentatively concluded that technological progress in an industry may be determined more by the industry's scientific character and "technological opportunities" than by its market structure. There may simply be more ways to progress in the computer industry than in the brickmaking industry, regardless of whether they are organized competitively or oligopolistically.

## ☐ COUNTERVAILING POWER

Aside from the technological progress issue, there is another reason to argue that the performance of oligopolies and monopolies might be more socially acceptable than traditional economic analysis would lead one to believe. Galbraith has developed the notion that many oligopolies (and monopolies) tend to induce the development of oligopolies (and monopolies) on the opposite side of the market.[10] That is, the existence of a monopolistic (or oligopolistic) seller tends to stimulate the growth of a monopsonistic (or oligopsonistic) buyer, and vice versa. More specifically, there is a tendency for *countervailing power* to evolve on the opposite side of those markets in which strong positions of "original power" have already developed. The development of countervailing power is *not* a matter of chance. It stems, on the one hand, from the desire of resource suppliers or customers to protect themselves from any abuses of the original-power position and, on the other hand, from the desire to share in the profits of the original-power position. Stated differently, for both defensive and offensive reasons, countervailing power is self-generating. Oligopoly begets oligopoly on the opposite side of the market. Oligopoly, in effect, generates its own antidote.

### △  Significance

The significance of countervailing power is that this "across-the-market" competition can be an important competitive force in those

very markets in which "same-side-of-the-market" rivalry is weak. Oligopolistic sellers may be restrained by a few large buyers. The Big Four of the tire industry face the Big Three of the automobile industry; chain grocery stores and mail-order houses buy in quantity from oligopolistic food processors and manufacturers. Oligopsonistic buyers may be faced with a small number of sellers. Labor unions face gigantic employers; agricultural marketing cooperatives sell to large food processors. Now, to the degree that these opposed positions of market power are successful in checking or restraining the power of one another, the socially desirable operation of a market system characterized by oligopoly will be furthered. The market power of oligopolistic buyers and sellers may be largely self-canceling, and the resulting compromise price and output close to the competitive level. Countervailing power is allegedly an important regulatory force in American capitalism and makes the economy more competitive than any discussion limited to same-side-of-the-market competition would lead one to conclude.[11]

### △  Limitations

Countervailing power, however, is not devoid of shortcomings and criticisms.

**1** One shortcoming is that it is not universally present. In the automobile industry, for example, dealers are highly dependent upon manufacturers and thus in a poor position to bargain for lower automobile prices which may benefit both themselves and consumers. In other cases—for example, the petroleum industry—manufacturers are increasingly integrated vertically down to the consumer, thus excluding the possibility of countervailing power.

**2** It has also been contended that countervailing power may prove to be of little or no benefit to consumers. What is there to guar-

---

[10]Galbraith, op. cit., chap. 9.

[11]The reader should consult the "bilateral monopoly model" of Chapter 31 for the theoretical details of countervailing power as it might apply to the labor market.

antee that price reductions obtained by strong buyers will be passed along to consumers? The consequence of countervailing power may merely be the redistribution of profits among giant buyers and sellers.

## ☐ AUTOMOBILES: A CASE STUDY[12]

The automobile industry provides an informative case study of oligopoly, illustrating many of the points made in this chapter. Although there were over eighty auto manufacturers in the early 1920s, a number of mergers (most notably the combining of Chevrolet, Pontiac, Oldsmobile, Buick and Cadillac into General Motors), a number of failures during the Great Depression of the 1930s, and the increasing importance of entry barriers, all tended to reduce numbers in the industry. Currently, three large firms clearly dominate the market for domestically produced automobiles. General Motors (GM) is preeminent with 55 to 60 percent of the market; Ford has 25 to 30 percent; and Chrysler has 10 to 15 percent. American Motors hangs on precariously with perhaps 2 to 3 percent of the market. These firms are gigantic: According to *Fortune* magazine, GM, Ford, and Chrysler were the second, fourth, and seventeenth largest manufacturing companies in the United States in 1979. And all three are leading truck manufacturers, produce a variety of household appliances, are involved in defense contracting, and have extensive overseas interests. GM has a virtual monopoly in producing buses and diesel locomotives in the United States.

Entry barriers are substantial as is evidenced by the fact that it has been about six decades since an American firm successfully entered the automobile industry. The primary barrier is economies of scale. It is estimated that the minimum efficient size for a producer is about 500,000 units of output per year.

However, given the uncertainties of consumer tastes, experts feel that a truly viable firm must produce at least two different models. Hence, to have a reasonable prospect of success a new firm would have to produce about 1,000,000 autos per year. In the mid-1970s the estimated cost of the required land, buildings, machinery, and investment in design would be about $2 billion! Other entry barriers include extensive advertising and the established reputations of existing firms for reliability and service. A newcomer would face the expensive task of overcoming existing brand loyalties. Given that the automobile industry spent $665 million on advertising in 1979, this is no small matter. There would also be the additional cost and effort involved in establishing a system of retail dealerships.

The indicated industry structure—a few firms with high entry barriers—is fertile ground for collusive or coordinated pricing. In practice, price leadership has characterized the industry for the past fifty years. GM has been the price leader since World War II. Each fall, when the new models are introduced, GM establishes prices for its basic models and Ford and Chrysler set the prices of their comparable models accordingly. (The details of how GM establishes its prices were outlined in the earlier section on cost-plus pricing). It is interesting to note that, even when Chrysler was in a rather critical financial position in the late 1950s and early 1960s, it did *not* resort to price cutting to improve its market position. Price leadership has been very profitable. The auto industry as a whole has enjoyed profit rates almost twice as great as all manufacturing corporations taken as a group.

In addition to advertising, nonprice competition has centered upon styling and technological advance. In practice the former has been stressed over the latter. As early as the 1920s GM recognized that the replacement market was becoming increasingly important as compared to the market for first-time purchasers. Therefore, their strategy—later adopted by the other manufacturers—became one of annual styling changes accompanied by

[12]This section draws heavily upon Lawrence J. White, "The Automobile Industry," in Walter Adams (editor), *The Structure of American Industry,* fifth edition (New York: The Macmillan Company, 1977), pp. 165–220.

model proliferation. The purpose is to achieve higher sales and profits by encouraging consumers to replace their autos with greater frequency.

Technological progress in the industry presents a mixed picture. With respect to manufacturing processes, the industry has not altered its basic production techniques since Ford's introduction of the moving assembly line some sixty years ago. However, the industry has done a good job of adapting and improving upon new production technologies which others have pioneered.

> Performance with respect to automotive technology offers a different picture. Since the 1920s, the industry's main attention has been on styling, not on engineering innovation. Progress has occurred. Cars in 1975 are clearly superior to those of 1925. But progress has been slow, the sources of innovations have frequently been supplier firms or foreign automobile manufacturers, and American manufacturers have often been slow to adopt improvements. The major changes have been in power brakes and steering, automatic transmission, and air conditioning, and even in these areas the pioneering work was frequently done elsewhere. Until the 1970s, there had been no fundamental changes in the basic engine, carburation, ignition, and suspension systems. Some manufacturers abroad have been more innovative in this area, offering diesel engines, Wankel engines, stratified charge engines, fuel injection, and pneumatic suspension systems. Other entrepreneurs have proposed fundamental alternatives to the internal combustion engine, such as steam and electric vehicles. Turbines frequently appeared to be a potential alternative. Yet, until pollution control requirements tightened in the 1970s, the auto companies showed at most only sporadic interest in fundamental changes and alternatives.

> If the large size and tight concentration of the automobile companies had any special value for technological progress, it should have been in these risky areas of fundamental change. Yet, the record of the industry, particularly in the post-war period, is woefully lacking.[13]

A number of economists feel that a more competitive structure in the auto industry would result in lower prices, lower profits, and perhaps a more impressive rate of technological progress. A specific recommendation is that, because (1) the industry sells 9 or 10 million autos per year and (2) an efficient firm need only produce 1 million units per year, the industry could support 9 or 10 efficient firms. That is, GM might be split into four or five separate firms, Ford into two or three, which, along with Chrysler and American Motors, would yield nine or ten domestic producers. The added competition might be beneficial to society, if not to GM stockholders.

[13]Ibid., p. 205.

## Summary

**1** Oligopolistic industries are characterized by the presence of few firms, each of which has a significant fraction of the market. Firms thus situated are mutually interdependent; the behavior of any one firm directly affects, and is affected by, the actions of rivals. Products may be virtually uniform or significantly differentiated. Underlying reasons for the evolution of oligopoly are economies of scale and the advantages of merger.

**2** There are four major variants of oligopoly *a.* the kinked-demand model, *b.* collusive oligopoly, *c.* price leadership, and *d.* cost-plus pricing.

**3** Noncollusive oligopolists in effect face a kinked demand curve. This curve and the accompanying marginal-revenue curve help explain the price rigidity which characterizes such markets; they do not, however, explain the level of price.

**4** The uncertainties inherent in noncollusive pricing are conducive to collusion. There is a tendency for collusive oligopolists to maximize joint profits—that is, to behave somewhat like pure monopolists. Demand and cost differences, the presence of a "large" number of firms, "cheating" through secret price concessions, recessions, and the antitrust laws, are all obstacles to collusive oligopoly.

**5** Price leadership is a less formal means of collusion whereby the largest or most efficient firm in the industry initiates price changes and the other firms follow.

**6** With cost-plus or markup pricing oligopolists estimate their unit costs at some target level of output and add a percentage "markup" to determine price.

**7** Market shares in oligopolistic industries are usually determined on the basis of nonprice competition. Oligopolists emphasize nonprice competition because **a.** advertising and product variations are less easy for rivals to match, and **b.** oligopolists frequently have ample financial resources to finance nonprice competition.

**8** The traditional view holds that the price-output results of oligopoly are similar to those of pure monopoly. The Schumpeter-Galbraith view is that oligopoly is conducive to technological progress and therefore results in better products, lower prices, and larger levels of output and employment than if the industry were organized more competitively.

**9** Although subject to important limitations, the presence of countervailing power may improve the price-output behavior of oligopolists.

## Questions and Study Suggestions

**1** Key terms and concepts to remember: oligopoly; homogeneous and differentiated oligopoly; kinked demand curve; price war; collusive oligopoly; cartel; gentlemen's agreement; price leadership; cost-plus pricing; traditional and Schumpeter-Galbraith views; countervailing power.

**2** What features distinguish oligopoly from monopolistic competition?

**3** "Fewness of rivals means mutual interdependence, and mutual interdependence means uncertainty as to how those few rivals will react to a price change by any one firm." Explain. Of what significance is this for determining demand and marginal revenue? Other things being equal, would you expect mutual interdependence to vary directly or inversely with the degree of product differentiation? With the number of firms? Explain.

**4** What assumptions concerning a rival's responses to price changes underlie the kinked demand curve? Why is there a gap in the marginal-revenue curve? How does the kinked demand curve help explain oligopolistic price rigidity? What are the shortcomings of the kinked-demand model?

**5** Why is there a tendency for price collusion to occur in oligopolistic industries? Assess the economic desirability of collusive pricing. Explain: "If each firm knows that the price of each of its few rivals depends on its own price, how can the prices be determined?" What are the main obstacles to collusion?

**6** Explain how price leadership might evolve and function in an oligopolistic industry. Is cost-plus pricing compatible with collusion?

**7** "Oligopolistic industries have both the means and the inclination for technological progress." Do you agree? Explain.

**8** How does countervailing power differ from ordinary competition? Why is it self-generating? What are its limitations?

**9** Using Figure 29-2, explain how a collusive oligopolist might increase its profits by offering secret price concessions to buyers. Indicate the amount of additional profits which the firm may realize on the diagram. What are the risks involved in such a policy?

## Selected References

Adams, Walter (ed.): *The Structure of American Industry,* 5th ed. (New York: The Macmillan Company, 1977), chaps. 3, 5, 13.

Bain, Joe S.: *Industrial Organization,* 2d ed. (New York: John Wiley & Sons, Inc., 1968), chap. 9.

Colberg, Marshall R., Dascomb R. Forbush, and Gilbert R. Whitaker, Jr.: *Business Economics: Principles and Cases,* 4th ed. (Homewood, Ill.: Richard D. Irwin, Inc., 1970), chap. 12.

Galbraith, John K.: *American Capitalism,* rev. ed. (Boston: Houghton Mifflin Company, 1956), chaps. 7, 9.

Koch, James V.: *Industrial Organization and Prices* (Englewood Cliffs, N.J.: Prentice-Hall, Inc., 1974), chaps. 9, 12, 13.

Scherer, F. M.: *Industrial Pricing: Theory and Evidence* (Chicago: Rand McNally & Company, 1970).

Shepherd, William G.: *Economics of Industrial Organization* (Englewood Cliffs, N.J.: Prentice-Hall, Inc., 1979), chaps. 14, 15, and 21.

Weiss, Leonard W.: *Case Studies in American Industry,* 3d ed. (New York: John Wiley & Sons, 1980), chap. 4.

# LAST WORD
## Auto Rentals: Trying Too Hard?

Collusive behavior by oligopolists is typically to the detriment of smaller competitors.

Travelers renting cars at most U.S. airports can choose to drive away the Fords of Hertz, the Plymouths of Avis or the Chevies of National Car Rental. Last week the Federal Trade Commission charged that the Big Three of the auto-rental business had combined to make sure that consumers got no other choice. Hertz, Avis and National, said the FTC, have been conspiring since 1968 to freeze competitors out of airport trade, which constitutes 70% of the $700 million-a-year business, and to keep car-rental prices artificially high.

The FTC alleged that Hertz, Avis and National conspired to submit identical bids for concession rights at airports, and persuaded airport managers to set requirements for concessions that disqualified competitors. One rule they are alleged to have promoted requires that "concessionaires have a nationwide reservations network." The FTC also accused the three companies of fixing rental prices and stated that smaller competitors kept out of the airports charged 10% to 40% less.

The commission further charged the rental companies with "entering into anticompetitive arrangements" with automakers—Hertz with Ford, Avis with Chrysler and National with General Motors. According to the complaints, the arrangements provide the rental companies with advertising subsidies from the automakers that average $5 million a year to each, and "have the effect of increasing barriers to entry" to smaller companies, which do not get such large subsidies.

The three rental concerns denied the charges. The FTC chose not to accuse the automakers of any violation, but a spokesman for Ford denied that the advertising agreements were anticompetitive and said the company had similar agreements with some of Hertz's smaller competitors.

A trial of the case before an FTC administrative-law judge may be a year off and the companies could appeal any unfavorable ruling through the federal courts. If the FTC eventually prevails, the three companies could be forced to pay triple damages to any competitors or consumers who win lawsuits. The FTC might also seek to have one or more of the three big rental companies booted out of some airports and replaced by smaller competitors.

# Production and the Demand for Economic Resources

chapter 30

The preceding four chapters have been concerned with the pricing and output of goods and services under a variety of product market structures. In producing any commodity, a firm must hire productive resources which, directly or indirectly, are owned and supplied by households. It is appropriate that we now turn from the pricing and production of goods to the pricing and employment of resources needed in accomplishing production. In terms of our circular flow diagram of the economy (Chapter 3), we now shift our attention from the bottom loop of the diagram, where firms supply and households demand products, to the top loop, where households supply and businesses demand resources. It is in part this reversal of roles which makes necessary a separate discussion of resource pricing.

## □ SIGNIFICANCE OF RESOURCE PRICING

There are a number of intertwined reasons for studying resource pricing.

**1 Money Incomes** The most basic fact about resource prices is that they constitute a major determinant of money incomes. The expenditures which businesses make in acquiring economic resources flow as wage, rent, interest, and profit incomes to those households which in turn supply the human and property resources at their disposal.

**2 Resource Allocation** Another important aspect of resource pricing is that, just as product prices ration finished goods and services to consumers, so resource prices allocate scarce resources among various industries and firms. An understanding of the manner in which resource prices negotiate the allocation of resources is particularly significant in view of the fact that in a dynamic economy, the efficient allocation of resources over time calls for continuing shifts in resources among alternative uses.

**3 Cost Minimization** To the firm, resource prices are costs, and to realize maximum profits a firm must produce the profit-maximizing output with the most efficient (least costly) combination of resources. Given technology, it is resource prices which play the major role in determining the quantities of land, labor, capital, and entrepreneurial ability that are to be combined in the productive process.

**4  Ethical Aspects**  Finally, aside from these objective facets of resource pricing, there are a myriad of ethical questions and public policy issues surrounding the resource market. In particular, the amoral nature of resource prices results in considerable inequality in the personal distribution of income. Too, the age-old question of the sizes of the income shares going to specific groups is still very much alive. What is the proper distribution of the national income between profits and wages? What shares should go to farmers, factory workers, white-collar employees? Much of Part 6 of this book is concerned with endeavors—both public and private—to alter the distribution of income. Chapter 37 is concerned specifically with the facts and ethics of income distribution.

## □  COMPLEXITIES OF RESOURCE PRICING

Economists are in substantial agreement as to the basic principles of resource pricing. Yet there exists considerable disagreement and sometimes an element of confusion as to the variations in these general principles which must be made as they are applied to specific resources and particular markets. While economists are in general agreement that the pricing and employment of economic resources, or factors of production, are a supply and demand phenomenon, they also recognize that in particular markets, resource supply and demand may assume strange and often complex dimensions. This is further complicated by the fact that the operation of supply and demand forces may be muted or even largely supplanted by the policies and practices of government, business firms, or labor unions, not to mention a host of other institutional considerations.

Our major objective in this chapter is a limited one: to explain the basic factors which underlie the demand for economic resources. We shall couch our discussion in terms of labor, recognizing that the principles we outline are also generally applicable to land, capital, and entrepreneurial ability. In Chapter 31 we shall combine our understanding of resource demand with a discussion of labor supply in analyzing wage rates. Then in Chapter 32 we shall emphasize the supply side of the market for property resources.

## □  MARGINAL PRODUCTIVITY THEORY OF RESOURCE DEMAND

The least complicated approach to resource demand is that which assumes a firm is hiring some specific resource in a competitive market and in turn is selling its product in a competitive market. The simplicity of this situation lies in the fact that under competition the firm can dispose of as little or as much output as it chooses at the going market price. The firm is selling such a negligible fraction of total output that it exerts no influence whatever on product price. Similarly, in the resource market, competition means that the firm is hiring such a small fraction of the total supply of the resource that its price is unaffected by the quantity the firm purchases.

### △  Resource Demand as a Derived Demand

Having specified these simplified conditions, we can note the most crucial point: the demand for resources is a *derived demand,* that is, derived from the finished goods and services which resources help produce. Resources do not directly satisfy consumer wants, but do so indirectly by producing goods and services. No one wants to consume an acre of land, an International Harvester tractor, or the labor services of a farmer, but households do want to consume the various food and fiber products which these resources help produce.

△   **Marginal Revenue Product (MRP)**

The derived nature of resource demand correctly implies that the strength of the demand for any resource will depend upon (1) the capability of the resource in producing a good, and (2) the market value of the good it is producing. In other words, a resource which is highly productive in turning out a commodity highly valued by society will be in great demand. On the other hand, demand will be very weak for a relatively unproductive resource which is only capable of producing some good not in great demand by households. There will be no demand for a resource which is phenomenally efficient in the production of something which no one will want to purchase!

The roles of productivity and product value in determining resource demand can be brought into sharper focus through Table 30-1. Here it is assumed that a firm is adding one variable resource—labor—to its fixed plant. Columns 1 through 3 remind us that the law of diminishing returns will be applicable in this situation, causing the marginal physical product (MPP) of labor to fall beyond some point.[1] For simplicity's sake, it is here assumed that diminishing marginal physical product sets in with the first worker hired.

---

[1] It might be helpful to review the subsection entitled "Law of Diminishing Returns" in Chapter 25 at this point.

But we have already emphasized that the derived demand for a resource depends not only upon the productivity of that resource but also upon the price of the commodity it produces. Column 4 adds this price information. Note that product price is constant, in this case at $2, because we are supposing a competitive product market. Multiplying column 2 by column 4, we get the total-revenue data of column 5. From these total-revenue data we can readily compute *marginal revenue product (MRP)—the increase in total revenue resulting from the use of each additional variable input (labor, in this case)*. This is indicated in column 6.

△   **Rule for Employing Resources:**
    **MRP = MRC**

*The MRP schedule—columns 1 and 6—constitutes the firm's demand schedule for labor.* To explain why this is so, we must first discuss the rule which guides a profit-seeking firm in hiring any resource. *To maximize profits, a firm should hire additional units of any given resource so long as each successive unit adds more to the firm's total revenue than it does to its total costs.* Economists have special terms which designate what each additional unit of a resource adds to total cost and what it adds to total revenue. We have just noted that, by definition, MRP measures how much

**TABLE 30-1**
**The Demand for a Resource: Pure Competition in the Sale of the Product**
(*hypothetical data*)

| (1) Units of resource | (2) Total product | (3) Marginal physical product (MPP), or Δ(2) | (4) Product price | (5) Total revenue, or (2) × (4) | (6) Marginal revenue product (MRP), or Δ(5) |
|---|---|---|---|---|---|
| 1 | 7 | 7 | $2 | $14 | $14 |
| 2 | 13 | 6 | 2 | 26 | 12 |
| 3 | 18 | 5 | 2 | 36 | 10 |
| 4 | 22 | 4 | 2 | 44 | 8 |
| 5 | 25 | 3 | 2 | 50 | 6 |
| 6 | 27 | 2 | 2 | 54 | 4 |
| 7 | 28 | 1 | 2 | 56 | 2 |

each successive worker adds to total revenue. The amount which each additional unit of a resource adds to the firm's total (resource) cost is called *marginal resource cost* (MRC). Thus we can restate our rule for hiring resources as follows: *It will be profitable for a firm to hire additional units of a resource up to the point at which that resource's MRP is equal to its MRC.* If the number of workers a firm is currently hiring is such that the MRP of the last worker exceeds his or her MRC, the firm can clearly profit by hiring more workers. But if the number being hired is such that the MRC of the last worker exceeds the MRP, the firm is hiring workers who are not "paying their way," and it can thereby increase its profits by laying off some workers. The reader will recognize that this MRP = MRC rule is very similar to the MR = MC rule employed throughout our discussion of product pricing. The rationale of the two rules is the same, but the point of reference is now *inputs* of resources, rather than *outputs* of product.

### △ MRP is a Demand Schedule

Just as product price and marginal revenue are equal in a purely competitive product market, so *resource price and marginal resource cost are equal when a firm is hiring a resource competitively.* In a purely competitive labor market the wage rate is set by the total, or market, supply of, and the market demand for, labor. Because it hires such a small fraction of the total supply of labor, a single firm cannot influence this wage rate. This means that total resource cost increases by exactly the amount of the going wage rate for each additional worker hired; the wage rate and MRC are equal. It follows that so long as it is hiring labor competitively, *the firm will hire workers to the point at which their wage rate (or MRC) is equal to their MRP.*

Accordingly, employing the data in column 6 of Table 30-1, we find that if the wage rate is $13.95, the firm will hire only one worker. This is so because the first worker adds $14 to total revenue and slightly less— $13.95—to total costs. For each successive

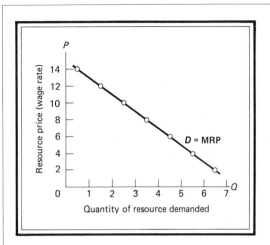

**FIGURE 30-1 THE PURELY COMPETITIVE SELLER'S DEMAND FOR A RESOURCE**

The MRP curve is the resource demand curve. The location of the curve depends upon the marginal productivity of the resource and the price of the product. Under pure competition product price is constant; therefore, it is solely because of diminishing marginal productivity that the resource demand curve is downsloping.

worker, however, we find that MRC exceeds MRP, indicating that it will not be profitable to hire any of those workers. If the wage rate is $11.95, we apply the same reasoning and discover that it will pay the firm to hire both the first and second workers. Similarly, if the wage rate is $9.95, three will be hired. If $7.95, four. If $5.95, then five. And so forth. It is evident that *the MRP schedule constitutes the firm's demand for labor, because each point on this schedule (curve) indicates the number of workers which the firm would hire at each possible wage rate which might exist.* This is shown graphically in Figure 30-1.[2]

[2]The rationale employed here is familiar to us. Recall in Chapter 26 that we applied the price-equals-marginal cost or $P = MC$ rule for the profit-maximizing *output* to discover that the portion of the competitive firm's short-run marginal-cost curve lying above average variable cost is the short-run *product* supply curve (Figure 26-6). Presently we are applying the MRP = MRC rule for the profit-maximizing *input* to the firm's MRP curve and determining that this curve is the input or *resource* demand curve.

△ **Resource Demand Under Imperfect Competition**

Our analysis of labor demand becomes slightly more complex when we assume that the firm is selling its product in an imperfectly competitive market. Pure monopoly, oligopoly, and monopolistic competition in the product market all mean that the firm's product demand curve is downsloping; that is, the firm must accept a lower price in order to increase its sales. Table 30-2 takes this into account. The productivity data of Table 30-1 are retained, but it is now assumed in column 4 that product price must be lowered in order to sell the marginal product of each successive worker. The MRP of the purely competitive seller falls for one reason: marginal physical product diminishes. But the MRP of the imperfectly competitive seller falls for two reasons: marginal product diminishes, *and* product price falls as output increases.

It must be emphasized that the lower price which accompanies every increase in output applies in each case not only to the marginal product of each successive worker but also to all prior units which otherwise could have been sold at a higher price. To illustrate: The second worker's marginal product is 6 units. These 6 units can be sold for $2.40 each or, as a group, for $14.40. But this is not the

MRP of the second worker. Why? Because in order to sell these 6 units, the firm must take a 20-cent price cut on the 7 units produced by the first worker—units which could have been sold for $2.60 each. Thus the MRP of the second worker is only $13.00 [= $14.40 − (7 × 20 cents)]. Similarly, the third worker's MRP is $8.40. Although the 5 units this worker produces are worth $2.20 each in the market, the third worker does not add $11.00 to the firm's total revenue when account is taken of the 20-cent price cut which must be taken on the 13 units produced by the first two workers. In this case the third worker's MRP is only $8.40 [= $11.00 − (13 × 20 cents)]. And so it is for the other figures in column 6.

The net result is obvious: The MRP curve—the resource demand curve—of the imperfectly competitive producer tends to be less elastic than that of a purely competitive producer. At a wage rate or MRC of $11.95, both the purely competitive and the imperfectly competitive seller will hire two workers. But at $9.95, the competitive firm will hire three and the imperfectly competitive firm only two. And at $7.95, the purely competitive firm will take on four employees and the imperfect competitor only three. This difference in elasticity can be readily visualized by graphing the MRP data of Table 30-2 as in

**TABLE 30-2**
**The Demand for a Resource: Imperfect Competition in the Sale of the Product (*hypothetical data*)**

| (1) Units of resource | (2) Total product | (3) Marginal physical product (MPP), or Δ(2) | (4) Product price | (5) Total revenue, or (2) × (4) | (6) Marginal revenue product (MRP), or Δ(5) |
|---|---|---|---|---|---|
| 1 | 7 | 7 | $2.60 | $18.20 | $18.20 |
| 2 | 13 | 6 | 2.40 | 31.20 | 13.00 |
| 3 | 18 | 5 | 2.20 | 39.60 | 8.40 |
| 4 | 22 | 4 | 2.00 | 44.00 | 4.40 |
| 5 | 25 | 3 | 1.90 | 47.50 | 3.50 |
| 6 | 27 | 2 | 1.80 | 48.60 | 1.10 |
| 7 | 28 | 1 | 1.70 | 47.60 | −1.00 |

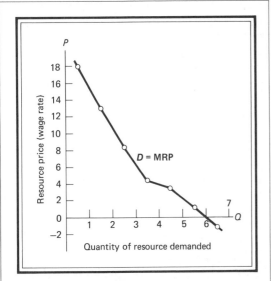

**FIGURE 30.2 THE IMPERFECTLY COMPETITIVE SELLER'S DEMAND FOR A RESOURCE**

An imperfectly competitive seller's resource demand curve slopes downward because marginal product diminishes and product price falls as output increases.

more employment, and lower prices in the long run than would a purely competitive market. The resource demand curve in these instances obviously would not be restricted.

### △   Market Demand for a Resource

Can we now derive the market demand curve for a resource? Yes, we can. You will recall that the total, or market, demand curve for a product is developed by summing the demand curves of all individual buyers in the market. Similarly, the market demand curve for a particular resource can be derived in essentially the same fashion, that is, by summing the individual demand or MRP curves for all firms hiring that resource.[3]

### ☐   CHANGES IN RESOURCE DEMAND

What will alter the demand for a resource, that is, shift the demand curve? The very derivation of resource demand immediately suggests two related factors—the resource's productivity and the market price of the product it is producing. And our previous analysis of changes in product demand (Chapter 4) suggests another factor—changes in the prices of other resources.

Figure 30-2 and comparing them with Figure 30-1.

It is not surprising that the imperfectly competitive producer is less responsive to wage cuts in terms of workers employed than is the purely competitive producer. The relative reluctance of the imperfect competitor to employ more resources and thereby produce more output when resource prices fall is merely the resource market reflection of the imperfect competitor's tendency to restrict output in the product market. Other things being equal, the imperfectly competitive seller will produce less of a product than would a purely competitive seller. In producing this smaller output, it will demand fewer resources.

But one important qualification is pertinent. We noted in Chapters 27 and 29 that the market structures of pure monopoly and oligopoly *might* be conducive to technological progress and to a higher level of production,

[3] The matter is actually not quite this simple. The resource demand, or MRP, curve *for each firm* is drawn on the assumption that product price is constant. However, if a lowering of resource price causes *all firms* in the industry to hire more of the resource and thereby expand total output, we can expect product price to decline. The result is that the resource market demand curve will not be quite identical with the sum of the individual firms' demand curves for that resource. Recall that the resource demand curve of Figure 30-2 is steeper or less elastic than the curve of Figure 30-1 *because* the latter is based on a constant product price and the former upon the assumption that product price falls as output or product supply increases. So it is for the case at hand. A simple horizontal summing of the resource demand curves of the individual firms is unrealistically based upon an unchanging product price. The true market demand curve takes cognizance of the fact that product price will fall as *industry* output expands, and, hence, this curve will be steeper or less elastic than that based upon a constant product price. For details consult Richard B. Freeman, *Labor Economics* (Englewood Cliffs, N.J.: Prentice-Hall, Inc., 1972), pp. 60–62.

△   **Changes in Product Demand**

Because resource demand is a derived demand, it is obvious that any change in the demand for the product will affect product price and therefore the MRP of the resource. In Table 30-1, assume an increase in product demand which boosts product price to $3. If you calculate the new labor demand curve and plot it in Figure 30-1, you will find that it lies to the right of the old curve. Similarly, a drop in product demand and price will shift the labor demand curve to the left. Real-world example: In late 1973 the gasoline shortage and rapidly rising gasoline prices twisted the demand for automobiles away from larger models toward compacts and subcompacts. As a result, workers in the large-car plants were being furloughed and small-car workers were working overtime!

△   **Productivity Changes**

Changes in productivity will also cause resource demand to shift. The productivity of any resource can be altered in several ways (Chapter 20). (1) The marginal productivity data for, say, labor will depend upon the quantities of other resources with which it is combined. The greater the amount of capital and land resources with which labor is combined, the greater will be the marginal productivity and the demand for labor. (2) Technological improvements will have the same effect. The better the quality of the capital, the greater the productivity of labor. Steelworkers employed with a given amount of real capital in the form of modern oxygen furnaces are more productive than when employed with the same amount of real capital embodied in the old open-hearth furnaces. (3) Improvements in the quality of the variable resource itself— labor—will increase the marginal productivity and therefore the demand for labor. In effect, we have a new demand curve for a different, more skilled kind of labor.

All these considerations, incidentally, are important in explaining why the average level of (real) wages is higher in the United States than in most foreign nations. American workers are generally healthier and better trained than those of foreign nations, and in most industries they work with a larger and more efficient stock of capital goods and more abundant natural resources than do the workers of most other countries. This spells a strong demand for labor. On the supply side of the market, labor is *relatively* scarce as compared with most foreign nations. A strong demand and a relatively scarce supply result in high wage rates. This will be discussed further in Chapter 31.

△   **Prices of Other Resources**

Just as changes in the prices of other products will change the demand for a specific commodity, so changes in the prices of other resources can be expected to alter the demand for a particular resource. And just as the effect of a change in the price of product X upon the demand for product Y depends upon whether X and Y are substitute or complementary goods, so the effect of a change in the price of resource A upon the demand for resource B will depend upon their substitutability or their complementariness.

Within limits, resources are typically substitutes for one another. A drop in the price of machinery may prompt a firm to substitute machinery for labor; this is the obvious adjustment to make if the firm seeks to produce any given output in the least costly fashion. At given wage rates, less labor will now be employed. The demand for labor will have fallen. But this *substitution effect* may be offset wholly or in part by an accompanying *output effect*. Because the price of machinery has fallen, the cost of producing various outputs will also have declined. And with lower costs, the firm will find it profitable to produce and sell a larger output. This greater output will tend to increase the demand for all resources, including labor. The net effect of a decline in the price of machinery upon the demand for labor will depend upon the sizes of these two opposed effects. If the substitution effect outweighs the output effect, the demand for labor will decline. If the reverse holds true, the demand for labor will increase.

When resources are complementary or jointly demanded, the situation is a bit more clear-cut. In some situations the nature of the productive process allows little or no room for substituting resources; resources are combined in fixed proportions. Suppose, for example, that a small manufacturer of metal products uses punch presses as its basic piece of capital equipment. Each press is designed to be operated by one worker; the machine is not automated—it won't run itself—and a second worker would be wholly redundant.

Assume that a significant technological advance in the production of these presses substantially reduced their costs. Now there can be no negative substitution effect because labor and capital must be used in fixed proportions, one person for one machine. Capital cannot be substituted for labor. But there is a positive output effect for labor. Other things being equal, the reduction in the price of capital goods means lower production costs. It will therefore be profitable to produce a larger output. In doing so the firm will use both more capital and more labor.

## □ ELASTICITY OF RESOURCE DEMAND

The considerations just discussed are responsible for shifts in the location of resource demand curves. Such changes in demand are to be carefully distinguished from a change in the quantity of a resource demanded. The latter, you will recall, does not entail a shift in the resource demand curve but rather a movement from one point to another on a stable resource demand curve, because of a change in the price of the specific resource under consideration. To illustrate: An increase in the wage rate from $5.95 to $7.95 will reduce the quantity of labor demanded from five to four workers, as can be seen in Table 30-1 and Figure 30-1.

This raises a question: What determines the sensitivity of producers to changes in resource prices? Or, more technically, what determines the elasticity of resource demand? Several long-standing generalizations provide some important insights in answering this question.

**1  Rate of MPP Decline**  A purely technical consideration—the rate at which the marginal physical product of the variable resource declines—is important. *If the marginal product of labor declines slowly as it is added to a fixed amount of capital, the MRP, or demand curve for labor, will decline slowly and tend to be highly elastic.* A small decline in the price of such a resource will give rise to a relatively large increase in the amount demanded. Conversely, if the marginal productivity of labor declines sharply, the MRP, or labor demand curve, will decline rapidly. This means that a relatively large decline in the wage rate will be accompanied by a very modest increase in the amount of labor hired; resource demand will be inelastic.

**2  Ease of Resource Substitutability**  The degree to which resources are substitutable for one another is a highly important determinant of elasticity. *The larger the number of good substitute resources available, the greater will be the elasticity of demand for a particular resource.* If a furniture manufacturer finds that some five or six different types of wood are equally satisfactory in making coffee tables, a rise in the price of any one type of wood may cause a very sharp drop in the amount demanded as the producer readily substitutes other woods. At the other extreme, it may be impossible to substitute; bauxite is absolutely essential in the production of aluminum ingots. This means that the demand for it tends to be very inelastic.

**3  Elasticity of Product Demand**  The elasticity of demand for any resource will depend upon the elasticity of demand for the product which it helps produce. *The greater the elasticity of product demand, the greater the elasticity of resource demand.* The derived nature of resource demand would lead us to expect this relationship. A small rise in the price of a product with great elasticity of demand will give rise to a sharp drop in output and therefore a relatively large decline in the amounts of the various resources demanded. Indeed, our comparisons of resource demand when output is being sold competitively (Table 30-1 and Figure 30-1) on the one hand, and under imperfectly competitive conditions (Table 30-2 and Figure 30-2) on the other, have already suggested that, other things being the same, the greater the elasticity of product demand, the greater the elasticity of resource demand.

**4 Labor Cost–Total Cost Ratio** *Finally, the larger the portion of total production costs accounted for by a resource, the greater will be the elasticity of demand for that resource.* The rationale here is rather evident. In the extreme, if labor costs were the only production cost, then a 20 percent increase in wage rates would shift the firm's cost curves upward by 20 percent. Given the elasticity of product demand, this substantial increase in costs would cause a relatively large decline in sales and a sharp decline in the amount of labor demanded. Labor demand would tend to be elastic. But if labor costs were only 50 percent of production costs, then a 20 percent increase in wage rates would only increase costs by 10 percent. Given the same elasticity of product demand, a small decline in sales and therefore in the amount of labor would result. The demand for labor would tend to be inelastic.

## ☐ OPTIMUM COMBINATION OF RESOURCES

We know that the production of any good will involve the use of several inputs. It is therefore important to consider what combination of resources a firm will employ. While our analysis will proceed on the basis of two resources, it can readily be extended to any number one chooses to consider.

Our discussion focuses upon two interrelated questions:

**1** What is the least-cost combination of resources to use in producing *any* given level of output?
**2** What combination of resources will maximize a firm's profits?

### △ The Least-Cost Rule

When is a firm producing *any* given output with the least costly combination of resources? The answer is: When the last dollar spent on each resource entails the same marginal physical product. That is, *the cost of any output is minimized when the marginal physical product per dollar's worth of each resource used is the same.* If we are thinking in terms of just two resources, labor and capital, the cost-minimizing position occurs where

$$\frac{\text{MPP of labor}}{\text{price of labor}} = \frac{\text{MPP of capital}}{\text{price of capital}} \quad (1)$$

It is not difficult to see why the fulfillment of this condition means least-cost production. Suppose, for example, that the prices of capital and labor are both $1 per unit, but that capital and labor are currently being employed in such amounts that the marginal physical product of labor is 9 and the marginal physical product of capital is 5. Our equation immediately tells us that this is clearly *not* the least costly combination of resources: $\text{MPP}_L/P_L$ is 9/1 and $\text{MPP}_C/P_C$ is 5/1. If the firm spends a dollar less on capital and shifts that dollar to labor, it will lose the 5 units of output produced by the marginal dollar's worth of capital, but will gain the 9 units of output from the employment of an extra dollar's worth of labor. *Net* output will increase by 4 ( = 9 − 5) units for the same total cost. Note that this shifting of dollars from capital to labor will push the firm down its MPP curve for labor and back up its MPP curve for capital, moving the firm toward a position of equilibrium wherein equation (1) is fulfilled. At that point the MPP of both labor and capital might be, for example, 7.

Whenever the same total cost results in a greater total output, it obviously means that cost per unit—and therefore the total cost of any given level of output—is being reduced. Stated somewhat differently, to be able to produce a *larger* output with a *given* total-cost outlay is the same thing as being able to produce a *given* output with a *smaller* total cost outlay. And as we have seen, the cost of producing any given output can be reduced so long as $\mathrm{MPP}_L/P_L \neq \mathrm{MPP}_C/P_C$. But when dollars have been shifted among capital and labor to the point at which equation (1) holds, then there are no further changes in the amounts of capital and labor employed which will further reduce costs. The least-cost combination of capital and labor is being realized for that output.

*All the long-run[4] cost curves developed in Chapter 25 and applied in the ensuing product market chapters implicitly assume that each possible level of output is being produced with the least costly combination of inputs.* If this were not the case, then presumably there would exist lower attainable positions for the cost curves, and consequently there would be some other (larger) output and lower price at equilibrium.

Note that the producer's least-cost rule is analogous to the consumer's utility-maximizing rule of Chapter 24. In achieving the utility-maximizing collection of goods, the consumer considers both his or her preferences as reflected in diminishing marginal-utility data *and* the prices of the various products. Similarly, a producer obviously wants to minimize costs, just as the consumer seeks to maximize utility. In pursuing this combination of resources, the producer must consider both the productivity of the resource as reflected in diminishing marginal physical–productivity data *and* the prices (costs) of the various resources. A firm may well find it profitable to employ very small amounts of an extremely productive resource if its price is particularly high. Conversely, it may be sensible to hire large amounts of a relatively unproductive resource if its price should turn out to be sufficiently low.

△   **The Profit-maximizing Rule**

In order to maximize profits it is not sufficient to simply minimize costs. There are many different levels of output which a firm can produce in the least costly way. But there is only one unique output which will maximize profits. Recalling our earlier analysis of product markets, this profit-maximizing *output* is where marginal revenue equals marginal cost (MR = MC). Our task now is to derive a comparable rule from the standpoint of resource *inputs.*

The derivation of such a rule is quite simple. In deriving the demand schedule for labor early in this chapter we determined that the profit-maximizing quantity of labor to employ is that quantity at which the wage rate, or price of labor ($P_L$), equals the marginal revenue product of labor ($\mathrm{MRP}_L$) or, more simply, $P_L = \mathrm{MRP}_L$.

The same rationale applies to any other resource—for example, capital. Capital will also be employed in the profit-maximizing amount when its price equals its marginal revenue product, or $P_C = \mathrm{MRP}_C$. Thus, in general, we can say that when hiring resources in competitive markets, a firm will realize the profit-maximizing combination of resources when each input is employed up to the point at which its price equals its marginal revenue product:

$$P_L = \mathrm{MRP}_L$$

$$P_C = \mathrm{MRP}_C$$

---

[4] We specify long run because the application of the least-cost rule assumes that the quantities of both labor and capital are variable.

This rule is sometimes alternatively expressed as

$$\frac{\text{MRP}_L}{P_L} = \frac{\text{MRP}_C}{P_C} = 1 \qquad (2)$$

Note in equation (2) that it is not sufficient that the MRPs of the two resources be *proportionate to* their prices; the MRPs must be *equal to* their prices and the ratios therefore equal to 1. For example, if $\text{MRP}_L = \$15$, $P_L = \$5$, $\text{MRP}_C = \$9$, and $P_C = \$3$, the firm would be underemploying both capital and labor even though the ratios of MRP to resource price were identical for both resources. That is, the firm could expand its profits by hiring additional amounts of both capital and labor until it had moved down their downsloping MRP curves to the points at which $\text{MRP}_L$ was equal to \$5 and $\text{MRP}_C$ was \$3. The ratios would now be 5/5 and 3/3 and obviously equal to 1.

A subtle, but significant, point must be added: Although we have separated the two for discussion purposes, the profit-maximizing position of equation (2) subsumes the least-cost position of equation (1).[5] That is, a firm which is maximizing its profits *must* be producing the profit-maximizing output with the least costly combination of resources. If it is *not* using the least costly combination of labor and capital, then it could obviously produce the same output at a smaller total cost and realize a larger profit! Thus, a necessary condition for profit-maximization is the fulfillment of equation (1). But equation (1) is not a sufficient condition for profit maximization. It is quite possible for a firm to produce the "wrong" output, that is, an output which does not maximize profits, but to produce that output with the least costly combination of resources. Question 7 at the end of this chapter stresses the distinction between the profit-maximizing and the least-cost combination of resources.

## △ Modifications for Imperfect Competition

Our development of the least-cost and profit-maximizing rules assumes purely competitive markets and therefore constant input prices. We shall find in Chapter 31 that, when a firm is hiring resources under imperfectly competitive conditions, its decision to hire more inputs will affect resource prices. Specifically, if a firm is large relative to a resource market, it will have to increase the current resource price to attract more inputs. And this higher price must be paid not only to the extra inputs employed, but also to all units of the resource already in the employment of the firm. This means that marginal resource cost (MRC)—the cost of an extra input—is actually greater than resource price. The fact that MRC exceeds resource price when resources are hired or purchased under imperfectly competitive conditions calls for appropriate adjustments in equations (1) and (2). Specifically, in making marginal decisions to determine the least-cost and profit-maximizing combination of resources, the firm must substitute MRC for resource price in the denominators of our two equations. That is, with imperfect competition in the hiring of both labor and capital, equation (1) becomes

$$\frac{\text{MPP}_L}{\text{MRC}_L} = \frac{\text{MPP}_C}{\text{MRC}_C} \qquad (1')$$

and equation (2) is restated as

$$\frac{\text{MRP}_L}{\text{MRC}_L} = \frac{\text{MRP}_C}{\text{MRC}_C} = 1 \qquad (2')$$

As a matter of fact, equations (1) and (2) can be regarded as special cases of (1') and (2') wherein firms happen to be hiring under purely competitive conditions and resource price is therefore equal to, and can be substituted for, marginal resource cost.

## ☐ MARGINAL PRODUCTIVITY THEORY OF INCOME DISTRIBUTION

Our discussion of resource pricing provides us with the cornerstone of the view that economic

[5] Note that if we divide the MRP numerators in equation (2) by product price we obtain equation (1).

justice is one of the outcomes of a competitive capitalist economy. Recall that Table 30-1 tells us, in effect, that each unit of labor receives an income payment equal to the marginal contribution which it makes to the firm's revenue. Bluntly stated, labor is paid what it is worth. Therefore, if one is willing to accept the ethical proposition "To each according to what one creates," the marginal productivity theory seems to provide a fair and equitable distribution of income. Because the marginal productivity theory is equally applicable to capital and land, the distribution of all incomes can be held as equitable.

At first glance an income distribution whereby workers and owners of property resources are paid in accordance with their contribution to output sounds eminently fair. But there are serious criticisms of the marginal productivity theory of income distribution.

**1**   Critics argue that the distribution of income resulting from the marginal productivity theory is likely to be highly unequal because productive resources are very unequally distributed in the first place. Aside from differences in genetic endowments, individuals encounter substantially different opportunities to enhance their productivity through education and training. Some members of society may not be able to participate in production at

all because of mental or physical handicaps and would obtain no income under a system of distribution based upon marginal productivity. The ownership of property resources is also highly unequal. Many landlords and capitalists obtain their property by inheritance rather than through their own productive effort. Hence, income from inherited property resources is at odds with the "To each according to what one creates" proposition. This line of reasoning can lead one to advocate the substitute proposition "To each according to one's needs."

**2**   The marginal productivity theory rests upon the assumption of competitive markets. We will find in Chapter 31 that labor markets, for example, are riddled with imperfections. Large employers exert monopsony power in hiring workers. And workers, through labor unions and professional associations, brandish market power in selling their services. Indeed, the process of collective bargaining over wages suggests a power struggle over the division of income. In this struggle market forces—and income shares based upon marginal productivity—are pushed into the background. In short, we will find that, because of real world market imperfections, wage rates and other resource prices frequently do *not* measure contributions to national output.

## Summary

**1**   Resource prices are a major determinant of money incomes, and simultaneously perform the function of rationing resources to various industries and firms.

**2**   Though economists agree that resource pricing is a supply and demand phenomenon, they frequently disagree as to the exact characteristics of, and the operation of, supply and demand in particular resource markets.

**3**   The fact that the demand for any resource is derived from the product it helps produce correctly suggests that the demand for a resource will depend upon its productivity and the market value (price) of the good it is producing.

**4**   The marginal revenue product schedule of any resource is the demand schedule for that resource. This follows from an application of the rule that a firm operating under competitive conditions will find it most profitable to hire a resource up to the point at which the price of the resource equals its marginal revenue product.

5   The demand curve for a resource is downsloping, because the marginal physical product of additional inputs of any resource declines in accordance with the law of diminishing returns.   When a firm is selling in an imperfectly competitive market, the resource demand curve will fall, too, because product price must be reduced in order to permit the firm to sell a larger output.   The market demand for a resource can be derived by summing the demand curves of all firms hiring that resource.

6   The demand for a resource will change, that is, a resource demand curve will shift, as the result of *a.* a change in the demand for, and therefore the price of, the product the resource is producing; *b.* changes in the productivity of the resource due either to increases in the quantity or improvements in the quality of the resources with which a given resource is being combined, or improvements in the quality of the given resource itself; and *c.* changes in the prices of other resources.

7   A decline in the price of resource A will typically give rise to a reduction in the demand for resource B (the substitution effect).   But this reduction may be offset by the fact that the decline in the price of A will lower production costs, increasing the equilibrium output and therefore the demand for resource B (the output effect).   There is no substitution effect, only an output effect, for resources which are complementary or jointly demanded.

8   The elasticity of resource demand will be greater *a.* the slower the rate at which the marginal physical product of the resource declines, *b.* the larger the number of good substitute resources available, *c.* the greater the elasticity of demand for the product, and *d.* the larger the proportion of total production costs attributable to the resource.

9   Any level of output will be produced with the least costly combination of resources when the marginal *physical* product per dollar's worth of each input is the same, that is, when

$$\frac{\text{MPP of labor}}{\text{price of labor}} = \frac{\text{MPP of capital}}{\text{price of capital}}$$

10   A firm will employ the profit-maximizing combination of resources when the price of each resource is equal to its marginal *revenue* product or, algebraically, when

$$\frac{\text{MRP of labor}}{\text{price of labor}} = \frac{\text{MRP of capital}}{\text{price of capital}} = 1$$

11   Imperfect competition in hiring labor and capital is accounted for by substituting the marginal resource costs of labor and capital for their prices in the least-cost and profit-maximizing equations.

## Questions and Study Suggestions

1   Key terms and concepts to remember: derived demand; marginal physical product; marginal revenue product; marginal resource cost; MRP = MRC rule; substitution and output effects; least-cost combination of resources; profit-maximizing combination of resources; marginal productivity theory of income distribution.

2   What is the significance of resource pricing?   Explain in detail how the factors determining resource demand differ from those underlying product demand.   Explain the meaning and significance of the notion that the demand for a resource is a *derived* demand. Why do resource demand curves slope downward?

3   Complete the following labor demand table for a firm which is hiring labor competitively and selling its product in a competitive market.

| Units of labor | Total product | Marginal physical product | Product price | Total revenue | Marginal revenue product |
|---|---|---|---|---|---|
| 1 | 17 |  | $2 | $ _____ | $ _____ |
| 2 | 31 | _____ | 2 | _____ | |
| 3 | 43 | _____ | 2 | _____ | _____ |
| 4 | 53 | _____ | 2 | _____ | _____ |
| 5 | 60 | _____ | 2 | _____ | _____ |
| 6 | 65 | _____ | 2 | _____ | _____ |

*a.* How many workers will the firm hire if the going wage rate is $27.95? $19.95? Explain why the firm will not hire a larger or smaller number of workers at each of these wage rates.

*b.* Show in schedule form and graphically the labor demand curve of this firm.

*c.* Now redetermine the firm's demand curve for labor on the assumption that it is selling in an imperfectly competitive market and that, although it can sell 17 units at $2.20 per unit, it must lower product price by 5 cents in order to sell the marginal physical product of each successive worker. Compare this demand curve with that derived in question 3*b.* Explain any differences.

4  Distinguish between a change in resource demand and a change in the quantity of a resource demanded. What specific factors might give rise to a change in resource demand? A change in the quantity of a resource demanded?

5  Using the substitution and output effects, explain how a decline in the price of resource A *might* cause an increase in the demand for substitute resource B.

6  What factors determine the elasticity of resource demand? What effect will each of the following have upon the elasticity *or* the location of the demand for resource C, which is being used in the production of commodity X? Where there is any uncertainty as to the outcome, specify the causes of that uncertainty.

*a.* An increase in the demand for product X.

*b.* An increase in the price of substitute resource D.

*c.* An increase in the number of resources which are substitutable for C in producing X.

*d.* A technological improvement in the capital equipment with which resource C is combined.

*e.* A decline in the price of complementary resource E.

*f.* A decline in the elasticity of demand for product X due to a decline in the competitiveness of the product market.

7  Suppose the productivity of labor and capital are as shown below. The output of these resources sells in a purely competitive market for $1 per unit. Both labor and capital are hired under purely competitive conditions at $1 and $3 respectively.

| Units of capital | MPP of capital | Units of labor | MPP of labor |
|---|---|---|---|
| 1 | 24 | 1 | 11 |
| 2 | 21 | 2 | 9 |
| 3 | 18 | 3 | 8 |
| 4 | 15 | 4 | 7 |
| 5 | 9 | 5 | 6 |
| 6 | 6 | 6 | 4 |
| 7 | 3 | 7 | 1 |
| 8 | 1 | 8 | $\frac{1}{2}$ |

    ***a.***   What is the least-cost combination of labor and capital to employ in producing 80  *7* units of output? Explain.

    ***b.***   What is the profit-maximizing combination of labor and capital for the firm to employ? Explain. What is the resulting level of output?

    ***c.***   When the firm is employing the profit-maximizing combination of labor and capital as determined in 7b, is this combination also the least costly way of producing the profit-maximizing output? Explain.

    **8**   If each input is paid in accordance with its marginal revenue product, will the resulting distribution of income be ethically just?

## Selected References

Bellante, Don, and Mark Jackson: *Labor Economics: Choice in Labor Markets* (New York: McGraw-Hill Book Company, 1979), chap. 2.

Burtt, Everett Johnson: *Labor in the American Economy* (New York: St. Martin's Press, 1979), chap. 4.

Kreps, Juanita M., Gerald G. Somers, and Richard Perlman: *Contemporary Labor Economics* (Belmont, Calif.: Wadsworth Publishing Company, Inc., 1974), chap. 11.

Leftwich, Richard H.: *The Price System and Resource Allocation,* 6th ed. (Hinsdale, Ill.: The Dryden Press, Inc., 1976), chaps. 14, 15.

Mansfield, Edwin: *Microeconomics: Theory and Applications,* 3d ed. (New York: W. W. Norton & Company, Inc., 1979), chaps. 13, 14.

Marshall, F. Ray, Allan G. King, and Vernon M. Briggs, Jr.: *Labor Economics: Wages, Employment, and Trade Unionism,* 4th ed. (Homewood, Ill.: Richard D. Irwin, Inc., 1980), chap. 9.

# LAST WORD
## "I'm Worth $5.9 Million"

A strong demand for a rather unique resource can result in extremely high incomes.

KANSAS CITY, Mo. (AP)—Relief pitcher Al Hrabosky says he's worth the $5.9 million he'll receive over the next five seasons from the Atlanta Braves "because they're paying it to me."

"The most obvious answer is 'no you're not,'" the former Kansas City Royal said when asked if he was worth millions. "But somebody's willing to pay it; then yes you are. I didn't set that salary. They did."

However, the Mad Hungarian, who struck it rich in the free agent market after playing out his option with the Royals last season, does see himself as a valuable gate attraction.

"When I came to the Royals, they came off their highest attendance they ever had—1,855,000," he said. "That first year, they went to 2,255,000. That's a 400,000 increase.

"I definitely paid my salary (in Kansas City)."

The Royals apparently didn't agree. They refused to offer more than three years on a contract calling for $1 million.

"I'm Worth $5.9 Million Since They'll Pay It," *Lincoln Evening Journal*, December 7, 1979.

# The Pricing and Employment of Resources: Wage Determination

chapter **31**

Armed with some understanding of the strategic factors underlying resource demand, we must now introduce supply as it characterizes the markets for labor, land, capital, and entrepreneurial ability to see how wages, rents, interest, and profits are determined. For two reasons, we discuss wage rates prior to other resource prices.

First, the marginal productivity theory of resource demand is probably more applicable to an explanation of wage rates than to the pricing of other resources.

Second, to the vast majority of households the wage rate is the most important price in the economy; it is the sole or basic source of income. About three-fourths of the national income is in the form of wages and salaries.

Our basic objectives in discussing wage determination are to: (1) understand the forces underlying the general level of wage rates in the United States; (2) see how wage rates are determined in particular labor markets by pre-

senting several representative labor market models; (3) discuss the economic effects of the minimum wage; (4) analyze the impact of unions upon the structure and level of wages; (5) explain wage differentials; and (6) introduce and briefly discuss the concept of investment in human capital.

Throughout this chapter we shall rely upon the marginal productivity theory of Chapter 30 as an explanation of labor demand.

## ☐ MEANING OF WAGES

Wages, or wage rates, are the price paid for the use of labor. Economists often employ the term "labor" broadly to apply to the payments received by (1) workers in the popular sense of the term, that is, blue- and white-collar workers of infinite variety; (2) professional people—physicians, lawyers, dentists, teachers, and so forth; and (3) owners of small businesses—barbers, plumbers, television repairmen, and a host of retailers—for the labor services they provide in operating their own businesses.[1]

Though in practice wages may take the form of bonuses, royalties, commissions, and monthly salaries, we shall use the term "wages" to mean wage rates per unit of time—per hour, per day, and so forth. This designation has the advantage of reminding us that the wage rate is a price paid for the use of units of labor service. It also permits us to distinguish clearly between "wages" and "earnings," the latter depending upon wage rates *and* the number of hours or weeks of labor service supplied in the market.

It is important, too, to make a distinction between money wages and real wages. *Money wages* are the amount of money received per hour, per day, per week, and so on. *Real wages,* on the other hand, are the quantity of goods and services which one can obtain with one's money wages; real wages are the "purchasing power" of money wages. Obviously one's real wages depend upon one's money wages and the prices of the goods and services one buys. Note that money wages and real wages need not move together. For example, money wages may rise and real wages simultaneously decline *if* product prices rise more rapidly than do money wages. Unless otherwise indicated, our discussion will be couched in terms of real wage rates by assuming that the level of product prices is constant.

## ☐ GENERAL LEVEL OF WAGES

Wages tend to differ among nations, among regions, among various occupations, and among individuals. Wage rates are vastly higher in the United States than in China or India; they are generally higher in the North and East of the United States than in the South; plumbers are paid more than cotton pickers; physician Abrams may earn twice as much as physician Bennett for the same number of hours of work. Wage rates also differ by sex and race.

Our approach will involve moving from the general to the specific. In this section we are concerned with explaining why the general level of wages is higher in the United States than in most foreign nations. This explanation will be largely applicable to regional wage differences within nations. In the following section we shall seek to explain wages in terms of markets for specific types of labor. In both these discussions a supply and demand approach will offer the most fruitful results.

The general level of wages, like the general level of prices, is a composite concept encompassing a wide range of different specific wage rates. This admittedly vague concept is a useful point of departure in making and explaining international and interregional wage comparisons. Statistical data indicate that the general level of real wages in the United States is among the highest in the world. The simplest explanation of this fact is that in the United States the demand for labor has been great in relation to the supply.

### △  Role of Productivity

Let us look behind these forces of demand and supply. We know that the demand for labor—or any other resource—depends upon its productivity. In general, the greater the productivity of labor, the greater the demand for it. And, given the total supply of labor, the stronger the demand, the greater the level of real wages. The demand for American labor has been high because it is highly productive. But why the high productivity? The reasons are several:

**1  Capital**  American workers are used in conjunction with large amounts of capital equipment. For example, the average American factory worker is assisted by some $41,000 worth of machinery and equipment.

---

[1] This broad definition of labor, incidentally, encompasses individuals who would be considered as profit receivers in national income accounting. Hence, under this definition, wages would clearly amount to more than three-fourths of the national income.

**2   Natural Resources**   Natural resources are very abundant in relation to the size of the labor force. The United States is richly endowed with arable land, basic mineral resources, and—at least until the emergence of recent energy problems—ample sources of industrial power. The fact that American workers have large amounts of high-quality natural resources to work with is perhaps most evident in agriculture where, historically, the growth of productivity has been dramatic (Chapter 35).

**3   Technology**   The level of technological advance is generally higher in the United States than in foreign nations. American workers in most industries use not only more capital equipment but better (that is, technologically superior) equipment than do foreign workers. Similarly, work methods are steadily being improved through detailed scientific study and research.

**4   Labor Quality**   The health, vigor, education and training, work attitudes, and adaptability of American workers to the disci-

pline of factory production have been generally superior to those of the labor of other nations. This means that, even with the same quantity and quality of natural and capital resources, American workers typically would be somewhat more efficient than most of their foreign counterparts.

**5   Other Factors**   Less tangible, yet important, items underlying the high productivity of American labor are (*a*) the efficiency and flexibility of American management; (*b*) a business, social, and political environment which puts great emphasis upon production and productivity; and (*c*) the vast size of the domestic market, which provides the opportunity for firms to realize mass-production economies.

The reader will recognize that the aforementioned factors are merely a restatement of the cornerstones of economic growth (Chapter 19). It is also notable that the productivity of labor depends to a very great degree upon considerations other than the quality of labor itself, that is, upon the quantity and quality of the property resources at the worker's disposal.

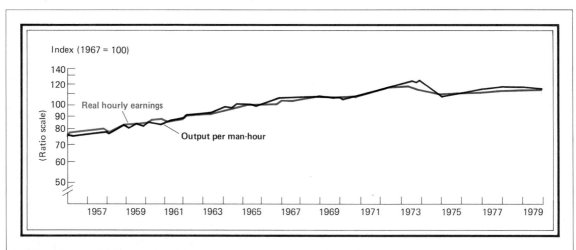

FIGURE 31-1 OUTPUT PER HOUR AND REAL AVERAGE HOURLY EARNINGS

Over a long period of years there has been a close relationship between real hourly wages and output per man-hour. (Department of Labor, *Employment and Earnings*).

### △  Real Wages and Productivity

The dependence of real hourly wages upon the level of productivity is indicated in Figure 31-1. Note the relatively close relationship in the long run between real hourly wages and output per labor-hour in nonfarm private industries. When one recalls that real income and real output are two ways of viewing the same thing, it is no surprise that *income per worker can increase only at about the same rate as output per worker.*

### △  Secular Growth

But simple supply and demand analysis suggests that, even if the demand for labor is strong in the United States, increases in the supply of labor will cause the general level of wages to decline over time. It is certainly true that the American population and the labor force have grown significantly over the decades. However, these increases in the supply of labor have been more than offset by increases in the demand for labor stemming from the productivity-increasing factors discussed above. The result has been a long-run, or secular, increase in wage rates, as suggested by Figure 31-2. One authoritative study indicates that, for the 1889–1969 period, labor productivity, as measured by output per labor-hour, grew at an annual rate of 2.4 percent. This rate of growth translates into a doubling of real output and real wage rates in about thirty years (recall the "rule of 70"), and for the entire eighty-year period under consideration, something in excess of a sixfold increase in real wages per labor-hour.[2]

### ☐  WAGES IN PARTICULAR LABOR MARKETS

We now turn from the general level of wages to the wage structure, that is, to the system of

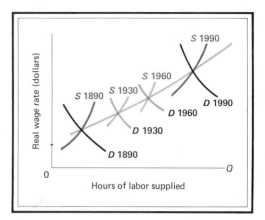

**FIGURE 31-2  THE SECULAR TREND OF REAL WAGES IN THE UNITED STATES**

The productivity of American labor has increased substantially in the long run, causing the demand for labor to increase in relation to the supply. The result has been increases in real wages.

specific wage rates which the general level of wages comprises. The question now is this: What determines the wage rate received by some specific type of worker? Demand and supply analysis again provides the most revealing approach. Our analysis covers some half-dozen basic market models.

### △  Competitive Model

Let us suppose that there are many—say, 200—firms demanding a particular type of semiskilled or skilled labor.[3] The total, or market, demand for this labor can be determined by summing the labor demand curves (the MRP curves) of the individual firms, as suggested in Figure 31-3a and b. On the supply side of the picture, we assume there is no union; workers compete freely for available jobs. The supply curve for a particular type of labor will be upsloping, reflecting the fact that,

---

[2]Solomon Fabricant, *A Primer on Productivity* (New York: Random House, Inc., 1969), p. 14. The reader might find it worthwhile to review the earlier (Chapter 19) discussion of the recent slowdown in the rate of productivity growth.

[3]These firms need not be in the same industry; industries are defined in terms of the products they produce and not of the resources they employ. Thus firms producing wood-frame furniture, window and door frames, and cabinets will all demand carpenters.

in the absence of unemployment, hiring firms as a group will be forced to pay higher wage rates to obtain more workers. Why? Because the firms must bid these workers away from other industries and other localities. Within limits, workers have alternative job opportunities; that is, they may work in other industries in the same locality, or they may work in their present occupations in different cities or states. In a full-employment economy the group of firms in this particular labor market must pay higher and higher wage rates to attract this type of labor away from these alternative job opportunities.

The equilibrium wage rate and the equilibrium level of employment for this type of labor are obviously determined by the intersection of the labor demand and labor supply curves. In Figure 31-3*b* the equilibrium wage rate is $W_c$ ($6), and the number of workers hired is $Q_c$ (1000). To the individual firm the wage rate $W_c$ is given. Each of the many hiring firms employs such a small fraction of the total available supply of this type of labor that none can influence the wage rate. Technically, the supply of labor is perfectly elastic to the individual firm, as shown by $S$ in Figure 31-3*a*. Each individual firm will find it profitable to

**TABLE 31-1**
**The Supply of Labor: Pure Competition in the Hire of Labor (*hypothetical data*)**

| (1) Units of labor | (2) Wage rate | (3) Total labor cost (wage bill) | (4) Marginal resource (labor) cost |
|---|---|---|---|
| 1 | $6 | $ 6 | $6 |
| 2 | 6 | 12 | 6 |
| 3 | 6 | 18 | 6 |
| 4 | 6 | 24 | 6 |
| 5 | 6 | 30 | 6 |
| 6 | 6 | 36 | |

hire workers up to the point at which the going wage rate is equal to labor's MRP. This is merely an application of the MRP = MRC rule developed in Chapter 30. (Indeed, the demand curve in Figure 31-3*a* is based upon Table 30-1.) As Table 31-1 indicates, *because resource price is given to the individual competitive firm, the marginal cost of that resource (MRC) will be constant and equal to resource price.* In this case the wage rate and hence the marginal cost of labor are constant to the individual firm. Each additional worker hired adds precisely his or her wage rate to the firm's total

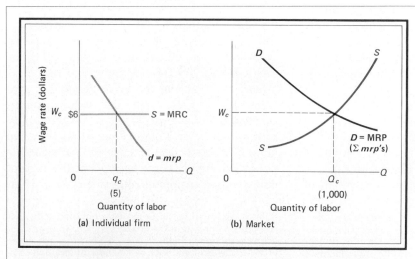

**FIGURE 31-3 THE SUPPLY OF, AND THE DEMAND FOR, LABOR IN A SINGLE COMPETITIVE FIRM (a) AND IN A COMPETITIVE MARKET (b)**

In a competitive labor market the equilibrium wage rate $W_c$ and number of workers employed $Q_c$ are determined by supply *SS* and demand *DD*, as shown in (b). Because this wage rate is given to the individual firm hiring in the market, its labor supply curve, *S* = MRC, is perfectly elastic, as in (a). The firm finds it most profitable to hire workers up to the MRP = MRC point.

resource cost. The firm then will maximize its profits by hiring workers to the point at which their wage rate, and therefore marginal resource cost, equals their marginal revenue product. In Figure 31-3a the "typical" firm will hire $q_c$ (five) workers.

△ **Monopsony Model**

But in many labor markets workers are not hired competitively. Rather, employers are *monopsonists;* that is, they have some monopolistic buying power. In some instances the monopsonistic power of employers is virtually complete in the sense that there is only one major employer in a labor market. For example, the economies of some towns and cities depend almost entirely upon one major firm. A silver-mining concern may be the basic source of employment in a remote Colorado town. A New England textile mill, a Wisconsin paper mill, or a farm-belt food processor may provide a large proportion of the employment in its locality. Anaconda Mining is the dominant employer in Butte, Montana. In other cases *oligopsony* may prevail; three or four firms may each hire a large portion of the supply of labor in a particular market. Our study of oligopoly correctly suggests that there is a strong tendency for oligopsonists to act in concert—much like a monopsonist—in hiring labor.

The market for professional athletes is characterized by ingenious collusive devices by which employers have attempted with considerable success to limit competition in the hire of labor. The National Football League, the National Basketball Association, and the American and National Baseball Leagues have established systems of rules which tend to tie a player to one team and prevent him from selling his talents to the highest bidder on the open (competitive) market. In particular, through the new player draft, the team which selects or "drafts" a player has the exclusive right to bargain a contract with that player. Furthermore, the so-called reserve clause in each player's contract gives his team the ex-

clusive right to purchase his services for the next season. Though recent court cases have tended to make the labor markets for professional athletes slightly more competitive, collusive monopsony persists.[4]

The important point is this: When a firm hires a considerable portion of the total available supply of a particular type of labor, its decision to employ more or fewer workers will affect the wage rate paid to that labor. Specifically, *if a firm is large in relation to the labor market, it will have to pay a higher wage rate in order to obtain more labor.* For simplicity's sake let us suppose there is only one employer of a particular type of labor in a specified geographic area. Obviously, the labor supply curve to that firm and the total supply curve for the labor market are identical. This supply curve, for reasons already made clear, is upsloping, indicating that the firm must pay a higher wage rate to attract more workers. This is shown by SS in Figure 31-4. The supply curve is in effect the average-cost-of-labor curve from the firm's perspective; each point on it indicates the wage rate (cost) per worker which must be paid to attract the corresponding number of workers.

But the higher wages involved in attracting additional workers will also have to be paid to all workers currently employed at lower wage rates. If not, labor morale will surely deteriorate, and the employer will be plagued with serious problems of labor unrest because of the wage-rate differentials existing for the same job. As for cost, the payment of a uniform wage to all workers will mean that the cost of an extra worker—the marginal resource (labor) cost (MRC)—will exceed the wage rate by the amount necessary to bring the wage rate of all workers currently employed up to the new wage level. Table 31-2 illustrates this point. One worker can be hired at a wage rate

[4]The interested reader should consult Janice M. Westerfield, "Restrictive Labor Practices in Baseball: Time for a Change?" *Business Review,* Federal Reserve Bank of Philadelphia, June 1975, pp. 17–26.

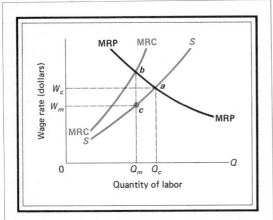

FIGURE 31-4   THE WAGE RATE AND LEVEL OF
EMPLOYMENT IN A MONOPSONISTIC LABOR
MARKET

In a monopsonistic labor market the employer's
marginal resource (labor) cost curve (MRC) lies above the
labor supply curve (S). Equating MRC with labor demand
MRP at point b, the monopsonist will hire $Q_m$ workers
(as compared with $Q_c$ under competition) and pay the
wage rate $W_m$ (as compared with the competitive wage $W_c$).

of $6. But the hire of a second worker forces
the firm to pay a higher wage rate of $7. Mar-
ginal resource (labor) cost is $8—the $7 paid
the second worker plus a $1 raise for the first
worker. Similarly, the marginal labor cost of
the third worker is $10—the $8 which must be
paid to attract this worker from alternative
employments plus $1 raises for the first two

**TABLE 31-2**

The Supply of Labor: Monopsony in the Hire of Labor
(*hypothetical data*)

| (1) Units of labor | (2) Wage rate | (3) Total labor cost (wage bill) | (4) Marginal resource (labor) cost |
|---|---|---|---|
| 1 | $ 6 | $ 6 | $ 6 |
| 2 | 7 | 14 | 8 |
| 3 | 8 | 24 | 10 |
| 4 | 9 | 36 | 12 |
| 5 | 10 | 50 | 14 |
| 6 | 11 | 66 | 16 |

workers. The important point is that *to the
monopsonist, marginal resource (labor) cost
will exceed the wage rate.* Graphically, the
MRC curve (columns 1 and 4 in Table 31-2)
will lie above the average cost, or supply, curve
of labor (columns 1 and 2 in Table 31-2). This
is shown graphically in Figure 31-4.

How much labor will the firm hire, and
what wage rate will it pay? To maximize profits the firm will equate marginal resource
(labor) cost with the MRP. The number of
workers hired by the monopsonist is indicated
by $Q_m$, and the wage rate paid, $W_m$, is indicated
by the corresponding point on the resource
supply, or average-cost-of-labor, curve. It is
particularly important to contrast these results with those which a competitive labor
market would have yielded. With competition
in the hire of labor, the level of employment
would have been greater ($Q_c$), and the wage
rate would have been higher ($W_c$). It simply
does not pay the monopsonist to hire workers
up to the point at which the wage rate and
labor's MRP are equal. Other things being
equal, the monopsonist maximizes its profits
by hiring a smaller number of workers and
thereby paying a less-than-competitive wage
rate. In the process, society gets a smaller
output,[5] and workers get a wage rate less by $bc$
than their marginal revenue product. Just as a
monopolistic seller finds it profitable to restrict
product output to realize an above-competitive
price for its goods, so the monopsonistic employer of resources finds it profitable to restrict
employment in order to depress wage rates and
therefore costs, that is, to realize below-com-
petitive wage rates.[6]

[5]This is analogous to the monopolist's restricting output as
it sets product price and output on the basis of marginal
revenue, not product demand. In this instance, resource
price is set on the basis of marginal labor (resource) cost,
not resource supply.
[6]Will a monopsonistic employer also be a monopolistic
seller in the product market? Not necessarily. The New
England textile mill may be a monopsonistic employer, yet
face severe domestic and foreign competition in selling its
product. In other cases—for example, the automobile and
steel industries—firms have both monopsonistic and monopolistic (oligopolistic) power.

## △ Some Union Models

Thus far, we have been content to assume that workers are actively competing in the sale of their labor services. In a good many markets, workers "sell" their labor services collectively through unions. To envision the economic impact of unions in the simplest context, let us suppose a union is formed in an otherwise competitive labor market. That is, a union is now bargaining with a relatively large number of employers. Later we shall consider the case where the union faces a large single employer, that is, a monopsonist.

Unions seek many goals. The basic economic objective, however, is to raise wage rates. The union can pursue this objective in several different ways.

**Increasing the Demand for Labor**   From the union's point of view, the most desirable technique for raising wage rates is to increase the demand for labor. As shown in Figure 31-5, an increase in the demand for labor will result in *both* higher wage rates and more jobs. The relative sizes of these increases will depend

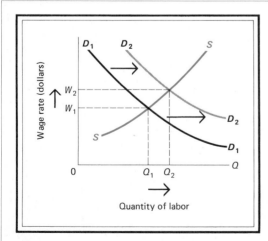

FIGURE 31-5 UNIONS AND THE DEMAND FOR LABOR

When unions can increase the demand for labor ($D_1 D_1$ to $D_2 D_2$), higher wage rates ($W_1$ to $W_2$) and a larger number of jobs ($Q_1$ to $Q_2$) can be realized.

upon the elasticity of labor supply. Classic examples are the International Ladies' Garment Workers Union and the Amalgamated Clothing Workers Union, both of which have assisted clothing firms to increase their productivity. The New York locals of the ILGWU have even helped employers in financing advertising campaigns to bolster the demand for their products. And it is no accident that some unions have vigorously supported their employers in seeking to maintain protective tariffs designed to exclude competing foreign products. The American Watch Workers Union is a case in point. Some unions have sought to expand the demand for labor by forcing make-work, or "featherbedding," rules upon employers. Prior to fairly recent court rulings, the Railway Brotherhoods forced railroads to hire train crews of a certain minimum size; diesel engines had to have a fireman even though there was no fire.

But the opportunity for unions to increase the demand for labor is limited. The main reason is obvious: As noted in our earlier discussion of the general level of wages, the basic forces underlying the productivity of, and therefore the demand for, labor are largely outside the control of labor unions. The quantity and quality of the capital equipment with which labor is combined are the basic determinants of labor productivity in most firms, and this is a matter over which unions typically have little or no control. It should be noted, too, that in many of the instances in which unions have pleaded for tariff protection and have practiced featherbedding, the situation has been that of a union's attempting to offset or forestall declines in the demand for labor rather than actually to increase the existing demand for a particular type of labor. This comment seems pertinent to the garment-makers, the watchmakers, and the Railway Brotherhoods, all of which find themselves in the unfortunate position of being employed in declining industries or faced with job-destroying technological advances. In view of these considerations, it is not surprising that union efforts to increase wage rates have concentrated upon the supply side of the market.

**Exclusive or Craft Unionism**   Unions may boost wage rates by reducing the supply of labor, that is, by shifting the supply curve of a particular type of labor to the left. Historically, the labor movement has favored policies designed to restrict the supply of labor to the economy as a whole in order to bolster the general level of wages. Labor unions have supported legislation which has (1) restricted immigration, (2) reduced child labor, (3) encouraged compulsory retirement, and (4) enforced a shorter workweek.

More relevant for present purposes is the fact that specific types of workers have adopted through unions a host of techniques designed to restrict their numbers. This has been especially true of *craft unions*—that is, unions which comprise workers of a given skill, such as carpenters, bricklayers, plumbers, and printers. These unions have in many instances forced employers to agree to hire only union workers, thereby giving the union virtually complete control of the supply of labor. Then, by following restrictive membership policies—long apprenticeships, exorbitant initiation fees, the limitation or flat prohibition of new members—the union causes an artificial restriction of the labor supply. As indicated in Figure 31-6, this results in higher wage rates. For obvious reasons, this approach to achieving wage increases might be called *exclusive unionism*. Higher wages are the result of excluding workers from the union and therefore from the supply of labor. This chapter's Last Word is a brief case study of how the American Medical Association has successfully practiced exclusive unionism.

**Occupational Licensure**   This is an increasingly important means by which workers have been able to restrict entry to certain occupations. Here a group of workers in an occupation will pressure state government to pass a law which provides that, say, barbers (plumb-

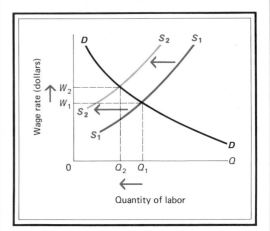

**FIGURE 31-6  EXCLUSIVE OR CRAFT UNIONISM**

By reducing the supply of labor ($S_1S_1$ to $S_2S_2$) through the use of restrictive membership policies, exclusive unions achieve higher wage rates ($W_1$ to $W_2$). However, the restriction of labor supply also reduces the number of workers employed ($Q_1$ to $Q_2$).

ers, beauticians, egg graders, pest controllers) can practice their trade only if they meet certain specified requirements. These requirements might specify the level of educational attainment, amount of work experience, the passing of an examination, and personal characteristics ("the practitioner must be of good moral character"). The licensing board which administers the law is typically dominated by members of the licensed occupation. The obvious result is self-regulation which is conducive to policies that reflect self-interest. In short, the imposition of arbitrary and irrelevant entrance requirements or the construction of an unnecessarily stringent examination can restrict the number of entrants to the occupation. The effect is to protect the job opportunities and wage scales of those already in the occupation. Furthermore, licensing requirements often specify a residency requirement which tends to inhibit the interstate movement of qualified workers. It is estimated that over 550 occupations are now licensed in the United States.

**Inclusive or Industrial Unionism**  Most unions, however, do not attempt to limit their membership. On the contrary, they seek to organize all available or potential workers. This is characteristic of the so-called *industrial unions*—unions, such as the automobile workers and steelworkers, which include all unskilled, semiskilled, and even skilled workers in a given industry. A union can afford to be exclusive when its members are skilled craftsmen for whom substitute workers are not readily available in quantity. But a union that comprises largely unskilled and semiskilled workers will undermine its own existence by limiting its membership and thereby causing numerous highly substitutable nonunion workers to be readily available for employment.

If an industrial union is successful in including virtually all workers in its membership, firms will be under great pressure to come to terms at the wage rate demanded by the union. Why? Because by going on strike the union can obviously deprive the firm of its entire labor supply.

*Inclusive unionism* is illustrated graphically in Figure 31-7. Initially, the competitive equilibrium wage rate is $W_c$, and the level of employment is $Q_c$. Now suppose an industrial union is formed, and it imposes a higher, above-equilibrium wage rate of, say, $W_u$. The imposition of this wage rate changes the supply curve of labor to the firm from the preunion $SS$ curve to the postunion $W_u aS$ curve shown by the heavy orange line.[7] No workers will be forthcoming at a wage rate less than that demanded by the union. If the employers decide

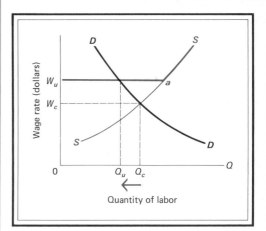

**FIGURE 31-7 INCLUSIVE OR INDUSTRIAL UNIONISM**

By organizing virtually all available workers and thereby controlling the supply of labor, inclusive industrial unions may impose a wage rate, such as $W_u$, which is above the competitive wage rate $W_c$. The effect is to change the labor supply curve from $SS$ to $W_u aS$. At the $W_u$ wage rate, employers will cut employment from $Q_c$ to $Q_u$.

it is better to pay this higher wage rate than to suffer a strike, they will cut back on employment from $Q_c$ to $Q_u$. In other words, the above-equilibrium wage rate will cause some unemployment of union workers in this particular labor market.

Needless to say, this unemployment effect constitutes an important restraining influence upon the union in formulating its wage demands. A union cannot expect to maintain solidarity within its ranks if it seeks a wage rate so high that the result will be joblessness for 20, 30, or 40 percent of its members. The elasticity of labor demand is the basic consideration in determining the amount of unemployment which will accompany a wage hike: the more inelastic the demand for labor, the smaller will be the resulting unemployment. You will recall from Chapter 30 that the determinants of the elasticity of labor demand include the elasticity of demand for the product, the portion of total costs for which wages account, and the substitutability of other re-

---

[7]Technically, the imposition of the wage rate $W_u$ makes the labor supply curve perfectly elastic over the $W_u a$ range in Figure 31-7. If employers hire any number of workers within this range, the union-imposed wage rate is effective and must be paid, or the union will supply no labor at all—the employers will be faced with a strike. If the employers want a number of workers in excess of $W_u a$ (which they never will when the union sets an above-equilibrium wage rate), they will have to bid up wages above the union's minimum.

sources for labor. It is notable that substituta-bility and hence elasticity vary directly with time. That is, over a short period—say a few weeks or months—a firm may hire about the same number of workers after a pay hike as it did before. But then, as the months pass, em-ployers have sufficient time to substitute la-borsaving capital equipment for workers. The practical significance of this is that, as substi-tution occurs, workers will be *gradually* unem-ployed and typically will drift into other jobs and other geographic areas. And with the ab-sence of job opportunities, new workers enter-ing the labor force will be discouraged from entering this line of work. For these reasons the unemployment restraint upon union wage demands may be less pressing than it first ap-pears to be.[8]

Even though industrial unions encourage rather than restrict membership, there is clearly a restrictive aspect to this analysis. But, in contrast to the practices of exclusive unionism, the restriction of employment here is made not by directly influencing labor sup-ply, but by enforcing an above-equilibrium wage rate and allowing the market to restrict the number of jobs available. The United Mine Workers is an excellent historical exam-ple of an inclusive union which was willing to sacrifice jobs for higher wages.[9]

△  **Bilateral Monopoly Model**

Now let us suppose that a strong indus-trial union is formed in a labor market which is monopsonistic rather than competitive. In other words, let us combine the monopsony model with the inclusive unionism model. The result is a case of *bilateral monopoly*. The union is a monopolistic "seller" of labor in that

it can exert an influence over wage rates; it faces a monopsonistic employer (or combina-tion of oligopsonistic employers) of labor who can also affect wages. Is this an extreme or special case? Not at all. In such important industries as steel, automobiles, meatpacking, and farm machinery, "big labor"—one huge industrial union—bargains with "big busi-ness"—a few huge industrial giants.

This situation can be shown graphically as in Figure 31-8, which merely superimposes Fig-ure 31-7 upon 31-4. The monopsonistic em-ployer will seek the wage rate $W_m$ and the union presumably will press for some above-equilibrium wage rate such as $W_u$. Which of these two possibilities will result? We cannot say with any certainty. The outcome is logi-cally indeterminate in the sense that economic theory does not explain what the resulting wage rate will be. We should expect the re-sulting wage to lie somewhere between $W_m$ and $W_u$. Beyond that, about all we can say is that the party with the most bargaining power and the most effective bargaining strategy will be able to get its opponent to agree to a wage close to the one it seeks.[10]

These comments suggest another impor-tant feature of the bilateral monopoly model. The kind of labor market we are here describ-ing may be an important manifestation of countervailing power. If either the union or management prevailed in this market—that is, if the actual wage rate were determined at $W_u$ or $W_m$—employment would be restricted to $Q_m$, which is obviously below the competitive level. But now let us suppose the countervail-ing power of the union roughly offsets the orig-inal monopsony power of management and a bargained wage rate of about $W_c$, which is the competitive wage, is agreed upon. Once man-

---

[8] In fact, in a growing economy the demand curves for most kinds of labor will be gradually shifting to the right through time, tending to offset unemployment effects. Instead of an absolute decline in the number of jobs in this market, the result may be a decline in the rate of growth of job opportunities.

[9] See Gordon F. Bloom and Herbert R. Northrup, *Eco-nomics of Labor Relations,* 5th ed. (Homewood, Ill.: Rich-ard D. Irwin, Inc., 1965), pp. 469–472.

[10] Economists have developed a number of bargaining the-ories. The ambitious reader should consult Bevars D. Mabry, *Economics of Manpower and the Labor Market* (New York: Intext Educational Publishers, 1973), chap. 13; and Albert Rees, *The Economics of Work and Pay,* 2d ed. (New York: Harper & Row, Publishers, Incorporated, 1979), chaps. 8 and 9.

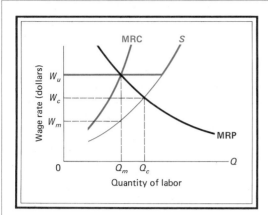

**FIGURE 31-8  BILATERAL MONOPOLY IN THE LABOR MARKET**

When a monopsonistic employer seeks the wage rate $W_m$ and the inclusive union he faces seeks an above-equilibrium wage rate such as $W_u$, the actual outcome is logically indeterminate.

agement agrees to this wage rate, its incentive to restrict employment disappears; no longer can the employer depress wage rates by restricting employment. Thus management equates the bargained wage rate $W_c$ ($= $ MRC) with MRP and finds it most profitable to hire $Q_c$ workers. In short, with monopoly on both sides of the labor market, it may be possible that the resulting wage rate and level of employment will be closer to competitive levels than if monopoly existed on only one side of the market.

### △  The Minimum-Wage Controversy

Since the passage of the Fair Labor Standards Act in 1938, the United States has had a Federal minimum wage. The analysis of the effects of union wage-fixing raises the much-debated question of the efficacy of this minimum-wage legislation as an antipoverty device.

**Case against the Minimum Wage**  Critics, reasoning in terms of Figure 31-7, contend that the imposition of effective (above-equilibrium)

minimum wages will simply push employers back up their MRP or labor demand curves because it is now profitable to hire fewer workers. The higher wage costs may even force some firms out of business. The result is that many of the poor, low-wage workers whom the minimum wage was designed to help will now find themselves out of work. Is it not obvious, critics query, that a worker who is unemployed at a minimum wage of $3.35 per hour is clearly worse off than if he or she were employed at the market wage rate of, say, $2.50 per hour? Some discharged workers may drift off into other labor markets and find employment, but in so doing they increase the supply of labor in these markets and tend to depress wage rates therein.

**Case for the Minimum Wage**  Advocates allege that critics have analyzed the impact of the minimum wage in an unrealistic context. Figure 31-7, advocates claim, assumes a competitive and static market. The imposition of a minimum wage in a monopsonistic labor market (Figure 31-8) suggests that the minimum wage can increase wage rates without causing unemployment; indeed, higher minimum wages may even result in more jobs by eliminating the monopsonistic employer's motive to restrict employment. Furthermore, the imposition of an effective minimum wage may increase labor productivity, shifting the labor demand curve to the right and offsetting any unemployment effects which the minimum wage might otherwise induce. But how might a minimum wage increase productivity? First, a minimum wage may have a *shock effect* upon employers. That is, firms using low-wage workers may tend to be inefficient in the use of labor; the higher wage rates imposed by the minimum wage will presumably shock these firms into using labor more efficiently, and so the productivity of labor rises. Second, it is argued that higher wages will tend to increase the incomes and therefore the health, vigor, and motivation of workers, making them more productive.

**Evidence** Which view is correct? It is hard to say, because empirical studies of the effects of increases in the minimum wage run into the problems of distinguishing the effects of the minimum wage per se from the effects of other developments—growth, inflation, recession—occurring in the economy. On balance, however, the evidence seems to suggest that periodic increases in the minimum wage are followed by employment declines in affected industries. Empirical studies suggest that the unemployment effect is particularly pronounced among teenage workers. The other side of the coin, of course, is that those who remain employed receive higher incomes and tend to escape poverty. The overall antipoverty effect of the minimum wage may thus be a mixed, ambivalent one. Those who lose their jobs are plunged deeper into poverty; those who remain employed tend to escape poverty.[11]

△ **Do Unions Raise Wages?**

Our union models (Figures 31-5, 31-6, and 31-7) all imply that unions have the capacity to raise wage rates. Has unionization in fact caused wage rates to be higher than otherwise? On the face of it, this might seem to be a naïve question, the answer to which must be an unqualified "Yes." Don't we persistently read of specific unions successfully bargaining for substantial wage gains? And doesn't casual observation suggest that the average wage for organized workers is higher than for unorganized workers?

**Complications** Yet, one may have second thoughts. For example, we know that the long-run trend of real wages in the United

States has been upward (Figure 31-2). So the real question is not solely whether unions successfully bargain for wage increases, but rather, whether these increases are larger than, smaller than, or about the same as those which the subtle, undramatic workings of the market would have brought about. Although the UAW now negotiates wage increases in the automobile industry, we must keep in mind that wages rose in the industry long before it was organized in 1938–1941 and undoubtedly would have risen substantially in the past several decades had the industry remained unorganized. Furthermore, there is the historical fact that unions have been most successful in organizing the more prosperous industries. Many of the now-unionized high-wage industries were also high-wage industries *before* they were organized. Again the automobile industry is a good illustration. Thus one may legitimately ask if the fact that unionized industries pay higher wages than unorganized industries is the result of unionization or, alternatively, if unions are getting credit for wage increases attributable to favorable market forces.

As with the minimum wage, empirical studies which attempt to compare union and nonunion wages encounter severe conceptual obstacles, and their conclusions are invariably questionable. For example, if it is found that unionized carpenters get $8.00 per hour in city X while unorganized carpenters earn only $6.00 per hour in city Y, can we say with certainty that the differential is attributable to unionization or to some other variable? Perhaps city X is a dynamic, growing economic area, while city Y is in a depressed area where wage rates are generally low.

**Two Generalizations** Given such difficulties, it is not too surprising that labor economists offer a tentative two-part response to the question "Do unions raise wages?" The first portion of the response compares union with nonunion wages; the second is concerned with the impact of unions upon the wage level of all workers.

[11]See Lloyd G. Reynolds, *Labor Economics and Labor Relations,* 7th ed. (Englewood Cliffs, N.J.: Prentice-Hall, Inc., 1978), pp. 103–107; James F. Ragan, Jr., "The Failure of the Minimum Wage Law," *Challenge,* May–June 1978, pp. 61–65; and Steven P. Zell, "The Minimum Wage and Youth Unemployment," *Economic Review,* Federal Reserve Bank of Kansas City, January 1978, pp. 3–16.

**1** *Unionized workers have probably achieved wage rates which average 10 to 15 percent higher than those received by nonunion workers in the same occupation.*[12] Although this is not an insignificant accomplishment, the advantage is not so large as to imply that the formation of unions and the determination of wages through collective bargaining somehow permit labor to break free of market restraints and to establish wage rates largely at their discretion. In particular, higher wages tend to mean fewer jobs, and this inverse relationship between wages and employment acts as an important constraint upon the wage-raising activities of labor unions.

**2** *Unions have probably had little or no perceptible impact upon the average level of real wages received by labor—both organized and unorganized—taken as a whole.*

At first glance these two conclusions may seem inconsistent. But they need not be if the wage gains of organized workers are at the expense of unorganized workers. Imagine an economy divided into two sectors which are identical except that one is unionized and the other is not. Now, consistent with generalization 1 above, suppose the organized sector realizes a 10 percent money-wage increase. Assuming constant productivity, unit production costs and the price level will rise by 10 percent in the organized sector and, given constant prices in the unorganized sector, the overall price level will rise by 5 percent. This will obviously mean that real wages have risen by 5 percent in the organized sector, because money wages have gone up 10 percent, and the price level by only 5 percent. But it also means a *fall* in real wages in the unorganized sector, where money-wage rates have assumedly remained constant while the price level has gone up by 5 percent. This tendency for higher union (real) wages to result in lower nonunion (real) wages may be reinforced by shifts in labor supply. Higher wages in the organized

sector will tend to reduce employment therein; these unemployed workers may then seek jobs in the unorganized sector. This increase in the supply of labor will tend to depress the money and real wages of workers in the unorganized sector. In short, higher real wage rates for organized workers may well be at the expense of unorganized workers with the result that the average level of real wages for labor as a whole is unaltered. Stated differently, the tight relationship between productivity and the average level of real wages shown in Figure 31-1 correctly suggests that unions have little power to raise real wage rates for labor as a whole. But Figure 31-1 is an average relationship and is therefore compatible with certain groups of (union) workers getting higher relative wages if other (nonunion) workers are simultaneously getting lower real wages.

## ☐ WAGE DIFFERENTIALS

We have discussed the general level of wages and the role of supply and demand in a series of specific labor market situations. Yet, the wage differences which persist between different occupations and different individuals in the same occupations still have not been explained. Why does a corporate executive or a movie actor receive $300,000 per year while laundry workers and retail clerks get a paltry $6000 or $7000 per year? Table 31-3 indicates the substantial wage differentials which exist among certain common occupational groups. Our problem is to explain these kinds of differences.

Once again the forces of supply and demand provide a general answer. If the supply of a particular type of labor is very great in relation to the demand for it, the resulting wage rate will be low. But if demand is great and the supply very small, wages will be very high. Though it is a good starting point, this supply and demand explanation is not particularly revealing. We want to know *why* supply and demand conditions differ in various labor markets. To do this we must probe those fac-

[12] Albert Rees, *The Economics of Trade Unions* (Chicago: The University of Chicago Press, 1962), p. 79.

**TABLE 31-3**
Average Hourly and Weekly Earnings in Selected Industries, November 1979

| Industry | Average hourly gross earnings | Average weekly gross earnings |
| --- | --- | --- |
| Bituminous coal | $10.41 | $430.97 |
| Motor vehicles | 9.14 | 362.86 |
| Contract construction | 8.38 | 294.14 |
| Chemicals | 7.86 | 330.91 |
| Printing and publishing | 7.10 | 269.09 |
| Fabricated metals | 7.00 | 286.30 |
| Food products | 6.50 | 260.65 |
| Retail trade | 4.62 | 140.45 |
| Apparel and finished textiles | 4.32 | 153.79 |
| Laundries and dry cleaning | 4.22 | 145.17 |
| Hotels and motels | 4.10 | 124.64 |

Source: U.S. Department of Labor, *Earnings and Employment,* January 1980.

tors which lie behind the supply and demand of particular types of labor.

*If* (1) all workers were homogeneous, (2) all jobs were equally attractive to workers, and (3) labor markets were perfectly competitive, all workers would receive precisely the same wage rate. As such, this is not a particularly startling statement. It merely suggests that in an economy having one type of labor and in effect one type of job, competition will result in a single wage rate for all workers. The statement is important in that it suggests the reasons why wage rates do differ in practice. (1) Workers are not homogeneous. They differ in capacities and in training and, as a result, fall into noncompeting occupational groups. (2) Jobs vary in attractiveness; the nonmonetary aspects of various jobs are not the same. (3) Labor markets are typically characterized by imperfections.

△ **Noncompeting Groups**

Workers are not homogeneous; they differ tremendously in their mental and physical capacities and in their education and training. Hence, at any point in time the labor force can be thought of as falling into a number of *noncompeting groups,* each of which may be composed of one or several occupations for which

the members of this group qualify. For example, a relatively small number of workers have the inherent abilities to be brain surgeons, concert violinists, and research chemists, and even fewer have the financial means of acquiring the necessary training. The result is obviously that the supplies of these particular types of labor are very small in relation to the demand for them and that the consequent wages and salaries are high. These and similar groups do not compete with one another or with other skilled or semiskilled workers. The violinist does not compete with the surgeon, nor does the garbage collector or retail clerk compete with either the violinist or the surgeon.

This is not to say that each of the thousands of specific occupations in the United States constitutes a noncompeting group of workers or that workers fall into isolated occupational compartments. A number of unskilled or semiskilled occupations may well fall into one noncompeting group. For example, gasoline station attendants, farmhands, and unskilled construction workers may all be classified in the same group, because each is capable of doing the others' jobs. Yet none of the workers in this group currently offers effective competition for printers or electricians, who find themselves in other, more exclusive groups.

It should be noted, too, that the lack of competition among noncompeting groups of workers is actually a matter of degree. *Within limits* unskilled construction workers can be substituted for printers and electricians. Furthermore, this substitutability will be greater over a period of time than it is in the short run; over time, workers may move from one noncompeting group to another as they are able to develop their native capacities through education and training. The assembly-line worker who has an IQ of 130 may become an accountant or a lawyer by going to night school. But here another obstacle arises: higher education is a costly business. Our ambitious but low-income laborer does not have the same opportunity of entering the higher-paid occupational groups as do the offspring of the lawyers and accountants who are already in those groups. And, needless to say, differences in inherent capacities provide an even more permanent obstacle to occupational mobility. In short, both native capacity and the opportunity to train oneself are unequally distributed, causing the wage differentials of noncompeting groups to persist.

The concept of noncompeting groups is a flexible one; it can be applied to various subgroups and even to specific individuals in a given group. Some especially skilled surgeons are able to command fees considerably in excess of their run-of-the-mill colleagues who perform the same operations. Kareem Abdul-Jabbar, Larry Bird, and Earvin "Magic" Johnson, and a few others demand and get salaries many times that of the average professional basketball player. Why? Because in each instance their colleagues are only imperfect substitutes.

△   **Equalizing Differences**

Now, if a group of workers in a particular noncompeting group is equally capable of performing several different jobs, one might expect that the wage rate would be identical for each of these jobs. But this is not the case. A group of high school graduates may be equally capable of becoming bank clerks or unskilled construction workers. But these jobs pay different wages. In virtually all localities, construction laborers receive better wages than do bank clerks.

These differences can be explained on the basis of the *nonmonetary aspects* of the two jobs. The construction job involves dirty hands, a sore back, the hazard of accidents, and irregular employment, both seasonally and cyclically. The banking job entails a white shirt, pleasant air-conditioned surroundings, and little fear of injury or layoff. Other things being equal, it is easy to see why workers will prefer picking up a deposit slip rather than a shovel. The result is that construction contractors must pay higher wages than banks pay to compensate for the unattractive nonmonetary aspects of construction jobs. These wage differentials are sometimes called *equalizing differences* because they must be paid to compensate for the nonmonetary differences in various jobs.

△   **Market Imperfections**

The notion of noncompeting groups helps explain wage differentials between various jobs for which limited numbers of workers are qualified. Equalizing differences aid in understanding wage differentials on certain jobs for which workers in the same noncompeting group are equally qualified. Market imperfections in the form of various immobilities help explain wage differences paid on identical jobs.

**1   Geographic Immobilities**   Workers take root geographically. They are reluctant to leave friends, relatives, and associates, to force their children to change schools, to sell their houses, and to incur the costs and inconveniences of adjusting to a new job and a new community. Geographic mobility is likely to be particularly low for older workers who have seniority rights and substantial claims to pension payments upon retirement. Then, too, workers who may be willing to move may simply be ignorant of job opportunities and wage rates in other geographic areas. As Adam Smith noted two centuries ago, "A man is of all sorts of luggage the most difficult to be transported." The reluctance or inability of workers to move obviously causes geographic wage differentials for the same occupation to persist.

**2  Institutional  Immobilities**  Geographic immobilities may be reinforced by artificial restrictions on mobility which are imposed by institutions. In particular, we have already noted that craft unions find it to their advantage to restrict their membership. After all, if carpenters and bricklayers become plentiful, the wages they can command will decline. Thus the low-paid nonunion carpenter of Brush, Colorado, may be willing to move to Chicago in the pursuit of higher wages. But his chances of successfully doing so are slim. He may be unable to get a union card; and no card, no job. The professions impose similar artificial restraints. For example, at most universities individuals lacking advanced degrees are automatically not considered for employment as teachers. Quite apart from one's competence as a teacher and one's command of the subject matter, a "union card"—an M.A. or a Ph.D.—is the first requisite for employment.

**3  Sociological  Immobilities**  Finally, we must acknowledge sociological immobilities. Despite recent legislation to the contrary, women workers frequently receive less pay than men working at the same job. The consequence of racial and ethnic discrimination is that blacks, Hispanics, and other minority groups are often forced to accept lower wages on given jobs than fellow workers receive. We shall have more to say on the matter of discrimination in Chapters 37 and 38.

A final point: It is more than likely that all three of these considerations—noncompeting groups, equalizing differences, and market imperfections—will play a role in the explanation of actual wage differentials. For example, the differential between the wages of a physician and a construction worker is largely explainable on the basis of noncompeting groups. Physicians fall into a noncompeting group where, because of mental and financial requisites to entry, the supply of labor is small in relation to demand, and wages are therefore high. In construction work, where mental and financial prerequisites are much less significant, the supply of labor is great in relation to demand and wages are low when compared with those of physicians. However, were it not for the unpleasantness of the construction worker's job and the fact that his craft union pursues restrictive membership policies, the differential would probably be even greater than it is.

☐  **INVESTMENT IN HUMAN CAPITAL**
We have just seen that the concept of noncompeting groups is a very important part of the explanation of wage differentials. Let us probe more carefully the question of why these noncompeting groups exist.

△  **The Concept**
According to human capital theory, noncompeting groups—and therefore wage differentials—exist to a large extent because of differing amounts of investment in human capital. Generally speaking, investments in human capital are of three kinds. Each of them is for the purpose of increasing the productivity of workers and thereby of expanding their wages and incomes.

First, expenditures on *education*—including general and specific education, formal and informal education, on-the-job training, and so forth—are the most obvious and perhaps most important kind of investment in human capital. Education contributes to a labor force which is more skilled and more productive. Second, expenditures on *health* are also significant. Better health—the consequence of expenditures on preventive medicine and medical care, improved diet, and better housing—gives rise to greater vigor, longevity, and higher productivity among workers. Finally, expenditures on *mobility* which shifts workers from relatively low to relatively high productivity uses are a less obvious form of investment in human capital. Like education, the geographic movement of workers may raise the market value of their labor services. In short, employable persons have embodied within themselves a future flow of labor services. According to human capital theory, the productivity and therefore the market value of labor services (one's wages) are determined to a great degree by the amount which the individual, his or her family, and society have chosen to invest in education and training, health, and location.

### △  The Investment Decision

It may seem odd or even repugnant to analyze investment in manpower in the same way one would explore the decision to buy a machine. But, in fact, the two decisions are very similar. The purchase of a machine (real capital) will give rise to a flow of additional net revenues over the estimated years of life of the machine. Potential investors can discount this lifetime flow of earnings, compare their present value with the cost of the machine, and determine a rate of return on the investment. By comparing this rate of return with the interest rate (that is, the financial cost of investing), a firm can rationally decide whether the purchase of this machine is profitable.[13] Similarly, one might subject the decision to invest in, say, a four-year college education to the same analysis. Figure 31-9 suggests that the families of those with larger investments in education achieve higher incomes initially and throughout their work careers than do those who have made smaller educational investments. The economic return from investment in a college education can therefore be regarded as the *additional* lifetime earnings which the college

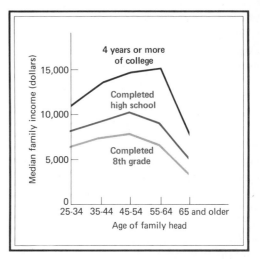

**FIGURE 31-9  EDUCATION LEVELS AND FAMILY INCOME**

Investment in education yields a return in the form of an income differential enjoyed both initially and throughout one's worklife. (*U.S. Bureau of the Census.*)

graduate will earn as compared with the earnings of a high school graduate. The present value of this difference in lifetime earnings can be determined and compared with the cost of the education, and the rate of return on the investment in the college education can be calculated. This rate will be useful to the individual in determining whether investment in additional education is economically justifiable. It will also be helpful to society in determining the proper balance between investment in people and investment in machinery.[14]

### △  Explanatory Value

Proponents contend that the theory of human capital explains a number of phenom-

---

[13]The reader may find it helpful to review the derivation of the investment-demand curve in Chapter 11.

[14]For a discussion of the many problems in estimating the returns from investment in human capital, see the articles by Theodore W. Schultz, Harry G. Shaffer, and William G. Bowen in M. Blaug (ed.), *Economics of Education 1* (Baltimore: Penguin Books, 1968). Also see Howard R. Bowen, *Investment in Education* (San Francisco: Jossey-Bass Publishers, 1977), chap. 12.

ena which would otherwise be minor mysteries. Why do we educate younger, rather than older, people? Why are younger people more mobile than older people? Answer to both questions: Younger people have a longer expected working life over which to realize returns on their investments in education or mobility. The fact that wages in the South have been persistently lower than in the rest of the country is partly the result of different levels of spending on education. The concept of human capital is also a part of the explanation of the rising level of real wages which the United States has enjoyed historically (Figure 31-2). If our economy had the same natural resources and real capital we now possess, but a completely uneducated and untrained labor force or even a labor force with the educational and skill levels of, say, 1929, our GNP and real wage levels would obviously be much lower than they now are. Recall (see Table 20-3, page 399) that improved education and training are of considerable importance in explaining the economic growth which our economy has enjoyed.

## △ Recent Criticism

In recent years enthusiasm for human capital theory has abated somewhat. The primary reason for this tarnished image has to do with the apparent failure of various human capital programs of the 1960s to lessen income inequality.

Human capital theory assumes the existence of a direct and significant relationship between investment in human capital and productivity. Specifically, the hypothesized cause-effect chain is:

Investment in human capital
(expenditures on education)
   *causes*
Increases in worker productivity
   *which cause*
Higher wage rates and higher earnings

Now, if these relationships are valid, it follows that the incomes of poor people can be increased by providing them with more human capital, that is, more education and training. This thinking was consistent with, and an endorsement of, a host of manpower programs (for example, the Job Corps) which were introduced in the 1960s as a part of the "war on poverty." Although economists still debate the efficacy of manpower programs, there is empirical evidence which questions the success of these programs and, more importantly, the cause-effect chain assumed by human capital theory. For example, government statistics indicate that, in fact, the degree of income inequality has *not* changed in recent years (Chapter 37). And studies of ghetto labor markets, at which many of the manpower programs were specifically directed, revealed that—contrary to what human capital theory would suggest—the better educated workers did *not* receive higher wages or experience less unemployment. Furthermore, much-discussed studies of a more global character have tended to downgrade and question the existence of a positive and significant relationship between public expenditures on education and an individual's ability to perform in school and in the labor market. For example, James S. Coleman and his associates found that the socioeconomic status of one's family—not the quantity of education—is the critical influence upon an individual's academic and labor market achievements.[15] Similarly, Christopher Jencks found only a modest relationship between schooling, on the one hand, and income, on the other.

> Economic success seems to depend on varieties of luck and on-the-job competence that are only moderately related to family background, schooling, or scores on standardized tests. The definition of competence varies greatly from one job to another, but it seems in most cases to

[15]James S. Coleman, *Equality of Educational Opportunity* (Washington: U.S. Department of Health, Education, and Welfare, 1966).

depend more on personality than on technical skills.[16]

If we accept this empirical evidence and thereby reject the cause-effect chain of human capital theory, how can we explain the fact (Figure 31-9) that people with "more" education *do* receive higher earnings than people with "less" education? One explanation is the argument that human capital theory has reversed the true relationship; perhaps high incomes cause families to spend more on education, just as they cause people to spend more on clothing, automobiles, and housing. A more complex explanation holds that

> . . . the only reason that education is correlated with income is that the combination of ability, motivation, and personal habits that it takes to succeed in education happen to be the same combination that it takes to be a productive worker.[17]

[16]Christopher Jencks et al., *Inequality: A Reassessment of the Effect of Family and Schooling in America* (New York: Basic Books, Inc., Publishers, 1972), p. 8.
[17]Alice M. Rivlin, "Income Distribution—Can Economists Help?" *American Economic Review,* May 1975, p. 10.

According to this view, the high-income "4 years or more of college" group of Figure 31-9 would have received high incomes even if they had chosen not to invest in a college education. The reason? They possess the ability and motivation—not to mention family connections—to succeed in the labor market; the fact that they attended college is incidental to this success. Stated differently, if it is in fact a combination of inherent ability, motivation, and personal habits that is rewarded in the labor market, then the subsidization of individuals who do not possess these characteristics to enable them to stay in school longer or to enroll in manpower training programs will not affect their ultimate earnings.

The essence of our argument is not that human capital theory should be flatly rejected. Indeed, it is the basis for many valuable insights into the workings of the labor market, the causes of economic growth, and so forth. Rather, the point is that the concept should be used judiciously and, more specifically, it has apparent limitations for making policy decisions.

## Summary

1  Wages are the price paid per unit of time for the services of labor.

2  The general level of wages in the United States is higher than in most foreign nations because the demand for labor is great in relation to the supply. The strong demand for American labor is based upon its high productivity, which in turn depends upon the quantity and quality of the capital equipment and natural resources used by labor, the quality of the labor force itself, the efficiency of management, a favorable sociopolitical environment, and the vast size of the domestic market. Over time these factors have caused the demand for labor to increase in relation to the supply, accounting for the long-run rise of real wages in the United States.

3  The determination of specific wage rates depends upon the structure of the particular labor market. In a competitive market the equilibrium wage rate and level of employment will be determined by the intersection of labor supply and demand.

4  Under monopsony, however, the marginal-resource-cost curve will lie above the resource supply curve, because the monopsonist must bid up wage rates in hiring extra workers and pay that higher wage to *all* workers. The monopsonist will hire fewer workers than it will under competitive conditions in order to achieve less-than-competitive wage rates (costs) and thereby greater profits.

**5**  A union may raise competitive wage rates by *a.* increasing the derived demand for labor, *b.* restricting the supply of labor through exclusive unionism, and *c.* directly enforcing an above-equilibrium wage rate through inclusive unionism.

**6**  In many important industries, the labor market takes the form of bilateral monopoly; that is, a strong union "sells" labor to a monopsonistic employer. Although the outcome of this labor market model is logically indeterminate, it might entail an important manifestation of the concept of countervailing power.

**7**  Economists disagree about the desirability of the minimum wage as an antipoverty mechanism. While it causes unemployment for some low-income workers, it raises the incomes of others who retain their jobs.

**8**  Unionized workers have probably realized wage rates 10 to 15 percent higher than would otherwise have been the case; but there is little evidence to suggest that unions have been able to raise the average level of real wages for labor as a whole.

**9**  Wage differentials are largely explainable in terms of *a.* noncompeting groups, that is, differences in the capacities and training of different groups of workers; *b.* equalizing differences, that is, wage differences which must be paid to offset nonmonetary differences in jobs; and *c.* market imperfections in the form of geographic, artificial, and sociological immobilities.

**10**  Investment in human capital takes the form of expenditures on education and training, health, and location. Despite limitations, the concept of human capital is useful in explaining, for example, the long-run rise in the average level of real wages and geographic wage differentials.


## Questions and Study Suggestions

**1**  Key terms and concepts to remember: money and real wage rates; competitive labor market; monopsony; marginal resource cost; exclusive and inclusive unionism; occupational licensure; bilateral monopoly; the minimum wage; wage differentials; noncompeting groups; equalizing differences; investment in human capital.

**2**  Explain why the general level of wages is higher in the United States than in most foreign nations. What is the most important single factor underlying the long-run increase in the average real wage rates in the United States? What, if anything, does this suggest concerning the ability of unions to raise real wages?

**3**  *a.*  Describe wage determination in a labor market in which workers are unorganized and many firms are actively competing for the services of labor. Show this situation graphically, using $W_1$ to indicate the equilibrium wage rate and $Q_1$ to show the number of workers hired by the firms as a group.

  *b.*  Suppose now that the formerly competing firms form an employers' association which hires labor as a monopsonist would. Describe verbally the impact upon wage rates and employment. Adjust the graph drawn for question 3a, showing the monopsonistic wage rate and employment level as $W_2$ and $Q_2$, respectively.

**4**  Describe the techniques which unions might employ to raise wages. Evaluate the desirability of each from the viewpoint of *a.* the union, and *b.* society as a whole. Explain: "Craft unionism directly restricts the supply of labor; industrial unionism relies upon the market to restrict the number of jobs."

**5**  Assume a monopsonistic employer is paying a wage rate of $W_m$ and hiring $Q_m$ workers, as is indicated in Figure 31-8. Now suppose that an industrial union is formed and that it forces the employer to accept a wage rate of $W_c$. Explain verbally and graphically why in this instance the higher wage rate will be accompanied by an *increase* in the number of workers hired.

**6**  Complete the following labor supply table for a firm hiring labor competitively.

| Units of labor | Wage rate | Total labor cost (wage bill) | Marginal resource (labor) cost |
|---|---|---|---|
| 1 | $14 | $_____ | $_____ |
| 2 | 14 | _____ | _____ |
| 3 | 14 | _____ | _____ |
| 4 | 14 | _____ | _____ |
| 5 | 14 | _____ | _____ |
| 6 | 14 | _____ | _____ |

   **a.**   Show graphically the labor supply and marginal resource (labor) cost curves for this firm.  Explain the relationships of these curves to one another.
   **b.**   Compare these data with the labor demand data of question 3 in Chapter 30.  What will the equilibrium wage rate and level of employment be?  Explain.
   **c.**   Now redetermine this firm's supply schedule for labor on the assumption that it is a monopsonist and that, although it can hire the first worker for $14, it must increase the wage rate by $1 to attract each successive worker.  Show the new labor supply and marginal labor cost curves graphically and explain their relationships to one another.  Compare these new data with those of question 3 for Chapter 30.  What will be the equilibrium wage rate and the level of employment?  Why does this differ from your answer to question 6b?
   **7**   A critic of the minimum wage has contended, "The effects of minimum wage legislation are precisely the opposite of those predicted by those who support them.  Government can legislate a minimum wage, but cannot force employers to hire unprofitable workers.  In fact, minimum wages cause unemployment among low-wage workers who can least afford to give up their small incomes."  Do you agree?  What bearing does the elasticity of labor demand have upon this assessment?  What factors might possibly offset the unemployment effects of a minimum wage?
   **8**   Explain: "Although unions have altered the wage structure, they have not been successful in raising the average real wage of the American labor force."
   **9**   What are the basic considerations which help explain the wage differentials between particular labor markets?
   **10**   What is meant by investment in human capital?  Use this concept to explain **a.** wage differentials, and **b.** the long-run rise in real wage rates in the United States.  What criticisms are made of human capital theory?


# Selected References

Bellante, Don, and Mark Jackson: *Labor Economics: Choice in Labor Markets* (New York: McGraw-Hill Book Company, 1979).

Bloom, Gordon F., and Herbert R. Northrup: *Economics of Labor Relations,* 8th ed. (Homewood, Ill.: Richard D. Irwin, Inc., 1977), chaps. 8–12.

Freeman, Richard B.: *Labor Economics,* 2d ed. (Englewood Cliffs, N.J.: Prentice-Hall, Inc., 1979), chaps. 1–5.

Levitan, Sar A., and Richard S. Belous: *More than Subsistence: Minimum Wages for the Working Poor* (Baltimore: The Johns Hopkins University Press, 1979).

Marshall, F. Ray, Allan G. King, and Vernon M. Briggs, Jr.: *Labor Economics: Wages, Employment, and Trade Unionism,* 4th ed. (Homewood, Ill.: Richard D. Irwin, Inc., 1980), chaps. 7–11.

Rees, Albert: *The Economics of Work and Pay,* 2d ed. (New York: Harper & Row, Publishers, Incorporated, 1979).

Reynolds, Lloyd G.: *Labor Economics and Labor Relations,* 7th ed. (Englewood Cliffs, N.J.: Prentice-Hall, Inc., 1978), chaps. 1–8, 12, 22.

# LAST WORD
## Why Doctors Earn So Much

The average earnings of physicians are 70 to 80 percent greater than those of lawyers and Ph.D. scientists. The high incomes of physicians can be partially explained in terms of the American Medical Association (AMA) functioning as an exclusive union.

The medical profession attained the incomparable income levels of the post-World War II period through its trade union powers. The AMA is perhaps the strongest trade union in the United States. It has virtually complete control over the supply of doctors, and actively uses this control to restrict supply and raise doctors' incomes. The source of AMA power lies in the fact that practicing physicians must be licensed and that licenses are given only to graduates from schools in the United States that are approved by the AMA's Council on Medical Education and Hospitals. When doctors' incomes fell during the Depression, the AMA sought to reduce admissions.

Restrictionist policies cut the number of medical school acceptances from 7578 in 1933 to 6211 in 1939 and kept the number below the 1933 "peak" for some 20 years. In 1926, 64% of applicants to medical school were accepted; in 1952, 52%; in 1973 just 35%. While there was a moderate increase in the number of M.D.s conferred (and in approved medical schools) through 1960, and a more rapid increase thereafter, medical schools are the only major segment of higher education that did not expand rapidly in the post-World War II years. In 1950, 5.2% of postbaccalaureate degrees were awarded in medicine; in 1972, 2.9%. In 1950 doctors, dentists, and related practitioners constituted 3.9% of the professional work force; in 1974, 2.8%. Medical incomes were raised and maintained by the AMA's control over supply.

The economic position of doctors was enhanced even further in the 1960s and 1970s by federal subsidization of medical services under Medicare and Medicaid. Because the increased demand brought about by federal spending had relatively little impact on the output of doctors from American medical schools, the price of doctors' services and their incomes increased greatly. From 1959 to 1969, physicians fees grew at twice the rate of the consumer price index. Median net earnings of physicians rose by 80%. By contrast, the average hourly earnings of production workers grew by just 50%.

Richard B. Freeman, *The Over-Educated American* (New York: Academic Press, 1976), pp. 118–120, abridged. Reprinted by permission.

# The Pricing and Employment of Resources: Rent, Interest, and Profits

chapter **32**

The discussion of wages in Chapter 31 is rather lengthy. In contrast, the discussions of the income shares—rent, interest, and profits—found in the present chapter are relatively brief. There are two reasons for this difference in emphasis.

**1** Wage incomes are clearly the major component of the national income. As we will find in the concluding section of this chapter, 70 to 80 percent of the national income is in the form of wage and salary incomes, the remainder accruing as rent, interest, and profit incomes.

**2** The economic theories of rent, interest, and profit are very unsettled; there are honest differences among authorities as to definitions, explanations, and implications where nonwage incomes are concerned. For these two reasons we shall concentrate upon the basic features of rent, interest, and profit determination and forgo the many controversial points and the often ambiguous details which are encountered

in more advanced discussions of these income shares.

## □ ECONOMIC RENT

To most people the term "rent" means the seemingly exorbitant sum one must pay for a two-bedroom apartment or a dormitory room. To the business executive, "rent" is a payment made for the use of a factory building, machinery, or warehouse facilities. Closer examination finds these commonsense definitions of rent to be confusing and ambiguous. Dormitory room rent, for example, includes interest on the money capital the university has borrowed from the government or private individuals in financing the dormitory's construction, wages for custodial and maid service, utility payments, and so forth. Economists therefore use the term "rent" in a narrower but less ambiguous sense: *Economic rent is the price paid for the use of land and other natural resources which are completely fixed in total supply.* It is the unique supply conditions of land and other natural resources—their fixed supply—which make rental payments distinguishable from wage, interest, and profit payments.

Let us examine this feature and some of its implications through simple supply and demand analysis. To avoid complications, assume, first, that all land is of the same grade or quality—in other words, that each available acre of land is equally productive. Suppose, too, that all land has just one use, being capable of producing just one product—say, corn. And assume that land is being rented in a competitive market—that many corn farmers are demanding and many landowners offering land in the market.

In Figure 32-1, $SS$ indicates the supply of arable farmland available in the economy as a whole and $D_2$ the demand of farmers for the use of that land. As with all economic re-

sources, demand is a derived demand. It is downsloping because of the law of diminishing returns and the fact that, for farmers as a group, product price must be diminished to sell additional units of output.

The unique feature of our analysis is on the supply side: For all practical purposes the supply of land is perfectly inelastic, as reflected in $SS$. Land has no production cost; it is a "free and nonreproducible gift of nature." The economy has so much land, and that's that. It is true, of course, that within limits existing land can be made more usable by clearing, drainage, and irrigation. But these programs constitute capital improvements and not changes in the amount of land as such. Furthermore, such variations in the usability of land are a very small fraction of the total amount of land in existence and therefore do not undermine the basic argument that land and other resources are in virtually fixed supply.

The fixed nature of the supply of land means that demand is the only active determinant of land rent; supply is passive. And what determines the demand for land? Those factors discussed in Chapter 30—the price of the product grown on the land, the productivity of land (which depends in part upon the quantity and quality of the resources with which land is combined), and the prices of those other resources which are combined with land. If, in Figure 32-1, the demand for land should increase from $D_2$ to $D_1$ or decline from $D_2$ to $D_3$, land rent would change from $R_2$ to $R_1$ or $R_3$, but the amount of land supplied would remain unchanged at $OS$. Changes in economic rent will have no impact upon the amount of land available; the supply of land is simply not augmentable. In technical terms, there is a large price effect and no quantity effect when the demand for land changes. If demand for land is only $D_4$, land rent will be zero; land will be a "free good" because it is not scarce enough in relation to demand for it to command a price. This situation was approximated in the free-land era of American history.

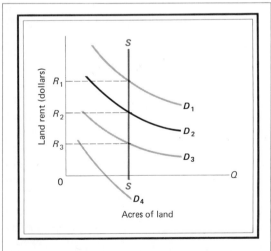

**FIGURE 32-1 THE DETERMINATION OF LAND RENT**

Because the supply of land and other natural resources is perfectly inelastic ($SS$), demand is the sole active determinant of land rent. An increase ($D_2$ to $D_1$) or decrease ($D_2$ to $D_3$) in demand will cause considerable changes in rent ($R_2$ to $R_1$ and $R_2$ to $R_3$). If demand is very small ($D_4$) relative to supply, land will be a "free good."

△  **Land Rent is a Surplus**

The perfect inelasticity of the supply of land must be contrasted with the relative elasticity of such property resources as apartment buildings, machinery, and warehouses. These resources are *not* fixed in total supply. A higher price will give entrepreneurs the incentive to construct and offer larger quantities of these property resources. Conversely, a decline in their prices will induce suppliers to allow existing facilities to depreciate and not be replaced. The same general reasoning applies to the total supply of labor. Within limits, a higher average level of wages will induce more workers to enter the labor force, and lower wages will cause them to drop out of the labor force. In other words, the supplies of nonland resources are upsloping, or, stated differently, the prices paid to such resources perform an *incentive function.* A high price provides an incentive to offer more; a low price, to offer less.

Not so with land. Rent serves no incentive function, because the total supply of land is fixed. If rent is $10,000, $500, $1, or $0 per acre, the same amount of land will be available to society to make a contribution to production. Rent, in other words, could be eliminated without affecting the productive potential of the economy. For this reason economists consider rent to be a *surplus,* that is, a payment which is not necessary to ensure that land will be available to the economy as a whole.[1]

△  **A Single Tax on Land?**

If land is a free gift of nature, costs nothing to produce, and would be available even in

the absence of rental payments, why should rent be paid to those who by historical accident or inheritance happen to be landowners? Socialists have long argued that all land rents are unearned incomes. Therefore, they argue, land should be nationalized—owned by the state—so that any payments for its use can be utilized by the state in furthering the well-being of the entire population rather than by a landowning minority. The Last Word section of this chapter pokes fun at private ownership and land rent.

In the United States, criticism of rental payments has taken the form of a *single-tax movement* which gained considerable support in the late nineteenth century. Spearheaded by Henry George's provocative book *Progress and Poverty* (1879), this reform movement centered upon the notion that economic rent might be taxed away completely without impairing the available supply of land or, therefore, the productive potential of the economy as a whole.

George observed that as population grew and the geographic frontier closed, landowners came to enjoy larger and larger rents from their landholdings. These increments in rent were simply the result of a growing demand for a resource whose supply was perfectly inelastic; some landlords were receiving fabulously high incomes, not through rendering any productive effort, but solely as the result of holding advantageously located land. Henry George took the position that these increases in land rent belonged to the economy as a whole; he held that land rents should be taxed away and spent for public uses.

To illustrate: If the relevant supply and demand conditions for land are as shown by *SS* and $D_2$ in Figure 32-1, land rent will be $OR_2$ per acre. Suppose government imposes a tax equal to, say, half the rent per acre. That is, a tax of $R_2R_3$ per acre is levied where $R_2R_3 = \frac{1}{2}OR_2$. Now, you will recall from Chapter 23 the generalization that the more inelastic the supply of a product (or resource), the larger will be the portion of a tax borne by the producer (or

[1] The alert reader will have observed that a portion—in some instances a major portion—of wage and salary incomes may be a surplus in that these incomes exceed the minimum amount necessary to keep an individual in his or her current line of work. For example, a professional basketball superstar may receive $200,000 or more per year, whereas his next best occupational option as, say, a high school coach, would earn him only $15,000 or $18,000 per year. Most of his income is therefore a surplus. Observe that in the twilight of their careers, professional athletes sometimes accept sizable salary reductions rather than seek employment in alternative occupations.

resource owner). In the case of land, the supply is completely inelastic, so all the tax must be borne by the landowner; it is impossible to shift any part of the tax to renters. Of course, the landowner could withdraw the land from production, but this would simply mean no rental income at all!

As George saw it, the fact that the tax burden remained on the landowner was perfectly justifiable; land rent, after all, was unearned income. Population growth and the closing of the geographic frontier were conferring windfall rental income upon landowners, and government was fully justified in taxing away such rental income. Indeed, George held that there was no reason to tax away only 50 percent of the landowner's unearned rental income. Why not take 70 or 90 or 99 percent? In seeking popular support for his ideas on land taxation, Henry George proposed that taxes on rental income be the only tax levied by government.

**Criticisms**   Critics of the single tax on land make these points: First, current levels of government spending are such that a land tax alone would clearly not bring in enough revenue; it cannot be considered realistically as a *single* tax. Second, as noted earlier, in practice most income payments combine elements of interest, rent, wages, and profits. Land is typically improved in some manner by productive effort, and economic rent cannot be readily disentangled from payments for capital improvements. As a practical matter, it would be very difficult to determine how much of any given income payment is actually rent. Third, the question of unearned income goes beyond land and land ownership. One can readily argue that many individuals and groups other than landowners benefit from the receipt of "unearned" income associated with the overall advance of the economy. For example, consider the capital gains income received by an individual who, some fifteen or twenty years ago, chanced to purchase (or inherit) stock in a firm which has experienced rapid growth (say,

IBM or Xerox). How is this income different from the rental income of the landowner?

**Renewed Concern**   On the other hand, there is a renewed interest in land taxation on the part of urban economists, city planners, and public officials. Many of them contend that a strong case can be made on grounds of both equity and efficiency for a heavy tax on land values.

*1   Equity*   With respect to *equity,* they argue, like Henry George, that much of the value of urban land results from population growth, community development, and, very significantly, public decisions to invest in roads, schools, and water, gas, and sewer utilities. Furthermore, zoning changes made by public bodies can increase sharply the value of affected land overnight. As a result, landowners, who are typically high-income people initially, realize large "unearned increments" of income with little or no expenditure of effort or money. Because the value of urban land is largely determined by public decision and public investment, it is held that the community should recapture the resulting increases in land value through taxation and use these revenues for public purposes.

*2   Efficiency*   The *efficiency* argument is that a tax on land value has a neutral effect upon the allocation or use of land; unlike most other taxes, a tax on land value does *not* contribute to the malallocation of resources. For example, glancing back at Figures 23-7 and 23-8, we find that sales and excise taxes have the effect of increasing prices and reducing output. Assuming allocative efficiency initially, the allocation of resources to affected products would obviously be less efficient as a result of the tax. Assume now that Figure 23-7 shows the demand for and supply of labor in a competitive market. The imposition of an income tax of a certain amount per worker per day would have the effect of reducing the supply of labor, distorting the workers' preferred balance between work and leisure away from the optimum. The tax would cause workers to offer less productive effort and to take more leisure. In comparison, the complete inelasticity of the supply of land means that a tax on land rent has no effect on price or output and therefore does not alter resource allocation. "The most profitable use of the [land] site before the tax is imposed continues to be the most profitable use."[2] This outcome is in contrast to property taxes on buildings—the major alternative revenue source for cities—wherein there is an adverse incentive effect; that is, taxes on buildings lower their return to investors and discourage their construction. We will find in Chapter 36 that high property taxes on buildings have been an important factor in the physical deterioration of the central city of many major metropolitan areas. Hence, more and more urban economists favor greater use of taxes on land and less use of property taxes on buildings.

### △ Productivity Differences

Our analysis thus far has proceeded upon the assumption that all units of land are of the same grade. In practice, this is plainly not so. Different acres vary greatly in productivity. These productivity differences stem primarily from differences in soil fertility and such climatic factors as rainfall and temperature. It is these factors which explain why Iowa soil is excellently suited to corn production, the plains of eastern Colorado are much less so, and desert wasteland of New Mexico is incapable of corn production. These differences in productivity will be reflected in resource demand. Competitive bidding by farmers will establish a high rent for the very productive Iowa land. The less productive Colorado land will command a much lower rent, and the New Mexico land no rent at all. Location may be equally important in explaining differences in land rent. Other things being equal, renters will pay more for a unit of land which is strategically located with respect to materials, labor,

and customers than for a unit of land whose location is remote from these markets. Witness the extremely high land rents in large metropolitan areas.

The rent differentials to which quality differences in land would give rise can be easily seen by looking at Figure 32-1 from a slightly different point of view. Suppose, as before, that only one agricultural product, say corn, can be produced on four grades of land, *each* of which is available in the fixed amount $OS$. When combined with identical amounts of capital, labor, and other cooperating resources, the productivity—or, more specifically, the marginal revenue productivity—of each grade of land is reflected in demand curves $D_1$, $D_2$, $D_3$, and $D_4$. Grade 1 land is the most productive, as reflected in $D_1$, whereas grade 4 is the least productive, as is shown by $D_4$. The resulting rents for grades 1, 2, and 3 land will obviously be $R_1$, $R_2$, and $R_3$ respectively, the rent differentials mirroring the differences in the productivity of the three grades of land. Grade 4 land is so poor in quality that it would not pay farmers to bring it fully into production; it would be a "free" and only partially used resource.

### △ Alternative Uses

We have also supposed, thus far, that land has only one use. Actually, we know that land usually has a number of alternative uses. An acre of Iowa farmland may be useful in raising not only corn, but also wheat, oats, milo, and cattle, or it may be useful as a site for a house or factory. What is the importance of this obvious point? It indicates that, although land is a free gift of nature and has no production cost from the viewpoint of society as a whole, the rental payments of individual producers are *costs*. The total supply of land will be available to society even if no rent at all is paid for its use, but, from the standpoint of individual firms and industries, land has alternative uses, and therefore payments must be made by specific firms and industries to attract that land from those other uses. Such payments by

[2]Dick Netzer, *Economics and Urban Problems,* 2d ed. (New York: Basic Books, Inc., Publishers, 1974), p. 257.

definition are costs. Once again the fallacy of composition has entered our discussion. From the standpoint of society, there is no alternative but for land to be used by society. Therefore to society, rents are a surplus, not a cost. But because land has alternative uses, the rental payments of corn farmers or any other individual user are a cost; such payments are required to attract land from alternative uses.

## ☐  INTEREST

*The interest rate is the price paid for the use of money.* More precisely, the interest rate is the amount of money one is required to pay for the use of one dollar for a year. Two aspects of this income payment are immediately notable.

**1**   Because it is paid in kind, interest is typically stated as a percentage of the amount of money being borrowed rather than as an absolute amount. It is less clumsy to say that one is paying 12 percent interest than to proclaim that interest is "$120 per year per $1000." Furthermore, stating interest as a percentage facilitates the comparison of interest paid on loans of much different absolute amounts. By expressing interest as a percentage, we can immediately compare an interest payment of, say, $432 per year per $2880 and one of $1800 per year per $12,000. In this case both interest payments are 15 percent—a fact not at all obvious from the absolute figures. It is worth noting that a *Truth in Lending Act* was passed in 1969 which requires lenders to state in concise and uniform language the costs and terms of consumer credit. In particular, the act requires that interest must be stated as an annual rate.

**2**   Money is *not* an economic resource. As such, money is not productive; it is incapable of producing goods and services. However, businesses "buy" the use of money, because money can be used to acquire capital goods— factory buildings, machinery, warehouses, and so forth. And these facilities clearly do make a contribution to production. Thus, in hiring the use of money capital, business executives are ultimately buying the use of real capital goods.

## △  Range of Rates

Although we often refer to "the" interest rate, in fact there exists a whole range or continuum of rates. Recently (Spring 1980) interest rates have been at extraordinarily high levels, the result of an extremely tight monetary policy which is intended to restrain an accelerating rate of inflation. The Federal government currently borrows at 11 percent on its long-term securities. Corporate bonds may pay 12 to 13 percent. Mortgage loans may entail interest rates of 12 to 13 percent. Bank loans to consumers for automobile or refrigerator puchases may run from 15 to 18 percent. Those whose credit standing forces them to borrow from consumer finance companies may pay extremely high rates—24 or 36 percent is not uncommon. Why the differences?

**1**   The varying degrees of *risk* on loans are important. The greater the chance the borrower will not repay the loan, the more interest the lender will charge to compensate for this risk.

**2**   The *length* of a loan also affects the interest rate. Other things being equal, long-term loans usually command higher rates of interest than do short-term loans, because the long-term lender suffers the inconvenience and possible financial sacrifice of forgoing alternative uses for his or her money for a greater period of time.

**3**   Given two loans of equal length and risk, the interest rate will be higher on the smaller of the two loans. This is so because the *administrative costs* of a large and a small loan are about the same absolutely.

**4**   *Market imperfections* are also important in explaining some interest rate differentials. The small-town bank which monopolizes the local money market may charge high interest rates on loans to consumers because households find it inconvenient to "shop around" at banks in somewhat distant cities. The large corporation, on the other hand, is able to survey a number of rival investment houses in disposing of a new bond issue and thereby secure the lowest obtainable rate. To circumvent the difficulties involved in discussing the whole structure of interest rates, economists talk of "the" interest rate or the *pure rate of interest.* This pure rate is best approximated by the interest paid on long-term, virtually riskless bonds such as the long-term bonds of the United States government or of American Telephone and Telegraph. This interest payment can be thought of as being made solely for the use of money over an extended time period, because the risk factor and administrative costs are negligible and the interest on such securities is not distorted by market imperfections. The pure interest rate is currently (Spring 1980) about 10 or 11 percent. Again, note that the high rate reflects a very tight money policy.

△  **Determining the Interest Rate**

The theory of interest rate determination and its relationship to aggregate investment has been presented in Part 3 and need only be summarized at this point.[3] Glancing back at Figure 16-1, we recall in Figure 16-1a that the total demand for money is comprised of the transaction and asset demands. The former is directly related to the level of money NNP, while the latter is inversely related to the interest rate. Graphed against the interest rate, the total demand for money curve is downsloping. The money supply is a vertical line on the assumption that the monetary authorities determine some stock of money (money supply) independent of the rate of interest. The intersection of the demand for money curve and the money supply curve determines the equilibrium rate of interest.

Now consider Figure 16-1b which shows how the interest rate relates to the purchase of real capital. You may remember that the investment–demand curve is constructed by aggregating all possible investment projects and ranking them from highest to lowest in terms of their expected rates of net profits.

[3]It is recommended that the reader review the following sections: "The Demand for Money" in Chapter 14; "Monetary Policy and Equilibrium NNP: A Restatement" in Chapter 16; and "Investment" in Chapter 11.

Chapter 30's discussion of resource demand provides us with a fuller understanding as to why the investment–demand curve is downsloping. Given available quantities of other resources (labor and land), real capital is subject to the law of diminishing returns. That is, the marginal revenue product of capital will decline as the amount of capital is increased in relation to these other inputs.

By projecting the equilibrium interest rate of Figure 16-1a off the investment–demand curve of Figure 16-1b, we determine the amount of investment which the business sector will find profitable to undertake. That is, all investment projects whose expected rate of net profits exceeds the equilibrium interest rate will be undertaken.

Although Figure 16-1b is in terms of the business sector as a whole, the analysis is equally applicable to an individual firm. Indeed, the discussion is highly reminiscent of that associated with Figure 31-3. We saw there that, given the wage rate, it would be profitable for a firm to hire labor up to the point at which that wage rate is equal to labor's MRP. Imagine now that Figure 16-1b is for a single firm which has arrayed its investment opportunities from those with the highest expected MRP to those with the lowest expected MRP. The equilibrium interest rate is given to the individual firm and, in effect, constitutes a perfectly elastic supply of capital curve to the firm. The firm can borrow financial capital (with which to purchase real capital) at the market-determined interest rate which the firm cannot influence or manipulate. For example, if the interest rate is 12 percent, then it costs $12 to acquire $100 of money capital which can be used to obtain $100 worth of real capital. The firm will obviously be purchasing the profit-maximizing amount of financial and real capital where the interest rate (supply of capital) and the MRP (demand for capital) are equal.

△  **Role of the Interest Rate**

The interest rate is an extremely important price in that it simultaneously affects both the *levels* and *composition* of investment goods production.

**Interest and National Output**  Our discussion of Figure 16-1 reminds us that, other things being equal, a change in the equilibrium rate of interest will move businesses along the aggregate investment–demand curve, thereby changing the level of investment and the equilibrium level of NNP. Indeed, the big message of Chapter 16 was that the interest rate is an "administered price." This means, of course, that the monetary authorities purposely manipulate the supply of money in order to influence the interest rate and thereby the levels of output, employment, and prices.

**Interest and the Allocation of Capital**  Prices, you will recall, are rationing devices. The interest rate is no exception; it performs the function of allocating money capital and therefore real capital to various firms and investment projects. It rations the available supply of money or liquidity to those investment projects whose rate of return or expected profitability is sufficiently high to warrant payment of the going interest rate. If the expected rate of net profits of additional real capital in industry X is 14 percent and the required funds can be secured at an interest rate of 10 percent, industry X will be in a position, in terms of profit, to borrow and expand its capital facilities. On the other hand, if the expected rate of net profits of additional capital in industry Y is expected to be only 8 percent, it will be unprofitable for this industry to accumulate more capital goods. In short, the interest rate allocates money, and ultimately real capital, to those industries in which it will be most productive and therefore most profitable. Such an allocation of capital goods is obviously in the interest of society as a whole.

But the interest rate does not perform perfectly the task of rationing capital to its most productive uses. Large oligopolistic borrowers are in a better position than competitive borrowers to pass interest costs on to consumers by virtue of their ability to manipulate their prices. And, too, the sheer size and prestige of large industrial concerns might allow them to obtain money capital on favorable terms, whereas the market for money capital screens out less-well-known firms whose profit expectations might actually be superior.

## ☐ BUSINESS PROFITS AND ECONOMIC PROFITS

As is the case with rent, economists find it advantageous to define profits more narrowly than do business entrepreneurs or accountants. To most business entrepreneurs, "profit" is what remains of a firm's total revenue after it has paid individuals and other firms for materials, capital, and labor supplied to the firm. To the economist, this conception is too broad and therefore ambiguous. The difficulty, as the economist sees it, is that this view of profits takes into account only *explicit* costs, that is, payments made by the firm to outsiders. It therefore ignores *implicit* costs, that is, payments to similar resources which are owned and self-employed by a firm. In other words, this concept of profits fails to allow for implicit wage, rent, and interest costs. *Economic,* or *pure, profits* are what remain after *all* opportunity costs—both explicit and implicit wage, rent, and interest costs and a normal profit— have been subtracted from a firm's total revenue (Chapter 25). Economic profits may be either positive or negative (losses).

An example may sharpen these comments. As the economist sees it, a farmer who owns his land and equipment and provides all his own labor is grossly overstating his economic profits if he merely subtracts his payments to outsiders for seed, insecticides, fertilizer, gasoline, and so forth, from his total receipts. Actually, much or possibly all of what remain are the implicit rent, interest, and wage costs which the farmer forgoes in deciding to self-employ the resources he owns rather than make them available in alternative employments. Interest on the capital or wages for the labor contributed by the farmer himself are no more profits than are the payments which would be made if outsiders had supplied these resources. In short, the business executive's definition and the economist's definition of profits are compatible only if the business executive includes both explicit and implicit costs in determining total costs. Economic profits are a residual—the total revenue remaining after *all* costs are taken into account.

### △ Economic Profits and the Entrepreneur

Speaking very generally, the economist views profits as the return to a very special type of human resource—entrepreneurial ability. The functions of the entrepreneur were summarized in Chapter 2. They entail (1) taking the initiative to combine other resources in the production of some good or service; (2) making the basic, nonroutine policy decisions for the firm; (3) introducing innovations in the form of new products or production processes; and (4) bearing the economic risks associated with all the aforementioned functions.

A part of the entrepreneur's return, you will recall, is called a *normal profit.* This is the minimum return or payment necessary to retain the entrepreneur in some specific line of production. By definition, this normal profit payment is a cost (Chapter 25). However, we know that a firm's total revenue may exceed its total costs (explicit, implicit, and inclusive of a normal profit). This extra or excess revenue above all costs is an *economic,* or *pure, profit.* This residual—which is *not* a cost because it is in excess of the normal profit required to retain the entrepreneur in the industry—accrues to the entrepreneur. The entrepreneur, in other words, is the residual claimant.

Economists offer several theories to explain why this residual of economic profit might occur. As we will see in a moment, these explanations relate to:

**1**   The risks which the entrepreneur necessarily bears by functioning in a dynamic and therefore uncertain environment or by undertaking innovational activity.

**2**   The possibility of attaining monopoly power.

### △ Sources of Economic Profit

Our understanding of economic profits and the entrepreneur's functions can be both deepened and widened by describing an artificial economic environment within which pure profits would be zero. Then, by noting real-world deviations from this environment, we can lay bare the sources of economic profit.

In a purely competitive, static economy, pure profits would be zero. By a static economy we mean one in which all the basic data—resource supplies, technological knowledge, and consumer tastes—are constant and unchanging. A static economy is a changeless one in which all the determinants of cost and supply data, on the one hand, and demand and revenue data, on the other, are constant. Given the static nature of these data, the economic future is perfectly foreseeable; economic uncertainty is nonexistent. The outcome of price and production policies is accurately predictable. Furthermore, the static nature of such a society precludes any type of innovational change. Under pure competition any pure profits (positive or negative) which might have existed initially in various industries will disappear with the entry or exodus of firms in the long run. All costs—both explicit and implicit—will therefore be precisely covered in the long run, leaving no residual in the form of pure profits.

The notion of zero economic profits in a static, competitive economy enhances our understanding of profits by suggesting that the presence of profits is linked to the dynamic nature of real-world capitalism and the accompanying uncertainty. Furthermore, it indicates that economic profits may arise from a source apart from the directing, innovating, risk-bearing functions of the entrepreneur. And that source is the presence of some degree of monopoly power.

**Uncertainty, Risk, and Profits**  In a dynamic economy the future is always uncertain. This means that the entrepreneur necessarily assumes risks. Profits can be thought of in part as a reward for assuming these risks.

In linking pure profits with uncertainty and risk bearing, it is important to distinguish between risks which are insurable and those which are not. Some types of risks—for example, fires, floods, theft, and accidents to employees—are measurable in the sense that actuaries can estimate their average occurrence with considerable accuracy. As a result, these risks are typically insurable. Firms can avoid, or at least provide for, them by incurring a small known cost in the form of an insurance premium. It is the bearing of uninsurable risks, then, which is a potential source of economic profits.

What are such uninsurable risks? Basically, they are uncontrollable and unpredictable changes in demand (revenue) and supply (cost) conditions facing the firm. Some of these uninsurable risks stem from unpredictable changes in the general economic environment or, more specifically, from the business cycle. Prosperity brings substantial windfall profits to most firms, whereas depression means widespread losses. In addition, changes are constantly taking place in the structure of the economy. Even in a full-employment, noninflationary economy, changes are always occurring in consumer tastes, resource supplies, and so forth. These changes continually alter the revenue and cost data faced by individual firms and industries, leading to changes in the structure of the business population as favorably affected industries expand and adversely affected industries contract. Changes in government policies are pertinent at both levels. Appropriate fiscal and monetary policies of government may reverse a recession, whereas a tariff may alter significantly the demand and revenue data of the protected industry.

The point is this: Profits and losses can be associated with the assumption of uninsurable risks stemming from both cyclical and structural changes in the economy.

**Uncertainty, Innovations, and Profits**  The uncertainties just discussed are external to the firm; they are beyond the control of the individual firm or industry. One other extremely important dynamic feature of capitalism—innovation—occurs at the initiative of the entrepreneur. Business firms deliberately introduce new methods of production and distribution to affect their costs favorably and new products to influence their revenue favorably. The entrepreneur purposely undertakes to upset existing cost and revenue data in a way which hopefully will be profitable.

But once again, uncertainty enters the picture. Despite exhaustive market surveys by well-established firms, new products or modifications of existing products may prove to be economic failures. Three-dimensional movies, not to mention Edsel and Corvair automobiles, come readily to mind as product failures. Nor is it known with certainty whether a new machine will actually provide the cost economies predicted for it while it is still in the blueprint stage. Innovations purposely undertaken by entrepreneurs entail uncertainty, just as do those changes in the economic environment over which an individual enterprise has no control. In a sense, then, innovation as a source of profits is merely a special case of risk bearing.

Under competition and in the absence of patent laws, innovational profits will be temporary. Rival firms will imitate successful (profitable) innovations, thereby competing away all economic profits. Nevertheless, innovational profits may always exist in a progressive economy as new, successful innovations replace those older innovations whose associated profits have been eroded or competed away.

**Monopoly Profits**  Thus far, we have emphasized that profits are related to the uncertainties and uninsurable risks surrounding dynamic events which enterprises are exposed to or initiate themselves. The existence of monopoly in some form or another is a final source of economic profits. As explained previously, because of its ability to restrict entry, a monopolist may persistently enjoy economic profits, provided demand is strong relative to cost (Figure 27-2). This profit stems from the monopolist's ability to restrict output and influence product price to its own advantage.

There are both a causal relationship and a notable distinction between uncertainty, on the one hand, and monopoly, on the other, as sources of profits. The causal relationship involves the fact that an entrepreneur can reduce uncertainty, or at least manipulate its effects, by achieving monopoly power.[4] The competitive firm is unalterably exposed to the vagaries of the market; the monopolist, however, can control the market to a degree and thereby offset or minimize potentially adverse effects of uncertainty. Furthermore, innovation is an important source of monopoly power; the short-run uncertainty associated with the introduction of new techniques or new products may be borne for the purpose of achieving a measure of monopoly power.

The notable distinction between profits stemming from uncertainty and from monopoly has to do with the social desirability of the two sources of profits. Bearing the risks inherent in a dynamic and uncertain economic environment and the undertaking of innovations are socially desirable functions. The social desirability of monopoly profits, on the other hand, is very doubtful. Monopoly profits typically are founded upon output restriction, above-competitive prices, and a contrived misallocation of resources.

△   **Functions of Profits**

Profit is the prime mover, or energizer, of the capitalistic economy. As such, profits influence both the level of resource utilization and the allocation of resources among alternative uses. It is profits—or better, the *expectation* of profits—which induce firms to innovate. And innovation stimulates investment, total output, and employment. Innovation is a fundamental aspect of the process of economic growth, and it is the pursuit of profit which underlies most innovation. We know from our previous analysis of the determination of national income that profit expectations are highly volatile, with the result that investment, employment, and the rate of growth have been unstable. Profits have functioned imperfectly as a spur to innovation and investment.

Perhaps profits perform more effectively the task of allocating resources among alternative lines of production. Recall the message of Chapter 5: Entrepreneurs seek profits and shun losses. The occurrence of economic profits is a signal that society wants that particular industry to expand. Indeed, profit rewards are more than an inducement for an industry to expand; they also are the financial means by which firms in such industries can add to their productive capacities. Losses, on the other hand, signal society's desire for the afflicted industries to contract; losses penalize businesses which fail to adjust their productive efforts to those goods and services most preferred by consumers. This is not to say that profits and losses result in an allocation of resources which is now and forever attuned to consumer preferences. In particular, the pres-

---

[4]The extensive efforts of large corporations to avoid risk and uncertainty constitute a major theme running through John Kenneth Galbraith's writings. He argues as follows: In resource markets, corporations vertically integrate their structure so as to guarantee themselves reliable sources of materials. Similarly, they finance their capital investment internally to insulate themselves from the vagaries of capital markets. The modern corporation reduces product market uncertainty by supplanting consumer sovereignty with "producer sovereignty," using advertising and other sales techniques to "manage" consumers so they will buy those goods corporations want to sell at the prices they want to charge. Finally, uncertainties of a larger sort—economic fluctuations—are mitigated indirectly by inducing government to undertake appropriate countercyclical policies. Galbraith's *Economics and the Public Purpose* (Boston: Houghton Mifflin Company, 1973) and *The New Industrial State* (Boston: Houghton Mifflin Company, 1967) are relevant.

ence of monopoly in both product and resource markets impedes the shiftability of firms and resources, as also do the various geographic, artificial, and sociological immobilities discussed in Chapter 31.

## ☐ INCOME SHARES

The discussions of Chapters 31 and 32 would be incomplete without a brief empirical summary as to the importance of wages, rent, interest, and profits as proportions or relative shares of the national income. Table 32-1 provides an historical look at income shares in terms of the income categories used in our national income accounts. Unfortunately, these accounting conceptions of income do not neatly fit the economist's definitions of wages, rent, interest, and profits. In particular, the national income-accounting conceptions are often mixtures of these four types of income. Notable example: Much of "proprietors' income" is wages and salaries, but most unincorporated businesses provide their own capital and entrepreneurial talent and, in the case of farming, their own land. Hence, a portion of proprietors' income is interest, profits, and

rent. Recognizing this kind of limitation, what do our national income data tell us about the relative size and trends of income shares?

## △ Current Shares

Looking at the most recent 1971–1979 figures in the table, we note immediately the dominant role of labor income. Defining labor income narrowly as "wages and salaries," labor currently receives about 76 percent of the national income. But some economists argue that since proprietors' income is largely comprised of wages and salaries, it should be added to the official "wages and salaries" category to determine labor income. When we use this broad definition, labor's share rises to 83 percent of national income. Interestingly, although we label our system a "capitalist economy," the capitalist share of national income—which we will define as the sum of "corporate profits," "interest," and "rent"—is substantially less than 20 percent of the national income.

## △ Historical Trends

What can be deduced from Table 32-1 with respect to historical trends? Let us concen-

**TABLE 32-1**
Relative Shares of National Income, 1900–1979 (*decade or period averages of shares for individual years*)

| (1)<br>Decade | (2)<br>Wages and salaries | (3)<br>Proprietors' income | (4)<br>Corporate profits | (5)<br>Interest | (6)<br>Rent | (7)<br>Total |
|---|---|---|---|---|---|---|
| 1900–1909 | 55.0% | 23.7% | 6.8% | 5.5% | 9.0% | 100% |
| 1910–1919 | 53.6 | 23.8 | 9.1 | 5.4 | 8.1 | 100 |
| 1920–1929 | 60.0 | 17.5 | 7.8 | 6.2 | 7.7 | 100 |
| 1930–1939 | 67.5 | 14.8 | 4.0 | 8.7 | 5.0 | 100 |
| 1939–1948 | 64.6 | 17.2 | 11.9 | 3.1 | 3.3 | 100 |
| 1949–1958 | 67.3 | 13.9 | 12.5 | 2.9 | 3.4 | 100 |
| 1954–1963 | 69.9 | 11.9 | 11.2 | 4.0 | 3.0 | 100 |
| 1963–1970 | 71.7 | 9.6 | 12.1 | 3.5 | 3.2 | 100 |
| 1971–1979 | 76.0 | 7.4 | 8.5 | 5.9 | 2.3 | 100 |

*Source:* Irving Kravis, "Income Distribution: Functional Share," *International Encyclopedia of Social Sciences,* vol. 7 (New York: The Macmillan Company and Free Press, 1968), p. 134, updated.

trate on the dominant wage share. Using the narrow definition of labor's share as simply "wages and salaries," we note an increase from about 55 to 76 percent in this century. Although there are several tentative explanations of this growth, one prominent theory stresses the structural changes which have occurred in our economy. Two specific points are made. First, noting the relative constancy of the capitalist share (the sum of columns 4, 5, and 6)—which was roughly 20 percent in both the 1900–1909 and the 1971–1979 periods—we find that the expansion of labor's share has come primarily at the expense of the share going to proprietors. This suggests that the evolution of the corporation as the dominant form of business enterprise (Chapter 7) is an important explanatory factor. Put bluntly, individuals who would have operated their own corner groceries in the 1920s are the hired managers of corporate supermarkets in the 1970s or 1980s. Second, the changing output-mix and therefore the industry-mix which have occurred historically have tended to increase labor's share. Overall, there has been a long-term change in the composition of output and industry which has been away from land- and capital-intensive production and toward labor-intensive production. Again, crudely stated, there has been an historical reallocation of labor from agriculture (where labor's share is quite low) to manufacturing (where labor's share is rather high) and, finally, to private and public services (where labor's share is very high). These shifts account for much of the growth of labor's share reflected in column 2 of Table 32-1.

One is tempted to explain an expanding wage share in terms of the growth of labor unions. But there are difficulties with this approach. First, the growth of the labor movement in the United States does not fit very well chronologically with the growth of labor's share of the national income. Much of the growth of "wages and salaries" occurred between 1900 and 1939; much of the growth in the labor movement came in the last few years

of the 1930s and the war years of the early 1940s. Second, recall from Chapter 31 the possibility that wage increases for union members may come at the expense of the wages of unorganized workers. That is, in obtaining higher wages, unions restrict employment opportunities (Figures 31-6 and 31-7) in organized industries. Unemployed workers and new labor force entrants therefore seek jobs in the nonunion sectors. The resulting increases in labor supply tend to depress wage rates in nonunion jobs. If this scenario is correct, then higher wages for union workers may be achieved, not at the expense of the capitalist share, but rather, at the expense of the nonunion wage share. Overall, the total labor share—union plus nonunion—could be unaffected by unions. Finally, if the national income is disaggregated into industry sectors (as in Table 7-5) and the historical trend of the wage share in each sector is examined, we reach a curious conclusion. Generally speaking, labor's share has grown more rapidly in those sectors where unions are weak than in sectors which are highly unionized!

Other economists perceive substantial stability in the shares of national income that go to labor and capital. That is, if we recognize that most of "proprietors' income" is wages and therefore define labor's share broadly as the sum of "wages and salaries" and "proprietors' income," we note a fairly high degree of stability in labor's share historically. Labor's share, defined as the sum of columns 2 and 3, and the capitalist share, composed of columns 4, 5, and 6, have divided the national income roughly on an 80–20 percent basis throughout the entire period. Economists who have treated the statistics in this way have attempted to explain the stability of labor's share. The *pursuit and escape theory,* for example, is an intriguing explanation with considerable intuitive appeal. It draws upon a number of ideas developed in Chapter 18. Labor and business are envisioned in effect as being engaged in a contest of pursuit and escape. Labor attempts to encroach upon the capitalist share—profits, in particular—by increasing money wages. But businesses can escape this encroachment in either of two ways: (1) through increasing productivity, which has the effect of absorbing increases in money wages and preserving profits; and (2) by increasing product prices as a means of passing increases in wage costs on to consumers. According to the theory, it has been the effective use of these two escape techniques which explains the perceived historical stability of labor's share.[5]

[5] See Clark Kerr, "Labor's Income Share and the Labor Movement," in George W. Taylor and Frank C. Pierson (eds.), *New Concepts in Wage Determination* (New York: McGraw-Hill Book Company, 1957), pp. 260–298.

## Summary

**1** Economic rent is the price paid for the use of land and other natural resources whose total supplies are fixed.

**2** Rent is a surplus in the sense that land would be available to the economy as a whole even in the absence of all rental payments. The notion of land rent as a surplus gave rise to the single-tax movement of the late 1800s. Currently, many urban economists and planners advocate a tax on land value on both equity and efficiency grounds.

**3** Differences in land rent are explainable in terms of differences in productivity due to the fertility and climatic features of land and in its location.

**4** Land rent is a surplus rather than a cost to the economy as a whole; however, because land has alternative uses from the standpoint of individual firms and industries, rental payments of firms and industries are correctly regarded as costs.

**5** Interest is the price paid for the use of money. The theory of interest envisions a total demand for money comprised of transactions and asset demands. The supply of money is primarily the consequence of monetary policy.

**6** The equilibrium interest rate influences the level of investment and helps ration financial and real capital to specific firms and industries.

**7** Economic, or pure, profits are the difference between a firm's total revenue and its total costs, the latter defined to include implicit costs and a normal profit. Profits accrue to entrepreneurs for assuming the uninsurable risks associated with the organizing and directing of economic resources and innovating. Profits also result from monopoly power.

**8** Profit expectations influence innovating and investment activities and therefore the level of employment. The basic function of profits and losses, however, is to induce that allocation of resources which is in general accord with the tastes of consumers.

**9** The largest share of the national income goes to labor. Narrowly defined as "wages and salaries," labor's relative share has increased through time. When more broadly defined to include "proprietors' income," labor's share has been about 80 percent and the capitalist share about 20 percent of national income since 1900.

## Questions and Study Suggestions

**1** Key terms and concepts to remember: economic rent; incentive function; single-tax movement; the pure rate of interest; Truth in Lending Act; theory of interest; transactions and asset demands for money; economic or pure profit; static economy; insurable and uninsurable risks; pursuit and escape theory.

**2**   How does the economist's usage of the term "rent" differ from everyday usage? "Though rent need not be paid by society to make land available, rental payments are very useful in guiding land into the most productive uses." Explain.

**3**   Explain why economic rent is a surplus to the economy as a whole but a cost of production from the standpoint of individual firms and industries. Explain: "Rent performs no 'incentive function' in the economy." What arguments can be made for and against a heavy tax on land?

**4**   If money capital, as such, is not an economic resource, why is interest paid and received for its use? What considerations account for the fact that interest rates differ greatly on various types of loans? Use these considerations to explain the relative size of the interest rates charged on the following: *a.* a long-term $1000 government bond; *b.* a $20 pawnshop loan; *c.* an FHA mortgage loan on a $67,000 house; *d.* a $6500 commercial bank loan to finance the purchase of an automobile; and *e.* a $100 loan from a personal finance company.

**5**   What are the major economic functions of the interest rate? Of economic profits? How might the fact that more and more businesses are financing their investment activities internally affect the efficiency with which the interest rate performs its functions?

**6**   How do the concepts of business profits and economic profits differ? Why are economic profits smaller than business profits? What are the three basic sources of economic profits? Classify each of the following in accordance with these sources: *a.* the profits acquired by a firm from developing and patenting a ball-point pen containing a permanent ink cartridge; *b.* the profit of a restaurant which results from construction of the interstate highway past its door; *c.* the profit received by a firm benefiting from an unanticipated change in consumer tastes.

**7**   Why is the distinction between insurable and uninsurable risks significant for the theory of profits? Carefully evaluate: "All economic profits can be traced to either uncertainty or the desire to avoid it."

**8**   Explain the absence of economic profit in a purely competitive, static economy. Realizing that the major function of profits is to allocate resources in accordance with consumer preferences, evaluate the allocation of resources in such an economy.

**9**   What has happened to the wage, profit, interest, and rent shares of national income over time? Explain the alleged growth of labor's share in terms of structural changes in the economy. Explain the alleged stability of labor's share in terms of the "pursuit and escape" theory. What are the implications of this theory for the rate of inflation?

## Selected References

Clower, Robert W., and John F. Due: *Microeconomics* (Homewood, Ill.: Richard D. Irwin, Inc., 1972), chaps. 13–16.

Hansen, Alvin: *A Guide to Keynes* (New York: McGraw-Hill Book Company, 1953), chaps. 6, 7.

Humphrey, Thomas M.: "Income Distribution and Its Measurement: Distribution among the Factors of Production," *Monthly Review* (Federal Reserve Bank of Richmond, August 1971).

Stonier, Alfred W., and Douglas C. Hague: *A Textbook of Economic Theory,* 3d ed. (New York: Longmans, Green & Co., Inc., 1964), chaps. 13–15.

# LAST WORD
## Land Rent Goes Ape

An American poet, Edmund Vance Cooke (1866–1932), satirizes the private-property, land-rent issue.

### UNCIVILIZED

An ancient ape, once on a time,
Disliked exceedingly to climb,
And so he picked him out a tree
And said, "Now this belongs to me.
I have a hunch that monks are mutts
And I can make them gather nuts
And bring the bulk of them to me,
By claiming title to this tree."

He took a green leaf and a reed
And wrote himself a title deed,
Proclaiming pompously and slow:
"All monkeys by these presents know."
Next morning when the monkeys came
To gather nuts, he made his claim:
"All monkeys climbing on this tree
Must bring their gathered nuts to me,
Cracking the same on equal shares;
The meats are mine, the shells are theirs."

"But by what right?" they cried, amazed,
Thinking the ape was surely crazed.
"By this," he answered; "if you'll read
You'll find it is a title deed,
Made in precise and formal shape
And sworn before a fellow ape,
Exactly on the legal plan
Used by that wondrous creature, man,
In London, Tokyo, New York,
Glengarry, Kalamazoo and Cork.

Unless my deed is recognized,
It proves you quite uncivilized."

"But," said one monkey, "you'll agree
It was not you who made this tree."
"Nor," said the ape, serene and bland,
"Does any owner make his land,
Yet all of its hereditaments
Are his and figure in the rents."

The puzzled monkeys sat about;
They could not make the question out.
Plainly, by precedent and law,
The ape's procedure showed no flaw;
And yet, no matter what he said,
The stomach still denied the head.

Up spoke one sprightly monkey then:
"Monkeys are monkeys, men are men;
The ape should try his legal capers
On men who may respect his papers.
We don't know deeds; we do know nuts,
And spite of 'ifs' and 'ands' and 'buts,'
We know who gathers and unmeats 'em,
By monkey practice also eats 'em.
So tell the ape and all his flunkies
No man tricks can be played on monkeys."
Thus, apes still climb to get their food,
Since monkeys' minds are crass and crude,
And monkeys, all so ill-advised,
Still eat their nuts, uncivilized.

From *The Public,* May 24, 1919, p. 546.

# General Equilibrium: The Price System and Its Operation[1]

chapter 33

It is the basic purpose of this chapter to draw together the discussion of product and resource markets which has been the dominant theme of Part 5. We have analyzed the various categories of individual product and resource markets in some detail. Our present goal is to reemphasize that the many diverse markets of our economy are interwoven into a highly complex *price system*. This price system is responsible for the production of about four-fifths or more of our national product and therefore for the allocation of a comparable proportion of available resources. It is imperative that we grasp how this price system works.

## □ PARTIAL AND GENERAL EQUILIBRIUM

Thus far, our discussion of prices has been compartmentalized; we have examined representative product and resource prices one at a time, in isolation, and apart from any detailed interrelationships each may bear to the other. In the jargon of the economist, we have been concerned with *partial equilibrium analysis*—a study of equilibrium prices and outputs in the many specific markets which are the component *parts* of the price system.

But the economy is not merely a myriad of isolated and unrelated markets. On the contrary, it is an interlocking network of prices wherein changes in one market are likely to elicit numerous and significant changes in other markets. Hence, our vantage point now shifts from individual markets and prices in isolation to an analysis of the price system as a whole. In technical language, our discussion now shifts to *general equilibrium analysis*—an overall big-picture view of the interrelationships among all the various prices (parts) which make up the price *system*.

[1] As a prologue to the present chapter, it might be helpful for the reader to scan Chapter 5 and the concluding section of Chapter 26, which evaluates competitive pricing.

We shall attempt to grasp the interrelatedness of various industries and markets through a series of three general equilibrium illustrations. We begin with an intuitive model of the automobile industry wherein the many possible repercussions of a change in demand are traced. Next we turn to a hypothetical model of two industries which makes explicit use of the formal analytical tools of microeconomics. At this point we will digress to summarize the implications of the functioning of a purely competitive price system for allocative efficiency and to recall some real-world complications. A third and final model views the interdependence of the various sectors of the economy through what is called input-output analysis. The chapter closes with a discussion of the relevance of general equilibrium analysis for economic understanding.

## ☐ MARKET INTERRELATIONSHIPS: AUTOMOBILES[2]

Suppose initially that general equilibrium exists—in other words, that all product and resource markets are "at rest." Now assume there occurs an increase in the demand for automobiles. What will be the effects?

The immediate impact is obviously an increase in automobile prices. As automobile manufacturers react by increasing production, an increase will occur in the derived demands for, and therefore the prices of, all those resources used in the production of automobiles. These interrelationships between product and resource prices are not new to us; they were a key point in our analysis of resource demand (Chapter 30). In any event, the prospect of higher earnings in the automobile industry will attract resources to it. Industries losing labor to the automobile industry may find it necessary to pay higher wages to counteract this loss, and these higher wage costs imply declin-

ing profits for the affected industries. Furthermore, if the shift of labor to the automobile industry involves a geographic relocation of workers and their families, we can expect repercussions upon a number of other industries. For example, the residential construction industry—and therefore cement, lumber, and glass suppliers in the area—will experience an increase in the demand for their products. Too, the demand for the services of various skilled and semiskilled construction workers will increase, imposing additional changes on the other labor markets. A similar analysis would apply to nonlabor resources. An increase in the demand for automobiles will increase the demand for steel, and we know that the list of firms and industries using substantial amounts of steel reads like a *Who's Who* of American industry. In brief, innumerable other industries using the same types of land, labor, and capital as the automobile industry will find that their costs have increased. This will give rise to increases in the prices and declines in the sales of the products produced by these industries.

But we must not conclude that the effects of an increase in the demand for automobiles emanate solely from the resource market. An increase in the price of automobiles will affect the demand for, and prices of, other goods. The demand for, and prices of, such products as gasoline, motor oil, and tires will increase in response to the initial increase in the demand for automobiles. The demand for, and prices of, the services provided by bus lines, interurban railways, and taxis will tend to decline. And these changes in the prices of goods and services will be communicated back into the resource markets relevant to all these industries.

This is still not all: An equally subtle series of price alterations will emanate in the resource market from the initial price increases of resources used by the automobile industry. To illustrate: If the increase in the automobile industry's derived demand for steel significantly increases the price of steel, automobile

[2]This illustration follows the excellent example discussed in Francis E. Hyde et al., *A New Prospect of Economics* (Liverpool: Liverpool University Press, 1958), chap. 9.

manufacturers may substitute aluminum where possible for engine and body parts. Many other industries using steel may make similar substitutions. As the prices of resources change, all industries and firms employing these resources will tend to shuffle the quantities of the various resources used to reachieve the least costly combination of resources (Chapter 30). This will affect the demand for, and prices of, these resources.

Noteworthy, too, is the fact that all the changes in resource prices which we have sketched will affect the personal distribution of income. In our example, automobile workers will find themselves moving into higher income brackets as the result of the initial increase in the demand for automobiles. They may well react by demanding more superior, or normal, goods such as butter and steak and less of such inferior goods as lard and potatoes. Indeed, they may even decide to buy still more automobiles, prompting a whole new series of price interactions such as we have already outlined.

The reader will readily note many loose ends in our discussion. If one had the patience and inclination, these price interrelationships could be pursued almost indefinitely. But our discussion is sufficiently detailed to emphasize our major point. Individual prices are interrelated in a number of both evident and subtle ways. Our basic point is that *any initial disturbance such as a change in demand, a change in technology, or a change in resource supply will set off a highly complex economic chain reaction.*

## ☐ GENERAL EQUILIBRIUM: A TWO-INDUSTRY MODEL

Let us now consider a hypothetical illustration which explicitly embodies the formal tools of economic analysis. In Figure 33-1, which is merely a somewhat sophisticated version of Figure 3-2, the discussion focuses upon two product markets, X and Y. And although each industry would actually employ a number of different inputs, it will facilitate our analysis to

concentrate only upon the labor market relevant to each industry. It is assumed that industry X uses type A labor and Y uses type B labor.

### △ Behind the Curves

A word or two is in order to remind us of the concepts which underlie the demand and supply curves of both product and resource markets. The product demand curves are downsloping because of *diminishing marginal utility* (Chapter 24). Successive units of a given product yield less and less additional satisfaction or utility to buyers, so that consumers will purchase more of that product only if its price falls. The upsloping product supply curves are based upon the concept of *increasing marginal costs* (Chapter 25). Because extra units of output are more costly, firms must receive a higher price before it will be profitable for them to produce this extra output. The downsloping labor demand curves are based upon the law of diminishing returns or *diminishing marginal physical productivity* (Chapter 30). Beyond some point, the addition of labor or any other variable resource to fixed resources will result in smaller and smaller increases in total output. And as we recall these concepts from earlier chapters, do not overlook the obvious link between the upsloping product supply curve and the downsloping resource demand curve. It is the diminishing marginal productivity of the resource which *causes* marginal costs to increase as output is increased. If each successive unit of labor (hired at a constant wage cost) adds less and less to output, then the cost of *each* successive unit of output must be more and more. Finally, the upsloping labor supply curves reflect the *work-leisure preferences* of individuals. A firm or an industry must pay higher and higher wage rates to obtain larger amounts of labor service.

We assume long-run equilibrium initially, so that $P_{x1}$ and $w_{a1}$ are the equilibrium product price and wage rate for industry X, and $P_{y1}$ and $w_{b1}$ represent the equilibrium price and wage

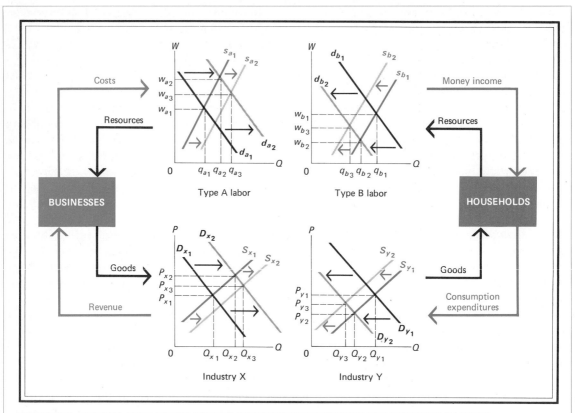

**FIGURE 33-1　GENERAL EQUILIBRIUM AND THE INTERACTION OF PRODUCT AND RESOURCE MARKETS**

These diagrams show the short-run and long-run adjustments resulting from an assumed increase in the demand for product X and assumed decline in the demand for product Y. Emphasis here is upon product and resource market interactions, and the diagrams therefore conceal many of the less obvious repercussions. For example, the given changes in demand for X and Y will affect the demands for substitute and complementary goods and alter the distribution of income.

for industry Y. Firms are making normal profits, and there is no reason for either industry to expand or contract. The two labor markets are similarly "at rest"; there is no incentive for workers to move out of or into either market.

Suppose now that something happens to upset this equilibrium. What will be the character of the resulting adjustments? Specifically, let us say that a change occurs in consumer preferences or tastes so that consumer demand for X increases and consumer demand for Y simultaneously decreases.

△　**Short-run Adjustments**

What short-run adjustments will occur in response to these changes in consumer demand? First of all, production, which was normally profitable in industry X before demand rose from $D_{x1}$ to $D_{x2}$, now results in economic profits. Firms in industry X, faced with the new higher price of $P_{x2}$, find it profitable to move to some point further up and to the right on their marginal-cost curves (Figure 26-6). Collectively, these marginal-cost curves are the supply curve $S_{x1}$ for the industry. Thus, in

Figure 33-1 existing firms find it profitable to expand output as a group from $Q_{x1}$ to $Q_{x2}$.

But to expand output, the firms in industry X must acquire more resources, such as type A labor. Remembering that the demand for resources is a *derived demand,* it is no surprise that the expansion of output by firms in X will increase the demand for labor from $d_{a1}$ to, say, $d_{a2}$. Workers in this labor market are willing to offer more of their services, perhaps by working longer hours or more days per week, moving up $s_{a1}$ in response to the higher wage rate $w_{a2}$.

An opposite set of short-run adjustments will be experienced in industry Y. Product demand falls to, say, $D_{y2}$, causing price to fall from $P_{y1}$ to $P_{y2}$. At this lower price, individual firms incur losses. These firms will react by moving down and to the left on their marginal-cost curves as they seek their loss-minimizing positions. The decline in demand for product Y is reflected back in the resource market. In particular, the demand for type B labor falls from $d_{b1}$ to $d_{b2}$, causing the equilibrium wage rate to decline to $w_{b2}$.

△ **Long-run Adjustments**

But we have only traced the first round of market adjustments. At the conclusion of these short-run adjustments, the production of X still yields an economic profit, while losses persist in industry Y. This means that, given sufficient time, new firms will enter industry X, while firms will fall into bankruptcy and fail in industry Y. That is, the presumed changes in consumer demand have made X a prosperous, expanding industry and Y an unprosperous, declining industry.

As new firms enter X, the industry supply curve will shift to the right from $S_{x1}$ to, say, $S_{x2}$. This increase in supply tends to bring price back down to, say, $P_{x3}$. Equilibrium output of X has further increased to $Q_{x3}$. If $P_{x3}$ and $Q_{x3}$ represent a new long-run equilibrium, as we assume is the case, we can note in passing that industry X must be an increasing-cost industry. Why? Because the new long-run

equilibrium entails a higher price than the initial equilibrium price $P_{x1}$ (Figure 26-11). If this were a constant-cost industry, the new price would be the same as the old price. It is to be emphasized that, in the new equilibrium position, consumers are getting a larger output of X—which is, of course, precisely what they wanted. In other words, these adjustments are a manifestation of *consumer sovereignty.*

Losses in industry Y force firms to leave the industry. As they do, industry supply will decline from $S_{y1}$ to, say, $S_{y2}$. This raises price somewhat from $P_{y2}$ to $P_{y3}$. If we assume industry Y is also an increasing-cost industry, contraction of the industry will lower unit costs. Thus, in the new long-run equilibrium position at $P_{y3}$, price will be lower than originally, production will be normally profitable once again, and industry size will be stabilized.

These long-run adjustments have counterparts in the resource markets. The supply curve for type B labor, $s_{b1}$, is drawn on the assumption that other wage rates—for example, the wage rate received by type A labor—are given. The same holds true for the type A labor supply curve, $s_{a1}$. But our short-run changes in the demand for labor have increased the wage rate for type A labor and reduced the wage rate for type B labor. The stage is set for type B labor to shift from industry Y, where job opportunities and wage rates have been declining, to industry X, where employment has been expanding and wage rates have been increasing. Thus we would expect the supply of type A labor to increase from $s_{a1}$ to, say, $s_{a2}$ and the supply of type B labor to fall from $s_{b1}$ to, say, $s_{b2}$. As a result, wage rates for type A labor fall somewhat from $w_{a2}$ to $w_{a3}$. And for type B labor, wage rates tend to go back up from $w_{b2}$ to, say, $w_{b3}$.

But note several related points about these labor market adjustments. First, we are assuming that type B labor can become qualified as type A labor without too much difficulty and retraining. In practice, occupational shifts may actually be complicated and costly to achieve. A second and closely related point is that supply shifts might take a substantial period of time. As suggested, type B workers may in fact require additional education, job retraining, and geographic relocation before becoming type A workers. Finally, because of various immobilities (Chapter 31), we would not expect the supply curve shifts to be sufficiently great to restore the wage rates of the original equilibrium. The new equilibrium wage rate will be $w_{a3}$ (higher than $w_{a1}$) for type A labor and $w_{b3}$ (lower than $w_{b1}$) for type B labor. Indeed, these long-run wage adjustments are consistent with, and a factor in, the assumed increasing-cost character of industries X and Y.

△  **Further Adjustments**
But this is only the beginning of the repercussions which stem from our original change in the structure of consumer demand. There are innumerable more subtle adjustments which we might take into account.

**Other Industries**   Consider now a third industry—call it industry Z. Will the initial increase in the price of X have any impact upon industry Z? It might! Recall that one of the determinants of the demand for Z are the prices of related goods, and X just might be "related" to Z. But any shift in the demand for Z which stems from the increase in the price of X depends on precisely how products X and Z are related. Recall (Chapter 4) that any two products might be *substitutes* (butter and oleo), *complements* (gas and oil), or substantially *independent* (raisins and wristwatches). If X and Z are independent, then a rise in the price of X will have no significant effect on the demand for Z. But if X and Z are substitutes, the rise in the price of X will increase the demand for Z. Therefore, a series of adjustments will be precipitated in the product and resource markets for Z similar to those just sketched for X. And if X and Z are complements, the higher price for X will lower the demand for Z. This would precipitate adjustments in Z like those already traced for industry Y.

**Other Resources**   The initial changes in the demands for type A and type B labor may have an impact upon other resource markets. Suppose that technology in industry X is such that labor and capital must be used in virtually fixed proportions, for example, one machine is needed for every two workers. This means that the expansion in the employment of type A labor will stimulate the demand for relevant kinds of capital goods.

**Income Distribution**   It is also quite evident that our short-run and long-run adjustments will alter the distribution of income. Workers and entrepreneurs associated with industry X will receive higher incomes; those in industry Y, lower incomes. It is realistic to assume some differences in tastes which will be transformed into further changes in the structure of consumer demand. These new changes in demand will trigger new rounds of short-run and long-run adjustments.

We could go on, but the basic point is clear. The adjustments stemming from our initial changes in demand are much more complex and go far beyond the simple supply and demand shifts portrayed in Figure 33-1.[3]

☐  **ECONOMIC WELFARE AND THE PRICE SYSTEM**
Now that we have some appreciation of the mechanics of the price system and the many complex market interrelationships it implies, we must inquire once again as to the efficiency of the system. How effectively does the price system function?

Although there is no unequivocal answer to this question, we can certainly say some things on behalf of a competitive price system. The fundamental argument for it is that *its operation is conducive to an efficient allocation of resources.* More precisely, *given the distribution of income among consumers, purely competitive product and resource mar-*

---

[3]A challenge for the ambitious student: Use the discussion of Figure 33-1 to analyze this chapter's Last Word.

*kets tend to give rise to the production of that collection of goods and services which maximizes the satisfactions of consumers.* Earlier discussion, particularly in Chapters 5 and 26, provided the analytical grounding for this claim of allocative efficiency. The following three technical points simply suggest that the price system provides economically desirable answers to the questions: What should the economy produce? How should that output be produced? For whom should it be produced?

**1**   Self-interest drives purely competitive firms to produce that output at which price equals marginal cost. Remember that the price of a product reflects its value or worth to society, while marginal cost measures the value of the resources needed in its production. This means that additional units of any product are produced as long as they are valued by society more highly than are the alternative products which the needed resources could otherwise have produced. In other words, the "right" or most desirable output of each commodity—and therefore the best mixture of goods and services—gets produced.

**2**   Pure competition also results in the production of each good at minimum average cost (Figure 26-12). In terms of the resource market, competition forces producers to use the least costly combination of resources; that is, the combination wherein the last dollar spent on each resource entails the same marginal physical product (Chapter 30).[4]

**3**   Not only does competition cause the right collection of goods and services to be produced and production to be at least cost, but free choice by consumers in competitive markets will result in the distribution of this output so as to maximize consumer satisfactions. *Given his or her income and tastes,* each consumer will purchase that collection of

goods and services which is most satisfying. Technically speaking, the consumer will buy various products in such amounts that the last dollar spent on each item yields equal amounts of extra satisfaction or marginal utility.[5]

And finally, remember that these desirable consequences follow from the free decisions of participants made in their own self-interest. Business executives are motivated in their decision making to maximize profits; resource suppliers, to increase their incomes; consumers, to maximize their satisfactions. Quite miraculously, the overall outcome of these freely rendered decisions, once coordinated and synchronized by the price system, is in the public interest. Scarce resources are apparently used with maximum efficiency.

☐   **THE REAL WORLD AND IMPERFECT COMPETITION**

Having discussed the adjustments of a purely competitive price system in moving toward long-run equilibrium and the consequences of these adjustments for allocative efficiency, we must now understand that the competitive price system is clearly a rough approximation of reality. The competitive model is essentially a simplified way of envisioning the operation of a market economy; it does not purport to be a description of reality.

One basic way in which the real world differs from our model is that, in actuality, most product and resource markets are imperfectly competitive; they deviate in varying degrees from the purely competitive model. As a result, resources may well be allocated less efficiently than under pure competition. Imperfectly competitive producers find it in their private interest as profit seekers to produce short of the price-equals-marginal-cost output,

---

[4] If any two resources—labor and capital—are being employed, then costs will be minimized when they are used in such amounts that

$$\frac{\text{MPP of labor}}{\text{price of labor}} = \frac{\text{MPP of capital}}{\text{price of capital}}$$

[5] If the consumer is buying just two products, X and Y, he or she will maximize utility by purchasing them in such quantities that

$$\frac{\text{MU of product X}}{\text{price of X}} = \frac{\text{MU of product Y}}{\text{price of Y}}$$

and an underallocation of resources to the production of such goods will occur. The private interest of the imperfectly competitive firm is at odds with society's interest in allocative efficiency. Similarly, monopsony (Figure 31-4) or monopoly (Figure 31-7) can cause prices in the resource market to vary from the competitive level and impair allocative efficiency.

Imperfect competition also means that adjustments of the type described in our general equilibrium models will be more sluggish and less complete. This is not to say the price system won't make generally appropriate adjustments. It will. But under imperfect competition, these adjustments will be only rough approximations of those described in our two-industry model. In general, most economists are willing to conclude that with imperfect competition, resource allocation is less efficient and the price system less responsive to changes in tastes, technology, or resource availability than if pure competition prevailed. On the other hand, the possibility of more rapid technological progress and the alleged advantages stemming from greater product variety under imperfectly competitive conditions must be regarded as potential offsets to diminished allocative efficiency (Chapter 28).

□  OUTPUT, INCOME, AND ETHICS

Even if the purely competitive model of the price system were an accurate portrayal of the real world, we would nevertheless be justified in questioning its capacity to allocate resources efficiently. This is so for at least two reasons.

△  **Allocative Activities of Government**

In the first place, we know that the production of certain products may entail benefits and costs which are external to the demand and supply curves of the market. If substantial *spillover benefits* are involved in the production or consumption of some good or service (for example, education), the market will understate the demand for such goods, and resources will be underallocated to their pro-

duction. Conversely, if the production or consumption of some good entails significant *spillover costs* (for example, air pollution), the market supply curve will understate costs, and resources will be overallocated to that commodity's production. Legislation and the imposition of special excise taxes (Chapters 6 and 23) are ways of correcting for this overallocation of resources which accompanies spillover costs. Recall that special public subsidies can be useful in correcting the underallocation of resources which characterizes the production of goods whose spillover benefits are substantial. Furthermore, the price system would ignore or grossly neglect the production of such *social goods* as national defense, streets and highways, flood control, and courthouses.

△  **Government and Distributive Justice**

A most perplexing question—to which economists as social scientists do not know the answer—now looms before us. The question is this: What is the "best" or optimal distribution of income?

Let us back up a moment and reexamine our claim that, aside from social goods and instances of substantial spillover benefits and costs, a competitive price system will negotiate that allocation of resources which maximizes consumer satisfaction. This claim is predicated upon a "given" or "assumed" distribution of income. Money income is presumably distributed among consumers in a certain way, and on the basis of their incomes, consumers make their wants effective in the various markets by expenditures for different goods. This is what we rather quaintly termed "dollar voting" in Chapter 5. In any event, these consumer decisions, based upon money income, are reflected in the product demand curves of our general equilibrium models. Given the structure of demand which results from this distribution of income, we have seen that it is a primary virtue of the price system that it brings about the allocation of resources and resulting product-mix which best fulfills the wants of consumers.

This is all well and good. But now an awkward question arises. *If* we were now to suppose, or bring about, a *different* distribution of money income so as to get a *different* structure of consumer demand, would not the competitive price system negotiate a new allocation of resources and a new product-mix which would result in the maximum satisfaction of this new pattern of consumer demand? The answer is: Yes, this is exactly what the price system would do! This answer leads inevitably to a further question: Which of these two allocations of resources—the one which is "most efficient" for the first income distribution or the one which is "most efficient" for the second income distribution—is truly optimal or best?

Economists have been unable to provide a satisfactory answer because they cannot measure and compare the ability of various individuals to derive satisfaction or utility from money income. If every individual were precisely identical in the capacity to enjoy income, economists would say that income should be distributed equally and that the allocation of resources which is most efficient in response to *that* distribution of income would result in the greatest possible level of consumer satisfaction. But people differ by virtue of their inherited physical and mental characteristics, not to mention their education, training, environment, experiences, and so forth. And we cannot meaningfully gauge the extent to which they are different; the capacity to derive satisfaction or utility is a highly subjective, psychological thing, elusive of measurement. So how can we determine whether some distribution of income, other than the existing one, is superior or inferior? In short, the whole question of what is the optimum distribution of income remains an ethical one. We will return to this question of distributive justice in Chapter 37 and discuss in some detail the ways in which government has altered the distribution of income from that which the unmodified price system would have provided. Indeed, most of the chapters of Part 6 bear upon the question of income distribution.

## ☐ GENERAL EQUILIBRIUM: INPUT-OUTPUT ANALYSIS

The relatively simple general equilibrium models thus far explored serve the major purpose of emphasizing the interrelatedness of the many decision makers who comprise the economy. Further appreciation of the intricate interrelationships between the various sectors or industries of the economy can be gained through an input-output table.

### △   Input-Output Table

Table 33-1 is a very much simplified hypothetical input-output table for an economy.[6] Listed down the left side of the table are the five producing sectors (industries) of the economy. Column 6 shows the total output associated with each of the five sectors; the metal sector produces 100 units, the machine sector 200 units, and so on. These same five sectors are also the consuming sectors of the economy and are shown in this capacity across the top of the table. Looking across each of the horizontal rows of figures, we can see how the total output of each sector is disposed of, or consumed, among the five sectors. For example, of the 200 units of output of the machinery sector, 40 units go to the metal sector, 25 to the machinery sector itself (because it takes machines to produce machines!), and 35, 75, and 25 units go to the fuel, agriculture, and household sectors, respectively, thereby exhausting the units produced.

Following through on this disposition-of-output procedure for all five sectors, we find that each vertical column must and does show the units of output of each producing sector which are consumed as inputs by the five sec-

---

[6] Wassily W. Leontieff is largely responsible for input-output analysis. See his simplified discussion of "Input-Output Economics," *Scientific American,* October 1951, pp. 15–21. Table 33-1 and portions of the accompanying discussion are from Francis M. Boddy, "Soviet Economic Growth," in Robert T. Holt and John E. Turner (eds.), *Soviet Union: Paradox and Change* (New York: Holt, Rinehart and Winston, Inc., 1962), pp. 77–79, with permission of the publisher.

**TABLE 33-1**
**A Simplified Input-Output Table (*hypothetical data*)**

| Producing sectors | Consuming or using sectors | | | | | |
| --- | --- | --- | --- | --- | --- | --- |
| | (1) Metal | (2) Machinery | (3) Fuel | (4) Agriculture | (5) Households (labor) | (6) Total output |
| (1) Metal | 10 | 65 | 10 | 5 | 10 | **100** |
| (2) Machinery | 40 | 25 | 35 | 75 | 25 | **200** |
| (3) Fuel | 15 | 5 | 5 | 5 | 20 | **50** |
| (4) Agriculture | 15 | 10 | 50 | 50 | 525 | **650** |
| (5) Labor (households) | 100 | 200 | 100 | 550 | 50 | **1000** |

tors. For example, we find in column 2 that to produce 200 units of machinery, inputs of 65 units of metal, 25 of machinery, 5 of fuel, 10 of agricultural products, and 200 of labor are required. In this way, the table vividly reveals the highly interdependent character of the various sectors or industries. Any given industry or sector employs the outputs of other sectors—and indeed, some of its own output—as its inputs! And the outputs of that given sector are similarly the inputs of the other sectors. To cite a real-world example: While outputs of steel are inputs in the production of railroad cars, these railroad cars are, in turn, used to transport both finished steel and the various inputs—coke, pig iron, and so forth—which are necessary to the production of steel.

△ **Interdependencies**

The interdependence of the economy's sectors or industries can be further demonstrated by tracing the repercussions of an assumed change in the output of some commodity.

Consider, for example, the repercussions of a 20-unit (10 percent) increase in machinery production. This means that a 10 percent increase in the production of all the outputs which are used as inputs in the production of machinery is required.[7] These inputs, as we

know, are listed in column 2 of the table. Applying the 10 percent figure, we find that 6.5 additional units (outputs) of metal, 2.5 units of machinery, 0.5 unit of fuel, 1 unit of agricultural products, and 20 units of labor will be needed to produce another 20 units of machinery.

But this is just the beginning: obviously, a myriad of further adjustments are also required. Because each sector which supplies inputs to the machinery sector must expand its output, these supplying sectors in turn will require more inputs from other sectors. Example: The additional 6.5 units of metal needed as inputs to produce the extra 20 units of machinery will in turn call for an appropriate—6.5 percent, in this case—increase in the production of all the inputs shown in column 1 to be needed in producing metal. The same reasoning, of course, is applicable to the fuel, agriculture, and labor sectors. That is, the 0.5-unit increase in fuel production required in producing the extra 20 units of machinery will call for an appropriate (1 percent) increase in the production of all the inputs listed in column 3, and similarly for the agricultural and labor sectors. Furthermore, note that the production of 20 more units of machinery output requires as inputs the production of 2.5 units of machinery. This 2.5-unit increase will require "second-round" increases (of 1.25 percent in this case) in the inputs of all the resources shown in column 2 in the same general fashion as did the initial 20-unit increase in machinery output.

[7]We invoke here one of the simplifying assumptions underlying the input-output table, namely, that production occurs under conditions of constant returns to scale (see Chapter 25).

The reader will clearly recognize that the chain reaction is by no means at an end. All the repercussions cited in these examples call for still further adjustments similar to those already described. The crucial point, of course, is that, because of the high degree of interrelatedness among the sectors of the economy, a change in the figure in any one "cell" or "box" of the input-output table will precipitate an almost endless series of adjustments in other figures. In our illustration, the expansion of production in one sector has nearly innumerable repercussions which reach into virtually every nook and cranny of the economy.

## ☐ GENERAL EQUILIBRIUM AND ECONOMIC UNDERSTANDING

General equilibrium analysis can be very useful in evaluating the overall operation of the economy, in understanding specific economic problems, and in formulating policies. A failure to recognize price and sector interrelationships is an important source of misunderstanding and faulty reasoning about major economic problems. Furthermore, input-output analysis lends itself to an abundance of practical applications.

### △ Some Illustrations

Some examples will clarify these points. One might expect that the effect of a general or widespread wage cut is to reduce the costs of specific firms. And, other things being equal, lower costs will cause a firm to lower prices, increase production, and hire more workers. But general equilibrium analysis suggests that this seemingly obvious conclusion is of doubtful validity. Lower wages mean lower incomes, which are communicated into the product market as general declines in the demand for, and prices of, products. These price declines are then projected back into the resource market once again as declines in resource demand. And these declines in resource demand will mean unemployment. The immediate impact of wage cuts (more employment), which partial equilibrium analysis suggests, may be swallowed up by the secondary effects (less employment), which are discernible only by an understanding of general equilibrium analysis.

Another example: Many people favor protective tariffs levied on, say, Japanese or German toys, because the immediate and obvious effect is to increase the price of foreign toys and therefore increase the demand for American-made toys. The result is that output and employment rise in the American toy industry. But this ignores the fact that incomes in Japan and Germany will decline as a result of their inability to sell toys in the United States. And with smaller incomes they will be less able to buy from American industries exporting machine tools, chemicals, grains, and so forth. The obvious increase in employment in the protected industry may well be offset, wholly or in part, by the indirect, subtle declines in employment in American export industries. As a matter of fact, apart from any decline in domestic employment stemming from tariff-induced declines in exports, general equilibrium analysis reminds us that the extra resources which are shifted into the expanding toy industry must come from other industries. That is, in a full-employment economy the tariff-inspired expansion of the toy industry will entail a contraction in the production of other goods.

### △ Forecasting and Planning

Input-output analysis has resulted in empirical measurement of the various interactions between sectors of the economy, and these measurements have proved of considerable value as an instrument of economic forecasting and planning. Assume for the moment a much more detailed input-output table containing 50 or even 500 individual sectors with each box filled with accurate empirical data. Now, for example, if the government should decide to undertake the production of fifty new supersonic bombers, the impact of this decision upon affected sectors could be quite accurately predicted; we can forecast quantitatively "what it will take" in terms of the outputs of all the many affected industries to fulfill this goal. Input-output analysis also has considerable relevance for the less developed nations, many of which seek growth through some form of planning (Chapter 21) and for more advanced centrally planned systems, such as the Soviet Union (Chapter 45). By revealing the quantitative interrelationships among various sectors of the economy, input-output analysis allows the planners to determine how realistic—how feasible—planned production targets actually are. By tracing the repercussions of, say, a planned increase in steel production of 10 percent, the Central Planning Board of the U.S.S.R. can determine what outputs of coal, iron ore, transportation, manpower, relevant capital equipment, and all other inputs used in the production of steel will be needed to fulfill this target. In this way, potential bottlenecks to the realization of this goal (or others) may be uncovered; for example, transportation problems may be revealed, or it may be found that the additional plant capacity required conflicts severely with the planned production of housing or the planned expansion of the chemicals industry. Appropriate adjustments

may therefore be made in the production targets for steel or other products to make the plan more realistic and more consistent with the constraints imposed by technology and overall scarcities of economic resources.

General equilibrium analysis provides a broader perspective for analyzing the effects of given economic disturbances or policies than does partial equilibrium analysis. Partial equilibrium analysis shows merely "the big splash" of an initial disturbance; general equilibrium analysis traces the waves and ripples emanating from the big splash. In some instances the waves and ripples are relatively unimportant; in others they may prove to be a tidal wave which completely changes conclusions one would draw from the big splash viewed in isolation. As we noted in Chapter 1, a basic task of the economist is that of ascertaining which waves and ripples are important to the analysis of a given question and which can be safely ignored. In any event, a grasp of the general equilibrium point of view is essential in understanding and evaluating our economy.

## Summary

1   General equilibrium analysis is concerned with the operation of the entire price system and the interrelationships among different markets and prices. These interrelationships are important in that they might modify or negate the immediate effects of economic disturbances or policies which partial equilibrium analysis reveals.

2   A purely competitive price system would tend to allocate resources so as to provide the maximum satisfaction of consumer wants.

3   The fact that imperfect competition generally exists in both product and resource markets detracts from the price system's capacity to allocate resources efficiently.

4   Efficient resource allocation would depend on an active role for government even if the price system were purely competitive. The price system would underproduce goods which entail substantial spillover benefits and overproduce those which embody substantial spillover costs. Also, the price system would tend to ignore the production of social goods.

5   Because of the inability to measure and compare the capacity of various individuals to derive satisfaction from income, economists are unable to define the optimum distribution of income.

6   The input-output table provides a kind of general equilibrium analysis which reveals the overall fabric of the economy by focusing upon the interdependencies that exist among the various sectors or industries which it comprises. Input-output analysis has practical applications to economic forecasting and planning.

## Questions and Study Questions

**1** Key terms and concepts to remember: partial equilibrium analysis; general equilibrium analysis; input-output analysis.

**2** Compare partial and general equilibrium analysis. In what respect is each useful?

**3** Trace through the price system the economic effects of: **a.** the development of a synthetic fiber which never wears out, fades, or stains; **b.** a permanent increase in the demand for leather; **c.** a sharp decline in the size of the labor force; **d.** the development of a new production technique which cuts the cost of color television by 50 percent; **e.** the imposition of a 20 percent excise tax on shoes; **f.** the discovery of an effective vaccine for the common cold.

**4** Explain the following statements:

**a.** "Allocative efficiency does not mean distributive justice."

**b.** "There is an 'efficient' or 'optimal' allocation of resources for every conceivable distribution of money income."

**5** What is an input-output table? Using Table 33-1, trace some of the repercussions of a 5-unit (10 percent) increase in fuel production. What insights might input-output analysis provide as to the operation of a capitalistic system? How might input-output analysis be used as a "mechanism of coordination" in a centrally planned system?

**6** Assume the United States is confronted with a 10 percent annual reduction in the amount of gasoline available. List some of the economic repercussions of this reduction. Would you advocate reliance upon the price system or governmental policies to deal with this problem? If the latter, indicate the nature and implications of the policies you recommend.

## Selected References

Brennan, Michael J.: *Theory of Economic Statics,* 2d ed. (Englewood Cliffs, N.J.: Prentice-Hall, Inc., 1970), chap. 25.

Brue, Stanley L., and Donald R. Wentworth, *Economic Scenes: Theory in Today's World,* 2d ed. (Englewood Cliffs, N.J.: Prentice-Hall, Inc., 1980), chap. 20.

Köhler, Heinz: *Welfare and Planning* (New York: John Wiley & Sons, Inc., 1966), particularly chaps. 1–5.

Miernyk, William H.: *The Elements of Input-Output Analysis* (New York: Random House, Inc., 1965).

Phelps-Brown, E. H.: *The Framework of the Pricing System* (London: Chapman & Hall, Ltd., 1936).

Ryan, W. J. L.: *Price Theory* (New York: St. Martin's Press, Inc., 1958), chap. 8.

Stigler, George J.: *The Theory of Price,* rev. ed. (New York: The Macmillan Company, 1952), chap. 16.

# LAST WORD
# The English Cotton Famine

The relevance of general equilibrium analysis is illustrated by the myriad effects of the marked decline of American cotton exports to England during the Civil War.

The Civil War led to a near suspension of English imports of American cotton, which in 1860 had accounted for about four-fifths of the English supply. The price of cotton at Liverpool rose from 8 pence per pound in June of 1860 to a peak of 31½ pence in July of 1864. The effects of this cotton famine provide some notion of the interrelationships of prices: the famine was severe (imports of cotton fell by three-fifths from 1861 to 1862) and the cotton industry was very large (employing about 500,000 people in a total labor force of 9 million), so wide effects are noticeable.

The famine led to a great decrease in the demand for cotton fabrication, and hence in the demand for the services of cotton mills and their laborers. The margin between the prices of raw cotton and cloth (taking 39-inch shirtings as an example) declined from 7 pence a pound in 1860, almost equal to the cost of the raw cotton, to 1 or 2 pence in 1862 and 1863. Wage (piece) rates fell an unknown amount, and workers' earnings fell much more when they were forced to work with the inferior Surat cotton.

Of course a large expansion took place in rival fabrics. The production of flax quadrupled between 1861 and 1864 in Ireland, and yarn imports rose greatly; even so, prices of linen goods rose about 60 per cent between 1862 and 1864. Similarly, the wool industry experienced a great boom: imports of wool rose by a third during the period, and raw wool prices rose more than 40 per cent, but the Yorkshire industry was overtaxed and processing margins increased by half. Some migration of cotton workers and entrepreneurs to Yorkshire, and of weaving of woolens to Lancashire, helped the latter area.

The unemployment in Lancashire caused great distress. The big decrease in consumer expenditures in the area hit shopkeepers hard, and landlords even harder: families doubled up, marriages fell by more than a third, and poor rates increased. By 1863 about one-fourth of the families requiring public assistance were not directly connected with the textile industry.

Of course the effects reached to industries for which cotton textiles was an important customer. The textile machinery industry had a bad slump until 1864, and the warehouses of the region suffered also. The Lancashire and Yorkshire Railway, unlike other English roads, had a decline in both freight and passenger traffic in 1862 and 1863.

We could cast our net farther to uncover more relationships of substitution and complementarity and buyer and seller, and subject only to the limitations of imagination and energy, we shall continue to find them. In Birmingham, to give only one example, the button and needle industries had to discharge many workers, but the edged-tool industry expanded greatly to provide tools for new cotton plantings in India and Egypt.

Perhaps this brief and highly incomplete sketch is sufficient to illustrate the basis for the economist's faith, for such it is, in the general interdependence of economic phenomena. It does not seem bold to conjecture that everyone in England was somehow affected by the cotton famine: as a consumer, in the price of clothing; as a laborer, in the altered directions of consumer spending; in the effects on transport, banking, and commerce; as a capitalist, in the return on investments in textiles and other industries.

# CURRENT ECONOMIC PROBLEMS

# PART SIX

# Antitrust and Regulation

# chapter 34

In earlier chapters two contrasting points have been made. First, many important American industries—such as those shown in Table 29-1 —possess considerable monopoly power. Second, one of the basic economic functions of government is to preserve competition as a key mechanism of control in the economy (Chapter 6). It is therefore imperative that we explore in some detail how government deals with the problem of business monopolies.

The scope of this chapter is as follows. After considering some definitional matters, the debate over the desirability of business monopoly is summarized. Next, we examine government policy toward business monopoly, considering both antitrust legislation and the *economic* regulation of industries which are "natural monopolies." Finally, we discuss the more recent and highly controversial *social* regulation of industry.

## ☐ BIG BUSINESS AND MONOPOLY

Before considering the pros and cons of business monopoly, we must pause to define our terminology.

In Chapters 22 and 27 we developed and applied a very strict definition of monopoly. A *pure,* or *absolute,* monopoly, we said, is a one-firm industry—a situation in which a unique product is produced entirely by a single firm, entry to the industry being blocked by certain insurmountable barriers. When a single firm controls an entire market, pure monopoly exists.

In the present chapter we shall find it convenient to use the term "monopoly" in a broader, generic sense. *Monopoly exists whenever a small number of firms controls all, or a large portion of, the output of a major industry.* This definition, which comes closer to the way most people understand monopoly, includes a large number of industries which we have heretofore designated under the category of oligopoly.

What is the difference between monopoly (as we have just defined it) and big business? The term "big business" may be defined in terms either of a firm's share of the total market for its product or of some absolute measure, such as the volume of its assets, sales, or profits, the number of workers employed, or the number of stockholders. A firm can obviously be large *in relation to* the size of the total market but small in an *absolute* sense. The Weeping Water General Store may almost completely dominate the local market for a good many products, yet be exceedingly small by any meaningful absolute standard. Conversely, a firm might be very large in the absolute sense but small in relation to the total market. For example, American Motors is large by most absolute standards one can employ. In 1979 its sales revenues were over $3 billion and some 28,400 employees were on its payroll. Yet American Motors sells only about 3 percent of all automobiles in the United States. Insofar as the automobile industry is concerned, American Motors is a small producer. However, *in a good many instances, absolute and relative bigness go hand in hand*. A firm which is large in absolute terms very frequently controls a significant portion of the market for its product. Thus, although "big business" and "monopoly" are not necessarily synonymous, they frequently do go together.

In using the term "business monopoly" in this chapter, we refer to those industries in which firms are large in absolute terms *and* in relation to the total market. Examples are the electrical equipment industry, where General Electric and Westinghouse, large by any absolute standard, dominate the market; the automobile industry, where General Motors and Ford are similarly situated; the chemical industry, dominated by du Pont, Union Carbide, and Allied Chemical; the aluminum industry, where three industrial giants—Alcoa, Reynolds, and Kaiser—reign supreme; and the cigarette industry, where the four giant firms of Reynolds, Brown and Williamson, American Brands, and Lorillard currently command the lion's share of this large market.[1]

□   MONOPOLY: GOOD OR EVIL?

It is not at all clear whether business monopolies are, on balance, advantageous or disadvantageous to the functioning of our economy.

△   **The Case against Monopoly**

The essence of the case against monopoly was stated in Chapter 27. Let us summarize and modestly extend those arguments.

**1   Inefficient   Resource   Allocation** Monopolists find it possible and profitable to restrict output and charge higher prices than would be the case if the given industry were organized competitively. Recall that with pure competition production occurs at the point where $P = MC$ (Chapter 26). This equality specifies an efficient allocation of resources because price measures the value or benefit to society of an extra unit of output, while marginal cost obviously reflects the cost or sacrifice of alternative goods. In maximizing profits the monopolist equates, not price, but marginal revenue with marginal cost. At this $MR = MC$ point, price will exceed marginal cost (Figure 27-2 and footnote 3 in Chapter 27), designating an underallocation of resources to the monopolized product. As a result, the economic well-being of society is less than it would be with pure competition.

**2   Income Inequality** Monopoly is also criticized as a contributor to income inequality. Because of entry barriers, the monopolist can charge a price above average cost and con-

[1] See George J. Stigler, "The Case against Bigness in Business," *Fortune,* May 1952, p. 123.

sistently realize economic profits.  These profits are realized by corporate stockholders and executives who are generally among the upper income groups.

**3  Unprogressive**  Critics hold that monopoly is neither essential for the realization of existing mass-production economies nor is it conducive to technological progress.

Empirical studies suggest that in the vast majority of manufacturing industries, fewness is not essential to the realization of economies of scale.  In most industries, firms need only realize a small percentage of the total market to achieve low-cost production; monopoly is *not* a prerequisite of productive efficiency.[2] Furthermore, the basic unit for technological efficiency is not the firm, but the individual plant.  Thus one can correctly argue that productive efficiency calls for, say, a large-scale, integrated steel-manufacturing plant.  But it is perfectly consistent to argue that there is no technological justification for the existence of U.S. Steel, which is essentially a giant business corporation composed of a number of geographically distinct plants.  Similarly, there are no efficiency grounds for the existence of huge conglomerate corporations engaged in the production of such widely divergent products as frozen foods, shoes, cosmetics, and office equipment.  In short, many existing monopolies have attained a size and structure far larger than necessary for the realization of existing economies of scale.

Nor does technological progress depend upon the existence of huge corporations with substantial monopoly power.  It is held that the evidence—one might review the closing pages of Chapter 29—does not support the view that large size and market power correlate closely with technological progress.  Indeed, the sheltered position of the monopolist is conducive to inefficiency and lethargy; there

[2]The classic study is Joe S. Bain, *Barriers to New Competition* (Cambridge, Mass.: Harvard University Press, 1956).

is no competitive spur to productive efficiency. Furthermore, monopolists are inclined to resist or suppress technological advances which may cause the sudden obsolescence of their existing machinery and equipment.

**4  Political Dangers**  A final criticism is based upon the assumption that economic power and political clout go hand in hand.  It is argued that giant corporations exert effective control over government, and this control is reflected in legislation and government policies which are congenial, not to the public interest, but rather, to the preservation and growth of these industrial giants.  Big businesses allegedly have exerted political power to become the primary beneficiaries of defense contracts, tax loopholes, patent policy, tariff and quota protection, and a variety of other subsidies and privileges.  Indeed, we have seen in recent years that multinational corporations may become an unofficial, disruptive, and highly controversial aspect of American "foreign policy."  Recall the 1972 scandal surrounding ITT's efforts to prevent the election of socialist Salvador Allende as President of Chile, prompted, of course, by ITT's fears that Allende would nationalize its assets in Chile.

△  **Defenses of Monopoly**

Business monopoly is not without significant defenses.

**1  "Workable Competition"**  One important defense is that, while the stringent conditions of pure competition are rarely met, most of the industries of our economy are effectively regulated by *workable competition*. For example, it is pointed out that, although only a small number of firms may produce certain specific products, these apparent monopolists may in fact face severe competition from firms producing distinct but highly substitutable products.  The fact that a handful of firms are responsible for the nation's output of aluminum belies the competition which aluminum faces in specific markets from steel, copper, wood, plastics, and other products. Furthermore, the development of new products and shifts in consumer demand continuously erode and destroy the market power of firms, making monopoly a precarious and transitory phenomenon. The Pullman Company's monopoly in producing railroad passenger cars was eclipsed by the evolution of auto and air travel. Witness the devastating competition which hand calculators have provided the manufacturers of slide rules in recent years. Similarly, digital watches threaten the markets held by conventional watchmakers.

**2   Countervailing Power**   Competition in the form of countervailing power must not be ignored (Chapter 29). If an original position of monopoly power induces the growth of monopoly power on the opposite side of the market, the consequent across-the-market competition can provide effective checks, or restraints, on both the original and the countervailing power position. Countervailing power can effectively prevent abuses of monopoly power in those very markets in which traditional same-side-of-the-market competition is weak.

**3   Technological Progress**   Perhaps the major defense of monopoly centers upon technology as an aspect of efficient industry performance. Two related arguments are made.

First, where existing technology is highly advanced, only large producers—firms which are large both absolutely and in relation to the market—can realize low unit costs and therefore sell to consumers at relatively low prices. In short, the traditional antimonopoly contention that monopoly means less output, higher prices, and an inefficient allocation of resources assumes that cost economies would be equally available to firms whether the industry's structure was highly competitive or quite monopolistic. In fact, this may not be the case; economies of scale may be accessible only if competition is absent.

Second, recall from Chapter 29 the *Schumpeter-Galbraith view* that monopolistic industries—in particular, three- and four-firm oligopolies—are conducive to a high rate of technological progress. Oligopolistic firms have both the financial resources *and* the incentives to undertake technological research.

Galbraith has extended this theme in his well-known book *The New Industrial State*.[3] He argues that "technological imperatives" have brought the corporate giant to a dominant role in the American economy. Production requires not only huge quantities of capital, but also a highly sophisticated technology, and this means that firms must be large to be efficient. Furthermore, the successful functioning of giant enterprises presumes detailed planning, not only of innovations and new productive processes, but also of the manipulation of consumer demand. According to Galbraith, the "technostructure"—the technicians and professional managers of the corporation—carry out these planning and decision-making functions.

A primary goal of the modern "mature" corporation is security and stability—the avoidance of risk. In seeking security the giant corporation attempts to insulate itself from the vagaries of free markets. Thus the corporation integrates vertically; that is, it creates, controls, or merges with materials suppliers. It engages in the internal financing of capital expansion to eliminate its dependence upon the capital market. On the demand side, the corporation controls its customers through advertising and sales techniques, thereby supplanting "consumer sovereignty" with "producer sovereignty." In these ways the corporation dominates both suppliers and consumers, thereby signaling the demise of the free-market system as traditionally conceived. Furthermore, the corporate giant, by virtue of

[3] John Kenneth Galbraith, *The New Industrial State* (Boston: Houghton Mifflin Company, 1967). This book is highly recommended reading; the terse summary presented here does not do justice to Professor Galbraith's arguments.

its size and crucial role in production, has achieved autonomy from government control. In fact, Galbraith feels that big business and government are in the process of establishing a tacit alliance to manage the economy. On the one hand, government plans and undertakes various functions—the stabilization of aggregate demand, the financing of research and development, the provision of highly educated manpower—which the technostructure and the corporate giants require for security and growth. On the other hand, the industrial giants assume responsibility for the planning of much of society's production. Galbraith feels that these trends are a "part of the broad sweep of economic development"; technological advance makes these developments necessary and immutable if productive efficiency is to be realized.

## □   THE ANTITRUST LAWS

In view of the sharp conflict of opinion over the relative merits of business monopoly, it is not surprising to find that government policy toward business monopolies has been something less than clear-cut and consistent. While the major thrust of Federal legislation and policy has been to maintain and promote competition, we shall examine later certain policies and acts which have furthered the development of monopoly.

### △   Historical Background

Historically, our economy, steeped in the philosophy of free, competitive markets, has been a fertile ground for the development of a suspicious and fearful public attitude toward business monopolies. Though relatively dormant in the nation's early years, this fundamental distrust of monopoly came into full bloom in the decades following the Civil War. The widening of local markets into national markets as transportation facilities improved, the ever-increasing mechanization of production, and the increasingly widespread adoption of the corporate form of business enterprise

were important forces giving rise to the development of "trusts"—that is, business monopolies—in the 1870s and 1880s. Trusts developed in the petroleum, meat-packing, railroad, sugar, lead, coal, whiskey, and tobacco industries, among others, during this era. Not only were questionable tactics employed in monopolizing the various industries, but the resulting market power was almost invariably exerted to the detriment of all who did business with these monopolies. Farmers and small businesses, being particularly vulnerable to the growth and tactics of the giant corporate monopolies, were among the first to censure their development. Consumers and labor unions were not far behind in voicing their disapproval of monopoly power.

Given the development of certain industries wherein market forces no longer provided adequate control to ensure socially tolerable behavior, two techniques of control have been adopted as substitutes for, or supplements to, the market. First, in those few markets where economic realities are such as to preclude the effective functioning of the market—that is, where there tends to be a "natural monopoly"—we have established public *regulatory agencies* to control economic behavior. Second, in most other markets wherein economic and technological conditions have not made monopoly essential, social control has taken the form of antimonopoly or *antitrust legislation* designed to inhibit or prevent the growth of monopoly. Let us first consider the major pieces of legislation which, as refined and extended by various amendments, constitute the basic law of the land with respect to corporate size and concentration.

### △   Sherman Act of 1890

Acute public resentment of the trusts which developed in the 1870s and 1880s culminated in the passage of the *Sherman Antitrust Act* in 1890. This cornerstone of antitrust legislation is surprisingly brief and, at first glance, directly to the point. The core of the act is embodied in two major provisions:

In Section 1:

> Every contract, combination in the form of a trust or otherwise, or conspiracy, in restraint of trade or commerce among the several states, or with foreign nations is hereby declared to be illegal. . . .

In Section 2:

> Every person who shall monopolize, or attempt to monopolize, or combine or conspire with any person or persons, to monopolize any part of the trade or commerce among the several states, or with foreign nations, shall be deemed guilty of a misdemeanor. . . .

The act had the effect of making monopoly and "restraints of trade" criminal offenses against the Federal government. Either the government or parties injured by business monopolies could file suits under the Sherman Act. Firms found in violation of the act could be ordered dissolved by the courts, or injunctions could be issued to prohibit practices deemed unlawful under the act. Fines and imprisonment were also possible results of successful prosecution. Further, parties injured by illegal combinations and conspiracies could sue for triple the amount of damages done them. The Sherman Act seemed to provide a sound foundation for positive government action against business monopolies.

However, early court interpretations raised serious questions about the effectiveness of the Sherman Act and it became clear that a more explicit statement of the government's antitrust sentiments was in order.

## △  Clayton Act of 1914

This needed elaboration of the Sherman Act took the form of the 1914 *Clayton Antitrust Act*. The following sections of the Clayton Act were designed to strengthen and make explicit the intent of the Sherman Act:

Section 2 *outlaws price discrimination* between purchasers when such discrimination is not justified on the basis of cost differences.

Section 3 *forbids exclusive,* or *"tying,"* *contracts* whereby a producer would sell a product only on the condition that the buyer acquire other products from the same seller and not from competitors.

Section 7 *prohibits the acquisition of stocks* of competing corporations when the effect is to lessen competition.

Section 8 *prohibits the formation of interlocking directorates*—the situation where a director of one firm is also a board member of another firm—in large corporations where the effect would be to reduce competition.

Actually, there was little in the Clayton Act which had not already been stated by implication in the Sherman Act. The Clayton Act merely attempted to sharpen and make clear the general provisions of the Sherman Act. Furthermore, the Clayton Act attempted to outlaw the techniques by which monopoly might develop and, in this sense, was a preventive measure. The Sherman Act, by contrast, was aimed more at the punishment of existing monopolies.

## △  Federal Trade Commission Act of 1914

The Federal Trade Commission Act was based on the belief that preventive rather than more punitive measures were needed to sustain competition. Specifically, the act was designed to prevent competition from assuming certain aggressive forms which would tend to undermine competition and bring about the development of monopoly power. The act created the Federal Trade Commission, a permanent five-member board, and charged it with the power to investigate unfair competitive practices on its own initiative or at the request of injured firms. The Commission could hold public hearings on such complaints and, if necessary, issue cease-and desist orders where "unfair methods of competition in commerce" were discovered.

The antitrust potential of the FTC has been limited by subsequent court rulings which have restricted the investigatory powers of the Commission and made it clear that the courts, not the FTC, have the final authority in interpreting the meaning of the antitrust laws. Then, in 1938, the *Wheeler-Lea Act* amended the Federal Trade Commission Act by prohibiting "unfair or deceptive acts or practices in commerce." As a result, a primary task of the FTC now is the prohibition of false and misleading advertising and the misrepresentation of products.

△  **Celler-Kefauver Act of 1950**

This act amended Section 7 of the Clayton Act which, you will recall, prohibits one firm from acquiring the *stock* of competitors when the acquisition would reduce competition. Firms could evade Section 7 by acquiring the physical *assets* (plant and equipment) of competing firms, rather than their stocks. The Celler-Kefauver Act plugged this loophole by prohibiting one firm from obtaining the physical assets of another firm when the effect would be to lessen competition.

The Celler-Kefauver Act also extended the coverage of the antitrust laws with respect to mergers. Earlier legislation was aimed at restricting *horizontal mergers,* that is, the combining of firms which produce the same product. The Celler-Kefauver Act also prohibited *vertical mergers* (firms at different stages in a given production process) and *conglomerate mergers* (firms producing unrelated products), provided that such mergers substantially lessen competition.

☐  **ANTITRUST: ISSUES AND IMPACT**

What has been the overall impact of the antitrust laws? The effectiveness of any law depends upon the vigor with which the government chooses to enforce it and how the law is interpreted by the courts. In fact, the Federal government has varied considerably in its willingness to apply the act. Administrations "friendly" toward big business have sometimes emasculated the act by the simple process of ignoring it or by cutting the budget appropriations of enforcement agencies. Similarly, the courts have run hot and cold in interpreting the antitrust laws. At times, the courts have applied them with vigor, adhering closely to the spirit and objectives of the laws. In other cases, the courts have interpreted the acts in such ways as to render them all but completely innocuous.

△  **Behavior or Structure?**

A comparison of two landmark court decisions reveals the existence of two distinct approaches in the application of antitrust. In the 1920 *U.S. Steel case* the courts applied the *rule of reason* which said in effect that *not* every contract or combination in the restraint of trade is illegal. Only those which "unreasonably" restrain trade are subject to antitrust action. The court held in this case that mere size was not an offense; although U.S. Steel clearly *possessed* monopoly power, it was innocent because it had not unreasonably used that power.

A quarter of a century later in the *Alcoa case* of 1945 the courts did a turnabout. The court held that, even though a firm's behavior might be legal, the mere possession of monopoly power (Alcoa had 90 percent of the aluminum ingot market!) was in violation of the antitrust laws.

These two cases point to a continuing controversy in antitrust policy. Should an industry be judged by its *behavior* or by its *structure?* Advocates of the latter contend that an industry which has a monopolistic structure will behave like a monopolist. Hence, the economic performance of industries with a monopolistic structure will be undesirable. Such industries are therefore legitimate targets for antitrust action. On the other hand, the "behavioralists" argue that the relationship between structure and performance is tenuous and unclear. They feel that a monopolistic industry may be technologically progressive and have an enviable record of providing products of increasing quality at reasonable prices. Therefore, if the industry has served society well and engaged in no anticompetitive practices, it should not be accused of antitrust violation simply because it is highly concentrated. Why use antitrust to penalize efficient, well-managed firms?

△ **Effectiveness**

Have the antitrust laws been effective? This is a difficult question, but some insight can be gained by noting how the laws have been applied.

> "Antitrust is rather strict toward cooperation and mergers, while being lenient toward existing concentrations. Thus a firm with a 60 percent market share is permitted to continue untouched, fixing prices pretty much as it pleases over more than half of the market. Meanwhile other firms may not merge to acquire as much as 10 percent of the market. Nor may they cooperate to fix prices on *any* part of the market."[4]

In other words, antitrust laws have *not* been used generally to attack the *existence* of monopoly power, but rather are applied only when *anticompetitive behavior* is evidenced. The giant corporation which already has vast market power is substantially immune from antitrust prosecution. But if substantially smaller firms in the same industry attempt to merge so as to compete more effectively with the dominant giant, they will run afoul of antitrust. Furthermore, by giving the public the illusion that the market remains a viable form of social control, the antitrust laws may protect the largest corporations from the alternative of public regulation.

It is also true that some of the government's most notable legal victories in applying the antitrust laws have proved to be economic defeats. That is, the guilty firms have agreed

to cease-and-desist orders or have been subject to minor penalties rather than forced to dissolve. Indeed, even when dissolution has occurred, the economic benefits have been dubious: When it comes to price and output policies, a tight three- or four-firm oligopoly is likely to behave much as the absolute monopoly which once comprised it.

On the positive side, there currently exists strong interest in antitrust enforcement. The electrical equipment price-fixing conspiracy of the early 1960s (Chapter 29) was successfully prosecuted. A suit against IBM was initiated in 1969, charging market dominance and anticompetitive pricing. Action was taken against Xerox in 1972 which resulted in a partial opening of Xerox patents to competing firms. The FTC has taken action against the manufacturers of breakfast cereals, charging that the advertising, product changes, and pricing behavior of these firms constitute a "shared monopoly." A 1974 suit seeks, among other things, to divest the Western Electric manufacturing branch of AT&T from its operating companies. The outcomes of the IBM, cereals, and AT&T cases are pending. But it can be said that antitrust policy is alive and reasonably well.

This recitation of recent antitrust activity may understate the importance of the antitrust laws in the sense that it does not take into account the extent to which the very existence of the laws may have positively influenced business behavior. United Gadget Corporation is more likely to avoid questionable price behavior if it entails a potential violation of the Sherman Act. It is often pointed out that the specter of Senator Sherman stalks the board room of America's corporate giants!

□ **RESTRICTING COMPETITION**

Let us now consider briefly the other side of the picture. Government has directly and indirectly promoted the growth of monopoly in several different ways. Consider some important examples.

[4]William G. Shepherd, *The Economics of Industrial Organization* (Englewood Cliffs, New Jersey: Prentice-Hall, Inc., 1979), p. 434.

## △   Exemptions to Antitrust

Over the years government has enacted certain laws which have either exempted certain specific industries or, alternatively, have excluded certain trade practices from antitrust prosecution. In doing so, the government has tended indirectly to foster the growth of monopoly power.

In 1918 the *Webb-Pomerene Act* exempted American exporters from the antitrust laws by permitting them to form export trade associations. Although the act was intended to put American exporters in a stronger competitive position with international cartels, the effect has probably been to reduce competition in both international and domestic markets.

Labor unions and agricultural cooperatives have been exempt, subject to limitations, from the antitrust laws. We shall see in the next chapter that Federal legislation and policy have attempted to provide some measure of monopolistic power for agriculture and have tended to keep agricultural prices above competitive levels. Similarly, in a subsequent chapter we shall discover that since 1930, Federal legislation on balance has generally promoted the growth of strong labor unions. This federally sponsored growth has resulted, according to some authorities, in the development of union monopolies whose goal is above-competitive wage rates. At state and local levels a wide variety of occupational groups have been successful in establishing licensure requirements which arbitrarily restrict entry to certain occupations, thereby keeping wages and earnings above competitive levels.

## △   Robinson-Patman Act of 1936

Although passed as an amendment to the price discrimination section of the Clayton Act, this act has had the effect of lessening competition at the retail level. Small independent grocers and druggists argued in the 1920s and 1930s that the growing number of chain stores were obtaining large and unjustified discounts from wholesalers because of their strong bargaining positions as buyers. By passing some of these cost savings on to consumers in the form of price reductions, the chains allegedly were driving their independent competitors into bankruptcy. The Robinson-Patman Act outlaws quantity discounts to large buyers when such discounts are not justified on the basis of actual cost economies arising from mass buying or when only a few buyers are large enough to take advantage of such discounts. Many economists feel that the effect of the act has been not so much to deter the growth of monopoly as to stifle price competition, particularly at the retail level, and therefore to sustain inefficient retailers who would otherwise succumb to more vigorous competition.

## △   Patent Laws

Technological research is a costly and risky procedure. American patent laws—the first of which was passed in 1790—are aimed at providing sufficient monetary incentive for innovators by granting them exclusive rights to produce and sell a new product or machine for a period of seventeen years. Patent grants have the effect of protecting the innovator from competitors who would otherwise quickly imitate this product and share in the profits, though not the cost and effort, of the research. Few contest the desirability of this particular aspect of our patent laws, particularly when it is recalled that innovation can weaken and undermine existing positions of monopoly power.

However, patents are a mixed blessing. The granting of a patent frequently amounts to the granting of monopoly power in the production of the patented item. Many economists feel that the length of patent protection—seventeen years—is much too long. Such an extended period of protection from competitors likely entrenches the innovator so firmly in a monopoly position that any potential competition can be successfully blocked after the patent expires. This is particularly true if the innovating firm extends its patent rights longer than seventeen years by patenting improved models of the original innovation. By this and similar procedures, innovating firms have often been able to extend their exclusive jurisdiction over a product for three or four decades!

When patents are licensed to competitors, the innovating firm has the right to specify the prices which these competitors may charge for the product, the markets in which they may sell, and even the amounts which they may produce. The result is that the innovator faces no genuine competition. The worst abuses of patent rights occur when one firm accumulates by research or purchase a large number of related patents or, alternatively, several firms in an industry "pool" the patents which they own and exclude potential rivals from their use. In such situations, patents can constitute a very formidable barrier to entry and thereby create and perpetuate monopoly power.

And finally, a patent monopoly is an excellent basis for a tying agreement and the subsequent extension of monopoly power. The classic case is that of the United Shoe Machinery Corporation, which leased the machinery over which it has exclusive patents only on the condition that shoe manufacturers would purchase all their other machinery from United. This practice stripped its competitors of their customers and firmly entrenched United as the dominant firm in the industry.

The importance of patent laws in the growth of business monopoly must not be underestimated. Such well-known firms as du Pont, General Electric, American Telephone and Telegraph, Eastman Kodak, Alcoa, and innumerable other industrial giants have attained various measures of monopoly power in part through their ownership of certain patent rights.[5]

[5]For a sophisticated and detailed discussion of this topic, see F. M. Scherer, *Industrial Market Structure and Economic Performance* (Chicago: Rand McNally & Company, 1970), chap. 16.

△ **Protective Tariffs**

Although we must postpone any detailed discussion of tariffs until a later chapter, it is relevant at this point to recognize that tariffs and similar trade barriers have the effect of shielding American producers from foreign competition. Protective tariffs are in effect discriminatory taxes against the goods of foreign firms. These taxes make it difficult and often impossible for foreign producers to compete in domestic markets with American firms. The result? A less competitive domestic market and an environment frequently conducive to the growth of domestic business monopolies.

□ **NATURAL MONOPOLIES AND THEIR REGULATION**

Antitrust is based upon the assumption that society will benefit by preventing monopoly from evolving or, alternatively, by dissolving monopoly where it already exists. We now consider a special case wherein there is an economic rationale for an industry to be organized monopolistically.

△ **Theory of Natural Monopoly**

A *natural monopoly* exists when economies of scale are so extensive that a single firm can supply the entire market at lower unit cost than could a number of competing firms. Such conditions exist for the so-called *public utilities,* such as electricity, water, gas, telephone service, and so on (Chapter 27). In these cases the fixed costs of producing and distributing the product are very large so that large-scale operations are necessary if low unit costs—and a low price—are to be realized (see Figure 25-7a). In this situation competition is simply uneconomic.

Two alternatives present themselves as possible means of ensuring socially acceptable behavior on the part of a natural monopoly. One is public ownership and the other is public regulation. Public ownership or some approximation thereof has been established in a few instances; the Postal Service, the Tennessee

Valley Authority, and Amtrak come to mind at the national level, while mass-transit, the water system, and garbage collection are typically public enterprises at the local level. But public regulation has been the option pursued most extensively in the United States. Table 34-1 lists the major Federal regulatory commissions and their areas of jurisdiction. All the states also have such regulatory bodies concerned with intrastate natural monopolies. The regulated sector is quantitatively important; it is estimated that about 10 percent of the GNP is produced by regulated industries.

The intent of "natural monopoly" legislation is to regulate such industries effectively and for the benefit of the public, to the end that consumers may be assured quality service at reasonable rates. The rationale is this: If competition is inappropriate, *regulated* monopolies should be established to avoid possible abuses of uncontrolled monopoly power. In particular, regulation should guarantee that consumers benefit from the economies of scale—that is, the lower per unit cost—which their natural-monopoly position allows public utilities to achieve. In practice, regulators seek to establish rates which will cover production costs and yield a "fair" or "reasonable" return to the enterprise. (The reader is urged to review the "Regulated Monopoly" section of Chapter 27 at this point.)

△   **Background: the ICC**

It is informative to consider for a moment the first of our Federal regulatory laws, the Interstate Commerce Act of 1887. This law was based on the supposition that competition was unworkable in the railroad industry. Certain industry characteristics ruled out the possibility of effective competition:

**1**   Relatively large fixed costs—for roadbed, track, engines, rolling stock, and so on—entailed the necessity of large-scale operations by each firm in order to achieve efficient, low-cost service.

**2**   The existence of several firms serving each city and town would entail the wasteful duplication of very costly capital facilities.

**3**   The service being supplied—transportation—was essential to many firms and individuals.

And, as a matter of fact, "competition" had not worked well in this industry. Price competition aimed at the fuller realization of economies of scale often degenerated into cutthroat competition and losses for all participants. The results would be either the elimination of the weaker competitors and the evolution of monopoly or the establishment of a collusive price agreement of some sort by which the competitors sought to improve their lot. If monopoly resulted, the exploitation of that power through discriminatory pricing—

**TABLE 34-1**
**The Main Federal Regulatory Commissions**

| Commission (year established) | Jurisdiction |
| --- | --- |
| Interstate Commerce Commission (1887) | Railroads, trucking, buses, water shipping, express companies, etc. |
| Federal Communications Commission (1934) | Telephones, television, cable television, radio, telegraph, CB radios, ham operators, etc. |
| Civil Aeronautics Board (1938) | Airlines (passenger and cargo), other carriers. |
| Federal Energy Regulatory Commission (1977) | Electricity, gas, gas pipelines, oil pipelines, water power sites. |

*Source:* Federal Power Commission, *Federal and State Commission Jurisdiction and Regulation* (Washington, D.C.: Federal Power Commission, 1973).

that is, charging what the traffic would bear—was likely. If a collusive price resulted, the industry would then operate in much the same manner as a pure monopoly, at least until another round of price warring was precipitated.

In view of such circumstances, the Interstate Commerce Act was passed by Congress to make railroads regulated monopolies. Although their management and actual operation remained in private hands, the Interstate Commerce Commission was established to regulate the rates and monitor the services of the railroads.

### △  Problems

While the logic of the theory of regulation rings true, there is considerable disagreement as to the effectiveness of regulation in practice. Let us briefly examine two of the major criticisms of regulation.

**1  Costs and Efficiency**  Regulatory experience suggests that there are a number of interrelated problems associated with cost containment and efficiency in the use of resources. For example, a major goal of regulation is to establish prices so that the regulated firms will receive a "normal" or "fair" return above their production costs. But this means, in effect, that the firms are operating on the basis of cost-plus pricing and, therefore, have no incentive to contain costs. On the contrary, higher costs will mean larger total profits. Why develop or accept new cost-cutting innovations if your "reward" will be a reduction in price? It is also recognized that a regulated firm may resort to accounting skulduggery to overstate its costs and thereby obtain a higher and unjustified profit. Furthermore, in many instances prices are set by the commission so that the firm will receive a stipulated rate of return based upon the value of its real capital. This poses a special problem. In order to increase profits the regulated firm will be inclined to make an uneconomic substitution of capital for labor, thereby contributing to an inefficient allocation of resources within the firm.

**2  Commission Deficiencies**  Another criticism is that the regulatory commissions function inadequately because they are frequently "captured" or controlled by the industries they are supposed to regulate. Commission members often were executives in these very industries! Hence, regulation is *not* in the public interest, but rather, it protects and nurtures the comfortable position of the natural monopolist. It is alleged that regulation typically becomes a means of guaranteeing profits and protecting the regulated industry from potential new competition which technological change might create.

> Though most government regulation was enacted under the guise of protecting the consumer from abuse, much of today's regulatory machinery does little more than shelter producers from the normal competitive consequences of lassitude and inefficiency. In some cases, the world has changed reducing the original threat of abuse. In other cases, the regulatory machinery has simply become perverted. In still other cases, the machinery was a mistake from the start. In any case, the consumer, for whatever presumed abuse he is being spared, is paying plenty in the form of government-sanctioned price fixing.[6]

An interesting illustration of how the development of competition outside of the jurisdiction of a regulatory agency can lead to the expansion of regulation to the competitors is provided by the ICC. As we have duly noted, the ICC was established to protect shippers against the monopoly power of the railroads.

> But by 1935, the nation had sprouted a network of highways, and the trucks which rolled over them were biting deeply into the market power of the railroads.
> With the trucking field still wide open to new entrants, this might logically have been the time

[6]Lewis A. Engman, address before the 1974 Fall Conference of the Financial Analysts Federation, Detroit, Michigan, October 7, 1974.

to dismantle the ICC. The railroad monopoly was broken, competition could take its course.

Did that happen? No sir. Instead of freeing the railroads from regulation, Congress, in the Motor Carrier Act of 1935, just cast the regulatory net wider to include the interstate truckers as well.

As a result, today we have a situation in whi. .iarket entry by new trucking firms is restricted by the ICC at the same time that rates are being fixed by the carriers who are given antitrust immunity to do so. . . .

And what is the result? Well, when the Supreme Court held some time ago that fresh dressed poultry was an agricultural commodity under the ICC Act and thus not subject to regulation, the average rate for shipping it fell by 33 percent. It is gratifying to note that the party who got the short end of the 5-4 decision was a certificated carrier who was trying to stamp out the competition of an uncertificated carrier who had the temerity to haul chickens without a license.[7]

Most economists agree that the trucking industry is *not* a natural monopoly; fixed costs are relatively small and economies of scale are not great. There is no economic reason for regulation. Indeed, one can make a convincing case that the transportation industry—including the railroads, trucking, barges, and so on—could have evolved into a workably competitive industry. But the expanded jurisdiction of the ICC prevented that from happening.

It is interesting that some economists have rejected the traditional *public interest theory* of regulation which presumes that the objective of regulation is to protect the public from the abuse of monopoly power. In its stead they offer a *supply-and-demand theory* of regulation. In the place of socially-minded statesmen *forcing* regulation upon natural monopolies to protect consumers, this view envisions practical politicians as supplying the "service" of regulation to firms which *want* to be regulated! Crudely put, in return for public support (including generous financial contributions), government officials provide or "supply"

regulation to various industries. Regulation is desired or "demanded" because it constitutes, in effect, a kind of legal cartel which can be highly profitable to the regulated firms. Specifically, the regulatory commission performs such functions as dividing up the market (for example, the CAB assigning routes to specific airlines) and restricting potential competition by enlarging the cartel (for example, adding the trucking industry to the ICC's domain). While private cartels tend to be unstable and subject to breakdown (Chapter 29), the special attraction of a government-sponsored cartel under the guise of regulation is that it tends to be enduring.

Proponents of the supply-and-demand theory of regulation call attention to the fact that the Interstate Commerce Act was supported by the railroads and that the trucking and airline industries both supported the extension of regulation to their industries on the grounds that unregulated competition was severe and destructive. The fact that fares have declined since the airlines were partially deregulated in 1978 is not inconsistent with the view that regulation approximates a legal cartel. Proponents also point to occupational licensure (Chapter 31) as the labor market manifestation of their theory. Certain occupational groups—barbers, pest controllers, or dietitians—demand licensure on the ground that it is necessary to protect the public from charlatans and quacks, but the real reason is to limit occupational entry so that practitioners may receive monopoly incomes.

☐  THE "NEW" SOCIAL REGULATION[8]

The "old" regulation just discussed has been labeled *industrial* or *economic regulation*.

[7] *Ibid.*

[8] This section is largely based upon George A. Steiner, "New Patterns in Government Regulation of Business," *MSU Business Topics,* Autumn 1978, pp. 51–61; William Lilley III and James C. Miller III, "The New 'Social Regulation,'" *The Public Interest,* Spring 1977, pp. 49–61; and Murray L. Weidenbaum, *The Costs of Government Regulation of Business* (Washington, D.C.: Government Printing Office, 1978).

Here government is concerned with the overall economic performance of a few specific industries, and concern focuses upon pricing and service to the public. Beginning in the early 1960s, government regulation of a new type evolved and experienced rapid growth. This new *social regulation* is concerned with the conditions under which goods and services are produced, the impact of production upon society, and the physical characteristics of goods themselves. Thus, for example, the Occupational Safety and Health Administration (OSHA) is concerned with protecting workers against occupational injuries and illnesses; the Consumer Products Safety Commission (CPSC) specifies minimum standards for potentially unsafe products; the Environmental Protection Agency (EPA) regulates the amount of pollutants manufacturers can emit; and the Equal Employment Opportunity Commission (EEOC) seeks to ensure that women and minorities have fair access to jobs.

Social regulation differs from economic regulation in several ways. In the first place, social regulation is applied "across the board" to virtually all industries and thereby directly affects far more people. While the Civil Aeronautics Board (CAB) focuses only upon the air transport industry, OSHA's rules and regulations apply to every employer! Secondly, the very nature of social regulation entails government involvement in the very details of the production process. For example, rather than simply specifying safety standards for products, CPSC mandates—often in detail—certain characteristics which products must embody. A final distinguishing feature of social regulation is its rapid expansion. Of the eighty-three Federal agencies involved in regulating business in 1976, thirty-four came into being after 1960. Between 1970 and 1975 legislation created seven major Federal regulatory agencies and, over the same period, some thirty important new laws were passed making significant alterations in the regulatory framework.

The above recitation of the names of a few of the better-known regulatory agencies sug-

gests the basic reason for their creation and growth: Much of our society had achieved a reasonably affluent level of living by the 1960s and attention thus shifted to the realization of improvements in the quality of life. This improvement called for safer and better products, less pollution, better working conditions, and greater equality of opportunity.

△ **Costs and Criticisms**

There is rather widespread agreement that the objectives of social regulation are laudable. But there is great controversy as to whether the benefits of these regulatory efforts justify the costs. It is generally agreed that social regulation has been costly. Professor Murray Weidenbaum, a staunch critic of social regulation, has estimated that the total cost of such regulation for 1979 was almost $103 billion![9] Cost estimates for specific types of regulations and for specific firms and industries are also revealing. It is estimated that the cost of pollution control alone for the 1974–1983 decade will be about $218 billion. Federally required safety and antipollution equipment increased the price of autos by $666 per car over the 1968–1978 period. Standard Oil of Indiana contends that it employs 100 employees at an average cost of $3 million per year to fill out some 4000 forms it must file each year with thirty-five different Federal agencies![10] The U.S. Office of Management and Budget has estimated that individuals and businesses spend over 143 million worker-hours each year filling out government forms.

Critics argue that the American economy is now subject to overregulation, that is, regulatory activities have been carried to the point where the marginal costs of regulation exceed the marginal benefits (Chapter 6). Why might this be the case? Why is social regulation allegedly inefficient? It is contended, in the first place, that some of the social regulation laws are poorly drawn so that regulators are virtu-

---

[9] Weidenbaum, op. cit., p. 5.
[10] These data and examples are from Steiner, op. cit., p. 54.

ally prohibited from making economically rational decisions and rules. "For example, the Clean Air Act of 1970 specifically instructs EPA to establish air-quality standards based on considerations of public health, and this has been interpreted within the agency to mean that other considerations, such as economics, simply cannot be considered."[11] More generally, regulatory objectives and standards are often stated in legal, political, or engineering terms which result in the pursuit of goals beyond the point at which marginal benefits equal marginal costs. Businesses complain that regulators press for small increments of improvement, unmindful of costs. A requirement to reduce pollution by an incremental 5 percent may cost as much as required to achieve the first 95 percent reduction. Secondly, decisions must often be made and rules promulgated on the basis of inadequate and sketchy information. CPSC officials may make sweeping decisions about the use of carcinogens in products upon the basis of very limited experiments with laboratory animals. Finally, it is contended that the regulatory agencies may tend to attract overzealous personnel who "believe" in regulation. It is often observed, for example, that the staff of EPA is comprised largely of "environmentalists" who are strongly inclined to punish polluters. "Treating all polluters as sinners is . . . much easier than making quantitative judgments about optimal levels of cleanliness in the air and water, but it leads to inefficient regulations, especially where government statutes imply rigid, national, uniform standards."[12] It is further argued that the bureaucrats of the new regulatory agencies are extremely sensitive to criticism by Congress or some special interest group, for example, consumerists, environmentalists, or organized labor. The result is bureaucratic inflexibility and the establishment of extreme or nonsensical regulations so that no watchdog group will question the agency's

commitment to its given social goal. OSHA's much-ridiculed specification of the shape of toilet seats and its proposal that farmers and ranchers provide toilet facilities within five minutes walking distance of any point where employees are at work are cases in point. In the words of one critic:

> No realistic evaluation of . . . government regulation comfortably fits the notion of benign and wise officials making altogether sensible decisions in the society's greater interests. Instead we find waste, bias, stupidity, concentration on trivia, conflicts among the regulators and, worst of all, arbitrary and uncontrolled power.[13]

△   **Economic Implications**

If overregulation does exist, what are its consequences? First of all, the new regulation contributes to inflation. It contributes directly because the costs of social regulation are passed on to consumers in the form of higher prices. Furthermore, social regulation is indirectly inflationary to the extent that it reduces labor productivity. Resources invested in antipollution equipment are not available for investment in new machinery to increase output per worker.[14] Secondly, the new regulation may have a negative impact upon the rate of innovation. The fear that a new, technologically superior plant will not meet with EPA approval or that a new product may run into difficulties with CPSC may be sufficient reason to persuade a firm to produce the same old product in the same old way. Finally, social regulation may have an anticompetitive effect in that it tends to be a relatively greater economic burden for small firms than for large firms. The costs of complying with the new regulation are, in effect, fixed costs. Smaller firms produce less output over which to distribute these costs and, hence, their compli-

---

[11]Lilley and Miller, op. cit., p. 57.
[12]Ibid., p. 58.

[13]Murray L. Weidenbaum, "The Cost of Overregulating Business," *Tax Review,* August 1975, p. 33.
[14]Productivity increases, you will recall (Chapter 18), tend to offset the inflationary effects of money wage increases.

ance costs per unit of output put them at a competitive disadvantage relative to their larger rivals. Bluntly put, the burden of social regulation is more likely to put small firms out of business and thereby contribute to the increased concentration of industry.

△  **In Support of Social Regulation**
Social regulation is not without its defenses. The problems with which social regulation contends are serious and substantial in scope.

In 1976 one of every 11 workers in private industry suffered from an accident or illness related to the job; 4,500 workers lost their lives from such causes. The Bureau of Labor Statistics estimated that over 39 million workdays were lost in the private sector in 1976 because of nonfatal occupational illness or accidents; and in the mining and construction trades, workers on the average lost more than one workday per year because of accidents and illness occasioned by the job.

Environmental problems are even more pervasive. Air pollution, produced by numerous industrial processes and the operation of transportation vehicles, has been clearly linked to many different illnesses. Adverse water quality has also proved to be dangerous. A recent study made by the Environmental Protection Agency (EPA) found the water of 80 cities to contain chemicals that are known to cause cancer in animals. [15]

After years of relative neglect, society cannot expect to cleanse the environment, enhance

the safety of the workplace, and improve economic opportunity without incurring substantial costs. Furthermore, cost calculations may paint too dim a picture of social regulation. Benefits tend to be taken for granted, are more difficult than costs to measure, and may accrue to society only over an extended period of time. But benefits have been substantial.

During the short time since their inception the social regulations have improved the conditions affecting the environment, health, and safety of Americans. For example, while the Nation's efforts to control water pollution are behind schedule and face some difficult problems, numerous bodies of water have been demonstrably improved. Because of mandated municipal and industrial waste treatment, aquatic life and recreational amenities have reappeared, and foul odors and visibly dirty water have disappeared in a number of the Nation's waterways.

Similarly marked progress has been achieved in reducing air pollution. Data collected by EPA and the Council on Environmental Quality (CEQ) at 280 locations around the country show significant improvements in ambient air quality between 1970 and 1976. [16]

Although we can expect social regulation to continue to be a matter of considerable controversy, it is generally agreed that the contested "question is not whether (social) regulation should occur, but how and when it should be used; how we can improve the system of regulation; and whether we are fully aware of the costs and benefits involved." [17]

[16] Ibid., p. 210.
[17] Testimony of Juanita M. Kreps in *The Cost of Government Regulation* (Washington, D.C., 1978), p. 7.

[15] *Economic Report of the President, 1978* (Washington, D.C.), p. 209.

## Summary

1  The case against business monopoly centers upon the contentions that business monopoly *a.* causes a misallocation of resources; *b.* promotes income inequality; *c.* retards the rate of technological advance; and *d.* poses a threat to political democracy.

2  The defense of business monopoly is built around the following points: *a.* "Workable competition" prevails in many industries in which large-numbers competition is absent;

**b.** countervailing power may compensate for an absence of same-side-of-the-market competition; and **c.** monopolies are technologically progressive and essential to the attainment of economies of scale.

3   The cornerstone of antitrust policy consists of the Sherman Act of 1890 and the Clayton Act of 1914. The Sherman Act specifies that "Every contract, combination . . . or conspiracy in the restraint of interstate trade . . . is . . . illegal," and that any person who monopolizes or attempts to monopolize interstate trade is guilty of a misdemeanor.

4   The Clayton Act was designed to bolster and make more explicit the provisions of the Sherman Act. To this end the Clayton Act declared that price discrimination, tying contracts, intercorporate stockholdings, and interlocking directorates are illegal when the effect of their use is the lessening of competition.

5   The Federal Trade Commission Act of 1914 created the Federal Trade Commission to investigate antitrust violations and to prevent the use of "unfair methods of competition." Empowered to issue cease-and-desist orders, the Commission now serves as a watchdog agency for the false and deceptive representation of products.

6   The Celler-Kefauver Antimerger Act of 1950 prohibits one firm from acquiring the assets of another firm where the result is a lessening of competition.

7   Government, however, has also done much to promote both directly and indirectly the concentration of economic power and the growth of monopoly. Industrial exceptions to antitrust laws include **a.** the exclusion of exporters by the Webb-Pomerene Act of 1918; **b.** partial exclusion of retailers by the Robinson-Patman Act of 1936; and **c.** the exemption of unions and agricultural cooperatives. Patent laws and protective tariffs also constitute bases for the development of business monopoly.

8   The objective of industrial regulation is to protect the public from the market power of natural monopolies by regulating prices and quality of service. Critics contend that industrial regulation is conducive to inefficiency and rising costs and that in many instances it constitutes a legal cartel for the regulated firms.

9   Social regulation is concerned with product safety, safer working conditions, less pollution, and greater economic opportunity. Critics contend that businesses are overregulated in that marginal costs exceed marginal benefits.


## Questions and Study Suggestions

1   Key terms and concepts to remember: monopoly; big business; workable competition; countervailing power; Sherman Act; Clayton Act; Federal Trade Commission Act; interlocking directorate; tying agreement; cease-and-desist order; Wheeler-Lea Act; Celler-Kefauver Act; U.S. Steel case; rule of reason; Alcoa case; Webb-Pomerene Act; Robinson-Patman Act; patent laws; industrial regulation; Interstate Commerce Act; public interest theory of regulation; supply-and-demand theory of regulation; social regulation.

2   "All big firms are monopolistic, but not all monopolistic firms are big." Appraise critically.

3   Suppose you are president of one of the Big Three automobile producers. Discuss critically the case against business monopoly. Now suppose you are a representative for a farm organization and are attempting to convince a congressional committee that the presence of business monopolies is a significant factor contributing to the farm problem. Critically evaluate the case for business monopoly.

4   Discuss the evolution and the social desirability of the giant corporation as envisioned in Galbraith's *The New Industrial State.*

5   Suppose a proposed merger of firms will simultaneously lessen competition and reduce unit costs through the greater realization of economies of scale. Do you feel such a merger should be allowed?

**6** "The social desirability of any given business enterprise should be judged not on the basis of the structure of the industry in which it finds itself, but rather, on the basis of the market performance and behavior of that firm." Analyze critically.

**7** What types of industries should be subjected to industrial regulation? Why might an inefficient combination of capital and labor be employed by a regulated natural monopoly?

**8** What are the economic implications of social regulation? Do you believe American industry is overregulated? Explain.

**9** "The antitrust laws serve to penalize efficiently managed firms." Do you agree?

## Selected References

Caves, Richard: *American Industry: Structure, Conduct, Performance,* 4th ed. (Englewood Cliffs, N.J.: Prentice-Hall, Inc., 1977).

MacAvoy, Paul W.: *The Regulated Industries and the Economy* (New York: W. W. Norton & Company, Inc., 1980).

Mullineaux, Donald J.: "Regulation: Whence it Came and Whether It's Here to Stay," *Business Review* (Federal Reserve Bank of Philadelphia), September-October, 1978, pp. 3–11.

Shepherd, William G.: *The Economics of Industrial Organization* (Englewood Cliffs, N.J.: Prentice-Hall, Inc., 1979), chaps. 23–24.

Sherman, Roger: *Antitrust Policies and Issues* (Reading, Mass.: Addison-Wesley Publishing Company, 1978).

Steiner, George A.: "New Patterns in Government Regulation of Business," *MSU Business Topics,* Autumn, 1978, pp. 53–61.

Weiss, Leonard, and Allyn D. Strickland: *Regulation: A Case Approach* (New York: McGraw-Hill Book Company, 1976).

# LAST WORD
## The Cost of Government Regulation of Business

Professor Murray Weidenbaum, a leading critic of governmental regulation of business, has estimated that the total cost of regulation was about $103 billion in 1979.

The impacts of government regulation of business are being felt in every part of the economy.

One: The taxpayer feels the effect. Government regulation literally has become a major growth industry, an industry supported by the taxpayer. . . . Outlays of 41 regulatory agencies are estimated to increase from $2.2 billion in the fiscal year 1974 to $4.8 billion in fiscal 1979, a growth of 115 percent.

Two: The motorist feels the effect. Federally mandated safety and environmental features increase the price of the average passenger car by $666 in 1978. . . . In addition, the added weight of the cars is increasing fuel consumption perhaps by about $3 billion annually.

Three: The businessman and businesswoman feel the effect. There are over 4,400 different Federal forms that the private sector must fill out each year. That takes over 143 million man-hours, the economic equivalent of a small army. The Federal Paperwork Commission recently estimated that the total cost of Federal paperwork imposed on private industry ranges from $25 billion to $32 billion a year and that a substantial portion of this cost is unnecessary.

Four: The homeowner feels the effect. Regulatory requirements imposed by Federal, State, and local governments are adding between $1,500 and $2,500 to the cost of a typical new house. The Government-imposed costs range from permit and inspection fees to wider and thicker required streets to time-consuming and excessively detailed environmental impact studies.

Five: The consumer feels the effect. The costs of complying with Government regulations are inevitably passed on by business to the consumer in the form of higher prices, that hidden tax of regulation.

Six: The worker feels the effect. Government regulation, albeit unintentionally, can have strongly adverse effects on employment. The minimum wage law has priced hundreds of thousands of people out of labor markets. . . . In addition, many industry facilities and entire factories have been closed down—with substantial but unmeasurable effects on employment—because of the high costs of meeting environmental, safety, and other regulatory requirements.

Seven: The investor feels the effect. Approximately $10 billion of new private capital spending is devoted each year to meeting governmentally mandated environmental, safety, and similar regulations rather than being invested in profitmaking projects.

Eight: The Nation as a whole feels the effect of Government regulation in a reduced rate of innovation and in many ways. . . . These undramatic but fundamental effects occur because of the diversion of management attention from traditional product development, production, and marketing efforts designed to provide new and better products and services to meeting governmentally imposed social requirements.

Testimony of Murray L. Weidenbaum in Joint Economic Committee, *The Cost of Government Regulation* (Washington, 1978), pp. 20–22, abridged.

# Rural Economics: The Farm Problem

chapter 35

Traditionally, American agriculture has been something of a paradox. Characterized by a rate of productivity growth substantially in excess of any other major sector of the economy, our agricultural abundance has been the envy of the world. But, ironically, farmers have typically received below-average incomes for their remarkable production feats. This irony is perhaps underscored by the fact that agriculture is the only major industry which approximates the purely competitive model of Chapter 26. We must try to discover why the functioning of competitive forces in farming has not yielded incomes comparable to those realized in nonfarm sectors of the economy.

The major objectives of this chapter are:

1 To describe "the farm problem" and outline its causes

2 To discuss public policy toward agriculture and comment upon its effectiveness

3 To inquire as to whether, in the 1970s and 1980s American agriculture has entered a new, more prosperous era

## □ HISTORY OF THE FARM PROBLEM

The two decades prior to World War I were exceedingly prosperous ones for agriculture; indeed, this period has been dubbed "the golden age of American agriculture." The demand for farm products, farm prices, and farm incomes all rose. World War I intensified these good times. Foreign demand for the output of American farmers skyrocketed during, and immediately following, the war. Foreign countries, diverting resources from agriculture to war goods production, turned to American agriculture for food and fiber. High prices and an almost insatiable demand were the happy lot of American farmers.

These highly favorable conditions were not to last. A sharp postwar depression in 1920 was a sudden and severe shock to agriculture. In particular, the large volume of mortgage indebtedness incurred during the previous years of prosperity proved a heavy burden. The economy as a whole quickly recovered from this downturn, however, and by 1921 the booming twenties were upon us. But agriculture failed to share in this prosperity to the extent that other segments of the economy did.

The reasons for this were several. European agriculture not only recovered from the war but also began to expand rapidly under the impetus of new technological advances. Hence, foreign demand for American farm goods began to level off and then to decline. American foreign trade policies also contributed to this deterioration in foreign demand. High tariffs on goods imported to the United States helped undermine foreign demand for American farm products. To the extent that foreigners could not sell to us because of trade restrictions, they were unable to earn the funds they needed to buy from American producers. Furthermore, the domestic demand for farm products did not rise very much in the twenties. Most American stomachs were full, and as a result, income increases were used to buy automobiles, refrigerators, and a host of new products of industry. Finally, on the supply side of the picture, technological advances boosted farm output markedly. The net result of a lagging, inelastic demand and a sharply increasing supply of farm products was low farm prices and incomes.

The Great Depression of the 1930s was a particularly acute blow to American agriculture. The highly competitive nature of agriculture makes it especially vulnerable to bad times. Unlike sellers who possess a modicum of monopoly power, farmers are unable to influence their prices. They are "price takers" at the mercy of the market. Therefore, when market demand declines as it did during the Depression, farm prices and farm incomes fall sharply. Ironically, farmers buy in markets which are basically noncompetitive. Hence, while their incomes fell by very large amounts, the prices of farmers' purchases declined very modestly. Farmers in the 1920s and 1930s found themselves in a harsh price-cost squeeze.

World War II provided welcome but temporary relief for the farmer. Both domestic and foreign demand for agricultural products boomed during the war, and prosperity returned to agriculture. Except for the 1948–1949 slump, the middle and the late forties were peak years for American farmers. Then in the 1950s a slow but certain relapse became evident, and agriculture was once again encountering difficulty.

☐  **FARM INCOMES**

The relative economic position of the farmer can be readily seen through income statistics. Indeed, low incomes are the most obvious symptom of the farm problem. Table 35-1 provides us with a comparison of per capita farm and nonfarm incomes since the mid-thirties. Generally speaking, farm incomes have been substantially less than nonfarm incomes. In 1978 per capita farm income was about 90 percent of per capita nonfarm income. Historically, the relationship has been much less favorable to farmers; for example, throughout the 1960s per capita farm incomes averaged less than two-thirds of nonfarm incomes.

But it would be a gross error to conclude that *all* farmers are poor. Table 35-2 indicates there is great income disparity *within* agriculture. These figures show that in 1978, 7 per-

**TABLE 35-1**

Per Capita Disposable Income of Farm and Nonfarm People, Selected Years, 1934–1978

| Year | Farm people | Nonfarm people |
|------|-------------|----------------|
| 1934 | $ 163 | $ 500 |
| 1937 | 283 | 638 |
| 1940 | 245 | 671 |
| 1944 | 630 | 1151 |
| 1948 | 913 | 1351 |
| 1952 | 949 | 1596 |
| 1956 | 877 | 1838 |
| 1960 | 1086 | 2014 |
| 1965 | 1692 | 2480 |
| 1970 | 2510 | 3390 |
| 1975 | 4520 | 5113 |
| 1978 | 6069 | 6673 |

*Source:* U.S. Department of Agriculture, *Farm Income Statistics.*

**TABLE 35-2**
Distribution of Commercial Farms by Economic
Class, 1978

| Value of farm products sold | Percent of total farms | Percent of total output |
|---|---|---|
| $100,000 or more | 7 | 56 |
| $40,000–$99,999 | 15 | 25 |
| $20,000–$39,999 | 12 | 10 |
| $10,000–$19,999 | 11 | 5 |
| $5,000–$9,999 | 11 | 2 |
| $2,500–$4,999 | 10 | 1 |
| Less than $2,500 | 34 | 1 |
| Total | 100 | 100 |

*Source:* U.S. Department of Agriculture, *Farm Income Statistics.*

cent of the farms in the United States accounted for 56 percent of total farm output. At the other extreme, cumulating the figures for the bottom two economic classes makes it clear that 44 percent of all farms sold less than $5000 worth of farm products in 1978 and that the output of these farms was a mere 2 percent of the total amount of farm products sold in that year. Note further that the 34 percent of our farms which market $20,000 or more each year produce 91 percent of all marketed farm products. The remaining 66 percent account for only 9 percent of marketed output. It is in this latter group that extremely low incomes—the main symptom of the difficulties which plague American agriculture—are predominant.

The data of Table 35-2 suggest a second point about which more will be said later: A substantial amount of human and property resources could leave agriculture without causing a very significant decline in total farm output.

## □  CAUSES OF THE FARM PROBLEM

It is a bit misleading to talk of "the" farm problem. Actually, the changes which have occurred in farm incomes suggest the presence of both a long-run problem and a short-run problem. The long-run problem concerns those forces which have tended to cause farm prices and incomes to lag behind the trends of prices and incomes for the economy as a whole. The short-run problem has to do with the extreme year-to-year instability of farm incomes.

## △  The Long-run Problem

Complex problems can rarely be stated accurately in brief terms. This is certainly true of the long-run problem which plagues American agriculture. Nevertheless, a workable picture of the problem can be portrayed through the economic tools of demand and supply. In these terms, we may say that the causes of the long-run farm problem are embodied in

**1**  The *price inelasticity* of the demand for agricultural products
**2**  The *shifts* which have occurred over time in the demand and supply curves for farm products
**3**  The relative *immobility* of agricultural resources

**The Inelastic Demand for Agricultural Products**  In most developed societies, the price elasticity of demand for agricultural products is low. For farm products in the aggregate, the elasticity coefficient is estimated to be from .20 to .25.[1] These figures suggest that the prices of agricultural products would have to fall by 40 to 50 percent in order for consumers to increase their purchases by a mere 10 percent. Consumers apparently put a low value on additional agricultural output as compared with alternative goods. Why is this so? You will recall that the basic determinant of elasticity of demand is substitutability. That is, when the price of a product falls, the consumer will tend to substitute *that* product for other products whose prices presumably have not fallen. But in wealthy societies this "substitution effect" (Chapter 24) is very mod-

[1] Dale E. Hathaway, *Problems of Progress in the Agricultural Economy* (Chicago: Scott, Foresman and Company, 1964), p. 10.

est. People simply do not switch from three to five or six meals each day in response to declines in the relative prices of agricultural products. An individual's capacity to substitute food for other products is subject to very real biological constraints. The inelasticity of agricultural demand can also be explained in terms of diminishing marginal utility. In a wealthy society, the population by and large is well fed and well clothed, that is, relatively saturated with the food and fiber of agriculture. Therefore, additional agricultural output entails rapidly diminishing marginal utility. Thus it takes very large price cuts to induce small increases in consumption. Curve $D$ in Figure 35-2 on page 684 portrays an inelastic demand.

**Technological Advance and Rapid Increases in Agricultural Supply**  An inelastic demand for farm products is, in and of itself, innocent enough. It is the accompanying fact that the supply of agricultural products has increased in relation to the demand for them that has spelled declining farm incomes.

On the supply side of the picture, a rapid rate of technological advance, particularly since World War I, has caused significant increases in the supply of agricultural products. This technological progress has many roots: the virtually complete electrification and mechanization of farms; improved techniques of land management and soil conservation; irrigation; the development of hybrid crops; the availability of improved fertilizers and insecticides; improvements in the breeding and care of livestock; and so forth.

How meaningful have these technological advances actually been? Very! The simplest index is the increasing number of people which a single farmer's output will support. In 1820 each farm worker produced enough food and fiber to support four persons. By 1979 each farmer produced enough to support about sixty! There can be no question but that productivity in agriculture has risen significantly. Since World War II, productivity in agriculture

has advanced at a rate which is *twice* as fast as that of the nonfarm economy.

Two additional important points must amend this discussion of the increasing productivity in American farming:

**1**  Most recent technological advances have not been initiated by farmers but are, rather, the result of government-sponsored programs of research and education and the work of farm machinery producers. Land-grant colleges, experiment stations, county agents of the Agricultural Extension Service, the inexhaustible supply of educational pamphlets issuing from the U.S. Department of Agriculture, and the research staffs of John Deere and International Harvester are the sources of technological advance in American agriculture.

**2**  Technological advance has not occurred evenly throughout agriculture. Many farmers are undermechanized, uninformed, and inefficient. It is no surprise that the low-productivity farmers are those on the bottom of Table 35-2's income ladder.

**Lagging Demand for Agricultural Products**  Increases in the demand for agricultural commodities have failed to keep pace with technologically inspired increases in their supply. Why? The answer lies in the two major determinants of agricultural demand—incomes and population.

In less developed countries, consumers must devote the bulk of their meager incomes to the products of agriculture—food and clothing—to sustain themselves. But as income expands beyond the subsistence level and the problem of hunger eventually gives way to one of obesity, consumers will increase their outlays on food and clothing at ever-declining rates. Once a consumer's stomach is filled, his or her thoughts turn to the amenities of life which industry, not agriculture, provides. Economic growth in the United States has boosted average per capita income far beyond the level of bare subsistence. As a result, *increases in the incomes of American consumers lead to less than proportionate increases in expenditures on farm products.* In technical terms, the demand for farm products is *income-inelastic;* that is, the demand for most agricultural products is quite insensitive to increases in income. Estimates indicate that a 10 percent increase in real per capita disposable income entails at the most an increase in the consumption of farm products of only 2 percent.[2] Certain specific farm products—for example, potatoes and lard—may be inferior goods; that is, as incomes increase purchases of these products decrease (Chapter 4).

Population is a somewhat different proposition. Despite the fact that, after a minimum income level is reached, each individual consumer's intake of food and fiber will become relatively fixed, more consumers obviously will mean an increase in the demand for farm products. And this increase has occurred. But population increases, added to the relatively small increase in the purchase of farm products which occurs as incomes rise, have simply not been great enough to match the concomitant increases in farm output.

**Graphic Portrayal**   When coupled with the inelastic demand for agricultural products, these shifts in supply and demand have tended to reduce farm incomes. This is illustrated in Figure 35-1, where a large increase in supply is shown against a very modest increase in demand. Because of the inelastic demand for farm products, these shifts have resulted in a sharp decline in farm prices accompanied by relatively small increases in sales. Farm incomes therefore tend to decline. Diagrammatically, income before the increase in supply occurs (measured by rectangle $OPAQ$) will exceed farm income after supply increases $(OP_1BQ_1)$. The income "loss" of $P_1PAC$ is not fully offset by the income "gain" of $QCBQ_1$. In summary, *given an inelastic demand for farm products, an increase in the supply of farm*

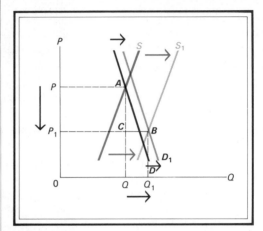

**FIGURE 35-1   A GRAPHIC SUMMARY OF THE LONG-RUN FARM PROBLEM**

In the long run, increases in the demand for agricultural products ($D$ to $D_1$) have not kept pace with the increases in supply ($S$ to $S_1$) which technological advances have permitted. Coupled with the fact that agricultural demand is inelastic, these shifts have tended to depress farm prices (as from $P$ to $P_1$) and incomes (as from $OPAQ$ to $OP_1BQ_1$).

*products relative to the demand for them has created persistent tendencies for farm incomes to fall.* This is not to say that farm incomes have fallen absolutely, but rather, that farm incomes have clearly lagged behind the nonfarm sector of the economy (Table 35-1). Furthermore, the prices which farmers have received for their output have declined relative to the prices farmers have had to pay for all the inputs used in farm production; that is, farmers have faced a chronic price-cost squeeze.

**Immobility of Resources**   Our previous discussion of the workings of the price system (Chapter 33) would certainly suggest an obvious and automatic solution to the long-run problem faced by agriculture. As noted earlier, agriculture is a highly competitive industry, characterized by large numbers of independent firms each of which produces a minute fraction

[2]Joint Economic Committee, *Staff Report on Employment, Growth, and Price Levels* (Washington, 1960), p. 190.

of the overall output of quite highly standardized products. One would expect declining farm prices and incomes to signal an exodus of resources from agriculture. Prices and incomes which are low in relation to the rest of the economy would seemingly prompt farmers to leave their farms in favor of more lucrative occupations. The adjustments of a competitive industry, as outlined in Chapters 5 and 26, indicate that this exodus of farmers would reduce industry supply in relation to demand, thereby boosting farm prices and incomes. This reallocation of resources away from agriculture and toward industry, one can assume, would bring farm incomes into rough accord with those of the rest of the economy.

Human resources *have* shifted out of agriculture in large numbers as the competitive market model would predict. But, except for the minute portion of total farmland which borders on metropolitan areas, most farmland has no real alternative uses. Farmers leave, but the land they leave stays in production. Hence, the mass outmigration of labor from agriculture, shown in Table 35-3, has failed to close the farm-nonfarm income gap embodied in Table 35-1. Furthermore, we must recognize that the farm-nonfarm disequilibrium is not the result of a single, one-shot imbalance. Hence, even as labor leaves agriculture in the pursuit of higher incomes in nonfarm sectors of the economy, the components of the long-run farm problem *continue* to depress farm incomes and to set the stage for a further exodus. Despite the remarkable secular decline in the farm population displayed in Table 35-3, agricultural economists still talk of surplus labor in the agricultural sector.

It is correct to say that, historically, the relative slowness of the reallocation of farmers from agriculture to industry is the crux of the farm problem. Ironically enough, in an industry long associated with the word "surplus," we find that the biggest and most fundamental farm surplus of all is the number of farmers. Indeed, the farm problem can be correctly envisioned as a problem of resource misalloca-

**TABLE 35-3**
The Declining Farm Population, Selected Years, 1910–1978

| Year | Farm Population, millions | Percentage of the total population |
|------|---------------------------|------------------------------------|
| 1910 | 32.1 | 35 |
| 1920 | 31.9 | 30 |
| 1930 | 30.5 | 25 |
| 1935 | 32.2 | 25 |
| 1940 | 30.5 | 23 |
| 1945 | 24.4 | 18 |
| 1950 | 23.0 | 15 |
| 1955 | 19.1 | 12 |
| 1960 | 15.6 | 9 |
| 1965 | 12.4 | 6 |
| 1970 | 9.7 | 5 |
| 1975 | 8.9 | 4 |
| 1978 | 8.0 | 4 |

*Source: Statistical Abstract of the United States.*

tion. It is the fact that too many farmers are sharing agriculture's shrinking slice of the national income pie that makes income per farmer small.

### △  The Short-run Problem

The lag of farm incomes behind the rest of the economy is evidence of the long-run agricultural problem. Substantial year-to-year fluctuations in farm prices and therefore in incomes reflect a short-run problem. This short-run instability can be traced back to the inelastic demand for agricultural products which contributes to the instability of farm prices and incomes in two different ways.

**Fluctuations in Output**  On the production side of the picture, the inelastic demand for farm products causes small changes in agricultural production to be magnified into relatively larger changes in farm prices and incomes. To understand this point, we must first note that farmers possess only limited control over their production. In the first place, floods, droughts, an unexpected frost, insect damage, and similar disasters can mean short crops. Conversely, an excellent growing season may mean bumper crops. Weather factors are beyond the control of farmers, yet they exert an important influence upon production. Second, the highly competitive nature of agriculture makes it virtually impossible for farmers to form a huge combination to control their production. If all the millions of widely scattered and independent producers should by chance plant an unusually large or abnormally small portion of their land, extra large or small outputs would result even if the growing season were normal.

Now, putting the instability of farm production together with an inelastic demand for farm products, we can readily discover why farm prices and incomes are highly unstable. Figure 35-2 is pertinent. Even if we assume that the market demand for agriculture products is stable at $D$, the inelastic nature of demand will magnify small changes in output into relatively large changes in farm prices and income. For example, assume that a "normal" crop of $Q_n$ results in a "normal" price of $P_n$ and a "normal" farm income of $OP_nNQ_n$. But a bumper crop or a short crop will cause large deviations from these normal prices and incomes; these results stem from the inelasticity of demand for farm products.

If an unusually good growing season occurs, the resulting bumper crop of $Q_b$ will cause farm incomes to *fall* from $OP_nNQ_n$ to $OP_bBQ_b$. Why? Because when demand is inelastic, an increase in the quantity sold will be accompanied by a *more than* proportionate decline in price. The net result is that total receipts, that is, total farm income, will decline. Similarly, for farmers as a group, a short crop caused by, say, drought may boost farm incomes. A short crop of $Q_s$ will raise total farm income from $OP_nNQ_n$ to $OP_sSQ_s$. Why? Because a decline in output will cause a *more than* proportionate increase in price when demand is inelastic. Ironically, for farmers as a group, a short crop may be a blessing and a bumper crop a hardship. Our conclusion is this: Given a stable market demand for farm products, the inelasticity of that demand will turn relatively small changes in output into relatively larger changes in farm prices and incomes.

**Fluctuations in Demand**   The other aspect of the short-run instability of farm incomes has to do with shifts in the demand curve for agricultural products. Let us suppose that somehow agricultural output is stabilized at the "normal" level of $Q_n$ in Figure 35-3. Now, because of the inelasticity of the demand for farm products, short-run fluctuations in the demand for these products will cause markedly different prices and incomes to be associated with this level of production that we assume to be constant. That is, a slight drop in demand from $D_1D_1$ to $D_2D_2$ will cause farm incomes to fall from $OP_1aQ_n$ to $OP_2bQ_n$. A relatively small decline in demand gives farmers a drastically reduced money reward for the same amount of production. (One can readily understand why President Carter's suspension of sales of agricultural products to the Soviet Union in early 1980 was a matter of grave concern to farmers!) Conversely, a slight in-

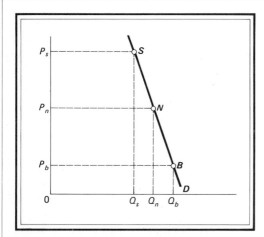

FIGURE 35-2   THE EFFECT OF OUTPUT CHANGES ON FARM PRICES AND INCOMES

Because of the inelasticity of demand for farm products, a relatively small change in output ($Q_n$ to $Q_s$ or $Q_b$) will cause relatively large changes in farm prices ($P_n$ to $P_s$ or $P_b$) and incomes ($OP_nNQ_n$ to $OP_sSQ_s$ or $OP_bBQ_b$).

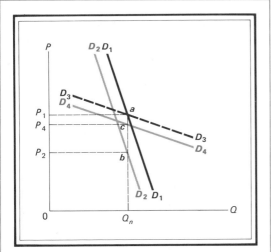

**FIGURE 35-3  THE EFFECT OF DEMAND CHANGES ON FARM PRICES AND INCOMES**

Because of the highly inelastic demand for agricultural products, a small shift in demand ($D_1D_1$ to $D_2D_2$) will cause drastically different levels of farm prices ($P_1$ to $P_2$) and farm incomes ($OP_1aQ_n$ to $OP_2bQ_n$) to be associated with a given level of production $Q_n$. Note that equal changes in a more elastic demand curve ($D_3D_3$ to $D_4D_4$) will be accompanied by much smaller price ($P_1$ to $P_4$) and income ($OP_1aQ_n$ to $OP_4cQ_n$) alterations.

crease in demand will bring an equally sharp increase in farm incomes for the same volume of output. These large price-income changes are linked to the fact that demand is inelastic. This relationship can be grasped by observing the much smaller price-income changes which accompany an equal shift in demand from the more elastic demand curve $D_3D_3$.[3] If demand drops from $D_3D_3$ to $D_4D_4$, price will fall very modestly from $P_1$ to $P_4$ and income will fall only from $OP_1aQ_n$ to $OP_4cQ_n$.

It is tempting to argue that the sharp declines in farm prices which accompany a decrease in demand will cause many farmers to close down in the short run, thereby reducing

[3]Though they may not appear so graphically, these two shifts in demand are equal in the sense that in each instance buyers want to purchase the same amount less at each possible price.

total output and alleviating these price-income declines. But farm production is relatively insensitive to price changes, because farmers' fixed costs are high compared with their variable costs. Interest, rental, tax, and mortgage payments on buildings and equipment are the major costs faced by the farmer. These are clearly fixed charges. Furthermore, the labor supply of the farmer and his family can also be regarded as a fixed cost. So long as he stays on his farm, the farmer cannot reduce his costs by firing himself! This means that his variable costs are for the small amounts of hired help he may employ, plus expenditures for seed, fertilizer, and fuel. As a result of this high volume of fixed costs, the farmer is almost invariably better off when working his land than when sitting idle and attempting to pay his fixed costs out of pocket. The other factors, noted previously, which contribute to the relative immobility of farmers are also pertinent. In particular, if a decline in the demand for farm output is part of an overall recession, there will be no real incentive for farmers to stop production in order to seek nonexistent jobs in industry. In fact, a migration in the opposite direction—from the city to the farm—often accompanies a full-scale depression. Note in Table 35-3 the absolute *increase* in the farm population which occurred between 1930 and 1935. Note, too, in Figure 10-3 that between 1929 and 1933, farm prices fell by 63 percent and farm output by a mere 6 percent.

△   **A Restatement**

Let us pause at this point to bring our knowledge of the causes of the long- and short-run farm problems into sharper focus. The long-run problem is the result of the unhappy combination of four factors.

**1**   The demand for agricultural commodities is inelastic.

**2**   Rapid technological advance has given rise to significant increases in the supply of farm products.

**3**  The demand for agricultural commodities has increased very modestly. This consideration, combined with factors 1 and 2, has resulted in a tendency for farm prices and incomes to fall or to grow only modestly.

**4**  The relatively fixed nature of agricultural resources—land, capital, and farmers themselves—has caused low prices and incomes to persist; resources have not been reallocated from agriculture rapidly enough to offset the tendency for agricultural prices and incomes to decline.

In the short run, the extreme sensitiveness of farm prices and incomes is based upon the inelastic demand for agricultural products which transforms small changes in farm output and demand into much larger changes in farm prices and incomes.

△  **Agriculture and Growth**

A slightly different perspective on this explanation of the long-run farm problem correctly puts emphasis upon resource misallocation and couches the problem in terms of a growing economy. Of necessity, primitive or underdeveloped countries have essentially agrarian economies. The total population of such a nation must devote its efforts to agricultural endeavors to provide enough food and fiber to sustain itself. But, as technological advance increases productivity per farmer, the economy can maintain or even increase its consumption of food and clothing and simultaneously transfer a portion of its population into nonagricultural pursuits. This is the path which any expanding, progressive economy follows. Indeed, the shift of resources from agricultural to industrial pursuits is the earmark of a growing economy. The experience of the United States is illustrative. About 90 percent of our population was devoted to agriculture in the eighteenth century. At present less than 4 percent of the population is in farming, the remaining 96 percent being free to produce refrigerators, furniture, automobiles, and the thousands of other goods and services which make up a high standard of living. But,

in our economy, the actual shift of resources to nonagricultural employments has not kept pace with the rate of reallocation which rapid technological advance permits. The result has been persistent downward pressure on farm prices and incomes.

☐  RATIONALE FOR PUBLIC POLICY

Historically, many arguments have been used in seeking and rationalizing public aid to agriculture. It has been contended, for example, that farming, and particularly the family farm, is a fundamental American institution and should be nurtured as "a way of life." Furthermore, farmers are subject to certain extraordinary hazards—floods, droughts, and invasion by hordes of insects—to which other industries are not exposed. It has been held, too, that agriculture is a major cog in the American economy, and therefore prosperity for farmers is a prerequisite for prosperity in the economy as a whole.

Two additional arguments for special aid to agriculture are of greater substance and merit more detailed consideration.

△  **Costs-of-Progress Argument**

While agriculture has made great contributions to the nation's economic growth, it has had to bear a disproportionately large share of the costs associated with this progress. The rapid rate of productivity growth in American agriculture has resulted in substantial and widespread benefits to the economy as a whole. The population has been able to get more and better food and fiber from agriculture in exchange for a smaller portion of its money income. Furthermore, over the years agriculture has been a major source of labor for industry (Table 35-3).[4]

Farm families have for years produced children well in excess of the numbers needed to replace retiring members of the farm labor force. This, together with the absolute decline in the number

[4]Hathaway, op. cit., p. 5.

of people on farms, means that a very substantial portion of our present productive nonfarm labor force was raised on a farm, educated in schools heavily dependent upon farm taxes, and migrated to the cities after finishing school.

On the other hand, the peculiar combination of economic circumstances already discussed—an inelastic demand for farm products, rapid technological progress, the slow growth of demand, and the relatively fixed nature of agricultural resources—has caused farm people to bear a large share of the costs of agricultural progress in the form of incomes substantially below those of nonfarm income receivers.

△ **Market-power Argument**

A second argument focuses upon the question of market power. Agriculture is a highly competitive industry, comprising hundreds of thousands of small, geographically dispersed producers. As a result, farmers have no control over the prices at which they must sell their products. Nonagricultural industries, on the other hand, have varying degrees of market power and, within limits, the capacity to adjust their prices. In particular, most of the firms from which farmers buy machinery, fertilizer, gasoline, and so forth, have some capacity to control their prices. Given the farmer's unenviable market position in comparison with the nonfarm sectors, it is not surprising that farmers get a disproportionately small share of the national income. It is argued on the basis of this rationale that a special farm program to help agriculture is justified as a means of compensating for the weak market position of farmers. Stated differently, agriculture is the last stronghold of pure competition in an otherwise imperfectly competitive economy; it warrants public aid to offset the disadvantageous terms of trade which result.

□ **FARM POLICY: OLD AND NEW**
On the basis of these arguments and the disproportionately large voice which farmers have

historically had in Congress, a detailed "farm program" concerning (1) farm prices, incomes, and output; (2) soil conservation; (3) agricultural research; (4) farm credit; (5) crop insurance; and other factors has come into being and persisted since the 1930s.

But the thrust of our farm policy has shifted through time. At the risk of oversimplification, our *traditional policies*—policies which prevailed during the 1930s, 1940s, and 1950s—were characterized by government market intervention. Specifically, traditional policy was largely designed to restrict farm production for the purpose of raising farm prices and incomes. These "price-centered" policies were a reflection of the excess productive capacity which characterized agriculture during most of this period. But, in the 1960s and particularly in the 1970s, the problems of excess productive capacity and chronically depressed farm incomes have diminished in importance, thanks largely to substantial increases in the overseas demand for American farm products. Hence, public policy in the 1960s and 1970s shifted away from market intervention and output restriction. The focus of *new policies* in the 1970s is toward freer farm markets and the realization of low-cost increases in agricultural production. We shall consider first the traditional policies, beginning with the concept of parity.

□ **TRADITIONAL POLICY: PARITY**
The *Agricultural Adjustment Act of 1933* established the concept of *parity* as a cornerstone of agricultural policy. The simple rationale of the parity concept can be readily envisioned in both real and money terms. In real terms, parity says that year after year for a given output of farm products, a farmer should be able to acquire a given total amount of goods and services. A given real output should always result in the same real income. "If a man could take a bushel of corn to town in 1912 and sell it and buy himself a shirt, he should be able to take a bushel of corn to town today and

buy a shirt." In money terms, *the parity concept suggests that the relationship between the prices received by farmers for their output and the prices they must pay for goods and services should remain constant.* The parity concept clearly implies that, if the price of shirts were to triple over some time period, then the price of corn should triple too.

A glance at Figure 35-4 indicates why farmers would benefit from having the prices of their products based upon 100 percent of parity. This graph shows the prices paid and received by farmers from 1910 to 1978 as percentages of the 1910 to 1914 base period. We observe that by 1978 prices paid had increased more than sixfold and prices received had increased about four and one half times as compared to the base period. The *parity ratio* shown in Figure 35-4 is merely the ratio of prices received relative to prices paid. In 1978 the parity ratio was about 75 percent ($=4.5 \div 6$), indicating that prices received in 1978 were about three-fourths as high relative to prices paid as they were in the 1910 to 1914 period. A farm policy calling for 100 percent of parity would entail substantially higher prices for farm products in order to bring the parity ratio up to 100.

△ **Price Supports**

The practical importance of the notion of parity prices is that it provides the rationale for government price supports on farm products. The fact that, in the long run, the market prices received by farmers have not generally kept abreast of prices paid by them means that to achieve parity or some percentage thereof, the government is likely to be required to establish above-equilibrium, or "support," prices on farm products.

Support prices have a number of significant effects. Suppose, in Figure 35-5, that the support price is $P_s$ as compared with the equilibrium price $P_e$.

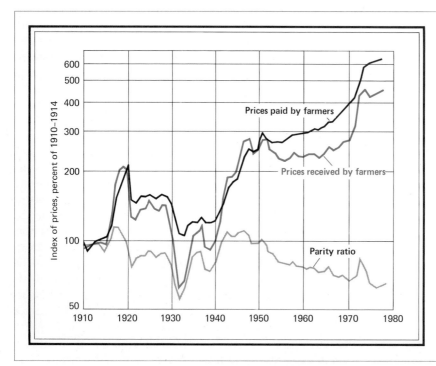

FIGURE 35-4 PRICES PAID AND RECEIVED BY FARMERS, 1910–1978

In the past three decades the prices paid by farmers have increased ahead of prices received. As a result, the parity ratio — which is simply the ratio of prices received to prices paid — has been less than 100 percent.

Index of prices, percent of 1910–1914

Prices paid by farmers

Prices received by farmers

Parity ratio

**1  Surplus Output**  The most obvious effect is that product surpluses will result. Private consumers will be willing to purchase only $OQ$ units at the supported price, while farmers will supply $OQ_s$ units. The amount $QQ_s$ is a surplus. What happens to this surplus? The government must buy it in order to make the above-equilibrium support price effective. Because of such purchases, huge surpluses accumulated during most of the 1950s and persisted until the late 1960s. These large accumulated surpluses were economically undesirable on two counts. First, their very existence indicates a misallocation of the economy's resources. Government-held surpluses reflect the fact that the economy is devoting large amounts of resources to the production of commodities which, *at existing supported prices,* are simply not wanted by consumers. Second, the storing of surplus products is an expensive undertaking which has added to the cost of the farm program and ultimately to the consumer's tax bill. Storage costs on surpluses have run as high as $1 billion per year when accumulated stocks were particularly large.

**2  Consumers' Loss**  Consumers "lose" in two ways. First, they will be paying a higher price ($P_s$ rather than $P_e$) and consuming less ($Q$ rather than $Q_e$) of the product. Second, they will be paying higher taxes to finance the government's purchase of the surplus. In Figure 35-5, this added tax burden will amount to the surplus output $QQ_s$, multiplied by its price $P_s$. Storage costs, of course, add to this tax burden.

**3  Farmers' Gain**  Farmers obviously gain from price supports. In Figure 35-5, gross receipts rise from the free market level of $OP_ebQ_e$ to the supported level of $OP_saQ_s$.

△  **Surplus Controls**

By what means might government cope with the surplus farm output which accompanies effective price supports? An elementary knowledge of the tools of supply and demand suggests that programs designed to reduce

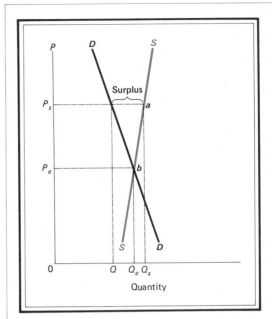

**FIGURE 35-5  EFFECTIVE PRICE SUPPORTS RESULT IN FARM SURPLUSES**

Application of the parity concept obligates government to support farm prices at above-equilibrium levels. These supported prices result in persistent surpluses of farm products.

market supply or increase market demand would help bring the market price up to the desired supported price, thereby reducing or eliminating farm surpluses (Figure 35-5).

**Restricting Supply**  On the supply side, public policy has long been aimed at restricting farm output. In particular, *acreage allotment programs* have accompanied the application of price supports. In return for the privilege of getting price supports on their crops, farmers must agree to limit the number of acres planted. Attempting to bring quantity supplied and quantity demanded into balance, the Department of Agriculture estimates the amount of each product which private buyers will take at the supported price. This amount is then translated into the number of acres of planting which will produce this amount. The total acreage figure is apportioned among states, counties, and ultimately individual farmers. Similarly, various *acreage reserve programs* have been employed whereby the Department of Agriculture makes direct payments to farmers for removing land entirely from crop production. For example, under the "soil bank" program, the government in effect rented land from farmers. Such idle land was to be planted in cover crops or timber, not in cash crops.

Have these supply-restricting programs been successful? It is difficult to give an unqualified answer. Certainly they have not eliminated surplus farm production. The basic reason is that acreage reduction invariably results in less than proportionate declines in production. Why? Farmers retire their worst land and keep their best in production. Those acres which are tilled are cultivated more intensively. The use of better seed, more and better fertilizer and insecticides, and more manpower will enhance output per acre. However, without these output controls, there is no doubt that accumulated farm surpluses and their associated costs would have been much greater than has actually been the case.

**Bolstering Demand**   Government has followed a number of paths in seeking to augment the demand for agricultural products.

**1**   Both government and private industry have spent considerable sums for research to uncover new uses for agricultural commodities. The production of "gasohol"—a blend of gasoline and alcohol made from grain—is a current and controversial attempt to create a new demand for agricultural output. Most experts conclude that at best we have only been modestly successful in such endeavors.

**2**   A variety of programs has been invoked to augment the domestic consumption of farm products. For example, the *food stamp program* is designed to distribute surplus farm products to low-income families. *School lunch programs* and the distribution of surpluses to welfare and charitable institutions have also

had the effect of enhancing the domestic demand for farm output.

**3**   A number of measures have been undertaken to increase foreign demand for American farm products. For example, our *Food for Peace program* under *Public Law 480* has permitted the less developed countries to buy our surplus farm products with their own currencies, rather than with dollars. Furthermore, in international trade bargaining, our negotiators have pressed hard to persuade foreign nations to reduce protective tariffs and other barriers against our farm products.

△   **Evaluation**

How successful has public policy been in resolving the long-run farm problem? Although it is difficult to offer an unequivocal answer, economists are generally critical of American farm policy. Let us note two major criticisms.

**Symptoms and Causes**   First and foremost, the farm program has failed to get at the causes of the farm problem. Public policy toward agriculture is designed to treat symptoms and not causes. The root *cause* of the farm problem has been a misallocation of resources between agriculture and the rest of the economy. Historically, the problem has been one of too many farmers. The effect or symptom of this misallocation of resources is low farm incomes. *For the most part, public policy in agriculture has been oriented toward supporting farm prices and incomes rather than toward alleviating the resource allocation problem, which is the fundamental cause of these sagging farm incomes.*

Some critics go further and argue that price-income supports have encouraged people to stay in agriculture when they otherwise would have migrated to some nonfarm occupation. That is, the price-income orientation of the farm program has deterred the very reallocation of resources which is necessary to resolve the long-run farm problem. On the other hand, one can argue that the extra income provided by price supports may have enabled farmers to provide more education for their children, thereby preparing them for better and higher-paying nonfarm jobs.

**Misguided Subsidies**  A second criticism is that price-income support programs have most benefited those farmers who least need government assistance. Assuming the goal of our farm program is the bolstering of low farm incomes, it follows that any program of government aid should be aimed at farmers at the bottom of the farm income distribution. But the poor, small-output farmer simply does not produce and sell enough in the market to get much aid from price supports. It is the large corporate farm which reaps the benefits by virtue of its large output. Individual subsidy checks running into hundreds of thousands of dollars are not easy to justify. If public policy must be designed to supplement farm incomes, a strong case can certainly be made for making those benefits vary inversely with one's position in the income distribution. An income-support program should be geared to *people,* not *commodities.* Many economists contend that, on equity grounds, direct income subsidies to poor farmers are highly preferable to indirect price support subsidies which go primarily to large and prosperous farmers.

The other side of the picture here is that our price support programs are also output-restricting programs. Remember that to receive price supports, a farmer must agree to restrict supply. If only small (low-income) farmers were eligible for price supports, little or no restricting of farm output would have occurred and our farm surplus problems would have been much more acute.

## ☐  THE SEVENTIES: WINDFALL OR WATERSHED?

In the 1970s, conditions in American agriculture changed quite dramatically. Against this backdrop of change, important alterations occurred in farm policy. What were these changes in agricultural conditions and policy?

## △  Exports: A New Era?

Recall that since World War II the basic problem in agriculture has been one of excess productive capacity. Consequently, farm policy has been essentially restrictive, that is, public policy has focused upon the restriction of farm output for the purpose of increasing farm prices and income. Thus, for example, since the early 1960s, about one-sixth of the nation's cropland has been held out of production.

But in 1972 and 1973 the agricultural picture was dramatically altered. Specifically, a number of interrelated factors accounted for a sharply increasing foreign demand for American agricultural products. As Figure 35-6 indicates, our agricultural exports spurted dramatically from about $6 billion in 1969 to almost $22 billion in 1975. Why did this happen?

**1**  On a worldwide basis—and especially in Western Europe and Japan—incomes have been expanding rapidly. But most countries have little or no excess capacity in agriculture; indeed, many countries were already large importers of food. Hence, much of their increased food and fiber demand has been for American output.

**2**  Dietary habits in Europe and Japan have been shifting toward the consumption of more red meat and poultry. Since it takes about 6 pounds of grain to produce 1 pound of meat, the increased demand for grains has been especially strong.

**3**  Poor harvests in many countries also accelerated the demand for American foodstuffs.

**4**  A further stimulus occurred in 1971 and another in 1973 as a result of the devaluation of the dollar in international trade. That is, dollars became less expensive in terms of other currencies, making American products—including farm products—cheaper for foreigners to buy (Chapter 44).

**5**  Finally, the opening of communist markets to American farm products bolstered demand. The controversial sale of over $1 bil-

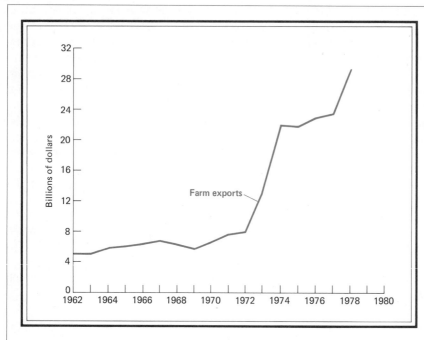

lion of grain to the Soviet Union in 1972–1973 was particularly significant.

In short, all these factors, coupled with a rather strong expansion of incomes domestically, sharply boosted agricultural demand, farm prices, and receipts (Figure 35-4).

### △  A New Farm Program

Many critics of past agricultural policy take the position that an ultimate solution to the farm problem must entail, in general, less government involvement in agriculture and, in particular, a return to freer markets.  Seizing upon the very favorable agricultural situation of the 1970s, Congress passed new farm legislation which tends to move in these directions. Specifically, the *Agriculture and Consumer Protection Act of 1973* embodied a program with the following basic features.

**1  Target Prices**  Price supports were replaced with *target prices*.  The target price is essentially a floor, or guaranteed minimum, price on basic agricultural products.  Target prices are stated in terms of dollars and cents, rather than as some percentage of parity.  The target prices were established substantially below the very high price levels of 1973, but generally above the support prices of prior legislation.  When market prices are above the targets, farmers receive no government subsidy.  But in years when market prices fall below target prices, government makes direct cash payments to farmers in the amount of the difference.

**2  All-out Production**  Although the new legislation extends the previously legislated authority to take land out of production, the implementation of this authority is now at the discretion of the Secretary of Agriculture. And, in fact, in the mid-1970s, the Secretary has given farmers the green light to produce as much as they choose.  Temporarily, at least, American agricultural policy has shifted from restriction to the encouragement of all-out production.

**3  Subsidy Ceilings**  The new program addressed the problem of paying huge subsidies to large, prosperous farmers by limiting total payments to $20,000 per individual farmer for all commodity programs combined.

In short, under the current farm legislation we are moving from price supports toward a more market-oriented policy, on the one hand, and from output restriction toward expanded production in response to market incentives, on the other.

△  **Consequences and Implications**

The upsurge in farm exports, along with the new agricultural policies, has a number of salient implications.

**1  Alleviated Income Problem**  There is no doubt that the expanded demand for agricultural products was of considerable benefit to farmers. But there were offsetting considerations. While the cash receipts of farmers from the sale of their products increased sharply, so did production costs (Figure 35-4). For example, livestock producers are major buyers of grains for feed; hence, rapidly rising grain prices mean higher costs for cattle production. And large quantities of oil are necessary to run farm equipment, to manufacture fertilizer, and to operate irrigation pumps. Hence, the prices paid by farmers have been greatly affected by the rising price of oil. Furthermore, historically, American farmers have obtained a substantial fraction of their incomes from government subsidies. But some of these subsidies vary inversely with the incomes farmers receive from the market. Thus, when market prices and incomes go up, farm income from public subsidy tends to fall. The point is that net farm incomes do *not* rise in proportion to gross farm receipts.

**2  End of Excess Capacity?**  Excess capacity in American agriculture *may* be disappearing. For example, under the new farm policy, some 60 million acres of land were released from acreage controls in the 1972–1974 period, but only 37 million acres were added to the nation's cultivated area in those years. This suggests that substantial investments are required to bring more land into production, and current farm prices are insufficient to justify that investment. Furthermore, much of the increase in export demand has been met by sales of grain from reserve stockpiles. As a result, these reserves have been substantially depleted. In 1973, total grain stocks reached their lowest levels since 1953.

**3  Domestic-Foreign Trade-off**  In the past, excess productive capacity and large grain reserves made it possible for the United States to increase food exports without significantly affecting domestic food prices. But in the current situation, as more foodstuffs are shipped abroad, available domestic supplies are reduced and prices rise. Rising food prices were a major factor in the domestic inflation of the early 1970s. In 1973, retail food prices rose at the most rapid rate in over a quarter of a century; in August 1973, food prices were 23 percent higher than they had been ten months earlier! It is no wonder that the issue of export embargoes on farm products was accorded considerable attention in the 1976 Presidential campaign and that President Carter's 1980 embargo on grain exports to the Soviet Union raised the ire of farmers.

**4  Greater Price Instability?**  Some experts feel that the problem of farm price instability may be aggravated in the present situation. Why so? Historically, price instability was cushioned by manipulating farm product reserves or changing the amount of land in production. Potential price increases could be softened by drawing on reserves and bringing more land into production. Conversely, a price fall could be offset by adding to reserves and withdrawing land from production. But fallow land reserves and surplus stocks are no longer available, at least to the degree they were under traditional farm policies. Furthermore, agricultural prices are obviously more exposed to the vagaries of international markets.

The domestic agricultural policies of the European Community and Japan inhibit the adjustments that can take place in their agricultural markets. Consequently, the burden of adjustment to changing conditions of demand and supply is pushed onto the United States and other exporting countries. In addition, the growing involvement of the U.S.S.R. in world trade in recent years has transmitted to world markets the shocks stemming from fluctuations in the relatively unstable agricultural sector of that country. Some 80 percent of the year-to-year fluctuations in the world wheat trade since 1960 have been accounted for by swings in Soviet wheat trade.[5]

**5  International Aspects**  Two implications of the growing role of export markets for American farm products merit comment at this point. First, the recent upsurge of our agricultural exports has been very helpful in dealing with our balance of payments problem (Chapters 43 and 44). Crudely put, the earnings from our growing farm exports have been helpful in financing our rapidly expanding imports of petroleum. Second, it is estimated that about two-thirds of our agricultural ex-

[5] *Economic Report of the President, 1975* (Washington), p. 173.

ports are subject to some form of restrictive trade barriers in foreign markets. It is obviously of great importance to the prosperity of American farmers that protected foreign markets be opened to our agricultural exports.

△  **Where Are We?**

By the mid-1970s the rise in farm prices leveled off. Indeed, bumper crops in 1976 and 1977 brought about declining prices for many crops and generated appeals for government aid. In response Congress passed the *Food and Agriculture Act of 1977* which resurrected price and income supports of the pre-1970s era and created a *grain reserve program*. Under this program output will be added to a reserve to cut market supply when prices are low and sales from the reserve will supplement supply when farm prices are unusually high. In short, the grain reserve is designed to stabilize farm prices and incomes around long-term market trends. Hence, as we enter a new decade, it is not at all clear that government involvement in agricultural markets will decrease in accordance with the underlying philosophy of the Agriculture and Consumer Protection Act of 1973 or whether we are returning to the price and income support programs of the 1950s and 1960s.

## Summary

1  Rapid technological advance, coupled with a highly inelastic and relatively constant demand for agricultural output, has caused low farm incomes. Because of the relatively fixed nature of both property and human resources, the price system has failed to correct the farm problem by reallocating sufficient amounts of resources out of agriculture. In the short run, the highly inelastic nature of agricultural demand translates small changes in output and small shifts in demand into large fluctuations in prices and incomes.

2  The two basic arguments for public assistance to agriculture are *a.* farmers have borne a disproportionately large share of the costs of economic progress, and *b.* farmers have little market power, compared with other sectors of the economy.

3  Historically, agricultural policy has been price-centered and based upon the parity concept. The application of price supports, based upon the parity concept, gives rise to surplus agricultural output. The government has pursued a variety of programs to reduce the supply of, and increase the demand for, agricultural products in order to limit the size of these surpluses.

**4**  Farm policy has been criticized for treating symptoms (low incomes) rather than causes (resource misallocation) and for maintaining the inverse relationship between the size of farm subsidies and economic need.

**5**  Owing largely to substantial increases in export demand, agriculture enjoyed considerable prosperity in the early 1970s. Consequences of this prosperity include rapidly rising domestic food prices and the reduction of excess productive capacity.

**6**  The Agriculture and Consumer Protection Act of 1973 shifted agricultural policy in the direction of freer markets, encourages all-out food production, and imposes a maximum $20,000 limit on commodity subsidies per farmer.

## Questions and Study Suggestions

**1**  Key terms and concepts to remember: long-run farm problem; short-run farm problem; Agricultural Adjustment Act of 1933; parity concept; parity ratio; price supports; Public Law 480; Food for Peace program; acreage allotment program; soil bank; Agriculture and Consumer Protection Act of 1973; target price; Food and Agriculture Act of 1977; grain reserve program.

**2**  Explain how each of the following contributes to the farm problem: *a.* the inelasticity of the demand for farm products, *b.* rapid technological progress in farming, *c.* the modest long-run growth in the demand for farm commodities, *d.* the competitiveness of agriculture, and *e.* the relative fixity or immobility of agricultural resources.

**3**  What relationship, if any, can you detect between the fact that the farmer's fixed costs of production are large and the fact that the supply of most agricultural products is generally inelastic? Be specific in your answer.

**4**  "The supply and demand for agricultural products are such that small changes in agricultural supply will result in drastic changes in prices. However, large changes in farm prices have modest effects on agricultural output." Carefully evaluate. *Hint:* A brief review of the distinction between *supply* and *quantity supplied* may be of assistance.

**5**  "The whole process of economic growth is one of making agriculture less fundamental in the economic system."[6] Evaluate this statement.

**6**  The key to efficient resource allocation is the shifting of resources from low-productivity to high-productivity uses. Given the high and expanding physical productivity of agricultural resources, explain why many economists want to get more resources out of farming in the interest of greater allocative efficiency.

**7**  "Industry complains of the higher taxes it must pay to finance subsidies to agriculture. Yet the fact that the trend of agricultural prices has been downward while industrial prices have been moving upward suggests that on balance agriculture is actually subsidizing industry." Explain and evaluate.

**8**  "Because consumers as a whole must ultimately pay the total incomes received by farmers, it makes no real difference whether this income is paid through free farm markets or through supported prices supplemented by subsidies financed out of tax revenues." Do you agree?

**9**  Suppose you are the president of a local chapter of one of the major farm organizations. You are directed by the chapter's membership to formulate policy statements for the chapter which cover the following topics: *a.* antitrust policy, *b.* monetary policy, *c.* fiscal policy, and *d.* tariff policy. Briefly outline the policy statements which will best serve the interests of farmers. What is the rationale underlying each statement? Do you see any conflicts or inconsistencies in your policy statements?

[6]Lauren Soth, *Farm Trouble* (Princeton, N.J.: Princeton University Press, 1957), p. 40.

**10**   Explain and evaluate the following statements:

*a.*   "Price supports intensify rather than resolve the farm problem."

*b.*   "The best farm program is the Employment Act of 1946."

*c.*   "The trouble with parity prices in agriculture is that they strip the price mechanism of its ability to allocate resources."

**11**   Reconcile these two statements: "The farm problem is one of overproduction." "Despite the tremendous productive capacity of American agriculture, plenty of Americans are going hungry."   What assumptions about the price system are implied in your answer?

**12**   Briefly describe the Agriculture and Consumer Protection Act of 1973.   Is it a significant departure from prior farm legislation?   Justify your answer.

**13**   What factors account for the great increase in American farm exports in the 1970s? Do you feel these factors are sustainable?

## Selected References

Duncan, Marvin R., Blaine W. Bickel, and Glenn H. Miller, Jr.: *International Trade and American Agriculture* (Federal Reserve Bank of Kansas City, 1976).

*Economic Report of the President, 1980* (Washington), pp. 147–155.

Goodwin, John W.: *Agricultural Economics* (Reston, Virginia: Reston Publishing Company, 1977), chaps. 5–14.

Halcrow, Harold G.: *Economics of Agriculture* (New York: McGraw-Hill Book Company, 1980), particularly chaps. 9 and 10.

Harshbarger, C. Edward, and Richard D. Rees: "The New Farm Program—What Does It Mean?" *Monthly Review,* Federal Reserve Bank of Kansas City, January 1974.

Joint Economic Committee: *Economic Problems of Rural America* (Washington, D.C., 1977).

Paarlberg, Don: *Farm and Food Policy: Issues of the 1980s* (Lincoln, Nebraska: University of Nebraska Press, 1980).

# LAST WORD
## Profess Faith, Do Otherwise

An expert on agricultural policy takes a critical look at the goals of farmers.

The *Des Moines Register* discovered recently that 76 percent of the farm men and women of Iowa favor a "free market economy" instead of government price supports and loans. This was based on interviews with a representative cross section of farm people.

But 76 percent of this same group said the government should not allow the importing of meat, and 71 percent said the government should raise its price support for corn.

It would be hard to think of a more glaring contradiction between political theory and practice. Are these farmers hypocrites? I think not. In saying they favor a free market, they are expressing a philosophy of independence and self-reliance—and faith in the theoretical virtues of a free-market economy, which is part of the American creed.

There's no real thought behind matters of faith. It's like professing faith in Christianity. Everybody understands that doesn't mean you have to practice it; or at least that you have latitude to define its doctrines as you please.

In the real world of farm politics, farmers see advantages for themselves in government intervention in the markets on their side, such as keeping out foreign competition or buying farm products to raise the price.

Some American Agriculture Movement enthusiasts argued fiercely that they did not want government supports or subsidies—they wanted 100 percent of parity "in the marketplace." How would they accomplish this? By having Congress enact a law requiring buyers of farm products to pay full parity prices.

Inconsistency (hypocrisy or ignorance, if you please) are not confined to people who live on farms. Steel industry executives do not even blush when they declare their devotion to "free enterprise" while exhorting the government to shield them from foreign competition. The same goes for the leaders of the shoe industry, the textile industry, the chemical industry—you name it.

Their eyes glaze over as they speak in hushed tones of the free market—especially oligopolists who fear an antitrust suit for price-fixing.

Everybody wants some sort of protection from the government. The cattle industry, of course, wants to stop imports of beef. But everybody advocates free markets in principle.

It is obvious that what most people mean by free markets is free markets for the other guy—the one you buy from. Make this fellow practice price competition and get his prices down; that's the American way.

Lauren Soth, "Profess Faith, Do Otherwise," *Lincoln Evening Journal,* April 27, 1979. Reprinted by permission.

# Urban Economics: The Problems of the Cities

# chapter 36

America's cities are a curious paradox. They are the depositories of great wealth and the source of abundant incomes; they are the nucleus of economic activity and opportunity. Yet these same cities simultaneously embody blighted neighborhoods, faltering school systems, an acutely deteriorating physical environment, and a growing sense of social unrest and alienation.[1]

> Fly over Manhattan or Nob Hill or the Chicago Loop and the breathtaking skyline will excite your pride with the very grandeur of the American achievement. These towering symbols give dramatic character to the core of our giant cities. But their shadows cannot hide the disgrace at their feet.

There we find the decayed and decaying center cities, traffic-clogged, smoke-polluted, crime-ridden, recreationally barren. It is there we find the segregated slum with its crumbling tenement house, waiting to crush the hope of the Negro and displaced farmer who has pursued his dream into the city. There too we find the suburbs ringing the cities in their rapid, undisciplined growth with ugly, congested webs of ticky-tacky houses and macadam-burst shopping centers. . . .

How have we built, or let build, this somewhat lacking, somehow defective, maculate home for man?

This chapter will explore a number of the paradoxes and problems posed by the dominant role of the city in American life. First, what is the economic rationale for the evolution of cities? Why have cities developed and grown? A second and closely related objective is to explain the more recent phenomenon of

[1]Terry Sanford, "The States and the Cities: The Unfinished Agenda," in Brian J. L. Berry and Jack Meltzer (eds.), *Goals for Urban America* (Englewood Cliffs, N.J.: Prentice-Hall, Inc., 1967), pp. 52–53.

suburban growth. What economic considerations underlie urban sprawl? Next, we will consider some problems which have been spawned by the dynamics of urban growth. These include transportation problems, environmental pollution, and central-city poverty. Finally, we will consider some possible solutions to the problems of the cities.

As a prelude to these questions and issues, we must first determine the extent to which the United States is urbanized. Today the United States is clearly an urban nation. But, as Table 36-1 indicates, this has not always been so. Musty records reveal that in 1790 some 95 percent of our population lived in rural areas, mostly on farms. But by 1920 a majority of the population had become urban. Currently, over three-fourths of our population is located in urban areas. While future demographic changes are difficult to forecast, there is no question that the United States is—and will continue to be—a nation of city dwellers.

**TABLE 36-1**
Urban Population Growth in the United States (*in millions*)

| Year | Urban population | Rural population | Urban as a percent of total population |
|------|------------------|------------------|----------------------------------------|
| 1790 | .2 | 3.7 | 5 |
| 1810 | .5 | 6.7 | 7 |
| 1830 | 1.1 | 11.7 | 9 |
| 1850 | 3.5 | 19.6 | 15 |
| 1870 | 9.9 | 28.7 | 25 |
| 1890 | 22.1 | 40.8 | 35 |
| 1910 | 42.0 | 50.0 | 46 |
| 1930 | 69.0 | 53.8 | 56 |
| 1950 | 96.5 | 54.2 | 64 |
| 1970 | 149.8 | 53.9 | 73 |
| 1975 | 155.9 | 57.3 | 73 |
| 1980* | 197.0 | 53.0 | 79 |

* Projected.
*Source:* U.S. Bureau of the Census. "Urban areas" are defined by the Census Bureau as cities and other incorporated places which have 2500 or more inhabitants.

## □ WHY CITIES DEVELOP

There are substantial economic reasons why modern cities have evolved and grown. Let us look at these reasons—the economic rationale for cities—in both general and specific terms. Consider first the production or supply aspect of this rationale.

### △ In General: Where to Produce?

The decision about where certain kinds of businesses should locate is as important as the decision to produce, say, more television sets and fewer radios. The very important question of business location was hidden in Chapter 5's discussion of the Five Fundamental Questions. In fact, the question of organizing production—*how* to produce?—implies the problem of location, or *where* to produce. Our analysis of the firm (particularly in Chapter 25) implicitly assumed that all production took place at some fixed geographic point. In effect, we supposed that the market for inputs was located at the firm's back door, and the market for outputs at its front door. This is obviously unrealistic; transportation or transfer costs are involved both in getting raw materials and other inputs to the plant and in delivering the finished product to buyers. Production decisions have a spatial or locational aspect.

Stated differently, one of the important costs in organizing resources for production is the cost of overcoming geographic space, that is, the amounts of time and resources necessary for transportation and communication. If producers locate close to those from whom they purchase inputs and to those to whom they sell their outputs, transportation and communication costs will obviously be reduced. Crudely put, there are economic advantages accruing to firms which agglomerate, that is, locate in proximity to one another and to their markets. These spatial advantages are fundamental to the economic rationale of urban growth.

### △ In Particular: Economies of Agglomeration

But let us back up and explain the economic reasons for the evolution of cities in more detail. In the first place, the necessary condition for the development of cities is the capacity of a nation's agriculture to produce surplus food and fiber. The rapidly expanding productivity of American agriculture, detailed in Chapter 35, has freed the vast majority of our population from farming so that this labor might turn to the production of nonagricultural goods and services. Because man is a social animal and because specialized industrial production demands large numbers of workers, it was only natural that labor, when released from an increasingly efficient agriculture, would cluster in villages, towns, and cities.

Although an increasingly efficient agricultural sector has "pushed" labor out of farming, it has been *economies of agglomeration* which have "pulled" population and industry to the villages, towns, and cities. What specifically are agglomeration economies? Generally speaking, agglomeration economies refer to the "cheapening" of production or marketing which results from the fact that firms locate relatively close to one another. The economies which result from such agglomeration are of several interrelated and admittedly overlapping types.

**Internal Economies of Scale**   Perhaps the simplest basis for spatial concentration is the economies of large-scale production. Recall that where economies of scale are substantial, reasonably efficient production will be possible only with a few producers relative to the total market. This suggests that one large producer can serve a number of market areas more cheaply than can many small, decentralized producers. Cities have large populations and therefore large potential markets which give producers the opportunity to move down their long-run average-cost curves and achieve low unit costs (Figure 25-7a).

**Locational (Transport) Economies**   The location of business enterprise is strongly influenced by the availability of transportation facilities. Transport costs will obviously be higher for a firm if required inputs and markets for outputs are not readily accessible. Hence, at any given time the locational choice of a firm will be strongly influenced by the existing transportation network. It is no accident that our major cities historically have grown around low-cost natural or man-made transportation nodes, that is, along seaboards (New York, San Francisco), on major rivers (St. Louis), or around railroad terminals (Chicago).

Perhaps less obvious as an incentive to agglomeration is the matter of "industrial linkages." Technological progress has caused the chain of goods production and assembly to become longer and more complex. The outputs of a growing number of firms and industries constitute the inputs of still other firms and industries. This growing specialization in production means that industrially linked firms can realize substantial economies in transportation and communication by locating in proximity. It is not difficult to see why the attraction of industry and therefore of population to the cities tends to be a self-perpetuating process. For obvious reasons, the location of an automobile assembly plant in a given city may induce tire and glass producers, for example, to locate plants in the same area. In turn, the existence of the glass and tire plants may induce still another automobile manufacturer to establish an assembly plant in the area. And so it goes.

**Urban Economies: Specialization and Infrastructure**   The foregoing discussion of internal economies of scale and locational economies is not sufficient to explain fully the phenomenon of urban growth. Nor does it explain why the larger cities have grown at the expense of the smaller cities. A more complete explanation involves *external economies of specialization* and the *infrastructure* of urban areas.

The economies of scale discussed earlier were labeled "internal economies of scale" because their realization depends solely upon the decisions and fortunes of individual firms. In other words, technology confronts the firm with a *given* average-cost curve which declines over a very substantial range, such as in Figure 25-7a, and it is entirely up to the firm to achieve the high levels of production prerequisite to low unit costs. Now we must consider scale economies of a different type. Specifically, there may exist certain economies which cause the average-cost curves of firms to *shift* downward. These downward shifts of the average-cost curves of individual firms depend upon the expansion of the entire *industry* or group of firms, not of the single *firm*. Therefore, such economies are called *external economies of scale,* for their realization lies beyond, or is external to, the actions and decisions of any single firm.

Specifically, as a number of firms agglomerate, they may *as a group* be able to realize lower input prices and therefore lower cost curves than if they were geographically dispersed. That is, as firms agglomerate, it tends to become profitable for specialized firms to perform certain functions for the industry on a larger scale—and therefore more cheaply—than can each firm internally. For example, prior to agglomeration a manufacturer may be forced to repair its own machinery or conduct its own technological or marketing research. But, as the number of firms in an industry, or even in different industries, concentrate in an area, the volume of repair or research business of the firms as a group becomes sufficient to support one or more firms specializing in these functions. The agglomerated firms can realize lower input prices—and lower unit costs—by "farming out" these functions to specialists rather than undertaking the tasks themselves.

This growing specialization obviously leads to an increased interdependence among various types of manufacturing and service establishments. Thus, the location of the individual establishments which are highly interdependent is, in a sense, determined simultaneously. Broadly speaking, producers of final goods must have easy access both to the inter-mediate goods and services needed as inputs and to the markets for their final product. Similarly, the suppliers of intermediate goods and services must have easy access to markets sufficient in scale to realize internal economies of large-scale production. It follows that the solution for both groups is the same—to cluster in cities that alone can provide both inputs and markets in sufficient scale and variety to meet their total needs. Thus, it is not difficult to see why the attraction of industry and therefore of population to the cities tends to be a self-perpetuating, cumulative process.

Another illustration: The geographic concentration of many firms requiring, say, unskilled and semiskilled labor may attract large pools of these kinds of labor to the area. The result? Lower wage rates for labor inputs and therefore lower average costs for the firms.

The *infrastructure* of an urban area is a source of economies or cost advantages not entirely unlike external economies of scale. Specifically, a city provides its firms with important services and facilities upon which producers rely and which would be costly for each firm to provide in the small amounts it alone needs. This infrastructure comprises such obvious things as ample water, electrical power, waste treatment facilities, transportation facilities, educational research and engineering facilities, financial and banking institutions, management and public relations consultants, and so forth.

A rich and varied infrastructure may be the strongest agglomerative force explaining the continuing and persistent growth of our largest urban areas. For example, one of the conclusions of a study of the New York metropolitan area is that even though the New York metropolitan area has lost nearly every industry it has ever had—flour mills, foundries, meat-packing plants, textile mills, and tanneries—the area continues to grow and earn above-average income. The report states that New York's propensity for growth and above-average income can be attributed to its rich infrastructure which attracts new enterprises that require highly specialized and sophisticated services.

## △  Demand Considerations

Aside from the importance of market demand as a requisite for firms and industries to realize both internal and external economies of scale, market demand plays another role in explaining urban growth. The large populations of the cities mean that a wider variety of products and services are available. Put bluntly, while the populations of Chicago and Philadelphia will generate a market demand sufficient to support Chinese restaurants and shops specializing in exotic imports, the demand for such products in Grand Mound, Iowa, or Eureka, Montana, is insufficient to make such enterprises profitable. Similarly, the live theater, symphony orchestras, highly specialized medical and professional facilities, and professional athletics are commercially feasible only in larger cities. In general, many of the refinements and amenities of modern life are urban-based because of adequate demand. This means that cities are places not only where goods and services can be produced more cheaply, but also where consumers can attain a higher level of satisfaction because of a finer matching of their wants with the wider variety of available goods and services.

## △  Deglomerative Forces

The advantages of agglomeration cannot be reaped indefinitely. Beyond some critical and difficult-to-specify point—a point which many of our larger cities have apparently passed—continued city growth and geographic concentration of industry will tend to create counterforces which give rise to higher production costs. That is, continued efforts to realize the economies of agglomeration may create certain offsetting diseconomies, or what might be termed *deglomerative forces*. Certain costs associated with geographic concentration are internal to, and therefore must be borne by, the producers themselves. For example, a growing concentration of industry in a given geographic area will mean higher land values and rents. (Figure 32-1 reminds us that a rising demand for a perfectly inelastic supply of centrally located sites will have a large price effect.) In turn, rising land values will make it increasingly costly for new firms to locate in an area or for existing firms to expand facilities. Furthermore, the intensified demand for labor which accompanies industrial agglomeration may be reflected in increased bargaining power for workers and rising wage costs.

*But many of the disadvantages and problems associated with urbanization stem from externalities or spillovers.* That is, within the context of the city the marketplace simply fails to correctly charge or reward individuals and businesses for their decisions. Consider spillover costs. As producers agglomerate in an urban area, air and water pollution may become so severe as to make the city a decidedly less attractive place for additional firms and households to locate. Similarly, beyond some point traffic congestion (a form of pollution) slows deliveries of both inputs and finished products, making the city a more costly environment in which to operate. Urban blight is largely a problem of spillover costs. Landlords who decide it is in their own self-interest to allow their properties to fall into disrepair are deteriorating the quality of the entire neighborhood, making it a less attractive place for households and businesses to locate. Rundown properties "pollute" a neighborhood in the same general way as do factory smokestacks.

Have deglomerative forces become sufficiently important in recent years so that they offset some of the advantages of agglomeration? Recent changes in urbanization patterns seem to indicate that this is the case. The growth of suburbia, the decentralization of central business districts, and the recent resurgence in the growth of smaller cities and towns are consistent with the notion that deglomerative forces are at work. Note, however, that the simple fact of urban growth will result in urban spread—the fanning out of people and businesses from the central city.

## ☐ THE FLIGHT TO THE SUBURBS: URBAN SPRAWL

This brief introduction to the economies and diseconomies of agglomeration helps explain the paradox stated at the outset of this chapter. The cities are centers of great wealth and income. They are centers of economic activity and for many people a magnet of economic opportunity. But the very growth and maturation of the modern city spawn spillover costs, not to mention the inevitable social tensions which characterize areas of high population density. These latter features of the cities obviously tend to make urban life less attractive. Hence, actual or potential urban residents—both businesses and households—ask themselves this question: How can the advantages and opportunities of the metropolitan area be realized without also incurring the disadvantages? How can one tap the economic activity of the city and realize a higher income *and* at the same time enjoy fresh air, space, privacy, and tranquillity?

Millions of more affluent Americans have answered: Move to the suburbs! It is significant that the percentage of our population living in the central city has actually been declining since the turn of the century; virtually all our metropolitan population growth has been in the suburbs. Many factors have contributed to this rapid growth. Rising postwar incomes, abetted by governmentally guaranteed mortgage credit, have made suburban living accessible to more and more families. Automobile ownership, as a convenient means of commuting, has been an important permissive factor.

Suburban growth has resulted not merely in the relocation of people, but also in the movement of businesses. The reasons for this are complex and diverse.[2] In the first place, it is easy to see why many of the retail and personal service industries—groceries, hardware

and furniture stores, laundries and cleaners, barber and beauty shops—have moved to the suburbs. Such establishments must be close to people; in particular, to people who have money! But many manufacturing firms have also fled the central city. We have already hit upon a couple of reasons for such shifts. Rising land costs make plant expansion very costly in the central city. And spillover costs make downtown locations less attractive. Firms which are large enough to have their own truck transportation encounter costly problems of traffic congestion, loading and parking, and so forth. In addition, technological changes have encouraged many manufacturers to migrate to the suburbs. The rapid development of truck transportation has freed many firms from the need to locate near downtown railroad terminals and harbor facilities. Perhaps more important is the great emphasis that modern production technology has put upon highly integrated, continuous processes which assume an extensive one-story plant layout. Space for the utilization of this technology is not available—or only available at prohibitive cost—in the central city.

This is not to suggest that *all* major businesses have fled to the suburbs. Certain kinds of businesses have remained—and prospered—in the central cities:[3]

> These are the highly specialized areas of finance, business services, and central office administration, whose inputs are skill or knowledge or information, whose outputs are not goods but service or advice or decisions. It is these establishments—banks and law offices, advertising agencies and central administrative offices, consulting firms and government agencies—which are filling more and more of the central cities of most urban areas, and are becoming the primary function of . . . the city's central business district.

Overall, however, the trend has been to the suburbs.

---

[2]The following discussion is based upon Benjamin Chinitz (ed.), *City and Suburb* (Englewood Cliffs, N.J.: Prentice-Hall, Inc., 1964), pp. 23–27.

[3]Ibid., p. 26.

△   **Political Fragmentation**

This dramatic flight to the suburbs has been accompanied by the political balkanization of our large cities. That is, the central cities have become encircled with a large number of new suburbs, each of which is a separate political entity. Figure 36-1 shows the case of St. Louis. The St. Louis urban area is served by 474 local governments which are almost equally divided between Illinois and Missouri. These 474 governmental units include over 100 separate municipalities. St. Louis is hardly an exceptional case. There are over 1400 separate units of government in the New York City metropolitan area and almost 1000 in the San Francisco Bay area.

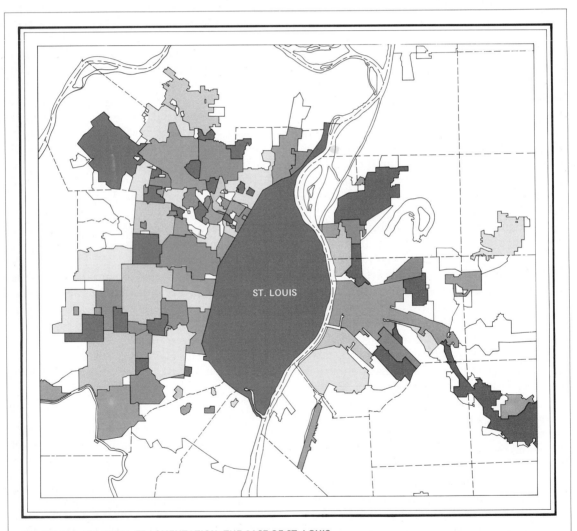

FIGURE 36-1  POLITICAL FRAGMENTATION: THE CASE OF ST. LOUIS

The dynamics of urban expansion has given rise to the growth of numerous politically distinct subdivisions around the central city. The 474 units of local government which comprise the St. Louis metropolitan area are quite typical of this political balkanization. (*Advisory Commission on Intergovernmental Relations, Urban America and the Federal System, Washington, 1969, p. 85.*)

△ **Economic Imbalance and Cumulative Decline**

Political fragmentation is the source of many urban problems. But it is particularly troublesome because the process of urban decentralization or suburban growth has brought about a highly unequal distribution of wealth and incomes geographically. The more prosperous people and many of the newer and more profitable industries have fled the central city in favor of the suburbs. By and large, the poor people and many of the less profitable industries have been left behind in the central city.

This dramatic process of change in the structure of metropolitan areas has been self-reinforcing and cumulative. The migration of both the wealthier people and businesses to new political entities in the suburbs seriously erodes the property tax base of the central cities.[4] New plants and new housing are built in the suburban ring, not in the central cities. To maintain public services, property tax *rates* must be increased in the central city. But these rising rates further motivate households and businesses to flee to the suburbs.

Furthermore, the poor, predominantly black families who by virtue of their poverty and discrimination are left behind in the central cities, are "high cost" citizens. An unusually high percentage are on welfare. Children are numerous, and education costs are high. High population densities—New York's Harlem has 67,000 people per square mile—mean that the costs of governing, of collecting garbage, of maintaining law and order are high.

All this is complicated and given further impetus by the fact that central-city decay, or urban blight, tends to be a cumulative process.[5]

The older structures concentrated near the city center lose their economic usefulness as the functions of the downtown areas change. Extensive conversion, rehabilitation, and reconstruction are needed. If a few buildings need to be replaced or renovated in an otherwise prosperous area, the market provides private developers and builders with sufficient incentives to undertake the work. However, when a pattern of decay permeates a large area, the dilapidation of neighboring buildings reduces the profitability of improving a particular property. A large area must then be improved as a single unit, and the cost and difficulties of acquiring and redeveloping a large tract of central city land are likely to deter private investors from the undertaking.

To summarize: The basic consequence of the dynamics of urban growth and the accompanying political fragmentation has been "to forge a white, middle- and high-income noose around the increasingly black and poor inner city. . . ." The losers in the flight to politically splintered suburbs have been the central cities, saddled with an inadequate and shrinking tax base and the burgeoning expenditure demands "incident to the governing, educating, and 'welfaring' of an increasing proportion of relatively poor [and usually] black families."[6] The winners, on the other hand, have been the more wealthy white suburban localities wherein income and wealth have been sufficient to underwrite viable public services with relatively modest tax efforts.

The dynamics of urban growth and the crazy quilt of political entities which has accompanied this growth have spawned a host of acute and interrelated problems. Let us now briefly survey some of these problems and sketch possible avenues for their resolution. Although the problems of the cities are manifold and not subject to simple classification, we will concentrate on three main problem areas: urban transportation, the ghettos and central-city poverty, and pollution.

---

[4] Recall from Table 8-4 that property taxes are the main source of revenue for local units of government.
[5] *Economic Report of the President, 1965,* pp. 149–150.

[6] Advisory Commission on Intergovernmental Relations, *Urban America and the Federal System* (Washington, 1969), pp. 2, 8.

## ☐ THE URBAN TRANSPORTATION PROBLEM

We have seen that one fundamental characteristic of urban growth is the direct relationship one finds between distance from the central city and income and wealth. Generally speaking, those living furthest from "downtown" are the professional, technical, and white-collar workers. A large proportion of these higher-income people work downtown; that is, they are employed in the banking and financial firms, the legal and consulting firms, and the advertising agencies which have remained in the central city. On the other hand, we have seen that many kinds of manufacturing, wholesale, retail, and personal service industries—industries which require blue-collar and less skilled workers—have moved to suburbia. The result is a significant locational mismatch of jobs and labor force between suburbs and central city. This mismatch creates the need for an effective transportation system to negotiate the required cross-hauling of the population.

But the need for efficient transportation is even more pervasive. Accessibility is the *sine qua non* of effective participation in urban life. Most of the cultural and social advantages of city life can only be efficiently realized through a viable transportation system. Museums, art galleries, and concert halls are indivisible, or "lumpy," social goods; since they cannot be divided and taken home by consumers, the consumer must go to them. Similarly, comparative shopping in the city assumes adequate transportation.

Given the convenience of private automobile travel, most suburbanites have chosen this form of transportation. Furthermore, large Federal subsidies to highway construction have created a substantial financial bias in favor of the automobile. But, ironically, dramatic increases in metropolitan automobile use and highway construction—Los Angeles is the classic case—have not solved the transportation problem. Indeed, the expanded use of auto transportation has given rise to increasingly acute problems of traffic congestion, not to mention the automobile's substantial contribution to air pollution. The response to traffic congestion, of course, has been to construct more highways. But the additional highways permit the growth of still more distant suburbs and elicit more traffic. Alas, more highways beget more autos. So mammoth highway construction programs have been accompanied by more—not less—traffic congestion and parking problems. We have witnessed a vicious cycle of more autos, more highways which induce more autos, and the construction of still more highways.

The other side of the coin has been the general deterioration of the mass-transit systems of the cities. The vast geographic dispersion of population throughout the suburbs has made it difficult for mass-transit systems to realize the heavy trunk-line operations requisite to their prosperity or survival. Again, we encounter a cumulative process. As patronage declines, unit costs rise and commuter fares must be increased, on the one hand, and the quality of both equipment and service deteriorates, on the other. So more people choose to drive their cars to work, and the process repeats itself.

Unfortunately, not all people can afford the automobile–mass-transit choice. The poor and less skilled of the central city must rely upon mass transit. Shrinkage and service deterioration of the transit system, accompanied by the shift of blue-collar jobs to the suburbs, unfortunately leave many of the central-city residents isolated from the economic opportunities of the metropolitan area.

## ☐ IMPROVING URBAN TRANSPORTATION

In considering possible solutions, it is both convenient and meaningful to consider the urban transport problem in two parts: the short-run problem and the long-run problem.

△  **The Short Run: User Charges and Peak Pricing**

First, there is a short-run problem: *Given existing transportation facilities and technology,* how can this transportation "plant" be used most efficiently? What is the best way of utilizing *existing* freeway–street-parking and mass-transit facilities? We have already noted that, historically, governmental subsidies have been heavily biased in favor of automobile transportation. Specifically, urban freeway and street construction has been heavily subsidized by Federal grants; financing also comes from state gasoline-tax revenues. A number of urban economists feel that a system of *user charges* on drivers would be very useful in achieving a better balance in the use of mass transit and auto transportation and, in particular, in alleviating the problem of traffic congestion. They contend that the city's streets and highways are overused and congested because drivers do not bear the full cost of driving; they are in fact subsidized by society (taxpayers) at large. More specifically, it is argued that automobile drivers should be confronted "as near as possible in time and place to the act of making the decision to drive" with a price—a user charge—which covers the full cost of driving. By "full cost" is meant not only the cost of highway construction and repair but also the cost of traffic control devices and traffic police and even automobile pollution costs. Price, after all, is a rationing device or disciplining mechanism, and traffic congestion is a symptom of quantity demanded in excess of quantity supplied at the going price. "Surely, we would have traffic jams in the aisles of food stores and 'shortages' of food if we tried to administer free food stores supported by general taxation. The food shortages would be analogous to the shortages of street space per automobile (traffic jams) and the shortages of parking places that characterize our underpriced and tax-supported urban transportation industry."[7]

What specifically will be the effects of a system of user charges on drivers? First, some will be rationed out of the "driving market"; that is, they will use the public transportation system or, if they have the option, will make fewer trips downtown. This response, of course, has the desired effect of relieving traffic congestion. Second, those who continue to drive will contribute more funds for the expansion and improvement of highway and parking facilities.

Recognizing that the morning and evening rush hours are the focal points of the urban transportation problem, many advocates of user charges also contend that the pricing of both auto and mass-transit facilities should vary according to the time of day. That is, *peak pricing* should be used; charges should be higher during the peak or rush hours and lower during off-peak hours. The purpose, of course, is to "ration out" travelers whose need to travel during rush hours is less pressing or less necessary. For example, shoppers might be induced by a system of peak prices to alter the timing of their trips to and from downtown so that they do not coincide with the travel times of commuting workers.

Those who favor user charges admit that significant problems of application exist. For example, how does one calculate the costs of air pollution, noise, and delay, and the opportunity cost of the land used in freeway and street construction in determining the full cost of an automobile trip to the downtown area? Then, too, there is the difficult problem of assessing and collecting user charges from drivers; can tolls be collected without creating toll station bottlenecks? Or is it possible to "include highly sophisticated electronic sensing devices mounted on cars and in the streets, which could result in computer-written monthly bills to motorists . . . , charging them more for the use of congested routes in crowded hours"?[8]

---

[7] Wilbur R. Thompson, *A Preface to Urban Economics* (Baltimore: The Johns Hopkins Press, 1965), pp. 340–341.

[8] Dick Netzer, *Economics and Urban Problems,* 2d ed. (New York: Basic Books, Inc., Publishers, 1974), p. 211.

### △  The Long Run: Mass Transit

This brings us to the long-run aspect of the urban transportation problem: What should be the character of future public investments in urban transportation facilities? For a variety of reasons, there has been a revival of interest in the revitalization and development of public mass-transit systems—commuter railroads, subways, buses, monorails, and so forth. First, given projections of suburban population growth and the consequent possibility that the volume of urban automobile traffic may double in the next twenty years, many city planners and public officials feel that effective alternatives to auto transportation are imperative. This is particularly so in view of the previously noted point that increased investment in streets and freeways often seems to induce a higher volume of traffic, rather than relieve congestion. Second, the energy crisis and soaring gasoline prices have made private automobile transportation decidely less attractive. Third, interest in public mass transit has been stimulated by the recognition that past transportation subsidies have favored the automobile and that there is now a need to achieve a better balance between auto and mass transit. Finally, it is felt that an expanded and improved mass-transit system can yield substantial social benefits in terms of (1) a viable and revitalized central city with an expanding property tax base, (2) greater accessibility to suburban jobs for the central-city poor, and (3) avoidance of an increasingly acute pollution problem which an expansion of automobile transportation is likely to entail.

Recent Federal mass transit legislation has provided substantial funds for the revitalization and technological improvement of public transportation systems. It should be emphasized, however, that the solution—if there is one—to the urban transportation problem will not entail an either-or choice; some workable combination of automobile and public mass transit will be essential to a viable transportation system.

### ▢  THE POLLUTION PROBLEM: THE EFFLUENT SOCIETY?

Cities do not have a monopoly on the pollution problem. Yet, the high population densities and high levels of industrial concentration which are the earmarks of urban life make pollution problems most acute in the cities.

### △  Dimensions of the Problem

The seriousness of water, air, and solid-waste pollution has been well documented in the popular press and needs only brief review here. We know that rivers and lakes have been turned into municipal and industrial sewers. Not only has Lake Erie deteriorated into a national cesspool, but the Cuyahoga River which feeds into it has become so permeated with sludge and oil that it has been labeled a fire hazard! Leaks from offshore wells have plagued the Southern California and Gulf coasts. The drainage of DDT into streams and lakes has imperiled our fish and bird populations. Almost half our population drinks water of dubious quality. Air pollution contributes to lung cancer, emphysema, pneumonia, and other respiratory diseases. The toxic substances in New York City's air make a day's walking and breathing the equivalent of smoking two packages of cigarettes.[9] Cynics tell us that one wakes up in Los Angeles to the sound of birds coughing. Each American accounts for some 2000 pounds of solid wastes—including, for example, 250 tin cans per person—each year.

---

[9] In a penetrating satire on New York City ("fume city"), Dick Schaap made this observation in *New York* magazine (April 15, 1968):

> Beyond its natural loveliness, pollution serves the city of New York in so many ways. It helps keep the City from becoming over-populated; it insures that only the fittest survive and the rest move to the suburbs. It helps keep the City from becoming overgrown with foliage; it kills roses and tulips and other harmful weeds. It provides employment for window washers and car-washers and eager little shoe-shine boys. And it saves money: it provides all the joys of cigarette smoking without any of the expenses.

Possible longer-run consequences of environmental pollution are even more disturbing. Competent scientists suggest that if current trends in automobile use continue, large, densely populated areas of our country may become uninhabitable, the source of certain suffocation. Some scientists contend that the concentrations of industry, people, structures, and cement which constitute cities might create air and heat pollution sufficient to cause irreversible and potentially disastrous changes in the earth's climate and weather patterns.

### △  Causes: Materials Balance Approach

The roots of the pollution problem can best be envisioned through the *materials balance approach,* which is the simple notion that the weight of the inputs (fuels, raw materials, water, and so forth) used in the economy's production processes will ultimately result in a roughly equivalent residual of wastes. For example, each year:[10]

> The economy . . . takes in about . . . [a] billion tons of minerals and food and forest products. Consumers use these goods in the form they receive them, or further transform them (e.g., by eating), but must sooner or later dispose of the end product, whether it be empty tin cans, "throw away" bottles, worn-out refrigerators, plastic toys or human excreta.

Fortunately, the ecological system—Nature, if you are over thirty—has the self-regenerating capacity which allows it, within limits, to absorb or recycle such wastes. But the volume of such residuals has tended to outrun this absorptive capacity.

Why has this happened? Why do we have a pollution problem? Causes are manifold, but perhaps four are paramount.

**1  Population Density**   There is the simple matter of population growth. An ecological system which may accommodate 50 or 100 million people may begin to break down under the pressures of 200 or 300 million. As noted, the absorptive capacity of our natural environment, an increasingly scarce resource, is most evident in urban areas where the concentration of population and economic activity is so great.

**2  Rising Incomes**   Per capita incomes have been rising. Industrial production, for example, has been growing at $4\frac{1}{2}$ percent per year, which means that industrial output will increase almost tenfold between 1969 and the year 2020.[11] The materials balance approach reminds us that, barring significant changes in technology or the composition of output, the total weight of wastes generated will also increase tenfold. Paradoxically, the affluent society helps to spawn the effluent society. A rising GNP (gross national product) means a rising GNG (gross national garbage). Thus a high standard of living permits Americans to own some 100 million automobiles. But autos are a primary source of air pollution and, concomitantly, give rise to the hard problem of disposing of some 7 or 8 million junked autos each year. Furthermore, the fact that more leisure has been a component of our rising standard of living has increased public awareness of the pollution problem. When you have time to spend on a beach or at a lake, you become concerned that the water may be unfit for swimming or that the fish may have been killed by thermal or chemical pollution.

**3  Technology**   Technological change is another contributor to pollution. For example, the expanded use of pesticides, herbicides, and insecticides has proved to be a deadly enemy of our fish and bird populations. The addition of lead to gasoline poses a serious threat to human health. The development and widespread use of "throw-away" containers made of virtually indestructible aluminum or plastic add substantially to the solid-waste crisis. Detergent soap products have been highly resistant to sanitary treatment and recycling.

---

[10]U.S. Department of Health, Education and Welfare, *Toward a Social Report* (Washington, 1969), p. 28.

[11]Ibid., p. 28.

**4  Incentives**  A final and crucial factor concerns economic incentives. Specifically, businesses find their private production costs will be lowered by polluting. In technical terms, pollution is a problem in spillover costs (Chapters 6 and 26). Profit-seeking manufacturers choose the least-cost combination of inputs and will find it advantageous to bear only unavoidable costs. If they can dump waste chemicals into rivers and lakes rather than pay for expensive treatment and proper disposal, businesses will be inclined to do so. If manufacturers can discharge smoke and the hot water used to cool machinery rather than purchase expensive abatement and cooling facilities, they will tend to do so. The result is air and water pollution—both chemical and thermal—and, in the economist's jargon, the shifting of certain costs to the community at large as spillover costs. Enjoying lower "internal" costs than if they had not polluted the environment, the producers can sell their products more cheaply, expand their production, and realize larger profits. The supply curve of a polluting firm or industry lies too far to the right because it omits the cost which society bears in the form of a debased environment. The result is an overallocation of resources to the polluter's commodity.

But it is neither just nor accurate to lay the entire blame for pollution at the door of industry. On the one hand, a well-intentioned firm which wants to operate in a socially responsible way with respect to pollution finds itself in an awkward position. If an individual firm "internalizes" all its external or spillover costs by installing, say, water-treatment and smoke-abatement equipment, the firm will find itself at a cost disadvantage in comparison to its polluting competitors. The socially responsible firm will have higher costs and will be forced to raise its product price. The "reward" for the pollution-conscious firm is a declining market for its product, diminished profits, and, in the extreme, the prospect of bankruptcy. This correctly suggests that effective action to combat pollution must be undertaken collectively through government. On the other hand, given that an important function of government is to correct the misallocation of resources which accompany spillover costs (Chapter 6), it is ironic that most major cities are heavy contributors to the pollution problem. Municipal power plants are frequently major contributors to air pollution; many cities discharge untreated or inadequately treated sewage into rivers or lakes because it is cheap and convenient to do so. Similarly, individuals avoid the costs of proper refuse pickup and disposal by burning their garbage. We also find it easier to use throw-away containers rather than recycle "return" containers.

△  **Antipollution Policies**

Because environmental pollution is a problem in spillover or external costs,[12] the task of antipollution policy is to devise ways of "internalizing" the external costs of pollution. The objective is to make the polluter pay *all* the costs associated with its activities. In terms of Figure 6-1*b* we want to eliminate the discrepancy between private and total costs by shifting $SS$ to, or at least toward, $S_tS_t$.

**1  Legislated Standards**  One obvious approach is for governmental units to pass legislation which prohibits or regulates pollution. Legislation may establish minimum standards for air and water which polluters must observe or face legal sanctions. The legislation of pollution standards will presumably force polluters to install water-treatment and air-filter equipment and thereby to bear costs which would otherwise be shifted to society. A much-publicized illustration of this approach is Federal legislation requiring automobile manufacturers to meet exhaust-emission standards. On a broader front, the Environmental Protection Agency was established by Congress in 1969 to develop quality standards for air and water in cooperation with state and local governments.

[12] Rereading the section entitled "Spillovers or Externalities" in Chapter 6 may be useful at this point.

**2  Special Taxes: Emission Fees**  A second approach is to levy special charges or taxes—emission or effluent fees—on polluters. That is, a special tax or fee should be assessed per ton of pollutant discharged into the air or water. Ideally, fees would be set so that spillover costs would be exactly covered and each producer's cost curve would reflect *all* production costs.

For example, suppose a chemical plant is polluting a river. The resulting external costs are manifold: Other manufacturers and municipalities located downstream must pay to purify the water prior to use; businesses based upon fishing or recreational uses of the river will be injured; individuals will suffer the loss of recreational uses; the river may become a health hazard; and so forth. If a special tax or emission fee covering these spillover costs is imposed upon the chemical plant, these external costs will become internalized to the plant. The chemical firm must recalculate its cost alternatives. On the one hand, it can purchase pollution-abatement equipment and thereby reduce or eliminate the payment of emission fees. Or it can continue to pollute and pay the required fees. In the second case, government can use the revenue from the emission fees to cleanse the downstream water or to compensate injured parties. A system of water pollution fees has been used effectively in Germany's Ruhr River basin for some time.

**3  A Market for Pollution Rights**  One of the more novel policy suggestions is to create a market for pollution rights.[13] The rationale for this proposal is that the air, rivers, lakes, oceans, and public lands, such as parks and streets, are all primary objects for pollution because the *rights* to use these resources are either held "in common" by society or are unspecified by law. As a result, no specific private individual or institution has any incentive to restrict the use or maintain the purity or qual-

ity of these resources because he or she does not have the right to realize a monetary return from doing so. One maintains the property one owns—you paint and repair your home periodically—because you will capture the value of these improvements at the time of resale. But, as long as the "rights" to air, water, and certain land resources are commonly held and these resources made freely available, there will be no incentive to maintain them or restrict their use. Hence, these natural resources are "overconsumed" and thereby polluted.

The proposal is therefore made that an appropriate pollution-control agency should determine the amount of pollutants which can be discharged into the water or air of a given region each year and still maintain the quality of the water or air at some acceptable standard. For example, the agency may determine that 500 tons of pollutants may be discharged into Metropolitan Lake and be "recycled" by Nature. Hence, 500 pollution rights, each entitling the owner to dump 1 ton of pollutants into the lake in the given year, are made available for sale each year. The resulting supply of pollution rights is fixed and therefore perfectly inelastic, as shown in Figure 36-2. The demand for pollution rights will take the same downsloping form as will the demand for any other input. At high prices, polluters either will stop polluting or will pollute less by acquiring pollution-abatement equipment. Thus, a market price for pollution rights—in this case $100—will be determined at which an environment-preserving quantity of pollution rights will be rationed to polluters. Note that without this market, 750 tons of pollutants would be discharged into the lake and it would be "overconsumed," or polluted, in the amount of 250 tons. And over time, as human and business populations expand, demand will increase, as from $D_{1981}$ to $D_{1991}$. *Without* a market for pollution rights, pollution would occur in 1991 in the amount of 500 tons beyond that which can be assimilated by Nature. *With* the market for pollution rights, price will now rise from $100 to $200 and the amount of pollutants will

---

[13]J. H. Dales, *Pollution, Property and Prices* (Toronto: University of Toronto Press, 1968).

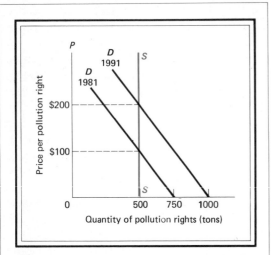

**FIGURE 36-2 THE MARKET FOR POLLUTION RIGHTS**

Pollution can be controlled by having a public body determine the amount of pollution which the atmosphere or a body of water can safely recycle and sell these limited rights to polluters. The effect is to make the environment a scarce resource with a positive price. Economic and population growth will increase the demand for pollution rights over time, but the consequence will be an increase in the price of pollution rights rather than more pollution.

remain at 500 tons—the amount which the lake can recycle.

This proposal has a number of advantages. Potential polluters are confronted with an explicit monetary incentive not to pollute. Conservation groups can fight pollution by buying up and withholding pollution rights, thereby reducing actual pollution below governmentally determined standards. As the demand for pollution rights increases over time, the growing revenue from the sale of the given quantity of pollution rights could be devoted to environment improvement. Similarly, with time the rising price of pollution rights should stimulate the search for improved techniques to control pollution.

**Problems** The problems involved in establishing and administering these antipollution proposals are both numerous and sub-

stantial. First, pollution standards are difficult to establish because of incomplete and disputed technological and biological information. We simply do not know with certainty the effects—the economic and human costs—of certain pollutants. Witness the prolonged dispute over the use of DDT. This lack of information is important because it is not economically rational to prohibit or flatly eliminate pollution, but rather to use benefit-cost analysis (Chapter 6) to determine the optimum extent to which antipollution programs should be pursued. This entails the very difficult problem of calculating the marginal benefits and marginal costs of such programs. Second, the administration and enforcement of legislated controls or standards can be both difficult and costly. Finally, governmental units—the very institutions we would expect to create and enforce antipollution policies—are themselves major polluters![14]

## ☐ THE GHETTOS: APARTHEID AMERICAN STYLE[15]

A combination of complex and interrelated forces—many of which are pointedly discussed in the Last Word section of this chapter—have given rise to central-city ghettos, populated disproportionately by blacks and other minority groups. The poverty and debased conditions of life which are pervasive in the ghettos are well known. The oldest, most deteriorated, and most crowded housing is in the central-city ghetto. In general, schools are grossly inadequate, and, as a result, ghetto students fall further behind nonghetto students with each level of school completed. Mortality rates

[14] If you are inclined to pursue the economics of pollution, you will find Thomas D. Crocker and A. J. Rogers, III, *Environmental Economics* (Hinsdale, Ill.: The Dryden Press, Inc., 1971), to be entertaining reading. Maurice F. Strong (ed.), *Who Speaks for Earth?* (New York: W. W. Norton & Company, Inc., 1973), is also recommended.

[15] The organization and content of this section follows Dick Netzer, *Economics and Urban Problems*, 2d ed. (New York: Basic Books, Inc., Publishers, 1974), chaps. 3 and 4. Netzer's book, which is both readable and perceptive, is recommended reading.

are high, the result of inadequate nutrition, high incidence of disease, drug use, insufficient medical care, deplorable levels of sanitation, and so forth. Social disintegration is acute and crime rates are high. And, perhaps most important, ghetto income levels are abysmally low; nearly 40 percent of central-city blacks live in poverty.

What combination of circumstances accounts for the ghettos? Most important, the whole process of urban decentralization is very much involved. Historically, the better-educated, better-trained, more prosperous whites have moved in large numbers from the central city to the suburbs, leaving behind obsolete housing in decaying neighborhoods. Their places have been taken by poorly educated, unskilled, low-income blacks migrating largely from the rural South, by Puerto Ricans, by Chicanos, and by Indians. Secondly, the dynamics of urban growth have shifted: "The activities which have been the traditional points of labor force entry for the urban un-skilled—manufacturing, wholesale and retail trade, construction—are precisely those that have been suburbanizing most rapidly, making entry for the central-city poor difficult indeed."[16] And this movement of jobs to the suburbs is particularly adverse because of the previously noted deterioration of the public transportation system; it is both difficult and costly for central-city residents—many of whom do not own cars—to get to the suburbs for jobs.

But, from a long-run viewpoint, racial discrimination is perhaps the most important force underlying the black ghettos. The Kerner Commission put the matter quite bluntly in asserting that past and present policies of discrimination have divided the nation into two societies, "one largely Negro and poor, located in the central cities; the other, predominantly white and affluent, located in the suburbs and outlying areas."[17] Discrimination

has taken many forms: Blacks have been denied adequate education; they have been denied entry to certain occupations; they have been paid lower wages than whites on given jobs; and they have been the last hired and the first fired (Chapter 37).

Given the complexity of the problems of the ghettos, our discussion of remedies will necessarily be brief and incomplete. To facilitate matters we will treat the human (poverty) and the physical (housing) aspects of the ghetto problem separately; in fact, they are obviously very closely interrelated.

△   **The Human Aspect:**
**Alleviating Ghetto Poverty**

How can the poverty which is endemic to the black ghetto be alleviated? The causes and characteristics of the ghettos imply possible solutions.

**1   More and Better Jobs**   Unemployment among central-city blacks is notoriously high and a major cause of poverty. The unemployment rate for nonwhites is generally twice that for whites. Black teenagers face a chronic depression; their unemployment rates are typically 25 to 35 percent! Given the present education and qualifications of the ghetto labor force, how can the unemployment situation be improved?

Two complementary approaches present themselves: Bring ghetto residents to existing jobs in the suburbs, *and* bring new jobs to the ghettos. Consider the first approach. Mobility in terms of residence is extremely difficult for ghetto dwellers. On the one hand, the incomes of most central-city blacks are so low that they simply cannot afford to move to the suburbs. On the other hand, those who can afford suburban housing are confronted with severe problems of discrimination. Real estate agencies and landlords have used a variety of both crude and subtle techniques for prohibiting or restricting these moves. Many suburban areas have purposely zoned for large minimum lot sizes and have enacted strict building and

[16] Ibid., p. 29.
[17] *Report of the National Advisory Commission on Civil Disorders* (New York: Bantam Books, 1968), p. 22.

housing codes which push up housing prices to prohibit any influx of lower-income (black) families from the central city.

Another means of making suburban employment opportunities more accessible to the ghetto labor force is to provide improved transportation facilities. We have already discussed the urban transportation problem and noted that the renewed interest in mass transit is partially motivated by the ghetto worker's need for greater accessibility to jobs located in suburban areas.

The second approach is to create new job opportunities in the ghettos. *Black capitalism* is a generic term which refers to the creation of new businesses, owned and operated by blacks, in ghetto areas. A variety of proposals—a few of which have become operational—have been made in support of black capitalism. These proposals advocate governmentally sponsored programs to provide liberal credit, tax incentives and subsidies, managerial assistance and training, and so forth, to present or potential black entrepreneurs. Related proposals urge subsidies to major corporations which are willing to build plants in the ghettos and to train black workers to staff them. The fundamental criticisms of black capitalism are twofold. First, the concept is flatly at odds with the strong economic forces which underlie the decentralization of economic activity in urban areas. Second, the types of industries which will be attracted to the ghetto are likely to be low-wage operations which provide largely "dead-end" jobs.

**2   Income Maintenance**   But a large fraction—perhaps as much as one-half—of the ghetto poor will not be helped by improved employment opportunities. The aged, the disabled, and the mothers of dependent children can be assisted effectively only by some sort of income maintenance program. The deficiencies of our present welfare programs and new proposals for a comprehensive income maintenance program will be discussed in Chapter 37.

**3   Improved  Education  and  Training**
Many of the ghetto blacks who are fully employed nevertheless live in poverty. The reason? They have not had access to sufficient education and training to qualify for jobs which pay higher wages. The major piece of Federal legislation in this area is the Comprehensive Employment and Training Act of 1973. CETA provides grants to state and local governments, but allows state and municipal governments to develop manpower training programs appropriate to their needs and to spend the Federal funds accordingly. Training programs typically involve institutional training to provide basic academic skills, on-the-job training, or some combination of the two. Program enrollees are overwhelmingly from low-income families. Young workers who have not completed high school dominate the programs and minorities are heavily represented.

But education and training should not be viewed as a panacea for ghetto dwellers. In fact, recent empirical work suggests that, although ghetto blacks have been obtaining more education, they have *not* been able to translate their efforts into an improved economic status because of a deficiency of suitable job opportunities.[18]

> . . . as a short-run antipoverty policy instrument, education without a supply of jobs which utilize and reward the capabilities of ghetto workers is unlikely to have much impact. The prevalence of ghetto unemployment, involuntary parttime employment, and substandard wages, . . . strongly suggests that existing urban labor markets under-utilize ghetto workers and do not permit these individuals to realize their potential productivities. If this interpretation is correct, then the remedy must be sought in opening up *new* urban job markets to the ghetto poor, markets whose jobs are physically accessible to ghetto residents, whose availability is made known to them, and whose entry level wages and promotional possibilities will in fact lead to a significant improvement in their levels of living.

[18] Bennett Harrison, "Education and Underemployment in the Urban Ghetto," *American Economic Review*, December 1972, p. 811.

## △  The Physical Aspect:
## Housing and Urban Renewal

The urban ghetto is not only a visible and potentially explosive concentration of poverty. It is also characterized by extensive deterioration of the physical environment; much of the housing and many commercial buildings are substandard and dilapidated. Many buildings have simply been abandoned by their owners.

Why has urban blight occurred? The reasons are manifold and include the following:

**1  Exodus and Externalities**  The physical decay of the central cities is a legacy of the flight to the suburbs. As the more prosperous households and businesses leave, so do the financial resources required for the maintenance of housing and commercial buildings. And as physical deterioration begins, the problem of external or spillover costs arises to reinforce the process. When landlord X allows his property to fall into disrepair, this decision contributes to the overall deterioration of the neighborhood and imposes costs upon other landlords in that neighborhood. Because of X's decision, there will be a smaller economic payoff to landlords Y and Z in maintaining their properties. Hence, a neighborhood can fall into a cumulative cycle of deterioration and decline. It is this externality problem, incidentally, which provides an economic rationale for government action.

**2  Property Tax Spiral**  The process of urban blight is also reinforced by rising property tax rates. As properties deteriorate and are abandoned, the central city property tax base shrinks. At the same time, the poor central city areas become increasingly costly to govern. Welfare costs, the costs of police and fire protection, the costs of public hospitals and clinics, all tend to rise. Given the dependence of municipalities upon the property tax, the inevitable result is higher property tax rates which provide a further inducement for landlords to neglect or abandon properties. In contrast, property owners in the more affluent suburbs usually enjoy better-quality schools and other public services *while paying lower tax rates*. This is the case because the value of suburban property is so much higher. A 5 percent tax on a $100,000 home in a relatively wealthy suburb will generate $5000 of tax revenue. A 15 percent tax on a $20,000 home in a deteriorating central city area will only generate $3000 of revenue.

**3  Discrimination**  Discrimination in housing has been a basic consideration in restricting blacks and other minorities to the decaying ghettos of the central cities. It is true that the incomes of many central-city blacks are so low that they cannot afford to move to the suburbs. But some could and would if housing were available to them.

One need merely recall the simple tools of supply and demand to grasp the impact of discrimination upon housing prices and rents. The immediate effect is to make available a disproportionately small supply of housing to blacks. This restricted supply means higher housing prices and rents. One result is that blacks are forced to use a very high proportion of their income for housing. But even so, the housing is likely to be of inferior quality. High rents induce ghetto families to "double up" on available housing. Landlords respond on the supply side by subdividing apartments. And, needless to say, a captive market provides little incentive for owners to repair or improve their property. The overall consequence is typically high rents for crowded and dilapidated housing.

**4  Rent Controls**  The fixing of rents by government at below-equilibrium levels has also contributed to urban blight. Once a New York City phenomenon (see Chapter 23's Last Word), rent controls have been adopted by Los Angeles, Boston, and Washington, D.C., and are under consideration by a number of other major cities. At first glance the objective of rent controls—to protect tenants from the skyrocketing increases in rents caused by demand increasing faster than supply—seems laudable. But there is rather overwhelming evidence that the actual long-run consequences tend to be much different.

As a direct consequence of rent controls, landlords receive a below-normal return on their housing investments. This prompts them to shift their financial capital to other kinds of investments or into geographic areas where controls do not exist. The amount of new housing constructed will thereby decline. Similarly, the low return on rental housing makes it unprofitable to maintain existing structures and so the existing stock of housing will deteriorate. Rather than resolve the housing scarcity, rent controls tend to aggravate that problem! Housing is now even scarcer; at the controlled—below equilibrium—price, quantity demanded exceeds quantity supplied so that a true shortage now exists. It is a useful exercise for the reader to construct a simple supply and demand diagram for housing units to verify these points.

If rent controls have such counterproductive effects, why have they persisted and tended to spread? The answer is that tenants outnumber landlords and builders. Current tenants who benefit from controls constitute a sizable and effective special interest group (Chapter 6).

**Policy Failures**  Given the fact that all levels of government have long and varied histories of involvement in the housing industry, the persistence and spread of urban blight may come as something of a surprise. For many years government—working through such agencies as the Federal Housing Administration (FHA) and the Veterans Administration (VA)—has attempted in a variety of ways to reduce the cost and increase the availability of mortgage funds to finance housing purchases. Since the late 1930s the Federal government has heavily subsidized the efforts of state and local governments to provide low-rent public housing for the poor. Urban renewal programs—again, subsidized with Federal funds—have attempted to reverse the spread of urban blight by rebuilding central-city areas.

Why have we failed? Why do we seem to be losing the battle against urban blight? In many instances our housing programs have been inappropriate or inadequate to the task. Mortgage subsidies, for example, have been most helpful to middle- and high-income groups in obtaining good housing. But low-income people have generally not been able to enjoy the low FHA and VA interest rates (nor the tax deductibility of mortgage interest payments) because they simply have not been able to qualify for such loans. Lofty statements of goals to the contrary, some housing programs have foundered for the lack of adequate financing. Public housing and rent subsidy programs have undoubtedly helped some low-income families, but the poorest families cannot afford even the subsidized rental payments.

Ironically, on balance, urban renewal programs have *reduced* the supply of housing available to low-income families. Some urban renewal efforts have not been primarily concerned with housing, but rather, the strategy has been to shore up the vitality of the central city by replacing slum neighborhoods with new office buildings to house both public services and private enterprises. This tendency helps explain the paradox that many ghetto dwellers are opposed to urban renewal. Witness the slogan: "Urban renewal is Negro removal." Furthermore, some families have been uprooted several times by public housing projects which have in fact increased the supply of housing available to middle-income families, but reduced it for low-income families.

□  SOLVING URBAN PROBLEMS: THE PREREQUISITES

We have outlined the general character of certain problems of the cities and have indicated specific remedies. We must now recognize that there exist certain institutional and financial prerequisites to these solutions. An obvious prerequisite to all proposed solutions is sufficient financial resources. This is not to say that urban problems will automatically disappear if we simply "throw money at them." Our knowledge of appropriate techniques and strategies for dealing effectively with the problems of the cities is embryonic and deficient. Nevertheless, adequately financed programs are essential. Furthermore, certain institutional changes may be required, not only to obtain adequate financing, but also to provide an effective and efficient decision-making environment.

△   **Political Consolidation**

Most urbanologists agree that one of the basic prerequisites to resolving urban problems is political consolidation. In particular, the design of efficient and equitable solutions to the problems of the cities depends in good measure on overcoming the political fragmentation which now exists in most cities.

Urban areas are in fact highly integrated and highly interdependent economic units. Most urban problems—transportation; discrimination in housing, employment, and education; pollution; land use—are clearly areawide in character. The individual, fragmented political units of the cities do not have effective jurisdiction over these problems; in our large cities, the local units of government have been losing the capacity to govern effectively. The realization of efficient and equitable—as opposed to politically feasible—solutions to urban problems depends upon coordinated, areawide action, that is, upon political consolidation.

**Efficiency**   Looked at from the economist's point of view, political consolidation can stimulate more efficient decision making in dealing with urban problems for several reasons.

**1**   Small political subdivisions will frequently be unable to realize economies of scale in providing certain public facilities, such as water and sewage systems. Levels of output will be low and these facilities will operate at points high on their unit-cost curves (Figure 25-7a).

**2**   A closely related point is that in such endeavors as police and fire protection, street construction, and public transit, political fragmentation results in the loss of certain qualitative advantages which would stem from the planning and coordination of these public services at the metropolitan level. "The case for bigness in public services probably rests more on quality than on cost; an areawide police force is better coordinated for traffic control and hot pursuit, and big enough to afford scientific crime detection facilities and specialists in juvenile and race problems."[19] Similarly, although the actual unit cost (per mile) of producing streets may be roughly the same whether provided by many small, independent municipalities or by a large metropolitan government, there are obvious advantages in having an overall plan to coordinate a given volume of street construction in the interest of maximum effectiveness.

**3**   Still another reason why most urban economists favor political consolidation is that, because of the small geographic size of existing urban political units, many of the benefits associated with the provision of needed public facilities in such areas as, say, education, recreation, and environmental improvement will accrue to individuals and businesses residing in other political units. For example, a small urban political unit which builds an excellent school system, provides for the treatment of sewage and industrial wastes, and constructs ample recreational facilities will be providing benefits which in part spill over its political boundaries, that is, are external to it in that they are realized by the residents of other political units. Many of the graduates of its school system will take jobs in other areas. And those living in other political subdivisions will use its parks and playgrounds and benefit from its antipollution activities. The crucial

[19]Thompson, op. cit., pp. 267–268.

point is that, when spillover benefits are large, a good or service will tend to be underproduced (Figure 6-1c). More specifically, the voters in each small political entity will not be anxious to tax themselves heavily to provide services and facilities whose benefits accrue in significant amounts to others.

**Equity**   The case for political consolidation also rests on grounds of equity. We have emphasized that political fragmentation has created serious fiscal disparities within the urban areas. Resources and needs have become separated in the political jungle of the cities:[20]

> Most of America's wealth and most of America's domestic problems reside in the metropolitan areas. Why, then, cannot this vast wealth be applied through vigorous social measures to meet the growing problems? Because the resources exist in one set of jurisdictions within the metropolitan areas and the problems in another. . . . This disparity between needs and resources is the disparity between the central city and its suburbs.

Political consolidation would obviously have the desirable effect of putting resources and needs within the same political jurisdiction.

**Avenues of Consolidation**   Political consolidation can be achieved in a variety of ways: the annexation of surrounding suburban areas by the city; the consolidation of city and county governments; the establishment of special regional authorities to deal with such particular problems as transportation or pollution.

But it would be unrealistic to expect that consolidation will be easily and quickly achieved. The "haves" of the wealthier suburbs have shown little inclination to assume the moral and financial responsibility for the

glaring problems of the "have nots" in the central city. Nor can we expect the officials of local governmental units to be eager to give up their power and functions. More positively, one can make counterarguments in favor of the present fragmented system. First, small local government is likely to be more conducive to personal political participation and more responsive to the needs and aspirations of its constituents than is a metropolitanwide government. A specific example: Some blacks feel that with fragmentation, they at least can gain political control of those geographic areas wherein they are numerically dominant, whereas, with consolidation, they are destined to be a largely ignored minority. Second, "bureaucracy"—inefficiencies in public administration—may tend to offset assumed cost economies in the provision and coordination of public goods and services by a consolidated urban government (Chapter 6). Finally, some would argue that small local governments contribute to the heterogeneity of urban living areas in that they provide residents with a variety of choices as to levels of local taxes and amounts and quality of public services. Thus, although most urbanologists endorse political consolidation, the case is not as clear-cut as one might at first suppose.

### △   The Larger Fiscal Problem

The much-publicized financial crises of New York City and Cleveland are symptomatic of the fiscal difficulties faced by many large cities. Causes are manifold. The equity argument for political consolidation focuses upon the problem of residential segregation by income and the urban fiscal dilemma it creates: Public service needs are divorced from the tax base. Although political consolidation will put resources and needs within the same political jurisdiction, a larger fiscal question remains. Even with political consolidation, it is questionable that the tax resources of the urban areas will be sufficient to meet the rising costs of urban governments. Consider some specific factors which have made urban gov-

[20] Advisory Commission on Intergovernmental Relations, op. cit., p. 1.

ernment very costly. Most big cities are old and, as a result, their physical plant—public buildings, sewer and electrical systems, streets, and so forth—is costly to maintain. Given the central city's dense concentrations of low-income and minority populations, it is no surprise that crime rates—and hence law-enforcement costs—are high. Welfare costs are very high and the public provision of many basic services (for example, medical care) is extensive. Financially troubled mass-transit systems require public subsidies. More recently, strong government employee unions have evolved and have aggressively pushed up wages and fringe benefits, including ofttimes-generous pension systems. Civil service or collective bargaining contracts restrict or impair the altering of job descriptions or reallocations of public workers in the interest of greater efficiency. The sheer size of big city bureaucracies may lead to inefficiencies which would not arise in smaller cities and towns. Empirical data show that the number of municipal workers per 1000 of population grows steadily as city size increases. It may also be that the kinds of services provided by cities are simply not susceptible to large productivity increases. For example, social workers, correctional officials, teachers, and public health physicians are all involved in direct person-to-person contact. In comparison to the mass production of air conditioners or automobiles, there is relatively little opportunity to save manpower through mechanization and technological progress. This means in turn that there is little or no productivity increase to offset the increases in the money wages and salaries of municipal workers. In brief, a significant part of the rapid rise in the cost of municipal services may stem from the fact that these services are inherently characterized by small and sporadic productivity increases. Finally, the combination of high rates of inflation and unemployment which has plagued much of the 1970s has intensified the budget difficulties of municipal governments.

There are a number of proposed solutions to the revenue crisis faced by local governments: (1) Federal revenue sharing, (2) the shifting of certain fiscal burdens to the Federal government, and (3) the restructuring of the property tax.[21]

**Federal Revenue Sharing**   We are already familiar with the first proposal (Chapter 8) and its underlying rationale. The Federal government has great tax-raising ability but limited responsibilities for public spending on civilian goods and services. Local governments, on the other hand, are largely responsible for spending on civilian public needs, but are obstructed by the severe revenue-raising limitations associated with their heavy dependence upon property taxation. The enactment of Federal revenue sharing in 1972 and its 1976 extension have helped to ease the fiscal crunch faced by many cities.

**Shifting Financial Responsibility**   Another recommendation is to have the Federal or state governments assume the financial responsibility for meeting certain urban problems and obligations. In Chapter 37 we will discuss the suggestion that the Federal government establish and finance an income maintenance program to relieve poverty, thereby reducing the heavy welfare costs now borne by city governments. Similarly, the shifting of all local costs of elementary and secondary education to the Federal government would not only relieve the fiscal crisis of the cities, but might also help to ensure greater equality of educational opportunity.

**Overhauling the Property Tax**   Like sin, everyone deplores the property tax. It is regressive because low-income people spend a larger proportion of their incomes for rental housing than do high-income people. It is difficult and costly to administer. Equitable assessment of property is difficult. Furthermore,

---

[21] This discussion generally follows the recommendations of the Advisory Commission on Intergovernmental Relations, ibid.

we have seen that rising property-tax rates have been a part of the self-reinforcing process by which wealthy people and prosperous businesses have fled to the suburbs. Yet the property tax is clearly the main source of revenue for local governments (Table 8-4) and is likely to remain so. It is therefore relevant to ask: Is it possible to restructure and revitalize the property tax so as to provide more revenue, on the one hand, and to reduce its harmful economic effects, on the other?

The basic proposal here is to shift the property-tax emphasis from buildings to land. We noted in Chapter 32 the reasons for a renewed interest in land-value taxation. The equity argument is that much of the value of urban land reflects public decisions with respect to zoning and the provision of roads, schools, and utilities. Most of the dramatic increases in urban land values are windfall gains in the sense that they are not the consequence of the efforts or expenditures of landowners. It would seem fair for society to tax away much of the increase in land value which society's decisions and expenditures have provided. The efficiency argument is that a tax on land has a neutral effect upon the use or allocation of land; a land-value tax does not contribute to a malallocation of land.

In the cities the present arrangement of relatively high property taxes on buildings and relatively low taxes on land tends to have perverse effects upon incentives. Specifically, heavy taxes on buildings harm the incentives of builders and property owners to construct new buildings and improve existing ones. This fact helps to explain central-city decay and blight. The relatively light taxes on land mean that landowners find the tax costs involved in holding vacant land to be comparatively small, and so they are encouraged to withhold land from productive uses in order to speculate on increases in its value. Such action—or inaction—prevents growth of the property-tax base and contributes to the fiscal problems of the cities. But higher taxes on land values are advocated for reasons that go beyond the rais-

ing of additional revenue for city government:[22]

> There is poetic justice in heavy land value taxation: at present land is typically taxed at rates, relative to market value, that are less than half those applied to buildings. We now, perversely, favor the speculator who impedes development and discourage the investor in new and better buildings.

△ **New Cities**

Some observers—dismayed at our apparent inability to cope with specific urban problems, dubious about the prospects for political consolidation and fiscal relief for the cities, and alarmed at the prospect of 100 million new city dwellers within the next thirty years—argue for the development of entirely new cities. These new cities might be satellites within the socioeconomic orbit of existing metropolitan areas, or they might be new, independent cities which are self-contained and distant from existing urban areas. In either event the prospect of "starting from scratch," and thereby avoiding the costly task of reversing the historical trends of urban dynamics and the associated problems, is appealing. High central-city land values would be circumvented, as would the burden of prevailing building-code and zoning regulations. And there would be a number of more positive advantages.[23]

> Designing and building a new community from the ground up provides a unique opportunity to plan for orderly growth with the most desirable location, timing, and sequence. It is possible to relate the new community development to area-wide, regional, and national urban development plans and objectives. The continuous planning process required permits adjustments between the actual rate of growth of a new community and job opportunities within or near the community and the need for public facilities, transportation,

[22] Netzer, op. cit., p. 258.
[23] Advisory Commission on Intergovernmental Relations, *Urban and Rural America: Policies for Future Growth,* (Washington, 1968), pp. 99–100.

public services, and commercial and retail establishments. Public investments can be related both to a projected and an actual rate of growth and anticipated need and capacity can be incorporated into current construction, thereby avoiding the necessity for later costly replacement or upgrading.

Planning and design in a new community can be on a large enough scale to incorporate features which are difficult to obtain on a piecemeal design basis. For example, an improved relationship between work and residential locations can be established through balanced development and distribution of economic activity. Greater ease of internal movement can be planned by separating types of motor vehicle traffic and in turn isolating them from pedestrians. Moreover, the size and location of commercial and public buildings and other facilities can be more easily related to traffic patterns in order to minimize congestion.

The large-scale planning required for a new

community can also produce an improved esthetic environment and provide amenities not otherwise available.

Despite the potential attractiveness of the "new cities" approach, it has been subjected to thoughtful criticism. Is the new cities concept merely a copout, a means of running away from the problems which our cities now face? The vast bulk of our population will continue to live in existing cities. Is it realistic to expect that model cities can make significant contributions to the problems confronting these people? Furthermore, existing cities have evolved and grown for compelling economic reasons. Can we expect contrived model cities—constructed to get away from the problems of existing cities—to have a viable economic base?[24]

[24]See, for example, William Alonso, "The Mirage of New Towns," *The Public Interest,* Spring 1970, pp. 3–17.

## Summary

**1** The economies of agglomeration are significant in explaining the growth of cities. Similarly, deglomerative forces account for the shift of population and economic activity from the central city to the suburbs. Political fragmentation and pronounced economic imbalances have accompanied urban sprawl.

**2** The short-run urban transportation problem is concerned with the most efficient use of existing transportation facilities. Although administrative problems are substantial, user charges and peak pricing are advocated by many economists. The long-run problem is concerned with the character of future investment in transportation facilities. For a variety of reasons, city planners and public officials tend to favor expanded and improved mass-transit systems.

**3** Pollution is a problem of spillover or external costs. Most proposed solutions— legislated controls and standards, emission fees, and markets for pollution rights—seek to internalize these spillover costs to offending firms.

**4** The central-city ghettos are heavily populated by blacks and other minorities who, because of low incomes and discrimination, cannot escape to suburban areas. Enlarged job opportunities, income-maintenance programs, and improved education and training are obvious ways of reducing ghetto poverty. Urban renewal and public housing programs have met with limited success in revitalizing the central-city areas and generally have done little to increase the supply of low-income housing.

**5** Because of the areawide character of urban problems and the unequal distribution of income and wealth between central city and suburbs, political consolidation would be very helpful in resolving many of the problems of the cities.

**6**  Even if political consolidation is realized, fiscal assistance in such forms as Federal revenue sharing and the shifting of fiscal responsibility for certain specific urban problems and obligations to the Federal government may be necessary.  The cities may reduce the harmful effects of property taxation and simultaneously obtain more revenue by shifting the relative burden of the property tax away from buildings and toward land.

**7**  Some observers argue that many advantages may be realized by planning and building entirely new cities to accommodate future population growth.

## Questions and Study Suggestions

**1**  Key terms and concepts to remember: economies of agglomeration; internal and external economies of scale; infrastructure; deglomerative forces; urban sprawl; political fragmentation; user charges; peak pricing; materials balance approach; emission fees; market for pollution rights; CETA; black capitalism.

**2**  Explain: "To agglomerate is to economize."  What, specifically, are the economies of agglomeration?  Distinguish between internal and external economies of scale.  What is the urban infrastructure?  Discuss the demand aspects of urban growth.

**3**  What socioeconomic forces underlie urban sprawl?  Explain in detail why the process of urban sprawl has been to the economic and fiscal disadvantage of the central city.  Of what significance is the fact that suburbs are typically separate political entities?  What arguments can be made for and against political consolidation?

**4**  "If cities are too large to be efficient or are poorly organized, the problem can be traced in large part to a failure to charge people for all the costs they impose or to reward them fully for the benefits of their action."  Explain.  Do you agree?

**5**  What is the nature of the urban transportation problem?  Explain: "Although improved transportation has been a necessary condition for decentralization and urban sprawl, this decentralization has also created acute transportation problems."

**6**  What are the main causes of environmental pollution?  Explain: "Clean air and water have become increasingly scarce and valuable resources precisely because they have been treated in the past as if they were free and unlimited in supply."  What methods might be used to internalize spillover costs?  Describe the operation of a market for pollution rights.

**7**  What is the role of racial discrimination in explaining the poverty of central cities?  Analyze the economics of the ghetto housing market.  Explain: "Urban blight—the cumulative deterioration of entire neighborhoods or areas—occurs because individual owners have little or no economic incentive to improve their property."

**8**  "We can go far to solve the central-city housing crisis by simply changing tax policy.  First, tax unused land at higher rates than land with buildings on it.  Second, tax new and improved housing at low rates and dilapidated and old housing at high rates."  Do you think these policies would have the indicated results?  Explain.

**9**  "Increases in the value of land in cities are the consequence of public decisions about zoning and investment in public utilities and facilities, not the result of individual efforts by owners.  Therefore, the city should recapture the unearned incomes from rising land values by taxation and use these revenues for public purposes."  Do you agree?

**10**  Analyze the fiscal problems of the cities.  What solutions do you recommend?  "The purpose of user charges is to confront decision-makers with the social or spillover costs of their decisions and in so doing cause them to alter their decisions."  Explain and illustrate this statement in terms of the urban transportation and pollution problems.

## Selected References

Baumol, William J.: *Economics, Environmental Policy, and the Quality of Life* (Englewood Cliffs, N. J.: Prentice-Hall, Inc., 1979).

Committee for Economic Development: *An Approach to Federal Urban Policy* (CED, December, 1977).

Downs, Anthony: *Urban Problems and Prospects,* 2d ed. (Chicago: Rand McNally & Company, 1976).

Emerson, M. Jarvin, and F. Charles Lamphear: *Urban and Regional Economics: Structure and Change* (Boston: Allyn and Bacon, Inc., 1975).

Joint Economic Committee: *Is the Urban Crisis Over?* (Washington, D.C., 1979).

Netzer, Dick: *Economics and Urban Problems,* 2d ed. (New York: Basic Books, Inc., Publishers, 1974).

Richardson, Harry W.: *Urban Economics* (Hinsdale, Illinois: The Dryden Press, 1978).

Winger, Alan R.: *Urban Economics: An Introduction* (Columbus, Ohio: Charles E. Merrill Publishing Company, 1977).

# LAST WORD
## The Ghetto as an Economic Subsystem

Professor Daniel R. Fusfeld of the University of Michigan explains why the urban ghettos persist as underdeveloped areas within a generally prosperous national economy.

The ghetto economy differs markedly from the rest of the economic system. It is the home of the bulk of our urban poverty. It is permanently depressed, with unemployment rates normally at the high levels that are characteristic of depressions when they occur in the national economy. It is backward and underdeveloped, lacking the dynamic, progressive changes that bring advancement to the rest of the economy. Its manpower is employed in the low wage sector of the economy, primarily, and provides a pool of low skilled labor for an economy in which this resource is needed less and less. Within the ghetto an irregular economy functions, partly legal and partly illegal, which provides many of the services needed by the low income ghetto residents which they cannot afford to pay for in the normal channels of commerce or which the regular economy does not provide at all.

When we look at the relationships between the ghetto and the progressive sector of the economy, two phenomena quickly become evident. First, there is a continuous drain of income and other resources out of the ghetto. Second, there is a continuing accretion of people into it, cast off as unuseable by the progressive sector, which wholly or partially counterbalances those who are able to climb up and out.

The drain of resources includes savings, income, physical capital and human resources. The savings of ghetto residents, small though they may be, are deposited in financial institutions whose loans are made to business firms or mortgage borrowers outside the ghetto, with a much smaller flow of capital into the ghetto for these purposes, leaving a net outflow. The size of the net outflow is unknown, but its presence is acknowledged by those who are familiar with the financial institutions that serve the ghetto.

Income is drained out in more easily observed ways. Products sold in the ghetto and to ghetto residents are produced outside the ghetto. The owners of the retail stores that sell these products and gain the profits live largely outside the ghetto. The same is true of the wholesale and shipping firms, advertising media and other elements of the economy that service retail establishments. A large portion of the employees of ghetto retail firms live outside the ghetto, although this has been less true after the 1967–68 riots than before.

Physical capital flows out of the ghetto largely through failure to replace depreciation of housing and public facilities. The ghetto landlord takes a large portion of his gains in the form of capital withdrawals that come from failure to maintain his property. This drain is large. Typically, 70 to 80 percent of ghetto residents rent their housing (as compared with 22% in the nation as a whole) and rent takes some 35 to 60 percent of family income (as compared with 25 to 30 percent in the economy as a whole). A large portion of those rental payments represent a drain of capital out of housing. Public facilities are subject to the same outward flow, through failure to maintain schools, streets, sidewalks, parks and other public facilities in ghetto areas.

Manpower also leaves, when it can. Many persons move up and out of the urban ghetto through education, skill, initiative and luck. They move out primarily through education and jobs in the high wage sector of the economy, and take with them a large part of the entrepreneurship and skill that any substantial population group generates.

The net result of the drain of income and resources from the urban ghetto is the poor, backward, undeveloped slum that continues to exist in the midst of a growing and progressive society. It is drained of all those resources which might form the base for economic development. When this is added to a weak community structure, inadequate public services, and relatively few professional skills, it is not hard to understand why the urban ghetto has been such an intractable problem.

From Daniel R. Fusfeld, "Transfer Payments and the Ghetto Economy," in Kenneth E. Boulding, Martin Pfaff, and Anita B. Pfaff (eds.), *Transfers in an Urbanized Economy: Theories and Effects of the Grants Economy* (Belmont, Calif.: Wadsworth Publishing Company, 1973), pp. 85–87. Reprinted by permission.

# The Economics of Income Distribution: Inequality and Poverty

chapter 37

The question of how income should be distributed has a long and controversial history in both economics and philosophy. Should our national income and wealth be more or less equally distributed than is now the case? Or, in terms of Chapter 5, is society making the proper response to the "For whom" question? The egalitarian debate has produced a wide spectrum of responses and positions. At one extreme we are urged to believe that greater equality is the basic prerequisite of capitalism's survival. At the other, we are warned that the "rush toward equality" will undermine the system and lead to its demise.

In this chapter we begin by surveying some basic facts concerning the distribution of income in the United States. Next, we consider some causes of income inequality. Third, we examine the debate over income inequality and the trade-off between equality and efficiency implied by this debate. Fourth, we will look at the poverty problem and the way in which poverty is related to racial discrimination. Finally, we consider public policy; existing income-security programs are outlined and the possibility of introducing a negative income tax to alleviate poverty is discussed.

## ☐ INCOME INEQUALITY: THE FACTS

How equally—or unequally—is income distributed in the United States? How wide is the gulf between rich and poor? Has the degree of income inequality increased or lessened over time?

### △ Personal Income Distribution

Average income in the United States is among the highest in the world. The median income for all families was $15,060 in 1978. But now we must envision how income is distributed around the average. Table 37-1 is instructive. At the low end of the scale we find

**TABLE 37-1**
The Distribution of Personal Income by Families, 1978

| (1) Personal income class | (2) Percentage of all families in this class | (3) Percentage of total personal income received by families in this class | (4) Percentage of all families in this class and all lower classes | (5) Percentage of income received by this class and all lower classes |
|---|---|---|---|---|
| Under $5,000 | 15 | 2 | 15 | 2 |
| $5,000–$9,999 | 18 | 8 | 33 | 10 |
| $10,000–$14,999 | 17 | 12 | 50 | 22 |
| $15,000–$19,999 | 15 | 15 | 65 | 37 |
| $20,000–$24,999 | 12 | 15 | 77 | 52 |
| $25,000–$49,999 | 20 | 36 | 97 | 88 |
| $50,000 and over | 3 | 12 | 100 | 100 |
|  | 100 | 100 |  |  |

*Source:* Bureau of the Census, *Money Income in 1978 of Households in the United States,* Current Population Reports, Series P-60, No. 121, February, 1980.

that 15 percent of all families receive about 2 percent of total personal income. Only 10 percent of the total income went to the 33 percent of the families receiving under $10,000 per year in 1978. At the top of the income pyramid we find that 23 percent of the families received incomes of $25,000 or more per year; this group received about 48 percent of total personal income. These figures suggest *there is considerable income inequality in the United States.*

△ **Trends in Income Inequality**

We know from Chapter 20 that economic growth has raised incomes: *Absolutely,* the

entire distribution of income has been moving upward over time. Has this changed the *relative* distribution of income? Incomes can move up absolutely, and the degree of inequality may or may not be affected. Table 37-2 is instructive on the relative distribution of income. In the table we divide the total number of income receivers into five numerically equal groups, or *quintiles,* and show the percentage of total personal income received by each.

These data suggest that a significant reduction in income inequality occurred between 1929 and 1947. Note in Table 37-2 the declin-

**TABLE 37-2**
Percentage of Total Before-Tax Income Received by Each One-fifth, and by the Top 5 Percent, of Families, Selected Years

| Quintile | 1929 | 1935–1936 | 1947 | 1955 | 1962 | 1972 | 1978 |
|---|---|---|---|---|---|---|---|
| Lowest } | 12.5 | 4.1 | 5.0 | 4.8 | 5.0 | 5.4 | 4.3 |
| Second } |  | 9.2 | 11.8 | 12.2 | 12.1 | 11.9 | 10.3 |
| Third | 13.8 | 14.1 | 17.0 | 17.7 | 17.6 | 17.5 | 16.9 |
| Fourth | 19.3 | 20.9 | 23.1 | 23.7 | 24.0 | 23.9 | 24.7 |
| Highest | 54.4 | 51.7 | 43.0 | 41.6 | 41.3 | 41.4 | 43.9 |
| Total | 100.0 | 100.0 | 100.0 | 100.0 | 100.0 | 100.0 | 100.0 |
| Top 5 percent | 30.0 | 26.5 | 17.2 | 16.8 | 15.7 | 15.9 | 16.6 |

*Source:* U.S. Bureau of the Census data. Details may not add up to totals because of rounding.

ing percentage of personal income going to the top quintile and the increasing percentage received by the other four quintiles during this period. Many of the forces at work during World War II undoubtedly contributed to this decline in inequality. War-born prosperity eliminated the many low incomes caused by the severe unemployment of the 1930s, brought a reduction of wage and salary differentials, boosted depressed farm incomes through sharp increases in farm prices, temporarily diminished discrimination in employment, was accompanied by a decline in property incomes as a share of the national income, and so forth.

But the data since 1947 tell a different story. *The relative distribution of income has been basically stable since World War II.* Apparently, the forces making for greater equality during the war ceased to be of great import after the war. Note that since 1947 the richest fifth of all families has received about eight times as much income as the poorest fifth.

△  **The Lorenz Curve**

The degree of income inequality can be envisioned through a *Lorenz curve* as shown in Figure 37-1. Here we cumulate the "percent of families" on the horizontal axis and the "percent of income" on the vertical axis. The theoretical possibility of a completely equal distribution of income is represented by a diagonal line because such a line indicates that any given percentage of families receives that same percentage of income. That is, if 20 percent of all families receive 20 percent of total income, 40 percent receive 40 percent; 60 percent receive 60 percent, and so on; all these points will fall on the diagonal line.

By plotting the 1978 data from Table 37-2 we locate the Lorenz curve to visualize the actual distribution of income. We find that the bottom 20 percent of all families received about 4.3 percent of the income as shown by point *a*; the bottom 40 percent received 14.6 percent (= 4.3 + 10.3) as shown by point *b*;

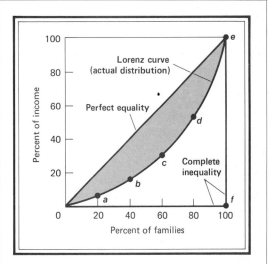

**FIGURE 37-1   THE LORENZ CURVE**

The Lorenz curve is a convenient means of visualizing the degree of income inequality. Specifically, the shaded area between the line of perfect equality and the Lorenz curve reflects the degree of income inequality.

and so forth. The shaded area, determined by the extent to which the resulting Lorenz curve sags away from the line of perfect equality, indicates the degree of income inequality. The larger this area or gap, the greater the degree of income inequality. If the actual income distribution was perfectly equal, the Lorenz curve and the diagonal would coincide and the gap would disappear. At the opposite extreme is the situation of complete inequality where 1 percent of the families have 100 percent of the income and the rest have none! In this case the Lorenz curve would coincide with the horizontal and right vertical axes of the graph, forming a right angle at point *f* as indicated by the heavy blue lines. The degree of inequality would be indicated by the entire area southeast of the diagonal.

The Lorenz curve can be used to contrast the distribution of income at different points in time, among different groups (for example, blacks and whites), or among different countries. As already observed, the data of Table

37-2 tell us that the Lorenz curve has not shifted significantly since World War II. Comparisons with other nations suggest that the distribution of income in the United States is less equal than in most other industrially advanced countries.

### △   Of Taxes, Time, and Transfers

The perceptive reader may raise several objections about our data.

**Taxes**   Tables 37-1 and 37-2 are both in terms of before-tax incomes. Is after-tax income more equally distributed? The answer is no. *In the United States the before-tax and after-tax distributions of income are not noticeably different.* Recalling Table 8-6, we see that the overall tax system is proportional. Hence, taxes reduce everyone's income by about the same percentage, and as a result, relative incomes are unchanged.[1]

**Time**   A second possible objection is that our annual data on inequality might well conceal the shifting of families up and down the income ladder, so when a time dimension is added to our analysis, the distribution of income is more nearly equal. For example, is the lifetime distribution of income more nearly equal than the annual distribution because of economic mobility? What are the chances, in Table 37-1, that a family falling in, say, the "under $5,000" class will progress to the "$10,000–$14,999" class next year, five years, or a generation from now?

**1   *Intragenerational   mobility***   Although data are sketchy, the evidence suggests that, in the short run, economic mobility is not great. For example, one study[2] indicates that 70 percent of the families who are living in poverty in any given year will also be in poverty the next year. Of the remaining 30 percent, 11 percent will have been dissolved as the result of death or other reasons. Of the 19 percent who escape poverty, most will hover close to the poverty line. Similar observations apply to high-income receivers. In fact, experts have concluded that "distributions of income would probably not be noticeably different if they were collected on a lifetime rather than on an annual basis."[3]

**2   *Intergenerational   mobility***   But what about the long run? Does the income status of families change from one generation to the next? Intergenerational income mobility is important because it provides some indication as to the degree of economic opportunity. If the sons and daughters of the rich all end up being rich, and, similarly, the children of the poor remain poor, then the implication is that our society is falling far short of the goal of equal economic opportunity. Data are limited and research findings are ambiguous. Yet one major study has concluded that:

> . . . there does not seem to be *any* mechanism available to most upper-middle class parents for maintaining their children's privileged economic position. Insofar as incomes are relative rather than absolute, most upper-middle class children simply end up worse off than their parents. Among men born into the most affluent fifth of the population, for example, we estimate that less than half will be part of this same elite when they grow up. Of course, it is also true that very few will be in the bottom fifth. Rich parents can at least guarantee their children that much. Yet if we follow families over several generations, even this will not hold true. Affluent families often have at least one relatively indigent grandparent in the background, and poor families, unless they are black or relatively recent immigrants, have often had at least one prosperous grandparent.[4]

[1] Lester C. Thurow and Robert E. B. Lucas, *The American Distribution of Income: A Structural Problem,* Joint Economic Committee (Washington: Government Printing Office, 1972), pp. 4–5.
[2] *Economic Report of the President, 1965* (Washington), pp. 164–165.

[3] Thurow and Lucas, op. cit., p. 13.
[4] Christopher Jencks et al., *Inequality: A Reassessment of the Effect of Family and Schooling in America* (New York: Basic Books, Inc., Publishers, 1972), p. 216.

Furthermore, one-third of the children of top-quintile parents received below-average incomes and, conversely, one-third of the children of bottom-quintile parents achieve above-average incomes. This study suggests that one's income status is not generally inherited; a reasonable degree of economic opportunity seems to exist.

**Transfers**   Edgar K. Browning has criticized the official Census Bureau data of Table 37-2 for its treatment of transfer payments. While including cash or money transfers (such as social security payments and unemployment compensation), the data exclude non-monetary or *in-kind transfers,* that is, transfers of goods and services which take place under such programs as Medicare, Medicaid, housing assistance, food stamps, and job-training programs. Browning points out that in-kind transfers have increased dramatically in the past fifteen years and that, when these are taken into account, we find a much more equal distribution in each year *and* "a marked trend toward equality" over the past twenty years.[5]

☐  **INCOME INEQUALITY: CAUSES**

Why does the United States have the degree of income inequality evidenced in Tables 37-1 and 37-2? In general, we note that the price system is an impersonal mechanism. It has no conscience, and it does not cater to any set of ethical standards concerning what is an "equitable," or "just," distribution of income. In fact, the basically individualistic environment of the capitalist economy is more than permissive of a high degree of income inequality. Some of the more specific factors contributing to income inequality include:

**1   Ability Differences**   People have different mental, physical, and aesthetic talents. Some individuals have had the good fortune to

inherit the exceptional mental qualities essential to entering the relatively high-paying fields of medicine, dentistry, and law. Others, rated as "dull normals" or "mentally retarded," are assigned to the most menial and low-paying occupations or are incapable of earning income at all. Some are blessed with the physical capacity and coordination to become highly paid professional athletes. A few have the aesthetic qualities prerequisite to becoming great artists or musicians. In brief, native talents put some individuals in a position to make contributions to total output which command very high incomes. Others are in much less fortunate circumstances.

**2   Education and Training**   In Chapter 31 we discussed investment in human capital, that is, expenditures on education and training. The point to be made here is that individuals differ significantly in the amounts of education and training they have obtained and, hence, in their capacities to earn income. In part, these differences are a matter of voluntary choice. Smith chooses to enter the labor force upon high school graduation, while Jones decides to attend college. On the other hand, such differences may be involuntary: Smith's family may simply be unable to finance a college education.

**3   Job Tastes and Risks**   Incomes differ because of differences in "job tastes." Individuals who are willing to take arduous, unpleasant jobs and to work long hours with great intensity will tend to earn more. Some individuals boost their incomes by "moonlighting," that is, by holding two jobs. Individuals also differ in their willingness to assume risk. We refer here not only to the steeplejack, but to entrepreneurial risk. Though most fail, the fortunate few who gamble successfully on the introduction of a new product or service may realize very substantial wealth.

**4   Property Ownership**   The ownership of property resources, and hence the receipt of

---

[5] Edgar K. Browning, "How Much More Equality Can We Afford?" *The Public Interest,* Spring 1976, pp. 90–110.

property incomes, is very unequal. The vast majority of households own little or no property resources, while the remaining few supply very great quantities of machinery, real estate, farmland, and so forth. For example, a study of the ownership of private assets indicates that, in 1962, the poorest 25 percent of all families had no net worth, that is, their debts equaled their assets, while the wealthiest 20 percent of the population owned over 75 percent of all private assets. Furthermore, the richest 8 percent of the population owned 60 percent, and the wealthiest 1 percent owned over 26 percent, of all private assets.[6] Basically, property incomes account for the position of those households at the very pinnacle of the income pyramid. The right of inheritance and the fact that "wealth begets wealth" reinforce the role played by unequal ownership of property resources in determining income inequality.

**5 Market Power** Ability to "rig the market" on one's own behalf is undoubtedly a major factor in accounting for income inequality. Certain unions and professional groups have adopted policies which limit the supplies of their productive services, thereby boosting the incomes of those "on the inside." Legislation which provides for occupational licensure for barbers, beauticians, accountants, taxi drivers, and so forth can also be a basis for exerting market power in favor of the licensed group. The same holds true in the product market: profit receivers in particular stand to benefit when their firm develops some degree of monopoly power.

**6 Luck, Connections, Misfortune, Discrimination** There are obviously other important forces which play a part in explaining income inequality. Luck, chance, and "being in the right place at the right time" have all

caused individuals to stumble into fortunes. Discovering oil on a run-down farm, meeting the right press agent, and making a favorable impression on the boss's daughter have accounted for many high incomes. Nor can personal contacts and political influence be discounted as means of attaining the higher income brackets. On the other hand, a host of economic misfortunes in such forms as prolonged illness, serious accident, death of the family breadwinner, and unemployment may plunge a family into relative poverty. The burden of such misfortunes is borne very unevenly by the population and hence contributes to the degree of income inequality. Discrimination is such a significant cause of inequality that we treat it in some detail later in this chapter.

☐  **EQUALITY VERSUS EFFICIENCY**
The critical policy issue concerning income inequality is: What is the optimal amount? While there is no generally accepted answer to this question, much can be learned by exploring the cases for and against greater equality.

△  **The Case for Equality:**
    **Maximizing Utility**
    *The basic argument in the case for an equal distribution of income is that income equality is necessary if consumer satisfaction or utility is to be maximized.* The rationale for this argument can be seen in terms of Figure 37-2 wherein it is assumed that the money incomes of two individuals, Anderson and Brooks, are subject to diminishing marginal utility (Chapter 24). In any time period income receivers spend the first dollars received on those products which they value most, that is, on products whose marginal utility is high. As their most pressing wants become satisfied, consumers then will spend additional dollars of income on less important, lower marginal utility, goods. The identical diminishing "marginal utility from income" curves reflect the

---

[6]Dorothy S. Projector, "Survey of Financial Characteristics of Consumers," *Federal Reserve Bulletin,* March 1964, pp. 285–293.

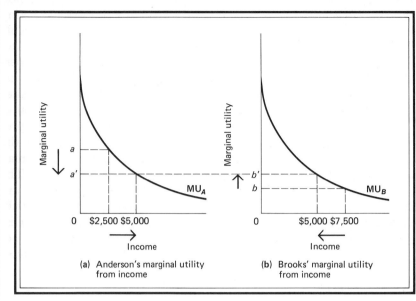

**FIGURE 37-2  THE OPTIMAL DISTRIBUTION OF INCOME**

Proponents of income equality argue that, given identical "marginal utility from income" curves, Anderson and Brooks will maximize their combined utility when any given income (say $10,000) is equally distributed. If income is unequally distributed ($2,500 to Anderson and $7,500 to Brooks), the marginal utility derived from the last dollar will be greater for Anderson (0a) than for Brooks (0b) and, hence, a redistribution toward equality will result in a net increase in total utility. When equality is achieved, the marginal utility derived from the last dollar of income will be equal for both consumers (0a' = 0b') and, therefore, there is no further redistribution of income which will increase total utility.

(a)  Anderson's marginal utility
     from income

(b)  Brooks' marginal utility
     from income

assumption that Anderson and Brooks have the same capacity to derive utility from income.

Now suppose there is, say, $10,000 worth of income (output) to be distributed between Anderson and Brooks. What is the best or optimal distribution? The answer: An equal distribution which causes the marginal utility of the last dollar to be the same for both persons. We can prove this by demonstrating that, for an initially unequal distribution of income, the combined total utility of the two individuals can be increased by moving toward equality. For example, suppose that initially the $10,000 of income is distributed unequally so that Anderson gets only $2500 and Brooks receives $7500. We observe that the marginal utility from the last dollar received by Anderson is high (0a) and the marginal utility from Brooks' last dollar of income is low (0b). Clearly the redistribution of a dollar's worth of income from Brooks to Anderson—that is, toward greater equality—would increase (by 0a − 0b) the combined total utility of the two

consumers. Anderson's utility gain exceeds Brooks' loss. This will continue to be the case until income is equally distributed with each person receiving $5000. At this point the marginal utility of the last dollar is identical for Anderson and Brooks (0a' = 0b') and, hence, further redistribution cannot increase total utility.

△  **The Case for Inequality:
Incentives and Efficiency**

Although the logic of the argument for equality is impeccable, critics attack its fundamental assumption that there exists some fixed amount of income to be distributed.[7] Critics of income equality argue that *the way in which income is distributed is an important determi-*

---

[7] Incidentally, the case for income equality does *not* rest upon the assumption of identical "marginal utility from income" curves. If these curves are different for Anderson and Brooks, it can be argued on probability grounds that an equal distribution of income is most likely to maximize consumer satisfactions. See Abba Lerner, *The Economics of Control* (New York: The Macmillan Company, 1944), chapter 3.

*nant of the amount of income produced and available for distribution.* That is, in moving toward equality in Figure 37-2, society (government) must *tax* away some of Brooks' income and *transfer* it to Anderson. This tax-transfer process will allegedly diminish the income rewards of high-income Brooks and raise the income rewards of low-income Anderson and in so doing reduce the incentives of both to *earn* high incomes. Why should Brooks work hard, save and invest, or undertake entrepreneurial risks, when the rewards from such activities will be reduced by taxation? And why should Anderson be motivated to increase his income through market activities when government stands ready to transfer income to him? In the extreme, argue the defenders of income inequality, imagine a situation wherein government levies a 100 percent tax on income and distributes the tax revenue equally to its citizenry. Why work hard? Indeed, why work at all? Why assume business risks? Why save—that is, forgo current consumption—in order to invest? The economic incentives to "get ahead" will have been removed and we can expect the productive efficiency of the economy—and hence the amount of income to be distributed—to diminish. The way the income pie is distributed affects the size of that pie! *The basic argument for income inequality is that it is essential to maintain incentives to produce output and income.*

△  **The Big Trade-off**[8]

The essence of the income (in)equality debate is that there exists a fundamental trade-off between equality and efficiency.

The contrasts among American families in living standards and in material wealth reflect a system of rewards and penalties that is intended to encourage effort and channel it into socially productive activity. To the extent that the system succeeds, it generates an efficient economy. But

[8]This section is based directly upon Arthur M. Okun, *Equality and Efficiency: The Big Tradeoff* (Washington, D.C.: The Brookings Institution, 1975).

that pursuit of efficiency necessarily creates inequalities. And hence society faces a trade-off between equality and efficiency.[9]

Thus the problem for a society inclined toward egalitarianism is how to achieve a given redistribution of income in such a way as to minimize the adverse effects upon economic efficiency. Consider this leaky-bucket analogy. Assume society agrees to shift income from the rich to the poor. But the money must be transferred from affluent to indigent in a leaky bucket. How much leakage will society accept and continue to endorse the redistribution? In other words, if cutting the income pie in more equal slices tends to shrink the pie, what amount of shrinkage will society tolerate? Is a loss of one cent on each redistributed dollar acceptable? Five cents? Twenty-five cents? Forty cents? This is obviously a critical, value-laden question which will permeate future political debates over extensions and modifications of our income maintenance programs.

☐  **THE DISMAL ECONOMICS OF POVERTY**

Many people are less concerned with the larger question of income distribution than they are with the more specific issue of income inadequacy. Therefore, armed with some background information on income inequality, let us now turn to the poverty problem. How extensive is poverty in the United States? What are the characteristics of the poor? And what is the best strategy to take to lessen poverty?

△  **Who Are the Poor?**

Poverty does not lend itself to precise definition. But, as a broad generalization, we might say that a family lives in poverty when its basic needs exceed its available means of satisfying them. A family's needs have many

[9]Ibid., p. 1.

determinants: its size, its health, the ages of its members, and so forth. Its means include currently earned income, transfer payments, past savings, property owned, and so on. The definitions of poverty accepted by concerned government agencies are based on family size. Hence, in 1977 an unattached individual receiving less than $3267 per year was living in poverty. For a family of four the poverty line was $6270. For a family of six, it was about $8680. Applying these definitions to income data for the United States, it is found that *slightly less than 12 percent of the nation lives in poverty.*

Who are these 25 million or so souls who live in poverty? Unfortunately for purposes of public policy, the poor are heterogeneous; they can be found in all geographic regions, they are whites and nonwhites, they include large numbers of both rural and urban people, they are both old and young. Yet, despite this pervasiveness, poverty is far from randomly distributed:[10]

> ... the poverty population has a greater proportion of the elderly, female-headed families, blacks, the poorly educated, and unrelated individuals (especially elderly unrelated individuals) than the general population. For example, 46 percent of poor families are headed by a female, and children in female-headed families are about 6 times as likely to be poor as children in male-headed families (52 percent vs. 9 percent). Blacks are more than 3 times as likely as whites to be poor; blacks comprise almost one-third of the poor population, compared to only 11 percent of the total population. About 16 percent of the elderly are poor, compared to a poverty rate of 12 percent for the general population, and the elderly constitute 14 percent of the poverty population. Only one-third of poor persons over 14 years have a high-school diploma. Although about two-thirds of poor families receive some earnings, employment tends to be unstable; only 19 percent of poor families have full-time, year round employment.

[10]U.S. Department of Health, Education, and Welfare, *The Measure of Poverty* (Washington, 1976), pp. 111–112.

## △ The "Invisible" Poor

These facts and figures on the extent and character of poverty may be a bit difficult to accept. After all, ours is presumably the affluent society. How does one square the depressing statistics on poverty which permeate both government and private reports with everyday observations of abundance? The answer lies in good measure in the fact that much American poverty is hidden; it is largely invisible. First of all, poverty is increasingly isolated in the hearts of large cities, because the middle and upper classes have migrated away from them to suburbia. Poverty persists in the slums and ghettos not readily visible from the freeway or subway. Secondly, much poverty embraces the aged and infirm, who rarely venture from their meager rented rooms. Thirdly, rural poverty and the chronically depressed areas of Appalachia are also off the beaten path. Finally, and perhaps most important,[11]

> The poor are politically invisible. . . . [They] do not, by far and large, belong to unions, to fraternal organizations, or to political parties. They are without lobbies of their own; they put forward no legislative program. As a group they are atomized. They have no face; they have no voice.

Indeed, the American poor have been labeled "the world's least revolutionary proletariat."

## □ DISCRIMINATION AND POVERTY

Noting that blacks bear a disproportionately large burden of poverty, it is important that we consider the economic aspects of discrimination. Assuming genetic similarity among all races and ethnic groups, the degree of discrimination can be measured by comparing the incomes of those who are favored and those who are injured by discrimination. The comparison

[11]Michael Harrington, *The Other America* (Baltimore: Penguin Books, Inc., 1962), p. 14. This admirable and disturbing little book is required reading for anyone seriously interested in the poverty problem.

of median income figures of whites and non-whites gives us a rough index of the degree of discrimination. As Table 37-3 indicates, the median income of nonwhite families is only 65 percent that of white families.

△  **Dimensions of Discrimination**

There is compelling evidence that this large income differential is firmly rooted in a number of different types of discrimination, some of which are reflected in Table 37-3.

**1** *Wage discrimination* occurs when black and other minority workers are paid less than whites for doing the same work. This kind of discrimination is of declining importance because of its unsubtle character and the fact that it clearly violates Federal law.

**2** *Employment discrimination* means that unemployment is concentrated among minorities. Blacks are frequently the last hired and the first fired. Hence, for the past fifteen or twenty years the unemployment rate for blacks has been roughly double that for whites (Table 37-3).

**3** *Occupational discrimination* means that minority workers have been arbitrarily restricted or prohibited from entering the more desirable, higher-paying occupations. Black executives and salesmen, not to mention electricians, bricklayers, and plumbers, are few and far between. Many craft unions have effectively barred blacks from membership and hence from employment. Simple supply and demand analysis suggests how occupational discrimination contributes to income disparity between whites and blacks. Imagine two occupations—say, carpenters and dockworkers—for which blacks and whites are equally well qual-

**TABLE 37-3**
Selected Measures of Discrimination and Inequality of Opportunity, 1978

| Selected measure | Whites | Blacks and other nonwhite races |
|---|---|---|
| *Income* | | |
| Median income of families | $15,660 | $10,130 |
| Percent of households in poverty | 7 | 28 |
| Percent of families with incomes of $10,000 or more | 69 | 51 |
| *Education* | | |
| Percent of labor force 16 years and over completing 4 years of high school or more | | |
| Males | 73 | 56 |
| Females | 78 | 64 |
| Percent of labor force 16 years and over completing 4 years of college or more | 18 | 9 |
| *Employment* (percent of total civilian employment) | | |
| White-collar occupations | 52 | 36 |
| Craftsmen-foremen occupations | 14 | 9 |
| *Unemployment rate* (percent of civilian labor force)* | | |
| Adult males | 3.6 | 8.4 |
| Adult females | 5.0 | 10.1 |
| Teenagers† | 13.9 | 33.6 |

*Unemployment data are for 1979.
†Males and females, 16–19 years old.
*Sources: Statistical Abstract of the United States and Manpower Report of the President, 1979 (Washington).*

ified. Now assume that carpentry becomes a "white man's job" and blacks are effectively barred by either the union or construction firms. This means that the supply of carpenters will decline and the wages of carpenters—all of whom are white—will rise. Conversely, blacks, who can no longer obtain employment as carpenters, will shift into the dockworkers' labor market, increasing labor supply and causing wages to decline. This model of occupational discrimination and its consequences can be pursued by referring to the "Women in the Labor Market" section of Chapter 38.

**4** *Human-capital discrimination* occurs when investments in education and training are lower for blacks than for whites. The smaller amount (Table 37-3) and inferior quality of the education received by blacks have had the obvious effect of denying them the opportunity to increase their productivity and qualify for better jobs. Unfortunately, a vicious circle seems to exist here. Many blacks are poor because they have acquired little human capital. Being poor, blacks have less financial ability to invest in education and training. They also have less economic motivation to invest in human capital: Facing the very real possibility of wage, employment, and occupational discrimination, blacks tend to receive a lower rate of return on their investments in education and training.

**5** *Other forms of discrimination* may make the nonwhite's economic status even worse than Table 37-3 suggests. A number of recent studies have demonstrated that the nonwhite generally gets less for his or her dollar than does the white consumer. In particular, the supply of housing available to blacks is sharply restricted, forcing them to pay higher rents for poorer housing than do whites. Ironically, urban renewal has typically resulted in a net reduction in the supply of housing for low-income blacks. In addition to housing, the limited consumer, banking and credit, insurance, and legal facilities found in urban ghettos have the effect of limiting supply, causing blacks to pay higher prices for these goods and services than do whites.

△ **Costs of Discrimination**

Given the diverse types of discrimination, naturally the economic costs of discrimination are difficult to estimate. However, the Council of Economic Advisers[12] has estimated that if economic and social policies were successful in lowering the black unemployment rate to the level of the white rate, and if education and training opportunities were made available to the black labor force so that the average productivity of black labor became equal to that of white workers, the total output of the economy would rise by about 4 percent. For 1979 the economic cost of racial discrimination would be on the order of $90 to $95 billion!

□ **THE INCOME MAINTENANCE SYSTEM**

The existence of a wide variety of income maintenance programs (Table 37-4) is evidence that the alleviation of poverty has been accepted as a legitimate goal of public policy. Basically, our income maintenance system consists of two kinds of programs. On the one hand, *social insurance programs* partially replace earnings lost due to retirement and temporary unemployment. "Social security" and unemployment compensation, the main social insurance programs, are financed out of earmarked payroll taxes. Benefits are viewed as earned rights and do not carry the stigma of public charity. On the other hand, *public assistance,* or *welfare, programs* provide benefits for those who are unable to earn income because of permanent handicaps or dependent children. These programs are financed out of general tax revenues and are regarded as public charity. Individuals and families must demonstrate low incomes in order to qualify for aid.

Total spending for income maintenance

---

[12]*Economic Report of the President, 1966* (Washington), p. 110.

**TABLE 37-4**
Characteristics of Major Income-Maintenance Programs

| Program | Basis of eligibility | Source of funds | Form of aid | Fiscal 1977 | |
|---|---|---|---|---|---|
| | | | | Expenditures* (billions of dollars) | Beneficiaries (millions) |
| OASDI | Age, disability, or death of parent or spouse Individual earnings | Federal payroll taxes on employers and employees | Cash | $71.3 | 28.5 |
| Medicare | Age or disability | Federal payroll tax on employers and employees | Subsidized health insurance | 20.8 | 25.4 |
| Unemployment compensation | Unemployment | State and Federal payroll tax on employers | Cash | 14.3 | 9.8 |
| Supplemental security income (SSI) | Age or disability Income | Federal revenues | Cash | 6.2 | 4.3 |
| AFDC | Certain families with children Income | Federal-state-local revenues | Cash and services | 9.8 | 11.2 |
| Food stamp | Income | Federal revenues | Vouchers | 5.0 | 17.1 |
| Medicaid | Persons eligible for AFDC, or SSI and medically indigent | Federal-state-local revenues | Subsidized health services | 16.3 | 21.6 |

*Expenditures by Federal, state, and local governments; excludes administrative expenses.
*Source: Economic Report of the President, 1978* (Washington), p. 222.

has expanded from about 4 percent of GNP in 1940 to about 10 percent of GNP currently. The Federal government finances virtually all the social insurance programs and about two-thirds of the welfare program expenditures.

△ **OASDI and Medicare**

OASDI—old age, survivors, and disability insurance—is essentially a gigantic social insurance program financed by compulsory payroll taxes levied upon both employers and employees. Generically known as "social security," the program is designed to replace earnings lost because of a worker's retirement, disability, or death. A payroll tax of 6.65 percent is levied on both worker and employer and applies to the first $29,700 of wage income. Workers may retire at 65 with full benefits or at 62 with reduced benefits. When the worker dies, benefits accrue to the survivors. Special provisions provide benefits for disabled workers. Currently, social insurance covers over 90 percent of all employed persons in the United States. In 1977 some 29 million people were receiving OASDI checks averaging about $245 per month. *Medicare* was appended to OASDI in 1965. The hospital insurance it provides for the elderly and disabled is financed out of the payroll tax. Medicare also makes available a low-cost voluntary insurance program which helps pay doctor fees.

There has been considerable controversy recently concerning both the short-term and long-term problems of financing OASDI. The program is financed essentially on a pay-as-you-go basis whereby benefits paid this year are derived primarily from this year's contributions. The *short-term problem* stems from the unseemly combination of inflation and unemployment which we have experienced in the 1970s. On the one hand, legislation has tied benefits to the cost of living; hence, rapid inflation has increased disbursements to beneficiaries. On the other hand, unemployment has eroded payroll tax payments into the program. The *long-term problem* is largely a reflection of demographic trends. Declining birth rates suggest that in the future there will be fewer workers contributing to the program at a time when the number of retirees will have increased substantially. While there are currently about nineteen retired persons for every 100 persons aged 20 through 64, that number is estimated to rise to thirty-four by the year 2030!

△  **Unemployment Compensation**

All fifty states sponsor unemployment insurance programs. These programs are financed by taxes on employers which average about $1\frac{1}{2}$ percent of covered payrolls. Any insured worker who becomes unemployed can, after a short waiting period (usually a week), become eligible for benefit payments. Almost 90 percent of all civilian workers are covered by the program. Size of payments and the number of weeks they may be received vary considerably from state to state. Generally speaking, benefits approximate one-half a worker's wage up to a certain maximum payment, which in many states is about $90. Obviously, the number of beneficiaries and the level of total disbursements vary greatly over the business

cycle. It is to be recalled that unemployment compensation benefits are one of our important built-in stabilizers.

△  **The Welfare Programs**

Many needy persons who do not qualify for OASDI or unemployment compensation are assisted through other programs. Beginning in 1972 Federal grants to states for public assistance to the aged, the blind, and the disabled were terminated and a new Federally financed and administered *Supplemental Security Income (SSI) program* was created. The purpose of SSI is to establish a uniform, nationwide minimum income for these three categories of workers who are unable to work. Over half the states provide additional income supplements to the aged, blind, and disabled.

The *Aid to Families with Dependent Children (AFDC) program* is state-administered, but is partly financed with Federal grants. The purpose is to provide aid to families in which dependent children do not have the financial support of a parent, usually the father, because of death, disability, divorce, or desertion.

The *food stamp program,* which has grown very rapidly in recent years, is designed to provide all low-income Americans with a "nutritionally adequate diet." Under the program eligible households receive monthly allotments of coupons which are redeemable for food. The amount of food stamps received varies inversely with a family's earned income.

*Medicaid* helps finance medical expenses of individuals participating in the SSI and AFDC programs.

△  **"The Welfare Mess"**

There can be no doubt that the social security system—not to mention local relief, housing subsidies, minimum-wage legislation, agricultural subsidies, veterans' benefits, and private transfers through charities, pensions, supplementary unemployment benefits, and so forth—provides important means of alleviating poverty. Indeed, as Figure 37-3 indicates, the

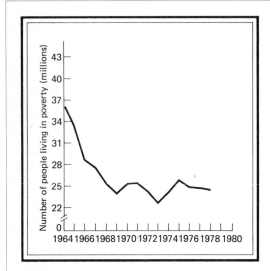

**FIGURE 37-3  THE DECLINE OF POVERTY**

Since the mid-1960s there has been a substantial decline in the number of people living in poverty. Note, however, that recently high unemployment rates have reversed the trend. (*U.S. Bureau of the Census*)

growth of the income maintenance system, along with overall economic progress, has substantially reduced the number of people living in poverty. On the other hand, the system has been subject to a wide variety of criticisms in recent years.

**1  Administrative Inefficiencies**  Critics charge that the willy-nilly growth of our welfare programs has created a clumsy and inefficient system, characterized by red tape and dependent upon a huge bureaucracy for its administration. Administrative costs account for relatively large portions of the total budget of many programs.

**2  Inequities**  Serious inequities arise in welfare programs in that people with similar needs may be treated much differently.

Benefit levels vary widely among States and among different demographic and family groups. Geographic differentials arise primarily

because benefits under the two major public assistance programs—AFDC and Medicaid—are essentially controlled by the States. As a result, sharp disparities in benefit levels exist between the poorer, rural States and the wealthier, more urban areas. . . .in 1976 a single-parent family of four with no earnings could obtain combined welfare benefits in New York City that were more than 2½ times larger than those available to the same family in Mississippi.[13]

Furthermore, control of the system is fragmented and some low-income families "fall between the slats" while other families collect benefits to which they are not entitled.

**3  Work Incentives**  A major criticism is that most of our income maintenance programs impair incentives to work. This is the case because all welfare programs are constructed so that a dollar's worth of earned income yields less than a dollar of net income. As earned income increases, program benefits are reduced. It is easy to understand why efforts to encourage AFDC mothers to work and become self-supporting have been largely unsuccessful. Since $0.67 of benefits will be lost for every $1 earned, there is little incentive to become a productive member of society. In fact, an individual or family participating in several welfare programs may find that, when the loss of program benefits and the effect of payroll taxes on earnings are taken into account, the individual or family is absolutely worse off by working! In effect, the marginal tax rate on earned income exceeds 100 percent!

There are other criticisms: AFDC regulations encourage family breakup. Various programs foster social divisiveness between welfare recipients and low-income workers. In-kind transfers interfere with freedom of consumer choice. And so forth.

□  **NEGATIVE INCOME TAX (NIT)**

There has emerged from this array of criticism support for a new approach to income mainte-

---

[13]*Economic Report of the President, 1978,* pp. 225–226.

nance. The contention is that the entire patchwork of existing welfare programs should be replaced by a *negative income tax* (NIT). The term NIT suggests that, just as the present (positive) income tax calls for families to "subsidize" the government through taxes when their incomes rise *above* a certain level, the government should subsidize households with NIT payments when household incomes fall *below* a certain level.

△  **Comparing Plans**

Let us examine the two critical elements of any NIT plan. First, a NIT plan specifies a *guaranteed annual income* below which family incomes would not be allowed to fall. Second, the plan embodies a *benefit-loss rate* which indicates the rate at which subsidy benefits are reduced or "lost" as a consequence of earned income. Consider Plan One of the three illustrative plans shown in Table 37-5. In Plan One the guaranteed annual income is assumed to be $4000 and the benefit-loss rate is 50 percent. Hence, if the family earns no income, it will receive a NIT subsidy of $4000. If it earns $2000, it will lose $1000 ($2000 of earnings *times* the 50 percent benefit-loss rate) of subsidy benefits and total income will be $5000 (= $2000 of earnings *plus* $3000 of subsidy). If $4000 is earned, the subsidy will fall to $2000, and so on. Note that at $8000 the NIT subsidy becomes zero. The level of earned income at

which the subsidy disappears and at which normal (positive) income taxes apply to further increases in earned income is called the *break-even income.*

But one might criticize Plan One on the grounds that a 50 percent benefit-loss rate is too high and therefore does not provide sufficient incentives to work. Hence, in Plan Two the $4000 guaranteed income is retained, but the benefit-loss rate is reduced to 25 percent. We observe, however, that the break-even level of income increases to $16,000 and many more families would now qualify for NIT subsidies. Furthermore, a family with any given earned income will now receive a larger NIT subsidy. For both of these reasons, a reduction of the benefit-loss rate to enhance work incentives will raise the cost of a NIT plan.

Examining Plans One and Two, still another critic might argue that the guaranteed annual income is too low in that it does not get families out of poverty. Plan Three raises the guaranteed annual income to $8000 and retains the 50 percent benefit-loss rate of Plan One. While Plan Three obviously does a better job of raising the incomes of the poor, it too yields a higher break-even income and would therefore be more costly than Plan One. Furthermore, if the $8000 income guarantee of Plan Three were coupled with Plan Two's 25 percent benefit-loss rate to strengthen work incentives, the break-even income level would

**TABLE 37-5**
The Negative Income Tax: Three Plans (*hypothetical data for a familiy of four*)

| Plan One ($4000 guaranteed income and 50% benefit-loss rate) | | | Plan Two ($4000 guaranteed income and 25% benefit-loss rate) | | | Plan Three ($8000 guaranteed income and 50% benefit-loss rate) | | |
|---|---|---|---|---|---|---|---|---|
| Earned income | NIT subsidy | Total income | Earned income | NIT subsidy | Total income | Earned income | NIT subsidy | Total income |
| $   0 | $4,000 | $4,000 | $   0 | $4,000 | $ 4,000 | $   0 | $8,000 | $ 8,000 |
| 2,000 | 3,000 | 5,000 | 4,000 | 3,000 | 7,000 | 4,000 | 6,000 | 10,000 |
| 4,000 | 2,000 | 6,000 | 8,000 | 2,000 | 10,000 | 8,000 | 4,000 | 12,000 |
| 6,000 | 1,000 | 7,000 | 12,000 | 1,000 | 13,000 | 12,000 | 2,000 | 14,000 |
| 8,000* | 0 | 8,000 | 16,000* | 0 | 16,000 | 16,000* | 0 | 16,000 |

*Indicates break-even income. Determined by dividing the guaranteed income by the benefit-loss rate.

shoot up to $32,000 and add even more to NIT costs.[14]

### △ Goals and Conflicts

The point to be derived by comparing these three plans is that there are conflicts or trade-offs among the goals of an "ideal" income maintenance plan. First, a plan should be effective in getting families out of poverty. Second, it should provide adequate incentives to work. Third, the plan's costs should be reasonable. Table 37-5 tells us that these three objectives conflict with one another and that compromises or trade-offs are necessary. Plan

[14]The alert reader may have sensed the generalization that, given the guaranteed income, the break-even level of income varies *inversely* with the benefit-loss rate. Specifically, the break-even income can be found by dividing the guaranteed income by the benefit-loss rate. Hence, for Plan One, $4000/.50 = $8000. Can you also demonstrate that, given the benefit-loss rate, the break-even level of income varies *directly* with the guaranteed income?

One, with a low guaranteed income and a high benefit-loss rate, keeps costs down. But the low-income guarantee means it is not very effective in eliminating poverty and the high benefit-loss rate weakens work incentives. In comparison, Plan Two has a lower benefit-loss rate and therefore stronger work incentives. But it is more costly because it involves a higher break-even income and therefore pays benefits to more families. Compared to Plan One, Plan Three entails a higher guaranteed income and is clearly more effective in eliminating poverty. While work incentives are the same as with Plan One, the higher guaranteed income makes the plan more costly. The problem is to find the magic numbers which will provide a "decent" guaranteed income, maintain "reasonable" incentives to work, and entail "acceptable" costs! While abolishing most of our current income maintenance programs in favor of the NIT might be an improvement, the NIT should not be regarded as a panacea.

## Summary

**1**  The distribution of personal income in American capitalism reflects considerable inequality. Though income inequality lessened quite significantly between 1929 and the end of World War II, little change has occurred in the postwar period. The Lorenz curve shows the degree of income inequality graphically.

**2**  Causes of income inequality include differences in abilities, education and training, job tastes, property ownership, and market power.

**3**  The basic argument for income equality is that it maximizes consumer satisfaction from a given income. The main argument against income equality is that equality undermines incentives to work, invest, and assume risks, thereby tending to reduce the amount of income available for distribution.

**4**  Current statistics suggest that about 12 percent of the nation lives in poverty. Although the poor are a heterogeneous group, poverty is concentrated among the poorly educated, the aged, and families headed by women. The incomes of blacks and other minorities are very substantially below those of whites, primarily because of wage, employment, occupational and human-capital discrimination.

**5**  Our present income maintenance system is comprised of social insurance programs (OASDI, Medicare, and unemployment compensation) and public assistance programs (SSI, AFDC, food stamps, and Medicaid). Many economists feel that a negative income tax would provide a superior income maintenance system.

## Questions and Study Suggestions

**1**   Key terms and concepts to remember: income inequality; Lorenz curve; optimal distribution of income; equality-efficiency trade-off; wage, employment, occupational, and human-capital discrimination; OASDI; food stamp program; unemployment compensation; Medicare; Medicaid; AFDC; SSI; negative income tax; guaranteed annual income; benefit-loss rate.

**2**   Assume Al, Beth, Carol, David, and Ed receive incomes of $500, $250, $125, $75, and $50 respectively.  Construct and interpret a Lorenz curve for this five-person economy.

**3**   Briefly discuss the major causes of income inequality.  With respect to income inequality, is there any difference between inheriting property and inheriting a high IQ?  Explain.

**4**   Use the "leaky-bucket analogy" to discuss the equality-efficiency trade-off.  As compared to our present income maintenance system, do you feel that a negative income tax would reduce the leak?

**5**   Should a nation's income be distributed to its members according to their contributions to the production of that total income or to the members' needs?  Should society attempt to equalize income *or* economic opportunities?  Are the issues of "equity" and "equality" in the distribution of income synonymous?  To what degree, if any, is income inequality equitable?

**6**   Comment upon or explain:

*a.*   "To endow everyone with equal income will certainly make for very unequal enjoyment and satisfaction."

*b.*   "Equality is a 'superior good'; the richer we become, the more of it we can afford."

*c.*   "The mob goes in search of bread, and the means it employs is generally to wreck the bakeries."

*d.*   "Under our welfare system we have foolishly clung to the notion that employment and receipt of assistance must be mutually exclusive."

*e.*   "Some freedoms may be more important in the long run than freedom from want on the part of *every* individual."

*f.*   "Capitalism and democracy are really a most improbable mixture.  Maybe that is why they need each other—to put some rationality into equality and some humanity into efficiency."

**7**   Compare and account for differences in the economic status of whites and non-whites.  Distinguish between the various kinds of economic discrimination.  Do you believe on balance that the distribution of education and training in our society alleviates, or contributes to, income inequality?  Explain.

**8**   What are the essential differences between social insurance and public assistance programs?  What are the major criticisms of our present income maintenance system?  What is the negative income tax proposal?  "The dilemma of the negative income tax is that you cannot bring families up to the poverty level on the one hand, and simultaneously preserve work incentives and minimize program costs on the other."  Explain in detail.

## Selected References

Galbraith, John Kenneth: *Nature of Mass Poverty* (Cambridge, Mass.: Harvard University Press, 1979).

Harrington, Michael: *The Other America: Poverty in the United States,* rev. ed. (New York: The Macmillan Company, 1970).

Munnell, Alicia H.: *The Future of Social Security* (Washington, D.C.: The Brookings Institution, 1977).

Okun, Arthur M.: *Equality and Efficiency: The Big Tradeoff* (Washington, D.C.: The Brookings Institution, 1975).

Rejda, George E.: *Social Insurance and Economic Security* (Englewood Cliffs, N.J.: Prentice-Hall, Inc., 1976).

Rivlin, Alice M.: "Income Distribution—Can Economists Help?" *American Economic Review,* May 1975, pp. 1–15.

Schiller, Bradley R.: *The Economics of Poverty and Discrimination,* 3d ed. (Englewood Cliffs, N.J.: Prentice-Hall, Inc., 1980).

Taubman, Paul: *Income Distribution and Redistribution* (Reading, Mass.: Addison-Wesley Publishing Company, 1978).

# LAST WORD
## Dangers of the Welfare State

In his farewell address as Secretary of Health, Education, and Welfare, Casper W. Weinberger offered some sobering thoughts on America's welfare state.

Federal spending has shifted away from traditional Federal functions such as defense and toward programs that reduce the remaining freedom of individuals and lessen the power of other levels of government.

The shift in Federal spending has transformed the task of aiding life's victims from a private concern to a public obligation. There are benefits and burdens in this:

One benefit is that the care of the less fortunate is guaranteed under law. The sweep of our social program commitments has brought secure incomes for the elderly, the ill, those who are alone, and those who are disabled. We have provided health care for millions and opened the doors of college to young people whose families could not otherwise have given their sons and daughters this opportunity.

But in the process of pouring out all of these compassionate and humanitarian blessings and institutionalizing our social obligations, we have built an edifice of law and regulation that is clumsy, inefficient and inequitable. Worst of all, the unplanned, uncoordinated and spasmodic nature of our responses to these needs—some very real, some only perceived—is quite literally threatening to bring us to national insolvency.

We are also creating a massive welfare state that has intruded into the lives and personal affairs of our citizens. This intrusion affects both those it seeks to help and those who do the helping. The entire human resources field is under the lash of Federal law—doctor, hospital, teacher, college president, student, voluntary agency, city hall and State capital.

There is another overriding danger inherent in the growth of an American welfare state. The danger simply is that we may undermine our whole economy. If social programs continue growing for the next two decades at the same pace they have in the last two, we will spend more than half of our whole Gross National Product for domestic social programs alone by the year 2000.

Should that day ever come, half of the American people will be working to support the other half. At that point, government would be like a gigantic sponge, sopping up all the Nation's surplus capital needed for industrial growth and modernization. Lacking funds for these vital purposes, we would no longer have enough surplus capital left to invest in job producing activities in the private sector—and it is that kind of investment which has always pulled us out of recessions and depressions in the past. In all likelihood, we could not maintain our free enterprise, incentive capitalistic economy, if 50 percent of the whole GNP had to be used to pay for domestic social programs alone. And if we lose our free enterprise, incentive system, we will have destroyed, by inaction, the system that has brought more benefits to more people at home and throughout the world than any other system since recorded history began.

Those who urge still more social programs view the problem upside down. It is not more social programs that will solve our Nation's ills, but more economic growth. Growth alone provides the jobs that reduce social ills.

What we do have to limit is the growth of the welfare state in America. We must summon up a common determination as a people to change drastically our present approach because it is not only not working—it can ruin all of us. Only a wave of public sentiment in this direction can give Congress the nerve to say "no" to more social programs.

Above all, we must recognize that personal freedoms diminish as the welfare state grows. The price of more and more public programs is less and less private freedom.

It is also the propensity of welfare states to spend beyond their means, leaving the day of fiscal reckoning to another generation. The news today is that we *are* that other generation.

Caspar W. Weinberger, "A View of the Federal Government," speech before the Commonwealth Club of San Francisco, July 21, 1975, excerpts.

# Unionism, Collective Bargaining, and Women at Work

## chapter 38

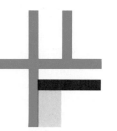

About 21 million workers—roughly 25 percent of the nonagricultural labor force—now belong to labor unions. Bare statistics, however, may understate the importance of unions. The wage rates, hours, and working conditions of nonunionized firms and industries are influenced by those determined in organized industries. Unions are clearly permanent and powerful institutions of American capitalism.

In this chapter we seek, first, an understanding of the historical background and the present status of labor unions. Attainment of this objective necessarily involves a discussion of government policy toward organized labor, because labor legislation and union growth are intimately related. A friendly government and prolabor legislation cause unions to flourish and grow; an indifferent government and unfavorable legislation can result in stagnation and decay of the labor movement. Second, we want to analyze labor-management relations, focusing upon the process of collective bargaining. Finally, we will discuss the increas-

ingly important role of women in the labor market and the discrimination which they have encountered.

## ☐ BRIEF HISTORY OF AMERICAN UNIONISM

The history of the labor movement in America is long, colorful, and flavored with violence.

In terms of national labor policy the American labor movement has gone through three phases: repression (1790 to 1930), encouragement (1930 to 1947), and intervention (1947 to date). Though the dates are somewhat arbitrary, these three phases serve as an excellent guide for our discussion.[1]

[1] The following are highly recommended: U.S. Department of Labor, *Brief History of the American Labor Movement* (1970); Richard B. Morris (ed.), *The American Worker* (Washington: Government Printing Office, 1976); Foster Rhea Dulles, *Labor in America,* 3d ed. (New York: Thomas Y. Crowell Company, 1960); and Joseph G. Rayback, *A History of American Labor* (New York: The Free Press, 1966).

△ **Repression Phase: 1790 to 1930**

Labor unions have existed in the United States for over 180 years. The shoemakers, carpenters, printers, and other skilled craftsmen formed unions of some permanence in the early 1790s. As Figure 38-1 indicates, despite this early start, union growth was relatively slow and sporadic until the 1930s. Two considerations go far to account for this meager progress: (1) the hostility of the courts toward labor unions, and (2) the extreme reluctance of American business to recognize and bargain with unions.

**Unions and the Courts**  It was not until the 1930s that legislation spelled out the Federal government's policy toward labor unions. In the absence of a national labor policy, it was up to the courts to decide upon specific union-management conflicts. And, much to the dismay of organized labor, the courts were generally hostile toward unions. Their hostility had two sources. First, most judges had propertied-class backgrounds. Secondly, the courts are inherently conservative institutions charged with the responsibility of protecting *established* property rights. Unions, throughout the 1800s and the early decades of the 1900s, were in the unenviable position of seeking rights for labor at the expense of the *existing* rights of management.

The hostility of the courts was first given vent in the *criminal conspiracy doctrine.* This doctrine, "imported" by the American courts from English common law at the turn of the nineteenth century, was unbelievably narrow by modern standards. The doctrine flatly concluded that combinations of workers to raise wages were criminal conspiracies and hence illegal. Though weakened by subsequent court rulings in the 1840s, the shadow of the conspiracy doctrine hung heavy over organized labor throughout most of the 1800s. Although unions, as such, were later recognized by the courts as legal organizations, the techniques employed by unions to press their demands—strikes, picketing, and boycotting—were generally held to be illegal. And, in the latter part of the 1800s, the courts employed both antitrust laws and injunctions in such a way as to impede the labor movement significantly.

Although Congress passed the Sherman

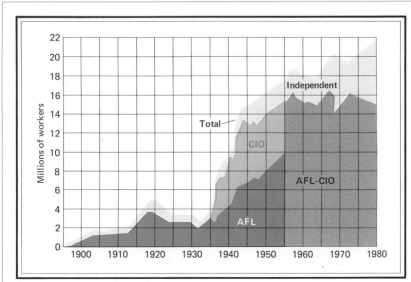

**FIGURE 38-1  THE GROWTH OF UNION MEMBERSHIP**

Most of the growth in organized labor has occurred since 1935. (*U.S. Bureau of the Census and Bureau of Labor Statistics.*)

Act of 1890 for the express purpose of thwart- ing the growth of business monopolies, the courts interpreted the loose wording of the act to include labor unions as conspiracies in restraint of trade and frequently so applied the act.

A simpler and equally effective antiunion device was the *injunction*. An injunction, or restraining order, is a court order directing that some act not be carried out, on the ground that irreparable damage will be done to those affected by the action. The attitude of the courts toward unions was such that it was extremely easy for employers to obtain injunc- tions from the courts, prohibiting unions from enforcing their demands by striking, picketing, and boycotting. Stripped of these weapons, unions were relatively powerless to obtain the status and rights they sought.

To summarize: The courts employed the criminal conspiracy doctrine, the Sherman Act, and injunctions, to the end that union growth was greatly retarded during the 1790– 1930 period.

**Antiunion Techniques of Management**
American business did not rely entirely upon the courts in its attempt to impede the growth of unions. The business community, hostile to unions from their inception, developed a group of techniques to undermine unions. A start- lingly simple antiunion technique was that of ferreting out and firing prounion workers. Too, many employers felt it their duty to inform fellow employers that the discharged workers were "troublemakers" and "labor agitators" and not fit to be hired. This combination of *discriminatory discharge* and *blacklisting* made it extremely risky for workers even to think in terms of organizing a union. One's present and future employment opportunities were at stake.

Another potent weapon in management's struggle to keep unions down was the *lockout*, management's counterpart of the strike. By closing up shop for a few weeks, employers were frequently able to bring their employees to terms and to destroy any notions they might have about organizing a union. In some cases this might prove a bit costly to the em- ployer in the short run. In other cases, when business was slack, the lockout was a good means of killing two birds with one stone— working off excess inventories and undermin- ing worker attempts to organize. Remember: Workers of the late 1800s and early 1900s were not blessed with savings accounts or multi- million-dollar strike funds to draw upon in such emergencies.

Where workers were determined to orga- nize, pitched battles often ensued. Rocks, clubs, shotguns, and an occasional stick of dynamite were the shadowy ancestors of col- lective bargaining. Some of the darkest pages of American labor history concern the violent clashes between workers and company-hired *strikebreakers*. The Homestead strike of 1892, the Pullman strike of 1894, and the Ludlow Massacre of 1914 are cases in point. Less dra- matic skirmishes erupt down to the present time.

But management tactics were often more subtle than a cracked skull. The *yellow-dog contract* was one of the more ingenious anti- union devices fostered by management. In such contracts workers agreed to remain non- union as a condition of employment. They often had little choice but to sign such con- tracts—no contract, no job. Violation of a yellow-dog contract exposed a worker to a law- suit by his employer, the result of which might be a court-imposed fine or even imprisonment.

As a last resort, an employer might shower his work force with such amenities as group insurance and pension programs and stock ownership and profit-sharing schemes to con- vince them that employers would look after the interests of the workers as effectively as would unions established by "outsiders." The next step beyond such *paternalism* was em- ployee-representation schemes or *company unions,* that is, employer-dominated "dummy" unions which, it was hoped, would discourage the establishment of genuine unions. Paternalism and company unions were decidedly effective in retarding union growth as late as the 1920s.[2]

**Evolution of Business Unionism**  The growth which occurred in the labor movement during the 1800s not only was modest, but it also embodied a variety of union philosophies. The mid-1800s were in effect a laboratory wherein American labor experimented with alternative forms of unionism—Marxism, utopianism, reformism, and a host of other isms. But such unions usually foundered in the span of a few short years because of the internal conflict between the workers' interest in short-run practical goals (higher wages and shorter hours) and the long-run utopian goals (producer cooperatives, creation of a labor party, and so forth) of the union leaders.

Then, in 1886, a new labor organization—the *American Federation of Labor*—which was to dominate the labor movement for the next fifty years was formed. Under the leadership of Samuel Gompers, labor charted a conservative course which has been very influential down to the present date.[3] Appropriately honored as "the father of the American labor movement," Gompers preached three fundamental ideas: (1) practical business unionism, (2) political neutrality for labor, and (3) the autonomy of each trade or craft.

**1  Business unionism**  Gompers was firmly convinced that "safe and sane" business

unionism was the only course for American labor to follow.  In 1903 he declared:[4]

> I want to tell you, Socialists, that I have studied your philosophy; read your works on economics . . . studied your standard works. . . . I have heard your orators and watched the work of your movement the world over.  I have kept close watch upon your doctrines for thirty years; have been closely associated with many of you, and know how you think and what you propose.  I know, too, what you have up your sleeve.  And I want to say that I am entirely at variance with your philosophy.  I declare it to you, I am not only at variance with your doctrines, but with your philosophy.  Economically, you are unsound; socially, you are wrong; industrially, you are an impossibility.

Gompers flatly rejected long-run idealistic schemes entailing the overthrow of the capitalistic system.  He spurned intellectuals and theorizers and emphasized that unions should be concerned with practical short-run economic objectives—higher pay, shorter hours, and improved working conditions.  In the words of one scholar, Gompers felt that "you must offer the American working man bread and butter in the here and now instead of pie in the sky in the sweet by and by."[5]

**2  Political neutrality**  In addition to espousing "bread and butter" unionism, Gompers had strong opinions on labor's role in politics and the basis upon which workers should be organized.  Insofar as politics was concerned, Gompers was convinced that government should keep its nose out of labor-management relations and collective bargaining.  Although he recognized that governmental interference on behalf of labor might be a boon

---

[2]During a prolonged strike in the bituminous coal industry in 1902, a spokesman for the mine operators, George F. Baer, issued the classic statement of business paternalism: "The rights and interests of the laboring man will be protected and cared for—not by the labor agitators, but by the Christian men to whom God in His infinite wisdom has given the control of the property interests of this country."
[3]This is not to say that all unions have followed conservative paths since Gompers first espoused the virtues of business unionism. The Industrial Workers of the World, founded in 1905, advocated a decidedly revolutionary brand of left-wing unionism. And in the late thirties and early forties, Communists infiltrated a number of CIO unions. In 1949 and 1950, the CIO expelled eleven affiliated unions whose leadership had come to be dominated by Communists.

[4]From the *Proceedings* of the 1903 AFL convention, reprinted in George P. Shultz and John R. Coleman, *Labor Problems: Cases and Readings,* 2d ed. (New York: McGraw-Hill Book Company, 1959), pp. 16–17.
[5]Charles C. Killingsworth, "Organized Labor in a Free Enterprise Economy," in Walter Adams (ed.), *The Structure of American Industry,* 3d ed. (New York: The Macmillan Company, 1961), p. 570.

to union growth, Gompers was equally certain that antiunion government policies could stifle the progress of the entire labor movement. In pursuing the idea of political neutrality, Gompers cautioned organized labor not to align itself with any political party. Preoccupation with long-run political goals, he argued, merely causes labor to lose sight of the short-run economic objectives it ought to seek. Gompers admonished organized labor to follow one simple principle in the political arena: Reward labor's friends and punish its enemies at the polls without regard to political affiliation.

**3 Trade autonomy** Finally, Gompers was firmly convinced that "autonomy of the trade," that is, unions organized on the basis of specific crafts, was the only permanent foundation for the labor movement. Unions composed of many different crafts lack the cohesiveness, he argued, that is essential to strong, hard-hitting, business unionism. These craft unions should then be affiliated in a national federation. "One union to each trade, affiliated for one labor movement."

This philosophy—conservative business unionism, political "neutrality," and the craft principle of union organization—was destined to dominate the AFL and the entire labor movement for the next half-century. Indeed, the AFL, operating under Gompers's leadership, met with considerable success—at least for a time. AFL membership hit a high-water mark of about 4 million members by the end of World War I. Then a combination of circumstances arose in the 1920s which forced the AFL into an eclipse (see Figure 38-1). One factor was a strong antiunion drive by employers. Spearheaded by the National Association of Manufacturers, businesses waged a last-ditch effort to stem the rising tide of organized labor. Then, too, many firms introduced employee representation plans, company unions, and a host of paternalistic schemes to convince workers that employers were better prepared to look out for their employees' interests than were labor leaders. Finally, the AFL clung

tenaciously to the craft principle of union organization, thereby ignoring the ever-increasing number of unskilled workers employed by the rapidly expanding mass-production industries—the automobile and steel industries in particular.

△ **Encouragement Phase: 1930 to 1947**

Two significant events occurred in the 1930s which revived the labor movement and inaugurated a period of rapid growth. Most important, the attitude of the Federal government toward unions changed from one of indifference, not to say hostility, to one of encouragement. Also, a major structural change in the labor movement accompanied the founding of the Committee (later the Congress) of Industrial Organizations in 1936. Both events, coupled with the wartime prosperity of the 1940s, greatly swelled the ranks of organized labor.

**Prolabor Legislation of the 1930s** Against the background of the depressed thirties, the Federal government enacted two decidedly prolabor acts. In part, the passage of these acts reflects the strong opposition of organized labor to the previously described weapons employed by the courts and by management to suppress unions. In part, they reflect a Democratic administration replacing a Republican administration. In part, they echo the widely held opinion that strong unions, by achieving higher wages through collective bargaining, would increase total spending—or at least prevent it from falling—and help alleviate the Great Depression.

The *Norris–La Guardia Act* of 1932 did much to clear the path for union growth by outlawing two of the more effective antiunion weapons. Specifically, the act

**1** Made it decidedly more difficult for employers to obtain injunctions against unions

**2** Declared that yellow-dog contracts were unenforceable

Three years later, in 1935, the Federal government took more positive steps to encourage union growth. The *Wagner Act* (officially the National Labor Relations Act) guaranteed the "twin rights" of labor: the right of self-organization and the right to bargain collectively with employers. The act listed a number of "unfair labor practices" on the part of management. Specifically it

1 Forbade employers from interfering with the right of workers to form unions

2 Outlawed company unions

3 Prohibited antiunion discrimination by employers in hiring, firing, and promoting

4 Outlawed discrimination against any worker who files charges or gives testimony under the act

5 Obligated employers to bargain in good faith with a union duly established by their employees

The Wagner Act was clearly "labor's Magna Charta."

A National Labor Relations Board was established by the act and charged with the authority to investigate unfair labor practices occurring under the act, to issue cease-and-desist orders in the event of violations, and to conduct worker elections in deciding which specific union, if any, the workers might want to represent them.

The Wagner Act was tailored to accelerate union growth. It was extremely successful in achieving this goal. The protective umbrella provided to unions by this act in conjunction with the Norris–La Guardia Act played a major role in causing the ranks of organized labor to mushroom from about 4 million in 1935 to 15 million in 1947.

**Industrial Unionism**  We have already noted that one of the causes of stagnation in the AFL during the 1920s was its unwillingness to organize the growing masses of unskilled assembly-line workers. Though the majority of AFL leaders chose to ignore the unskilled workers, a vocal minority under the leadership of John L. Lewis contended that craft union-

ism would be completely ineffective as a means of organizing the hundreds of thousands of workers in the growing mass-production industries. According to Lewis and his followers, the basis for organization should be shifted from *craft unionism* to *industrial unionism,* that is, away from unions which only encompass a specific type of skilled workers to unions which include all workers—both skilled and unskilled—in a given industry or group of related industries.[6] This conflict came to a head, and in 1936 Lewis and his sympathizers withdrew their unions (and were simultaneously expelled) from the AFL.

The withdrawing unions established themselves as the *Congress of Industrial Organizations.* The CIO met with startling success in organizing the automobile and steel industries. So great was this success that the AFL also moved in the direction of organizing on an industrial basis. By 1940, total union membership approximated 9 million workers.

△  **Intervention Phase: 1947 to Date**

Since World War II there has been a decided increase in government regulation of, and intervention in, labor-management relations. It is important to understand the background of this governmental interference.

The prolabor legislation of the 1930s, the birth of industrial unionism, and the booming prosperity of the war years brought rapid union growth (see Figure 38-1). As unions gathered strength—both numerical and financial—it became increasingly evident that labor unions could no longer be regarded as the weak sister or underdog in their negotiations with management. Just as the growing power of business monopolies brought a clamor for public control in the 1870s and 1880s, the upsurge of union power in the 1930s and 1940s brought a similar outcry for regulation. This pressure for union control came to a head in the years immediately following World War II.

---

[6]Figures 31-6 and 31-7 compare the techniques employed by craft and industrial unions in attempting to raise wages.

Many people felt that the wartime strike record of American labor left much to be desired. Despite no-strike pledges, work stoppages reached a new high at the height of the war effort in 1944. Equally harmful to the favorable climate of public opinion which labor enjoyed in the 1930s was the series of nationwide strikes which broke out during the reconversion period in such basic industries as steel, coal, meat-packing, and railway transportation. People felt that these strikes not only slowed the reconversion process but also inaugurated the severe wage-price inflationary spiral which was to plague the immediate postwar years. Many in the business community, needless to say, were happy to fan the flames of public resentment. By the mid-forties the prolabor climate of the prior decade had done a virtual turnabout.

**Taft-Hartley Act of 1947**   This growing public hostility toward unions was crystallized in the *Taft-Hartley Act* (officially the Labor–Management Relations Act) in 1947. A very detailed piece of legislation, this act mirrors the increasing complexity of labor-management relations. Generally its specific provisions fall under four headings: (1) provisions which designate and outlaw certain "unfair union practices"; (2) provisions which regulate the internal administration of unions; (3) provisions which specify collective bargaining procedures and regulate the actual contents of bargaining agreements; and (4) provisions for the handling of strikes imperiling the health and safety of the nation.

**1   Unfair union practices**   You will recall that the Wagner Act outlined a number of "unfair labor practices" on the part of management. A new and crucial feature of the Taft-Hartley Act was that it listed a number of "unfair labor practices" on the part of unions. These unfair practices, which constitute some of the most controversial sections of the act, are as follows: (*a*) Unions are prohibited from coercing employees to become union members.

(*b*) *Jurisdictional strikes* (disputes between unions over the question of which has the authority to perform a specific job) are forbidden, as are *secondary boycotts* (refusing to buy or handle products produced by another union or group of workers) and certain *sympathy strikes* (strikes designed to assist some other union in gaining employer recognition or some other objective). (*c*) Unions are prohibited from charging excessive or discriminatory initiation fees or dues. (*d*) *Featherbedding,* a mild form of extortion wherein the union or its members receive payment for work not actually performed, is specifically outlawed. (*e*) Unions cannot refuse to bargain in good faith with management.

**2   Union administration**   Taft-Hartley also imposes significant controls on the internal processes of labor unions: (*a*) Unions are obligated to make detailed financial reports to the National Labor Relations Board and to make such information available to its members. (*b*) Unions are prohibited from making political contributions in elections, primaries, or conventions which involve Federal offices. (*c*) Originally, union officials were required to sign non-Communist affidavits.

**3   Contract contents**   Other Taft-Hartley provisions are designed to control the actual collective bargaining process and the contents of the work agreement resulting therefrom: (*a*) The *closed shop* (which requires that a firm hire only workers who are already union members) is specifically outlawed for workers engaged in interstate commerce; that is, a closed-shop arrangement cannot be written into a collective bargaining agreement. (*b*) The *checkoff* (whereby union dues are deducted from the workers' paychecks by the employer and turned over to the union in a lump sum) cannot be written into a bargaining agreement unless authorized in writing by individual workers. (*c*) Collective bargaining agreements must provide that, where they exist, welfare and pension funds are kept separate from other union funds and jointly administered by the union and management. (*d*) Bargaining agreements must contain termination or *reopening clauses* whereby both labor and management must give the other party 60 days' notice of the intent to modify or terminate the existing work agreement.

**4  "Health and safety" strikes**  Finally, the Taft-Hartley Act outlines a procedure for avoiding major strikes which might disrupt the entire economy and thereby imperil the health or safety of the nation. According to this procedure, the President may obtain an injunction to delay such strikes for an 80-day "cooling off" period. Within this period the involved workers are polled by the NLRB as to the acceptability of the last offer of the employer. If the last offer is rejected, the union can then strike. The government's only recourse—one of questionable legality—is seizure of the industry.

The Taft-Hartley Act is difficult to evaluate.[7] It has been a subject of heated debate since its enactment. Unions have condemned Taft-Hartley as a "slave labor act," claiming that it has undermined the status of unions and imperiled many of organized labor's basic weapons. Most employers feel that the act is merely a step in the right direction—a long-overdue attempt to restore a better balance of power between labor and management.

This much is agreed upon: The Taft-Hartley Act represented a marked shift in public policy. This shift is essentially one from "government-sponsored" collective bargaining to "government-regulated" collective bargaining. The underlying philosophy of the Wagner Act was that a balance of bargaining power between labor and management should be established. This balance would be conducive to effective collective bargaining free of government intervention. The Taft-Hartley Act, however, envisioned a need for detailed and continuous government control of collective bargaining to assure labor-management relations which are not unduly injurious to the welfare of the general public. Most objective observers feel that this shift in public policy was a necessary one. Disagreement persists, however, with respect to the form these controls should take and the manner in which they should be applied.

**Landrum-Griffin Act of 1959**  Government regulation of the internal processes of labor unions was extended by passage of the *Landrum-Griffin Act* (officially the Labor-Management Reporting and Disclosure Act) in 1959. This act places regulations upon union elections and union finances and guarantees certain rights of union members. Specifically, the act regulates union elections by requiring regularly scheduled elections of officers and the use of secret ballots; restrictions are placed upon ex-convicts and Communists in holding union offices. Furthermore, union officials are now held strictly accountable for union funds and property. Officers handling union funds must be bonded; the embezzlement of union funds is made a Federal offense; and close restrictions are placed upon a union's loans to its officers and members. The act is also aimed at preventing autocratic union leaders from infringing upon certain rights of their constituents. The individual worker's rights to attend and participate in union meetings, to vote in union proceedings, and to nominate officers are guaranteed. The act permits a worker to sue his union if it denies him these rights. Under the act the Secretary of Labor is given broad powers in investigating violations of the act.

△ **Labor Unity**

In 1955 unity was formally reestablished in the American labor movement with the merger of the AFL and the CIO. Many forces were significant in closing the breach which had existed between the two for almost two decades:

---

[7]See "The Taft-Hartley Act after Ten Years: A Symposium," *Industrial and Labor Relations Review,* April 1958.

**1** The AFL's increased willingness to accept and practice industrial unionism lessened the original structural differences between the AFL and the CIO.

**2** The political and legislative setbacks which labor has encountered since the prolabor era of the 1930s convinced labor leaders that unity in the labor movement was a necessary first step toward bolstering the political influence of organized labor.

**3** Failure to achieve the desired rate of growth in the ranks of organized labor in the post-World War II years made evident to organized labor that a concerted, unified effort was needed to organize currently nonunion firms and industries.

**4** Then, too, considerable turnover in top leadership in both the AFL and the CIO pushed into the background certain personality conflicts which had proved to be a significant obstacle to reunification of the labor movement at an earlier date.

△ **Labor Movement Stagnation**

The achievement of labor unity seemed to set the stage for vigorous growth of the labor movement. In fact, the period since the AFL-CIO merger has *not* been characterized by a resurgence of organized labor. Union membership was virtually constant between 1955 and 1965. Membership increased by some 2 million in the next five years, but there has been virtually no further growth since 1970. Union membership has actually been declining as a percentage of the labor force. One must conclude that the American labor movement is in a period of stagnation with respect to membership.

Observers have cited a variety of explanatory factors. First, consumer demand and employment patterns have shifted away from traditional union strongholds. Specifically, employment has shifted from manufacturing (where unions are traditionally strong) to service industries (where unions are typically weak). Secondly, an unusually large proportion of the increase in employment in recent years has been concentrated among women, youths, and part-time workers, groups which are not easily organized because of their less permanent attachment to the labor force. Third, the energy crunch and other factors have encouraged the migration of industry to the Sun Belt and the South has traditionally been a "hard-to-organize" area. Fourth, in some instances employment and union membership in highly organized industries such as steel have been reduced as the result of import competition. Lastly, organized labor seems to have suffered from a deteriorating public image. Some liberal observers contend that labor's traditional progressive stance has given way to conservativism, complacency, and bureaucracy. Many unions—the craft unions in particular—have followed membership policies which foster racial discrimination. Furthermore, the growing number of public sector strikes, involving schoolteachers, garbage collectors, and municipal transit workers, has entailed more direct adverse effects upon the public than is usually the case with private sector strikes. Hence, such strikes have contributed to public impatience and dissatisfaction with unions.

The main bright spot in the picture has been the rather dramatic increase in public sector employees in recent years. The number of unionized public sector workers grew from 2,155,000 in 1968 to 3,625,000 in 1978. The fact that the public sector has been providing an expanding proportion of total employment has undoubtedly been conducive to this surge of union growth. Moreover, many public employees have sought to offset the adverse effects of the inflation which has persisted since the mid-1960s upon their real incomes by joining unions.

The rapid development of public sector bargaining has a number of interesting and important implications. First, in general, strikes by public employees are legally prohibited. Should public employee strikes—strikes by transit workers, schoolteachers, garbage collectors, and police and firemen—be legal-ized? Second, the unionization of public employees has been accompanied by traumatic redistributions of power and sovereignty. Decisions which were once made unilaterally by agency chiefs or school boards are now subject to worker protest and bilateral review. Third, public sector bargaining has probably contributed substantially to cost-push inflationary pressures. Partially because of unionization, wage rates have been increasing rapidly in some public sector areas. However, it is generally agreed that productivity advances in the public sector have been modest. As we recall from Chapter 18, the combination of substantial wage increases and small productivity increases means significant cost-push pressures.[8]

At present the AFL-CIO boasts some 17 million members. Independent unions, of which the Teamsters, the United Auto Workers, and the United Mine Workers are the major ones, add another 4 million members. Hence, the ranks of organized labor now embody about 21 million workers, which is slightly more than one-fourth of the nonfarm labor force.

## ☐  COLLECTIVE BARGAINING

Given the importance of labor unions, collective bargaining has become a way of life in labor-management relations. It is estimated that over 175,000 collective bargaining agreements are now in force in the United States.

### △  The Bargaining Process

To the outsider, collective bargaining is a dramatic clash every two or three years between labor and management. And it is easy to get the impression from the newspapers that labor and management settle their differences only with strikes, picketing, and not infrequent acts of violence.

[8] The interested reader should consult George H. Hildebrand, *American Unionism: An Historical and Analytical Survey* (Reading, Massachusetts: Addison-Wesley Publishing Company, 1979), chapters 6 and 8.

These impressions are largely inaccurate. Collective bargaining is a somewhat less colorful process than most people believe. In negotiating important contracts, the union is represented by top local and national officials, duly supplemented with lawyers and research economists. Management representatives include top policy-making executives, plant managers, personnel and labor relations specialists, lawyers, and staff economists. The union usually assumes the initiative, outlining its demands. These take the form of specific adjustments in the current work agreement. The merits and demerits of these demands are then debated. Typically, a compromise solution is reached and written into a new work agreement. Strikes, picketing, and violence are clearly the exception and not the rule. Over 95 percent of all bargaining contracts are negotiated without resort to work stoppages. In recent years it has generally held true that less than one-fifth of 1 percent of all working time has been lost each year as a result of work stoppages resulting from labor-management disputes! *Labor and management display a marked capacity for compromise and agreement.* We must keep in mind that strikes and labor-management violence are newsworthy, whereas the peaceful renewal of a work agreement hardly rates a page-5 column.

### △  The Work Agreement

Collective bargaining agreements assume a variety of forms. Some agreements are amazingly brief, covering two or three typewritten pages; others are highly detailed, involving 200 or 300 pages of fine print. Some agreements involve only a local union and a single plant; others set wages, hours, and working conditions for entire industries. There is no such thing as an "average" or "typical" collective bargaining agreement. Nevertheless, the following skeleton agreement, based on an actual contract, provides a fairly accurate notion of the scope and content of collective bargaining.

☐ CONTRACT AND AGREEMENT

△ Sample Agreement

**Article I. Intent, union status, management prerogatives** *Section 1* This agreement entered into June 30, 1981, between the Deep South Manufacturing Company, hereinafter referred to as the "Employer," and the International Brotherhood of Boilermakers, Iron Shipbuilders, and Helpers of America, Local No. 167, hereinafter referred to as the "Union." It is the intent and purpose of the parties hereto that this Agreement will promote and improve industrial relations between the Employer and the Union.

*Section 2* The Employer recognizes the Union as the sole and exclusive bargaining agency for the purpose of determining rates of pay, hours of employment, and all other conditions of employment for all the Employer's production and maintenance employees. It is understood and agreed that the Union shall designate a representative who is duly authorized and will be consulted in all matters pertaining to the application of this agreement.

*Section 3* The Employer shall have the sole right of determining plant layout, the means of manufacturing and distributing products, the scheduling of production operations, and the setting of work shifts.

*Section 4* Upon receipt of a written authorization by an employee the Employer shall deduct from the first pay each month and remit to the local Union such sum as the employee shall specify in said authorization.

**Article II. Wages, hours of work, holidays** *Section 1* The minimum wage rates per hour shall be as follows:

| | |
|---|---|
| Layout men | $8.50 |
| Welders | 7.80 |
| Tackers | 5.90 |
| Painters | 5.75 |
| Riveting machine operators | 5.50 |
| Truck drivers | 5.10 |
| Helpers | 4.75 |

*Section 2* Wage rates shall be adjusted every three (3) months in accordance with changes in the U.S. Department of Labor's Index of Consumer Prices. For each one (1) point change upward in the Index, there shall be a five (5) cent per hour raise in wages.

*Section 3* Forty (40) hours shall constitute the workweek, from Monday to Friday, inclusive. The established schedule of hours shall be from 8 A.M. to 12 noon and from 12:30 noon to 4:30 P.M.

*Section 4* Time and one-half shall be paid for work performed in excess of eight (8) hours in one day and for hours worked on Saturday. Double time shall be paid for hours worked on Sunday.

*Section 5* When the following legal holidays—New Year's Day, Memorial Day, Fourth of July, Labor Day, Veteran's Day, Thanksgiving Day, and Christmas Day—occur or are celebrated during the employee's workweek, he/she shall receive said holidays off duty with his/her regular straight-time pay, provided that he/she shall have been in the employ of the Employer at least thirty (30) calendar days. If said holiday falls on Saturday, it shall be celebrated on Friday, and if it falls on Sunday, celebration shall be on Monday. In the event an employee is required to work on one of the above-named holidays, he/she shall receive double time for time worked in addition to his/her regular holiday pay. However, if any employee shall refuse to work on a holiday if he/she is requested by the Employer, he/she shall forfeit his holiday pay, but only if he/she refuses for other than a legitimate reason.

*Section 6* All overtime work shall be divided among the workers according to seniority.

*Section 7* All employees within the bargaining unit of the Union who shall have been in the service of the company one (1) year and less than three (3) years shall receive a paid vacation of five (5) days; those who have been in the service of the company three (3) years or more shall receive a paid vacation of ten (10) days.

**Article III. Seniority and job opportunities** *Section 1* Seniority is defined as the principle that if, because of lack of work, the Employer deems it advisable to reduce the work force, the last person hired shall be the first person laid off, and, in rehiring, the last person laid off shall be the first person rehired, until the list of former employees is exhausted.

*Section 2* Seniority shall be the determining factor regarding layoff and reemployment, transfers, demotions, promotions, or other job changes where the necessary skill and ability are present to perform the work required.

*Section 3* Seniority shall be lost for the following reasons: (*a*) voluntary quitting; (*b*) discharge for cause; (*c*) layoff for twelve (12) months; (*d*) if laid-off employee is notified by the Employer by registered mail sent to his/her last known address to return and fails to do so within five (5) days of mailing the letter, unless a reasonable excuse shall be established.

*Section 4* A seniority list shall be maintained and kept up to date by the Employer and shall be available to the Union at all times.

**Article IV. Grievance procedure** *Section 1* In the event a grievance arises between an employee or group of employees and the Employer, such grievance shall be handled as follows:

*Section 2* The employee or employees having a grievance shall report the same in a signed statement to the Shop Steward, who will in turn take up the grievance with the Foreman verbally. The Foreman will attempt to make a satisfactory settlement and will advise the Steward of his/her decision.

*Section 3* If the Steward and employee are not satisfied with the decision of the Foreman, the Steward shall then submit the grievance to the Plant Superintendent verbally. The Superintendent shall make his/her decision within ten (10) days of the time the grievance is submitted to him/her. If the Steward or employee is not satisfied with the decision of the Superintendent, the Steward shall report the grievance to the Union's President, who shall submit the grievance to the management within ten (10) days and endeavor to reach an agreement.

*Section 4* If no agreement is reached within ten (10) days, the grievance shall be submitted to an impartial arbitrator. The arbitrator shall be jointly selected by the Employer and the Union. The arbitrator shall be required to hand down a decision within thirty (30) days. This decision shall be binding, so long as it does not change the terms of this Agreement in any way.

**Article V. Termination** *Section 1* This Agreement shall remain in full force and effect until June 30, 1983, and thereafter from year to year unless, within the ten (10) day period immediately preceding the sixty (60) days prior to the day of expiration, notice is given in writing to the other party indicating a desire to change the agreement.

*Section 2* Anything in this Agreement found to be contrary to any state or national law shall be automatically voided.

. . . . . . . . . .

International Brotherhood of Boilermakers, Iron Shipbuilders, and Helpers of America, Local 167
Deep South Manufacturing Company

△ **Basic Contract Areas**

This contract is representative in that it covers four basic areas: (1) the degree of recognition and status accorded the union and the prerogatives of management (Article I); (2) wages and hours (Article II); (3) seniority and job opportunities (Article III); and (4) a procedure for settling grievances (Article IV).

**Union Status and Managerial Prerogatives** Unions enjoy differing degrees of recognition from management. Listed in order of the union's preference are (1) the closed shop, (2) the union shop, and (3) the open shop.

Prior to being outlawed by the Taft-Hartley Act, the *closed shop* afforded the greatest security to a union. Under a closed shop a worker must be a member of the union before being hired. A *union shop,* on the other hand, permits the employer to hire nonunion workers but provides that these workers must join the union in a specified period—say, thirty days—or relinquish their jobs. Since it is not specified to the contrary, we may assume, in our sample contract, that an *open shop* exists (Article I, section 2). Management may apparently hire union or nonunion workers. Those who are nonunion are not obligated to join the union; they may continue on their jobs indefinitely as nonunion workers. In this contract, the union is the bargaining agent for *all* the firm's production and maintenance workers. In other cases the union may bargain only for union members. In some instances union or open-shop status will be supplemented with *preferential hiring.* Management agrees to hire union members so long as they are available; then it can hire nonunion workers. Finally, we must also mention the *nonunion shop.* Here no union exists, and the employer makes a conscious effort to hire those workers who are least inclined to form or join a union.

One of the most controversial aspects of union status has grown out of the (in)famous section 14(b) of the Taft-Hartley Act. Section 14(b) makes the union shop a legal form of union status *unless* prohibited by state legislation. Some twenty states now have so-called *right-to-work laws* which make compulsory union membership, and therefore the union shop, illegal.

Proponents of these laws (mainly employers) hold that an individual should be free to refrain from joining any organization without being denied access to a job. No worker, as a condition of employment, should be forced to join and support financially an organization whose principles he or she may hold to be unacceptable or which he or she feels is corrupt. Opponents (mainly organized labor)

counter that employer support of right-to-work laws is motivated more by the desire to undermine unions than by an urge to protect the freedom of workers. Furthermore, the union shop is held to be a desirable means of eliminating "free riders"—nonunion workers who benefit from, but do not, financially or otherwise, support the union. Finally, opponents of the right-to-work laws argue that an open-shop union, which must constantly strive to secure its position and gain wider worker support, is frequently forced to make unreasonable demands as a means of obtaining this support; a union whose existence is secure through a union shop can approach collective bargaining more reasonably and responsibly. No easy resolution of the right-to-work controversy is apparent. Chances are that it will remain a prominent bone of contention in labor-management relations for some time to come.

The other side of the union-status coin is the issue of *managerial prerogatives.* Many business executives fear that in time the expansion of the scope of collective bargaining may reach the point where certain fundamental management decisions will become matters to be decided jointly by management and labor. It is felt by business that such an eventuality will "tie the hands" of management to the extent that efficient business operation may be jeopardized. For this reason, at the insistence of management most work agreements contain clauses outlining certain decisions which are to be made solely by management. These managerial prerogatives usually cover such matters as the size and location of plants, products to be manufactured, types of equipment and materials used in production, and the scheduling of production (Article I, section 3). Frequently the hiring, transfer, discipline, discharge, and promotion of workers are decisions made solely by management but are subject to the general principle of seniority and to challenge by the union through the grievance procedure.

**Wages and Hours**   The focal point of any bargaining agreement is wages and hours. Our skeleton agreement is representative of most contracts in that basic hourly pay rates, length of workweek, overtime rates, holidays, and vacations are all specified (Article II).

Both labor and management tend to be highly pragmatic in wage bargaining. The standards, or "talking points," most frequently invoked by labor in demanding (and by management in resisting) wage boosts are (1) "what others are getting," (2) productivity, (3) ability to pay, and (4) cost of living. If a given firm has basic rates below those of comparable firms, the union is likely to stress that wages should be increased to bring them into line with what workers employed by other firms are getting. Similarly, if the firm has had a very profitable year, the union is likely to demand high wages on the ground that the company has ample ability to grant such increments. In recent years unions have achieved considerable success in tying wages to the cost of living. It is estimated that work agreements covering some 8 to 9 million workers embody some kind of "escalator clause." This is true of our sample agreement (Article II, section 2). Some contracts link wage rates to productivity; wages automatically increase in terms of an estimated "improvement factor."

Three points should be made in connection with the aforementioned wage criteria. In the first place, they are clearly two-edged propositions. For example, the cost-of-living criterion is invoked by the union only when prices are hurrying upward; unions conveniently ignore this criterion when prices are stable or declining. Similarly, the union considers the ability-to-pay argument to be of importance only when profits are large. Management is equally inconsistent in the evaluation it places on the various wage-bargaining standards.

Secondly, these wage criteria are considerably less objective than might first appear. Most people might agree that it is only fair that wage rates be adjusted for increases in productivity and the cost of living. But then arises the difficult question, "By how much?" What wage boost should accompany, say, a 2-point increase in the Consumer Price Index? Furthermore, productivity increases—particularly in the area of services—can be very difficult to measure.

A third noteworthy point: Wage changes—either increases or declines—based on these criteria are not necessarily desirable on either economic or equity grounds. Many economists fear, for example, that the widespread use of the cost-of-living criterion will cause a wage-price inflationary bias to be built into our economy.

**Seniority and the Control of Job Opportunities**   The uncertainty of employment in a capitalistic economy, coupled with the fear of antiunion discrimination on the part of employers, has made workers and their unions decidedly "job-conscious." The explicit and detailed provisions covering job opportunities which most work agreements contain reflect this concern. The importance of *seniority* as the guiding principle in controlling job opportunities is apparent from Article III of our work agreement. It should be noted, however, that in many cases seniority is not rigidly applied. Strategic workers, or "key" personnel, will often be exempt from seniority regulations. And unions are typically willing to recognize that, particularly where promotion is concerned, ability must take precedence over seniority (Article III, section 2).

**Grievance Procedure**   It has been quipped that a collective bargaining agreement is to labor relations what the wedding ceremony is to domestic relations—only the beginning. Despite formal agreements, it is the "living together" that counts. It is unthinkable that even the most detailed and comprehensive work agreement can anticipate all the issues and problems which might occur during its life. What if Local 167 members show up for work on a Monday morning to find that for some reason—say, a mechanical failure—the plant is closed down? Should they be given "show-up" pay amounting to, say, two or four hours' pay? This event is not covered in the contract and would therefore be a problem which might be ironed out through the grievance machinery. Then, too, there may be some disagreement in interpreting points covered in the work agreement. For example, our skeleton work agreement poses some possible questions of interpretation which may necessitate invoking the grievance procedure. What is a "legitimate reason" for refusing to work on a holiday (Article II, section 5)? Exactly how are "necessary skill and ability" to be defined in specific cases (Article III, section 2)? What is meant by "discharge for cause" (Article III, section 3)?

As a result, virtually all agreements contain a more-or-less explicit procedure for the handling of disputes which arise during the life of an agreement. In our sample agreement, a very complete four-step procedure is clearly outlined. In this instance the grievance machinery culminates in *arbitration,* that is, a neutral third party is designated to render a decision by which both labor and management must abide.

△   **Three Implications**
Three points implicit in our discussion of collective bargaining merit emphasis:

**1**   Collective bargaining is concerned not only with wage rates but also with the security and status of workers and of the union itself. Man does not live by bread alone. Workers seek protection from arbitrary actions by management; they seek a voice in determining the conditions under which they must work; they seek a means of voicing their grievances; they seek the status and dignity which accompany membership in economically powerful institutions. These objectives are fulfilled wholly or in part by membership in unions.

**2**   Collective bargaining is a continuous process. True, the *negotiation* of an agreement

is an important and often dramatic point of departure. But this is followed by the equally important and continuing tasks of *administering* and *interpreting* (through the grievance procedure) the agreement. Collective bargaining involves much more than a periodic clash of labor and management.

**3**   Finally, labor-management relations occur in a dynamic climate. Technological advance, business fluctuations, population changes, changes in the legislative framework, and changes in the character of business and of unions themselves constitute some of the obvious dynamic aspects of the environment in which bargaining occurs. Changes such as these virtually preclude the reaching of final, once-and-for-all solutions to labor-management problems. At best, collective bargaining provides short-run, temporary adjustments to labor-management conflicts—adjustments which the changing economic milieu is likely to render obsolete in a relatively short span of time. In view of this observation, the previously cited paucity of work stoppages due to labor-management disputes is all the more remarkable.

☐   **WOMEN IN THE LABOR MARKET** [9]
Perhaps the most profound labor market development since World War II has been the increasingly important role of women in the labor force. As the figures in Table 38-1 clearly indicate, not only has a growing percentage of all working-age women entered the labor market, but women have become a rising proportion of the total labor force. In fact, in the 1950–1979 period 23 million women entered the labor force as compared to only 15 million men!

△   **Increased Participation Rate**
What influences have caused this increase in the rate at which women participate in the

---

[9]This section draws heavily upon chapter 4 of the *Economic Report of the President, 1973* (Washington).

**TABLE 38-1**
Women in the Labor Force, 1900–1979

| Year | Women in labor force (thousands) | Women in labor force as percent of | |
|------|------|------|------|
| | | Total labor force | All women of working age |
| 1900 | 5,114 | 18.1 | 20.4 |
| 1920 | 8,180 | 20.4 | 23.3 |
| 1940 | 12,845 | 24.3 | 25.4 |
| 1945 | 19,270 | 29.6 | 35.7 |
| 1955 | 20,634 | 30.2 | 35.7 |
| 1965 | 26,232 | 34.0 | 39.3 |
| 1970 | 31,560 | 36.7 | 43.4 |
| 1973 | 34,510 | 38.9 | 45.7 |
| 1976 | 39,117 | 40.9 | 48.0 |
| 1979 | 43,391 | 42.2 | 51.0 |

*Source:* U.S. Bureau of Labor Statistics.

labor force? An incomplete list of factors includes the following.

**1   Opportunities and Needs**   The rising wage rates and expanding job opportunities which have accompanied economic growth have provided obvious economic incentives for women to seek paid employment. In particular, the service sector of the economy, which contains a disproportionately large number of "women's jobs," has expanded rapidly since World War II. Interestingly, one might think that the substantial increases in husbands' earnings that have occurred since World War II would induce married women—who, incidentally, compose the lioness's share of female labor force entrants—to stay out of the job market. But once it is recognized that a woman's entry into the labor force means, not a substitution of work for leisure, but rather, the substitution of paid work in the market for unpaid work at home, the wholesale entry of women into paying jobs is easily understood. Furthermore, although the pursuit of greater economic independence is an important reason that some women enter the labor force, for many women work is a matter of sheer economic necessity. About two-fifths of all working women are either single, divorced, sepa-

rated, or widowed; they must in large measure support themselves. Similarly, the adverse impact of recent inflation upon real incomes has induced many married women to take jobs as a means of maintaining family living levels.

**2   Education**   Like men, women have been acquiring more education, thereby increasing their productivity and earning capacity in the labor market. Statistics make it clear that the more education a woman has, the more likely she is to work.

**3   Family Size**   The improvement of birth control technology, coupled with changing attitudes toward family size, has tended to increase the labor force participation rate for women. Not only has the average number of children per family diminished historically, but the timing of births has been altered to expedite a mother's labor-force career.

**4   Increased Working Life**   A related point is that the expected working life of women has been rising because of longer life expectancy and the tendency of today's women to complete their childbearing at an earlier age. "This lengthening of a woman's expected working life is significant because it increases her return on her investment in training and education; the greater the number of years in which to collect the return, the greater is the return."[10] Indeed, many educated women are choosing career over marriage and making a permanent commitment to the labor force.

**5   Substituting Capital for Labor at Home**   It has become increasingly economic to substitute capital for labor in the home, thereby freeing women from housework and permitting them to enter the labor market. The development of relatively low-cost, time-saving household appliances, for example, dishwashers, vacuum cleaners, and microwave ovens, is illustrative. As the opportunity cost

[10] Ibid., p. 93.

to homemakers, that is, the earnings women forgo by not entering the labor force, has risen, it has become more and more rational in economic terms to purchase and substitute this household capital for women's work at home in order that they may enter the labor force.

### △  Economic Status of Women

Are women in the labor force accorded a status equal to that of men? There is convincing evidence of substantial economic bias against women workers. For example, in 1977 median earnings for full-time male workers were $14,626; the comparable figure for females was only $8,618. Stated differently, the average female earned only 59 percent as much as the average male worker. Furthermore, this 59 percent figure has remained virtually unchanged over the past ten years; women have *not* been closing the earnings gap.

Figure 38-2 is instructive in that it reveals substantial income differentials when men and women of the same age and education are compared. In addition, these differentials widen through much of the working lives of men and women. Note that men with a *high school* education earn more, over much of their working lives, than do women with a *college* education!

### △  Occupational Segregation: The Crowding Hypothesis

The various forms of discrimination encountered by women are essentially the same as those confronting blacks (Chapter 37), but studies of discrimination against women single out the importance of job segregation, that is, male-female occupational differences which reflect deeply ingrained attitudes about the labor market characteristics and capabilities of women. More specifically, the *crowding hypothesis* asserts that occupational discrimination has crowded women workers into a limited number of occupations, causing labor supply to

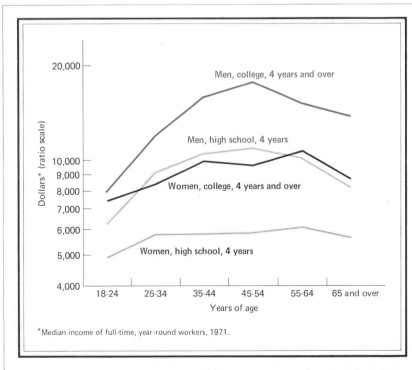

**FIGURE 38-2  ANNUAL INCOME BY AGE FOR MALE AND FEMALE HIGH SCHOOL AND COLLEGE GRADUATES**

Men receive a substantial income advantage over women with the same amount of education; this differential tends to widen over much of the working lives of men and women. During almost all their working years, men with a high school education are paid more than are women with a college education. (*U.S. Department of Commerce.*)

*Median income of full-time, year-round workers, 1971.

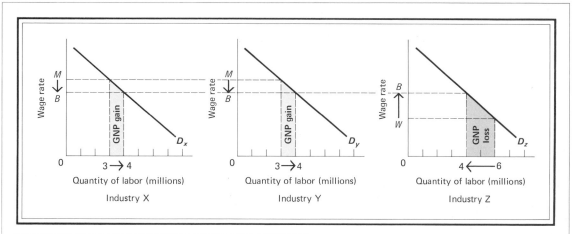

**FIGURE 38-3  THE SIMPLE ECONOMICS OF SEX DISCRIMINATION**

By crowding women into one industry, men enjoy high wage rates of *OM* in industries *X* and *Y* while women receive low wages of *OW* in industry *Z*. The abandonment of discrimination will equalize wage rates at *OB and* result in a net increase in national output.

be great relative to demand and therefore wage rates and incomes to be low.

The division of labor on the basis of sex appears to be a universal characteristic of every society. . . . Moreover, occupational segregation by sex within the labor market mirrors the traditional relations of women and men within the family unit. Within the family, the work of women and men is generally viewed as complementary rather than competitive. Sexual segregation of the labor market and the resultant division of female and male workers into two noncompeting groups preserves this basic characteristic that governs the relations of women and men in the family. . . .

The force of these institutional factors operates on both the supply and demand side to restrict the employment opportunities of women.

On the supply side, girls are socialized to aspire to and train for what are considered to be appropriate female occupations. The educational system frequently further intensifies this problem by channeling women into traditionally feminine pursuits. . . .

On the demand side, there is no reason to assume that employers as a group should be free

from socially prevalent attitudes as to what constitutes appropriate female tasks. . . .[11]

Thus we find women disproportionately represented in elementary teaching, retail sales, clerical jobs, and nursing. Men dominate medicine, dentistry, law, engineering, blue-collar craft jobs, and virtually all business positions which entail significant decision making and supervisory authority.

△  **Crowding: A Simple Model**

The character and consequences of occupational discrimination can be revealed through a very simple supply and demand model.[12] We make the following simplifying assumptions.

**1**  The labor force is equally divided between males and females (or white and black)

---

[11] Francine Blau Weisskoff, "'Women's Place' in the Labor Market," *American Economic Review,* May 1972, pp. 163–164.

[12] This portrayal is a slight modification of the analysis of sex discrimination presented in Paul A. Samuelson, *Economics,* 11th ed. (New York: McGraw-Hill Book Company, 1980), pp. 739–740.

workers. Let us say there are 6 million male and 6 million female workers.

**2** The economy is comprised of three industries (occupations), each having identical labor demand curves as shown in Figure 38-3.

**3** Men and women (whites and blacks) are homogeneous with respect to their labor force characteristics; each of the three industries' labor force needs could be filled equally well by men or women.

Suppose now that, as a consequence of irrational discrimination, the 6 million women are excluded from industries (occupations) X and Y and crowded into industry (occupation) Z. Men distribute themselves equally among industries X and Y so there are 3 million male workers in each industry and the resulting common wage rate for men is OM. (Assuming no barriers to mobility, any initially different distribution of males between X and Y would result in a wage differential which would prompt labor shifts from low- to high-wage industry until wage equality was realized.) Note that women, on the other hand, are crowded into industry Z and, as a consequence of this occupational segregation, receive a much lower wage rate OW. Given the reality of discrimination, this is an "equilibrium" situation. Women *cannot,* because of discrimination, reallocate themselves to industries X and Y in the pursuit of higher wage rates.

Assume at this point that through legislation or sweeping changes in social attitudes, discrimination disappears. What are the results? Women, attracted by higher wage rates, will shift from Z to X and Y. Specifically, 1 million women will shift into X and another 1 million into Y, leaving 4 million workers in Z. At this point 4 million workers will be in each industry and wage rates will be equal to OB in all three industries. This new, nondiscriminatory equilibrium is to the obvious advantage of women, who now receive higher wages, and to the disadvantage of men, who now receive lower wages. Women were initially exploited through discrimination to the benefit of men; the termination of discrimination corrects that situation.

But that's not all: There is a net gain to society. Recall that the labor demand curve reflects labor's marginal revenue product (Chapter 30) or, in other words, labor's contribution to the national output.[13] Hence, the shaded areas for industries X and Y show the *increases* in national output—the market value of the marginal or extra output—realized by adding 1 million women workers in each of those two industries. Similarly, the shaded area for industry Z shows the *decline* in national output caused by the shifting of the 2 million women workers from industry Z. By inspection we note that the sum of the two additions to national output exceed the subtraction from national output when discrimination is ended. This is to be expected: After all, women workers are reallocating themselves from industry Z, where their contribution to national output (their MRP) is relatively low, to alternate employments in X and Y, where their contributions to national output (their MRPs) are relatively high. Conclusion: *Society gains from a more efficient allocation of resources when discrimination is abandoned.*

△ **Nondiscriminatory Factors**

How can the inferior economic position of women—for example, the fact that their earnings are roughly 40 percent below those of men—be explained? Is this disparity simply a reflection of discrimination? Or are other factors at work? Some researchers have argued that nondiscriminatory factors explain a part of the earnings differential. The typical work-life cycle of married women who have children involves a continuous period of work until birth of the first child, then a five- to ten-year period of nonparticipation or partial participation in the labor force related to childbearing and child care, followed by a more continuous period of work experience when the mother is in her late thirties or early forties. The net result is that, on the average, married women have accumulated only about half the labor-

---

[13]Technical note: This assumes pure competition in product and resource markets.

force experience as men in the same age group.[14] Hence, on the average they are less productive workers and are therefore paid lower wage rates. Furthermore, family ties provide married women with less geographical mobility in job choice than is the case with males. In fact, married women may give up good positions to move with husbands who decide to accept jobs located elsewhere. And some married women may put convenience of job location and flexibility of working hours ahead of occupational choice.[15]

But even after adjustments are made for factors such as these, that is, when male and female workers with equal amounts of education and work experience are compared, large earnings differentials remain. These differences must be attributable to discrimination. Furthermore, cause and effect are difficult to unravel as one tries to analyze labor-market behavior. A self-fulfilling prophecy may occur which works to the disadvantage of women. Employers, believing married women are more

likely to quit their jobs in order to follow their husbands to a new job location or to have children, deny them access to on-the-job training and assign them to dead-end jobs at low rates of pay. However, these are the very kinds of jobs where quit rates for *all* workers tend to be high. Thus women do leave these kinds of jobs in relatively large numbers, reaffirming the initial beliefs of employers.

It is difficult to forecast whether the relative economic position of women will improve significantly in the forseeable future. The large number of female labor-force entrants in recent years has undoubtedly tended to sustain, if not widen, the income differential between men and women. But counter influences are at work. The Women's Liberation Movement has played a positive role in publicizing the discriminatory treatment of women in the labor force. On the legal front the Civil Rights Act of 1964 prohibits discrimination on the basis of sex, as well as of race, religion, and ethnic background. Finally, proponents of the controversial Equal Rights Amendment, which provides that "equality of rights under the law shall not be denied or abridged by the United States or by any State on account of sex," contend that it would go far to eliminate the differential treatment of women.

---

[14]U.S. Department of Labor, *Manpower Report of the President, 1974* (Washington), p. 119.
[15]Sar A. Levitan, Garth Mangum, and Ray Marshall, *Human Resources and Labor Markets,* 2d ed. (New York: Harper & Row, Publishers, Incorporated, 1976), pp. 85, 88.

## Summary

**1** The growth of labor unions was slow and irregular until the 1930s. The repression of unions by the courts and by management was an important factor in accounting for this retarded growth. The courts employed the conspiracy doctrine, injunctions, and the antitrust laws against unions. Management invoked such varied antiunion techniques as discriminatory discharge, blacklisting, lockouts, strikebreakers, yellow-dog contracts, paternalism, and company unions in slowing the development of unions.

**2** The AFL dominated the American labor movement from 1886 until the CIO was formed in 1936. Its philosophy was essentially that of Samuel Gompers—business unionism, political neutrality, and craft unionism.

**3** Union growth was rapid in the 1930s and 1940s. The shift toward industrial unionism, triggered by the formation of the CIO in 1936, was a significant factor in this growth. Equally important were the prolabor legislation passed by the Federal government in the 1930s and the wartime prosperity of the 1940s.

**4**   The Norris–La Guardia Act of 1932 rendered yellow-dog contracts unenforceable and sharply limited the use of injunctions in labor disputes. The Wagner Act of 1935—"labor's Magna Charta"—guaranteed labor the rights to organize and to bargain collectively with management. The act prohibited certain "unfair labor practices" on the part of management, thereby paving the way for unions to organize, unimpeded by management.

**5**   The Taft-Hartley Act of 1947 brought about a shift from government-sponsored to government-regulated collective bargaining. The act *a.* specifically outlaws certain "unfair practices" of unions; *b.* regulates certain internal operations of unions; *c.* controls the content of collective bargaining agreements; and *d.* outlines a procedure for handling "national health and welfare" strikes.

**6**   The Landrum-Griffin Act of 1959 was designed to regulate the internal processes of unions—in particular the handling of union finances and the union's relationships with its members.

**7**   At the present time about 21 million workers are union members; this constitutes about one-fourth of the nonfarm labor force. Although the labor movement has been relatively stagnant overall, rapid unionization of public employees has occurred in the past decade.

**8**   Labor and management "live together" under the terms of collective bargaining agreements. These work agreements cover four major topics: *a.* union status and managerial prerogatives; *b.* wages and hours; *c.* seniority and job control; and *d.* a grievance procedure. Experience indicates that both labor and management are very willing to compromise and reach agreement short of work stoppages.

**9**   Historically, an increasing percentage of all working-age women have entered the labor market, and women constitute a rising percentage of the total labor force.

**10**   The median income of full-time female workers is about 59 percent that of males. This differential is partially the result of discrimination and, in particular, job segregation.

## Questions and Study Suggestions

**1**   Key terms and concepts to remember: criminal conspiracy doctrine; injunction; discriminatory discharge; blacklisting; lockout; yellow-dog contract; company union; business unionism; Norris–LaGuardia Act of 1932; Wagner Act of 1935; National Labor Relations Board; Taft-Hartley Act of 1947; jurisdictional strike; sympathy strike; secondary boycott; featherbedding; closed shop; union shop; open shop; nonunion shop; right-to-work law; checkoff; Landrum-Griffin Act of 1959; preferential hiring; seniority; arbitration; American Federation of Labor (AFL); Congress of Industrial Organizations (CIO); craft and industrial unions; female participation rate; occupational discrimination; crowding hypothesis.

**2**   Briefly describe the repression, encouragement, and intervention phases of the American labor movement. "In the 1930s public opinion was prolabor, but by the mid-1940s the public was of an antilabor disposition." Account for this turnabout.

**3**   What are the major provisions of the Taft-Hartley Act? If you had the power to revise this act, what changes would you make? In what ways has the Taft-Hartley Act directly affected the sample work agreement studied in this chapter? Be specific.

**4**   It has been said that the Taft-Hartley Act was passed to achieve three major goals: *a.* to reestablish an equality of bargaining power between labor and management to maintain industrial peace; *b.* to protect "neutrals," that is, third parties who are not directly concerned with a given labor-management dispute; *c.* to protect the rights of individual workers in their relations with unions. Review the Taft-Hartley provisions as outlined in this chapter, and relate each to these three major goals.

**5**   Summarize the controversy surrounding the so-called right-to-work laws.

**6**   Suppose you are the president of a newly established local union which is about to bargain with an employer for the first time.  Make a list of those points which you would want to be covered explicitly in the work agreement.  Assuming the economic climate which exists at this moment, what criteria would you use in backing your wage demands? Explain.

**7**   "There are legislative, executive, and judicial aspects to collective bargaining." Explain.

**8**   Explain the increasing participation rate for women in the labor force.  Use demand and supply to explain the economic impact of job segregation by sex upon the relative earnings of men and women.  How might society benefit from the elimination of sex discrimination?

**9**   Evaluate and comment:

*a.*   "In general, women are simply less productive workers than men.  And, in particular, there are certain kinds of jobs in which women are not physically or temperamentally equipped to perform."

*b.*   "Equal pay legislation may not be very helpful to women because such laws tend to further reduce on-the-job training opportunities for women and thereby reinforce job segregation."

## Selected References

Chamberlain, Neil W., Donald E. Cullen, and David Lewin: *The Labor Sector,* 3d ed. (New York: McGraw-Hill Book Company, 1980).

Gregory, Charles O., and Harold A. Katz: *Labor and the Law,* 3d ed. (New York: W. W. Norton & Company, Inc., 1979).

Hildebrand, George H.: *American Unionism: An Historical and Analytical Survey* (Reading, Mass.: Addison-Wesley Publishing Company, 1979).

Levitan, Sar A., Garth L. Mangum, and Ray Marshall: *Human Resources and Labor Markets,* 2d ed. (New York: Harper & Row, Publishers, Incorporated, 1976), chaps. 5, 23.

Reynolds, Lloyd G., Stanley H. Masters, and Collette H. Moser (eds.): *Readings in Labor Economics and Labor Relations,* 2d ed. (Englewood Cliffs, N.J.: Prentice-Hall, Inc., 1978), parts 5 and 6.

U.S. Department of Labor, *Monthly Labor Review.*  Contains statistics and articles of current interest on collective bargaining and industrial relations.

# LAST WORD
## Return of the Sweatshops

While the wage rates and working conditions of most workers are effectively protected by legislation and unions, some workers are less fortunate.

(Reprinted from *U.S. News & World Report.*)

From the back alleys of Lower Manhattan to the heart of Los Angeles, federal investigators are mounting a nationwide offensive against what they view as a revival of sweatshops.

The squalid and oppressive working conditions uncovered recently by these Labor Department officials are reminiscent of the early days of the Industrial Revolution. As Assistant Labor Secretary Donald E. Elisburg says: "Nobody's seen working conditions like these, except in the history books."

Chief target of the government's crackdown are the operators of tiny garment factories that allegedly ignore laws governing minimum wage, overtime and child labor. Also under suspicion are some motels and hotels, restaurants, retail stores, janitorial services, fast-food shops, building contractors, farms and waterfront enterprises. . . .

One of the most common violations found by federal investigators is the employer's failure to keep a record of the hours worked by employees. Failure to pay the minimum wage and failure to provide overtime pay at $1\frac{1}{2}$ times the regular hourly rate for work beyond 40 hours a week also are common complaints. In a typical case opened recently in the Houston area, the government found that a construction firm failed to pay $130,000 to its employees in overtime wages.

In the past few years, federal officials say, violations have become more flagrant. One example: A Houston landscaping nursery paid less than the minimum wage and no overtime to a dozen illegal aliens. The nursery's foreman also required each worker to pay him a $25 kickback every week. Federal officials estimated the foreman received $7,000 in kickbacks before he was stopped.

The employees of the landscaping firm were forced to live in shacks with bare wooden floors, no inside plumbing, no sanitary facilities and a single water faucet outside. Their bedding consisted of plastic cushions on the floor. The foreman also charged the workers $1 to cash their paychecks and another sum for transportation to a store to buy food and supplies.

The most widespread pattern of abuses has been found in garment factories in New York, Los Angeles and elsewhere. Some Chinatown factories are accused of paying as little as $1.50 an hour. Children between the ages of 10 and 12 are employed to sweep floors and move boxes while their mothers operate sewing machines. Often employees will work from 7 a.m. to 8 p.m., although they punch in at 9 a.m. and out at 5 p.m. to make it appear that they are complying with the law. . . .

Health and safety violations also are commonplace in these shops, according to government officials. . . . "I would call it 19th-century working conditions," says Edmund M. Sullivan, wage-and-hour division chief in Los Angeles. "Most of the garment shops are in lofts, on the top floors of old buildings. The skylight windows are so heavily encrusted with dirt that you can't see through them. They quit providing light in the 1920s. It's filthy and enormously crowded. Between 40 and 80 workers, mostly women, are stooped and bent over machines. Bare dangling bulbs, or sometimes fluorescent tubes, light the room. The floors are wooden. It's incredibly hot in the summer and cold in the winter. There is one toilet for all the workers.". . .

# The Economics of the Energy Crisis

chapter 39

Energy—the source of the United States' industrial preeminence and its high standard of living—has become its most pressing problem. The basic goal of this chapter is to achieve an overview of "the energy crisis" and to assess its economic and political implications.

Our discussion will adhere to the following outline. First, some basic factual information on the sources and uses of energy in the United States will be presented. This will lead us into a thumbnail historical sketch of the energy problem and our growing dependence upon imported oil. Next, the economic and political effects of the energy problem will be examined. Finally, we will consider policy options with emphasis upon the Carter Administration's proposals.

Two caveats are in order. First, the energy problem and energy policies are not separate and distinct topics for analysis. We will soon discover that the energy problem is in part the result of past and current government policies. Secondly, attempts to comprehend the energy problem and to formulate effective policies are complicated by a spectrum of unknowns. How vast—or meager—are the yet undiscovered energy sources in the United States and worldwide? Are new technologies in the offing which will "bail us out" of the energy problem? What are the elasticities of demand and supply for various forms of energy? What is the likelihood that future political crises in the Middle East will trigger embargoes, or, in the case of a growing Soviet presence, the permanent loss of imported oil? Will the Organization of Petroleum Exporting Countries (OPEC) cartel survive as a price-fixing institution? What are the environmental costs associated with coal and nuclear power? These are all questions to which individuals of goodwill might provide vastly different answers! It is not difficult to understand why the energy problem is a fertile ground for disagreement and debate.

## ☐ FACTUAL OVERVIEW: USES AND SOURCES

The United States, embodying about 6 percent of the world's population and 6 percent of its land mass, consumes almost a third of the world's total energy production. To what uses do we put this vast amount of energy? And what are its sources? Figure 39-1 provides us with aggregative answers to these questions. In 1978 residential and commercial users accounted for 37 percent of the total energy consumed. In both instances this energy was used for space and water heating, lighting, air conditioning, cooking, and so forth. Industrial users—manufacturers of all types—also used approximately 37 percent. Finally, transportation users accounted for the remaining 26 percent. It is worthy of note that transportation accounts for over one-half of the demand for petroleum.

On the sources or supply side of the energy equation, we observe the dominant role of oil,

which provides 47 percent of America's energy. While natural gas and coal are also important energy sources, it is clear that at this point in time hydroelectric and nuclear energy are relatively insignificant.

Oil will be the focal point of the ensuing discussion. The reasons for this are twofold: (1) Oil is clearly prominent in the energy equation of Figure 39-1, and (2) oil is at the center of the energy problem. Economists are in general agreement that the Western world's energy problems are tied intimately to its growing dependence upon imported oil and, in particular, the oil which the industrial nations must purchase from the nations which comprise the OPEC cartel. Most of the known oil reserves are located outside the major oil-consuming countries. The United States, the Western European nations, and Japan consume almost two-thirds of the world's oil output, while their proven reserves are only 8 percent. The Middle East nations hold over half the world's oil reserves, but consume only 2 percent of current output. To repeat: The essence of the energy problem for the industrial nations is that they must import larger and larger quantities of crude oil, the availa-

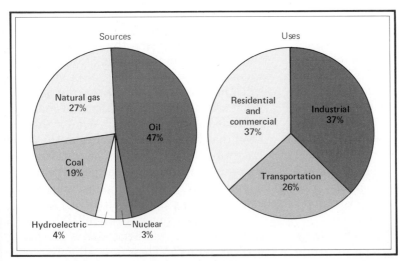

**FIGURE 39-1 AMERICA'S ENERGY EQUATION**

Oil accounts for nearly one-half of the United States' energy consumption. Approximately one-half of the oil we use currently is imported.

bility and price of which are determined by the OPEC cartel. Stated differently, most economists agree that the energy crisis is *not* that the world is "running out of oil" a la the Doomsday model of Chapter 20. The basic problem is one of the allocation, price, and availability of oil.

## ☐ THE ENERGY CRISIS: A BACKWARD GLANCE

You are undoubtedly familiar with the energy-related events of the 1970s. In 1973–1974 OPEC imposed an embargo on oil exports to the United States and subsequently quadrupled the price of our imported oil. Energy shortages quickly appeared as evidenced by long lines at the gas pumps and the temporary closing of factories and schools. The petroleum market more or less stabilized for the next several years, but again in late 1978 the Iranian revolution disrupted that country's exports and OPEC pushed oil prices above $20 per barrel to generate another energy crisis. Imported oil which could be purchased for about $2 per barrel prior to the 1973–1974 crisis was selling for over $32 per barrel in early 1980 with signs of further increases on the horizon!

How did all of this come about? Why has the United States economy become so dependent upon foreign oil? And wherein does OPEC derive its price-fixing power? The answers to these questions are complex, but they center upon (1) United States policies which historically have been conducive to low-priced energy, and (2) political and economic developments which caused American companies to lose control over foreign sources of cheap oil.

### △ Cheap Energy Policies

Though perhaps not designed with that goal in mind, Federal policies with respect to taxation, regulation, and pollution generally encouraged low energy prices in the post-World War II period. Over the quarter-century from 1946 to 1970 the price of crude oil remained extremely stable. This stability is

remarkable in view of the fact that the consumption of oil increased threefold over this period. Indeed, over the 1957–1970 period the price of oil in real terms actually *decreased* about 30 percent![1] In the postwar period up to the early 1970s petroleum products were available at bargain prices.

The government's low-priced energy "policy" had several facets. First, special tax subsidies in the form of depletion allowances were accorded oil and natural gas firms for the purported purpose of compensating them for the inherent risks involved in oil and gas exploration. Secondly, the government has applied price controls (ceilings) to both natural gas and oil at various times, thereby making energy available to consumers at below-equilibrium prices. A third and less obvious "policy" which contributed to cheap energy was the absence of significant environmental legislation. Until quite recently society was allowed to ignore the external or spillover costs associated with energy production and consumption; as a result, the supply of energy was greater and the price lower than would otherwise have been the case (Figure 6-1*b*).

What were the consequences of the low price of energy?

> Consumers responded by purchasing homes, automobiles, and appliances that required substantial inputs of energy; firms substituted energy and capital for labor in constructing buildings and factories and in manufacturing their goods. The entire American way of life, from the spread of the suburbs to the popularity of large automobiles, has been conditioned by low-cost energy.[2]

Thus, in the pre-OPEC days of the early 1970s, the United States was firmly and increasingly locked into stocks of capital goods, housing, and consumer durables geared to low-cost petroleum and natural gas. Furthermore, Amer-

[1] Fred C. Allvine and Fred A. Tarpley, Jr., *The New State of the Economy* (Cambridge, Mass.: Winthrop Publishers, Inc., 1977), pp. 111–112.
[2] *Economic Report of the President, 1978,* p. 180.

ican demand for oil was growing more or less proportionately with the growth of our real GNP. In brief, low energy prices and industrial growth generated a voracious appetite for energy in general and for petroleum in particular.

△  **Cheap Foreign Oil**

Observe in Figure 39-2 that the United States did not become a net importer of oil until about 1948. Since then our oil dependence has grown steadily to the extent that we now (1980) import about one-half of our oil! Our dependence upon foreign oil is not solely the consequence of a domestic cheap-energy policy; it also reflects the discovery of vast quantities of low-cost oil in the Middle East after World War II.[3] Strongly aided in their efforts by the United States government, American oil companies obtained concessions to explore for, and to produce, oil in the Middle

[3] Middle East oil is less costly than American oil primarily because Middle Eastern wells are much more productive. The typical well in Saudi Arabia, for example, may produce thousands of barrels of oil per day as compared to 20 or 30 barrels for an average American well.

East and in other less-developed countries throughout the world.

The biggest prize of all . . . was the Middle East. There the U.S. drive [for control] succeeded admirably. The United States pushed the British aside, prevented the French from expanding their small interests, and then defended the region (or most of it) from Russian encroachment. In a thirty-year period, from the mid-1920's to the mid-1950's, U.S. companies, starting with no base, gained a dominant position in the area that was to hold the future of the world's oil supply. It was one of the most stunning examples of economic expansion in history. The Middle East nations themselves (at the time, some were scarcely nations) were often a little more than spectators to Great Power competition.[4]

By 1955 the dominant position of American firms in international oil reached its peak. Five major American firms produced about two-thirds of the oil for the world oil market;

[4] Robert Stobaugh and Daniel Yergin (eds.), *Energy Future* (New York: Random House, 1979), p. 20. Chapter 2 of *Energy Future* is the basis for the historical summary presented here.

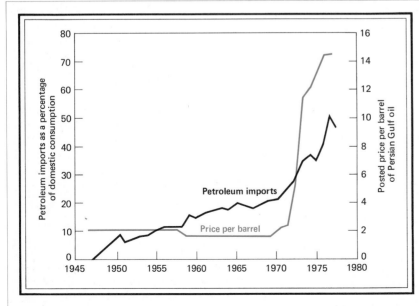

FIGURE 39-2 OIL IMPORTS AND THE PRICE OF IMPORTED OIL

Greatly expanding imports of low-priced foreign oil in the post-World War II period were an important factor in sustaining the cheap-energy era. Although prices rose abruptly in the early 1970s when the OPEC oil cartel became effective, our oil imports continued to rise. (Department of the Interior and the Federal Energy Administration.)

two British firms dominated the remaining share. As Figure 39-2 suggests, steadily expanding imports of low-priced foreign oil over the 1946–1970 period were of great importance in sustaining the United States' era of cheap and plentiful energy.

### △   Enter OPEC

But we observe in Figure 39-2 that in the early 1970s these circumstances changed abruptly. A series of events led to the formation of OPEC and the subsequent end of the cheap oil era. Let us pinpoint two of the important economic factors which depressed the international oil market and set the stage for the development of the OPEC cartel. On the one hand, by the late 1950s the United States government had prevailed upon the "major" oil companies to permit American "independent" oil companies a share of Middle East production. The added supply contributed to a decline in world oil prices. A second major economic factor was that a coalition of domestic oil producers and refiners was successful in 1959 in persuading Congress to impose import quotas upon foreign oil. These import quotas (Chapter 42) restricted the importation of foreign oil to a fixed percentage of the domestic oil market. The net effect was that the American demand for foreign oil was effectively constrained. The combination of increased supply and restricted demand put downward pressure upon world oil prices.[5] Price cuts were announced unilaterally by the American international oil firms. These cuts outraged the oil-producing countries for the simple reason that their oil revenues were a fixed percentage of oil prices. The immediate response of the oil-producing nations was a banding together to form OPEC in 1960 to protect their common interests.

We observe in Figure 39-2, however, that OPEC was *not* successful in raising oil prices during the 1960s. But by the early 1970s the

stage was set for OPEC to flex its economic muscle. In particular, the world oil market was becoming very tight, largely as the result of a rapidly expanding demand for oil. This surging demand was primarily a reflection of rapid economic growth in the Western nations and Japan. Coincidentally, the United States lifted its previously mentioned import quotas, adding significantly to the demand for Middle East oil. Against the backdrop of this very tight oil market, OPEC used the occasion of the 1973–1974 Egyptian-Israeli war to generally cut exports, to impose a six-month oil embargo on nations considered hostile to the Arab cause (including the United States), and to quadruple the price of Middle East oil.

Amidst the resulting economic trauma, it became evident that the OPEC nations—which account for about 90 percent of world oil exports—had successfully achieved a dramatic shift in power vis-à-vis the international oil companies. Acting in concert, the oil-producing OPEC nations effectively established control over both production and prices. The status of the international oil companies had been reduced to that of sales agents and suppliers of technical services.

To summarize: The combination of domestic policies and American control of vast quantities of cheap foreign oil provided the American economy with cheap energy throughout most of the post-World War II era. But during that period the United States in effect traded energy self-sufficiency for cheap foreign oil (Figure 39-2). Then the evolution of OPEC dislodged American oil companies from their domination of world oil markets. Hence, since the 1973–1974 crisis the United States has been faced with dramatically higher oil prices and a growing dependence upon uncertain foreign supplies.

### □   ECONOMIC EFFECTS

The economic ramifications of OPEC have been manifold. Most obviously, OPEC curtailed the production of oil and thereby greatly

[5] For a more detailed discussion see Jai-Hoon Yang, "The Nature and Origins of the U.S. Energy Crisis," *Review* (Federal Reserve Bank of St. Louis), July, 1977.

increased oil prices. This brought about a number of other interrelated effects. The shock of dramatically higher oil prices contributed to stagflation in the United States and other oil-producing nations. Higher oil prices have also precipitated a massive real income transfer from oil-importing nations to oil-producing nations. These income transfers have aggravated American international balance of payments deficits and thereby threatened the viability of the international monetary system. Finally, our dependence upon OPEC oil makes the United States, not only economically, but also politically and militarily vulnerable to OPEC decisions. United States foreign policy decisions, for example, must now be attuned to possible OPEC reactions. Let us consider this agenda of implications in the order stated.

△   **OPEC and the Oil Market**

We know from Chapter 27 that the effect of a monopoly or cartel is to restrict production or supply and to thereby obtain a higher price (Figure 27-2 and footnote 2 on page 548). In the case of the international oil market as portrayed in Figure 39-3, a relatively small restriction of output is accompanied by a relatively large price increase, because the demand for oil is relatively *inelastic*. That is, in 1973–1974 OPEC was able to obtain a dramatic increase in per barrel oil prices and only incur a very modest decline in sales due to the inelasticity of demand.

But why is the demand for oil inelastic rather than elastic? The answer in part is that few energy substitutes are immediately available. Automobiles run only on gasoline; a home with an oil furnace must be heated with fuel oil, and so on. Furthermore, remember that during the earlier years of cheap energy, American consumers and producers acquired large stocks of energy-intensive durable and investment goods. That is, with gas selling at about 50 cents per gallon in the 1970–1972 period, it was not unreasonable to buy a large gas-guzzling automobile. It would not be eco-

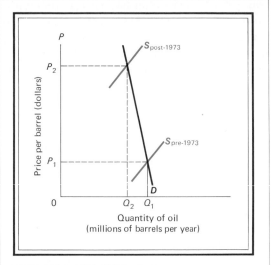

FIGURE 39-3 OPEC AND THE WORLD OIL MARKET

Because of the inelasticity of the demand for oil, in 1973–1974 the OPEC cartel was able to obtain a dramatic increase in the price of oil ($P_1$ to $P_2$) accompanied by only a very modest decline in production and sales ($Q_1$ to $Q_2$).

nomically rational to sell that relatively new automobile in 1973 or 1974 in the face of a substantial increase in gas prices. Hence, it is not surprising that the "short-run" elasticity of demand for gasoline is estimated to be in the .20 to .40 range. That is, a 10 percent increase in the price of gasoline will only result in a 2 to 4 percent decrease in consumption.[6] Similarly, most of our present stock of residential and commercial buildings was constructed during the cheap energy period; hence, they were built with a rather cavalier attitude concerning the use of insulation, weatherstripping, thermopane windows, and so forth. And pre-1973 low energy prices made it rational for producers to

[6]The "short run" is defined here as an adjustment period of one year. "Long-run" estimates, wherein consumers have five years in which to make adjustments, suggest that the elasticity of demand for gasoline is on the order of .60 to .80. The reason for this lesser inelasticity is that it *does* make sense to shift from a gas-guzzler to a fuel-efficient auto when the time comes to replace your old car. Elasticity data are from *Economic Report of the President, 1980*, p. 108.

equip their workers with large amounts of energy-intensive machinery and equipment. In brief, in the "short run" our economy is locked in to stocks of durable and investment goods which we continue to use at about the same intensity, regardless of the price of oil. Hence, the demand for oil is inelastic. The important point is that the inelastic demand is highly advantageous to the OPEC cartel. Given an inelastic demand, higher oil prices mean increased total revenue to producers. The accompanying smaller output means lower production costs. The combination of more revenue and lower costs obviously results in greater profits.

△  **Stagflation**

The post-OPEC realities of the oil market spawned a series of additional effects, the most obvious and widely discussed of which was its contribution to stagflation. In 1973–1974 American industries found their production costs suddenly skyrocketing because of rising fuel prices. Most reacted by increasing the prices of their products. In short, a substantial and pervasive dose of cost-push inflation was imposed upon the American economy. Workers reacted to this sharply rising cost of living and the consequent erosion of their real incomes by demanding higher money wages. But higher wages fueled further increases in production costs and, needless to say, further price increases. In other words, the initial cost-push inflation caused by OPEC helped initiate a cumulative wage-price spiral.

Furthermore, as suggested in Chapter 18, the OPEC price increases simultaneously contributed to rising unemployment and the stagnation of the growth of real GNP. On the one hand, some firms found themselves unable to shift their higher production costs on to consumers and remain profitable. Such firms simply went out of business and discharged their workers. More generally, the OPEC price boost was the equivalent of a gigantic excise tax levied upon imported oil. American consumers and producers were forced to pay the

tax and the OPEC nations served as tax collectors. This "OPEC tax" had the same contractionary effect as any other tax. American consumers and businesses found themselves with less "after tax" income to spend on domestic consumer and investment goods. The result was a decline in aggregate demand, a falling real output, and rising unemployment.

Aside from this "tax" aspect, the higher price of energy has entailed more subtle contractionary effects. First, higher energy prices have rendered obsolete the plants and equipment of many firms and industries. In some cases the impact is a direct result of higher operating costs; capital goods which were economic and usable when oil was $2 per barrel became uneconomic when oil was priced at $10, $15, or $20 per barrel. In other instances the obsolescence reflects the impact of higher energy prices upon the structure of demand. The hard times now being faced by the American automobile industry is a relevant illustration. The plants of General Motors, Ford, and Chrysler are heavily committed to the production of large fuel-inefficient automobiles, the demand for which is lagging as consumers switch to more fuel-efficient imports. The net result in both cases is that larger amounts of investment in new facilities are required merely to sustain current rates of production. Secondly, the new realities and uncertainties concerning OPEC policies—and hence the future course of the American economy—undoubtedly have had adverse effects upon business and consumer confidence. Economic uncertainty and pessimism are conducive to retrenchment in both investment and consumer spending (Chapter 11).

Key economic data for the early 1970s clearly reflect stagflation. The consumer price index rose from 133 to 161—about 21 percent—in the 1973–1975 period. Real GNP actually declined from $1235 to $1202 billion in the same period, while the unemployment rate rose from 4.9 to 8.5 percent! Although the impact of the OPEC oil price increase was not the only force at work, there is no doubt that it has been an important contributor to stagflation.

## △ International Economic Effects

The higher price of imported oil has given rise to gigantic transfers of purchasing power from the oil-importing nations to OPEC and other oil-exporting countries. The United States is currently paying an annual amount on the order of $50 billion for its oil imports!

In real terms these transfers are a reflection of the fact that higher oil prices have shifted the terms of trade sharply against the oil-importing nations and in favor of the oil-exporting nations. The United States and other oil importers must exchange larger amounts of their real output to obtain a barrel of imported oil than was previously the case.

But the purely financial aspects of these transfers also pose problems. In financial terms the transfers have contributed greatly to the United States' international balance of payments deficits (Chapters 43 and 44). Crudely put, the United States for many years has failed to "pay its way" in its goods, services, and financial transactions with the rest of the world. The large boosts in the price of imported oil have exacerbated this problem. Conversely, the OPEC nations are incurring balance of payments surpluses; they are more than paying their way in international trade and finance because of their sharply increased earnings from crude oil exports.

Given that the OPEC countries are underdeveloped, the obvious solution to these international payments imbalances is for the oil-exporting countries to spend or "recycle" the dollars earned from their oil exports (called *petrodollars*) on the capital and consumer goods of the oil-importing countries. And to a substantial extent this recycling of petrodollars has occurred. But these income transfers have been so large that it has been impossible for the economies of many oil-exporting nations to absorb efficiently such large quantities of goods and services. OPEC nations have therefore accumulated large quantities of dol-

lars and assets, the value of which is denominated in terms of dollars. Hence, international payments imbalances persist and reassert themselves whenever OPEC decides upon a further increase in the price of its oil. It has been estimated that between 1978 and 1980 the OPEC payments surplus will rise by over $90 billion vis-à-vis the industrialized free-world oil importing nations as a group![7]

A variety of interrelated problems emanate from these payments imbalances. First, and in anticipation of Chapter 44, problems arise for the international monetary system. In particular, the international value of the dollar—that is, the price of dollars in terms of other currencies—is determined (largely) by the forces of supply and demand. Therefore, when OPEC raises oil prices, the resulting increases in United States expenditures for its oil imports will increase the supply of dollars in international money markets. This increase in the supply of dollars relative to demand tends to reduce the price or value of dollars in comparison to other currencies; that is, the international value of the dollar declines. Because the dollar is the key currency in the present international monetary system, this decline in the value of the dollar is a threat to the existing system.

Secondly, the decline in the dollar's value contributes to domestic inflation by increasing the prices of all goods which Americans import. When the value of the dollar declines, it takes more dollars to buy a given amount of a foreign currency and, therefore, more dollars to buy a foreign product. (A British woolen suit, selling for £50 in Britain will cost an American buyer only $100 when a dollar is worth half a pound. That same suit will cost an American $200 if the value of the dollar falls to one-fourth of a pound.) A decline in the international value of the dollar increases the prices of *all* imported goods and contributes to domestic inflation.

Finally, an inflationary-causing "feed-

<hr>

[7] *Economic Report of the President, 1980,* pp. 168–169.

back" effect may occur. Consider this simple scenario. OPEC increases oil prices. This causes inflation in the United States—*directly* by raising production and transportation costs and *indirectly* by reducing the international value of the dollar and increasing the prices of American imports. But American inflation means that the real value or purchasing power of the petrodollars held by OPEC nations is consequently reduced. The OPEC nations use the decline in the value of their dollars to justify another increase in the price of their oil. Hence, a vicious circle of OPEC oil price increases, followed by United States inflation, and further increases in oil prices may tend to occur.

While our discussion has focused upon the economic implications of the energy crisis for the United States, we would be remiss not to recognize that in relative terms the economic burden of higher oil prices is greater for many other nations. Most of our Western European allies are more dependent upon imported oil than we are. Japan, at the extreme, imports virtually all its energy supplies. And clearly the impact of OPEC has been most devastating for the non-oil producing, less-developed countries of Asia, Africa, and Latin America. They are unable to develop their economies without petroleum. But by paying the rising price for oil, they must sacrifice, not only sorely needed consumer goods, but also the capital goods requisite to long-term economic development.

△   **The Political Arena**

Our discussion of the international economic implications of the energy crisis inevitably shades into some of its more salient political aspects. Let us briefly document three political implications.

**1   Foreign Policy Constraint**   First and most obviously, American foreign policy will undoubtedly be constrained and distorted by our dependence upon OPEC oil. After all, the 1973–1974 oil embargo and price increase was largely a form of political punishment for the

United States' support of Israel in its conflicts with neighboring Arab nations. As long as our energy dependence persists, we can expect that future United States foreign policy decisions will be formulated and tempered with anticipated OPEC reactions in mind.

**2   International Divisiveness**   The post-OPEC world is a more fertile ground for suspicion and hostility *among* Western oil-importing nations. Example: Suppose another round of large boosts in the price of OPEC oil occurs, triggering both stagflation and increasingly acute balance of payments problems for the United States and other Western nations. One tempting way of dealing with these problems is to use trade barriers—for example, tariffs and import quotas—to restrict imports (Chapter 42).[8] By making foreign goods more expensive, tariffs cut a nation's imports and tend to correct its payments deficit. Furthermore, domestic demand is deflected from foreign to domestic goods, thereby alleviating the domestic problems of unemployment and slow growth. But why is this divisive? The problem is that a decline in one nation's *imports* is a decline in some other nation's *exports!* That is, if the United States imposes higher tariffs to ease its payments deficits and to stimulate output and employment, our trading partners will experience an intensification of *their* payments problems and contractionary effects upon employment and economic growth. Such policies—appropriately labeled "beggar-thy-neighbor" policies—are therefore shortsighted and tend to foment political disunity among otherwise friendly nations. Indeed, nations adversely affected by one nation's tariff policies can be expected to retaliate by increasing their own trade barriers, to the end that both economic and political cooperation among Western nations is impaired. The added economic disadvantage is that artificial obstacles

---

[8]Note the growing political pressure of the United Automobile Workers in 1980 to restrict imports of foreign cars as unemployment has increased in the ailing United States automobile industry.

to international trade entail the loss of the efficiency gains associated with specialization (Chapters 3 and 41).

We must recognize the critical leadership role played by the United States as the world's largest consumer (in absolute terms) of imported oil. Whether or not the world oil market is tight—and therefore conducive to frequent and sizable OPEC price increases—depends heavily upon our ability to constrain our demand for imported oil. It is not unreasonable for our major trading partners to feel chagrined that, despite the crises of 1973–1974 and 1978–1979, the United States has yet to establish an effective program for restricting its dependence upon foreign oil.

**3  Domestic Political Infighting**  The energy problem has also fueled domestic political conflicts. For example, OPEC price hikes have brought about a staggering $800 billion increase in the value of known reserves of crude oil and natural gas. The bitter controversies over the windfall profits tax on oil producers and price controls on oil and gas are political battles over how this gigantic bounty should be distributed. Environmental issues surrounding the various energy sources have also been pushed into the political spotlight. Beyond the Three Mile Island drama, potentially cataclysmic problems associated with the emission of carbon dioxide and sulfur dioxide in burning coal are debated daily in the national press.

□  **POLICY OPTIONS**
What should be done in the area of public policy? What are the best means for coping with our energy problems?

If we are essentially correct in assuming that the essence of the energy crisis lies in (1) the growing dependence of the major industrial nations upon OPEC oil, and (2) the twin facts that OPEC oil is increasingly costly and of uncertain supply, then it follows that the focal point of public policy should be to

weaken or undermine the OPEC cartel. And, recalling that OPEC became economically effective in the context of a very tight market for its oil, it is reasonable that public policy should be designed to (1) reduce the demand for OPEC oil, (2) increase the oil supply of non-OPEC countries and (3) develop alternative energy sources which will have the effects of reducing the demand for oil and increasing the overall supply of energy. The specific policy options which we are about to examine can best be understood with this framework in mind.

△  **Policy in Retrospect:
Price Controls**
It is helpful at the outset to have some understanding of what *not* to do by way of public policy. As the result of legislation passed in 1973 and 1975, the United States has applied price controls to domestic crude oil which, economists generally agree, has had adverse consequences. Price controls tend simultaneously to *increase* domestic oil consumption and *decrease* domestic production, thereby *increasing* our dependence upon imported oil! These are particularly ironic consequences in view of the fact that our avowed policy since the 1973–1974 oil crisis has been to reduce our dependence upon imported oil.

The problem can be envisioned in simplified form[9] through the supply and demand analysis of Figure 39-4. We assume here that $D_d$ and $S_d$ reflect domestic demand for and domestic supply of crude oil. Let us also suppose that OPEC is able and willing to provide as much crude oil as we want to purchase at a per barrel price of $P_o$. Note that OPEC oil is presumably cheaper $(P_o)$ than is free-market domestic oil $(P_d)$. In the absence of price controls the oil supply curve to American users is the heavy kinked orange line, $soeS_o$. This supply curve, which is a combination of domestic $(so)$ and foreign $(oeS_o)$ supplies, intersects domestic demand at $e$, where equilibrium price

[9]For details see Yang, op. cit.

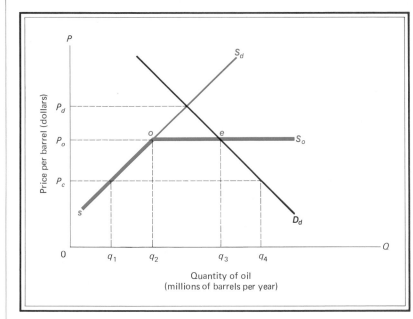

**FIGURE 39-4   THE EFFECTS OF PRICE CONTROLS ON THE DOMESTIC OIL MARKET**

In the absence of price controls American users would purchase the quantity $q_2$ from domestic producers and import the amount $q_2q_3$. A ceiling price of $P_c$ on domestic oil will reduce domestic production to $q_1$ while increasing the quantity of oil consumed domestically to $q_4$. Oil imports will therefore rise from $q_2q_3$ to $q_1q_4$.

is $P_o$ and equilibrium quantity is $q_3$. Observe that the quantity $q_2$ will be purchased from those more efficient American producers who can profitably supply oil below the OPEC price. The remaining quantity demanded, $q_2q_3$, will be imported from OPEC.

But now assume government imposes a ceiling price upon American crude oil of $P_c$.[10] Note carefully the effects. First, at the new lower price domestic producers will cut back on their production by $q_1q_2$, that is, domestic production declines from $Oq_2$ to $Oq_1$. Secondly, domestic consumers will increase the amount of oil consumed by $q_3q_4$, that is, domestic consumption will increase from $Oq_3$ to $Oq_4$. Finally, the amount $q_1q_4$, as compared to the smaller quantity $q_2q_3$ before controls, is filled by imports purchased at the price $P_o$. As noted at the outset, the imposition of controls discourages American production, encourages

American consumption, and thereby increases our dependence upon oil imports. Recall from Figure 39-2 that oil imports increased in the late 1970s despite sharply rising OPEC prices. Most economists feel that the ill-advised system of price controls just described contributed to that unusual development. We will note momentarily that price controls on both domestic oil and natural gas are being phased out.

△   **The Market Alternative**

Given the counterproductive effects of price controls shown in Figure 39-4, it is hardly surprising that some economists believe that the most effective means of adjusting to the world's new energy realities is to rely upon the free market. It is argued that the basic solution to the energy problem is to acknowledge that the demand for energy in general, and for petroleum in particular, has increased relative to supply. The real cost of energy has risen, but the impact of this fact need not be catastrophic if we will simply let the price of energy

[10] Policy goals of price controls on domestic oil include the restraining of overall price inflation *and* the avoidance of a substantial income transfer from consumers to the large oil companies.

rise and thereby signal appropriate adjustments. What are these adjustments?

**1   Voluntary Conservation**   On the demand side of the market, higher prices will provide consumers with an incentive to conserve in the use of gasoline, heating oil, natural gas, and so on. Witness the recent redirection of consumer demand away from large gas-guzzling automobiles and toward subcompact fuel-efficient cars.[11] Similarly, consumers will be prompted to set thermostats at lower levels in the winter and higher levels in the summer.

**2   Production-Exploration  Responses**
On the supply side higher prices will increase the profits of energy producers and induce them to (1) produce more energy from existing sources, and (2) more actively explore for new sources. As oil prices rise, it will now be profitable for oil firms to use more expensive meth-

[11]A glance back at the diagram in Chapter 1's Last Word reminds us that, over time, consumers are quite responsive to changes in gasoline prices.

ods—for example, the injection of steam or water into old wells—to achieve more recovery from existing oil fields. Similarly, higher prices will induce oil firms to explore for new oil in less accessible and less promising areas which were ignored when prices were lower. Market advocates contend that supply responses should not be underestimated. Figure 39-5 shows how the sharp increases in crude oil prices in 1973–1974 stimulated well-drilling activity.

**3   Substitutes and Innovations**   As the price of oil rises, there will be a greater economic incentive to use existing substitutes and to develop new ones. Witness the "comeback" of wood-burning stoves for home heating. Also observe the burgeoning interest in solar heating for homes and commercial buildings, the increased interest in developing new methods for deriving crude oil and natural gas from shale rock, the interest in developing synthetic fuels, and so on.

In short, market proponents stress that

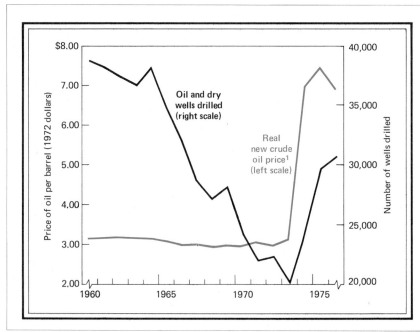

FIGURE 39-5 OIL PRICES AND DRILLING ACTIVITY

Prior to the 1973–1974 oil crisis, the relatively low price of crude oil was an impediment to well drilling activity. The much higher prices following the crisis was a great stimulus to oil exploration. However, declining output from exisitng wells has offset the rise in output from new discoveries, and United States oil production declined in the 1970s. (*Economic Report of the President, 1978*, p. 183.)

appropriate adjustments to a growing relative scarcity of oil can be made, *provided* government does not impede the required price changes with price controls and other counterproductive programs. Advocates of the market alternative also stress that these adjustments will be *voluntary* and consistent with the preferences of each consumer. Government decrees which mandate that thermostats be set at certain levels, or that newly manufactured automobiles must meet certain miles-per-gallon standards are *coercive* and unnecessarily in conflict with consumer tastes. Confronted with higher energy prices, consumer Schultz may prefer to conserve by living in a cool house in the winter while continuing to drive a large gas-inefficient auto. Consumer Smythe may conserve by shifting to a gas-efficient car and maintaining a warm house in the winter. To each his own, with the result that individual tastes are most satisfactorily fulfilled, while at the same time energy is conserved![12] Note, too, that all these responses—consuming less oil, producing more oil, and the development of new energy sources—tend to reduce our dependence upon OPEC oil and are consistent with undermining the OPEC cartel.

But there are well-known objections to a market-centered solution to the energy crisis. First, sharply increasing energy prices have particularly harsh effects upon low-income families. The retired, fixed-income couple living in Bangor, Maine, should not be forced to shiver through a harsh winter because they are unable to cope with the soaring price of fuel oil. Second, given the short-run inelasticity of demand for oil and other energy sources, higher prices will generate large windfall profits for the big oil companies. It is pointed out that the potential transfer of income from energy users to energy producers is not inconsequential. As already noted, the OPEC price hike increased the value of proven United States reserves of crude oil and natural gas by

some \$800 billion, a figure that amounts to about \$10,000 for each American family![13] Third, critics of the market solution point out that unfettered increases in energy prices have been an important ingredient in inflation, or, worse yet, stagflation. A market solution to our energy problem will merely enhance our inflationary problem and that trade-off is not particularly attractive. It should be observed that market advocates have responses to these criticisms. They contend that it is most efficient to aid the poor by direct income transfers rather than by interfering with product (energy) prices, that inflation is more the result of faulty stabilization policies than rising energy prices, and that the profits of the large oil companies have not been significantly higher than those of other large corporations.

△  **Need for Public Policy**

Aside from undesirable redistributive and inflationary effects, a more serious objection to the market alternative is that it will not *by itself* bring about a satisfactory solution to the energy problem. Many economists believe that, in practice, market outcomes will be decidedly less acceptable than those described by the simple theory of supply and demand. Consider the following points. First, oil markets may reflect market failure (Chapter 6) in that certain costs are not taken into account. These *external costs* include the political costs associated with the possibility of "oil blackmail" or import disruptions resulting from Middle East political instability, in addition to the economic costs of stagflation and slower economic growth. Such external costs provide legitimate grounds for market intervention by government. Secondly, critics question the speed with which the market will respond. The point is that a pure market solution to the energy problem will involve substantial amounts of *time.* But the problem is acute and pressing; hence, society cannot afford the luxury of waiting for the market to elicit adjust-

---

[12] See Richard H. Leftwich and Ansel M. Sharp, *Economics of Social Issues,* 4th ed. (Dallas, Texas: Business Publications, Inc., 1980), chap. 4 and particularly pp. 110–111.

[13] Stobaugh and Yergin, op. cit., p. 217.

ments. For example, while petroleum users will tend to purchase more fuel-efficient autos, houses, and factories as oil prices rise, it will take many years before our auto fleet and our stocks of dwellings and factory buildings can be upgraded for greater fuel efficiency. In the meantime, our economy is exposed to the tender mercies of OPEC. Thirdly, it is contended that special obstacles may impede the anticipated market adjustments. For example, while it is quite correct to suggest that higher oil prices will stimulate the search for energy alternatives, the economic *risks* associated with such endeavors may be so great as to make the task unattractive to even a corporate giant like Exxon. A firm might be required to invest hundreds of million of dollars in an attempt to develop, say, new synthetic fuels or a more efficient process for extracting oil from shale. Even if these efforts are technologically successful, they may become uneconomic overnight as the result of the demise of OPEC and a consequent plummeting of the price of imported oil.[14] Only the public sector is in a position to assume such formidable risks. Similarly, although Figure 39-5 does accurately show that rising oil prices did in fact stimulate oil-well drilling, it fails to reveal that net domestic production has failed to increase. "Declining output from existing wells more than offset the rise in new discoveries, producing a decline in total crude oil production in the lower 48 States between 1970 and 1977."[15] Proven reserves of oil in the United States have *declined* in the past decade. Contrary to the predictions of the market model, price in-

centives seem to be doing little, if anything, to stimulate domestic oil production. In summary, a case can be made that at a minimum the market mechanism may need a public sector nudge or two if it is to respond appropriately and with reasonable speed and efficiency to the energy crisis.

### △  Carter Administration Policies

While the policies of the Carter Administration have shifted ground over time, the current program is eclectic in that it relies both upon the market *and* upon governmentally sponsored incentives and policies.[16] The Carter program considers the task of an energy policy to be twofold: "to promote over the long run an efficient and orderly adjustment to a world of scarcer and more costly energy supplies, and in the interim to reduce the Nation's vulnerability to the transitional costs of sudden increases in oil prices and disruptions in supply."

**Reducing Short-Run Vulnerability**  In order to ameliorate the effects of a sudden cutoff in imports, two programs are proposed. The first is a *strategic petroleum reserve* designed to stockpile some 750 million barrels of oil, or roughly the equivalent of a 90-day supply of imported oil. This reserve will "buy time" in the event of an import disruption to allow mandatory conservation measures to be put into effect. The second proposal is a standby *"white market" motor fuel rationing plan*. This plan would be used only when a major supply interruption—defined as a 20 percent or more shortfall—was confronted. The plan is called a "white market" plan because it would be legal for motorists to sell ration coupons which they chose not to use. (This is in contrast to the illegal "black mar-

---

[14] A kind of paradox may be at work which enhances the risk that progress in the production of synthetic fuels will cause world oil prices to fall and thereby make the production of synthetic fuels uneconomic. "The more OPEC countries are convinced that high oil prices will bring a large synthetic fuels industry into existence, the more their own decisions are likely to lead to moderate pricing. But the more potential investors fear this reaction from OPEC, the less likely they are to make investments needed for developing a large-scale synthetic fuels industry on their own." *Economic Report of the President, 1980,* p. 113.
[15] *Economic Report of the President, 1978* (Washington, 1978), p. 183.

[16] The following discussion is largely a synopsis of the section entitled "Meeting the Energy Challenge," from the *Economic Report of the President, 1980* (Washington, 1980), pp. 105–116. No attempt is made to offer an exhaustive presentation or critique of the Administration's energy proposals.

ket" sale of coupons which occurred during World War II.)

Any rationing proposal is imbued with complex equity problems (Chapter 23). The basic question is how should ration coupons—entitlements to purchase gasoline and diesel fuel—be allocated? Is it most equitable to allocate coupons by the number of drivers in a family? By the number of cars? Should the mileage efficiency of cars be taken into account? The first criterion might prompt a family to increase its coupons by obtaining a driver's license for a senile grandmother, while the second might shore up the used-car market! If the owner of a Chrysler station wagon is entitled to more coupons than a Rabbit or a Honda owner, then are we penalizing the latter for his or her conservation efforts? Should drivers in "long-distance" states like Wyoming and Montana be entitled to extra coupons? The point is that rationing schemes which start out simple have a tendency to become extremely complex and the associated administration costs tend to escalate accordingly.

**Facilitating Long-Run Adjustments**
Over the long run the Administration's goal is to lessen substantially our dependence upon foreign oil. President Carter has pledged that the United States will never import more oil than it did in 1977—8½ million barrels per day. This is to be accomplished by (1) decontrolling domestic crude oil and natural gas prices, and (2) a series of specific programs designed to stimulate the domestic conservation and production of energy.

*Decontrol and rational pricing*  "A key aim in the Administration's energy program is to move as quickly as feasible to a rational pricing policy for energy. Price controls are being removed from domestic oil and natural gas so that the market can direct efficient use of energy and encourage the production of additional supplies." Beginning in June of 1979 the Administration inaugurated a program to decontrol domestic oil prices, which is to be completed by October of 1981. At this

point the price of domestic oil will coincide with world oil prices. Similarly, Congress enacted in 1978 the Administration's proposal to deregulate natural gas prices; decontrol is occurring gradually and will be completed by 1985.

While the Administration predicts that higher oil and natural gas prices will have the desired effects upon consumption and production, it also envisions side effects sufficiently adverse to justify public action. In particular, the decontrol of oil prices will involve a very substantial windfall transfer of income from oil consumers to oil producers. Why "windfall"? Because the additional profits will *not* be the result of any socially useful or productive activity by the oil companies, but rather the simple consequence of a change in public policy. The Carter Administration therefore advocates a *windfall profits tax* which will take over half of these additional oil profits and divert them "to public uses that will help the economy to adjust to higher oil prices." These proposed uses include the financing of research and development activity to discover new energy sources and technologies, the subsidization of public mass transit systems, and offsetting "the drain on the incomes of poor households from higher energy prices. . . ."

*Stimulating conservation and production*  While recognizing the importance of decontrolling domestic energy prices, the Carter Administration also believes that the market may need some public prodding to achieve the goals of greater conservation and production of energy with more speed and certainty than would otherwise be the case. It is believed that ". . . a strong case can be made for supplementary measures to push conservation and supply decisions beyond what the market dictates."

Consider one or two of the Administration's proposals to promote greater conservation of energy. First, in addition to imposing a 55-mph speed limit, the government has required that automobile manufacturers upgrade substantially the fuel efficiency of their products. Thus, by 1985 the average fuel efficiency of new cars must reach 27½ miles per gallon as measured by EPA tests. The Department of Energy is in the process of imposing similar requirements upon the manufacturers of electrical appliances. Secondly, a number of tax incentives have been established to induce homeowners to increase the fuel efficiency of homes. In particular, a 15 percent tax credit is available on the first $2000 a household spends for the installation of insulation, weatherstripping, storm doors, and special fuel-saving heating equipment. Similarly, builders of new residences or commercial buildings which incorporate solar heating are eligible for substantial tax credits.

On the supply side government has increased the financing of a variety of energy-related R & D programs designed to reduce the pollution effects of greater coal usage, to improve solar and nuclear technologies, to improve the extraction of oil from shale, and so forth. In 1979 President Carter proposed the establishment of an *Energy Security Corporation* to provide financial assistance to private firms in the development of synthetic fuels.

△ **Conservation: The Ultimate Energy Source?**

There is a great deal of disagreement as to which of the various governmental actions and proposals will be most helpful in resolving the energy problem. As noted earlier, some put their faith in the market solution while others favor government programs to stimulate energy production and conservation.

The Harvard Energy Project—a six-year study at the Harvard Business School—concludes that, for the immediate future, conservation is the primary avenue which the United States must pursue. It is argued that increases in energy supplies from domestic oil, natural gas, coal, and nuclear sources will be modest in the next decade or so. Oil and natural gas reserves have *not* expanded since the 1973–1974 crisis, despite greatly intensified exploration (Figure 39-5). Coal and nuclear energy entail serious environmental, technological, and political obstacles to expanded production. This leaves us essentially with the options of increasing dependence upon foreign oil, on the one hand, or conservation, on the other. It is stressed that "conservation is no less an energy alternative than oil, coal, or nuclear." Furthermore,

> Conservation may well be the cheapest, safest, most productive energy alternative readily available in large amounts. By comparison, conservation is a quality energy source. It does not threaten to undermine the international monetary system, nor does it emit carbon dioxide into the atmosphere, nor does it generate problems comparable to nuclear waste.[17]

The link between economic growth and energy use is held to be elastic and flexible. Hence, the conclusion that "If the United States were to make a serious commitment to conservation, it might well consume 30 to 40 percent less energy than it now does, and still enjoy the same or an even higher standard of living."[18]

[17]Stobaugh and Yergin, op. cit., p. 137.
[18]Ibid., p. 136.

## Summary

1   The United States enjoyed low energy prices throughout most of the post-World War II period as the result of *a.* domestic tax, regulation, and pollution policies; and *b.* the ready availability of cheap, American-controlled foreign oil.

2   An energy crisis was created in 1973–1974 when the OPEC cartel became effective. Faced with an inelastic demand for oil, OPEC was able to increase prices and profits very substantially as a consequence of very modest curtailments in oil production.

**3** OPEC price and production policies have contributed to stagflation in, and serious balance of payments imbalances among, the industrialized nations. The payments imbalances have tended to reduce the international value of the dollar and threaten the viability of the international monetary system.

**4** Political aspects of the energy crisis include *a.* the modification of United States foreign policy for anticipated OPEC reactions, *b.* international divisiveness among the industrial nations as a result of stagflation and payments imbalances, and *c.* heightened domestic political tensions surrounding such issues as oil company profits and the environmental implications of coal and nuclear energy.

**5** Price controls on domestic crude oil in the 1970s have aggravated our energy problems by encouraging greater domestic consumption of oil, discouraging domestic oil production, and increasing our dependence upon imported oil.

**6** A number of economists recommend a free-market adjustment to the energy crisis. They contend that rising oil prices will *a.* induce voluntary conservation, *b.* encourage the production of more domestic oil, and *c.* stimulate the search for alternate energy sources.

**7** Other economists believe that external costs associated with oil dependence, the relative slowness of market responses, and the magnitude of the economic risks associated with the search for new energy sources justify an array of public policies to deal with our energy problems.

**8** The Carter Administration's program involves policies to reduce *a.* our short-run vulnerability to an OPEC embargo, and *b.* our long-run dependence upon foreign oil. The former include the establishment of reserve stocks of petroleum and a standby rationing program for gasoline and diesel fuel. The latter entail decontrolling the prices of domestic oil and natural gas, government regulations with respect to speed limits and automobile fuel efficiency, tax incentives for energy conservation, and the funding of synthetic fuel development.

## Questions and Study Suggestions

**1** Key terms and concepts to remember: OPEC; cheap-energy era; "OPEC tax"; balance of payments deficits and surpluses; petrodollars; international value of the dollar; beggar-thy-neighbor policies; price controls; Strategic Petroleum Reserve; motor fuel rationing plan; windfall profits tax; Energy Security Corporation.

**2** What was the role of governmental tax, regulatory, and pollution policies in contributing to the energy crisis? Could the 1973–1974 energy crisis have been avoided?

**3** Since the mid-1950s the price of natural gas has been regulated in the United States. What effect would you expect this policy to have upon *a.* the demand for oil, and *b.* the price of oil? How does your answer relate to the United States' energy problems in the 1970s and 1980s?

**4** Of what significance is the elasticity of demand for oil for the functioning of OPEC? Why might the "long-run" demand for oil be more elastic than the "short-run" demand? Is this difference of any practical significance?

**5** Assume that tomorrow OPEC doubles the price of its oil. Trace the likely domestic and international consequences.

**6** What are the basic means by which a cartel such as OPEC can be weakened or dissolved?

**7** Use an appropriate diagram to demonstrate how a ceiling price on domestic oil which is below the price of imported oil will *a.* increase domestic consumption of oil, *b.* decrease domestic production of oil, and *c.* increase that economy's dependence upon foreign oil.

**8**   If the flow of Middle East oil is disrupted in the future, would you recommend rationing by price or by coupons? Indicate the advantages and shortcomings associated with both options.

**9**   "There is a rather simple solution to our energy problems. It is that the government withdraw from the markets for energy resources. When prices are permitted to rise to their equilibrium levels, shortages disappear. Government energy programs become unnecessary." Do you agree? Can you provide any economic justification for government energy programs?

**10**   What is your evaluation of each of the following components of the Carter Administration's energy program?

   *a.*   The 55-mph speed limit

   *b.*   Financial assistance to firms seeking to develop synthetic fuels

   *c.*   The establishment of a Strategic Oil Reserve

   *d.*   The standby fuel rationing plan

   *e.*   Deregulation of domestic oil and natural gas prices

   *f.*   A windfall profits tax on domestic oil companies

   *g.*   Tax credits for insulating homes and commercial buildings

**11**   It has recently been proposed that a $.50 per gallon tax be imposed on gasoline. What is the rationale for this proposal? Do you favor it?

**12**   What impact would the development of synthetic fuels and other new forms of energy have upon the elasticity of demand for oil? What effect might this change in elasticity have upon OPEC's price policies?

**13**   How does a "windfall profit" differ from an ordinary profit? Are windfall profits necessary to induce American oil companies to intensify their search for oil?

**14**   On what grounds does the Harvard Energy Project conclude that conservation is the best means of coping with the energy crisis?

## Selected References

*Economic Report of the President, 1978*, pp. 179–194.

*Economic Report of the President, 1980*, pp. 105–116.

Goodman, John C., and Edwin G. Dolan: *Economics of Public Policy* (St. Paul: West Publishing Company, 1979), chaps. 3, 9, and 10.

Grayson, Leslie E. (ed.): *Economics of Energy* (Princeton, N. J.: The Darwin Press, 1975).

Leftwich, Richard H., and Ansel M. Sharp: *Economics of Social Issues*, 4th ed. (Dallas: Business Publications, Inc., 1980), chap. 4.

Lowinger, Thomas C.: "U.S. Energy Policy: A Critical Assessment," *MSU Business Topics*, Winter 1980, pp. 15–22.

Miller, Robert Leroy: *The Economics of Energy: What Went Wrong?* (Glen Ridge, N. J.: Thomas Horton and Daughters, 1974).

Stobaugh, Robert, and Daniel Yergin: *Energy Future* (New York: Random House, 1979).

Yang, Jai-Hoon: "The Nature and Origins of the U.S. Energy Crisis," *Review,* Federal Reserve Bank of St. Louis, July, 1977.

# LAST WORD
## Predicting the Price of OPEC Oil

Increases in the price of OPEC oil have had highly disruptive effects upon the industrialized nations. What factors influence OPEC price decisions?

The member nations of OPEC, accounting for over 90 percent of the world exports of oil, by and large have taken over ownership of the oil concessions within their territories and continue to set prices unilaterally. . . .

One country dominates OPEC—Saudi Arabia. It is favored by a unique conjunction of huge reserves, extraordinary ease of exploitation, and a population so tiny (5 or 6 million people) that domestic revenue needs at current prices have no practical effect on the level of oil production. Saudi Arabia is the largest producer in OPEC, with 30 percent of total production and 34 percent of total reserves. . . . The pricing system for OPEC oil itself shows the importance of Saudi Arabia, for all other OPEC oil is priced in relation to Saudi "marker crude."

[A] difficulty in predicting world oil prices with much certainty stems from the fact that Saudi Arabia dominates OPEC and thereby sets the world oil price. But there is no way to determine exactly on what basis the Saudis set the price. It is reasonable to assume that the most fundamental goal of the present ruling family is survival, that is, to keep themselves in power. There are forces pushing them in different directions. On the one hand, they desire good relations with the United States, and want to avoid creating economic conditions in Western Europe that would lead to left-wing governments. They fear that higher prices will augment the arms-buying potential of their neighbors, such as Iraq. On the other hand, they are not anxious to sell their only real asset—oil—at too low a price. Furthermore, they are becoming increasingly wary of producing substantially greater quantities of oil in order to pay for massive industrial development, especially with Iran as an object lesson. Also, the Saudis are under pressure from the more radical Arabs to raise oil prices and not increase production.

Thus, predicting oil prices is as much art as it is science, requiring sensitivity to political nuance as much as dexterity in mathematical analyses.

Robert Stobaugh and Daniel Yergin (eds.), *Energy Future* (New York: Random House, 1979), pp. 31, 223, abridged. Reprinted by permission.

# The Radical Critique: The Economics of Dissent

chapter 40

The basic purpose of this book is to present the orthodox—the "traditional" or "mainstream"—view of how capitalism operates, the sources of its problems, and the various policies which might be appropriate in alleviating those problems. The general tenor of this presentation is acceptable to the vast majority of economists; they agree that it is a rough approximation of reality.

But in the 1960s and 1970s there emerged a relatively small group of economists—variously labeled "New Left," neo-Marxist, or radical economists, who envision the American economy and its problems much differently. Although radical economics encompasses an important intellectual tradition which traces back to Karl Marx, its recent growth is rooted in the apparent inability of capitalistic society to resolve a number of deeply rooted problems such as the unequal distribution of income, wealth, and power both domestically and internationally; the wasteful use of resources; the

deterioration of the environment; discrimination; the urban malaise; and the stagflation dilemma. More specifically, radical economists flatly reject the portrayal of capitalism presented in this textbook; they regard it essentially as an apology for, or a legitimization of, the existing system. Furthermore, the radicals are pessimistic about the prospects for reform of the existing society from within for the simple reason that those who benefit most from the status quo dominate and control the political system.

The basic objective of the present chapter is to present—in as systematic and objective a fashion as possible—those basic ideas and contentions which constitute radical economics. This is not an easy task. On the one hand, just as there are many different postures or schools of thought within orthodox economics, so there are many divergent views within the radical position. On the other hand, the literature of radical economics is vast and far-ranging;

hence, the summary statement offered here is necessarily abrupt and incomplete.[1]

The agenda is as follows. First, a thumbnail sketch of Marxian economics—the historical predecessor of radical economics—is presented. Next, we shall examine certain fundamental differences between orthodox and radical economics in the areas of methodology and problem perception. Third, our main task will be to outline in some detail a radical model of modern capitalism. Finally, we shall consider the orthodox rebuttal to the economics of dissent.

## □  THE MARXIAN HERITAGE: THE "OLD LEFT"

The roots of the radical critique of capitalism go back to Karl Marx (1818–1883). An intellectual of the first rank, Marx was both a radical journalist and an active revolutionary. Expelled from continental Europe for his activities, Marx spent some thirty-five years in England engaged in scholarly research.

During this period he was eyewitness to the depressing picture presented by the industrial revolution in capitalistic England.[2]

> Workers in the new factories were paid low wages. . . . Hours of work were long, women and children were employed in substantial numbers and often in hard and dangerous jobs, factory discipline was often harsh and rigorous, and in some areas company-owned stores profited from exclusive selling rights among employees. Particularly in the textile and coal industries,

competition kept selling prices low, and firms competed with each other by squeezing labor costs whenever possible.

> The realities of industrial life created sharp contrasts between the growing wealth of the new industrialists and bankers and the poverty of those without property who formed the work force in the factories of the slum-ridden cities. . . .

> . . . industrialization promised abundance. For the first time it seemed as though it might be possible to produce everything men could want and that the great struggle for existence could be resolved. Yet the gray slums of Manchester and the black country of the coal mines told a different story. The promise and the reality were vastly different.

Marx grasped the inconsistencies of capitalism and, in particular, the promise of abundance and the reality of widespread poverty. Hence, in his great work *Capital,* Marx's attention was devoted primarily to an explanation of how the dynamic forces and contradictions within capitalism would cause the system to break down. In capsule form, Marx's theory of capitalistic development and collapse runs as follows.

### △  The Class Struggle

To Marx the economist, mankind is engaged in a struggle with nature. Initially, this is a struggle to wrest subsistence from the physical resources which nature provides. But over time the development of factory production and improved machine technology increase man's ability to obtain material wealth from nature and pose the prospect of economic abundance. However, to Marx the social philosopher, there is a simultaneous struggle which pits person against person. Human beings as workers are also a part of nature; they, too, are productive resources. Hence, it is possible for some individuals to improve their material well-being by wresting output from other individuals. Pointing to the slave-based economies of ancient societies and the serfdom

---

[1] Most radical economists belong to the Union for Radical Political Economics (URPE), which publishes the quarterly *Review of Radical Political Economics.* The *Monthly Review* is also an important outlet of radical thought. The references at the end of this chapter present important summaries and critiques of the radical view. For an excellent summary of "the major tenets and general orientation" of radical thought by two radical economists, consult Raymond S. Franklin and William K. Tabb, "The Challenge of Radical Political Economics," *Journal of Economic Issues,* March 1974, pp. 127–150.

[2] Daniel R. Fusfeld, *The Age of the Economist,* 3d ed. (Glenview, Ill.: Scott, Foresman and Company, 1977), p. 57.

of the Middle Ages, Marx argued that this man-versus-man struggle has been a central theme of history. In Marx's time, this class struggle centered upon the wage system of capitalism—a system based upon the private ownership of capital.

### △ Private Property and the Exploitation of Labor

In the man-against-man struggle Marx envisioned two great groups of protagonists—capitalists (the bourgeoisie) and workers (the proletariat). The former, thanks to the capitalistic institution of private property, own the machinery and equipment necessary for production in an industrial society. The propertyless working class is therefore dependent upon the capitalists for employment and for its members' livelihood. Given the worker's inferior bargaining position and the capitalist's pursuit of profits, the capitalist will exploit labor by paying a daily wage which is much less than the value of the worker's daily production. In short, the capitalist can and will pay workers a subsistence wage and expropriate the remaining fruits of their labor as profits, or what Marx called *surplus value*.

### △ Capital Accumulation and Its Consequences

The dynamics of the capitalistic system, however, put pressures upon the capitalist-entrepreneur. In the early stages of capitalism, there exist severe competitive pressures which force the capitalist to become more efficient, more productive. Capitalists react to these pressures by investing the profits they have expropriated from labor in additional and technologically superior machinery and equipment. The capitalist who fails to accumulate capital faces the prospect of losing out to those rivals who do; the capitalist must accumulate or be accumulated.

This *law of capitalist accumulation* has a number of consequences in the capitalist system.

1 First and expectedly, it is a basic source of the expanding national output which capitalism is potentially able to produce. Marx, it should be noted, expressed great admiration for the productive potential of the capitalistic system. His hostility toward the system was based on the belief that, although labor was the ultimate source of all output, a large portion of this output was denied labor by property-owning capitalists.

2 Capital accumulation results in the substitution of capital for labor in the productive process; Marx argued that capital accumulation would cause technological unemployment and give rise to a growing body of unemployed workers, which he termed the *industrial reserve army*. This unemployment would be aggravated by the growing productive capacity of capitalism, coupled with the inadequate purchasing power of the masses of low-wage workers.

3 Finally and paradoxically, Marx held that the capitalist's investment in machinery and equipment, motivated by the desire to preserve profits, would in fact *lower* the rate of profits. Why so? Because the capitalist's source of surplus value or profits is (the exploitation of) the labor force and not capital goods. Therefore, as capitalists substitute machinery for labor, a growing proportion of their outlays is for nonprofitable machinery and a declining proportion for profit-generating labor. Hence, the *rate* of profits must fall.

### △ Increasing Degradation of the Working Class

An inevitable consequence of these developments is the increased immiseration of the working class. Consider the forces bearing upon workers. The institution of private property divorces them from the means of production—machinery and equipment—and allows the capitalist to pay a subsistence wage and expropriate much of their production as profits. The substitution of capital for labor, coupled with the growing divergence between capitalism's capacities to produce and consume, leads to a growing body of unemployed workers. Finally, in an effort to offset falling profit rates, capitalists will increase their exploitation of labor by increasing the intensity of work, lengthening the work day, and bringing more women and children into the labor force.

△ **Monopoly Capitalism
and Imperialism**

The forces of capitalistic development also impose serious changes upon the capitalist class. In particular, the competition which characterizes the early stages of capitalism will give way to the increased monopolization of industry in its later stages. Bluntly put, the falling rate of profits and the growing gap between production and consumption will force the weaker capitalists out of business. Hence, over time the ownership and control of industry will become increasingly concentrated in the hands of a diminishing number of capitalists. The smaller and financially weaker business owners who have succumbed to the forces of capitalistic development will join the ranks of the working class. The combined impact of the increased degradation of the working class and the monopolization of industry yields Marx's famous assertion that under capitalism, the rich get richer (and fewer in number) and the poor get poorer (and increasingly numerous).

These circumstances would give rise to *imperialism,* the final stage of capitalistic development.[3] That is, faced with falling profits, diminishing ability to further exploit the domestic labor force, and increasing difficulty in selling their products domestically because of the inadequate incomes and purchasing power of the masses of workers, monopoly capitalists will inevitably turn their attention to the exploitation of the less developed countries. The underdeveloped areas are typically characterized by abundant and therefore cheap labor and, frequently, cheap raw materials. Fur-

thermore, their primitive state of economic development makes them lucrative targets for capitalist investment or accumulation. These developments allegedly explain the colonization and domination of the world's underdeveloped areas by "imperialistic powers," a process which reached its peak in the period between 1890 and World War II. The important point is that imperialism transforms the class struggle from a domestic to a worldwide conflict.

△ **Revolution and Socialism**

But the imperialistic phase merely prolongs capitalism's life span. The ultimate results of the internal contradictions—falling profit rates, difficulties in finding markets for output, and especially the increasing exploitation of labor—inevitably culminate in worker revolution and the overthrow of capitalism. Consider the impassioned prose of Marx's *Capital:*

> Along with the constantly diminishing number of the magnates of capital, who usurp and monopolize all advantages of this process of transformation, grows the mass of misery, oppression, slavery, degradation, exploitation; but with this too grows the revolt of the working-class, a class always increasing in numbers, and disciplined, united, organized by the very mechanism of the process of capitalist production itself. . . . Centralization of the means of production and socialization of labour at last reach a point where they become incompatible with their capitalist integument. This integument bursts asunder. The knell of capitalist private property sounds. The expropriators are expropriated.

Marx envisioned the political state in capitalism as a means through which the capitalist class will sustain its capacity to exploit the working class. The period following the worker revolution would be characterized by a "dictatorship of the proletariat," or working class; its primary task would be to socialize the means of production and thereby to abolish the capitalist class. The specific program for trans-

---

[3]Lenin, not Marx, was responsible for the analysis of the imperialistic stage of capitalism.

forming society under proletariat leadership was presented by Marx and his lifelong associate Friedrich Engels (1820–1895) in *The Communist Manifesto*. Specific measures included the nationalization (socialization) of all basic productive resources, including land, factories, and the banking, transportation, and communication systems. A heavily progressive income tax was advocated and the right of inheritance was to be canceled. Child labor was also to be abolished and free public education provided for all children. But in time the establishment of a classless society would mean the elimination of the primary function of the state—the oppression of one class (labor) by another (capitalist)—and hence the state would "wither away" and some unspecified form of communism would evolve.

Given this terse outline of the economics of the Old Left, let us now consider its modernization by the New Left.

## □ ORTHODOX AND RADICAL ECONOMICS: BASIC DIFFERENCES

In the radical or New Left view, the methodological shortcomings of orthodox economics render it incapable of understanding, and dealing effectively with, the "big problems" of capitalist society. Radicals envision two related methodological deficiencies: First, orthodox economists have a naïve and incorrect conception of the realities—the institutions and operations—of the capitalistic system; second, orthodox economics is too narrow a discipline to permit a clear understanding of real-world problems. Let us consider these two criticisms in the order stated.

### △  Harmony or Conflict?

Consider the comments of a leading Marxist on the first point:[4]

> Orthodox economics takes the existing social system for granted, much as though it were a part

of the natural order of things. Within this framework it searches for harmonies of interest among individuals, groups, classes, and nations; it investigates tendencies toward equilibrium; and it assumes that change is gradual and non-disruptive.

But it is contended that capitalist reality is not so placid:

> . . . the world we live in is not one of harmonies of interest, tendencies to equilibrium, and gradual change. . . . Conflicts of interest, disruptive forces, abrupt and often violent change—these are clearly the *dominant* characteristics of capitalism on a world-wide scale today.

Orthodox economists, in other words, envision a basic harmony in capitalism which allows the system to realize a satisfactory and workable reconciliation of divergent interests. Where product and resource markets are reasonably competitive, the market system promotes a rough identity of private and social interests through the "invisible hand" (Chapter 5). In other cases, monopoly is countered with monopoly—big business faces big labor—so that market outcomes are usually socially tolerable. Where the market fails—for example, in the cases of unbridled monopoly, public goods, spillover costs, and income inequality—a benevolent government will intervene so as to protect and promote the general welfare. Modern capitalism is a pluralistic system wherein power is rather widely dispersed among business, labor, consumers, and government so that consensus decisions are reached which are consistent with the general welfare. Hence, argue mainstream economists, the system's problems and shortcomings can be ameliorated or resolved within its present institutional and ideological framework. Indeed, they contend that the system is not only viable, but in most respects and at most times works well.

But the radical economists see in modern capitalism the deep class conflicts envisioned by Marx. In particular, in capitalist reality,

[4] Paul M. Sweezy, *Modern Capitalism and Other Essays* (New York: Monthly Review Press, 1972), pp. 53–55.

power lies with the giant, monopolistic corporation—with the capitalist class—which dominates the productive system of industrialized capitalism. Furthermore, rather than functioning as a catalyst in the resolution of conflicts of interest, the public sector is dominated by, and is an instrument of, the large corporations. Rather than promote socioeconomic harmony and further the general welfare, the public sector is essentially a tool by which the capitalists preserve and promote their own selfish interests—both domestically and internationally—to the detriment of the rest of society. Following Marx, the radicals conclude that the system is laden with contradictions and irrationalities and therefore is beyond redemption. The "solution" to capitalism's problems lies in a radical change in the ideology and institutions upon which it is based; in particular, the private ownership of capital goods and reliance upon the market system as a decision-making mechanism must be eliminated in favor of some form of socialism.

△  **Disciplinary Narrowness**
A related criticism centers upon the disciplinary narrowness of economics. The radicals charge that orthodoxy concentrates upon the purely economic aspects of society and turns its back upon the critical interactions among economic, political, sociological, and technological facets of modern society. Orthodox economists, argue the radicals, devote their energies to the technical treatment of highly specialized and esoteric matters which are remote from the real problems of the day. A primary example of this shortcoming is the failure of orthodox economics to recognize the political character of the modern corporation:[5]

> When the modern corporation acquires power over markets, power in the community, power over the state, power over belief, it is a political instrument, different in form and degree but not in kind from the state itself.

[5]John Kenneth Galbraith, "Power and the Useful Economist," *The American Economic Review,* March 1973, p. 6. Galbraith is not considered a radical economist.

The net result is that fundamental questions surrounding the distribution and use of *power* in capitalist society are largely ignored by orthodox economists. This neglect allegedly results in a failure to understand the root causes of most of the problems which plague modern capitalism.

☐   **THE RADICAL CONCEPTION OF CAPITALISM**
Modern radical economists have constructed a model of American capitalism which is essentially an extension and updating of Marxian thought. Let us outline the main features of the radical conception.

△  **Corporate or Monopoly Capitalism**
The radical view holds that capitalism has reached an advanced stage in the United States wherein huge monopolistic corporations dominate the economy. Small corporations have succumbed through merger or bankruptcy. Proprietorships and partnerships flourish only on the relatively unimportant fringes of the economy. Even agriculture is increasingly dominated by corporate farming. The dynamics of capitalist expansion has resulted in gigantic multiproduct enterprises, frequently of a multinational character. All major industries are now characterized by a high degree of concentration of economic activity among a small number of giant corporations. And, most importantly, the two hundred or so largest industrial, financial, and commercial corporations shape and define the character of our economy and society.[6]

> The reality is we now have an integrated industrial economy dominated by corporate collectives with resources greater than those of most States and many nations. These control technological innovation, administer prices, generate unending consumer wants, while expanding to an international scale. . . . Highly accomplished profit

[6]Statement by Robert Engler in *Controls or Competition,* Hearings before the Senate Subcommittee on Antitrust and Monopoly (Washington, 1972), p. 261.

gatherers, they are able to shift risk and social costs to the consumer, the taxpayer and the less powerful.

## △ Domination of the State

The evolution of corporate giants might not be such an ominous development if appropriate public surveillance through antitrust or regulation were to yield socially satisfactory (near-competitive) results. The radical view, however, is that the corporate giants have come to dominate the political state; hence, rather than control corporate power in socially desirable ways, the public sector has become the handmaiden of the corporate giants. Or, at a minimum, a situation of mutual interdependence—a symbiotic relationship—has developed between the corporate giants and government. The success of political parties in realizing and maintaining power depends upon the financial support of wealthy corporations; in turn, government follows policies which are responsive to the needs of the large corporations. The radicals contend that there is substantial evidence of this mutual dependence of big business and government. Consider some of the ways by which government has catered to the corporate giants.

**Failure of Social Control**  The regulatory commissions which are designed to control natural monopolies are ineffective for the simple reason that they are controlled by the very corporate monopolies they are supposed to regulate! Witness, for example, the assessment of government regulation offered by a former chairman of the Federal Trade Commission:[7]

Though most government regulation was enacted under the guise of protecting the consumer from abuse, much of today's regulatory machinery does little more than shelter producers from normal competitive consequences of lassitude and inefficiency. In some cases, the world has

[7] Lewis A. Engman, speech before the 1974 Fall Conference, Financial Analysts Federation, Detroit, Oct. 7, 1974.

changed reducing the original threat of abuse. In other cases, the regulatory machinery has simply become perverted. In still other cases, the machinery was a mistake from the start. In any case, the consumer, for whatever presumed abuse he is being spared, is paying plenty in the form of government-sanctioned price fixing.

The fact of the matter is that most regulated industries have become federal protectorates, living in the cozy world of cost-plus, safely protected from the ugly specters of competition, efficiency and innovation.

Similarly, antitrust legislation is applied half-heartedly, if at all, to large corporations; at best, the flagrant violations of antitrust by giant enterprises result in harmless admonitions or token penalties.

**Public Subsidies**  The radical economists also argue that the public sector uses tax revenues derived from a substantially regressive tax system to subsidize the corporate giants in a variety of ways. For example, the tax-supported educational system provides corporate enterprise with the technical, scientific, and administrative manpower which it needs to operate profitably. Similarly, government finances most of the new scientific and technological developments upon which corporate enterprise depends. Governmentally sponsored construction of streets and highways has amounted to a tremendous subsidy to the automobile industry and all the related industries which feed inputs to it. The radicals emphasize that, in striking contrast, underprivileged minorities are powerless to obtain quality education, decent health care, and, frequently, adequate housing and food from the public treasury.

**Provision of Markets**  Government has also played a primary role, both directly and indirectly, in providing markets for the output of the corporate giants. High levels of military spending—currently in excess of $100 billion per year—have created major markets for many of the large corporations. Similarly, monetary and fiscal policies have tended to eliminate or mitigate recessions, the major source of financial losses for corporate monopolies. Finally, the government has assisted corporations in establishing and expanding their overseas markets through various "imperialistic" measures.

△ **Dynamics of Capitalist Expansion**

Despite the friendly affiliation of monopoly capitalists with the state, capitalist expansion does involve dynamics that pose a serious problem for the corporate capitalists. Competition among capitalists compels them to protect themselves against rivals by producing more goods, accumulating more capital, and realizing more profits. This process, the radicals argue, spawns a variety of evils and irrationalities within the capitalistic system. The problem is this: As Marx foresaw, the accumulation of real capital by the corporate giants increases their productive capacity; therefore, their continued prosperity depends upon ever-expanding markets.[8]

> The pressure created by the necessity to find markets for expanding production constitutes one of the most fundamental characteristics of capitalism. . . . competition induces capitalists to expand sales and production of goods in order to realize profits. Greater output leads to expanded profits and capital accumulation. . . , but in order to realize profits on the newly accumulated capital, even greater sales of output are required.

According to the radicals, the consequences of corporate capitalism and capitalist expansion are manifold and uniformly bad. The domination of society—including the political state—by huge, powerful, profit-seeking corporations creates a variety of "big" problems and inhibits the resolution of others. The

problems allegedly spawned or aggravated by corporate capitalism run the gamut from worker exploitation, income inequality, and alienation to militarism and imperialism.

△ **Exploitation**

Orthodox economics explains the distribution of income largely in terms of marginal productivity. That is, under competitive conditions any resource, say some particular kind of labor, will be employed up to the point at which its wage rate equals its marginal revenue product (Chapters 30 and 31). Putting the matter very simply, this implies that any specific kind of labor is paid in accordance with its contribution to the national output at the margin. The theory can also be applied to land or capital so that all resources are rewarded in accordance with what they have produced or contributed to the national output. Furthermore, it is a situation wherein one class of resources cannot possibly exploit or take advantage of another. Note: Neither radical economists nor most mainstream economists believe the resulting distribution of income is equitable or just. For example, we know from Chapter 37 that, even under pure competition, differences in natural abilities and the random (unequal) distribution of misfortune can result in a highly unequal distribution of wage incomes.

Radical economists stress three basic defects in the marginal productivity theory of income distribution.

**1** They point out, first, that this theory rests upon the assumption of competitive markets, while in fact monopoly has replaced competition in both labor and product markets. Corporate capitalists thus have the power to exploit workers in both labor and product markets. In labor markets, the competitive model of Figure 31-3 has given way to the monopsony model of Figure 31-4, and monopsonistic employers—the large corporations—find it profitable to pay workers an amount *less* than their marginal revenue productivity (MRP). Similarly, the markets for most prod-

[8]Richard C. Edwards, Michael Reich, and Thomas A. Weisskopf (eds.), *The Capitalist System: A Radical Analysis of American Society* (Englewood Cliffs, N.J.: Prentice-Hall, Inc., 1972), p. 98.

ucts are dominated by a few large corporations which use their market power to "rig" the market against workers as consumers.

**2**   A second point is less obvious. Even if all markets are competitive and labor resources are paid their marginal revenue product, the ability of workers to generate MRP may be constrained arbitrarily by exploitative or discriminatory factors. That is, if the opportunity of individuals to develop their natural abilities through education and training is arbitrarily and unequally distributed *or* if society discriminates among workers on the basis of race or sex, then those workers are exploited in that their "actual" MRP and hence their wage payments will be arbitrarily held below their "potential" MRP.

**3**   Radical economists challenge the legitimacy of income payments to the owners of real capital. Their reasoning goes thus: To be sure, physical capital is productive; when combined with labor, machinery and equipment obviously enhance total output. *But* the productivity of real capital—created, incidentally, by the past efforts of labor—must be distinguished from the capitalist owner's ability to command profit income from the productive contribution of real capital.[9]

> Radicals admit that a machine may increase production, that workers need them, and that they increase the worker's productivity. . . . But it is the physical capital that is productive (jointly with the worker), *not* the capitalist. The capitalist owns the capital, but he is not himself the machine. The machine does the work (with the worker); the capitalist gets the profit.

Stated somewhat differently, the mere owning of capital is *not* a productive activity and the income derived from capital ownership is unearned and unjustified.

## △   Inequality

The factual characteristics of income inequality in the United States have already been examined (Chapter 37). Recall that the personal distribution of income has *not* changed significantly since 1947 (Table 37-2). The point stressed by radicals is that capitalistic institutions create most of this inequality and cause it to persist. Hence, the following comments on inequality tie in closely with the discussion of exploitation.

**Unearned Income and Power**   First, by providing unearned incomes to capitalist owners, the institution of private property is a basic source of income inequality. Wealth is even more highly concentrated than is income. One authoritative study, for example, concluded that 1.6 percent of the adult population owns 27.6 percent of the nation's total personal wealth, while at the other extreme one-half the adult population owns only 8.3 percent.[10] Radicals hold that weak and easily avoided inheritance taxes allow the economic inequality arising from private property to be perpetuated through time.

In the second place, inequality is created and fostered by the exercise of economic power by one group against other groups. As the comments on exploitation indicate, in corporate capitalism giant firms can use their market power in both labor and product markets to the detriment of noncapitalists as workers and consumers. As a result, monopoly profits accrue and income inequality is reinforced.

Third, political power has sustained economic inequality. Given the domination of the state by the monopoly capitalists, it is no surprise that big business has benefited from a variety of tax loopholes and subsidies, from protection against foreign competition, and from lucrative government contracts. The progressivity of the Federal tax system has

[9] E. K. Hunt and Howard J. Sherman, *Economics: An Introduction to Traditional and Radical Views* (New York: Harper & Row, Publishers, Incorporated, 1972), p. 226.

[10] Robert J. Lampman, *The Share of Top Wealth-Holders in National Wealth: 1922–1956* (Princeton, N.J.: Princeton University Press, 1962), p. 213.

been eroded over time and, when coupled with regressive state and local tax systems, the overall tax structure turns out at best to be proportional. Therefore, the tax system has failed to function as a "great equalizer" of incomes. And the so-called welfare system has been underfinanced and of little benefit to those groups most deeply mired in poverty. Indeed, American capitalism has displayed no propensity to alter significantly the distribution of income which the market provides.

These factors which cause and sustain income inequality, argue the radicals, are cumulative and self-reinforcing. The very high concentration of wealth fattens the bank accounts of those at the top of the income distribution. And it is only these high-income receivers who are able to save in substantial amounts. What do they do with their saving? They invest it in more income-producing assets from which they receive still more income, which they reinvest in still more property resources, and so on.

Much the same holds true with respect to economic opportunity. Education—particularly higher education—is traditionally viewed as an income equalizer; college is the ladder by which the children of the poor presumably gain the human capital—the skills and training—to climb out of poverty and into higher income brackets. Not so, say the radicals. The rich have not only more real capital, but also greater access to human capital. Those who go to college are increasingly the youth from higher income groups. The poor and middle-income groups find it increasingly difficult to afford college training, not merely because of the rising out-of-pocket costs associated with higher education, but because the opportunity cost—the income forgone by not entering the labor market—is relatively high. Crudely stated, poor families attach greater relative importance to the income which a son or daughter could earn by *not* attending college. Thus the educational system has become a mechanism for the intergenerational perpetuation of economic inequality. And, finally, the college graduate from the rich family is likely to get a better job than the graduate from the poor family because of his or her "connections." One starts out higher and moves up more rapidly in the business world if Daddy owns the business!

**Dual Labor Markets**  In the past several years the foregoing explanation of capitalist inequality has been supplemented by the concept of *dual* or *segmented labor markets*. In abbreviated form, the radical view is that labor markets are increasingly of two distinct types. The *primary labor market* is characterized by relatively high and rising wage rates, employment stability, good and well-defined opportunities for advancement, and the presence of advanced production techniques and efficient management. The *secondary labor market* embraces the opposite characteristics: Wages are low and stagnant; employment is casual and unstable; available jobs are "dead ends"; relevant technology is archaic; and management is inefficient and exploitative.

The historical reasons for the evolution of these two distinct labor markets are diverse and largely complementary.

**1**  One view is that dual labor markets are essentially a reflection of the alleged duality found in product markets. That is, the giant corporations which dominate major industries give rise to primary labor markets, whereas the competitive fringes of the economy are conducive to secondary labor markets.

**2**  Another position is of a more conspiratorial nature: Labor-market segmentation is the result of an historical effort by capitalists to retard the evolution of a homogeneous and unified labor force which might threaten and overthrow capitalist dominance of the economy.

**3**  A third interpretation is that the characteristics of both primary and secondary labor markets are self-reinforcing and over time cause the two markets to diverge. The features of the primary labor market lead to a benign cycle of progress; those of the secondary labor market spawn a vicious cycle of perpetual stagnation and poverty. That is, the high wages of the primary labor markets put firms under constant pressure to innovate and use technologically advanced capital goods. But such progress calls for more skills, and management invests in the training of its work force. Improved real capital and investment in labor's human capital both increase labor's productivity and lead to further wage increases which cause the cycle to repeat itself. Similarly, the fact that employers have invested in the training of their work force gives them a vested interest in greater employment stability; a firm must keep labor turnover low to realize a return on its investment in human capital. Hence, a self-reinforcing cycle of events occurs which allows those workers fortunate enough to be in the primary labor market to be relatively well off and to share to some extent in the gains of general economic advance.

Substantially the opposite occurs in the secondary labor market. At poverty wage rates there is no reason for a firm to be labor-saving or technologically innovative; technology and capitalization languish. Indeed, secondary labor markets are typically highly competitive and, motivation aside, firms are financially unable to invest in real or human capital. Workers therefore tend to be unskilled and relatively unproductive. And high worker turnover is acceptable to the firm; indeed, it may be helpful in discouraging unionization. In fact, a kind of symbiotic relationship evolves wherein worker behavior mirrors the characteristics of the secondary labor market. Employment is unstable, so workers become "unreliable." Because production is technologically backward, workers have no motivation to upgrade their education and skills. The important point is that, while workers in the primary labor market achieve some economic progress, those in the secondary labor market are confined to a vicious cycle of stagnation and poverty. Furthermore, as the two labor markets diverge, it is increasingly difficult for

workers to achieve mobility between the markets. The growing skill gap between the two markets, reinforced by discrimination based on race and sex and the geographic segregation of many secondary labor markets in urban ghettos, makes upward occupational mobility less and less likely for secondary labor market workers. In the radical view this scenario is meaningful in explaining the persistence of income inequality and poverty through time.

△  **Alienation**

Radical economists argue that the institutions and operations of capitalism are a major source of *alienation*. That is, under corporate capitalism, individuals have less and less control over their lives and activities; the masses of people are increasingly remote from the decision-making processes which determine the character and quality of their lives.[11]

> In general, people in capitalist society do not participate in making the basic decisions that affect their lives; instead, these decisions are made through capitalist institutions over which most individuals have little or no control. The actual decisions are likely, if not inevitably, independent of the interests of the persons involved, and the consequences of these decisions will be contrary to their needs.

The causes and forms of alienation are manifold. First, corporate dominance has largely eliminated the possibility of achieving independence and autonomy by going into business for oneself. Second, the sheer size of corporations and their bureaucratic structure put most workers—both blue- and white-collar—in positions where they have little or no decision-making power. Both blue- and white-collar workers have jobs which are segmented and subject to authoritarian direction. Even middle managers feel that they have no influence upon the organizational decisions which they are obligated to implement. In

---

[11] Edwards, Reich, and Weisskopf, op. cit., p. 255.

general, the sheer size of corporations is conducive to jobs which are constrained by inflexible work rules and procedures. Third, radicals envision a fundamental contradiction between an individual's desire for "self-realization" and creativity, on the one hand, and the progressive division of labor which accompanies technological advance, on the other. Blue-collar workers in particular are confronted with the dehumanization of assembly-line production. In general, in their drive for profits, corporations ride roughshod over the individual's needs and his or her desire for self-fulfillment and meaningful participation. The dynamics of capitalism entails mass-production technology, boring and stultifying jobs, and a highly constraining work environment.

### △  The Irrational Society:
### Production for Waste

Orthodox economists generally argue that one of the great virtues of capitalism is the capacity of the market system to allocate resources with considerable efficiency. Radical economists, however, cite what they feel is overwhelming evidence that resources are used most irrationally under capitalism. Furthermore, this wasteful production is rooted in the institutions of capitalism and, ironically, in the price system itself.

The radical position is that simple evidence of the eye makes clear that capitalism uses its resources irrationally. The economy produces incredible quantities of automobiles, television sets, cosmetics, and alcoholic beverages while, at the same time, many households are without adequate housing, medical care, or diet. The fact that over $44 billion is squandered each year on advertising is ample evidence that the production of many consumer goods fails to fulfill the true needs of consumers. At a time when the nation spends $100 billion or more per year on military hardware and the maintenance of overseas military bases, such areas as urban decay, mass transit, and social services are woefully ignored. Fur-

thermore, environmental pollution has been an inevitable by-product of capitalist production.

Why do these apparent irrationalities—this gross misuse of scarce resources—occur under capitalism? The answer, according to the radical position, lies basically in the dynamics of capitalist expansion abetted by the system's emphasis upon market signals, individual profit incentives, and its highly unequal distribution of income and wealth.

The essence of capitalistic expansion is that the pursuit of profits induces the giant corporations to expand their productive capacities. But this enhanced capacity necessitates ever-expanding markets if this additional productive capacity is to be profitably utilized. "The pursuit of profits and the desire to accumulate lead to more and more production for the sake of production. . . ."[12] The consequences are quite obvious. In the first place, the great emphasis upon industrial growth and materialism in capitalism exacerbates the problem of environmental deterioration. Resources are devoured and waste products are dumped into the environment at an accelerating rate (Chapter 20). The monopoly capitalist's concern is solely with private benefits and internal costs; spillover or external costs are uniformly ignored. Second, an ever-expanding demand is required if the expanding productive capacity of the monopoly capitalists is to be profitably utilized. Capitalists attempt to assure themselves of an adequate demand for their products both directly and indirectly. Direct efforts center upon want-creating, consumer-manipulating activities. Given the highly unequal distribution of income under capitalism, the poor cannot afford to partake of an expanding output. The rich, in contrast, are already glutted with most goods. Hence, the heavy hand of advertising and the technique of "planned obsolescence" are mustered to induce the consumption of essentially unneeded output. The demand for capitalistic production is supported indirectly by the pub-

---

[12] Ibid., p. 363.

lic sector. Starkly put, government engages in wasteful and unnecessary military spending to absorb the output of the capitalistic system. Furthermore, government engages in imperialistic activities on a global basis to create and sustain overseas markets and to secure cheap sources of inputs. The basic point is that under capitalism, production priorities are determined not on the basis of the real needs of the people, but rather in accordance with what is profitable to the capitalist class. The outcome is the irrational use of resources, on the one hand, and the creation of a "commodity fetish culture" with undue emphasis upon rank materialism, on the other. Capitalism, so to speak, is producing more and enjoying it less.

△  **Imperialism**

Given the dynamics of capitalism, it is inevitable that monopoly capitalism will transcend national boundaries to dominate and exploit the less developed areas of the world. This "internationalization of capitalism" is, of course, imperialism.

Radicals envision orthodox explanations of underdevelopment as hoaxes. In particular, they argue that it is patently incorrect to explain underdevelopment in terms of overpopulation or natural resource deficiencies. High population density and economic growth do *not* correlate significantly and, in fact, the underdeveloped countries are a major source of natural resources. Similarly, the familiar "vicious circle of poverty"—the argument that in poor countries, incomes are so low that there is no economic surplus to invest in capital goods with which to increase productivity and per capita incomes—is rejected by radical economists.[13]

> In the radical view . . . the main obstacles to development are *not* natural or biological factors inherent in the underdeveloped countries, and *not* sexual desires and procreation, laziness, low intelligence or lack of natural resources. The

obstacles are in the present social relationships of man to man: the fact that all the peasants' and workers' surplus over immediate need is extracted from them by the landlords, moneylenders, tax collectors, and foreign corporations.

Furthermore, orthodox theories of underdevelopment provide

> the perfect defense against the suspicion of these peoples that their problems are due to antiquated social systems, rapacious ruling classes and—above all—foreign domination and exploitation.[14]

More specifically, radicals contend that imperialism is the basic obstacle to the development of poor nations.

**1**  In the first place, capitalist aid supports reactionary ruling classes (landlords, moneylenders, and the government itself) who in turn expropriate the economic surplus of workers and peasant farmers. For what purposes? For luxury consumption, for showcase (nonproductive) construction projects, for investment in advanced nations, and for military goods to repress domestic "liberation" movements.

**2**  Contrary to the Marxian view that imperialism entails a flow of investment from mature capitalist countries to the underdeveloped areas of the world, modern radicals hold that the underdeveloped countries have, in fact, made very substantial contributions to the capital accumulation of the United States and other imperialistic countries. That is, over time the imperialistic countries derive profit incomes from their overseas investments which far exceed the value of these investments, thereby contributing to a growing income gap between the have and have-not nations.

**3**  Finally, trade between the advanced capitalist nations and the poor countries occurs on terms which are highly favorable to the former; in addition, the pattern of that trade tends to inhibit growth in the underdeveloped countries. That is, the underdeveloped coun-

---

[13]Howard Sherman, *Radical Political Economy* (New York: Basic Books, Inc., 1972), pp. 151–152.

[14]Ibid., p. 152.

tries are essentially exporters of raw materials and importers of finished goods, a trade pattern which fosters economic dependence rather than industrialization and growth.

It is perhaps in connection with imperialism or neocolonialism that the domination of the state by monopoly capitalists is most apparent.

> On the international front, U.S. trade and especially foreign investments grew enormously throughout the capitalist world during the postwar period and became increasingly important as sources of profits for U.S. corporations. Successive national administrations protected these expanding profitable international activities by the general policy of keeping as much of the world as possible open for trade, investment, and raw materials acquisition by giant corporations. This aim was pursued by economic aid to "friendly" governments (that is, those receptive to U.S. direct investment and trade or those in strategic positions to further the global aims of the U.S.), partly to strengthen them economically, partly to provide supporting overhead capital for U.S. private enterprise, and partly to increase export markets for U.S. corporations. Postwar administrations have also extended military aid to "friendly" governments, for the purposes of fostering the weapons and aircraft output of U.S. corporations and of protecting these client governments from the militant opposition of some of their own people. The U.S. has, moreover, conducted counterinsurgency operations throughout the underdeveloped capitalist world, and when all has failed, it has used military force in pursuit of its basic aim—the maximization of the area of the world that is open for profitable corporate activities.[15]

△  **Socialist Visions**

What kind of new society do the radicals envision or advocate? The heterogeneity of the radical critique becomes most apparent at this point:

> . . . every radical in the United States has his own view of exactly what socialism should be like. All agree that there should be no private profit, that it should be decent and human, that it should be based on a genuinely democratic process. But beyond that, there is disagreement on every particular.[16]

A few radical economists are attracted to the Soviet model (Chapter 45), but most are repulsed by its repressive features. Others recommend market socialism, that is, public ownership and the preservation of the price system. A few are content to advocate anarchism; many espouse some new form of economic organization based upon producer cooperatives. Some kind of socioeconomic organization along the lines of China's communes appeals to many radicals. Still others advocate "participatory socialism":[17]

> Most fundamentally, socialism means democratic, decentralized and *participatory* control for the individual: it means having a say in the decisions that affect one's life. Such a participatory form of socialism certainly requires equal access for all to material and cultural resources, which in turn requires the abolition of private ownership of capital and the redistribution of wealth. But it also calls for socialist men and women to eliminate alienating, destructive forms of production, consumption, education and social relations. Participatory socialism requires the elimination of bureaucracies and all hierarchical forms and their replacement, not by new state or party bureaucracies, but by a self-governing and self-managing people with directly chosen representatives subject to recall and replacement. Participatory socialism entails a sense of egalitarian cooperation, of solidarity of people with one another; but at the same time it respects individual and group differences and guarantees individual rights. It affords to all individuals the freedom to exercise human rights and civil liberties that are not mere abstractions but have concrete day-to-day meaning.

[15] John G. Gurley, "The Future of American Capitalism," *Quarterly Review of Economics and Business,* Autumn 1972, pp. 7–8.

[16] Hunt and Sherman, op. cit., 564.
[17] Edwards, Reich, and Weisskopf, op. cit., p. 520.

# □ THE ORTHODOX REBUTTAL

The radical critique of capitalism is not merely an enumeration of this or that sin, but rather a unified and systematic frontal attack on the whole system. That is, the entire spectrum of socioeconomic problems—exploitation, inequality, alienation, pollution, militarism, imperialism, and so forth—has a common cause. That cause, of course, is the ideology of capitalism; the private ownership of property resources and the functioning of the price system have spawned monopolistic corporations and their ultimate domination of the state and society. Let us briefly consider the response of orthodox economists to the economics of dissent.

## △  Invalid Perceptions

We have seen that radical economics rejects the orthodox perception of modern capitalism as a pluralistic system characterized by a socially responsive public sector. Similarly, orthodox economists reject the radical model of capitalism as a grossly distorted caricature; the radical view, they argue, is inconsistent with commonsense observation and therefore not realistic and believable.

Consider, for example, the following points. If worker exploitation depends directly upon the degree of monopsony power possessed by a firm, why is it that the large corporations generally pay the highest wages? How can radical economics square the upward drift of labor's share of national income and the virtual constancy of the corporate profit share (Table 32-1) with their contention that monopoly capitalists are exploiting labor? Where do such phenomena as the social security and welfare systems, Medicare, and minimum-wage legislation fit into the conception of government as handmaiden of the monopoly capitalists? Similarly, how does the long-term decline in protective tariffs square with government as a protector and promoter of capitalist profits? Is the radical notion that militarism is necessary to sustain aggregate demand credible in view of the fact that inflation, not overproduc-

tion and unemployment, has been the primary problem of capitalist countries since World War II? How is prosperous, capitalistic Japan, with its minimum military establishment, to be reconciled with the radical notion of militarism as an economic prop? As for imperialism,[18]

> It seems to be a mistake to believe that the business society generally considers foreign-policy confrontations advantageous to the business community. This is certainly suggested by the declines in stock exchange prices that usually accompany international political crisis and the rises that usually follow rumors of peace.

At a more philosophical level, orthodox economists reject the radicals' deterministic conception of capitalism, that is, the view that the problems and contradictions of modern capitalism are the *inevitable* consequences of the laws of capitalist production. The underlying mode of production, so say the radicals, *necessarily* results in a highly unequal distribution of income, wealth, and power; in worker alienation; in wasteful production; and in imperialism and militarism. Orthodox economists are unwilling to accept this deterministic interpretation of capitalism. Furthermore, even if this deterministic interpretation were correct, would it not transcend ideological and institutional arrangements and therefore also apply to alternative (socialistic) systems? In fact, there may be more-or-less inevitable consequences of socialistic systems, for example, that the seizure of power by force (socialist revolution) may be conducive to the selection of an "authoritarian and cruel" leadership, and that viable socialistic systems are necessarily highly centralized and bureaucratic.

## △  Nonobjectivity

Orthodox economists have grave reservations concerning the methodology of radical

---

[18] Assar Lindbeck, *The Political Economy of the New Left* (New York: Harper & Row, Publishers, Incorporated, 1971), p. 21.

economics; radicals, they contend, are strongly inclined to substitute rhetoric for reasoning. The claim is that radical economics is doctrinaire, dogmatic, and deficient in scientific objectivity. Put uncharitably, radicals are alleged to employ a "cowboys and Indians mentality" in their interpretation of capitalism. Any and all actions by capitalists or government are envisaged within a conspiratorial framework for they are the "bad guys." The "good guys"—those who ultimately suffer from the actions of monopoly capitalists and government—are, of course, "the people." The radical method, argue orthodox economists, is to interpret current problems and policies to fit their preconceived conception of capitalist society, rather than to modify or retreat from their conception when the problems and policies in fact do *not* fit. Radicals, it is alleged, display a cavalier disregard for facts—both statistical and anecdotal—and for alternative explanations which are at odds with the neo-Marxist framework.[19] In interpreting problems to dovetail with the radical model, great reliance is placed upon simple two-variable analysis to explain issues and situations which are decidedly more complex. For example, to the radical economist the pollution problem is clearly the consequence of profit-hungry corporations shifting costs to society, an indirect form of exploitation. Alternative explanations, for example, those centering upon population growth and its geographic concentration, are conveniently ignored. Similarly, we have seen that the radical conceives of the relationships between rich and poor countries entirely within an imperialistic framework, stressing the flow of benefits (capital) from the underdeveloped to the advanced capitalistic nations. The concept of comparative advantage and the consequent possibility that international intercourse could be *mutually* advantageous is carefully excluded from their thinking.

---

[19]Radical reply: Transpose "orthodox" and "radical" in the foregoing statements and you have a basic radical criticism of orthodox economics.

△ **Importance of Ideology**

Orthodox economists are highly skeptical of the radical assertion that each and every problem present in American capitalism is traceable to the ideological-institutional bases of the system. Other world economies with very different ideological bases seem to suffer from the same kinds of problems. Consider, for example, the question of income inequality. What is there to guarantee that the socialization of any economy will result in greater income equality? Socialization might merely redistribute income from private to public sectors and not from rich to poor. Furthermore, empirical studies show that a substantial portion of income inequality in the United States results from differences in the distribution of *human,* rather than *property* or *real,* capital. Hence, the nationalization of real capital would lessen, but not resolve, the inequality issue. We note, incidentally, that wage income is unequally distributed in the Soviet Union, perhaps as much so as in the United States.

Consider imperialism. Can one seriously argue that imperialism correlates highly with the private ownership of resources and monopoly capitalism?

> Preindustrial and precapitalist societies certainly have been characterized by militarism, aggressive foreign policy, and imperialism—and present day noncapitalist societies are hardly free of a military-industrial complex and an aggressive nationalist foreign policy![20]

Soviet policy toward Estonia, Latvia, and Lithuania, Hungary, Czechoslovakia, and Afghanistan among others, makes it abundantly clear that monopoly capitalism does not have a monopoly on imperialism.

What about the critical problem of the distribution of *power?* One might concede the existence of casual evidence suggesting that the distribution of power has become increasingly concentrated in the United States. But by what means is the nationalization of property resources going to alleviate the problem?

---

[20]Lindbeck, op. cit., p. 62.

We would expect the problem to be accentuated, for then the bulk of economic power over physical assets would be concentrated in the one hand which also happens to exert political and military power: that is, the hand of centrally placed politicians and administrators.[21]

Similarly, there is ample evidence of environmental pollution, alienation, discrimination, not to mention repression, in other systems with widely varying ideological bases and institutions. The point is this: Radical economics offers no convincing evidence that the ideological-institutional changes which it prescribes will provide the will, the resources, and the social technology to remedy the problems and contradictions it envisions in capitalism. Is the ideological-institutional structure of a society really the crucial determinant of its character and the source of its shortcomings? Or are such problems as inequality, imperialism, alienation, pollution, and so on, indigenous to any complex social system?

△   **Viable Options**

It is relatively easy to criticize the existing system; it is much more difficult to set forth a viable system which will effectively overcome the fancied and real deficiencies of modern capitalism. The essence of rational choice calls for the objective comparison of realistic and attainable alternatives. The radical economists are therefore obliged to state clearly and in detail the nature of the alternative system which they advocate. This they have not done.[22]

> What the New Left lacks . . . is a practical, comprehensive solution. . . . The radicals know what must come down, but not what should be left standing or what should go up. . . . revolutionaries call for destruction first and experimentation afterward. One may be reluctant to sign up for such an uncertain future.

[21]Ibid., pp. 59–60.
[22]Charles Perrow, (ed.), *The Radical Attack on Business* (New York: Harcourt Brace Jovanovich, Inc., 1972), p. 4.

Orthodox economists argue that the radical position is bankrupt insofar as viable alternatives are concerned. Specifically, most radicals reject *both* the market system *and* the bureaucracy of government as means of providing a satisfactory solution to the economic problem. Since the price system and the public bureaucracy are the only two basic alternatives for economic decision making, the rejection of both leaves an operational vacuum. The orthodox economist says, in effect, "reread the earlier statement on the character of participatory socialism and attempt to discern how that system would actually operate." How would the system respond to the everyday questions which are at the core of *any* economy's functioning? How, specifically, would it decide what to produce? How would production be organized? What productive techniques would be selected? How would output be distributed? How would the "What, How, and For Whom" decisions be coordinated? Would resources be fully employed? How would resources be reallocated over time from uses of declining importance to those of increasing importance? And what incentives would exist for citizens to undertake all the required tasks and decisions? Radical conceptions of idyllic communal societies (wherein the distinction between director and worker is obliterated and "self-fulfillment" is given priority over materialistic objectives) are superficially attractive, but they fail to respond to the hard question: "How do you plan to run the steel industry?"

Radical response: We are not irresponsible, scatterbrained critics. Our movement is relatively new and our energies have been absorbed in uncovering and articulating the shortcomings of the existing system and in developing a critique of orthodox economic analysis. Radicals are just now getting seriously into the formidable task of framing meaningful, workable alternatives which will avoid the evils of both the market system and the bureaucracy. It is not a simple matter to create a viable system based upon equality and egalitarianism, cooperation, and self-realization as opposed to inequality, competition, and alienation. But give us time!

The evidence is quite clear that radical economics has established itself as an alternative, competing explanation of socioeconomic phenomena. And whether one greets the economics of dissent with delight or dismay, there is no doubt that a nodding acquaintance with the radical view contributes a new, skeptical dimension to one's interpretation of the economic, political, and social milieu. Furthermore, whether one finds their answers relevant or unreasonable, the radical economists perform a useful service in underscoring some of the perennial problems associated with advanced capitalism. Finally, radical economics is useful in reminding us that economics, narrowly defined, provides only a limited perspective on the real world and that this perspective is not always the most relevant for understanding.

## Summary

1   Radical economics is essentially a modernization and an extension of Marxian economics.

2   Radical economists criticize the method of orthodox economics for accepting the existing ideological-institutional framework, for stressing harmony of interests and conflict resolution, and for its disciplinary narrowness.

3   In the radical view, giant monopolistic corporations dominate capitalistic society, including the political state. The dynamics of capitalist expansion entails the continual pursuit of profits within a context of expanding productive capacity.

4   According to the radical position, capitalist expansion creates or intensifies a variety of problems: for example, the exploitation of labor, income inequality, alienation, irrational or wasteful production, and imperialism.

5   Radical visions of a new society range from anarchy to centralized socialism; "participatory socialism" is a frequently discussed possibility.

6   Orthodox economists criticize the radical position on the grounds that it *a.* embraces an inaccurate interpretation or portrayal of modern capitalism; *b.* lacks scientific objectivity; *c.* overemphasizes ideology and institutions as the source of socioeconomic problems; and *d.* fails to offer viable alternatives to the market system or the public bureaucracy.

## Questions and Study Suggestions

1   Key terms and concepts to remember: Marxian economics; radical economics; class struggle; bourgeoisie and proletariat; surplus value; law of capitalist accumulation; industrial reserve army; monopoly capitalism; exploitation; dual labor markets; alienation; imperialism; participatory socialism.

2   Briefly summarize Marxian economics, using the concepts of class struggle, exploitation, and the increasing degradation of the working class in your discussion.

3   How might a radical economist explain or interpret *a.* income inequality, *b.* environmental pollution, *c.* the military budget, *d.* minimum-wage legislation, *e.* the social security system and *f.* the Employment Act of 1946? How might an orthodox economist interpret the same phenomena?

4   "The activities and policies of the American national state are responsive to the needs and objectives of the capitalist class." Cite both supporting and conflicting evidence.

**5** Critically evaluate each statement:

*a.* "Human behavior and the ultimate character of any society are determined by its economic ideology and institutions."

*b.* "The economic processes in a capitalistic system inevitably generate irreconcilable conflicts between the various groups in society who have contradictory goals and needs."

*c.* "Under the banners of free enterprise, democracy, and the protection of underdeveloped countries from communism, the United States has waged imperialistic wars, exploited foreign labor, stripped underdeveloped countries of their material resources, and supported unpopular and undemocratic governments."

*d.* "The trouble with the radical position is twofold: First, too many government policies clearly *are* in the public interest, and second, they offer no operationally viable system which will eliminate the alleged *evils* of capitalism."

**6** Explain how radical economists use the concept of dual labor markets to explain income inequality and the persistence of poverty in the United States.

**7** In the radical view, what are the specific relationships between exploitation and income inequality? Capitalist expansion and militarism? Capitalist expansion and imperialism? Explain the radical argument that capitalism results in a grossly inefficient allocation of resources.

# Selected References

Edwards, Richard C., Michael Reich, and Thomas E. Weisskopf (eds.): *The Capitalist System: A Radical Analysis of American Society,* 2d ed. (Englewood Cliffs, N.J.: Prentice-Hall, 1978).

Franklin, Raymond S.: *American Capitalism: Two Visions* (New York: Random House, 1977).

Freeman, Harold: *Toward Socialism in America* (Cambridge, Mass.: Schenkman Publishing Company, 1979).

Hunt, E. K., and Howard J. Sherman: *Economics: An Introduction to Traditional and Radical Views,* 2d ed. (New York: Harper & Row, Publishers, Incorporated, 1975).

Lindbeck, Assar: *The Political Economy of the New Left* (New York: Harper & Row, Publishers, Incorporated, 1971).

Mermelstein, David (ed.): *Economics: Mainstream Readings and Radical Critiques,* 2d ed. (New York: Random House, Inc., 1973).

Sherman, Howard J.: *Radical Political Economy: Capitalism and Socialism from a Marxist-Humanist Perspective* (New York: Basic Books, Inc., 1972).

Sherman, Howard J.: *Stagflation: A Radical Theory of Unemployment and Inflation* (New York: Harper & Row, Publishers, Incorporated, 1976).

Weaver, James H. (ed.): *Modern Political Economy* (Boston: Allyn and Bacon, Inc. 1973).

# LAST WORD
## Monopoly Capitalism at Work

This excerpt is an extension of Chapter 7's Last Word. This testimony before a government committee provides anecdotal evidence to support the radical argument that huge corporations dominate government as a means of exploiting both human and property resources.

[The conditions in West Virginia] result, in large measure, from the domination, economically and politically, of the coal industry which in turn is controlled by a handful of large out-of-State corporations. . . .

West Virginia is comprised of 55 counties containing less than 1,900,000 people. The nine southernmost counties contain approximately 30 percent of the State's total population and produce about 70 percent of the State's coal. Nine corporations own more than 33 percent of these nine counties with real estate holdings worth over $90 million at grossly underassessed values. The top 25 landowners in the nine counties control more than one-half the total land area through their collective ownership of more than 1,600,000 acres of land. Of these nine corporations, only one is a West Virginia corporation doing business principally within the State.

The effects of this corporate giantism have been devastating in many ways. Despite the fact that coal, oil and gas entrepreneurs have prospered almost beyond measure, the land and its inhabitants have not. West Virginia is not a poor State—it is a rich State inhabited by poor people. Employment in the coal industry has dropped from a high of 135,000 to barely 40,000 with automation. Coal production, on the other hand, is soaring. Contrary to the prevailing myth, the company's size is no index of safety. The most recent mine disaster at Farmington, W. Va., took the lives of 78 miners employed by Consolidation Coal Company, the largest producer in the State. Aside from the continuing high rate of injuries, the toll of black lung victims has been dramatically increased by virtue of the continuous miner—a formidable machine developed by the corporate giants.

The magnitude of the wealth of the huge companies which own many areas of West Virginia is matched only by the magnitude of the poverty of the people who live in these same areas. There are counties in West Virginia where one out of every four families is on the welfare program—an inadequate program at that. In the last 20 years, West Virginia has lost 15 percent of its population and the people are still leaving. Our streams are badly polluted from coal wastes and acid mine drainage. Our air is filthy from burning gob piles and slag heaps. Factories and power plants dump their industrial garbage with little restraint. . . .

Public services such as education, health care, environmental protection and public welfare are in a condition not dissimilar to the land itself—shabby. Through the coal industry's heavy influence in the State legislature, combined with the power of the manufacturers and the utilities, State taxes are kept so regressive and so unproductive that all services which are dependent upon public revenues are doomed to remain inadequate. Until recently the entire coal industry paid less in taxes to the State of West Virginia than the State collected from cigarette smokers. West Virginia coal production at the same time, approximated 150 million tons per year.

Not only is the private government of the giant corporations beyond the reach of the citizenry, but it is beyond the State itself. The total annual budget of the State of West Virginia approximates $500 or $600 million a year. The total annual budget for any one of the giant corporations which compose the private government of West Virginia far exceeds that total. Members of the West Virginia Legislature just last year received a raise from $1,500 to $3,000 per year. The legislature meets only a few months out of the year. Staff facilities available to them are severely limited; they do not even have an office. On the other hand, lobbyists for the private government of the corporate giants are paid upwards of $25,000 per year and are supported by lawyers, researchers, and experts in abundance.

The West Virginia Public Service Commission which is supposed to control all public utilities and common carriers operating in the State is required by law to be supported financially by the very corporations it is supposed to regulate, and its funding is minimal. Most of the State regulatory agencies are required by law to include corporate representatives on their governing boards, their appeal boards, or their advisory boards.

Until recently, the president of Amherst Coal Company was also chairman of the State air pollution control commission, for example. He is still on the commission. An executive vice president of the Continental Oil-Consolidation Coal setup is a former State tax commissioner. The executive secretary of the West Virginia Coal Association is a former speaker of the West Virginia House of Delegates. His predecessor with the coal association was a former president of the West Virginia Senate. A high official of Continental Oil Company was once director of the West Virginia Department of Natural Resources, our conservation commission. The chairman of the State senate commission on natural resources is in the oil and gas business, as was the immediate past president of the West Virginia Senate. I could go on and on.

In short, however, the State and its people are ill equipped to deal with the corporate giants which have tremendous power over their lives. . . .

From *Controls or Competition,* Hearings before the Subcommittee on Antitrust and Monopoly of the Committee on the Judiciary, U.S. Senate, 92d Congress, 1st Session, Washington, 1972, pp. 143–144. Statement by Paul Kaufman, Director, Appalachian Research and Defense Fund, Inc.

# INTERNATIONAL ECONOMICS AND THE WORLD ECONOMY

# PART SEVEN

# International Trade and Comparative Advantage

chapter 41

Thus far, our analysis of American capitalism has been based upon the assumption that it is an isolated or *closed economy*. This is obviously not true. Ours is an *open economy* in that it is linked to other nations of the world through a complex network of international trade and financial relationships. It is the purpose of this and the following three chapters to describe and analyze these relationships and to assess both the advantages and the problems associated with them.

The goals of the present chapter are modest in number, but of fundamental importance. First, we will look briefly at the volume and unique characteristics of international trade. Next, we want to explain the basis for international trade and to assess its microeconomic impact. Our third objective is to analyze the macroeconomic implications of world trade.

## ☐ IMPORTANCE OF WORLD TRADE

Is the volume of world trade sufficiently great, or are its characteristics so unique, as to merit special consideration?

### △ Quantitative Aspects

Table 41-1 provides us with a rough index of the importance of world trade for a number of representative countries. Many nations which have restricted resource bases and limited domestic markets simply cannot produce with reasonable efficiency all the goods they want to consume. For such countries, exports may run from 30 to 35 percent or more of their GNP. Other countries—the United States and the Soviet Union, for example—have rich and highly diversified resource bases and vast internal markets and are therefore less dependent upon world trade.

But even in the case of the United States,

**TABLE 41-1**
Exports as a Percentage of Gross National Product,
Selected Countries, 1978

| Country | Exports | |
| --- | --- | --- |
| | Percentage of GNP | Total volume (billions of dollars) |
| The Netherlands | 38 | $ 37.5 |
| Canada | 24 | 47.9 |
| Italy | 24 | 56.1 |
| United Kingdom | 23 | 71.7 |
| West Germany | 22 | 142.5 |
| France | 17 | 79.4 |
| Japan | 10 | 98.4 |
| United States | 7 | 141.1 |
| Soviet Union | 4 | 52.4 |

*Source:* Central Intelligence Agency, *Handbook of Economic Statistics, 1979.*

where exports and imports are a small proportion of total output, international trade can be extremely important.

**1  Volume**  In the United States, 7 percent of the GNP is a very large figure in absolute terms.  In 1978, for example, American exports of goods totaled about $141 billion, and imports were about $172 billion.  Though there are nations which derive a third or more of their national incomes from international trade, *the absolute volume of American imports and exports exceeds that of any other nation.*

**2  Dependence**  Despite the versatility of our economy, we are almost entirely dependent upon other countries for our supplies of specific commodities.  Bananas, cocoa, coffee, spices, tea, raw silk, nickel, tin, natural rubber, and diamonds are cases in point.  Casual observation suggests that imported goods compete strongly in many of our domestic markets: Japanese cameras and tape recorders, French and Italian wines, English bicycles, and Japanese motorcycles are a few cases in point.  Foreign cars have made persistent gains in American markets and now account for about

20 percent of total sales in the United States.  Perhaps most apparent is the growing dependence of the United States upon foreign oil.  Even the great American pastime—baseball—relies heavily upon imported gloves!

But world trade is a two-way street, and a host of American industries are highly dependent upon foreign markets.  Almost all segments of agriculture rely heavily upon foreign markets—rice, wheat, cotton, and tobacco exports vary from one-fourth to more than one-half of total output.  The chemical, automobile, machine tool, and computer industries are only a few of many American industries which sell significant portions of their output in international markets.  Table 41-2 shows some of the major commodity exports and imports of the United States.

**3  Level of Output**  Changes in net exports, that is, in the difference between the value of a nation's exports and that of its imports, have multiple effects upon the level of national income in roughly the same fashion as do fluctuations in the various types of domestic spending.  A small change in the volume of American imports and exports can have magnified repercussions upon the domestic levels of income, employment, and prices.

With these points in mind, we need not belabor the significance of international trade for such nations as the Netherlands, Japan, Australia, and Great Britain, whose volumes of international trade constitute substantial fractions of their national incomes.

△  **Unique Aspects**
Aside from essentially quantitative considerations, world trade has certain unique characteristics which require us to devote special attention to it.

**1  Mobility Differences**  Though the difference is a matter of degree, the mobility of resources is considerably less among nations than it is within nations.  American workers, for example, are free to move from Iowa to

**TABLE 41-2**
Principal Commodity Exports and Imports of the United States, 1978 (*in millions*)

| Exports | Amount | Percentage of total | Imports | Amount | Percentage of total |
|---|---|---|---|---|---|
| Machinery | $ 37,022 | 26 | Petroleum and products | $ 39,109 | 23 |
| Transport equipment | 22,248 | 16 | Automobiles and parts | 20,631 | 12 |
| Chemicals | 12,618 | 9 | Iron and steel products | 7,259 | 4 |
| Grains, cereals, etc. | 11,634 | 8 | Chemicals | 6,427 | 4 |
| Soybeans | 5,210 | 4 | Electrical machinery | 5,171 | 3 |
| Iron and steel products | 1,714 | 1 | Coffee | 3,728 | 2 |
| All other exports | 50,708 | 36 | All other imports | 89,700 | 52 |
| Total | $141,154 | 100 | Total | $172,025 | 100 |

*Source:* U.S. Department of Commerce, *Survey of Current Business,* February 1980, pp. S-22 and 24. Details may not add to totals because of rounding.

California or from Maine to Texas. If workers want to move, they can do so. Crossing international boundaries is a different story. Immigration laws, not to mention language and cultural barriers, put severe restrictions upon the migration of labor between nations. Different tax laws, different governmental regulations, different business practices, and a host of other institutional barriers limit the migration of real capital over international boundaries.

*International trade is a substitute for the international mobility of resources.* If human and property resources do not move readily among nations, the movement of goods and services can provide an effective substitute.

**2  Currency Differences**  Each nation uses a different currency. This poses complications (Chapter 43). For example, in buying a British automobile you must first buy British pounds sterling (£) and then spend these pounds on the Jaguar or MG of your choice.

**3  Politics**  As we will note shortly, international trade is subject to political interferences and controls which differ markedly in degree and kind from those applying to domestic trade.

## ☐  THE ECONOMIC BASIS FOR TRADE

But why do nations trade? What is the basis for trade between nations? Stated most generally, international trade is a means by which nations can specialize, increase the productivity of their resources, and thereby realize a larger total output than otherwise. Sovereign nations, like individuals and regions of a nation, can gain by specializing in those products which they can produce with greatest relative efficiency and by trading for those goods they cannot produce efficiently.

While the above rationale for world trade is quite correct, it in a sense begs the question. A more sophisticated answer to the question "Why do nations trade?" hinges upon two points. First, the distribution of economic resources—natural, human, and capital goods—among the nations of the world is quite uneven; nations are substantially different in their endowments of economic resources. Second, the efficient production of various goods requires different technologies or combinations of resources.

The character and interaction of those two points can be readily illustrated. Japan, for example, has a large and quite well-educated labor force; skilled labor is abundant and therefore cheap. Hence, Japan can produce efficiently (at low cost) a variety of goods whose production requires much skilled labor: cameras, transistor radios, and tape recorders are some examples of such *labor-intensive* commodities. In contrast, Australia has vast amounts of land in comparison with its human and capital resources and hence can cheaply produce such *land-intensive* commodities as wheat, wool, and meat. Brazil possesses the soil, tropical climate, rainfall, and ample supplies of unskilled labor requisite to the efficient low-cost production of coffee. Similarly, the United States and other industrially advanced nations are in a strategic position to produce cheaply a variety of *capital-intensive* goods, for example, automobiles, agricultural equipment, machinery, and chemicals.

It is important to emphasize that the economic efficiency with which nations can produce various goods can and does change over time. Both the distribution of resources and technology can change so as to alter the relative efficiency with which goods can be produced by various countries. For example, in the past forty to fifty years the Soviet Union has substantially upgraded the quality of its labor force and has greatly expanded its stock of capital. Hence, although Russia was primarily an exporter of agricultural products and raw materials a half-century ago, it now exports large quantities of manufactured goods. Similarly, the new technologies which gave rise to synthetic fibers and rubber drastically altered the resource-mix needed to produce these goods and thereby changed the relative efficiency of nations in manufacturing them. In short, as national economies evolve, the size and quality of their labor forces may change, the volume and composition of their capital stocks may shift, new technologies will develop, and even the quantity and quality of land and natural resources may be altered (Chapter 19). As these changes occur, the relative efficiency with which a nation can produce various goods will also change.

## ☐  SPECIALIZATION AND COMPARATIVE ADVANTAGE

Let us now introduce the concept of comparative advantage and employ it in analyzing the basis for international specialization and trade. We employ a simplified trade model to reveal most clearly the basic principles involved.

### △  Two Isolated Nations

Suppose the world economy is composed of just two nations, say, the United States and Brazil. Assume further that each is capable of producing both steel and coffee, but at differing levels of economic efficiency. To be specific, let us suppose that the United States and Brazilian domestic production possibilities curves for coffee and steel are as shown in Figure 41-1a and b. Two characteristics of these production possibilities curves must be stressed.

**1  Constant Costs**  We have purposely drawn the "curves" as straight lines, in contrast to the concave-from-the-origin type of production possibilities boundaries introduced in Chapter 2. That is, we have in effect replaced the law of increasing costs with the assumption of constant costs. This simplification will greatly facilitate our discussion. With increasing costs, the comparative costs of the two nations in producing coffee and steel would obviously vary with the amounts produced, and comparative advantages might even change. The assumption of constant costs permits us to complete our entire analysis without having to shift to different comparative-cost ratios with every variation in output. The constant-cost assumption will not seriously impair the validity of our analysis and conclusions. We shall note later in our discussion the effect of the more realistic assumption of increasing costs.

**2  Different Costs**  The production possibilities lines of the United States and Brazil are obviously different, reflecting different resource mixes and differing levels of technologi-

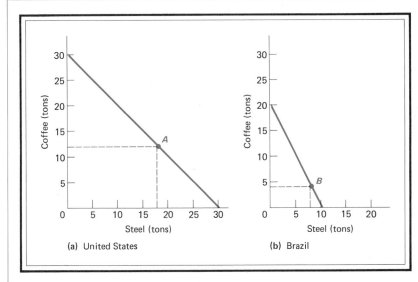

**FIGURE 41-1 PRODUCTION POSSIBILITIES FOR THE UNITED STATES AND BRAZIL**

The two production possibilities lines show the amounts of coffee and steel the United States **(a)** and Brazil **(b)** can produce domestically. The production possibilities for both countries are straight lines because we are assuming constant costs. The different cost ratios—$1S = 1C$ for the United States and $1S = 2C$ for Brazil—are reflected in the different slopes of the two lines.

(a) United States

(b) Brazil

cal progress. More specifically, the opportunity costs of producing steel and coffee differ between the two nations. We note in Figure 41-1a that under full-employment conditions, the United States can increase its output of steel 1 ton by forgoing 1 ton of coffee output. That is to say, in the United States the domestic exchange ratio or *cost ratio* for the two products is 1 ton of steel for 1 ton of coffee, or simply $1S = 1C$. The United States, in effect, can "exchange" a ton of steel for a ton of coffee domestically by shifting resources from steel to coffee. Our constant-cost assumption means that this exchange or cost ratio prevails for all possible shifts on the United States' production possibilities curve. Brazil's production possibilities line in Figure 41-1b reveals a different exchange or cost ratio. In Brazil the domestic cost ratio for the two goods is 1 ton of steel for 2 tons of coffee, or $1S = 2C$.

If the United States and Brazil are isolated and therefore self-sufficient, each must choose some output-mix on its production possibilities line. Let us assume that point A in Figure 41-1a is regarded as the optimum output-mix in the United States. The choice of

this combination of 18 tons of steel and 12 tons of coffee is presumably rendered through the price system, as described in Chapters 5 and 33. Suppose Brazil's optimum product-mix is 8 tons of steel and 4 tons of coffee, as indicated by point B in Figure 41-1b. These choices are also reflected in column 1 of Table 41-3.

△ **Specialization According to Comparative Advantage**

Given these different cost ratios, is there any rule or guideline which will tell us the products in which the United States and Brazil should specialize? Yes, there is: The *principle of comparative advantage* says that total output will be greatest when each good is produced by that nation which has the lower opportunity cost. For our illustration, the United States' opportunity cost is lower for steel, that is, the United States need only forgo 1 ton of coffee to produce 1 ton of steel, whereas Brazil must forgo 2 tons of coffee for 1 ton of steel. *The United States, therefore, has a comparative (cost) advantage in steel, and it should specialize in steel production.* The "world" (the United States and Brazil) obvi-

**TABLE 41-3**
International Specialization According to Comparative Advantage and the Gains from Trade
(*hypothetical data; in tons*)

| Country | (1) Outputs before special- ization | (2) Outputs after special- ization | (3) Amounts exported (−) and imported (+) | (4) Outputs available after trade | (5) Gains from special- ization and trade |
|---|---|---|---|---|---|
| United States | 18 steel | 30 steel | −10 steel | 20 steel | 2 steel |
|  | 12 coffee | 0 coffee | +15 coffee | 15 coffee | 3 coffee |
| Brazil | 8 steel | 0 steel | +10 steel | 10 steel | 2 steel |
|  | 4 coffee | 20 coffee | −15 coffee | 5 coffee | 1 coffee |

ously is *not* economizing in the use of its resources if a given product (steel) is produced by a high-cost producer (Brazil) when it could have been produced by a low-cost producer (the United States). To have Brazil produce steel would mean that the world economy would have to give up more coffee than is necessary to obtain a ton of steel.

Conversely, Brazil's opportunity cost is lower for coffee, that is, Brazil must sacrifice only ½ ton of steel in producing 1 ton of coffee, whereas the United States must forgo 1 ton of steel in producing a ton of coffee. *Brazil has a comparative advantage in coffee, and therefore it should specialize in coffee production.* Again, the world would *not* be employing its resources economically if coffee were produced by a high-cost producer (the United States) rather than a low-cost producer (Brazil). If the United States produced coffee, the world would be giving up more steel than would be necessary to obtain each ton of coffee. *Economizing—using given quantities of scarce resources so as to obtain the greatest total output—requires that any particular good be produced by that nation which has the lower opportunity cost, that is, which has the comparative advantage.* In our illustration, the United States should produce steel and Brazil should produce coffee.

By looking at column 2 of Table 41-3, we can quickly verify that specialized production

in accordance with the principle of comparative advantage does, indeed, allow the world to get more output from given amounts of resources. By specializing completely in steel, the United States can produce 30 tons of steel and no coffee. Similarly, by specializing completely in coffee, Brazil produces 20 tons of coffee and no steel. We note that the world has more steel—30 tons as compared with 26 (= 18 + 8) tons—*and* more coffee—20 tons as compared with 16 (= 12 + 4) tons—than in the case of self-sufficiency or unspecialized production.

△   **Terms of Trade**

But the consumers of each nation will want *both* steel and coffee. Specialization implies the need to trade or exchange the two products. What will be the *terms of trade*? That is, at what exchange ratio will the United States and Brazil trade steel and coffee? We know that because $1S = 1C$ in the United States, the United States must get *more than* 1 ton of coffee for each ton of steel exported or it will not pay the United States to export steel in exchange for Brazilian coffee. That is, the United States must get a better price (more coffee) for its steel in the world market than it can get domestically, or else trade will not be advantageous. Similarly, because $1S = 2C$ in Brazil, we know that Brazil must be able to get 1 ton of steel by exporting some amount *less than* 2 tons of coffee. Brazil must be able to pay a lower price for steel in the world market than it must pay domestically, or it will not wish to engage in international trade. Thus we can be certain that the international exchange ratio or *terms of trade* must lie somewhere between

$$1S = 1C$$

and

$$1S = 2C$$

But where will the actual world exchange ratio fall between the $1S = 1C$ limit (established by cost conditions in the United States) and the $1S = 2C$ limit (determined by cost conditions in Brazil)? This question is very important, because the exchange ratio determines how the gains from international specialization and trade are divided among the two nations. Obviously, the United States will prefer a rate close to $1S = 2C$, say, $1S = 1\frac{3}{4}C$. Americans want to get a great deal of coffee for each ton of steel they export. Similarly, Brazil desires a rate approximating $1S = 1C$, say, $1S = 1\frac{1}{4}C$. Brazil wants to export as little coffee as possible for each ton of steel it receives in exchange.

The actual exchange ratio that will materialize between the two limits depends upon world supply and demand conditions for the two products. If the overall world demand for coffee is weak relative to its supply and the demand for steel is strong relative to its supply, the price of coffee will be low and that of steel high. The exchange ratio will settle near the $1S = 2C$ figure preferred by the United States. Under the opposite world supply and demand conditions, the ratio will settle near the $1S = 1C$ level most favorable to Brazil.

## △  The Gains from Trade

Let us arbitrarily suppose that the international exchange ratio or terms of trade are actually $1S = 1\frac{1}{2}C$. The possibility of trading on these terms permits each nation to supple-

ment its domestic production possibilities line with a *trading possibilities line.* This can be seen in Figure 41-2a and b. Just as a production possibilities line shows the options that a full-employment economy has in obtaining one product by shifting resources from the production of another, so a trading possibilities line shows the options that a nation has by specializing in one product and trading (exporting) its speciality to obtain the other product. The trading possibilities lines in Figure 41-2 are drawn on the assumption that both nations specialize in accordance with comparative advantage and therefore that the United States specializes completely in steel (point $S$ in Figure 41-2a) and Brazil completely in coffee (point $c$ in Figure 41-2b). Now, instead of being constrained by its domestic production possibilities line and having to give up 1 ton of steel for every ton of coffee it wants as it moves up its domestic production possibilities line from point $S$, the United States, through trade with Brazil, can get $1\frac{1}{2}$ tons of coffee for every ton of steel it exports to Brazil as it moves up the trading line $SC'$. Similarly, we can think of Brazil as starting at point $c$, and instead of having to move down its domestic production possibilities line and thereby having to give up 2 tons of coffee for each ton of steel it wants, it can now export just $1\frac{1}{2}$ tons of coffee for each ton of steel it wants by moving down its $cs'$ trading possibilities line. Specialization and trade give rise to a new exchange ratio between steel and coffee which is reflected in a nation's trading possibilities line. This new exchange ratio is superior to the self-sufficiency exchange ratio embodied in the nation's production possibilities line. By specializing in steel and trading for Brazil's coffee, the United States can obtain *more than* 1 ton of coffee for 1 ton of steel. Similarly, by specializing in coffee and trading for the United States' steel, Brazil can get 1 ton of steel for *less than* 2 tons of coffee.

The crucial fact to note is that by specializing according to comparative advantage and trading for those goods produced with the least relative efficiency domestically, both the

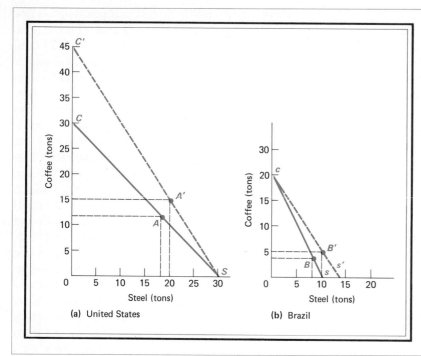

**FIGURE 41-2 TRADING POSSIBILITIES LINES AND THE GAINS FROM TRADE**

As a result of international specialization and trade, the United States and Brazil can both realize levels of output superior to those attainable on their domestic production possibilities curves. For example, the United States in (a) can move from point $A$ on its domestic production possibilities line to point $A'$ on its trading possibilities line; similarly, Brazil in (b) can move from $B$ to $B'$.

United States and Brazil can realize combinations of steel and coffee which lie beyond their production possibilities boundaries. *Specialization according to comparative advantage results in a more efficient allocation of world resources, and larger outputs of both steel and coffee are therefore available to the United States and Brazil.* To be more specific, suppose that at the $1S = 1\frac{1}{2}C$ terms of trade, the United States exports 10 tons of steel to Brazil and Brazil in return exports 15 tons of coffee to the United States. How do the new quantities of steel and coffee available to the two nations compare with the optimum product-mixes that existed before specialization and trade? Point $A$ in Figure 41-2a reminds us that the United States chose 18 tons of steel and 12 tons of coffee originally. Now, by producing 30 tons of steel and no coffee, and by trading 10 tons of steel for 15 tons of coffee, the United States can enjoy 20 tons of steel and 15 tons of coffee. This new, superior combination of steel and

coffee is shown by point $A'$ in Figure 41-2a. Compared with the nontrading figures of 18 tons of steel and 12 tons of coffee, the United States' gains from trade are 2 tons of steel and 3 tons of coffee. Similarly, we assumed Brazil's optimum product-mix was 4 tons of coffee and 8 tons of steel (point $B$) before specialization and trade. Now, by specializing in coffee and thereby producing 20 tons of coffee and no steel, Brazil can realize a combination of 5 tons of coffee and 10 tons of steel by exporting 15 tons of its coffee in exchange for 10 tons of American steel. This new position is shown by point $B'$ in Figure 41-2b. Brazil's gains from trade are 1 ton of coffee and 2 tons of steel. *As a result of specialization and trade, both countries have more of both products.* Table 41-3 is a summary statement of all these figures and merits careful study by the reader.

The fact that points $A'$ and $B'$ are positions superior to $A$ and $B$ is extremely important. You will recall from Chapters 2 and 19 that the only ways a given nation can penetrate its production possibilities boundary are (1) to expand the quantity and improve the quality of its resources or (2) to realize technological progress. We have now discovered a third means—international trade—by which a nation can circumvent the output constraint imposed by its production possibilities curve. The effects of international specialization and trade are tantamount to having more and better resources or discovering improved production techniques.

△   **Increasing Costs**

In formulating a straightforward statement of the principles underlying international trade, we have invoked a number of simplifying assumptions. Our discussion was purposely limited to two products and two nations in order to minimize verbiage; multination and multiproduct examples yield similar conclusions. The assumption of constant costs, on the other hand, is a more substantive simplification. Let us therefore pause to consider the significance of increasing costs (concave-from-the-origin production possibility curves) for our analysis.

Suppose, as in our previous constant-cost illustration, that the United States and Brazil are at positions on their production possibilities curves where their cost ratios are initially $1S = 1C$ and $1S = 2C$ respectively. As before, comparative advantage indicates that the United States should specialize in steel and Brazil in coffee. But now, as the United States begins to expand its steel production, its $1S = 1C$ cost ratio will *rise;* that is, it will have to sacrifice *more than* 1 ton of coffee to get 1 additional ton of steel. Resources are no longer perfectly shiftable between alternative uses, as the constant-cost assumption implied. Resources less and less suitable to steel production must be allocated to the American steel industry in expanding steel output, and this means increasing costs—that is, the sacrifice of larger and larger amounts of coffee for each additional ton of steel. Similarly, Brazil,

starting from its $1S = 2C$ cost ratio position, expands coffee production. But as it does, it will find that its $1S = 2C$ cost ratio begins to *fall.* Sacrificing a ton of steel will free resources which are only capable of producing something *less than* 2 tons of coffee, because these transferred resources are less suitable to coffee production.

Hence, as the American cost ratio rises from $1S = 1C$ and Brazil's falls from $1S = 2C$, a point may be reached at which the cost ratios are equal in the two nations, for example, at $1S = 1\frac{1}{2}C$. At this point the underlying basis for further specialization and trade—differing cost ratios—has obviously disappeared, and further specialization is uneconomic. And most important, this point of equal cost ratios may be realized where the United States is still producing *some* coffee along with its steel and Brazil is producing *some* steel along with its coffee. *The primary effect of increasing costs is to make specialization less than complete.*

☐   **MICROECONOMIC EFFECTS OF WORLD TRADE**

What are the major economic effects of international specialization and trade?

△   **Resource Allocation and Output**

We are familiar with the impact of specialization and trade upon resource allocation and output. International specialization causes each country to shift resources away from that product in which it has a comparative disadvantage and toward that product in which it has a comparative advantage. In our example, the United States shifts resources from coffee to steel and Brazil reallocates its resources from steel to coffee. These reallocations of resources in accordance with comparative advantage give rise to more efficient production; that is, a larger world output results from fixed inputs of resources.

△   **Product Prices**

International specialization and trade

bring about the redirection of demand so that product prices in the trading countries move toward equality. Recall that prior to trade, steel was relatively cheap in the United States; it would take only 1 ton of coffee to get a ton of steel in the United States. Conversely, steel was relatively expensive in Brazil; it would take 2 tons of coffee to obtain a ton of steel in Brazil. With specialization and trade, Brazilians redirected their demand for steel from their domestic steel to American steel. The consequence was that the total demand (domestic plus foreign) for American steel rose, pulling up the price of American steel. Or, looking at the matter from the other vantage point, as American exports of steel augmented domestic supplies in Brazil, the price of steel in Brazil fell. Take your choice: Either approach implies an equalization of the price of steel in the two countries as the result of trade. That is, a single world market and therefore a single world price for steel will result.[1] Recall that, in real terms, the price of 1 ton of steel before trade was 1 ton of coffee in the United States and 2 tons of coffee in Brazil. With trade, the price of a ton of steel became $1\frac{1}{2}$ tons of coffee in both countries. The same rationale applies to coffee.

△  **Resource Prices**

Specialization and trade will also *tend* to equalize resource prices in the two countries. Capital is presumably relatively abundant and land relatively scarce in the United States. Conversely, in Brazil land is apparently relatively abundant and capital relatively scarce. It is these differences in resource endowments which give rise to the different domestic production costs and give the United States a comparative advantage in steel (a capital-intensive good) and Brazil a comparative advantage in coffee (a land-intensive good). These differences in resource availability will be mirrored in resource prices: the price of

capital is relatively low in the United States, while the price of land is relatively high. The opposite is true in Brazil where the price of capital is relatively high and that of land relatively low.

International trade obviously permits both the United States and Brazil to specialize in that good whose production demands the relatively abundant resource. That is, trade allows the United States to increase its output of steel, a capital-intensive good. Brazil produces more coffee, a land-intensive good. The stimulus for this redirection of production is a redirection of demand. Through trade, the United States' domestic demand for steel is now supplemented by the foreign (Brazilian) demand for American steel. This increased demand for American steel is reflected in the resource market as an increase in the demand for capital. Hence, the price of capital in the United States rises. Conversely, as a result of opening up trade with Brazil, American demand for coffee is redirected from domestic to Brazilian coffee. In the American resource market, this is reflected in a decline in the demand for land, and the price of land therefore falls.

Similar forces exist in Brazil, causing the demand for, and price of, land to rise *and* the demand for, and price of, capital to fall.

Note carefully what is happening here: In both countries the prices of abundant, relatively cheap resources (capital in the United States and land in Brazil) tend to rise while the prices of the scarce, relatively expensive resources (land in the United States and capital in Brazil) tend to fall. In short, international trade shifts demand from the scarce toward the abundant resource in both countries, *tending* to equalize resource prices in the two countries.

△  **Other Considerations**

Two final points merit emphasis.

**1  Trade versus Mobility**  We noted earlier that international trade is a substitute for

---

[1] We are simplifying here in that we ignore transportation costs, tariffs, and market imperfections.

the international mobility of resources. The meaning of this assertion should now be evident. If capital resources, for example, could move freely between the United States and Brazil, capital would actually flow from the United States (where its price is initially low) to Brazil (where its price is initially high), and this would obviously increase the price of capital in the United States and lower it in Brazil. This flow would continue until the price of capital was equal in the two countries. While capital has not moved between the two countries, free trade has brought about similar changes in capital prices. The redirecting of Brazil's steel demand from its domestic producers to the United States has increased the price of capital in the United States and simultaneously reduced the price of capital in Brazil. In this sense, trade is a substitute for resource mobility.

**2   Assumptions**   Our discussion of the impact of trade upon commodity and resource prices rests on a number of simplifying assumptions. We have assumed (as noted) that there are no transportation costs or barriers to trade—for example, tariffs and quotas. Further, both economies are presumably at full employment, and domestic product and resource markets are highly competitive. To the extent that these conditions are not realized, the weaker will be the tendency for product and resource prices to move toward equality.

## ☐   MACROECONOMIC EFFECTS OF WORLD TRADE

Not only does world trade affect the allocation of resources and the structure of product and resource prices, but it can also alter aggregate demand and thereby the levels of output, income, and employment. If world trade increases a nation's aggregate demand, then domestic income, output, and employment will rise. If trade diminishes aggregate demand, then income, output, and employment will fall.

### △   Net Exports and Aggregate Demand

First, consider exports. Recall from Chapter 9 that—like consumption, investment, and government purchases—exports $(X)$ give rise to domestic production, income, and employment. Even though the goods and services produced in response to such spending flow abroad, foreign spending on American goods increases production and creates jobs and incomes in the United States. Exports must therefore be added as a new component of aggregate demand. Conversely, when an economy is open to international trade, we must acknowledge that a portion of its consumption, investment, and government spending will be for goods and services which were produced abroad rather than in the United States. Hence, in order not to overstate the value of domestic production, we must in effect reduce the sum of consumption, investment, and government expenditures for the portions which were expended on imported goods. That is, in measuring aggregate demand for domestic goods and services, it is necessary to make a subtraction for expenditures on imports. In short, for a nontrading or closed economy, aggregate demand is $C_a + I_n + G$. But for a trading or open economy, aggregate demand is $C_a + I_n + G + (X - M)$. Or, recalling from Chapter 9 that net exports $(X_n)$ equals $(X - M)$, we can say that aggregate demand for an open economy is $C_a + I_n + G + X_n$.

Now we must ask: What determines the volume of a nation's exports and imports? What determines whether the net export figure added to aggregate demand is positive or negative? The answers are complex. The basic consideration, we know, is comparative costs and the terms of trade. And we will find in Chapter 42 that trade barriers can be significant. But given these considerations, the volume of American exports will depend primarily and directly upon the levels of incomes in foreign nations. That is, if such major trading partners as Japan, Britain, and West Germany are prosperous, they will purchase much from us and American exports will be relatively large. But if these economies are depressed, their purchases from the United States— American exports—will be relatively small. Note that American exports are independent of the level of *domestic* national income. On the other hand, it is reasonable to assume that any nation's imports will vary directly with domestic income in the same general fashion as does domestic consumption. That is, as our domestic net national product (NNP) rises, we can expect households to buy, not only Fords and more Schlitz, but also more Ferraris and more Scotch.

### △  Exports, Imports, and NNP

Let us now add exports and imports to our discussion of income determination as presented in Part 2. Columns 1 and 2 of Table 41-4 merely repeat columns 2 and 9 from Table 13-1, where the equilibrium NNP for a closed economy was $490 billion. In column 3, we have added exports of $30 billion, which are dependent upon the incomes of foreign countries and therefore independent of domestic NNP. Imports are added in column 4; it is assumed that imports increase by $2 billion for every $20 billion increase in domestic national

income. Column 5 combines exports and imports to show net exports. In column 6, we have adjusted the domestic aggregate demand of column 2 for net exports, giving us aggregate demand for an open economy.

The particular export and import figures we have selected are such that foreign trade leaves the equilibrium NNP unchanged. That is, net exports are zero at the closed economy's equilibrium NNP of $490 billion, so aggregate demand for the open economy (column 6) equals aggregate supply (column 1) at $490 billion. Figure 41-3 portrays these results graphically. The $C_a + I_n + G$ schedule is aggregate demand for the closed economy, plotted from column 2 of Table 41-4. The $(C_a + I_n + G + X_n)_0$ schedule is aggregate demand for the open economy and reflects the figures of column 6. Observe that aggregate demand for the open economy intersects aggregate supply at the same point as does aggregate demand for the closed economy and therefore the $490 billion equilibrium NNP is unaltered in this case by world trade.

But there is no reason why net exports will have a neutral effect on equilibrium NNP. For example, by *either* reducing exports by $7

**TABLE 41-4**
Determination of the Equilibrium Levels of Output and Income: Private, Public, and Foreign Sectors (*hypothetical data*)

| (1) Possible levels of aggregate supply (NNP = NI = PI), billions | (2) Aggregate demand for closed economy $(C_a + I_n + G)$, billions | (3) Exports, billions | (4) Imports, billions | (5) Net exports, billions (3) − (4) | (6) Aggregate demand for open economy $(C_a + I_n + G + X_n)$, billions (2) + (5) |
|---|---|---|---|---|---|
| $370 | $400 | $30 | $18 | $12 | $412 |
| 390 | 415 | 30 | 20 | 10 | 425 |
| 410 | 430 | 30 | 22 | 8 | 438 |
| 430 | 445 | 30 | 24 | 6 | 451 |
| 450 | 460 | 30 | 26 | 4 | 464 |
| 470 | 475 | 30 | 28 | 2 | 477 |
| 490 | 490 | 30 | 30 | 0 | 490 |
| 510 | 505 | 30 | 32 | −2 | 503 |
| 530 | 520 | 30 | 34 | −4 | 516 |
| 550 | 535 | 30 | 36 | −6 | 529 |

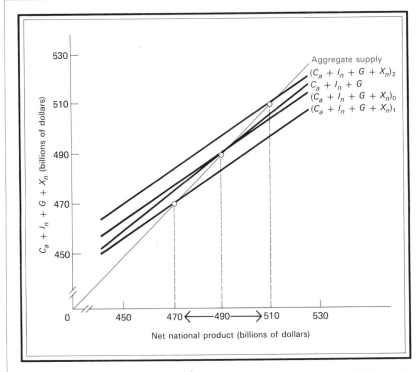

**FIGURE 41-3 NET EXPORTS AND THE EQUILIBRIUM NNP**

An increase in net exports raises the aggregate demand schedule as from $(C_a + I_n + G + X_n)_0$ to $(C_a + I_n + G + X_n)_2$ and increases the equilibrium NNP. Conversely, a decrease in net exports shifts the aggregate demand schedule downward as from $(C_a + I_n + G + X_n)_0$ to $(C_a + I_n + G + X_n)_1$ and lowers the equilibrium NNP. Note also that net exports reduce the slope of the aggregate demand schedule which implies a smaller multiplier.

billion (from $30 to $23 billion) *or* increasing imports by $7 billion at each level of NNP, we would find that net exports would be *minus* $7 billion at the $490 billion NNP. Recalculating aggregate demand in column 6 of Table 40-4, we see that the resulting new equilibrium NNP will be $470 billion. Graphically, the new open-economy aggregate demand schedule is shown by $(C_a + I_n + G + X_n)_1$ in Figure 41-3. This schedule lies $7 billion below $(C_a + I_n + G + X_n)_0$, reflecting the assumed $7 billion decline in net exports. Hence, at the original $490 billion equilibrium NNP, a contractionary gap of $7 billion exists which causes the equilibrium NNP to decline to $470 billion.

Conversely, by *either* increasing exports by $7 billion (from $30 to $37 billion) *or* decreasing imports by $7 billion at each NNP level, one discovers that net exports are now *plus* $7 billion at the original $490 billion

NNP. Again, the recalculation of aggregate demand in column 6 of Table 41-4 reveals that the equilibrium NNP will shift from $490 to $510 billion. In Figure 41-3 the new open economy aggregate demand line is $(C_a + I_n + G + X_n)_2$, which lies $7 billion above $(C_a + I_n + G + X_n)_0$ because of the assumed $7 billion increase in net exports. This creates a $7 billion gap at the original $490 equilibrium NNP, and, as a result, the equilibrium NNP increases to $510 billion. As shown in Figure 12-5b, this increase may be in terms of money NNP or real NNP, depending upon whether the economy is currently at full employment.

The generalizations which can be distilled from these examples are quite obvious. A decline in net exports—that is, a decrease in exports or an increase in imports—decreases aggregate demand and has a contractionary effect on domestic NNP. Conversely, an increase in net exports—the result of either an increase in exports or a decrease in imports—increases aggregate demand and has an expansionary effect on domestic NNP.

## △  Open-Economy Multiplier

A final and rather technical point: You undoubtedly noted in Figure 41-3 that the slope of the aggregate demand schedule is reduced by the introduction of international trade. This diminished slope correctly implies a smaller multiplier. Specifically, in the above illustrations we noted that a $7 billion change in net exports would cause a $20 billion change in equilibrium NNP, indicating a multiplier of $2\frac{6}{7}$ ($= \$20/\$7$). Why does this new *open-economy multiplier* differ from the multiplier of 4 associated with the closed economy of Table 13-1 and columns 1 and 2 of Table 41-4?

Recall that for the closed economy the multiplier is $1/\text{MPS}$ or, for our data, $1/.25$, or 4. In other words, the multiplier is the reciprocal of the MPS, where we define the MPS as

the fraction of any change in national income which "leaks" into saving. Now in moving to an open economy, we add a second leakage in the form of expenditures on imports. That is, saving and imports are similar in that both are ways of disposing of income other than spending it on *domestically* produced goods. Defining the *marginal propensity to import* (MPM) as the fraction of any change in national income which is spent on imports, we can add the MPM to the MPS in the denominator of the multiplier formula so that the multiplier becomes $\dfrac{1}{\text{MPS} + \text{MPM}}$ for an open economy. For the data of Table 41-4 the MPM is $\frac{2}{20}$, or .10. Hence,

$$\frac{1}{\text{MPS} + \text{MPM}} = \frac{1}{.25 + .10} = 1/.35 = 2\tfrac{6}{7}$$

To repeat: Because it entails another leakage from the domestic income-expenditures stream, international trade tends to reduce the size of the multiplier.

## Summary

1   International trade is important, quantitatively and otherwise, to most nations. World trade is vital to the United States in several respects.  *a.* The absolute volumes of American imports and exports exceed those of any other single nation.  *b.* The United States is completely dependent upon trade for certain commodities and materials which cannot be obtained domestically.  *c.* Changes in the volume of net exports can have magnified effects upon the domestic levels of output and income.

2   International and domestic trade differ in that *a.* resources are less mobile internationally than domestically; *b.* each nation uses a different currency; and *c.* international trade is subject to more political controls.

3   World trade is ultimately based upon two considerations: the uneven distribution of economic resources among nations, and the fact that the efficient production of various goods requires particular techniques or combinations of resources.

4   Mutually advantageous specialization and trade are possible between any two nations so long as the cost ratios for any two products differ. By specializing according to comparative advantage, nations can realize larger real incomes with fixed amounts of resources. The terms of trade determine how this increase in world output is shared by the trading nations. Increasing costs impose limits upon the gains from specialization and trade.

5   In addition to reallocating resources toward those products in which a nation has a comparative advantage, international specialization creates tendencies for both product and resource prices in trading countries to move toward equality.

6   An increase in a country's exports or a decrease in its imports will have an expansionary effect upon its NNP.  Conversely, a decline in exports or an increase in imports will have a contractionary impact on NNP.

7   Because imports are a leakage, the multiplier for an open economy is equal to the reciprocal of the sum of the marginal propensities to save and import.

## Questions and Study Suggestions

1   Key terms and concepts to remember: open economy, labor- (land-, capital-) intensive commodity; cost ratio; comparative advantage; terms of trade; gains from trade; trading possibilities line; net exports; marginal propensity to import; open-economy multiplier.

2   In what ways are domestic and foreign trade similar?  In what ways do they differ?

3   The following are production possibilities tables for Japan and Hawaii.  Assume that prior to specialization and trade, the optimum product-mix for Japan is alternative B and for Hawaii alternative D.

| Product | Japan's production alternatives | | | | | |
|---|---|---|---|---|---|---|
| | A | B | C | D | E | F |
| Radios (in thousands) | 30 | 24 | 18 | 12 | 6 | 0 |
| Pineapples (in tons) | 0 | 6 | 12 | 18 | 24 | 30 |

| Product | Hawaii's production alternatives | | | | | |
|---|---|---|---|---|---|---|
| | A | B | C | D | E | F |
| Radios (in thousands) | 10 | 8 | 6 | 4 | 2 | 0 |
| Pineapples (in tons) | 0 | 4 | 8 | 12 | 16 | 20 |

*a.*   Are comparative-cost conditions such that the two nations should specialize?  If so, what product should each produce?

*b.*   What is the total gain in radio and pineapple output which results from this specialization?

*c.*   What are the limits of the terms of trade?  Suppose the actual terms of trade are 1 unit of radios for 1½ units of pineapples and that 4 units of radios are exchanged for 6 units of pineapples.  What are the gains from specialization and trade for each nation?

*d.*   Can you conclude from this illustration that specialization according to comparative advantage results in the more efficient use of world resources?  Explain.

4   Assume that by using all its resources to produce X, nation A can produce 80 units of X; by devoting all its resources to Y, it can produce 40 Y.  Comparable figures for nation B are 60 X and 60 Y.  Assuming constant costs, in which product should each nation specialize?  Why?  Indicate the limits of the terms of trade.  Explain the effects of trade upon resource and product prices in the two nations.

5   "The United States can produce product X more efficiently than can Great Britain.  Yet we import X from Great Britain."  Explain.

**6** The data in columns 1 and 2 of the following table are for a closed economy.

| (1) Aggregate supply (NNP = DI), billions | (2) Aggregate demand, closed economy, billions | (3) Exports, billions | (4) Imports, billions | (5) Net exports, billions | (6) Aggregate demand, open economy, billions |
|---|---|---|---|---|---|
| $200 | $240 | $20 | $18 | $ _____ | $ _____ |
| 250 | 280 | 20 | 22 | _____ | _____ |
| 300 | 320 | 20 | 26 | _____ | _____ |
| 350 | 360 | 20 | 30 | _____ | _____ |
| 400 | 400 | 20 | 34 | _____ | _____ |
| 450 | 440 | 20 | 38 | _____ | _____ |
| 500 | 480 | 20 | 42 | _____ | _____ |
| 550 | 520 | 20 | 46 | _____ | _____ |

*a.* Use columns 1 and 2 to determine the equilibrium NNP and the multiplier for the closed economy.

*b.* Now open this economy for international trade by including the export and import figures of columns 3 and 4. Determine the equilibrium NNP and the multiplier for the open economy. Explain why these figures differ from those for the closed economy.

*c.* Given the import figures of column 4, what would be the level of equilibrium NNP if exports were $48 billion? $6 billion? What generalization concerning the level of exports and the equilibrium NNP can you derive from these examples?

*d.* Given the original $20 billion level of exports, what would be the equilibrium NNP if imports were $14 billion larger at each level of NNP? Or $14 billion smaller at each level of NNP? What generalization concerning the level of imports and the equilibrium NNP is illustrated by these examples?

## Selected References

Baldwin, Robert E., and J. David Richardson (eds.): *International Trade and Finance: Readings* (Boston: Little, Brown and Company, 1974), part 1.

Caves, Richard E., and Ronald W. Jones: *World Trade and Payments: An Introduction,* 2d ed. (Boston: Little, Brown and Company, 1977), chaps. 1–4.

Hogendorn, Jan S., and Wilson B. Brown: *The New International Economics* (Reading, Mass.: Addison-Wesley Publishing Company, 1979), chaps. 10–11.

Humphrey, Thomas M.: "Changing Views of Comparative Advantage," *Monthly Review* (Federal Reserve Bank of Richmond, July 1972).

Kenen, Peter B., and Raymond Lubitz: *International Economics,* 3d ed. (Englewood Cliffs, N.J.: Prentice-Hall, Inc., 1971), particularly chaps. 1, 2, 4.

Pen, Jan: *A Primer on International Trade* (New York: Random House, Inc., 1967).

Snider, Delbert A.: *Introduction to International Economics,* 7th ed. (Homewood, Ill.: Richard D. Irwin, Inc., 1979), chaps. 1–6.

# LAST WORD
## Imperialism and
## World Trade

Orthodox economics employs the notion of comparative advantage to explain mutually advantageous trade between nations. Radical or Marxist economics explains trade in terms of capitalist nations exploiting less developed areas of the world.

. . . according to Marxists, foreign trade continues to play an important role as capitalism develops. By means of this trade, older capitalistic countries can take advantage of both larger markets for their manufactures and cheaper sources of foodstuffs and raw materials. To regulate the terms of this trade, however, so that they can obtain the major benefits from trade, the mature capitalistic nations tighten and extend their control over poorer areas by building up colonial empires. In other words, Marxists maintain that colonialism is designed to increase the degree of exploitation in the poorer countries for the benefit of the advanced capitalistic nations.

Foreign markets become even more important as capitalism moves into what Marxists term its monopoly stage. This occurs when the concentration and centralization of capital gradually eliminate most areas of free competition in the economy. At this stage imperialism emerges. As Lenin says, "Imperialism is capitalism in that stage of development in which the dominance of monopolies and finance capital has established itself; . . . in which the division of the world among the international trusts has begun; in which the division of all territories of the globe among the great capitalist powers has been completed."

At this point in capitalist development, so argue the Marxists, the forces of stagnation in the form of a low rate of profit and chronic overproduction are conditions that press ever harder upon the economy. The older capitalistic countries turn more and more to the foreign sector in order to postpone their final destruction. The export of capital to backward areas in which the rate of profit is higher becomes a major means of attempting to lessen the tendency towards stagnation. This also becomes a means for encouraging the export of commodities which relieves the pressures of overproduction at home.

According to the Marxist view, further domination of the poorer countries by the advanced capitalist countries accompanies this export of capital. There are resistances to be overcome within these areas, if foreigners are to find profitable outlets and exploit the people. Each capitalist power also desires to exclude competition from other capitalist nations who are in similar difficulties. Consequently, the governments of the great powers step in and forcibly create conditions favorable to the process of exploitation. In all this, the people of the poorer regions benefit little, if any. Traditional habits and customs are destroyed; handicraft industries are wiped out by cheap manufacturing imports; and the masses are stripped of their means of production. In short, "Finance capital and the trusts are increasing instead of diminishing the differences in the rate of development of the various parts of world economy."

Gerald M. Meier and Robert E. Baldwin, *Economic Development: Theory, History, Policy* (New York: John Wiley & Sons, Inc., 1957), pp. 59–60. Copyright © 1957 by John Wiley & Sons, Inc. Reprinted by permission of John Wiley & Sons, Inc.

# The Economics of Free Trade and Protection

chapter **42**

The fundamental conclusion of Chapter 41 is that nations can enjoy an expanded world output by specializing in accordance with comparative advantage and by freely engaging in trade. Despite the apparent advantages of uninhibited world trade, nations embrace a variety of policies which restrict such trade. Hence, the goals of this chapter are to (1) restate the case for free trade; (2) discuss trade barriers and their economic consequences; (3) set forth and critically evaluate the arguments for protectionism; and (4) summarize the evolution of international trade policy.

## ☐ THE CASE FOR FREE TRADE

The compelling logic of the case for free trade is hardly new. Indeed, in 1776 Adam Smith got to the heart of the matter by asserting:[1]

It is the maxim of every prudent master of a family, never to attempt to make at home what it will cost him more to make than to buy. The taylor does not attempt to make his own shoes, but buys them of the shoemaker. The shoemaker does not attempt to make his own clothes but employs a taylor. The farmer attempts to make neither the one nor the other, but employs those different artificers. All of them find it for their interest to employ their whole industry in a way in which they have some advantage over their neighbors, and to purchase with a part of its produce, or what is the same thing, with the price of a part of it, whatever else they have occasion for.

In modern jargon, the case for free trade comes down to this one potent argument. *Through free trade based upon the principle of comparative advantage, the world economy can achieve a more efficient allocation of resources and a higher level of material well-being.* The resource mixes and technological knowledge of

[1] Adam Smith, *The Wealth of Nations* (New York: Modern Library, Inc., 1937), p. 424.

each country are different. Therefore, each nation can produce particular commodities at different real costs. Each nation should produce goods for which its costs are low relative to those of other nations and exchange these specialties for products for which its costs are high relative to those of other nations. If each nation does this, the world can realize fully the advantages of geographic and human specialization. That is, the world—and each free-trading nation—can realize a larger real income from the given supplies of resources available to it. Protection—barriers to free trade—lessens or eliminates the gains from specialization. If nations cannot freely trade, they must shift resources from efficient (low-cost) to inefficient (high-cost) uses in order to satisfy their diverse wants.

A collateral benefit of free trade also should be noted: Unimpeded international trade deters the establishment of domestic business monopolies. As opposed to free trade, protection from foreign competition creates a domestic economic environment more conducive to the development of monopoly and the host of restrictive practices associated therewith.

It is fair to say that the vast majority of economists embrace the case for free trade as an economically valid position. However, economists do, as we shall note shortly, acknowledge the relevance of short-run and politically motivated exceptions to the case for free trade.

## □   TRADE BARRIERS

No matter how compelling the logic of the case for free trade, in fact a wide variety of barriers to free trade do exist. The discussion that follows will center upon the two most widely used barriers.

### △   Protective Tariffs and Import Quotas

Tariffs are simply excise taxes on imported goods; they may be imposed for purposes of revenue or protection. *Revenue tariffs* are usually applied to products which are not produced domestically, for example, tin, coffee, and bananas in the case of the United States. Rates on revenue tariffs are typically modest. *Protective tariffs,* on the other hand, are designed to shield domestic producers from foreign competition. Although protective tariffs are usually not high enough to prohibit the importation of foreign goods, they obviously put foreign producers at a competitive disadvantage in selling in domestic markets.

*Import quotas* specify the maximum amounts of specific commodities which may be imported in any period of time. Frequently, import quotas are more effective in retarding international commerce than are tariffs. A given product might be imported in relatively large quantities despite high tariffs; low import quotas, on the other hand, completely prohibit imports once the quotas are filled. We will emphasize protective tariffs in the following discussion of protectionism.

### △   Motivations

The imposition of protective tariffs and import quotas is rooted in several motivations.

**1   Special Interests**   While nations as a whole gain from free international trade, particular industries and groups of resource suppliers can be hurt. In Chapter 41's comparative advantage example, specialization and trade adversely affected the American coffee industry and the Brazilian steel industry. It is easy to see why such groups may seek to preserve or improve their economic positions by persuading the government to impose tariffs or quotas to protect them from the deleterious effects of free trade. Such groups have sometimes been highly vocal and politically powerful.

**2   Domestic Stimulus**   During depressions or recessions, nations have sometimes attempted to stimulate their domestic economies by controlling or manipulating their world trade. In particular, as we have seen in

Chapter 41, a decline in imports tends to shift the aggregate demand schedule upward, thereby increasing domestic income and employment.

**3   Defense**   Post-World War II international tensions prompted nations to use tariffs and quotas to protect domestic producers of materials and goods essential to mobilization and war.

**4   Industrialization**   In Chapter 21 we found that underdeveloped nations have sometimes turned to tariffs and quotas in attempting to industrialize and diversify their economies.

### △   Economic Impact of Tariffs

Let us now employ simple supply and demand analysis to examine the economic effects of the most widely used trade barrier—protective tariffs. The $D_d$ and $S_d$ curves in Figure 42-1 show domestic demand and supply for a product in which the United States has a comparative *dis*advantage, for example, cassette recorders. In the absence of world trade, the domestic price and output would be $OP_d$ and $Oq$, respectively.

Assume now that the domestic economy is opened to world trade, and that the Japanese, who have a comparative advantage in cassette recorders and dominate the world market, begin to sell their recorders in the United States. We assume that with free trade the domestic price cannot differ from the lower world price, which here is $P_w$. We observe at $P_w$ that domestic consumption is $Od$, domestic production is $Oa$, and the difference between the two, $ad$, reflects imports.

Next we assume that the United States imposes a tariff of $P_wP_t$ per unit on the imported recorders. This will raise the domestic price from $OP_w$ to $OP_t$ and will have a variety of effects. First, the consumption of recorders in the United States will decline from $Od$ to $Oc$ as the higher price moves buyers up their de-

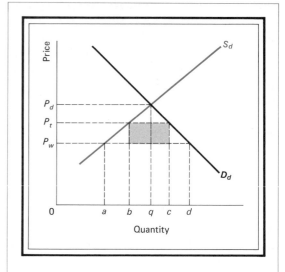

**FIGURE 42-1  THE ECONOMIC EFFECTS OF A PROTECTIVE TARIFF**

A tariff of $P_wP_t$ will reduce domestic consumption from *Od* to *Oc*. Domestic producers will be able to sell more output (*Ob* rather than *Oa*) at a higher price ($OP_t$ rather than $OP_w$). Foreign exporters are injured because they are able to sell less output (*bc* rather than *ad*) in the United States. The orange area indicates the amount of tariffs paid by American consumers.

mand curve. American consumers are clearly injured by the tariff. The tariff prompts consumers to buy fewer recorders and to reallocate their expenditures to less desired substitute products. Second, American producers—who are *not* subject to the tariff—will receive a higher price of $OP_t$ per unit. Because this new price is higher than the pretariff or world price of $OP_w$, the domestic recorder industry will move up its supply curve $S_d$, increasing domestic output from $Oa$ to $Ob$. Domestic producers will enjoy both a higher price and expanded sales. These effects obviously explain the interest of domestic producers in lobbying for protective tariffs. From a social point of view, however, the expanded domestic production of *ab* reflects the fact that the tariff permits domestic producers of recorders to bid resources away from other, more efficient, industries. Third, Japanese producers will be hurt. Although the sales price of recorders is higher by $P_wP_t$, that increase accrues to the United States government and not to Japanese producers! The after-tariff price remains at $OP_w$, while the volume of United States imports (Japanese exports) falls from $ad$ to $bc$. Finally, note that the orange rectangle indicates the amount of revenue which the tariff yields. That is, total revenue from the tariff is determined by multiplying the tariff of $P_tP_w$ per unit by the number of imported recorders, $bc$. This tariff revenue is essentially a transfer of income from consumers to government and does not represent any net change in the nation's economic well-being; government gains what consumers lose.

There are more subtle effects of tariffs which go beyond our simple supply and demand diagram. Because of diminished sales of recorders in the United States, Japan will now earn fewer dollars with which to buy American exports. That is, American export industries—industries in which the United States has a comparative advantage—will cut production and release resources. These are highly efficient industries, as is evidenced by their comparative advantage and their ability to sell goods in world markets. In short, tariffs directly promote the expansion of relatively inefficient industries which do not have a comparative advantage *and* indirectly cause the contraction of relatively efficient industries which do have a comparative advantage. This obviously means that tariffs cause resources to be shifted in the wrong direction. This is not surprising. The big message of Chapter 41 was that specialization and unfettered world trade based on comparative advantage would lead to the efficient use of world resources and an expansion of the world's real output. The purpose and effect of protective tariffs are to reduce world trade. Therefore, aside from their specific effects upon consumers and foreign and domestic producers, tariffs diminish the world's real output.

## ☐ THE CASE FOR PROTECTION: A CRITICAL REVIEW

Although free-trade advocates tend to prevail in the classroom, protectionists often dominate the halls of Congress. What arguments do protectionists make to justify trade barriers? Of what validity are these arguments?

### △ Military Self-Sufficiency Argument

The argument here is not economic, but rather, it is of a political-military nature: Protective tariffs are needed to preserve or strengthen industries producing strategic goods and materials essential for defense or war. It very plausibly contends that in an uncertain world, political-military objectives (self-sufficiency) must take precedence over economic goals (efficiency in the allocation of world resources).

Unfortunately, there is no objective criterion for weighing the relative worth of the increase in national security on the one hand, and the decrease in productive efficiency on the other, which accompany the reallocation of resources toward strategic industries when such tariffs are imposed. The economist can only call attention to the fact that certain economic costs are involved when tariffs are levied to enhance military self-sufficiency.

Although we might all agree that it is probably not a good idea to import our missile guidance systems from the Soviet Union, the self-sufficiency argument is nevertheless open to serious abuse. Virtually every industry can directly or indirectly claim a contribution to national security. Can you name an industry which did *not* contribute in some small way to the execution of World War II? Aside from abuses, are there not means superior to tariffs which will provide for needed strength in strategic industries? When achieved through tariffs, self-sufficiency gives rise to costs in the form of higher domestic prices on the output of the shielded industry. Hence, the cost of enhanced military security is apportioned arbitrarily among those consumers who buy the industry's product. Virtually all economists agree that a direct subsidy to strategic industries, financed out of general tax revenues, would entail a more equitable distribution of these costs.

### △  Protect Domestic Living Standards

Proponents of tariff protection frequently argue that tariffs are essential to *protect high wages and the high standard of living* now enjoyed in our domestic economy. Cheap foreign labor, it is contended, will cause cheap foreign goods to flow into the United States. As a result, the prices of American goods and ultimately wage rates and the level of living will be driven down by this competition.

This appeal is tempting. But the argument falsely assumes that low foreign wages will automatically mean low prices on foreign goods and that high domestic wages mean high prices on domestic goods. This is not necessarily the case. Indeed, the argument conveniently ignores the fact that wage rates and per unit production costs are related through productivity. Hourly wage rates may be high and unit costs and product price low, provided productivity is high. And what determines the productivity of labor? Basically, the quality of labor and the quality and quantity of the capital with which it is equipped (Chapters 19 and 20). As compared with most other nations, American labor is high in quality and is extremely well equipped. The consequence is that high wages in the United States usually are accompanied by relatively low unit costs and relatively low product prices. As we have already discovered (Chapter 31), wages are high in the United States for the simple reason that productivity is high!

These comments, of course, do not rule out the fact that in the production of certain articles, higher American productivity is more than offset by the low money wages paid foreign workers. This is particularly likely to be true where production of a commodity requires much hand labor and little capital equipment, for example, Swiss watches or Japanese toys.

Is protection warranted under these circumstances? Not on economic grounds. These nations will simply have a comparative advantage in these lines of production. Furthermore, limiting American imports of such goods by imposing tariffs will also curtail American exports; in the long run, other nations must be able to sell to us in order to earn dollars so they can buy from us. The result is that American workers will be released from efficient, high-productivity export industries and absorbed in relatively inefficient, low-productivity industries which can survive only under an umbrella of protective tariffs. This reallocation will lower, not increase, real wages domestically and impair the domestic standard of living.

### △  Increase Domestic Employment

This argument for tariffs becomes increasingly fashionable as an economy encounters a recession. It is rooted in the macro analysis of Chapter 41. Aggregate demand in an open economy is comprised of $C_a + I_n + G + X - M$. By reducing imports, $M$, aggregate demand will rise, stimulating the domestic economy by boosting income and employment. In the short run this policy may work, but there are important shortcomings.

**1**  It is obvious that all nations cannot simultaneously succeed in this endeavor. The exports of one nation must be the imports of another. To the extent that one country is able to stimulate its economy through an excess of exports over imports, some other economy's unemployment problem is worsened by the resulting excess of imports over exports. It is no wonder that tariff boosts and the imposition of import quotas for the purposes of achieving domestic full employment are termed "beggar my neighbor" policies.

**2**  Nations adversely affected by tariffs and quotas are likely to retaliate, causing a competitive raising of trade barriers which will choke off trade to the end that all nations are worse off. It is not surprising that the Smoot-Hawley Tariff Act of 1930, which imposed the highest tariffs ever enacted in the United States, backfired miserably. Rather than stimulate the American economy, this tariff act only induced a series of retaliatory restrictions by adversely affected nations. This caused a further contraction of international trade and tended to lower the income and employment levels of all nations.

**3** Lastly, in the long run an excess of exports over imports is doomed to failure as a device for stimulating domestic employment. Remember: It is through American imports that foreign nations earn dollars with which to purchase American exports. In the long run a nation must import in order to export. Hence, the long-run impact of tariffs is not to increase domestic employment but at best to reallocate workers away from export industries and toward protected domestic industries. This shift implies a less efficient allocation of resources. Tariffs shift resources away from those industries in which production is so efficient as to provide a comparative advantage. There is little doubt that intelligent, well-timed monetary and fiscal policies are preferable to tariff and quota adjustments as anticyclical techniques.

△  **Diversification for Stability**

Closely related to the increase-domestic-employment argument for tariff protection is the diversification-for-stability argument. The point here is that highly specialized economies—for example, Brazil's coffee economy or Cuba's sugar economy—are highly dependent upon international markets for their incomes. Wars, cyclical fluctuations, and adverse changes in the structure of industry will force large and frequently painful readjustments upon such economies. It is therefore alleged that tariff and quota protection is needed in such nations to induce greater industrial diversification and consequently less dependence upon world markets for one or two products. This will help insulate the domestic economy from international political developments, depressions abroad, and from random fluctua-

tions in world supply and demand for one or two particular commodities, thereby providing greater domestic stability.

There is some truth in this argument. There are also serious qualifications and shortcomings. (*a*) The argument has little or no relevance to the United States and other advanced economies. (*b*) The economic costs of diversification may be great; one-crop economies may be highly inefficient in manufacturing.

△  **Infant-Industry Argument**

The infant-industry argument contends that protective tariffs are needed for the purpose of allowing new domestic industries to establish themselves. Temporarily shielding young domestic firms from the severe competition afforded by more mature and therefore currently more efficient foreign firms will give the infant industries a chance to develop and become efficient producers. This argument for protection rests upon an alleged exception to the case for free trade. The exception is that all industries have not had, and in the presence of mature foreign competition, will never have, the chance to make long-run adjustments in the direction of larger scale and greater efficiency in production. The provision of tariff protection for infant industries will therefore correct a current misallocation of world resources now perpetuated by historically different levels of economic development between domestic and foreign industries.

Though the infant-industry argument has logical validity, these qualifying points must be noted. (*a*) This argument is not particularly pertinent to industrially advanced nations such as the United States. (*b*) In the underdeveloped nations it is very difficult to determine which industries are the infants capable of achieving economic maturity and therefore deserving of protection. (*c*) Unlike old soldiers, protective tariffs rarely fade away, but rather, tend to persist and increase even after industrial maturity has been realized. (*d*) Most economists feel that if infant industries are to be subsidized, there are better means than tariffs for doing it. Direct subsidies, for example, have the advantage of making explicit which industries are being aided and to what degree.

## △ A Summing Up

One should obviously not judge an issue by simply counting the number of arguments pro and con. The arguments for protection are numerous, but they are not weighty. Under proper conditions, the infant-industry argument stands as a valid exception, justifiable on economic grounds. And on political-military grounds, the self-sufficiency argument can be used to validate protection. Both arguments, however, are susceptible to severe abuses, and both neglect alternative means of fostering industrial development and military self-sufficiency. Most other arguments are semiemotional appeals in the form of half-truths and outright fallacies. These arguments note only the immediate and direct consequences of protective tariffs. They ignore the plain truth that in the long run a nation must import in order to export.

The arguments for free trade are not numerous, but their logic is compelling. Unimpeded international trade permits greater specialization, the more efficient utilization of world resources, and the realization of higher standards of living. The increased competition provided by foreign producers forces domestic firms to be innovative and progressive with respect to both production methods and product quality. And free trade provides consumers with a wider range of products from which to choose.

## □ INTERNATIONAL TRADE POLICIES

As Figure 42-2 makes clear, tariffs in the United States have had their ups and downs.[2]

[2]Technical footnote: Average tariff-rate figures understate the importance of tariffs by not accounting for the fact that some goods are *excluded* from American markets because of existing tariffs. Then, too, average figures conceal the high tariffs on particular items: watches, china, hats, woolens, scissors, wine, jewelry, glassware, and so forth.

Generally speaking, the United States tended to be a high-tariff nation over much of its history. Note that the Smoot-Hawley Tariff Act enacted in 1930 embodied some of the highest tariff rates ever imposed by the United States.

Given the case for free trade, this high-tariff heritage may be a bit surprising. If tariffs are economically undesirable, why has Congress been so willing to employ them? The answer lies in the political realities of tariff making. Recall Chapter 6's special-interest effect as an aspect of public sector failure. A small group of domestic producers who will receive large economic gains from tariffs and quotas will press vigorously for protection through well-financed and well-informed political lobbyists. The large number of consumers who individually will have small losses imposed upon them will be generally uninformed and indifferent. Indeed, the public may be won over, not only by the vigor, but also by the apparent plausibility ("Cut imports and prevent domestic unemployment") and the patriotic ring ("Buy American!") of the protectionists. Alleged tariff benefits seem immediate and clear-cut to the public. The adverse effects cited by economists appear ever so obscure and widely dispersed over the economy. Then, too, the public is likely to stumble on the fallacy of composition: "If a protective tariff on Swiss watches will preserve profits and employment in the American watch industry, how can it be detrimental to the economy as a whole?" When political logrolling is added in—"You back tariffs for industry X in my state and I'll do the same for industry Y in your state"—the sum can be protective tariffs and import quotas.

## △ Reciprocal Trade Act and GATT

The downward trend of tariffs since Smoot-Hawley was inaugurated with the *Reciprocal Trade Agreements Act of 1934*. Specifically aimed at tariff reduction, the act had two main features:

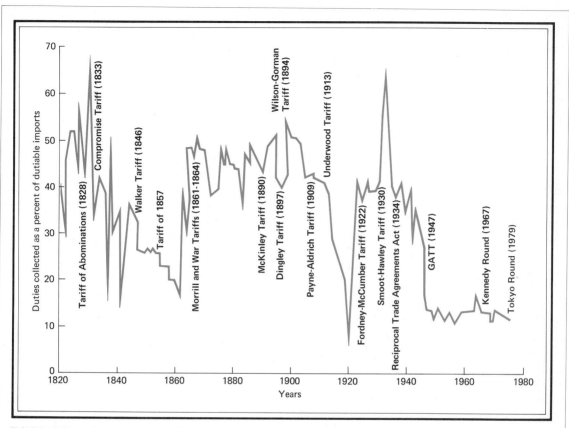

**FIGURE 42-2   UNITED STATES TARIFF RATES, 1820-1980.**

American tariff rates have fluctuated historically. But beginning with the Reciprocal Trade Agreements Act of 1934, the trend has been downward. (*U.S. Department of Commerce data.*)

**1   Negotiating Authority**   It authorized the President to negotiate agreements with foreign nations which would reduce American tariffs up to 50 percent of the existing rates. Tariff reductions were to hinge upon the willingness of other nations to reciprocate by lowering tariffs on American exports.

**2   Generalized Reductions**   By incorporating *most-favored-nation clauses* in these agreements, the resulting tariff reductions not only would apply to the specific nation negotiating with the United States, but they would be *generalized* so as to apply to all nations.

But the Reciprocal Trade Act gave rise to only bilateral (two-nation) negotiations. This approach was broadened in 1947 when twenty-three nations, including the United States, signed a General Agreement on Tariffs and Trade (GATT). GATT is based on three cardinal principles: (1) equal, nondiscriminatory treatment for all member nations; (2) the reduction of tariffs by *multilateral* negotiations; and (3) the elimination of import quotas. Basically, GATT is a forum for the negotiation of reductions in tariff barriers on a multilateral basis. One hundred eleven nations now belong to GATT, and there is little doubt but that it has been an important force in the trend toward liberalized trade. Under its sponsorship, seven "rounds" of negotiations to reduce trade barriers have been completed in the post-World War II period. We will consider two of these negotiating rounds momentarily.

### △ Economic Integration: The Common Market

Another crucial development in trade liberalization has taken the form of economic integration. The most dramatic illustration is the European Economic Community (EEC), or the Common Market, as it is popularly known. The EEC was begun in 1958 with France, West Germany, Italy, Belgium, the Netherlands, and Luxembourg as members. Britain, Denmark, and Ireland joined in 1973; Greece and Turkey are "associate members."

**Goals** The Common Market calls for (1) the gradual abolition of tariffs and import quotas on all products traded among the nine participating nations; (2) the establishment of a common system of tariffs applicable to all goods received from nations outside the Common Market; (3) the eventual free movement of capital and labor within the Market; and (4) the creation of common policies with respect to a number of other economic matters of joint concern, for example, agriculture, transportation, and restrictive business practices.

**Results** Motives for creating the Common Market were both political and economic. The primary economic motive, of course, was to gain the advantages of freer trade for members. While it is difficult to determine the extent to which rapid postwar growth (Table 20-2) has been due to economic integration, it is clear that integration creates the mass markets which are essential to Common Market industries if economies of large-scale production are to be realized. More efficient production for a large-scale market permits European

industries to realize the lower costs which small, localized markets have historically denied them.

The effects upon nonmember nations, such as the United States, are even less certain. On the one hand, a peaceful and increasingly prosperous Common Market makes member nations better potential customers for American exports. On the other hand, American firms encounter tariffs which make it difficult to compete in EEC markets. For example, *before* the establishment of the Common Market, American, German, and French automobile manufacturers all faced the same tariff in selling their products to, say, Belgium. However, with the establishment of internal free trade among EEC members, Belgian tariffs on German Volkswagens and French Renaults fell to zero, but an external tariff still applies to American Chevrolets and Fords. This obviously puts American firms and those of other nonmember nations at a serious competitive disadvantage.

### △ The Kennedy Round

Against this background, it became increasingly evident in the early 1960s that, if the United States' economic isolation from the Common Market and potential political disunity were to be avoided, the United States should take the initiative to reduce trade barriers against the Common Market. This initiative took the form of the *Trade Expansion Act of 1962,* which provided the President with broad powers to negotiate reciprocal trade reductions. In particular, the act gave American negotiators the authority to reduce tariffs up to 50 percent on broad classes of industrial products and to eliminate tariffs completely on goods where tariffs have been only 5 percent or less. The reductions were to be made by reciprocal negotiations and to embody "most-favored-nation" clauses, automatically extending the lower tariffs to many other countries.

The Trade Expansion Act was the legislative basis for the "Kennedy Round" of tariff negotiations under the auspices of GATT, which were concluded in 1967.[3] The Kennedy Round was generally successful in that it achieved tariff cuts averaging more than 35 percent of some $40 billion worth of goods. The underdeveloped nations also benefited from the negotiations in that special efforts were made to reduce tariffs on products of particular interest to these nations without requiring full reciprocity. The main disappointment from the United States' viewpoint was the EEC's reluctance to reduce tariffs on agricultural products because American competition in foodstuffs would jeopardize the Common Market's program of agricultural price supports.

△   **The Tokyo Round**

In 1973, representatives of some 100 nations established the groundwork for a new round of trade negotiations which was completed in 1979. Known as the "Tokyo Round," the agreements embody a further substantial reduction of 30 to 35 percent in average tariff levels. These reductions are to be phased in over an eight-year period to facilitate domestic economic adjustments. Equally important, however, is the attention given to *nontariff barriers* (NTBs) to trade. While many tariffs were substantially reduced or eliminated under the previous six rounds of trade negotiations, trade has been impeded by a variety of NTBs in the form of import quotas, licensing requirements, unreasonable standards for product quality, unnecessary red tape in customs procedures, and so forth. To illustrate: Japan and the European countries frequently require importers to obtain licenses. By restricting the issuance of licenses, imports can be effectively restricted. Great Britain bars the importation of coal in this way. Similarly, unrealistic health and safety standards may be applied to

foreign products to the end that their importation is discouraged. The United States has "Buy American" legislation which puts restrictions on the Federal government's purchasing foreign goods. Unnecessarily complex procedures in the administration of customs can also reduce the flow of trade. A unique feature of the Tokyo Round is agreement to a variety of "codes of conduct" which are intended to mitigate the use and abuse of NTBs. The agreement also provides for new mechanisms designed to settle disputes which might arise over the application of NTBs. While the effectiveness of the codes remains to be determined, the mere fact that the participating nations have explicitly recognized the need to reduce the trade obstacles inherent in NTBs is encouraging.

△   **United States–Communist Trade**

Since World War II, American policy has leaned toward greater trade liberalization with respect to noncommunist countries. But over most of this period, our policies toward trade with communist countries—the Soviet Union and its Eastern European satellites, China, and North Korea—have been highly restrictive. In the late 1960s, for example, United States trade with the communist nations accounted for less than 1 percent of both our trade and their trade. In particular, the United States has severely restricted exports to communist nations for the purpose of preventing these nations from acquiring goods and technologies which might enhance their industrial-military capacities.

But, beginning in 1969, United States policy began to change. And for several reasons. First, the political climate between the United States and the communist countries began to ease; the reestablishment of American political contact with the People's Republic of China is particularly notable. Second, the Soviet Union began to display a growing interest in both American capital goods and industrial products. Underlying this interest is a declining

---

[3] So called because this sixth "round" of trade negotiations came about largely at the initiative of President Kennedy.

Soviet growth rate and the hope that imports embodying advanced Western technology will provide a stimulus to Soviet productivity and growth. Third, rather persistent Soviet agricultural shortfalls have resulted in agreements to buy substantial quantities of American grain. Finally, recognition was growing that the restrictionist American policy was unrealistic and substantially a failure. There was increasing awareness, on the one hand, that the sale of consumer and capital goods to the communist countries would benefit our economy—not to mention our balance of payments—as much as theirs. On the other hand, other nations of Western Europe as well as Japan *were* liberalizing their trade with the communists and supplying the goods and technologies which the United States was withholding. Why should not American firms get a piece of the action?

**Opportunities**  The potential for United States–communist trade is considerable. For example, the Soviet Union is clearly an important new market for American grains and other farm products. And, as just noted, the U.S.S.R. is interested in American capital and technological knowledge which can further its industrial growth and help develop its enormous natural resources in the areas of oil, natural gas, timber, and nonferrous metals. The United States, of course, could alleviate its energy, natural gas, and lumber shortages by sharing in expanded Soviet production. Hence, there is some basis for an expanding complementary trade. In fact, some attention has been given to "coproduction agreements" whereby American firms would provide the capital, technology, and managerial expertise to develop certain fuel and mineral resources in the Soviet Union in return for a share of the resulting production. Similarly, the communist systems of Eastern Europe embody growing markets for many consumer goods in which American manufacturers have a comparative advantage. Finally, China could become an export market for American machinery, com-

puters, chemical fertilizers, and certain food products. Aside from the mutual economic benefits of an expanding East-West trade, important political benefits can also accrue. Trade can lead to mutual interdependence and greater communication, not to mention enhanced scientific-technical and cultural interaction, all of which contribute to mutual understanding and encourage a rational approach to the resolution of areas of disagreement.

**Problems**  But the problems involved in establishing and sustaining a prosperous flow of East-West trade are substantial. First, the market-oriented economies of the West do business in ways which are a far cry from the practices and policies of the centrally planned communist economies. Western nations typically engage in multilateral trade wherein X may send goods to Y in order to get other goods from Z (Figure 3-1); the communist countries find bilateral trade much more compatible with central planning. Second, the communist and the Western nations march to different drummers with respect to copyright and patent protection, the settlement of commercial disputes, and so forth. For example, how can an American firm which has licensed technological knowledge in the Soviet Union be certain it is receiving proper compensation when Soviet production and sales data are held secret? Third, the communist nations do not belong to either GATT or the international monetary institutions to which Western nations subscribe. Can the rules of the international trading and financial game as practiced by the capitalistic nations be modified so as to facilitate East-West trade, or must entirely new institutions and techniques be evolved? Fourth, Soviet ideology is steeped in the notion of autarchy—of self-reliance and economic independence from the surrounding capitalistic world. Hence, the rapid growth of East-West trade would be at the cost of some ideological disruption. Finally, both the Soviet Union and the People's Republic of China have had balance of payments problems which make it difficult for them to finance an increasing volume of Western imports.

**Trade Growth**   What does the record show? There *has* been a substantial absolute increase in the volume of United States–Soviet trade in the 1970s. In 1978 the volume of trade between the two nations was twelve times its 1971 level! But two caveats are in order. First, about two-thirds of American exports to the Soviet Union are agricultural products, the purchase of which depends upon the vagaries of Soviet harvests. Second, in relative terms our trade with the Soviet Union is minuscule, amounting to about one percent of the total.

The future trend of United States–Soviet trade is most difficult to predict for the simple reason that political developments overshadow economic considerations. Both the United States and the Soviet Union have demonstrated a willingness to use international trade as a political weapon. In recent years com-

mercial relations between the two countries have been buffeted by Soviet and Cuban activities in Africa, problems associated with the SALT negotiations, and human rights problems within the Soviet Union. Witness the United States' embargo of grain exports to the Soviet Union in response to the invasion of Afghanistan. At present the United States denies the Soviet Union most-favored-nation treatment and the accessibility to export credit. Legislation continues to restrict the export of certain goods and technologies which would prove detrimental to the national security of the United States. It may be that the evolution of a more cordial political relationship is the fundamental prerequisite to the continued expansion of East-West trade.[4]

[4]The interested reader should consult Hertha W. Heiss, Allen J. Lenz, and Jack Brougher, "United States–Soviet Commercial Relations Since 1972," in Joint Economic Committee, *Soviet Economy in a Time of Change,* vol. 2 (Washington, 1979), pp. 189–207.

## Summary

1   The basic argument for free trade is that it fosters a more efficient allocation of resources and a higher standard of living for the world as a whole.

2   The most common trade barriers take the form of protective tariffs and quotas. Supply and demand analysis reveals that protective tariffs increase the prices and reduce the quantities demanded of affected goods. Foreign exporters find their sales diminish. Domestic producers, however, enjoy higher prices and enlarged sales. Tariffs promote a less efficient allocation of domestic and world resources.

3   When applicable, the strongest arguments for protection are the infant-industry and military self-sufficiency arguments. Most of the other arguments for protection are half-truths, emotional appeals, or fallacies which typically emphasize the immediate effects of trade barriers while ignoring long-run consequences.

4   The Reciprocal Trade Agreements Act of 1934 was the beginning of a trend toward lower American tariffs. In 1947 the General Agreement on Tariffs and Trade was formed *a.* to encourage nondiscriminatory treatment for all trading nations, *b.* to achieve tariff reduction, and *c.* to eliminate import quotas.

5   Economic integration is an important means of liberalizing trade. The outstanding illustration is the European Common Market wherein internal trade barriers are abolished, a common system of tariffs is applied to nonmembers, and the free internal movement of labor and capital is perceived. The Kennedy Round of reciprocal tariff reductions under GATT was initiated to make the Common Market more accessible to American producers. The Tokyo Round embodies further tariff reductions and pays special attention to the problem of nontariff barriers to trade.

**6**   The United States has begun to relax its highly restrictive trade policies with communist nations and, while many problems exist, there are signs of a growing mutually advantageous trade with the Soviet Union, the People's Republic of China, and the Eastern European nations.

## Questions and Study Suggestions

**1**   Key terms and concepts to remember: revenue and protective tariffs; import quotas; Reciprocal Trade Agreements Act of 1934; most-favored-nation clause; General Agreement on Tariffs and Trade (GATT); economic integration; European Economic Community (Common Market); Trade Expansion Act of 1962; Kennedy Round; Tokyo Round; nontariff barriers (NTBs).

**2**   State the economist's case for free trade.  Given this case, how do you explain the existence of artificial barriers to international trade?

**3**   Draw a domestic supply and demand diagram for a product in which the United States does not have a comparative advantage.  Indicate the impact of foreign imports upon domestic price and quantity.  Now show a protective tariff which eliminates approximately one-half the assumed imports.  Indicate the price-quantity effects of this tariff to **a.** domestic consumers, **b.** domestic producers, and **c.** foreign exporters.

**4**   Carefully evaluate the following statements:

**a.**   "Protective tariffs limit both the imports and the exports of the nation levying tariffs."

**b.**   "The extensive application of protective tariffs destroys the ability of the international price system to allocate resources efficiently."

**c.**   "Apparent unemployment can often be reduced through tariff protection, but by the same token disguised unemployment typically increases."

**d.**   "Given the rapidity with which technological advance is dispersed around the world, free trade will inevitably yield structural maladjustments, unemployment, and balance of payments problems for industrially advanced nations."

**e.**   "Free trade can improve the composition and efficiency of domestic output.  Only the Volkswagen forced Detroit to make a compact car, and only foreign success with the oxygen process forced American steel firms to modernize."

**5**   "The most valid arguments for tariff protection are also the most easily abused."  What are these arguments?  Why are they susceptible to abuse?

**6**   Suppose the existing American tariffs on Swiss watches were abolished.  What would be the short-run economic effects upon the American and Swiss watch industries?  Upon total American exports to and imports from Switzerland?  What would be the long-run effects of this abolishment upon **a.** the volume of employment, **b.** the allocation of resources, and **c.** the standard of living in the two nations?

**7**   Carefully evaluate the use of artificial trade barriers, such as tariffs and import quotas, as a means of achieving and maintaining full employment.

**8**   Use the "economies of scale" analysis of Chapter 25 to explain why the Common Market has enabled many European industries to compete more effectively in international markets.  Explain: "Economic integration leads a double life: it can further free trade for members, but pose serious trade obstacles for nonmembers."

**9**   "The future of United States trade with the communist nations depends primarily upon political, not economic considerations."  Do you agree?  What are some of the practical problems involved in increasing East-West trade?

# Selected References

Gray, H. Peter: *International Trade, Investment, and Payments* (Boston: Houghton Mifflin Company, 1979), chaps. 7–10.

Humphrey, Thomas M.: "Changing Views of Comparative Advantage," *Monthly Review* (Federal Reserve Bank of Richmond, July 1972).

Institute for Contemporary Studies: *Tariffs, Quotas, and Trade: The Politics of Protectionism* (San Francisco: Institute for Contemporary Studies, 1979).

Joint Economic Committee: *Issues in East-West Commercial Relations* (Washington, D.C., 1979).

Kenen, Peter B., and Raymond Lubitz: *International Economics,* 3d ed. (Englewood Cliffs, N.J.: Prentice-Hall, Inc., 1971), particularly chaps. 1, 2, 4.

Pen, Jan: *A Primer on International Trade* (New York: Random House, Inc., 1967).

Snider, Delbert A.: *Introduction to International Economics,* 7th ed. (Homewood, Ill.: Richard D. Irwin, Inc., 1979), chaps. 9–12.

# LAST WORD
## Petition of the Candlemakers, 1845

The French economist Frédéric Bastiat (1801–1850) devastated the proponents of protectionism by satirically extending their reasoning to its logical and absurd conclusions.

PETITION of the Manufacturers of Candles, Wax-lights, Lamps, Candlesticks, Street Lamps, Snuffers, Extinguishers, and of the Producers of Oil Tallow, Rosin, Alcohol, and, Generally, of Everything Connected with Lighting.

TO MESSIEURS THE MEMBERS OF THE CHAMBER OF DEPUTIES.

Gentlemen,—You are on the right road. You reject abstract theories, and have little consideration for cheapness and plenty. Your chief care is the interest of the producer. You desire to emancipate him from external competition, and reserve the *national market* for *national industry*.

We are about to offer you an admirable opportunity of applying your—what shall we call it? your theory? No; nothing is more deceptive than theory; your doctrine? your system? your principle? but you dislike doctrines, you abhor systems, and as for principles, you deny that there are any in social economy: we shall say, then, your practice, your practice without theory and without principle.

We are suffering from the intolerable competition of a foreign rival, placed, it would seem, in a condition so far superior to ours for the production of light, that he absolutely *inundates* our *national market* with it at a price fabulously reduced. The moment he shows himself, our trade leaves us—all consumers apply to him; and a branch of native industry, having countless ramifications, is all at once rendered completely stagnant. This rival . . . is no other than the Sun.

What we pray for is, that it may please you to pass a law ordering the shutting up of all windows, sky-lights, dormerwindows, outside and inside shutters, curtains, blinds, bull's-eyes; in a word, of all openings, holes, chinks, clefts, and fissures, by or through which the light of the sun has been in use to enter houses, to the prejudice of the meritorious manufactures with which we flatter ourselves we have accommodated our country,—a country which, in gratitude, ought not to abandon us now to a strife so unequal.

If you shut up as much as possible all access to natural light, and create a demand for artificial light, which of our French manufactures will not be encouraged by it?

If more tallow is consumed, then there must be more oxen and sheep; and, consequently, we shall behold the multiplication of artificial meadows, meat, wool, hides, and, above all, manure, which is the basis and foundation of all agricultural wealth.

The same remark applies to navigation. Thousands of vessels will proceed to the whale fishery; and, in a short time, we shall possess a navy capable of maintaining the honour of France, and gratifying the patriotic aspirations of your petitioners, the undersigned candlemakers and others.

Only have the goodness to reflect, Gentlemen, and you will be convinced that there is, perhaps, no Frenchman, from the wealthy coalmaster to the humblest vender of lucifer matches, whose lot will not be ameliorated by the success of this our petition.

Frédéric Bastiat, *Economic Sophisms* (Edinburgh: Oliver and Boyd, Tweeddale Court, 1873), pp. 49–53, abridged.

# The Balance of Payments and Exchange Rates

chapter **43**

Chapter 41 was concerned with comparative advantage as the basis for international trade; Chapter 42 stressed the fact that free trade would tend to maximize the potential gains from international specialization. The present chapter, building upon these notions, has the following specific objectives: (1) to introduce explicitly the monetary or financial aspects of international trade, (2) to define, analyze, and interpret the international balance of payments, and (3) to explain the various mechanisms for correcting a balance of payments disequilibrium.

## ☐ FINANCING INTERNATIONAL TRADE

Although the particular techniques of financing international transactions are rather detailed, their general nature can be readily grasped. The basic feature which distinguishes international from domestic payments is that two different national currencies are obviously

involved. Thus, for instance, when American firms export goods to British firms, the American exporter will want to be paid in dollars. But the British importers have pounds sterling. The problem, then, is to exchange pounds for dollars to permit the American export transaction to occur.

### △ American Export Transaction

Suppose our American exporter agrees to sell $30,000 worth of computers to a British firm. Assume that the *rate of exchange*—that is, the rate or price at which pounds can be exchanged for, or converted into, dollars, and vice versa—is $2 for £1. This means that the British importer must pay £15,000 to the American exporter. Let us summarize what occurs in terms of simple bank balance sheets (Figure 43-1) such as those employed in Part 3.

*a.* To pay for the American computers, the British buyer draws a check on its demand deposit in a London bank for £15,000.

LONDON BANK

| Assets | Liabilities and net worth |
|---|---|
| | Demand deposit of British importer  −£15,000(a) |
| | Deposit of New York bank  +£15,000(c) |

NEW YORK BANK

| Assets | Liabilities and net worth |
|---|---|
| Deposit in London bank  +£15,000(c) ($30,000) | Demand deposit of American exporter  +$30,000(b) |

FIGURE 43-1  FINANCING A U.S. EXPORT TRANSACTION

American export transactions create a foreign demand for dollars.  The satisfaction of this demand increases the supplies of foreign monies held by American banks.

**b.** The British firm then sends this £15,000 check to the American exporter. But the rub is that the American exporting firm must pay its employees and materials suppliers, as well as its taxes, in dollars, not pounds. So the exporter sells the £15,000 check or draft on the London bank to some large American bank, probably located in New York City, which is a dealer in foreign exchange. The American firm is given a $30,000 demand deposit in the New York bank in exchange for the £15,000 check.

**c.** And what does the New York bank do with the £15,000? It in turn deposits it in a correspondent London bank for future sale. To simplify, we assume this correspondent bank is the same bank from which the British firm obtained the £15,000 draft.

Note these salient points. First, American exports create a foreign demand for dollars, and the satisfaction of this demand increases the supply of foreign monies—pounds, in this case—held by American banks and available to American buyers. Second, the financing of an American export (British import) reduces the supply of money (demand deposits) in Britain and increases the supply of money in the United States by the amount of the purchase.

△ **American Import Transaction**

But a question persists: Why would the New York bank be willing to give up dollars for pounds sterling? As just indicated, the New York bank is a dealer in foreign exchange; it is in the business of buying—for a fee—and, conversely, in selling—also for a fee—pounds for dollars. Having just explained that the New York bank would buy pounds with dollars in connection with an American export transaction, we shall now examine how it would sell pounds for dollars in helping to finance an American import (British export) transaction. Specifically, suppose that an American retail concern wants to import £15,000 worth of woolens from a British mill. Again we rely on simple commercial bank balance sheets to summarize our discussion (Figure 43-2).

**a.** Because the British exporting firm must pay its obligations in pounds rather than dollars, the American importer must somehow exchange dollars for pounds. It can obviously do this by going to the New York bank and purchasing £15,000 for $30,000—perhaps the American importer purchases the very same £15,000 which the New York bank acquired in the previous American export transaction. This purchase reduces the American importer's demand deposit in the New York bank by $30,000 and, of course, the New York bank gives up its £15,000 deposit in the London bank.

**b.** The American importer sends its newly purchased check for £15,000 to the British firm, which deposits it in the London bank.

| LONDON BANK | | NEW YORK BANK | |
|---|---|---|---|
| Assets | Liabilities and net worth | Assets | Liabilities and net worth |
| | Demand deposit of British exporter +£15,000(*b*) | Deposit in London bank −£15,000(*a*) ($30,000) | Demand deposit of American importer −$30,000(*a*) |
| | Deposit of New York bank −£15,000(*a*) | | |

FIGURE 43-2 FINANCING A U.S. IMPORT TRANSACTION

American import transactions create an American demand for foreign monies. The satisfaction of that demand reduces the supplies of foreign monies held by American banks.

Note that American imports create a domestic demand for foreign monies (pounds sterling, in this case) and that the fulfillment of this demand reduces the supplies of foreign monies held by American banks. Moreover, an American import transaction increases the supply of money in Britain and reduces the supply of money in the United States.

By putting these two transactions together, a further point comes into focus. American exports (in this case, computers) make available, or "earn," a supply of foreign monies for American banks, and American imports (British woolens, in this instance) create a demand for these monies. That is, in a broad sense, *any nation's exports finance or "pay for" its imports.* Exports provide the foreign currencies needed to pay for imports. From Britain's point of view, we note that its exports of woolens earn a supply of dollars, which are then used to meet the demand for dollars associated with its imports of computers.

Postscript: Although our examples are confined to the exporting and importing of goods, demands for and supplies of pounds also arise from transactions involving services and the payment of interest and dividends on foreign investments. Thus Americans demand pounds not only to finance imports, but also to purchase insurance and transportation services from the British, and to pay dividends and

interest upon British investments in the United States.

## ☐ THE INTERNATIONAL BALANCE OF PAYMENTS

The generalization that "exports finance imports" is only a first approximation, because the economic relationships among nations involve much more than the exporting and importing of goods and services. The spectrum of international transactions is reflected in a nation's balance of payments. Specifically, nations of the world systematically record and summarize *all* the transactions which take place between their residents (including individuals, businesses, and governmental units) and the residents of all other foreign nations and present them in an annual accounting statement called the *international balance of payments.* Despite its name, this statement is more like a business firm's profit and loss statement than a balance sheet. Like a profit and loss statement a nation's balance of payments records its sales to, and purchases from, all other nations, and it accounts for any differences between its sales (receipts) and its purchases (expenditures). A simplified balance of payments for the United States in 1978 is presented in Table 43-1. Let us analyze this accounting statement to see what it reveals about American international trade and fi-

**TABLE 43-1**
The United States Balance of Payments, 1978 *(in billions)*

| | | | |
|---|---|---:|---:|
| (1) | United States exports. . . . . . . . . . . . . . . . . . . . . . . . . . . . . . . . | | $+221.3 |
| | (a) Goods . . . . . . . . . . . . . . . . . . . . . . . . . . . . . . . | $+142.3 | |
| | (b) Services . . . . . . . . . . . . . . . . . . . . . . . . . . . | +35.5 | |
| | (c) Income from United States investments abroad . . . . . . . . . . . . . . | +43.5 | |
| (2) | United States imports . . . . . . . . . . . . . . . . . . . . . . . | | −229.4 |
| | (a) Goods. . . . . . . . . . . . . . . . . . . . . . . . . . . . . . | $−175.8 | |
| | (b) Services . . . . . . . . . . . . . . . . . . . . . . . . . . | −31.7 | |
| | (c) Income from foreign investments in United States . . . . . . . . . . | −21.9 | |
| (3) | Net balance due United States on exports and imports . . . . . . . . . . | | $  −8.1 |
| (4) | Net remittances. . . . . . . . . . . . . . . . . . . . . . . | | −1.9 |
| (5) | Net government transactions: grants, loans, etc. . . . . . . . . . . . . . . | | −3.4 |
| (6) | Net capital movements. . . . . . . . . . . . . . . . . . . . . . . | | −30.3 |
| | (a) United States capital outflow . . . . . . . . . . . . . . . . . . . | $ −60.3 | |
| | (b) Foreign capital inflow to United States. . . . . . . . . . . . . . . . . | +30.0 | |
| (7) | Errors and omissions . . . . . . . . . . . . . . . . . . . . . . | | +10.7 |
| (8) | Balance due United States (+) or rest of world (−) . . . . . . . . . . . . | | $ −33.0 |
| (9) | Financing (balancing) transactions. . . . . . . . . . . . . . . . . . | | |
| | (a) Decrease in United States holdings of foreign currencies* . . . . . . . . | | +2.0 |
| | (b) Increase in liquid dollar balances held by foreigners . . . . . . . . . . . | | +31.0 |
| | | | $    0.0 |

*Includes SDR allocation.
*Source: Survey of Current Business,* March 1980. Details may not add to totals because of rounding.

nance. Specifically, what does it tell us about our position in world trade and finance?

△ **Exports and Imports of Goods and Services**

The most obvious and perhaps most basic segment of the balance of payments involves the export and import of goods and services. As items 1 and 2 in Table 43-1 indicate, exports and imports are broadly defined. There is no question about the inclusion of items 1a and b as a part of American exports. As with domestic trade, international trade involves the exchange of both goods and services. The United States exports not only machinery, automobiles, and farm products, but also sells transportation services, insurance, and brokerage services to residents of foreign nations. Note, however, that one of the very special services which foreigners get from the United States consists of the services of American money capital which has been invested abroad. As

item 1c indicates, the dividend and interest income received from the use of American capital which has been invested in foreign nations is a payment for the American "export" of the services of this capital. United States imports, item 2, obviously include three analogous items. Americans import goods and services, including the services of foreign money capital which has been invested in the United States.

In Table 43-1 we have designated American exports with *plus* signs and American imports with *minus* signs. You will recall from our earlier discussion of foreign exchange that American exports entail payments of dollars from foreign buyers to the United States. These transactions, which involve dollar "inpayments" to the United States, have been marked plus (+). Conversely, American imports require that Americans make dollars available to foreigners. Such transactions, which involve dollar "outpayments" from the United States, have been marked minus (−).

Thus the fact that the balance-due figure is a *minus* $8.1 billion indicates that net outpayments of that amount are due the rest of the world from the United States (item 3).

### △   Remittances

A second component of the United States' balance of payments involves remittances—item 4 in Table 43-1. These are private gifts or grants: for example, immigrants' remittances sent to their families in the "old country," contributions to overseas missions, and pensions going to American citizens who are now living abroad. Note that net remittances to the rest of the world amounted to some $1.9 billion during 1978.

### △   Government Transactions

Item 5 reflects the fact that the United States government makes substantial loans and grants to many nations. These loans and grants are for economic and military aid and in part reflect our ideological competition with the Soviet Union (Chapter 45). In 1978 these government transactions entailed dollar outpayments of $3.4 billion. That is, American government transactions were a source of that many dollars to foreign nations. The United States government was, in effect, "importing" claims against foreign nations in the case of loans and goodwill or, as it has been facetiously put, "thank-you notes" in the case of grants.

### △   Net Capital Movements

Americans—both individuals and businesses—may choose to make investments in, and extend loans to, other nations. For example, many American corporations have become multinational by purchasing or constructing plants or outlets in foreign countries. Or Americans may buy the securities—stocks and bonds—of foreign firms. Or American individuals or firms may make dollar deposits in foreign banks.

All such transactions involve capital outflows in monetary or real form. That is, just like American imports of goods, these Ameri-can investing and lending transactions provide foreigners with American dollars. Indeed, it is quite appropriate to think of American investors and lenders as importing securities—claims of ownership to foreign assets, claims against foreign borrowers, and passbook claims against foreign banks. As item 6a indicates, American capital flows going abroad amounted to $60.3 billion in 1978.

Of course, foreigners can and do engage in similar capital transactions. They may purchase real assets in the United States, buy American stocks and bonds, make deposits in United States banks, and so forth. In these instances, the United States is in effect exporting securities and claims and, as with merchandise or service exports, getting inflows or inpayments of dollars in return. In 1978 capital inflows to the United States were $30.0 billion, as shown by item 6b.

It is appropriate to ask: Why did the United States experience a *net* capital outflow of $30.3 billion in 1978? Why don't Americans make all their investments in, and loans to, American firms rather than foreign firms? The answer is that Americans invest and lend abroad when they expect the rates of return from these foreign loans and investments to be greater than they can realize domestically. Given the rapid pace of economic expansion experienced by the countries of Western Europe and by Japan (Table 20-2), we have simply found it profitable to channel a large volume of loans and investments overseas.

### △   Errors and Omissions

The gathering of data for the balance of payments statement is a complex and highly imperfect process. Hence, an "errors and omissions" item will invariably appear. Item 7 is essentially a bookkeeping entry which simply reflects the difference between all known inpayment and outpayment items. In 1978 errors and omissions were unusually large at $10.7 billion. It is generally agreed that most of this item reflects unrecorded capital inflows (note the plus sign) to the United States.

Let us now summarize our discussion to this point. Taking items 1 through 7 into account, we find that in 1978 the United States imported more goods and services than it exported and, as a result, "owed" other countries $8.1 billion. However, as the consequence of American remittances abroad, United States government grants and loans, private net capital outflows from this country, and taking the errors and omissions item into account, the United States owed $33.0 billion to the rest of the world.

### △  Financing Transactions

The $33.0 billion shown as item 8 measures the United States' *balance of payments deficit* for 1978. This deficit, which we shall define in more detail shortly, means that the United States provided more dollars to the world as a result of its imports, remittances, grants, and net public and private capital outflows than it earned back through its exports. That is, our exports were not sufficiently large to finance the sum of our imports, public and private grants and remittances, and public and private capital outflows.

What must the United States do to settle up the $33.0 billion difference? Briefly stated, the United States' $33.0 billion payments deficit can be financed in essentially two ways. First, it may expend some of its international monetary reserves, that is, some of the foreign currencies which it may have on hand.[1] Certain currencies—for example, German marks and Japanese yen—are widely acceptable as an international medium of exchange and therefore can be used to finance deficits. As item 9(a) in Table 43-1 indicates, the United States drew down some $2.0 billion of these reserves.

A second way in which the United States payments deficit can be handled is simply for foreign countries to hold a part or all of the surplus dollars which reflect the deficit. That

is, the United States can increase its outstanding dollar liabilities as is indicated by item 9(b). These dollar balances represent claims against the future output of the United States economy. Hence, in holding larger dollar balances, foreign countries are in effect granting us credit; they are saying to us: "We'll settle up later." In 1978 foreign holdings of dollars increased by $31.0 billion.

### ☐  INTERNATIONAL DISEQUILIBRIUM

The meaning of international disequilibrium or, in the present instance, the meaning of a payments deficit, merits further discussion. The balance of payments statement must always balance, for the simple reason that every transaction must be settled, or accounted for, in one way or another. But the fact that this accounting statement balances is of little economic significance. The really important aspect of the balance of payments is the means by which that balance is achieved.

### △  An Analogy

Consider a crude analogy comparing two families. Family 1's earnings or income substantially exceeds its expenditures on goods and services. It uses its unconsumed income to buy stocks and bonds (make loans), to buy real assets such as real estate (make investments), perhaps to make some grants, and to add to its monetary reserves. We would agree that all is well with family 1; it is in good financial shape. Moreover, this family is in equilibrium in the sense that it can indefinitely maintain this position.

Family 2 is in a different situation. Its expenditures exceed the sum of its earnings plus any loans or grants it might be fortunate enough to receive. Family 2 is in financial difficulty; it is "living beyond its income" and must draw upon its monetary reserves or must borrow to finance the shortfall of its receipts relative to its expenditures. Note that in an accounting sense, inpayments and outpayments are in balance for both families; each

---

[1] In Chapter 44 we will find that a nation with a payments deficit can finance it by borrowing, within rather strict limits, from the International Monetary Fund (IMF).

family's "balance of payments" with the rest of the economy is in balance. Yet family 2 is clearly in a nonmaintainable or disequilibrium position. Its monetary reserves are presumably limited, and so is its credit, and it therefore cannot continue indefinitely to spend in excess of its receipts. Family 2 will be obliged to get its financial house in order.

### △  Autonomous and Accommodating Transactions

The same general kind of comparison can be applied to nations. Once again, the important consideration is not the fact that the balance of payments balances, but what kinds of transactions occur in achieving that balance. To pursue this point, we must distinguish between autonomous transactions, on the one hand, and accommodating or compensating transactions, on the other.

*Autonomous transactions* are independent of the balance of payments in the sense that they arise from, or are caused by, factors lying outside the balance of payments statement itself. Five of the items discussed in Table 43-1 (items 1, 2, 4, 5, and 6) are generally considered to be autonomous: exports, imports, remittances, public transactions, and net capital movements. Thus Americans buy goods and services from, and sell goods and services to, foreign nations because of differences in comparative costs. Remittances and government grants and loans are based upon humanitarian, political, or military considerations. Capital movements occur on the expectation that the income earned abroad on investments and loans will exceed the income which is anticipated domestically.

*Accommodating transactions* occur in order to account or compensate for differences between the inpayments and outpayments which arise from a nation's autonomous transactions. Accommodating transactions can be thought of as balancing transactions, that is, transactions which take place to accommodate or finance payment imbalances associated with the autonomous transactions. Illustration:

Suppose a nation's autonomous transactions are such that its exports are $10 billion and its imports are $15 billion; it receives remittances of $1 billion and public grants and loans of another $1 billion; finally, it receives net capital inflows of $1 billion. The outpayments associated with these autonomous transactions are $15 billion, and the inpayments or receipts are only $13 (= $10 + $1 + $1 + $1) billion. The country has a $2 billion *dis*equilibrium or, more specifically, a $2 billion deficit, in its balance of payments. The nation must undertake $2 billion worth of financing or accommodating transactions to account for the difference between autonomous outpayments and inpayments. These financing transactions will involve reductions in its balances of foreign monies or increases in the balances of its currency held by other nations.

We can therefore say that the occurrence of accommodating or financing transactions is evidence of a balance of payments disequilibrium. In Table 43-1, items 9a and 9b are accommodating transactions and are evidence of the United States payments deficit. They indicate that the United States is not "paying its way" internationally. And although the United States has been realizing deficits for a period of years, these accommodating transactions cannot be maintained indefinitely. In the next chapter we shall discover that in the early 1970s, our persistent deficits precipitated fundamental changes in the international monetary system.

### □  INTERNATIONAL EQUILIBRIUM AND EXCHANGE RATES

Both the size of balance of payments deficits and the means by which these imbalances are resolved will depend upon the functioning of exchange rates. There are two polar options: (1) a system of *flexible* or *floating exchange rates* where the rates at which national currencies exchange for one another are determined by demand and supply; and (2) a system of rigidly *fixed exchange rates* wherein governmental intervention in foreign exchange markets or some other mechanism offsets the changes in exchange rates which fluctuations in demand and supply would otherwise cause.

### △ Freely Floating Exchange Rates

Freely floating exchange rates are determined by the unimpeded forces of demand and supply. Let us examine the rate, or price, at which American dollars might be exchanged for, say, British pounds sterling. As indicated in Figure 43-3, the demand for pounds will be downsloping, and the supply of pounds will be upsloping. Why? The downsloping demand for pounds shown by *DD* indicates that, if pounds become less expensive to Americans, British goods will become cheaper to Ameri-

cans. This fact causes Americans to demand larger quantities of British goods and therefore larger amounts of pounds with which to buy those goods. The supply of pounds is upsloping, as *SS*, because, as the dollar price of pounds *rises* (that is, the pound price of dollars *falls*), the British will be inclined to purchase more American goods. The reason, of course, is that at higher and higher dollar prices for pounds, the British can obviously get more American dollars and therefore more American goods per pound. Thus, American goods become cheaper to the British, inducing the British to buy more of these goods. Such purchases, we have seen, will make larger and larger quantities of pounds available to Americans.

The intersection of the supply and demand for pounds will determine the dollar price of pounds. In this instance the equilibrium rate of exchange is $2 to £1.

**Depreciation and Appreciation**   An exchange rate which is determined by free market forces can and does change frequently. When the dollar price of pounds increases, for example, goes from $2 for £1 to $3 for £1, we say that the value of the dollar has *depreciated* relative to the pound. More generally, currency depreciation means that it takes more units of a country's currency (dollars) to buy a single unit of some foreign currency (pounds). Conversely, when the dollar price of pounds decreases—goes from $2 for £1 to $1 for £1— the value of the dollar has *appreciated* relative to the pound. In general terms, currency appreciation means that it takes fewer units of a country's currency (dollars) to buy a single unit of some foreign currency (pounds).

Observe in our American-British illustrations that when the dollar depreciates the pound necessarily appreciates and vice versa. When the exchange rate between dollars and pounds changes from $2 = £1 to $3 = £1, it now takes *more* dollars to buy £1 and the dollar has depreciated. But it now takes *fewer* pounds to buy a dollar. That is, at the initial

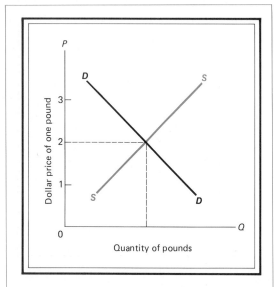

**FIGURE 43-3 THE MARKET FOR FOREIGN EXCHANGE**

The American demand for pounds is downsloping because, as pounds become less expensive, all British goods and services become cheaper to Americans. The supply of pounds to Americans is upsloping because at higher dollar prices for pounds the British will want to purchase larger quantities of American goods and services. The intersection of the demand and supply curves will determine the equilibrium rate of exchange.

rate it took £½ to buy $1; at the new rate it only takes £⅓ to buy $1. The pound has obviously appreciated relative to the dollar.

**Determinants of Exchange Rates**  Why are the demand for and the supply of pounds located as they are in Figure 43-3? Stated differently, what forces will cause the demand and supply curves for pounds to change and thereby cause the dollar to appreciate or depreciate? Consider briefly some of the more important factors.

*1  Relative income changes*  If the growth of a nation's national income is more rapid than other countries, its currency is likely to depreciate. Recall from Table 41-1 that a country's imports vary directly with its level of income. If the United States economy is expanding rapidly and the British economy is stagnant, American imports of British goods—and therefore American demand for pounds—will increase. The dollar price of pounds will rise and this means the dollar has depreciated.

*2  Relative price changes*  If domestic prices rise rapidly in the United States and remain constant in Britain, American consumers will seek out relatively low-priced British goods thereby increasing the demand for pounds. Conversely, the British will be less inclined to purchase American goods, reducing the supply of pounds. This combination of an increase in the demand for, and a reduction in the supply of, pounds will cause the dollar to depreciate.

*3  Relative interest rates*  Suppose an easy money policy keeps interest rates down in the United States, while a tight money policy raises interest rates in Britain. Seeking higher returns, Americans will demand more pounds in order to purchase high-yield British securities. Conversely, British investors will reduce their supplies of pounds because American investments are less attractive to them. Again, the dollar will depreciate.

**Flexible Rates and the Balance of Payments**  Proponents of flexible exchange rates argue that such rates embody a compelling virtue: flexible rates *automatically* adjust so as to eliminate balance of payments deficits or surpluses. We can explain this by looking at *SS* and *DD* in Figure 43-4 which merely restate the demand for, and supply of, pounds curves from Figure 43-3. The resulting equilibrium exchange rate of $2 = £1 correctly suggests that there is no balance of payments deficit or surplus. At the $2 = £1 exchange rate the quantity of pounds demanded by Americans in order to import British goods, buy British transportation and insurance services, and to

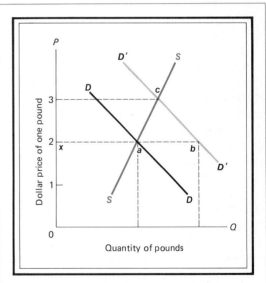

**FIGURE 43-4** ADJUSTMENTS UNDER FLEXIBLE EXCHANGE RATES, FIXED EXCHANGE RATES, AND THE GOLD STANDARD

Under flexible rates an American trade deficit at the $2-for-£1 rate would be corrected by an increase in the rate to $3 for £1. Under fixed rates the *ab* shortage of pounds would be met out of international monetary reserves. Under the gold standard the deficit would cause changes in domestic price and income levels which would shift the demand for pounds (*D'D'*) to the left and the supply (*SS*) to the right, reestablishing equilibrium at the $2-for-£1 rate.

pay interest and dividends on British investments in the United States is equal to the amount of pounds supplied by the British in buying American exports, purchasing services from Americans, and making interest and dividend payments on American investments in Britain. More succinctly, the accommodating transactions 9a and 9b in Table 43-1 would be zero.

Now let us suppose there is a change of tastes such that Americans decide to buy more small, gas-efficient British automobiles. Or we might assume that the American price level has increased relative to Britain or that interest rates have fallen in the United States as compared to Britain. In all instances, the American demand for British pounds will increase from DD to, say, D'D' in Figure 43-4. We observe that *at the initial $2 = £1 exchange rate* an American balance of payments deficit has been created in the amount ab. That is, there is a shortage of pounds in the amount ab to Americans. American export-type transactions will earn xa pounds, but Americans will want xb pounds to finance import-type transactions. Because this is a free competitive market, the shortage will change the exchange rate (the dollar price of pounds) from $2 = £1 to say, $3 = £1; that is, the dollar will depreciate.

At this point it must be emphasized that the exchange rate is a very special price which links *all* domestic (United States) prices with *all* foreign (British) prices. A change in the exchange rate therefore alters the prices of all British goods to Americans and all American goods to potential British buyers. Specifically, this particular change in the exchange rate will alter the relative attractiveness of American imports and exports in such a way as to restore equilibrium in the balance of payments of the United States. From the American point of view, as the dollar price of pounds changes from $2 to $3, the Triumph automobile priced at £1500, which formerly cost an American $3000, now costs $4500. Other British goods will also be more expensive to Americans.

Hence, American imports of British goods and services will tend to decline. Graphically, this is shown as a move from point b toward point c in Figure 43-4.

Conversely, from Britain's standpoint the exchange rate, that is, the pound price of dollars, has fallen (from £$\frac{1}{2}$ to £$\frac{1}{3}$ for $1). The international value of the pound has *appreciated*. The British previously got only $2 for £1; now they get $3 for £1. American goods are therefore cheaper to the British, and as a result American exports to Great Britain tend to rise. In Figure 43-4 this is indicated by the move from point a toward point c. The two adjustments described—a decrease in American imports from Great Britain and an increase in American exports to Great Britain—are precisely those needed to correct the American balance of payments deficit. (The reader should reason through the operation of freely fluctuating exchange rates in correcting an initial American balance of payments surplus in its trade with Great Britain.) In short, the free fluctuation of exchange rates in response to shifts in the supply of, and demand for, foreign monies tends to restore international equilibrium automatically. As a matter of fact, if floating rates worked perfectly, a balance of payments disequilibrium would not occur.

**Disadvantages**  Though freely fluctuating exchange rates automatically correct a balance of payments disequilibrium, they may entail several significant problems:

*1  Uncertainty and diminished trade* The risks and uncertainties associated with flexible exchange rates may discourage the flow of trade. To illustrate: Suppose an American automobile dealer contracts to purchase ten Triumph cars for £25,000. At the current exchange rate of, say, $2 for £1, the American importer expects to pay $50,000 for these automobiles. But if in the two- or three-month shipping period the rate of exchange shifts to $3 for £1, the £25,000 payment contracted by the American importer will now amount to

$75,000. Obviously, this unheralded increase in the dollar price of pounds may easily turn the potential American importer's anticipated profits into substantial losses. Aware at the outset of the possibility of an adverse change in the exchange rate, the American importer may simply not be willing to assume the risks involved. The American firm therefore confines its operations to domestic automobiles, with the result that international trade does not occur in this item.

The same rationale applies to investment. Assume that, when the exchange rate is $3 to £1, an American firm invests $30,000 (or £10,000) in a British enterprise. It estimates a return of 10 percent, that is, it anticipates earnings of $3000 or £1000. Suppose these expectations prove correct in the sense that the British firm earns £1000 the first year on the £10,000 investment. But suppose that during the year, the value of the dollar appreciates to $2 = £1. The absolute return is now only $2000 (rather than $3000) and the rate of return falls from the anticipated 10 percent to only 6⅔ percent (= $2000/$30,000). Investment is inherently risky. The added risk posed by adverse changes in exchange rates may persuade the potential American investor to shy away from overseas ventures.[2]

**2  *Terms of trade***  A nation's terms of trade will tend to be worsened by a decline in the international value of its currency. For example, an increase in the dollar price of pounds will mean that the United States must export a larger volume of goods and services to finance a given level of imports from Britain.

**3  *Instability***  Freely fluctuating exchange rates may also have destabilizing effects upon the domestic economy as wide fluctuations stimulate and then depress those industries producing internationally traded goods. If the American economy is operating

at full employment and the international value of its currency depreciates as in our illustration, the results will be inflationary. This is so for two reasons. First, foreign demand for American goods will increase. Second, the prices of all American imports will increase. (Recall from Chapter 18 that in the early 1970s a decline in the international value of the dollar was a factor in the rightward shift of the Phillips Curve.) Conversely, appreciation of the dollar could lower exports and increase imports, tending to cause unemployment. Looked at from the vantage point of policy, acceptance of floating exchange rates may complicate the use of domestic fiscal and monetary policies in seeking full employment and price stability. This is especially so for those nations whose exports and imports may amount to 20 to 30 percent of their GNPs (Table 41-1).

△  **Fixed Exchange Rates**

At the other extreme nations have often fixed or "pegged" their exchange rates in an effort to circumvent the disadvantages associated with floating rates. To analyze the implications and problems associated with fixed rates, let us assume that the United States and Britain agree to maintain a $2 = £1 exchange rate.

The basic problem, of course, is that a governmental proclamation that a dollar will be worth so many pounds does *not* mandate stability with respect to the demand for, and the supply of, pounds. As demand and supply shift over time, government must intervene directly or indirectly in the foreign exchange market if the exchange rate is to be stabilized. Consider Figure 43-4 once again. We assume that the American demand for pounds increases from *DD* to *D'D'* and an American payments deficit of *ab* arises. This obviously means that the American government is committed to an exchange rate ($2 = £1) which is below the equilibrium rate ($3 = £1). How can the United States prevent the shortage of pounds—reflecting an American balance of

---

[2]At modest cost and inconvenience, a *trader* can circumvent the risk of unfavorable exchange rate fluctuations by "hedging" in the "futures market" for foreign exchange. However, there is no long-term *investment* futures market; hence, the *investor* must bear the risk.

payments deficit—from driving the exchange rate up to the equilibrium level? The answer clearly is to alter market demand or supply or both so that they continue to intersect at the $2 = £1 rate of exchange. There are several means by which this can be achieved.

**1  Use of Reserves**  The most desirable means of pegging an exchange rate is to manipulate the market through the use of reserves. International monetary *reserves* are simply stocks for foreign monies owned by a particular government. How do reserves originate? Let us conveniently assume that in the past the opposite market condition prevailed wherein there was a surplus, rather than a shortage, of pounds, and the United States government had acquired that surplus. That is, at some earlier time the United States government spent dollars to buy surplus pounds which were threatening to reduce the $2 = £1 exchange rate to, say, $1 = £1. By now selling a part of its reserve of pounds, the United States government could shift the supply of pounds curve to the right so that it intersects $D'D'$ at $b$, thereby maintaining the exchange rate at $2 = £1.

Historically nations have used gold as "international money" or, in other words, as reserves. Hence, in our example the United States government might sell some of the gold which it owns to Britain for pounds. The pounds thus acquired could be used to augment the supply earned through American trade and financial transactions to shift the supply of pounds to the right in order to maintain the $2 = £1 exchange rate.

Note that it is obviously critical that the amount of reserves be enough to accomplish the required increase in the supply of pounds. This is *not* a problem if deficits and surpluses occur more or less randomly and are of approximately equivalent size. That is, last year's balance of payments surplus with Britain will increase the United States' reserve of pounds and this reserve can be used to "finance" this year's deficit. But, anticipating Chapter 44, if the United States encounters persistent and sizable deficits for an extended period of time, the reserves problem can become critical and force the abandonment of a system of fixed exchange rates. Or, at least, a nation whose reserves are inadequate must resort to less appealing options if it hopes to maintain exchange rate stability.

**2  Domestic Macroeconomic Adjustments**  Another means of maintaining a stable exchange rate is to use domestic fiscal and monetary policies in such a way as to eliminate the shortage of pounds. In particular, restrictive fiscal and monetary measures will reduce the United States' national income relative to Britain's and thereby restrain our demand for British goods and therefore for pounds. (Recall from Table 41-4 that imports vary directly with the level of national income.) To the extent that these contractionary policies cause our price level to decline relative to Britain's, American buyers of consumption and investment goods will divert their demands from British to American goods, also restricting the demand for pounds. Finally, a restrictive (tight) money policy will increase United States interest rates as compared to Britain and, hence, reduce American demand for pounds to make investments in Britain. From Britain's standpoint lower prices on American goods and higher American interest rates will increase British imports of American goods and stimulate British financial investment in the United States. Both developments will increase the supply of pounds. The combination of a decrease in the demand for and an increase in the supply of pounds will obviously tend to eliminate the initial American payments deficit. In terms of Figure 43-4 the new supply and demand curves will intersect at some new equilibrium point on the broken $ab$ line where the exchange rate persists at $2 = £1.

This means of maintaining pegged exchange rates is hardly appealing. The "price" of exchange rate stability for the United States is falling output, employment, and price levels—in other words, a recession! Achieving a balance of payments equilibrium and realizing domestic stability are both important national economic objectives; but to sacrifice the latter for the former is to let the tail wag the dog.

**3  Trade Policies**  A third set of policy options entails measures designed to control directly the flows of trade and finance. The United States might undertake to maintain the $2 = £1 exchange rate in the face of a shortage of pounds by discouraging imports (thereby reducing the demand for pounds) and by encouraging exports (thereby increasing the supply of pounds). Specifically, imports can be reduced by imposing tariffs or import quotas (Chapter 42). Similarly, special taxes may be levied on the interest and dividends which Americans receive for foreign investments. On the other hand, the United States government might subsidize certain American exports and thus increase the supply of pounds.

The fundamental problem with these policies is that they reduce the volume of world trade and distort its composition or pattern away from that which is economically desirable. That is, tariffs, quotas, and the like can be imposed only at the sacrifice of some portion of the economic gains or benefits attainable from a free flow of world trade based upon the principle of comparative advantage. These effects should not be underestimated; remember that the imposition of exchange or trade controls can elicit retaliatory responses from other nations which are adversely affected.

**4  Exchange Controls: Rationing**  A final possibility is exchange controls or rationing. Under exchange controls the United States government would handle the problem of a pound shortage by requiring that all pounds obtained by American exporters be sold to it. Then, in turn, the government allocates or rations this short supply of pounds ($xa$

in Figure 43-4) among various American importers who demand the quantity $xb$. In this way the American government would be restricting American imports to the amount of foreign exchange earned by American exports. American demand for British pounds in the amount $ab$ would simply be unfulfilled. Government forces a balance of payments equilibrium by restricting imports to the value of exports.

There are many objections to exchange controls. First, like trade policies—tariffs, quotas, and export subsidies—exchange controls distort the pattern of international trade away from that based upon comparative advantage. Second, the process of rationing scarce foreign exchange necessarily involves discrimination among importers. Serious problems of equity and favoritism are implicit in the rationing process. Third, controls impinge upon freedom of consumer choice. Americans who prefer Scotch may be forced to buy bourbon. The business opportunities of some American importers will necessarily be impaired because imports are being constrained by government. Finally, there are likely to be enforcement problems. The market forces of demand and supply indicate there are American importers who want foreign exchange badly enough to pay *more* than the $2 = £1 official rate; this sets the stage for extralegal or "black market" foreign exchange dealings.

Recapitulation: Proponents of fixed exchange rates contend that such rates lessen the risks and uncertainties associated with international trade and finance. Fixed rates are thereby said to be conducive to a large and expanding volume of mutually advantageous trade and financial transactions. However, the viability of a fixed rate system hinges upon two interrelated conditions: (1) the availability of adequate amounts of reserves and (2) the random occurrence of payments deficits and surpluses which are of modest size. Large and persistent deficits may deplete a nation's reserves. A nation with inadequate reserves is confronted with less desirable options. On the one hand, it may have to submit to painful and politically unpopular macroeconomic adjustments in the form of inflation or recession. On the other hand, that nation may have to resort to protectionist trade policies or exchange controls, both of which inhibit the volume of international trade and finance.

## ☐ HISTORICAL POSTSCRIPT: THE GOLD STANDARD

Over the 1879 to 1934 period—with the exception of the World War I years—the United States and most other industrialized nations participated in an international monetary system known as the *gold standard*.[3] This system provided for essentially fixed exchange rates and a backward glance at its operation and ultimate downfall is instructive with respect to some of the problems associated with fixed-rate systems.

### △ Conditions

A nation is on the gold standard when it fulfills two conditions:

**1** It must define its monetary unit in terms of a certain quantity of gold and stand ready to convert gold into paper money and paper money into gold at the rate stipulated in its definition of the monetary unit.

**2** It must allow gold to be freely exported and imported.

If each nation defines its monetary unit in terms of gold, the various national currencies will have a fixed relationship to one another. For example, suppose the United States defines a dollar as being worth, say, 25 grains of gold and Britain defines its pound sterling as being worth 50 grains of gold. This means that a British pound is worth $50/25$ dollars or, simply, £1 equals $2.

[3]We will examine the more recent Bretton Woods and "managed float" systems in the next chapter.

### △ Gold Flows

Now, if we momentarily ignore the costs of packing, insuring, and shipping gold between countries, under the gold standard the rate of exchange would not vary from this $2-for-£1 rate. And the reason is clear: No one in the United States would pay more than $2 for £1, because one could always buy 50 grains of gold for $2 in the United States, ship it to Britain, and sell it for £1. Nor would an Englishman pay more than £1 for $2. Why should you, when you could buy 50 grains of gold in England for £1, send it to the United States, and sell it for $2?

Of course, in practice the costs of packing, insuring, and shipping gold must be taken into account. But these costs would only amount to a few cents per 50 grains of gold. For example, if these costs were 3 cents for 50 grains of gold, Americans wanting pounds would pay up to $2.03 for a pound rather than buy and export 50 grains of gold to get that pound. Why? Because it would cost them $2 for the 50 grains of gold plus 3 cents to send it to England to be exchanged for £1. This $2.03 exchange rate, above which gold would begin to flow out of the United States, is called the *gold export point*. Conversely, the exchange rate would fall to $1.97 before gold would flow into the United States. Englishmen wanting dollars would accept as little as $1.97 in exchange for £1, because from the $2 which they could get by buying 50 grains of gold in England and reselling it in the United States, 3 cents must be subtracted to pay shipping and related costs. This $1.97 exchange rate, below which gold would flow into the United States, is called the *gold import point*. Our basic conclusion is that *under the gold standard the flow of gold between nations would result in exchange rates which for all practical purposes are fixed.*

### △ Domestic Adjustments

But the stabilization of exchange rates under the gold standard required some mechanism for the correction of any persistent balance of payments deficits or surpluses which a nation might encounter. Under the gold standard the relevant mechanism was macroeconomic adjustments in the domestic economies of the gold standard nations.

Suppose, once again, that the United States incurs a balance of payments deficit by importing more from Great Britain than it exports to her. The immediate result is that the dollar price of pounds will move up to the $2.03 gold export point and gold will flow from the United States to Great Britain to settle the deficit. But as gold leaves the United States, the amount of money in circulation will decline, credit availability will be lessened, and interest rates tend to rise. Other things being unchanged, this is conducive to a decline in aggregate demand and therefore in national income and, perhaps, the price level in the United States. The opposite occurs in Great Britain; the inflow of gold expands the money supply, lowering interest rates and causing aggregate demand, national income, and the price level to rise. Declining American prices and incomes and rising British prices and incomes will both encourage American exports to, and discourage American imports from, Great Britain, thereby tending to correct the initial American payments deficit. Similarly, the rise in United States interest rates relative to British interest rates will encourage Americans to invest at home *and* the British to buy bonds in the United States.

Note that all of these indicated changes are such as to reduce the American demand for pounds *and* to increase the supply of pounds. In terms of Figure 43-4 the $D'D'$ curve will shift toward the left and the $SS$ curve toward the right, providing a new intersection (equilibrium) point somewhere on the broken line between points $a$ and $b$. At such a point, the initial balance of payments deficit has been eliminated.

△   **Evaluation**

The gold standard entails obvious advantages:

**1**   The stable exchange rates the gold standard fosters reduce uncertainty and risk and thereby stimulate the volume of international trade.

**2**   The gold standard automatically corrects balance of payments disequilibria. International equilibrium under the gold standard does not require the action of governmental bodies; inevitable gold flows adjust trade deficits or surpluses to the end that a balance of payments disequilibrium will be resolved.

The basic drawback of the gold standard is apparent from our discussion of the adjustment processes it entails. Nations on the gold standard must accept domestic adjustments in such distasteful forms as unemployment and falling incomes, on the one hand, or inflation, on the other. In playing the gold standard game nations must be willing to submit their domestic economies to painful macroeconomic adjustments.

△   **Demise**

The worldwide Great Depression of the 1930s signalled the end of the gold standard. As national outputs and employment plummeted, the restoration of prosperity became the primary goal of afflicted nations. You will recall from Chapter 42 that protectionist measures—for example, the United States' Smoot-Hawley Tariff—were enacted as the various nations sought to increase net exports and thereby stimulate their domestic economies. And each nation was fearful that its economic recovery would be aborted by a balance of payments deficit which would lead to an outflow of gold and consequent contractionary effects. Indeed, the various gold standard nations attempted to devalue their currencies in terms of gold so as to make their exports more attractive and imports less attractive. These devaluations undermined a basic condition of the gold standard and the system simply broke down. As we shall see in Chapter 44, a new fixed exchange rate system was created at the end of World War II.

## Summary

**1** American exports create a foreign demand for dollars and make a supply of foreign exchange available to Americans. Conversely, American imports simultaneously create a demand for foreign exchange and make a supply of dollars available to foreigners. Generally speaking, a nation's exports earn the foreign currencies needed to pay for its imports.

**2** The balance of payments is an annual accounting statement of all a nation's international trade and financial transactions. In 1978 the United States' imports exceeded its exports by $8.1 billion. Remittances from the United States, government loans and grants, and net capital movements from the United States totaled $24.9 billion, resulting in a balance of payments deficit of $33.0 billion. Payments deficits have been common to the United States since the early 1950s.

**3** In general, a balance of payments disequilibrium occurs when the inpayments and outpayments resulting from a nation's autonomous transactions do not balance. This imbalance necessitates accommodating or financing transactions. In the case of a deficit, financing transactions typically involve reductions in the nation's holdings of foreign monies and increases in the amount of its liquid liabilities to nonresidents—mostly foreign central and commercial banks.

**4** A flexible or floating exchange rate will depreciate or appreciate as the result of relative changes in incomes, price levels, and interest rates as between any two nations.

**5** Floating exchange rates correct balance of payments disequilibria by changing the relative attractiveness of foreign and domestic goods, services, and investments.

**6** Maintenance of fixed exchange rates requires adequate reserves to accommodate periodic payments deficits. If reserves are inadequate, nations must endure domestic macroeconomic adjustments, invoke protectionist trade policies, or engage in exchange controls.

**7** Historically, the gold standard provided exchange rate stability until its disintegration during the 1930s. Under this system, gold flows between nations precipitated sometimes painful changes in price, income, and employment levels in bringing about international equilibrium.

## Questions and Study Suggestions

**1** Key terms and concepts to remember: export and import transactions; balance of payments; remittances; net government transactions; net capital movements; financing transactions; balance of payments deficit and surplus; autonomous and accommodating transactions; flexible (floating) exchange rates; currency depreciation and appreciation; fixed exchange rates; international monetary reserves; foreign exchange controls; international gold standard; gold export and import points.

**2** Explain how an American automobile importer might finance a shipment of Renaults from France. Explain: "American exports earn supplies of foreign monies which Americans can use to finance imports."

**3** "A rise in the dollar price of pesos necessarily means a fall in the peso price of dollars." Do you agree? Illustrate and elaborate: "The critical thing about exchange rates is that they provide a direct link between the prices of goods and services produced in all trading nations of the world."

**4** Indicate whether each of the following creates a demand for, or a supply of, French francs in foreign exchange markets:
   **a.** An American importer purchases a shipload of Bordeaux wine
   **b.** A French automobile firm decides to build an assembly plant in Los Angeles
   **c.** An American college student decides to spend a year studying at the Sorbonne

   **d.** A French manufacturer exports machinery to Morocco on an American freighter

   **e.** The United States incurs a balance of payments deficit in its transactions with France

   **f.** A United States government bond held by a French citizen matures

   **5** "Exports pay for imports. Yet in 1978 the rest of the world exported about $8.1 billion more worth of goods and services to the United States than were imported from the United States." Resolve the apparent inconsistency of these two statements.

   **6** Use the distinction between autonomous and accommodating transactions to explain the notion of international disequilibrium.

   **7** Assuming a system of floating exchange rates between Mexico and the United States, indicate whether each of the following would cause the Mexican peso to appreciate or depreciate:

   **a.** The United States unilaterally reduces tariffs on Mexican products

   **b.** Mexico encounters severe inflation

   **c.** Deteriorating political relations reduces American tourism in Mexico

   **d.** The United States economy moves into a severe recession

   **e.** The Board of Governors embarks upon a tight money policy

   **f.** Mexican products become more fashionable to Americans

   **g.** The Mexican government invites American firms to invest in Mexican oil fields

   **h.** The rate of productivity growth in the United States diminishes sharply

   **8** Explain in detail the means or mechanisms by which a balance of payments surplus would be resolved under **a.** flexible exchange rates, **b.** fixed exchange rates, and **c.** the gold standard. Now trace the resolution of a payments deficit. What are the advantages and shortcomings of each system of exchange rates?

   **9** "The operation of the international gold standard undermines domestic full-employment policies, and, conversely, the active pursuit of full employment domestically is inimical to the operation of the gold standard." Explain and evaluate this statement.


## Selected References

Hogendorn, Jan S., and Wilson B. Brown: *The New International Economics* (Reading, Mass.: Addison-Wesley Publishing Company, 1979), chaps. 2–4.

Ingram, James C.: *International Economic Problems,* 3d ed. (Santa Barbara, Calif.: John Wiley and Sons, 1978), chaps. 4 and 5.

Kreinin, Mordechai E.: *International Economics: A Policy Approach,* 3d ed. (New York: Harcourt Brace Jovanovich, Inc., 1979), chaps. 1–6.

Richardson, J. David: *Understanding International Economics: Theory and Practice* (Boston: Little, Brown and Company, 1980), chaps. 1–3.

Snider, Delbert A.: *Introduction to International Economics,* 7th ed. (Homewood, Ill.: Richard D. Irwin, Inc., 1979), chaps. 13–15.

# LAST WORD
## Are Floating Exchange Rates Desirable?

In early 1973 the international monetary system changed from fixed to flexible or floating exchange rates. Dr. Arthur F. Burns, former Chairman of the Board of Governors of the Federal Reserve System, questions the long-term desirability of floating rates.

For the longer run, thinking of a reformed international monetary system, I remain skeptical about the desirability of a general system of floating exchange rates. I hold this view even though I recognize the usefulness of floating rates in particular situations, such as the present. Some reasons for my skepticism are as follows:

First, in my judgment, the floating exchange-rate system that has figured so heavily in academic discussions is a dream that will continue to elude us. Even for a country with as low a ratio of international trade to gross national product as that of the United States, the repercussions of exchange-rate changes on the domestic economy can be substantial. Under a floating exchange-rate system, governments are always apt to be subject to political pressure by business, agricultural, and labor interests for protection against large movements of exchange rates—which may mean new controls or central bank intervention or both. . . .

Second, a system of floating exchange rates may lead to political friction and competitive national economic policies. From time to time suspicions will be generated that this or that country has been manipulating its exchange rate at the expense of the interests of its trading partners. In such an atmosphere, whether for defensive or retaliatory reasons, governments may impose controls on capital flows or on current transactions. It is true, of course, that suspicion and political friction may be present under any type of exchange-rate regime. And we know from experience that governments often imposed controls on international transactions when they were trying to defend fixed exchange rates that were unrealistic. Nonetheless, I fear that such problems would be greater with widespread permanent floating of the major currencies.

Third, the uncertainties associated with floating exchange rates may lead in time to some erosion of international trade, particularly in the case of equipment purchases that require long-term financing and when profit margins are slim. These uncertainties may also weaken private foreign investment—especially in long-term bond issues.

Fourth, exchange-rate fluctuations under a floating regime may add further to the difficulties that some governments already have in carrying out suitable fiscal and monetary policies. There is danger, for example, that a temporary exchange-rate depreciation will get translated into permanent price-level increases through upward revisions of nominal [money] wages. Moreover, floating exchange rates may themselves become a tool of business-cycle policy, and thereby lead at times to neglect of appropriate domestic policies.

From *How Well Are Fluctuating Exchange Rates Working?*, Hearings before the Subcommittee on International Economics of the Joint Economic Committee, 93d Congress, 1st Session, Washington, 1973, p. 173, abridged.

# International Trade and Finance: Problems and Policies

chapter **44**

With the elements of international trade and finance in mind, we are now in a position to examine some more recent developments in the areas of international trade and finance. In particular, we want to examine the evolution of the international monetary system in the postwar period and to relate this evolution to United States balance of payments problems.

## ☐ A BACKWARD GLANCE

At the conclusion of Chapter 43 we observed that the Great Depression forced an abandonment of the fixed exchange rate system known as the international gold standard. Recall, too, from Chapter 42 that the depression spawned protectionist trade policies. World War II was similarly disruptive to international trade and finance. At the outset of hostilities the European belligerents sought to mobilize as many resources as possible—both domestic and for-

eign—for war goods production. This meant cutting exports and increasing imports and, as a consequence, large payments deficits. The war also brought differing rates of inflation which aggravated payments imbalances. In short, as World War II came to its conclusion it was evident that international trade and financial relationships were in a shambles.

The interrelated problems involved in rebuilding the world economy were both evident and formidable:

**1 Trade Liberalization** The artificial barriers which accompanied and contributed to the disintegration of world trade in the 1930s had to be dismantled. The postwar liberalization of trade through the General Agreement on Tariffs and Trade (GATT) and economic integration has been outlined in Chapter 42.

**2  Postwar Reconstruction**  The most immediate problem was to rebuild the war-devastated economies of Europe. Because the United States emerged from the holocaust with a much greater productive capacity than when it had entered the war, it was not surprising that American economic aid would play an important role in rebuilding the European economies. Indeed, an economically strong Europe was essential to American economic and political welfare. Hence, the *European Recovery Program,* popularly known as the *Marshall Plan,* came into being in 1948 as a means of channeling some $10 billion in United States aid to our European allies. By the early 1950s European economic recovery was substantially achieved.

**3  International Monetary System**  The remaining problem was that of establishing an international monetary system which would facilitate the reconstruction and growth of international trade and finance.

☐  **THE BRETTON WOODS SYSTEM**

In order to lay the groundwork for such a system, an international conference of Allied nations was held at Bretton Woods, New Hampshire, in 1944. Out of this conference evolved a commitment to an *adjustable-peg system* of exchange rates, sometimes called the Bretton Woods system. Furthermore, the conference created the *International Monetary Fund* (IMF) to make the new exchange rate system feasible and workable. This international monetary system, emphasizing relatively fixed exchange rates and managed through the IMF, prevailed with modifications until 1971.

△  **IMF and Adjustable Pegs**

What was the Bretton Woods adjustable-peg system? Why was it evolved? What caused its demise? Consider the second question first. Recall that during the depressed 1930s, various countries resorted to the practice of devaluing their currencies in the hope of

stimulating domestic employment. For example, if the United States was faced with growing unemployment, it might devalue the dollar by *increasing* the dollar price of pounds from $2.50 for £1 to, say, $3 for £1. This action would make American goods cheaper to the British and British goods dearer to Americans, increasing American exports and reducing American imports. The resulting increase in the net exports, abetted by the multiplier effect, would stimulate output and employment in the United States. But the problem was that every nation can play the devaluation game, and most gave it a whirl. The resulting rounds of competitive devaluations benefited no one; on the contrary, they actually contributed to the demoralization of world trade. Nations at Bretton Woods therefore agreed that the postwar monetary system must provide for overall exchange rate stability whereby disruptive currency devaluations could be avoided.

What was the adjustable-peg system of exchange rates like? First, reminiscent of the gold standard, each member of the IMF was obligated to define its monetary unit in terms of gold (or dollars), thereby establishing par rates of exchange between its currency and the currencies of all other members. Each nation was further obligated to keep its exchange rate stable vis-à-vis any other currency. But how was this obligation to be fulfilled? As we found in Chapter 43, fixed rates can only be maintained if sufficient international monetary reserves are available. Under the Bretton Woods system these reserves were of two kinds.

**1  Stabilization Funds**  Each member nation established a stabilization fund, affiliated with its central bank or treasury, which holds supplies of both foreign and domestic monies and gold. These monies and gold are used to augment the supply of, or demand for, any currency required to avoid or restrict fluctuations in the rate of exchange. For example, if the dollar appreciates in value, the United States government can augment the supply by offering extra dollars for sale. This action restricts the rise in the price of dollars. Conversely, if the dollar depreciates in value, the government can use some of the foreign currencies it has on hand to buy dollars. This bolsters the demand for dollars and limits the decline in the price of the dollar.

**2  IMF Credit**  The IMF plays a major role in stabilizing exchange rates. Specifically, the IMF is empowered to make short-term loans to nations faced with temporary, or short-run, balance of payments deficits. These loans are made out of currencies and gold contributed by the participating nations on the basis of size of national income, population, and volume of trade. If Great Britain or France, for example, faces a temporary shortage of dollars, it can borrow the needed dollars from the Fund by supplying its own currency as collateral. The dollars so acquired are in the form of a loan, not a grant, and must be repaid with interest in a relatively short period. Presumably in the near future, the borrowing country's trade deficit with the United States will be corrected so that it can obtain the gold or dollars needed to retire its IMF loan.

△  **Disequilibria: Adjusting the Peg**

While stabilization funds and IMF credit are the primary means of avoiding *short-run* fluctuations in exchange rates, the adjustable-peg system—as its name implies—provided for the *orderly* alteration of exchange rates to cope with international disequilibrium stemming from *long-run,* or fundamental, causes. It was recognized that if a nation's currency is overvalued[1] in relation to other

[1] The problem of an overvalued dollar can be envisioned by referring back to Figure 43-4. Assume the supply of and the demand for pounds are *SS* and *D'D'* and the United States is obligated to keep its exchange rate fixed at $2 = £1. The dollar will be overvalued in that its fixed exchange rate is below the market or equilibrium rate. In other words, the market rate indicates that a dollar is worth only one-third of a pound, while at the fixed rate a dollar is worth one-half of a pound. The fixed rate obviously overstates the worth of the dollar as compared to the market rate; the dollar is overvalued.

currencies, that nation will encounter severe difficulties in exporting. Hence, it will persistently be faced with a payments deficit. To cope with such situations, the Fund allowed each member nation to alter the value of its currency by 10 percent without explicit permission from the Fund in order to correct a deeply rooted balance of payments deficit. Larger exchange rate changes required the sanction of the Fund's board of directors. By requiring approval of significant rate changes, the Fund attempted to guard against arbitrary and competitive currency devaluation prompted by nations seeking a temporary stimulus to their domestic economies or the solution to a payments deficit.

The objective of the adjustable-peg system was to realize a world monetary system which embraced the best features of both a fixed exchange rate system (such as the old international gold standard) and a system of freely fluctuating exchange rates. By reducing risk and uncertainty, short-run exchange rate stability—pegged exchange rates—stimulates trade and is conducive to the efficient use of world resources. Periodic exchange rate adjustments—adjustment of the pegs—made in an orderly fashion through the IMF, and on the basis of permanent or long-run changes in a country's payments position, provided a mechanism by which international payments disequilibria could be resolved by means other than painful changes in domestic levels of output and prices.

△  **International Monetary Reserves**

The effective functioning of an essentially fixed-exchange rate monetary system, such as the Bretton Woods system, requires the availability of sufficient quantities of international monetary reserves. We have noted that as nations incur short-run payments deficits, they need monetary reserves if exchange rates are to be kept stable while domestic adjustments in output and employment are avoided.

Throughout most of the postwar period, gold and certain *key currencies* functioned as international monetary reserves. The dollar has been the primary key currency, although other currencies—the British pound, the German mark, and the Japanese yen, for example—have functioned in that capacity at various times.

The acceptability of gold bullion as an international medium of exchange was derived from its role under the international gold standard of an earlier era. But why did the dollar become acceptable as money internationally? The answer has historical roots. The United States emerged from World War II as the free world's strongest economy; hence it became the center of international trade and finance. Furthermore, before and during the war the United States accumulated vast amounts of gold, and between 1934 and 1971 it maintained a policy of buying gold from, and selling gold to, foreign monetary authorities at a fixed price of $35 per ounce. Thus the dollar was convertible into gold on demand; the dollar came to be regarded as a substitute for gold and therefore "as good as gold."

△   **Dilemma: Dollars and Deficits**
But the role of the dollar as a key currency—as a component of international monetary reserves—contained the seeds of a dilemma. Consider the situation as it developed in the 1950s and 1960s. The problem with gold as international money was a quantitative one. The growth of the world's money stock depends upon the amount of newly mined gold, less any amounts hoarded for speculative purposes or used for industrial and artistic purposes. Unfortunately, the growth of the gold stock lagged behind the rapidly expanding volume of international trade and finance. Thus the dollar came to occupy an increasingly important role as an international monetary reserve. Question: How do economies of the world acquire dollars as reserves? Answer: As the result of United States balance of payments deficits. As Figure 44-1 reveals, the United States has obligingly incurred deficits over the past three decades! Figure 44-2 indi-

cates that these deficits were financed in part by drawing down American gold reserves. But for the most part United States deficits were financed by growing foreign holdings of American dollars which, remember, were "as good as gold" until 1971.

Figure 44-2 also reveals a problem: As the amount of dollars held by foreigners soared and as our gold reserves dwindled, other nations inevitably began to question whether the dollar was really "as good as gold." The ability of the United States to maintain the convertibility of the dollar into gold became increasingly doubtful, and, therefore, so did the role of the dollar as a key currency. Hence, the dilemma: ". . . to preserve the status of the dollar as a reserve medium, the payments deficit of the United States had to be eliminated; but elimination of the deficit would mean a drying up of the source of additional dollar reserves for the system."[2]

☐   **UNITED STATES PAYMENTS DEFICITS**
Let us pause at this point to examine the causes of our chronic payments deficits and to indicate some potential cures. We shall then consider how the noted dilemma posed by these deficits forced the abandonment of the Bretton Woods monetary system.

△   **Causes**
A number of interlaced factors have given rise to our payments deficits.

**1   Military Expenditures and Economic Aid**   Substantial American economic grants and loans in the form of both military and economic aid have been an important contributor to our payments deficit. One might think at first glance that American dollar aid would tend to increase our exports and therefore not contribute to our payments deficit. But it has

[2]Delbert A. Snider, *Introduction to International Economics,* 7th ed. (Homewood, Ill.: Richard D. Irwin, Inc., 1979), p. 352.

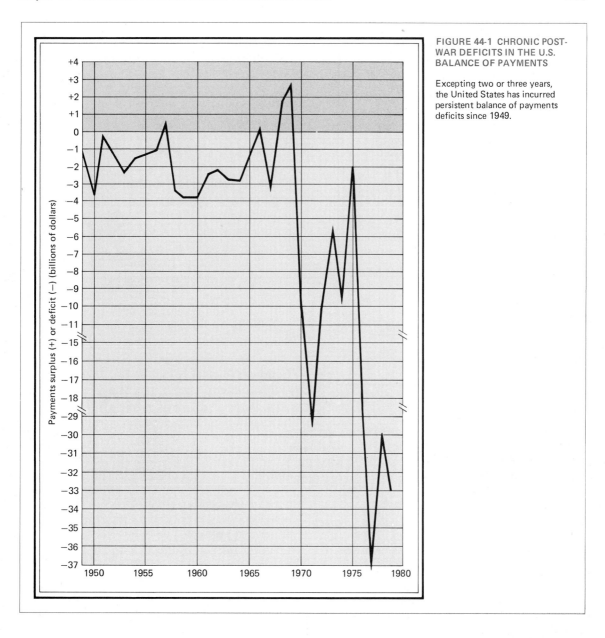

FIGURE 44-1 CHRONIC POST-WAR DEFICITS IN THE U.S. BALANCE OF PAYMENTS

Excepting two or three years, the United States has incurred persistent balance of payments deficits since 1949.

worked this way only to a limited degree. Some American aid dollars have been spent on American goods, thereby increasing our exports. But other American aid dollars have been spent on, say, German and French goods, ultimately converging on the central banks of these countries and therefore not being respent on American exports. Thus foreign aid and military spending have entailed dollar outflows not fully matched by dollar inflows resulting from aid-induced expenditures on American exports. In this way, aid and military outlays have contributed to our payments deficit. Overseas expenditures associated with the

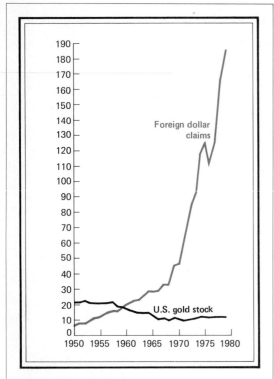

**FIGURE 44-2** THE U.S. GOLD STOCK AND FOREIGN DOLLAR CLAIMS SINCE 1950

Chronic balance of payments deficits for over two decades have drained off much of the United States' gold reserves and have resulted in large foreign holdings of dollar claims. (*Federal Reserve Bulletin.*)

Vietnam war in the late 1960s exacerbated our balance of payments difficulties.

**2   Private Capital Outflows**   This outflow of public dollars has been accompanied by substantial outflows of American private capital. Private capital outflows have been expanding since the mid-1950s. Growth in the outflow of long-term capital has occurred in response to the burgeoning profit opportunities available in the more rapidly expanding economies of the world, particularly those of Western Europe. Americans have found that the expected return on foreign investment has ex-

ceeded that on domestic investment, so they have invested abroad. Note in Table 43-1 that net capital outflows were $30.3 billion in 1978.

**3   Foreign Productivity Increases**   The rate of productivity increase of our major trading partners—the Western European nations and Japan—has been more rapid than in the United States. This has meant a relative lowering of production costs and prices for foreign goods as compared to American goods. Our exports have therefore tended to fall and our imports to rise. Witness the flood of imported automobiles and television sets and the decline of our domestic steel industry.

Why has this happened? The manifold causes of our productivity slowdown were detailed in Chapter 19 and will not be restated here. It is important to add, however, that rapidly rising foreign productivity has undoubtedly been caused in part by economies of scale associated with the formation of the Common Market (Chapter 42). It may also be attributable to the United States' assumption of a large share of the free world's defense burden, freeing high-level manpower and other crucial resources for the task of modernizing the domestic industries of Japan and Western Europe.

**4   Domestic Inflation**   Other things being equal, domestic inflation tends to price American products out of international export markets and simultaneously to make imported goods more attractive. Fortunately for the United States, other things have *not* been equal. Most of our trading partners have also experienced inflation, in some instances more severe than in the United States. Nevertheless, there is no doubt that our rapid inflation of the post-1965 Vietnam war period contributed substantially to our deteriorating balances of trade and payments.

**5   OPEC**   The United States and many other oil-importing countries experienced a sharp deterioration in their balance of payments positions as a result of the formation of the Organization of Petroleum Exporting Countries (OPEC) and the subsequent increase in oil prices. The price of imported crude oil rose from about $2 per barrel in 1973 to the $30 to $32 range by mid-1980. Given our expanding dependence upon imported oil, these dramatic price increases have contributed heavily to our payments deficits. In recent years the annual outpayments required for foreign oil have been on the order of $45 to $50 billion per year!

### △ Cures

Our discussion of the causes of our lingering balance of payments problem implies the thrust of basic corrective measures. A basic line of attack is to reverse our productivity slowdown. This implies, among other things, the need for a higher level of investment spending, a resurgence of research and development activities, a thorough reexamination of our tax and regulatory policies, and perhaps greater labor-management cooperation. Similarly, the more effective use of fiscal, monetary, and incomes policies in controlling inflation would undoubtedly strengthen our position in world trade. And we might seek to have our allies bear a larger share of the costs of the mutual defense effort. Finally, we might more vigorously petition those nations with whom we have the largest and most persistent deficits—Japan and West Germany in particular—to reduce or remove existing barriers to American exports. It is obvious that these cures are much easier to state than to accomplish.

Of course, we know from Chapter 43 that there is another option. And that is to abandon the essentially fixed exchange rates of the Bretton Woods system in favor of floating exchange rates. This option became a reality in the early 1970s. Let us return to the dilemma mentioned earlier to see precisely how it led to the breakdown of the Bretton Woods monetary system and its replacement by a system involving greater exchange rate flexibility.

## □ DEMISE OF THE BRETTON WOODS SYSTEM

The demise of the Bretton Woods system in the early 1970s stemmed from two problems: (1) a reserves or liquidity problem and (2) an adjustment problem. Both these problems were intimately linked to the United States' payments deficits we have just discussed.

### △ The Reserves Problem

Recall the dilemma posed earlier. Gold production in the 1950s and 1960s did not keep pace with the need for additional international monetary reserves; hence, gold became less significant as international money. The dollar, however, became a key currency—in effect, an international money—because of the economic preeminence of the United States and its commitment to convert dollars into gold at a fixed price. But our chronic deficits dramatically increased the amount of dollars held by foreigners and simultaneously reduced our gold reserves (Figure 44-2). The willingness and ability of the United States to maintain its convertibility commitment became increasingly doubtful. Hence, the previously noted dilemma: The United States had to reduce or eliminate its payments deficits to preserve the dollar's status as an international medium of exchange. But success in this endeavor would limit the expansion of international reserves or liquidity and therefore tend to restrict the growth of international trade and finance. This dilemma was central to the reserves or liquidity problem.

### △ The Adjustment Problem

The other basic problem of the Bretton Woods system was that it did not provide an effective means by which a nation could resolve serious, long-run balance of payments deficits. As noted in our discussion of the United States' payments deficits, trading partners may grow apart over time in terms of their productivities, price and income levels, interest rates, and so forth. This means that fundamental realignments of their exchange rates will be necessary if chronic payments disequilibria are to be avoided. While the Bretton Woods system offered a procedure for orderly currency devaluation to correct a deeply rooted deficit, in reality the system did not work very effectively in this respect. Exchange rate pegs were rarely adjusted, and the system in fact became one of rigid exchange rates. A nation's IMF commitment to stabilize its exchange rate and the availability of loans to help achieve this objective were both conducive to the deferring of exchange rate adjustments. Furthermore, there were also political obstacles to exchange rate realignments. When a nation requested the IMF to adjust the exchange rate pegs so that its money would be worth less vis-à-vis other currencies, its political leaders were in effect confessing their inability to manage domestic economic affairs so that the nation could pay its way in international trade and finance. Conversely, leaders in surplus countries would not be anxious to have their currencies revalued upward because the result would be a fall in net exports and rising domestic unemployment.

Thus, in practice, many deficit nations—including the United States—tended to put off the use of Bretton Woods mechanisms to change their exchange rates in the hope that in time their deficit would somehow correct itself. Typically, the disequilibrium became worse, rather than better, and the use of Bretton Woods adjustment mechanisms became even more distasteful. There was another reason why deficit nations were hesitant to "adjust the peg," that is, to devalue their currencies. In the absence of free markets for foreign exchange, there is no way of knowing by how much the value of a currency should be reduced to correct a "fundamental disequilibrium." Obviously, a devaluation which is too small will not restore equilibrium.

△ **Shattering of the System**

These problems came to a head in the early 1970s and precipitated the breakdown of the Bretton Woods system. The chronic balance of payments deficits of the United States, which averaged $2 or $3 billion per year in the 1950s and 1960s, increased sharply in the early 1970s (Figure 44-1). Faced with this situation, President Nixon suspended the dollar's convertibility into gold on August 15, 1971. This suspension abrogated the policy to exchange gold for dollars at $35 per ounce, which had existed for thirty-seven years. This new policy severed the link between gold and the international value of the dollar, thereby "floating" the dollar and allowing its value to be determined by market forces. Such profound action was taken on the assumption that, under the basically stable exchange rates of the postwar international monetary system, the dollar had come to be substantially overvalued in relation to the currencies of our major trading partners—Japan and most of the Common Market countries. We know the consequences of devaluation. Exchange rates link the entire price structures of nations. Therefore, a decline in the international value of the dollar means that all American goods will be cheaper to foreigners and, conversely, all foreign goods will be more expensive to Americans. In short, the devaluation of the dollar means that the United States' exports will rise and its imports will fall, tending to correct our payments deficit. More importantly, the floating of the dollar withdrew American support from the old Bretton Woods system of fixed exchange rates and sounded the death knell for that system.

□ **EMERGENCE OF FLOATING RATES**

The system of exchange rates which has since evolved is not easily described; it can probably best be labeled a system of *managed floating exchange rates*. On the one hand, it is recognized that changing economic conditions among nations require continuing changes in exchange rates to avoid persistent payments deficits or surpluses; exchange rates must be allowed to float. On the other hand, short-term changes in exchange rates—perhaps accentuated by purchases and sales by speculators—can cause frequent and significant exchange rate fluctuations which tend to disrupt and discourage the flow of trade and finance. Hence, it is generally agreed that the central banks of the various nations should buy and sell foreign exchange to smooth out these day-to-day fluctuations in rates. In other words, central banks should "manage" or stabilize short-term speculative variations in their exchange rates. These characteristics were formalized by a leading group of IMF nations in 1976. Thus, ideally, the new system will entail not only the needed long-term exchange rate flexibility to correct fundamental payments disequilibria, but also sufficient short-term stability of rates to sustain and encourage international trade and finance.

### △ Liquidity and Special Drawing Rights

The shift from the Bretton Woods system of essentially fixed exchange rates to a new system of basically floating rates will presumably help significantly in dealing with "the adjustment problem." That is, a nation experiencing a payments deficit will find its currency depreciating under a floating rate system. Its exports will rise and its imports will fall, tending automatically to adjust its balance of payments toward equilibrium. But what of "the liquidity problem" which played a critical role in the dissolution of the Bretton Woods system?

Recall, first, that under a fixed rate system a nation incurring a payments deficit was required to draw upon its international reserves to cover the deficit. That is, to play the fixed exchange rate game, large quantities of international reserves or liquidity are essential. But with a floating rate system, changing exchange rates automatically tend to correct or ameliorate deficits and thereby lessen the need for reserves. Second, the IMF endorsed in 1967 a plan providing for a new international money called *Special Drawing Rights,* or simply *SDRs*. Popularly referred to as "paper gold," SDRs are created at the initiative of the directors of the IMF, but only with the approval of an 85 percent majority of the voting power of Fund participants. SDRs are made available to Fund members in proportion to their IMF quotas and can be used, as gold was once used, to settle payments deficits or satisfy reserve needs.

Special Drawing Rights are created and function in this way. Assume the IMF is authorized to make available, say, $5 billion in SDRs to member nations. Each nation is allocated, not pieces of paper similar to dollars, marks, or pounds, but IMF accounts. Each nation's SDR account, as noted, is in proportion to its IMF quota. In other words, SDRs consist of bookkeeping entries at the IMF, conceptually similar to your demand deposit in a commercial bank. Now assume that Italy, for example, incurs a payments deficit and does not have sufficient quantities of, say, dollars, marks, and yen to cover the deficit. Italy may simply transfer some of its SDR credits to the SDR accounts of the United States, Germany, and Japan in order to finance its deficit. The basic point is that SDRs constitute an important new source of international monetary reserves.

What backs the SDRs? The answer is simply that they are fiat money. They are international reserves because IMF members have agreed to accept them as such. How are SDRs valued? What are they worth? When first issued in 1970, SDRs were valued in terms of the dollar; one SDR was defined as being worth one dollar. But because of fluctuations (primarily declines) in the value of the dollar and its downgrading as a key currency in the 1970s, the value of the SDR since 1974 has been determined by a weighted average of the international value of the currencies of the sixteen major trading nations. There is safety in numbers: The average international value of this "basket" of sixteen currencies is less likely to fluctuate than might the value of any single currency, for example, the dollar. The stable value of SDRs has contributed to their acceptability as international monetary reserves.

## △  Demonetization of Gold?

Reform of the international monetary system has also involved the intentional downgrading of the role of gold. Recall (Chapter 14) that close ties between gold and domestic money systems of the various nations were severed long ago. Why? Because there is no particular logic in arbitrarily linking the monetary system to gold or any other commodity; it is much more rational to manage the monetary system so as to accommodate changing levels of economic activity.

What actions has the IMF taken toward the demonetization of gold? First, the creation of SDRs has provided an apparently acceptable replacement for gold as international money. Furthermore, gold has been replaced by SDRs as the official IMF unit of account. Finally, the IMF is in the process of disposing of one-third of its gold holdings. Specifically, one-sixth of its total gold stock is being "restituted," that is, sold back to member nations in proportion to their IMF quotas. Another one-sixth is being sold at public auction over a four-year period. The profits from this auction are being put in a trust fund to aid countries that are less developed. Whether gold will be completely demonetized remains to be seen.

## △  Evaluation of the Managed Float

How well has the managed floating system worked? Although our experience with this system is historically too short for a definitive assessment, the system has both proponents and critics.

Proponents argue that the system has functioned quite well, particularly in view of the diverse and disruptive economic developments of the 1970s. Internationally diverse rates of inflation and growth, shortfalls in agricultural production, varying amounts of unemployment, and dramatic oil price increases were important forces which tended to generate substantial international disequilibria. It is contended that flexible rates facilitated international adjustments to these develop-

ments, whereas the same events would have put unbearable pressures upon a fixed-rate system.

But there is still considerable sentiment in favor of a system characterized by greater exchange rate stability. Those favoring stable rates envision problems with the current system.

**1  Reinforcement of Inflation?**  A controversial criticism of the managed float is that it tends to reinforce a nation's inflationary pressures. Much simplified, the argument is as follows. Assume a nation—Britain, for example—experiences domestic inflation as the result of, say, inappropriate stabilization policies or cost-push pressures. As a consequence, the British pound will depreciate in value. But this depreciation, by stimulating British exports and diminishing its imports, will increase aggregate demand in Britain and reinforce its inflationary problem. This additional dose of inflation will contribute to the further depreciation of the pound and the process repeats itself. To repeat: this "vicious circle" theory of inflation through exchange rate adjustments is quite new and a source of considerable disagreement among economists.

**2  A "Nonsystem"?**  Skeptics feel that the managed float is basically a "nonsystem"; that is, the rules and guidelines circumscribing the behavior of each nation vis-à-vis its exchange rate are not sufficiently clear or constraining to make the system viable in the long run. Bluntly put, the various nations will inevitably be tempted to intervene in foreign exchange markets, not merely to smooth out short-term or speculative fluctuations in the value of their currencies, but to prop up their currency if it is chronically weak or to purposely manipulate the value of their currency to achieve domestic stabilization goals. In short, there is fear that in time there may be more "managing" and less "floating" of exchange rates, and this may be fatal to the present loosely defined system.

## △ **The European Monetary System**

Evidence of a latent desire for exchange rate stability is reflected in the proposed new European Monetary System (EMS). Under this arrangement Common Market nations will attempt to achieve fixed exchange rates with one another, while their monetary unit would vary in value vis-à-vis nonmember currencies. The proposal essentially is for fixed exchange rates internally, but flexible rates externally. The evolution of EMS is obviously consistent with the Common Market's long-run objective of economic and political unification.

But previous attempts to establish such a system have encountered difficulties because of the problems inherent in a system of fixed rates such as the Bretton Woods system. Specifically, as changes in growth, inflation, and interest rates occur between participating nations, the currencies of individual countries come to be overvalued or undervalued. Hence, the success of EMS will ultimately depend upon reasonably compatible macroeconomic developments between the participating economies and this in turn implies the need for coordinated macroeconomic policies. The other requirement, of course, is sufficient reserves or credit to finance short-run balance of payments disequilibria.

## △ **Whither the Dollar?**

How has the dollar fared under the managed float? As Figure 44-3 indicates, the value of the dollar has declined in comparison to (a trade-weighted average of) some ten other currencies. The decline of the dollar in the early 1970s was expected. After all, it was the fact that the dollar came to be chronically overvalued under the Bretton Woods system which was instrumental in the demise of that system.

**Crisis of 1977–1978** But Figure 44-3 also reflects a serious "dollar crisis" which developed in 1977–1978. We note here a dramatic plunge of almost 20 percent in the value of the dollar between the late summer of 1977 and the fall of 1978. This downward slide was accompanied by considerable day-to-day volatility of exchange rates.

The causes of the dollar plunge were manifold and interrelated. First, despite its chronic payments deficits, the United States managed to export more goods and services than it imported in most years through the early 1970s.[3] This situation reversed itself in 1977 and 1978; United States merchandise imports exceeded exports. The reason for this, paradoxically, was that our economy grew more rapidly than did our major trading partners and, hence, our imports expanded rapidly. Secondly, relatively high interest rates in Europe prompted large net outflows of money capital from the United States. Third, inflation accelerated in the United States. Not only did this inflationary spurt tend to lower our exports and increase our imports, but it also raised questions both at home and abroad as to whether the United States government was willing and able to install an effective anti-inflation program. Finally, the convergence of the aforementioned factors prompted speculators to anticipate that the value of the dollar would fall. This meant that speculators holding dollars could make a profit by selling them now (when the price is still high) and buying them back later (when the price is low). The sale of dollars by speculators increased the supply of dollars in foreign exchange markets and helped *cause* the value of the dollar to decline!

**Policy Response** On November 1, 1978, the Carter Administration announced a new program to strengthen the dollar. The rationale for the government's program was that the selling of dollars by speculators was an important factor in the dollar's decline; that is, the dollar's plunge was "not justified by economic

---

[3] Our payments deficits resulted from outpayments in the form of remittances, grants, and net capital outflows. See Table 43-1.

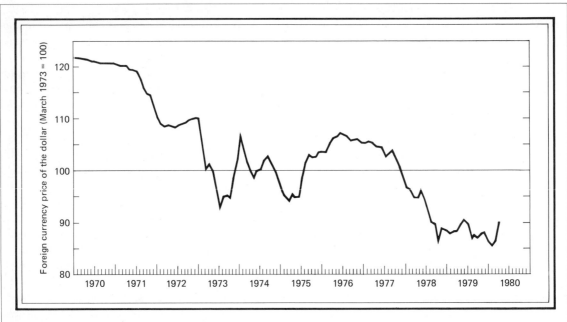

**FIGURE 44-3** THE DECLINE OF THE DOLLAR IN THE SEVENTIES

As compared to ten major currencies (weighted by the amount of trade we carry on with each country), the long-term trend under the managed floating system of exchange rates has been for the dollar's international value to decline. The extremely sharp decline in 1977–1978 prompted special policies to support the dollar's exchange value. (*Board of Governors of the Federal Reserve System.*)

conditions" and "had become disorderly." While the new program was complex and diverse, the essential elements are as follows:

**1**  The Federal Reserve raised the discount rate from $8\frac{1}{2}$ to $9\frac{1}{2}$ percent. The intended effects were threefold. First, this tight money measure would indicate to the world that the United States intended to do a better job of controlling its domestic price level and therefore correcting its payments deficit. Second, the higher interest rates would tend to restrain growth of the United States national income and therefore the growth of its imports. Finally, by boosting the whole structure of interest rates it was hoped that the net outflow of American capital would be discouraged. Specifically, higher interest rates in the United States would make it relatively less attractive for Americans to invest abroad and

relatively more attractive for foreigners to invest in the United States.

**2**  The United States also mobilized some $30 billion worth of international reserves to be used as required in support of the dollar. What were the sources of this "intervention package"? First, the United States borrowed marks and yen from the IMF. Secondly, the central banks of West Germany, Japan, and Switzerland exchanged or "swapped" some $15 billion of their currencies for dollars. These reserves were then drawn upon by the United States to increase the demand for dollars in foreign exchange markets and thereby to bolster the value of the dollar.

These steps were successful in resolving the immediate crisis. The dollar's decline ceased and its value began to rise. The jury is out, however, as to the long-run course of the dollar. Much obviously depends upon our ability to cope with the interrelated problems of stagflation and chronic balance of payments deficits.

## ☐ COMPATIBILITY OF DOMESTIC AND INTERNATIONAL POLICIES

Depending upon the particular combination of circumstances facing a nation with respect to domestic conditions and its balance of payments, domestic and international economic policies may be compatible or in conflict. Hence, the thrust of the final section of this chapter is that neither the domestic goal of full employment with reasonable price stability nor the international goal of balance of payments equilibrium should be viewed in isolation. Policies designed to achieve domestic stability will affect the balance of payments, and vice versa. Let us therefore consider briefly various combinations of domestic and international conditions and determine whether appropriate policy in, say, the domestic area is consistent with our balance of payments objectives. Table 44-1 summarizes the four possible cases to be considered.

Suppose the domestic economy is sluggish and characterized by unemployment and slow growth, on the one hand, and that we face a payments deficit, on the other (row 1). Appropriate domestic policy would entail an expansionary fiscal policy—more government spend-ing and lower taxes—and an easy money (low interest rate) policy. Unfortunately, these expansionary policies would be inconsistent with the resolution of a payments deficit; indeed, domestic economic expansion is likely to intensify the deficit. Why so? First, recall that rising domestic income will mean an expanding volume of imports (Table 41-4). Second, given the Phillips Curve and the likelihood of premature inflation, our domestic products will tend to become less and less competitive in world markets, so exports will fall. Third, the decline in interest rates engendered by an easy money policy will prompt outflows of capital to other nations where interest rates are now higher, further contributing to the payments deficit. Incidentally, the situation just described is very similar to that faced by the United States in the early 1960s. The policy decision was made to stimulate the domestic economy by cutting taxes, but this stimulus was at odds with the resolution of our balance of payments disequilibrium.

On the other hand, if the problems are domestic inflation coupled with a payments deficit, there is no policy conflict (row 2). On the domestic front, contractionary monetary and fiscal measures are in order. The resulting restraint on income growth will curtail imports, and the halting or diminution of inflation will tend to stimulate exports. Finally, rising interest rates will stop outflows of capital and tend to encourage inflows. Similarly,

**TABLE 44-1**
**Compatibility and Conflict Between Domestic and International Economic Policies**

| Domestic problem | International (balance of payments) problem | Appropriate domestic policy | Appropriate international policy | Relationship between domestic and international policies |
|---|---|---|---|---|
| (1) Unemployment | Deficit | Expansionary | Contractionary | Conflicting |
| (2) Inflation | Deficit | Contractionary | Contractionary | Compatible |
| (3) Unemployment | Surplus | Expansionary | Expansionary | Compatible |
| (4) Inflation | Surplus | Contractionary | Expansionary | Conflicting |

*Source:* Adapted from Mordechai E. Kreinin, *International Economics: A Policy Approach,* 2d ed. (New York: Harcourt Brace Jovanovich, Inc., 1975), p. 92.

the reader should verify that domestic measures to eliminate unemployment are in accord with the correction of a payments surplus (row 3). Finally, domestic policies to combat inflation are inconsistent with alleviating a payments surplus (row 4).

A final comment: There is an evident and quite understandable propensity for policy makers in the United States to accord priority to domestic stability when that objective conflicts with the realization of a balance of payments equilibrium. On the one hand, the Congress and the Administration recognize that the general public is highly sensitive to the "bread-and-butter" issues of unemployment and inflation. On the other hand, given the fact that international trade is small relative to the size of our domestic economy, according first priority to international equilibrium would be to let the tail wag the dog.

## Summary

**1**    In the 1929–1945 period, the Great Depression and World War II severely disrupted the volume and pattern of world trade. The immediate world economic problem after World War II was to achieve European economic recovery. A large flow of United States aid to Europe through the Marshall Plan contributed to this goal.

**2**    The post-World War II international monetary system—the Bretton Woods system— was committed to an "adjustable-peg" system of exchange rates. In particular, the International Monetary Fund was created ***a.*** to make short-term foreign currency loans to help nations meet temporary payments deficits, and ***b.*** to provide for an orderly adjustment of exchange rates to help correct fundamental payments deficits. As the world's monetary system evolved after the war, gold and certain key currencies—particularly American dollars and British pounds—served as international monetary reserves.

**3**    Since about 1950 the United States has been faced with large and persistent balance of payments deficits. The growing productivity of Western Europe and Japan, American inflation, large outflows of investment capital, substantial American foreign aid and overseas military expenditures, and, more recently, oil price increases under OPEC have all contributed to these deficits.

**4**    The use of the dollar as a key currency—as international monetary reserves—in the Bretton Woods system created a dilemma. On the one hand, needed growth in monetary reserves depended upon the persistence of United States payments deficits; on the other hand, these chronic deficits raised doubts as to the continued convertibility of the dollar into gold and therefore as to the status of the dollar as a key currency. Sharp increases in our payments deficit in 1971 forced the abandonment of dollar convertibility into gold, shattering the Bretton Woods system.

**5**    The new system is one of managed floating exchange rates. Central banks buy and sell foreign currencies to smooth out or "manage" short-term fluctuations, but exchange rates are allowed to float or fluctuate in response to more fundamental changes in a nation's exports and imports. The international value of the dollar has declined under this new system of exchange rates.

**6**    Special Drawing Rights (SDRs) have been successfully introduced by the IMF to provide greater international liquidity. At the same time, the IMF has been moving toward the demonetization of gold.

**7**    Some economists feel that, given the turbulent economic conditions of the 1970s, the managed floating system has functioned well. Others are more critical, arguing that the system ***a.*** has an inflationary bias and ***b.*** may be prone to breakdown because the behavioral guidelines and constraints of the system are poorly defined.

## Questions and Study Suggestions

**1**   Key terms and concepts to remember: Marshall Plan; Bretton Woods system; adjustable pegs; International Monetary Fund (IMF); international monetary reserves; key currencies; SDRs; managed floating exchange rates; European Monetary System.

**2**   What factors underlay the disintegration of international trade and finance in the 1930s and 1940s? Explain the impact of each. Briefly describe the Marshall Plan.

**3**   Describe the Bretton Woods monetary system, identifying the role of the IMF and the adjustable-peg system of exchange rates. What constituted international reserves under this system?

**4**   What have been the major causes of the United States' chronic balance of payments deficits? How did these deficits contribute to the demise of the Bretton Woods system?

**5**   How do SDRs function as international monetary reserves? Comment on the statement: "The creation of SDRs is part of the IMF's program to demonetize gold."

**6**   Explain the adjustments which would occur in response to a chronic payments deficit under *a.* the Bretton Woods system and *b.* the managed float.

**7**   Explain and illustrate:

*a.*   "Policies that stimulate the domestic economy tend to cause a trade deficit."

*b.*   "A balance of payments deficit imposes severe constraints upon domestic economic policies."

*c.*   "Balance of payments equilibrium will quickly result for all nations if their relative prices are in proper relationship to one another. The only systematic means of achieving these proper relationships is through a system of freely fluctuating exchange rates."

*d.*   "Monetarily, gold is a barbaric relic of the past which should be given no role in an efficient international monetary system."

## Selected References

Carlozzi, Nicholas: "Pegs and Floats: The Changing Face of the Foreign Exchange Market," *Business Review* (Federal Reserve Bank of Philadelphia), May–June, 1980, pp. 13–23.

*Economic Report of the President* (Washington). Annual reports contain a chapter on current international issues and policies.

Fried, Edward R., and Philip H. Trezise: "The United States in the World Economy," in Henry Owen and Charles L. Schultz (eds.), *Setting National Priorities: The Next Ten Years* (Washington: The Brookings Institution, 1976).

*IMF Survey,* current issues.

*International Economic Report of the President, 1977* (Washington).

Snider, Delbert A.: *Introduction to International Economics,* 7th ed. (Homewood, Ill.: Richard D. Irwin, Inc., 1979), chaps. 17–20.

Triffin, Robert: "The American Response to the European Monetary System," *Challenge,* March–April, 1980, pp. 17–25.

Wallich, Henry C.: "Evolution of the International Monetary System," *Challenge,* January–February, 1979, pp. 13–17.

# LAST WORD
## Multinational Corporations: For Good or Evil?

What have been the effects of the rapid growth of multinational corporations upon our domestic economy? Compare the following labor and business views.

*Labor's view: George Meany, President, AFL-CIO:*

. . . operations by American [multinational] companies obviously displace United States produced goods in both American markets and world markets. These companies export American technology—some of it developed through the expenditure of Government funds paid by American taxpayers. Their biggest export, of course, is United States jobs. . . .

The multinational firms can juggle their bookkeeping and their prices and their taxes. Their export and import transactions are within the corporation, determined by the executives of the corporation—all for the benefit and profit of the corporation. This is not foreign trade. Surely it is not foreign competition.

The complex operations of multinationals—with the aid of Madison Avenue advertising—have utterly confused the picture of national origin of products. For example, Ford's Pinto has been heralded as the U.S. answer to imported small cars. But the engines are imported from England and Germany, and the standard transmissions are imported from Europe.

This phenomenon is far different from the development of corporations here in America during the last 100 years. The multinational is not simply an American company moving to a new locality where the same laws apply and where it is still within the jurisdiction of Congress and the Government of the United States. This is a runaway corporation, going far beyond our borders. This is a runaway to a country with different laws, different institutions, and different labor and social standards. In most instances, even the name changes. . . .

Ironically, these are the same multinational corporations who have sought to influence U.S. trade legislation in the name of "free trade."

Meanwhile, back in the United States, expansion of large national corporations has been tempered to a degree by Government regulations, standards, and controls. And, in the past few decades, large U.S. corporations have had to meet responsibilities to their employees through labor unions. Moreover, the multinationals' global operations are beyond the reach of present U.S. law or the laws of any single nation.

*Business' view: Dr. N. R. Danielian, President, International Economic Policy Association:*

The multinational corporations are caught in the contradictions of our policies in defense, aid, and trade. Their alleged sins are now being decried among academicians, certain spokesmen of labor and even in ministerial conferences in Europe. These corporations are accused of exporting jobs; but they seldom receive credit for the jobs they create from exports—as in fact they produce one-fourth of the total U.S. exports with their shipments to their overseas affiliates.

The implication that "runaway" U.S. companies serve the U.S. market with cheap, foreign labor simply is inaccurate in all but a few cases. To take one example: Of the 1,321,000 foreign cars imported during 1970, only 123,299, or 9.3 percent, were made by U.S. subsidiaries abroad. The rest were Volkswagens, Toyotas, Fiats, and the like, all produced by foreign-owned companies. In the case of the 13 million short tons of iron and steel imported during 1970, hardly any could be attributed to American-owned subsidiaries abroad.

If all U.S. investments abroad were suddenly eliminated, the United States would be worse off by nearly $17 billion in its international receipts, two-thirds in exports and one-third in investment income, not including the $1.5 billion income from royalties and fees. As sympathetic as I am to labor's viewpoint in the matter of employment, I sincerely believe that they are whipping the wrong horse in attacking international or multinational corporations. Most of our imports come from foreign-owned enterprises; and if third-country markets could not be supplied by U.S. subsidiaries abroad, they would simply be supplied by foreign competitors. . . .

Many people, who should know better, blame American companies for the recent [international] currency crisis. Multinational corporations are in the business of manufacturing and selling products, not gambling with huge cash reserves. They would not be in business long if they speculated with a magnitude of liquid assets which could shake the foundations of the combined central banks of Europe.

From *Foreign Trade:* Hearings before the Subcommittee on International Trade of the Senate Committee on Finance, 91st Congress, 1st Session, Washington, 1971, pp. 169–171 and 126–127, abridged.

# The Economy of the Soviet Union

chapter **45**

Despite expanding economic relations, the negotiation of arms limitations agreements, and persistent hopes of achieving political détente, the fact remains that the United States and the Soviet Union are, and will continue to be, ideological and political rivals. Witness the comments of Party Secretary Mikhail A. Suslov:[1]

> We Communists have no illusions about the antipopular nature and policy of imperialism. . . . The assertion of the principles of peaceful coexistence in international affairs in no way signifies the weakening of the class struggle . . . or a "conciliation" between socialism and capitalism. . . . Now when the imperialists are increasingly realizing the impossibility of overthrowing socialism by force, this struggle is more frequently being transferred to the spheres of ideology, politics and economics.

[1] As quoted in Paul K. Cook, "The Political Setting," in Joint Economic Committee, *Soviet Economic Prospects for the Seventies* (Washington, 1973), p. 2.

We turn, then, in this final chapter to an analysis of this rival economy. We want to survey its institutions, understand its goals, evaluate its performance, and appreciate the challenge it poses for the West. There are two notable by-products of this endeavor. First, the Soviet economy is a fascinating case study in forced economic growth; the accomplishments and shortcomings of the Soviet system in vigorously pursuing economic growth provide invaluable lessons. Second, by examining an economy at the opposite end of the ideological spectrum, we cannot help but deepen our understanding of the capitalistic system.

## ☐ INSTITUTIONS OF THE COMMAND ECONOMY

There are two outstanding institutional characteristics of the Soviet economy: (1) state ownership of property resources, and (2) authoritarian central economic planning.

## △  State Ownership

The new Soviet constitution of 1977 makes the pervasiveness of public ownership of property resources quite clear:

> Socialist ownership of the means of production, in the form of state ownership (that of all the people) . . . is the foundation of the USSR's economic system. . . .
>
> The land, its mineral wealth, the waters and the forests are the exclusive property of the state.  The principal means of production in industry, construction and agriculture, means of transport and communication, banks, the property of trade, municipal-service and other enterprises organized by the state and the bulk of the urban housing stock, as well as other property necessary to carry out the state's tasks, belong to the state.

The Soviet state owns all land, natural resources, transportation and communication facilities, the banking system, and virtually all industry.  Most retail and wholesale enterprises and most urban housing are governmentally owned.  In agriculture many farms are state-owned; most, however, are government-organized collective farms, that is, essentially cooperatives to which the state assigns land "for free use for an unlimited time."  A near exception to state ownership is the small plot of land which each collective farm family has set aside for its personal use: "Citizens may have the use of plots of land . . . for auxiliary farming operations (including the keeping of livestock and poultry), the growing of fruit and vegetables, and also for individual housing construction."  And, of course, clothing, household furnishings, and small tools and implements used by craftsmen are privately owned.  Workers in rural areas and farmers typically own their homes, as do over one-third of all urban families.

## △  Central Economic Planning

Despite a highly democratic constitution, in practice the government of Soviet Russia is a strong dictatorship.  The Communist Party, although limited in membership to the most dedicated 4 or 5 percent of the total population, stands unchallenged.  Indeed, the party and the government can be regarded as virtually synonymous.

As the constitution makes clear, the Soviet economy is based upon central economic planning:

> The economy of the USSR is a single national-economic complex embracing all elements of social production, distribution, and exchange. . . .  Management of the economy is carried out on the basis of state plans of economic and social development. . . .

In contrast with the decentralized market economy of the United States, that of the Soviet Union is a centralized, "command" economy functioning in terms of a detailed economic plan.  The Soviet economy is government-directed rather than price-directed.

## △  Circumscribed Freedom

The dominant roles of state ownership and central planning correctly imply that it is not the free decisions of consumers and business-owners which determine the allocation of resources and the composition of total output in the Soviet Union.  Yet, subject to the restraints imposed by the central planners, consumers and laborers have a degree of free choice.

The concept of consumer sovereignty as we know it does not exist in the Soviet Union.  The preferences of individual consumers, as reflected in the size and structure of consumer demand, do *not* determine the volume and composition of consumer goods production in Soviet Russia; this determination is made by the government and implemented through the plan.  However, consumers are free to spend their money incomes as they see fit on those consumer goods for which the central plan provides.

Similarly, although the Soviet Union has a history of compulsory job assignment, harsh labor codes, and, in the extreme, slave labor, much greater reliance has been put upon free occupational choice in recent years. But again, there are overall restraints imposed by the central plan. The composition of output as determined by the plan establishes the number and kinds of jobs available. Then the government planners set wage rates so as to attract the needed number and types of workers to the various occupations. If the plan assigns great importance to steel and a low priority to shoes, jobs will be plentiful and wage rates established at a relatively high level in the steel industry. Conversely, few jobs will be available and wages will be relatively low in the shoe industry. In short, workers are largely free to change jobs in response to wage differentials; the differentials, however, are designed and manipulated to bring about an allocation of labor, both geographically and occupationally, which is consistent with the goals of the plan.

## ☐   CENTRAL PLANNING

Perhaps the most dramatic feature of the Soviet economy is its use of central planning. In the Soviet Union the means of answering the Five Fundamental Questions is central planning. Choices made primarily through the market in our United States economy must be consciously made by bureaucratic decision in the U.S.S.R. The overall character of the Soviet Five-year Plans has been succinctly described in these words:[2]

> The Soviet economic plan is a gigantic, comprehensive blueprint that attempts to govern the economic activities and interrelations of all persons and institutions in the U.S.S.R., as well as the economic relations of the U.S.S.R. with other countries. To the extent that the plan actually controls the development of events, all the manifold activities of the Soviet economy are coordinated as if they were parts of one incredibly enormous enterprise directed from the central headquarters in Moscow.

[2]Harry Schwartz, *Russia's Soviet Economy,* 2d ed. (Englewood Cliffs, N.J.: Prentice-Hall, Inc., 1954), p. 146.

Now let us probe below the surface. What are the goals of the plans? How are the plans constructed and implemented? What problems does central planning entail?

### △   Planning Goals

The Soviet government—in reality the Communist Party—sets the basic objectives for the Russian economy. These objectives have varied somewhat as succeeding Five-year Plans have been formulated, but emphasis has been upon rapid economic growth through the development of heavy industry. The attainment of a high level of military strength is a closely correlated goal. Lip service is invariably accorded the goal of a higher standard of living for consumers, but the lower priority assigned to this goal means that it is frequently sacrificed to achieve the objectives of industrial expansion and military strength.

### △   Basic Planning Problem: Coordination

It is no simple matter to sweep away the guiding function of the market system, as the Soviet Union has done, and replace it with an effective central plan. After all, we have found that the market system is a powerful organizing force which coordinates millions upon millions of individual decisions by consumers, entrepreneurs, and resource suppliers and fosters a reasonably efficient allocation of resources. Is central planning a satisfactory substitute for the market?

The core of the planning problem is revealed by the input-output table (Table 33-1). Input-output analysis, you will recall, reveals the highly interdependent character of the various industries or sectors of the economy. Each industry employs the outputs of other industries as its inputs; in turn its outputs are inputs to still other firms. This means that a planning decision to increase the production of machinery by, say, 10 percent is not a single, isolated directive, but rather, a decision which implies a myriad of related decisions for fulfillment. For example, in terms of Table 33-1, if planners do not make the related decisions to increase metal output by 6.5 units, fuel by 0.5 units, agricultural products by 1 unit, and to provide an extra 20 units of labor (not to mention additional second-round increases in all these inputs because 2.5 more inputs of machinery are also needed to increase machinery output!), bottlenecks will develop, and the planned increase in machinery output cannot be realized.

Let us look at the matter from a slightly different vantage point: Even if an internally consistent set of decisions—a perfectly coordinated plan—could be constructed by the central planners, the failure of any single industry to fulfill its output target would cause an almost endless chain of adverse repercussions. If iron mines—for want of machinery or labor or transportation inputs—fail to supply the steel industry with the required inputs of iron ore, the steel industry in turn will be unable to fulfill the input needs of the myriad of industries dependent upon steel. All these steel-using industries will be unable to fulfill their planned production goals. And so the bottleneck chain reaction goes on to all those firms which use steel parts or components as inputs.

It must be emphasized that our illustrative input-output table (Table 33-1) is a gross oversimplification of the problem of coordinating a command economy. There are now some 200,000 industrial enterprises producing goods in the Soviet Union. The central planners must see to it that all the resources needed by these enterprises to fulfill their assigned production targets are somehow allocated to them.[3]

> The literally billions of planning decisions that must be made to achieve consistency result in a complex and complete interlocking of macro- and micromanagement. . . . The number of planned interconnections increases more rapidly than the size of the economy. . . . Even with the

most sophisticated mathematical techniques and electronic computers, the task of interrelating demands and factor inputs for every possible item by every possible subcategory becomes impossible for the central planners alone.

△ **Coordination Techniques**

Despite the gargantuan character of the coordination problem, Soviet central planning has worked, and in some respects has functioned remarkably well. It is certainly legitimate to inquire: Why? What techniques do Soviet planners employ to achieve the level of coordination sufficient to make central planning workable? The answers lie substantially in the way the plans are constructed and implemented.

**1  Planning by Negotiation**  Given the overall economic objectives established by the Communist Party, it is the task of the State Planning Commission, or *Gosplan,* to construct a detailed economic blueprint designed to bring about the realization of these goals. In formulating a plan, the Gosplan collects voluminous amounts of statistical data from a host of subordinate ministries, each of which is concerned with the operation of certain industries. From these data, a tentative plan is constructed. The projected Five-year Plan is divided into Annual Plans, the latter being more relevant for actual operating purposes. The Annual Plan is then submitted to the various units of the Soviet administrative hierarchy for study, evaluation, and criticism. This criticism, it must be noted, concerns the specific details of the economic plan and anticipated problems in its fulfillment, not the overall goals which the plan seeks.

Let us illustrate this procedure. Note, first, that there are two obvious organizational alternatives for a planned economy: geographical (regional) and functional (industrial). All enterprises in a given region may be grouped for planning purposes, or all enterprises in a given industry may be grouped for planning regardless of their location. Over time the

[3]Barry M. Richman, *Soviet Management* (Englewood Cliffs, N.J.: Prentice-Hall, Inc., 1965), p. 17.

Soviet Union has used both alternatives and mixtures of the two. Currently the emphasis is upon the industrial approach; thus a number of countrywide ministries—for example, the ministries of construction, machine tools, automobiles, and tractors—are subordinate to Gosplan in the planning hierarchy. The important point is that relevant segments of the overall plan are submitted to the subordinate agencies, which exercise operational control. Thus the Annual Plan is evaluated at the industrywide level, by the trusts and combines—that is, groups of plants which are combined for administrative purposes—and ultimately by the individual plants or enterprises. At each level the plan is analyzed, suggestions are made for revision, and perhaps alterations are proposed in production goals or planned allocations of inputs. These evaluations are passed back up the planning hierarchy to Gosplan. Taking into account those suggestions and criticisms which it feels are worthy, Gosplan then draws up a final plan. When rubber-stamped by the party and the government, this becomes the official Annual Plan.

The point to be emphasized is this: By breaking the overall plan into its component parts and subjecting these detailed segments to considerable critical examination by subministries, combines, and plants, the Gosplan is able to establish a final plan which is more realistic and workable than would otherwise be the case. Soviet planners apparently recognize their limitations in obtaining and digesting masses of detailed information. The "down-and-up" evaluation of the tentative plan by the administrative hierarchy and its subsequent revision is aimed at obtaining on-the-spot knowledge and an understanding of immediate, detailed facts and circumstances which a relatively small group of planners could not otherwise grasp. To the extent that the resulting plan is more realistic and feasible, the chance is less that problems of coordination—in particular, bottlenecks—will arise to jeopardize plan fulfillment.

**2 Priority Principle** A second means of making central planning workable is embodied in the priority principle of resource allocation. Not all production goals established by Gosplan are held to be of equal importance. The goals of certain "leading links" sectors or industries (machinery, chemicals, steel) are given high priority; other industries (clothing, automobiles) in effect are assigned low priorities. Thus, when bottlenecks arise in the actual operation of the national plan, resources or inputs are shifted from low-priority to high-priority sectors of the economy. Coordination and plan fulfillment are sacrificed in low-priority production in order to maintain coordination and fulfill production targets in high-priority sectors. This accounts for the unevenness with which the goals of the various central plans have been fulfilled. Planned increases in housing and consumer goods are typically sacrificed to realize the planned increases in industrial and military goods production.

**3 Reserve Stocks** To some extent, coordination problems—bottlenecks and the chain reactions they precipitate—can be avoided by drawing upon reserve stocks of various inputs. Inventories, in other words, are used as a cushion or buffer to resolve specific bottlenecks or input deficiencies before they can trigger a chain of production shortfalls.

Although all these techniques contribute in varying degrees to the workability of Soviet central planning, they by no means ensure a high degree of efficiency. There is a great amount of evidence gathered from Soviet sources to indicate that bottlenecks do occur with rather alarming regularity. The result is frequent production stoppages and underfulfillment of production plans.[4]

△ **Executing the Plan: Control Agencies**

Setting up detailed production goals and making some provision for their internal bal-

[4]Ibid., p. 123.

ance are one thing; achieving those objectives may be something else again.

The Soviet government is not inclined to sit back, after each industrial plant and farm has been assigned its production targets, and hope for favorable results. On the contrary, an abundance of control agencies supervises the carrying out of each plan. Most obvious, of course, is the Gosplan and the various subordinate planning groups affiliated with it. These administrative units keep a running check on the progress of the plan. The Central Committee of the Communist Party and a variety of subordinate party organizations function as watchdog agencies by uncovering, reporting, and helping to correct deviations from the plan. The control functions of the infamous secret police are well known. And, too, a less formal type of control is exercised through a much-publicized program of "criticism and self-criticism," whereby the Soviet citizenry is encouraged to register complaints concerning deviations from, and violations of, the plan.

Perhaps the most vital enforcement agency is the state banking system, or *Gosbank*. The Gosbank, with its thousands of branches, supervises the financial aspects of each plant's production activities and in this manner has a running account of each plant's performance. More precisely, this supervision—called *control by the ruble*—works something like this: The government establishes prices on all resources and finished products. As a greatly simplified example, the Leningrad Machine Tool Plant may require 1000 tons of steel and 100 workers to produce 5000 units of output per year. If steel costs 60 rubles per ton and each worker is paid 1000 rubles per year, the total cost of the 5000 units of output will be 160,000 rubles. Gosplan then directs the Gosbank to make this amount of credit available to the plant over the course of the year. Now, because all the plant's financial transactions—both receipts and expenditures—must be completed through the use of checks, the Gosbank will have an accurate record (in effect, a running audit) of the plant's progress, or

lack thereof, in fulfilling the production targets assigned by the Five-year Plan. Should the plant achieve its assigned output at an expense less than 160,000 rubles, it will have overfulfilled its production goal. Inefficient, wasteful production will cause the plant to exhaust its bank credit before its production goal is reached. Either eventuality will be reflected in the plant's account with the Gosbank.

△ **Incentives**

How are the various economic units motivated toward fulfillment of the Annual Plan? A combination of monetary and nonmonetary incentives, on the one hand, and coercive techniques, on the other, are employed to this end.

**Monetary Incentives**   The Soviet government relies quite heavily upon monetary incentives to obtain the maximum productive effort from labor. In particular, wages are geared to skill and productivity. The resulting wage differentials are considerable. Great emphasis is put upon piecework, more so than in the United States. Probably as much as four-fifths of the Soviet labor force works under a piecework plan of one sort or another. Elaborate systems of bonuses and premiums induce workers to exceed normal production rates. However, in the last two decades there has been a narrowing of wage differentials in the Soviet Union, the impact of which upon incentives is not clear. Keep in mind, too, that Soviet income receivers, though not free to determine the portion of total output which is to take the form of consumer goods, are able to spend their incomes as they wish on the consumer goods which the Gosplan makes available to them. This means that differences in money incomes are generally reflected in real income differentials.

**Nonmonetary Incentives**   A variety of nonmonetary inducements also exist to stimulate labor to greater productivity. A rather comprehensive system of awards and decorations exists to cite exemplary workers. These are closely correlated with material rewards. For example, a "Hero of Socialist Labor" is likely to be accorded certain tax exemptions, monthly bonuses, low rental on state housing, free use of transportation facilities, government-supplied vacations at a Crimean resort, and so forth. The real standard of living of the average Soviet citizen is roughly half that of an American counterpart, so that the value of such benefits is considerable. Much publicity accompanies these awards. A member of the "Order of Lenin" may enjoy fame and prestige comparable to that of a professional baseball player or movie star in the United States. In addition, "socialist competitions" are encouraged by the party, pitting the productive capacities of various groups of workers against one another.

The labor unions to which the vast majority of Soviet workers belong bear little or no resemblance to their American counterparts. In effect, Russian labor unions are essentially functionaries of the state; their basic goals are to encourage a high level of productivity among their members in carrying out the economic plan, to train new workers, to aid in the solution of labor discipline problems, and to administer the social security system. Wage rates are set by the government; collective bargaining as we know it does not exist; and strikes simply do not occur. Soviet labor unions do, however, prevent undue exploitation of their members by plant managers eager to fulfill their assigned production quotas. They also play an active role in providing recreational and cultural programs for workers.

**Coercion**  Monetary and nonmonetary inducements are duly supplemented by a variety of coercive techniques. (Indeed, the old Soviet constitution of 1936 flatly stated that, "Work in the U.S.S.R. is a duty and a matter of honor for every able-bodied citizen, in accordance with the principle 'He who does not work, neither shall he eat.'") But labor discipline has at times been very poor: absenteeism, tardiness, and worker indifference are common

problems. The rate of labor turnover has also been a major difficulty. Plant managers frequently "pirate" the personnel of one another to ensure a labor force adequate for fulfillment of their output targets. Workers seem very willing to change jobs, however slight the resulting improvement in their standard of living might be. The net result is a chronic problem of low levels of labor productivity.

Soviet authorities have taken action to cope with such problems. Fines, pay reductions, dismissal, eviction from state housing, the freezing of workers to their jobs, and discriminatory treatment with respect to social insurance benefits all hang over the head of the bungling, the lazy, the indifferent, and the overly mobile worker. In extreme cases, "spies" and "wreckers," along with political dissidents, may be subject to the wrath of the secret police and assigned to "correctional labor camps" in Siberia or similarly remote areas. The Last Word section of this chapter is a grim reminder of this aspect of Soviet society.

Comparable monetary and nonmonetary inducements and compulsory techniques bear upon plant managers. High salaries, bonuses, awards, and promotion await those who fulfill their production targets. Failure exposes the plant manager to investigation and reassignment to a less palatable position. A good many plant managers are party members and therefore inspired by party doctrines.

△ **Planning and Prices**

Let us now look at the way in which prices have been traditionally used in Soviet planning. Then we shall examine some important microeconomic shortcomings of Soviet planning and relatively recent reforms designed to meet these problems.

To say that the Soviet system is a command economy rather than a market economy is not to say that prices have no role to play in the centrally planned system. Although Soviet prices are not employed as a guiding mechanism in determining the structure of output, they are used in *implementing* the production objectives established by the state. *Soviet prices are government-manipulated to aid in the achievement of state-established goals; capitalistic prices, although often subject to serious market imperfections, are more market-oriented and more sensitive to individual wants.*

Actually, the function of prices in the Soviet Union has differed considerably between the production process, on the one hand, and the sale of final products to consumers, on the other. In the first instance, prices are merely accounting devices which facilitate checking the efficiency with which products are manufactured. In the latter case, prices are employed as rationing devices to distribute products to consumers without the use of government rationing.

**Producer Prices**  In producing, say, a television set, a Soviet plant will be faced with certain governmentally established prices for component parts, labor, and other needed resources. And, similarly, the government will determine the price of the final product. Generally speaking, the basic principle in establishing these prices is that a plant or an industry of average efficiency would realize total receipts from its production which will cover its total costs and yield a "planned profit" of 5 to 10 percent. If production is less efficient than that deemed average by the plan, planned profits will not be achieved and losses may result. Greater-than-average efficiency will result in unplanned profits.[5] In short, the prices of resources and components are used as accounting costs to assess the efficiency with which various plants and industries operate. Except for the fact that capitalistic prices are essentially market-determined rather than government-determined, this role of the Soviet

price system parallels that of its capitalistic counterpart. But here—for two reasons—the similarity ends.

**1**  In a capitalistic economy, losses call for a contraction of output and a release of resources by the affected industry; profits signal industry expansion and the absorption of resources. Not so in the Soviet Union. Expansion and contraction of industry are determined by the government, not by the price system. Therefore, a relatively inefficient industry which is considered vital by the state may be expanded despite losses. Similarly, a highly efficient, profit-realizing industry may be purposely contracted by state planning.

**2**  Despite market imperfections, input prices in a capitalistic system should reflect with some reasonable degree of accuracy the relative scarcity of resources and their value in alternative uses. Thus, to minimize money costs in the production of a product is to minimize real costs, that is, to get a given good produced with a minimum sacrifice of alternative goods (Chapter 26). But in the Soviet Union prices are governmentally determined and therefore do not accurately reflect the relative scarcity of resources. Hence, the minimization of money costs in a Soviet enterprise does not mean that real costs of production are being minimized.

**Consumer Prices**  Whereas prices in the production process are essentially accounting devices used to gauge plan fulfillment, the prices of finished goods are established to serve as rationing devices. In other words, the government attempts to set consumer goods prices at levels which will clear the market so there will be no persistent shortages or surpluses. As a result, the price of television sets which is used for accounting purposes may vary considerably from the price which is charged consumers who purchase them. The difference typically takes the form of what the Russians call a *turnover tax,* which is very roughly similar to an excise tax.

To illustrate: Suppose the accounting

---

[5]For the most part, these profits will accrue to the government as revenue from state-owned enterprises. A part may be used to expand the industry, if such expansion is consistent with the objectives of the plan. Another portion may be shared by the plant's workers and executives as a bonus for their efficiency.

price of a finished television set is 200 rubles. This price is used by the Gosplan in judging the efficiency of the assembly plant. But because of the low priority assigned to consumer goods, consumer demand in the Soviet Union has persistently exceeded the available supply of many consumer goods. This means that, if shortages and government rationing are to be avoided, the price charged by the state in selling television sets to consumers must be higher than the accounting price. Suppose the government estimates that the consumer price of television sets must be 400 rubles to bring the quantity demanded into balance with the quantity available. This is accomplished by adding a 100 percent turnover tax to television sets. At this price the market will be cleared and government rationing avoided.

Turnover taxes—which, incidentally, are the major source of government revenue in Russia—vary widely among various products. High turnover taxes on particularly scarce goods greatly discourage their consumption and force the amounts demanded into accord with the modest quantities allowed by the plan. Lower rates on abundantly available consumer staples—for example, potatoes and certain other vegetables—encourage their consumption. In general, the greater the relative scarcity of a product, the higher the turnover tax placed upon it. The total prices of such products will necessarily be higher and purchases discouraged. Lower tax rates on more abundant products give them lower relative prices and encourage their consumption. In this way inflation-causing income is taxed away, and the pattern of consumer spending is forced into rough accord with the planned composition of consumer goods output. Furthermore, the use of differential turnover tax rates tends to make *real* income differentials less than *money* income differentials. That is, turnover taxes tend to be higher on "luxury goods" than on "necessities."[6]

[6]For a discussion of Soviet pricing, see Morris Bornstein, "The Soviet Price System" in Morris Bornstein (ed.), *Comparative Economic Systems: Models and Cases* (Homewood, Ill.: Richard D. Irwin, Inc., 1965), pp. 278–309.

## ☐ RECENT PROBLEMS AND REFORMS

Let us now review some of the operational difficulties of Soviet planning and summarize recent economic reforms designed to resolve these problems.

### △ Microeconomic Problems

As the Soviet economy has grown and become more sophisticated and complex, detailed central planning has encountered rather severe microeconomic problems.

In the first place, lacking a genuine price system to communicate the wants of consumers and producers, central planners have frequently directed enterprises to produce goods for which there is little or no demand. The result is unwanted inventories of unsalable goods. Secondly, the major "success indicator" for Soviet enterprise managers has been the quantity of output; the enterprise's main goal is to fulfill or overfulfill its assigned production target. Production costs and product quality are secondary considerations at best. Indeed, planners have found it very difficult to state a quantitative production target without unintentionally eliciting ridiculous "distortions" in output. Example: If an enterprise manufacturing nails has its production target stated in terms of weight (tons of nails), it will tend to produce all large nails. But if its target is a numerical one (thousands of nails), it will be motivated to produce all small nails! Furthermore, the Soviet press persistently denounces the poor quality of both consumer goods and many producer goods. Least-cost production is virtually impossible in the absence of a system of genuine prices which accurately reflect the relative scarcity of the various resources. Finally, Soviet enterprise managers have been highly resistant to innovation. Managers are more concerned with "bargaining" for realistic production targets and fulfilling their output goals so that they can achieve bonuses. New production processes invariably mean higher and often unrealistic targets, underfulfillment, and loss of bonuses.

## △  **Reforms of 1965: Libermanism**

The Soviet government responded to these problems by introducing important reforms in 1965. The reforms stem in large measure from the proposals of Professor E. Liberman of Kharkov University and are sometimes referred to as "Libermanism." The reforms called for the introduction of a modified "profit motive" as the primary success indicator in an enterprise; for greater decentralization of decision making and greater autonomy for enterprise managers; and for some degree of "planning from below."

Under the reforms, enterprises can take orders from customers (retailers or other enterprises) which specify the types (colors, sizes, styles) and amounts of each product. This "planning from below" provides "direct links" to consumer or producer demand and is obviously designed to bring about a better matching of output with the structure of demand. Management also negotiates with other firms for the purchase of needed inputs. Furthermore, the management of each enterprise has restricted authority in setting prices, including rates of pay for its labor force.

The enterprise's major success indicator was no longer to be physical output, but rather, "profitability" calculated in relation to the fixed and working capital of the enterprise. The management and labor force of an enterprise were to receive bonuses in direct relation to profitability. This reorientation of goals meant that enterprises would be penalized for the production of goods which were unsalable because they were of shoddy quality or, in the case of producer goods, because they did not fit the input requirements of purchasing enterprises. That is, enterprises must be concerned not only with production, but also with the sale of output. Moreover, the emphasis upon profitability means that greater attention should be paid to production costs and technological improvements.

But the performance of the Soviet economy did not improve significantly in the post-1965 period and the Soviet government has tended to back away from the reforms. In fact, the cards were stacked against the reforms from the start. On the one hand, there is strong ideological resistance to market-oriented reforms. "Old guard" central planners regard the market as alien to the system, contrary to the tasks of central planning, and a threat to the existing power structure. On the other hand, piecemeal modifications—such as the 1965 reforms—are almost doomed to failure.

> . . . the system has an inner logic which resists *partial* change. Thus if one frees an industry—say clothing—from central control, then what would happen to the industries which provide it with inputs? Unless they too responded to market stimuli (i.e., based their production on orders from the clothing industry), there would be acute problems in ensuring that they produce what is needed. The traditional system ensured—though imperfectly—that the central planners transmitted the input requirements in the form of production and delivery instructions, backed (most of the time) by the necessary inputs for the input-providing enterprises, and so on. A missing link in this chain disrupts the system. Consequently, the easiest way out of the resulting confusion would be to put the clothing industry back into the centralized system.[7]

The fact is that the Soviet economy remains one wherein central planning is paramount and the associated microeconomic problems persist.

## ☐  **SOVIET ECONOMIC GROWTH**

In view of our foregoing discussion of the Soviet Union's microeconomic problems, it is fair to say that the system has been quite unsuccessful in realizing the goal of allocative efficiency. But we know there are other measures in terms of which an economy's performance might be judged. The alternative and essentially macroeconomic goal which has been paramount with the Soviet leadership is *rapid* economic growth. Soviet Russia has pursued

---

[7] Alec Nove, *The Soviet Economic System* (London: George Allen & Unwin, Ltd., 1977), pp. 313–314.

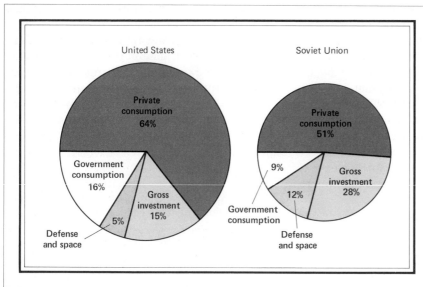

**FIGURE 45-1 SIZE AND COMPOSITION OF GNP IN THE UNITED STATES AND THE SOVIET UNION**

Soviet Russia's GNP is roughly one-half the size of the United State's GNP.  As compared with the United States, the Soviet Union puts relatively greater emphasis on investment goods than on consumer goods. [Imogene Edwards, Margaret Hughes, and James Noven, "U.S. and U.S.S.R.:  Comparisons of GNP," in *Soviet Economy in a Time of Change* (Washington, D.C.:  U.S. Printing Office, 1979, pp. 391–392; and *Economic Report of the President*, 1980 (Washington, D.C.:  U.S. Printing Office, 1980), p. 203.)

with great vigor the goal of rapid growth and the political-military strength derived therefrom. These two concepts of efficiency may be in conflict in certain important ways.[8] In particular, because Soviet planning seeks very rapid growth, it results in highly ambitious production targets and the overcommitment of resources. And ambitious targets and over-committed resources are the source of many of the coordination problems discussed earlier. In any event, we know that historically the Soviet economy has performed well in terms of the objective of growth. Let us now consider the rate of growth achieved by the Soviet Union, the sources of this growth, and the prospect of its maintenance.

△   **Growth Comparisons**

Authoritative estimates put the Soviet GNP at slightly more than one-half that of the United States. Figure 45-1 shows this relationship and indicates the relative composition of the national outputs of the two nations.

Experts also agree that the Soviet growth rate has generally exceeded that of the United States in the post-World War II period as a whole. For the 1948–1974 period the Soviet Union's annual growth rate was 5.9 percent as compared with 3.6 percent for the United States. But there is evidence of convergence in recent years: Soviet annual growth was 4.9 percent in the 1960–1974 period, while the United States enjoyed a 3.8 percent rate. Both economies performed poorly in the first half of the 1970s as reflected in a 3.5 percent annual rate for the Soviet Union and a 2 percent rate here at home.[9]

△   **Sources of Soviet Growth**

Let us first pinpoint certain factors which have contributed to the Soviet Union's historically high growth rates.

**1   Natural Resource Base**   The Soviet Union has a generous and varied natural resource base. Although they differ significantly

[8]The interested reader should consult Albert O. Hirschman, *The Strategy of Economic Development* (New Haven, Conn.: Yale University Press, 1959).

[9]Herbert Block, "Soviet Economic Power Growth—Achievements under Handicaps," in Joint Economic Committee, *Soviet Economy in a New Perspective* (Washington, 1976), p. 268.

in composition, it is not inaccurate to say that the natural resource endowments of the U.S.S.R. are roughly comparable with those of the United States. There are two major exceptions to this generalization. First, U.S. agricultural resources are much superior to those of the U.S.S.R. Much of the Soviet Union's most fertile soil lies in regions susceptible to drought and short growing seasons. The Soviets are much more vulnerable to substantial fluctuations in agricultural output. Second, the Soviet Union is the world's only major industrial nation which is self-sufficient in energy. Whether this will persist, as we shall note later, is a matter of some controversy.

**2   Totalitarianism and Allocation**   Because the Soviet Union is a totalitarian state, the government can and does exercise tight political control over the allocation of resources. That the government has, with little hesitation or reservation, exerted a strong and often brutal "will to develop" is reflected in its efforts to indoctrinate, regiment, push and prod its citizenry, and structure its institutions to the overriding goal of economic growth. The Soviet economy has aptly been described as "totalitarianism harnessed to the task of rapid industrialization and economic growth."[10]   To be more specific, we may say that the will to develop has been expressed most explicitly in the high-volume and growth-oriented composition of Soviet investment. The Soviet Union devotes about 28 percent of its total output to investment, compared with 15 percent for the United States (Figure 45-1). Furthermore, the composition of Soviet investment has put emphasis upon those industries most crucial to the growth process. Retail and wholesale distributional facilities, for example, have been largely ignored in favor of steel, petroleum, chemicals, and machine tools.

**3   Surplus Farm Labor**   You may recall from Chapter 21 that it is characteristic of

[10] Robert W. Campbell, *The Soviet-type Economies,* 3d ed. (Boston: Houghton Mifflin Company, 1974), p. 3.

underdeveloped countries to have a sizable amount of surplus or underemployed labor in agriculture. This was true of the Soviet Union at the time of the revolution. Under central planning, much of this low-productivity farm labor was shifted to newly created industries, where its productivity was substantially higher. In 1925, 84 percent of the Soviet labor force was in agriculture; currently, about 25 percent are so employed. This reallocation has resulted in significant increases in the Soviet GNP.

**4   Technological Gap**   Rapid expansion in Soviet production has stemmed in good measure from the adoption of the superior technological knowledge pioneered by the Western nations. The Soviet Union has eagerly, unashamedly, and quite effectively borrowed and skillfully applied the superior techniques of other nations. In this manner, the U.S.S.R. has quickly and very inexpensively bridged a long period of research and development activity in many key industries.

**5   Full Employment**   The Soviet economy's growth rate, unlike those of the United States and other capitalistic nations, has benefited in that, since about 1930, Soviet economic planning has virtually eliminated cyclical unemployment. Unlike the United States, the Soviet Union has *not* had to count years of zero or negative growth due to recession in calculating its long-term rate of growth.

△   **Retarding Factors**
Why has the Soviet growth rate diminished? What growth-retarding forces have come into play since the late 1960s?

**1   Diversion of Resources**   A frequently cited reason for the slowing down of Soviet growth is that expanding defense expenditures in recent years have diverted resources from more growth-effective uses. In particular, growing defense outlays have caused declines in both the quantity and quality of industrial investment. Rising defense expenditures have become an "onerous burden" upon the Soviet economy because of their direct competitiveness with civilian investment and therefore economic growth. Furthermore, the "policy of channeling superior management and the best scientists and engineers into defense research and production denies prime innovative resources to civilian oriented investment"[11] and has adversely affected technological progress and the quality (productivity) of investment in the civilian sector.

The "onerous burden" hypothesis may apply not only to the military, but also to the consuming sector:[12]

> Soviet leaders are finding it increasingly difficult to reject or postpone the satisfaction of consumers' wants. Revolutionary enthusiasm, it is said, no longer is sufficient to make sacrifices of consumer welfare acceptable either to the population at large or to many Communist Party members and leaders. The very sizable improvements that have been made in consumer welfare in recent years have not relieved universal dissatisfaction with living conditions, but rather may have whetted the general appetite for further gains.

It is significant that in the 1970s the Soviet Union spent billions of dollars to import grain when its domestic harvests were low. These grain purchases were financed with funds which otherwise would have been used primarily to import capital goods.

The basic point is that emphasis upon military production and the need to improve living standards has made it difficult for the Soviet Union to sustain the high levels of investment which have been a key factor in its past growth.

**2   Labor Shortage**   Whereas much of the Soviet Union's earlier growth was attributable to shifts of surplus labor from agriculture to industry, the Soviet Union is finding it increasingly difficult to make additional labor shifts without significantly imperiling the output of an already troubled agricultural sector. Indeed, the overall picture in the Soviet Union is now one of labor scarcity. Shortages of labor reflect both the dramatic manpower losses associated with World War II and the declining birthrates which have accompanied urbanization. Estimates suggest that the decline in the number of new labor force entrants is destined to become more acute in the early and mid-1980s. The basic point is that the relatively easy means of increasing GNP by employing more labor inputs is less available to the Soviets; they are faced with the more demanding task of expanding their GNP by increasing labor productivity, that is, output per worker.

**3   Agricultural Drag**   By Western standards Soviet agriculture is something of a monument to inefficiency and now constitutes a drag upon economic growth, engulfing as it does some 25 percent of the labor force. The low productivity of Soviet agriculture is attributable to many factors: the relative scarcity of good land; vagaries in rainfall and length of growing season; the limited use of chemical fertilizers; serious errors in planning and administration; and perhaps most important, the failure to construct an effective incentive system. Given the relatively large size of the agricultural sector, a poor growing season can have highly adverse effects upon the Soviet growth rate. For example, the poor harvest of 1975 was a major factor in pulling that year's growth rate down to 2.5 percent.

**4   Productivity Slowdown**   It is estimated that growth in Soviet labor productivity fell by nearly one-half between the 1960s and the first half of the 1970s.[13] There are two

---

[11]Stanley H. Cohn, "General Growth Performance of the Soviet Economy," in Joint Economic Committee, *Economic Performance and the Military Burden in the Soviet Union* (Washington, 1970), p. 12.
[12]Terence E. Byrne, "Recent Trends in the Soviet Economy," in ibid., p. 5.

[13]Joint Economic Committee, *Soviet Economic Problems and Prospects* (Washington, D.C., 1977), p. 3.

predominant reasons for this slowdown. First, the Soviet Union may now have reached the stage of development where it must resort increasingly to inferior and less accessible natural resources. In particular, ores, fuels, electric power, and timber are becoming increasingly costly, largely because reserves in the industrialized western Soviet Union are being depleted, and it is very costly to develop resources in Siberia and Central Asia for existing industrialized areas. The CIA has made a controversial forecast that the Soviet Union's previously noted self-sufficiency in energy will soon end and it will shift from being an exporter to an importer of oil. This would mean that an important source of foreign exchange for the purchase of productivity-increasing capital goods and technology from the West would disappear.

The second main factor contributing to the productivity slowdown are previously discussed planning problems. These problems are linked in part to the development of the Soviet economy itself. Early planning under Stalin was not unlike the wartime planning of Western nations: A limited number of key production goals were established, and resources were centrally directed toward the fulfillment of these goals regardless of costs or consumer welfare. But the past success of such "campaign planning" has resulted in a complex, industrially advanced economy. The planning techniques which were more-or-less adequate for the Stalinist era are less efficient in the more sophisticated economy of the 1970s and 1980s. To state the situation quite simply, the Soviet economy has tended to outgrow its planning mechanisms. This fact has posed serious questions concerning the allocative efficiency of the system and its capacity to sustain its growth rate. And, as we shall see momentarily, Soviet planning has not performed well in devising incentives which effectively stimulate innovation and technological progress. Evidence of Party awareness of planning deficiencies is reflected in the more-or-less contin-

uous restructuring of the production hierarchy.[14]

△  **Future Growth**

What of the future? Will the Soviet growth rate persist at comparatively low levels? Or will the rather spectacular rates of the 1950s be reachieved?

There is some agreement that Soviet growth would be accelerated if (1) military production were curtailed and scientific-technical personnel, along with other strategic resources, were reallocated to civilian uses; (2) planning institutions and managerial mechanisms were simplified and improved; and (3) commercial relationships with capitalistic nations were expanded to facilitate the transfer of superior technology to the Soviet Union. On the last point, it is acknowledged that a basic motivation behind growing Soviet trade with the Western economies is to acquire high-technology plants and equipment. "Soviet leaders hope that imported plant and equipment embodying advanced Western technology will permit rapid growth of selected key outputs, raise the productivity of labor and capital, and provide spinoff examples that can spread widely throughout the Soviet economy."[15]

But there are serious obstacles to realizing these three means of growth. Improved economic performance may call for a higher degree of ideological and bureaucratic flexibility than currently prevails in the U.S.S.R.:[16]

Deemphasis of the military and heavy industry run counter to the entrenched interests of important segments of the Soviet elite. Significant

[14] See, for example, Alice C. Gorlin, "Industrial Reorganization: The Associations," in Joint Economic Committee, *Soviet Economy in a New Perspective* op. cit., pp. 162–188.
[15] Holland Hunter, M. Mark Earle, Jr., and Richard B. Foster, "Assessment of Alternative Long-Range Soviet Growth Strategies," in Joint Economic Committee, ibid., p. 200.
[16] John P. Hardt, "Summary," in Joint Economic Committee, *Soviet Economic Prospects for the Seventies* (Washington, 1973), p. xvii.

changes in planning and management would result in a diffusion or redirection of economic power and control in the Soviet system. Thus the economic role of the Party might be at stake. Changes in relations between the Soviet economy and the non-Communist world might mean renouncing the Stalinist concept of autarky and isolation and joining the international commercial and financial community. Thus, the political costs for improved economic performance might be high, perhaps too high.

It is also recognized that the Soviet planning hierarchy and incentive system are resistant to the technological progress needed by the economy to restore its vitality.

> The bureaucratic immobility of the Soviet decision-making mechanism smothers a great deal of the volatility present in a normal market economy. Established procedures regularly grind out standard forms of output, while conventional methods enlarge capital stocks embodying orthodox technology. This stability has, of course, its advantages, but it also means that unfavorable conditions and unsatisfactory performance are hard to remedy. Where new procedures are required in order to produce new forms of output involving altered capital stocks embodying unfamiliar technology, the Soviet system responds poorly. The rewards and penalties that motivate Soviet managers and workers serve admirably to replicate and enlarge the existing economy. These same rewards and penalties act negatively, however, with the effect of protecting the system against changes—even if the needed changes are improvements.[17]

Thus a recent authoritative research study concludes, "The gradual decline in output growth rates since 1958 . . . seems destined to continue in the future. . . . The slacking off of labor-force increments, declining effectiveness of capital investment, and other forces underlying the tapering growth of the last 15 years, cast their influence forward into the baseline projection for the coming 15 years as

well." The study's basic prediction is that Soviet real GNP will grow at 3.7 percent per year in the 1980–1985 period, and at only 3.3 percent over 1985–1990.[18] *If* these projections turn out to be correct, they will reflect a marked slowdown in Soviet growth. On the other hand, the projected rates are quite comparable to those recently achieved by industrially advanced capitalistic nations (Table 20–2).

## ☐   GENERAL EVALUATION

Our discussion thus far has centered upon central planning and the growth performance which planning has fostered. A more complete evaluation of the Soviet system calls for the consideration of several other accomplishments and shortcomings.

### △   Accomplishments

**1   Education**   Though circumscribed by Communist doctrine and shaped in terms of government goals, Soviet Russia has made tremendous strides in increasing the quantity and quality of education. Free public education has been a high-priority goal of the Soviet regime from the outset. Much has also been done to encourage cultural pursuits, again within limits imposed by the party.

**2   Economic Security**   In keeping with socialist tradition, the Soviet Union has developed a quite complete system of social insurance. Medical care is virtually free and disability and sick leave benefits are provided, as are maternity benefits. Rental payments are heavily subsidized and amount to only about 4 or 5 percent of a worker's income. Retirement pensions are available for industrial workers and have recently been extended to collective farmers. Although benefit payments are not overly generous by American standards, they are sufficient in terms of the Soviet standard of living.

---

[17]Hunter, op. cit., p. 212.

[18]Ibid., p. 203.

△ **Shortcomings**

Generally speaking, the major shortcomings of the Soviet system are the offspring of its accomplishments. Two major points merit emphasis.

**1   Standard of Living**   The costs of rapid industrialization and economic growth have been great, and have been borne for the most part by consumers. This is reflected in both the quantity and quality of Soviet consumer goods. Living standards are much lower than in the United States:[19]

> Soviet city life is similar to life in Western cities fifty years ago. People live in crowded apartments, use public transportation, wear drab clothing, and eat a starchy diet. . . . Soviet rural life compares with still earlier European experience, though the presence of large machinery and trucks hampers comparison. The general pattern in both city and country is still "old fashioned," yet elements of modernization run all through it.

Recent improvements in the Soviet standard of living have been significant. For example, during the first eight years of the Brezhnev regime (1965–1972), per capita consumption rose by 5 percent per year, in contrast to 3 percent per year in the Khrushchev era (1956–1964). Unfortunately, the recent overall decline in the Soviet growth rate has had adverse effects upon consumption. In the 1971–1975 period the average annual growth rate for consumption has fallen back to about 3 percent. As far as the consumer is concerned, the Soviet Union is far from being a society of abundance.

**2   Freedom**   The decisions which determine the overall economic, political, social, and cultural environment are made by the Soviet dictatorship. Only within governmentally prescribed limits is individual freedom tolerated.

Consumers and wage earners are "free" to choose from the goods and jobs that planners decide to provide. In general, artists and writers must conform to the party line in their creative efforts. The confinement, harassment, and ultimate expulsion of writer Aleksandr Solzhenitsyn vividly illustrate the Soviet system's intolerance of dissident voices.

It must be emphasized that the Soviet Union, viewed in broader perspective, is a dictatorship based ultimately upon coercion, terror, or the effective threat thereof. Though there has been a general relaxation of the tensions which surrounded Stalinist tyranny, the threat of force is omnipresent. Elections are a farce, the press is essentially a propaganda organ of the government, and the role of the secret police in maintaining allegiance and conformity continues to be substantial.[20]

☐ **THE CONVERGENCE HYPOTHESIS**

Some economists envision a long-term decline in the differences between the capitalistic and communistic systems. Certain fundamental forces, they argue, are at work to promote convergence. The essence of the *convergence hypothesis* is that as capitalistic and communistic systems evolve, they encounter experiences and problems which induce the adoption of similar institutions and policies. That is, industrialization results in the reallocation of population from rural to urban areas; in greater education and concern for consumer welfare; in greater dependence upon technology and innovation; and so forth. Regardless of ideology, these developments induce behavioral patterns, values, and even institutional changes which tend to make the two types of economies increasingly similar.

---

[19]Clair Wilcox, Willis D. Weatherford, Jr., Holland Hunter, and Morton S. Baratz, *Economies of the World Today,* 3d ed. (New York: Harcourt Brace Jovanovich, Inc., 1976), pp. 126–127.

[20]For a short study of the history and strategy of communism, the reader should consult Andrew Gyorgy, *Communism in Perspective* (Boston: Allyn and Bacon, Inc., 1964). Andrei D. Sakharov's *Progress, Coexistence, and Intellectual Freedom* (New York: W. W. Norton & Company, Inc., 1968) is also of great interest. Sakharov, who was largely responsible for the development of Russia's atomic bomb, appeals to the party to democratize the Soviet system. The Soviet government exiled Sakharov from Moscow in early 1980.

Consider the communistic systems. As they develop economically, complex problems arise with respect to allocative efficiency. To deal with such problems, these systems turn more and more to the use of markets and prices. Recall that the Soviet reforms of the 1960s put greater reliance upon the "profitability" of output. And other communistic systems, Yugoslavia, for example, have gone much further than the Soviet Union in upgrading the role of the price system in their economies. Conversely, as capitalistic systems evolve, the public sector becomes increasingly important; government plays a more active role in economic affairs. The provision of social goods and governmental modification of the price system for significant externalities become commonplace. Government also provides a welfare system to temper income inequality and ensure against various personal risks. Finally, government's responsibility to "manage" the economy so as to avoid severe economic instability is well accepted and, more recently, incomes policies have become commonplace. Indeed, some economies of the West—of France, for example—have adopted a loose form of central planning. In short, the argument is that the imperfections of the communistic economies call for a reduced governmental role and increased reliance upon prices and markets, while the shortcomings of capitalistic economies demand less reliance upon the market system and an expanded public sector. The net result is convergence. To promote greater economic efficiency and improve the well-being of their populations, the two systems edge their way toward some common middle ground between the extremes of laissez faire capitalism and authoritarian central planning.

There may well be an important element of truth to the convergence hypothesis. But differences between the two systems are immense and, in fact, evidence of movement toward convergence may be more apparent than real. For example, some economists point out that the Soviet reforms of the 1960s were designed to strengthen central planning and not to move the economy in the direction of a market system. Furthermore, there is little or no evidence of convergence with respect to certain basic institutional features, such as property ownership. In the Soviet Union, state ownership is not merely a matter of economic ideology, but also a means of political control. That is, to permit the private ownership of farmland and capital would be to diminish political control over a large portion of the Soviet population. There is no evidence that such a dramatic institutional change is in the thinking of the Soviet leadership. Similarly, while the issue of public versus private ownership of large-scale enterprises is open to debate, there is little question on economic grounds that small-scale enterprises should be privately owned. Yet the Soviet Union shows no inclination to move toward private small-scale enterprises. Finally, basic and perhaps insurmountable differences remain between East and West in noneconomic spheres. The nature of the political state, the sources of its power, and the relationship between the individual and the state are viewed in fundamentally different ways in the ideologies of East and West. In brief, there may be forces working toward convergence, but its realization may be far beyond the horizon.

## Summary

1 The vivid contrast which the Soviet economy provides to American capitalism, the economic challenge it presents to the Western world, and the rapid economic growth achieved in Soviet Russia are important reasons for studying the Soviet economic system.

**2**   Virtually complete state ownership of property resources and authoritarian central planning are the outstanding institutional features of the Soviet economy.  The major goals of the Five-year Plans, as determined by the government, have been rapid industrialization, growth and military strength.

**3**   The basic problem of central planners is to achieve coordination or internal consistency in their plans so as to avoid bottlenecks and the chain reaction of production failures which they cause.  The evaluation of preliminary plans by the administrative hierarchy, the assignment of priorities to planned goals, and reserve stocks are used to prevent or alleviate coordination problems in the U.S.S.R.

**4**   Many agencies check upon the actual execution of the Five-year Plans—the planning hierarchy, the Communist Party and its numerous officials, and the secret police.  The most important of these agencies is the Gosbank, which exerts "control by the ruble."

**5**   In the production process, governmentally determined prices on resources and components and on finished products serve as accounting devices to evaluate the efficiency of production.  In consumer goods markets, prices are adjusted through the turnover tax to ration products to consumers, that is, to balance the amount demanded with available supplies.

**6**   As the Soviet economy has become more complex, certain microeconomic problems—the production of unwanted goods, a distorted product-mix, and resistance to innovation—have developed.  The 1965 reforms, emphasizing profitability of production, "planning from below," and greater decentralization of decision making, were adopted in response to these problems.

**7**   Although the Soviet GNP is only one-half as large as that of the United States, the Soviet GNP has grown more rapidly than ours.  A generous natural resource base, great emphasis upon capital formation, the transfer of surplus agricultural labor to industry, the adoption of superior production techniques from the West, and the planning away of cyclical unemployment are factors which have contributed to this high growth rate.

**8**   A number of factors suggest a future decline in the Soviet growth rate: the diversion of resources from growth-inducing uses, a shortage of industrial labor, the stagnation of agriculture, and declining productivity growth.  Authoritative estimates suggest the Soviet growth rate may fall to about 3.5 percent in the 1980s.

**9**   In addition to proving the feasibility of central planning and achieving an historically high growth rate, the Soviet Union has made significant advances in education and has established a comprehensive social security system.  On the other hand, the Soviet standard of living is not enviable by Western standards, and freedom is closely circumscribed by party objectives.

## Questions and Study Suggestions

**1**   Key terms and concepts to remember: state ownership; central economic planning; Gosplan; priority principle; Gosbank; "control by the ruble"; turnover tax; reforms of 1965; convergence hypothesis.

**2**   Compare the institutional framework of the Soviet economy with that of American capitalism.  Contrast the manner in which production is motivated in these two economic systems.

**3**   "So long as a central planning board, as opposed to society as a whole, sets the economic goals, there can be no freedom of occupational or consumer choice."  Explain.

**4**   Compare the sources of insecurity which face an American and a Soviet steelworker.

**5**  "It has become increasingly difficult for thoughtful men to find meaningful alternatives posed in the traditional choices between socialism and capitalism, planning and the free market, regulation and laissez faire, for they find their actual choices neither simple nor so grand."[21] Explain and evaluate.

**6**  How does Soviet planning attempt to cope with the Five Fundamental Questions which all economies must face? Discuss the problem of coordination. What mechanisms do Soviet planners use to avoid and correct problems of coordination? Explain: "Soviet planning problems mainly arise from the fact that the command economy is rooted in the logic of haste."

**7**  Evaluate carefully the level of efficiency which has been achieved in Soviet economic planning. Discuss the background and character of the 1965 reforms.

**8**  Compare the size, composition, and rate of growth of the GNPs of the United States and the Soviet Union. What have been the major sources of Soviet economic expansion? Do you feel that the Soviet Union will be able to reachieve its past growth performance? Explain.

**9**  Carefully contrast the role of the price system in Soviet Russia and the United States, distinguishing between resource and product markets. Explain the use of turnover taxes. How is the number of automobiles to be produced determined in American capitalism? In the Soviet Union? How are these decisions implemented in the two economies?

**10**  Briefly discuss the convergence hypothesis, indicating evidence for and against its validity.

## Selected References

Bergson, Abram, "The Soviet Economic Slowdown," *Challenge,* January–February 1978, pp. 22–27.
Bornstein, Morris, and Daniel R. Fusfeld (eds.): *The Soviet Economy,* 4th ed. (Homewood, Ill.: Richard D. Irwin, Inc., 1974).
Campbell, Robert W.: *The Soviet-type Economies,* 3d ed. (Boston: Houghton Mifflin Company, 1974).
Joint Economic Committee: *Soviet Economy in a New Perspective* (Washington, 1976).
NATO, *The USSR in the 1980s* (Brussels: NATO, 1978).
Nove, Alec: *The Soviet Economic System* (London: George Allen & Unwin, Ltd., 1977).
Wilczynski, J.: *The Economics of Socialism,* 3d ed. (London: George Allen & Unwin, Ltd., 1977).

[21] Robert A. Dahl and Charles E. Lindblom, *Politics, Economics and Welfare* (New York: Harper & Row, Publishers, Incorporated, 1953), p. 1.

# LAST WORD
# The Testimony of Avraham Shifrin

A refugee from a Soviet prison camp recalls camp conditions, prisoner uprisings, and the important role of prison labor in the economy of the U.S.S.R. Elsewhere in his testimony Mr. Shifrin estimates that there are currently some 5 to 10 million prison laborers in the Soviet Union today.

In 1953, 1954, it was awful conditions in concentration camps. It is hard to explain how bad it was. It was a time when people worked without holidays or any days when they can rest—10, 12, sometimes 15 hours in a day, with one letter to their relatives in the year. One to the year. And without meeting relatives, without any salary, with such bad food that when I came to the concentration camp, I have seen prisoners which have only bones and skin. Each day in our concentration camp, I do not remember a day when it was less than 30, 35 people—less than 35—which died from starvation. People died from scurvy, from pellagra also, a sort of scurvy, and from other diseases, because the body can't work in these conditions when men are so hungry. And that is why people was in such a condition that one day, in Vorkuta, in this district, which you can see on this map up near the polar circle—it was in these days, maybe some millions prisoners in this district—spontaneously, they began to strike. Then they asked some prisoners to speak with the guards, with officers. And they stopped the work in all the coal mines. . . .

This coal mining, it is very important in the U.S.S.R. because industry works on this coal. That is why came to them Khrushchev, Bulganin, Voroshilov, many members of the government, the General Procurator of the U.S.S.R., with members of the Supreme Court, with members of the Supreme Soviet of Ministers. They came to these concentration camps and spoke with these prisoners, but the prisoners answered, "We would work in these coal mines if you would take away these numbers and you would permit us first to live like people; and then you would examine our files again, because we are innocent." And they refused to do this. And these conversations was maybe 20, 25, 30 days in some concentration camps.

Then the government sent bombers and then they sent tanks. They sent troops, and they drowned this uprising in the blood. Thousands and thousands of prisoners was killed. . . .

In Norilsk, there was big uprising. In Norilsk is big mining for molybdenum and uranium and they need uranium in industry. That is why in Norilsk, they tried to speak for weeks; and then these killers sent big guns and tanks and they crushed these people. Thousands of prisoners were killed in Norilsk.

Norilsk is a place in which, before there came prisoners to Norilsk, it was mountains and plain with snow. You could not find there any buildings. Then prisoners build the city for 300,000 or 400,000 people. Now it is a big city. And all this city was built by prisoners. . . .

Building Volga-Don Canal, it was a half million prisoners in the center of the U.S.S.R.

Belomorsky Canal here [pointing to map]—also prisoners.

I talked to you about this Omsk refinery [pointing to map]—also built by prisoners. I talked to you about this biggest power station, Bratsk—also prisoners. I can show you here it was in Angarsk [pointing to map] they brought from Germany one of the biggest in Germany refinery, artificial gasoline. And it was here—I have had many friends here—100,000 people for 5 years, they build this synthetic refinery.

They built all the Kolyma gold mines with the hands of prisoners.

You can see on all these places from which they think to send to the United States these rockets, all these missile bases and airfields—all built by prisoners. All the railways in the country—only prisoners. Highways—all prisoners. All lumber cutting—only prisoners.

I have seen many times—I have heard, excuse me, please—I have seen twice myself and I have heard many times when prisoners cut their own hands and put them in the cars with lumber. They said to me, "We want that people in the freedom in the West will know who cut this lumber." You know—this lumber goes to free world. When I came to the West and I asked some people which make trade with the U.S.S.R. in this lumber, I asked these people: "It was such cases when came lumber with cut hands?" They answered me, "Yes; it was. . . ."

In all the U.S.S.R., these slaves work without salary, only because prisoners want to live. They work in this industry, in this lumber cutting, in all this country. . . .

I was once in train and Khrushchev was here in the United States, and I was in a special car for prisoners, with guards, with soldiers, and so on. And Khrushchev here in the U.N. made this speech, "I have finished with all the concentration camps in the U.S.S.R.; now we have no prisoners in the U.S.S.R.; we are finished with all the crimes of Stalin." And in a corridor in another stage of this cage stayed an officer. He smoked, smiled, and said to us: "When we come to the station, I will release you because you are not here."

You see, in the U.S.S.R., no one believes the government, because they lie in the eyes of people. People in U.S.S.R. used to all this. I know—I am sure that my father was innocent. I was sure of this when he was arrested. He never was an anti-Soviet man. He was a simple civil engineer. And then came this great purge. He was sent to the prison and died after 10 years. And in 1958, they sent to my mother so little letter, "Your husband, Shifrin, Itzak, was innocent and today he is rehabilitated after death."

Sad. You enjoy here your rights. We also have rights in U.S.S.R. And one of our rights is "after death rehabilitation;" such sad joke in U.S.S.R. you can hear.

Once in such a prisoner railway car, a soldier asked a prisoner, "Why do you sit here in the prison?" And the prisoner answered "I am innocent; for nothing."

"And how many years they gave you?"

The prisoner answered "25 years."

And the soldier said to the prisoner, "Ah, you liar! If men are innocent, they always give only 10 years!"

You understood me?

From *U.S.S.R. Labor Camps,* Hearings before the Subcommittee to Investigate the Administration of the Internal Security Act and Other Internal Security Laws of the Committee on the Judiciary, U.S. Senate, 93d Congress, 1st Session, Washington, 1973, pp. 71–75, abridged.

# Index

# Index

# NATIONAL INCOME AND RELATED STATISTICS FOR YEARS, 1957–1979

National income statistics are in billions of current dollars. Details may not add to totals because of rounding.

| | | | 1957 | 1958 | 1959 | 1960 | 1961 | 1962 | 1963 | 1964 | 1965 | 1966 |
|---|---|---|---|---|---|---|---|---|---|---|---|---|
| THE SUM OF | 1 | Personal consumption expenditures | $280.4 | $289.5 | $310.8 | $324.9 | $335.0 | $355.2 | $374.6 | $400.4 | $430.2 | $464. |
| | 2 | Gross private domestic investment | 69.2 | 61.9 | 77.6 | 76.4 | 74.3 | 85.2 | 90.2 | 96.6 | 112.0 | 124.5 |
| | 3 | Government purchases of goods and services | 87.1 | 95.0 | 97.6 | 100.3 | 108.2 | 118.0 | 123.7 | 129.8 | 138.4 | 158. |
| | 4 | Net exports | 6.1 | 2.5 | .6 | 4.4 | 5.8 | 5.4 | 6.3 | 8.9 | 7.6 | 5. |
| EQUALS | 5 | Gross national product | 442.8 | 448.8 | 486.5 | 506.0 | 523.3 | 563.8 | 594.7 | 635.7 | 688.1 | 753. |
| LESS | 6 | Capital consumption allowances | 42.0 | 44.0 | 46.1 | 47.7 | 49.1 | 50.5 | 52.2 | 54.5 | 57.5 | 61. |
| EQUALS | 7 | Net national product | 400.8 | 404.8 | 440.4 | 458.3 | 474.2 | 513.3 | 542.5 | 581.2 | 630.6 | 691. |
| LESS | 8 | Indirect business taxes | 38.5 | 40.8 | 43.3 | 46.3 | 50.0 | 55.9 | 59.7 | 62.0 | 64.6 | 69. |
| EQUALS | 9 | National income | 362.3 | 364.0 | 397.1 | 412.0 | 424.2 | 457.4 | 482.8 | 519.2 | 566.0 | 622. |
| LESS | 10 | Social security contributions | 14.9 | 15.2 | 18.0 | 21.1 | 21.9 | 24.3 | 27.3 | 28.7 | 30.0 | 38. |
| | 11 | Corporate income taxes | 21.4 | 19.0 | 23.7 | 22.7 | 22.8 | 24.0 | 26.2 | 28.0 | 30.9 | 33. |
| | 12 | Undistributed corporate profits | 9.2 | 7.1 | 12.4 | 11.0 | 10.8 | 16.5 | 17.9 | 21.7 | 27.1 | 29. |
| PLUS | 13 | Transfer payments | 32.5 | 36.7 | 39.1 | 42.5 | 46.2 | 48.0 | 51.7 | 54.9 | 59.1 | 64. |
| EQUALS | 14 | Personal income | 349.3 | 359.3 | 382.1 | 399.7 | 414.9 | 440.7 | 463.1 | 495.7 | 537.0 | 584. |
| LESS | 15 | Personal taxes | 42.4 | 42.2 | 46.0 | 50.3 | 52.0 | 56.8 | 60.3 | 58.7 | 64.8 | 74. |
| EQUALS | 16 | Disposable income | 306.9 | 317.1 | 336.1 | 349.4 | 362.9 | 383.9 | 402.8 | 437.0 | 472.2 | 510. |
| | 17 | Real gross national product (in 1972 dollars) | 680.9 | 679.5 | 720.4 | 736.8 | 755.3 | 799.1 | 830.7 | 874.4 | 925.9 | 981. |
| | 18 | Percent change in real GNP | 1.8 | –.2 | 6.0 | 2.3 | 2.5 | 5.8 | 4.0 | 5.3 | 5.9 | 5.9 |
| | 19 | Real GNP per capita | 4031 | 3885 | 4051 | 4078 | 4112 | 4284 | 4390 | 4557 | 4765 | 499 |

| RELATED STATISTICS | | | 1957 | 1958 | 1959 | 1960 | 1961 | 1962 | 1963 | 1964 | 1965 | 1966 |
|---|---|---|---|---|---|---|---|---|---|---|---|---|
| | 20 | Consumer price index (1967 = 100) | 84.3 | 86.6 | 87.3 | 88.7 | 89.6 | 90.6 | 91.7 | 92.9 | 94.5 | 97.2 |
| | 21 | Index of industrial production (1967 = 100) | 61.9 | 57.9 | 64.8 | 66.2 | 66.7 | 72.2 | 76.5 | 81.7 | 89.8 | 97.8 |
| | 22 | Supply of money (in billions of dollars) | 135.9 | 141.1 | 143.4 | 144.2 | 148.7 | 150.9 | 156.5 | 163.7 | 171.3 | 175.7 |
| | 23 | Population (in millions) | 172.0 | 174.9 | 177.8 | 180.7 | 183.7 | 186.5 | 189.2 | 191.9 | 194.3 | 196.6 |
| | 24 | Civilian labor force (in millions) | 66.9 | 67.6 | 68.4 | 69.6 | 70.4 | 70.6 | 71.8 | 74.0 | 74.4 | 75.8 |
| | 25 | Unemployment (in millions) | 2.9 | 4.6 | 3.7 | 3.9 | 4.7 | 3.9 | 4.1 | 3.8 | 3.4 | 2.9 |
| | 26 | Unemployment as a % of the civilian labor force | 4.3 | 6.8 | 5.5 | 5.5 | 6.7 | 5.5 | 5.7 | 5.2 | 4.5 | 3.8 |
| | 27 | Total consumer credit outstanding (in millions of dollars) | 52.2 | 52.7 | 60.7 | 65.1 | 67.6 | 73.9 | 82.8 | 92.6 | 103.2 | 109.7 |